SOMETHING ABOUT THE AUTHOR®

Something about
the Author *was named
an* **"Outstanding
Reference Source,"**
*the highest honor given
by the American
Library Association
Reference and Adult
Services Division.*

ISSN 0276-816X

SOMETHING ABOUT THE AUTHOR®

**Facts and Pictures about Authors
and Illustrators of Books for Young People**

volume 201

GALE
CENGAGE Learning

Detroit • New York • San Francisco • New Haven, Conn • Waterville, Maine • London

GALE
CENGAGE Learning

Something about the Author, Volume 201

Project Editor: Lisa Kumar

Editorial: Dana Ferguson, Amy Elisabeth Fuller, Michelle Kazensky, Jennifer Mossman, Joseph Palmisano, Mary Ruby, Marie Toft

Permissions: Jermaine Bobbitt, Jacqueline Flowers, Robyn Young

Imaging and Multimedia: John Watkins, Robyn Young

Composition and Electronic Capture: Amy Darga

Manufacturing: Drew Kalasky

Product Manager: Janet Witalec

Gale
27500 Drake Rd.
Farmington Hills, MI, 48331-3535

LIBRARY OF CONGRESS CATALOG CARD NUMBER 62-52046

ISBN-13: 978-1-4144-3498-8
ISBN-10: 1-4144-3498-7

ISSN 0276-816X

This title is also available as an e-book.
ISBN-13: 978-1-4144-5747-5
ISBN-10: 1-4144-5747-2
Contact your Gale, Cengage Learning sales representative for ordering information.

Printed in the United States of America
1 2 3 4 5 6 7 13 12 11 10 09

Contents

Authors in Forthcoming Volumes vii

Introduction ix

SATA Product Advisory Board xi

Illustrations Index 207

Author Index 239

A

Alma, Ann 1946- 1

Anderson, Scoular 1946- 2

Anderson, Thomas Scoular
    See Anderson, Scoular 2

Arihara, Shino 1973- 8

Averbeck, Jim 1963- 8

B

Bauer, A.C.E. 10

Bernheimer, Kate 11

Bloor, Edward 1950- 12

Bloor, Edward William
    See Bloor, Edward 12

Bogan, Paulette 1960- 16

Bowman, Catherine
    See Smith, Cat Bowman 182

Braasch, Gary 18

Broyles, Anne 1953- 19

C

Caple, Laurie 1958- 21

Cline-Ransome, Lesa 22

Craste, Marc 24

Cutbill, Andy 1972- 24

D

Dezern, Chad 26

Dodds, Dayle Ann 1952- 26

Donohue, Moira Rose 1954- 31

Dunmore, Helen 1952- 32

E

Edmund, Sean
    See Pringle, Laurence 127

Elliott, David 1947- 36

Evans, Nate 40

F

Farmer, Philip José 1918-2009
    Obituary Notice 42

Farmer, Philip Jose
    See Farmer, Philip José

Farmer, Philipé Jos
    See Farmer, Philip José 42

Fehler, Gene 1940- 43

Feiffer, Jules 1929- 45

Fotheringham, Ed
    See Fotheringham, Edwin 52

Fotheringham, Edwin 52

Freeman, Martha 1956- 53

G

Gibbons, Gail 1944- 57

Grobler, Piet 1959- 64

H

Harper, Lee 67

Harris, Joe 1928- 68

Hawkes, Kevin 1959- 68

Henderson, Lauren 1966- 72

Hibbert, Arthur Raymond
    See Hibbert, Christopher 75

Hibbert, Christopher 1924-2008
    Obituary Notice 75

J

James, Matt 76

Jarrett, Clare 1952- 76

Jennings, Christopher S. 1971(?)- 78

Jennings, C.S.
　See Jennings, Christopher S. 78

K

Kim, David 1977- 79

Kitamura, Satoshi 1956- 80

Kodman, Stanislawa 85

Kruusval, Catarina 1951- 86

L

Lanagan, Margo 1960- 88

Lechner, Jack 90

Lenain, Thierry 1959- 91

Levin, Betty 1927- 92

Lord, Michele 98

Luján, Jorge 99

M

MacDonald, Ross 1957- 102

Macken, JoAnn Early 1953- 104

MacLeod, Doug 1959- 107

McDonald, Rae A. 1952- 108

Meltzer, Milton 1915- 109

Miglio, Paige 1966- 117

Mueller, Miranda R. 120

N

Nobati, Eugenia 1968- 121

North, Sherry 121

P

Pastel, Elyse 122

Pham, LeUyen 1973- 123

Pringle, Laurence 1935- 127
　Autobiography Feature 136

Pringle, Laurence Patrick
　See Pringle, Laurence 127

R

Rauh, Sherry
　See North, Sherry 121

Reeve, Philip 157

Rey, Luis V. 1955- 161

Rovetch, L. Bob
　See Rovetch, Lissa 163

Rovetch, Lissa 163

S

Serafini, Frank 165

Shepherd, Amanda 166

Shusterman, Neal 1962- 167

Singer, Marilyn 1948- 174

Smith, Cat Bowman 1939- 182

Soo, Kean 185

Suarez, Maribel 1952- 186

T

Tamaki, Jillian 1980- 188

Townsend, Wendy 1962- 189

Trout, Kilgore
　See Farmer, Philip José 42

U

Ulmer, Wendy K. 1950- 190

V

Vail, Rachel 1966- 191

van Lieshout, Maria 195

Votaw, Carol 1961- 196

W

Watson, John H.
　See Farmer, Philip José 42

Weigelt, Udo 1960- 197

Winston, Sherri 1964(?)- 200

Wummer, Amy 1955- 201

Y

Young, Selina 1971-2006 203

Authors in Forthcoming Volumes

Below are some of the authors and illustrators that will be featured in upcoming volumes of *SATA*. These include new entries on the swiftly rising stars of the field, as well as completely revised and updated entries (indicated with *) on some of the most notable and best-loved creators of books for children.

*Wayne Anderson ▮ An award-winning British illustrator who works in colored pencil, acrylic ink, water color, and graphite, Anderson has provided the artwork for more than forty children's books, including such modern classics as Christopher Logue's *Ratsmagic*, L. Frank Baum's *The Wizard of Oz*, and Helen Ward's *Moon Dog*. In addition to creating art for a host of other writers, such as Ben Butterworth, Joan Aiken, Philippa Pearce, and A.J. Wood, Anderson also produced the self-illustrated picture books *Dragon* and *The Perfect Match*, which draw on his interest in fantasy.

*Raúl Colón ▮ Inspired to become an artist by the drawings in his favorite comic books, Colón has illustrated several children's books, including titles by such noted authors as Jane Yolen, Robert D. San Souci, Frank McCourt, and Robert Burleigh. His collaboration with McCourt, the author of the highly acclaimed memoir *Angela's Ashes*, resulted in *Angela and the Baby Jesus*, a picture book that features Colón's stylized soft-toned water color and graphite images, which have been praised for imbuing the picture-book text with warmth and optimism.

*Kate DiCamillo ▮ DiCamillo's writing career is the stuff of literary fantasy: her first novel, *Because of Winn-Dixie*, was published while its author was working at a Minneapolis bookstore and went on to win a Newbery Honor Book award and become a popular feature film. With a gift for setting and dialogue, the versatile DiCamillo proved that luck had nothing to do with it when her fanciful third novel, *The Tale of Despereaux* won the prestigious Newbery Medal.

Simon James ▮ James is a British author and illustrator whose picture-book credits include such award-winning titles as *Leon and Bob, Sally and the Limpet,* and the quirkily titled *Baby Brains: The Smartest Baby in the Whole World*. In *Leon and Bob* an imaginary friend helps a boy deal with his transition to a new neighborhood, while an infant is given an education before he is even born in *Baby Brains*. James brings each of his humorous stories to life in animated ink and watercolor illustrations.

John Lekich ▮ Lekich, a Canadian journalist and film reviewer, is the author of the young-adult novels *The Losers' Club* and *King of the Lost and Found*. Before turning to YA literature, Lekich won several national awards for his contributions to major U.S. and Canadian periodicals. Reflecting its author's serious approach, *The Losers' Club* explores the teen concerns of bullying and peer pressure.

Jimmy Liao ▮ Liao is well known as an artist and writer for children in his native Taiwan, and his popularity has prompted his works to be translated for English-language readers. His self-illustrated titles include *The Sound of Colors: A Journey of the Imagination, The Blue Stone: A Journey through Life,* and *When the Moon Forgot,* while Liao's artwork has been paired with texts by Jerry Spinelli and Joyce Dunbar.

Diane Palmisciano ▮ A prolific illustrator, Palmisciano is known for her colorful illustrations featuring bright, primary colors and engaging characters. In addition to her work for Ellen Conforth's popular "Jenny Archer" beginning reader series, Palmisciano has created cartoon artwork for texts by authors ranging from Fran Manushkin and Cari Best to Steven Kroll.

*Ann Rinaldi ▮ Known for writing historical fiction with fully developed characters and compelling plots, Rinaldi candidly addresses social, cultural, and moral issues in her work. Her unique and spirited young heroines make consequential personal decisions regarding public events during the Revolutionary War era, as in *Time Enough for Drums* and *The Secret of Sarah Reeve*, or in the Civil War era, as in *The Last Silk Dress*. Additionally, Rinaldi presents a dramatic retelling of British history in *Mutiny's Daughter* and explores the life of Queen Elizabeth I in *The Redheaded Princess*.

Hope Anita Smith ▮ In her award-winning books *The Way a Door Closes* and *Keeping the Night Watch* poet and teacher Smith explores the emotions of a young black teen as he comes to terms with the realities of his future after his father abandons the family. Smith, who began writing poetry while growing up in Ohio, has been greatly influenced by writers such as Maya Angelou and Edna St. Vincent Millay and also shares her love of writing in workshops for both adults and children.

*Ian Whybrow ▮ The author of more than a hundred books, Whybrow writes humorous stories for children that range from the whimsical and poignant to the raucous and slightly naughty. His books for the storybook set, including *Quacky Quack-Quack!, Harry and the Bucketful of Dinosaurs,* and *Little Wolf's Book of Badness,* have been praised for capturing typical childhood emotions in simple tales with satisfying conclusions. Whybrow's middle-grade novel *The Unvisibles* is more serious in tone; here he melds humor with compassion in his story about a special friendship.

Introduction

Something about the Author (*SATA*) is an ongoing reference series that examines the lives and works of authors and illustrators of books for children. *SATA* includes not only well-known writers and artists but also less prominent individuals whose works are just coming to be recognized. This series is often the only readily available information source on emerging authors and illustrators. You'll find *SATA* informative and entertaining, whether you are a student, a librarian, an English teacher, a parent, or simply an adult who enjoys children's literature.

What's Inside *SATA*

SATA provides detailed information about authors and illustrators who span the full time range of children's literature, from early figures like John Newbery and L. Frank Baum to contemporary figures like Judy Blume and Richard Peck. Authors in the series represent primarily English-speaking countries, particularly the United States, Canada, and the United Kingdom. Also included, however, are authors from around the world whose works are available in English translation. The writings represented in *SATA* include those created intentionally for children and young adults as well as those written for a general audience and known to interest younger readers. These writings cover the entire spectrum of children's literature, including picture books, humor, folk and fairy tales, animal stories, mystery and adventure, science fiction and fantasy, historical fiction, poetry and nonsense verse, drama, biography, and nonfiction. Obituaries are also included in *SATA* and are intended not only as death notices but also as concise overviews of people's lives and work. Additionally, each edition features newly revised and updated entries for a selection of *SATA* listees who remain of interest to today's readers and who have been active enough to require extensive revisions of their earlier biographies.

Autobiography Feature

Beginning with Volume 103, many volumes of *SATA* feature one or more specially commissioned autobiographical essays. These unique essays, averaging about ten thousand words in length and illustrated with an abundance of personal photos, present an entertaining and informative first-person perspective on the lives and careers of prominent authors and illustrators profiled in *SATA*.

Two Convenient Indexes

In response to suggestions from librarians, *SATA* indexes no longer appear in every volume but are included in alternate (odd-numbered) volumes of the series, beginning with Volume 57.

SATA continues to include two indexes that cumulate with each alternate volume: the Illustrations Index, arranged by the name of the illustrator, gives the number of the volume and page where the illustrator's work appears in the current volume as well as all preceding volumes in the series; the Author Index gives the number of the volume in which a person's biographical sketch, autobiographical essay, or obituary appears in the current volume as well as all preceding volumes in the series.

These indexes also include references to authors and illustrators who appear in *Gale's Yesterday's Authors of Books for Children, Children's Literature Review,* and *Something about the Author Autobiography Series.*

Easy-to-Use Entry Format

Whether you're already familiar with the *SATA* series or just getting acquainted, you will want to be aware of the kind of information that an entry provides. In every *SATA* entry the editors attempt to give as complete a picture of the person's life and work as possible. A typical entry in *SATA* includes the following clearly labeled information sections:

PERSONAL: date and place of birth and death, parents' names and occupations, name of spouse, date of marriage, names of children, educational institutions attended, degrees received, religious and political affiliations, hobbies and other interests.

ADDRESSES: complete home, office, electronic mail, and agent addresses, whenever available.

CAREER: name of employer, position, and dates for each career post; art exhibitions; military service; memberships and offices held in professional and civic organizations.

MEMBER: professional, civic, and other association memberships and any official posts held.

AWARDS, HONORS: literary and professional awards received.

WRITINGS: title-by-title chronological bibliography of books written and/or illustrated, listed by genre when known; lists of other notable publications, such as plays, screenplays, and periodical contributions.

ADAPTATIONS: a list of films, television programs, plays, CD-ROMs, recordings, and other media presentations that have been adapted from the author's work.

WORK IN PROGRESS: description of projects in progress.

SIDELIGHTS: a biographical portrait of the author or illustrator's development, either directly from the biographee—and often written specifically for the *SATA* entry—or gathered from diaries, letters, interviews, or other published sources.

BIOGRAPHICAL AND CRITICAL SOURCES: cites sources quoted in "Sidelights" along with references for further reading.

EXTENSIVE ILLUSTRATIONS: photographs, movie stills, book illustrations, and other interesting visual materials supplement the text.

How a *SATA* Entry Is Compiled

SATA editors examine a wide variety of published sources to gather information for an entry. Biographical and bibliographic sources are consulted, as are book reviews, feature articles, published interviews, and material sometimes obtained from the biographee's family, publishers, agent, or other associates. Whenever possible, the author or illustrator is sent a copy of the entry to check for accuracy and completeness.

Entries that have not been verified by the biographees or their representatives are marked with an asterisk (*).

Contact the Editor

We encourage our readers to examine the entire *SATA* series. Please write and tell us if we can make *SATA* even more helpful to you. Give your comments and suggestions to the editor:

Editor
Something about the Author
Gale, Cengage Learning
27500 Drake Rd.
Farmington Hills MI 48331-3535

Toll-free: 800-877-GALE
Fax: 248-699-8070

Something about the Author Product Advisory Board

The editors of *Something about the Author* are dedicated to maintaining a high standard of excellence by publishing comprehensive, accurate, and highly readable entries on a wide array of writers for children and young adults. In addition to the quality of the content, the editors take pride in the graphic design of the series, which is intended to be orderly yet inviting, allowing readers to utilize the pages of *SATA* easily and with efficiency. Despite the longevity of the *SATA* print series, and the success of its format, we are mindful that the vitality of a literary reference product is dependent on its ability to serve its users over time. As literature, and attitudes about literature, constantly evolve, so do the reference needs of students, teachers, scholars, journalists, researchers, and book club members. To be certain that we continue to keep pace with the expectations of our customers, the editors of *SATA* listen carefully to their comments regarding the value, utility, and quality of the series. Librarians, who have firsthand knowledge of the needs of library users, are a valuable resource for us. The *Something about the Author* Product Advisory Board, made up of school, public, and academic librarians, is a forum to promote focused feedback about *SATA* on a regular basis. The nine-member advisory board includes the following individuals, whom the editors wish to thank for sharing their expertise:

Eva M. Davis
Director,
Canton Public Library,
Canton, Michigan

Joan B. Eisenberg
Lower School Librarian,
Milton Academy,
Milton, Massachusetts

Francisca Goldsmith
Teen Services Librarian,
Berkeley Public Library,
Berkeley, California

Susan Dove Lempke
Children's Services Supervisor,
Niles Public Library District,
Niles, Illinois

Robyn Lupa
Head of Children's Services,
Jefferson County Public Library,
Lakewood, Colorado

Victor L. Schill
Assistant Branch Librarian/Children's Librarian,
Harris County Public Library/Fairbanks Branch,
Houston, Texas

Caryn Sipos
Community Librarian,
Three Creeks Community Library,
Vancouver, Washington

Steven Weiner
Director,
Maynard Public Library,
Maynard, Massachusetts

something ABOUT the AUTHor

ALMA, Ann 1946-

Personal

Born 1946, in Uit-huiz-er-meeden, Netherlands; immigrated to Canada, 1970. *Hobbies and other interests:* Writing, walking in the mountains with her dog, gardening, traveling, singing, skiing, reading.

Addresses

Home and office—S8 C5, RR. No. 1, South Slocan, British Columbia V0G 2G0, Canada. *E-mail*—annalma@shaw.ca.

Career

Writer. Public school teacher in Holland, Canada, Japan, and Zambia until 1992.

Member

Writers' Union of Canada, Canadian Children's Book Centre, Canadian Society of Children's Authors, Illustrators, and Performers, Children's Writers and Illustrators of British Columbia.

Awards, Honors

Silver Birch Regional award, and Chocolate Lily Award nomination, both 2003, and Red Cedar Award nomination, and Diamond Willow nomination, both 2004, all for *Summer of Changes;* Silver Birch Award nomination, 2008, for *Skateway to Freedom;* Silver Birch Award nomination, 2009, and and Chocolate Lily Award nomination, 2010, both for *Brave Deeds.*

Writings

Camping with Children: A How-to Guide for Teachers, Teachers' Federation Lesson Aids Service (Vancouver, British Columbia, Canada), 1991.

Skateway to Freedom, Orca (Victoria, British Columbia, Canada), 1993, reprinted, Dundurn (Toronto, Ontario, Canada), 2008.

Under Emily's Sky, Beach Holme (Vancouver, British Columbia, Canada), 1997.

Something to Tell, Riverwood (Newmarket, Ontario, Canada), 1998.

Summer of Changes, Sono Nis (Victoria, British Columbia, Canada), 2001.

Summer of Adventures, Sono Nis (Winlaw, British Columbia, Canada), 2002.

Brave Deeds: How One Family Saved Many from the Nazis, Groundwood Books (Toronto, Ontario, Canada), 2008.

Adaptations

Skateway to Freedom was adapted as an audiobook, Library Services Branch (Burnaby, British Columbia, Canada), 2000.

Sidelights

Canadian author Ann Alma was born in the Netherlands and worked there as an educator before moving to Canada in 1970. She was a full-time teacher in Canada before relocating to a new home in the Kootenay mountains of British Columbia and she became a full-time writer in 1992. During her teaching career, Alma also taught in Japan and Zambia. As a writer, Alma continues to teach; as Mary Thomas noted in her *Canadian Review of Materials* appraisal of Alma's novel *Under Emily's Sky,* the time-travel story "is attempting to be painlessly instructive, and, in large part, it succeeds."

In *Under Emily's Sky* a modern-day girl named Lee goes back in time to 1936 and meets noted Canadian artist Emily Carr. Lee is also an artist, and her art helps her deal with the crumbling marriage between her parents as a result of her father's alcoholism. During a camping trip the day after Lee's father is kicked out of their house by her mother, Lee trips over a tree root and falls unconscious. When she wakes up, she encounters Carr camping in the wilderness and studying the natural world as material for her paintings. Lee takes the opportunity to learn from Carr and as she encounters the many homeless people who are also living in the mountains due to joblessness and the depressed economy of the 1930s, she begins to gain perspective on her own situation.

Alma's highly praised "Summer" series, which includes *Summer of Changes* and *Summer of Adventures,* deals with the complex subject of schizophrenia. Eleven-year-old Anneke is coping with the woman's mental illness. When her mother begins to wander off, Anneke decides to strike off on her own and she moves to a nearby cave for the summer so that she will not be placed in foster care. *Summer of Adventures* finds the preteen living with foster parents Larry and Eileen, a couple that truly cares for her. However, Anneke fights the relationship because she does not want to admit that her mother may no longer be able to live a normal life. *Summer of Changes* "is full of pathos, optimism, and love written in a very realistic and appealing style," Rosemary Anderson concluded in *Resource Links.* "Despite the heavy emotional content . . . , the ['Summer'] books are very much adventure driven," observed Liz Greenaway in the *Canadian Review of Materials,* the critic adding that both novels "are fast-paced and extremely well written."

In *Brave Deeds: How One Family Saved Many from the Nazis* Alma turns to history, recounting a story of World War II through the voice of a fictional character. The Braal family, which lived in Alma's native Netherlands, was part of the Dutch resistance movement. They actively sought to help Jews escape from the Nazis to safety. Their story is supplemented with many photographs, maps, and notes for young readers to better understand the role of the Braals in history. Betty Klassen, writing in the *Canadian Review of Materials,* called *Brave Deeds* "a tribute to people of courage, and a challenge to those who wonder if they would ever have such courage." Noting that Alma interviewed members of the Braal family, who were friends, in the process of writing her book, Kim Dare wrote in *School Library Journal* that the author's "tribute to an ordinary family who took extraordinary risks is commendable."

Biographical and Critical Sources

PERIODICALS

Biography, summer, 2008, Susan Perren, review of *Brave Deeds: How One Family Saved Many from the Nazis,* p. 504.
Booklist, April 1, 2008, Hazel Rochman, review of *Brave Deeds,* p. 42.
Canadian Review of Materials, April 24, 1998, Mary Thomas, review of *Under Emily's Sky;* April 25, 2003, Liz Greenaway, reviews of *Summer of Changes* and *Summer of Adventures;* April 18, 2008, Betty Klassen, review of *Brave Deeds.*
Kliatt, April 1, 2008, review of *Brave Deeds.*
Resource Links, February, 2002, Rosemary Anderson, review of *Summer of Changes,* p. 9; April, 2003, Shannon Danylko, review of *Summer of Adventures,* p. 11.
School Library Journal, September, 2008, Kim Dare, review of *Brave Deeds,* p. 198.

ONLINE

Ann Alma Home Page, http://www.annalma.ca (May 13, 2009).
Canadian Society of Children's Authors, Illustrators, and Performers Web site, http://www.canscaip.org/ (May 13, 2009).

* * *

ANDERSON, Scoular 1946- (Thomas Scoular Anderson)

Personal

Born February 10, 1946, in Scotland. *Education:* Attended art school in Glasgow, Scotland. *Hobbies and other interests:* Gardening, playing the guitar, cooking, walking.

Addresses

Home—Dunoon, Argyll, Scotland. *E-mail*—mail@scoularanderson.co.uk.

Career

Writer and illustrator. Former illustrator for London University, London, England; art instructor.

Writings

SELF-ILLUSTRATED; FOR CHILDREN

My First Joke Book, Young Corgi (London, England), 1986.

(With Chris Powling) *The Phantom Carwash,* A. & C. Black (London, England), 1986, reprinted, Barn Owl (London, England), 2001.

A-Z of Animal Jokes, Young Corgi (London, England), 1987.

The Enormous Chocolate Pudding, Dent (London, England), 1987.

(With Chris Powling) *Hiccup Harry,* A. & C. Black (London, England), 1988, Dutton Children's Books (New York, NY), 1990.

The Daring Dot-to-Dot Dinosaur, Young Corgi (London, England), 1989.

The Knock Knock Joke Book, Hippo (London, England), 1989.

A Journey down the Clyde, Drew (England), 1989.

A Plunder of Pirates, Puffin (London, England), 1989, published as *Project Pirates: Amazing Facts! Amazing Fun!,* Viking (London, England), 1994.

The Spider and Chips Joke Book, Young Corgi (London, England), 1989.

(With Chris Powling) *Harry's Party,* A. & C. Black (London, England), 1989.

Never Keep a Python as a Pet, Dent (London, England), 1990.

The Really Revolting Puzzle Book, Piccolo (England), 1990.

Wendy's Wheels, Ginn (England), 1990.

(With Chris Powling) *Harry with Spots On,* A. & C. Black (London, England), 1990.

Why Did the Chicken Cross the Road?, Hippo (London, England), 1991.

The Magic Boomerang; The Magic Present, Macmillan Children's (London, England), 1991.

School Jokes for Aliens, Young Corgi (London, England), 1991.

The Puffin Book of Royal London, Puffin (London, England), 1991.

Dreamy Daniel, Brainy Bert, Simon & Schuster Young Books (Hemel Hempstead, England), 1992.

The Curse of Hackjaw Island, Puffin (London, England), 1992.

Changing Charlie, A. & C. Black (London, England), 1992.

Land Ahoy! The Story of Christopher Columbus, Puffin (London, England), 1992.

Puzzling People, Puffin (London, England), 1992.

The Elephant Joke Book, Scholastic (London, England), 1993.

The Haunted Dot-to-Dot Hotel, Young Corgi (London, England), 1993.

The Puffin Factfile of Kings and Queens, Puffin (London, England), 1993.

(With Chris Powling) *Harry Moves House,* A. & C. Black (London, England), 1993.

Clogpots in Space, A. & C. Black (London, England), 1994.

A Puzzling Day at Castle MacPelican, Walker Books (London, England), 1994, Candlewick Press (Cambridge, MA), 1995.

The Survival Guide to Parents, Lions (London, England), 1994.

The Amazing Mark in Creepstone Castle, Viking (London, England), 1994.

The Survival Guide to Pets, Lions (London, England), 1995.

Finlay MacTrebble and the Fantastic Fertiliser, A. & C. Black (London, England), 1995.

Plotting and Chopping: Tudors and Stuarts with a Few Gory Bits, Puffin (London, England), 1995.

(With Chris Powling) *Harry the Superhero,* A. & C. Black (London, England), 1995.

Backseat's Special Day, Hippo (London, England), 1996.

A Puzzling Day in the Land of the Pharaohs, Candlewick Press (Cambridge, MA), 1996.

The Survival Guide to Food, Collins (London, England), 1996.

(With Chris Powling) *Harry on Holiday,* A. & C. Black (London, England), 1997.

1314 and All That, Canongate Books (Edinburgh, Scotland), 1998.

MacPelican's American Adventure, Candlewick Press (Cambridge, MA), 1998.

Ghost Docs on Patrol, Collins Children's (London, England), 1998.

Raiding and Trading: Vikings with a Few Gory Bits, Puffin (London, England), 1998.

Fun: The Awful Truth, Hodder Children's (London, England), 1999.

Grown-ups: The Awful Truth, Hodder Children's (London, England), 1999.

School: The Awful Truth, Hodder Children's (London, England), 1999.

Ghost Docs at School, Collins Children's (London, England), 1999.

(With Chris Powling) *Rover Goes to School,* A. & C. Black (London, England), 1999.

(With Chris Powling) *Rover Shows Off,* A. & C. Black (London, England), 1999.

(With Chris Powling) *Rover the Champion,* A. & C. Black (London, England), 1999.

(With Chris Powling) *Rover's Birthday,* A. & C. Black (London, England), 1999.

(With Chris Powling) *The Book about Books,* A. & C. Black (London, England), 2000.

1745 and All That: The Story of the Highlands, Berlinn (Edinburgh, Scotland), 2001.

The Bin Bears, Corgi Pups (London, England), 2001.

My First Knock Knock Joke Book, Young Corgi (London, England), 2001.

Rob the Roman Gets Eaten by a Lion (Nearly), Hippo (London, England), 2001.

Trev the Tudor Gets the Chop (Nearly), Scholastic (London, England), 2001.

Stan and the Major Makeover, A. & C. Black (London, England), 2002, published as *Stan the Dog and the Major Makeover,* Picture Window Books (Minneapolis, MN), 2007.

Stan and the Sneaky Snacks, A. & C. Black (London, England), 2002, published as *Stan the Dog and the Sneaky Snacks,* Picture Window Books (Minneapolis, MN), 2007.

Stan and the Golden Goals, A. & C. Black (London, England), 2002, published as *Stan the Dog and the Golden Goals,* Picture Window Books (Minneapolis, MN), 2007.

Stan and the Crafty Cats, A. & C. Black (London, England), 2002, published as *Stan the Dog and the Crafty Cats,* Picture Window Books (Minneapolis, MN), 2007.

Teacher Taming, Puffin (London, England), 2003.

The Mean Team from Mars, A. & C. Black (London, England), 2003, Picture Window Books (Minneapolis, MN), 2006.

Space Pirates and the Treasure of Salmagundy, Frances Lincoln Children's (London, England), 2004, published as *Space Pirates: A Map-reading Adventure,* Annick Press (Toronto, Ontario, Canada), 2004.

Super Splosh, HarperCollins Children's (London, England), 2005.

Scary Dog, Walker (London, England), 2005.

Spookball Champions, A. & C. Black (London, England), 2005, Picture Window Press (Minneapolis, MN), 2006.

Superdog Stan, A. & C. Black (London, England), 2006, published as *Stan the Dog Becomes Superdog,* Picture Window Books (Minneapolis, MN), 2007.

Lovely, Lovely Pirate Gold, Evans (London, England), 2006.

Space Pirates and the Monster of Malswomp, Frances Lincoln (London, England), 2007.

Some of Anderson's books have been translated into Spanish.

"WIZARD BOY" SERIES; AND ILLUSTRATOR

The Perfect Pizza, A. & C. Black (London, England), 2000.

The Posh Party, A. & C. Black (London, England), 2000.

The Potty Panto, A. & C. Black (London, England), 2000.

The Muddled Monsters, A. & C. Black (London, England), 2000.

"WIZBANG WIZARD" SERIES; AND ILLUSTRATOR

Bubble Trouble, HarperCollins Children's (London, England), 2006.

Dragon Danger; and Grasshopper Glue, HarperCollins Children's (London, England), 2007.

ILLUSTRATOR

Sybil Marshall, *Polly at the Window,* Puffin (Harmondsworth, England), 1975.

Charles Dickens, *Oliver Twist,* adapted by Norman Wymer, Collins (London, England), 1979.

Charles Dickens, *Hard Times,* adapted by Viola Huggins, Collins (London, England), 1979.

Viola Huggins, *Five Ghost Stories,* Collins (London, England), 1980.

WAC Ghosts, Monsters, and Legends, Corgi (London, England), 1986.

WAC Jokes, Corgi (London, England), 1986.

David Pugh, editor, *The Grisly Joke Book,* Armada (London, England), 1986.

Jennifer Kavanagh, editor, *The Methuen Book of Humorous Stories,* Methuen (London, England), 1987.

Brian Ball, *The Quest for Queenie,* Macdonald (England), 1988.

Corley Byrne, *Kipper & Co.,* Dent (London, England), 1988.

Dick Cate, *Alexander and the Star Part,* Macmillan Children's (London, England), 1988.

Ruth Manning-Sanders, editor, *A Cauldron of Witches* (short stories), Methuen (London, England), 1988.

Jennifer Curry and Graeme Curry, *Down Our Street,* Methuen (London, England), 1988.

Victor Osborne, *Rex, the Most Special Car in the World,* Dent (London, England), 1988, Carolrhoda Books (Minneapolis, MN), 1989.

Phillip Schofield, *The Phillip Schofield Fun File,* Bantam (England), 1988.

Miranda Seymour, *Pierre and the Pamplemousse,* Hodder & Stoughton (London, England), 1989.

Dick Cate, *Alexander and the Tooth of Zaza,* Macmillan Children's (London, England), 1989.

Dick Cate, *Scared!,* Macdonald (England), 1989.

Carol Vorderman, *Dirty, Loud, and Brilliant Too,* Knight (England), 1989.

Paul Jackson, *Flying Mobiles,* [England], 1989, Watermill Press (Mahwah, NJ), 1990.

Mary Danby, *How to Halt a Hiccup,* Knight (England), 1990.

Corley Byrne, *Kipper & Co. Strike Again!,* Dent (London, England), 1990.

Robert Swindells, *Tim Kipper,* Macmillan Children's (London, England), 1990, new edition, 1992.

John Dinneen, *Super-Challenge 2,* HarperCollins, 1991.

Saviour Pirotta, *Pineapple Crush,* Hodder & Stoughton (London, England), 1991.

Peter Hayward, *Nature File,* Puffin (London, England), 1992.

Christina Noble, *The Story of Loch Fyne Oysters,* Oyster Ideas (Cairndow, Scotland), 1993.

Robert Swindells, *The Siege of Frimly Prim,* Methuen Children's (London, England), 1993.

Theresa Breslin, *Bullies at School,* Canongate Books (Edinburgh, Scotland), 1994.

Roy Apps, *Nigel the Pirate,* Simon & Schuster Young Books (Hemel Hempstead, England), 1994.

Sam McBratney, *The Stranger from Somewhere in Time,* Heinemann (London, England), 1994.

Hazel Townson, *The Armband Band,* Collins Educational (London, England), 1995.

Wes Magee, *The Scumbagg School Scorpion,* Orchard (London, England), 1995.

Sam McBratney, *The Firetail Cat,* Macdonald Young Books (Hemel Hempstead, England), 1995.

Wes Magee, *The Spook Spotters of Scumbagg School,* Orchard (London, England), 1996.

Wes Magee, *Sports Day at Scumbagg School,* Orchard (London, England), 1996.

Elisabeth Jane McNair, *Robert Burns: Maker of Rhymes,* Viking (London, England), 1996.

Dick Cate, *Bernard's Prize,* Walker Books (London, England), 1996.

Sally Grindley, *Jimjams and the Ratnappers,* Macdonald Young Books (Hove, England), 1997.

Judy Allen, *The Most Brilliant Trick Ever,* Walker Books (London, England), 1997.

Jack Marlowe, *Explorers,* Hodder Children's (London, England), 1997.

Jack Marlowe, *Inventors,* Hodder Children's (London, England), 1997.

Jack Marlowe, *Scientists,* Hodder Children's (London, England), 1997.

Jack Marlowe, *Writers: Truly Terrible Tales,* Hodder Children's (London, England), 1997.

Dick Cate, *Bernard's Magic,* Walker Books (London, England), 1997.

Dick Cate, *Bernard's Gang,* Walker Books (London, England), 1998.

Hazel Richardson, *How to Split the Atom: The Hands-on Guide to Being a Science Superstar,* Oxford University Press (Oxford, England), 1999, Franklin Watts (New York, NY), 2001.

Hazel Richardson, *How to Build a Rocket,* 1999, Franklin Watts (New York, NY), 2001.

Jeremy Strong, *Problems with a Python,* Barrington Stoke (Edinburgh, Scotland), 1999.

Dyan Sheldon, *Leon Loves Bugs,* Walker Books (London, England), 2000.

Margaret McAllister, *Doughnut Dilemma,* Oxford University Press (Oxford, England), 2000.

Margaret McAllister, *The Worst of the Vikings,* Oxford University Press (Oxford, England), 2000.

Jeremy Strong, *Living with Vampires,* Barrington Stoke (Edinburgh, Scotland), 2000, Stone Arch Books (Minneapolis, MN), 2007.

K.M. Briggs, *Hobberdy Dick* (new edition), Jane Nissen (London, England), 2000.

Clive Gifford, *How to Live on Mars,* Franklin Watts (London, England), 2000, Franklin Watts (New York, NY), 2001.

Timothy de Jongh Scott, *History Hoaxes,* Hodder Children's (London, England), 2000.

Clive Gifford, *How to Meet Aliens,* Franklin Watts (New York, NY), 2001.

Barbara Taylor, *How to Save the Planet,* Franklin Watts (New York, NY), 2001.

David Shenton, *A Day in the Life of a Roman Charioteer,* Pearson Education (Harlow, England), 2001.

Pat Thomson, *Pirates, Gold, and Custard,* Oxford University Press (Oxford, England), 2001.

Garry Kilworth, *Monster School,* A. & C. Black (London, England), 2002.

Jeremy Strong, *Mad Iris,* Barrington Stoke (Edinburgh, Scotland), 2002.

Jeremy Strong, *Don't Go into the Cellar,* Barrington Stoke (Edinburgh, Scotland), 2003, new edition, 2004, Stone Arch Book (Mankato, MN), 2006.

Rachel Anderson, *Hugo and the Long Red Arm,* A. & C. Black (London, England), 2004.

Jeremy Strong, *The Smallest Horse in the World,* Barrington Stoke (Edinburgh, Scotland), 2005.

Martin Waddell, *The Ghost Ship,* Oxford University Press (Oxford, England), 2006.

Jeremy Strong, *Mad Iris Goes Missing,* Barrington Stoke (Edinburgh, Scotland), 2006.

Susan Gates, *Robo-Vac,* Oxford University Press (Oxford, England), 2006.

Allan Burnett, *Robert the Bruce and All That,* Birlinn (Edinburgh, Scotland), 2006.

Allan Burnett, *Bonnie Prince Charlie and All That,* Birlinn (Edinburgh, Scotland), 2006.

Allan Burnett, *Mary, Queen of Scots and All That,* Birlinn (Edinburgh, Scotland), 2006.

Allan Burnett, *William Wallace and All That,* Birlinn (Edinburgh, Scotland), 2006.

Allan Burnett, *Robert Burns and All That,* Birlinn (Edinburgh, Scotland), 2007.

Allan Burnett, *Rob Roy and All That,* Birlinn (Edinburgh, Scotland), 2007.

Allan Burnett, *Macbeth and All That,* Birlinn (Edinburgh, Scotland), 2007.

Carolyn Bear, *Town Dog,* Oxford University Press (Oxford, England), 2007.

Illustrator of numerous other children's books.

OTHER

(Self-illustrated) *Images of Dunoon and the Cowal Peninsula,* Argyll Publishing (Gendaruel, Argyll, Scotland), 1998, foreword of Emma Thomson, 2007.

A Day in the Life of a Roman Charioteer (for children), illustrated by David Shenton, Pearson Education (Harlow, England), 2001.

Contributor of short stories to journals, including *Puffin Post.*

Sidelights

Scoular Anderson is the author and illustrator of more than seventy books and the illustrator of at least a hundred more. He enjoys writing history books because it allows him to read widely and search for fascinating and little-know facts to share with readers. Many of Anderson's history books are illustrated with his own cartoons, and some couch their lessons in puzzle series that readers can solve along the way. His work is popular among young readers, some as young as age six or seven, and his humorous cartoon illustrations make Anderson's work appealing to older, reluctant readers as well. Asked on his home page where his ideas come from, Anderson quipped: "I have a brain like a huge net which catches all sorts of rubbish. Now and again, one of these bits of rubbish gives me a nudge and says: 'Don't you think I'm a totally excellent idea for a story?'"

Scoular Anderson's humorous cartoons are a feature of My First Joke Book. (Illustration copyright © by Scoular Anderson. Reproduced by permission of Random House Group, Ltd.)

One of Anderson's early successes, *A Plunder of Pirates,* relates the stories of several famous pirates, both male and female. From these tales the reader learns interesting background information about how people came to be pirates, how they dressed and talked, what daily life was like aboard a pirate ship, and about the ships and their armaments as well. The book proved popular enough to merit a redesign and reprint titled *Project Pirates: Amazing Facts! Amazing Fun!,* which Stuart Hannabuss referred to in *School Librarian* as a witty and "light-hearted" presentation for young readers. Although a *Junior Bookshelf* reviewer cautioned that *Project Pirates* "include[s] some chilling details," Kevin Steinberger praised the reprint in *Magpies* as full of facts so "engaging" and "comically presented" that children will be inspired "to read it [from] cover to cover."

In *Land Ahoy! The Story of Christopher Columbus,* Anderson introduces young readers to the self-styled "admiral of the ocean sea." In a humorous narrative, punctuated by lively cartoons, maps, and other line drawings, the author/illustrator presents a great deal of biographical and historical detail and even offers his views on what might have compelled the explorer to risk his life and the lives of his crew, not once, but four times in his futile quest to reach the East Indies. Although Barbara Roberts reported "some minor discrepancies" in her *Science Books & Films* review of the book, Ingrid Broomfield commended Anderson in *School Librarian* for creating an account that is "factu-

ally accurate without being . . . boring." In *Books for Keeps,* Veronica Holliday noted the book's "carefully balanced . . . blend of humour and factual information," and went on to recommend *Land Ahoy!* for its "refreshingly lively, anecdotal style."

Anderson has penned and illustrated several popular children's histories about the British Isles, each of which is brought to life in his trademark cartoon illustrations. Important moments in Scottish history are the focus of *1314 and All That* (1314 being the year the Scots won their independence from England at the Battle of Bannockburn) and *1745 and All That: The Story of the Highlands.* He describes daily life in other times in *Trev the Tudor Gets the Chop (Nearly)* and *Rob the Roman Gets Eaten by a Lion (Nearly),* both of which contain facts about historical events as well as humorous anecdotes and obscure trivia about the people and the times in which they lived.

Anderson sometimes disguises history in puzzle books. He introduces inventor Hector MacPelican in *A Puzzling Day at Castle MacPelican,* a book that takes readers on a treasure hunt full of puzzles to solve, mazes to explore, and tiny details of evidence to spot in the cartoon-style illustrations. In her *School Librarian* review, Elizabeth J. King cited the "amazing amount of detail" to be discovered in Anderson's art work and the "sheer fun" of pursuing the hidden treasure. In *MacPelican's American Adventure* the inventor leads readers—along with the whole MacPelican family—on a tour of the United States as it appeared in 1898, the year of the "Grand Louisiana Exhibition." Readers with the "patience, fortitude, and great vision" required to solve the puzzles in this book, observed Susan Pine in *School Library Journal,* will also be treated to a scenic tour of America at the end of the nineteenth century. In *A Puzzling Day in the Land of the Pharaohs* the adventurous reader travels back in time with Mrs. Pudget and her students to ancient Egypt. In what *School Library Journal* critic Jane Claes called a "lighthearted romp around an ancient world," readers learn about Egyptian history while searching for the clues they need to solve puzzles that will return them to their own world and time.

In addition to history, Anderson has also created many works of self-illustrated fiction. In his "Wizard Boy" series, which include *The Perfect Pizza, The Posh Party, The Potty Panto,* and *The Muddled Monsters,* he focuses on the adventures of Eric and his dad, a bumbling wizard whose attempts at magic often stray far afield. In *The Perfect Pizza* Dad attempts to spruce up dinner with a magic spell that ends up turning pizza dough into snow and transforming the family's pets beyond recognition, not to mention creating a mess in the kitchen. Therefore, when Dad offers to substitute for a birthday-party magician in *The Posh Party,* Eric has some anxious reservations. In *The Potty Panto* Dad is assigned to provide special effects for a children's play, while *The Muddled Monsters* finds him attempting to repair a ride at the Mighty Monster Theme Park. Mar-

garet Mallett, in a *School Librarian* review of *The Perfect Pizza,* described the combination of page layout, narrative, and cartoon-style illustrations as "cleverly matched" to "add energy and interest." The series is meant for beginning readers, and Mallett predicted that the books will encourage children toward the joy of reading and the joy of learning as well.

Geared for beginning readers, *Dreamy Daniel, Brainy Bert* introduces a daydreamer who is not much interested in either reading or learning. During idle moments in class, Daniel begins to notice a little mouse who lives in the classroom. Sherbert the mouse is no daydreamer; he can read and write. The boy and the mouse become friends, and "Bert" offers a series of tips to help Daniel with his studies, including a trip to the school library. While *Dreamy Daniel, Brainy Bert* is intended to motivate reluctant readers, Frances Ball pointed out in *School Librarian* that Bert is a well-rounded, engaging little fellow, "and the advice about reading is nicely disguised."

In addition to aiding beginning readers, Anderson helps hone navigational skills in *Space Pirates: A Map-reading Adventure,* a book published in England as *Space Pirates and the Treasure of Salmagundy.* With the help of their space ship's computer, a diverse group of four passengers led by Captain Tosca on the starship *Sleepy Sheep* explores a new planet and recovers several caches of pirate treasure. Praising *Space Pirates* as an "entertaining offering," Anne L. Tormohlen added in *School Library Journal* that the book will appeal to "fans of puzzle books," while *Resource Links* contributor Antonia Gisler concluded that "older fans of 'Where's Waldo?' will be delighted to discover [Anderson's] . . . book." Mazes and more treasure fuel the plot of *Space Pirates and the Monster of Malswomp,* in which Anderson's detailed cartoon art contains humorous lessons in reading a compass and following directions. According to a *Kirkus Reviews* writer, this *Space Pirates* follow-up "painlessly impart[s] map-reading skills." Anderson is also noted for the sense of humor he demonstrates in numerous joke books for young readers and his "awful truth" books, in which he offers fun facts and quasi-facts about school, grownups, and other aspects of childhood that sometimes puzzle and frustrate young readers everywhere.

For the very young Anderson has written and illustrated *The Enormous Chocolate Pudding,* about a king with an incongruous problem. Somehow the palace garden sprouted a chocolate pudding that is so huge that it is blocking the king's view from his window. What to do? The king tries everything, to no avail. The court jester finds an answer and the solution unfolds in a colorful two-page spread that requires no narrative explanation. A *Books for Keeps* contributor remarked that Anderson's story, with its detailed illustrations, provides "plenty to laugh about," and Elizabeth J. King enthusiastically recommended *The Enormous Chocolate Pud-*

ding in a *British Book News* review, writing that its "good story line" and "funny, expressive illustrations" demonstrate the author's sense of "visual and verbal humour."

Biographical and Critical Sources

PERIODICALS

Books, October, 1989, review of *The Knock Knock Joke Book,* p. 22; July, 1991, Tony Bradman, review of *The Puffin Book of Royal London,* p. 8.

Books for Keeps, May, 1989, review of *The Enormous Chocolate Pudding,* p. 8; March, 1992, review of *The Magic Boomerang; The Magic Present,* p. 9; May, 1992, Veronica Halliday, review of *Land Ahoy! The Story of Christopher Columbus,* p. 22; July, 1992, review of *Dreamy Daniel, Brainy Bert,* p. 11; May, 1995, review of *The Amazing Mark in Creepstone Castle,* p. 11; November, 1999, review of *MacPelican's American Adventure,* p. 24.

British Book News, December, 1987, review of *The Enormous Chocolate Pudding,* p. 11.

Junior Bookshelf, June, 1995, review of *Project Pirates: Amazing Facts! Amazing Fun!,* p. 98.

Kirkus Reviews, October 15, 2007, review of *Space Pirates and the Monster of Malswomp.*

Magpies, May, 1995, Kevin Steinberger, reviews of *A Plunder of Pirates* and *Project Pirates,* p. 36.

Publishers Weekly, August 5, 1996, review of *A Puzzling Day in the Land of the Pharaohs,* p. 442.

Resource Links, February, 2005, Antonia Gisler, review of *Space Pirates: A Map-reading Adventure,* p. 11.

School Librarian, August, 1992, review of *Dreamy Daniel, Brainy Bert,* p. 99; August, 1992, review of *Land Ahoy!,* p. 105; May, 1995, Elizabeth J. King, review of *A Puzzling Day at Castle MacPelican,* p. 62; May, 1995, Stuart Hannabuss, review of *Project Pirates,* p. 68.

School Library Journal, May, 1990, Carolyn Jenks, review of *Hiccup Harry,* p. 90; June, 1995, JoAnn Rees, review of *A Puzzling Day at Castle MacPelican,* p. 76; October, 1996, Jane Claes, review of *A Puzzling Day in the Land of the Pharaohs,* p. 120; August, 1998, Susan Pine, review of *MacPelican's American Adventure,* p. 132; spring, 2001, Margaret Mallett, review of *The Perfect Pizza,* p. 17; summer, 2001, Carol Woolley, review of *The Bin Bears,* p. 73; April, 2002, Jean Lowery, review of *How to Live on Mars,* p. 172; January, 2005, Anne L. Tormohlen, review of *Space Pirates,* p. 101.

Science Books & Films, November, 1992, Barbara Roberts, review of *Land Ahoy!,* p. 244.

ONLINE

Scoular Anderson Home Page, http://www.scoularanderson.co.uk (March 8, 2009).

OTHER

Storybook TV: A Video Collection of Eight Well-loved Children's Picture Books, Introduced and Read by Their Authors, Scottish Council for Educational Technology, 1999.*

*   *   *

ANDERSON, Thomas Scoular
See ANDERSON, Scoular

*   *   *

ARIHARA, Shino 1973-

Personal

Born 1973; married. *Education:* Attended Art Center College of Design.

Addresses

Agent—Gerald and Cullen Rapp, Artist Representatives, 420 Lexington Ave., New York, NY 10170. *E-mail*—shinoillustration@gmail.com.

Career

Illustrator.

Awards, Honors

Bronze medal, Society of Illustrators Los Angeles Illustration West 41 competition.

Illustrator

Christopher Phillips, *Ceci Ann's Day of Why,* Tricycle Press (Berkley, CA), 2006.
Michelle Lord, *A Song for Cambodia,* Lee & Low Books (New York, NY), 2008.
Betsy Franco, *Zero Is the Sound of Snowflakes,* Tricycle Press (Berkley, CA), 2009.

Sidelights

American illustrator Shino Arihara is making a name for herself through her use of gouache in helping tell tales. Gouache is a form of opaque water color that is prepared using gum as a binding agent. Arihara uses this media in two of the picture books she has illustrated: Michelle Lord's *A Song for Cambodia* and Christopher Phillips' *Ceci Ann's Day of Why.*

In *A Song for Cambodia* Lord tells the story of Arn Chorn, a Cambodian musician who survived internment at a forced labor camp under the Khmer Rouge. The Khmer Rouge, led by dictator Pol Pot, was the ruling communist party of Cambodia from 1975 until 1979, when it was toppled by a Vietnamese invasion. Its rule directly caused one of the worst genocides of the twentieth century, killing an estimated one-fifth of the population of Cambodia. As a child, Chorn survived camp internment under this deadly government by learning to play the *khim,* a traditional Cambodian instrument, before escaping into the jungle. Linda Perkins, writing for *Booklist,* described Arihara's contributions to *A Song for Cambodia* as "realistic gouache illustrations [that] depict the terrors of war but refrain from showing graphic violence." A reviewer for *Children's Bookwatch* maintained that Lord's text and Arihara's illustrations merge tastefully and that "the result is a high-quality picturebook." Monika Schroeder, reviewing *A Song for Cambodia* in *School Library Journal,* noted that Arihara's images "underscore the changing mood of Chorn-Pond's story," and a *Kirkus Reviews* contributor maintained that "Arihara crafts somber scenes in broad brushstrokes to illustrate this important story of devastation and rebuilding."

Reflecting the book's upbeat theme, Arihara creates brightly colored gouache images in *Ceci Ann's Day of Why.* This story by Phillips follows a girl who wonders about the world around her. A *Publishers Weekly* reviewer noted that, "using Phillip's spare, Zen-like rhymes as a springboard, newcomer Arihara takes flight with her gouache spreads of everyday childhood situations," and *Booklist* contributor Jennifer Mattson concluded that Arihara's "buoyant images provide little ones with plenty to look at and talk about."

Biographical and Critical Sources

PERIODICALS

Booklist, January 1, 2007, Jennifer Mattson, review of *Ceci Ann's Day of Why,* p. 115; April 1, 2008, Linda Perkins, review of *A Song for Cambodia,* p. 43.
Children's Bookwatch, April, 2008, review of *A Song for Cambodia.*
Kirkus Reviews, February 15, 2008, review of *A Song for Cambodia,.*
Publishers Weekly, October 30, 2006, review of *Ceci Ann's Day of Why,* p. 61; March 10, 2008, review of *A Song for Cambodia,* p. 81.
School Library Journal, April, 2008, Monika Schroeder, review of *A Song for Cambodia,* p. 166.

ONLINE

Shino Arihara Home Page, http://www.shinoillustration. com (May 13, 2009).*

*   *   *

AVERBECK, Jim 1963-

Personal

Born 1963. *Education:* Case Western Reserve University, B.S. (civil engineering); attended University of California, Berkeley.

Addresses

Home—San Francisco, CA. *E-mail*—inablueroom@gmail.com.

Career

Writer and illustrator. Peace Corps, served in Cameroon, 1990-94.

Member

Society of Children's Book Writers and Illustrators (former regional advisor for San Francisco Bay Area).

Awards, Honors

Charlotte Zolotow Honor Award, CCBC, 2009, and Marion Vannett Rideway Award, both for *In a Blue Room.*

Writings

In a Blue Room, illustrated by Trisha Tusa, Harcourt (Orlando, FL), 2008.
except if, Atheneum (New York, NY), 2011.
The Market Bowl, Charlesbridge (New York, NY), 2012.

Sidelights

Beginning his studies in children's literature at the University of California at Berkeley, San Francisco-based writer Jim Averbeck achieved success with his very first picture book, *In a Blue Room.* The winner of a 2009 Charlotte Zolotow Honor Book award, *In a Blue Room* is an imaginative bedtime story that Averbeck described to Web writer Tina Nichols Coury as "a lyrical bedtime book about the relationship between a mother and daughter" that "has a subtle environmental message and a magical twist at the end."

In a Blue Room introduces a young girl named Alice who has no intention of falling asleep at bedtime. She hopes to postpone the inevitable by making demands of her mother that everything in her room be blue in color. Mother adds scented flowers, a cup of hot tea, and a cozy quilt, all of which are not blue, but by the time the lights go out and nighttime creates its blue magic, Alice has fallen asleep. Describing *In a Blue Room* as "the perfect final selection for a pajama storytime," Marian Drabkin noted in her *School Library Journal* review that Averbeck's text "doesn't have a single unnecessary word." In addition to citing the story as "an inventive introduction to color," a *Kirkus Reviews* writer praised Tricia Tusa's gouache, ink, and watercolor art as "the perfect touch," and in *Booklist* Ilene Cooper concluded of *In a Blue Room* that Averbeck "provides a spare, charming text for the talented Tusa to work her artistic magic." "If bedtime books were dances," maintained a

Jim Averbeck's gentle bedtime story **In a Blue Room** *features engaging artwork by Tricia Tusa.* (Illustration copyright © 2008 by Tricia Tusa. Reproduced by permission of Harcourt.)

Publishers Weekly critic, *In a Blue Room* "would be a pas de deux; prose and pictures partner each other effortlessly all the way to the last page."

Biographical and Critical Sources

PERIODICALS

Booklist, April 1, 2008, Ilene Cooper, review of *In a Blue Room,* p. 55.
Bulletin of the Center for Children's Books, May, 2008, Deborah Stevenson, review of *In a Blue Room,* p. 372.
Kirkus Reviews, March 15, 2008, review of *In a Blue Room.*
Publishers Weekly, March 31, 2008, review of *In a Blue Room* p. 62.
School Library Journal, June, 2008, Marian Drabkin, review of *In a Blue Room,* p. 94.

ONLINE

Jim Averbeck Home Page, http://jimaverbeck.com (May 15, 2009).
Jim Averbeck Web log, http://jimaverbeck.blogspot.com (May 15, 2009).
Tina Nichols Coury Web log, http://www.tinanicholscoury blog.com/ (April 15, 2008), Tina Nichols Coury, interview with Averbeck.

B

BAUER, A.C.E.

Personal
Born in Montreal, Quebec, Canada; married; children: two. *Education:* Attended law school.

Addresses
Home—Cheshire, CT (winter); Quebec, Canada (summer).

Career
Writer. Formerly worked as an attorney.

Awards, Honors
Tassy Walden Award for New Voices in Children's Literature finalist, 2002, and Rainbow List citation, American Library Association, 2009, both for *No Castles Here.*

Writings

No Castles Here, Random House (New York, NY), 2007.

Sidelights
Canadian-born author A.C.E. Bauer, who lives part of the year in southern New England, is the author of the middle-grade novel *No Castles Here,* a story that combines fantasy with the everyday as it describes the life of a shy, oft-bullied preteen growing up in a scrappy, drug-infested city environment.

In *No Castles Here* readers meet Augie Boretski, an eleven year old who lives with his single mom in an upstairs apartment in a rough area of the depressed city of Camden, New Jersey. Augie's theft of a possibly magical book of fairy tales reaps surprising consequences, especially after his school—the bookish boy's

refuge—is damaged in an ice storm and slated to be shut down. In addition, he must deal with such everyday issues as interactions with his new mentor from Big Brothers and his forced membership in a local musical

Cover of A.C.E. Bauer's young-adult novel No Castles Here, *featuring artwork by Danny "casroc" Casu.* (Illustration copyright © 2007 by Danny "casroc" Casu. All rights reserved. Reproduced by permission of Random House Children's Books, a division of Random House, Inc.)

chorus. A *Kirkus Reviews* writer commented of *No Castles Here* that "complex characters and an infinitely readable text make this one of the strongest titles of the year," while in *Booklist,* Kathleen Odean deemed Bauer's story "heartwarming." Norah Piehl, writing for *KidsReads* online, noted that combining fairy tales and a Camden setting seems ambitious, but, "remarkably, Bauer fulfills the task seemingly with ease, resulting in a story in which magic can seem real but in which the real magic occurs in the relationships between people." *School Library Journal* contributor Lillian Hecker called *No Castles Here* "a successful mingling of genres and a testament to the truths in timeless tales."

Biographical and Critical Sources

PERIODICALS

Booklist, December 1, 2007, Kathleen Odean, review of *No Castles Here,* p. 42.
Kirkus Reviews, September 15, 2007, review of *No Castles Here.*
School Library Journal, October, 2007, Lillian Hecker, review of *No Castles Here,* p. 144.

ONLINE

KidsReads Web site, http://www.kidsreads.com/ (May 13, 2009), Nora Piehl, review of *No Castles Here.**

*   *   *

BERNHEIMER, Kate

Personal

Female. *Education:* Wesleyan University, B.A.; University of Arizona, Tucson, M.F.A.

Addresses

Home—Tuscaloosa, AL.

Career

Writer and editor. *Fairy Tale Review,* founder and editor.

Writings

FICTION

The Complete Tales of Ketzia Gold (adult novel), Fiction Collective Two (Tallahassee, FL), 2001.

The Complete Tales of Merry Gold (adult novel), Fiction Collective Two (Tuscaloosa, AL), 2006.
The Girl in the Castle inside the Museum (picture book), illustrated by Nicoletta Ceccoli, Schwartz & Wade (New York, NY), 2008.
The Lonely Book, Schwartz & Wade (New York, NY), 2010.

EDITOR

Mirror, Mirror on the Wall: Women Writers Explore Their Favorite Fairy Tales, Anchor (New York, NY), 1998, second edition, 2002.
Brothers and Beasts: An Anthology of Men on Fairy Tales, Wayne State University Press (Detroit, MI), 2007.

Editor of a fairy-tale anthology for Penguin Books, 2010.

Sidelights

Teacher and scholar Kate Bernheimer has wrapped fairy tales into many aspects of her writing. In addition to original works, she has served as an editor of essay collections featuring the thoughts of notable writers such as Julia Alvarez and bell hooks in *Mirror, Mirror on the Wall: Women Writers Explore Their Favorite Fairy Tales* and Neil Gaiman and Gregory Maguire in *Brothers and Beasts: An Anthology of Men on Fairy Tales.* Discussing *Mirror, Mirror on the Wall* in *Herizons,* a critic noted that "anyone with an interest in fairy tales, from the casual reader to the academic, should find something worthwhile here," and *Library Journal* reviewer Katherine K. Koenig called the collection "a refreshingly honest took at the genre on a realistic and personal level." Bernheimer is also the editor of the annual literary journal, *Fairy Tale Review,* which features contemporary prose and poetry inspired by traditional tales. Each issue is assigned a color, much like nineteenth-century anthologist Andrew Lang's *Blue Fairy Book* and its many-hued sequels. "If 'The Blue Issue' is representative of the annual volumes to come," wrote Jennifer Orme in evaluating *Fairy Tale Review* for *Marvels and Tales* online, then readers interested in the impact of fairy tales on modern literature "have something to look forward to."

Bernheimer uses fairy-tale motifs to explore modern life in her adult novels *The Complete Tales of Ketzia Gold* and its sister novel *The Complete Tales of Merry Gold.* Inspired by tales from Germany and Russia, as well as Yiddish stories, Bernheimer recounts the unsettled marriage of Katzia Gold, whose husband fills some of the tropes of the eerie "Blue-beard" story. Evelin Sullivan, writing in the *Review of Contemporary Fiction,* called *The Complete Tales of Ketzia Gold* an "intriguing first novel" and a "captivating debut." In *Marvels and Tales* Helen Pilinovsky found Bernheimer's book to be "a fascinating exploration of the many levels that fairy tales influence in the human psyche."

The Complete Tales of Merry Gold is more comedic than *The Complete Tales of Ketzia Gold*, but it has the same dark subtext; as Pedro Ponce observed in the *Review of Contemporary Fiction*, Bernheimer "evokes childhood and its aftermath in all their often-overlooked complexity" in this work.

With *The Girl in the Castle inside the Museum*, Bernheimer shares her love of fairy tales with a new audience: young readers. In the story, which is illustrated by Italian artist Nicoletta Ceccoli, a little girl lives in a castle in a snow globe that sits in a toy museum. Children who look hard enough can see into the girl's world, and when the girl looks out at her visitors, she asks them for a picture to hang on her lonely, empty wall. A *Kirkus Reviews* contributor maintained that the museum serves as an allegory for forgotten fairy tales, as well as a plea for children to read the old stories, calling *The Girl in the Castle inside the Museum* "an invitation too good to decline for the fairy-tale lovers among us." As a *Publishers Weekly* critic concluded, "young fans of fantasy will be spellbound," and Jon Kindig wrote in *School Library Journal* that Bernheimer's "unusual book will jump-start the imaginations of all who are lucky enough to enter it."

Biographical and Critical Sources

PERIODICALS

Booklist, June 1, 2008, Ilene Cooper, review of *The Girl in the Castle inside the Museum*, p. 88.

Herizons, spring, 1999, review of *Mirror, Mirror on the Wall: Women Writers Explore Their Favorite Fairy Tales*, pp. 35-36.

Kirkus Reviews, February 1, 2008, review of *The Girl in the Castle inside the Museum*.

Library Journal, June 15, 1998, Katherine K. Koenig, review of *Mirror, Mirror on the Wall*, p. 80.

Marvels and Tales, April, 2003, Helen Pilinovsky, review of *The Complete Tales of Ketzia Gold*, p. 175; April, 2007, Jennifer Orme, review of *Fairy Tale Review*, p. 149.

Publishers Weekly, September 3, 2001, review of *The Complete Tales of Ketzia Gold*, p. 64; February 4, 2008, review of *The Girl in the Castle inside the Museum*, p. 56.

Review of Contemporary Fiction, spring, 2002, Evelin Sullivan, review of *The Contemporary Tales of Ketzia Gold*, p. 125; spring, 2007, Pedro Ponce, review of *The Complete Tales of Merry Gold*, p. 165.

School Library Journal, February, 2008, Joan Kindig, review of *The Girl in the Castle inside the Museum*, p. 82.

ONLINE

Fairy Tale Review Online, http://www.fairytalereview.com/ (May 13, 2009).

BLOOR, Edward 1950-
(Edward William Bloor)

Personal

Born October 12, 1950, in Trenton, NJ; son of Edward William and Mary Bloor; married Pamela Dixon (a teacher), August 4, 1984; children: Amanda Kristin, Spencer Dixon. *Education:* Fordham University, B.A., 1973.

Addresses

Home—Winter Garden, FL. *E-mail*—ebloor@edward-bloor.net.

Career

Novelist and editor. English teacher in Florida public high schools, 1983-86; Harcourt Brace School Publishers, Orlando, FL, senior editor, beginning 1986.

Awards, Honors

Books in the Middle Outstanding Titles listee, Pick of the List designation, American Booksellers Association, and included among 100 Titles for Reading and Sharing, New York Public Library, all 1997, and Top Ten Best Books for Young Adults and Best Books for Young Adults citations, both American Library Association, and Edgar Allan Poe Award nomination for Best Young Adult Novel, Mystery Writers of America, both 1998, all for *Tangerine;* Silver Medal in Young-Adult Fiction, Florida Book Awards, 2007, for *Taken;* First Place award in YA Hardcover category, Bookbinders' Guild of New York, 2008, for *London Calling.*

Writings

Tangerine, Harcourt Brace (San Diego, CA), 1997.
Crusader, Harcourt Brace (San Diego, CA), 1999.
Story Time, Harcourt (Orlando, FL), 2004.
London Calling, Harcourt (Orlando, FL), 2005.
Taken, Alfred A. Knopf (New York, NY), 2007.

Contributor to anthologies, including *Dear Author: Letters of Hope, What a Character!,* and *Guys Write for Guys Read,* edited by Jon Scieszka.

Author's work has been translated into Italian and French.

Adaptations

Several of Bloor's novels were adapted as audiobook, including *Tangerine,* Recorded Books, 2001. *Crusader* was optioned for film by CrushFilm, Ltd.

Sidelights

A former high school English teacher, Edward Bloor managed to establish his career as a writer while working as a book editor at a major publishing house and

Edward Bloor (Reproduced by permission of Edward Bloor.)

helping to raise his two children. His well-received novels for teen readers include *Crusader, Story Time, Taken,* and his award-winning debut novel *Tangerine.* As Bloor once told *SATA,* "My teaching job led to a job in educational publishing, where I was actually required to sit and read young adult novels all day long. So I decided to try it myself."

Born in 1950, Bloor was raised in Trenton, New Jersey, and recalled that, during his childhood, soccer reigned supreme. "Different ethnic communities—Poles, Italians, Germans, Ukrainians—all had their kids' soccer clubs. Parents of the children on these teams raged and howled at the games as if their national pride was at stake. I was one of those little kids trying desperately to kick a soccer ball amidst the multilingual howling. I continued my soccer playing through high school, on a really good team, and into college, on a really bad team." Bloor's memories of the game eventually found their way into his fiction.

In the meantime, Bloor graduated from college, then worked for three years as a teacher. He began his career in children's publishing in 1986, and came up with the idea for his first novel while commuting to work on Florida's back roads west of Orlando. As he once recalled: "To my dismay, I watched the daily destruction of the citrus groves along this route. This is how it happens: The citrus trees are uprooted and bulldozed into piles; the piles are set on fire; the charred remains of the trees are buried, and tons of white sand are dumped over their graves. After that, a completely different place is created, a place as fictional as any novel. A developer

erects a wall, thinks of a theme, and gives the place a name. Then the place fills up with large houses and with people whose only common bond is that they qualified for the same amount of mortgage money." Upset by the changing landscape, Bloor asked himself: "Who are the people who used to make a go of it here? Who are the people now making their exit while we're making our entrance? And how do they feel about all this?"

Bloor addresses such questions in his debut novel, 1997's *Tangerine.* Set in the tangerine-growing region of Florida, the novel touches on environmental and social issues while exploring the trials of its legally blind, soccer-playing protagonist, Paul Fisher. As Bloor once explained: "Paul lives in constant fear of his evil older brother, Erik. Paul also struggles mightily to lead a normal life and to see things as they really are despite the thick-framed glasses that cover his injured eyes. Playing goalie in soccer is at the core of Paul's life, and he gets to do it on two teams, one of which is a mixture of boys and girls. It is the clash of these two teams, these two schools, and these two worlds that brings about the climactic scenes of the novel."

Bulletin of the Center for Children's Books reviewer Deborah Stevenson praised *Tangerine* as "a richly imag-

Cover of Bloor's middle-grade novel **Tangerine,** *featuring artwork by Joel Peter Johnson.* (Illustration copyright © 1997 by Joel Peter Johnson. Reproduced by permission of Harcourt, Inc.)

ined read about an underdog coming into his own," while a *Kirkus Reviews* critic cited "a series of gripping climaxes and revelations" as among the book's strengths. Noting that well-rounded characterization and a humorous edge add to the appeal of the book, *Booklist* reviewer Kathleen Squires asserted that "this dark, debut novel proves that Bloor is a writer to watch."

Bloor also draws readers to southern Florida in his second novel, *Crusader*. Here he focuses on fifteen-year-old Roberta, who works in her uncle's virtual-reality arcade in a seedy suburban strip mall. Roberta has felt helpless since her mother's murder seven years ago, and the strangeness of her home life and the virulent atmosphere at the arcade make her loneliness and adolescent growing pains even more painful. When a brutal new racist video game called Crusader taps into the ethnic hatreds of the arcade's customers and brings in an even more violent clientele, Roberta begins to see how distorted her world is. She breaks from her family's traditions, and begins to take action to track down her mother's murderer, in addition to furthering her own career as a journalist.

While some reviewers noted that the novel's multiple plot lines sometimes tangle, Frances Bradburn wrote in *Booklist* that Bloor's message in *Crusader*—that life holds "no easy answers"—makes the novel "a stretch book in the truest sense." Praising the novel as "ambitious," a *Publishers Weekly* reviewer added that its "characters are sharply drawn" and concluded that in *Crusader* Bloor's storyline is "deeper, denser, and more complex than most YA fare." Echoing the praise of these reviewers, a *Horn Book* contributor noted that the novel's "situations and characters are both intriguing and unsettling," and that Bloor successfully supplies readers with "palpable atmosphere and a fascinating range of undeniable human characters."

Story Time draws on Bloor's quirky sense of humor as well as his short tenure as a public-school teacher. In this darkly comic, quasi-ghost story, eighth grader Kate Melvil and her very bright, slightly younger uncle George are unexpectedly transferred into the Whittaker Magnet School. There they expect to be challenged by advanced classwork in the county's "Leave No High-Scoring Child Behind" program. Instead, they spend much of the time in the school's basement, where they are barraged by an endless stream of practice tests, horrid health-food concoctions, exercise regimens designed to keep them in top testing shape, administrative mumbo jumbo from a controlling principal who plays favorites, and a malevolent presence emanating from a collection of old books in the school's upper regions. Large vocabulary words are memorized, but their meanings are never understood; the principal's quest is for higher test scores, not education. As Bloor noted in an interview posted on the Harcourt Books Web site, the message behind *Story Time* is that "standarized testing is not really about [students] . . . at all. It is about real estate and politics and money, but not about them. Therefore,

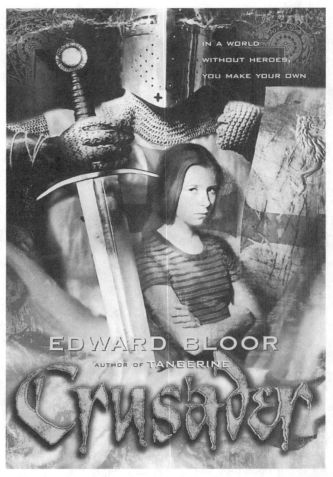

Cover of Bloor's historical novel Crusader, *featuring artwork by Cliff Nielson.* (Illustration copyright © 1999 by Cliff Nielsen. Reproduced by permission of Harcourt, Inc.)

they should not let such tests upset them. They should concentrate on discovering and developing their God-given talents."

Story Time was praised by several reviewers, *Kliatt* critic Paula Rohrlick describing the novel as "a funny, offbeat, often Gothic tale." While, as a *Kirkus Reviews* contributor noted, adult readers "will relish this wild satire on modern education," Bloor's novel addresses readers on more than one level; the engaging characters, bizarre plot twists, and haunted library setting balance what a *Publishers Weekly* contributor dubbed as "a no-holds-barred, deeply subversive tale about modern education." While Mary R. Hofmann wrote in her *School Library Journal* review that *Story Time* is "overly ambitious" in its attempt to combine "social satire, black comedy, fantasy/humor, and extreme situations," she added that Bloor nonetheless creates an "expansive and engrossing tale" on the order of works by writers Roald Dahl and *Peter Pan* author J.M. Barrie.

In *London Calling* the initial setting is the exclusive New Jersey college preparatory school that eighth-grader Martin Conway attends on a scholarship. To avoid the derision of his more-affluent peers, Martin

signs up for an independent study project he can work on at home: the study of the bombing of London, England, during World War II. A 1940s radio that once belonged to his grandmother brings Martin into contact with a boy from that era, and while returning to the past to help the boy, Martin also finds solutions to many of his problems from his own present. Bloor's "evocative descriptions and elegant phrasings make the writing most enjoyable," noted *School Library Journal* contributor Cheri Dobbs, the critic adding that the first-person narration in *London Calling* helps readers "feel Martin's turmoil and angst." Although noting that Bloor "demands much of his readers," such as an understanding of the complex diplomatic relationships during wartime, Jennifer Mattson added in *Booklist* that the novel is "provocative and open-ended," and *Kliatt* critic Paula Rohrlick predicted that "Martin's determination and the vivid scenes of London during the Blitz are sure to appeal" to middle-grade history buffs.

While *London Calling* transports readers into the recent past, *Taken* takes them forward in time to the year 2036, where they encounter a society where the wealthy have become targets of kidnappers and now live in isolation. Charity Meyers, the daughter of a wealthy widowed father living in Florida, now joins the growing number of kidnap victims, despite the standard survival training she has received from her home-based schooling. When the ransom exchange goes awry, however, the girl must rely on her wits—as well as the help of a sympathetic kidnapper who is not of her socioeconomic class—in order to return to her family. Her experiences cause Charity to reconsider the value system that she had inherited from her distant, self-involved parents, resulting in what *Kliatt* contributor Janice Flint-Ferguson dubbed "a compelling story with enough suspense to keep readers guessing." "Bloor has written another dark thriller," noted Sharon Senser McKellar in describing *Taken* in *School Library Journal*, and in *Publishers Weekly* a reviewer found the book to be both "deftly constructed" and "as riveting as it is thought-provoking." Calling Bloor's young protagonist "an appealing observer" who gains in social awareness, Lynn Rutan added in her *Booklist* review of *Taken* that the novel "will grab readers at the outset."

Biographical and Critical Sources

PERIODICALS

Booklist, May 15, 1997, Kathleen Squires, review of *Tangerine,* p. 1573; November 15, 1999, Frances Bradburn, review of *Crusader,* p. 614; March 15, 2004, Jennifer Mattson, review of *Story Time,* p. 1306; July 1, 2006, Jennifer Mattson, review of *London Calling,* p. 48; September 1, 2007, Lynn Rutan, review of *Taken,* p. 118.

Bulletin of the Center for Children's Books, March, 1997, Deborah Stevenson, review of *Tangerine,* p. 241.

Horn Book, July-August, 1997, review of *Tangerine,* p. 449; January, 2000, review of *Crusader,* p. 70.

Journal of Adolescent and Adult Literacy, May, 2008, Kathryn Jackson, review of *Taken,* p. 695.

Kirkus Reviews, February 1, 1997, review of *Tangerine,* p. 219; February 15, 2004, review of *Story Time,* p. 174; September 1, 2006, review of *London Calling,* p. 900; October 1, 2007, review of *Taken.*

Kliatt, March, 2004, Paula Rohrlick, review of *Story Time,* p. 6; September, 2006, Paula Rohrlick, review of *London Calling,* p. 8; September, 2007, Janis Flint-Ferguson, review of *Taken,* p. 6.

Publishers Weekly, March 24, 1997, review of *Tangerine,* p. 84; November 8, 1999, review of *Crusader,* p. 69; February 16, 2004, review of *Story Time,* p. 174; September 11, 2006, review of *London Calling,* p. 56; September 3, 2007, review of *Taken,* p. 60.

St. Petersburg Times, February 18, 2002, Holly Atkins, interview with Bloor.

School Library Journal, April, 1997, review of *Tangerine,* p. 1334; March, 2002, Sarah Flowers, review of *Tangerine,* p. 87; April, 2004, Mary R. Hofmann, review of *Story Time,* p. 148; September, 2006, Cheri Dobbs,

Cover of Bloor's novel **London Calling,** *featuring artwork by Ericka O'Rourke.* (Reproduced by permission of Alfred A. Knopf, a division of Random House, Inc.)

review of *London Calling,* p. 200; December, 2007, Sharon Senser McKellar, review of *Taken,* p. 119.

ONLINE

Edward Bloor Home Page, http://www.edwardbloor.net (May 15, 2009).
Harcourt Books Web site, http://www.harcourtbooks.com/ (July 2, 2004), interview with Bloor.*

* * *

BLOOR, Edward William
See BLOOR, Edward

* * *

BOGAN, Paulette 1960-

Personal
Born October 2, 1960, in Pt. Pleasant, NJ; daughter of Howard (a fishing boat captain) and Lucille (a homemaker) Bogan; married Charles Johnston, February 29, 1992; children: Sophia, Rachael, Lucille. *Education:* Attended University of Miami (Miami, FL); Parsons School of Design, B.F.A. (illustration), 1983.

Addresses
Home—New York, NY. *E-mail*—paulettebogan@gmail. com.

Career
Freelance illustrator and writer, 1983—. Parsons School of Design, New York, NY, instructor, 1992-95. *Exhibitions:* Works exhibited in solo and group gallery shows in New York, NY, 1989-94, and Society of Illustrators Original Art Show, 2000.

Awards, Honors
Children's Book Council (CBC) Children's Choice award, 2001, for *Spike in the City;* International Reading Association/CBC Children's Choice designation, 2002, for *Spike in the Kennel; Book Sense* Children's Pick, 2005, for *Chicks and Salsa* by Aaron Reynolds.

Writings

SELF-ILLUSTRATED

Spike, Putnam (New York, NY), 1998.
Spike in the City, Putnam (New York, NY), 2000.
Spike in the Kennel, Putnam (New York, NY), 2001.
Spike in Trouble, Putnam (New York, NY), 2003.

Paulette Bogan (Reproduced by permission.)

Goodnight Lulu, Bloomsbury Children's Books (New York, NY), 2003.
Momma's Magical Purse, Bloomsbury Children's Books (New York, NY), 2004.
Lulu the Big Little Chick, Bloomsbury Children's Books (New York, NY), 2009.

ILLUSTRATOR

Ben Farrell, *Dad Saves the Day,* Silver, Burdett & Ginn, 1992.
Penny Coleman, *One Hundred One Ways to Do Better in School,* Troll Associates (Mahwah, NJ), 1994.
Helen Lester, *Help! I'm Stuck,* Celebration Press (Glenview, IL), 1996.
Jokes, Riddles, and Poems, Scholastic (New York, NY), 1998.
Tracey West, *Teaching Tall Tales across the Curriculum,* Scholastic (New York, NY), 1998.
Kathleen Weidner Zoehfeld, *Fossil Fever,* Golden Books (New York, NY), 2000.
Kathleen Weidner Zoehfeld, *Amazon Fever,* Golden Books (New York, NY), 2001.
Aaron Reynolds, *Chicks and Salsa,* Bloomsbury Children's Books (New York, NY), 2005.
Aaron Reynolds, *Buffalo Wings,* Bloomsbury Children's Books (New York, NY), 2007.

Contributor of illustrations to periodicals, including *New York Times, Ladies' Home Journal, Business Week, Parents, Family Circle, Los Angeles Times Magazine,* and *Billboard.*

Sidelights
Early in her career, Paulette Bogan contributed illustrations to such periodicals as the *New York Times, Ladies'*

Home Journal, Business Week, and *Parents.* She also worked for the book publishers Harcourt Brace Jovanovich, Simon & Schuster, and Scholastic. After the birth of her first two children, however, she decided to make a career change and turned her focus to children's books. In 1992 Bogan broke into children's book illustration with her work for Ben Farrell's picture book *Dad Saves the Day.* Reflecting her talent for storytelling, Bogan has also created several original self-illustrated stories, include a series of picture books about a dog named Spike. As an illustrator, her artwork continues to appear alongside texts by writers such as Kathleen Weidner Zoehfeld, Helen Lester, and Aaron Reynolds. Reviewing the collaborations between Bogan and Reynolds, which include *Chicks and Salsa* and *Buffalo Wings,* a *Publishers Weekly* critic wrote of the former title that the artist's "fiesta-bright comic watercolors evoke the spirit of vintage Warner Bros. animation." "Bogan's humorous illustrations keep the action moving," noted Susan E. Murray in a *School Library Journal* review, and in *Kirkus Reviews* a contributor concluded that the illustrator's "big cartoon scenes capture the increasing excitement" of Reynolds' rhyming text.

The daughter of a fishing-boat captain, Bogan grew up in Brielle, New Jersey. Since the second grade, she wanted to be an artist, and her mother encouraged this interest. During a family outbreak of chicken pox, Bogan and her siblings were allowed to paint a mural on their playroom wall. With such encouragement, the young artist continued to paint throughout her school years. After attending the University of Miami, Bogan went on to earn a degree at the prestigious Parsons School of Design in 1983, and then taught there for several years.

In *Spike,* Bogan introduces her canine hero and describes how Spike, dissatisfied with being a dog, attempts to change himself. After trying out the lives of a horse, a bird, and a fish, Spike learns that he is happy being a dog, and Shannon's dog at that. *Spike in the City* shows what kind of adventures a dog might have visiting the city: he rides an elevator, gets messy with gum, and plays Frisbee in the park. In *Spike in the Kennel* readers follow Spike as he stays overnight at a kennel for the very first time, and *Spike in Trouble* finds the spunky pup getting blamed for things that he did not do.

Bogan's "Spike" books caught the attention of several reviewers. According to a *Kirkus Reviews* contributor, the first book in the series is enlivened by Bogan's "amiable illustrations with strong lines," and *School Library Journal* contributor Shawn Brommer praised the "lively, engaging cartoonlike illustrations" and brisk pacing in *Spike in the City.* Also writing for *School Library Journal,* Marlene Gawron was impressed with Bogan's accurate portrayal of emotions and humor in *Spike in the Kennel.*

Other original picture books in which Bogan pairs story and art include *Momma's Magical Purse, Goodnight Lulu,* and *Lulu the Big Little Chick,* the last two which star a spunky little chicken. In *Goodnight Lulu* the chick is nervous about heading to bed alone in the dark, conjuring up a host of potential worries, until Mother Hen convinces Lulu that all is safe. Determined to prove her independence as a grown-up chick, Lulu heads away from the farm in *Lulu the Big Little Chick,* a picture book with a story that independent-minded toddlers can relate to. In addition to Bogan's "humorous" text, the author/illustrator creates "vibrant watercolor-and-ink illustrations . . . in rich shades," wrote *School Library Journal* critic Linda M. Kenton in a review of *Goodnight Lulu,* while a *Kirkus Reviews* writer compared Bogan's cartoon art to the work of noted illustrator Sandra Boynton. The picture book "is guaranteed to generate giggles, guffaws, and . . . a drowsy 'good night,'" the critic added.

A mother's preparedness for whatever comes is the focus of *Momma's Magical Purse.* Here a kitten named Rachel joins cousin David the dog and Momma Cat on a picnic, only to encounter a series of setbacks. First Rachel hurts her knee, and then raindrops threaten to make the picnic a wash, but Momma manages to solve all these setbacks by pulling the perfect solution from her large, lumpy handbag. Praising the story's rotund feline star as "a hip mama cat with double-pierced ears," *Booklist* critic Lauren Peterson added that *Momma's Magical Purse* features "offbeat humor, campy characterizations, and [an] expressive illustrative style," while in *School Library Journal* Linda L. Walkins praised the picture book's "humorous details" and "paintings that capture the emotions of the characters."

Aaron Reynolds' story of a farmyard with an unusual menu, **Chicks and Salsa** *features amusing artwork by Bogan.* (Illustration copyright © 2005 by Paulette Bogan. Reprinted by permission of Bloomsbury USA. All rights reserved.)

Biographical and Critical Sources

PERIODICALS

Booklist, June 1, 2004, Lauren Peterson, review of *Momma's Magical Purse,* p. 1738.

Family Life, April, 1998, Christine Loomis, "Children's Hour."

Kirkus Reviews, December 1, 1997, review of *Spike,* p. 1773; May 15, 2003, review of *Goodnight Lulu,* p. 746; March 15, 2004, review of *Momma's Magical Purse,* p. 266; October 1, 2005, review of *Chicks and Salsa,* p. 1987; October 1, 2007, review of *Buffalo Wings.*

Publishers Weekly, April 14, 2003, review of *Goodnight Lulu,* p. 69; November 15, 2005, review of *Chicks and Salsa,* p. 68.

School Library Journal, March, 1998, Christine A. Moesch, review of *Spike,* p. 166; May, 2000, Shawn Brommer, review of *Spike in the City,* p. 130; June, 2001, Marlene Gawron, review of *Spike in the Kennel,* p. 102; July, 2003, Linda M. Kenton, review of *Goodnight Lulu,* p. 88; September, 2004, Linda L. Walkins, review of *Momma's Magical Purse,* p. 154; November, 2005, Susan E. Murray, review of *Chicks and Salsa,* p. 104; December, 2007, Lee Bock, review of *Buffalo Wings,* p. 98.

ONLINE

Paulette Bogan Home Page, http://www.paulettebogan. com (May 30, 2009).*

*   *   *

BOWMAN, Catherine
See SMITH, Cat Bowman

*   *   *

BRAASCH, Gary

Personal

Born in Omaha, NE.

Addresses

Home and office—Gary Braasch Environmental Photography, P.O. Box 1465, Portland, OR 97207. *E-mail*—gary@braaschphotography.com.

Career

Photojournalist. *Exhibitions:* Photographs included in the permanent design collection at the Library of Congress.

Member

International League of Conservation Photographers (fellow and board member).

Awards, Honors

Ansel Adams award for conservation photography; Top Fifty designation for environmental books and DVDs, *Vanity Fair* magazine, 2007, for *Earth under Fire;* Best Middle-Grade Science Book designation (with Lynn Cherry), American Association for the Advancement of Science, 2009, for *How We Know What We Know about Our Changing Climate;* Nikon Legend behind the Lens citation.

Writings

(And photographer) *Photographing the Patterns of Nature,* Amphoto (New York, NY), 1990, revised and updated edition, 1999.

(And photographer) *Williamette University,* Harmony House (Louisville, KY), 1992.

(And photographer) *Earth under Fire: How Global Warming Is Changing the World,* University of California Press (Berkley, CA), 2007.

(With Lynne Cherry; and photographer) *How We Know What We Know about Our Changing Climate: Scientists and Kids Explore Global Warming,* Dawn Publications (Nevada City, CA), 2008.

PHOTOGRAPHER

David Kelly, *Secrets of the Old Growth Forest,* Gibbs-Smith (Salt Lake City, UT), 1988.

Bruce Brown, *The Northwest: Pacific Coast and Cascades,* Rizzoli (New York, NY), 1988.

Kim Robert Stafford, *Entering the Grove,* Peregrine Smith Books (Salt Lake City, UT), 1990.

Contributor to journals, including *Time, Life, Discover, Audubon, National Wildlife, Smithsonian, Scientific American, International Wildlife, Natural History, Sierra, Animals, Terre Sauvage, Photo* (French edition), *Outdoor Photographer, Photo District News, 2wice, BBC Wildlife,* and *Animan.*

Sidelights

Award-winning photojournalist Gary Braasch does not limit himself to working in his native United States; in his quest to document the effects of rapid climate change, Braasch has visited China, Australia, Tuvalu, Antarctica, and the Arctic. He has also photographed ecosystems in Alaska, Hawaii, Florida, Tennessee, Peru, and Venezuela, studying, with his camera, everything from Mount St. Helens to a single tree.

Braasch's books on climate change include *Earth under Fire: How Global Warming Is Changing the World* and *How We Know What We Know about Our Changing Climate: Scientists and Kids Explore Global Warming,* the latter coauthored with Lynne Cherry. *Earth under Fire* documents environmental evidence of possible

global climate change, such as changing polar bear habitats, disappearing islands, coral-reef bleaching, and receding glaciers. In *E* Jim Motavalli commented that "beyond the striking photographs are clearly written essays" by contributing scientists and a *Science News* writer described the work as a collection of "eyewitness accounts of the detrimental effects of global warming through a combination of stark photography and detailed text." In *Booklist* Pamela Crossland wrote that, in spite of the complex science surrounding global warming, the scientific theory's "impact is made comprehensible in this richly photographic blend of memoir and reportage."

Geared for a younger audience, *How We Know What We Know about Our Changing Climate* explains the science that led to man's awareness of climate change. As Kathy Piehl explained in *School Library Journal,* "Small color photographs show the fieldwork and experiments of scientists and students," and a *Kirkus Reviews* writer dubbed Braasch and Cherry's book "a must for school libraries." Ilene Cooper, writing for *School Library Journal,* commented that Braasch's "intriguing color photographs are thoughtful and upbeat," and a *Publishers Weekly* reviewer concluded that *How We Know What We Know about Our Changing Climate* is a "beautifully photographed global guide [that] offers a look at how research in diverse fields leads to an understanding of the warming climate."

Biographical and Critical Sources

PERIODICALS

Booklist, October 15, 2007, Pamela Crossland, review of *Earth under Fire: How Global Warming Is Changing the World,* p. 10; February 15, 2008, Ilene Cooper, review of *How We Know What We Know about Our Changing Climate: Scientists and Kids Explore Global Warming,* p. 88.

E, March-April, 2008, Jim Motavalli, "Danger Signs," p. 60.

Horn Book, September-October 2008, Danielle J. Ford, review of *How We Know What We Know about Our Changing Climate,* p. 609.

Kirkus Reviews, March 1, 2008, review of *How We Know What We Know about Our Changing Climate.*

Publishers Weekly, March 10, 2008, review of *How We Know What We Know about Our Changing Climate,* p. 83.

School Library Journal, June, 2008, Kathy Piehl, review of *How We Know What We Know about Our Changing Climate,* p. 155.

Science News, October 13, 2007, review of *Earth under Fire,* p. 239.

Science Scope, April-May 2008, Suzanne Flynn, review of *How We Know What We Know about Our Changing Climate,* p. 75.

ONLINE

Gary Braasch Home Page, http://www.braaschphoto graphy.com (May 14, 2009).*

* * *

BROYLES, Anne 1953-

Personal

Born 1953, in Tucson, AZ; married Larry Peacock (a minister), 1977; children: Trinity, Justus. *Education:* University of Arizona, graduated; Garrett-Evangelical Theological Seminary, degree, 1979. *Religion:* Methodist.

Addresses

Home—Eastern MA. *E-mail*—annebroyles@anne broyles.com.

Career

Minister and author. Malibu United Methodist Church, Malibu, CA, co-pastor until 1999; full-time author.

Awards, Honors

Notable Social Studies Trade Book for Young People designation, 2001, and Teachers' Choice Award, *Learning* magazine, 2002, both for *Shy Mama's Halloween;* Notable Social Studies Trade Book for Young People designation, and Best Children's Books of the Year, Bank Street College of Education, both 2008, both for *Priscilla and the Hollyhocks.*

Writings

FOR CHILDREN

Shy Mama's Halloween, illustrated by Leane Morin, Tilbury House (Gardiner, ME), 2000.

Priscilla and the Hollyhocks, illustrated by Anna Alter, Charlesbridge (Watertown, MA), 2008.

OTHER

Meeting God through Worship, Abingdon Press (Nashville, TN), 1992.

Growing Together in Love: God Known through Family Life, Upper Room Books (Nashville, TN), 1993.

Journaling: A Spiritual Journey, Upper Room Books (Nashville, TN), 1999.

At Home with God: Family Devotions for the School Year, Upper Room Books (Nashville, TN), 2002.

Contributor to books, including *Prayers for Our Country: Daily Prayer Book,* Publications international, Ltd. (Lincolnwood, IL), 2002.

Sidelights

A Christian minister, Anne Broyles began writing as a way of sharing her faith with others in books such as *Meeting God through Worship* and *At Home with God: Family Devotions for the School Year.* She also entertains young readers in the picture books *Shy Mama's Halloween* and *Priscilla and the Hollyhocks,* both of which are set during an interesting time in U.S. history. *Shy Mama's Halloween,* for example, focuses on the Halloween holiday and how it is experienced by a woman who has recently emigrated from Russia to Ellis Island with her four children. Broyles' second picture book, *Priscilla and the Hollyhocks,* is set in the American south during the U.S. Civil War and features artwork by Anne Alter.

In *Priscilla and the Hollyhocks,* which is based on a true story, Broyles introduces a young girl who works as a house slave until her master dies. After she watches her mother being purchased by a new owner, Priscilla is sold to a Native-American family. As the years pass, the girl experiences the difficulties faced by the Cherokee, including their eventual expulsion to an arid reservation, before being given her freedom by a long-time friend. Although they never meet again, Priscilla's memories of her mother are unleashed when she sees the beautiful flowers of the tall hollyhock. Reviewing *Priscilla and the Hollyhocks, School Library Journal* critic Julia R. Ranelli noted that Broyles' story is narrated "in descriptive language" and "offers a unique perspective on slavery." In *Booklist* Kristen McKulski praised "Broyles' poetic and colloquial narrative," while in *School Library Journal* Bina Williams concluded that the author's use of "details in both the text and the artwork set the story firmly in the past."

On her home page, Broyles discussed the inspiration for her writing. "Ideas flit in and out of my mind all day long," she admitted. "I've also awakened from dreams with a book titles and plots in mind—it can be quite distracting! If I hear a story or read a newspaper article, my mind automatically jumps to, 'How would this story have been different if. . .?' My imagination may be sparked by an interesting figure of speech, an unusual person, or a desire to learn more about a particular place or time. I always keep a notebook with me so I can write down bits and pieces of stories to work on later. Like most writers, I look at the world through the lens of 'What if. . . .'"

Biographical and Critical Sources

PERIODICALS

Booklist, November 15, 2000, John Peters, review of *Shy Mama's Halloween,* p. 646; February 1, 2008, Kristen McKulski, review of *Priscilla and the Hollyhocks,* p. 60.

Kirkus Reviews, February 15, 2008, review of *Priscilla and the Hollyhocks.*

Publishers Weekly, September 25, 2000, Elizabeth Devereaux, review of *Shy Mama's Halloween,* p. 64.

School Library Journal, January, 2001, Bina Williams, review of *Shy Mama's Halloween,* p. 91; March, 2008, Julie R. Ranelli, review of *Priscilla and the Hollyhocks* p. 155.

ONLINE

Anne Broyles Home Page, http://www.annebroyles.com (May 15, 2009).*

C

CAPLE, Laurie 1958-

Personal

Born 1958; married; children: two sons. *Education:* Michigan Technological University, earned degree.

Addresses

Home—WI. *Agent*—Sheldon Fogelman Agency, 10 E. 40th St., Ste. 3205, New York, NY 10016. *E-mail*—lcaple@charter.net.

Career

Artist and illustrator. Artist-in-residence, Hamline University's Center for Global Environmental Education; former creative consultant for *Once upon a Tree* television series.

Awards, Honors

Best Books for Children inclusion, *Science Books and Films* magazine, 1999, for *Bug Watching with Charles Henry Turner* and *Bird Watching with Margaret Morse Nice.*

Illustrator

Margaret K. Wetterer, *Clyde Tombaugh and the Search for Planet X,* Carolrhoda (Minneapolis, MN), 1996.

Michael Elsohn Ross, *Bird Watching with Margaret Morse Nice,* Carolrhoda (Minneapolis, MN), 1997.

Michael Elsohn Ross, *Bug Watching with Charles Henry Turner,* Carolrhoda (Minneapolis, MN), 1997.

Michael Elsohn Ross, *Flower Watching with Alice Eastwood,* Carolrhoda (Minneapolis, MN), 1997.

Michael Elsohn Ross, *Wildlife Watching with Charles Eastman,* Carolrhoda (Minneapolis, MN), 1997.

Caroline Arnold, *Giant Shark,* Clarion (New York, NY), 2000.

Caroline Arnold, *Dinosaurs with Feathers: The Ancestors of Modern Birds,* Clarion (New York, NY), 2001.

Caroline Arnold, *When Mammoths Walked the Earth,* Clarion (New York, NY), 2002.

Laurie Caple

Pat Brisson, *Mama Loves Me from Away,* Boyds Mills (Honesdale, PA), 2004.

Caroline Arnold, *Pterosaurs: Rulers of the Skies in the Dinosaur Age,* Clarion (New York, NY), 2004.

Kathy-Jo Wargin, *The Legend of Old Abe, a Civil War Eagle,* Sleeping Bear Press (Chelsea, MI), 2006.

Caroline Arnold, *Giant Sea Reptiles of the Dinosaur Age,* Clarion (New York, NY), 2007.

Kathy-jo Wargin, *North Star Numbers: A Minnesota Number Book,* Sleeping Bear Press (Chelsea, MI), 2008.

Caroline Arnold, *Global Warming and the Dinosaurs: Fossil Discoveries at the Poles,* Clarion (New York, NY), 2009.

Contributor of illustrations to *American Girl* and *Cricket* magazines.

Sidelights

Illustrator Laurie Caple grew up in Michigan's Upper Peninsula, a landscape that gave her an appreciation for nature that she carries over into her artwork. Caple's interest in capturing the natural world with her art has led to her position as artist-in-residence at Hamline University's Center for Global Environmental Education. When not working on her illustrations, Caple spends time near her Wisconsin home, hiking and photographing the natural world or watching wildlife from her studio.

Caple began her career as an illustrator by creating art for Michael Elshon Ross's children's-book biographies of famous naturalists and scientists, two of which were named to the Best Books for Children list of *Science Books and Film* magazine. She has continued to illustrate nonfiction titles for children, contributing artwork to picture books such as Caroline Arnold's *Dinosaurs with Feathers: The Ancestors of Modern Birds.* In her illustrations for this work, Caple illustrates the similar features that are shared by both birds and feathered dinosaurs, an interesting phenomenon considering that the two species are not related. "Caple's watercolors are clear and lively, and not overly dramatic," wrote Stephen Engelfried in a *School Library Journal* review of *Dinosaurs with Feathers.*

The era of the dinosaurs has been the setting for many of Caple's nonfiction books, most of them written by Arnold. The duo profiles the pterosaur, the only flying reptile, in *Pterosaurs: Rulers of the Skies in the Dinosaur Age.* Here "Caple's neatly labeled watercolors emphasize clarity over drama," wrote Jennifer Mattson in *Booklist,* the critic adding that the weird features of the pterosaurs that are depicted in Caple's art "will draw kids into the diorama-like tableaus." Sandra Welzenbach noted in *School Library Journal* that "Caple keeps the watercolor paintings subtle and subdued" in *Giant Sea Reptiles of the Dinosaur Age,* another collaboration between Arnold and Caple, and in *Horn Book* Danielle J. Ford found Caple's illustrations for this same book to be "finely detailed."

Caple and Arnold explore the ice age and introduce readers to the extinct mastodon in *When Mammoths Walked the Earth.* Of Caple's work in this book, Ellen Heath wrote in *School Library Journal* that the "watercolors are realistic, detailed, and surprisingly beautiful." In *Horn Book* Ford praised the book's "precise illustrations," which "convey a sense of the pristine vastness of ancient landscapes."

Along with her educational nonfiction, Caple has illustrated a counting book and the retelling of an old legend, both by Kathy-Jo Wargin, as well as an original picture book by Pat Brisson titled *Mama Loves Me from Away.* Brisson's tale finds a mother and daughter separated when the mother is sent to prison. "Caple's realistic watercolors focus on the child's face, portraying a sense of deep sadness, confusion, and loss," wrote a *Kirkus Reviews* contributor in reviewing the poignant picture book.

Biographical and Critical Sources

PERIODICALS

Booklist, October 1, 2001, John Peters, review of *Dinosaurs with Feathers: The Ancestors of Modern Birds,* p. 313; August, 2002, Julie Cummins, review of *When Mammoths Walked the Earth,* p. 1952; December 1, 2004, Jennifer Mattson, review of *Pterosaurs: Rulers of the Skies in the Dinosaur Age,* p. 665; December 15, 2004, review of *Mama Loves Me from Away,* p. 746; August, 2007, Ilene Cooper, review of *Giant Sea Reptiles of the Dinosaur Age,* p. 67.
Childhood Education, summer, 2006, Isabel Killoran, review of *Mama Loves Me from Away,* p. 244.
Horn Book, November-December, 2002, Danielle J. Ford, review of *When Mammoths Walked the Earth,* p. 772; January-February, 2008, Danielle J. Ford, review of *Giant Sea Reptiles of the Dinosaur Age,* p. 105.
Kirkus Reviews, July 15, 2002, review of *When Mammoths Walked the Earth,* p. 1026; October 15, 2004, review of *Mama Loves Me from Away,* p. 1002; November 15, 2004, review of *Pterosaurs,* p. 1087.
Publishers Weekly, December 6, 2004, review of *Mama Loves Me from Away,* p. 60.
School Library Journal, November, 2001, Steven Engelfried, review of *Dinosaurs with Feathers,* p. 140; October, 2002, Ellen Heath, review of *When Mammoths Walked the Earth,* p. 136; February, 2005, Holly T. Sneeringer, review of *Mama Loves Me from Away,* p. 94; September, 2007, Sandra Welzenbach, review of *Giant Sea Reptiles of the Dinosaur Age,* p. 213.

ONLINE

Children's Literature Network Web site, http://www.childrensliteraturenetwork.org/ (May 13, 2009), profile of Caple.
Laurie Caple Home Page, http://www.lauriecaple.com (May 13, 2009).
Sleeping Bear Press Web site, http://www.sleepingbearpress.com/ (May 13, 2009), profile of Caple.*

*   *   *

CLINE-RANSOME, Lesa

Personal

Born in MA; daughter of nurses; married James E. Ransome (an illustrator); children: Jaime, Maya, Malcolm, Leila. *Education:* Pratt Institute, degree; New York University, M.A. (early childhood and elementary education).

Addresses

Home—Rhinebeck, NY. *E-mail*—info@lesaclineran some.com.

Career

Author. Lord & Taylor, New York, NY, member of advertising staff; former elementary teacher.

Awards, Honors

(All with James E. Ransome) Notable Book designation, American Library Association (ALA), Bank Street College of Education Best Children's Book of the Year designation, Children's Literature Choice listee, and Notable Social Studies Trade Book designation, National Council for the Social Studies/Children's Book Council, all 2000, all for *Satchel Paige;* Capitol Choices listee, 2004, for *Major Taylor, Champion Cyclist;* Image Award nomination, National Association for the Advancement of Colored People, 2008, for *Young Pelé.*

Writings

Satchel Paige, illustrated by James E. Ransome, Simon & Schuster Books for Young Readers (New York, NY), 2000.

Quilt Alphabet, illustrated by James E. Ransome, Holiday House (New York, NY), 2001.

Quilt Counting, illustrated by James E. Ransome, Seastar Books (New York, NY), 2002.

Major Taylor, Champion Cyclist, illustrated by James E. Ransome, Atheneum Books for Young Readers (New York, NY), 2004.

Young Pelé: Soccer's First Star, illustrated by James E. Ransome, Schwartz & Wade (New York, NY) 2007.

Helen Keller: The World in Her Heart, illustrated by James E. Ransome, HarperCollins (New York, NY), 2008.

Joseph Boulogne, Chevalier de Saint-George, illustrated by James E. Ransome, Schwartz & Wade (New York, NY), 2010.

Sidelights

Lesa Cline-Ransome would likely have become involved in children's literature even if she did not harbor a lifelong love of writing; her husband, James E. Ransome, is a noted illustrator of children's books. Encouraged by James to follow her interest, Cline-Ransome has created several picture-book texts that have been paired with her husband's paintings. Focusing on sports figures, *Satchel Paige, Major Taylor, Champion Cyclist,* and *Young Pelé: Soccer's First Star* encourage budding athletes through stories of perseverence, while in *Quilt Alphabet* and *Quilt Counting* husband and wife pair colorful paintings and simple rhymes to capture a family-centered, rural feel. In *Helen Keller: The World in Her Heart* Cline-Ransome introduces new generations of children to the pivotal childhood experiences of

a woman who lived an exemplary life of service despite the challenges created by being both blind and deaf. In *School Library Journal* Kathleen Kelly MacMillan described *Helen Keller* as "an excellent, accessible introduction to a fascinating woman," and a *Kirkus Reviews* writer concluded that Cline-Ransome's "rhythmic text" effectively "evoke[s Keller's] . . . shuttered-in world to sighted and hearing children."

One of the most famous African-American baseball players in the United States is the subject of *Satchel Paige,* the first collaboration between Cline-Ransome and her artist husband James. Leroy "Satchel" Paige was the first African-American player to stand on the pitcher's mound during the World Series. In her book Cline-Ransome recounts the development of Paige's unique pitching style, as well as his other contributions to baseball history during his long career, creating what *Black Issues Book Review* contributors Khafre K. Abif and Kelly Ellis described as an "engaging story . . . told with a warm regard for baseball lore." The author "plays up the mythic elements" of Paige's life story, wrote *Booklist* critic Bill Ott, and the paintings created by Cline-Ransome's artist husband "jump off the page with bright colors and startling contrasts." Citing Cline-Ransome's "leisurely down-home style and . . . comfort in storytelling," Martha V. Parravano added in her *Horn Book* review of *Satchel Paige* that the author "packs the text with valuable information." In *Publishers Weekly* a critic dubbed the husband-and-wife collaboration "an informal, anecdotal profile" that features a "conversational and flavorful" text and "boldly hued oil paintings." "Written with a storyteller's sense of rhythm and pacing, Paige's history will be best appreciated as a read-aloud," concluded *School Library Journal* contributor Alicia Eames.

Satchel Paige was followed by the picture-book biography *Major Taylor, Champion Cyclist,* which follows a young boy from Indianapolis who worked hard to gain the speed to win an international bicycle race in the last year of the nineteenth century. Beginning in the early 1890s, Taylor gained skill and speed as a stunt rider, and in 1899 he defeated the reigning world-champion cyclist in Paris, battling racial prejudice all the way. Ironically, the athlete died a pauper at age fifty-three, his accomplishments all but forgotten by the world. Cline-Ransome imbues Taylor's story with "all the elements of a traditional sports tale, complete with a climactic showdown . . . and a triumphant ending," noted *Booklist* contributor Jennifer Mattson, and in *School Library Journal* Lauralyn Persson concluded that *Major Taylor, Champion Cyclist* features a text that is "smoothly written and greatly enhanced by [James E.] Ransome's vivid and accomplished paintings."

South American soccer star Pelé is the focus of *Young Pelé,* and in her picture-book biography Cline-Ransome describes how the noted athlete—born Edson Arates do Nascimento—got his start growing up as part of a poor family in Bauru, Brazil in the 1940s and kicking rocks

and playing with soccer balls made of household rags bound together with string. Praising the book's "handsome oil paintings and . . . stirring story," Hazel Rochman added in her *Booklist* review of *Young Pelé* that Cline-Ransome's tale "will first grab children with its action." The book's "text is focused and cohesive," wrote *Horn Book* contributor Martha V. Parravano, and the author's depiction of Pelé's "struggles and triumphs" is reflective in James E. Ransome's "lush oil paintings" in tones of blue and yellow.

"I always knew that I wanted to be a writer, I just didn't know that I wanted to be a chidren's book writer," Cline-Ransome admitted in an interview posted on her home page. "When I was young, I had hoped to be a journalist, writing investigative pieces for newspapers like the *Boston Globe* or the *New York Times*. And then I realized I was too shy to conduct interviews." "I write biographies because I am fascinated by the lives of others," she added. "I enjoy discovering how a person's childhood impacts their adult lives. I especially love finding the most interesting parts of a person's life, piecing them together and creating a new story for a new group of readers."

Biographical and Critical Sources

PERIODICALS

Booklist, December 15, 1999, Bill Ott, review of *Satchel Paige,* p. 782; September 1, 2001, Ellen Mandel, review of *Quilt Alphabet,* p. 111; February 15, 2004, Jennifer Mattson, review of *Major Taylor, Champion Cyclist,* p. 1077; September 1, 2007, Hazel Rochman, review of *Young Pelé: Soccer's First Star,* p. 136.

Black Issues Book Review, November, 2001, Khafre K. Abif and Kelly Ellis, review of *Satchel Paige,* p. 81.

Horn Book, March, 2000, Martha V. Parravano, review of *Satchel Paige,* p. 207; November-December, 2007, Martha V. Parravano, review of *Young Pelé,* p. 695.

Kirkus Reviews, August 1, 2001, review of *Quilt Alphabet,* p. 1119; July 1, 2002, review of *Quilt Counting,* p. 951; December 15, 2003, review of *Major Taylor, Champion Cyclist,* p. 1448; September 1, 2007, review of *Young Pelé;* June 1, 2008, review of *Helen Keller: The World in Her Heart.*

Publishers Weekly, January 10, 2000, review of *Satchel Paige,* p. 68; December 22, 2003, review of *Major Taylor, Champion Cyclist,* p. 60.

School Library Journal, March, 2000, Alicia Eames, review of *Satchel Paige,* p. 223; November, 2001, Alice Casey Smith, review of *Quilt Alphabet,* p. 143; November, 2002, Catherine Threadgill, review of *Quilt Counting,* p. 119; February, 2004, Lauralyn Persson, review of *Major Taylor, Champion Cyclist,* p. 128; August, 2007, Blair Christolon, review of *Young Pelé,* p. 97; August, 2008, Kathleen Kelly MacMillian, review of *Helen Keller,* p. 109.

ONLINE

Lesa Cline-Ransome Home Page, http://www.lesaclineransome.com (May 15, 2009).*

*   *   *

CRASTE, Marc

Personal

Born in England.

Addresses

Home—England. *Office*—Studio AKA, 30 Berwick St., London W1F 8RH, England.

Career

Animation director and illustrator. Worked in animation studios in Australia and Belgium; Studio aka, London, England, senior animation director.

Awards, Honors

Best Animated Short Film award, British Association for Film and Television Actors, Best Animated Short Film award, Clermont-Ferrand Film Festival (France), and Aspen Short Film Festival Jury Prize, all 2004; Illustrator of the Year Award, AOI.

Writings

(Illustrator) Helen Ward, *Varmints,* Candlewick Press (Cambridge, MA), 2008.

Author of screenplay and animator for films, including *Varmints* and *Jojo in the Stars.*

Biographical and Critical Sources

PERIODICALS

Creative Review, December 3, 2007, review of *Varmints,* p. 16.
Kirkus Reviews, February 15, 2008, review of *Varmints.*

ONLINE

LumenEclipse Web site, http://www.http://222.lumeneclipse.com/ (May 29, 2009), "Marc Craste."*

*   *   *

CUTBILL, Andy 1972-

Personal

Born 1972, in London, England; married; children: one daughter, one son. *Education:* Oxford Brookes University, B.A. (with honors), 1994; graduate studies in art direction.

Addresses

Home—London, England.

Career

Children's author, illustrator, and television series creator; writer of television commercials; freelance copywriter and editor.

Awards, Honors

Best Young Writer of the Year for TV and Film designation, *Broadcast* magazine, 2002; awards for best children's television series, British Animation Festival, and Bradford International Animation Festival, both 2002, and Annecy International Animation Festival, 2003.

Writings

Albie, Collins (London, England), 2002.
The Beast of Baloddan, Hodder (London, England), 2003.
A Beastly Feast at Baloddan Hall, Hodder (London, England), 2003.
(Self-illustrated, with Mark Stacey) *Albie and the (Superduper, Intergalactic) Space Rocket,* Collins (London, England), 2003.
(Self-illustrated, with Mark Stacey) *Albie and the Big Race,* HarperCollins (London, England), 2004.
The Cow That Laid an Egg, illustrated by Russell Ayto, HarperCollins (New York, NY), 2008.
The Cow That Was the Best Mother, illustrated by Russell Ayto, HarperCollins (New York, NY), 2009.

Creator and developer of animated children's television series *Albie,* for Children's Independent Television.

Sidelights

British children's author and illustrator Andy Cutbill has written several books for children and also created the animated television series *Albie.* Cutbill began his television career by writing commercials before transitioning into creating work geared for children. He followed a similar path as a writer, working as a freelance copywriter and editor in addition to publishing books for young readers. Along with his middle-grade "Albie" books, Cutbill has also penned the novels *The Beast of Baloddan* and *A Beastly Feast at Baloddan Hall,* which tap into many preteens' interest in tales of the supernatural,

Cutbill's first picture book for children to appear in the United States, *The Cow That Laid an Egg* features illustrations by Russell Ayto. The story follows Marjorie, a bovine who feels that her talents pale in comparison with those of other cows in her herd. Sensing her melancholy mood, the chickens set on a plan to boost Marjorie's spirits by slipping an egg with black-and-white cow-like markings underneath her and making it appear that she laid the egg herself. While the ruse makes Marjorie the talk of the barnyard, other Holsteins on the farm doubt the cow's new-found egg-laying ability. By story's end, however, the newly hatched chick utters such a deep "moo" that even skeptics begin to believe. Comparing *The Cow That Laid an Egg* to Dr. Seuss's *Horton Hatches the Egg, School Library Journal* critic Lee Bock predicted that Cutbill's "funny book . . . will delight children." *Booklist* reviewer Hazel Rochman deemed *The Cow That Laid an Egg* "a great comic take on the Ugly Duckling tale," while a contributor to *Kirkus Reviews* suggested that the combination of Cutbill's narrative and Ayto's artwork "creates a merry farmstead farce that will tickle young audiences."

Biographical and Critical Sources

PERIODICALS

Booklist, February 15, 2008, Hazel Rochman, review of *The Cow That Laid an Egg,* p. 85.
Kirkus Reviews, February 1, 2008, review of *The Cow That Laid an Egg.*
Publishers Weekly, February 4, 2008, review of *The Cow That Laid an Egg,* p. 56.
School Library Journal, February, 2008, Lee Bock, review of *The Cow That Laid an Egg,* p. 84.*

D

DEZERN, Chad

Personal
Male.

Addresses
Home—Pasedena, CA. *Office*—Insomniac Games, 2255 N. Ontario St., Ste. 550, Burbank, CA 91504. *E-mail*—cmd@insomniacgames.com.

Career
Illustrator and game developer. Game credits include the "Rachet and Clank" series. Insomniac Games, Burbank, CA, currently art director.

Illustrator
Andy Stanton, *You're a Bad Man, Mr. Gum!* (U.S. edition), HarperCollins (New York, NY), 2008.

Andy Stanton, *Mr. Gum and the Biscuit Billionaire* (U.S. edition), HarperCollins (New York, NY), 2008.

Andy Stanton, *Mr. Gum and the Goblins* (U.S. edition), HarperCollins (New York, NY), 2009.

Biographical and Critical Sources

PERIODICALS

Kirkus Reviews, January 1, 2008, review of *You're a Bad Man, Mr. Gum!*

ONLINE

Chad Dezern Home Page, http://www.wingedrobots.com (May 15, 2009).*

DODDS, Dayle Ann 1952-

Personal
Born June 14, 1952, in Ridgewood, NJ; daughter of Theodore (a lawyer) and Edith (a homemaker) Bruinsma; married Glen Dodds (an architect), December 6, 1976; children: Jaime, Greg. *Education:* California State Polytechnic University, San Luis Obispo, B.S. (childhood development; with honors); elementary teaching credential.

Addresses
Home—Carmel, CA. *Agent*—Ginger Knowlton, Curtis Brown, Ltd., 10 Astor Pl., New York, NY 10003.

Career
Writer of books for children. Teacher and teacher's aide for kindergarten, first through third grades, and art classes in Palo Alto, CA, 1975-78; administrative assistant for a publishing company in Palo Alto, 1978-80; freelance proofreader, 1980-82; writer, beginning 1989.

Member
Society of Children's Book Writers and Illustrators, Independent Media Artists Group.

Awards, Honors
Bay Area Book Reviewers Association nomination, 1989, for *Wheel Away!; Parenting* magazine Award of Excellence; American Booksellers Pick of the List designation; *School Library Journal* Best Books designation.

Writings

Wheel Away!, illustrated by Thatcher Hurd, Harper & Row (New York, NY), 1989.

On Our Way to Market, illustrated by John Gurney, Simon & Schuster (New York, NY), 1991.

Do Bunnies Talk?, illustrated by Arlene Dubanevich, HarperCollins (New York, NY), 1992.

The Color Box, illustrated by Giles Laroche, Little, Brown (Boston, MA), 1992.

Sardines, illustrated by Jerry Smath, Simon & Schuster (New York, NY), 1993.

The Shape of Things, Candlewick Press (Cambridge, MA), 1994.

Someone Is Hiding: A Lift-the-Flap Counting Game, Simon & Schuster (New York, NY), 1994.

Sing, Sophie!, Candlewick Press (Cambridge, MA), 1994.

Ghost and Pete, illustrated by Matt Novak, Random House (New York, NY), 1995.

The Great Divide: A Mathematical Marathon, illustrated by Tracy Mitchell, Candlewick Press (Cambridge, MA), 1999.

Pet Wash, illustrated by Tor Freeman, Candlewick Press (New York, NY), 2001.

The Kettles Get New Clothes, illustrated by Jill McElmurry, Candlewick Press (New York, NY), 2002.

Where's Pup?, illustrated by Pierre Pratt, Dial Books (New York, NY), 2003.

Henry's Amazing Machine, illustrated by Kyrsten Brooker, Farrar, Straus & Giroux (New York, NY), 2004.

Minnie's Diner: A Multiplying Menu, illustrated by John Manders, Candlewick Press (Cambridge, MA), 2004.

Hello, Sun!, illustrated by Sachiko Yoshikawa, Dial Books (New York, NY), 2005.

Teacher's Pets, illustrated by Marylin Hafner, Candlewick Press (Cambridge, MA), 2006.

Full House: An Invitation to Fractions, illustrated by Abby Carter, Candlewick Press (Cambridge, MA), 2007.

The Prince Won't Go to Bed!, illustrated by Kyrsten Brooker, Farrar, Straus & Giroux (New York, NY), 2007.

Sidelights

Trained as an educator and with a strong background in publishing, Dayle Ann Dodds creates picture books that entertain on two levels: both as entertaining read-alouds and beginning readers in which challenging vocabulary words are made clear in her story's context. "One of my writing friends calls me the 'noisiest writer I know,'" Dodds once told *SATA*. "I love words, I love sounds, I love how words sound, alone and together." Praising her book *Hello, Sun!,* which focuses on a change in the weather, Carolyn Phelan wrote in *Booklist* that Dodds' "easy rhymes and bouncing rhythms . . . set a brisk pace," while in *Teacher's Pets* her "fresh and engaging" tale was described by the same critic as "gracefully written" and "gently amusing."

"As a child," Dodds once told *SATA*, "I enjoyed reading stories of fantasy most of all. *Grimms' Fairy Tales* were

Dayle Ann Dodds joins illustrator Pierre Pratt to tell a fanciful tale in **Where's Pup?**

probably my favorite, especially 'The Twelve Dancing Princesses,' who sneaked off into the night without being caught and danced their shoes to pieces. I was the youngest child in my family, and in many of the Brothers Grimm tales, the youngest child grew to become the smartest after all the others failed. I also loved the story of the table cloth that became covered with luscious food when the boy commanded 'Spread yourself.' What a wonderful treasure that would be to own! I read *The Wizard of Oz* over and over and the tales of Hans Christian Andersen, then my tastes took a turn to the whimsical and humorous. I loved Homer Price's misadventures, especially the donut-making machine that went out of control, and the ball of string that grew bigger and bigger. I carried this love for cumulative, building and 'out-of-control' happenings into my own stories later on.

"Drawing and riding horses were my favorite pastimes as a child. I was lucky to have my own horse, and most days after school were filled with galloping escapes through the canyons of our Southern California community, still largely rural at that time. I also loved 'putting things together.' Magazine scraps and glue became illustrated books. Light bulbs taped to soda pop bottles were transformed into brightly painted papier-mâché animals. Bits of leather were cut and woven into saddles and bridles for my stable of toy horses. My favorite spot in the house was the junk drawer in the kitchen, where my mother stashed everything from magnets to glitter to broken watches. These were the jewels my treasures were made of.

"It wasn't until college that the thought of writing books for children came to me. A class on children's literature sparked a longing to relive the excitement of the stories of my youth. I found myself reading children's books once again. After all, my chosen career was teaching young children, wasn't it? I had every right to choose Robert McCloskey or Theodor Geisel as my weekend reading. I had a lovely excuse for returning to the world of children's books.

"The arrival of my first child, daughter Jaime, gave me the green light to begin writing my own children's books. I had taken a leave from teaching to work for an educational publishing company, where I gained some valuable experience about the putting together of illustrated books. Now I had someone to write for: my own child. I found myself getting up at 5 a.m. to have time to work before the baby woke up. I wrote every chance I got (which isn't much with a new baby), and I found great pleasure in knowing I had my own creative secret: I was writing children's books and no one else knew. For the first year, I literally worked in my upstairs closet, my special space where my thoughts and ideas were my own.

"My first published story, 'The Carrot Corporation,' concerned two boys who started a carrot cake business in their mother's kitchen. I got so excited that I could write something that could be published, that I began

thinking along the lines of a book. For three years, I worked on story after story, making all the mistakes beginners do. My first stories were too long, too complicated, not easily illustrated as picture books.

"Next, my son Greg was born. Although a busy mother, I refused to give up on my dream to write books for children. As the children grew, my world centered around strollers, wagons, roller skates, bicycles: wheels. *Wheel Away!* was one of those ideas that comes out of nowhere and everywhere at the same time. As I stood in the shower (I did most of my creative thinking in the shower in those days), I could see the cover of the book in front of me. What resulted was a simple, cumulative tale of a wheel that gets loose from a boy's bicycle and makes a funny, noisy journey through the town. I submitted the story to Harper & Row, and to my delight, they bought it. My wishes had been answered, my dreams had come true. I was a children's book author."

Dodds' books feature illustrations created by a variety of artist. In *Where's Pup?,* for example, Pierre Pratt brings to life her story about a circus clown that hunts for his puppy, only to find the animal at the very top of an elaborate fold-out spread. Writing for *School Library Journal,* Linda M. Kenton deemed *Where's Pup?* "a visually exciting charmer for storytime," and *Horn Book* reviewer Betty Carter declared it to be "an engaging story for beginning readers."

Dodds has drawn praise for incorporating mathematics into several of her picture books, among them *The Shape of Things,* an introduction to basic shapes, and *The Great Divide: A Mathematical Marathon,* a study of simple division. In *School Library Journal* Ruth Semrau called *The Shape of Things* "an effective concept book," while *Booklist* contributor Ilene Cooper complimented its "appealing, crisp design . . . [and] choice of kid-appealing subjects." *The Great Divide* wraps its lesson into an around-the-world race that ends with a surprising twist. A *Kirkus Reviews* writer concluded of Dodds' book that "few readers will notice that they've just finished a math problem, and most will want to go over all the action again," while a *Publishers Weekly* reviewer quipped of *The Great Divide:* "All lessons should be this gratifying."

In *Minnie's Diner: A Multiplying Menu,* which features artwork by John Manders, Dodds' lesson about "doubling goes down easy," according to *Horn Book* contributor Martha V. Parravano. In the book, a family of brothers leave the family farm after a long day of work and winds up at Minnie's Diner, where each McFay brother orders double the food ordered by the brother arriving ahead of him. After all five brothers are lined up at the counter, Minnie's abilities as a short-order cook are sorely taxed, so when Papa McFay arrives to hustle his boys back to the farm she is relieved. Parravano praised the "jaunty rhyme scheme . . . and chantable refrain" in *Minnie's Diner,* while in *Booklist* Hazel Rochman predicted that young readers will relish "the math, the slapstick, and the words." Lynda Ritterman

Dodds focuses on the close relationship between teachers and their young students in **Teacher's Pets,** ***featuring artwork by Marylin Hafner.*** (Illustration copyright © 2006 by Marylin Hafner. Reproduced by permission of the publisher Candlewick Press, Inc., Somerville, MA.)

cited Dodds' use of "jaunty rhyme" in *Minnie's Diner,* adding that the book provides youngsters with "a fun first look at multiplication."

Featuring what *School Library Journal* critic Judy Chichinski described as "fresh, whimsical watercolor illustrations," *Full House: An Invitation to Fractions* is

Kyrsten Brooker brings to life a palace in a hubub in her illustrations for Dodds' picture book **The Prince Won't Go to Bed!** (Illustration copyright © 2007 by Kyrsten Brooker. Reproduced by permission of Farrar, Straus & Giroux, a division of Farrar, Straus & Giroux, LLC.)

another of Dodds' math-themed books, this time harnessing the author's characteristic whimsy and humor to teach a lesson about portions less than a whole. In the story, Miss Bloom keeps the Strawberry Inn, and she fills her six vacant rooms with a wacky assortment of guests in a book that features a lesson on fractions related via "repetitious phrasing and rollicking rhymes," according to a *Kirkus Reviews* writer. In *Booklist* Phelan had praise for the "jovial pencil-and-watercolor artwork" contributed by Ann Carter, going on to dub *Full House* "colorful" and "upbeat."

Some of Dodds' books are less about learning and more about having fun. In *Pet Wash,* for instance, two enterprising boys bathe an array of animals, from rhinos and alligators to an ant, before facing their biggest challenge: a customer's baby brother. "Young readers will be in stitches," Laurie Edwards warned in her *School Library Journal* review of the work. A similar spirit animates *The Kettles Get New Clothes,* in which a dog family finds that its formerly no-nonsense clothing shop has been transformed into a chic boutique. After trying on a series of gaudy outfits, the Kettles finally opt for the useful, if drab, clothes they always buy—except for the youngest Kettle, who revels in the designer duds. A *Publishers Weekly* reviewer concluded of *The Kettles Get New Clothes* that Dodds' "engaging book will earn giggles from kids who love a good joke."

One of two stories by Dodds that features artwork by Kyrsten Brooker, *The Prince Won't Go to Bed!* finds a royal household in a royal hullabaloo when the young princeling refuses to go quietly to bed. Martha V. Parravano wrote in *Horn Book* that Dodds' "uproarious and kid-pleasing" tale pairs effectively with Brooker's "expansive multimedia collages full of movement and amusing detail." Full of "merriment and mayhem," according to Joan Kindig in *School Library Journal, The Prince Won't Go to Bed!* serves up a treat for "children who soak up rhyme and fun wherever they can."

Biographical and Critical Sources

PERIODICALS

Booklist, August, 2004, Hazel Rochman, review of *Minnie's Diner: A Multiplying Menu,* p. 1941; September 1, 2004, Julie Cummins, review of *Henry's Amazing Machine,* p. 130; June 1, 2005, Carolyn Phelan, review of *Hello, Sun!,* p. 1820; May 15, 2006, Carolyn Phelan, review of *Teacher's Pets,* p. 49; October 1, 2007, Julie Cummins, review of *The Prince Won't Go to Bed!,* p. 66; December 1, 2007, Carolyn Phelan, review of *Full House: An Invitation to Fractions,* p. 58.

Bulletin of the Center for Children's Books, July, 1997, Pat Mathews, review of *Sing, Sophie!,* p. 392.

Emergency Librarian, November-December, 1995, Teri S. Lesesne, review of *The Shape of Things,* p. 56.

Horn Book, March-April, 2003, Betty Carter, review of *Where's Pup?,* p. 201; January-February, 2005, Martha V. Parravano, review of *Minnie's Diner,* p. 75; January-February, 2008, Martha V. Parravano, review of *The Prince Won't Go to Bed!,* p. 70.

Kirkus Reviews, November 15, 1999, review of *The Great Divide: A Mathematical Marathon,* p. 1808; July 1, 2002, review of *The Kettles Get New Clothes,* p. 952; January 15, 2003, review of *Where's Pup?,* p. 141; July 15, 2004, review of *Minnie's Diner,* p. 683; April 15, 2006, review of *Teacher's Pets,* p. 404; October 15, 2007, reviews of *Full House* and *The Prince Won't Go to Bed!*

Publishers Weekly, December 13, 1999, review of *The Great Divide,* p. 82; September 17, 2001, review of *Pet Wash,* p. 78; July 22, 2002, review of *The Kettles Get New Clothes,* p. 177; August 30, 2004, review of *Henry's Amazing Machine,* p. 53; September 6, 2004, review of *Minnie's Diner,* p. 62; February 7, 2005, review of *The Great Divide,* p. 62; June 12, 2006, review of *Teacher's Pets,* p. 52; November 26, 2007, review of *The Prince Won't Go to Bed!,* p. 51.

School Library Journal, February, 1995, Ruth Semrau, review of *The Shape of Things,* p. 90; March, 1996, Sharron McElmeel, review of *Ghost and Pete,* p. 173; November, 1999, Kathleen M. Kelly MacMillan, review of *The Great Divide,* p. 114; October, 2001, Laurie Edwards, review of *Pet Wash,* p. 114; July, 2003, Linda M. Kenton, review of *Where's Pup?,* p. 95; August, 2004, Lynda Ritterman, review of *Minnie's Diner,* p. 85; September, 2004, Marge Loch-Wouters, review of *Henry's Amazing Machine,* p. 158; June, 2005,

Kathleen Simonetta, review of *Hello, Sun!,* p. 108; May, 2006, Gloria Koster, review of *Teacher's Pets,* p. 86; December, 2007, Joan Kindig, review of *The Prince Won't Go to Bed,* p. 87, and Judy Chichinski, review of *Full House,* p. 106.

ONLINE

Dayle Ann Dodds Home Page, http://dayleanndodds.com (June 2, 2009).*

* * *

DONOHUE, Moira Rose 1954-

Personal

Born December 26, 1954, in New York, NY; married; husband's name Rob (an attorney); children: Peter, Rose. *Education:* Mississippi University for Women, B.A.; University of Santa Clara, J.D. *Hobbies and other interests:* Dogs, old movies, opera, tap dancing.

Addresses

Home—VA. *E-mail*—moira@moirarosedonohue.net.

Career

Author and playright. Formerly worked as an attorney. Presenter at schools.

Member

Society of Children's Book Writers and Illustrators (Mid-Atlantic chapter).

Writings

Alfie the Apostrophe, illustrated by JoAnn Adinolfi, Albert Whitman (Morton Grove, IL), 2006.

Moira Rose Donahue's fascination with punctuation inspired her picture book Penny and the Punctuation Bee, *featuring artwork by Jenny Law.* (Illustration copyright © 2008 by Jenny Law. All rights reserved. Reproduced by permission.)

The Three Bears versus Goldi Locks, Contemporary Drama Service, 2007.

Penny and the Punctuation Bee, illustrated by Jenny Law, Albert Whitman (Morton Grove, IL), 2008.

Contributor of play "An Alphabet Story" to *Plays* magazine; contributor to *Chicken Soup for the Kid's Soul II;* contributor to periodicals, including *Pockets* and *Wee Ones* online.

Sidelights

A self-described "punctuation geek," Moira Rose Donohue shares her passion for good grammar in her picture books *Alfie the Apostrophe* and *Penny and the Punctuation Bee.* In *Alfie the Apostrophe* a spunky blue punctuation mark joins his friends in a friendly talent-show competition where heavily punctuated jokes, riddles, and exclamations abound. Although Alfie is nervous, he makes it through his act performing such magic tricks as transforming two words into one through the use of a hyphen and changing the meaning of a phrase by using the possessive. According to *Booklist* critic Carolyn Phelan, Donohue salts her story "with sly bits of punctuation-mark-based humor and even a bit of ancient history," while JoAnn Adinolfi's colorful art contributes "a certain verve reminiscent of children's own artwork." Also praising both art and text, Sally R. Dow wrote in *School Library Journal* that Adinolfi's "fanciful" art for *Alfie the Apostrophe* "capture[s] the whimsy of this original, instructional story."

Readers are introduced to a chatty exclamation point in *Penny and the Punctuation Bee,* Donohue's second book for children. In a story brought to life in Jenny Law's colorful art, Elsie brags that she will win the school's upcoming punctuation bee. Penny the period and Quentin the question mark decide that they, too, have a chance, and their practicing may pay off when the field of contestants narrows down to three. Praising Donohue's text for its "humor and verve," Phelan added that *Penny and the Punctuation Bee* may inspire teachers to play a similar game in their classrooms. Law's paintings bring to life Donhue's characters in what a *Kirkus Reviews* writer described as "a bright world populated by colorful, easily recognizable punctuation of all sorts."

Biographical and Critical Sources

PERIODICALS

Booklist, August 1, 2006, Carolyn Phelan, review of *Alfie the Apostrophe,* p. 86; July, 1, 2008, Carolyn Phelan, review of *Penny and the Punctuation Bee,* p. 73.

Kirkus Reviews, February 1, 2006, review of *Alfie the Apostrophe;* March 1, 2008, review of *Penny and the Punctuation Bee.*

School Library Journal, August, 2006, Sally R. Dow, review of *Alfie the Apostrophe,* p. 80; May, 2008, Jayne Damron, review of *Penny and the Punctuation Bee,* p. 94.

ONLINE

Goodreads Web site, http://www.goodreads.com/ (May 20, 2009).

Moira Rose Donohue Home Page, http://www.moirarose donohue.net (May 15, 2009).*

*   *   *

DUNMORE, Helen 1952-

Personal

Born 1952, in Yorkshire, England; married; husband an attorney; children: one daughter, one son, one stepson. *Education:* York University, B.A., 1973.

Addresses

Home—Bristol, England.

Career

Writer. Has worked as reader, performer and, teacher of poetry and creative writing. Teacher in Finland, beginning 1973; associated with Arvon Foundation and Poetry Society's Writer-in-Schools program; instructor at University of Glamorgan, University of Bristol's Continuing Education Department, and Open College of the Arts. Contributes to arts programs on BBC Radio.

Member

Royal Society of Literature (fellow), British Society of Authors (member of ruling committee, 2002-05, chairman, 2005-08).

Awards, Honors

Alice Hunt Bartlett Award, 1987, for *The Sea Skater;* McKitterick Prize, 1994, for *Zennor in Darkness;* Signal Poetry Award, 1995, for *Secrets;* Orange Prize for fiction, 1996, for *A Spell of Winter;* T.S. Eliot Prize shortlist, for *Bestiary;* Whitbread Novel Award shortlist, 2001, and Orange Prize for Fiction, 2002, both for *The Siege;* Cardiff International Poetry Prize.

Writings

POETRY

The Apple Fall, Bloodaxe Books (Newcastle upon Tyne, England), 1983.

The Sea Skater, Bloodaxe Books (Newcastle upon Tyne, England), 1986.

The Raw Garden, Bloodaxe Books (Newcastle upon Tyne, England), 1988.

Short Days, Long Nights: New and Selected Poems, Bloodaxe Books (Newcastle upon Tyne, England), 1991.

Helen Dunmore

Recovering a Body, Bloodaxe Books (Newcastle upon Tyne, England), 1994.
Secrets: A Collection of Poems from Hidden Worlds (for children), Bodley Head (London, England), 1994.
Bestiary, Dufour Editions (Chester Springs, PA), 1997.
(With Jo Shapcott and Matthew Sweeney) *Penguin Modern Poets 12,* Penguin (London, England), 1997.
Snollygoster and Other Poems (for children), Scholastic (London, England), 2001.
Out of the Blue: Poems, 1975-2001, Bloodaxe Books (Tarset, Northumberland, England), 2001.
Rose, 1944, Penguin (London, England), 2005.
Glad of These Times, Bloodaxe Books (Tarset, Northumberland, England), 2007.

FICTION; FOR ADULTS

Going to Egypt, MacRae (London, England), 1992.
Zennor in Darkness, Penguin (London, England), 1993.
Burning Bright, Penguin (London, England), 1994.
A Spell of Winter, Viking (London, England), 1995, Atlantic Monthly Press (New York, NY), 2001.
Talking to the Dead, Little, Brown (Boston, MA), 1996.
Love of Fat Men (short stories), Viking (London, England), 1997.
Your Blue-eyed Boy, Little, Brown (Boston, MA), 1998.
With Your Crooked Heart, Atlantic Monthly Press (New York, NY), 1999.
The Siege, Grove Press (New York, NY), 2001.

Mourning Ruby, Viking (London, England), 2003, Putnam (New York, NY), 2004.
(Author of foreword) F. Scott Fitzgerald, *The Popular Girl,* Hesperus (London, England), 2005.
House of Orphans, Fig Tree (New York, NY), 2006.
Counting the Stars, Fig Tree (New York, NY), 2008.

FICTION; FOR CHILDREN

In the Money, Red Fox (London, England), 1993.
Allie's Apples, Methuen (London, England), 1995.
Go Fox!, Young Corgi (London, England), 1996.
Fatal Error, Yearling (New York, NY), 1996.
Clyde's Leopard (Cambridge reading series), Cambridge University Press (Cambridge, England), 1998.
Great-Grandma's Dancing Dress (Cambridge reading series), Cambridge University Press (Cambridge, England), 1998.
Allie's Rabbit, Mammoth (London, England), 1999.
Brother, Brother, Sister, Sister (for teens), Scholastic (London, England), 1999.
Ice Cream (short stories) Grove Press (New York, NY), 2000.
Aliens Don't Eat Bacon Sandwiches, Mammoth (London, England), 2000.
Allie Away, Mammoth (London, England), 2000.
Zillah and Me, Scholastic (London, England), 2000.
The Zillah Rebellion (for adolescents), Scholastic (New York, NY), 2001.
Amina's Blanket, illustrated by Paul Dainton, Crabtree (New York, NY), 2003.
The Silver Bead, Scholastic (London, England), 2003.
The Seal Cove, Scholastic (London, England), 2004.
The Lilac Tree, Scholastic (London, England), 2004.
Tara's Tree House, illustrated by Karin Littlewood, Egmont (London, England), 2004, Crabtree (New York, NY), 2006.
Ingo, HarperCollins (London, England), 2005, HarperCollins (New York, NY), 2006.
The Tide Knot: A Return to Ingo, HarperCollins (London, England), 2006, HarperCollins (New York, NY), 2008.
The Deep, HarperCollins (London, England), 2007.
The Crossing of Ingo, HarperCollins (London, England), 2008.

OTHER

(With others) *Poetry Quartet 5* (audio), Bloodaxe Books 1999.
(Author of introduction) D.H. Lawrence, *The Fox; The Captain's Doll; The Ladybird,* edited by Dieter Mehl, Penguin (London, England), 2006.

Contributor of reviews to London *Times* and London *Observer.*

Adaptations

Burning Bright was serialized on BBC Radio's *Woman's Hour. Zennor in Darkness* was optioned for film.

Sidelights

Helen Dunmore is an award-winning English author with diverse talents and credits; she has published poetry collections, adult novels, and fiction as well as stories and verse for children and a trilogy of fantasy novels for preteens. Her adult novel *Talking to the Dead,* a Freudian tale of two sisters who share a haunted past, appeals to both adult and teen readers, while younger children have enjoyed Dunmore's poetry collections *Snollygoster and Other Poems* and *Secrets: A Collection of Poems from Hidden Worlds.*

In *Ingo,* the first novel in her fantasy trilogy, Dunmore mixes the perennial fascination with the sea's mystery and the intriguing science-fiction theme of parallel worlds. In the novel, narrator Sapphire, age eleven, and her older brother Conor, live in a coastal Cornwall village where their father, Matthew, works as a fisherman. Then Matthew disappears and is believed to have been lost at sea. A year after their loss, the siblings meet Mer children Elvira and Faro, who live in the underwater world of Ingo. Taught by the mer children to breathe underwater and commune with the fishes, Sapphire realizes that her love of the sea is due to the fact that she is part Mer, and the preteen begins to be conflicted between the Air and Mer worlds. Praising Dunmore's middle-grade fantasy, Anne O'Malley wrote in *Booklist* that *Ingo* proves that the author "is as adept at writing books for children as she is at writing adult fiction and poetry." In *Horn Book* Anita L. Burkam dubbed *Ingo* "a spellbinding tale," while in *Publishers Weekly* the critic wrote that Dunmore effectively "captures Sapphy's lonely struggle." "The pull of Mer life versus" the girl's love of her human family "persist[s] to the tale's end and beyond," the critic added.

Sapphire and Conor return in *The Tide Knot: A Return to Ingo,* as the siblings continue to be drawn into the world of the Merfolk they have met through their friendship with Faro and Elvira. Matthew soon reveals himself and explains that he was pulled from the Air world by the call of the sea. Their father also delivers a warning: when the tide knot is released, and no longer holds back the seas, the Air world of humans will be threatened. Living with a foot in two worlds has a cost, as well, and both Conor and Sapphire must decide where their ultimate loyalties lie in a novel that *Kliatt* contributor Cara Chancellor wrote "will introduce a wonderful, enthralling world the reader can dive into again and again." According to Elizabeth Bird, a reviewer for *School Library Journal,* in *The Tide Knot* Dunmore crafts a "mature and thoughtful" tale of Merfolk, and the story's "strong characters and . . . consistently enticing plot make this a cut above the rest." O'Malley described the middle-grade fantasy as "a worthy follow-up" to *Ingo,* adding that the story "will capture returning readers from its first wet, magical shimmer."

Although she has written many books for younger readers, Dunmore is perhaps best known for her adult novels, many of which are inspired by her interest in history. Titles include *Your Blue-eyed Boy, With Your Crooked Heart, The Siege,* and the award-winning *Zennor in Darkness,* a book that focuses on the experiences of British novelist D.H. Lawrence and his German-born wife Frieda during World War I.

In *Your Blue-eyed Boy* Simone is a thirty-something mother of two young boys who is struggling to keep her family financially solvent while also grappling with recurring memories of a childhood trauma. She accepts a position as district judge in her remote seaside village in a desperate effort to keep the family out of bankruptcy, while her unemployed and depressed husband cares for their sons. Simone's already-stressful life takes a turn for the worse when Michael, an American with whom she once had a relationship, starts sending her compromising letters. As a *Publishers Weekly* reviewer noted, "the novel's marsh-country setting . . . is a fearsome metaphor for a life abundant with insecurity and tension," and Vanessa Bush concluded in *Booklist* that *Your Blue-eyed Boy* is "a compelling novel about reconciling desires of the past with responsibilities of the present."

Rebecca, the narrator of Dunmore's novel *Mourning Ruby,* is an orphan who was raised by unloving adoptive parents. When she shares a flat with a writer friend named Joe, Rebecca experiences both true companionship and a devastating tragedy. In *The Siege* Dunmore takes readers to 1941 and the fall of Leningrad, as a middle-class family attempts to survive Nazi efforts to wage a war of deprivation during a bitter Russian winter, while in *Counting the Stars* she transports readers to ancient Rome and the mythic love affair between the poet Catullus and the beautiful and wealthy aristocratic Clodia Metelli.

Biographical and Critical Sources

BOOKS

Contemporary Poets, St. James Press (Detroit, MI), 2001.

PERIODICALS

Booklist, May 1, 1997, GraceAnne DeCandido, review of *Talking to the Dead,* p. 1477; May 15, 1998, Vanessa Bush, review of *Your Blue-eyed Boy,* p. 1594; December 15, 1999, Michelle Kaske, review of *With Your Crooked Heart,* p. 756; February 1, 2004, Carol Haggas, review of *Mourning Ruby,* p. 949; September 1, 2006, Anne O'Malley, review of *Ingo,* p. 126; January 1, 2008, Anne O'Malley, review of *The Tide Knot: A Return to Ingo,* p. 84.
Childhood Education, summer, 2007, Tom Smith, review of *Ingo,* p. 240.
Entertainment Weekly, August 8, 1997, Carmela Ciuraru, review of *Talking to the Dead,* p. 75.

History Today, April, 2008, Martin Evans, interview with Dunmore.

Horn Book, September-October, 2006, Anita L. Burkam, review of *Ingo,* p. 581.

Kirkus Reviews, April 1, 1997, review of *Talking to the Dead;* April 15, 1998, review of *Your Blue-eyed Boy.*

Kliatt, May, 2005, Nancy Zachary, review of *Mourning Ruby,* pp. 23-25; January, 2008, Cara Chancellor, review of *The Tide Knot,* p. 6.

Library Journal, May 15, 1998, Caroline M. Hallsworth, review of *Your Blue-eyed Boy,* p. 113; July 1, 2007, Louis McKee, review of *Glad of These Times,* p. 96.

New York Times Book Review, June 1, 1997, Carol Kino, review of *Talking to the Dead;* March 12, 2000, Dana Kennedy, review of *With Your Crooked Heart.*

People, September 29, 1997, Paula Chin, review of *Talking to the Dead,* p. 45.

Publishers Weekly, May 5, 1997, review of *Talking to the Dead,* p. 194; April 27, 1998, review of *Your Blue-eyed Boy* p. 44; November 29, 1999, review of *With Your Crooked Heart,* p. 50; January 21, 2002, Sybil Steinberg, interview with Dunmore, p. 59; February 9, 2004, review of *Mourning Ruby,* p. 55; October 15, 2006, review of *Ingo,* p. 54.

School Library Journal, February, 2008, Elizabeth Bird, review of *The Tide Knot,* p. 113.

ONLINE

Bloodaxe Books Web site, http://www.bloodaxebooks.com/ (October 28, 2003), "Helen Dunmore."

Contemporary Writers Web site, http://www.contemporary writers.com/ (June 2, 2009), "Helen Dunmore."*

E-F

EDMUND, Sean
    See PRINGLE, Laurence

       *   *   *

ELLIOTT, David 1947-

Personal

Born 1947; married; children: Eli. *Education:* School of International Training, M.A.

Addresses

Home—Warner, NH. *E-mail*—delliott@conknet.com.

Career

Author and educator. Colby-Sawyer College, New London, NH, instructor and director of English language and American culture program.

Writings

An Alphabet of Rotten Kids, illustrated by Oscar de Mejo, Philomel (New York, NY), 1991.

The Cool Crazy Crickets, illustrated by Paul Meisel, Candlewick Press (Cambridge, MA), 2000.

The Cool Crazy Crickets to the Rescue, illustrated by Paul Meisel, Candlewick Press (Cambridge, MA), 2001.

The Transmogrification of Roscoe Wizzle, Candlewick Press (Cambridge, MA), 2001.

Hazel Nutt, Mad Scientist, illustrated by True Kelley, Holiday House (New York, NY), 2003.

And Here's to You!, illustrated by Randy Cecil, Candlewick Press (Cambridge, MA), 2004.

Evangeline Mudd and the Golden-haired Apes of the Ikkinasti Jungle, illustrated by Andréa Wesson, Candlewick Press (Cambridge, MA), 2004.

Hazel Nutt, Alien Hunter, illustrated by True Kelley, Holiday House (New York, NY), 2004.

Evangeline Mudd and the Great Mink Escapade, illustrated by Andréa Wesson, Candlewick Press (Cambridge, MA), 2006.

One Little Chicken: A Counting Book, illustrated by Ethan Long, Holiday House (New York, NY), 2007.

Jeremy Cabbage and the Living Museum of Human Oddballs and Quadruped Delights, Alfred A. Knopf (New York, NY), 2008.

Knitty Kitty, illustrated by Christopher Denise, Candlewick Press (Cambridge, MA), 2008.

On the Farm, illustrated by Holly Meade, Candlewick Press (Cambridge, MA), 2008.

Wuv Bunnies from Outer Pace, illustrated by Ethan Long, Holiday House (New York, NY), 2008.

What the Grizzly Knows, illustrated by Max Grafe, Candlewick Press (Cambridge, MA), 2008.

Finn Throws a Fit, illustrated by Timothy Basil Ering, Candlewick Press (Somerville, MA), 2009.

Elliott's titles have been translated into German and Italian.

Sidelights

David Elliott, an instructor at Colby-Sawyer College in New Hampshire, stumbled into his second career as a children's-book author while at a party with friends. In a conversation with a woman named Amy Ehrlich, he began to discuss ideas for an alphabet book, unaware that Ehrlich was a retired editor from Dial Books. She got him in contact with some other editors, and not long after, Elliott's name was on the title page of his first published book, *An Alphabet of Rotten Kids.* The book introduces readers to twenty-six naughty children, and, according to some reviewers, Elliott's humor is reminiscent of that in Edward Gorey's macabre alphabet book *The Gashlycrumb Tinies.* "The humor is silly enough to appeal to kids," commented a reviewer for *Publishers Weekly.* Not all parents appreciated *An Alphabet of Rotten Kids,* however, and Elliott's first book was banned in at least one U.S. city on moral grounds. The author was disappointed in the book himself; he was surprised that the illustrator had depicted the children as all one race. "I joke that the book should have

been banned because it's so bad," he told an interviewer for the Colby-Sawyer College Web site.

The mixed reception of his first book did not deter Elliott from further writing. In his *The Cool Crazy Crickets* four friends of diverse racial backgrounds decide to form a club, and over the course of the story, decide the club's name, find their clubhouse, vote on a mascot, and put together a reason for their club's existence. *The Cool Crazy Crickets* contains "quick-paced dialogue, brief sentences and a generous smattering of art," according to a *Publishers Weekly* reviewer, adding that these qualities will make Elliott's book appeal to young readers transitioning from picture books to chapter books. In *Booklist* John Peters called *The Cool Crazy Crickets* a "light, good-humored tale."

The four friends return in *The Cool Crazy Crickets to the Rescue,* in which the club members are looking for ways to earn money. Through enterprises such as baby sitting, pet sitting, and building a lemonade stand, the four begin to earn some money and discuss how they will spend it. Then a sickly cat moves into their club-house, and they quickly decide upon the best way to spend their money: taking their new housemate to the veterinarian. Roxanne Burg, reviewing *The Cool Crazy Crickets to the Rescue* for *School Library Journal,* called Elliott's story "an easygoing tale about summer days."

Three unlikely elements—fast food, science-fiction, and modern German writer Franz Kafka—mix in Elliott's *The Transmogrification of Roscoe Wizzle,* in which the title character begins to turn into a bug after eating too much food from the ominous restaurant Gussy's. When Roscoe begins to investigate, he discovers that Gussy's may also be the reason that several children from his town have gone missing, and it is soon up to him and vegetarian friend Kinshasa to solve the mystery. A *Publishers Weekly* reviewer noted that Elliott combines "sassy first-person narration and snappy dialogue" to create a story skewed "a few thoroughly enjoyable degrees off normal." Eva Mitnick, writing in *School Library Journal,* felt that "the wacky plot and quirky details" in the book "will appeal to young and reluctant readers."

A needle-wielding feline is the star of David Elliott's **Knitty Kitty,** *a picture book illustrated by Christopher Denise.* (Illustration copyright © 2008 by Christopher Denise. All rights reserved. Reproduced by permission of the publisher, Candlewick Press, Inc., Somerville, MA.)

Elliott introduces a determined young heroine in **Hazel Nutt, Alien Hunter,** ***a picture book featuring suitably quirky cartoon illustrations by True Kelley.*** (Illustration copyright © 2004 by True Kelley. All rights reserved. Reproduced by permission of Holiday House, Inc.)

Elliott introduces popular character Hazel Nutt in *Hazel Nutt, Mad Scientist,* a story clearly inspired by old horror movies and the author's love of puns. Hazel Nutt is determined to cross a vampire with an opera singer; when she brings her creation to life, she calls it "Dracula-la-la." The townspeople are not thrilled with having a mad scientist in their neighborhood, however, and they approach with torches, ready to drive Hazel out. Instead, the girl invites them to a concert where Dracula-la-la is accompanied by a living piano named "Frankensteinway." "Children with a good sense of humor should appreciate this book," recommended Kristin de Lacoste in her review for *School Library Journal,* while a reviewer for *Publishers Weekly* quipped that the story's "transmonsterfied piano is a hoot."

Hazel goes through a career change in *Hazel Nutt, Alien Hunter,* as she and her crew land their spaceship directly on top of the leader of Planet Wutt. Much confusion ensues, from an Abbott-and-Costello-like discussion about the planet's name to Hazel giving the aliens a ladder. When the ship leaves, the Wuttite leader is miraculously revived. "Elliott's story is nonsensical goofiness," noted a *Kirkus Reviews* contributor, while Lisa Gangemi predicted that *Hazel Nutt, Alien Hunter* "will be a hit with younger fans" of other goofy authors, including Dav Pilkey (author of *Captain Underpants*) and Jon Scieszka (author of the "Timewarp Trio" series).

A young girl raised by primatologists is the heroine of another pair of humorous books by Elliott. Introduced in *Evangeline Mudd and the Golden-haired Apes of the Ikkinasti Jungle,* Evangeline is raised by anthropologist parents in the same way golden-haired apes raise their young. As a result, the girl can use her toes to eat, swing from tree to tree, and complete other daring ape-type tasks. When Evangeline is eight years old, her par-

ents leave on a research trip and deposit her at her uncle's house. A mink rancher, the uncle is unkind to both animals and the environment, and he is also possibly plotting against Evangeline's parents! When Dr. Aphrodite Pikkaflee warns the girl that her parents have vanished, it is up to Evangeline and a new friend to save the day. The "madcap adventures will appeal to kids with a taste for silliness," noted a *Publishers Weekly* critic and B. Allison Gray wrote in *School Library Journal* that in *Evangeline Mudd and the Golden-haired Apes of the Ikkinasti Jungle* "everything is sorted out neatly, but not facilely, in the end."

Evangeline returns in *Evangeline Mudd and the Great Mink Escapade,* which finds her busy staging another animal rescue. A group of minks are threatened because their fur is desired for ballet costumes, and Evangeline is determined to change their fate. Joining with noted young dancer Alexy Alexy, the girl tracks down the ballet promoter, who turns out to be her own distant cousin Melvin Mudd. Saving the minks starts Evangeline on a succession of selfless acts, one of which is helping Alexy escape the control of maniacal dance master Ratsputin. "Elliott doesn't miss any opportunity to toss bucketfuls of humor into his farcical plot," wrote *Booklist* critic Todd Morning in a review of *Evangeline Mudd and the Great Mink Escapade,* and in *School Library Journal* Terrie Dorio deemed the book a "rollicking adventure" with "an underlying theme of respect for all living things."

Although most of his books are beginning readers geared for the early elementary grades, Elliott has also created texts for several picture books. Featuring a rhyming text, *And Here's to You!* toasts the creatures of land and sea, from birds to bugs to fish to humans. Cows, sheep, rabbits, and chickens are among the stars

of *On the Farm,* which pairs Elliott's rhyming text with Holly Meade's pictures, while *Knitty Kitty* recalls a popular nursery rhyme in its story about a mother cat who busily knits wintertime garments—including the traditional mittens—for her three kittens. Andrea Tarr deemed *And Here's to You!* "a powerful package," while a critic for *Kirkus Reviews* noted that the work "will have young readers and listeners calling for another round." In *Horn Book* Susan Dove Lempke noted that *On the Farm* "will make an unusually interesting choice for farm-animal storytimes," and in *School Library Journal* Jane Marino wrote of *Knitty Kitty* that the author "tells the story in economical, repetitive and rhythmic words and phrases that . . . lull and comfort" its intended preschool audience.

He also addresses older children in the novel *Jeremy Cabbage and the Living Museum of Human Oddballs and Quadruped Delights.* Here readers meet an eleven-year-old orphan who feels lucky to be saved from a dismal orphanage, even though his new parents are rather odd. In fact, Jeremy's parents Bo and Ba are cloons: people suffering from a genetic condition in which they actually possess the big feet, bulbous red nose, and other features characteristic of circus clowns. When cloons and other misfits are banished from town by their city's dictator, Jeremy also comes under government scrutiny and must work to keep the family he has come to love. Although Robyn Gioia expressed concern in her *School Library Journal* review that the unfolding plot might be difficult for readers to follow due to its many flashbacks, the "unique characters" peopling Elliott's tale "make their pieces of the puzzle fun to read." In *Booklist,* Kay Weisman praised *Jeremy Cabbage and the Living Museum of Human Oddballs and Quadruped Delights* as a "madcap fantasy full of quirky characters and outrageous adventures" on the order of the author's other popular books for children.

Other books by Elliott that are geared for pre-readers include two titles featuring artwork by Ethan Long. In *One Little Chicken: A Counting Book* numbers from one to ten are featured as chubby chickens take to the stage in ten different dance performances. Goofy jokes are the source of the humor in *Wuv Bunnies from Outer Pace,* in which a group of floppy-eared space travelers are determined to save Earth from a race of bad bunnies. According to a *Kirkus Reviews* writer, *Wuv Bunnies from Outer Pace* "is perfectly pitched to its audience and guaranteed to garner groans from the grown-ups," and *One Little Chicken* was described by *Booklist* critic Julie Cummins as "clever preschool chick lit that you can count on to be a favorite." Elliott also teams up with illustrator Max Grafe for *What the Grizzly Knows,* a story that a *Kirkus Reviews* writer described as a "lyrical" picture book about a teddy bear that transforms into a grizzly bear during a young boy's dream. Elliott's "spare, poetic" text for *What the Grizzly Knows* "creates a believable childlike dream world," the *Kirkus Reviews* critic added, while also praising Grafe's characteristic hazy, warm-toned art.

While Elliott's books are lighthearted and zany, their genesis is not necessarily instantaneous; sometimes takes months for an idea to arrange itself as a story. Young people continue to be his readership of choice; as he told an interviewer on the Candlewick Press Web site: "I love kids. I love their raw intelligence, their unfiltered, almost savage honesty, their Roman sense of justice. Kids still believe that bad guys get done in. I also love how almost pathologically conspiratorial children are. As a writer, who could ask for a better audience?"

Biographical and Critical Sources

PERIODICALS

Booklist, September 15, 2000, John Peters, review of *The Cool Crazy Crickets,* p. 240; October 15, 2003, Todd Morning, review of *Hazel Nutt, Mad Scientist,* p. 418; February 15, 2006, review of *Evangeline Mudd and*

Another engaging—and unusual—heroine is featured in Elliott's middle-grade novel **Evangeline Mudd and the Great Mink Escapade,** *which features art by Andréa Wesson.* (Illustration copyright © 2006 by Andréa Wesson. All rights reserved. Reproduced by permission of the publisher, Candlewick Press, Inc., Somerville, MA.)

the Great Mink Escapade, p. 98; March 15, 2007, Kay Weisman, review of *Jeremy Cabbage and the Living Museum of Human Oddballs and Quadruped Delights,* p. 50; November 15, 2007, Julie Cummins, review of *One Little Chicken: A Counting Book,* p. 50; May 15, 2008, Jennifer Mattson, review of *On the Farm,* p. 44; November 1, 2008, Shelle Rosenfeld, review of *What the Grizzly Knows,* p. 50.

Children's Bookwatch, October, 2004, review of *Hazel Nutt, Alien Hunter.*

Horn Book, March-April, 2008, Susan Dove Lempke, review of *On the Farm,* p. 223.

Kirkus Reviews, February 1, 2004, review of *Evangeline Mudd and the Golden-haired Apes of the Ikkinasti Jungle,* p. 132; March 15, 2004, review of *And Here's to You!,* p. 268; August 15, 2004, review of *Hazel Nutt, Alien Hunter,* p. 805; May 1, 2008, review of *Wuv Bunnies from Outer Pace;* September 15, 2008, review of *What the Grizzly Knows.*

People, August 26, 1991, review of *An Alphabet of Rotten Kids!,* p. 31.

Publishers Weekly, May 24, 1991, review of *An Alphabet of Rotten Kids!,* p. 58; June 25, 2000, review of *The Cool Crazy Crickets,* p. 75; May 7, 2001, review of *The Transmogrification of Roscoe Wizzle,* p. 247; October 13, 2003, review of *Hazel Nutt, Mad Scientist,* p. 77; March 15, 2004, review of *Evangeline Mudd and the Golden-haired Apes of the Ikkinasti Jungle,* p. 75; March 3, 2008, review of *On the Farm,* p. 44; June 30, 2008, review of *Knitty Kitty,* p. 183.

School Library Journal, August, 2000, Kate McLean, review of *The Cool Crazy Crickets,* p. 154; June, 2001, Eva Mitnick, review of *The Transmogrification of Roscoe Wizzle,* p. 112; July, 2001, Roxanne Burg, review of *The Cool Crazy Crickets to the Rescue!,* p. 75; March, 2004, Kristin de Lacoste, review of *Hazel Nutt, Mad Scientist,* p. 156, B. Allison Gray, review of *Evangeline Mudd and the Golden-haired Apes of the Ikkinasti Jungle,* p. 156; May, 2004, Andrea Tarr, review of *And Here's to You!,* p. 109; October, 2004, Lisa Gangemi, review of *Hazel Nutt, Alien Hunter,* p. 112; March, 2006, Terrie Dorio, review of *Evangeline Mudd and the Great Mink Escapade,* p. 186; December, 2007, Mary Jean Smith, review of *One Little Chicken,* p. 88; June, 2008, Robyn Gioia, review of *Jeremy Cabbage and the Living Museum of Human Oddballs and Quadruped Delights,* p. 138; September, 2008, Jane Marino, review of *Knitty Kitty,* p. 145; October, 2008, Joanna K. Fabicon, review of *Wuv Bunnies from Outer Pace,* p. 106.

ONLINE

Candlewick Press Web site, http://www.candlewick.com/ (May 20, 2009), "David Elliott."

David Elliott Home Page, http://www.davidelliottbooks.com (May 20, 2009).*

*   *   *

EVANS, Nate

Personal

Married.

Addresses

Home—Statesboro, GA.

Career

Author and illustrator of children's books. Formerly worked as an artist at a greeting-card company.

Writings

(Self-illustrated) *The Mixed-up Zoo of Professor Yahoo,* Junior League of Kansas City, Missouri (Kansas City, MO), 1992.

(And illustrator; coauthor with Paul Hindman) *Dragon Bones,* Random House (New York, NY), 1997.

(With Laura Numeroff) *Sherman Crunchley,* illustrated by Tim Bowers, Dutton (New York, NY), 2003.

(With Laura Numeroff) *The Jellybeans and the Big Dance,* illustrated by Lynn Munsinger, Harry Abrams (New York, NY), 2008.

(And illustrator with Vince Evans; coauthor with Paul Hindman) *The Mystery of Merlin and the Gruesome Ghost,* Sourcebooks Jabberwocky (Naperville, IL), 2008.

(And illustrator with Vince Evans; coauthor with Paul Hindman) *Humpty Dumpty, Jr., Hardboiled Detective, in the Case of the Fiendish Flapjack Flop,* Sourcebooks Jabberwocky (Naperville, IL), 2008.

ILLUSTRATOR

Margo Lundell, *My Book of Funny Valentines,* Scholastic (New York, NY), 1993.

Carol Thompson, *Monster Maker,* Cartwheel Books (New York, NY), 1994.

Marjorie Weinman Sharmat, *Tiffany Dino Works Out,* Macmillan (New York, NY), 1995.

Katharine Ross, *Fuzzy Monsters,* Random House (New York, NY), 1995.

Sara Hoagland Hunter, *Rondo's Stuff,* Aladdin (New York, NY), 1996.

Richie Chevat, *No Blue Food!,* Aladdin (New York, NY), 1996.

Roberta Edwards, *Space Kid,* Grosset & Dunlap (New York, NY), 1996.

H.B. Gilmour, *The Amazing Zoo,* Aladdin (New York, NY), 1996.

Ellen Weiss, *First Day at Day Care,* Aladdin (New York, NY), 1996.

Way out in Space, Grosset and Dunlap (New York, NY), 1996.

Mary Packard, *I Am Not a Dinosaur,* Scholastic (New York, NY), 1997.

Judith Bauer Stamper, *Monster Town,* Scholastic (New York, NY), 1997.

Hugh Westrup, *Bite Size Science: 150 Facts You Won't Believe,* Scholastic (New York, NY), 1997.

Michael Ratnett, *Horrible Holly's Pet Raptor,* Troll/Bridgewater Books (Mahwah, NJ), 1997.

Judith Bauer Stamper, *Monster Town Fair,* Scholastic (New York, NY), 1998.

Artie Bennett, *The Dinosaur Joke Book: A Compendium of Pre-hysteric Puns,* Random House (New York, NY), 1998.

Laura Numeroff, *Monster Munchies,* Random House (New York, NY), 1998.

Sarah Albee, *My Best Friend Is out of This World,* Golden Books (New York, NY), 1998.

Ted Pedersen and Francis Moss, *Make Your Own Web Page!: A Guide for Kids,* Price Stern Sloan (New York, NY), 1998.

Sarah Albee, *My New Pet Is the Greatest,* Golden Books (New York, NY), 1999.

Alexa Witt, *It's Great to Skate!: An Easy Guide to In-line Skating,* Simon & Schuster (New York, NY), 2000.

Tui Sutherland, *Monster Party,* Grosset & Dunlap (New York, NY), 2000.

Carol Molski, *A Little Taste of God's Love: Bible Story Recipes and Activities,* Concordia Publishing House (St. Louis, MO), 2001.

Dana Meachen Rau, *Clown Around,* Compass Point Books (Minneapolis, MN), 2001.

Laura Numeroff, *Laura Numeroff's Ten-Step Guide to Living with Your Monster,* Laura Geringer Books (New York, NY), 2002.

Sidelights

Beginning his art career as an illustrator of greeting cards, Nate Evans spent a decade in that position before deciding to devote his energies full-time to creating children's books. As he remarked on his home page, "Finally I decided that I had to do the thing that I loved most: I had to try to write and illustrate books for kids (kids like me, who love to read and look at funny pictures)." While much of Evans's early efforts were spent illustrating the books of other authors, his work began to diversify when he teamed up with other authors to write not only picture books, but also short mystery novels featuring the son of children's nursery rhyme character Humpty Dumpty.

In 1998, with the publication of Evans's artwork in *Monster Munchies,* the artist began what would become a productive collaboration with author Laura Numeroff. Five years later, the pair co-wrote *Sherman Crunchley,* the story of a canine police officer who is tapped to fill his retiring father's position as police chief. Unfortunately for Sherman, his greatest job satisfaction comes from wearing a police hat, not from being a police officer. Unsure of how to break the news to his sure-to-be disappointed dad, the dog decides to relay his decision to turn down the promotion by designing a series of special hats to be worn at the elder Crunchley's retirement bash. Much to Sherman's surprise, however, his father delights at the decision, as the elder officer did not actually want to step down. Several reviewers commended the book's message about the importance of being able to say no in spite of the fear of disappointing others. Writing in *School Library Journal,* Sheilah Kosco predicted that young readers will "enjoy this funny tale, and they might even learn a lesson about life in the process." A *Kirkus Reviews* contributor wrote that *Sherman Crunchley* provides children a reassuring story about choosing to say no, because "the house will not fall down and family and friends will not flee" just because one decides against other people's wishes. A *Publishers Weekly* critic similarly claimed that Numeroff and Evans "have crafted a mild-mannered, humorous tale about handling a difficult situation."

Numeroff and Evans team up again in *The Jellybeans and the Big Dance,* a picture book featuring illustrations by Lynn Munsinger. When young Emily the dog signs up for dance lessons, she becomes disappointed to learn that the other students in the class do not share her unbounded enthusiasm for dancing: one would rather be playing soccer, another painting pictures, and another reading a book. Sensing her daughter's unhappiness over her dance partners, Emily's mom suggests a trip to the candy store where a jelly-bean snack inspires the young canine to figure out how to incorporate everyone's special interest into a unique performance at the dance recital. For a *Kirkus Reviews* contributor, *The Jellybeans and the Big Dance* provides a "timely tale of forging connections despite seemingly insurmountable differences." Finding the narrative "well paced" with "clever, whimsical touches," *Booklist* reviewer Gillian Engberg predicted that Evans and Numeroff's book about resolving differences will be "a sure hit with kids on the dance-recital circuit."

Nate Evans joins coauthor Laura Numeroff and illustrator Tim Bowers to create the imaginative picture-book adventure **Sherman Crunchley.**

Coauthors Evans and Laura Numeroff combine their talents in a colorful picture-book outing, The Jellybeans and the Big Dance, *featuring artwork by Lynn Munsinger.* (Illustration copyright © 2008 by Lynn Munsinger. All rights reserved. Reproduced by permission.)

Biographical and Critical Sources

PERIODICALS

Booklist, November 15, 1995, Susan Dove Lempke, review of *Tiffany Dino Works Out,* p. 566; April 15, 2008, Gillian Engberg, review of *The Jellybeans and the Big Dance,* p. 49; October 1, 2008, Ian Chipman, review of *Humpty Dumpty, Jr., Hardboiled Detective, in the Case of the Fiendish Flapjack Flop,* p. 44.

Kirkus Reviews, August 15, 2003, review of *Sherman Crunchley,* p. 1077; February 15, 2008, review of *The Jellybeans and the Big Dance.*

Publishers Weekly, September 1, 1997, review of *Holly's Pet Raptor,* p. 104; February 25, 2002, review of *Laura Numeroff's Ten-Step Guide to Living with Your Monster,* p. 65; October 13, 2003, review of *Sherman Crunchley,* p. 77; February 11, 2008, review of *The Jellybeans and the Big Dance,* p. 69.

School Library Journal, April, 2000, Kate Kohlbeck, review of *It's Great to Skate!: An Easy Guide to In-line Skating,* p. 128; August, 2001, Melinda Piehler, review of *Clown Around,* p. 158; June, 2002, John Sigwald, review of *Laura Numeroff's Ten-Step Guide to Living with Your Monster,* p. 106; December, 2003, Sheilah Kosco, review of *Sherman Crunchley,* p. 122; June, 2008, Julie R. Ranelli, review of *The Jellybeans and the Big Dance,* p. 112.

ONLINE

Nate Evans Home Page, http://www.nateevans.com (May 5, 2009).*

* * *

FARMER, Philipé Jos
See FARMER, Philip José

* * *

FARMER, Philip José 1918-2009
(Philip Jose Farmer, Philipé Jos Farmer, Kilgore Trout, John H. Watson)

OBITUARY NOTICE—

See index for *SATA* sketch: Born January 26, 1918, in North Terre Haute, IN; died February 25, 2009, in Peoria, IL. Technical writer, novelist, and short-story writer. Farmer was not well known to the general public as one of the giants of science fiction, but to millions of science-fiction readers around the world he was warmly regarded as a major architect of the genre as it is known today. Like many science-fiction writers of his generation, Farmer was extraordinarily prolific, but he worked as a technical writer for several years before his fiction provided a sustainable living. When he became a full-time writer, his output was even more prodigious. Some critics faulted him for working at such a breakneck pace that errors and rambling plots sometimes made it

into print, but even his critics excused such lapses in order to experience his breathtaking flights of imagination. Farmer introduced at least two elements into the science-fiction genre that were new. He dared to write about sex (between human and alien, no less) in a genre that had been surprisingly prudish until then, and that was one of many controversial topics he invited readers to explore. He also blended elements of mystery, romance, historical fiction, and other genres that had traditionally been kept apart. Though he wrote dozens of stand-alone novels and hundreds of short stories, Farmer excelled at creating worlds so complex and compelling that they supported long-running series. "Riverworld," which began in 1971 with the novel *To Your Scattered Bodies Go,* is set on a planet with a million-mile river, to which every human who ever lived and others who did not—from Odysseus to Cyrano de Bergerac—is reincarnated at the same time to pursue a universal quest to find the headwaters of the river. *To Your Scattered Bodies Go* received one of Farmer's three Hugo awards from the World Science Fiction Convention. Another series, "Worlds of Trier," beginning with *The Maker of Universes: The Enigma of the Many-leveled Cosmos* (1980), and features a futuristic race of men so technically advanced that each one (including, perhaps, God himself) could create a unique, complete world for his personal enjoyment. *Dayworld* (1985) and its companion volumes explores a world so overcrowded that each inhabitant spends only one day each week awake and the other six days asleep, waiting his turn—until one of them fakes seven identities so that he can experience every single day. One of Farmer's stand-alone novels, *Venus on the Half-Shell* (1975), was published under the pseudonym Kilgore Trout, supposedly as a tribute to author Kurt Vonnegut, Jr., who created the character. Vonnegut, who supposedly approved the project initially, was not amused; Farmer was chagrined. He also wrote in the persona of Sherlock Holmes's sidekick John H. Watson. Farmer explored so many creative themes in his fifty-year career that they cannot be summarized, except through the prestigious awards that came his way, including the Nebula Grand Master Award of the Science Fiction and Fantasy Writers of America and a World Fantasy award for lifetime achievement. Farmer's last novel was *The City beyond Play* (2007).

OBITUARIES AND OTHER SOURCES:

PERIODICALS

Chicago Tribune, February 27, 2009, sec. 1, p. 29.
Los Angeles Times, March 4, 2009, p. A26.
New York Times, February 27, 2009, p. B1.

*   *   *

FARMER, Philip Jose
    See FARMER, Philip José

FEHLER, Gene 1940-

Personal

Surname is pronounced "*fay*-ler"; born September 30, 1940, in Savanna, IL; son of Franklin and Hazel (Ashpole) Fehler; married Polly Diane Eggert (a nurse educator), December 26, 1964; children: Timothy Gene, Andrew Scott. *Education:* Northern Illinois University, B.S., 1962, M.S., 1968. *Religion:* Protestant. *Hobbies and other interests:* Baseball, golf, tennis, playing board and card games, old movies.

Addresses

Home—Seneca, SC. *E-mail*—Fehler@nctv.com.

Career

Educator and author. Kishwaukee College, Malta, IL, English teacher and writer-in-residence, 1969-80; teacher at Park College, Austin, TX, Austin Community College, Austin, Auburn University at Montgomery, Montgomery, AL, and at high schools in Illinois, Texas, and Georgia. Visiting poet at artist-in-education programs in Alabama, Texas, and South Carolina.

Member

National Federation of State Poetry Societies, Society for American Baseball Research, Texas Poetry Society, Austin Poetry Society.

Awards, Honors

Jim Harrison Award, *Spitball* magazine, 1984, for outstanding contributions to baseball literature.

Writings

Center Field Grasses: Poems from Baseball, McFarland & Co. (Jefferson, NC), 1991.
I Hit the Ball!: Baseball Poems for the Young, illustrated by Mike Schact, McFarland & Co. (Jefferson, NC), 1996.
Tales from Baseball's Golden Age (nonfiction), Sports Publishing, 2000.
Let the Poems Begin!: A Poet's Guide to Writing Poetry, Good Apple, 2000.
Dancing on the Basepaths: Baseball Poetry and Verse, McFarland & Co. (Jefferson, NC), 2001.
More Tales from Baseball's Golden Age (nonfiction), Sports Publishing, 2002.
(With Robert Harrison) *Goblin Giggles: A Ghastly Lift-the-Flap Book,* illustrated by Lee Calderon, Little Simon (New York, NY), 2005.
Beanball (young-adult verse novel), Clarion (New York, NY), 2008.
Change-up: Baseball Poems, illustrated by Donald Wu, Clarion (New York, NY), 2009.

Contributor of poems and short stories to periodicals and anthologies, including *Baseball, I Gave You All the Best Years of My Life,* North Atlantic Books, 1978; *Baseball Diamonds,* Anchor Press, 1980; *From Hide and Horn,* Eakin Press, 1985; *Light Year '86,* Bits Press, 1985; *Light Year '87,* Bits Press, 1986; *The Bedford Introduction to Literature,* St. Martin's Press (New York, NY), 1987; *Writing Poems,* Little, Brown (Boston, MA), 1987; *The Best of Spitball,* Pocket Books (New York, NY), 1988; and *At the Crack of the Bat,* Hyperion (New York, NY), 1992. Work featured in documentary film *When It Was a Game II,* produced by Home Box Office.

POETRY CHAPBOOKS

The Day Willy Missed the Bus, Mailbox Press, 1979.
But Nobody Slam-Dunked, Mailbox Press, 1979.
By Book or by Crook, Mailbox Press, 1985.
When Main Street Was One Block Long: Poems from a Small-Town Childhood, Mailbox Press, 1999.
Breaking into a Smile: Poems with a Light Touch, Mailbox Press, 1999.
The Silly (and Sometimes Serious) Side of Sports: Sports Poems, Mailbox Press, 1999.

Sidelights

Baseball is a subject very close to Gene Fehler's heart, and he shares his affection and enthusiasm for the All-American sport in poems for both old and young. Pee Wee players are introduced to the rudiments of the game in *I Hit the Ball!: Baseball Poems for the Young,* an anthology that Steve Gietschier described in *Sporting News* as full of "beauty, whimsy, fantasy, and memory." Adults are the intended readers of *Center Field Grasses: Poems from Baseball* and *Dancing on the Basepaths: Baseball Poetry and Verse,* while Fehler turns to a teen readership in *Beanball,* his first verse novel.

In *Beanball* Fehler introduces Luke "Wizard" Wallace, a high schooler who seems to have it all—good grades, a popular girlfriend, and a top spot on the school baseball team—until a wild fastball hits him head-on and propels the teen into a three-day coma, partial blindness, and a medical nightmare from which he may never emerge. Luke's ordeal is recounted from the viewpoint of over two dozen different viewpoints—witnesses, friends, family members, players from the rival team, his girlfriend, and his coach—all of which are expressed in free verse. While *Booklist* critic Linda Perkins wrote that some of the book's characters are stereotypical, in *Beanball* Fehler creates a teen protagonist who is "real and believable," according to the critic. A *Publishers Weekly* reviewer cited the author's "clear grasp of the dedicated athlete's mind" and his ability to capture the emotions such a person would feel upon being "suddenly and seemingly permanently sidelined." In *Kliatt* Paula Rohrlick praised *Beanball,* calling it a "moving" story and a "swift read [that] will appeal to . . . reluctant readers" as well as fans of America's favorite pastime.

Cover of Gene Fehler's young-adult novel Beanball, *featuring photography by Chris Mooney.* (Clarion Books, 2008. Cover photographs copyright by Chris Mooney/Getty Images (baseball), and SW Productions/Getty Images (pitcher).)

Fehler once told *SATA:* "I grew up in Thomson, Illinois, a town of five hundred people. My wife and sons and I moved to the South in 1980; yet if I have a personal voice as a writer, it is a Midwestern voice, shaped by growing up within sight of [Mark] Twain's Mississippi; shaped by forty years of having lived and taught in Illinois; shaped by attending a tiny country Methodist church whose yard bordered and joined with ours, a yard where I spent hour upon pleasant hour with my two sons playing baseball and tossing a football. That big backyard in the shadow of a church steeple and surrounded by cornfields was not only 'Our Yankee Stadium,' as I described it in my poem 'Backyard Glory'—it was our own field of dreams.

"Most of my fondest memories of my childhood and teen years are of playing baseball, basketball, and sandlot football. And reading. Our village library was open only a few hours a week, on Wednesday evenings and Saturday afternoons. I loved to browse through the children's and young-adult collections. Each visit would excite me with a new discovery, a new book or series with its unique colors and smell and feel and story. In

high school, I think I managed to read every sports novel in our public and school libraries.

"I started to write poetry only when I realized it was entirely permissible to enjoy a poem even without being able to decipher its meaning. For a long time I had worried that I wasn't very good at understanding poetry. I was thirty-three years old before I learned that the understanding isn't as important as enjoying the sounds and images and emotions. I like what Dylan Thomas said of poetry: 'All that matters is the enjoyment of it.' The understanding of it is merely a nice bonus. . . .

"Some say poetry is 'a lie that tells the truth.' That's true of most of my poems, especially those in which I've drawn from my own experiences yet strayed from the truth in order to create a particular effect. I try to write the kind of poems I most like to read: poems about people (almost all of my poems, even my baseball poems, have people in them), poems that tell stories, poems that stir the emotions, poems with pleasing sounds—yet always poems that illustrate a careful attention to craft. Almost everything I write goes through many drafts as I search for the best words and the best form. I would offer young writers this advice: don't be afraid to revise. You must cross out passages, add details, rethink, reshape. But most of all—write, and write often. You might have to write ten or twenty poems or stories that fail for each one that works. But creating one that works makes the effort worthwhile.

"While I continue to write poems, much of my writing time is spent working on picture books for children and on young adult novels. And while baseball and other sports play a major role in some of the books, those books are not so much 'sport' books as they are books about the people whose lives just happen to be in some way touched by the world of sport."

Biographical and Critical Sources

PERIODICALS

Booklist, February 15, 2008, Linda Perkins, review of *Beanball*, p. 75.
Kliatt, January, 2008, Paula Rohrlick, review of *Beanball*, p. 6.
Publishers Weekly, February 4, 2008, review of *Beanball*, p. 58.
School Library Journal, May, 2008, Marilyn Taniguchi, review of *Beanball*, p. 122.
Sporting News, May 20, 1996, Steve Gietschier, review of *I Hit the Ball!: Baseball Poems for the Young*, p. 8.

ONLINE

Gene Fehler Home Page, http://www.genefehler.com (June 2, 2009).*

FEIFFER, Jules 1929-

Personal

Born January 26, 1929, in Bronx, NY; son of David (a dental technician, then salesman) and Rhoda (a fashion designer) Feiffer; married Judith Sheftel (a motion picture executive), September 17, 1961 (divorced 1983); married Jennifer Allen (a journalist), September 11, 1983; children: (first marriage) Kate; (second marriage) Halley, Julie. *Education:* Attended Art Students' League, 1946, and Pratt Institute, 1947-48, 1949-51.

Addresses

Home—New York, NY; Martha's Vineyard, MA. *Agent*—Royce Carlton Inc., 866 United Nations Plaza, New York, NY 10017. *E-mail*—julesfeiffer@gmail.com.

Career

Playwright, cartoonist, and author/illustrator. Assistant to cartoonist Will Eisner, 1946-51; drew syndicated cartoon series "Clifford," 1949-51; held various art jobs, 1953-56, including making slide films, as writer for Terrytoons, and as designer of booklets for an art film; cartoons syndicated by Publishers-Hall Syndicate and distributed to more than one hundred newspapers in the United States and abroad, 1956-2000. Member of faculty at Yale University School of Drama, 1972-73, Northwestern University, 1996, and Southampton College, 1999—; senior fellow of national arts journalism program, Columbia University, 1997. *Exhibitions:* Retrospective staged at University of Wisconsin-Milwaukee, 2003. *Military service:* U.S. Army, Signal Corps, 1951-53; worked in cartoon-animation unit.

Member

Authors League of America, Dramatists Guild (member of council), PEN, Writers Guild of America, East.

Awards, Honors

Academy Award for Best Short-Subject Cartoon, Academy of Motion Picture Arts and Sciences, 1961, for *Munro;* Special George Polk Memorial Award, 1961; most promising playwright award, New York Drama Critics, 1966-67, Best Foreign Play of the Year designation, London Theatre Critics, 1967, and Outer Critics Circle Award, and Off-Broadway Award, *Village Voice,* both 1969, all for *Little Murders;* Outer Critics Circle Award, 1970, for *The White House Murder Case;* Pulitzer Prize, 1986, for editorial cartooning; Best Screenplay honor, Venice Film Festival, 1989, for *I Want to Go Home;* elected to American Academy of Arts & Letters, 1995; honorary D.H.L., Long Island University, 1999; Red Colver Children's Choice Picture Book Award, 2000, for *Bark, George;* Milton Caniff Lifetime Achievement Award, National Cartoonists Society, 2003; Ian McLellan Hunter Award for Lifetime Achievement in Writing, Writers Guild of America, East, 2004;

Jules Feiffer (Photograph by Lawrence Lucier/Getty Images.)

Harold Washington Literary Award, 2004; Patricia A. Barr Shalom Award, Americans for Peace Now, 2004; named Creativity Foundation laureate, 2006; Writers Guild Award award for lifetime achievement, 2007.

Writings

The Man in the Ceiling, HarperCollins (New York, NY), 1993.

A Barrel of Laughs, a Vale of Tears, HarperCollins (New York, NY), 1995.

Meanwhile . . . , HarperCollins (New York, NY), 1997.

I Lost My Bear, Morrow (New York, NY), 1998.

Bark, George, HarperCollins (New York, NY), 1999.

I'm Not Bobby!, Hyperion (New York, NY), 2001.

By the Side of the Road, Hyperion (New York, NY), 2002.

The House across the Street, Hyperion (New York, NY), 2002.

The Daddy Mountain, Hyperion (New York, NY), 2004.

A Room with a Zoo, Michael di Capua Books (New York, NY), 2005.

FOR CHILDREN; ILLUSTRATOR

Norton Juster, *The Phantom Tollbooth,* Random House (New York, NY), 1961, published with an appreciation by Maurice Sendak, Random House (New York, NY), 1996.

Florence Parry Heide, *Some Things Are Scary,* Candlewick Press (Cambridge, MA), 2000.

Jenny Allen, *The Long Chalkboard and Other Stories,* Pantheon (New York, NY), 2006.

Kate Feiffer, *Henry, the Dog with No Tail,* Simon & Schuster (New York, NY), 2007.

FOR ADULTS; CARTOONS, UNLESS OTHERWISE NOTED

Sick, Sick, Sick: A Guide to Non-confident Living, McGraw (New York, NY), 1958, with introduction by Kenneth Tynan, Collins (London, England), 1959.

Passionella and Other Stories, McGraw (New York, NY), 1959.

(Illustrator) Robert Mines, *My Mind Went All to Pieces,* Dial (New York, NY), 1959.

The Explainers, McGraw (New York, NY), 1960.

Boy, Girl, Boy, Girl, Random House (New York, NY), 1961.

Feiffer's Album, Random House (New York, NY), 1963.

Hold Me!, Random House (New York, NY), 1963.

Harry, the Rat with Women (novel), McGraw (New York, NY), 1963.

(Compiler and annotator) *The Great Comic Book Heroes,* Dial (New York, NY), 1965, revised edition, Fantagraphics Books (Seattle, WA), 2003.

The Unexpurgated Memories of Bernard Mergendeiler (also see below), Random House (New York, NY), 1965.

The Penguin Feiffer, Penguin (London, England), 1966.

Feiffer on Civil Rights, Anti-Defamation League (New York, NY), 1966.

Feiffer's Marriage Manual, Random House (New York, NY), 1967.

Pictures at a Prosecution: Drawings and Text from the Chicago Conspiracy Trial, Grove (New York, NY), 1971.

Feiffer on Nixon: The Cartoon Presidency, Random House (New York, NY), 1974.

Ackroyd (novel), Simon & Schuster (New York, NY), 1977.

Tantrum: A Novel-in-Cartoons, Knopf (New York, NY), 1979.

Feiffery: Jules Feiffer's America from Eisenhower to Reagan, Knopf (New York, NY), 1982.

Marriage Is an Invasion of Privacy, and Other Dangerous Views, Andrews McMeel (Kansas City, MO), 1984.

Feiffer's Children: Including Munro, Andrews McMeel (Kansas City, MO), 1986.

Ronald Reagan in Movie America: A Jules Feiffer Production, Andrews McMeel (Kansas City, MO), 1988.

Feiffer: The Collected Works, Volume 1, Fantagraphics Books (Seattle, WA), 1989.

Feiffer: The Collected Works, Volume 2, Fantagraphics Books (Seattle, WA), 1989.

Feiffer: The Collected Works, Volume 3, Fantagraphics Books (Seattle, WA), 1991.

Feiffer: The Collected Works, Volume 4, Fantagraphics Books (Seattle, WA), 1997.

Explainers: The Complete Village Voice Strips, Volume 1: *1956-1966,* Fantagraphics Books (Seattle, WA), 2008.

Contributor of cartoons, including "Explainer" strip to *Village Voice,* 1956-97, and cartoons to London *Observer,* 1958-66, 1972-2000, and *Playboy,* beginning 1959. Ghost-writer for comic-book series "The Spirit," 1949-51. Contributor to periodicals, including *Ramparts.*

Feiffer's books have been translated into German, Swedish, Italian, Dutch, French, and Japanese.

PLAYS

The Explainers (satirical review; based on his comic strip), produced in Chicago, IL, 1961.

Crawling Arnold (one-act; produced in Spoleto, Italy, 1961; produced by WEAV-TV, 1963), Dramatists Play Service (New York, NY), 1963.

The World of Jules Feiffer, produced in New Jersey, 1962.

The Unexpurgated Memoirs of Bernard Mergendeiler (based on Feiffer's cartoons; produced in Los Angeles, CA, 1967; produced off-Broadway as part of *Collision Course,* 1968), published in *Collision Course,* edited by Edward Parone, Random House (New York, NY), 1968.

Little Murders (two-act comedy; produced on Broadway, 1967; produced by Royal Shakespeare Company, London, England, 1967; revived off-Broadway, 1969), Random House (New York, NY), 1968.

God Bless, produced in New Haven, CT, 1968; produced by Royal Shakespeare Company, 1968.

Feiffer's People: Sketches and Observations, (produced in Edinburgh, Scotland, 1968; produced in Los Angeles, CA, 1971), Dramatists Play Service (New York, NY), 1969.

Dick and Jane (one-act; also see below; revised by Kenneth Tynan and produced in New York, NY, in *Oh! Calcutta!* 1969), published in *Oh! Calcutta!,* edited by Tynan, Grove (New York, NY), 1969.

The White House Murder Case [and] *Dick and Jane* (*The White House Murder Case* produced in New York, NY, 1970), Grove (New York, NY), 1970.

(With others) *The Watergate Classics,* produced in New Haven, CT, 1973.

Knock-Knock (produced in New York, NY, 1974), Hill & Wang (New York, NY), 1976.

Hold Me! (produced in New York, NY, 1977), Dramatists Play Service (New York, NY), 1977.

Grown-ups (produced in New York, NY, 1981), Samuel French (New York, NY), 1982.

A Think Piece, produced in Chicago, IL, 1982.

Feiffer's America, produced in Evanston, IL, 1988.

Carnal Knowledge, produced in Houston, TX, 1988.

Elliot Loves (produced in Chicago, IL, 1988), Grove (New York, NY), 1990.

Anthony Rose, produced in Philadelphia, PA, 1989.

E-mail (one-act), produced in New York, NY, as part of *Short Talks on the Universe,* 2002.

A Bad Friend (produced in New York, NY, 2003) Dramatists Play Service (New York, NY), 2005.

SCREENPLAYS

Little Murders, Twentieth Century-Fox, 1971.

(With Israel Horovitz) *VD Blues* (produced by Public Broadcasting Service, 1972), Avon (New York, NY), 1974.

Popeye, Paramount, 1980.

(Adapter) *Puss in Boots,* Columbia Broadcast System/Fox Video, 1984.

I Want to Go Home, Marvin Karmitz Productions, 1989.

Contributor of sketches to productions of DMZ Cabaret, New York; writer for *Steve Allen Show,* 1964; author of episode "Kidnapped" for *Happy Endings* (series), American Broadcasting Company, Inc., 1975.

Adaptations

Munro, an animated cartoon based on Feiffer's story, was produced by Rembrandt Films, 1961; *The Apple Tree,* a musical by Jerry Bock and Sheldon Harnick, contains a playlet based on Feiffer's "Passionella," and was produced in New York, NY, 1966; *Harry, the Rat with Women* was adapted as a play produced at the Detroit Institute of Arts, 1966; *Carnal Knowledge* was adapted as a motion picture, Avco Embassy, 1971; *Grown-Ups* was adapted for film and produced by PBS-TV, 1986; *Popeye, the Movie Novel,* based on Feifer's screenplay, was edited and adapted by Richard J. Anobile, Avon, 1980; *Bark, George* was adapted as an animated film narrated by John Lithgow, Weston Woods, 2003.

Sidelights

Decades before he published his first self-illustrated children's book in 1993, Pulitzer Prize-winning cartoonist Jules Feiffer was well known to young readers as the illustrator of Norman Juster's classic 1961 novel *The Phantom Tollbooth.* During the intervening years, Feiffer became known to adult readers as the creator of satiric cartoons published in hundreds of newspapers, while his plays appeared on numerous stages and several, along with the artist/playwright's original screenplays, were adapted for film.

In the early 1990s Feiffer came more than full circle in his creative life, beginning a new phase of his career as a children's book author as well as illustrator. With books such as *By the Side of the Road, The House across the Street,* and *A Room with a Zoo,* he has won new fans who enjoy his sketchy pen-and-ink drawings and quirky texts. In 2008, with the publication of *Henry, the Dog with No Tail,* Feiffer also entered a family collaboration by bringing to life a story by his writer

Feiffer's illustrations for Norton Juster's classic novel **The Phantom Tollbooth** ***started his career in children's books.*** (Illustration copyright © 1961 and renewed 1989 by Jules Feiffer. Used by permission of Random House Children's Books, a division of Random House, Inc. and in the UK by the illustrator.)

daughter Kate Feiffer in what a *Publishers Weekly* contributor described as "insouciant, loose-lined charcoal and watercolor illustrations" featuring the tale's doggy characters.

Born in the Bronx, New York, in 1929, Feiffer was the son of a Polish mother and a father whose unsuccessful business ventures caused money worries to haunt the Feiffer household. The trials of the Great Depression did not help matters, and young Jules reacted by escaping into books—more specifically comic books such as

"Detective Comics"—and drawing. When Feiffer was approximately seven years of age, he won a gold medal in an art contest sponsored by a New York City department store. Knowing that a good job would help him avoid the financial plight of his parents, he decided to become a cartoonist. As Feiffer recalled in *The Great Comic Book Heroes:* "I . . . drew sixty-four pages in two days, sometimes one day, stapled the product together, and took it out on the street where kids my age sat behind orange crates selling and trading comic books. Mine went for less because they weren't real."

Feiffer studied the comic strips in the pages of the *New York Times* and the *World-Telegram* that his father brought home after work, salvaged newspapers from garbage cans, and got friends to bring him the comics sections from the newspapers their parents discarded. "To see 'Terry and the Pirates,'" Feiffer explained, "we'd have to get the *Daily News,* which my family wouldn't allow in the house." The reason: his parents—both Jewish and both Democrats—believed that the publisher of the New York *Daily News* was anti-Semitic.

At age fifteen Feiffer enrolled at the Art Students' League, then studied at the Pratt Institute for a year, taking night courses. Meanwhile, in 1946, through a stroke of luck, he became an assistant to noted cartoonist Will Eisner. "He said I was worth absolutely nothing, but if I wanted to hang out there, and erase pages or do gofer work, that was fine," Feiffer recalled to Gary Groth in *Comics Journal.* Eisner eventually assigned Feiffer the writing and layout for the comic strip "The Spirit," and in exchange let his young apprentice have the space on the last page of his current strip. Thus, the "Clifford" comic strip was born.

"Clifford" came to a close in 1951, when Feiffer was drafted into the U.S. Army during the Korean War. His experiences as part of the military provided him with the subject he would satirize for most of his remaining career: the workings of the U.S. government. "It was the first time I was truly away from home for a long period of time," Feiffer explained to Groth, "and thrown into a world that was antagonistic to everything I believed in, on every conceivable level. In a war that I was out of sympathy with, and in an army that I despised; [an army that] displayed every rule of illogic and contempt for the individual and mindless exercise of power. [That] became my material."

Released from duty in 1953, Feiffer was at work creating a weekly comic strip for the *Village Voice* by 1956. "We cut a stiff deal," the cartoonist recalled to a writer for *Dramatists Guild Quarterly* of his early attempt to get published. "They would publish anything I wrote and drew as long as I didn't ask to be paid." As he planned, Feiffer got a call from an editor at a different publication, who, as the cartoonist recalled, "said, 'oh boy, this guy is good, he's in the *Voice*,' and accepted the same stuff his company had turned down when I had come to their offices as an unpublished cartoonist."

With the security of regular cartoon assignments, Feiffer could now refine his style, which was already influenced by the work of illustrator William Steig. By the late 1950s, his cartoons appeared regularly in *Playboy,* the London *Observer,* and in newspapers across the United States. Many of these strips have been collected in books such as *Feiffer's Album, Feiffer on Nixon: The Cartoon Presidency,* and *Feiffer's Children: Including Munro.* In 1986 Feiffer was honored with a Pulitzer Prize for editorial cartooning. He continued to create

comic strips on a regular basis for several decades, finally ending his syndicated comic strip in the summer of 2000.

While working as a syndicated cartoonist, Feiffer also began penning plays, and his first drama, *Little Murders,* was produced on Broadway in 1967. The play was a popular and critical success, winning an Outer Critics' Circle award and a *Village Voice* Off-Broadway award, among others. Through the 1980s Feiffer wrote a number of other plays, as well as several screenplays that were produced as major motion pictures. His film *Popeye,* starring Robin Williams, was released in 1980, and his stage works, which include the autobiographical *Grown-ups, The White House Murder Case,* and with *A Bad Friend,* have been produced both in the United States and in Europe.

Feiffer's debut as a children's author came in the early 1990s with *The Man in the Ceiling,* a story about ten-year-old Jimmy Jibbett and his efforts to win the friendship of the popular Charlie Beemer by expressing a willingness to translate Charlie's stories into cartoons. Cathryn M. Camper noted in *Five Owls* that *The Man in the Ceiling* "recognizes that a large part of the for-

Cover of Feiffer's middle-grade novel The Man in the Ceiling. (Illustration copyright © 1993 by Jules Feiffer. Used by permission of HarperCollins Publishers.)

Feiffer's characteristic scratch cartoon art is a feature of his quirky picture book **I'm Not Bobby.** (Illustration copyright © 2001 by Jules Feiffer. Reproduced by permission of Hyperion Books for Children and the illustrator.)

mation of an artist takes place in his or her youth. . . . Feiffer conveys . . . this with a sense of humor, combining samples of Jimmy's comics to help tell the tale."

In *A Room with a Zoo* Feiffer once again gears his tale to an upper-elementary-grade audience, and this time he weaves himself into the tale. Eight-year-old Julie loves animals, and her habit of bringing home new pets makes life in her family's Manhattan apartment rather trying for her adoptive parents, the Feiffers. While some pets fit in with life in the big city, others create problems, and *A Room with a Zoo* focuses on "the less rewarding moments in pet ownership" as much as it depicts Julie's caring and generous nature, according to a *Publishers Weekly* contributor. In *Booklist* Ilene Cooper praised the book as "briskly written with lots of amusing moments," adding that "Feiffer's distinctive drawings delectably capture" the story's action. Sarah Ellis, reviewing *A Room with a Zoo* for *Horn Book,* called Feiffer's final scene "a rollicking tour de force" that crowns the author's "delicate portrayal, in words and line-and-wash drawings, of an interracial family."

Some of Feiffer's children's books feature their creator's characteristic mature satire even as they entertain younger readers with a humorous tale. *A Barrel of Laughs, a Vale of Tears* was described by a *Publishers*

Weekly contributor as "a sophisticatedly silly fairy tale that relaxes storytelling conventions." The topic of road rage prompted by long-distance family auto trips is the focus of *By the Side of the Road,* which finds the parents of an unruly eight year old making good on their threat: "If you don't stop that now you'll end up on the side of the road." Actually deposited on the side of the road and abandoned, the boy makes a new life for himself, is joined by another abandoned child, and grows to adulthood, occasionally receiving visits from his family and becoming the subject of envy by his stay-at-home brother. While noting that *By the Side of the Road* is "really for parents," *New York Times Book Review* contributor Cynthia Zarin wrote that Feiffer "is in top form here."

Feiffer turns to more traditional tales for children with *Meanwhile . . . , The Daddy Mountain,* and *Bark, George,* the last a reversal of the old-lady-who-swallowed-a-fly story. *Meanwhile . . .* draws on a fantasy tradition of a modern sort, as comic-book fan Raymond, pursued by his angry mother, decides to pull the "Meanwhile. . ." dialogue balloon out of his comic book to see if it will transport him somewhere else in a hurry. "Frantic action and the clever theme make this a great read-aloud," concluded *School Library Journal* contributor Lisa S. Murphy. In *The Daddy Mountain,* which narrates a small girl's successful attempt at a daunting ascent up onto her father's shoulders, the author captures what *Booklist* reviewer Jennifer Mattson described as "daddies' special fondness for roughhousing" in illustrations that "are vintage Feiffer," according to Grace Oliff in *School Library Journal.*

A young dog who goes "meow" instead of "arf" is the focus of Feiffer's award-winning *Bark, George,* which finds a pup's distressed mother hurrying her son off to the local vet to find the source of the problem: he has swallowed a cat. Praising *Bark, George* as the "pairing of an ageless joke with a crisp contemporary look," a *Publishers Weekly* contributor dubbed Feiffer's simply drawn illustrations for the book "striking" and "studies in minimalism and eloquence." *Booklist* reviewer Stephanie Zvirin praised Feiffer's "easy to follow" text and added that the author/illustrator's "characters are unforgettable . . . and the pictures burst with the sort of broad physical comedy that a lot of children just love."

I'm Not Bobby finds a young boy determined to be someone else. Refusing to respond to calls for Bobby, he pretends to be a horse, a car, a dinosaur, a giant, and even a space ship in an effort to tune out his mother's calls. Finally, dinner time and fatigue make being Bobby by far the best option in a book that features "Feiffer's exuberantly drawn signature illustrations," according to a *Horn Book* contributor.

Dissatisfaction is also the subject of *The House across the Street,* which finds a young boy wishing he lived in the larger house of a neighborhood friend. While imag-

ining that a wealth of wonderful toys, fabulous dogs, and even a dolphin-filled swimming pool must exist in that amazing house, the boy also conjures up a family in which parents never fight, happy friends come and go, and rooms ring with laughter, giving *The House across the Street* a poignant note while it also captures the whining note of many a "common childhood tune," according to a *Kirkus Reviews* writer. Noting that Feiffer captures "a child's anger about . . . adult authority," *Booklist* contributor Hazel Rochman also praised the book for expressing "a child's loneliness and his soaring imaginative power."

Biographical and Critical Sources

BOOKS

Cohen, Sarah Blacher, editor, *From Hester Street to Hollywood: The Jewish-American Stage and Screen,* Indiana University Press (Bloomington, IN), 1983.

Contemporary Dramatists, 5th edition, St. James Press (Detroit, MI), 1993.

Contemporary Literary Criticism, Volume 64, Gale (Detroit, MI), 1991.

Dictionary of Literary Biography, Gale (Detroit, MI), Volume 7: *Twentieth-Century American Dramatists,* 1981, Volume 44: *American Screenwriters,* 1986.

Encyclopedia of World Biography, 2nd edition, Gale (Detroit, MI), 1998.

Feiffer, Jules, *The Great Comic Book Heroes,* Dial (New York, NY), 1965.

PERIODICALS

American Theatre, May-June, 2003, "Twenty Questions: Jules Feiffer," p. 88.

Back Stage, June 27, 2003, Irene Backalenick, review of *A Bad Friend,* p. 48.

Booklist, November 15, 1993, Elizabeth Bush, review of *The Man in the Ceiling,* p. 620; December 1, 1997, Stephanie Zvirin, review of *Meanwhile . . . ,* p. 636; August 19, 1999, Stephanie Zvirin, review of *Bark, George,* p. 2052; June 1, 2002, Hazel Rochman, review of *By the Side of the Road,* p. 1742; December 1, 2002, Hazel Rochman, review of *The House across the Street,* p. 673; May 1, 2004, Jennifer Mattson, review of *The Daddy Mountain,* p. 1562; September 15, 2005, review of *A Room with a Zoo,* p. 66.

Comics Journal, August, 1988, Gary Groth, "Memories of a Pro Bono Cartoonist"; winter, 2004, "A Thirst for Storytelling."

Dramatists Guild Quarterly, winter, 1987, Christopher Duran, "Jules Feiffer, Cartoonist-Playwright."

Editor & Publisher, May 31, 1986, David Astor, "An Unexpected Pulitzer for Jules Feiffer"; May 29, 2000, Dave Astor, "Feiffer Focus No Longer on Syndication," p. 35.

Five Owls, January-February, 1994, Cathryn M. Camper, review of *The Man in the Ceiling,* pp. 66-67.

Horn Book, March-April, 1998, Lauren Adams, review of *I Lost My Bear,* p. 212; January, 2001, review of *Some Things Are Scary,* p. 83; November-December, 2001, review of *I'm Not Bobby!,* pp. 735-736; May-June, 2002, Kristi Beavin, review of *The Man in the Ceiling,* p. 353; May-June, 2004, Joanna Rudge Long, review of *The Daddy Mountain,* pp. 310-311; December, 2005, Sarah Ellis, review of *A Room with a Zoo,* p. 718.

Kirkus Reviews, November 1, 2002, review of *The House across the Street,* p. 1611; April 1, 2004, review of *The Daddy Mountain,* p. 328; September 15, 2007, review of *The Dog with No Tail.*

Library Journal, July, 2003, Steve Raiteri, review of *The Great Comic Book Heroes,* pp. 69-70.

Los Angeles Times, September 30, 1993, Lawrence Christon, "Jules Feiffer Fine-toons His Career," p. E1; June 17, 2000, John J. Goldman, "Swan Song for Feiffer's Dancer," p. D1.

New Leader, July-August, 2003, Stefan Kanfer, "Family Affairs," pp. 41-43.

New Yorker, December 12, 2005, review of *A Room with a Zoo,* p. 109.

New York Post, May 26, 2002, "Still Quick on the Draw," p. 62.

New York Times, May 29, 1997, Elisabeth Bumiller, "Jules Feiffer Draws the Line at No Pay from *The Voice,*" p. B1; January 23, 2000, Josh Schonwald, "Laughs and Learning with Jules Feiffer," p. P2; June 17, 2000, Sarah Boxer, "Jules Feiffer, at Seventy-one, Slows down to a Gallop," p. B1; March 4, 2003, Mel Gussow, "Jules Feiffer, Freed of His Comic Strip Duties, Finds a New Visibility," p. E1; June 10, 2003, Bruce Weber, "Uncle Joe Smiles down on a Family of Old Lefties," p. E1.

New York Times Book Review, November 14, 1993, Jonathan Fast, review of *The Man in the Ceiling,* p. 57; December 31, 1995, Daniel Pinkwater, review of *A Barrel of Laughs, a Vale of Tears;* March 15, 1998, Constance L. Hays, review of *Meanwhile . . . ,* p. 24; May 17, 1998, Krystyna Poray Goddu, review of *I Lost My Bear,* p. 22; August 15, 1999, review of *Bark, George,* p. 24; November 19, 2000, Jeanne P. Binder, "Things That Go Squish in the Night," p. 44; November 18, 2001, Dwight Garner, "'Better Not Call Me Again. I'm a Monster,'" p. 25; September 29, 2002, Cynthia Zarin, "The Boy Who Willed One Thing," p. 27; October 29, 2002, Cynthia Zarin, review of *By the Side of the Road;* June 8, 2003, Andrea Stevens, "Jules Feiffer's Communist Manifesto," p. 5.

New York Times Magazine, May 16, 1976, Robin Brantley, "'Knock Knock' 'Who's There?' 'Feiffer'"; June 15, 2003, Deborah Solomon, "Playing with History," p. 13.

Print, May-June, 1998, Steven Heller, interview with Feiffer, pp. 40-41; May-June, 1999, Carol Stevens, "Baby Teeth," p. 50; September, 2000, Steven Heller, "Feiffer's Last Dance," p. 26.

Publishers Weekly, October 25, 1993, review of *The Man in the Ceiling,* p. 62; November 27, 1995, review of *A Barrel of Laughs, a Vale of Tears,* p. 70; January 26, 1998, review of *I Lost My Bear,* p. 91; June 21, 1999,

review of *Bark, George,* p. 66; October, 2000, review of *Some Things Are Scary,* p. 76; August 20, 2001, review of *I'm Not Bobby,* p. 78; May 13, 2002, review of *By the Side of the Road,* p. 69; October 14, 2002, review of *The House across the Street,* p. 82; June 30, 2003, review of *The Great Comic Book Heroes,* p. 59; April 5, 2004, review of *The Daddy Mountain,* p. 60; August 22, 2005, review of *A Room with a Zoo,* p. 64; October 8, 2997, review of *Henry, the Dog with No Tail,* p. 51.

School Library Journal, September, 1997, Lisa S. Murphy, review of *Meanwhile . . . ,* p. 180; March, 1998, Julie Cummins, review of *I Lost My Bear,* p. 179; September, 1999, p. 182; January 1, 2001, Maryann H. Owen, review of *Some Things Are Scary,* p. 101; November, 2001, review of *I'm Not Bobby!,* pp. 119-120; May, 2002, Wendy Lukehart, review of *By the Side of the Road,* p. 152; February, 2003, Wendy Lukehart, review of *The House across the Street,* p. 111; May, 2003, Steve Weiner, "A Found Feiffer," p. 33; June, 2004, Grace Oliff, review of *The Daddy Mountain,* p. 108 November, 2005, Susan Hefler, review of *A Room with a Zoo,* p. 90.

Time, May 21, 2001, Francine Russo, "A Matter of Medium," p. G8.

ONLINE

Jules Feiffer Home Page, http://www.julesfeiffer.com (June 8, 2009).

Public Broadcasting System Web site, http://www.pbs.org/ (March 15, 1998), "The Art of Jules Feiffer"; (August 10, 2000) "Power of the Pen."*

*   *   *

FOTHERINGHAM, Ed
See FOTHERINGHAM, Edwin

*   *   *

FOTHERINGHAM, Edwin
(Ed Fotheringham)

Personal

Male. *Education:* Attended University of Washington School of Art.

Addresses

Home—Seattle, WA. *E-mail*—efotheringham@mac.com.

Career

Commercial and children's picture-book illustrator. Clients include Macy's department store and Levi-Straus clothing company; illustrator of compact disc covers for musical groups and musicians, including Mudhoney, Bo Diddley, and Elvis Costello.

Awards, Honors

Nonfiction Honor Book designation, *Boston Globe/Horn Book* Award, 2008, Children's Notable Book selection, American Library Association (ALA), and Robert Sibert Honor Book designation, ALA, both 2009, all for *What to Do about Alice.*

Illustrator

(As Ed Fotheringham) Karen Salmansohn, *Even God Is Single: (So Stop Giving Me a Hard Time),* Workman (New York, NY), 2000.

Barbara Kerley, *What to Do about Alice: How Alice Roosevelt Broke the Rules, Charmed the World, and Drove Her Father Teddy Roosevelt Crazy!,* Scholastic (New York, NY), 2008.

Shana Corey, *Mermaid Queen: The Spectacular True Story of Annette Kellerman, Who Swam Her Way to Fame, Fortune, and Swimsuit History!,* Scholastic (New York, NY), 2009.

Contributor to periodicals, including *Vanity Fair, Wall Street Journal,* and *New Yorker.*

Sidelights

After spending his childhood in Australia, illustrator and commercial artist Edwin Fotheringham traveled across the Pacific Ocean to attend the University of Washington School of Art. Establishing a career as a fine artist in Seattle, Washington, following graduation, Fotheringham began taking on commercial clients in the early 1990s, and his artwork has since been displayed around the United States in periodicals such as *Vanity Fair* and the *Wall Street Journal,* as well as in advertising campaigns for clients that include the department store Neiman Marcus.

In 2008, Fotheringham expanded his talents to include illustrating children's books, his first images appearing in Barbara Kerley's picture-book biography *What to Do about Alice: How Alice Roosevelt Broke the Rules, Charmed the World, and Drove Her Father Teddy Roosevelt Crazy!* Focusing on the spirited antics of President Theodore Roosevelt's oldest child, *What to Do about Alice* shares with young readers the daring activities Alice attempted, often to the dismay of her father. Neither sledding down the White House stairs on trays nor greeting guests with her favorite pet snake was out of bounds for the spirited child, a girl who eventually matured into one of her father's trusted advisors. Writing in *School Library Journal,* Grace Oliff maintained that Fotheringham's pictures "not only enhance but are frequently the source of humor," calling them "a superb match for the text." In addition to suggesting that the illustrator's artwork "perfectly evoke[s] the retro styles of an earlier age," a *Kirkus Reviews* critic concluded that Fotheringham enhances Kerley's narrative because the artist "takes every opportunity to develop Alice's character further."

Another illustration project, Fotheringham's work for *Mermaid Queen: The Spectacular True Story of Annette Kellerman, Who Swam Her Way to Fame, Fortune, and*

Swimsuit History! enlivens a brief biography by Shana Corey that focuses on a woman who refused to be constrained by society's view of appropriate female behavior. Annette Kellerman, an Australian, is credited with being the first female to attempt swim the English Channel, and she also designed a "daring" one-piece swimsuit for women. As a child, Kellerman was encouraged to exercise her legs by swimming, leading to a lifelong love of the water. She ultimately earned acclaim due to her aquatic ability and even landed leading roles in several Hollywood movies. Several reviewers wrote that Fotheringham's illustrations for the book aptly capture Kellerman's energetic nature, a *Publishers Weekly* critic observing that the artist's "punchy graphics suggest a woman in perpetual motion." In addition to writing that the book's artwork depicts the swimmer as "a strong but feminine competitor," a *Kirkus Reviews* contributor observed of *Mermaid Queen* that Fotheringham uses "both fiery and cool colors [to] pay homage to this vibrant woman."

Biographical and Critical Sources

PERIODICALS

Booklist, January 1, 2008, Ilene Cooper, review of *What to Do about Alice: How Alice Roosevelt Broke the Rules, Charmed the World, and Drove Her Father Teddy Roosevelt Crazy!,* p. 79.

Horn Book, March-April, 2008, Betty Carter, review of *What to Do about Alice,* p. 227.

Kirkus Reviews, February 1, 2008, review of *What to Do about Alice;* March 1, 2009, review of *Mermaid Queen: The Spectacular True Story of Annette Kellerman, Who Swam Her Way to Fame, Fortune, and Swimsuit History!*

Publishers Weekly, March 31, 2008, review of *What to Do about Alice,* p. 61; January 26, 2009, review of *Mermaid Queen.*

School Library Journal, October, 2008, Grace Oliff, review of *What to Do about Alice,* p. 185.

ONLINE

Edwin Fotheringham Home Page, http://www.edfotheringham.com (May 7, 2009).*

*   *   *

FREEMAN, Martha 1956-

Personal

Born February 25, 1956, in Whittier, CA; daughter of Leslie F. (a fine artist) and Barbara Freeman; married Russell B. Frank (a journalist), October, 1995; children: Sylvie, Rosa, Ethan. *Education:* Stanford University, B.A. (with distinction), 1978.

Martha Freeman (Reproduced by permission.)

Addresses

Home—State College, PA. *Agent*—Jane Jordan Browne, 410 S. Michigan Ave., Chicago, IL 60605.

Career

Writer. Freelance reporter/editor in Sonora, CA, 1980-95.

Writings

Stink Bomb Mom, Delacorte (New York, NY), 1996.

The Year My Parents Ruined My Life, Holiday House (New York, NY), 1997.

The Polyester Grandpa, Holiday House (New York, NY), 1998.

Fourth Grade Weirdo, Holiday House (New York, NY), 1999.

The Trouble with Cats, illustrated by Cat Bowman Smith, Holiday House (New York, NY), 2000.

The Spy Wore Shades, HarperCollins (New York, NY), 2001.

The Trouble with Babies, illustrated by Cat Bowman Smith, Holiday House (New York, NY), 2002.

Who Is Stealing the Twelve Days of Christmas?, Holiday House (New York, NY), 2003.

Who Stole Halloween?, Holiday House (New York, NY), 2005.

Mrs. Wow Never Wanted a Cow, illustrated by Steven Salerno, Random House (New York, NY), 2006.

The Trouble with Twins, illustrated by Cat Bowman Smith, Holiday House (New York, NY), 2007.

1,000 Reasons Never to Kiss a Boy, Holiday House (New York, NY), 2007.

Who Stole Uncle Sam?, Holiday House (New York, NY), 2008.

Who Stole Grandma's Million-Dollar Pumpkin Pie?, Holiday House (New York, NY), 2009.

Adaptations

Several of Freeman's books have been adapted for audiocassette.

Sidelights

Humorous middle-grade novels with likeable characters and "this could happen to you" scenarios are a specialty of Pennsylvania-based author Martha Freeman. "After years of reporting and editing on real life, I turned to fiction, which is preferable because I get to make it all

Cover of Freeman's middle-grade novel The Year My Parents Ruined My Life, *featuring artwork by Eric Brace.* (Bantam, 1997. Used by permission of Random House Children's Books, a division of Random House, Inc.)

up," Freeman once told *SATA*. "My inspiration comes from my childhood, my kids, my friends and the stories people tell me. If you ever meet me, watch out—you may find yourself in the next book." Freeman's novels for preteen readers include *Stink Bomb Mom, The Year My Parents Ruined My Life,* and *The Trouble with Twins,* while beginning readers are entertained by *Mrs. Wow Never Wanted a Cow* and her "The Trouble with. . ." books featuring artwork by Cat Bowman Smith. Praising Freeman's use of "spare and natural" use of one-syllable words in *Mrs. Wow Never Wanted a Cow,* Bobbee Pennington added in *School Library Journal* that the "brightly colored cartoon illustrations" by artist Steve Salerno "amplify the text's humor."

Stink Bomb Mom concerns the travails of twelve-year-old Rory. Rory has a menagerie of pets that includes Agnes the dog, as well as an absentee dad and a New-Age mom who earns a living selling aromatherapy products—or, as Rory's friends call them, "stink bombs." When Agnes bites Rory's best friend, Rory thinks of a clever way to save the day using her mom's stink bombs. In a review for *School Library Journal,* Carrie A. Guarria noted that Freeman writes about issues most young people can relate to, including "relationships with parents who can be embarrassing, the serious responsibility of pet ownership, friendship, and the consequences of divorce." *Bulletin of the Center for Children's Books* reviewer Susan S. Verner maintained that "Freeman's brisk pace and agreeably sarcastic dialogue keeps the . . . plot whizzing satisfactorily along, propelled by human buffoonery and canine angst."

Freeman continues in the same vein with *The Year My Parents Ruined My Life.* When Kate Sommers and her parents move the family from sunny California to cold, rainy Pennsylvania, Kate has to adjust to a new house and new schoolmates in addition to a much-different climate. When she decides to escape to her best friend's home back on the West Coast, pandemonium ensues. A reviewer in *Publishers Weekly* praised Freeman's "personable characters, dry sense of humor and understanding of the adolescent mind," while Janice M. Del Negro asserted in a review for the *Bulletin of the Center for Children's Books* that "Freeman gives Kate a strong voice and some realistic (but not overwhelming) adolescent angst that is bound to keep readers chuckling."

Self-proclaimed oddball Dexter Plum is the protagonist of Freeman's chapter book *Fourth Grade Weirdo.* Dexter carries a briefcase to class, consumes only black jelly beans, and loves to fill out math worksheets. When his absentminded teacher, Mr. Ditzwinkle, misplaces school funds and comes under fire from an angry school board candidate, Dexter and his pals help their teacher save face. According to a critic in *Publishers Weekly,* "most of the entertainment stems from Dexter's ability to laugh at himself." Christina Dorr, reviewing *Fourth Grade Weirdo* for *School Library Journal,* noted that Freeman's "quirky characters who work to right the problems of friends and family will appeal to young readers."

Freeman teams up with artist Cat Bowman Smith to create the chapter book **The Trouble with Cats.** (Illustration copyright © 2000 by Cat Bowman Smith. Reprinted by permission of Holiday House, Inc.)

Part of Freeman's "The Trouble with" series, *The Trouble with Cats* introduces Holly, a third grader whose life changes dramatically after her mother remarries and moves the family into her new husband's tiny San Francisco apartment. Along with attending a new school and making new friends, Holly must deal with her stepfather's four mischievous cats as they constantly chew up her socks, eat her cookies, and escape from the apartment. *The Trouble with Cats* "is filled with incidents in which the protagonist makes adjustments common to many youngsters," wrote Denise Brna in *School Library Journal.* *Booklist* contributor Carolyn Phelan called Freeman successful at "establishing Holly as a sympathetic narrator with some real problems and the gumption to work them out for herself."

In *The Trouble with Babies* readers become reacquainted with Holly as she and her family move to a new neighborhood. Here Holly befriends Xavier, a boy who lives with his two dads, and Annie, whose baby sister is too gross for Annie's tastes. Hoping to impress Annie, Xavier creates a "deyuckkifying" machine to clean up the baby, but Annie, with Holly's assistance, finally learns to accept her little sister. Holly then gets a pleas-

ant surprise: her own mother is pregnant. In *School Library Journal* Marilyn Ackerman wrote that *The Trouble with Babies* offers a "good, nonjudgmental portrayal of alternative family lifestyles." While writing that the plotlines involving Xavier are "silly," *Booklist* reviewer Hazel Rochman added that "the better story line is Holly's adapting to her new situation."

Holly's adventures continue in *The Trouble with Twins,* as the girl takes over party-planning duties from her mom when brothers Dylan and Jeremy turn three. With over a dozen preschoolers in the house, things turn ugly until Holly's best friend comes up with an entertaining solution that calms even the most rambunctious youngsters. Holly's upbeat personality is "charming," wrote a *Kirkus Reviews* writer, the critic also praising the "simplicity and realism" in Freeman's chapter-book story. In *School Library Journal,* Katheen Meulen described *The Trouble with Twins* as "a winning portrait of a family struggling with everyday concerns."

Freeman combines mystery with humor in *Who Is Stealing the Twelve Days of Christmas?*, the first in a series of chapter books featuring eleven-year-old Alex and his young neighbor Yasmeen. Each holiday season the neighbors on Chickadee Court decorate their homes according to the stanzas in "The Twelve Days of Christmas." When the birds—a partridge, goose, calling bird, and French hen—disappear from neighbors' yards, Alex and friend Yasmeen decide to track down the thief. "The amiable story is entertaining and moves at a brisk pace," noted Kitty Flynn in *Horn Book.* A critic in *Kirkus Reviews* found the work "breezy and humorous, with chatty dialogue and huge kid appeal," and Susan Patron wrote in *School Library Journal* that the mystery is "cleverly choreographed and unfolds dynamically."

Alex and Yasmeen return in *Who Stole Halloween?* and *Who Stole Uncle Sam?,* two more sleuthing adventures. In *Who Stole Halloween?* it is not the holiday that has gone missing; it is the neighbor's black cat. When several other cats do not return home, the children worry that history is repeating itself: a century ago several cats went missing at the same time that two local murders were committed and never solved. "With kids always hungry for mysteries," *Who Stole Halloween?* "is a good one to have on the shelf," concluded *Booklist* critic Ilene Cooper, and Debbie Stewart Hoskins wrote in *School Library Journal* that Freeman's "characters are well drawn." Series sequel *Who Stole Uncle Sam?* also ranked as "fine fare for summer reading," in the opinion of a *Kirkus Reviews* writer, and Freeman's story about a missing baseball coach and an accidental explosion of 4th of July fireworks that may have been no accident are featured in the book's "well-paced narrative."

Older teen readers are Freeman's focus in *1,000 Reasons Never to Kiss a Boy,* a young-adult novel about Jane, a sixteen year old who decides to give up on love after fickle boyfriend Elliot moves on. With the help of

supportive best friends and the generous advice of caring adults, the teen ultimately decides to give romance another go in a story that *Booklist* critic Abby Nolan dubbed a "breezy" story full of "laugh-out-loud humor." *1,000 Reasons Never to Kiss a Boy* is "solid chick-lit," according to a *Kirkus Reviews* writer, as well as "a wholesome read that will undoubtedly be popular with female teen readers."

Freeman turns to fantasy in *The Spy Wore Shades.* In the work, Dougie Minners encounters a strange girl while exploring the hills near his home in Calaveras County, California. The girl, named Varloo, explains that she lives in Hek, an underground civilization that sends a spy to the earth's surface every fifty years to monitor how society has changed. Dougie and Varloo form an unlikely friendship, and together they discover that a new housing development threatens the very existence of Hek. "The concept of a secret civilization existing in hidden caves is appealing," remarked Kay Weisman in *Booklist.* "While perhaps a bit far-fetched," Susan L. Rogers wrote in *School Library Journal, The Spy Wore Shades* "is still a good fantasy that's grounded with fascinating true facts."

Biographical and Critical Sources

PERIODICALS

Booklist, December 1, 1998, John Peters, review of *The Polyester Grandpa,* p. 666; March 15, 2000, Carolyn Phelan, review of *The Trouble with Cats,* p. 1376; October 1, 2001, Kay Weisman, review of *The Spy Wore Shades,* p. 318; July, 2002, Ilene Cooper, review of *The Trouble with Babies,* p. 1844; August, 2005, Ilene Cooper, review of *Who Stole Halloween?,* p. 2028; December 1, 2007, Ilene Cooper, review of *The Trouble with Twins,* p. 41.

Bulletin of the Center for Children's Books, February, 1997, Susan S. Verner, review of *Stink Bomb Mom,* p. 204; February, 1998, Janice M. Del Negro, review of *The Year My Parents Ruined My Life,* p. 201.

Horn Book, November-December, 2003, Kitty Flynn, review of *Who Is Stealing the Twelve Days of Christmas?,* p. 744.

Kirkus Reviews, June 15, 2002, review of *The Trouble with Babies,* p. 880; November 1, 2003, *Who Is Stealing the Twelve Days of Christmas?,* p. 1316; September 15, 2005, review of *Who Stole Halloween?;* May 15, 2007, review of *1,000 Reasons Never to Kiss a Boy;* November 15, 2007, review of *The Trouble with Twins;* July 1, 2008, review of *Who Stole Uncle Sam?*

Los Angeles Times, January 1, 2004, Josh Getlin, "Trouble with Gay Characters," p. A1.

Publishers Weekly, September 15, 1997, review of *The Year My Parents Ruined My Life,* p. 77; November 30, 1998, review of *The Polyester Grandpa,* p. 72; January 10, 2000, review of *Fourth Grade Weirdo,* p. 68; July 9, 2001, review of *The Spy Wore Shades,* p. 68; September 22, 2003, review of *Who Is Stealing the Twelve Days of Christmas?,* p. 72.

School Library Journal, December, 1996, Carrie A. Guarria, review of *Stink Bomb Mom,* p. 122; December, 1998, Marlene Gawron, review of *The Polyester Grandpa,* p. 122; January, 2000, Christina Dorr, review of *Fourth Grade Weirdo,* p. 96; July, 2000, Denise Brna, review of *The Trouble with Cats,* p. 72; August, 2001, Susan L. Rogers, review of *The Spy Wore Shades* p. 178; August, 2002, Marilyn Ackerman, review of *The Trouble with Babies,* p. 155; October, 2003, Susan Patron, review of *Who Is Stealing the Twelve Days of Christmas?,* p. 63; October, 2005, Debbie Stewart Hoskins, review of *Who Stole Halloween?,* p. 160; June, 2006, Bobbee Pennington, review of *Mrs. Wow Never Wanted a Cow,* p. 112.

ONLINE

Martha Freeman Home Page, http://www.marthafreeman.com (June 8, 2009).

Random House Web site, http://www.randomhouse.com/ (March 16, 2004), "Martha Freeman."*

G-H

GIBBONS, Gail 1944-

Personal

Born August 1, 1944, in Oak Park, IL; daughter of Harry George (a tool and die designer) and Grace Ortmann; married Glenn Gibbons, June 25, 1966 (died May 20, 1972); married Kent Ancliffe (a builder), March 23, 1976; children: (stepchildren) Rebecca, Eric. *Education:* University of Illinois, B.F.A., 1967.

Addresses

Home and office—Corinth, VT.

Career

Freelance writer and illustrator of children's books, 1975—. WCIA-Television, Champaign, IL, artist, 1967-69; WMAQ-TV, Chicago, IL, promotions and animation artist, 1969; Bob Howe Agency, Chicago, staff artist, 1969-70; WNBC-Television, House of Animation, New York, NY, staff artist, 1970-76; United Press International, New York, NY, freelance artist, 1977-88.

Awards, Honors

New York City Art Director Club award, 1979, for *The Missing Maple Syrup Sap Mystery;* American Institute of Graphic Arts award, 1979, for *Clocks and How They Go;* National Science Teachers Association/Children's Book Council Award, 1980, for *Locks and Keys,* and 1982, for *Tool Book;* certificate of appreciation from U.S. Postmaster General, 1982, for *The Post Office Book;* Notable Book designation, American Library Association, 1983, for *Cars and How They Go,* and 1985, for *The Milk Makers; Washington Post*/Children's Book Guild Award, 1987, for contribution to nonfiction children's literature; Notable Children's Trade Book in the Field of Social Studies designation, National Council of Social Studies, 1983, 1987, 1989, 1990, 1992; Outstanding Science Trade Books for Children designation, National Science Teachers Association, 1983, 1987,

Gail Gibbons (Reproduced by permission.)

1991, 1998; Children's Choice Award, International Reading Association, 1989, 1995; American Bookseller Pick of the Lists designation, 1992.

Writings

SELF-ILLUSTRATED; JUVENILE NONFICTION, UNLESS NOTED

Willy and His Wheel Wagon, Prentice-Hall (New York, NY), 1975.
Things to Make and Do for Halloween, Franklin Watts (New York, NY), 1976.
Salvador and Mister Sam: A Guide to Parakeet Care, Prentice-Hall (New York, NY), 1976.

Things to Make and Do for Columbus Day, Franklin Watts (New York, NY), 1977.

Things to Make and Do for Your Birthday, Franklin Watts (New York, NY), 1978.

Clocks and How They Go, Crowell (New York, NY), 1979.

Locks and Keys, Crowell (New York, NY), 1980.

The Too Great Bread Bake Book, Warne, 1980.

Trucks, Crowell (New York, NY), 1981.

Tool Book, Holiday House (New York, NY), 1982.

The Post Office Book: Mail and How It Moves, Crowell (New York, NY), 1982.

Christmas Time, Holiday House (New York, NY), 1982.

Boat Book, Holiday House (New York, NY), 1983.

Thanksgiving Day, Holiday House (New York, NY), 1983.

New Road!, Crowell (New York, NY), 1983.

Sun up, Sun Down, Harcourt (New York, NY), 1983.

Department Store, Crowell (New York, NY), 1984.

Fire! Fire!, Crowell (New York, NY), 1984.

Halloween, Holiday House (New York, NY), 1984, revised as *Halloween Is . . . ,* Holiday House (New York, NY), 2002.

The Seasons of Arnold's Apple Tree, Harcourt (New York, NY), 1984.

Tunnels, Holiday House (New York, NY), 1984.

Check It Out: The Book about Libraries, Harcourt (New York, NY), 1985.

Lights! Camera! Action! How a Movie Is Made, Crowell (New York, NY), 1985.

Fill It Up! All about Service Stations, Crowell (New York, NY), 1985.

The Milk Makers, Macmillan/Collier (New York, NY), 1985.

Playgrounds, Holiday House (New York, NY), 1985.

Flying, Holiday House (New York, NY), 1986.

From Path to Highway: The Story of the Boston Post Road, Crowell (New York, NY), 1986.

Happy Birthday!, Holiday House (New York, NY), 1986.

Up Goes the Skyscraper!, Four Winds Press (New York, NY), 1986.

Valentine's Day, Holiday House (New York, NY), 1986.

Deadline! From News to Newspaper, Crowell (New York, NY), 1987.

Dinosaurs, Holiday House (New York, NY), 1987.

The Pottery Place, Harcourt (New York, NY), 1987.

Trains, Holiday House (New York, NY), 1987.

Weather Forecasting, Four Winds Press (New York, NY), 1987.

Zoo, Crowell (New York, NY), 1987.

Dinosaurs, Dragonflies and Diamonds: All about Natural History Museums, Four Winds Press (New York, NY), 1988.

Farming, Holiday House (New York, NY), 1988.

Prehistoric Animals, Holiday House (New York, NY), 1988.

Sunken Treasure, Crowell (New York, NY), 1988.

Easter, Holiday House (New York, NY), 1989.

Catch the Wind!: All about Kites, Little, Brown (Boston, MA), 1989.

Marge's Diner, Crowell (New York, NY), 1989.

Monarch Butterfly, Holiday House (New York, NY), 1989.

Beacons of Light: Lighthouses, Morrow (New York, NY), 1990.

Weather Words and What They Mean, Holiday House (New York, NY), 1990.

How a House Is Built, Holiday House (New York, NY), 1990.

The Puffins Are Back!, HarperCollins (New York, NY), 1991.

From Seed to Plant, Holiday House (New York, NY), 1991.

Surrounded by Sea: Life on a New England Fishing Island, Little, Brown (Boston, MA), 1991.

Whales, Holiday House (New York, NY), 1991.

The Great St. Lawrence Seaway, Morrow (New York, NY), 1992.

Sharks, Holiday House (New York, NY), 1992.

Recycle! A Handbook for Kids, Little, Brown (Boston, MA), 1992.

Say Woof!: The Day of a Country Veterinarian, Macmillan (New York, NY), 1992.

Stargazers, Holiday House (New York, NY), 1992.

Caves and Caverns, Harcourt Brace (New York, NY), 1993.

Frogs, Holiday House (New York, NY), 1993.

Pirates: Robbers of the High Seas, Little, Brown (Boston, MA), 1993.

The Planets, Holiday House (New York, NY), 1993, third edition, 2008.

Puff—Flash—Bang!: A Book about Signals, Morrow (New York, NY), 1993.

Spiders, Holiday House (New York, NY), 1993.

Christmas on an Island, Morrow (New York, NY), 1994.

Country Fair, Little, Brown (Boston, MA), 1994.

Emergency!, Holiday House (New York, NY), 1994.

Nature's Green Umbrella: Tropical Rain Forests, Morrow (New York, NY), 1994.

St. Patrick's Day, Holiday House (New York, NY), 1994.

Wolves, Holiday House (New York, NY), 1994.

Bicycle Book, Holiday House (New York, NY), 1994.

Knights in Shining Armor, Little, Brown (Boston, MA), 1995.

Planet Earth/Inside Out, Morrow (New York, NY), 1995.

The Reasons for Seasons, Holiday House (New York, NY), 1995.

Sea Turtles, Holiday House (New York, NY), 1995.

Cats, Holiday House (New York, NY), 1996.

Deserts, Holiday House (New York, NY), 1996.

Dogs, Holiday House (New York, NY), 1996.

Click!: A Book about Cameras and Taking Pictures, Little, Brown (Boston, MA), 1997.

Gulls . . . Gulls . . . Gulls, Holiday House (New York, NY), 1997.

The Honey Makers, Morrow (New York, NY), 1997.

The Moon Book, Holiday House (New York, NY), 1997.

Paper, Paper Everywhere, Harcourt Brace (New York, NY), 1997.

Marshes and Swamps, Holiday House (New York, NY), 1998.

Soaring with the Wind: The Bald Eagle, Morrow (New York, NY), 1998.

Yippee-Yay!: A Book about Cowboys and Cowgirls, Little, Brown (Boston, MA), 1998.

The Art Box, Holiday House (New York, NY), 1998.

Penguins!, Holiday House (New York, NY), 1998.

The Quilting Bee, Morrow (New York, NY), 1999.

Exploring the Deep, Dark Sea, Little, Brown (Boston, MA), 1999.

Behold—the Dragon!, Morrow (New York, NY), 1999.

Pigs, Holiday House (New York, NY), 1999.

The Pumpkin Book, Holiday House (New York, NY), 1999.

Santa Who?, Morrow (New York, NY), 1999.

Rabbits, Rabbits, and More Rabbits, Holiday House (New York, NY), 2000.

My Soccer Book, HarperCollins (New York, NY), 2000.

My Football Book, HarperCollins (New York, NY), 2000.

My Basketball Book, HarperCollins (New York, NY), 2000.

My Baseball Book, HarperCollins (New York, NY), 2000.

Apples, Holiday House (New York, NY), 2000.

Polar Bears, Holiday House (New York, NY), 2001.

Ducks, Holiday House (New York, NY), 2001.

Christmas Is . . . , Holiday House (New York, NY), 2001.

Behold—the Unicorns!, Morrow (New York, NY), 2001.

Tell Me, Tree: All about Trees for Kids, Little, Brown (Boston, MA), 2002.

Giant Pandas, Holiday House (New York, NY), 2002.

The Berry Book, Holiday House (New York, NY), 2002.

Horses!, Holiday House (New York, NY), 2003.

Grizzly Bears, Holiday House (New York, NY), 2003.

Chicks and Chickens, Holiday House (New York, NY), 2003.

Thanksgiving Is . . . , Holiday House (New York, NY), 2004.

Mummies, Pyramids, and Pharaohs: A Book about Ancient Egypt, Little, Brown (Boston, MA), 2004.

Dinosaur Discoveries, Holiday House (New York, NY), 2005.

From Sheep to Sweater, Holiday House (New York, NY), 2005.

Owls, Holiday House (New York, NY), 2005.

Surrounded by Sea: Life on a New England Fishing Island, Holiday House (New York, NY), 2005.

Ice Cream: The Full Scoop, Holiday House (New York, NY), 2006.

Valentine's Day Is . . . , Holiday House (New York, NY), 2006.

Coral Reefs, Holiday House (New York, NY), 2007.

Galaxies, Galaxies!, Holiday House (New York, NY), 2007.

Groundhog Day!, Holiday House (New York, NY), 2007.

The Vegetables We Eat, Holiday House (New York, NY), 2007.

Corn, Holiday House (New York, NY), 2008.

Gibbons combines colorful art and an engaging story about creativity in her picture book **The Art Box.** (Copyright © 1998 by Gail Gibbons. Reproduced by permission.)

Dinosaurs!, Holiday House (New York, NY), 2008.
Elephants of Africa, Holiday House (New York, NY), 2008.
Tornadoes!, Holiday House (New York, NY), 2009.

SELF-ILLUSTRATED; FICTION

The Missing Maple Syrup Sap Mystery, Warne, 1979.
The Magnificent Morris Mouse Clubhouse, Franklin Watts (New York, NY), 1981.

ILLUSTRATOR

Jane Yolen, *Rounds about Rounds,* Franklin Watts (New York, NY), 1977.
Judith Enderle, *Good Junk,* Dandelion Press, 1979.
Catharine Chase, *Hot and Cold,* Dandelion Press, 1979.
Catharine Chase, *My Balloon,* Dandelion Press, 1979.
Catharine Chase, *Pete, the Wet Pet,* Dandelion Press, 1979.
Donna Lugg Pape, *The Mouse at the Show,* Elsevier/Nelson, 1981.
Joanna Cole, *Cars and How They Go,* Crowell (New York, NY), 1983.

Adaptations

Several of Gibbons' books have been adapted as film-strips and cassettes, including *Thanksgiving Day, Christmas Time,* and *Valentine's Day,* all by Live Oak Media; *Dinosaurs* and *Check It Out!* were adapted as filmstrips with cassettes by Listening Library.

Sidelights

A prolific author and illustrator of nonfiction books for curious-minded young readers, Gail Gibbons has answered questions about everything from clocks, locks, and post offices to grizzly bears and owls. Name a topic—milk, paper, news-reporting, puffins—and odds are that Gibbons has addressed it in one of her many award-winning books, each of which feature a clearly written text and vibrant design. In according Gibbons the 1987 *Washington Post*/Children's Book Guild Award for nonfiction, the judges noted: "The enormous breadth of subjects that Gail Gibbons has brought to life is astonishing," and her books "are free-flowing fountains of information."

Readers in the five-to-nine-year-old group are Gibbons' focus, and she was one of the first author/illustrators to bring vitality and visual excitement into children's nonfiction books for that age group. Beginning with her first book, 1975's *Willy and His Wheel Wagon,* she has gathered ideas from many sources: from suggestions from family and friends, from editors, and from children at schools where she speaks, but mostly from her own insatiable curiosity.

Born in Oak Park, Illinois, in 1944, Gibbons exhibited artistic talent at an early age. As she wrote in an entry for *Something about the Author Autobiography Series*

(*SAAS*), "there has always been a need for me to put words down on paper and draw and paint pictures." In kindergarten teachers noticed Gibbons' knack for drawing, and her love of painting and drawing increased throughout school. Soon with a reputation as the class artist, Gibbons created small books and "writing and drawing pictures of what I loved and where I wanted to be," as she recalled in *SAAS.*

While visits to the nearby Chicago Art Institute inspired her drawing, books became a passion for the young Gibbons as well, and each night she would read long past the time for lights out. By high school, art became a refuge for the shy teenager, and after graduation she applied and was accepted to the University of Illinois where she studied art. "I consider myself quite fortunate because I never had to debate with myself as to what I wanted to do with my life," Gibbons explained in *SAAS.* "The answer was always there. I wanted to be a writer and artist."

College was a revelation to Gibbons, and she was particularly inspired by one of her instructors, a professional illustrator of children's books who "became sort of an idol to me." She also grew closer and closer to a young man she had begun dating in high school, and she married Glenn Gibbons at age twenty-one. Helping to support the household while her husband finished his degree, Gibbons took her first job in television, working for a local station in Champaign, Illinois, doing set design, animations, and on-air graphics.

When the couple moved to Chicago, Gibbons continued her television work with WMAQ-TV and also worked at an advertising agency. After a 1969 move to New

Colorful springtime hues entertain readers of Gibbons' self-illustrated picture book **Apples.** (House 2000. Reproduced by permission of Holiday House, Inc.)

York, she worked for WNBC-TV creating graphics for news shows as well as for segments of *Saturday Night Live* and *Today.* In 1971 Gibbons became the graphic artist for the NBC children's program, *Take a Giant Step.* It was at this point in her career that she first thought about creating children's books, inspired by the children she was working with on air.

Gibbons' life took a radical turn in 1972, when her husband died in an accident. Emotionally distraught, she turned to her art. Picking an agent out of the yellow pages at random, she submitted her portfolio, and the agent encouraged her to get to work on a children's book. Deciding to take the subject of set theory as her topic, Gibbons discovered that her years in television came in very handy. "The bright colors I use come from my television background," she explained to *Booklist* contributor Stephanie Zvirin in an interview. "A television image is only on the screen for about ten seconds so it has to be very readable and simple." Expanding on this point, Gibbons told Jennifer Crichton in a *Publishers Weekly* interview that when she was working in television, a lot of people still had black-and-white sets, so that the artist had to be careful to use contrasting colors. "I can't put red next to black, for instance, because on black-and-white, the colors will come out a uniform gray. Bold, flat colors lend themselves to simplicity." As a result, the use of bright, flat colors and visual simplicity have become a Gibbons trademark.

After producing her first few books, Gibbons left New York for a part-time home on Cape Cod, and in 1976 married her Massachusetts landlord, Kent Ancliffe. With her husband and two stepchildren, she moved to Vermont, where Ancliffe built a house on two hundred and forty acres. After being advised to turn her hand to children's nonfiction, a bit of market research convinced Gibbons that this was a good idea. *Clocks and How They Go* was the first book to show Gibbons' new, simplified style. In this book she does not attempt to tell a story, but to explain concepts as clearly and vividly as possible.

Reviewing *Clocks and How They Go, Booklist* contributor Barbara Elleman wrote that the "inside movements of the weight and spring clock seemingly tick into action with Gibbons' concisely worded text and clean line work," while Ann A. Flowers wrote in *Horn Book,* that the work is an "admirable example of the kind of book that explains for the young reader how mechanical things work." The recipient of several awards, *Clocks and How They Go* set the tone for Gibbons' style through its simple text and clear illustration.

Other books on technology include *Locks and Keys,* which traces the history of such devices and shows the workings of various locks. Karen Jameyson, writing in *Horn Book,* noted that Gibbons "has once again skillfully combined a concise, clear text with explicit, at-

tractive illustrations to acquaint young readers with a mechanical subject." More things mechanical are served up in *Tool Book,* in which "Gibbons presents clear, attractive, and colorful drawings of common hand tools," according to Richard J. Merrill in *Science Books,* while a tasty concoction is given the Gibbons treatment in *Ice Cream: The Full Scoop.* Following ice cream from farm to large-scale manufacturing facility to your table, the book "delivers the scoop" on its history and ingredients "in cheerful watercolors and a lucid text," according to *Booklist* critic Jennifer Mattson.

Gibbons investigates other production processes, such as how apples grow, how honey and paper are made, and how milk gets from the cow to the supermarket, in several of her nonfiction titles. *The Seasons of Arnold's Apple Tree* does double service by showing the change of seasons as well as the development of apples on a tree. *School Library Journal* reviewer Harriet Otto commented that the book also "shows the close relationship between a boy and an apple tree," and went on to note that Gibbons' "colorful double-page spreads depict the changing seasons." Reviewing *Paper, Paper Everywhere,* a *Publishers Weekly* contributor commented that "Gibbons' works have been honored as innovations that entertain and teach children about things encountered in daily life."

More natural "manufacturing" is the focus of *The Honey Makers,* a book that looks at the workings of a hive by following a worker bee from birth through its many jobs. Reviewing that title in *Booklist,* Kay Weisman stated that "Gibbons' signature full-color artwork makes each page a visual delight, and numerous inset captions and labels add to the wealth of knowledge found in the text." With *The Milk Makers* Gibbons creates "an attractive, informative book on milk production for young readers," according to Eldon Younce in *School Library Journal.* "The Milk Makers is a perfect introduction for the class trip to a dairy farm or dairy plant and should also have great appeal for younger children," remarked Elizabeth S. Watson in *Horn Book.*

Exploring businesses and the world of commerce, Gibbons has illustrated the workings of post offices, diners, and newsrooms, among others. In *The Post Office: Mail and How It Moves* she explains the behind-the-counter activities of postal workers in a "bright and cheerful" format, according to George A. Woods in the *New York Times Book Review.* "Text and pictures greatly simplify a complex operation and reveal the postal system to be most expeditious," Woods concluded. In *Department Store* Gibbons tackles the workings of large-scale retail enterprises. According to Barbara S. Worth in *Children's Book Review Service,* the author/illustrator does "a remarkable job of bringing order and organization to a complex topic."

The work processes of a rural potter are presented in *The Pottery Place,* a book that supplies an "appealing introduction to pottery making for the preschool and

One of the most famous critters in the United States is the focus of Gibbons' picture book **Groundhog Day!**

elementary-school-aged child," according to Nancy Vasilakis in her review for *Horn Book*. Using a lightly fictionalized format, Gibbons illustrates the workings of a small restaurant in *Marge's Diner,* a book that *School Library Journal* contributor Mary Lou Budd dubbed a "delightful, charming presentation of how a hometown diner operates."

Gibbons gives young readers a peek behind the headlines in *Deadline!: From News to Newspaper,* in which she "explains in simple format the incredible amount of activity generated by a busy staff during six hours in the office of a daily newspaper," according to Martha Rosen in *School Library Journal*. "The colorful, cartoon-like illustrations reinforce the message of the text," Rosen added. From a modern newspaper to an ancient tomb is a manageable jump for Gibbons' readers. In *Mummies, Pyramids, and Pharaohs: A Book about Ancient Egypt* she outlines ancient Egyptian beliefs and customs, and also discusses their treatment of the dead in a volume that *School Library Journal* contributor Gloria Koster praised as showing the author's "usual flair for simplifying complex topics."

Few topics have escaped Gibbons' practiced eye. Cowboys and cowgirls come under her lens in *Yippee-Yay!,* a book focusing on the development of the so-called "Wild West" during the three decades following the U.S. Civil War. "Following her own tried-and-true layout, she has given youngsters yet another useful historical introduction to a popular topic," wrote John Sigwald in a *School Library Journal* review of the book. Environmentalism comes under scrutiny in *Recycle!,* the natural world is the focus of such books as *Owls, Coral Reefs, Corn,* and *The Food We Eat,* while a popular mode of transportation comes under scrutiny in *Bicycle Book. Booklist* critic Carolyn Phelan commented that *Bicycle Book* is one of Gibbons' "more engaging picture books" and one that introduces the history as well as design and care of bikes with clear, colorful illustrations in a "satisfying book." Featuring Gibbons' "clear, informative introduction" to basic food groups, *The Vegetables We Eat* serves as "a simple, effective approach to the topic," according to Kathy Piehl in her *School Library Journal* review of the educational work.

Gibbons' magpie curiosity finds subjects in everything she does. When she and her husband bought a house on a Maine island, she turned her attention to things of the sea, producing a book on lighthouses—*Beacons of Light;* on sea animals—including *Whales* and *The Puffins Are Back;* and life on such an island—*Surrounded by the Sea: Life on a New England Fishing Island.* She has looked at holidays from Halloween to St. Patrick's Day, at means of transport from trucks to boats, even at children's beloved dinosaurs and knights, and examined occupations from that of a veterinarian to a farmer. Kites caught her fancy, and books on wind and weather resulted. Stargazing, sharks, zoos, skyscrapers, dinosaurs, the solar system, and museums all have been fodder for her books.

Living the country life in northern New England over the years, Gibbons has also found many subjects in the natural landscape nearby. *Owls* focuses on the habitat, physiology, and unique hunting habits of one of the region's most interesting birds, while *Tell Me, Tree: All about Trees for Kids* follows a tree's life cycle from seed to harvest, and includes activities that allow budding naturalists to engage in some field work as well. Praising *Tell Me, Tree* as "sure to please" both adults and children, Phelan also cited Gibbons' "bright watercolor illustrations," while *Owls* was described as "a bright addition to owl lore" by Patricia Manning in *School Library Journal.*

"Nonfiction requires a tremendous amount of research," Gibbons noted in *SAAS.* "I want it to be accurate and contain up-to-date information." In addition to library research, she draws on personal experience and seeks out experts in the fields she is writing about. After several months of research, she writes the text, and has been known to make up to fifteen revisions for one book.

After the text comes a dummy, a fake copy of the format of the book with line sketches for illustrations. Once this is approved and she receives the typeset text, Gibbons creates the book's actual illustrations, using watercolors, black pen, acrylics, colored pencils, or a process called pre-separation in order to achieve her bright, flat colors. "I usually am working on a number of books all at the same time," she explained in *SAAS.* "I might be illustrating one, researching another, and working on the writing of another."

In addition to creating new books, Gibbons regularly visits schools where she talks with both children and educators. "Whenever I am speaking to children, teachers, and librarians, I always stress how much I feel that nonfiction is important," the author/illustrator concluded in *SAAS.* "I am constantly impressed in seeing what is happening in schools and libraries around the country. There is a sincere excitement about good literature coming from these places. I like to encourage others to write, hoping that it will be as exciting and rewarding to them as it has been to me."

Biographical and Critical Sources

BOOKS

Authors of Books for Young People, Scarecrow Press (Metuchen, NJ), 1990.
Children's Books and Their Creators, Houghton Mifflin (Boston, MA), 1995.
Children's Literature Review, Volume 8, Gale (Detroit, MI), 1985.
Something about the Author Autobiography Series, Volume 12, Gale (Detroit, MI), 1991, pp. 71-82.

PERIODICALS

Booklist, November 1, 1979, Barbara Elleman, review of *Clocks and How They Go,* p. 448; December 1, 1994, Stephanie Zvirin, interview with Gibbons, pp. 676-677; December 1, 1995, Carolyn Phelan, review of *Bicycle Book,* p. 630; March 15, 1997, Kay Weisman, review of *The Honey Makers,* p. 1245; August, 2000, Gillian Engberg, review of *Apples,* p. 2144; September 15, 2001, Gillian Engberg, review of *Polar Bears,* p. 225; April 1, 2002, Carolyn Phelan, review of *Tell Me Tree: All about Trees for Kids,* p. 1330; September 14, 2002, Carolyn Phelan, review of *Halloween Is . . . ,* p. 245; January 1, 2003, Karin Snelson, review of *Giant Pandas,* p. 897; July, 2003, Francisca Goldsmith, review of *Chicks and Chickens,* p. 1893; December 1, 2003, Hazel Rochman, review of *Grizzly Bears,* p. 680; December 15, 2003, Kay Weisman, review of *Horses!,* p. 751, and Jennifer Mattson, review of *The Quilting Bee,* p. 758; June 1, 2004, Gillian Engberg, review of *Mummies, Pyramids, and Pharaohs: A Book about Ancient Egypt,* p. 1735; March 15, 2005, Carolyn Phelan, review of *Owls,* p. 1298; October 1, 2005, Julie Cummins, review of *Dinosaur Discoveries,* p. 60; February 1, 2006, Ilene Cooper, review of *Valentine's Day Is . . . ,* p. 51; June 1, 2006, Jennifer Mattson, review of *Ice Cream: The Full Scoop,* p. 76; January 1, 2007, Ilene Cooper, review of *Groundhog Day,* p. 108; September 1, 2007, Gillian Engberg, review of *The Vegetables We Eat,* p. 122; December 1, 2007, Gillian Engberg, review of *Coral Reefs,* p. 56; February 15, 2008, John Peters, review of *Snakes,* p. 84; November 15, 2008, Linda Perkins, review of *Corn,* p. 47.
Childhood Education, summer, 2002, review of *Polar Bears,* p. 241; fall, 2004, Stacey Haley, review of *Horses!,* p. 47.
Children's Book Review Service, spring, 1984, Barbara S. Worth, review of *Department Store,* p. 122.
Children's Book Watch, August, 2004, review of *Mummies, Pyramids, and Pharaohs,* p. 1.
Horn Book, December, 1979, Ann A. Flowers, review of *Clocks and How They Go,* p. 676; December, 1980, Karen Jameyson, review of *Locks and Keys,* p. 653; July-August, 1985, Elizabeth S. Watson, review of *The Milk Makers,* pp. 463-464; November-December, 1987, Nancy Vasilakis, review of *The Pottery Place,* pp. 758-759; January, 2000, review of *Bats,* p. 97;

July-August, 2002, Danielle J. Ford, review of *Tell Me, Tree,* p. 484.

Kirkus Reviews, September 1, 2001, review of *Polar Bears,* p. 1289; March 1, 2002, review of *Tell Me, Tree,* p. 335; August 1, 2002, review of *Halloween Is . . . ,* p. 1129; November 15, 2002, review of *Giant Pandas,* p. 1692; November 1, 2003, review of *Horses!,* p. 1311; November 15, 2003, review of *Grizzly Bears,* p. 1359; January 1, 2004, review of *The Quilting Bee,* p. 36; May 15, 2004, review of *Mummies, Pyramids, and Pharaohs,* p. 491; February 15, 2005, review of *Owls,* p. 228; October 15, 2006, review of *Galaxies, Galaxies!,* p. 1071; October 15, 2007, review of *Coral Reefs;* February 15, 2008, review of *Snakes;* September 15, 2008, review of *Corn;* May 15, 2008, review of *Dinosaurs!;* November 15, 2008, review of *Elephants of Africa.*

New York Times Book Review, September 26, 1982, George A. Woods, review of *The Post Office Book: Mail and How It Moves,* p. 31.

Publishers Weekly, February 18, 1983, review of *Paper, Paper Everywhere,* p. 129; July 27, 1984, Jennifer Crichton, "Picture Books That Explain," pp. 88-89; March 20, 2000, review of *Rabbits, Rabbits, and More Rabbits,* p. 94; August 4, 2003, review of *Halloween Is,* p. 82.

School Library Journal, December, 1984, Harriet Otto, review of *The Seasons of Arnold's Apple Tree,* p. 70; April, 1985, Eldon Younce, review of *The Milk Makers,* p. 78; June-July, 1987, Martha Rosen, review of *Deadline!: From News to Newspaper,* p. 82; September, 1989, Mary Lou Budd, review of *Marge's Diner,* p. 226; March, 1998, John Sigwald, review of *Yippee-Yay!: A Book about Cowboys and Cowgirls,* p. 195; April, 1998, p. 116; March, 2000, Jill O'Farrell, review of *Rabbits, Rabbits, and More Rabbits!,* p. 224; September, 2000, Louise L. Sherman, review of *Apples,* p. 216; November, 2000, Meghan R. Malone, review of *My Basketball Book,* p. 142; September, 2001, Edith Chang, review of *Polar Bears,* p. 214; March, 2002, Anne Chapman Callaghan, review of *The Berry Book,* p. 214; December, 2002, Sally Bates Goodroe, review of *Giant Pandas,* p. 122; July, 2003, Shauna Yusko, review of *The Pumpkin Book,* p. 74, and Anne Champan Callaghan, review of *Chicks and Chickens,* p. 113; December, 2003, Carol Schene, review of *Horses!,* p. 134; March, 2004, Sally Bates Goodroe, review of *Grizzly Bears,* p. 193; May, 2004, Teri Markson, review of *The Quilting Bee,* p. 132; June, 2004, Gloria Koster, review of *Mummies, Pyramids, and Pharaohs,* p. 127; September, 2004, Gloria Koster, review of *Thanksgiving Is . . . ,* p. 186; April, 2005, Patricia Manning, review of *Owls,* p. 122; November, 2005, John Peters, review of *The Planets,* p. 115; February, 2006, Patricia Manning, review of *Dinosaur Discoveries,* p. 118; March, 2006, Blair Christolon, review of *Valentine's Day Is . . . ,* p. 208; August, 2006, Kara Schaff Dean, review of *Ice Cream,* p. 104; December, 2006, John Peters, review of *Galaxies, Galaxies!,* p. 122; March, 2007, Maura Bresnahan, review of *Groundhog Day!,* p. 195; July, 2007, Kathy Piehl, review of *The Vegetables We Eat,* p. 91; January, 2008, Nicki Clausen-Grace, review of *Coral Reefs,* p. 105; April, 2008, Patricia Manning, review of *Snakes,* p. 131; October, 2008, Anne L. Tormohlen, review of *Corn,* p. 131.

Science Books, January-February, 1983, Richard J. Merrill, review of *Tool Book,* p. 149.

ONLINE

Gail Gibbons Home Page, http://www.gailgibbons.com (June 8, 2009).*

* * *

GROBLER, Piet 1959-

Personal

Born September 26, 1959, in Nylstroom, Limpopo, South Africa; married; wife's name Marietjie (a music teacher); children: Catherina. *Education:* University of Pretoria, B.A., B.D., 1984; Stellenbosch University, B.A. (journalism; with honors), 1990, M.F.A. (cum laude), 2004; Cape Town Technical College, certificate in graphic design, 1993. *Hobbies and other interests:* Traveling, gardening, collecting picture books.

Addresses

Home and office—2B Ryneveld St., Stellenbosch 7600, South Africa. *Office*—24 Florida St., Paradyskloof, Stellenbosch 7600, South Africa. *E-mail*—pietg@iafrica. com.

Career

Freelance illustrator, 1996—. Hervormde Kerk, minister of religion, 1985-89; SANLAM Advertising and Publications, graphic designer and editor, 1991-96. Teacher of illustration at schools, including Cape Peninsula University of Technology and Stellenbosch University.

Member

Society of Children's Book Writers and Illustrators.

Awards, Honors

Tienie Holloway gold medal, South African Academy for Arts and Science, 1997, for *Rhinoscephants on the Roof;* silver medal, NOMA Concours (UNESCO), 1997, for *Here I Am,* and 2003, for *Sun Canary, Moon, Canary;* Octogone de Chêne, and bronze medal, Teheran International Biennale for Illustration, both 1999, and Primo Alpi Apuane, 2000, all for *Carnival of the Animals;* bronze medal, Biennial of Illustrations Bratislava, 2003; MER-Price, 2006, for *Mia se ma/ Mia's Mom;* Katrine Harries Award for Children's Book Illustrations, 1999-2001 and 2002-03, for *Toepa Toepa Towery, Net een Slukkie,* and *Padda and die spree met föte,* and 2004-05 for *Het vogeltjes ABC, Makwelane en die krokodil,* and *Mia's Mom.*

Writings

SELF ILLUSTRATED

The Story of Water, Prisma (Cape Town, South Africa), 1989.

Albert, Lizzie, en die Tasrekenaar, Juta (Kenwyn, South Africa), 1994.

Boontjie Kry Sy Loontjie, Juta (Kenwyn, South Africa), 1994.

Rainbow Birds, Kagiso (Pretoria, South Africa), 1997.

Please Frog, Just One Sip!, translated by Kobus Geldenhuys, Human & Rosseau (Cape Town, South Africa), 2002, published as *Hey, Frog!,* Front Street (Asheville, NC), 2002.

Little Bird's ABC, Front Street (Asheville, NC), 2005.

ILLUSTRATOR

Thea Brink, *Miracles of Jesus,* Prisma (Cape Town, South Africa), 1989.

Thea Brink, *Jesus Helps the Sick,* Prisma (Cape Town, South Africa), 1989.

Thea Brink, *Jesus and His Friends,* Prisma (Cape Town, South Africa), 1989.

Thea Brink, *Jesus Lives with Us,* Prisma (Cape Town, South Africa), 1989.

Thea Brink, *Joseph,* Prisma (Cape Town, South Africa), 1989.

Thea Brink, *David,* Prisma (Cape Town, South Africa), 1989.

Biebie de Villiers, *Each Day Has a Name,* Prisma (Cape Town, South Africa), 1989.

Biebie de Villiers, *Auntie Molly Must Give Me My Bath,* Prisma (Cape Town, South Africa), 1989.

Biebie de Villiers, *The World Is Filled with Clocks and Watches,* Prisma (Cape Town, South Africa), 1989.

Thea Brink, *Ruth and Samuel,* Prisma (Cape Town, South Africa), 1990.

Thea Brink, *Jesus, the Children's Friend,* Prisma (Cape Town, South Africa), 1990.

Thea Brink, *Jesus Teaches and Helps Us,* Prisma (Cape Town, South Africa), 1990.

Thea Brink, *When It All Began,* Prisma (Cape Town, South Africa), 1990.

Reviva Schermbrucker, *Almal Teken,* Juta (Kenwyn, South Africa), 1994, translated as *We All Draw,* Juta (Kenwyn, South Africa), 1997.

Annatjie Hanekom, *Kom kyk My Monsters,* Juta (Kenwyn, South Africa), 1994, translated as *Look at My Monsters,* Juta (Kenwyn, South Africa), 1997.

Philip de Vos, *Van Rand en sent tot insolvent,* Juta (Kenwyn, South Africa), 1994.

Madeleine Van Biljon, *Aan tafel met Nettie Pikeur,* Kiepersol (Cape Town, South Africa), 1994.

Janie Oosthuysen, *Kara en die blafdemper,* Human & Rosseau (Cape Town, South Africa), 1995.

Carmen Niehaus, *You Budget Beaters,* Human & Rosseau (Cape Town, South Africa), 1995.

Philip de Vos, *Moenie 'n Mielie kielie nie: en ander pittige uitinge,* Human & Rosseau (Cape Town, South Africa), 1995.

Marita van der Vyver, *Rhinocephants on the Roof,* Human & Rosseau (Cape Town, South Africa), 1996.

Janie Oosthuysen, *Grandma Duckitt and the Getaway Car,* Human & Rosseau (Cape Town, South Africa), 1996.

Ann Walton, *Hier is Ek,* Juta (Kenwyn, South Africa), 1996.

Ernst Conradie, *Rus vir die hele aarde: Wat doen ons aan onsself en die aarde?,* Lux Verbi (Cape Town, South Africa), 1996.

Janie Oosthuysen, *Grandma Duckitt and the Zeppelin,* Human & Rosseau (Cape Town, South Africa), 1996.

Karel Benjamin, *Staan uit die Water Uit!: 'n kaapse jeug,* Kwela Boeke (Roggebaai, South Africa), 1996.

Philip de Vos, *Die deng van Gauteng: en ander ordentlike limericke,* Human & Rosseau (Cape Town, South Africa), 1996.

Janie Oosthuysen, *Ms. Buggbuster and the Brainwashers,* Human & Rosseau (Cape Town, South Africa), 1996.

Hennie Aucamp, *Rampe in die ruigte: fabels vir almal,* Queillerie (Cape Town, South Africa), 1996.

Alex d'Angelo, *The Trouble with Sannie Langtand,* Tafelberg (Cape Town, South Africa), 1997.

Martie Preller, *Op die spoor van die Lesea-vanger: 'n kies-koes-kopkrapboek,* Juta (Cape Town, South Africa), 1997.

Sanet Groenewald, *Die geheim van Katjiepoetstraat 9,* Juta (Cape Town, South Africa), 1997.

Janie Oosthuysen, *Grandma Duckitt and the Dreadnought Mark III,* Human & Rosseau (Cape Town, South Africa), 1997.

Janie Oosthuysen, *Professor ExPerimento's Frightening Formulas,* Human & Rosseau (Cape Town, South Africa), 1997.

J.G.H. Combrink, *Kwinksinnig,* Tafelberg (Cape Town, South Africa), 1998.

Philip de Vos, *Carnival of the Animals,* Human & Rosseau (Cape Town, South Africa), 1998.

Janie Oosthuysen, *Grandma Duckitt and the Intergalactic V-919 Supercomet,* Human & Rosseau (Cape Town, South Africa), 1998.

Alex d'Angelo, *Sannie Langtand Rides Again,* Tafelberg (Cape Town, South Africa), 1998.

Ann Walton, *Mrs. Lulu Langtree: Local Spiderwoman,* Juta (Kenwyn, South Africa), 1998.

Janie Oosthuysen, *Sergeant Spoofer's Incredible Lie Detector,* Human & Rosseau (Cape Town, South Africa), 1998.

Karel Benjamin, *Pastor Scholls trek sy toga uit en ander stories,* Kwela (Roggebaai, South Africa), 1999.

Verna Vels, *Liewe Heksie en die rekenaar en ander nuwe liewe heksie-stories,* Human & Rosseau (Cape Town, South Africa), 1999.

Philip de Vos, *Kat se Blad: stuitige strokies,* Human & Rosseau (Cape Town, South Africa), 1999.

Petra du Preez, *Horoscope 2000,* Zebra (Rivonia, South Africa), 1999.

Philip de Vos, *Beware of the Canary,* Human & Rosseau (Cape Town, South Africa), 2000.

Roberto Piumini, *Doctor Me De Cin*, Front Street (Asheville, NC), 2001.

Verna Vels, *Die liewe heksie-omnibus*, Human & Rosseau (Cape Town, South Africa), 2002.

Annie M.G. Schmidt, *Die spree net Föte: Afrikaanse Verwerkings van Annie M.G. Schmidt-verse*, edited by Philip de Vos, Human & Rosseau (Cape Town, South Africa), 2002.

Anushka Ravishankar, *Today Is My Day*, Human & Rosseau (Cape Town, South Africa), 2003.

Lida Dijkstra, *Missy My Mousey*, Human & Rosseau (Cape Town, South Africa), 2003, published as *Little Mouse*, Front Street (Asheville, NC), 2003.

J.F. Spies, *Teopa teopa towery*, Protea (Pretoria, South Africa), 2003.

Philip de Vos, *Mallemeuleman: 'n Keur uit Philip de Vos se verseis*, Human & Rosseau (Cape Town, South Africa), 2004.

Pieter de Villiers, *Boerneef sing: komposisies van uitgesoekte Verse: 10 siklusse*, Litera (Pretoria, South Africa), 2004.

Philip de Vos, *Limericke vir die lekkerte*, Kagiso Education (Cape Town, South Africa), 2004.

Maria Hendricks, *Makwelane and the Crocodile*, Human & Rosseau (Cape Town, South Africa), 2004.

Marita van der Vyver, *Mia's Mom*, Human & Rosseau (Cape Town, South Africa), 2005.

Beverley Naidoo, *The Great Tug of War, and Other Stories*, Frances Lincoln (London, England), 2006.

Jorge Luján, *Accidente Celeste*, Fondo de Cultura Economica (Argentina), 2006, translated by Elisa Amado as *Sky Blue Accident/ Accidente Celeste*, Groundwood Books (Toronto, Ontario, Canada), 2007.

Jorge Luján, *Colors!/ Colores!*, Sudamericana (Mexico), 2006, translated by John Oliver Simon, Groundwood Books (Toronto, Ontario, Canada), 2008.

Katharine Quarmby, *Fussy Freya*, Human & Rosseau (Cape Town, South Africa), 2008.

Sidelights

South African illustrator Piet Grobler began his career in children's books while he was working as a minister in the Dutch Reformed Church. With a talent for art, he illustrated a series of Bible books by Thea Brink, and he enjoyed the project so much that when he left the ministry Grobler decided to pursue a career in journalism and graphic design. While working as a graphic designer he continued to illustrate children's books, and in 1996, with several illustration awards under his belt, he decided to work exclusively in the field of illustration and children's books. In recent years, Grobler has opened his own art studio, called Hoi Hannelore! and Other Stories, near his home in Stellenbosch, South Africa.

Grobler has worked with many authors during his career, and one of his most frequent collaborators is Philip de Vos. The artist earned critical acclaim for his illustrations for de Vos's *Carnival of the Animals*, and his artwork prompted GraceAnne A. DeCandido to note in *Booklist* "the nervous squiggles and dreamlike edginess

of Grobler's etchings." A *Publishers Weekly* critic described the same images as "kinetic etchings accented with splashes of muted watercolors." Grobler uses brighter ink and watercolor designs in his work for Roberto Piumini's *Doctor Me Di Cin*, and a *Kirkus Reviews* critic praised these illustrations as "a perfect match for the story." Catherine Threadgill expressed a similar view in her *School Library Journal* review of *Doctor Me Di Cin*, writing that "Grobler's simple, evocative illustrations do a wonderful job of setting the tone throughout the story."

In Lida Dijkstra's *Little Mouse*, a retelling of a folk tale, "Grobler's charming, stylized color illustrations are the highlight," according to *School Library Journal* critic Robin L. Gibson, and in *Booklist* Ilene Cooper cited the book's "stylized yet child-friendly artwork." According to a *Publishers Weekly* critic, "it's the giddy glee emanating from Grobler's artwork that makes the story magic." Another picture book, award-winning writer Beverly Naidoo's *The Great Tug of War, and Other Stories*, features eight retold folktales from southern Africa that are accompanied by Grobler's small-scale pen-and-ink drawings, while in his work for Katharine Quarmby's *Fussy Freya* Grobler injects folk-style elements to help tell the story about a child who is too picky with her food. A *Kirkus Reviews* critic described Grobler's art for *Fussy Freya* as "lightheartedly loose line-and-watercolor illustrations [that are] packed with fanciful culinary details."

Among his many picture-book collaborations, Grobler has teamed up with Argentine poet and architect Jorge Luján on the books *Sky Blue Accident/ Accidente Celeste* and *Colors!/ Colores!* In the fantasy story *Sky Blue Accident/ Accidente Celeste* Grobler combines chalk-and-crayon scribbles with gouache and pastel, resulting in "art that's sure to spark the imagination," according to Mary Elam in *School Library Journal*. A contributor to *Kirkus Reviews* called the same book "a vibrantly presented and provocative exploration of the imagination." For *Colors!/ Colores!* Grobler "interprets the verse through watercolor paintings that are as spare and fanciful as the writing," according to *Booklist* critic Carolyn Phelan. Madeline Walton-Hadlock, writing in *School Library Journal*, observed that the "elegant details in the art and design further unify the poems and colors."

In addition to his illustration work, Grobler is also the author of several original self-illustrated stories. *Hey Frog!*—originally published in South Africa as *Please Frog, Just One Sip!*—is a folk-style tale in which a greedy frog drinks all of the world's water. A group of indigenous South African animals try to convince Frog to open his mouth and release all the water: Lion, Crocodile, and Crow try scratching, frightening, and insulting the greedy amphibian in turn, but nothing works until Eel remembers that Frog is ticklish. Grobler "proposes a funny, creative solution to conflict in which no one is harmed," wrote a *Publishers Weekly* reviewer,

and in *Kirkus Reviews* a contributor praised the "whimsically clever art" that accompanies the gentle tale. Engberg also found the greatest appeal in the artwork, writing that Grobler's illustrations "really extend the laughs with quirky, slightly stylized depictions of animals and plants."

Another original picture book by Grobler, *Little Bird's ABC*, also features a host of animals—in this case, birds—that create sounds for every letter of the alphabet. Using aural expressions rather than descriptive-words in some cases, Grobler created a text that helps pre-readers sound out letters. Finding that the author/illustrator's "creative use of line and color makes each illustration a pleasant surprise," Steven Engelfried concluded in *School Library Journal* that *Little Bird's ABC* is "an inspired and original entry." Calling Grobler's book the "freshest primer" in years, a *Publishers Weekly* critic cited the combination of "elegantly impish watercolors and a soupçon of naughty humor."

Biographical and Critical Sources

PERIODICALS

Booklist, August, 2000, GraceAnne A. DeCandido, review of *Carnival of the Animals,* p. 2143; January 1, 2003, Gillian Engberg, review of *Hey Frog!,* p. 906; January 1, 2005, Ilene Cooper, review of *Little Mouse,* p. 868; November 15, 2005, Hazel Rochman, review of *Little Bird's ABC,* p. 49; April 1, 2008, Carolyn Phelan, review of *Colors!/ Colores!,* p. 51.

Kirkus Reviews, September 1, 2001, review of *Doctor Me Di Cin,* p. 1299; October 1, 2002, review of *Hey Frog!,* p. 1470; October 1, 2004, review of *Little Mouse,* p. 959; September 1, 2005, review of *Little Bird's ABC,* p. 973; March 1, 2007, review of *Sky Blue Accident/ Accidente Celeste,* p. 227; March 1, 2008, review of *Colors!/ Colores!*; September 15, 2008, review of *Fussy Freya.*

Publishers Weekly, October 28, 2002, review of *Hey Frog!,* p. 70; January 10, 2005, review of *Little Mouse,* p. 55; August 15, 2005, review of *Little Bird's ABC,* p. 56.

School Library Journal, July, 2000, Jane Marino, review of *Carnival of the Animals,* p. 93; October, 2001, Catherine Threadgill, review of *Doctor Me Di Cin,* p. 129; February, 2005, Robin L. Gibson, review of *Little Mouse,* p. 96; December, 2005, Steven Engelfried, review of *Little Bird's ABC,* p. 113; January, 2007, Susan Scheps, review of *The Great Tug of War, and Other Stories,* p. 119; July, 2007, Mary Elam, review of *Sky Blue Accident/ Accidente Celeste,* p. 80; May, 2008, Madeline Walton-Hadlock, review of *Colors!/ Colores!,* p. 116.

ONLINE

Children's Literature South Africa Web site, http://www.childlit.org.za/ (May 13, 2009), "Piet Grobler."

Piet Grobler Home Page, http://www.pietgrobler.com (May 13, 2009).

South African Illustrators Web site, http://www.illustrators.co.za/ (May 13, 2009), profile of Grobler.

Stellenbosch Artists Web site, http://www.stellenboschwriters.com/ (May 13, 2009), profile of Grobler.*

*   *   *

HARPER, Lee

Personal

Married; wife's name Krista; children: four. *Education:* Attended Pennsylvania Academy of Fine Arts.

Addresses

Home—Doylestown, PA. *E-mail*—lee@leeharper.com.

Career

Painter, sculptor, and illustrator.

Awards, Honors

Great Lakes Picture Book of the Year Award nomination, and Book Sense Pick, both 2008, both for *Woolbur* by Leslie Helakoski.

Writings

(And illustrator) *Snow! Snow! Snow!,* Simon & Schuster (New York, NY), 2009.

ILLUSTRATOR

Leslie Helakoski, *Woolbur,* HarperCollins (New York, NY), 2008.

Wendi J. Silvano, *Turkey Trouble,* Marshall Cavendish (Tarrytown, NY), 2009.

Walter Dean Myers, *The Easy Life,* HarperCollins (New York, NY), 2010.

Sidelights

Author and illustrator Lee Harper has been drawing since he was old enough to hold a pencil. He made good use of a friend's unlimited paper supply in elementary school and continued to draw through middle and high school. Harper's interest in art eventually led him to study at the Pennsylvania Academy of Fine Arts in Philadelphia, and since embarking on a career in illustration he has contributed to picture books by Leslie Helakoski, Wendi J. Silvano, and Walter Dean Myers. In addition, he has created the original self-illustrated story *Snow! Snow! Snow!*

Harper's first published illustrations appear in Helakoski's *Woolbur.* Woolbur is a young sheep who constantly worries his parents, Maa and Paa, by living his life

against the standards of the herd. As Maa and Paa try to get their "black sheep" to conform, Woolbur is determined to retain his individuality, and does so with the support of Grandpaa. A *Publishers Weekly* reviewer wrote of Harper's picture-book debut that he "meets the challenge of conceiving new ways to illustrate the patterned repetitions of the story, even if his characters are sometimes static." Abby Nolan, writing for *Booklist,* observed that "Helakoski turns out a charming story, supported by [Harper's] wonderful artwork," and a *Kirkus Reviews* writer noted that the illustrator's "lumpy, expressive ovines, especially the wild-wooled Woolbur, bring Helakoski's delightful tale of independence to life." Kara Schaff Dean, reviewing *Woolbur* in *School Library Journal,* commented that "Harper's amusing illustrations contribute to that fun with subtle details."

Biographical and Critical Sources

PERIODICALS

Booklist, January 1, 2008, Abby Nolan, review of *Woolbur* p. 96.
Kirkus Reviews, November 15, 2007, review of *Woolbur.*
Publishers Weekly, December 10, 2007, review of *Woolbur* p. 54.
School Library Journal, January, 2008, Kara Schaff Dean, review of *Woolbur,* p. 88.

ONLINE

Lee Harper Home Page, http://www.leeharperart.com (May 14, 2009).*

*   *   *

HARRIS, Joe 1928-

Personal
Born 1928; married (marriage ended); children: three daughters.

Addresses
Home—New York, NY.

Career
Animator, cartoonist, and illustrator. Dancer Fitzgerald Sample (advertising agency), New York, NY, supervisor of animation, c. 1950s; co-creator of cartoon television series, including *King Leonardo and His Short Subjects, Tennessee Tuxedo,* and *Underdog,* beginning 1964; J. Walter Thompson, New York, NY, pharmaceutical advertising copywriter.

Writings

The Belly Book, Random House Children's Books (New York, NY), 2008.
Halloween Ball, Random House (New York, NY), 2008.

Adaptations

Underdog inspired a life-action film, directed by Frederik du Chau, 2007.

Biographical and Critical Sources

PERIODICALS

Kirkus Reviews, December 1, 2007, review of *The Belly Book.*
School Library Journal, March, 2008, Gloria Koster, review of *The Belly Book,* p. 164.

ONLINE

About.com, http://animatedtv.about.com/ (July 23, 2007), Nancy Basile, interview with Harris.
Associated Content Web site, http://www.associatedcontent.com/ (July 30, 2007), Susan Mead, interview with Harris.*

*   *   *

HAWKES, Kevin 1959-

Personal
Born August 28, 1959, in Sherman, TX; son of Joseph (a military officer) and Carma (a homemaker) Hawkes; married Karen Perkes (a medical technologist), December 15, 1982; children: Spencer Morgan, Jessie Elizabeth, Ian David. *Education:* Utah State University, B.A., 1985. *Religion:* Church of Jesus Christ of Latter-Day Saints (Mormon). *Hobbies and other interests:* Bicycling, playing soccer, reading, gardening, painting furniture.

Addresses
Home—Gorham, ME. *E-mail*—info@kevinhawkes.com.

Career
Illustrator and author. Xam, Inc., Midvale, UT, animation assistant, 1985; Gibby Studios, Ogden UT, photo re-toucher, 1985-86; book store clerk in Boston, MA, 1986-87; freelance illustrator, 1987-90; children's illustrator and writer, 1990—.

Member
Society of Children's Book Writers and Illustrators.

Kevin Hawkes (Reproduced by permission.)

Awards, Honors

Boston Globe/Horn Book Award nomination in nonfiction, 2002, for *Handel, Who Knew What He Liked,* by M.T. Anderson; Lupine Award for Best Picture Book, 2007, for *Velma Gratch and the Way Cool Butterfly* by Alan Madison; Irma S. and James H. Black Award, Bank Street College of Education, 2008, for *The Wicked Big Toddlah.*

Writings

FOR CHILDREN; SELF-ILLUSTRATED

Then the Troll Heard the Squeak, Lothrop (Boston, MA), 1991.
His Royal Buckliness, Lothrop (Boston, MA), 1992.
The Wicked Big Toddlah, Alfred A. Knopf (New York, NY), 2007

ILLUSTRATOR

Marvin Terban, *Hey, Hay!: A Wagonful of Funny Homonym Riddles,* Clarion Books (New York, NY), 1991.
Walter de la Mare, *The Turnip,* David R. Godine (Boston, MA), 1992.

Joyce Maxner, *Lady Bugatti,* Viking (New York, NY), 1993.
Caroline Stutson, *By the Light of the Halloween Moon,* Lothrop, Lee & Shepard Books (New York, NY), 1993.
Kathryn Lasky, *The Librarian Who Measured the Earth,* Joy Street Books (Boston, MA), 1994.
Catherine Cowan, *The Nose,* Lothrop, Lee & Shepard (New York, NY), 1994.
M.L. Miller, *The Enormous Snore,* Putnam (New York, NY), 1995.
Roni Schotter, *Dreamland,* Orchard Books (New York, NY), 1996.
Bill Grossman, *My Little Sister Ate One Hare,* Crown Publishers (New York, NY), 1996.
Michelle Dionetti, *Painting the Wind,* Little, Brown (Boston, MA), 1996.
Elizabeth Loredo, *Boogie Bones,* Putnam (New York, NY), 1997.
Kathryn Lasky, *Marven of the Great North Woods,* Harcourt, Brace (San Diego, CA), 1997.
Dee Lillegard, *The Poombah of Badoombah,* Putnam (New York, NY), 1998.
Jack Prelutsky, *Imagine That!: Poems of Never-Was,* Alfred A. Knopf (New York, NY), 1998.
Jane Yolen and Linda Mannheim, *The Liars' Book,* Blue Sky Press (New York, NY), 1998.
Catherine Cowan, *My Friend the Piano,* Lothrop, Lee & Shepard (New York, NY), 1998.
Mary Ann Hoberman, *And to Think We Thought That We'd Never Be Friends,* Crown (New York, NY), 1999.
Paul Fleischman, *Weslandia,* Candlewick Press (Cambridge, MA), 1999.
Marion Dane Bauer, *Jason's Bears,* Hyperion (New York, NY), 2000.
Eva Ibbotson, *Island of the Aunts,* Dutton (New York, NY), 2000.
Philip Pullman, *I Was a Rat!,* Alfred A. Knopf (New York, NY), 2000.
Bill Grossman, *Timothy Tunny Swallowed a Bunny,* Laura Geringer Books (New York, NY), 2000.
A Christmas Treasury: Very Merry Stories and Poems, HarperCollins (New York, NY), 2001.
Eva Ibbotson, *Dial-a-Ghost,* Dutton (New York, NY), 2001.
Joan Aiken, *A Necklace of Raindrops and Other Stories,* Alfred A. Knopf (New York, NY), 2001.
M.T. Anderson, *Handel, Who Knew What He Liked,* Candlewick Press (Cambridge, MA), 2001.
Eva Ibbotson, *The Great Ghost Rescue,* Dutton (New York, NY), 2002.
Eva Ibbotson, *Journey to the River Sea,* Dutton (New York, NY), 2002.
Kathryn Lasky, *The Man Who Made Time Travel,* Melanie Kroupa Books (New York, NY), 2002.
Anne Lindberg, *Worry Week,* David R. Godine (Boston, MA), 2003.
Eva Ibbotson, *Not Just a Witch,* Dutton (New York, NY), 2003.
M.T. Anderson, *Me, All Alone, at the End of the World,* Candlewick Press (Cambridge, MA), 2004.

Lynne Bertrand, *Granite Baby,* Farrar, Straus & Giroux (New York, NY), 2004.

Paul Fleischman, *Sidewalk Circus,* Candlewick Press (Cambridge, MA), 2004.

Eva Ibbotson, *The Haunting of Hiram,* Dutton (New York, NY), 2004.

Bill Grossman, *My Little Sister Hugged an Ape,* Knopf (New York, NY), 2004.

Eva Ibbotson, *The Haunting of Granite Falls,* Dutton Children's Books (New York, NY), 2004.

Eva Ibbotson, *The Star of Kazan,* Dutton Children's Books (New York, NY), 2004.

Michelle Knudsen, *Library Lion,* Candlewick Press (Cambridge, MA), 2006.

Eva Ibbotson, *The Beasts of Clawstone Castle,* Dutton Children's Books (New York, NY), 2006.

Andrea Beaty, *When Giants Come to Play,* Abrams Books for Young Readers (New York, NY), 2006.

Lisa Trumbauer, *Mountain Manor Mystery,* Mondo (New York, NY), 2007.

Alan Madison, *Velma Gratch and the Way Cool Butterfly,* Atheneum Books for Young Readers (New York, NY), 2007.

Michael Ian Black, *Chicken Cheeks,* Simon & Schuster Books for Young Readers (New York, NY), 2008.

Kathleen Krull, *The Road to Oz: Twists, Turns, Bumps, and Triumphs in the Life of L. Frank Baum,* Alfred A. Knopf (New York, NY), 2008.

Robin Cruise, *Bartleby Speaks!,* Farrar, Straus & Giroux (New York, NY), 2009.

Caroline Stutson, *By the Light of the Halloween Moon,* Marshall Cavendish (New York, NY), 2009.

Karla Kuskin, *A Boy Had a Mother Who Bought Him a Hat,* Laura Geringer Books (New York, NY), 2010.

Michael Ian Black, *A Pig Parade Is a Terrible Idea,* Simon & Schuster Books for Young Readers (New York, NY), 2010.

Sidelights

After graduating from college with a degree in art, children's book illustrator and author Kevin Hawkes did his apprenticeship in the field by working in a bookstore where he paid attention to which books caught the eye of young readers and their parents. Getting his first illustration contract in the early 1990s from Boston-based publisher David R. Godine, Hawkes has gone on to a successful career that includes award-winning original picture books like *The Wicked Big Toddlah* as well as dozens of illustration projects to his credit. From Eva Ibbotson's popular "Ghost Family" series to Philip Pullman's comic *I Was a Rat!* to Kathryn Lasky's *Marven of the Great North Woods,* Hawkes's fanciful acrylic paintings bring to life a host of picture-book characters in bright, vibrant color and with droll humor. A characteristic response to his work was given by Wendy Lukehart, who wrote of the artist's work for Alan Madison's *Velma Gratch and the Way Cool Butterfly* that "Hawkes's sensitive but humorous" art "propels the narrative with seamless, rhythmic buoyancy"

"My characters come from places where lampposts are never straight, the hills are impossibly steep, and the skies are impossibly blue," Hawkes said on the StorybookArt Web site. His slightly offbeat perspective allows the artist to create realistic fantasy worlds, as he does for Paul Fleischman's *Weslandia,* about a creative, imaginative boy who refuses to fit in. "In vibrant, puckish acrylic paintings," a *Publishers Weekly* contributor noted, "Hawkes . . . introduces the outlandish elements so naturally that they seem organic" in a picture book "bursting at the seams with creativity." Another collaboration with Fleishchman, *Sidewalk Circus,* allows readers to join a girl on her walk down city streets where colorful posters announcing a traveling circus brighten the urban landscape. Praising Hawkes's "gorgeous" artwork, a *Kirkus Reviews* critic deemed *Sidewalk Circus* "a lovely tribute to the endless power of imagination" and *Booklist* critic Michael Cart described it as "a magical, inspired collaboration."

Hawkes's creative contributions to the works of such authors as Ibbotson, Lasky, and Pullman, as well as Bill Grossman, Kathleen Krull, Joan Aiken, M.T. Anderson, and others, have elicited consistent praise from reviewers. Commenting on Hawkes's paintings for Lasky's *Marven of the Great North Woods,* the story of a ten-year-old Jewish boy who is based on the author's grandfather, *New York Times Book Review* contributor Meg Wolitzer dubbed the illustrations "both exciting and tender," and their creator "as successful at depicting the gigantic, ursine men as he is at showing the existential

Hawkes created the animated artwork that brings to life Kathryn Lasky's old-world story Marven of the Great North Woods.

vastness of the great outdoors." In his humorous collaborations with Grossman in the concept books *My Little Sister Ate One Hare* and *My Little Sister Hugged an Ape,* the artist's "color-soaked caricatures and Grossman's good-natured text offer a lively view of a girl's creative attempt to show the animal kingdom some love," according to *Horn Book* critic Christine M. Heppermann. Krull's picture-book biography about the author of a beloved childhood classic, *The Road to Oz: Twists, Turns, Bumps, and Triumphs in the Life of L. Frank Baum,* features images that draw on the book's original art and "invoke the magic of Oz within the great author's real-world setting," according to Jane Damron in *School Library Journal.*

One of several collaborations with Anderson, *Handel, Who Knew What He Liked* relates the life of the eighteenth-century composer in a humorous way, and Hawkes echoes the author's perspective in his illustrations. In *General Music Today* contributor Richard Ammon dubbed the book's art as "strikingly handsome" and "refreshingly whimsical." Even more impressed, *Horn Book* contributor Mary M. Burns stated in her review that Hawkes's "superb interpretive illustrations" are "executed with respect for the text and understanding of the subject." Drawing on the story-book art of centuries past, *Me, All Alone at the End of the World* also pairs the visions of Hawkes and Fleishman, this time in a story about a boy whose boring home is transformed into a bustling carnival. Here the artist's "electric watercolor-and-acrylic paintings" capture the transformation from "mystical tranquility" to "dizzying views of soulless carnival amusements," according to *Booklist* critic Jennifer Mattson,

In addition to acrylic paintings, Hawkes also creates pen-and-ink and pencil illustrations in text-heavy books for older readers. Bringing to life Ibbotson's novel *Dial-a-Ghost,* about the conflicts that ensue between two spectral families when they are assigned by the Adopt-a-Ghost Agency to haunt the same building, he creates illustrations described as "elegantly comic" by a *Horn Book* contributor, while in *School Library Journal* Eva Mitnick maintained that Hawkes's "black-and-white illustrations have an eerie charm." A *Publishers Weekly* critic wrote that in *Island of the Aunts,* another "Ghost Family" series installment, the artist's "whimsical drawings perfectly capture the book's slapstick action and sly humor."

In addition to illustrating the works of others, Hawkes has also created artwork for his own picture-book texts. Featuring a humorous story, *Then the Troll Heard the Squeak* follows a little girl whose nocturnal habit of jumping on her bed eventually creates all manner of havoc in her creaky Victorian home. Ultimately, she not only disrupts her brother, parents, and grandmother, but even awakens a crotchety old troll which has made its home in a dark corner of the house's gloomy basement. A *Kirkus* reviewer praised the book as "witty, innovative, and lots of fun: a fine debut." In *Horn Book* Ann

A day of fun with supersized friends is captured in Hawkes's paintings for Andrea Beaty's picture book **When Giants Come to Play.** (Illustration copyright © 2006 by Kevin Hawkes. Reproduced by permission.)

A. Flowers praised Hawkes's "wonderfully ghoulish illustrations" while a *Publishers Weekly* contributor expressed equal enthusiasm for the "unusual, imaginative perspectives" adopted by the author/illustrator.

In *The Wicked Big Toddlah* Hawkes sets his story in his adopted state of Maine, as a super-duper-sized newborn arrives at the home of a local family, courtesy of a fatigued stork. The resulting stresses on the family are soon apparent: every diaper change requires fire hoses and protective gear, while an ice-cream treat requires the treat to be trucked in. In his artwork Hawkes "uses space and perspective to particular advantage," noted *School Library Journal* critic Marge Loch-Wouters, and "the sheer exuberance" of his artwork "will keep children's imaginations stoked."

"Much of my writing stems from the issues of my early childhood," Hawkes once noted. "My artwork often has a darker, European look to it, perhaps the result of my stay as a child in Europe. My work certainly reflects my own personal sense of humor."

Biographical and Critical Sources

PERIODICALS

Booklist, November 1, 1994, Carolyn Phelan, review of *The Librarian Who Measured the Earth,* p. 497; Sep-

tember 1, 1998, Julie Corsaro, review of *My Friend the Piano,* p. 124; July, 1999, Stephanie Zvirin, review of *Weslandia,* p. 1942; December 15, 1999, Ilene Cooper, review of *And to Think We Thought That We'd Never Be Friends,* p. 789; April 15, 2003, Carolyn Phelan, review of *Not Just a Witch,* p. 1466.

General Music Today, winter, 2002, Richard Ammon, review of *Handel, Who Knew What He Liked,* p. 31.

Horn Book, May, 1991, Ann A. Flowers, review of *Then the Troll Heard the Squeak,* p. 314; September, 2001, review of *Dial-a-Ghost,* p. 586; November-December, 2001, Mary M. Burns, review of *Handel, Who Knew What He Liked,* p. 767; April 15, 2004, Michael Cart, review of *Sidewalk Circus,* p. 1440; November-December, 2004, Christine M. Heppermann, review of *My Sister Hugged an Ape,* p. 697; May-June, 2005, Kitty Flynn, review of *Granite Baby,* p. 306; November 15, 2005, Jennifer Mattson, review of *Me, All Alone, at the End of the World,* p. 44; August 1, 2006, Gillian Engberg, review of *Library Lion,* p. 88; October 15, 2007, Gillian Engberg, review of *Velma Gratch and the Way Cool Butterfly,* p. 55.

Kirkus Reviews, February 15, 1991, review of *Then the Troll Heard the Squeak,* p. 248; November 1, 1992, review of *His Royal Buckliness,* p. 1377; October 1, 2001, review of *A Christmas Treasury: Very Merry Stories and Poems,* p. 1424; March 1, 2004, review of *Sidewalk Circus,* p. 221.

Library Journal, December, 1992, Judith Gloyer, review of *His Royal Buckliness.*

New York Times, November 18, 2001, Martha Chowning, review of *Handel, Who Knew What He Liked,* p. 42.

New York Times Book Review, November 16, 1997, Meg Wolitzer, review of *Marven of the Great North Woods,* p. 46; December 16, 2001, review of *A Christmas Treasury,* p. 20; March 20, 2002, review of *Journey to the River Sea,* p. 20; September 15, 2007, Julie Just, review of *The Wicked Big Toddlah,* p. 19.

Publishers Weekly, December 21, 1990, review of *Then the Troll Heard the Squeak,* pp. 55-56; July 5, 1991, Diane Roback, "Kevin Hawkes," p. 39; March 11, 1996, review of *Dreamland,* p. 64; May 24, 1999, review of *Weslandia,* p. 78; March 17, 2003, review of *The Man Who Made Time Travel,* p. 77; September 4, 2006, review of *Library Lion,* p. 66; October 23, 2006, review of *When Giants Come to Play,* p. 49; June 4, 2007, review of *The Wicked Big Toddlah,* p. 49.

School Library Journal, October, 2001, review of *A Christmas Treasury,* p. 65; December, 2001, Wendy Lukehart, review of *Handel, Who Knew What He Liked,* p. 117; April, 2003, Dona Ratterree, review of *The Man Who Made Time Travel,* p. 184; December, 2005, Linda L. Walkins, review of *Me, All Alone, at the End of the World,* p. 100; October, 2006, Sally R. Dow, review of *When Giants Come to Play,* p. 102; August, 2006, Kathy Krasniewicz, review of *Library Lion,* p. 91; June, 2007, Marge Loch-Wouters, review of *The Wicked Big Toddlah,* p. 107; September, 2008, Jayne Damron, review of *The Road to Oz: Twists, Turns, Bumps, and Triumphs in the Life of L. Frank Baum,* p. 165; December, 2007, Wendy Lukehart, review of *Velma Gratch and the Way Cool Butterfly,* p. 96.

ONLINE

Ingram Book Company Web site, http://www.ingrambook group.com/ (September 9, 2003), interview with Hawkes.

Kevin Hawkes Home Page, http://www.kevinhawkes.com (June 5, 2009).

StorybookArt, http://www.storybookart.com/ (September 9, 2003), "Kevin Hawkes."

*   *   *

HENDERSON, Lauren 1966-

Personal

Born 1966, in London, England; married. *Education:* Cambridge, University, degree (English literature). *Hobbies and other interests:* Traveling, movies, theatre, watching daytime television, static trapeze classes, cooking, wine tasting.

Addresses

Home—London, England; Italy. *Agent*—Anthony Goff, David Higham Literary Agency, 5-8 Lower John St., Golden Square, London W1F 9HA, England.

Alan Madison's Velma Gratch and the Way Cool Butterfly *is brought to life in Hawkes's colorful paintings.* (Illustration copyright © 2007 by Kevin Hawkes. Reproduced by permission of Schwartz & Wade Books, an imprint of Random House Children's Books, a division of Random House, Inc.)

Career
Novelist and journalist.

Awards, Honors
Anthony Award nomination, 2009, for *Kiss Me, Kill Me.*

Writings

FICTION

My Lurid Past, Downtown Press (New York, NY), 2003.
Don't Even Think about It, Downtown Press (New York, NY), 2004.
Exes Anonymous, Time Warner (New York, NY), 2005.

"SAM JONES" MYSTERY SERIES

Dead White Female, Hodder & Stoughton (London, England), 1996.
Too Many Blondes, Crown (New York, NY), 1996.
The Black Rubber Dress, Hutchinson (London, England), 1997.
The Strawberry Tattoo, Crown (New York, NY), 1999.
Chained!, Three Rivers Press, (New York, NY), 2000.
Pretty Boy, Three Rivers Press (New York, NY), 2002.

Author's books have been translated into over twenty languages.

"SCARLETT WAKEFIELD" MYSTERY SERIES; FOR YOUNG ADULTS

Kiss Me, Kill Me, Delacorte Press (New York, NY), 2008.
Kisses and Lies, Delacorte Press (New York, NY), 2009.
Kiss in the Dark, Delacorte Press (New York, NY), 2010.

OTHER

(Editor with Stella Duffy) *Tart Noir* (anthology), Berkley Prime Crime (New York, NY), 2002.
(Editor with Chris Manby and Sarah Mlynowski) *Girls' Night In,* Red Dress (Don Mills, Ontario, Canada), 2004.
Jane Austen's Guide to Dating, Hyperion (New York, NY), 2005.
Jane Austen's Guide to Romance: The Regency Rules, Hyperion (New York, NY), 2006.

Contributor to periodicals, including London *Observer, New Statesman, Cosmopolitan, Glamour, Marxism Today,* and *Lime Lizard.*

Sidelights
A London-based journalist and novelist, Lauren Henderson started her career as a writer after graduating from Cambridge University with a degree in English

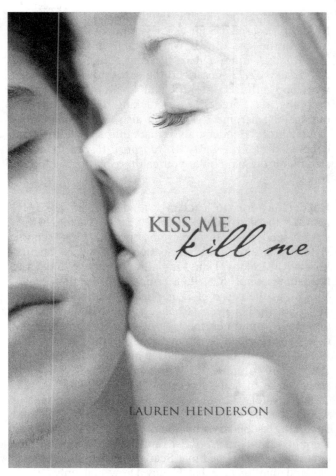

Cover of Lauren Henderson's Kiss Me, Kill Me, *a novel featuring a photograph by Jonathan Cavendish.* (Delacorte Press, 2008. Photograph © by Jonathan Cavendish/Corbis.)

literature. Her articles and essays have appeared in an eclectic mix of periodicals that includes the London *Observer;* mainstream magazines such as *Cosmopolitan, Glamour,* and *New Statesman;* and more specialized publications such as *Marxism Today* and the now-defunct indie music magazine *Lime Lizard.* Henderson's fictional oeuvre is equally versatile; her novels include the mysteries in her "Sam Jones" series, the young-adult novels in her "Scarlett Wakefield" saga as well as romantic comedies such as *My Lurid Past* and *Exes Anonymous.* In addition to gaining a mastery of the chick-lit genre, she also taps the wisdom of the great romantic writers in her nonfiction books *Jane Austen's Guide to Dating* and *Jane Austen's Guide to Romance: The Regency Rules.*

Henderson's "Sam Jones" series begins with *Dead White Female,* which finds metal sculptress Samantha Jones leaving her studio to look into murder. When the body of Lee Jackson is discovered after a nighttime party, the local police are willing to write the tragedy off as accidental death. Sam has other ideas, however; she is convinced that the man was murdered. Sam's adventures continue in *Freeze My Margarita, The Black Rubber Dress, Chained!,* and *Pretty Boy,* among other

tales featuring the likeable sleuth. *Booklist* critic Jenny McLarin described Sam as "a genuinely original heroine with the sass of V.I. Warshawski" in her review of *The Black Leather Dress.* Sharing McLarin's view, a *Publishers Weekly* described the same novel as "loaded with pop cultural, literary and fashion-world name-dropping, . . . breezy, wise-cracking dialogue and a[n outrageous] heroine." McClarin also cited *Chained!* as evidence of "Henderson's remarkable storytelling and concluded of *Freeze My Margarita:* "If you like your sleuths on the wild side, you can't go wrong with Sam Jones."

Henderson turns to a teenage readership in *Kiss Me, Kill Me,* the first volume in her "Scarlett Wakefield" series. A student at an upper-class private girls' school, sixteen-year-old, orphaned Scarlett experiences her first kiss with dreamy Dan McAndrew, only to have the handsome young man then crumple to the floor, dead. Viewed as the cause of Dan's death, Scarlett falls from grace among her peers. Change schools in order to put the death behind her, the teen also decides to solve the case herself, aided by good friend Taylor. Calling *Kiss Me, Kill Me* "a breezy blend of mystery and mean-girl fun," a *Kirkus Reviews* writer added that "Scarlett's sharp sense of self-deprecating humor shines." A seasoned mystery writer, Henderson creates a novel in which "pacing and exposition of clues are skillful, and intriguing secondary characters abound," according to Debbie Carton in *Booklist,* and a *Publishers Weekly* contributor maintained that Scarlett "has a natural glamour and intelligence that Nancy Drew can only dream of."

Both *Jane Austen's Guide to Dating* and *Jane Austen's Guide to Romance* tap *Pride and Prejudice, Emma,* and *Sense and Sensibility* to distill what Henderson calls the "Ten Principles of Dating." Dotted with the examples of Austen's beloved heroines, the books illustrate how patience, honesty, self-awareness, and the ability to speak one's mind will ultimately connect a modern woman with Mr. Right. Henderson also includes quizzes that guide the reader to the heroine she most resembles and also gauge whether their romantic partner is the appropriate hero. The quizzes in *Jane Austen's Guide to Dating* "are fun and will be particularly appealing," wrote *Library Journal* reviewer Deborah Bigelow. Henderson herself is the best endorsement for the book's accuracy: she used the same advice in finding and marrying her own Mr. Right.

Biographical and Critical Sources

PERIODICALS

Booklist, March 15, 1999, Jenny McLarin, review of *The Black Rubber Dress,* p. 1291; December 15, 1999, Jenny McLarin, review of *Freeze My Margarita,* p. 760; November 15, 2001, Jenny McLarin, review of *Chained!,* p. 557; September 1, 2002, Jenny McLarin, review of *Pretty Boy,* p. 63; September 15, 2004, Kristine Huntley, review of *Girls' Night In,* p. 220; November 15, 2004, Kristine Huntley, review of *Don't Even Think about It,* p. 567; February 1, 2008, Debbie Carton, review of *Kiss Me, Kill Me,* p. 42; July, 2000, Jenny McLarin, review of *Strawberry Tattoo,* p. 2013.

Kirkus Reviews, November 1, 2001, review of *Chained!,* p. 1520; August 15, 2002, review of *Pretty Boy,* p. 1178; September 15, 2003, review of *My Lurid Past,* p. 1145; December 1, 2007, review of *Kiss Me, Kill Me.*

Library Journal, January, 2002, Rex Klett, review of *Chained!,* p. 158; October 1, 2002, Rex E. Klett, review of *Pretty Boy,* p. 132; November 15, 2003, Stacy Alesi, review of *My Lurid Past,* p. 97; January 1, 2005, Deborah Bigelow, review of *Jane Austen's Guide to Dating,* p. 134.

New York Times Book Review, March 5, 2000, Marilyn Stasio, review of *Freeze My Margarita,* p. 34; September 10, 2000, review of *Strawberry Tattoo,* p. 74; February 17, 2002, Marilyn Stasio, review of *Chained!,* p. 21.

Publishers Weekly, May 3, 1999, review of *The Black Rubber Dress,* p. 69; January 17, 2000, review of

Henderson taps the wisdom of one of the most popular novelists of all time in Jane Austen's Guide to Dating, *featuring artwork by Roxanna Bikadoroff.* (Hyperion, 2005. Reproduced by permission of the illustrator.)

Freeze My Margarita, p. 46; November 19, 2001, review of *Chained!,* p. 50; September 2, 2002, review of *Pretty Boy,* p. 57; August 23, 2004, review of *Girls' Night In,* p. 37; January 21, 2008, review of *Kiss Me, Kill Me,* p. 172.
School Library Journal, March, 2008, Shelley Huntington, review of *Kiss Me, Kill Me,* p. 200.

ONLINE

Fantastic Fiction Web site, http://www.fantasticfiction.net/ (June 8, 2009), "Lauren Henderson."
Lauren Henderson Home Page, http://www.laurenhenderson.net (June 8, 2009).
Teen Reads Too, http://wwwteenreadstoo.com/ (June 8, 2009), interview with Henderson.*

*   *   *

HIBBERT, Arthur Raymond
See HIBBERT, Christopher

*   *   *

HIBBERT, Christopher 1924-2008
(Arthur Raymond Hibbert)

OBITUARY NOTICE—

See index for *SATA* sketch: Born March 5, 1924, in Enderby, England; died of bronchial pneumonia, December 21, 2008, in Henley-on-Thames, England. Real estate agent, historian, biographer, and author. Hibbert's life was steeped in history, and he had a gift for bringing history to life. He was working as a real-estate agent in his native Leicestershire in 1962, when one of his early literary efforts, *The Destruction of Lord Raglan,* won an award from the Royal Society of Literature. That proved to be sufficient incentive for him to change careers. For the next forty years Hibbert published at least one book a year on a wide range of historical topics, from sixty to more than one hundred titles in all, depending on the data source. His only specialty seemed to be a talent for writing history in the style of a novel, engaging the reader's curiosity and creating an aura of suspense, even regarding events already familiar to the reader. Hibbert wrote about England and Italy, China and Russia, the world of King Arthur and the world of Gilbert and Sullivan. If pressed to name a specialty, one might mention the genre of biography. Many of Hibbert's books related the lives of historical figures, and he even applied the description of "biography" to his histories of the cities of London, Rome, Venice, and Florence. Hibbert did not attempt historical analysis or detective work. He devoted himself instead to presenting an accurate story in an entertaining way. Some of his accounts did receive praise, however, for presenting a familiar historical topic from an unfamiliar perspective. An example would be his sympathetic account of the life of King George IV, Prince of Wales (1762-1830), who was most often remembered for his corpulent frame, his extravagant and hedonistic lifestyle, and his scandalous financial woes, but whose accomplishments were not completely without merit. Hibbert was credited especially for the attention he paid to the personal lives of public figures. His writings, all published under the nickname Christopher, include *The Dragon Wakes: China and the West, 1793-1911* (1970), *Redcoats and Rebels: The American Revolution through British Eyes* (1990), *Cavaliers and Roundheads: The English Civil War, 1642-1649* (1993), and *Disraeli: A Personal History* (2004).

OBITUARIES AND OTHER SOURCES:

PERIODICALS

New York Times, January 6, 2009, p. B11.

J

JAMES, Matt

Personal
Born in Ontario, Canada.

Addresses
Home—Toronto, Ontario, Canada. *E-mail*—info@matt james.ca.

Career
Painter, illustrator, musician, and actor. Performer with Wayne Omaha (band) and The Keep on Keepin' Ons. Actor in films, including (as Stoner Guy Number 1) *Goldirocks* and *Face Off. Exhibitions:* Work included in shows at Katherine Mulherin Contemporary Art Projects and BusGallery, Toronto, Ontario, Canada, and Art Gallery of Nova Scotia-Arena, and Harbourfront Centre, Nova Scotia, Canada, both 2008. Work included in private collections.

Illustrator
Pamela Porter, *Yellow Moon, Apple Moon,* Groundwood Books (Toronto, Ontario, Canada), 2008.

Contributor to periodicals, including *Outpost, Explore,* and *Utne.*

Work featuring James' illustrations has been translated into Spanish.

Biographical and Critical Sources

PERIODICALS

Kirkus Reviews, February 15, 2008, review of *Yellow Moon, Apple Moon.*
School Library Journal, May, 2008, Susan Weitz, review of *Yellow Moon, Apple Moon,* p. 106.

ONLINE

Matt James Home Page, http://www.mattjames.ca (May 15, 2009).*

*   *   *

JARRETT, Clare 1952-

Personal
Born 1952, in London, England; married; children: three. *Education:* Attended Chelsea School of Art and Royal College of Art (London, England).

Addresses
Home—Norfolk, England. *Agent*—Laura Cecil, 17 Alwyne Villas, London N1 2HG, England.

Career
Children's author and illustrator; fine artist. Royal College of Art, London, England, instructor, 1989-95.

Awards, Honors
Mother Goose Award, Books for Children (England), 1996, for *Catherine and the Lion.*

Writings

SELF-ILLUSTRATED

Catherine and the Lion, Collins (London, England), 1996, Carolrhoda Books (Minneapolis, MN), 1997.

Dancing Maddy, HarperCollins (London, England), 1999.

Jamie, Collins (London, England), 2001, published as *Jamie and the Lost Bird,* Collins (London, England), 2002.

The Best Picnic Ever, Candlewick Press (Cambridge, MA), 2004.

Arabella Miller's Tiny Caterpillar, Candlewick Press (Cambridge, MA), 2008.

OTHER

(Illustrator) Warren Lamb and Elizabeth Watson, *Body Code: The Meaning in Movement,* Routledge & Kegan Paul (London, England), 1979.

Sidelights

British children's author and illustrator Clare Jarrett has produced several well-received picture books, earning warm reviews in particular for *The Best Picnic Ever* and *Arabella Miller's Tiny Caterpillar.* In *The Best Picnic Ever* Jack initially feels disappointed that no other children are playing at the park when he and his mother visit to have a picnic. Rather than mope, however, the boy decides to use his imagination and call on a series of imaginary animal friends to keep him company. By story's end, Jack's mother has prepared a spread of pizza, strawberries, hot dogs, and chocolate cake, to which the little boy invites all of his pretend friends. "This paean to the joy of a robust imagination has great child appeal," noted *School Library Journal* critic Carol Ann Wilson. Writing in *Booklist,* Jennifer Mattson predicted that young readers "will love turning the oversize pages filled with Jarrett's scribbly, colored pencil drawings," while a *Publishers Weekly* critic claimed that, "with simple-hearted whimsy and celebratory, imaginative spirit, Jarrett lays out a treat" in *The Best Picnic Ever.*

Called "an engaging, exceptional picture book" by *Booklist* reviewer Julie Cummins, *Arabella Miller's Tiny Caterpillar* follows the metamorphosis of a striped caterpillar as it transforms into a colorful butterfly. When young Arabella Miller finds a caterpillar, she decides to keep it as a pet, creating a habitat for the creature in a shoe box. In each successive page of her story, Jarrett chronicles the development of the butterfly in "bouncy, well-constructed verse that imparts plenty of information," according to a *Publishers Weekly* critic. At the end of the story, the author/illustrator includes a two-page spread of supplemental material about the lifecycle of a butterfly. A *Kirkus Reviews* contributor described *Arabella Miller's Tiny Caterpillar* as "pleasing and useful, for storytimes as well as one-on-one sharing," while *School Library Journal* reviewer Mary Elam wrote that Jarrett's "lilting, rhythmic, patterned story has personal poetic expression and information."

Clare Jarrett combines a gentle story and her simple cartoon illustrations to produce the picture book **Arabella Miller's Tiny Caterpillar.**
(Copyright © 2008 by Clare Jarrett. All rights reserved. Reproduced by permission of the publisher, Candlewick Press, Inc., Somerville, MA, on behalf of Walker Books, Ltd., London.)

Biographical and Critical Sources

PERIODICALS

Booklist, December 15, 1996, Carolyn Phelan, review of *Catherine and the Lion,* p. 731; August, 2004, Jennifer Mattson, review of *The Best Picnic Ever,* p. 1942; March 1, 2008, Julie Cummins, review of *Arabella Miller's Tiny Caterpillar,* p. 66.

Kirkus Reviews, June 1, 2002, review of *Jamie,* p. 805; June 1, 2004, review of *The Best Picnic Ever,* p. 538; February 15, 2008, review of *Arabella Miller's Tiny Caterpillar.*

New York Times Book Review, June 6, 2004, Susan Marie Swanson, review of *The Best Picnic Ever,* p. 25.

Publishers Weekly, June 7, 2004, review of *The Best Picnic Ever,* p. 49; February 25, 2008, review of *Arabella Miller's Tiny Caterpillar,* p. 78.

School Library Journal, September, 2002, Meghan R. Malone, review of *Jamie,* p. 194; July, 2004, Carol Ann Wilson, review of *The Best Picnic Ever,* p. 78; April, 2008, Mary Elam, review of *Arabella Miller's Tiny Caterpillar,* p. 133.*

JENNINGS, Christopher S. 1971(?)-
(C.S. Jennings)

Personal

Born c. 1971. *Education:* Attended University of Central Oklahoma, 1989-94.

Addresses

Home—Austin, TX. *E-mail*—art@csjennings.com.

Career

Author and illustrator in print and video media. *Fort Worth Star Telegram,* Fort Worth, TX, sports editorial cartoonist for four years. Film work includes animation lead for *A Scanner Darkly;* art director for children's video.

Writings

(Self-illustrated) *Animal Band,* Sterling Publishing (New York, NY), 2007.

(Illustrator) Scott Nickel, *The Incredible Rockhead,* Stone Arch Books (Minneapolis, MN), 2010.

Contributor of editorial art to periodicals under name C.S. Jennings, including *Weekly Reader, Disney Adventures, Threads, Austin Chronicle, Oklahoma Gazette,* and *SHOUT!*

Biographical and Critical Sources

PERIODICALS

Kirkus Reviews, March 15, 2008, review of *Animal Band.*

ONLINE

Christopher Jennings Home Page, http://www.csjennings. com (May 15, 2009).*

*   *   *

JENNINGS, C.S.
See JENNINGS, Christopher S.

K

KIM, David 1977-

Personal

Born 1977, in São Paulo, Brazil; moved to United States. *Education:* Art Center College of Design. graduate. *Hobbies and other interests:* Animation, nature, cultures, surfing.

Addresses

E-mail—uakariart@gmail.com.

Career

Illustrator.

Illustrator

Mike Leonetti, *Swinging for the Fences: Hank Aaron and Me,* Chronicle Books (San Francisco, CA), 2008.

Sidelights

Brazilian-born artist David Kim started drawing at age two and never stopped. Originally an architecture student, Kim switched to an illustration major while en-

David Kim captures the magic of American sports legend Hank Aaron in his artwork for Mike Leonetti's **Swinging for the Fences.**

rolled at the Art Center College of Design in Pasadena, California. His other artwork encompasses graphic design, digital art, street painting, 3-D work, and modeling.

Kim's first children's-book project, created in conjunction with author Mike Leonetti, is *Swinging for the Fences: Hank Aaron and Me,* a story about Mark, a Little Leaguer with lessons to learn about teamwork. Mark's idol is Hank Aaron, a baseball player who is on his way to breaking Babe Ruth's home-run record. Mark gets to see Aaron hit his 700th home run, and a meeting between Mark and Aaron leads to some advice on teamwork and the gift of a book on hitting that helps Mark's own game. Marilyn Taniguchi, writing in *School Library Journal,* wrote that *Swinging for the Fences* "sports attractive acrylic spreads depicting games and indoor scenes," while a *Kirkus Reviews* writer commented that "Kim's bright, double-page spreads add some zest to the text." Writing in *Booklist,* Todd Morning observed that while some of Kim's illustrations seem stiff, "the paintings showing Aaron standing heroically in huge stadiums are very effective."

Biographical and Critical Sources

PERIODICALS

Booklist, May 15, 2008, Todd Morning, review of *Swinging for the Fences: Hank Aaron and Me,* p. 45.
Book World, March 16, 2008, Elizabeth Ward, review of *Swinging for the Fences,* p. 12.
Kirkus Reviews, March 15, 2008, review of *Swinging for the Fences.*
School Library Journal, May, 2008, Marilyn Taniguchi, review of *Swinging for the Fences,* p. 102.

ONLINE

David Kim Home Page, http://www.uakariart.com (May 14, 2009).*

*   *   *

KITAMURA, Satoshi 1956-

Personal

Born June 11, 1956, in Tokyo, Japan; moved to England, 1983; son of Testuo (a retail consultant) and Fusae (Sadanaga) Kitamura; married Yoko Sugisaki (an interior designer), December 15, 1987. *Education:* Attended schools in Japan.

Addresses

Home—London, England.

Satoshi Kitamura (Reproduced by permission.)

Career

Freelance illustrator and author, 1975—.

Awards, Honors

Mother Goose Award, Books for Children Book Club, 1983, for *Angry Arthur;* Signal Award, 1984, for *Sky in the Pie;* *New York Times* Notable Books designation, 1985, for *What's Inside*; Children's Science Book Award (Great Britain) and Children's Science Book Award, New York Academy of Sciences, both 1987, both for *When Sheep Cannot Sleep;* Smarties' Prize shortlist, 1989, and Bronze Award, 1997; Children's Literature Choice listee, 1997; National Art Library Award, Victoria & Albert Museum, 1999, for *A Ring of Words.*

Writings

SELF-ILLUSTRATED

What's Inside?: The Alphabet Book, Farrar, Straus (New York, NY), 1985.
Paper Jungle: A Cut-out Book, A. & C. Black (London, England), 1985, Holt, Rinehart (New York, NY), 1986.
When Sheep Cannot Sleep: The Counting Book, Farrar, Straus (New York, NY), 1986.
Lily Takes a Walk, Dutton (New York, NY), 1987.

Captain Toby, Dutton (New York, NY), 1987.

UFO Diary, Andersen (London, England), 1989, Farrar, Straus (New York, NY), 1990, reprinted, Andersen, 2007.

From Acorn to Zoo, Andersen (London, England), 1991, published as *From Acorn to Zoo and Everything in between in Alphabetical Order,* Farrar, Straus (New York, NY), 1992.

Sheep in Wolves' Clothing, Andersen (London, England), 1995, Farrar, Straus (New York, NY), 1996.

Paper Dinosaurs: A Cut-out Book, Farrar, Straus (New York, NY), 1995.

Squirrel Is Hungry, Farrar, Straus (New York, NY), 1996.

Cat Is Sleepy, Farrar, Straus (New York, NY), 1996.

Dog Is Thirsty, Farrar, Straus (New York, NY), 1996.

Duck Is Dirty, Farrar, Straus (New York, NY), 1996.

Bathtime Boots, Andersen (London, England), 1997, Farrar, Straus (New York, NY), 1998.

A Friend for Boots, Andersen (London, England), 1997, Farrar, Straus (New York, NY), 1998.

Goldfish Hide-and-Seek, Farrar, Straus (New York, NY), 1997.

Me and My Cat?, Andersen (London, England), 1999, Farrar, Straus (New York, NY), 2000.

Comic Adventures of Boots, Farrar, Straus (New York, NY), 2002.

Igor: The Bird Who Couldn't Sing, Farrar, Straus (New York, NY), 2005.

Pablo the Artist, Farrar, Straus (New York, NY), 2006.

Hello, Who's There?, Andersen Press (London, England), 2006.

Play with Me!, Andersen Press (London, England), 2007.

Stone Age Boy, Candlewick Press (Cambridge, MA), 2007.

Mila's Marvellous Hat, 2009.

Kitamura's books have been translated into Spanish.

ILLUSTRATOR

Hiawyn Oram, *Angry Arthur,* Harcourt (New York, NY), 1982.

Hiawyn Oram, *Ned and the Joybaloo,* Anderson (London, England), 1983, Farrar, Straus (New York, NY), 1989.

Roger McGough, *Sky in the Pie* (poems), Viking (New York, NY), 1983.

Hiawyn Oram, *In the Attic,* Andersen (London, England), 1984, Holt (New York, NY), 1985.

The Flying Trunk (anthology), Andersen (London, England), 1986.

Alison Sage and Helen Wire, compilers, *The Happy Christmas Book* (anthology), Scholastic (New York, NY), 1986.

Pat Thomson, *My Friend Mr. Morris,* Delacorte (New York, NY), 1987.

Andy Soutter, *Scrapyard,* A. & C. Black (London, England), 1988.

A Children's Chorus (anthology), Dutton (New York, NY), 1989.

Hiawyn Oram, *A Boy Wants a Dinosaur,* Andersen (London, England), 1990, Farrar, Straus (New York, NY), 1991, reprinted, 2004.

Hiawyn Oram, *Speaking for Ourselves* (poems), Methuen (London, England), 1990.

Carl Davis and Hiawyn Oram, *A Creepy Crawly Song Book,* Farrar, Straus (New York, NY), 1993.

Mick Fitzmaurice, *Morris Macmillipede: The Toast of Brussels Sprout,* Andersen (London, England), 1994.

Stephen Webster, *Inside My House,* Riverswift (London, England), 1994.

Stephen Webster, *Me and My Body,* Riverswift (London, England), 1994.

Richard Edwards, *Fly with the Birds: An Oxford Word and Rhyme Book,* Oxford University Press (Oxford, England), 1995, published as *Fly with the Birds: A Word and Rhyme Book,* Orchard Books (New York, NY), 1996.

Brenda Walpole, *Hello, Is There Anyone There?,* Riverswift (London, England), 1995.

Brenda Walpole, *Living and Working Together,* Riverswift (London, England), 1995.

John Agard, *We Animals Would Like a Word with You,* Bodley Head (London, England), 1996.

John Agard, *Points of View with Professor Peekaboo* (poems), Bodley Head (London, England), 2000.

John Agard, *Einstein, the Girl Who Hated Maths,* Hodder Wayland (London, England), 2002.

Colin McNaughton, *Once upon an Ordinary School Day,* Farrar, Straus (New York, NY), 2004.

Carnival of the Animals: Poems Inspired by Saint-Saëns' Music, edited by Judith Chernaik, Candlewick Press (Cambridge, MA), 2005.

Kathy Ashford, *The Jackdaw Jinx,* Andersen (London, England), 2006.

John Agard, *The Young Inferno,* 2008.

Adaptations

From Acorn to Zoo and Everything in between in Alphabetical Order was published in Braille and also made into a take-home literacy pack that includes an audiocassette and activity book. Several books featuring Kitamura's work have been translated into Braille, including *When Sheep Cannot Sleep* and Hiawyn Oram's *Ned and the Joybaloo.*

Sidelights

Praised for his ability to interweave Japanese and Western visual traditions within the engaging illustrations he creates for books by a variety of writers, Satoshi Kitamura has also become known as an author of children's books. With strong technical abilities and a gift for visual humor, Kitamura adds a whimsical, often unconventional touch to traditional children's book formats such as alphabet and counting books. He is widely recognized for his use of simplified, angular shapes and a rich palette of earth and sky tones. "I am interested in different angles of looking at things," Kitamura once told *SATA.* "I find great potential in picture books where visual and verbal fuse to experience and [I also] experiment with these angles. Also, there is an advantage of universality of expression in this medium due to the clarity required for young readers."

As David Wiesner noted in the *New York Times Book Review,* Kitamura's books "are suffused with both warmth and wit. . . . The simplicity of Mr. Kitamura's art is deceptive. A superb draftsman and colorist, he uses pen and brush to create remarkably lush and textured illustrations." Among the author/illustrator's well-received titles are the award-winning counting book *When Sheep Cannot Sleep: The Counting Book, Sheep in Wolves' Clothing, Pablo the Artist, Stone Age Boy,* and *UFO Diary.* In *Publishers Weekly* a critic noted of *Stone Age Boy* that Kitamura's "accomplished story" about a boy who travels from his sterile modern world into a lush, prehistoric landscape is "an imaginative way to kindle interest in, and admiration for, the people of a far distant era," while *School Librarian* contributor Sue Smedley praised *UFO Diary* as "a sophisticated book acknowledging that children deserve quality texts and illustrations."

Kitamura was born and raised in Tokyo, Japan. In 1983 he moved to England, making his permanent home in London. By the time he became a resident of Great Britain, Kitamura's first children's book illustration project, Hiawyn Oram's *Angry Arthur,* had already been published in both England and the United States. An award-winning book, *Angry Arthur* caused publishers to take notice of the young Japanese illustrator and his work; numerous projects were soon awarded to Kitamura in quick succession.

In 1985 Kitamura published *What's Inside?: The Alphabet Book,* the first of his many solo children's book projects. Full of visual clues to help lead young pre-readers through alphabetically ordered pairs of lower-cased letters, *What's Inside* was dubbed "gloriously exuberant" by a *Junior Bookshelf* critic and praised by *School Library Journal* contributor Patricia Homer as a book "which will delight readers who are up to a verbal and visual challenge." Denise M. Wilms echoed such praise in *Booklist,* maintaining that the "imaginative quality" of Kitamura's full-color line and wash illustrations "make for a fresh, engaging display of letters that will stand up to more than one close look."

In another alphabet book, Kitamura builds young readers' vocabulary, one letter at a time. *From Acorn to Zoo* features pages chock-full of illustrated objects that begin with the same letter, allowing children's vocabularies to be "expanded almost painlessly and [their] capacity for observation sharpened," in the opinion of a *Junior Bookshelf* reviewer. Each illustration features energetic pen-and-ink renderings of an unusual assortment of animals and objects, richly colored and positioned on the page in ways readers will find humorous. For example, on one page a hefty hippo tests the strength of a hammock by sitting in it and playing his harmonica while a harp and coat hanger can be found nearby. In a similar vein, Kitamura tackles introductory mathematics by illustrating the quandary of an insomniac named Woolly in *When Sheep Cannot Sleep,* a 1-2-3 book. Rather than lay about in the dark, Woolly goes on a search for ob-

jects grouped first in pairs, then in threes, fours, and so on up to twenty-two before tiring himself out and falling asleep in an abandoned country cottage. Kitamura does not make things any too easy for his reader, however; on each page the object Woolly finds must also be discovered by the reader and its quantity totaled up.

Calling *When Sheep Cannot Sleep* "a joy to look at," *Horn Book* contributor Anita Silvey added that Kitamura's "slightly primitive drawing style is delightful, making counting the objects or just looking at the book a great deal of fun." *Booklist* reviewer Ilene Cooper noted that the author/illustrator's "squared-off sheep has an endearingly goofy look that kids and adults will love," while Jane Doonan, writing in the *Times Literary Supplement,* dubbed *When Sheep Cannot Sleep* the "perfect picture book[—]free from stereotype images, [and] brimming with unforced humor." In *School Library Journal* Lorraine Douglas praised Kitamura for his "engaging and fresh approach." *School Librarian* reviewer Donald Fry also lauded *When Sheep Cannot Sleep,* concluding that no other such counting book is "so witty and enjoyable as this one."

Goofy looking sheep serve also as the focus of Kitamura's *Sheep in Wolves' Clothing.* Here sheep Hubert, Georgina, and Gogol hoof it on down to the seashore for one last dip in the ocean before the chill of winter sets in. Near the beach, they meet a group of wolves enjoying the fall afternoon by taking time off from work at their knitwear factory to play a round of golf. The wolves generously offer to watch the sheep's warm wool coats while the seabound swimmers take their plunge; not surprisingly, neither wolves nor wool are anywhere to be found when the soaked sheep return. Fortunately, the sheep call in the services of Elliott Baa, a fully fleeced ace detective, who follows the woolly trail to its conclusion. "Younger children will delight in the climactic brouhaha and will also find [*Sheep in Wolves' Clothing*] a satisfying mystery story," according to *Horn Book* reviewer Margaret Bush.

In *Lily Takes a Walk* young readers get a look at an overactive imagination and the divergent perceptions of dog and child. While on their routine evening walk, Nicky the puppy scares up shadows of everything from vampires to monsters, yet Nicky's leashholder, Lily, sees none of her pet's concerns. Several reviewers of the book praised Kitamura's combination of scariness and humor, a *Kirkus Reviews* writer calling *Lily Takes a Walk* "understated, subtle, and delightful." Kay E. Vandergrift dubbed the work a "clever idea with an appropriately humorous ending" in *School Library Journal,* and a *Publishers Weekly* contributor deemed the walk in Kitamura's picture book "well worth taking."

Other books by Kitamura that showcase his vivid imagination and ability to capture a child's attention include *UFO Diary,* the observations of an outer-space visitor who accidentally lands on Earth and is befriended by a young boy. Although never actually depicted in Kita-

Kitamura's original self-illustrated picture books include **Stone Age Boy.** (Copyright © 2007 by Satoshi Kitamura. Reproduced by permission of the publisher, Candlewick Press, Inc., Somerville, MA, on behalf of Walker Books, Ltd., London.)

mura's colorful drawings, the alien provides readers with an opportunity to "see our planet's natural abundance and beauty with fresh eyes," according to John Peters, a *School Library Journal* contributor. The book's other enthusiasts included *Times Literary Supplement* critic Liz Brooks, who praised both Kitamura's artistry and simplicity, and Susan Perren, who noted in *Quill & Quire* that the illustrations "say it all." In the words of *Horn Book* contributor Nancy Vasilakis, *UFO Diary* is an "unusual" work which constitutes a "beautiful, quiet, respectful reminder of who we are and whence we come."

The picture book *Captain Toby* is also unusual in showing the aplomb of a young boy who takes charge in his imagination after he becomes convinced that the storm raging outside his bedroom window has blown his house out to sea. According to *School Library Journal* critic Patricia Pearl, Kitamura's "clever premise is carefully realized in the illustrations," yet she found the plot less successful, particularly its denouement. On the other hand, a *Publishers Weekly* contributor called *Captain Toby* a "nautical romp," a voyage in which the creator melds "sweet charm and raucous revelry." Likening it to a film that scrolls from frame to frame, Margery Fisher described Kitamura's book as a "complete and believable fantasy" in her *Growing Point* review.

Cats play an important role in several of Kitamura's picture books. For example, *Me and My Cat?,* which

Booklist critic Amy Brandt described as "funny, frenetic, and insightful," revolves around the body-switch perpetrated by a witch's spell upon the boy Nicholas and his cat Leonardo. So while Leonardo in Nicholas's body goes off to school, Nicholas in Leonardo's body explores the varied activities of a cat with "high humor" and a "wickedly delightful twist at the end," to quote Ann Welton in *School Library Journal.* A reviewer for *Horn Book* also praised the story's humor, describing it as "dry" and the book as a whole a "farcical comedy." In addition, in *Goldfish Hide-and-Seek* a cat stalks a goldfish that has left his bowl in search of a missing playmate, in what Lynne Taylor of *School Library Journal* termed "original, playful, absurd, superlative, [and] inspired."

A cat slo stars in one of a quartet of cardboard books Kitamura has created for toddlers. Since they are geared to the youngest book users, *Cat Is Sleepy, Squirrel Is Hungry, Dog Is Thirsty,* and *Duck Is Dirty* feature fewer words and use illustrations that employ somewhat heavier lines than Kitamura's standard fare. Applauding these books for their appropriate humor and plots, *School Library Journal* contributor Ann Cook added: "No cutesy, patronizing stuff here." In fact, each story shows how an animal hero solves a simple, but not trivial, problem. According to a *Kirkus Reviews* writer, even the artwork in this quartet demonstrates more sophistication than is expected in books for such young readers.

Also reflecting Kitamura's interest in felines, a cat named Boots figures prominently in his fictional world. *Bathtime Boots, A Friend for Boots,* and *Comic Adventures of Boots* introduce readers to a memorable feline. The first two works are board books for toddlers in which a round-eyed cat tries to evade the bath and to find a friend, respectively. This duo "will hit home with small children" a *Kirkus Reviews* writer noted, because of their simple plot lines and the expressively depicted characters. For an older readership—children in grades two through four—*Comic Adventures of Boots* is a collection of three cat stories that, to quote *Booklist* reviewer Susan Dove Lempke, are "equally goofy and laugh-out-loud funny." The first story, "Operation Fish Biscuit," shows how Boots gets back his best napping place; in "Please to Meet You, Madam Quark" he takes swimming lessons from a duck, and in "Let's Play a Guessing Game" kittens play charades. The pages are broken up into panels like a comic book and use dialogue balloons. This busy visual style elicited comment from Linda M. Kenton, who expressed concern in *School Library Journal* that some readers might be put off by such cluttered pages; even so she praised the humor in *Comic Adventures of Boots* as "simultaneously sly and outrageous." Sometimes, as a *Kirkus Reviews* writer pointed out, words are unnecessary because Kitamura "captures an astonishing range of expressions and reactions" in his felines' features.

Other original picture books from Kitamura capture abstract concepts. In *Igor: The Bird Who Couldn't Sing,* for example, his story of a bird with a desire to sing that is not matched by ability "will show children that making music is a joyful experience, regardless of how it sounds," according to Kristen M. Todd in *School Library Journal.* Another resonant work, *Pablo the Artist,* finds a dapperly dressed elephant hoping to enter a painting in the upcoming Hoof Lane Art Club show. At the same time, Pablo is worried that he does not feel creatively inspired. "Kitamura's familiar cartoon style and wry humor pair perfectly in this original take on artist's block," concluded a *Kirkus Reviews* writer in a review of *Pablo the Artist,* while in *Publishers Weekly* a contributor noted that the author/illustrator's "signature choppy, shaky ink lines and saturated colors" successfully convey his story about "a character overcoming creative limitations."

In assessing the author/artist's contribution to children's literature for *Children's Literature,* Jane Doonan wrote: "Kitamura's work is notable . . . for the artist's material skills and for his distinctive relationship to the pictorial tradition of Japan. . . . In less than a decade Kitamura has made, and continues to make, a distinctive contribution to the art of the children's picture book. The fresh way of saying 'even something very commonplace' [to quote Maurice Sendak] is evident in all he does."

Biographical and Critical Sources

BOOKS

Children's Literature Review, Volume 60, Gale (Detroit, MI), 2000, pp. 82-103.

PERIODICALS

American Music Teacher, December, 2005, Midori Koga, review of *Igor: The Bird Who Couldn't Sing,* p. 64.
Booklist, September 1, 1985, Denise M. Wilms, review of *What's Inside?: The Alphabet Book,* p. 64; October 1, 1986, Ilene Cooper, review of *When Sheep Cannot Sleep,* p. 273; April 15, 1991, Stephanie Zvirin, review of *A Boy Wants a Dinosaur,* p. 1651; July, 1992, Deborah Abbott, review of *From Acorn to Zoo,* p. 1943; March 1, 2000, Amy Brandt, review of *Me and My Cat?,* p. 1250; October 1, 2002, Susan Dove Lempke, review of *Comic Adventures of Boots,* p. 326; March 15, 2006, Jennifer Mattson, review of *Carnival of the Animals: Poems Inspired by Saint Saëns' Music,* p. 48.
Books for Keeps, September, 1988, Liz Waterland, review of *When Sheep Cannot Sleep,* pp. 8-9; July, 1995, Wendy Cooling, review of *Sheep in Wolves' Clothing,* pp. 24-25, 28.
Children's Literature, Volume 19, 1999, Jane Doonan, "Satoshi Kitamura: Aesthetic Dimensions," pp. 107-137.
Growing Point, January, 1987, Margery Fisher, review of *When Sheep Cannot Sleep,* p. 4745; January, 1990, Margery Fisher, "Picture-Book Adventures," pp. 5269-5272.
Horn Book, November, 1986, Anita Silvey, review of *When Sheep Cannot Sleep,* pp. 736-737; March, 1990, Nancy Vasilakis, review of *UFO Diary,* pp. 190-191; May, 1992, Nancy Vasilakis, review of *From Acorn to Zoo,* p. 330; January, 1994, Nancy Vasilakis, review of *A Creepy Crawly Song Book,* p. 83; July, 1996, Margaret Bush, review of *Sheep in Wolves' Clothing,* p. 450; March, 2000, review of *Me and My Cat?,* p. 187; March-April, 2005, Joanna Rudge Long, review of *Once upon an Ordinary School Day,* p. 192; January-February, 2008, Elissa Gershowitz, review of *Stone Age Boy,* p. 74.
Junior Bookshelf, October, 1982, A. Thatcher, review of *Angry Arthur,* p. 183; October, 1985, R. Baines, review of *What's Inside?,* p. 212; February, 1991, S.M. Ashburner, review of *Speaking for Ourselves,* p. 26.
Kirkus Reviews, May 15, 1985, review of *What's Inside? The Alphabet Book,* p. J26; November 1, 1987, review of *Lily Takes a Walk,* pp. 1575-1576; June 15, 1996, review of *Duck Is Dirty,* p. 906; June 15, 1997, review of *Gold Fish Hide-and-Seek,* p. 951; January 1, 1998, review of *Bathtime Boots,* p. 58; June 1, 2002, review of *Comic Adventures of Boots,* p. 806; January 15, 2006, review of *Pablo the Artist,* p. 86.
New York Times Book Review, June 16, 1985, Karla Kuskin, review of *What's Inside?,* p. 30; May 21, 1989, John Cech, review of *Ned and the Joybaloo,* p.

41; May 19, 1991, Francine Prose, review of *A Boy Wants a Dinosaur,* p. 23; May 19, 1996, David Wiesner, "A Job for Elliott Baa, Private Eye," p. 27; May 14, 2000, David Small, review of *Me and My Cat?,* p. 21; June 1, 2002, review of *Comic Adventures of Boots,* p. 806; April 9, 2006, review of *Carnival of the Animals,* p. 21.

Publishers Weekly, February 22, 1985, review of *In the Attic,* p. 158; September 11, 1987, review of *Lily Takes a Walk,* p. 92; June 24, 1988, review of *Ned and the Joybaloo,* p. 110; September 30, 1988, review of *Captain Toby,* p. 65; March 25, 1996, review of *Fly with the Birds: A Word and Rhyme Book,* p. 82; May 6, 1996, review of *Sheep in Wolves' Clothing,* p. 80; June 24, 1996, "Animal Pragmatism," p. 62; June 9, 1997, review of *Goldfish Hide-and-Seek,* p. 44; March 20, 2000, review of *Me and My Cat?,* p. 91; July 17, 2000, review of *Sheep in Wolves' Clothing,* p. 198; March 14, 2005, review of *Once upon an Ordinary School Day,* p. 66; September 5, 2005, review of *Igor,* p. 61; January 30, 2006, review of *Pablo the Artist,* p. 69; December 3, 2007, review of *Stone Age Boy,* p. 69.

Quill & Quire, October, 1989, Susan Perren, review of *UFO Diary,* pp. 17-18.

School Librarian, December, 1986, Donald Fry, review of *When Sheep Cannot Sleep,* p. 337; February, 1988, Margaret Meek, review of *Lily Takes a Walk,* p.16; November, 1989, Sue Smedley, review of *UFO Diary,* p. 145; November, 1990, Angela Redfern, review of *Speaking for Ourselves,* p. 156; February, 1991, Val Booler, review of *A Boy Wants a Dinosaur,* p. 20; August, 1992, I. Anne Rowe, review of *From Acorn to Zoo,* p. 97; November, 1997, Lynne Taylor, review of *Goldfish Hide-and-Seek,* p. 187.

School Library Journal, September, 1982, Holly Sanhuber, review of *Angry Arthur,* p. 110; August, 1984, Joan Wood Sheaffer, review of *Ned and the Joybaloo,* p. 63; September, 1985, Patricia Homer, review of *What's Inside?,* p. 120; December, 1986, Lorraine Douglas, review of *When Sheep Cannot Sleep,* pp. 90-91; November, 1987, Kay E. Vandergrift, review of *Lily Takes a Walk,* pp. 93-94; March, 1989, Patricia Pearl, review of *Captain Toby,* p. 164; January, 1990, John Peters, review of *UFO Diary,* p. 84; July, 1992, Mary Lou Budd, review of *From Acorn to Zoo,* p. 60; January, 1994, Jane Marino, review of *A Creepy Crawly Song Book,* pp. 108-109; March, 1996, Sally R. Dow, review of *Fly with the Birds,* p. 173; August, 1996, Ann Cook review of *Cat Is Sleepy,* p. 124; August, 1996, Luann Toth, review of *Sheep in Wolves' Clothing,* p. 124; October, 1997, Karen James, review of *Goldfish Hide-and-Seek,* p. 100; March, 2000, Ann Welton, review of *Me and My Cat?,* p. 209; August, 2002, Linda M. Kenton, review of *Comic Adventures of Boots,* p. 159; March, 2005, review of *Once upon an Ordinary School Day,* p. 185; September, 2005, Kristen M. Todd, review of *Igor,* p. 175; February, 2006, Kara Schaff, review of *Pablo the Artist,* p. 104; April, 2006, Teresa Pfeifer, review of *Carnival of the Animals,* p. 124; January, 2008, Mary Jean Smith, review of *Stone Age Boy,* p. 90.

Times Educational Supplement, November 11, 1994, Mary Gribbin, review of *Inside My House,* p. 18.

Times Literary Supplement, November 28, 1986, Jane Doonan, review of *When Sheep Cannot Sleep,* p. 1345; July 7, 1989, Liz Brooks, "Picturing Pets," p. 757.*

*   *   *

KODMAN, Stanislawa

Personal

Female. *Education:* Cumberland College, B.A. (English); University of Kentucky, B.F.A. (studio arts).

Addresses

Home—Atlanta, GA. *Agent*—Alexander Pollard, Inc., 1678 Four Lakes, Dr., Madison, GA 30650. *E-mail*—stanis@stanislawakodman.com.

Career

Illustrator, photographer, and jewelry artist. Creative Circus, Atlanta, GA, instructor in design theory and illustration.

Awards, Honors

Best of the Best listee, Chicago Public Library, 2008, and Keystone Reading Book Award nomination, 2009, both for *Grow* by Juanita Havill.

Illustrator

Juanita Havill, *Grow: A Novel in Verse,* Peachtree (Atlanta, GA), 2008.

Stanislawa Kodman creates the whimsical artwork that brings to life the story in Juanita Havill's verse novel **Grow.** (Illustration © copyright by Stanislawa Kodman. All rights reserved. Reproduced courtesy of Peachtree Publishers.)

Contributor of artwork to periodicals, including *Atlanta Woman* and the *Wall Street Journal.*

Sidelights

Known for her unique pencil-and-ink-wash style, Stanislawa Kodman creates illustrations that have appeared in periodicals as well as in the pages of Juanita Havill's picture book *Grow: A Novel in Verse.* In the book, which is geared for readers in the early elementary grades, Havill describes how residents of an inner-city neighborhood band together, young and old, to transform a vacant lot full of trash and other discarded objects into a beautiful garden. The metamorphosis is described by twelve-year-old Kate after retired special-needs teacher Berneetha inspires some surprising people—including a local veterinarian, a firefighter, and a young gang member—into participating in the neighborhood renewal project.

Characterizing Kodman's illustrations for *Grow* as "quiet, scribbly drawings," Hazel Rochman added in *Booklist* that the artist's animated images "depict the power of working as a community." In *School Library Journal,* Anne Knickerbocker praised Havill's story as "beautifully written with pleasing alliteration and flowing lines," adding that Kodman's "whimsical line drawings add to the heartwarming story." The artist's "pencil illustrations add touches of whimsy and charm to the story," wrote a *Kirkus Reviews* writer, "and designate [*Grow*] . . . a work for a young audience."

Biographical and Critical Sources

PERIODICALS

Booklist, June 1, 2008, Hazel Rochman, review of *Grow: A Novel in Verse* p. 74.
Kirkus Reviews, March, 15, 2008, Juanita Havill, review of *Grow.*
School Library Journal, May, 2008, Anne Knickerbocker, review of *Grow,* p. 126.

ONLINE

Alexander Pollard Web site, http://www.alexanderpollard.com/ (May 15, 2009), "Stanislawa Kodman."
Stanislawa Kodman Home Page, http://stanislawakodman.com (May 15, 2009).*

* * *

KRUUSVAL, Catarina 1951-

Personal

Born 1951, in Sweden.

Addresses

Home—Molndal, Sweden.

Career

Illustrator and author of books for children.

Awards, Honors

Rabén & Sjögrens Tecknarstipendium, and Wettergrens Bokollon prize, both 1996; Ottilia Adelborg-stipendiet, 2000.

Writings

SELF-ILLUSTRATED

Sagan om eken och den vresiga gumman, Rabén & Sjögren (Stockholm, Sweden), 1995.
No Clothes Today!, R & S Books (New York, NY), 1995.
Ellen, Rabén & Sjögren (Stockholm, Sweden), 1996.
Ellen på stranden, Rabén & Sjögren (Stockholm, Sweden), 1996, translated as *Beach Day,* R & S Books (New York, NY), 1997.
Blommor från Ellen, Rabén & Sjögren (Stockholm, Sweden), 1996, translated as *Birthday Flowers,* R & S Books (New York, NY), 1997.
Ellens boll, Rabén & Sjögren (Stockholm, Sweden), 1997, translated as *Where's the Ball?,* R & S Books (New York, NY), 1997.
Egon och julgubben, Eriksson & Lindgren (Stockholm, Sweden), 1998.
Ellens ABC, Rabén & Sjögren (Stockholm, Sweden), 1999.
Ellen och Olle leker, Rabén & Sjögren (Stockholm, Sweden), 2002.
Ellen och Olle äter, Rabén & Sjögren (Stockholm, Sweden), 2002.
Ellens 1, 2, 3, Rabén & Sjögren (Stockholm, Sweden), 2002.
Ellens blombok, Rabén & Sjögren (Stockholm, Sweden), 2003.
Ellens visor och ramsor, Rabén & Sjögren (Stockholm, Sweden), 2004.
Lilla Tulla, Rabén & Sjögren (Stockholm, Sweden), 2004.
Lilla Tulla vill inte, Rabén & Sjögren (Stockholm, Sweden), 2004.
Lilla Tulla får en potta, Rabén & Sjögren (Stockholm, Sweden), 2005.
Lilla Tulla hjälper till, Rabén & Sjögren (Stockholm, Sweden), 2005.
Ellen och Olle badar, Rabén & Sjögren (Stockholm, Sweden), 2005.
Boken om Ellen, Rabén & Sjögren (Stockholm, Sweden), 2005.
Ellen och Olle åker, Rabén & Sjögren (Stockholm, Sweden), 2005.
Katten Bobby vandrar söderut, Eriksson & Lindgren (Stockholm, Sweden), 2005.
Boken om mig, Rabén & Sjögren (Stockholm, Sweden), 2005.

Boken om mig—Olle, Rabén & Sjögren (Stockholm, Sweden), 2006.

Ellens äppelträd, Rabén & Sjögren (Stockholm, Sweden), 2006, translated as *Ellen's Apple Tree,* R & S Books (New York, NY), 2008.

Fia och djuren, Rabén & Sjögren (Stockholm, Sweden), 2007, translated by Joan Sandin as *Franny's Friends,* R & S Books (New York, NY), 2008.

Fia och djuren på dagis, Rabén & Sjögren (Stockholm, Sweden), 2007.

En elefant balanserade, Rabén & Sjögren (Stockholm, Sweden), 2008.

Fjörnen sover, Rabén & Sjögren (Stockholm, Sweden), 2008.

Fia och djuren—Alla ska vara med!, Rabén & Sjögren (Stockholm, Sweden), 2008.

Djurpussel, Rabén & Sjögren (Stockholm, Sweden), 2009.

Ellen och Olle leker med bokstäver, Rabén & Sjögren (Stockholm, Sweden), 2009.

Ellen och Olle leker med siffror, Rabén & Sjögren (Stockholm, Sweden), 2009.

Fia och djuren går till sjöss, Rabén & Sjögren (Stockholm, Sweden), 2009.

I ett hus . . . , Rabén & Sjögren (Stockholm, Sweden), 2009.

ILLUSTRATOR

Lena Arro, *Fastrar och fullriggare!,* Rabén & Sjögren (Stockholm, Sweden), 1995.

Ann-Sofie Jeppson, *Det går framåt Pontus!,* Rabén & Sjögren (Stockholm, Sweden), 1997, translated as *You're Growing up, Pontus!,* R & S Books (New York, NY), 2001.

Ann-Sofie Jeppson, *Här kommer Pontus!,* Rabén & Sjögren (Stockholm, Sweden), 1997, translated by Frances Corry as *Here Comes Pontus!,* R & S Books (New York, NY), 2000.

Svante Björkum, *Elin och Erik,* Rabén & Sjögren (Stockholm, Sweden), 1998.

Lena Arro, *Gubbar ach galoscher!,* Rabén & Sjögren (Stockholm, Sweden), 2000, translated as *By Geezers and Galoshes!,* R & S Books (New York, NY), 2001

Lena Arro, *Godnatt alla djur,* Raben & Sjogren (Stockholm, Sweden), 2001, translated by Joan Sandin as *Good Night, Animals,* R & S Books (New York, NY), 2002.

Lena Arro, *Tomtegroöt och tulpaner!,* Rabén & Sjögren (Stockholm, Sweden), 2001.

Kristina Westerlund, *Åke går i valpskola,* Eriksson & Lindgren (Stockholm, Sweden), 2002.

Kristina Westerlund, *Åkes bästa pappa,* Eriksson & Lindgren (Stockholm, Sweden), 2003.

Alice Tegnér, *Bä, bä vita lamm,* Rabén & Sjögren (Stockholm, Sweden), 2007.

Alice Tegnér, *Ekorr'n satt i granen,* Rabén & Sjögren (Stockholm, Sweden), 2007.

Alf Proysen, *Sagan om mössens julafton,* Rabén & Sjögren (Stockholm, Sweden), 2008.

Adaptations

Several of Kruusval's books have been adapted for videotape.

Biographical and Critical Sources

PERIODICALS

Booklist, March 15, 2000, Connie Fletcher, review of *Here Comes Pontus!,* p. 1387; July, 2001, Denise Wilms, review of *By Geezers and Galoshes!,* p. 2016; December 15, 2002, Connie Fletcher, review of *Good Night, Animals,* p. 766; June 1, 2008, Hazel Rochman, review of *Franny's Friends,* p. 87.

Kirkus Reviews, September 1, 2001, review of *You're Growing up, Pontus!,* p. 1292; August 1, 2002, review of *Good Night, Animals,* p. 1121; March 1, 2008, review of *Franny's Friends.*

School Library Journal, Carol Schene, July, 2000, review of *Here Comes Pontus!,* p. 80; September, 2001, Kathleen Whalin, review of *By Geezers and Galoshes!,* p. 182; November, 2001, Jane Marino, review of *You're Growing up, Pontus!,* p. 124; May, 2008, Maura Bresnahan, review of *Franny's Friends,* p. 102.

ONLINE

Rabén & Sjögren Web site, http://www.norstedsforlags grupp.se/ (June 1, 2009), Catarina Kruusval.*

L

LANAGAN, Margo 1960-

Personal

Born 1960, in Newcastle, New South Wales, Australia; children: two sons. *Education:* Studied history at universities in Perth and Sydney.

Addresses

Home—Sydney, New South Wales, Australia.

Career

Freelance book editor, technical writer, and author.

Awards, Honors

World Fantasy Award for Best Short Fiction, 2005, and Michael L. Printz Award Honor Book designation, 2006, both for *Black Juice;* Top Choice designation, Children's Book Council of Australia, 2007, for *Red Spikes.*

Writings

WildGame, Allen & Unwin (North Sydney, New South Wales, Australia), 1991.

The Tankermen, Allen & Unwin (North Sydney, New South Wales, Australia), 1992.

The Best Thing, Allen & Unwin (St. Leonards, New South Wales, Australia), 1995.

Touching Earth Lightly, Allen & Unwin (St. Leonards, New South Wales, Australia), 1996.

Walking through Albert, Allen & Unwin (St. Leonards, New South Wales, Australia), 1998.

White Time (short stories), Allen & Unwin (Crows Nest, New South Wales, Australia), 2000, Eos (New York, NY), 2006.

Treasure Hunters of Quentaris, Lothian Books (South Melbourne, New South Wales, Australia), 2004.

Black Juice (short stories), Allen & Unwin (Crows Nest, New South Wales, Australia), 2004, Eos (New York, NY), 2005.

Red Spikes (short stories), Allen & Unwin (Crows Nest, New South Wales, Australia), 2006, Alfred A. Knopf (New York, NY), 2007.

The Singing Stones: A Tale of the Shimmaron, ABC Books (Sydney, New South Wales, Australia), 2007.

Tender Morsels, Alfred A. Knopf (New York, NY), 2008.

Stories included in anthologies, such as *Click,* Scholastic (New York, NY), 2007.

Sidelights

In addition to writing for children, author Margo Lanagan has worked as a freelance book editor as well as a technical writer. Growing up in the Hunter Valley and in Melbourne, Australia, she traveled extensively, in addition to studying history at universities in both Perth and Sydney. The insight and experiences gained from both her travels and her education have provided the inspiration for Lanagan's middle-grade and young-adult novels as well as for short-story collections such as *White Time, Black Juice,* and *Red Spikes.*

Black Juice, which includes stories such as "Earthly Uses," "Singing My Sister Down," "House of the Many," and "Sweet Pippit," was described by *Kliatt* contributor Sherry Hoy as "a powerful, evocative collection" that is "not for faint-hearted readers." In *School Library Journal* Sarah Couri wrote that each of the book's ten stories "is strange and startling," providing readers with "a glimpse into weird, wondrous, and sometmes terrifying worlds." Praised for containing "memorable characters a-plenty" by a *Kirkus Reviews* critic, the ten-story collection is a companion volume to Lanagan's *White Time* and was awarded a Michael L. Printz Award Honor Book designation following its publication in the United States.

Published after *Black Juice* in the United States but appearing first in the author's native Australia, *White Time* is another "magical, wondrous collection" that weaves speculative fiction and fantasy into stories that resonate with universal human themes, according to *Journal of*

Adolescent and Adult Literacy. Her short-story collection *Red Spikes,* which weaves together such disparate elements as monkeys, gods, and a changeling, coalesces through the author's "searing prose and bizarre, whimsical vision," according to a *Kirkus Reviews* writer. Also containing ten stories, *Red Spikes* captures the stuff of nightmares in a text that features what Baker characterized as "a mixture of earthly dialect and inventiveness that makes *Red Spikes* "mexmerizing, sometimes horrifying, and occasionally funny."

A longer work of fiction, *Tender Morsels* is a middle-grade novel in which Lanagan draws from the story of "Snow White and Rose Red." The story focuses on two sisters, Branza and Urdda, who live in isolation with their victimized mother, Liga, deep in the forest. Ultimately, a wild bear and a dwarf draw the girls out and force each sister to decide between remaining in isolation and accepting the risks and rewards of human society. While noting the novel's complexities, *Booklist* contributor Carolyn Lehman assured her readers that Lanagan's text is "beautifully written and surprising" in its exploration of "what it means to be human." The author's "trademark linguistic gyrations bring to life" her

Cover of Margo Lanagan's short-story collection **Red Spikes,** *featuring artwork by Jeremy Caniglia.* (Jacket art copyright © 2007 by Jeremy Caniglia. Reproduced by permission of Alfred A. Knopf, an imprint of Random House Children's Books, a division of Random House, Inc.)

"utterly fresh take" on the classic Grimms' Brothers story, according to a *Kirkus Reviews* writer, even as she "offers up difficult truths . . . that are as sobering as they are triumphant," according to Deirdre Baker in *Horn Book.*

Discussing her transition between writing novels and short fiction with Amy Fiske for the *Journal of Adolescent and Adult Literacy,* Lanagan explained: "Short stories are more instantly gratifying to write. Even when they don't work, you know soon whether a story idea is going to work on its own, or require some other idea and more time to animate it. Also, it doesn't take a lot of work to hold the story in its entirety in my head, which means that I can fit short stories into the rest of my life more easily. Writing novels, you really have to put aside good slabs of weeks to keep the thing operational."

Lanagan features children and teens as central characters in her books "because I'm interested in what it's like to piece together the world, to make connections and realize things for the first time. And there's a lot more room for adventure in children's and teenagers' lives, before they make the decisions that will set them on their path in adulthood."

"Inspiration is pretty much everywhere," Lanagan noted in an essay on the *Allen & Unwin Web site.* "I get it from reading both good and bad writing, from watching and listening to people, from landscapes and cityscapes, from wildlife documentaries and building sites and classrooms and music. My problem is not finding ideas but finding time to pin a few of them down to a page.

"I write because it's my way of making sense of the world," she added. "I've always loved reading, both to escape from real life and to make life more real, and I like doing both in my writing too, writing straight realistic and fantasy stories."

Biographical and Critical Sources

PERIODICALS

Booklist, April 15, 2005, Frances Bradburn, review of *Black Juice,* p. 1463; August 1, 2006, Holly Koelling, review of *White Time,* p. 75; October 1, 2007, Jennifer Mattson, review of *Red Spikes,* p. 58; August 1, 2008, Ian Chipman, review of *Tender Morsels,* p. 69.

Horn Book, May-June, 2005, Joanna Rudge Long, review of *Black Juice,* p. 330; July-August, 2006, Joanna Rudge Long, review of *White Time,* p. 445; November-December, 2007, Deirdre F. Baker, review of *Red Spikes,* p. 683; September-October, 2008, Deirdre F. Baker, review of *Tender Morsels,* p. 590.

Journal of Adolescent and Adult Literature, March, 2007, Amy Fiske, review of *White Time* and interview with Lanagan, pp. 506-508.

Cover of Lanagan's young-adult novel Tender Morsels, *featuring artwork by Jodi Hewgill.* (Reproduced by permission of Alfred A. Knopf, a division of Random House, Inc.)

Kirkus Reviews, February 1, 2005, review of *Black Juice,* p. 178; July 15, 2006, review of *White Time,* p. 725; October 1, 2007, review of *Red Spikes;* September 15, 2008, review of *Tender Morsels.*

Kliatt, July, 2006, Sherry Hoy, review of *Black Juice,* p. 24.

Publishers Weekly, October 1, 2007, review of *Red Spikes,* p. 59; September 8, 2008, review of *Tender Morsels,* p. 51.

School Library Journal, March, 2005, Sarah Couri, review of *Black Juice,* p. 213; November, 2006, Allison Follos, review of *White Time,* p. 139; November, 2008, Carolyn Lehman, review of *Tender Morsels,* p. 126.

ONLINE

Aussie Reviews Online, http://www.aussiereviews.com/ (March 19, 2005), Sally Murphy, review of *Black Juice.*

Margo Lanagan Web log, http://amongamidwhile.blogspot.com/ (June 9, 2008).

SFSite.com, http://www.sfsite.com/ (August, 2003), Trent Walters, interview with Lanagan.*

LECHNER, Jack

Personal

Married Sam Maser (a writer and film programmer). *Education:* Yale University, B.A.

Addresses

Home—501 W. 110th St., New York, NY 10025.

Career

Entertainment industry executive. Columbia Pictures, creative executive; Dirty Hands Productions, director of development, 1988-89; Art Linson Productions, vice president of development, 1990; Film on Four (film division of Channel Four), London, England, second in command, 1991-94; Home Box Office, former vice president of original programming; Miramax, executive vice president of production and development, 1996-99; @radical.media, director of motion-picture division, beginning 2000. Producer of television series and documentaries, including *Aretha Franklin: The Queen of Soul,* 1988, *Shots in the Dark,* 2001, *Parking Lot,* 2003, "Left of the Dial" (episode of *America Undercover*), 2005, and "Smoke Gets in Your Eyes"(episode of *Mad Men*), 2007; producer of film documentaries *The Fog of War: Eleven Lessons from the Life of Robert S. McNamara,* 2003; *Naked on the Inside,* 2007; *Very Young Girls,* 2007; and *Smile 'til It Hurts: The Up with People Story,* 2009.

Writings

The Ivy League Rock and Roll Quiz Book, Delilah (New York, NY), 1983.

Can't Take My Eyes off You: One Man, Seven Days, Twelve Televisions, Crown (New York, NY), 2000.

Mary Had a Little Lamp, illustrated by Bob Staake, Bloomsbury (New York, NY), 2008.

Sidelights

In addition to a twenty-year career in the entertainment industry, Jack Lechner has published three books, including *Can't Take My Eyes off You: One Man, Seven Days, Twelve Televisions,* a lighthearted look at programming in the age of cable television, and *Mary Had a Little Lamp,* an offbeat picture book for young readers that reinvents a traditional nursery rhyme. In *Can't Take My Eyes off You* Lechner recalls his experience devoting seven days of his life to watching television, keeping an eye on twelve screens during fifteen-hour viewing marathons. Imitating an earlier experiment by Charles Sopkin, who watched six televisions for a week in the late 1960s, Lechner expanded the range of viewing material by including the hundreds of cable channels available to the American audience by 1999. Writ-

ing in *Publishers Weekly,* a critic observed of the book that Lechner incorporates "highly intelligent, witty cultural criticism" with "endless quips and quirky, laugh-out-loud observations" to create a thoughtful commentary on the state of television in the United States. While pointing out that some readers may disagree with the author's conclusions, *Booklist* critic Mary Carroll nonetheless predicted that readers will "enjoy accompanying him on his televisual journey." *Library Journal* reviewer David M. Lisa offered a similar judgment of *Can't Take My Eyes off You,* suggesting that "everyone will have fun reading this tale of television viewing taken to extremes."

In *Mary Had a Little Lamp* Lechner revises the traditional "Mary Had a Little Lamb" nursery rhyme to include an appliance-loving girl. Wherever she is, Mary keeps her favorite flexible-necked lamp at her side, taking the light fixture to school, to the park, and even tucking it in bed with her at night. However, she leaves her bright companion at home when she attends summer camp, much to the relief of her parents who hope her bond with the lamp is short lived. Upon arriving home from camp, Mary realizes that she has outgrown the lamp and, instead, turns to a new appliance—a shiny electric toaster—for companionship. "Mother Goose fans will delight in this offbeat interpretation of the classic nursery rhyme," claimed *School Library Journal* critic Linda L. Walkins, while a *Kirkus Reviews* contributor commented that "Lechner's rhythm and rhyme are spot-on in adapting the beloved nursery favorite."

Biographical and Critical Sources

PERIODICALS

Booklist, November 1, 2000, Mary Carroll, review of *Can't Take My Eyes off You: One Man, Seven Days, Twelve Televisions,* p. 509.

Kirkus Reviews, March 15, 2008, review of *Mary Had a Little Lamp.*

Library Journal, November 1, 2000, David M. Lisa, review of *Can't Take My Eyes off You,* p. 84.

Publishers Weekly, August 28, 2000, review of *Can't Take My Eyes off You,* p. 62.

School Library Journal, March, 2008, Linda L. Walkins, review of *Mary Had a Little Lamp,* p. 170.

Variety, November 6, 2000, Paula Bernstein, review of *Can't Take My Eyes off You,* p. 31.

Washington Monthly, December, 2000, Joe Dempsey, review of *Can't Take My Eyes off You,* p. 56.*

*   *   *

LENAIN, Thierry 1959-

Personal

Born 1959, in France; children: Wahid (son).

Addresses

Home—Grenoble, France.

Career

Educator and author. *Citruille* (journal), cofounder and editor.

Awards, Honors

Prix Sorciéres roman, for *La fille du canal.*

Writings

FOR CHILDREN

Trouillard!, illustrated by Miles Hyman, Nathan Jeunesse (Paris, France), 1997.

Un marronnier sous les éltoiles, Syros (France), 1998.

Le soleil dans la poche, illustrated by Christophe Merlin, Casterman (Paris, France), 1999.

Au secours, les anges!, illustrated by Serge Bloch, Nathan Première (Paris, France), 1999.

Je ne suis plus un bébé, maman!, illustrated by Laurence de Kemmeter, Nathan (Paris, France), 1999.

Petit zizi, illustrated by Stéphane Poulin, Les 400 Coups (Paris, France), 2000, translated by Daniel Zolinsky as *Little Zizi,* Cinco Puntos Press (El Paso, TX), 2008

Un pacte avec le diable, Pocket Jeunesse (Paris, France), 2001.

Mademoiselle Zazie a-t-elle un zizi?, illustrated by Delphine Durand, Nathan Jeunesse (Paris, France), 2001.

Thomas-la-honte, illustrated by Stéphane Bourrières, Nathan Jeunesse (Paris, France), 2003.

Wahid, illustrated by Olivier Balez, Albin Michel Jeunesse (Paris, France), 2003.

Bouboule rêve, illustrated by Jean-Marc Mathis, Nathan Jeunesse (Paris, France), 2003.

Ma Maman à moi, illustrated by Julien Rosa, Nathan Jeunesse (Paris, France), 2005.

Zoé et la sorcière du quatrième, illustrated by Colonel Moutarde, Milan Jenuesse (Paris, France), 2005.

Julie Capable, illustrated by Anne Brouillard, Grasset (Paris, France), 2005.

L'amour Hérisson, illustrated by Françoise Malaval, Masala (France), 2006.

La fille du canal, Syros (France), 2006.

Mademoiselle Zazie et les femmes nues, illustrated by Magali Schmitzler, Où sont les Enfants (France), 2008.

Les baisers de Mademoiselle Zazie, illustrated by Delphine Durand, Nathan Jeunesse (Paris, France), 2008.

Author of young-adult novels and picture books published in French, including *Quand les chiens s'en vont, Pareil qu'avant, Une île mon ange,* and *Clair de loup.*

OTHER

La peinture des singes: histoire et esthétique, Syros/ Alternatives (Paris, France), 1990.

Pour une critique de la raison ludique: essai sur la problé-matique Nietzschéenne, J. Vrin (Paris, France), 1993.

Eric Rondepierre: un art de la Décomposition, Lettre volée (Brussells, Belgium), 1999.

Bernar Venet, 1961-1963: L'immanence mise en chantier, Presses de réel (France), 2003.

(With Thomas McEvilley) *Bernar Venet,* Flammarion (Paris, France), 2007.

Biographical and Critical Sources

PERIODICALS

French Resources, April, 2008, Suzanne Dagenais, review of *Au secours, les anges!,* p. 56.

Kirkus Reviews, March 15, 2008, review of *Little Zizi.*

Publishers Weekly, May 12, 2008, review of *Little Zizi,* p. 54.

School Library Journal, June, 2008, Blair Christolon, review of *Little Zizi,* p. 108.

ONLINE

Comptines Web site, http://www.comptines.fr/ (May 30, 2009), "Thierry Lenain."

Thierry Lenain Home Page, http://thierrylenain.hautefort. com (June 9, 2009).*

*   *   *

LEVIN, Betty 1927-

Personal

September 10, 1927, in New York, NY; daughter of Max (a lawyer and farmer) and Eleanor (a musician) Lowenthal; married Alvin Levin (a lawyer), August 3, 1947 (died, January 19, 1987); children: Katherine, Bara, Jennifer. *Education:* University of Rochester, A.B. (high honors), 1949; Radcliffe College, M.A., 1951; Harvard University, A.M.T., 1951. *Politics:* "Democrat or independent." *Religion:* Unitarian.

Addresses

Home—Lincoln, MA. *E-mail*—bettylevin@earthlink. net.

Career

Writer, educator, and sheep farmer. Museum of Fine Arts, Boston, MA, assistant in research, 1951-52; part-time teaching fellow, Harvard Graduate School of Education, 1953; creative writing fellow, Radcliffe Institute, 1968-70; Massachusetts coordinator, McCarthy Historical Archive, 1969; Pine Manor Open College, Chestnut Hill, MA, instructor in literature, 1970-75; Minute Man Publications, Lexington, MA, feature writer, 1972; Sim-

Betty Levin (Reproduced by permission of Betty Levin.)

mons College Center for the Study of Children's Literature, Boston, special instructor in children's literature, 1975-77, adjunct professor of children's literature, 1977-87; instructor at Emmanuel College, Boston, 1975, and at Radcliffe College, Cambridge, MA, beginning 1976. Member of steering committee, Children's Literature New England.

Member

Authors Guild, Authors League of America, Masterworks Chorale, Children's Books Authors (Boston), Middlesex Sheep Breeders Association.

Writings

FOR YOUNG PEOPLE; NOVELS

The Zoo Conspiracy, illustrated by Marian Parry, Hastings House, 1973.

The Sword of Culann, Macmillan (New York, NY), 1973.

A Griffon's Nest (sequel to *The Sword of Culann*), Macmillan (New York, NY), 1975.

The Forespoken (sequel to *A Griffon's Nest*), Macmillan (New York, NY), 1976.

Landfall, Atheneum (New York, NY), 1979.

The Beast on the Brink, illustrated by Marian Parry, Avon (New York, NY), 1980.

The Keeping-Room, Greenwillow (New York, NY), 1981.

A Binding Spell, Lodestar/Dutton (New York, NY), 1984.

Put on My Crown, Lodestar/Dutton (New York, NY), 1985.

The Ice Bear, Greenwillow (New York, NY), 1986.

The Trouble with Gramary, Greenwillow (New York, NY), 1988.

Brother Moose, Greenwillow (New York, NY), 1990.

Mercy's Mill, Greenwillow (New York, NY), 1992.

Starshine and Sunglow, illustrated by Jos. A. Smith, Greenwillow (New York, NY), 1994.

Away to Me, Moss!, Greenwillow (New York, NY), 1994.

Fire in the Wind, Greenwillow (New York, NY), 1995.

Gift Horse, Greenwillow (New York, NY), 1996.

Island Bound, Greenwillow (New York, NY), 1997.

Look Back, Moss, HarperCollins (New York, NY), 1998.

The Banished, HarperCollins (New York, NY), 1999.

Creature Crossing, HarperCollins (New York, NY), 1999.

Shadow-Catcher, HarperCollins (New York, NY), 2000.

That'll Do, Moss, HarperCollins (New York, NY), 2002.

Shoddy Cove, Greenwillow Books (New York, NY), 2003.

Thorn, Front Street Books (Asheville, NC), 2005.

The Unmaking of Duncan Veerick, Front Street Books (Asheville, NC), 2007.

Contributor to books, including *Innocence and Experience: Essays and Conversations on Children's Literature,* compiled and edited by Barbara Harrison and Gregory Maguire, Lothrop, 1987; *A Wizard's Dozen,* Harcourt, 1993; *Origins of Story,* edited by Barbara Harrison and Gregory Maguire, Simon & Schuster, 1999; and *Proceedings for Travelers in Time,* Green Bay Press, 1990. Also contributor of articles to periodicals, including *Harvard Educational Review, Horn Book,* and *Children's Literature in Education.*

Levin's manuscripts are housed in the Kerlan Collection, University of Minnesota, Minneapolis.

Sidelights

Novelist Betty Levin develops her young-adult characters in either realistic or fantastic settings, sometimes overlapping the two. Ancient myths and real historical events are both important elements of her novels, as is magic. Among the real settings Levin uses in her stories are modern-day Maine in *The Trouble with Gramary,* ancient Ireland in *The Sword of Culann,* and the Orkney Islands in *The Forespoken.* Her characters often unravel mysteries and reach a higher level of maturity by the end of their adventures. "Levin is not an easy writer," stated Adele M. Fasick in *Twentieth-Century Children's Writers,* but, she added, readers of her works "who are willing to immerse themselves in the strange settings and to struggle to understand the significance of mysterious events will find themselves embarking on an enriching experience. Levin's work grows in strength and scope with each book published."

And so it is with the author's memories of the past; as Levin once noted, they grow in strength with each one remembered. Pieces of Levin's childhood come to her on a regular basis in the form of memory fragments: the day her best friend's older sister knocked her down and sat on her, or the day she went skating with her older brothers but never got to skate because it took her too long to put her skates on properly. "Early memories are like scraps of trash set loose by a space capsule," observed Levin. "Detached fragments continue to orbit, but outside the scheme that spawned them. They are so unfixed that it is often impossible to date them. Yet they float across our consciousness. When we recognize the truth of them, we suspect that in some way they are still a part of us."

Levin grew up with her two older brothers in three different places: a farm in Bridgewater, Connecticut; in New York City; and in Washington, DC. Other family members included Levin's parents; Kitty Healy, who came from Ireland to live with the family; and Robby, who had grown up on a farm in Virginia. Kitty served as a sort of older sister to Levin, at least until she married Walter Beck and had her first child, Katherine. The early stories that left lasting impressions on Levin were told to her by both her mother and by Kitty; among her absolute favorites were those dealing with animals. This love of animals became a reality for Levin when she acquired a puppy, to be joined by a rabbit, a cat, and a pony while growing up. "Looking back, it seems to me that I spent a large part of my childhood with real and pretend animals," Levin once said. On her family's farm she first learned of the partnership possible between a human and a dog, and this relationship has helped Levin numerous times throughout her life, especially in her adult career as a sheep farmer.

Levin's childhood was touched by other experiences as well, the most significant arising from World War II. Her mother worked with an organization that helped European refugees, and her father began spending more and more time in Washington, DC, until the family moved there in the fall of 1940. Leaving all her friends behind during her transition from childhood to adolescence was hard for Levin, but she maintained ties with these friends through the books they all read. The books they shared included some that were considered "real" literature, like *Caddie Woodlawn* and *Oliver Twist,* and others that offered the pleasures of "junk" reading, such as *Gone with the Wind.* "It didn't entirely replace good literature," Levin once asserted, "but it had a strong grip on me, along with movies and movie magazines. . . . Romanticism saved me from absolute degradation. When I discovered Emily Brontë's *Wuthering Heights,* I found even more to satisfy than the sudsy romance of books like *Gone with the Wind.*"

The real world of these years was far removed from the romances Levin read, and she was very aware of the effects on her community emanating from the growing power of Hitler and Germany's Third Reich. Also, racism became a part of daily life. "I had grown up with friends of all backgrounds," Levin revealed. "I had hardly been aware of racial differences. That first year

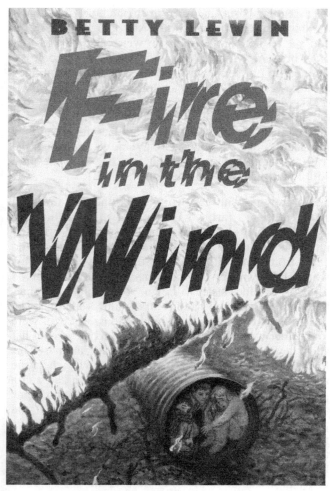

Cover of Levin's young-adult novel Fire in the Wind, *featuring cover art by Jos. A. Smith.* (Jacket art © 1995 by Jos. A. Smith. Used by permission of HarperCollins Publishers.)

in Washington was a shock. . . . I was struggling, and not very well, with the realization that people really can systematically hurt other people." Levin's mother helped during this period of adjustment, taking her daughter to a performance by African-American contralto Marian Anderson and enrolling her in the National Cathedral School. In this place of serious academic pursuit, Levin learned with a multicultural student body and was encouraged to pursue her interest in writing.

Because of the U.S. role in the relocation of displaced persons and the restoration of property to war victims during World War II, Levin's father traveled to Europe before the end of the war, and her mother continued her work for the War Department. Thus, it took time for the family to move back to New York, but Levin was sent ahead to start her senior year at the Lincoln School with her friend Andy Wolf. "Lincoln was academically undemanding and socially fantastic," Levin pointed out. "I lived for the weekends, for parties and dates." In the midst of her social activities Levin was accepted into the University of Rochester and, joined by her parents, moved into a new apartment. The summer between high

school and college was filled with a variety of advertising jobs on Madison Avenue. At the end of the summer Levin was offered a full-time job at an agency but instead set off for college.

Originally planning to major in voice, Levin quickly decided that she was out of her league and changed her studies to history and literature. The majority of her friends were interested in books, poetry, and politics, and it was through this circle of friends that Levin met her future husband, Alvin Levin. Having been in the army, her fiancée wanted to get married more quickly than Levin did, but she decided he was more important than her freedom and they married the summer before their junior year of college. Living in a one-room apartment, the Levins finished college in Rochester and spent the summer working before joining Levin's family at the farm.

Levin's husband received a scholarship from Harvard Law School, and the couple moved to Boston in the summer of 1949. Halfway through this first year in Boston, Levin started graduate school. "It was for a seminar on the American city that I wrote a 250-page paper on literature about New York City," she recalled. "I discovered and included children's books in that study. It was the beginning of my interest in the history of children's literature."

Living in a variety of apartments, Levin held numerous jobs while her husband completed law school. Among these were a job at the Museum of Fine Arts, a part-time teaching fellowship, and a research job for a historian. When Levin inherited a bit of money at the same time that her husband was between his clerkship and his new job, she was able to finance a trip to Scotland and England. Traveling with their young daughter Kathy, the Levins were welcomed into several homes and visited both historic sites and places that were of interest only to sheepdog enthusiasts. By the time they returned home the Levins were determined to build their own small farm near the home of some good friends in Lincoln.

During her second summer in Lincoln, and after the birth of her second child, Bara, Levin was diagnosed with polio during an epidemic of the disease in Boston; her husband contracted the disease two weeks later. Levin was lucky enough to suffer no lasting effects from the disease, but her husband suffered with it for two years before he was able to return home. When their third child, Jennifer, was born, "we had to learn new ways of living and being parents, because Alvin never did recover the use of his legs and arms and much of his upper torso," the author explained. "And the children grew up learning how to help him with his daily needs in countless ways." As the children grew, so did the Levin household as more sheep, puppies, stray cats, and a pony joined the family.

This happy home was eventually lost, however, when the Minute Man National Historical Park was estab-

lished and the Levins were forced to sell their home. Around the same time the family began spending part of each summer in Maine. Staying mostly in coastal towns, the Levin family spent many days on their small sailboat and explored the islands of the bay. They also passed summers on the family farm, where everyone congregated, including Levin's brothers and their families.

By the 1960s and early 1970s Levin had become increasingly active in civil rights and the movement to end the Vietnam War. Sharing her political interests, her husband eventually served as a delegate at the Democratic Convention. Just as her political activity brought new friends into Levin's life, so did the sheep and sheepdogs she raised. These activities and influences finally led her to write juvenile novels. She followed up a fellowship in creative writing at the Bunting Institute from 1968 to 1970 with a teaching career and then wrote a fantasy trilogy containing elements of Celtic and Norse mythology.

In all three books of Levin's early trilogy—*The Sword of Culann*, *A Griffon's Nest*, and *The Forespoken*—the

Cover of **The Trouble with Gramary,** *a teen adventure novel by Levin that features cover art by David Monteiel.* (Greenwillow Books, 1988. Used by permission of HarperCollins Children's Books, a division of HarperCollins Publishers.)

protagonist Claudia, who lives on an island off the coast of Maine, travels back in time through the use of an ancient sword hilt. In the first two stories she is accompanied by her stepbrother Evan, and they visit both ancient Ireland during the historical struggle between Queen Medb and Cuchulain (the House of Culann) and the Orkney Islands during medieval times. In the final story, *The Forespoken*, Claudia alone returns to the Orkney Islands, arriving during the nineteenth century in search of the crow that belongs to the old man who originally gave her the sword hilt.

"Levin is skillful in writing of the physical realities of both worlds, especially the cold, dampness, dirt, and hard physical labor," observed Fasick in reviewing the trilogy. A *Kirkus Reviews* contributor wrote of *The Sword of Culann*: "The characters are stirring creations, . . . and although the plot is labyrinthian it's well worth staying on for the surprises and layered revelations at every turn." Finding the use of symbols, magic, and historical events to be implausible in *A Griffon's Nest*, another *Kirkus Reviews* contributor concluded that, "for the agile mind," Levin's story is "an unusual adventure in time travel." In a *School Library Journal* review of the final novel of the trilogy, *The Forespoken*, Andrew K. Stevenson found the numerous subplots confusing but asserted that the "characterization is good, and the mystery and brutality of the islands is powerfully conveyed."

Maine is again the setting in Levin's mystery/fantasy *A Binding Spell*. Very unhappy about her family's move to a farm in Maine, Wren seems to be the only one able to glimpse a ghost horse in the mist around the farm. Her two brothers are already too busy with their new friend Larry to notice anything, so Wren must investigate on her own. These inquiries lead her to Larry's reclusive Uncle Axel, the original owner of the ghost horse. Through her efforts to bring Axel back into reality, Wren is able to rid him of his haunted past, and the ghost horse disappears. "Levin's characters are meticulous, and intermittent scenes are quite vivid," noted Denise M. Wilms in *Booklist,* and a *School Library Journal* reviewer maintained that *A Binding Spell* features "an evocative prose which turns even the commonplace into something magical."

The Ice Bear is one of the first fantasy books in which Levin constructs her story in only one world. Set in the primitive kingdom of Thyrne, the novel focuses on Wat, a bakeshop boy, and Kaila, a silent girl from the north, as they flee to the Forest of Lythe to defend a white Ice Bear. Wat hopes to gain a reward from the king for protecting the precious animal, but Kaila wants only to return to her home in the north with the bear. During their journey both Wat and Kaila face many dangers and learn the consequences of their actions and the true meaning of freedom. "As always in Levin's work a poignant tone underlies the action," stated Ruth S. Vose in *School Library Journal.* Zena Sutherland asserted in the

Bulletin of the Center for Children's Books that *The Ice Bear* "has a good pace and sweep; the characters change and grow; the setting is roundly conceived."

The Banished, a prequel to *The Ice Bear*, stars Siri, who lives in the Land of the White Falcons and listens to her grandmother's tales of their ancient island homeland. Because they can return only by giving an ice bear to their king, and Siri is forced to undertake the journey. Writing in *Booklist*, Shelle Rosenfeld praised Levin's detailed world-building, drama and suspense, and well-developed characters, describing *The Banished* as "wonderfully detailed."

Another story set in prehistoric times, *Thorn,* follows the slow extinction of the People of the Seal as infants are stillborn or die young of birth defects. To save the tribe, Seal women of childbearing age are treated with great care to preserve their health. When a boy with a malformed leg is abandoned on the tribe's island home, villagers take him in but isolate him as a genetic threat. Thorn grows up under the care of Willow, the tribe's young Keeper of Story, and from Thorn Willow gains the advanced knowledge of engineering and medicine that he learned before being banished from his own tribe. Praising *Thorn* as "a challenging story about superstition, death, and friendship," Frances Bradburn recommended the novel in *Horn Book* as a good choice "for reflective readers." "Strongly lyrical writing, the unusual structure and provocative themes distinguish a stimulating work," concluded a *Kirkus Reviews* critic in an appraisal of *Thorn.*

Continuing to set her books in just one genre and time period, Levin crafts the stories in *The Trouble with Gramary* and *Starshine and Sunglow* against a realistic backdrop. Fourteen-year-old Merkka lives in a Maine seaside village with her mother, father, younger brother, and grandmother in *The Trouble with Gramary*. As the town becomes a tourist attraction, Merkka's family is pressured to move from their home because of the welding business her grandmother, Gramary, runs out of the backyard. At first upset by the move, Merkka eventually learns to appreciate her grandmother's nonconformity. "Although Merkka doesn't always understand her grandmother, the natural affinity between the two is unmistakable," noted Nancy Vasilakis in *Horn Book*. Eleanor K. MacDonald described *The Trouble with Gramary* in her *School Library Journal* review as "a novel in which place, character, and circumstance mesh into a believable and satisfying whole."

Starshine and Sunglow also realistically fuses character and setting. Young Ben, Kate, and Foster come to the rescue in this story when their neighbors, the Flints, decide not to grow sweet corn for the first time in many years. Having supplied this corn to the neighborhood for as long as the children can remember, the Flints are tired of dealing with the many animals that raid their fields. The children decide to organize the growing of the corn, setting up two scarecrows made out of an old mop and an old broom—Starshine and Sunglow—at opposite ends of the field. As the crops grow, however, the scarecrows mysteriously move to different locations in the field and are dressed in different clothes. In the meantime, the children and others in the community band together to grow the corn and stop the critters from stealing it. "Accurate information about the challenges of farming are woven into the plot," observed Lee Bock in *School Library Journal*. A *Kirkus Reviews* contributor, pointing out that the focus in *Starshine and Sunglow* "is on the nurturing of community spirit," concluded that "Levin has honed her easily read story with a grace and subtle humor."

Mercy's Mill is a time-travel story in which three characters from three different periods—Mercy from the colonial period, Jethro from the nineteenth century, and modern-day Sarah—find that they are able to interact with each other at an old mill and house in Massachusetts. Both Jethro and Mercy were slaves who managed to escape their unhappy lives by traveling through time: Mercy traveled through time to meet Jethro, and Jethro moved forward in time to cross paths with Sarah. Sarah, who dislikes her new stepfather and home, is also unhappy with her life, and she finds the prospect of escaping through time appealing. As she learns more about the mill and its history, however, she becomes troubled by Jethro's secrets. When Sarah tells her family's social worker about Jethro, she is assured that the boy is likely attempting to escape an unhappy reality. Levin's readers have to decide for themselves whether Jethro's tale is true; meanwhile, Sarah grows to become less self-involved and more caring about her family through her experiences at the mill.

In the same way that *Mercy's Mill* is more than a time-travel story, the novel series that includes *Away to Me, Moss!, Look Back, Moss,* and *That'll Do, Moss* is more than a dog story. In the "Moss" books Levin uses her own extensive knowledge of sheepdogs and herding to create a "heartfelt and satisfying portrayal" of the understanding bond between dogs and people, as Wendy E. Betts put it in her *Five Owls* review of *Away to Me, Moss!* In the first "Moss" novel Rob Catherwood has suffered a stroke and can no longer give the commands his border collie, Moss, needs to herd sheep. As a result, the dog has become unmanageable because of its frustration in not being able to do the work it has been bred for. In trying to help Moss and Rob, young Zanna learns all about sheep herding and discovers, to her surprise, that she loves the work. Levin complicates her tale with subplots involving Zanna's parents' trial separation and the pressure on Rob to give up Moss to help pay for his rehabilitation.

Moss returns in *Look Back, Moss* and *That'll Do, Moss.* The dog is injured when his new owner enlists it in a failed effort to "rescue" sheep from a sheep-dog trial in *Look Back, Moss,* while *That'll Do, Moss* finds Moss living on Prager farm and helping a girl named Diane locate some stray lambs during an outbreak of rabies.

Critics praised Levin's adept handling of the complicated plot in *Away to Me, Moss!,* Betsy Hearne writing in the *Bulletin of the Center for Children's Books* that "the stress of both Zanna's and Rob's families is skillfully paralleled" in the novel. "Levin sketches adult problems adroitly," remarked a *Kirkus Reviews* contributor in a review of the same book, ". . . while never losing focus on Zanna and Moss." The "intriguing setting" in *Look Back, Moss* "will attract animal lovers," predicted *Booklist* critic Debbie Carton, and in *That'll Do, Moss* Levin creates a compelling story "about people drawn together by need, responsibility, love, and even fear," according to fellow *Booklist* critic Ellen Mandel.

Island Bound is a supernatural story about two teenagers on a mysterious island who find an old journal. The book tells the story of a girl who was left on the island during her Irish family's attempt to immigrate illegally to the United States some 150 years before. John Peters wrote in *Booklist* that in the novel Levin "expertly develops characters, pushes them past brushes with danger, and doles out pieces of a puzzle."

Shadow-Catcher tells the story of Jonathan, who is apprenticed to his grandfather, a photographer, to learn the trade in 1800s rural Maine. Besides exploring the family dynamics and daily life of the time, Levin presents a mystery that "slowly unravels through the rest of the story," according to Carol A. Edwards in *School Library Journal.*

Runaways living in different eras are the focus of *Shoddy Cove,* which spans the modern era and the 1830. Clare is unhappy helping out her mother in her job as a costumed reenactor at a local historical settlement museum. Then she meets May and Adam, two children who are hiding out at the settlement in order to avoid being separated and sent to live with different relatives. Soon the children discover that the building where the children are hiding once harbored another group of runaways: runaway slaves traveling north on the Underground Railroad. In addition to a surprising conclusion, Levin weaves into her storyline "eerily elusive, possibly ghostly strangers," according to *Booklist* critic John Peters.

The Unmaking of Duncan Veerick, another middle-grade novel by Levin, finds a boy enmeshed in a multicultural mystery when he assists an elderly woman living in his small town. After eighth grader Duncan agrees to help befuddled Astrid Valentine store some unusual objects acquired by her late husband—including an Inca mummy and several Inuit sculptures—the woman is hospitalized. When a mysterious fire threatens the object shortly afterward, the police become involved and soon the teen finds himself suspected of being part of a ring of thieves. In *School Library Journal* Nora G. Murphy wrote that *The Unmaking of Duncan Veerick* features a hard-working and "likable" protagonist, and Kat Corliss noted in the *Journal of Adolescent and Adult*

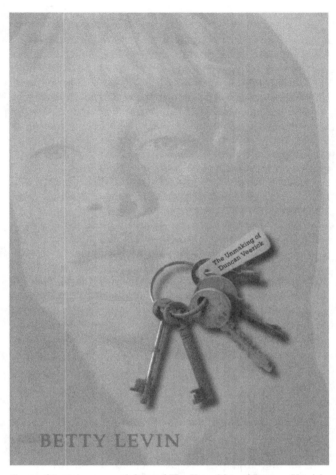

Cover of Levin's young-adult novel The Unmaking of Duncan Veerick, *in which a multigenerational friendship is complicated by a mystery.* (Front Street, 2007. Reproduced by permission.)

Literacy that Levin's "wonderfully entertaining novel . . . makes for an anxious rollercoaster ride of emotions and events."

Although Levin's work presents a variety of settings and messages, the author sees a connection between all her works. "The themes I'm drawn to and the situations I explore through fiction reflect not only the places and people and ways of life I love, but also the baffling aspects of the human condition—human traits that sadden and trouble me. I see connections between some of the tiny experiences in my early childhood and unavoidable truths about callousness and cruelty."

Biographical and Critical Sources

BOOKS

Pendergast, Sara, and Tom Pendergast, editors, *St. James Guide to Children's Writers,* fifth edition, St. James Press (Detroit, MI), 1999.
Something about the Author Autobiography Series, Volume 84, Gale (Detroit, MI), 1996.

PERIODICALS

Booklist, November 15, 1984, Denise M. Wilms, review of *A Binding Spell,* p. 449; July, 1997, John Peters, review of *Island Bound,* p. 1819; August, 1998, Debbie Carton, review of *Look Back, Moss,* p. 2006; March 1, 1999, Shelle Rosenfeld, review of *The Banished,* p. 1214; August, 2002, Ellen Mandel, review of *That'll Do, Moss,* p. 1964; July, 2003, John Peters, review of *Shoddy Cove,* p. 1890; December 15, 2005, Frances Bradburn, review of *Thorn,* p. 41.

Bulletin of the Center for Children's Books, January, 1987, Zena Sutherland review of *The Ice Bear,* p. 91; December, 1994, Betsy Hearne, review of *Away to Me, Moss!,* p. 135.

Five Owls, February, 1995, Wendy E. Betts, review of *Away to Me, Moss!,* p. 63.

Horn Book, May-June, 1988, Nancy Vasilakis, review of *The Trouble with Gramary,* p. 353; January-February, 1993, Maeve Visser Knoth, review of *Mercy's Mill,* p. 92; March-April, 1996, Maeve Visser Knoth, review of *Fire in the Wind,* p. 196; January, 1999, review of *Look Back, Moss,* p. 67; May, 1999, review of *Creature Crossing,* p. 331; November, 1999, Jennifer M. Brabander, review of *The Banished,* p. 742; July, 2000, review of *Shadow-Catcher,* p. 461.

Journal of Adolescent and Adult Literacy, December, 2007, Kat Corliss, review of *The Unmaking of Duncan Veerick,* p. 361.

Kirkus Reviews, November 1, 1973, review of *The Sword of Culann,* p. 1212; April 15, 1975, review of *A Griffon's Nest,* p. 465; May 15, 1994, review of *Starshine and Sunglow,* p. 702; October 15, 1994, review of *Away to Me, Moss!,* p. 1410; May 1, 2002, review of *That'll Do, Moss,* p. 660; April 15, 2003, review of *Shoddy Cove,* p. 609; October 15, 2005, review of *Thorn,* p. 1141; October 1, 2007, review of *The Unmaking of Duncan Veerick.*

Publishers Weekly, June 5, 2000, review of *Shadow-Catcher,* p. 95.

School Library Journal, October, 1976, Andrew K. Stevenson, review of *The Forespoken,* p. 118; December, 1984, review of *A Binding Spell,* p. 101; October, 1986, Ruth S. Vose, review of *The Ice Bear,* p. 192; April, 1988, Eleanor K. MacDonald, review of *The Trouble with Gramary,* p. 102; June, 1994, Lee Bock, review of *Starshine and Sunglow,* p. 132; July, 2000, Carol A. Edwards, review of *Shadow-Catcher,* p. 106; January, 2006, Melissa Moore, review of *Thorn,* p. 136; December, 2007, Nora G. Murphy, review of *The Unmaking of Duncan Veerick,* p. 134.*

*   *   *

LORD, Michele

Personal

Married; children: three.

Addresses

Home—New Braunfels, TX. *E-mail*—theelords@satx.rr.com.

Career

Author.

Writings

Little Sap and Monsieur Rodin, illustrated by Felicia Hoshino, Lee & Low (New York, NY), 2006.

A Song for Cambodia, illustrated by Shino Arihara, Lee & Low (New York, NY), 2008.

Sidelights

Michele Lord was inspired to write her first picture book, *Little Sap and Monsieur Rodin,* after a trip to Cambodia to adopt her first daughter. Based by a drawing by turn-of-the-twentieth-century artist August Rodin, the story finds the niece of a Cambodian laundress selected to train as a palace dancer. When Little Sap excels at her art, she is chosen to perform in France, where she meets the famous artist. Lord's picture book "presents a rare look at Cambodian culture through the eyes of a winning heroine," announced a *Publishers Weekly* contributor in a review of *Little Sap and Monsieur Rodin,* while in *Kirkus Reviews* a critic dubbed the book "charming" and noted that artist Felicia Hoshino's "mixed-media illustrations . . . illuminate the lyrical text." Susan Scheps echoed the view of other critics, writing in *School Library Journal* that Lord's story treats readers to "an inviting glimpse at Cambodian dance and a sweet tidbit of art history."

Michelle Lord's adventure-filled picture book **A Song for Cambodia** *is brought to life in artwork by Shino Arihara.* (Illustration copyright © 2008 by Shino Arihara. All rights reserved. Reproduced by permission of Lee & Low Books, Inc.)

Based on actual events surrounding the rise to power of ruthless dictator Pol Pot, *A Song for Cambodia* presents Lord's biography of a young boy named Arn Chorn-Pond. Raised in a small village in Cambodia, Arn was forced to join others in his village who are employed in the rice paddies at a children's work camp following the invasion of his home by Khymer Rouge revolutionaries in 1975. Fortunately for the boy, his talent for music was recognized by his captors and he was taken from the rice fields and trained to play a string instrument called a *khim*. Arn eventually escaped and found a new home with an American family, but he has since returned to his native country as an adult and dedicated himself to reviving Cambodia's native culture. Describing *A Song for Cambodia* as "an age-appropriate view of a subject rarely visited in children's books," a *Publishers Weekly* critic noted that Lord's text is "more educational than engaging." However, in *School Library Journal* Monika Schroeder dubbed *A Song for Cambodia* a "solid picture-book biography" and a *Kirkus Reviews* critic called Lord's book a "sensitive reconstruction" that draws on both interviews and copious research.

Biographical and Critical Sources

PERIODICALS

Booklist, May 1, 2006, Jennifer Mattson, review of *Little Sap and Monsieur Rodin*, p. 92; April 1, 2008, Linda Perkins, review of *A Song for Cambodia*, p. 43.

Children's Bookwatch, July, 2006, review of *Little Sap and Monsieur Rodin*.

Kirkus Reviews, April 1, 2006, review of *Little Sap and Monsieur Rodin*, p. 351; February 15, 2008, review of *A Song for Cambodia*.

Publishers Weekly, May 29, 2006, review of *Little Sap and Monsieur Rodin*, p. 58; March 10, 2008, review of *A Song for Cambodia*, p. 81.

School Library Journal, September, 2006, Susan Scheps, review of *Little Sap and Monsieur Rodin*, p. 178; April, 2008, Monika Schroeder, review of *A Song for Cambodia*, p. 166.

ONLINE

Cynsations Web site, http://cythialeitichsmith.blogspot.com/ (April, 2006), Cynthia Leitich Smith, interview with Lord.

Lee & Low Web site, http://www.leeandlow.com/ (May 20, 2009), "Michele Lord."

Voice of America Web site, http://www.voanews.com/Khmer/ (January 22, 2007), Manilene Ek, "The Making of 'Little Sap and Monsieur Rodin.'"*

*   *   *

LUJÁN, Jorge

Personal

Born in Córdoba, Argentina; immigrated to Mexico, 1978; children: two children. *Education:* University of Córdoba, degree (architecture); attended Antioch College; U.N.A.M., degree (Hispanic studies).

Addresses

Home—Mexico City, Mexico. *E-mail*—jorge_lujan555@yahoo.com; jorge_lujan@prodigy.net.mx.

Career

Writer, musician, and architect. Harrison & Abramovitz (architecture firm), New York, NY, associate; Casa Lamm, Mexico D.F., instructor in master's program in creative writing; teacher on educating children through music and poetry; presenter at creative-writing workshops. Performer in concerts at various venues, including Columbia University and George Washington University.

Awards, Honors

Fullbright scholarship in architecture; Children's Poetry Prize, Asociatión de Literatura Infantil y Juvenil Argentina, 1995; Best Children's Show of the Year prizes, Unión de Críticos y Cronistas de México; Premio Virginia Fábregas; Highly Recommended distinction, International Board on Books Brasil, 2009, for *Los gemelos del Popol Vuh*.

Writings

Arico iris de sueños, Nafinsa-Amaroma (Mexico), 1995.

Más allá de mi brazo, illustrated by Istvan, Cronopio azul (Argentina), 1997, translation by Elisa Amado as *Beyond My Hand*, illustrated by Georgina Quintana, Groundwood Books (Toronto, Ontario, Canada), 2002.

Vaca Roja, illustrated by Francisco Nava, Santillana (Miami, FL), 2000.

La gitana de las flores (title means, "The Flower Gypsy"), illustrated by Francisco Nava, Santillana (Miami, FL), 2000.

Alba y ocaso, illustrated by Manuel Monroy, 2003, translated as *Daybreak, Nightfall*, Groundwood Books (Berkeley, CA), 2003.

Tic Tac, illustrated by Isol, Alfaguara Infantil (Mexico), 2003.

Rooster/ Gallo, illustrated by Manuel Monroy, translated by Elisa Amado, Groundwood Books (Toronto, Ontario, Canada), 2004.

Los gemelos del Popol Vuh, illustrated by Oscar Rojas, Sudamericana (Argentina), 2004.

En la Colina, Artes de Mexico y del Mundo, 2005.

Mi cuerpo y yo, illustrated by Isol, Artes de Mexico y del Mundo (Mexico), 2005.

Tarde de invierno, illustrated by Mandana Sadat, Kókinos (Madrid, Spain), 2005, translated by Elisa Amado as *Tarde de invierno/ Winter Afternoon*, Groundwood Books (Toronto, Ontario, Canada), 2006.

Como atrapar una estrella, illustrated by Olivia Jeffers, Fondo de Cultura Economica (Argentina), 2006.

Perdido y encontrado, illustrated by Olivia Jeffers, Fondo de Cultura Economica (Argentina), 2006.

Accidente Celeste, illustrated by Piet Grobler, Fondo de Cultura Economica (Argentina), 2006, translated by Elisa Amado as *Sky Blue Accident/ Accidente Celeste,* Groundwood Books (Toronto, Ontario, Canada), 2007.

Colors!/ Colores!, illustrated by Piet Grobler, Sudamericana (Mexico), 2006, translated by John Oliver Simon, Groundwood Books (Toronto, Ontario, Canada), 2008.

Numeralia, illustrated by Isol, Fondo de Cultura Economica (Argentina), 2007.

Equis y Zeta (graphic novel; two volumes), illustrated by Isol, Sudamericana (Argentina), 2008.

Contributor to anthologies, including *Poetry inside out,* 2003, 2004; and *Keys to Learning,* 2004. Translator of books from English to Spanish.

Author's work has been translated into several languages, including Korean, Polish, Italian, French, and Portuguese.

Sidelights

Jorge Luján is an Argentine writer and musician. Originally training to be an architect, Luján returned to the University of Córdoba to study music composition and film, but was forced to leave his home country by a military coup in 1976. Immigrating to Mexico, he settled in Mexico City, where he now lives and works. Luján received a Fullbright scholarship for architecture, as well as a children's poetry prize from the Argentine Association of Children's Literature. In addition to offering writing workshops and performing in concerts throughout North America, Luján has also created poetry and picture-book stories for young readers.

Piet Grobler's color-washed illustrations are featured in Argeninian author Jorge Luján's bilingual picture book Sky Blue Accident/ Accidente Celeste. (Illustration copyright © 2006 by Piet Grobler. All rights reserved. Reproduced by permission of Groundwood Books.)

One of Luján's earliest children's books to be released in the United States, *Daybreak, Nightfall* was originally published in Spanish as *Alba y ocaso.* The book includes two free-verse poems by Luján, each of which is accompanied by Manuel Monroy's artwork. Noting that the surreal imagery conjured up by the poet's language can be frightening, Judith Constantinides wrote in *School Library Journal* that *Daybreak, Nightfall* "offers a lot for a class to discuss," and Antonia Gisler commented in her *Resource Links* review that "adults may find this book of poetry useful when introducing the genre to children." While predicting that some young readers would need to have some of the book's themes explained, a *Publishers Weekly* critic concluded of *Daybreak, Nightfall* that "both poems wittily resolve the terror they evoke."

Luján's picture book *Rooster/ Gallo* is geared for a younger audience. In its Spanish and English text, it tells a story in only three sentences, the spare text spread across the pages. Despite its simplicity, "there's a sense of wonder here that will entice children," wrote Ilene Cooper in *Booklist.* "The repeated words . . . enhance a sense of continuity in the cycle" of day and night, Joanna Rudge Long noted in *Horn Book,* and a *Kirkus Reviews* contributor called *Rooster/Gallo* "imagistically vivid" and full of "sharp, evocative language" that would be equally pleasing to children and adult readers. In *Resource Links* Denise Parrott noted that Luján's simple text "is a welcome addition to bilingual picture book collections."

In *Sky Blue Accident/ Accidente Celeste,* Luján tells the story of a boy who has a very bad bicycle accident. Sent flying into the sky, which he accidentally breaks, the boy then has a series of misadventures with both clouds and the moon. "The story is quite short, about sixteen lines in the original Spanish, but evocative in its surrealistic dream world," wrote a *Kirkus Reviews* critic.

Colors!/ Colores! is a bilingual collection of eleven of Luján's poems about colors. The poems are presented in English first, and then in their original Spanish on the next page. Calling the text "charming," a *Kirkus Reviews* contributor wrote that the poetry and images combine to effectively "convey the colors of the natural world with simple yet sophisticated grace."

Biographical and Critical Sources

PERIODICALS

Booklist, May 15, 2004, Ilene Cooper, review of *Rooster/ Gallo,* p. 1625; April 1, 2008, Carolyn Phelan, review of *Colors!/ Colores!* p. 51.

Horn Book, March-April, 2004, Joanna Rudge Long, review of *Rooster/ Gallo,* p. 173.

Kirkus Reviews, March 1, 2004, review of *Rooster/ Gallo,* p. 226; March 1, 2007, review of *Sky Blue Accident/ Accidente Celeste,* p. 227; March 1, 2008, review of *Colors!/ Colores!*

Publishers Weekly, March 31, 2003, review of *Daybreak, Nightfall,* p. 67.

Resource Links, October, 2003, Antonia Gisler, review of *Daybreak, Nightfall,* p. 6; October, 2004, Denise Parrott, review of *Rooster/ Gallo,* p. 6; June, 2007, Maria Forte, review of *Sky Blue Accident/ Accidente Celeste,* p. 4.

School Library Journal, April, 2003, Judith Constantinides, review of *Daybreak, Nightfall,* p. 152; September, 2004, Ann Welton, review of *Rooster/ Gallo,* p. 197; July, 2007, Mary Elam, review of *Sky Blue Accident/ Accidente Celeste,* p. 80; May, 2008, Madeline Walton-Hadlock, review of *Colors!/ Colores!,* p. 116.

ONLINE

Jorge Luján Home Page, http://www.jorgeLujan.com (May 13, 2009).

M

MacDONALD, Ross 1957-

Personal
Born 1957; married; children: two.

Addresses
Home—CT. *Agent*—Pippin Properties, Inc., 155 E. 38th St., Ste. 2H, New York, NY 10016. *E-mail*—bright work@earthlink.net.

Career
Printer, illustrator, and cartoonist. Creator of props for films, including *National Treasure: Book of Secrets, Infamous,* and *Seabiscuit.* Founder, Brightwork Press, 1993.

Writings

SELF-ILLUSTRATED

Another Perfect Day, Roaring Brook Press (Brookfield, CT), 2002.
Achoo! Bang! Crash!: A Noisy Alphabet, Roaring Brook Press (Brookfield, CT), 2003.
Bad Baby, Roaring Brook Press (Brookfield, CT), 2005.

ILLUSTRATOR

Sally Cook and James Charlton, *Hey Batta, Batta, Swing!: The Wild Old Days of Baseball,* Margaret K. McElderry Books (New York, NY), 2007.
Alison McGhee, *Bye-bye, Crib,* Simon & Schuster (New York, NY), 2008.
Marc Tyler Nobleman, *Boys of Steel: The Creators of Superman,* Knopf (New York, NY), 2008.
Heather Henson, *Grumpy Grandpa,* Atheneum (New York, NY), 2009.

OTHER

Contributor of illustrations and cartoons to numerous publications, including *New York Times, Forbes, Virginia Quarterly Review, Kiplinger's, Mother Jones,* and *Wall Street Journal.* Contributing editor, *Virginia Quarterly Review.*

Sidelights
Enjoying a varied career as a printer, illustrator, and cartoonist, Ross MacDonald expanded his talents to include children's books with the publication of 2002's *Another Perfect Day.* In the pages of *Another Perfect Day,* the author/illustrator juxtaposes a simple narrative with fanciful, dramatic illustrations that share with readers the early-morning dreams of a young boy. For instance, Jack dreams about commuting to his job as an ice-cream tester in his own airplane, defeating a monster, and catching a moving train with his bare hands. Strange things begin to occur, however, as a pink tutu and baby bonnet replace Jack's blue suit, causing the young boy to want to wake from his dream. "Simple text contrasts delightfully with the energy of the illustrations," remarked *School Library Journal* critic Mary Ann Carcich, the reviewer going on to predict that Mac-Donald's first effort will likely "satisf[y] the unabashed superhero in all children." A *Kirkus Reviews* contributor thought "children will roar at the droll swerves that fill this broad, hilarious episode," while *Booklist* reviewer Ilene Cooper praised MacDonald's artwork, concluding of *Another Perfect Day:* "The art is the thing in this delicious parody of a businessman's day."

MacDonald adds his own twist to the conventional alphabet book in *Achoo! Bang! Crash!: A Noisy Alphabet.* Here alphabetical sound are matched up along a series of humorous illustrations, creating a book that "is hard to ignore, easy to appreciate, and sure to delight the young," according to *School Library Journal* critic Jody McCoy. MacDonald captions his pictures with both actual and invented words, incorporating much slapstick comedy into the illustrations, such as when a

tiny cat startles a much larger cow and a lion chases a hunter, eventually exposing his backside. Several reviewers commented favorably on the comical pictures in *Achoo! Bang! Crash!* The author/illustrator displays "a pleasingly silly sense of humor in this idiosyncratic alphabet book," remarked a *Publishers Weekly* critic. "This alphabet book explodes with raucous humor," claimed *Horn Book* contributor Susan Dove Lempke, the critic also predicting that young readers "will roar over every boisterous detail."

Jack returns in *Bad Baby,* accompanied by his new baby sister. Originally looking forward to having a new playmate, Jack instead finds the infant to be a challenge as she grows, breaking his toys, coloring on the walls, and generally annoying Jack. While the young boy appeals to his parents for help, Jack realizes that they find nothing wrong with their youngest child's behavior, much to his aggravation. Writing in *Kirkus Reviews,* a critic thought that *Bad Baby* would appeal to readers with younger siblings, calling the book "a new and very funny take on a perennially relevant subject." MacDonald's combination of text and pictures again earned positive recognition from critics, with *Booklist* contributor Michael Cart observing that the "richly imaginative, highly stylized pictures invest a deadpan text with laugh-out-loud humor."

In addition to his own works, MacDonald has also provided the illustrations for several other picture books, including two recounting perennial childhood favorites: baseball and comic books. Written by Sally Cook and James Charlton, *Hey Batta, Batta, Swing!: The Wild Old Days of Baseball* relates trivia about the early days of the sport, sharing with readers slang, historical facts, and oddities of the game as it came to be popularized across the United States. Once again, MacDonald received high marks for his artwork, with a *Publishers Weekly* critic deciding the "watercolor and pencil crayon illustrations pleasingly convey the text's lighthearted tone," while in her *School Library Journal* review, Marilyn Taniguchi noted that MacDonald's "pictures have an old-fashioned flavor and add plenty of detail and slapstick humor."

The history of the two men who created the comic-book hero Superman is recounted in *Boys of Steel: The Creators of Superman,* a picture-book biography written by Marc Tyler Nobleman. Featuring MacDonald's art, *Boys of Steel* shares with readers the story of two quiet high-school friends, writer Jerry Siegel and illustrator Joe Shuster, who turned their creative talents into one of the most recognizable characters in comic-book history. "MacDonald's retro illustrations . . . are the perfect foil for Superman's story," believed *Horn Book* contributor Robin L. Smith. Finding MacDonald's artwork well matched with Nobleman's text, *Booklist* reviewer Jennifer Mattson thought the illustrations "capture the look of 1930s comics with their sepia-toned, stylized imagery."

Biographical and Critical Sources

PERIODICALS

Booklist, November 1, 2002, Ilene Cooper, review of *Another Perfect Day,* p. 509; November 1, 2003, Diane Foote, review of *Achoo! Bang! Crash!: A Noisy Alphabet,* p. 502; October 1, 2005, Michael Cart, review of *Bad Baby,* p. 52; January 1, 2007, GraceAnne A. DeCandido, review of *Hey Batta, Batta, Swing!: The Wild Old Days of Baseball,* p. 84; April 15, 2008, Jennifer Mattson, review of *Bye-bye, Crib,* p. 48; June 1, 2008, Jennifer Mattson, review of *Boys of Steel: The Creators of Superman,* p. 102.

Horn Book, January-February, 2004, Susan Dove Lempke, review of *Achoo! Bang! Crash!,* p. 71; September-October, 2005, Christine M. Heppermann, review of *Bad Baby,* p. 564; March-April, 2007, Vicky Smith, review of *Hey Batta, Batta, Swing,* p. 213; July-August, 2008, Robin L. Smith, review of *Boys of Steel,* p. 471.

Kirkus Reviews, July 1, 2002, review of *Another Perfect Day,* p. 958; September 1, 2003, review of *Achoo! Bang! Crash!,* p. 1127; August 1, 2005, review of *Bad Baby,* p. 853; January 15, 2007, review of *Hey Batta, Batta, Swing!,* p. 71; February 15, 2008, review of *Bye-bye, Crib.*

Publishers Weekly, August 19, 2002, review of *Another Perfect Day,* p. 89; August 11, 2003, review of *Achoo! Bang! Crash!,* p. 277; August 22, 2005, review of *Bad Baby,* p. 63; January 8, 2007, review of *Hey Batta, Batta, Swing!,* p. 50; February 25, 2008, review of *Bye-bye, Crib,* p. 77; June 23, 2008, review of *Boys of Steel,* p. 54.

Resource Links, April, 2003, Heather Hamilton, review of *Another Perfect Day,* p. 4.

Ross MacDonald captures the birth of super-hero comics in his illustrations for Marc Tyler Nobleman's picture book **Boys of Steel.** (Alfred A. Knopf, 2008. Illustrations copyright © 2008 by Ross MacDonald. All rights reserved. Reproduced by permission of Alfred A. Knopf, an imprint of Random House Childrens Books, a division of Random House, Inc.)

School Library Journal, September, 2002, Mary Ann Car-cich, review of *Another Perfect Day,* p. 201; December, 2003, Jody McCoy, review of *Achoo! Bang! Crash!,* p. 119; September, 2005, Marie Orlando, review of *Bad Baby,* p. 177; March, 2007, Marilyn Taniguchi, review of *Hey Batta, Batta, Swing!,* p. 225; February, 2008, Kathy Krasniewicz, review of *Bye-bye, Crib,* p. 92; October, 2008, Kim T. Ha, review of *Boys of Steel,* p. 173.

ONLINE

Ross MacDonald Home Page, http://ross-macdonald.com (May 12, 2009).*

*   *   *

MACKEN, JoAnn Early 1953-

JoAnn Early Macken (Reproduced by permission.)

Personal

Born 1953; married; children: two sons. *Education:* University of Wisconsin-Milwaukee, B.A. (economics); Vermont College, M.F.A. (writing for children and young adults). *Hobbies and other interests:* Reading, walking, gardening, canoeing, photography.

Addresses

Home and office—Shorewood, WI. *E-mail*—joann@joannmacken.com.

Career

Writer and educator. Mount Mary College, Milwaukee, WI, adjunct professor; previously worked as a technical writer and an editor for educational children's books.

Writings

Cats on Judy, illustrated by Judith DuFour Love, Whispering Coyote (Boston, MA), 1997.

Zebras, Weekly Reader Early Learning (Milwaukee, WI), 2002.

African Animals, illustrated by Paul Hess, Gareth Stevens (Milwaukee, WI), 2002.

Bears, Weekly Reader Early Learning (Milwaukee, WI), 2002.

Camels, Weekly Reader Early Learning (Milwaukee, WI), 2002.

Elephants, Weekly Reader Early Learning (Milwaukee, WI), 2002.

Farm Animals, Gareth Stevens (Milwaukee, WI), 2002.

Giraffes, Weekly Reader Early Learning (Milwaukee, WI), 2002.

Hippos, Weekly Reader Early Learning (Milwaukee, WI), 2002.

Lions, Weekly Reader Early Learning (Milwaukee, WI), 2002.

Monkeys, Weekly Reader Early Learning (Milwaukee, WI), 2002.

Penguins, Weekly Reader Early Learning (Milwaukee, WI), 2002.

Polar Animals, Gareth Stevens (Milwaukee, WI), 2002.

Rain Forest Animals, Gareth Stevens (Milwaukee, WI), 2002.

Sea Lions, Weekly Reader Early Learning (Milwaukee, WI), 2002.

Snakes, Weekly Reader Early Learning (Milwaukee, WI), 2002.

Tigers, Weekly Reader Early Learning (Milwaukee, WI), 2002.

(Editor) Vanessa Lee, *Welcome to Sri Lanka,* Gareth Stevens (Milwaukee, WI), 2003.

Crossing Guard, illustrated by Gregg Andersen, Weekly Reader Early Learning (Milwaukee, WI), 2003.

Mail Carrier, illustrated by Gregg Andersen, Weekly Reader Early Learning (Milwaukee, WI), 2003.

Nurse, illustrated by Gregg Andersen, Weekly Reader Early Learning (Milwaukee, WI), 2003.

Sanitation Worker, illustrated by Gregg Andersen, Weekly Reader Early Learning (Milwaukee, WI), 2003.

Teacher, illustrated by Gregg Andersen, Weekly Reader Early Learning (Milwaukee, WI), 2003.

Veterinarian, illustrated by Gregg Andersen, Weekly Reader Early Learning (Milwaukee, WI), 2003.

Goldfish, Weekly Reader Early Learning (Milwaukee, WI), 2004.

Guinea Pigs, Weekly Reader Early Learning (Milwaukee, WI), 2004.

Kittens, Weekly Reader Early Learning (Milwaukee, WI), 2004.

Parakeets, Weekly Reader Early Learning (Milwaukee, WI), 2004.

Puppies, Weekly Reader Early Learning (Milwaukee, WI), 2004.

Rabbits, Weekly Reader Early Learning (Milwaukee, WI), 2004.

Sing-along Song, illustrated by LeUyen Pham, Viking (New York, NY), 2004.

Moose, Weekly Reader Early Learning (Milwaukee, WI), 2005.

Music Lessons, Weekly Reader Early Learning (Milwaukee, WI), 2005.

Ocean Floors, Weekly Reader Early Learning (Milwaukee, WI), 2005.

Opossums, Weekly Reader Early Learning (Milwaukee, WI), 2005.

Owls, Weekly Reader Early Learning (Milwaukee, WI), 2005.

Pigs, Weekly Reader Early Learning (Milwaukee, WI), 2005.

Porcupines, Weekly Reader Early Learning (Milwaukee, WI), 2005.

Sheep, Weekly Reader Early Learning (Milwaukee, WI), 2005.

Swimming, Weekly Reader Early Learning (Milwaukee, WI), 2005.

Art Classes, Weekly Reader Early Learning (Milwaukee, WI), 2005.

Bike Riding, Weekly Reader Early Learning (Milwaukee, WI), 2005.

Black Bears, Weekly Reader Early Learning (Milwaukee, WI), 2005.

Chickens, Weekly Reader Early Learning (Milwaukee, WI), 2005.

Cows, Weekly Reader Early Learning (Milwaukee, WI), 2005.

Deer, Weekly Reader Early Learning (Milwaukee, WI), 2005.

Goats, Weekly Reader Early Learning (Milwaukee, WI), 2005.

Gymnastics, Weekly Reader Early Learning (Milwaukee, WI), 2005.

Horses, Weekly Reader Early Learning (Milwaukee, WI), 2005.

Karate, Weekly Reader Early Learning (Milwaukee, WI), 2005.

Spring, Weekly Reader Early Learning (Milwaukee, WI), 2006.

Summer, Weekly Reader Early Learning (Milwaukee, WI), 2006.

Vultures, Weekly Reader Early Learning (Milwaukee, WI), 2006.

Wetlands, Weekly Reader Early Learning (Milwaukee, WI), 2006.

Winter, Weekly Reader Early Learning (Milwaukee, WI), 2006.

(With Louis Sabin) *The Wright Brothers: The Flight to Adventure,* Scholastic (New York, NY), 2006.

(With Louis Sabin) *Thomas Edison: Incredible Inventor,* Scholastic (New York, NY), 2006.

The Life Cycle of a Hummingbird, Weekly Reader Early Learning (Milwaukee, WI), 2006.

The Life Cycle of a Moth, Weekly Reader Early Learning (Milwaukee, WI), 2006.

Seas, Weekly Reader Early Learning (Milwaukee, WI), 2006.

Mountain Goats, Weekly Reader Early Learning (Milwaukee, WI), 2006.

Mountains, Weekly Reader Early Learning (Milwaukee, WI), 2006.

Ocean Floors, Weekly Reader Early Learning (Milwaukee, WI), 2006.

Plains, Weekly Reader Early Learning (Milwaukee, WI), 2006.

Rattlesnakes, Weekly Reader Early Learning (Milwaukee, WI), 2006.

Rivers, Weekly Reader Early Learning (Milwaukee, WI), 2006.

Roadrunners, Weekly Reader Early Learning (Milwaukee, WI), 2006.

Elk, Weekly Reader Early Learning (Milwaukee, WI), 2006.

Gary Paulsen: Voice of Adventure and Survival, Enslow (Berkeley Heights, NJ), 2006.

Gila Monsters, Weekly Reader Early Learning (Milwaukee, WI), 2006.

Golden Eagles, Weekly Reader Early Learning (Milwaukee, WI), 2006.

Jackrabbits, Weekly Reader Early Learning (Milwaukee, WI), 2006.

Lakes ("Water Habits" series), Weekly Reader Early Learning (Milwaukee, WI), 2006.

The Life Cycle of a Bat, Weekly Reader Early Learning (Milwaukee, WI), 2006.

The Life Cycle of a Cicada, Weekly Reader Early Learning (Milwaukee, WI), 2006.

The Life Cycle of a Dragonfly, Weekly Reader Early Learning (Milwaukee, WI), 2006.

The Life Cycle of a Flamingo, Weekly Reader Early Learning (Milwaukee, WI), 2006.

Autumn, Weekly Reader Early Learning (Milwaukee, WI), 2006.

Beaches, Weekly Reader Early Learning (Milwaukee, WI), 2006.

Bighorn Sheep, Weekly Reader Early Learning (Milwaukee, WI), 2006.

Condors, Weekly Reader Early Learning (Milwaukee, WI), 2006.

Coral Reefs, Weekly Reader Early Learning (Milwaukee, WI), 2006.

Cougars, Weekly Reader Early Learning (Milwaukee, WI), 2006.

Coyotes, Weekly Reader Early Learning (Milwaukee, WI), 2006.

Deserts, Weekly Reader Early Learning (Milwaukee, WI), 2006.

(With Keith Brandt) *Abraham Lincoln: Road to the White House,* illustrated by John Lawn, Scholastic (New York, NY), 2007.

(With Keith Brandt) *Paul Revere, Son of Liberty,* illustrated by Francis Livingston, Scholastic (New York, NY), 2007.

(With Francine Sabin) *Abigail Adams: Young Patriot,* illustrated by Yoshi Miyake, Scholastic (New York, NY), 2007.

(With Francine Sabin) *Elizabeth Blackwell, the First Woman Doctor,* illustrated by Ann Toulmin-Rothe, Scholastic (New York, NY), 2007.

(With Laurence Santrey) *Ben Franklin: Extraordinary Inventor, Brave Leader,* Scholastic (New York, NY), 2007.

(With Laurence Santrey) *George Washington: Founding Father,* illustrated by William Ostrowsey, Scholastic (New York, NY), 2007.

(Coauthor) *Daniel Boone,* Scholastic (New York, NY), 2007.

(Coauthor) *Davy Crockett,* Scholastic (New York, NY), 2007.

(Coauthor) *Babe Ruth,* Scholastic (New York, NY), 2007.

(Coauthor) *Roberto Clemente,* Scholastic (New York, NY), 2007.

Building a Road, Capstone (Mankato, MN), 2008.

Building a Skyscraper, Capstone (Mankato, MN), 2008.

Construction Crews, Capstone (Mankato, MN), 2008.

Construction Tools, Capstone (Mankato, MN), 2008.

Demolition, Capstone (Mankato, MN), 2008.

Digging Tunnels, Capstone (Mankato, MN), 2008.

Flip, Float, Fly: Seeds on the Move, illustrated by Pam Paparone, Holiday House (New York, NY), 2008.

Building a Bridge, Capstone (Mankato, MN), 2009.

Building a House, Capstone (Mankato, MN), 2009.

Waiting out the Storm, illustrated by Susan Gaber, Candlewick (Somerville, MA), 2010.

A Day on the Town, Black Rabbit Books (Mankato, MN), 2010.

The Dinosaur Museum, Black Rabbit Books (Mankato, MN), 2010.

Road Signs, Black Rabbit Books (Mankato, MN), 2010.

Shopping at the Mall, Black Rabbit Books (Mankato, MN), 2010.

Flags around the World, Black Rabbit Books (Mankato, MN), 2011.

Landmarks around the World, Black Rabbit Books (Mankato, MN), 2011.

Contributor to magazines, including *Cricket, Ladybug,* and *Highlights for Children;* to the anthology, *Stories from Where We Live: The Great Lakes;* and to *Children's Writer's and Illustrator's Market,* 2006, 2008, 2009.

Adaptations

Several of Macken's books have been published in bilingual editions.

Sidelights

Wisconsin author JoAnn Early Macken has written more than a hundred books for young readers, including picture books, poetry collections, novels, and educational titles. As one of seven girls in her family, Macken grew up surrounded by music, and she sang in a band with her sisters during college. Despite her musical talent, early on Macken discovered a passion for writing. "My mother saved a story I wrote in second grade about how much I loved walking our neighbor's dog, Zsa Zsa," the prolific author recalled on her home page. "I know my imagination was working when I wrote that story because that dog was mean!"

The picture book *Cats on Judy* marked the start of Macken's writing career. A story about cats instead of a dog, it started as a poem she wrote in college. When Macken had married and was raising her children, she edited it and submitted it to several publishers. Macken has written several other books with rhyming texts, among them *Sing-along Song.* "Maybe you can't base a whole book on good cheer, but this makes a run at it," wrote Ilene Cooper in describing *Sing-along Song* for *Booklist.* The picture book features a cheerful narrator who greets every creature and person he meets throughout his day, singing a cheerful song when the mood strikes. Marianne Saccardi, writing for *School Library Journal,* noted that the "rhythm, repetition, and tongue twisting silliness of the text," together with the illustrations by Judith DuFour Love, "will entice even the youngest listeners." Citing the potential for added sound effects in *Sing-along Song,* a *Kirkus Reviews* contributor found that Macken's "bouncy, rhyming text invites a creative read-aloud interpretation."

The majority of Macken's books are series nonfiction titles that explain basic concepts to very young readers. She had produced a number of texts about animals for Weekly Reader Early Learning, several of which have been published in bilingual editions. *School Library Journal* critic Ann Welton pointed out the "kid-friendly small size" of several of these: *Tigers, Snakes,* and *Monkeys.* Noting that works such as *Rattlesnakes* and *Roadrunners* are intended as added resources for elementary students, Maria Otero-Boisvert observed in her *School Library Journal* review that "fun and interesting facts abound" in Macken's books. In one series, the "After School Fun" books released by Scholastic, Macken explores activities that children can pursue after their school day ends in *Karate, Art Classes,* and *Bike Riding.* For Capstone Press, she has produced a sequence of books about building and construction. Noting that Macken's simple text is accompanied by large photographs, Gillian Engberg wrote in her *Booklist* reveiw of *Digging Tunnels* that the book is "just right for beginning readers seeking nonfiction choices."

Macken sometimes combines educational elements into picture books. *Flip, Float, Fly: Seeds on the Move,* for example, introduces the concept of seed distribution through a rhyming text. Carolyn Phelan, reviewing it for *Booklist,* noted that Macken's descriptions "provide information succinctly" by making use of "internal rhyme or onomatopoeic words" to give "verbal punch to the presentation." In *School Library Journal* Patricia Manning described Macken's text for *Flip, Float, Fly* as "crisp."

"Growing up in a large family, I learned the importance of sticking together," Macken recalled to *SATA.* "That feeling, along with music, shows up in much of my fiction." *Waiting out the Storm,* her rhyming picture book, reveals a conversation between a mother and child about watching and listening to the weather from a safe place indoors. "I want children to be able to hear a reassuring voice when they are frightened," the author explained.

Biographical and Critical Sources

PERIODICALS

Booklist, July, 2004, Ilene Cooper, review of *Sing-along Song,* p. 1848; April 15, 2008, Carolyn Phelan, review of *Flip, Float, Fly: Seeds on the Move,* p. 48; August 1, 2008, Gillian Engberg, review of *Digging Tunnels,* p. 74.

Kirkus Reviews, May 1, 2004, review of *Sing-along Song,* p. 444; March 15, 2008, review of *Flip, Float, Fly.*

School Library Journal, February, 2003, Cathie Bashaw Morton, reviews of *Tigers* and *Zebras,* both p. 136; June, 2004, Marianne Saccardi, review of *Sing-along Song,* p. 114; September, 2004, Ann Welton, reviews of *Bears, Elephants,* and *Penguins,* all p. 197; May, 2005, Ann Welton, reviews of *Monkeys, Snakes,* and *Tigers,* all p. 119; August, 2005, Lynda Ritterman, reviews of *Art Classes, Bike Riding,* and *Karate,* all p. 114; June, 2006, Maria Otero-Boisvert, reviews of *Bighorn Sheep, Cougars, Golden Eagles,* and *Mountain Goats,* all p. 144, and reviews of *Gila Monsters, Jackrabbits, Rattlesnakes,* and *Roadrunners,* all p. 145; August, 2006, Eldon Younce, reviews of *Deserts, Mountains, Rivers,* and *Seas,* all p. 106; December, 2006, Karen Wehner, reviews of *The Life Cycle of a Cicada, The Life Cycle of a Hummingbird,* and *The Life Cycle of a Moth,* all p. 125; May, 2008, Patricia Manning, review of *Flip, Float, Fly,* p. 116; August, 2008, Eldon Younce, reviews of *Demolition* and *Digging Tunnels,* both p. 112.

ONLINE

JoAnn Early Macken Home Page, http://www.joannmacken.com (May 13, 2009).

Teaching Authors Web log, http://www.teachingauthors.com/ (June 9, 2009), "JoAnn Early Macken."

* * *

MacLEOD, Doug 1959-

Personal

Born October 13, 1959, in Melbourne, New South Wales, Australia; son of Donald Frank (a breeder of Shetland ponies) and Marian Eva (an ethnic garment maker) MacLeod. *Education:* Victorian College of Arts, diploma of arts, 1982

Addresses

Home—North Carlton, Victoria, Australia.

Career

Australian Children's Puffin Club, Melbourne, New South Wales, Australia, co-editor of *Puffinalia,* 1981-88; The Comedy Co., head writer, 1988. Presenter of *RAVE,* Australian Broadcasting Corp., 1982-93. Member of state steering committee for International Youth Year, 1985; writer-in-residence at Playbox Theatre Co., Melbourne, 1987.

Member

Fellowship of Australian Writers, Actors' Equity Association.

Awards, Honors

Young Australian Best Book of the Year Younger Honor designation, and Australian Children's Book Award Honor Book designation, both 1987, both for *Sister Madge's Book of Nuns.*

Writings

Hippopotabus, Outback Press, 1976.
The Story of Admiral Sneeze, Beatrice Publications, 1977.
Tales of Tuttle, Penguin (Camberwell, Victoria, Australia), 1980.
Knees, Penguin (Camberwell, Victoria, Australia), 1981.
In the Garden of Badthings, illustrated by Peter Thomson, Penguin (New York, NY), 1982
The Fed up Family Album, illustrated by J. Brierley, Penguin (New York, NY), 1983.
Frank Boulderbuster: The Last of the Great Swagmen, illustrated by M. Atchison, Puffin (Camberwell, Victoria, Australia), 1986.
Sister Madge's Book of Nuns, illustrated by Craig Smith, Omnibus Books (Adelaide, New South Wales, Australia), 1986
(With Terry Denton) *Ten Monster Island,* Omnibus (Norwood, South Australia, Australia), 1987.
My Son the Lawyer Is Drowning, Dramatic Pub. Co. (Woodstock, IL), 1990
Birdsville Monster, illustrated by Craig Smith, Penguin (Camberwell, Victoria, Australia), 2000.
On the Cards, illustrated by Craig Smith, Puffin (Camberwell, Victoria, Australia), 2002.
Tumble Turn, Puffin (Camberwell, Victoria, Australia), 2004.
Spiky, Spunky, My Pet Monkey; and Other Weird and Wicked Rhymes, illustrated by Craig Smith, Penguin (Camberwell, Victoria, Australia), 2004.
Leon Stumble's Book of Stupid Fairytales, illustrated by Craig Smith, Working Title Press (Kingswood, South Australia, Australia), 2005.
I'm Being Stalked by a Moonshadow, Penguin (Camberwell, Victoria, Australia), 2005, Front Street Books (Asheville, NC), 2007.

Author of column in *Age.* Author of comedy scripts and children's stories for Australian Broadcasting Corp.

Sidelights

Doug MacLeod is a popular Australian children's author, playwright, and columnist who has also won fans in the United States through his entertaining young-

adult novel *I'm Being Stalked by a Moonshadow*. Featuring what *Horn Book* contributor Sarah Ellis described as a "vivid cast of comic characters," the novel finds fourteen-year-old Seth Parrot caught between the competing egos of his own flower-child dad and his new girlfriend's very straight-laced father. While the teen attempts to win over his beloved despite such disadvantages as a home built of environmentally friendly but unsightly mud bricks and dried manure, as well as a quirky brother, his lack of romantic expertise may prove to be his ultimate undoing in MacLeod's lighthearted tale. *I'm Being Stalked by a Moonshadow* "is . . . studded with comedy, fun, and a good-natures pleasure in human quirkiness," according to Ellis, and in *School Library Journal* Rhona Campbell called Seth "an unassumingly innocent character whose lack of artifice brings a lighthearted humor to his . . . dialogue." Hoping that "more of MacLeod's charm and humor crosses the ocean," a *Kirkus Reviews* writer dubbed the novel's young hero "irresistible," and in *Booklist* Hazel Rochman predicted of *I'm Being Stalked by a Moonshadow* that "the conflicts of loyalty and love will attract teens as much as the farce" in MacLeod's "fast, funny" tale.

"I wrote a monthly column in *Age,* Melbourne's newspaper, at the age of thirteen," MacLeod once commented, in discussing his career as a writer. "My work was published in book form when I was sixteen. This early success cemented my desire to become a children's author. I have also performed in numerous children's shows and have written pantomimes. I am a keen advocate of the need to perform poetry in the classroom.

"My books are, in general, works of comic verse. I list as my two greatest sources of inspiration the works of C.J. Dennis (an Australian author, poet, and collector of indigenous slang) and Ogden Nash, whose 'Custard the Dragon' was a childhood favorite. Although a full-time writer, I do not like to consider myself chained to the typewriter. I spend a good deal of time performing my work at schools, libraries, and other venues all over Australia. I particularly like performing in country areas and have used my experiences of country towns in compiling my 'Frank Boulderbuster' anthology. Most of the stories about Frank the swagman are based on real events—many of the goings-on in the Australian outback being so bizarre that no embellishment is necessary. For example, a story featuring a race meeting where shingleback lizards are substituted for racehorses is based on an actual event which happens annually in the Queensland town of Cunnamulla.

"I feel it necessary to stress that I do not write 'nonsense' verse. The lame limericks of Edward Lear prove consistently disappointing to me. Rather, I tell stories in verse, making strong use of wordplay and intricate rhyming patterns. I have tried to make the 'sting in the tail' another hallmark of my style. These final 'twists' are so important to me that I frequently write my pieces backwards; that is to say, I write the conclusion before I write the premise.

"The reader will notice that I have been careful to avoid referring to my work as 'poetry.' I do not consider myself to be a poet. At the same time, I consider my work to be something better than doggerel. 'Comic verse' is the best label I can use to describe the from of writing which I am best at and which I find the most enjoyable."

Biographical and Critical Sources

PERIODICALS

Booklist, October 1, 2007, Hazel Rochman, review of *I'm Being Stalked by a Moonshadow,* p. 45.
Horn Book, January-February, 2008, Sarah Ellis, review of *I'm Being Stalked by a Moonshadow,* p. 90.
Kirkus Reviews, September 15, 2007, review of *I'm Being Stalked by a Moonshadow.*
School Library Journal, January, 2008, Rhona Campbell, review of *I'm Being Stalked by a Moonshadow,* p. 122.

ONLINE

Penguin Books Australia Web site, http://www.penguin.com.au/ (June 8, 2009), "Doug MacLeod."*

*   *   *

McDONALD, Rae A. 1952-

Personal

Born 1952, in MN.

Addresses

Home—WA. *E-mail*—raeAmcdonald@comcast.net.

Career

School librarian and author.

Member

Authors Guild, Society of Children's Book Writers and Illustrators.

Writings

A Fishing Surprise, illustrated by Kathleen Kemly, North-Word Books (Minnetonka, MN), 2007.

Biographical and Critical Sources

PERIODICALS

Children's Bookwatch, July, 2007, review of *A Fishing Surprise.*

Kirkus Reviews, September 15, 2007, review of *A Fishing Surprise.*

ONLINE

Rae A. McDonald Home Page, http://www.raemcdonald. com (May 15, 2009).*

*   *   *

MELTZER, Milton 1915-

Personal

Born May 8, 1915, in Worcester, MA; son of Benjamin and Mary Meltzer; married Hilda Balinky, June 22, 1941; children: Jane, Amy. *Education:* Attended Columbia University, 1932-36.

Addresses

Home—New York, NY. *Agent*—Harold Ober Associates, 425 Madison Ave., New York, NY 10017.

Career

Federal Theatre Project of the Works Projects Administration, New York, NY, staff writer, 1936-39; Columbia Broadcasting System Inc. (CBS-Radio), New York, NY, researcher and writer, 1946; Public Relations Staff of Henry A. Wallace for President, 1947-49; Medical and Pharmaceutical Information Bureau, New York, NY, account executive, 1950-55; Pfizer Inc., New York, NY, assistant director of public relations, 1955-60; Science and Medicine Publishing Co. Inc., New York, NY, editor, 1960-68; full-time writer of books, 1968—. Consulting editor, Thomas Y. Crowell Co., 1962-74, Doubleday & Co. Inc., 1963-73, and Scholastic Book Services, 1968-72; University of Massachusetts, Amherst, adjunct professor, 1977-80; lecturer at universities in the United States and England and at professional meetings and seminars; writer of films and filmstrips. *Military service:* U.S. Army Air Force, 1942-46; became sergeant.

Member

Authors Guild, Authors League of America, PEN, Organization of American Historians.

Awards, Honors

Thomas Alva Edison Mass Media Award for special excellence in portraying America's past, 1966, for *In Their Own Words: A History of the American Negro,* Volume 2, *1865-1916;* National Book Award nominations for children's literature, 1969, for *Langston Hughes: A Biography,* 1975, for both *Remember the Days* and *World of Our Fathers,* and 1977, for *Never to Forget;* Christopher Award, 1969, for *Brother, Can You Spare a Dime?,* and 1980, for *All Times, All Peoples;* Charles Tebeau

Milton Meltzer (Reproduced by permission of Milton Meltzer.)

Award, Florida Historical Society, 1973, for *Hunted like a Wolf;* Jane Addams Peace Association Children's Honor Book designation, 1975, for *The Eye of Conscience,* and 1989, for *Rescue; Boston Globe/Horn Book* Nonfiction Honor Book, 1976, for *Never to Forget,* and 1983, for *The Jewish Americans;* Association of Jewish Libraries Book Award, 1976, Jane Addams Peace Association Children's Book Award, 1977, Charles and Bertie G. Schwartz Award for Jewish Juvenile Literature, National Jewish Book Awards, 1978, Hans Christian Andersen Honor listee, 1979, and American Library Association (ALA) Best of the Best Books 1970-1983 selection, all for *Never to Forget;* Washington Children's Book Guild award honorable mention, 1978 and 1979, and Nonfiction Award, 1981, all for body of work; American Book Award nomination, 1981, for *All Times, All Peoples;* Carter G. Woodson Book Award, National Council for Social Studies, 1981, for *The Chinese Americans;* Jefferson Cup Award, Virginia State Library Association, 1983, for *The Jewish Americans;* Children's Book Award special citation, Child Study Children's Book Committee, 1985, Olive Branch Award, Writers' and Publishers' Alliance for Nuclear Disarmament, Jane Addams Peace Association Children's Book Award, and New York University Center for War, Peace, and the News Media award, all 1986, all for *Ain't Gonna Study War No More;* John Brubaker Memorial Award, Catholic Library Association, 1986; Golden Kite Award for nonfiction, Society of Children's Book Writers and Illustrators, 1987, for *Poverty in America;* Regina Medal, Catholic Library Association, 2000;

Laura Ingalls Wilder Award, 2001. Meltzer's books have been selected as best books of the year by the American Library Association, Library of Congress, *Horn Book, School Library Journal,* and *New York Times;* and designated a Notable Children's Trade Book in Social Studies by the National Council for Social Studies/Children's Book Council.

Writings

NONFICTION; FOR YOUNG READERS

A Light in the Dark: The Life of Samuel Gridley Howe, Crowell (New York, NY), 1964.

In Their Own Words: A History of the American Negro, Crowell (New York, NY), Volume 1: *1619-1865,* 1964, Volume 2: *1865-1916,* 1965, Volume 3: *1916-1966,* 1967, abridged edition published as *The Black Americans: A History in Their Own Words, 1619-1983,* Crowell (New York, NY), 1984.

Tongue of Flame: The Life of Lydia Maria Child, Crowell (New York, NY), 1965.

Time of Trial, Time of Hope: The Negro in America, 1919-1941 (includes teacher's guide), illustrated by Moneta Barnett, Doubleday (New York, NY), 1966.

Thaddeus Stevens and the Fight for Negro Rights, Crowell (New York, NY), 1967.

Bread—and Roses: The Struggle of American Labor, 1865-1915, Knopf (New York, NY), 1967, reprinted, Facts on File (New York, NY), 1991.

Langston Hughes: A Biography, Crowell (New York, NY), 1968.

Brother, Can You Spare a Dime? The Great Depression, 1929-1933, Knopf (New York, NY), 1969.

(With Lawrence Lader) *Margaret Sanger: Pioneer of Birth Control,* Crowell (New York, NY), 1969.

Freedom Comes to Mississippi: The Story of Reconstruction, Follett, 1970, reprinted, Modern Curriculum, 1991.

Slavery, Cowles, Volume 1: *From the Rise of Western Civilization to the Renaissance,* 1971, Volume 2: *From the Renaissance to Today,* 1972, updated edition published in one volume as *Slavery: A World History,* Da Capo Press (New York, NY), 1993.

To Change the World: A Picture History of Reconstruction, Scholastic Book Services, 1971.

Hunted like a Wolf: The Story of the Seminole War, Farrar, Straus (New York, NY), 1972, reprinted, Pineapple Press (Sarasota, FL), 2004

The Right to Remain Silent, Harcourt (Boston, MA), 1972.

(With Bernard Cole) *The Eye of Conscience: Photographers and Social Change,* Follett, 1974.

World of Our Fathers: The Jews of Eastern Europe, Farrar, Straus (New York, NY), 1974.

Remember the Days: A Short History of the Jewish American, illustrated by Harvey Dinnerstein, Doubleday (New York, NY), 1974.

Bound for the Rio Grande: The Mexican Struggle, 1845-1850, Knopf (New York, NY), 1974.

Taking Root: Jewish Immigrants in America, Farrar, Straus (New York, NY), 1974.

Violins and Shovels: The WPA Arts Projects, Delacorte (New York, NY), 1976.

Never to Forget: The Jews of the Holocaust (includes teacher's guide), Harper (New York, NY), 1976.

The Human Rights Book, Farrar, Straus (New York, NY), 1979.

All Times, All Peoples: A World History of Slavery, illustrated by Leonard Everett Fisher, Harper (New York, NY), 1980.

The Chinese Americans, Crowell (New York, NY), 1980.

The Truth about the Ku Klux Klan, F. Watts (New York, NY), 1982.

The Hispanic Americans, illustrated with photographs by Morrie Camhi and Catherine Noren, Crowell (New York, NY), 1982.

The Jewish Americans: A History in Their Own Words, 1650-1950, Crowell (New York, NY), 1982.

The Terrorists, Harper (New York, NY), 1983, revised as *The Day the Sky Fell: A History of Terrorism,* Random House (New York, NY), 2002.

A Book about Names: In Which Custom, Tradition, Law, Myth, History, Folklore, Foolery, Legend, Fashion, Nonsense, Symbol, Taboo Help Explain How We Got Our Names and What They Mean, illustrated by Mischa Richter, Crowell (New York, NY), 1984.

Ain't Gonna Study War No More: The Story of America's Peace Seekers, Harper (New York, NY), 1985, reprinted, Random House (New York, NY), 2002.

Mark Twain: A Writer's Life, F. Watts (New York, NY), 1985.

Betty Friedan: A Voice for Women's Rights ("Women of Our Time" series), illustrated by Stephen Marchesi, Viking (New York, NY), 1985.

Dorothea Lange: Life through the Camera ("Women of Our Time" series), illustrated by Donna Diamond, photographs by Dorothea Lange, Viking (New York, NY), 1985.

The Jews in America: A Picture Album, Jewish Publication Society, 1985.

Poverty in America, Morrow (New York, NY), 1986.

Winnie Mandela: The Soul of South Africa ("Women of Our Time" series), illustrated by Stephen Marchesi, Viking (New York, NY), 1986.

George Washington and the Birth of Our Nation, F. Watts (New York, NY), 1986.

Mary McLeod Bethune: Voice of Black Hope ("Women of Our Time" series), illustrated by Stephen Marchesi, Viking (New York, NY), 1987.

The Landscape of Memory, Viking (New York, NY), 1987.

The American Revolutionaries: A History in Their Own Words, 1750-1800, Crowell (New York, NY), 1987.

Starting from Home: A Writer's Beginnings, Viking (New York, NY), 1988.

Rescue: The Story of How Gentiles Saved Jews in the Holocaust, Harper (New York, NY), 1988.

Benjamin Franklin: The New American, F. Watts (New York, NY), 1988.

American Politics: How It Really Works, illustrated by David Small, Morrow (New York, NY), 1989.

Voices from the Civil War: A Documentary History of the Great American Conflict, Crowell (New York, NY), 1989.

The Bill of Rights: How We Got It and What It Means, Harper (New York, NY), 1990.

Crime in America, Morrow (New York, NY), 1990.

Columbus and the World around Him, F. Watts (New York, NY), 1990.

The American Promise: Voices of a Changing Nation, 1945-Present, Bantam (New York, NY), 1990.

Thomas Jefferson: The Revolutionary Aristocrat, F. Watts (New York, NY), 1991.

The Amazing Potato: A Story in Which the Inca, Conquistadors, Marie Antoinette, Thomas Jefferson, Wars, Famines, Immigrants, and French Fries All Play a Part, HarperCollins (New York, NY), 1992.

Andrew Jackson and His America, F. Watts (New York, NY), 1993.

Lincoln: In His Own Words, illustrated by Stephen Alcorn, Harcourt (San Diego, CA), 1993.

Gold: The True Story of Why People Search for It, Mine It, Trade It, Fight for It, Mint It, Display It, Steal It, and Kill for It, HarperCollins (New York, NY), 1993.

Cheap Raw Material: How Our Youngest Workers Are Exploited and Abused, Viking (New York, NY), 1994.

The Mexican-American War, Jackdaw Publications (Amawalk, NY), 1994.

Reconstruction, Jackdaw Publications (Amawalk, NY), 1994.

Who Cares?, Walker (New York, NY), 1994.

Theodore Roosevelt and His America, F. Watts (New York, NY), 1994.

Frederick Douglass: In His Own Words, Harcourt (San Diego, CA), 1995.

Hold Your Horses!, HarperCollins (New York, NY), 1995.

A History of Jewish Life from Eastern Europe to America, Jason Aronson (New York, NY), 1996.

Tom Paine: Voice of Revolution, F. Watts (New York, NY), 1996.

Weapons and Warfare: From the Stone Age to the Space Age, illustrated by Sergio Martinez, HarperCollins, (New York, NY), 1996.

The Many Lives of Andrew Carnegie, F. Watts (New York, NY), 1997.

Langston Hughes: An Illustrated Edition, Millbrook Press (New York, NY), 1997.

Food, Millbrook Press (New York, NY), 1998.

Ten Queens: Portraits of Women in Power, Penguin Putnam (New York, NY), 1998.

Witches and Witch-hunts: A History of Persecution, Blue Sky Press, (New York, NY), 1999.

Carl Sandburg: A Biography, Millbrook Press (New York, NY), 1999.

They Came in Chains: The Story of the Slave Ships, Marshall Cavendish (Tarrytown, NY), 1999.

Driven from the Land: The Story of the Dust Bowl, Marshall Cavendish (Tarrytown, NY), 2000.

Case Closed: The Real Scoop on Detective Work Life, Orchard Books (New York, NY), 2001.

In the Days of the Pharaohs: A Look at Ancient Egypt, Franklin Watts (New York, NY), 2001.

Piracy and Plunder: A Murderous Business, illustrated by Bruce Waldman, Dutton Children's Books (New York, NY), 2001.

There Comes a Time: The Struggle for Civil Rights, Random House (New York, NY), 2001.

Bound for America: The Story of the European Immigrants, Benchmark Books (New York, NY), 2002.

Mark Twain Himself: A Pictorial Biography, University of Missouri Press (Columbia, MO), 2002.

Ten Kings: And the Worlds They Ruled, illustrated by Bethanne Andersen, Orchard Books (New York, NY), 2002.

Captain James Cook: Three Times around the World, Benchmark Books (New York, NY), 2002.

Ferdinand Magellan: First to Sail around the World, Benchmark Books (New York, NY), 2002.

Walt Whitman: A Biography, Twenty-first Century Books (Brookfield, CT), 2002.

Edgar Allan Poe: A Biography, Twenty-first Century Books (Brookfield, CT), 2003.

Hour of Freedom: American History in Poetry, Wordsong/Boyds Mills Press (Honesdale, PA), 2003.

Hear That Train Whistle Blow!: How the Railroad Changed the World, Random House (New York, NY), 2004.

The Cotton Gin, Benchmark Books (New York, NY), 2004.

The Printing Press, Benchmark Books (New York, NY), 2004.

Francisco Pizarro: The Conquest of Péru, Benchmark Books (New York, NY), 2005.

Emily Dickinson: A Biography, Twenty-first Century Books (Minneapolis, MN), 2006.

Herman Melville: A Biography, Twenty-first Century Books (Minneapolis, MN), 2006.

Henry David Thoreau: A Biography, Twenty-rirst Century Books (Minneapolis, MN), 2007.

Nathaniel Hawthorne: A Biography, Twenty-first Century Books (Minneapolis, MN), 2007.

Albert Einstein: A Biography, Holiday House (New York, NY), 2008.

John Steinbeck: A Twentieth-Century Life, Viking (New York, NY), 2008.

Willa Cather: A Biography, Twenty-first Century Books (Minneapolis, MN), 2008.

OTHER

(With Langston Hughes) *A Pictorial History of the Negro in America,* Crown (New York, NY), 1956, fifth revised edition, also with C. Eric Lincoln, published as *A Pictorial History of Black Americans,* 1983, revised as *African American History: Four Centuries of Black Life,* Scholastic Textbooks (New York, NY), 1990, new revised edition, also with Jon Michael Spencer, published as *A Pictorial History of African Americans,* 1995.

Mark Twain Himself, Crowell (New York, NY), 1960, reprinted, University of Missouri Press (Columbia, MO), 2002.

(Editor) *Milestones to American Liberty: The Foundations of the Republic,* Crowell (New York, NY), 1961, revised edition, 1965.

(Editor, with Walter Harding) *A Thoreau Profile,* Crowell (New York, NY), 1962.

(Editor) *Thoreau: People, Principles, and Politics,* Hill & Wang (New York, NY), 1963.

(With Langston Hughes) *Black Magic: A Pictorial History of the Negro in American Entertainment,* Prentice-Hall (Englewood Cliffs, NJ), 1967, revised as *Black Magic: A Pictorial History of the African-American in the Performing Arts,* introduction by Ossie Davis, Da Capo Press (New York, NY), 1990.

Underground Man (novel), Bradbury, 1972, reprinted, Harcourt (Orlando, FL), 2006.

Dorothea Lange: A Photographer's Life, Farrar, Straus (New York, NY), 1978.

(Editor, with Patricia G. Holland and Francine Krasno) *The Collected Correspondence of Lydia Maria Child, 1817-1880: Guide and Index to the Microfiche Edition,* Kraus Microform, 1980.

(Editor, with Patricia G. Holland) *Lydia Maria Child: Selected Letters, 1817-1880,* University of Massachusetts Press (Amherst, MA), 1982.

Nonfiction for the Classroom: Milton Meltzer on Writing, History, and Social Responsibility, edited by Wendy Saul, Teachers College Press (New York, NY), 1994.

Milton Meltzer: Writing Matters, Franklin Watts (New York, NY), 2004.

Tough Times (novel), Clarion Books (New York, NY), 2007.

Editor of "Women of America" series, Crowell, 1962-74, "Zenith Books" series, Doubleday, 1963-73, and "Firebird Books" series, Scholastic Book Services, 1968-72. Author of introduction for *Learning about Biographies: A Reading-and-Writing Approach,* by Myra Zarnowski, National Council of Teachers of English, 1990. Also script writer for documentary films, including *History of the American Negro* (series of three half-hour films), Niagara Films, 1965; *Five,* Silvermine Films, 1971; *The Bread and Roses Strike: Lawrence, 1912* (filmstrip), District 1199 Cultural Center, 1980; *The Camera of My Family,* Anti-Defamation League, 1981; and *American Family: The Merlins,* Anti-Defamation League, 1982. Author of scripts for radio and television.

Contributor to periodicals, including *New York Times Magazine, New York Times Book Review, English Journal, Virginia Quarterly Review, Library Journal, Wilson Library Bulletin, School Library Journal, Microform Review, Horn Book, Children's Literature in Education, Lion and the Unicorn, Social Education, New Advocate,* and *Children's Literature Association Quarterly.* Member of U.S. editorial board of *Children's Literature in Education,* beginning in 1973, and of *Lion and the Unicorn,* beginning 1980.

Sidelights

Honored with the 2001 Laura Ingalls Wilder Award for his career-long contribution to literature for children, Milton Meltzer is best known for his comprehensive nonfiction studies of the oppressed peoples, social concerns, and historical events that occupied the hearts and minds of many Americans during the twentieth century. As the American Library Association's Wilder Award committee noted in its presentation, as posted on its Web site: "Meltzer's commitment to his art form, and his respect for his readers empowers young people to think creatively and critically and take an active role in a socially challenging world." Many critics have praised Meltzer's approach to complex issues, noting that the author never "talks down" to his young audience. In an essay for the *Something about the Author Autobiography Series (SAAS),* Meltzer explained why he writes about controversial people and themes: "My subjects choose action. . . . Action takes commitment, the commitment of dedicated, optimistic individuals. I try to make readers understand that history isn't only what happens to us. History is what we *make* happen. Each of us. All of us."

Meltzer gained an interest in social issues during childhood when, as a first-generation American, he was able to see first hand the difficulties faced by many immigrants. His Austrian-born parents, for example, tried to assimilate into American society as much as possible; this action would later cause identity problems for their son. An early influence on his literary career was his introduction to the works of American author Henry David Thoreau during high school. Thoreau's transcendentalist message of simplicity and spiritual rebirth would stay with Meltzer into adulthood.

As a teen, Meltzer began to feel a keen sense of loss with regard to his Eastern European/Jewish roots. "Perhaps [my parents] wanted to forget the world they had left behind," he reflected in *SAAS.* "Or because they knew I had no interest in their culture. I didn't realize until much later how much meaning their early life would have for me. When at last I had the sense to want to know about it, it was too late. They were gone."

After attending Columbia University, Meltzer went to work for a time for the federal government's Works Projects Administration (WPA). After serving in the U.S. Army Air Force during World War II, he worked in public relations for fifteen years. This was followed by another career in editing before he finally became a full-time writer in 1968. His first publications were geared for adults, until, at the request of his daughter, he wrote *A Light in the Dark: The Life of Samuel Gridley Howe,* the book that launched his long and rewarding career as a writer of nonfiction books for children.

Meltzer has used some key periods and events in his life, such as the Great Depression of the 1930s and his job with the government-sponsored WPA, as fodder for books such as *Brother, Can You Spare a Dime? The Great Depression, 1929-1933* and *Violins and Shovels: The WPA Arts Projects,* as well as for his novel *Tough Times,* a story set during the Depression that finds a high schooler trying to survive by riding the rails. Ultimately, the teen travels to Washington, DC, to join

World War I veterans in their ill-fated march demanding the bonus monies once promised them by the U.S. government. In *Brother, Can You Spare a Dime?,* he presents "a tremendously powerful and moving account of the Depression years," as Judy Silverman declared in the *Voice of Youth Advocates. The Day the Sky Fell: A History of Terrorism,* a revision of Meltzer's 1983 book *The Terrorists,* was inspired by a more-recent personal experience: the terrorist attacks of September 11. Reviewing *Tough Times,* Lynn Rutan noted in *Booklist* that Meltzer describes the history of the 1932 Bonus March "with particular poignancy," and a *Kirkus Reviews* contributor maintained that the author's own memories of the period "will make this a memorable story for its audience."

In *Driven from the Land: The Story of the Dust Bowl,* Meltzer details the origins of the Dust Bowl that forced so many farmers off their land in the early 1930s. Here he "offers a fascinating and well-chosen perspective," wrote Steven Engelfried in a *School Library Journal* review, the critic also noting also that his "well-chosen statistics emphasize the destruction" of the environmental disaster. In *Cheap Raw Material: How Our Youngest Workers Are Exploited and Abused* Meltzer follows the phenomenon of child labor from ancient times to the present. He "effectively uses quotes from numerous youngsters from different eras," wrote Marilyn Long

Graham in a *School Library Journal* review of the book, and his "vivid and captivating" writing makes the work "an excellent resource." *Booklist* critic Stephanie Zvirin called *Cheap Raw Material* an "extraordinary book . . . relevant, passionate, consciousness-raising." In *Who Cares?* Meltzer presents a partial answer to such injustices, documenting altruism through the ages. This "may be the most comprehensive history of volunteerism ever written for young adults," declared Melissa Ducote Shepherd in *Voice of Youth Advocates,* the critic predicting that *Who Cares?* "should inspire more [young adults] to take part" in the volunteer effort.

Meltzer has gained a reputation for effectively incorporating eyewitness accounts and personal documents such as diaries, letters, and speeches into his work. He noted in a *School Library Journal* article that "the use of original sources . . . is a giant step out of the textbook swamp. Working with the living expression of an era . . . you get close to reliving those experiences yourself." Starting with *In Their Own Words,* a three-volume history of African Americans, Meltzer has brought to life the stories of various ethnic groups, including Jewish, Chinese, and Hispanic Americans, as well as historical events and people, such as the American Revolution, the U.S. Civil War, and President Abraham Lincoln. In *The American Revolutionaries: A History in Their Own Words, 1750-1800,* Meltzer is "careful to in-

Meltzer's picture-book biography Langston Hughes *features artwork by Stephen Alcorn that reflects its subject's early-twentieth-century roots.* (Illustration © 1997 by Stephen Alcorn. Reprinted with permission of Millbrook Press, a division of Lerner Publishing Group, Inc., and the author. All rights reserved. No part of this excerpt may be used or reproduced in any manner whatsoever without the prior written permission of Lerner Publishing Group, Inc.)

Cover of Meltzer's **Tough Times,** *a profile of life during the Great Depression of the 1930s.* (Illustration copyright © 2007 by Robert Barrett. Reproduced by permission of Houghton Mifflin Company.)

corporate various points of view and to give a balanced perspective in the narrative with which he pieces together the primary sources," as *Bulletin of the Center for Children's Books* critic Betsy Hearne wrote. *Voices from the Civil War: A Documentary History of the Great American Conflict* similarly contains "a good cross-section" of Union and Confederate viewpoints, according to *School Library Journal* contributor Elizabeth M. Reardon, a reviewer who also found Meltzer's narrative to be "clear, concise, and well-written, putting these turbulent times into perspective."

Meltzer's choice of material has sometimes come as a surprise to the author himself. "In those first years I wrote books without any great self-consciousness about the subjects I chose," he recalled in *SAAS.* "Then one day a reviewer described me as a writer known for his interest in the underdog. A pattern had become obvious. It was not a choice deliberately made." This interest has been manifested in several studies of oppression, such as *Slavery; All Times, All Peoples: A World History of Slavery;* and *Never to Forget: The Jews of the Holocaust.* He also examines the ways people have fought oppression in *Rescue: The Story of How Gentiles Saved Jews in the Holocaust.* a book that details the efforts of the many non-Jews who risked their lives to protect their Jewish neighbors from the Nazi death camps of the 1940s. Including histories of anti-Semitism in Europe, *Rescue* is "a historical study as well as a series of exciting stories about individual courage," Christine Behrmann noted in *School Library Journal.*

Meltzer has continued to deal with racism and its effects throughout his career. In *They Came in Chains: The Story of the Slave Ships* he tells the story of the slave ships and slavery in America, from the capture of slaves in Africa through their transportation during the Civil War era and emancipation. Laura Glaser, writing in *School Library Journal,* noted that "firsthand accounts, black-and-white photographs and reproductions, and excerpts from newspapers and speeches dramatically convey the horrors of slavery." In *There Comes a Time: The Struggle for Civil Rights* Meltzer follows the history of the civil-rights movement from slavery through reconstruction and Jim Crow and on to school desegregation, sit-ins, and the assassination of Reverend Martin Luther King, Jr. Reviewing the title in *School Library Journal,* Eunice Weech called *There Comes a Time* a "concise, informational overview" and a "perceptive account [that] will cause readers to think critically about where we have been and where we are going as a nation." A contributor for *Publishers Weekly* called the same study an "impressive survey."

Meltzer also brings context to his studies of individual lives. *Benjamin Franklin: The New American,* which is about the noted Revolutionary American inventor and politician, "incorporates much historical background," Mary Mueller observed in *School Library Journal;* the author "shows him as a real person, pointing out many of Franklin's faults and indiscretions as well as his strengths." Meltzer's biography "is a smooth selection, condensation, and explanation of the events and significance of a complex life," *Horn Book* reviewer Mary A. Bush said. Likewise, Julie Corsaro commented in *Booklist* that in *Columbus and the World around Him* "Meltzer moves beyond his subject . . . to a well-integrated history of intellectual, scientific, and social ideas." In addition, the author includes information about the exploitation of Native Americans that was brought about by Christopher Columbus's voyages. "Readers cannot complete his book without an embarrassing appreciation for the great price paid by all humanity in the exploration and settlement of the new world," stated Frances Bradburn in *Wilson Library Journal.*

In some of his biographies, Meltzer lets the subjects speak for themselves. Thus. in *Lincoln: In His Own Words* and *Frederick Douglass: In His Own Words,* he presents a plethora of primary sources, including speeches and letters, that are woven together by brief descriptions and narratives to paint a firsthand portrait. Reviewing the work on Douglass, the most renowned black leader of the nineteenth century, *Horn Book* contributor Mary M. Burns noted that Meltzer brings "a historian's sensibility to his work as well as an innate

sensitivity to his subject." *School Library Journal* critic Joanne Kelleher concluded of the same work, "Douglass's words live again in this volume, invoking young people to never give up the struggle for freedom and equality for all." In a review of *Lincoln*, Mueller remarked of the book *School Library Journal* that *Frederick Douglass* is a "fine book [that] introduces Lincoln to readers through his [Douglass's] own words."

Meltzer deals with movers and shakers in the political sphere in several of his biographies. *Thomas Jefferson: The Revolutionary Aristocrat* presents a "rich and multifaceted" portrait of the noted constitutionalist president and statesman, according to *Horn Book* reviewer Anita Silvey, the critic adding that the author treats young readers "with respect and evidences a belief in their intelligence." Meltzer does "his usual skillful job" in a further biography of an early revolutionary, according to Nancy Eaton, reviewing *Tom Paine: Voice of Revolution* in *Voice of Youth Advocates*. "The complex ideas presented . . . are essential to understanding the background of the American Revolution and the evolution of our political system," Eaton concluded. In *Andrew Jackson and His America* Meltzer contextualizes his subject, creating a life-and-times approach to this military man, land-speculator, slave-holder, and president. "Meltzer's biographies always teach us as much about the history of the period as they do about his subject," commented Chris Sherman in a *Booklist* review of *Andrew Jackson,* and in *Voice of Youth Advocates* Laura L. Lent dubbed the book "fascinating and informative from start to finish." In *Andrew Jackson,* Lent added, Meltzer "makes the persona of Jackson come alive," warts and all.

Ten Queens: Portraits of Women in Power contains biographical accounts of female monarchs ranging from Cleopatra to Catherine the Great of Russia. The women Meltzer portrays were not accidental queens—regents who married kings—but rather women who held and wielded real power. Dubbing Meltzer "one of children's literature's foremost writers of nonfiction," *Booklist* critic Ilene Cooper noted that in *Ten Queens* the author employs a "wonderful narrative device; he writes in a tone that is almost chatty, one that engages readers." In *Publishers Weekly* a contributor dubbed the same book an "enticing mix of history and biography."

Similar in format, *Ten Kings: And the Worlds They Ruled* profiles a range of influential powerbrokers, including Mesopotamia's Hammurabi, Alexander the Great, Attila the Hun, French king Louis IX, Russia's Peter the Great, the Incan ruler Atahualpa, and Mali's Mansa Musa. Featuring maps along with stories and facts regarding the man and his accomplishments, the book "would be especially useful to beginning researchers," noted *School Library Journal* contributor Shauna Yusko. As he did in *Ten Queens,* in *Ten Kings* Meltzer "employs an inviting tone that draws readers in," observed Cooper, the *Booklist* contributor adding that report writers who find the book will "surely be tempted to read on."

Turning to life's commercial sphere, Meltzer provides insightful looks at people ranging from Andrew Carnegie and Albert Einstein to notable seabound explorers such as Francisco Pizarro, Captain James Cook, and Ferdinand Magellan. In *The Many Lives of Andrew Carnegie* he documents the steelmaker's rise from his humble Scottish origins to his accomplishments as a wealthy U.S. captain of industry, presenting readers with a "fascinating portrait [that] makes a lively read," according to *Booklist* contributor Anne O'Malley. In *Albert Einstein: A Biography* Meltzer "offers a sound, cogent introduction" to the scientist who revolutionized man's understanding of physical laws, in the opinion of *Booklist* contributor Carolyn Phelan.

In the literary world, the lives of Carl Sandburg, John Steinbeck, Emily Dickinson, Herman Melville, Walt Whitman, Edgar Allan Poe, and Langston Hughes are given Meltzer's consideration. The poet and biographer of Lincoln is profiled in *Carl Sandburg: A Biography,* a "probing, inspirational study," according to a critic for *Kirkus Reviews,* while in *Emily Dickinson* Meltzer "profiles a poet whose nonconformist spirit speaks strongly to many teens," according to *Booklist* critic Jennifer Mattson. In *School Library Journal* Pat Bender cited the biographer's "clear and succinct writing" in his profile of nineteenth-century New England poet Dickinson. Discussing the biography of Steinbeck, who is best known as the author of *The Grapes of Wrath,* Mattson also noted that Meltzer's work "will enhance appreciation of any of Steinbeck's frequently assigned titles."

In all his books, Meltzer evidences his passion and viewpoint on his subjects and society. In his history of pacifism, *Ain't Gonna Study War No More: The Story of America's Peace Seekers,* for example, he "is openly partisan, urging readers to learn from history and courageously oppose the false heroism of war," related Hazel Rochman in *Booklist.* Likewise, as Elizabeth S. Watson observed in *Horn Book,* Meltzer's *American Politics: How It Really Works* "is a thoughtfully created" work in which the "widely read, articulate" author "has decided to share his knowledge of and views on politics with young people." With *Witches and Witch-hunts: A History of Persecution* Meltzer chronicles the human impulse to scapegoat that has surfaced throughout history, during medieval witch trials and twentieth-century "witch-hunts" such as those against the Jews in Nazi Germany and against communists in postwar McCarthyite America. Kitty Flynn, writing in *Horn Book,* called *Witches and Witch-hunts* an "engaging and thought-provoking book," as well as a "provocative study from a seasoned historian." A critic for *Publishers Weekly,* in a review of the same book, felt that Meltzer "crams a lot of ideas and insights into his ambitious, unusually meaty survey."

Meltzer has extended his interest in social issues from writing to his private life by joining unions, campaigning for political candidates, parading, and lobbying. Additionally, in titles such as *The Amazing Potato: A Story*

in Which the Inca, Conquistadors, Marie Antoinette, Thomas Jefferson, Wars, Famines, Immigrants, and French Fries All Play a Part; Gold: The True Story of Why People Search for It, Mine It, Trade It, Fight for It, Mint It, Display It, Steal It, and Kill for It; and *Food,* he takes a particular topic and follows it across time and cultures to present an interdisciplinary nonfiction approach that integrates history, economics, science, and art. *The Amazing Potato* is, according to Sherman in another *Booklist* review, "a wonderful example of nonfiction writing at its best." Filled with anecdotes as well as hard research, the book traces the lowly potato from its origins in Peru through the Irish famine and on to today's French fries. Meltzer takes the same approach in *Gold,* in which the author "makes nonfiction an exciting story," according to Rochman. "Meltzer shows that the story of gold is one of great inventiveness and also one of human cruelty and greed," the critic concluded. A similar treatment informs *Food,* an "entertaining, historical overview," as Marilyn Fairbanks described it in *School Library Journal.*

"I try to be useful in the same way wherever and whenever I can," Meltzer related in his *SAAS* essay. "All my writing comes out of my convictions. I've never had to write about anything I didn't believe in." "Through his books, Meltzer asks young readers to think critically as he gives the opportunity to experience history firsthand," observed Carol Sue Harless in a *School Library Journal* review of *Nonfiction for the Classroom: Milton Meltzer on Writing, History, and Social Responsibility.* "It is writers like Meltzer who make the reading of history a pleasure."

Biographical and Critical Sources

BOOKS

Children's Books and Their Creators, edited by Anita Silvey, Houghton Mifflin (Boston, MA), 1995.

Children's Literature Review, Volume 13, Gale (Detroit, MI), 1987.

Contemporary Literary Criticism, Volume 26, Gale (Detroit, MI), 1983.

Dictionary of Literary Biography, Volume 61: *American Writers for Children since 1960: Poets, Illustrators, and Nonfiction Authors,* Gale (Detroit, MI), 1987.

Meltzer, Milton, *Starting from Home: A Writer's Beginnings,* Viking (New York, NY, 1988.

St. James Guide to Young-Adult Writers, 2nd edition, St. James (Detroit, MI), 1999.

Something about the Author Autobiography Series, Volume 1, Gale (Detroit, MI), 1986.

PERIODICALS

Booklist, May 1, 1985, Hazel Rochman, review of *Ain't Gonna Study War No More: The Story of America's Peace Seekers,* p. 1248; April 15, 1990, Julie Corsaro,

review of *Columbus and the World around Him,* p. 1634; July, 1992, Chris Sherman, review of *The Amazing Potato: A Story in Which the Inca, Conquistadors, Marie Antoinette, Thomas Jefferson, Wars, Famines, Immigrants, and French Fries All Play a Part,* p. 1939; January 1, 1994, Hazel Rochman, review of *Gold: The True Story of Why People Search for It, Mine It, Trade It, Fight for It, Mint It, Display It, Steal It, and Kill for It,* p. 815; January 15, 1994, Chris Sherman, review of *Andrew Jackson and His America,* p. 924; March 1, 1994, Stephanie Zvirin, review of *Cheap Raw Material: How Our Youngest Workers Are Exploited and Abused,* p. 1261; October 1, 1997, Anne O'Malley, review of *The Many Lives of Andrew Carnegie,* p. 316; April 15, 1998, Ilene Cooper, review of *Ten Queens: Portraits of Women in Power,* p. 1439; January 1, 1999, Stephanie Zvirin, review of *Food,* p. 868; July, 2002, Ilene Cooper, review of *Ten Kings: And the Worlds They Ruled,* p. 1840; October 15, 2002, Carolyn Phelan, review of *Ain't Gonna Study War No More,* p. 400; September 15, 2004, Michael Cart, review of *Hear That Train Whistle Blow! How the Railroad Changed the World,* p. 229; February 15, 2006, Jennifer Mattson, review of *Emily Dickinson,* p. 108; September 1, 2007, Lynn Rutan, review of *Tough Times,* p. 118; February 1, 2008, Carolyn Phelan, review of *Albert Einstein: A Biography,* p. 43; March 15, 2008, Jennifer Mattson, review of *John Steinbeck,* p. 46; April 15, 2008, Hazel Rochman, review of *Willa Cather,* p. 39.

Bulletin of the Center for Children's Books, July, 1987, Betsy Hearne, review of *The American Revolutionaries: A History in Their Own Words, 1750-1800,* p. 215.

Horn Book, May-June, 1986, Elizabeth S. Watson, review of *Poverty in America,* p. 341; March-April, 1989, Mary A. Bush, review of *Benjamin Franklin: The New American,* pp. 227-228; September-October, 1989, Elizabeth S. Watson, review of *American Politics: How It Really Works,* p. 641; January-February, 1993, Anita Silvey, review of *Thomas Jefferson: The Revolutionary Aristocrat,* pp. 98-99; July-August, 1995, Mary M. Burns, review of *Frederick Douglass: In His Own Words,* pp. 480-481; November-December, 1999, Kitty Flynn, review of *Witches and Witch-hunts: A History of Persecution,* p. 759; July-August, 2001, Wendy Saul, "Milton Meltzer," p. 431; September-October, 2004, Margaret A. Bush, review of *Hear That Train Whistle Blow!,* p. 606.

Kirkus Reviews, December 1, 1999, review of *Carl Sandburg: A Biography,* p. 1888; February 1, 2002, review of *Walt Whitman: A Biography,* p. 184; October 1, 2007, review of *Tough Times;* January 15, 2008, review of *Albert Einstein.*

Kliatt, March, 2003, Mary T. Gerrity, review of *Ain't Gonna Study War No More,* p. 50; September, 2003, Barbara Mckee, review of *Ten Queens,* p. 35.

Library Journal, February 1, 1994, review of *Slavery: A World History,* p. 116.

New York Times Book Review, August 11, 2002, review of *Ten Kings,* p. 18.

Publishers Weekly, April 6, 1998, review of *Ten Queens,* p. 80; September 6, 1999, review of *Witches and Witch-*

hunts, p. 105; December 11, 2000, review of *There Comes a Time: The Struggle for Civil Rights,* p. 85.

School Library Journal, October, 1968, Milton Meltzer, "The Fractured Image: Distortions in Children's History Books," pp. 107-111; August, 1988, Christine Behrmann, review of *Rescue: The Story of How Gentiles Saved Jews in the Holocaust,* pp. 110-111; January, 1989, May Mueller, review of *Benjamin Franklin,* p. 101; December, 1989, Elizabeth M. Reardon, review of *Voices from the Civil War: A Documentary History of the Great American Conflict,* p. 127; September, 1993, Mary Mueller, review of *Lincoln: In His Own Words,* p. 258; July, 1994, Marilyn Long Graham, review of *Cheap Raw Material,* p. 125; February, 1995, Joanne Kelleher, review of *Frederick Douglass,* p. 121; June, 1995, Carol Sue Harless, review of *Nonfiction for the Classroom: Milton Meltzer on Writing, History, and Social Responsibility,* p. 43; January, 1999, Marilyn Fairbanks, review of *Food,* p. 147; February, 2000, Steven Engelfried, review of *Driven from the Land: The Story of the Dust Bowl,* p. 130; February, 2000, Laura Glaser, review of *They Came in Chains: The Story of the Slave Ships,* p. 133; January, 2001, Eunice Weech, review of *There Comes a Time,* p. 151; March, 2002, Jane Halsall, review of *Walt Whitman,* p. 255; October, 2002, Shauna Yusko, review of *Ten Kings,* p. 189; October, 2004, Ginny Gustin, review of *Hear That Train Whistle Blow!,* p. 192; January, 2006, Kristen Oravec, review of *Herman Melville: A Biography,* p. 158; June, 2006, Pat Bender, review of *Emily Dickinson,* p. 181; November, 2006, Michael Santangelo, review of *Nathaniel Hawthorne: A Biography,* p. 162; May, 2007, Jill Heritage Maza, review of *Henry David Thoreau: A Biography,* p. 158; December, 2007, Quinby Frank, review of *Tough Times,* p. 136; March, 2008, Barbara Katz, review of *Albert Einstein,* p. 186.

Voice of Youth Advocates, June, 1991, Judy Silverman, review of *Brother, Can You Spare a Dime? The Great Depression, 1929-1933,* p. 128; February, 1994, Laura L. Lent, review of *Andrew Jackson and His America,* pp. 399-400; February, 1995, Melissa Ducote Shepherd, review of *Who Cares?,* p. 361; February, 1997, Nancy Eaton, review of *Tom Paine: Voice of Revolution,* p. 352.

ONLINE

Worcester (MA) Area Writers Web site, http://www.wpi.edu/ (June 5, 2009), "Milton Meltzer."

American Library Association Web site, http://www.ala.org/ (October 3, 2001), "Milton Meltzer Wins Laura Ingalls Wilder Award."*

       *   *   *

MIGLIO, Paige 1966-

Personal

Born 1966, in CT; children: two. *Education:* Rhode Island School of Design, B.A.

Addresses

Home and office—9 Highwood Rd., Milford, CT 06460. *E-mail*—paige@paigemiglio.com.

Career

Illustrator and designer. Previously worked as a book designer.

Illustrator

Gail Radley, *The Spinner's Gift: A Tale,* North-South (New York, NY), 1994.

Philemon Sturges, *Crocky Dilly,* Museum of Fine Arts (Boston, MA), 1998.

Rick Walton, *So Many Bunnies: A Bedtime ABC and Counting Book,* Lothrop, Lee & Shepard (New York, NY), 1998.

Rick Walton, *One More Bunny: Adding from One to Ten,* Lothrop, Lee & Shepard (New York, NY), 2000.

Mike Thaler, *Little Dinosaur,* Henry Holt (New York, NY), 2001.

Rick Walton, *Bunny Day: Telling Time from Breakfast to Bedtime,* HarperCollins (New York, NY), 2002.

Rick Walton, *Bunnies on the Go: Getting from Place to Place,* HarperCollins (New York, NY), 2003.

Rick Walton, *Bunny Christmas: A Family Celebration,* HarperCollins (New York, NY), 2004.

Rick Walton, *Bunny School: A Learning Fun-for-All,* HarperCollins (New York, NY), 2005.

Mike Thaler, *Pig Little,* Henry Holt (New York, NY), 2006.

Rick Walton, *What Do We Do with the Baby?,* HarperCollins (New York, NY), 2008.

Sidelights

Paige Miglio began her career in art as a book designer before deciding to move to the world of children's book illustration. Along with her work in children's books, where she works primarily in water color and pencil, Miglio also works from her home in Connecticut illustrating portraits and creating design motifs for walls, cabinets, and other furniture pieces.

The majority of Miglio's illustration projects have been written by Rick Walton and feature bunnies in various child-familiar scenarios. The series began with the concept books *So Many Bunnies: A Bedtime ABC and Counting Book* and *One More Bunny: Adding from One to Ten,* both of which incorporate basic math concepts. *Bunny Day: Telling Time from Breakfast to Bedtime* introduces young readers to telling time on clock faces. A *Publishers Weekly* critic wrote that the illustrations in *So Many Bunnies* are "chock-full of cozy details and possess a Victorian flair." In *Booklist* Connie Fletcher concluded that in *One More Bunny* "fun predominates" in Miglio's "springlike" art, and Lucinda Snyder Whitehurst wrote in *School Library Journal* that the same book's "illustrations sustain the mood of idealized childhood." Noting that *Bunny Day* actually begins with the

Paige Miglio's illustration projects includes the fanciful artwork for Rick Walton's toddler concept book **So Many Bunnies.** (Illustration © 1998 by Paige Miglio. Used by permission of HarperCollins Publishers.)

illustrations of Father Rabbit setting clocks in the beginning and end-papers, Susan Marie Pitard added in her *School Library Journal* review that "each spread is filled with humor and detail, and children will want to pore over the pictures."

In *Bunnies on the Go: Getting from Place to Place* Miglio depicts bunnies in cars, trains, and ferries as the bunny family goes on vacation. Her images "are bright, and the anthropomorphic rabbits are expressive," wrote a *Kirkus Reviews* contributor. According to Julie Cummins, writing in *Booklist,* young bookworms will "scru-tinize the picture scenes for hints about the mode of transportation the bunnies will choose." *Bunny School: A Learning Fun-for-All* features the little bunnies in their first day at school, and here "Miglio's terrific illustrations . . . tell the whole story," according to a contributor to *Kirkus Reviews.* Carolyn Phelan noted in *Booklist* that the artwork for *Bunny School* is "large in scale and quite detailed." A new baby bunny stars in *What Do We Do with the Baby?,* in which "part of the fun is turning the pages to see how the long-eared characters are dressed," according to *School Library Journal* critic Lynn K. Vanca.

Miglio has worked with several other authors on picture books for young readers. For *Crocky Dilly,* by Philemon Sturges, she contributes stylistic details drawn from ancient Egypt to help better place the main character, an Egyptian crocodile, in the story's setting. "The artwork blends the lightness of the verse with historically accurate embellishments," wrote Susan Dove Lempke in *Booklist,* and in *Publishers Weekly* a contributor praised the illustrator's "idealized riverscape of fan-shaped papyrus plants, water lilies, blue-green water and sandy shores." Of *Pig Little,* which features Miglio's art along with a story by Mike Thaler, Marge Loch-Wouters wrote

in *School Library Journal* that, despite the story's cast of anthropomorphized pigs, children "will recognize themselves in the warm verse and illustrations."

Biographical and Critical Sources

PERIODICALS

Booklist, March 15, 1998, April Judge, review of *So Many Bunnies: A Bedtime ABC and Counting Book,* p. 1252; April 1, 1999, Susan Dove Lempke, review of *Crocky*

Miglio and Walton team up for a second dose of bunny-centered fun in **Bunny Day,** *which features the illustrator's detailed art.* (Illustration copyright © 2002 by Paige Miglio. Used by permission of the illustrator.)

Dilly, p. 1422; April 15, 2000, Connie Fletcher, review of *One More Bunny: Adding from One to Ten,* p. 1554; May 15, 2002, Ilene Cooper, review of *Bunny Day: Telling Time from Breakfast to Bedtime,* p. 1603; August, 2005, Carolyn Phelan, review of *Bunny School: A Learning Fun-for-All,* p. 2042; February 15, 2008, Ilene Cooper, review of *What Do We Do with the Baby?,* p. 87.

Kirkus Reviews, December 15, 2001, review of *Bunny Day,* p. 1764; December 1, 2002, review of *Bunnies on the Go: Getting from Place to Place,* p. 1775; June 15, 2005, review of *Bunny School,* p. 692; June 1, 2006, review of *Pig Little,* p. 581.

Publishers Weekly, January 26, 1998, review of *So Many Bunnies,* p. 90; November 16, 1998, review of *Crocky Dilly,* p. 73.

School Library Journal, July, 2000, Lucinda Snyder Whitehurst, review of *One More Bunny,* p. 90; December, 2001, Ann Cook, review of *Little Dinosaur,* p. 113; April, 2002, Susan Marie Pitard, review of *Bunny Day,* p. 126; March, 2003, Bina Williams, review of *Bunnies on the Go,* p. 210; September, 2005, Ely M. Anderson, review of *Bunny School,* p. 188; July, 2006, Marge Loch-Wouters, review of *Pig Little,* p. 95; March, 2008, Lynn K. Vanca, review of *What Do We Do with the Baby?,* p. 178.

ONLINE

HarperCollins Web site, http://www.harpercollins.com/ (May 13, 2009).
Paige Miglio Home Page, http://www.paigemiglio.com (May 13, 2009).*

MUELLER, Miranda R.

Personal

Married Andy Rommel, June, 2009. *Hobbies and other interests:* Organic vegetable gardening, wildlife habitat preservation, the outdoors, animal husbandry, travel, cooking, camping, kayaking.

Addresses

Home—Austin, TX. *E-mail*—mirandamueller@gmail. com.

Career

Illustrator and portrait artist.

Illustrator

Adrienne Ehlert Bashista, *Mishka: An Adoption Tale,* DRT Press (Pittsboro, NC), 2007.

Illustrator of phonics books for Frishco, Inc., 2008-09.

Biographical and Critical Sources

PERIODICALS

Children's Bookwatch, November, 2007, review of *Mishka: An Adoption Tale.*

ONLINE

Miranda R. Mueller Home Page, http://www.mirandamuel ler.com (May 15, 2009).
Miranda Mueller Web Log, http://mirandamueller/blogspot. com (May 9, 2009).

N-P

NOBATI, Eugenia 1968-

Personal
Born 1968, in Argentina.

Addresses
Home—Buenos Aires, Argentina. *Agent*—Libby Ford, 320 E. 57th St., Ste. 10B, New York, NY 10022.

Career
Illustrator.

Writings

SELF-ILLUSTRATED

En coche va una niña, Cantaro Editores, 2006.

ILLUSTRATOR

Graciela Beatriz Cabal, *Vidas de cuento: ayer y siempre,* Alfaguara Santillana (Miami, FL), 2001.

Luciana Fernandez, *Dame un Besito,* Cantaro Editores, 2006.

Isabel F. Ada and Alma Flor Ada, *Celebrate Mardi Gras with Joaquín, Harlequín,* Alfaguara Santillana (Miami, FL), 2006.

Graciela Repun, *Una bruja casi perfecta,* Unaluna, 2006.

Margaret Read MacDonald, *Bat's Big Game,* Albert Whitman (Morton Grove, IL), 2008.

Amy White, *A la búsqueda del tesoro!,* Alfaguara Santillana (Miami, FL), 2009.

Biographical and Critical Sources

PERIODICALS

Booklist, June 1, 2008, Shelle Rosenfeld, review of *Bat's Big Game,* p. 86.

Kirkus Reviews, February 15, 2008, Margaret MacDonald, review of *Bat's Big Game.*

School Library Journal, June, 2008, Donna Cardon, review of *Bat's Big Game,* p. 127.

ONLINE

Eugenia Nobati Web Log, http://eugenianobati-ilustracion. blogspot.com (June 8, 2009).*

* * *

NORTH, Sherry
(Sherry Rauh)

Personal
Born in NY; married; children: two. *Education:* University of Florida, B.A.; New York University, M.A. *Hobbies and other interests:* Travel, volunteer work, inline skating.

Addresses
Home—FL. *E-mail*—sherry@sherrynorth.com.

Career
Writer, journalist, and television producer.

Awards, Honors
NAPPA Gold Award, 2008, for *Because You Are My Baby.*

Writings

The School That Sank, illustrated by Diane Bowles, Macmillan Caribbean (Oxford, England), 2003.

Sherry North (Photo courtesy of Sherry North.)

Sailing Days, illustrated by Jim Eldridge, Macmillan Caribbean (Oxford, England), 2008.

Because You Are My Baby, illustrated by Marcellus Hall, Harry Abrams (New York, NY), 2008.

Contributor to anthology *Treasure House 1,* 2006. Contributor to periodicals, including *Highlights for Children* and *High Five.*

Sidelights

Sherry North started writing children's stories as a way to express her creative side. A journalist and producer for *CNN Headline News,* North had been working with facts for three years at the television news network, and she needed to refresh herself with something more creative. In addition to her new career as the author of picture books such as *Sailing Days* and *Because You Are My Baby,* North works in television under the name Sherry Rauh, where she produces and scripts programming and also writes educational videos and Web content.

Illustrated by Marcellus Hall, North's picture book *Because You Are My Baby* finds a mother with an expansive imagination telling her baby, in verse, all the things she would do for him while taking on outrageous careers. Janice Del Negro, writing in *Booklist,* commented that "North's rhyming text is occasionally forced, but her imagined motherly roles offer occasions for visualization of Baby's reactions." A *Kirkus Reviews* writer called *Because You Are My Baby* "an energetic and inspiring testament to motherhood," while Regan McMahon noted in the *San Francisco Chronicle* that "when a

book comes along that portrays this powerful love in a fresh and spirited way, that's truly cause for celebration."

North began her writing career with two books—*The School That Sank* and *Sailing Days*—for Macmillan Caribbean's "Hop, Step, Jump" series, a collection of child-centered books at three different language levels. She has also contributed to the same publisher's *Treasure House 1* anthology, and to several periodicals geared for young children.

North told *SATA:* "One of the best ways to get an idea for a story is to take something true and twist it in a fun way. The inspiration for my first book, *The School That Sank,* came from a real seaside school that was in danger of sinking. The inspiration for *Because You Are My Baby* was my own baby. I wanted to find an exciting, whimsical way to tell my son I would do anything for him."

Biographical and Critical Sources

PERIODICALS

Booklist, April 1, 2008, Janice Del Negro, review of *Because You Are My Baby,* p. 53.

Kirkus Reviews, March 1, 2008, review of *Because You Are My Baby,.*

Publishers Weekly, March 24, 2008, review of *Because You Are My Baby,* p. 69.

San Francisco Chronicle, April 27, 2008, Regan McMahon, review of *Because You Are My Baby.*

ONLINE

Sherry North Home Page, http://www.sherrynorth.com (May 15, 2009).

*   *   *

PASTEL, Elyse

Personal

Married; children: two.

Addresses

Home—Los Angeles, CA. *E-mail*—elyse.pastel@gmail.com.

Career

Illustrator, animator, and high-school art teacher. Worked for animation companies, including Marvel, Don Bluth, and Disney; on films, including *Pocahontas, The Black Caldron,* and *The Secret of NIMH;* and on

television shows, including *Muppet Babies* and *Ducktales.* Former children's product designer for Disney Consumer Products.

Illustrator

Lynn E. Hazen, *Cinder Rabbit,* Henry Holt (New York, NY), 2008.

Lara Bergen, *Tutu Twins,* innovativeKids (Norwalk, CT), 2008.

Sidelights

After enjoying a career in both animation and development of children's products, Elyse Pastel began a new path as a children's book illustrator with *Cinder Rabbit,* a chapter book for beginning readers that is written by Lynn E. Hazen. Excited at the prospect of playing the role of "Cinder Rabbit" in her school's spring play, Zoe looks forward to her upcoming performance and joins all of her classmates in preparing for the special day. When the young rabbit learns she must lead everyone in the bunny hop, however, Zoe becomes apprehensive about her part in the production, fearful that she might again embarrass herself. With the help of sympathetic friends, however, she learns how to overcome her anxi-

Elyse Pastel creates the amusing cartoon art that brings to life Lynn E. Hazen's picture-book text in Cinder Rabbit. (Illustration copyright © 2008 by Elyse Pastel. All rights reserved. Reprinted by arrangement with Henry Holt & Company, LLC.)

ety about hopping and enjoy her special night. According to *Booklist* critic Shauna Yusko, Pastel's "charming black-and-white illustrations will engage kids" as they separate the story into the smaller portions new readers can better comprehend. In *School Library Journal* Heather M. Campbell also thought that Pastel's artwork serves a useful purpose, writing that the "black-and-white illustrations on each spread expand on the characters," and a *Kirkus Reviews* contributor offered warm words for Pastel's "darling, expressive bunnies."

In an interview conducted by the author of *Cinder Rabbit,* Pastel remarked that the most important thing an aspiring illustrator can do is practice drawing. As she told Hazen on the *Cinder Rabbit Home Page,* "Draw everything. Don't worry about how the drawings look, just keep drawing and they will slowly get better."

Biographical and Critical Sources

PERIODICALS

Booklist, June 1, 2008, Shauna Yusko, review of *Cinder Rabbit,* p. 86.
Kirkus Reviews, March 15, 2008, review of *Cinder Rabbit.*
School Library Journal, March, 2008, Heather M. Campbell, review of *Cinder Rabbit,* p. 164.

ONLINE

Cinder Rabbit Home Page, http://wwwcinderrabbit.com/ (May 13, 2009), Lynn E. Hazen, interview with Pastel.
Elyse Pastel Home Page, http://elysepastel.com (May 13, 2009).*

*   *   *

PHAM, LeUyen 1973-

Personal

First name pronounced "Le-Win"; born September 7, 1973, in Saigon, Vietnam; daughter of Phong T. and LeHuong Pham; married Alexandre Puvilland (an artist), October 29, 2005. *Ethnicity:* "Vietnamese." *Education:* Attended University of California, Los Angeles, 1991-93; Art Center College of Design (Pasadena CA), B.A., 1996.

Addresses

Agent—Linda Pratt, Sheldon Fogelman Agency, 10 E. 40th St., New York, NY 10016. *E-mail*—leuyenp@sbcglobal.net.

Career

Children's book author and illustrator. Dreamworks Feature Animation, Glendale, CA, layout artist, 1996-99; Art Center College of Design, Pasadena, CA, in-

structor, 2000; Academy of Art University, San Francisco, CA, instructor; LeUyen Pham Illustration, San Francisco, freelance artist, 1999—. *Exhibitions:* Work exhibited at New York Society of Illustrators Original Art Show, 2005; and New York Society of Illustrators Spectrum Exhibition, 2005.

Member

Society of Illustrators.

Awards, Honors

American Booksellers Association Pick of the List designation, and Oppenheim Toy Portfolio Gold Award, both 2000, both for *Can You Do This, Old Badger?* by Eve Bunting; Best Children's Books of the Year designation, *Child* magazine, 2002, for *Whose Shoes?* by Anna Grossnickle Hines, and 2005, for *Big Sister, Little Sister;* 100 Titles for Reading and Sharing designation, and Oppenheim Toy Portfolio Gold Award, both 2004, both for *Twenty-one Elephants* by Phil Bildner; Society of Illustrators, Los Angeles, Bronze Medal in Children's Book Category; Texas 2x2 Reading List, 2004, for *Sing-along Song* by JoAnn Early Macken.

Writings

SELF-ILLUSTRATED

Big Sister, Little Sister, Hyperion Books for Children (New York, NY), 2005.

ILLUSTRATOR

Adrienne Moore Bond, *Sugarcane House, and Other Stories about Mr. Fat,* Harcourt Brace (San Diego, CA), 1997.

Eve Bunting, *Can You Do This, Old Badger?,* Harcourt (San Diego, CA), 1999.

Anna Grossnickle Hines, *Whose Shoes?,* Harcourt (San Diego, CA), 2001.

Eve Bunting, *Little Badger, Terror of the Seven Seas,* Harcourt (San Diego, CA), 2001.

Anna Grossnickle Hines, *Which Hat Is That?,* Harcourt (San Diego, CA), 2002.

Eve Bunting, *Little Badger's Just-about Birthday,* Harcourt (San Diego, CA), 2002.

Dori Chaconas, *One Little Mouse,* Viking (New York, NY), 2002.

Charlene Costanzo, *A Perfect Name,* Dial Books for Young Readers (New York, NY), 2002.

Karma Wilson, *Sweet Briar Goes to School,* Dial Books for Young Readers (New York, NY), 2003.

Kathryn Lasky, *Before I Was Your Mother,* Harcourt (San Diego, CA), 2003.

Kathi Appelt, *Piggies in a Polka,* Harcourt (San Diego, CA), 2003.

Esme Raji Codell, *Sing a Song of Tuna Fish: Hard-to-Swallow Stories from Fifth Grade,* Hyperion Books for Children (New York, NY), 2004.

Phil Bildner, *Twenty-one Elephants,* Simon & Schuster Books for Young Readers (New York, NY), 2004.

JoAnn Early Macken, *Sing-along Song,* Viking (New York, NY), 2004.

Esme Raji Codell, *Hanukkah, Shmanukkah!,* Hyperion Books for Children (New York, NY), 2005.

Karma Wilson, *Sweet Briar Goes to Camp,* Dial Books for Young Readers (New York, NY), 2005.

Alexander McCall Smith, *Akimbo and the Lions,* Bloomsbury Children's Books (New York, NY), 2005.

Alexander McCall Smith, *Akimbo and the Elephants,* Bloomsbury Children's Books (New York, NY), 2005.

Alexander McCall Smith, *Akimbo and the Crocodile Man,* Bloomsbury Children's Books (New York, NY), 2006.

Lenore Look's amusing middle-grade novel **Alvin Ho: Allergic to Girls, School, and Other Scary Things,** *is one of several books in the series that features LeUyen Pham's graphic-style illustrations.* (Illustration copyright © 2008 by LeUyen Pham. All rights reserved. Used by permission of Random House Children's Books, a division of Random House, Inc.)

Jabari Asim, *Whose Toes Are Those?,* Little, Brown (New York, NY), 2006.

Alexander McCall Smith, *Akimbo and the Snakes,* Bloomsbury Children's Books (New York, NY), 2006.

Bobbi Katz, *Once around the Sun,* Harcourt (Orlando, FL), 2006.

Jean Van Leeuwen, *Benny and Beautiful Baby Delilah,* Dial Books for Young Readers (New York, NY), 2006.

Jabari Asim, *Whose Knees Are These?,* Little, Brown (New York, NY), 2006.

Kelly S. DiPucchio, *Grace for President,* Hyperion Books for Children (New York, NY), 2007.

Bruce Coville, reteller, *William Shakespeare's The Winter's Tale,* Dial Books for Young Readers (New York, NY), 2007.

Charlotte Zolotow, *A Father like That,* HarperCollins (New York, NY), 2007.

Julianne Moore, *Freckleface Strawberry,* Bloomsbury Children's Books (New York, NY), 2007.

Archbishop Desmond Tutu, with Douglas Carlton, *God's Dream,* Candlewick Books (Cambridge, MA), 2008.

Alexander McCall Smith, *Akimbo and the Baboons,* Bloomsbury Children's Books (New York, NY), 2008.

(With husband Alex Puvilland) A.B. Sina, *Jordan Mechner's Prince of Persia* (graphic novel), First Second (New York, NY), 2008.

Lenore Look, *Alvin Ho: Allergic to Girls, School, and Other Scary Things,* Schwartz & Wade (New York, NY), 2008.

Charlotte Herman, *My Chocolate Year: A Novel with Twelve Recipes,* Simon & Schuster (New York, NY), 2008.

Julianne Moore, *Freckleface Strawberry and the Dodgeball Bully,* Bloomsbury (New York, NY), 2009.

Lenore Look, *Alvin Ho: Allergic to Camping, Hiking, and Other Natural Disasters,* Schwartz & Wade (New York, NY), 2009.

Sidelights

Vietnamese-born children's book author and illustrator LeUyen Pham has produced picture-book illustrations for texts by a number of writers, among them Alexander McCall Smith, Eve Bunting, Jean Van Leeuwen, and Karma Wilson. Earning her first illustration credit with the publication of Adrienne Moore Bond's *Sugarcane House, and Other Stories about Mr. Fat* in 1997, Pham's self-illustrated *Big Sister, Little Sister* earned her additional respect as an author when it was published seven years later.

Big Sister, Little Sister is told through the eyes of a little girl who compares her life to that of her older sister. While big sister wears lipstick and is orderly, little sister is always a little messy, and she is only allowed to wear lipstick at playtime. To accompany her story, Pham created full-page illustrations featuring striking inked brush-and-pen renderings. "Pham has beautifully captured the touch-and-go affection that is a verity of sibling life," commented a *Publishers Weekly* reviewer, going on to praise the author/illustrator's "bold, accomplished brush strokes." Writing in *School Library Jour-*

Pham joins noted South African mystery writer Alexander McCall Smith to illustrate his children's book **Akimbo and the Elephants.** (Illustration copyright © 2005 by LeUyen Pham. Used by permission.)

nal, Linda Ludke noted that, "with warmth and good humor, the ups and downs of sisterly love are perfectly conveyed" in Pham's art, while a *Kirkus Reviews* critic deemed *Big Sister, Little Sister* "a frothy fun tale that at its heart shows the depth and breadth of these relationships as something to be cherished."

As an illustrator, Pham has also earned the praise of many critics. The half-tone art she creates for McCall Smith's series of books about an African boy living with his ranger father were called "evocative" by a *Publishers Weekly* contributor in a review of *Akimbo and the Elephants,* and in *Kirkus Reviews* a critic wrote that Pham's illustrations for a new edition of Charlotte Zolotow's *A Father like That* "flow across each . . . spread and beautifully capture the spirit of the text." In *Jordan Mechner's Prince of Persia* Pham teams up with her husband, fellow artist Alex Puvilland, to illustrate a graphic novel based on a popular video game, producing a book that *School Library Journal* critic Andrea Lipinski praised for its "vibrant colors and stirring images." *Once around the Sun,* a picture book by Bobbi Katz, benefits from "large, color illustrations [by Pham that] are perfect for engaging youngsters in discussion"

about the seasons, according to *School Library Journal* contributor Teresa Pfeifer. Also features Pham's art, *God's Dream,* a picture book by Nobel Peace Prize-winner Archbishop Desmond Tutu, was commended by a *Publishers Weekly* critic who noted that the artist "nimbly sidesteps triteness through her velvety, saturated palette and the unassuming sweetness" of Tutu's multicultural cast of young characters.

Pham once told *SATA:* "When I first considered doing children's books, I was told, flat out by every art instructor I met, that one could 'never make a living at it.' Children's books has long been considered a field that one does for the pure love of, and not to find one's fortune, much less to make a simple living at.

"I have never been one to listen to such things, and I set about trying to prove everyone wrong. Besides which, I simply could not imagine doing anything else with my life.

"I think it was that single idea, the belief that I really had no other choice in my life other than to write and illustrate books, that has kept me motivated and going for all this time. And truth be told, it *is* an extremely

difficult field to be in, and one has to be quite prolific to stick around for very long. I might even wager to guess that my ability to ebb with the tide, to change my style from book to book to match the different mood of every story, has kept me adrift in this business, and has made it extremely challenging and enormously engaging in the process.

"It's interesting that in the field of illustration, one is encouraged to 'find one's voice', as if style is simply an ever-present constant. I supposed there's merit to thinking that one can become a rather reliable illustrator in this way, that there are no surprises to the work, and what you ask for is what you get each time. For myself, I never found this thought very appealing, and what's more, it's always seemed a bit derogatory to the text, as though the words themselves are as predictable as the artist's consistent work.

"Each time I receive a manuscript, I can't help but look for the uniqueness of the story, the voice that I haven't heard anywhere else that attracts and holds my imagination. If I find a story like that, my goal is to find a visual translation for it that is just as unique, just as attractive, to do the thing justice. So begins my journey—of finding a new style to translate the story.

"From book to book, I've made it a goal to try to be different than the book before, in everything from the medium to the rendering to the storytelling. Admittedly, this hasn't always been an easy task. It means feeling extremely insecure each time I start a new book, wondering if this style is working at all, if the graphic imagery is actually beneficial, or if it's taking away from the story. And of course, there is the matter of convincing the editor that this direction is the right direction. Somehow, I've been lucky enough to work with people who seem to really trust my instincts, and have let me express and change fluidly from book to book.

"Has this changing style been the reason for having done so many books in my short career? Heaven only knows there's no key to success. At least, I haven't found it yet. And all these years later, when I think back at my girlish stubbornness at sticking it out in this field, I can't help but laugh. Because somewhere, along the way, among the many, many books illustrated, and many stories, to tell, I discovered that what I was looking for wasn't a way to make a living—I was simply looking for a way to love living. Ain't it grand?"

Pham joins her husband, Alex Puvilland, to create the artwork for **Prince of Persia** *by Jordan Mechner.* (Artwork copyright © 2008 by LeUyen Pham and Alex Puvilland. All rights reserved. Reproduced by permission of:01 First Second.)

Biographical and Critical Sources

PERIODICALS

Booklist, March 15, 2003, Ilene Cooper, review of *Before I Was Your Mother,* p. 1332; July, 2004, Ilene Cooper, review of *Sing-along Song,* p. 1848; October 1, 2004, Karin Snelson, review of *Twenty-one Elephants,* p.

Pham's illustration projects include Esme Raji Codell's picture book **Sing a Song of Tuna Fish.** (Illustration copyright © 2004 by LeUyen Pham. All rights reserved. Reprinted by permission of Hyperion Books for Children.)

332; June 1, 2005, Jennifer Mattson, review of *Big Sister, Little Sister,* p. 1823; September 1, 2005, Kay Weisman, review of *Hanukkah, Shmanukkah!,* p. 131; September 1, 2005, Shelle Rosenfeld, review of *Akimbo and the Elephants,* p. 135; February 1, 2006, Ilene Cooper, review of *Benny and Beautiful Baby Delilah,* p. 59; April 15, 2006, Hazel Rochman, review of *Once around the Sun,* p. 49; May 15, 2007, Julie Cummins, review of *A Father like That,* p. 50; February 15, 2008, Ilene Cooper, review of *Grace for President,* p. 84.

Books, December 11, 2005, review of *Hanukkah, Shmanukkah!,* p. 2.

Bulletin of the Center for Children's Books, March, 2005, Karen Coats, review of *Sing a Song of Tuna Fish: Hard-to-Swallow Stories from Fifth Grade,* p. 285; September, 2005, Timnah Card, review of *Big Sister, Little Sister,* p. 36; May, 2006, Deborah Stevenson, review of *Benny and Beautiful Baby Delilah,* p. 426; July-August, 2006, Deborah Stevenson, review of *Once around the Sun,* p. 504.

Children's Bookwatch, May, 2004, review of *Piggies in a Polka,* p. 2.

Kirkus Reviews, March 1, 2003, review of *Before I Was Your Mother,* p. 257; July 15, 2003, review of *Piggies*

in a Polka, p. 961; May 1, 2004, JoAnn Macken, review of *Sing-along Song,* p. 444; October 1, 2004, review of *Twenty-one Elephants,* p. 956; June 15, 2005, review of *Big Sister, Little Sister,* p. 689; November 1, 2005, review of *Hanukkah, Shmanukkah!,* p. 1191; March 15, 2006, review of *Once around the Sun,* p. 293; May 1, 2007, review of *A Father like That;* September 15, 2007, review of *William Shakespeare's The Winter's Tale.*

Library Media Connection, August-September, 2005, Quinby Frank, review of *Big Sister, Little Sister,* p. 71; March, 2006, Pamela Ott, review of *Akimbo and the Elephants,* p. 64.

Publishers Weekly, January 27, 2003, review of *Before I Was Your Mother,* p. 257; August 25, 2003, review of *Piggies in a Polka,* p. 63; August 22, 2005, review of *Big Sister, Little Sister,* p. 64; September 5, 2005, review of *Akimbo and the Elephants,* p. 63; September 26, 2005, review of *Hanukkah, Shmanukkah!,* p. 85; April 3, 2006, review of *Akimbo and the Crocodile Man,* p. 76; July 31, 2006, review of *Sing a Song of Tuna Fish,* p. 77; January 14, 2008, review of *Grace for President,* p. 57; February 18, 2008, review of *My Chocolate Year,* p. 153; July 7, 2008, reviews of *God's Dream,* p. 57, and *Alvin Ho: Allergic to Girls, School, and Other Scary Things,* p. 58; July 28, 2008, review of *Jordan Mechner's Prince of Persia,* p. 58.

School Library Journal, May, 2003, Catherine Threadgill, review of *Before I Was Your Mother,* p. 122; September, 2003, Grace Oliff, review of *Piggies in a Polka,* p. 166; June, 2004, Marianne Saccardi, review of *Sing-along Song,* p. 114; November, 2004, Susan Lissim, review of *Twenty-one Elephants,* p. 90; September, 2005, Linda Ludke, review of *Big Sister, Little Sister,* p. 184; March, 2006, Martha Topol, review of *Benny and Beautiful Baby Delilah,* p. 204; May, 2006, Teresa Pfeifer, review of *Once around the Sun,* p. 114; June, 2006, Amelia Jenkins, review of *Whose Knees Are These?,* p. 104; February, 2008, Cheryl Ashton, review of *My Chocolate Year,* p. 116; September, 2008, Andrea Lipinski, review of *Jordan Mechner's Prince of Persia,* p. 219.

Washington Post Book World, December 11, 2005, Lori Smith, review of *Hanukkah, Shmanukkah,* p. 10.

ONLINE

LeUyen Pham Home Page, http://www.leuyenpham.com (May 20, 2009).

Web Esteem Web site, http://art.webesteem.pl/ (December 27, 2006), "LeUyen Pham."*

*   *   *

PRINGLE, Laurence 1935-
(Sean Edmund, Laurence Patrick Pringle)

Personal

Born November 26, 1935, in Rochester, NY; son of Laurence Erin (a real estate agent) and Marleah (a homemaker) Pringle; married Judith Malanowicz (a li-

Laurence Pringle (Photo courtesy of Laurence Pringle.)

brarian), June 23, 1962 (divorced, 1970); married Alison Newhouse (a freelance editor), July 14, 1971 (divorced, c. 1974); married Susan Klein (a teacher), March 13, 1983; children: (first marriage) Heidi, Jeffrey, Sean; (third marriage) Jesse, Rebecca. *Education:* Cornell University, B.S., 1958; University of Massachusetts, M.S., 1960; Syracuse University, doctoral studies, 1960-62. *Hobbies and other interests:* Photography, films, sports, surf fishing.

Addresses

Home—P.O. Box 252, W. Nyack, NY 10994. *E-mail*—octopushug@aol.com.

Career

Writer, photographer, wildlife biologist, and educator. Lima Central School, Lima, NY, high school science teacher, 1961-62; American Museum of Natural History, New York, NY, associate editor, 1963-65, senior editor, 1965-67, executive editor of *Nature & Science* (children's magazine), 1967-70; New School for Social Research (now New School University), New York, NY, faculty member, 1976-78; Kean College of New Jersey, Union, writer-in-residence, 1985-86; *Highlights for Children* Writers Workshop, faculty member, 1985-2004, 2007.

Awards, Honors

New Jersey Institute of Technology Award, 1970, for *The Only Earth We Have;* Special Conservation Award,

National Wildlife Federation, 1978; honor book designation, New York Academy of Sciences, 1980, for *Natural Fire;* Distinguished Alumnus Award, University of Massachusetts Department of Forestry and Wildlife Management, 1981; Eva L. Gordon Award, American Nature Society, 1983; John Burroughs List of Nature Books for Young Readers, 1991, for *Batman,* 1993, for *Jackal Woman,* and 1997, for *An Extraordinary Life;* A Book Can Develop Empathy Award, New York State Humane Association, 1991, for *Batman;* Orbis Pictus Honor Book designation for Outstanding Nonfiction for Children, National Council of Teachers of English, 1996, for *Dolphin Man,* and 1998, for *An Extraordinary Life;* Nonfiction Award, *Washington Post*/Children's Book Guild, 1999, for body of work; AAAS/Subaru SB&F Prize for Excellence in Science Books, 2005, for lifetime achievement; John Simon Guggenheim Memorial Foundation fellowship, 2007; dozens of Pringle's titles have been selected National Science Teachers Association Outstanding Science Trade Books for Children.

Writings

FOR YOUNG PEOPLE; NONFICTION

Dinosaurs and Their World, Harcourt (New York, NY), 1968.

The Only Earth We Have, Macmillan (New York, NY), 1969.

(Editor) *Discovering the Outdoors: A Nature and Science Guide to Investigating Life in Fields, Forests, and Ponds,* Natural History Press (New York, NY), 1969.

(Editor) *Discovering Nature Indoors: A Nature and Science Guide to Investigations with Small Animals,* Natural History Press (New York, NY), 1970.

(And photographer) *From Field to Forest: How Plants and Animals Change the Land,* World (New York, NY), 1970.

(And photographer) *In a Beaver Valley: How Beavers Change the Land,* World (New York, NY), 1970.

Cockroaches: Here, There, Everywhere, illustrated by James and Ruth McCrea, Crowell (New York, NY), 1970.

Ecology: Science of Survival, Macmillan (New York, NY), 1971.

One Earth, Many People: The Challenge of Human Population, Macmillan (New York, NY), 1971.

From Pond to Prairie: The Changing World of a Pond and Its Life, illustrated by Karl W. Stuecklen, Macmillan (New York, NY), 1972.

Pests and People: The Search for Sensible Pest Control, Macmillan (New York, NY), 1972.

This Is a River: Exploring an Ecosystem, Macmillan (New York, NY), 1972.

Estuaries: Where Rivers Meet the Sea, Macmillan (New York, NY), 1973.

Follow a Fisher, illustrated by Tony Chen, Crowell (New York, NY), 1973.

Into the Woods: Exploring the Forest Ecosystem, Macmillan (New York, NY), 1973.

Twist, Wiggle, and Squirm: A Book about Earthworms, illustrated by Peter Parnall, Crowell (New York, NY), 1973.

Recycling Resources, Macmillan (New York, NY), 1974.

Chains, Webs, and Pyramids: The Flow of Energy in Nature, illustrated by Jan Adkins, Crowell (New York, NY), 1975.

City and Suburb: Exploring an Ecosystem, Macmillan (New York, NY), 1975.

Energy: Power for People, Macmillan (New York, NY), 1975.

Water Plants, illustrated by Kazue Mizumura, Crowell (New York, NY), 1975.

Listen to the Crows, illustrated by Ted Lewin, Crowell (New York, NY), 1976.

The Minnow Family: Chubs, Dace, Minnows, and Shiners, illustrated by Dot and Sy Barlowe, Morrow (New York, NY), 1976.

Our Hungry Earth: The World Food Crisis, Macmillan (New York, NY), 1976.

Animals and Their Niches: How Species Share Resources, illustrated by Leslie Morrill, Morrow (New York, NY), 1977.

The Controversial Coyote: Predation, Politics, and Ecology, Harcourt (New York, NY), 1977.

Death Is Natural, Four Winds (New York, NY), 1977.

The Gentle Desert: Exploring an Ecosystem, Macmillan (New York, NY), 1977.

The Hidden World: Life under a Rock, illustrated by Erick Ingraham, Macmillan (New York, NY), 1977.

Dinosaurs and People: Fossils, Facts, and Fantasies, Harcourt (New York, NY), 1978.

The Economic Growth Debate: Are There Limits to Growth?, Franklin Watts (New York, NY), 1978.

Wild Foods: A Beginner's Guide to Identifying, Harvesting, and Cooking Safe and Tasty Plants from the Outdoors, illustrated by Paul Breeden, Four Winds Press (New York, NY), 1978.

Natural Fire: Its Ecology in Forests, Morrow (New York, NY), 1979.

Nuclear Power: From Physics to Politics, Macmillan (New York, NY), 1979.

Lives at Stake: The Science and Politics of Environmental Health, Macmillan (New York, NY), 1980.

Frost Hollows and Other Microclimates, Morrow (New York, NY), 1981.

What Shall We Do with the Land? Choices for America, Crowell (New York, NY), 1981.

Vampire Bats, Morrow (New York, NY), 1982.

Water: The Next Great Resource Battle, Macmillan (New York, NY), 1982.

Being a Plant, illustrated by Robin Brickman, Crowell (New York, NY), 1983.

"The Earth Is Flat"—and Other Great Mistakes, illustrated by Steve Miller, Morrow (New York, NY), 1983.

Feral: Tame Animals Gone Wild, Macmillan (New York, NY), 1983.

Radiation: Waves and Particles/Benefits and Risks, Enslow (Berkeley Heights, NJ), 1983.

Wolfman: Exploring the World of Wolves, Scribner (New York, NY), 1983.

Animals at Play, Harcourt (New York, NY), 1985.

Nuclear War: From Hiroshima to Nuclear Winter, Enslow (Berkeley Heights, NJ), 1985.

Here Come the Killer Bees, Morrow (New York, NY), 1986, revised edition published as *Killer Bees,* 1990.

Throwing Things Away: From Middens to Resource Recovery, Crowell (New York, NY), 1986.

Home: How Animals Find Comfort and Safety, Scribner (New York, NY), 1987.

Restoring Our Earth, Enslow (Berkeley Heights, NJ), 1987.

Rain of Troubles: The Science and Politics of Acid Rain, Macmillan (New York, NY), 1988.

The Animal Rights Controversy, Harcourt (New York, NY), 1989.

Bearman: Exploring the World of Black Bears, photographs by Lynn Rogers, Scribner (New York, NY), 1989.

Nuclear Energy: Troubled Past, Uncertain Future, Macmillan (New York, NY), 1989.

Living in a Risky World, Morrow (New York, NY), 1989.

The Golden Book of Insects and Spiders, illustrated by James Spence, Western Publishing (Racine, WI), 1990.

Global Warming: Assessing the Greenhouse Threat, Arcade (New York, NY), 1990.

Saving Our Wildlife, Enslow (Berkeley Heights, NJ), 1990.

Batman: Exploring the World of Bats, photographs by Merlin D. Tuttle, Scribner (New York, NY), 1991.

Living Treasure: Saving Earth's Threatened Biodiversity, illustrated by Irene Brady, Morrow (New York, NY), 1991.

Antarctica: The Last Unspoiled Continent, Simon & Schuster (New York, NY), 1992.

The Golden Book of Volcanoes, Earthquakes, and Powerful Storms, illustrated by Tom LaPadula, Western Publishing (Racine, WI), 1992.

Oil Spills: Damage, Recovery, and Prevention, Morrow (New York, NY), 1993.

Chemical and Biological Warfare: The Cruelest Weapons, Enslow (Berkeley Heights, NJ), 1993.

Jackal Woman: Exploring the World of Jackals, photographs by Patricia D. Moehlman, Macmillan (New York, NY), 1993.

Scorpion Man: Exploring the World of Scorpions, photographs by Gary A. Polis, Scribner (New York, NY), 1994.

Fire in the Forest: A Cycle of Growth and Renewal, illustrated by Bob Marstall, Simon & Schuster (New York, NY), 1995.

Dinosaurs! Strange and Wonderful, illustrated by Carol Heyer, Boyds Mills Press (Honesdale, PA), 1995.

Coral Reefs: Earth's Undersea Treasures, Simon & Schuster (New York, NY), 1995.

Vanishing Ozone: Protecting Earth from Ultraviolet Radiation, Morrow (New York, NY), 1995.

Dolphin Man: Exploring the World of Dolphins, Atheneum (New York, NY), 1995.

Taking Care of the Earth: Kids in Action, illustrated by Bobbie Moore, Boyds Mills Press (Honesdale, PA), 1996.

Smoking: A Risky Business, Morrow (New York, NY), 1996.

An Extraordinary Life: The Story of a Monarch Butterfly, illustrated by Bob Marstall, Orchard Books (New York, NY), 1997.

Elephant Woman: Cynthia Moss Explores the World of Elephants, photographs by Cynthia Moss, Atheneum (New York, NY), 1997.

Nature! Wild and Wonderful (autobiography), photographs by Tim Holmstrom, Richard C. Owen (Katonah, NY), 1997.

Everyone Has a Bellybutton: Your Life before You Were Born, illustrated by Clare Wood, Boyds Mills Press (Honesdale, PA), 1997.

Drinking: A Risky Business, Morrow (New York, NY), 1997.

Animal Monsters: The Truth about Scary Creatures, Marshall Cavendish (New York, NY), 1997.

One-Room School, illustrated by Barbara Garrison, Boyds Mills Press (Honesdale, PA), 1998.

Bats! Strange and Wonderful, illustrated by Meryl Henderson, Boyds Mills Press (Honesdale, PA), 2000.

The Environmental Movement: From Its Roots to the Challenges of a New Century, HarperCollins (New York, NY), 2000.

Sharks! Strange and Wonderful, illustrated by Meryl Henderson, Boyds Mills Press (Honesdale, PA), 2001.

A Dragon in the Sky: The Story of a Green Darner Dragonfly, illustrated by Bob Marstall, Orchard Books (New York, NY), 2001.

Scholastic Encyclopedia of Animals, photographs by Norbert Wu, Scholastic Reference (New York, NY), 2001.

Global Warming: The Threat of Earth's Changing Climate, SeaStar Books (New York, NY), 2001.

Strange Animals, New to Science, Marshall Cavendish (New York, NY), 2002.

Crows! Strange and Wonderful, illustrated by Bob Marstall, Boyds Mills Press (Honesdale, PA), 2002.

Dog of Discovery: A Newfoundland's Adventures with Lewis and Clark, Boyds Mills Press (Honesdale, PA), 2002.

Come to the Ocean's Edge: A Nature Cycle Book, illustrated by Michael Chesworth, Boyds Mills Press (Honesdale, PA), 2003.

Whales! Strange and Wonderful, illustrated by Meryl Henderson, Boyds Mills Press (Honesdale, PA), 2003.

Snakes! Strange and Wonderful, illustrated by Meryl Henderson, Boyds Mills Press (Honesdale, PA), 2004.

American Slave, American Hero: York of the Lewis and Clark Expedition, illustrated by Cornelius Van Wright and Ying-Hwa Hu, Calkins Creek Books (Honesdale, PA), 2006.

Penguins! Strange and Wonderful, illustrated by Meryl Henderson, Boyds Mills Press (Honesdale, PA), 2007.

Imagine a Dragon, illustrated by Eujin Kim Neilan, Boyds Mills Press (Honesdale, PA), 2008.

Alligators and Crocodiles! Strange and Wonderful, illustrated by Meryl Henderson, Boyds Mills Press (Honesdale, PA), 2009.

PICTURE BOOKS

Jesse Builds a Road, illustrated by Leslie Holt Morrill, Macmillan (New York, NY), 1989.

Octopus Hug, illustrated by Kate Salley Palmer, Boyds Mills Press (Honesdale, PA), 1993.

Naming the Cat, illustrated by Katherine Potter, Walker (New York, NY), 1997.

Bear Hug, illustrated by Kate Salley Palmer, Boyds Mills Press (Honesdale, PA), 2003.

OTHER

(And photographer) *Wild River* (adult nonfiction), Lippincott (Philadelphia, PA), 1972.

(With others) *Rivers and Lakes* (adult nonfiction), Time-Life Books (New York, NY), 1985.

(Author of foreword) Robert Few, *Macmillan Children's Guide to Endangered Animals,* Simon & Schuster (New York, NY), 1993.

Contributor to periodicals, including *Audubon, Ranger Rick's Nature Magazine* (sometimes under pseudonym Sean Edmund), *Highlights for Children,* and *Smithsonian;* contributor of essays to professional magazines on children's literature and education, including *Reading Teacher,* and to books, including *Celebrating Children's Books: Essays on Children's Literature in Honor of Zena Sutherland,* edited by Betsy Hearne and Marilyn Kaye, Lothrop, 1974; *The Voice of the Narrator in Children's Literature,* edited by Charlotte Otten and Gary Schmidt, Greenwood Press, 1989; *Nonfiction for Young Adults: From Delight to Wisdom,* edited by Betty Carter and Richard Abrahamson, Oryx, 1990; and *Vital Connections: Children, Science, and Books,* edited by Wendy Saul and Sybille Jagusch, Heinemann, 1991.

Sidelights

A prolific author of nonfiction, fiction, and picture books, as well as a photographer and science educator, Laurence Pringle has been praised as one of the top writers of informational books for readers from elementary through high school. Educated as a wildlife biologist, Pringle is noted for creating authoritative, well-researched works that inform readers about the natural sciences and the environment in a manner that critics have cited as accurate as well as interesting. He is noted for transforming complex material on scientific and ecological subjects into lucid, balanced overviews of sophisticated topics, some of which are not often treated in books for children. Several of the author's titles are regarded as definitive references and consistently cited as among the best books available on their respective subjects.

Pringle's works provide information on nature and the environment while also emphasizing the dangers that threaten Earth and its resources. While some of his books focus on the world's rivers, forests, oceans, and

deserts, others deal with man-made hazards such as nuclear energy, nuclear war, global warming, oil spills, pollution, acid rain, and radiation. Pringle includes constructive information, advising readers what they can do to protect their environment by recycling, fighting world hunger, and protecting biological diversity. In his wildlife-centered books he turns his attention to mammals, insects, birds, and fish as well as related topics, including the animal rights movement and what happens to tame animals that are released in the wild. Sometimes courting controversy, Pringle has also introduced younger readers to the ongoing debate between evolution and creationism, and has authored several biographies that introduce prominent naturalists and their work with animals such as wolves, scorpions, bats, dolphins, and elephants.

Born in Rochester, New York, Pringle grew up in Mendon, a rural town just south of his birthplace. In the family's isolated rural home, Pringle's mother learned to cook fish and game, while Pringle and his older brother explored woods, fields, and ponds. As a young boy, he was educated in a one-room schoolhouse, where one teacher handled the first through eighth grades; in 1998, he wrote a book based on his experience titled *One-Room School.* In 1945, Pringle transferred to a larger school in Honeoye Falls, a village of approximately 2,000 that provided him his first access to a library.

Spending many hours out of doors as a child, Pringle developed a love of nature. He soon began to focus on birds, attracting and identifying them and finding their nests; later, he began building birdhouses and subscribing to *Audubon* magazine, which he has credited with sparking his interest in wildlife photography.

In 1951 Pringle and his family moved to a new home in Rush, New York. Now in his teens, he enjoyed reading and baseball in addition to activities connected with nature. His interest led to writing and in 1952, he submitted an article to the "True Experiences and Camping Trips" section of *Open Road* magazine, a periodical similar to *Boys' Life.* The article described Pringle's observations of crow behavior and earned the future writer five dollars.

After graduating from high school, Pringle worked for a year in the kitchen of the local county hospital while continuing to hunt, trap, study birds, and follow baseball. In 1954 he enrolled at Cornell University, majoring in wildlife conservation, and his interest in nature was nurtured by his classes and by vacations with friends. For example, he spent winter holidays in the Adirondack Mountains following the trails of fishers—fox-sized members of the weasel family—and other wildlife; in 1973, he published *Follow a Fisher,* a work that shows how following a fisher's tracks leads to information about its hunting, eating, mating, and mothering habits. At Cornell Pringle also took two courses on writing nonfiction for magazines and won a campus

photography contest with a nature photo he had taken. Shortly after graduation, he had an article published in *The Conservationist,* the environmental magazine of New York State.

In 1958 Pringle enrolled in a master's degree program at the University of Massachusetts—Amherst. While his research on cottontails earned him a degree, he continued to pursue his interest in mammalian predators. While trapping, tagging, and releasing bobcats, Pringle captured and identified some of the first coyotes ever caught in Massachusetts. In 1977, he published *The Controversial Coyote: Predation, Politics, and Ecology,* which attempts to separate fact from fiction regarding coyotes and other predators. Pringle then enrolled at Syracuse University intending to earn his Ph.D. in wildlife biology, but changed his course of study when writing proved to be the greater attraction. His education was cut short, however; shortly after entering the Syracuse School of Journalism, Pringle contracted hepatitis.

After recovering from hepatitis at his family's home, Pringle began teaching science at Lima Central School in Lima, New York. In 1962, he took an education class at Syracuse as well as a course in writing magazine articles. In 1963, partly as a result of this course, he got a job as an assistant editor of the fledgling children's magazine *Nature & Science,* published by the American Museum of Natural History. He moved to senior editor and then executive editor before the magazine's demise in 1970. It was at *Nature & Science* that a fellow editor suggested to Pringle that he begin writing works for the young.

In 1968, Pringle published his first book, *Dinosaurs and Their World.* A basic treatment of selected dinosaurs, their evolution, and how paleontologists learn about them, *Dinosaurs and Their World* was praised by a reviewer in *Science Books:* "There are in print a great many dinosaur books for children, but this is one of the best because it is a well-researched and carefully written narrative." The reviewer continued: "Irrespective of how many dinosaur books elementary and public libraries own, they need this one." Pringle followed *Dinosaurs and Their World* with *The Only Earth We Have,* a work that outlines the dangers to the planet from pollution, solid wastes, pesticides, and the disruption of animal and plant communities. A contributor to *Kirkus Reviews* praised the book for including, "in summary form, what every conservationist would like every child to absorb." Pringle's book "is as good a way to get young or older people to react as any we have," the reviewer added. Pringle also explores the issue of human population growth in *One Earth, Many People,* which a *Kirkus Reviews* critic assigned as "required reading for the generation that stands to inherit the earth and its problems." A reviewer in *Science Books* noted: "Rarely does a book present so completely in so little space the basic components of population dynamics."

During the remainder of the 1970s, Pringle continued to publish well-received titles on the earth and its animals.

By 1974, he had become a freelance writer, and two years later *Listen to the Crows* became the first of several of his works to be named a notable book by the American Library Association. Through his explanation of the various forms of crow communication in this book, Pringle demonstrates that the oft-maligned crow is actually one of the most intelligent of birds. A contributor to *Kirkus Reviews* commented that in *Listen to the Crows* the author's "appreciation for the common but redoubtable crow avoids generalities and focuses on the amazing versatility of the bird's voice box."

Shortly afterward, Pringle wrote *Death Is Natural*. This work, which explains how death in the plant and animal worlds is a necessary part of nature's recycling process, was called a "remarkable book for children as well as some adults" by Gregory R. Belcher in *Appraisal*. In 1978 Pringle also earned a special conservation award from the National Wildlife Federation for being "the nation's leading writer of books on biological and environmental issues for young people."

In 1979, Pringle published two titles that were considered somewhat controversial: *Natural Fire: Its Ecology in Forests* and *Nuclear Power: From Physics to Politics*. In *Natural Fire,* he explains that, since forest fires are a natural force in the environment, we may be wrong to prevent fires and to put them out when they begin. Writing in *Horn Book,* Harry C. Stubbs concluded that Pringle "makes a very good case, and the book deserves to be read carefully and thoughtfully." Gregory R. Belcher noted in *Appraisal* that *Natural Fire* is a "provocative introduction" to the study of the role of fire within an ecological system. *Nuclear Power* provides an overview of the controversy surrounding its subject; although he admits to an antinuclear bias, here Pringle presents cases both for and against nuclear power in what David G. Hoag, in a review for *Appraisal,* called "unemotional language." The reviewer also commented: "If one feels that a children's science book may or should intermix science with politics, then this book ranks high." Writing in *School Library Journal,* Robert Unsworth noted that the author is "clear-headed, crisp, and always informative," and went on to write: "Pringle seems to have a sixth sense when it comes to knowing when enough information is enough."

In the early 1980s Pringle's subjects ranged from vampire bats and water to plants, radiation, and scientific misconceptions. He also continued his exploration of controversial issues in *Nuclear War: From Hiroshima to Nuclear Winter* and *Nuclear Energy: Troubled Past, Uncertain Future.* He also examined the composition and effects of acid rain in *Rain of Troubles: The Science and Politics of Acid Rain* and the animal-rights issue in *The Animal Rights Controversy.* Reviewers have consistently praised Pringle's objective overviews. For example, in his review of *Nuclear Energy* for *School Library Journal,* Alan Newman claimed that the author "gives an exceptionally knowledgeable and thoughtful

treatment of a difficult subject" and called the work a "savvy, well-written book on a subject often confused by hysteria and misinformation."

During the 1980s Pringle also began writing biographies of prominent scientists who work with animals, providing information about both the figure profiled and the animals he or she studies. In her review of *Batman: Exploring the World of Bats,* which focuses on mammalogist photographer Merlin Tuttle, Karey Wehner noted in *School Library Journal* that the book "offers a unique perspective on these gentle mammals." Pringle outlines the life and work of Cynthia Moss, a scientist without formal training, in *Elephant Woman: Cynthia Moss Explores the World of Elephants.* Writing in *School Library Journal,* Susan Oliver maintained that "Moss will fascinate young readers." "Elephants are extraordinary animals, Cynthia Moss is a great role model," the critic added, "and Pringle has brought them together in an exciting presentation." A contributor to *Kirkus Reviews* called *Elephant Woman* "an inspirational book for those interested in animal-related vocations."

Pringle espouses the preservation of the earth in books such as *What Shall We Do with the Land? Choices for America* and *Restoring Our Earth.* In her review of the first title for *Booklist,* Denise M. Wilms commented that the author's "environmentalist bent is quietly apparent throughout" and that his thought-provoking work is "a first-rate starting point for background on a topic that will be increasingly in the news." Julia Rholes noted in *School Library Journal* that land-use questions are important and that Pringle's "thoughtful, well-written book should be a must" wherever "the rights of society as a whole versus individual rights" are seriously discussed.

Pringle has created several books that highlight not only the damage being done to the earth but also the recuperative and preventative measures being taken on the planet's behalf. In *Living Treasure: Saving Earth's Threatened Biodiversity,* he discusses how millions of species are being destroyed, as well as how the damage can be stopped. Writing in the *Children's Literature Association Quarterly,* Mary Harris Veeder noted that because Pringle "can move beyond the notion of the rain forest as a pretty place, . . . his readers can begin to understand exactly why the destruction of the rain forest makes no sense."

In *The Environmental Movement: From Its Roots to the Challenges of a New Century,* Pringle "offers an accessible, wide-ranging overview of environmentalism in the U.S." at the end of the twentieth century, according to *Booklist* contributor Gillian Engberg. The author "deftly incorporates a wide range of topics from the establishment of national parks to the threat of global warming," noted Kathy Piehl in the *School Library Journal,* and he introduces some of the key figures in the environmental movement.

Come to the Ocean's Edge: A Nature Cycle Book depicts a day in the life of the creatures who inhabit coastal areas, including gulls, mole crabs, and bluefish. Reviewing *Come to the Ocean's Edge* in *School Library Journal*, Joy Fleishhacker praised the "poetic text" and "descriptive language" that fills the work. Focusing on the life surrounding more inland waters, Pringle follows a winged insect from its birth in a New York swamp to its death in a Florida pond in *A Dragon in the Sky: The Story of a Green Darner Dragonfly.* "Rarely do books of this nature delve so deeply into one species," observed a *Horn Book* contributor. *A Dragon in the Sky* is an "exemplary nature-study book—accurate, explicit, and satisfyingly complete," according to *School Library Journal* contributor Ellen Heath.

Dinosaurs! Strange and Wonderful was Pringle's first informational picture book for preschoolers and early primary graders. An introduction to the popular creatures that explains basic facts about them as well as recent discoveries by paleontologists, the book "lives up to its subtitle," according to Sally Erhard, who added in *Appraisal* that Pringle's text "is full of just the right amount of information about dinosaurs for the preschool level." Among the most highly praised of Pringle's books in this genre is *An Extraordinary Life: The Story of a Monarch Butterfly.* Recounting the life cycle of a female monarch—including her migration flight from New England to Mexico—the Orbis Pictus award-winning book was called "superb" and "well-researched" by a *Kirkus Reviews* contributor, who added that the volume "finds extraordinary science in the everyday life of a butterfly."

Like *Dinosaurs!,* the other volumes in Pringle's "Strange and Wonderful" series examine the behavior, anatomy, feeding habits, methods of communication, and other characteristics of several creatures. In *Booklist*, Hazel Rochman praised the "informal, fact-filled narrative" in *Crows! Strange and Wonderful,* while *School Library Journal* critic Patricia Manning dubbed *Sharks! Strange and Wonderful* an "eye-catching, edifying work." Reviewing *Whales! Strange and Wonderful* for *Booklist*, Carolyn Phelan stated that Pringle offers a "surprising amount of information in an interesting manner." Reviewing *Snakes! Strange and Wonderful,* Phelan called the volume an "excellent introduction to the subject," while in *Penguins! Strange and Wonderful,* "Pringle's succinct text provides an engaging overview," according to *Booklist* critic Kristen McKulski. Illustrated by Meryl Henderson, *Penguins!* is representative of the "Strange and Wonderful" series; it contains a wealth of scientific information, including information on penguins' habitats and reproduction. In a review for *School Library Journal,* Barbara Auerbach wrote that *Penguins!* "will satisfy report writers and browsers alike."

In another animal-centered title, *Strange Animals, New to Science,* Pringle provides descriptions of seventeen newly discovered species of animals, including a Vietnamese rhinoceros and a Tibetan horse. According to Phelan, *Strange Animals, New to Science* is an "informative book on an unusual topic that will open kids' minds." Discussing the same book in *School Library Journal*, Nancy Call remarked that in *Strange Animals, New to Science* "Pringle brings insight into the struggles and triumphs" of the scientists who search for new or extinct species.

A loyal and heroic canine is the focus of *Dog of Discovery: A Newfoundland's Adventures with Lewis and Clark,* which describes the explorations of the American West by Meriwether Lewis, William Clark, and the Corps of Discovery team between 1803 and 1806. Lewis and Clark were accompanied by a hunting and guide dog named Seaman, and the dog was mentioned frequently in the explorers' journals. *Dog of Discovery* "is a richly detailed and historically accurate account of the expedition," noted Janet Gillen in her review of the book for *School Library Journal.*

Pringle returns readers to the undiscovered Pacific Northwest in *American Slave, American Hero: York of the Lewis and Clark Expedition,* a book that should be placed "atop the teetering stack of Lewis and Clark titles," according to a *Kirkus Reviews* contributor. The book examines the life of Clark's personal slave, providing known facts about York's life and his role in the famous expedition that helped open U.S. expansion westward. "Pringle is meticulous about what is documented and what is 'probably' true," wrote Hazel Rochman in *Booklist. School Library Journal* contributor Pat Leach commented of *American Slave, American Hero* that the author "tells the story well."

In addition to his nonfiction titles, Pringle has created several picture books for younger children, among them *Jesse Builds a Road* and *Bear Hug. Jesse Builds a Road* was inspired by the author's son; it introduces readers to a small boy who, while playing with his trucks and bulldozers, imagines he is driving the real machines. Writing in *School Library Journal,* Judith Gloyer noted that Pringle's technique of "weaving in and out of the imagination and reality is engaging," and readers will be loath to be "pulled back to reality." The picture book *Naming the Cat* is also based on a family experience: while trying to name the stray cat that has entered their lives, several close calls make it apparent to family members that the cat should be dubbed Lucky. Writing in the *Bulletin of the Center for Children's Books,* Janice M. Del Negro called *Naming the Cat* a "light but engaging tale" that is "certain to have listeners bursting to tell the stories of how they named their own family pets."

Octopus Hug depicts two spirited youngsters, Jesse and Becky, who spend an evening playing with their father; Dad becomes a tree for climbing, then a mechanical horse; the book is a celebration of the delights of rough-housing. As a contributor to *Publishers Weekly* noted:

"The imaginative antics that tumble across these pages could constitute a manual for bored baby-sitters." In *Bear Hug,* a companion volume to *Octopus Hug,* Jesse and Becky go camping with their dad, and they spend the day hiking and exploring the woods, They worry about meeting a black bear. The creature does not appear, however, and at the end of their camping adventure the children's father gathers them in his arms for a huge bear hug. *School Library Journal* contributor Linda L. Walkins called *Bear Hug* "an atmospheric story that portrays the excitement of a family outing."

Pringle is also the author of two books relating his own life experiences: *Nature! Wild and Wonderful,* in which he presents interesting experiences from his life to readers in the early primary grades, and *One-Room School,* an informational picture book set in 1945, the final year of operation of Pringle's one-room schoolhouse. In a review of *Nature!,* Marlene Gawron described the work in *School Library Journal* as a memoir that "will entertain and inspire young readers," while Evelyn Butrico wrote of *One-Room School* in the same periodical that Pringle's "gentle story" also serves as a "good curriculum aid" for those studying "American history, the history of schools, or life in another era."

In an essay for *Celebrating Children's Books: Essays on Children's Literature in Honor of Zena Sutherland,* Pringle wrote: "The doing of science depends on such special human qualities as curiosity, passion, creativity, and veracity. Partly because of these characteristics, science has been called the greatest hope of the human race. Children's books have a vital role to play. They can make science and the universe more accessible to young people. They can stand for and appeal to the finest characteristics and highest aspirations of the human species."

Biographical and Critical Sources

BOOKS

Arbuthnot, May Hill, Dianne L. Monson, and Zena Sutherland, *Children and Books,* 6th edition, Scott, Foresman (Chicago, IL), 1981.

Children's Literature Review, Volume 4, Gale (Detroit, MI), 1984.

Hearne, Betsy, and Marilyn Kaye, editors, *Celebrating Children's Books: Essays on Children's Literature in Honor of Zena Sutherland,* Lothrop, Lee & Shepard (New York, NY), 1981.

St. James Guide to Children's Writers, 5th edition, St. James Press (Detroit, MI), 1999.

Silvey, Anita, editor, *Children's Books and Their Creators,* Houghton (Boston, MA), 1995.

PERIODICALS

Appraisal, winter, 1978, Gregory R. Belcher, review of *Death Is Natural,* pp. 39-40; winter, 1981, Gregory R. Belcher, review of *Natural Fire: Its Ecology in Forests,* p. 52; fall, 1980, David G. Hoag, review of *Nuclear Power: From Physics to Politics,* p. 54.

Booklist, October 1, 1981, Denise M. Wilms, review of *What Shall We Do with the Land? Choices for America,* p. 239; November 1, 1993, Chris Sherman, review of *Jackal Woman: Exploring the World of Jackals,* p. 520; January 15, 1995, Lauren Peterson, review of *Scorpion Man: Exploring the World of Scorpions,* p. 922; December 1, 1996, Susan Dove Lempke, review of *Smoking: A Risky Business,* p. 660; February 1, 2000, Carolyn Phelan, review of *Taste and Hearing,* p. 1021; March 15, 2000, Carolyn Phelan, review of *Bats! Strange and Wonderful,* p. 1373; April 1, 2000, Gillian Engberg, review of *The Environmental Movement: From Its Roots to the Challenges of a New Century,* p. 1459; April 1, 2001, Gillian Engberg, review of *Global Warming: The Threat of Earth's Changing Climate,* p. 1462; April 15, 2001, Carolyn Phelan, review of *Sharks! Strange and Wonderful,* p. 1548; July, 2002, Carolyn Phelan, review of *Strange Animals, New to Science,* p. 1841; November 1, 2002, Hazel Rochman, review of *Crows! Strange and Wonderful,* pp. 500-501; December 1, 2002, Carolyn Phelan, review of *The Dog of Discovery: A Newfoundland's Adventures with Lewis and Clark,* p. 666; March 15, 2003, Carolyn Phelan, review of *Whales! Strange and Wonderful,* p. 1326; February 1, 2004, Carolyn Phelan, review of *Come to the Ocean's Edge: A Nature Cycle Book,* p. 978; December 1, 2004, Carolyn Phelan, review of *Snakes! Strange and Wonderful,* p. 672; November 1, 2006, Hazel Rochman, review of *American Slave, American Hero: York of the Lewis and Clark Expedition,* p. 51; February 15, 2007, Kristen McKulski, review of *Penguins! Strange and Wonderful,* p. 75; March 1, 2008, Linda Perkins, review of *Imagine a Dragon,* p. 64.

Bulletin of the Center for Children's Books, November, 1993, review of *Jackal Woman,* p. 96; May, 1997, Susan S. Verner, review of *An Extraordinary Life: The Story of a Monarch Butterfly,* pp. 333-334; October, 1997, Janice M. Del Negro, review of *Naming the Cat,* p. 65; April, 1998, review of *One-Room School,* p. 293; September, 2002, review of *Strange Animals, New to Science,* p. 31.

Childhood Education, spring, 2003, Jovita Heist, review of *Crows!,* p. 177, and Kristen Weimer, review of *Dog of Discovery,* p. 179.

Children's Literature Association Quarterly, winter, 1994-95, Mary Harris Veeder, "Children's Books on Rain Forests: Beyond the Macaw Mystique," pp. 165-169.

Horn Book, December, 1979, Harry C. Stubbs, review of *Natural Fire,* p. 688; September-October, 1989, review of *Bearman: Exploring the World of Black Bears,* pp. 641-642; September-October, 1990, Margaret A. Bush, review of *Global Warming,* p. 620; November-December, 1995, Margaret A. Bush, review of *Coral Reefs: Earth's Undersea Treasures,* p. 757; May-June, 1997, Ellen Fader, review of *An Extraordinary Life,* p. 344; January-February, 1998, Margaret A. Bush, review of *Elephant Woman: Cynthia Moss Explores the World of Elephants,* p. 95; July, 2001, review of *A*

Dragon in the Sky: The Story of a Green Darner Dragonfly, p. 475; May-June, 2007, Danielle J. Ford, review of *Penguins!,* p. 303.

Kirkus Reviews, September 15, 1969, review of *The Only Earth We Have,* p. 1017; April 15, 1971, review of *One Earth, Many People: The Challenge of Human Population,* p. 448; October 1, 1976, review of *Listen to the Crows,* p. 1099; November 1, 1981, review of *What Shall We Do with the Land?,* p. 1350; February 15, 1997, review of *An Extraordinary Life,* p. 304; July 1, 1997, review of *Naming the Cat,* p. 1035; November 1, 1997, review of *Elephant Woman,* p. 1648; August 15, 2002, review of *Crows!,* p. 1232; March 1, 2003, review of *Whales!,* p. 396; August 15, 2004, review of *Snakes!,* p. 811; October 15, 2006, review of *American Slave, American Hero,* p. 1077; February 1, 2007, review of *Penguins!,* p. 128; January 1, 2008, review of *Imagine a Dragon.*

Language Arts, Richard M. Kerper, "Art Influencing Art," pp. 60-67.

Publishers Weekly, October 4, 1993, review of *Octopus Hug,* p. 79; January 2, 1995, review of *Dinosaurs! Strange and Wonderful,* p. 77; January 5, 1998, review of *One-Room School,* p. 67.

School Library Journal, December, 1981, Julia Rholes, review of *What Shall We Do with the Land?,* p. 72; April, 1989, Alan Newman, review of *Nuclear Energy,* pp. 124-125; February, 1990, Judith Gloyer, review of *Jesse Builds a Road,* p. 78; July, 1991, Karey Wehner, review of *Batman: Exploring the World of Bats,* p. 85; December, 1993, Susan Oliver, review of *Jackal Woman,* p. 130; January, 1994, Louise L. Sherman, review of *Octopus Hug,* p. 97; March, 1995, Karey Wehner, review of *Scorpion Man,* pp. 217-218; September, 1997, Marlene Gawron, review of *Nature! Wild and Wonderful,* p. 199; December, 1997, Susan Oliver, review of *Elephant Woman,* pp. 145-146; April, 1998, Evelyn Butrico, review of *One-Room School,* pp. 123-124; March, 2000, Peg Glisson, review of *Hearing,* p. 261; June, 2000, Kathy Piehl, review of *The Environmental Movement,* p. 170; June, 2000, Karey Wehner, review of *Bats!,* p. 135; June, 2001, Anne Chapman Callaghan, review of *Global Warming,* p. 178; August, 2001, Patricia Manning, review of *Sharks!,* and Ellen Heath, review of *A Dragon in the Sky,* both p. 172; August, 2002, Nancy Call, review of *Strange Animals, New to Science,* p. 216; September, 2002, Cynthia M. Sturgis, review of *Crows!,* p. 217, and Janet Gillen, review of *Dog of Discovery,* p. 231; February, 2003, Linda L. Walkins, review of *Bear Hug,* p. 120; April, 2003, Patricia Manning, review of *Whales!,* p. 154; August, 2003, Kathy Piehl, review of *The Environmental Movement,* pp. 116-117; October, 2003, Joy Fleishhacker, review of *Come to the Ocean's Edge,* p. 156; September, 2004, Karey Wehner, review of *Snakes!,* p. 191; January, 2007, Pat Leach, review of *American Slave, American Hero,* p. 119; April, 2007, Barbara Auerbach, review of *Penguins!,* p. 126.

Science Books, September, 1968, review of *Dinosaurs and Their World,* p. 114; September, 1971, review of *One Earth, Many People,* p. 144.

Scientific American, December, 1982, review of *Vampire Bats* and *Frost Hollows and Other Microclimates,* both p. 39; December, 1991, review of *Batman,* p. 150; December, 1993, review of *Jackal Woman,* p. 135.

Teaching K-8, April, 2003, Becky Rodia, "The Call of the Wild," pp. 42-44.

Voice of Youth Advocates, April, 1997, Mary B. McCarthy, review of *Smoking,* p. 60.

Wilson Library Bulletin, January, 1991, Frances Bradburn, review of *Global Warming,* p. 109; November, 1991, Frances Bradburn, review of *Living Treasure: Saving Earth's Threatened Biodiversity,* pp. 95-96.

ONLINE

Authors and Illustrators Who Visit Schools, http://www.authorsillustrators.com/ (September 19, 2004), "Laurence Pringle."

Boyds Mills Press Web site, http://www.boydsmillspress.com/ (April 15, 2008), "Laurence Pringle."

ChildrensLit.com, http://www.childrenslit.com/ (July 21, 2007), interview with Pringle.

Laurence Pringle Home Page, http://www.laurencepringle.com (July 21, 2007).

Autobiography Feature

Laurence Pringle

Pringle contributed the following autobiographical essay to *SATA*:

First sentences can be hard to write. I'll start by describing some old photographs, to ease my way into this, and to set the scene for you.

Two little boys outdoors, holding dead muskrats by their tails. A family posed outdoors, with a dead deer hanging in the background. Eleven kids in front of a white clapboard building; they're most of the student body, grades one through eight, of a one-room schoolhouse.

I was a country boy.

Although my father, Laurence Erin Pringle, was born in Brooklyn, New York, he was raised in farming country and in a culture that valued living off the land—not just by growing food but also by hunting, fishing, and trapping. About a year before I was born (on November 26, 1935) my family had moved from Rochester, New York, to a rural area south of there, in the town of Mendon. My father had an assembly-line job at Eastman Kodak. He stuck at it for twenty-one years to earn a small pension, but his heart was in the country.

My mother, whose maiden name was Marleah Rosehill, learned to cook fish and game. And my brother Gary (two years older) and I grew up in an environment that included bird dogs, vegetable gardens, chickens and sometimes hogs, goats, cows, and—in season—dead pheasants, rabbits, deer, and muskrats.

When I was four years old, we moved to a larger house on even-more-isolated Parrish Road in the town of Mendon. (How isolated? Well, if we heard a car coming along the gravel road, we usually moved to a window to look at it; only a few cars passed each day.) The house was in the heart of the Hopper Hills, a place where the last glacier had left a delightful landscape of big and little hills, and basins, some of which held ponds. We had little money but owned 120 acres of land, mostly pasture and woods. My father earned extra income by renting pasture, harvesting hay to sell to farmers, and selling muskrat pelts. Soon after moving to Parrish Road, I remember coming home from school to find the just-modernized indoor bathroom; the outhouse among the lilacs was retired.

School was a one-room schoolhouse, or actually one large classroom, a cloakroom for coats and boots, and a room where coal for the stove was stored. North privy for the boys, south privy for the girls. My brother and I walked nearly two miles one way to this school, where Miss Gladys Shackelton taught grades one through eight.

One-room schoolhouses were reputed to be good places to learn to work independently, and to concentrate with distractions around. I didn't learn these skills very well and for a time did poorly for another reason. Miss Shackelton suspected that something was wrong with my vision. An optometrist said no, but Miss Shackelton persisted and my parents sought a second opinion. I had a "lazy" eye and began wearing glasses, sometimes with a black patch over one lens to force the "lazy" eye to function normally. This strategy worked.

Laurence and brother, Gary, with muskrats, 1938 (Photo courtesy of Laurence Pringle.)

My memories of this little school include embarrassing, painful moments, of course. Once I threw a handful of gravel at some girls. Miss Shackelton took me to the cloakroom and closed the door. I knew what was coming, and vowed not to cry. She began whacking my outstretched palm with a ruler. Something got to me. Not the pain but perhaps the look on my teacher's face—was she about to cry? Or perhaps it was the enormity of what I had done; I had a big investment in being "good," and had stepped out of character. Anyway, I cried. Alas. I remember the crime and the punishment but not what prompted my gravel attack.

In the fall of 1942 or 1943 the students gathered scrap iron and steel, gradually making a huge pile of it in the school yard, as part of the recycling that was prompted by World War II. We also hiked along roads near school, collecting milkweed seedpods that were supposed to be used inside life preservers that would keep downed pilots afloat.

World War II is my favorite war. The good guys and the bad guys seemed so clearly defined. Of course I was just six years old when it began in 1941. When the news came over the radio (this was before television), my brother and I made silly rhymes of words like Manila and Pearl Harbor while my parents spoke in worried tones. My father was in the marine reserves, but Kodak began making bombsights and other devices for the military so he was not called to active service.

Overtime pay and night-shift work made life a bit more prosperous. News of the war's end came over the car radio one day in 1945. My father tooted the horn wildly in celebration. By then our family had grown, with the birth of Marleah Anne in 1943. Linda Mary was born in 1946.

The one-room schoolhouse closed in the spring of 1944. That fall my brother and I began to ride a bus to a central school in the nearest big village—Honeoye Falls, population about two thousand. I had to unlearn some of the math "skills" Miss Shackelton had taught me. I also suffered from culture shock, going from a fourth grade of four students at the one-room schoolhouse to a fifth grade of thirty-four at the central school. The latter had a library, however, that fed my hunger for books. As I edged toward adolescence, books became increasingly important. Whether fiction or nonfiction, they allowed me to escape from an often unhappy reality.

My father and mother had had rather wretched childhoods themselves, and were no doubt more giving than their parents had been. Nevertheless, they had difficulty expressing love openly. When I began raising kids of my own, my father offered this advice: "First teach them respect." I decided it would be pointless to tell him that respect isn't taught, it is earned, and that the predominant feeling he evoked in me as a child was fear. My brother Gary and I didn't get hit all that much, but the threat always seemed to be there in Dad's tyran-

Laurence and Gary with their father on the farm, about 1939 (Photo courtesy of Laurence Pringle.)

nical behavior. And I recall the time Gary and I cleaned out the chicken house and Dad praised the job we had done. This memory stands out, sadly, because praise was so seldom given.

Gary and I had some friendly times, but for the most part we were fierce competitors for attention and love. I fondly remember shooting him in the rear with a BB gun—a rare triumph in our ongoing power struggle.

I felt neglected, unappreciated, lonely. I found comfort outdoors, and spent many hours roaming the Hopper Hills, exploring its forests, springs, and ponds. I also found a different world in the home of my nearest playmate, Alison, who played the piano, and whose house was rich in books.

It was a book in my own home, however, that seemed to awaken a deepening interest in the natural world. One May day I noticed some little birds flitting among the half-formed leaves of an elm. Their colors were so striking; I wondered what they were. We didn't have many books, but did have one introductory guide to birds, and in it were the species of warblers I had seen. I was hooked. My curiosity became focused on birds, on identifying them, finding their nests, attracting them. Eventually, as a teenager, I built birdhouses that were occupied by eastern bluebirds and house wrens. For a time I subscribed to *Audubon* magazine, and that may have triggered my interest in wildlife photography.

One day, walking home alone from the school bus stop, I heard a noise down an embankment. I crept close and saw a colorful ring-necked pheasant a few feet away. "If only I had a camera," I thought. So I asked for one, and received a Kodak Baby Brownie Special for Christmas. (This was 1947; I was twelve years old.) Dream-

ing of great wildlife photos, I set out to take them that very cold and blustery day but saw only squirrel tracks in the snow. Great wildlife photos didn't come as easily as I had imagined, nor were many taken with a Baby Brownie or a Kodak Hawkeye, my second camera. I did the best I could, photographing bird nests and wild-flowers.

About that time I also received my first rifle, a routine step in that place and time, when virtually all boys (and a good many girls) were encouraged to become hunters. In the fall I set out alone with my .22 and shot a gray squirrel. I recall mixed feelings, including regret as I watched life fade from its eyes. The triumph was also diminished by facing the task of skinning and gutting the squirrel for the table. I cut myself badly and Gary was told to finish the job. Then and now, taking a life—even an insect's life—stirs in me a mixture of feelings, but hunting success earned respect in my environment and I was hungry to succeed at something.

Gary and I served a sort of apprenticeship, sometimes accompanying my father as he hunted, trapped, and fished. After my initial clumsiness with my first squirrel, I became adept at skinning and was paid ten cents apiece by Dad for each muskrat pelt I removed. I recall the excitement of being awakened well before dawn and tagging along on deer-hunting trips. Later, as a teenager and in my early twenties, I shot a few deer myself.

Is that the sound of stereotypes shattering? I am a naturalist, an environmentalist, so I must abhor hunting,

right? Wrong. I am not a hunter now, and haven't had a hunting license for at least two decades, but don't rule it forever out of my life. I own firearms but use them rarely, mostly for esthetic reasons, to maintain a starling-free zone around my home.

Since I live in a major metropolitan area, most of my friends are not only nonhunters but also oppose hunting. Their attitudes are understandable, given their experiences, or lack of experiences. Some seem to believe that their food comes from stores. All are content to let others kill the animals they eat, although they've been known to drop live lobsters into boiling water. In the midst of all these paradoxes, I give my greatest respect to those animal-rights advocates who refuse to eat meat and fish, and to those hunters who admit they do it for the meat and the challenge, not because they are helping wildlife populations. (This benefit may sometimes occur but that's not why people hunt.)

In early 1951, at age fifteen, I began to keep a nature journal. Some of my notes reveal a simplistic, black-and-white view of nature, of "good" and "bad" animals. Typical entry: "June 6, 1951—Shot a starling and 2 English sparrows." But I was already moving beyond the basic "what species is that?" level of interest to "why" and "how" questions about nature. That same summer, for example, I built a bird blind, took photos of wrens bringing food to their nest, and also wrote meticulous notes about differences in behavior of the male and female.

In August of 1951 my family moved from the Hopper Hills to the town of Rush, New York. I hated the move,

"At the one-room school" (Pringle is second from right), 1944 (Photo courtesy of Laurence Pringle.)

but Dad had become a real-estate agent and needed to be easily found by customers. At our new home I put hundreds of hours into habitat improvement on our five acres of land, actually digging a small pond with an earthen dam, building birdhouses and bird feeders, transplanting shrubs and wildflowers.

The great passions of my life were reading, nature, and baseball. Unfortunately, the lack of male playmates in the Hopper Hills and lack of sports interest by my parents had left me inept in most sports. Gym classes were often humiliating experiences. But the complexity and drama of baseball had captured me. Night after night I listened to radio play-by-play of the Rochester Redwings of the International League (then the Triple A farm team of the St. Louis Cardinals). Actually attending a game for the first time was a disappointing experience—the players looked so ordinary and human compared with their stature in my imagination.

Although living in Rush, I continued to attend high school in Honeoye Falls. I had one close friend, Ritchie Buckmann, and corresponded with a few other male teenagers who shared my interests. I had found their names and addresses in *Open Road* magazine, a periodical that then competed with *Boys' Life*. In the spring of 1952, I submitted a brief article to the "True Experiences and Camping Tips" page of *Open Road*. It described some crow behavior I had seen, and my interpretation of it. (Later I learned that my explanation was dead wrong.) That summer I received a letter of acceptance from the editor—"Deep-River Jim"—and a check for five dollars.

Though a published author at the age of sixteen, I felt no strong urge to become a writer. I was an ardent consumer of printed words, not a producer. Perhaps I showed a little writing talent; I was a favorite of Miss Jane McGuinness, English teacher during my junior and senior years. I am thankful for the encouragement she gave me, but being a favorite of any teacher is a mixed blessing. One day she mentioned to our class that I had a hobby she admired. I braced myself, knowing what was coming. I had asked for it, having written a term paper titled "Bird Watching—Strictly for the Birds?"

"Laurence is a bird-watcher," she said. True enough, but who wants a fact like that announced to fellow teenagers? Given the stereotypical notions about birdwatching, she might have just as well announced that I knitted doilies.

Miss McGuinness's class was, however, one of the few public places where I began to unleash my wit. Although I was not a total goody-goody—I had helped tip over an outhouse or two on Halloween, and cut classes on opening day of Redwing baseball—most of my classmates perceived me as a shy, unathletic bookworm who had little to do with girls. In their presence I usually felt ugly and incapable of conducting a conversation.

Father, Laurence Erin Pringle, about 1945 (Photo courtesy of Laurence Pringle.)

By the way, Miss McGuinness also erred in calling me Laurence. Then and now I prefer to be called Larry or just Laurence. In my family, however, it seemed there could be only one Larry—my father—so another name was found for me: Lornie. My dislike for this name grew until I declared to my parents, at about age sixteen, "Call me *anything* but Lornie. Call me. . ."—I groped for a name that seemed almost as offensive to me as Lornie, to demonstrate just how I hated it—"call me Zeke." They missed the point, and called me Zeke for several years.

In the late winter and early spring of my senior year I arose each day before dawn and rode a bike several miles to creeks and marshes, checking muskrat traps. By the end of March, trapping had earned me the extraordinary sum of $166.50, which enabled me to buy a better camera for wildlife photography. That spring also produced riches of anxiety, about the senior play, graduation, and life beyond.

In May the pressure built for me to be in the senior play, Cornelia Otis Skinner's *Our Hearts Were Young*

Mother, Marleah Rosehill Pringle, with Gary (left) and Laurence, 1938
(Photo courtesy of Laurence Pringle.)

and Gay. Not that I had shown any acting ability or interest; it was a matter of numbers. Our class of thirty-four included just nine males, and there was a small part for me, as a hotel window washer. I resisted and resisted, gave in, performed, survived.

Earlier, as a junior, my stage fright had been focused on the possibility that I would eventually be class salutatorian. That prospect—of giving a speech at graduation—so terrified me that I considered sabotaging my grades. This proved unnecessary, as Bob Francis moved to town, joined our class, and earned better grades.

The school at that time had only a part-time guidance worker. Knowing of my interest in nature, and that my hobbies included taxidermy (learned via a mail-order course), he urged me to apply for a museum job opening at the state capitol. But I wasn't yet eighteen, or otherwise well qualified, so that bubble of hope burst. Graduation approached, and I had only the vaguest idea of what I might do with the rest of my life. One thing seemed certain: I wasn't going to college.

I don't recall any discussions about college in my family, but it wasn't part of anyone's expectations. Neither of my parents had finished high school so they aimed to have their children accomplish that. The morning after graduation, some classmates and I applied for jobs at several Rochester industries. Nothing came of this for me, nor from my other efforts for a job, partly because I was not yet eighteen. In early July, however, I took the first job I found, working in the kitchen of the county hospital.

Aside from trapping, picking cucumbers or corn for farmers, or selling sweet corn or raspberries to passing motorists, this was my first job. I didn't enjoy mopping floors and washing pots and pans all that much, but other aspects of the work and the pay checks had some good effects. I bought and began driving Gary's 1949 Ford (he was with the U.S. Army in Korea). Perhaps most important, in the long run, was my friendship with a pair of young women who worked as dieticians at the hospital. Most of the kitchen workers were well along in years. These dieticians were recent college graduates, closer to me in age and interests. I began to learn how to talk with attractive young women, and when the time came, I received encouragement from them to move on, not just to another job, but to college.

I trace the germ of this idea to a September evening in 1953. While waiting at a service station in Honeoye Falls for tires to be put on my car, I met another customer, Raymond Francis, father of my former classmate. Bob was attending college; his father wondered why I wasn't. I don't recall the conversation, but know

Laurence with his mother, on the day of his First Communion (Photo courtesy of Laurence Pringle.)

that I was left with the notion that college might be attainable and affordable, and that Ray Francis (a school principal in Rochester) would help if I wanted to aim for it.

I did nothing about this for almost a year. I continued to work, study birds, hunt, trap, and follow the fortunes of the Rochester Redwings. I stopped being a sports spectator and spent countless hours batting and throwing with friends Ritchie and Willard Champlin. Ritchie and I "rodded around" in our cars, went to movies, and talked. Girls were a frequent subject, but we did little more than look at them.

In late June of 1954 I called Raymond Francis and went to his home: we talked for several hours about my college prospects. The following day he brought me a stack of college catalogs. In a few days my mother saw the catalogs when she cleaned my room, and this was the first inkling my family had of my interest.

My passion for the written word (if not writing) led me to consider studying journalism at Syracuse University. My passion for the outdoors led me to consider wildlife conservation at Cornell University. Economics tipped the scales; I applied to the then-tuition-free State College of Agriculture (now the College of Agriculture and Life Sciences) at Cornell. Finally apprised of my aim, my father willingly agreed to pay most of the costs.

I don't recommend applying on July 21 for September admission to college, but it worked for me. In September Dad and Mom delivered me to a freshman dorm at Cornell. In 1954 many freshmen males were housed for a few weeks in old wooden buildings while some new dormitories were completed. My immediate surroundings were plain, even shabby, and a reputed firetrap, but Cornell itself was magic. Perhaps it would have meant less if I had always expected to attend college. Many successes in my life—and a few disasters—have come as total surprises, as something I never dreamed of. Cornell was certainly an extraordinary surprise, one that has opened doors to so many adventures of mind, body, and spirit.

"Half of the students there will be dumber than you," a family friend had said in an attempt at encouragement. Maybe so, but I ranked 233 out of a class of 260 in my own college. I felt especially inferior to engineers, chemists, and mathematicians in other divisions at Cornell; my struggles with chemistry and physics twice put me on academic probation. Twice the probation scared me and my grades improved—not the last times that the outside world gave my own motivation an extra push.

Mark Twain said, "I have never let schooling interfere with my education," and I had a lot to learn outside of classrooms. The beginning of dating, for example, at age nineteen, when I was a fraternity pledge in the spring of my freshman year. I was having plenty of fun

"My father took this photo in the fall of 1947. Left to right: Gary, Linda in Mother's arms, 'Lornie,' and Marleah Anne in foreground"
(Photo courtesy of Laurence Pringle.)

with new friends, all of whom were independent, so I eventually withdrew from the fraternity. My dating activity went into temporary remission. That summer, whenever I was home from a camp naturalist job, the observation of young women by Ritchie and me reached new levels of intensity, particularly at a roller-skating rink on nearby Conesus Lake. Back at Cornell, I began corresponding with a high-school girl I met there. We didn't start going out until the spring of my sophomore year, when I experienced my first kiss at age twenty! Later that summer I suffered the pangs of first unrequited love for another young woman.

Part of my slow progress with the opposite sex can be credited to, or blamed on, Catholicism. The Pringles were Roman Catholics, and I took it seriously until my mid-thirties. One day after the local priest in Honeoye

"First nature journal, begun at age fifteen" (Photo courtesy of Laurence Pringle.)

Fails had spoken to the Catholics in my junior-high class, I overheard Billy Jenkins say to a companion, "You don't believe that stuff, do you?"

I was shocked. For some time after that I shunned Billy—the skeptic, the doubter, the first threat to my blind faith. In any event, I remained committed to Catholicism through high school, college, and beyond, and tried to honor church teaching, for example, that premarital sex and even conscious sexual fantasizing are mortal sins to be resisted at all cost. The costs were heavy, but a commitment to almost any goal or belief system brings rewards too.

At a gathering of Cornell Catholics in my junior year I met Patricia, a mathematics major and senior. The relationship—such a tame word—lasted about two years, and took me to levels of emotional ecstasy and agony I hadn't been anywhere near before. Being good 1950s Catholics, we saved most of the physical ecstasy for later, for our marriage, which didn't occur. My Catholic zeal reached a peak during this time; as a Cornell senior I often attended daily Mass.

At Cornell my interest in nature and the outdoors was nurtured not only by many courses but also by weekend and vacation adventures with friends. They included Ritchie Buckmann, who entered Cornell to study engineering the year after I began; L. David Mech, a fellow wildlife major; and Paul "Jorgie" Christensen, an engineering student and Dave's roommate. I experienced wilderness for the first time, as we spent winter vacations in New York's Adirondack Mountains, following on snowshoes the trails of fishers (fox-sized members of the weasel family) and other wildlife.

For two summers I was a counselor and hike leader at a conservation camp in the heart of the Adirondacks. I discovered a lake, and a special place on the shore of that lake, where I and various loved ones have camped for more than three decades. The ashes from my cremation may be scattered there (a tiny chemical antidote to the harm caused by acid rain).

At Cornell I searched for a way to excel at something, to somehow feel recognized and accepted by people. I entered a nature photograph in a campus photo contest and won a ribbon; I tried out for a position on the campus radio station but failed to get it. I took two courses on writing nonfiction for magazines and, not long after graduation, had an article published in New York State's environmental magazine, *The Conservationist.* Having a byline with an article and credit lines with photographs felt so good; I began to aim for national outdoor magazines.

In the spring of my senior year the job market for wildlife biologists was poor, and I was still vulnerable to being drafted into the armed forces. Without much hope, considering my grades, I applied to some graduate schools. Another surprise—in the autumn of 1958 I began a two-year master's degree study of the New England cottontail at the University of Massachusetts in Amherst. Although I was given financial support for rabbit research, I was more deeply interested in mammalian predators, and began an additional project on the bobcats of Prescott Peninsula, which lies within the boundaries of the vast Quabbin Reservoir lands. While trapping, tagging, and releasing bobcats, I also captured several coyotes—among the first to be caught and identified in Massachusetts.

My research on cottontails earned me a master's degree, but evidence was building that I wasn't meant to be a wildlife biologist. Nevertheless, college life held such appeal that I aimed for a doctorate in forest zoology at the State University College of Forestry at Syracuse University. My research subject was to be the fisher, my study area the heart of the Adirondack Mountains.

Despite this alluring prospect I left Massachusetts reluctantly, for I was also leaving Ruth. She was Jewish, I was Catholic, and our romance had a bittersweet quality based on a mutual assumption of "Alas, we can never get married." Our love endured for another year, but eventually that assumption and the miles between us took their toll.

At Syracuse I encountered the twin challenges of German and statistics, and fell behind in these requirements for a Ph.D. The long grind to a doctorate looked grim. More important, a few of my nonfiction articles and photos had been published. Syracuse's School of Journalism seemed to beckon. I had reached a turning point and made a choice I have never regretted—by early 1961 I had given up on the doctorate and was enrolled in journalism.

Hepatitis soon knocked me off the path to a writing career. By mid-March I was recuperating at home (then in Honeoye Falls) with my parents and sisters, and was advised by a doctor not to return to classes. I wrote articles and submitted them to magazines; nearly all came back. I obtained a union card and worked on some construction jobs, but earned far less than needed to return to journalism classes in the fall. Late that summer I learned that nearby Lima Central School needed a science teacher. Within a few days I was the entire science department of this small school, teaching physics, biology, general science, plus a half-year of science for the seventh and eighth grades. Despite all the preparation needed for these classes, and my continuing difficulties with physics, I liked teaching and was tempted to return to Lima.

In the summer of 1961, however, I had met Judith Malanowicz, a recent college graduate and school librarian. Two months after we met I proposed marriage: we were married in June of 1962. That summer I hedged my career bets—taking some education courses at Syracuse in case I returned to teaching, but also planning on further journalism courses in the fall and taking a two-weeks summer "article marketing" course taught by George Bush, a longtime editor with *Better Homes and Gardens.*

"At age sixteen, instead of trying to attract girls, I dug a pond to attract wildlife" (Photo courtesy of Laurence Pringle.)

Within a few days, George decided that most of his students, myself included, needed to learn how to write clear English sentences rather than how to find markets for articles. He changed the emphasis of the daily classes and conferences, and a bit of his writing wisdom rubbed off on me. Each of three articles I began in his class was published.

In early 1963 my writing was put to a test in an article assigned by Roy Gallant, editor of a new children's science magazine. This was no ordinary article assignment. I was job hunting. Judy and I expected a baby, and I had traveled to New York City in hopes of finding work with an outdoor or nature magazine. I found only one opportunity, with the fetal *Nature & Science,* which was to be published at the American Museum of Natural History. If I had found no openings, I might have given up on the dream of working for a magazine and become a science teacher. Or, if I had found a job with a magazine for adults, I might never have written for young readers. As it turned out, my four manuscript pages pleased Roy Gallant, and I became part of a small team of editors who launched *Nature & Science* in the fall of 1963.

The magazine was a critical success among educators, especially those teachers who used it in classrooms. But the science phobia of so many teachers in the middle grades kept *Nature & Science* from reaching the circulation needed for financial success. The magazine died in the spring of 1970, but its seven years of life were a time of extraordinary growth and change for me, both in and out of the office.

Nearly everyone on the *Nature & Science* staff shared a variety of tasks, and all editors, regardless of rank, edited the writing of the others. Roy Gallant returned to his career as a freelance science writer but continued as a consulting editor; I learned a great deal from him and his successor, Franklyn Lauden. Roy was already a well-known author of children's books about astronomy and the earth sciences, and it was he who suggested that I write a book for children. Roy's recommendation to a book editor brought me a contract that provided for an advance on royalties once I submitted an acceptable manuscript.

I had some reason for confidence, since I had been writing articles not just for *Nature & Science* but for other magazines as well. Also, the editor and I had agreed on a subject—dinosaurs—that intrigued me. There were and are many dinosaur books in print, but dinosaurs are far from a dead subject; new fossil discoveries and new ideas about how dinosaurs lived continue to fuel our fascination with them.

The dinosaur book was the longest piece I had attempted and was also homework at a time when there were few free hours. Judy and I were caring for Heidi Elizabeth (born in 1963) and Jeffrey Laurence (born in 1964). In addition, we were active in a church group

and I volunteered many hours to the management of a local nature center. The dinosaur book was set aside many times, and I missed its delivery deadline. With great relief I finally sent the manuscript of about 6,500 words to the publisher in mid-March, 1966. Even if it was published, I felt, the writing had been such a prolonged ordeal that I wouldn't try another book.

The mail of April Fools' Day brought an alarmingly large package: my manuscript and a letter of rejection that did not even suggest that I revise it and try again. Without my experience at *Nature & Science* I might have accepted the editor's judgment and given up. Instead, I set the manuscript aside for awhile, then read it as objectively as possible and decided to begin sending it to other publishers, particularly those that had no recently published juvenile dinosaur books.

This was a slow process, especially when editors held the manuscript for as long as two months before returning it. A year passed, then Margaret McElderry, of Harcourt, Brace & World, accepted the manuscript, which became the book *Dinosaurs and Their World*. Published in 1968, this book in both hardcover and paperback editions sold more than 70,000 copies and stayed in print long after some of my later titles had expired.

My second son, Sean Edmund, was born in the spring of 1966. Judy and I bought a house in Englewood, New Jersey. With three children under four years of age, we had little time for one another. My career as a writer and photographer was flourishing, but Judy and I were growing apart.

When Judy and I were divorced, I learned that a New Jersey man in the late l960s could not divorce a woman without also divorcing his children. During this time of crisis I belatedly decided that I needed help to sort out my confused feelings, and began to talk with psychiatrist Charles Oestreicher. You might say I was a slow learner, however, because I remarried and was divorced again within three years. Hindsight now shows that either of these marriages might have been saved, had both partners been committed to change and aided by professional counseling. Thus, the sum of my advice to troubled mates: get good help, give it a good try.

In the spring of 1973 I bought a house in Rockland County, New York, within a few miles of my children. The house had been advertised as an artist's or writer's retreat, and it was indeed a special woodsy place on a private lane. I retreated there to lick my wounds, and to temporarily avoid any serious involvement with a woman. It seemed like a good time to learn more about myself, to meet new people, and also to compensate for experiences missed earlier (this might be called sowing wild oats retroactively). I learned to cook, and focused on being a father to my children and a freelance writer.

At *Nature & Science* I had hoped to arrange a reduced work week in order to nurture my book-writing career. Demise of the magazine in 1970 gave me a choice: seek another editing job or try to survive as a freelancer. With several book contracts in hand or in the offing, I did not hesitate to choose the latter. Except for occasional income from part-time college teaching, I thereafter earned a living—or at least a surviving—from writing and photography.

I'm sometimes asked whether I have a favorite book. I do like some better than others, but each brings different experiences, challenges, satisfactions. One reward of any book or article is being paid to pursue my curiosity, as I explore a subject that interests me—mostly by reading, but also by direct contact with scientists and other experts.

I still record my own nature observations in a journal, but seldom include them in my writing; invariably there are individuals who have spent decades studying a subject, such as Nicholas Thompson of Clark University and his research on crow communication (caws and effect), which became the basis for my book *Listen to the Crows*. Most scientists are eager to have their work explained clearly and accurately to the public, and generously share their knowledge. One biologist claimed that my description of his work had a remarkable effect. I had written about Peter Moyle's intriguing study of minnows in *Animals and Their Niches* and in *Audubon* magazine. According to Moyle, his wife claimed that she had learned more about his work from that book than from living with him for many years.

"The people in Rush, New York, joked about the local mosquitoes, so I made a giant mosquito model and photographed Gary attacking it"
(Photo courtesy of Laurence Pringle.)

Graduation photo, Honeoye Falls Central School, 1953 (Photo courtesy of Laurence Pringle.)

Minnows are one of several subjects I've written about that can be traced back to early experiences in my life. In the Hopper Hills, Gary and I sometimes walked a mile to fish in a creek (or crick in the rural vernacular). We had worms for bait, and our basic tackle was a willow stick about five feet long, a few feet of string, and a bent pin. Sometimes we made bobbers from the spherical galls that form on goldenrod stems.

It was fun, fishing along the spearmint-lined banks of a creek that meandered through pastures. We usually released our catch. Decades later I learned that the fish were creek chubs and blacknose dace. Thus, research for a book in the 1970s shed light on experiences of the 1940s (this might be called understanding nature observations retroactively). My rural roots also led to writing *Wild Foods*. In its acknowledgment, I speculated about the origin of the book: "Perhaps it began in the 1940s in upstate New York where I picked black raspberries, some for pies my mother baked, some for sale for precious pocket money. My family also dined on rabbit potpie, venison, muskrat legs, and other game. The idea was planted: nature offers delicious wild foods."

Adventures on the trails of fishers in the Adirondacks became the basis for *Follow a Fisher*, although the book

was based more on the research of genuine wildlife biologists than on my experiences during college vacations. My fellow fisher tracker, Dave Mech, began his lifelong study of wolves after graduation from Cornell in 1958. I accompanied him in the field during visits to Isle Royale National Park, where he conducted his graduate studies, and later to northern Minnesota. He was my subject in *Nature & Science* articles and eventually in *Wolfman,* my fortieth book.

The economics of writing nonfiction for children and young adults do not allow for much research travel. Fortunately, firsthand experience with a subject is not a prerequisite for a wise, accurate book. In the fall of 1976, for example, I wrote a book about deserts of the Southwest, *The Gentle Desert,* without having visited a desert. I felt I could trust the writings of Edward Abbey, David Costello, and others as references to accurately describe this special environment. The following spring, however, I asked for early payment of some royalties and visited the Southwest for the first time. Taking photos for the book, I roamed deserts in California and Arizona for a week. I fell in love with the desert, and, incidentally, found no reason to change a word of text I had created from library research.

Early in my book-writing career I was an avid collector of books. I envisioned a time when I would rely mostly

Graduation photo, Cornell University, 1958 (Photo courtesy of Laurence Pringle.)

Heidi, Jeffrey, and Sean Pringle in Englewood, New Jersey, 1968 (Photo courtesy of Laurence Pringle.)

on my own bookshelves for information about almost any subject. Backed by an extraordinary personal library, I could live in the wilderness and still write nonfiction. As the years passed, however I found that I was out of shelf space and many books were in cardboard boxes in the attic, a situation that made information retrieval difficult. More important, I noticed that many books were out of date.

I came to rely more and more on libraries for contemporary knowledge. Most of my own once-vast library is gone, given away or sold at yard sales. Much as I love books, I seldom buy one for research. And when I travel and begin to fantasize about moving and living in, say, Tucson or Martha's Vineyard, I soon begin to wonder about the quality of the libraries—a vital factor in my work.

My second visit to the Southwest was especially sweet, as I traveled by train in March of 1978 with Jeffrey and Sean (then ages fourteen and twelve, respectively) to attend the awards banquet of the National Wildlife Federation in Phoenix. I received a Special Conservation Award for being, in the federation's words, "the nation's leading writer of books on biological and environmental issues for young people." The boys and I then spent several days exploring the Sonoran Desert before flying home.

Sometimes reviewers point out qualities in my books that I did not consciously put there, for example, saying that I "deduce principles, examine meanings, raise questions, and encourage observation." My approach to writing a book is like that of a teacher planning to present a subject to students—not "how many facts, dates, and definitions can I jam into their heads" but "what are the key ideas and how can I spark some enthusiasm about them."

As my knowledge of ecology has grown, so has my appreciation of diversity, complexity, and the interdependence of living and nonliving things. My books tend to encourage readers to feel a kinship with other living things, and a sense of membership in the earth ecosystem. I have also become an advocate of scientific thinking, or perhaps I should say just clear thinking.

Challenging authority and accepted truths is a basic part of the scientific process. It has influenced my choice of book subjects, as I have questioned popular but incorrect notions about forest fires, dinosaurs, vampire bats, wolves, coyotes, and killer bees. These books give readers the truth, to the extent we know it, and also demonstrate that the explorations of science aim at a better understanding of the world. As long as we keep exploring, that understanding can change.

I also encourage a skeptical attitude toward the fruits of technology and various vested interests that come into

play with such issues as nuclear power, environmental health, biocides, or acid rain. My books on such subjects are never neutral; sometimes I am tempted to lean heavily toward one side of an issue. The temptation to do so is strong when one side mainly represents short-term economic interests and the other mainly represents concern about public health, maintenance of natural diversity and beauty, and the quality of life for both present and future generations. Temptation is also fueled by the knowledge that students are often subjected to the biased publications and films (free to schools), and advertisements of powerful economic interests, and are ill-prepared to detect the distortions and omissions of these materials.

My books about controversial issues are not balanced—in the sense of equal space and weight applied to all sides—but are balanced by presenting arguments from the opposing interests, and a reading list that includes a diversity of views for those who want to explore the subject further.

It is said of writers, especially fiction writers, that any experience can become material for a story, novel, or other piece of writing. Nonfiction writers seldom infuriate relatives and others who recognize themselves in print, but we do find that any interest or hobby can eventually lead to articles or books. I expect this to occur as a result of an interest of mine that began in the spring of 1976.

That early May I read an article about morel mushrooms, considered by many to be the most delicious of all wild fungi. I knew morels and had eaten them—including some that Gary found growing under an elm as he mowed his lawn in Honeoye Falls—but had never tried to find them in the area northwest of New York City where I had settled. The article mentioned some habitat in which morels grow each spring, and I decided to hunt for them.

A friend and I hiked through shoulder-high poison ivy for an hour or two, searching the ground without success. Then Ruth asked, hesitantly, "Is that one?," pointing to a place I had just passed. It was! I found a few more that spring; by the following spring I was taking detailed notes, recording morel sites on a topographic map, and pursuing morels with the passion I had devoted as a teenager to bird-watching and baseball. (Fortunately, wild morels grow for only a few weeks a year, so I can turn to other matters in the long off-season.)

I have since found black morels growing on my own acre of woods, and with friends have collected as many as twenty pounds of morels in one day. For a few years a friend and I sold fresh morels to restaurants in New York City. The prospect of receiving up to twenty-five dollars a pound stimulated a successful search for even more morel sites, but I didn't like the other side effects of putting a price tag on each morel found so I stopped

selling. Morel hunting in my area can also be a disheartening experience, as each year developers destroy bosky havens where morels once flourished.

My research on morels included participation in the 1984 National Mushroom Hunting Championship at Boyne City, Michigan. My journal of morel observations and collection of morel photographs grows, so it is only a matter of time before this hobby yields a book. It will most likely be a cookbook, with a foreword about finding morels written by me, and recipes by former chef, fellow morel hunter, and longtime friend, Lois Murphy.

If I someday write about groundhogs and Groundhog Day, it will be partly because of my roots in the rural Hopper Hills but mostly because of my first divorce. As a country boy I was probably more conscious of this holiday than many city dwellers. Later, with a divorce in progress in early 1971, I was looking for ways to show my children that I still loved them. That year they received gifts from the Great Groundhog, who leaves presents in the basement and marks the package with a paw print.

They no longer search the cellar on February 2, but they and other loved ones usually receive some form of groundhog greetings from me. During my "single again"

"In an Easter snowfall, 1970. Left to right: Jeffrey, 'Bunny,' Sean, and me" (Photo courtesy of Laurence Pringle.)

"On a Maine vacation in 1978, with Jeffrey, Heidi, and Sean" (Photo courtesy of Laurence Pringle.)

stage Groundhog Day became the focus of an annual party. In southeastern New York the day has special meaning, not because of nonsense about shadows and weather prediction, but because bird songs and the lengthening days of early February show that spring is on the way—reason enough for a party.

My book *Animals at Play* was inspired in part by a special cat. Until my late thirties I had little experience with cats. My parents had had dogs as pets. Furthermore, as a result of my early simplistic view of nature, cats were "bad" because they sometimes killed birds. I stopped short of shooting cats but encouraged dogs to chase them.

Alison, my penultimate wife, was a cat lover, and so was I once I had shared a home with such memorable individuals as Mr. Big, Purr-vert, Shadow, and especially the Burmese Female (pronounced FEM-al-ee). Cat behavior fascinates me and may someday be the basis for a book, but my own behavior with cats is a disturbing reminder of the difficulty I and others have with emotional intimacy. My parents found it much easier to lavish affection on dogs than on their children, and I express love for a special cat more freely than love for my wife.

It is unlikely that I will write about my interest in baseball, the New York Mets, and volleyball. I still don't play the last all that well, but have developed a wicked

serve—a striking contrast to my embarrassing efforts in high-school gym classes (this might be called experiencing sports success retroactively). Surf fishing, however, will almost certainly lead to something in print, although John Hersey, in *Blues,* has written the definitive book about my favorite prey.

Aside from catching minnows as a boy and a bit of trout and perch fishing through the years, I reached the age of forty-five with little fishing experience. Then Susan Klein and I rented a place in Montauk, at the eastern end of Long Island, for August of 1980. We overindulged in guests but on Labor Day weekend found time for a bit of fishing, catching snappers (young bluefish) at an old fishing haunt of hers. Until then I had enjoyed ocean beaches for summer swimming, sunning, and sand sculpture, but that weekend I found a way to feel connected to the ocean's life and tides in all seasons (but especially in the autumn).

Susan Klein and I met in the late summer of 1976, and became deeply involved the following spring. She was thirty-three and childless when we became involved, and she wanted children. I was forty-two, had college expenses for three children looming ahead, and did not want further children.

Even without this conflict the relationship was stormy; twice it seemed to be over. Then Susan and I began liv-

Jeffrey, Sean, and Heidi, 1980 (Photo courtesy of Laurence Pringle.)

ing together, intermingling silverware and cats. Finally, on March 13, 1983, we were married.

About that time I heard a joke having to do with a priest, minister, and rabbi discussing when human life begins. The rabbi gives the punch line: that life begins when all of your children are out of college and the dog dies. Flying in the face of this wisdom, I helped start a new family. My third son, Jesse Erin Pringle, was born on December 31, 1983, and my second daughter, Rebecca Anne Pringle, on December 31, 1985.

People ask what it's like to become a father again at age forty-eight and fifty. It seems more exhausting; I do not have the energy to roughhouse as much as I did when Heidi, Jeffrey, and Sean were young. It also differs from my earlier experience because I was then a magazine editor and commuter, primarily a weekend father, and now my freelance life makes me more available to my children every day. Unfortunately, in order to get work done, I often have to shut myself off from Jesse and Becky. More than ever before, I write between the hours of 10 p.m. and 4 a.m.

People say that having children rather late in life helps keep one young. Adding "and broke," I agree. I take pleasure in correcting the people who assume I am Jesse and Becky's grandfather, and enjoyed winning a prize at my thirty-fourth high-school reunion for having the youngest children. The best prize of all is, of course, being witness to and an influence on the growth of two extraordinary children.

In the summer of 1987, while a faculty member of the *Highlights for Children* Writers Workshop at the Chautauqua Institution, I wondered aloud why some people choose to write for children. I speculated:

> It is easier, less demanding than writing for adults? Or perhaps we all have some psychological quirk, a character flaw that leads us to aim our efforts at kids rather than adults.
>
> Or perhaps in each of our personal histories there are experiences that have left us with a special regard for children. Perhaps we believe, more strongly than most, that what happens to kids is awfully important. Perhaps we feel that it is too late to influence most adults, but that everything that touches a child's life, including magazine articles and books, can make a difference in the future of that child, and in the future of the world.

Since nonfiction writers get much less mail from readers than do authors of fiction, I have little direct evidence that I have influenced the lives of children. I do know that focusing on children—thinking about their lives, and of course being a father of five children—has influenced me. For one thing, it has helped keep me a hopeful person.

I feel that some of the gloomy fiction written for teenagers is unconscionable. My writings deal with some tough issues and don't minimize the difficulties of ac-

"Thoroughly hooked on surf fishing, 1982" (Photo courtesy of Laurence Pringle.)

complishing social and political change, but usually conclude with the thought that people have the ability and power to effect change.

Beginning in the 1960s with Heidi, Jeffrey, or Sean on my lap, I've read many fiction picture books to young children. In the early 1970s I tried to write a story or two. One dealt with the efforts of a child to stop a parent from smoking. I thought it was subtle; editors found it didactic. (At the time, I didn't know the word. A dictionary told me it means "preachy.") I gave up. Recently, however, a child inspired me to write a story called *Jesse Builds a Road*. I had hoped it would be my fiftieth published book, but that honor went to *Home: How Animals Find Comfort and Safety* while the picture-book manuscript, like my very first nonfiction book, took a while to find its publishing home at Macmillan.

As I write this, the manuscript has just been accepted. I don't yet know who will illustrate it or how it will look. This is one of the frustrations of writing an autobiography in my fifty-second year. As I am fond of saying about many human matters, all the evidence isn't in. I want to know how things turn out. (I long ago gave up the prospect of an afterlife, but jokingly say I will sign up for any religion that guarantees me everlasting delivery of the *New York Times*.)

Take *Jesse Builds a Road* for example. It was inspired, of course, by my son. History may record that Jesse

and Becky, along with the memories they evoke of my other children, influenced me to venture into a whole new area of writing for children. All the evidence isn't in.

Pringle contributed the following update to *SATA* in 2008:

Twenty Years Later

Publication of *Jesse Builds a Road* did not launch a whole new career of picture-book fiction. This field is extremely competitive; more basically, my strengths in writing nonfiction don't help that much in creating wonderful stories. With one exception—*Bear Hug*—my published fiction picture books were rejected several times before I revised them into acceptable form. Even as I write this, two of such stories are at publishing houses. I hope they will be added to my short list of fiction titles.

Though few in number, my fiction titles are among my favorites because all were inspired by experiences with my children. Jesse's fascination with bulldozers, front-end loaders, and other machines led to *Jesse Builds a Road*. The joys of roughhousing, and camping, with all of my children inspired *Octopus Hug* and *Bear Hug*. Also, Jesse and Rebecca, along with my wife Susan and I, once struggled to pick a name for a kitten; this led to *Naming the Cat*. These books are also favorites

Wife, Susan Klein (Photo courtesy of Laurence Pringle.)

because they were more of a writing challenge, and thus more of an accomplishment.

Twenty years of parenting our "little ones" feels like a blur of meeting school buses, attending school events, dance recitals, countless soccer, basketball, and volleyball games—and more recently, giving driving lessons, touring colleges, and hauling many loads up to college dorm rooms or apartments. There was the adventure of everyday life, and farther away—vacations in the U.S., Mexico, Europe, and each August some special times on Martha's Vineyard.

For twenty years (1985-2004), my friend Kent Brown, Jr., invited me to serve on the faculty of the *Highlights for Children* Writers Workshop at Chautauqua. I worked, but each of these experiences—during the third week of each July—was also a delightful family vacation. Jesse first attended in a stroller; Rebecca in utero. In some ways these children grew up at the Chautauqua Institution, where they could roam freely and safely. For young or old, the Chautauqua experience is hard to describe. Historian David McCullough did it best: "There is no place like it. . . . it is at once, a summer encampment and a small town, a college campus, an arts colony, a music festival, a religious retreat and the village square."

Each year about a hundred people signed up to learn more about writing for children. Some of these "conferees," as they are called, have gone on to distinguished careers in children's literature. One notable example: Sharon Creech. I tended to meet and work with those writers with nonfiction leanings; this led to enduring friendships with authors Susan Quinlan, Sneed Collard III, and Gail Karwoski. At Chautauqua I also met scores of other authors, and editors, on the faculty. Writing is a very solitary activity, so most authors relish opportunities to talk with their peers. In 1989 I joined a group of authors who met irregularly on Long Island, New York, where most of them lived. This is not a typical writers group, in which members critique each other's work. It is more of a "support" group; we share good and bad news about work, editors, agents, and other aspects of a writer's life. On one memorable evening we spoke about people in our pasts who had played key roles along our paths toward being successful authors. We all had some of these mentors, but that evening I also learned of "anti-mentors"—people who had been obstacles to success. One group member, Pam Conrad, had two "anti-mentors," including a college professor who told her she had no writing talent. She wrote more than twenty highly praised novels and picture books. We were robbed of many more when her life was cut tragically short by cancer in 1996.

In my writers group, author Johanna Hurwitz coined a phrase: "pulling a Pringle." I feel a bit embarrassed by the term, since I'm sure many authors have "pulled" the same trick: legally selling the same book manuscript multiple times. Here is the story of how I "pulled a Pringle":

With Susan and children, 1987: daughter Rebecca, age two, and son Jesse, age four (Photo courtesy of Laurence Pringle.)

In November of 1988 I proposed the idea of a nonfiction book about dragons to a publisher. In January of 1989 I received a contract, and half of the advance money. About a year later, my manuscript was accepted (the editor called it "delightful") and I was paid the balance of the advance. Months later I was told that an illustrator had been found. However, in September, 1992, there was an editorial shakeup. The new editors decided to not publish my book. DISASTER! Well, maybe not, because I did not have to return the advance money, and I was free to sell the manuscript elsewhere.

I submitted the manuscript, which I called *Imagine a Dragon,* to a succession of publishers. By September of 1993 it had been rejected eight times. Then, in November, it was accepted and I was paid a full advance. However, just a few months later, the publishing house was bought by another publisher, which had its own dragon book in the works. Mine would not be published! ANOTHER DISASTER! Well, maybe not, because I did not have to return the advance money, and I was free to sell the manuscript elsewhere.

My so-far-unpublished book received another rejection in the fall of 1995. Then, in autumn, 1996, or spring, 1997, it was accepted for the third time. I received another advance. (Total from three publishers: $19,000.) At the third and last publisher, the manuscript sat idle

for a long time, partly because I was too busy with other book projects to urge action. Then I did, worked with an editor, and completed the final editing in September of 2003. Finally, in early 2005, Korean artist Eujin Kim Neilan was contracted to illustrate the book. *Imagine a Dragon,* my 106th title, was published in March of 2008. For writers, the moral of this saga is: if a piece of writing is good enough to be accepted once, but not published, there's a chance it will be accepted again and published—eventually.

More details of this book's long history are on my home page, www.laurencepringle.com, under the title *How to Get a Children's Book Published.* My home page was launched in 2004. It lacks the "bells and whistles" of many author sites, but has one strength: the story behind the creation of certain books. Readers often report that they enjoy learning about these background stories. Indeed, one pleasure of my work is that each project is a different experience—including meeting and working with different people.

My nonfiction relies on the wisdom and cooperation of many kinds of experts. Beginning with *Wolfman: Exploring the World of Wolves* (1983) and concluding with *Elephant Woman: Cynthia Moss Explores the World of Elephants* (1997), I wrote seven books about wildlife biologists and the animals they study. Each of

the scientists had extraordinary photographs to illustrate their books. In some cases I went "into the field" with them during the interview process. In each book I wrote about their childhoods, and traced the path—sometimes direct, sometimes roundabout—to their unusual careers.

More than a dozen scientists from all over North America helped with my eighty-eighth title, *An Extraordinary Life: The Story of a Monarch Butterfly.* The roots of this book lie in a 1993 talk with editor Harold Underdown. We both admired the books of Holling Clancy Holling, such as *Minn of the Mississippi,* which is about a snapping turtle, but much more. It is rich with connections—to other life, history, geography, ecology. We wanted to create a shorter, simpler book with some of the same richness. I considered several creatures; monarch butterflies, with their amazing migration, seemed the most intriguing to me.

I chose to tell the story of one individual monarch. The book is well-researched nonfiction, yet has a character that readers care about as they follow her life story. (Some readers have told of crying at the book's end— definitely not a common experience with nonfiction!) Some of the information woven into the story, or revealed in sidebars, was so fresh that it had not yet been published in scientific journals. While I didn't actually need to visit a monarch winter colony in order to write the book, I leaped at the chance to go to Mexico with artist Bob Marstall. This experience enabled me to add a special detail: that the fluttering of countless butterfly wings makes noise like a breeze through the forest.

Published in 1997, *An Extraordinary Life* was awarded the Orbis Pictus Award as the best children's nonfiction book published that year by the National Council of Teachers of English. Every autumn since, I continue to be deeply touched by monarchs. Wherever I am in the fall—looking out my office window at butterfly bushes, driving a car, fishing on an Atlantic Ocean beach—my heart leaps when I see monarchs doing their best to reach faraway Mexico.

Research of a very different kind helped in the creation of *One-Room School,* a memoir of the last year that my first school existed. Of course I had my own vivid memories of school life, but I learned more details by interviewing others who had attended the school, especially my brother and my classmates. For example, here are some *One-Room School* details about teacher Miss Shackelton: "She often wore dresses made with a flower pattern, and dusty rose nail polish. When she came close to my desk, I could smell her perfume. A girl said

Larry, Rebecca, Jesse, and Susan at Jesse's 2006 graduation from Penn State University (Photo courtesy of Laurence Pringle.)

"A framed picture of miniature jackets of my one hundred published books, a surprise gift from Susan at the 2003 party" (Photo courtesy of Laurence Pringle.)

it was called Tabu." As a guy, I did not pay much attention to nail polish or perfume. Fortunately those details came from "a girl"—classmate Lucille (Palmer) Pattison. Lucille's brother, Byron, had some desks from our long-closed school in his barn. He brought them outdoors so I could photograph them. These photos helped the book's artist draw the desks correctly.

Research for my ninety-ninth book led me to an extraordinarily wise and helpful expert in Oregon, Jay Rasmussen. He was president of the Oregon chapter of the Lewis and Clark Trail Heritage Foundation. The book: *Dog of Discovery: A Newfoundland's Adventures with Lewis and Clark.* Decades earlier I had learned that a Newfoundland dog named Seaman had accompanied the Lewis and Clark Expedition. "A good idea for a book," I thought. As the 200th-year celebration of the 1804-1806 expedition approached, I sought a publishing contract for such a book, and signed one. Later, as I dug deeply into the story of the dog, I learned that it is mentioned infrequently in the explorer's journals. (For one eight-month period, Seaman is not mentioned at all.)

So I had a choice: write a short book focusing on the known actions of the dog, or write a much-longer book about the whole expedition, focusing on the dog whenever possible. I chose the latter, partly because this gave me a good reason to read all of the expedition's richly detailed journals. (As usual, I enjoyed the research more than I did the writing.) Closer and closer to finishing the book, I wondered how I would end it. The fate of the dog had been a mystery for almost two centuries. Seaman was not mentioned in the journals after July 15, 1806, during the expedition's return from the Pacific. Historians had not found a shred of evidence about the fate of Seaman. I was about to write the last few pages of my book. Then, with exquisitely good timing, a historian announced in February, 2000, the discovery of the first evidence of what happened to Seaman. I was able to write what is likely a true ending for *Dog of Discovery.*

When this book was published in 2002, I assumed it would be my only title about the Lewis and Clark Expedition. But I noticed that there were at least a half-

dozen books about Seaman, and more than a dozen about Sacagawea, but only two about York—William Clark's personal servant. Moreover, one of the two York titles that existed in 2004 had major errors. It troubled me that young readers were being misled about York; I decided to write about him. Once again, historian Jay Rasmussen helped make my text, and the art, as accurate as possible. The artists had to re-do several drawings, as Jay pointed out problems in depicting clothing, weapons, landscapes, and so on. But Cornelius Wright and Ying-Hwa Hu responded well, and produced a gloriously colorful—and very accurate—book: *American Slave, American Hero: York of the Lewis and Clark Expedition.*

As 2003 approached, it became clear that one of my three books to be published that year would be my one-hundredth. Publisher Boyds Mills Press printed a special book jacket celebrating the event. Up till age thirty or so, I never expected to write one book, let alone a hundred. The dedication of *Whales!* reads: "Dedicated with deep gratitude to all who helped and inspired me on an amazing journey that now leads to publication of this, my one hundredth book. Far too numerous to mention by name, they include my parents, children, and wife Susan, friends, teachers, mentors, librarians, scientists, editors, book designers, artists, and fellow writers." Susan organized a delightful party in honor of the

"One of several little ponds dug in neighborhood swampy woods— waiting for rain to fill it, and eventually for spring peepers" (Photo courtesy of Laurence Pringle.)

event that was attended by a good number of the people referred to in the book's dedication. (To be fair, thanks also to wives Judy and Alison, who gave support and encouragement early in my career.)

Reaching this milestone was extraordinary, but my goal was never numbers. The total published could be much higher, had I skimped on research, had I cared less about accuracy. (Not all children's books authors do; most reviewers are librarians, who are understandably not expert enough to catch errors.) Quality is sometimes recognized: in 1999, the *Washington Post/ Children's Book Guild Award for Nonfiction*; in 2005, a lifetime achievement award from the American Association for the Advancement of Science (officially called the AAAS/Subaru SB&F Prize for Excellence in Science Books).

The most mind-boggling honor of all was a grant from the John Simon Guggenheim Memorial Foundation. Decades earlier I had proposed book projects (for adult readers) and had not won. In autumn, 2006, I sent another proposal, and in February of 2007 learned that I had been selected for a fellowship—a rare honor for a children's-book author. My proposal: to write at least two children's books about evolution.

Charles Darwin's ideas about how life evolves have stood the test of time—and countless investigations—to become the very foundation of modern biology. His ideas and evidence of a century ago could have been proved wrong by modern discoveries in genetics, biochemistry, and other sciences. Instead, they have been confirmed. Evidence continues to show that evolution occurred, and is occurring. Each year the theory of evolution grows stronger.

Those in the business of denying evolution pounce on that word: theory. "It is just a theory," they say. This reveals their ignorance about science, or their goal of exploiting the ignorance of others. In common use, the word "theory" can mean a hunch, an idea, a hypothesis. In science, the word has a very different meaning. In science, a theory is supported by an extraordinary amount of evidence. In science, saying that something is "only a theory" is nonsensical.

Evolution is one of the most solidly established theories in all of science. Nevertheless, in the United States some politicians and many citizens say they do not believe in evolution. Some call for schools to teach alternatives to the theory of evolution. (There are none in science.) The United States stands alone in this resistance to reality; in other industrialized nations, eighty percent or more of citizens accept evolution.

This sad situation, plus my long record of exploring complex, controversial subjects with depth and clarity, led the Guggenheim Foundation to support my proposed writings. One book is written; at least one more will follow. Among my goals is to explain the evolu-

Most of the family; (left to right) Heidi, Jesse, Rebecca, Sean, Susan, and Larry (Jeffrey was in California), 2007 (Photo courtesy of Laurence Pringle.)

tionary process—both what we know and how we know it. Once published, these books may be among the most important I've written.

In 2006, returning from a vacation in British Columbia, Canada, I remarked to friends that it has been delightful to visit a more-advanced, more-civilized nation. I had more than U.S. backwardness about evolution in mind. There was also U.S. government resistance to other scientific reality, especially the human role in global climate change. Two of my books, most recently *Global Warming: The Threat of Earth's Changing Climate* (2001), deal with this issue. Any person with a fifth-grade education, or higher, can understand the basic chemistry of climate change, and how the burning of long-buried fossil fuels is drastically affecting Earth's climate. Research by thousands of climate scientists add steadily to human understanding of this vital issue. Nevertheless, some U.S. politicians, editorial writers, and talk-radio ideologues continue to try to confuse the public. They preach that climate change is "a liberal hoax." Sometimes I am embarrassed to be from a nation where such anti-science propaganda flourishes.

One of my forthcoming books is about frogs, one of the many groups threatened by habitat changes caused by the coming climate disruptions. They are also appealing, fascinating creatures. However, I chose to write about frogs for a more personal reason: my own frog

habitat restoration project in the neighborhood. Springtime at my West Nyack home is delightful, with trilliums and other wild flowers in the woods, the songs of wood thrushes, and a chorus of spring peepers. These frogs gather in the swampy woods of my neighbors, mate, and then disperse into the forest.

Early in the new century the local spring peeper chorus ceased. Drought had dried up the vernal ponds (usually full only in the spring), preventing tadpoles from developing into adults. My restoration project began in 2003; I brought in peeper tadpoles from other wetlands and began to dig out the basins that had formerly been vernal ponds in the woods. (Digging into the clay on summer mornings, I recalled doing similar habitat improvement . . . as a teenager!) For several years I dug even more ponds, and deepened them all. Peeper calls now brighten my family's life each spring. The ponds may ensure that the frogs will survive droughts well into the future—long after I'm gone.

Way back in 1977 my book *Death Is Natural* was published. At that time I had not thought much about the end of life, but that reality can't be ignored by anyone in his or her seventies. The loss of loved ones also helps focus on one's own death; so does speaking at memorial services. My list of deceased loved ones includes a few cats, but especially my

father (1988), brother Gary (1994), best friend Lois Murphy (1994), and mother (1995).

Just after my name at the beginning of this entry in *Something about the Author,* there is a date and a dash: 1935—. People don't usually get to choose the date after the dash. It could be later this year (2008); it could be a much higher number. For many reasons, great and small, I prefer the latter. One odd reason: I want to experience another local emergence of seventeen-year cicadas. *Brood II* appeared in 1979 and 1996; I studied, photographed, and even transplanted these amazing insects, and hope to do the same in 2013. Less frivolous reasons: being in the lives of my wife and children as long as possible, being an active grandfather (should grandchildren ever appear!), doing genealogical re-

search, reading, traveling, and—yes, writing more books on favorite subjects, including cicadas!

As I wrote earlier, I do not believe in gods or an afterlife. The only hell or heaven people will have is right here on Earth, during their "dash"—the length of time between birth and death. I've experienced some hellish times, but much more of paradise, thanks in part to my unexpected life's work of writing for children.

* * *

PRINGLE, Laurence Patrick
See PRINGLE, Laurence

R

RAUH, Sherry
See NORTH, Sherry

*   *   *

REEVE, Philip

Personal
Born in Brighton, England; married; children: one son. *Hobbies and other interests:* Walking, drawing, writing, reading.

Addresses
Home—Devon, England.

Career
Illustrator, author, and bookseller. Children's book illustrator, 1994—. Producer and director of stage plays.

Awards, Honors
Whitbread Children's Book Award shortlist, and Gold Award, Nestlé Smarties Book Prize, both 2002, and Best Book of the Year designation, *Washington Post,* Best Book for Young Adults designation, American Library Association (ALA), and Blue Peter Book Award Book of the Year, all 2003, all for *Mortal Engines;* Best Book for Young Adults designation, ALA, and W.H. Smith People's Choice Award shortlist, 2004, for *Predator's Gold;* London *Guardian* Children's Fiction Prize, 2006, for *A Darkling Plain;* Carnegie Medal, 2008, for *Here's Lies Arthur.*

Writings

FOR CHILDREN

(Self-illustrated) *Horatio Nelson and His Victory* ("Dead Famous" series), Hippo (London, England), 2003.

Larklight: A Rousing Tale of Dauntless Pluck in the Farthest Reaches of Space, illustrated by David Wyatt, Bloomsbury (New York, NY), 2006.

Starcross; or, The Coming of the Moobs!; or, Our Adventures in the Fourth Dimension!: A Stirring Tale of British Vim upon the Seas of Space and Time, illustrated by David Wyatt, Bloomsbury (London, England), 2007, published as *Starcross; or, The Coming of the Moobs!; or, Our Adventures in the Fourth Dimension!: A Stirring Adventure of Spies, Time Travel, and Curious Hats,* Bloomsbury Children's Books (New York, NY), 2007.

Here Lies Arthur, Scholastic Press (London, England), 2007, Scholastic Press (New York, NY), 2008.

Mothstorm: The Horror from beyond Georgium Sidus!, illustrated by David Wyatt, Bloomsbury U.S.A. Children's Books (New York, NY), 2008.

Coauthor, with Brian P. Mitchell, of musical *The Ministry of Biscuits.*

"HUNGRY CITY CHRONICLES" SERIES; YOUNG-ADULT SCIENCE FICTION

Mortal Engines, Scholastic (London, England), 2001, HarperCollins (New York, NY), 2003.

Predator's Gold, Scholastic (London, England), 2003, Eos (New York, NY), 2004.

Infernal Devices, Eos (New York, NY), 2006.

A Darkling Plain, EOS (New York, NY), 2006.

"BUSTER BAYLISS" SERIES; FOR CHILDREN

Night of the Living Veg, illustrated by Graham Philpot, Scholastic Children's Books (London, England), 2002, new edition, illustrated by Steve May, 2006.

The Big Freeze, illustrated by Graham Philpot, Scholastic Children's Books (London, England), 2002, new edition, illustrated by Steve May, 2006.

Day of the Hamster, illustrated by Graham Philpot, Scholastic Children's Books (London, England), 2002.

Custardfinger, illustrated by Graham Philpot, Scholastic Children's Books (London, England), 2003.

ILLUSTRATOR

Terry Deary, *Wicked Words* ("Horrible Histories" series), Andre Deutsch (London, England), 1996.

Terry Deary, *Dark Knights and Dingy Castles* ("Horrible Histories" series), Andre Deutsch (London, England), 1997.

Terry Deary, *The Angry Aztecs* ("Horrible Histories" series), Andre Deutsch (London, England), 1997, published with *The Incredible Incas,* 2001.

Chris D'Lacey, *Henry Spaloosh!,* Hippo (London, England), 1997.

Michael Cox, *Awful Art* ("The Knowledge" series), Hippo (London, England), 1997.

Michael Cox, *Mind-Blowing Music* ("The Knowledge" series), Hippo (London, England), 1997.

Peter Corey, *Coping with Love,* Hippo (London, England), 1997.

Michael Cox, *Smashin' Fashion* ("The Knowledge" series), Hippo (London, England), 1998.

Kjartan Poskitt, *More Murderous Maths,* Hippo (London, England), 1998.

Chris D'Lacey, *Snail Patrol,* Hippo (London, England), 1998.

Terry Deary and Barbara Allen, *Space Race* ("Spark Files" series), Faber (London, England), 1998.

Terry Deary and Barbara Allen, *Shock Tactics* ("Spark Files" series), Faber (London, England), 1998.

Terry Deary and Barbara Allen, *Chop and Change* ("Spark Files" series), Faber (London, England), 1998.

Terry Deary and Barbara Allen, *Bat and Bell* ("Spark Files" series), Faber (London, England), 1998.

Kjartan Poskitt, *Isaac Newton and His Apple* ("Dead Famous" series), Hippo (London, England), 1999.

Hayden Middleton, *Come and Have a Go if You Think You're Cool Enough!,* Hippo (London, England), 1999.

Hayden Middleton, *Come and Have a Go if You Think You're Mad Enough!,* Hippo (London, England), 1999.

Alan MacDonald, *Henry VIII and His Chopping Block,* Scholastic (London, England), 1999.

Alan MacDonald, *Al Capone and His Gang,* Scholastic (London, England), 1999.

Terry Deary, *Rowdy Revolutions* ("Horrible Histories" series), Scholastic (London, England), 1999.

Terry Deary and Barbara Allen, *Magical Magnets* ("Spark Files" series), Faber (London, England), 1999.

Margaret Simpson, *Cleopatra and Her Asp,* Hippo (London, England), 2000.

Alan MacDonald, *Oliver Cromwell and His Warts* ("Dead Famous" series), Hippo (London, England), 2000.

Terry Deary and Barbara Allen, *The Secrets of Science* ("Spark Files" series), Faber (London, England), 2000.

Margaret Simpson, *Elizabeth I and Her Conquests,* Hippo (London, England), 2001.

Margaret Simpson, *Mary, Queen of Scots and Her Hopeless Husbands,* Hippo (London, England), 2001.

Kjartan Poskitt, *Do You Feel Lucky?: The Secrets of Probability* ("Murderous Maths" series), Hippo (London, England), 2001.

Mike Goldsmith, *Albert Einstein and His Inflatable Universe* ("Dead Famous" series), Hippo (London, England), 2001.

Michael Cox, *Elvis and His Pelvis,* Hippo (London, England), 2001.

Phil Robins, *Joan of Arc and Her Marching Orders* ("Dead Famous" series), Scholastic (London, England), 2002.

Kjartan Poskitt, *Vicious Circles and Other Savage Shapes* ("Murderous Maths" series), Hippo (London, England), 2002.

Kjartan Poskitt, *Professor Fiendish's Book of Diabolical Brainbenders* ("Murderous Maths" series), Hippo (London, England), 2002.

Kjartan Poskitt, *Numbers: The Key to the Universe* ("Murderous Maths" series), Hippo (London, England), 2002.

Kjartan Poskitt, *The Phantom X* ("Murderous Maths" series), Hippo (London, England), 2003.

Kjartan Poskitt, *The Magic of Pants: A Conjuror's Compendium of Underpants Tricks to Delight All Ages (and Sizes),* Scholastic (London, England), 2004, published as *Pantsacadabra! A Conjuror's Compendium of Underpants Tricks to Delight All Ages,* 2007.

Kjartan Poskitt, *The Fiendish Angletron* ("Murderous Maths" series), Hippo (London, England), 2004.

Kjartan Poskitt, *Urgum the Axeman,* Scholastic (London, England), 2006.

Kjartan Poskitt, *The Perfect Sausage,* Hippo (London, England), 2007.

Kjartan Poskitt, *Urgum and the Seat of Flames,* Scholastic (London, England), 2007.

Adaptations

The "Buster Bayliss" novels were adapted as audiobooks by Chivers Children's Audio Books, 2003. *Larklight* was scheduled to be adapted for a film, produced by Denise Di Novi, for Warner Brothers.

Sidelights

A former bookseller and a highly successful illustrator of children's books, Philip Reeve has earned fame and critical acclaim for his "Hungry City Chronicles" science-fiction series, which includes the novels *Mortal Engines, Predator's Gold, Infernal Devices,* and *A Darkling Plain.* Imaginative and clever, these novels have been compared to Philip Pullman's "His Dark Materials" trilogy, and have earned positive reviews as well as a large readership. In addition to his novels, as well as his humorous "Buster Bayliss" series for younger readers, Reeve is a popular cartoonist and illustrator who has contributed substantially to artwork for Terry Deary's popular "Horrible Histories" nonfiction series.

Mortal Engines takes place in a bleak time thousands of years in the future, "in which larger, faster cities literally gobble up the resources of smaller towns in order to feed the never-ending need for fuel," as Janice M. Del Negro explained in the *Bulletin of the Center for Children's Books.* In a mobile London, scavenger Thaddeus Valentine has discovered an ancient energy source that will enable his city to overwhelm the stationery but well-defended cities of Asia. When a horribly disfigured girl named Hester attempts to take Valentine's life, loyal

Cover of Mortal Engines, *Philip Reeve's fantasy novel that features artwork by David Frankland.* (Cover Illustration © 2001 by David Frankland. Reproduced with the permission of Scholastic, Ltd. All rights reserved.)

young apprentice historian Tom Natsworthy saves his mentor. To Tom's surprise, instead of rewarding him, Valentine shoves both he and Hester down a waste chute and out of London. Learning several unpleasant truths about Valentine—including that the man killed Hester's parents—Tom joins the girl's quest for vengeance as the two set out across a landscape rife with pirates and slave traders in pursuit of east-bound London.

"The grimy yet fantastical post-apocalyptic setting; the narrow escapes, deepening loyalties, and not-infrequent bitter losses—all keep readers' attention riveted," commented Anita L. Burkam in a review of *Mortal Engines* for *Horn Book. Kliatt* reviewer Paula Rohrlick described Reeve's "wildly imaginative British tale" as "full of marvelous details . . . humor, and grand adventures," and *Chronicle* contributor Don D'Ammassa found the book "well worth the time of readers of any age."

The second book in the "Hungry City Chronicles" series, *Predator's Gold,* finds Tom and Hester in Anchor-

age, Alaska, a city that, like many in Reeve's futuristic world, moves from place to place, searching for comfortable climes and incorporating smaller cities that cross its path. Anchorage is now under the control of a pretty young woman named Freya, and when she recalls the town's history and the lush fields it once controlled in its original stationary site in the old continental United States, she decides to take Anchorage on the perilous journey back across the ice wastes. When Hester sees Tom kissing Freya, a jealous rage causes her to betray Anchorage's location to the predatory city of Arkangel. At the same time, a gang of baddies known as the Lost Boys are spying on the city and trying to kidnap Tom, while the Anti-Traction League seeks to destroy Anchorage with the help of a horrible cyborg.

For *Horn Book* contributor Anita L. Burkam, "the technological wizardry" in *Predator's Gold* "will gratify young sci-fi gearheads, while the intense emotions drive the thrilling plot at top speed." In *Kliatt,* Rohrlick commended Reeve's "marvelous imagination and emotional depth, the sympathetic young protagonists, and the thrilling adventures," while *Booklist* contributor Sally Estes noted that, despite a complex plot and multiple characters, the story "is still easy to follow [and] gripping enough to leave readers anxious to find out what's to come."

Infernal Devices and *A Darkling Plain* finish up Reeve's "Hungry City Chronicles" saga featuring Tom and Hester. In *Infernal Devices* two decades have passed since the action in *Predator's Gold,* and the two protagonists now have a teenage daughter, Wren, who is being threatened by the same Lost Boys who once pursued her father. As the middle-aged Tom watches, Earth's population fractures into the competing Traction League and Green Storm in *A Darkling Plain*; meanwhile, a powerful weapon created by humans prior to the apocalyptic war that destroyed the first human civilization hangs in the sky, poised to destroy everything. "Reeve keeps the multiple plots moving with surprises, tragedy, and multiple betrayals," noted Tim Wadhams, reviewing *Infernal Devices* for *School Library Journal,* and in *Booklist* Sally Estes praised the book's culmination in "a thrilling climax and hint of more battles to come."

While commenting on the "fabulous streak of frivolity running through absolutely everything that Reeve writes," London *Guardian* contributor Josh Lacey added that the author also has a more serious side: "Municipal Darwinism. A perfect expression of the true nature of the world: that the fittest survive," as one character explains. While noting that the author's prose alternates between complex and "sparkling and witty," Lacey concluded that in the "Hungry City Chronicles" "Reeve has created an extraordinary imaginative achievement" that ends with a "cunning twist."

With his "Hungry City Chronicles" Reeve amassed some of England's top honors for children's literature, among them the 2002 Nestlé Children's Gold Award,

the 2003 Blue Peter Book of the Year award and, in 2006, the London *Guardian* Children's Fiction Prize for *A Darkling Plain*. In 2008 he also triumphed, receiving the Carnegie Medal for his book *Here Lies Arthur*, a new version of the legend of King Arthur. As narrated by a perceptive girl named Gwyna, Reeve's medieval Britain is a dark, unsettling place where a subtle magic and evil exist side by side. In this world Arthur claims himself to be king of a band of marauders, while Myddrin (Merlin) is a woman with a talent for disguise, subterfuge, and storytelling. Citing the "deep cynicism" that undergirds Reeve's tale, a *Publishers Weekly* contributor maintained that *Here Lies Arthur* resonates in the present, "neatly skewering the modern-day cult of spin and the age-old trickery behind it." Calling the novel "a study in balance and contradiction," *Horn Book* reviewer Claire E. Gross expressed a similar view, deeming Reeve's story "bleak yet tender; impeccably historical, yet distinctly timely in its driving sense of disillusionment." The legends of Camelot have "inspired many novels for young people," concluded *Booklist* critic Carolyn Phelan in her review of *Here Lies Arthur*, "but few as arresting as this."

Featuring illustrations by David Wyatt, Reeve's middle-school novels *Larklight: A Rousing Tale of Dauntless Pluck in the Farthest Reaches of Space* and *Starcross; or, The Coming of the Moobs!; or, Our Adventures in the Fourth Dimension!: A Stirring Tale of British Vim upon the Seas of Space and Time* take readers on a more lighthearted excursion into the author's imagination. Set in a Victorian alternate world where houses float in space, *Larklight* introduces siblings Myrtle and Art Mumby, who live in a floating house called Larklight along with their father. Separated from home during an attack of space spiders, the children begin an adventure that leads them from the moon and Venus to the pirate ship of Captain Jack Havock. From there, they travel to a scientific institute where they uncover a plot by a mad scientists that involves the invasion of hoards of the pesky spiders. With the help of Wyatt's detailed ink drawings, *Larklight* "melds deadpan comedy, anticolonial political satire, sci-fi epic, and pirate caper with aplomb," maintained Gross, while a contributor to *Kirkus Reviews* dubbed the novel "jolly good fun, all around." Calling Reeve's story "utterly entertaining," a *Publishers Weekly* critic added that the conclusion of *Larklight* "is an absolute hoot" and leaves readers craving more.

Dubbed a "dashing and outrageous sequel" by a *Publishers Weekly* writer, *Starcross* reunites readers with Art and Myrtle and send them off on another fanciful adventure in Reeve's alternate universe. Together with their half-alien-and-older-that-dirt Mum, the children travel to Starcross, a space resort, where they hope to take a rest. Such is not to be, however, when vicious sand crabs appear and another plot surfaces that threatens their free-floating world. "Tongue-in-cheek, hilarious, and wildly imaginative," according to Connie Tyrell Burns in *School Library Journal*, *Starcross* leaves

the story open for another sequel in Reeve's archly British saga: *Mothstorm: The Horror from beyond Georgium Sidus!*

Biographical and Critical Sources

PERIODICALS

Booklist, November 1, 2003, Sally Estes, review of *Mortal Engines*, p. 491; August, 2004, Sally Estes, review of *Predator's Gold*, p. 1920; May 15, 2006, Sally Estes, review of *Infernal Devices*, p. 61; November 1, 2007, Todd Morning, review of *Starcross*, p. 48; August 1, 2008, Carolyn Phelan, review of *Here Lies Arthur*, p. 69.

Bookseller, August 10, 2001, Tara Stephenson, review of *Mortal Engines*, p. 33; June 27, 2008, Caroline Horn, interview with Reeve, p. 10.

Bulletin of the Center for Children's Books, March, 2004, Janice M. Del Negro, review of *Mortal Engines*, p. 294; November, 2004, Timnah Card, review of *Predator's Gold*, p. 141.

Chronicle, January, 2004, Don D'Ammassa, review of *Mortal Engines*, p. 31.

Guardian (London, England), April 8, 2006, Josh Lacey, review of *A Darkling Plain*.

Horn Book, November-December, 2003, Anita L. Burkam, review of *Mortal Engines*, p. 755; September-October, 2004, Anita L. Burkam, review of *Predator's Gold*, p. 596; November-December, 2006, Claire E. Gross, review of *Larklight: A Rousing Tale of Dauntless Pluck in the Farthest Reaches of Space*, p. 724; November-December, 2008, Claire E. Gross, review of *Here Lies Arthur*, p. 713.

Kirkus Reviews, October 15, 2003, review of *Mortal Engines*, p. 1275; August 15, 2004, review of *Predator's Gold*, p. 216; September 15, 2006, review of *Larklight*, p. 965; October 15, 2008, review of *Here Lies Arthur*.

Kliatt, November, 2003, Paula Rohrlick, review of *Mortal Engines*, p. 10; September, 2004, Paula Rohrlick, review of *Predator's Gold*, p. 16; May, 2006, Paula Rohrlick, review of *Infernal Devices*, p. 13.

Magpies, May, 2002, review of *Mortal Engines*, p. 38; March, 2004, Rayma Turton, review of *Predator's Gold*, p. 43.

Publishers Weekly, October 27, 2003, review of *Mortal Engines*, p. 70; August 16, 2004, review of *Predator's Gold*, p. 64; August 28, 2006, review of *Larklight*, p. 54; November 5, 2007, review of *Starcross*, p. 64; October 6, 2008, review of *Here Lies Arthur*, p. 55.

School Librarian, winter, 2001, review of *Mortal Engines*, p. 214; winter, 2002, review of *Night of the Living Veg*, p. 202; spring, 2004, Michael Holloway, review of *Predator's Gold*, p. 34.

School Library Journal, December, 2003, Sharon Rawlins, review of *Mortal Engines*, p. 864; September, 2004, Sharon Rawlins, review of *Predator's Gold*, p. 216; June, 2006, Tim Wadham, review of *Infernal Devices*, p. 164; November, 2006, Rick Margolis, interview with Reeve, p. 33; December, 2007, Connie Tyrell Burns, review of *Starcross*, p. 142.

Tribune Books (Chicago, IL), November 23, 2003, review of *Mortal Engines*, p. 4.
Voice of Youth Advocates, October, 2004, Sarah Flowers, review of *Predator's Gold,* p. 318.

ONLINE

British Broadcasting Corporation Web site, http://www.bbc.co.uk/ (September 29, 2004), interview with Reeve.
ContemporaryWriters.com, http://www.contemporarywriters.com/ (June 8, 2009), "Philip Reeve."*

*   *   *

REY, Luis V. 1955-

Personal

Born 1955, in Mexico; immigrated to England. *Education:* San Carlos Academy, Universidad Nacional Autónoma de México, M.A. (visual arts), 1977.

Addresses

Home—London, England. *E-mail*—luisrey@ndirect.co.uk.

Career

Painter, sculptor, author, and illustrator. Amateur paleontologist; model designer and anatomist; Dinosaur art and anatomical consultant. Presenter at workshops. *Exhibitions:* Work included at exhibits at galleries in the United States, Great Britain, and Europe, including Denver Museum of Nature and Science, Dudley Museum and Art Gallery, EAA Air Venture Museum, and Houston Museum of Natural Science.

Member

Society of Vertebrate Paleontology, Dinosaur Society (UK).

Awards, Honors

Lanzendorf Award for best two-dimensional paleoart, Society of Vertebrate Paleontology, 2008.

Writings

SELF-ILLUSTRATED

Extreme Dinosaurs!, Chronicle Books (New York, NY), 2001.
(With Henry Gee) *A Field Guide to Dinosaurs: The Essential Handbook for Travelers in the Mesozoic,* Barron's (Hauppauge, NY), 2003.

Dinosaurs in the Round (pop-up book), Random House (New York, NY), 2008.

ILLUSTRATOR

Robert T. Bakker, *Maximum Triceratops,* Barron's (Hauppauge, NY), 2004.
Robert T. Bakker, *Dactyls!: Dragons of the Air,* Barron's (Hauppauge, NY), 2005.
Robert T. Bakker, *Dinosaurs!: An Introduction,* Random House (New York, NY), 2005.
(With others) Susanna Davidson, Stephanie Turnbull, and Rachel Firth, *The Usborne Internet-linked World Atlas of Dinosaurs,* Random House (San Francisco, CA), 2005.
Kelly Milner Halls, *The Random House Dinosaur Travel Guide,* Random House (New York, NY), 2006.
Anusuya Chinsamy-Turan, *The Microstructure of Dinosaur Bone,* Johns Hopkins Press (Baltimore, MD), 2006.
Thomas R. Holtz, *Dinosaurs: The Most Complete, Up-to-Date Encyclopedia for Dinosaur Lovers of All Ages,* Random House (New York, NY), 2007.
Robert T. Bakker, *Prehistoric Monsters!,* Random House (New York, NY), 2008.

Contributor to books, including *Dinosaurs: A Celebration,* Marvel Comics, 1992; Sue Maynes, *The Usborne Book of Dinosaurs,* Usborne, 1993; Dougal Dixon, *The Search for Dinosaurs,* Wayland, 1995; *Deinos-Saurus,* Universidad Nacional Autónoma de Méico (UNAM), 1999; Kenneth Carpenter, *Dinosaur Nests and Babies,* Indiana University Press, 1999; *Monsters,* Scintilla Editorial, 2000; *The Scientific American Book of Dinosaurs,* 2001; David Lambert, *Dorling Kindersley Guide to Dinosaurs,* Dorling Kindersley, 2000; Lambert and Darren Naish, and *Dorling Kindersley Prehistoric Animal Encyclopaedia,* 2001. Contributor to periodicals, including *National Geographic Kids, Discover, Journal of Morphology,* and *UNAM.*

Sidelights

Judging by his career as an artist, author, model maker, and amateur paleontologist, Luis V. Rey shares a common interest with many young boys: dinosaurs. A trained artist—the Mexican-born Rey earned a degree in the visual arts at the Universidad Nacional Autónoma de México—he relocated to London, England, where he continues to study, create his detailed paintings, and write about prehistoric creatures. In addition to contributing artwork to numerous nonfiction books and articles, as well as to the intricate 3-D pop-up book *Dinosaurs in the Round,* Rey has also coauthored *A Field Guide to Dinosaurs: The Essential Handbook for Travelers in the Mesozoic* with paleontologist Henry Gee, and created the self-illustrated book *Extreme Dinosaurs!* In *School Library Journal* Steven Engelfried wrote that *Extreme Dinosaurs!* features "eye-catching illustrations and an enthusiastic text" in which "the author's fascination with paleontology and art comes through."

In *A Field Guide to Dinosaurs* Rey and Gee draw readers into the puzzling world of those who attempt to decipher dinosaur bones. In black-and-white illustrations, Rey depicts dinosaur behaviors such as hunting, sleeping, and climbing trees, although Gee asserts in his text that modern paleontologists really do not know for sure how these creatures lived. Recognizing Rey as "a leading dinosaur artist," a *Publishers Weekly* contributor praised *A Field Guide to Dinosaurs* for leading "dinophiles [on an] . . . excursion into a vividly illustrated possible past world." In *Booklist,* Ed Sullivan dubbed the work "a fascinating mix of fact and fiction" that is brought to life in Rey's "stunning color illustrations," while Patricia Manning cited the volume's effective "field guide" divisions into Triassic, Jurassic, Early and Mid-Cretaceous, and late Cretaceous format in her *School Library Journal* review. "Handsome and engrossing," *A Field Guide to Dinosaurs* "should have a large and appreciative audience," Manning concluded.

As an illustrator, Rey has created detailed artwork for a number of well-respected dino-resources authored by paleontologists in the field, among them *Dinosaurs: The Most Complete, Up-to-Date Encyclopedia for Di-*

Dinosaur expert Luis V. Rey creates the detailed artwork that appears in nonfiction books such as **Dactyls!** *by anthropologist Robert T. Bakker.* (Illustration copyright © 2005 by Luis V. Rey. All rights reserved. Used by permission of Random House Children's Books, a division of Random House, Inc.)

nosaur Lovers of All Ages, by Thomas R. Holtz, and several species-specific dino-guides by well-known researcher Robert T. Bakker. While young dino fans might not recognize all the names—Guanlong, Zupaysaurus, Sinornithomimus, Supersaurus, Lurdosaurus, and Draconyx, among many others—Holtz's *Dinosaurs* "delivers a plethora of facts and discovers" in its forty-two chapters, according to *Booklist* critic Cheryl Ward. In addition to a chapter on the science behind dinosaur art, the book also discusses new dinosaur skeleton restorations, fossilization, dino-evolution, and what scientists know about the extinction of these creatures, making *Dinosaurs* an "eye-catching imagination grabber," according to Manning.

Bakker's *Dactyls!: Dragons of the Air* serves as "a read-a-bration of pterosaurs," according to *School Library Journal* critic Patricia Manning. Rey's colorful illustrations for the book reflect the artist's "sensible reasoning" about the winged dactyl species, according to Manning, and in *Kirkus Reviews* a writer concluded that the artwork "clearly support[s] . . . the text" of this "entirely winning" picture-book collaboration. Another book by Bakker and Rey, *Dinosaurs!* has an easy-to-read text highlighted by "brilliantly colored" paintings featuring dinos that are "probably the most dynamically posed of any in the tradition of paleoart," according to a *Natural History* critic.

Biographical and Critical Sources

PERIODICALS

Booklist, August, 2003, Ed Sullivan, review of *A Field Guide to Dinosaurs: The Essential Handbook for Travelers in the Mesozoic,* p. 1970; January 1, 2008, Cheryl Ward, review of *Dinosaurs: The Most Complete, Up-to-Date Encyclopedia for Dinosaur Lovers of All Ages,* p. 131.

Horn Book, January-February, 2008, Danielle J. Ford, review of *Dinosaurs!,* p. 112.

Kirkus Reviews, November 1, 2005, review of *Dactyls!: Dragons of the Air* p. 1181.

Natural History, May, 2005, review of *Dinosaurs!,* p. 63.

Publishers Weekly, February 24, 2003, review of *A Field Guide to Dinosaurs!,* p. 69.

School Library Journal, September, 2001, Steven Engelfried, review of *Extreme Dinosaurs,* p. 252; September, 2003, Patricia Manning, review of *A Field Guide to Dinosaurs,* p. 210; February, 2006, Patricia Manning, review of *Dactyls!,* p. 114; December, 2006, Cynde Suite, review of *A Field Guide to Dinosaurs,* p. 163; December, 2007, Patricia Manning, review of *The Most Complete, Up-to-Date Encyclopedia for Dinosaur Lovers of All Ages,* p. 153; October, 2008, John Peters, review of *Dinosaurs in the Round* p. 130.

ONLINE

Luis V. Rey Home Page, http://www.luisrey.ntilda.co.uk (May 15, 2009).*

ROVETCH, L. Bob
See ROVETCH, Lissa

*   *   *

ROVETCH, Lissa
(L. Bob Rovetch)

Personal

Daughter of Gerda Rovetch; children: Kia, Niko. *Education:* Parsons School of Design, B.F.A.; attended New School for Social Research (now New School University) and Otis College of Art and Design.

Addresses

Home—Fairfax, CA.

Career

Author and illustrator. California College of the Arts, San Francisco, instructor, 2008—.

Member

Society of Children's Books Writers and Illustrators.

Writings

Trigwater Did It, Morrow (New York, NY), 1989.
(Self-illustrated with Martha Weston) *Cora and the Elephants,* Viking (New York, NY), 1995.
Sweet Dreams, Little One, illustrated by Betina Ogden, Random House (New York, NY), 2001.
Ook the Book and Other Silly Rhymes, illustrated by Shannon McNeill, Chronicle Books (San Francisco, CA), 2001.
TLC Grow with Me!, illustrated by Chum McLeod, Kindermusik (Greensboro, NC), 2005.
1, 2, 3, Octopus and Me, illustrated by Claudine Gèvry, Kindermusik (Greensboro, NC), 2006.
Frog Went a-Dancing, illustrated by Holly Berry, Kindermusik (Greensboro, NC), 2006.
I Need a Kazoot!, illustrated by Carly Castillon, Kindermusik (Greensboro, NC), 2006.
(With Emily Whitman) *Sir Henry, the Polite Knight,* illustrated by Bryn Barnard, Kindermusik (Greensboro, NC), 2007.
(Illustrator) Gerda Rovetch, *There Was a Man Who Loved a Rat and Other Vile Little Poems,* Philomel (New York, NY), 2008.

Also author of *Cock-a-doodle Blue,* illustrated by Bob Barner, *Peekaboo, I Love You!,* illustrated by Paul Meisel, *Shoofly Pie,* illustrated by Kathi Ember, *Cowboy Baby,* illustrated by Cheryl Mendenhall, and *Zoo Train,* illustrated by Brian Lies, all for Kindermusik,

and *Mole's Huge Nose,* for Leapfrog. Columnist for periodicals, including *Highlights for Children, Highlights' High Five, Spider, Leapfrog's Leap's Pond,* and *Ta Daa!*

"HOT DOG AND BOB" SERIES; AS L. BOB ROVETCH

Hot Dog and Bob and the Seriously Scary Attack of the Evil Alien Pizza Person, illustrated by Dave Whamond, Chronicle Books (San Francisco, CA), 2006.
Hot Dog and Bob and the Particularly Pesky Attack of the Pencil People, Chronicle Books (San Francisco, CA), 2006.
Hot Dog and Bob and the Dangerously Dizzy Attack of the Hypno Hamsters, Chronicle Books (San Francisco, CA), 2007.
Hot Dog and Bob and the Exceptionally Eggy Attack of the Game Gators, illustrated by Dave Whamond, Chronicle Books (San Francisco, CA), 2007.
Hot Dog and Bob and the Surprisingly Slobbery Attack of the Dog-wash Doggies, illustrated by Dave Whamond, Chronicle Books (San Francisco, CA), 2007.
Hot Dog and Bob and the Ferociously Freaky Attack of the Foot Fighters, illustrated by Dave Whamond, Chronicle Books (San Francisco, CA), 2007.

Sidelights

In addition to authoring story columns for popular children's periodicals, author and illustrator Lissa Rovetch has also published picture books for young readers and the "Hot Dog and Bob" series of illustrated novels for the elementary-school set. When asked about her story ideas in an interview with *Highlights for Children,* Rovetch explained: "I remember a lot of things that happened in my childhood—especially when it comes to the times I felt nervous, embarrassed, or confused. I get story ideas from remembering those times." She also credits her own children with supplying her ideas for new stories as well as the young people who write to her with questions of their own.

One of Rovetch's first books, *Cora and the Elephants* is a collaboration with Martha Weston. An orphan child who is raised by two elephants in the African jungle, Cora decides that she would like to see from whence she came. The enterprising girl sells coconuts in order to earn money for her trip, her destination San Francisco, California. Unfortunately, Cora's only clue to her early life comes from printing on a life preserver, and this information leads to the location of the life preserver's manufacturer rather than her own home. Undaunted, Cora and her two elephant parents decide to remain in San Francisco, where Cora learns how to live like a human and her parents find jobs. When they begin to miss life in the wild, family members return home and Cora makes weekly trips into a nearby village as a way of satisfying her need to be around other humans. "Together words and illustrations stretch the imaginations of all who have wondered about their origins," observed *School Library Journal* critic Kathy Piehl, while in

Lissa Rovetch illustrates a text written by her mother, Gerda Rovetch, in There Was a Man Who Loved a Rat, and Other Vile Little Poems.
(Illustration copyright © 2008 by Lissa Rovetch. All rights reserved. Reproduced by permission of Philomel Books, a division of Penguin Putnam Books for Young Readers.)

Booklist Ilene Cooper called *Cora and the Elephants* "a delightful tale that proves the adage home is where the herd is."

Rovetch has also added her talents to other books, penning *Ook the Book and Other Silly Rhymes* and creating the illustrations for a book written by her mother, Gerda Rovetch, titled *There Was a Man Who Loved a Rat and Other Vile Little Poems. Ook the Book* offers young readers a series of humorous poems focusing on vowel and consonant sounds, resulting in "a useful and fun addition to easy-reader shelves," according to *School Library Journal* contributor Jane Marino. Funny poems also fill the pages of *There Was a Man Who Loved a Rat and Other Vile Little Poems,* and the verses are complemented by Lissa Rovetch's "comically serious illustrations," in the opinion of a *Kirkus Reviews* critic. Each of the book's fourteen poems features a black-and-white picture, with one element of the drawing accented with a splash of a single color. The artist "matches the exaggeration in her mother's work with her black ink cartoons," remarked a *Publishers Weekly* reviewer, the critic dubbing *There Was a Man Who Loved a Rat and Other Vile Little Poems* "good and gleeful."

Under the pen name L. Bob Rovetch, Rovetch has also teamed up with illustrator Dave Whamond to create a series of chapter books for beginning readers about Bob, a fifth-grade student, and a talking hot dog from the planet of Dogzalot. Sent to help Bob defend Earth from evil aliens, Hot Dog races to rescue the students of Lugenheimer Elementary School from a variety of sinister aliens, including a pizza-faced creature who eats students in *Hot Dog and Bob and the Seriously Scary Attack of the Evil Alien Pizza Person,* a barrage of overeager pencil erasers in *Hot Dog and Bob and the Particularly Pesky Attack of the Pencil People,* and a dog-napping duo bent on stealing pets in *Hot Dog and Bob and the Surprisingly Slobbery Attack of the Dog-wash Doggies.* In a review of *Hot Dog and Bob and the Seriously Scary Attack of the Evil Alien Pizza Person, School Library Journal* reviewer Jennifer Cogan described the book as an "off-the-wall, zany early chapter book," while a *Publishers Weekly* critic predicted that readers "who relish the zaniest sort of slapstick will eat this up" and look forward to new books featuring Rovetch and Whamond's unusual characters.

Biographical and Critical Sources

PERIODICALS

Booklist, January 15, 1995, Ilene Cooper, review of *Cora and the Elephants,* p. 938; January 1, 2008, Hazel Rochman, review of *There Was a Man Who Loved a Rat and Other Vile Little Poems,* p. 88.
Highlights for Children, February, 2008, "All about Arizona," interview with Rovetch, p. 22.
Kirkus Reviews, January 1, 2008, review of *There Was a Man Who Loved a Rat and Other Vile Little Poems.*
Publishers Weekly, May 1, 1995, review of *Cora and the Elephants,* p. 57; May 28, 2001, review of *Ook the Book and Other Silly Rhymes,* p. 86; July 31, 2006, review of *Hot Dog and Bob and the Seriously Scary Attack of the Evil Alien Pizza Person,* p. 75; March 3, 2008, review of *There Was a Man Who Loved a Rat and Other Vile Little Poems,* p. 46.
Resource Links, October, 2006, Myra Junyk, review of *Hot Dog and Bob and the Particularly Pesky Attack of the Pencil People,* p. 14; December, 2006, Evette Berry, review of *Hot Dog and Bob and the Seriously Scary Attack of the Evil Alien Pizza Person,* p. 23; October, 2007, Eva Wilson, review of *Hot Dog and Bob and the Dangerously Dizzy Attack of the Hypno Hamsters,* p. 21, and Linda Aksomitis, review of *Hot Dog and Bob and the Exceptionally Eggy Attack of the Game Gators,* p. 21; December, 2007, Teresa Hughes, review of *Hot Dog and Bob and the Surprisingly Slobbery Attack of the Dog-wash Doggies,* p. 23.
School Library Journal, April, 1995, Kathy Piehl, review of *Cora and the Elephants,* p. 116; August, 2001, Jane Marino, review of *Ook the Book and Other Silly Rhymes,* p. 172; September, 2006, Jennifer Cogan, review of *Hot Dog and Bob and the Seriously Scary Attack of the Evil Alien Pizza Person,* p. 183; May, 2008, Julie Roach, review of *There Was a Man Who Loved a Rat and Other Vile Little Poems,* p. 117.

ONLINE

Hot Dog and Bob Web site, http://www.hotdogandbob.com/ (May 14, 2009).*

S

SERAFINI, Frank

Personal

Male. *Education:* Fort Lewis College (Durango, CO), B.A. (business administration), 1984; Arizona State University, M.Ed. (elementary education), 1992, Ph.D. (reading education), 2001.

Addresses

Home—Scottsdale, AZ. *E-mail*—frank@frankserafini. com.

Career

Author, educator, musician, and photographer. Elementary School teacher, 1989-2000; Northern Arizona University, adjunct professor, 1997-2001; Arizona State University, adjunct professor, 1993-2001, associate professor of literacy education and children's literature, 2008—; Southwest Educational Consultants, president, beginning 1994; University of Nevada, Las Vegas, assistant, 2001-06, then associate professor of literacy education and children's literature, 2006-08. Presenter at conferences. Performer with Frankie and the Tornados.

Awards, Honors

University of Nevada, Las Vegas, New Investigator Award, and Distinguished New Faculty Award, both 2002, scholarship, 2003, distinguished teacher award, 2007; Society of School Librarians International Honors award, and Teacher's Choice Award nomination, International Reading Association, both for *Looking Closely: Along the Shore;* Arizona State University Alumni Faculty Teaching Achievement Award, 2009; Bank Street College of Education Best Book award, for *Looking Closely: Along the Shore* and *Looking Closely: Through the Forest.*

Writings

FOR CHILDREN

(With Ruth Devlin) *Desert Seasons: A Year in the Mojave,* Stephens Press (Las Vegas, NV), 2004.
Looking Closely: Along the Shore, Kids Can Press (Toronto, Ontario, Canada), 2008.
Looking Closely: Inside the Garden, Kids Can Press (Toronto, Ontario, Canada), 2008.
Looking Closely: Across the Desert, Kids Can Press (Toronto, Ontario, Canada), 2008.
Looking Closely: Through the Desert, Kids Can Press (Toronto, Ontario, Canada), 2008.
Looking Closely: Into the Rainforest, Kids Can Press (Toronto, Ontario, Canada), 2009.
Looking Closely: Around the Pond, Kids Can Press (Toronto, Ontario, Canada), 2009.

OTHER

The Reading Workshop: Creating Space for Readers, Heinemann (Portsmouth, NH), 2001.
(With Cyndi Giorgis) *Reading Aloud and Beyond: Fostering the Intellectual Life with Older Readers,* Heinemann (Portsmouth, NH), 2003.
Lessons in Comprehension: Explicit Instruction in the Reading Workshop, Heinemann (Portsmouth, NH), 2004.
(With Suzette Serafini-Youngs) *Around the Reading Workshop in 180 Days: A Month-by-Month Guide to Effective Instruction,* Heinemann (Portsmouth, NH), 2006.
(With Norma MacFarlane) *Reflections on Literacy,* Pearson Education Canada (Toronto, Ontario, Canada), 2006.
(With Suzette Youngs) *More (Advanced) Lessons in Comprehension: Expanding Students' Understanding of All Types of Texts,* Heinemann (Portsmouth, NH), 2008.
Interactive Comprehension Strategies: Fostering Meaningful Talk about Texts, Scholastic (New York, NY), 2009.

Contributor to books, including *The Fate of Progressive Language Policies and Practices,* edited by Marling and Edelsky, NCTE (Urbana, IL), 2001; *Talking Class-*

rooms: Shaping Children's Learning through Oral Language Instruction, edited by P.G. Smith, International Reading Association (Newark, DE), 2001; and *Talking beyond the Page: Reading and Responding to Contemporary Picture Books,* edited by J. Evans, Routledge (London, England), 2009. Contributor to periodicals, including *Academic Exchange Quarterly, Arizona State Reading Journal, California Reader, Current Issues in Education, English Quarterly Canada, Journal of Children's Literature, Journal of Educational Controversy, Journal of Reading, Writing, and Literacy, Language and literacy Spectrum, New England Journal of Reading and Literacy Instruction, Reading Teacher,* and *South Carolina English Teacher.*

Biographical and Critical Sources

PERIODICALS

Kirkus Reviews, March 15, 2008, review of *Looking Closely: Along the Shore.*
Reference and Research Book News, August, 2008, review of *More (Advanced) Lessons in Comprehension.*
School Library Journal, October, 2005, review of *Lessons in Comprehension,* p. 85; April, 2008, Susan Oliver, review of *Looking Closely: Along the Shore,* p. 136; September, 2008, Kathy Piehl, review of *Looking Closely: Across the Desert,* p. 169; October, 2008, review of *More (Advanced) Lessons in Comprehension,* p. 76.

ONLINE

Frank Serafini Home Page, http://www.frankserafini.com (May 15, 2009).

*   *   *

SHEPHERD, Amanda

Personal

Female.

Addresses

Home—Phoenix, AZ. *E-mail*—shepherd_amanda@yahoo.com.

Career

Illustrator.

Illustrator

Bridget Levin, *Rules of the Wild: An Unruly Book of Manners,* Chronicle Books (San Francisco, CA), 2004.
Patricia MacLachlan, *Who Loves Me?,* Joanna Colter Books (New York, NY), 2005.

Patricia MacLachlan and Emily MacLachlan Charest, *Fiona Loves the Night,* Joanna Colter Books (New York, NY), 2007.
Steffanie Lorig and Richard Lorig, *Such a Silly Baby!,* Chronicle Books (New York, NY), 2008.

Sidelights

Amanda Shepherd made her debut as a children's book illustrator in the pages of Bridget Levin's *Rules of the Wild: An Unruly Book of Manners.* Dubbing the book an "appealing offering" to storytime fans, *Rules of the Wild* benefits from "humorous" full-color drawings "rendered in oil and gesso," according to a *Kirkus Reviews* writer. "Shepherd's illustrations are witty and expressive," wrote *School Library Journal* writer Mary Hazelton, and her images contribute "lots of extra details" to the "clever, well-executed" picture book.

Other illustration projects by Shepherd includes Steffanie and Richard Lorig's humorous *Such a Silly Baby!* as well as two books by award-winning writer Patricia MacLaughlan: *Who Loves Me?* and *Fiona Loves the Night,* the latter coauthored by MacLaughlan's daughter Emily MacLachlan Charest. In her collaboration with the Lorigs, the artist creates "bright, wildly cartoonlike oil paintings [that] perfectly reflect the wackiness" of the story, according to *School Library Journal* contributor Kathleen Kelly MacMillan. A *Kirkus Reviews* critic echoed MacMillan's assessment, writing that Shepherd's "exuberant" paintings "cleverly build . . . in visual cues to help readers" follow the Lorigs' imaginative tale. Although a *Publishers Weekly* critic observed that the artist of *Such a Silly Baby!* "revels in buoyantly hued silliness and goofy visual asides," the critic added that, ultimately, "a firm hand . . . guides these compositions."

In *Fiona Loves the Night* the MacLachlans' story about a young girl's discovery of the natural world after dark is brought to life by Shepherd in what a *Publishers Weekly* critic described as "lush, comforting tones" that "convey the dappling moonlight" of the book's starlit setting. "Circles of color make the moon and stars soft and mysterious," wrote Mary Jean Smith in her *School Library Journal* review of *Fiona Loves the Night,* "and fireflies in the garden are as luminous as stars." In creating art for MacLachlan's *Who Loves Me?,* Shepherd uses warm shades of brown and gold, employing what *Booklist* critic Jennifer Mattson described as an "angular, folk-art style" of illustration. The artist's "deftly expressed gestures embellish" MacLachlan's reassuring bedtime story, wrote a contributor to *Kirkus Reviews,* and in *Publishers Weekly* a critic concluded of *Who Loves Me?* that "Shepherd's lovely, high-spirited pictures add a kookiness to MacLachlan's story that both readers and listeners will appreciate."

On her home page, Shepherd discussed the illustration process as well as her approach to her art when working with school groups. ""I like to think there are no

mistakes" she explained.. "All artists and writers write or draw things they don't like, Mistakes are changes in decisions: it's part of the learning process and part of the journey of writing and illustrating. Mistakes are ways to explore what we paint or write. They improve our work. Writers rewrite their stories hundreds of times. Illustrators make changes until there are stacks of drawing papers up to the rooftops (you should see my drawing room)! Mistakes—if you want to call them that—are a good thing."

Biographical and Critical Sources

PERIODICALS

Booklist, June 1, 2005, Jennifer Mattson, review of *Who Loves Me?,* p. 1822.

Kirkus Reviews, August 15, 2004, Bridget Levin, review of *Rules of the Wild: An Unruly Book of Manners,* p. 809; May 1, 2005, review of *Who Loves Me,* p. 542; August 1, 2007, review of *Fiona Loves the Night*; April 15, 2008, review of *Such a Silly Baby!*

New York Times Book Review, May 15, 2005, M.P. Dunleavey, review of *Who Loves Me?,* p. 23; November 9, 2008, Jessica Bruder, review of *Such a Silly Baby!,* p. 39.

Publishers Weekly, November 15, 2004, review of *Rules of the Wild,* p. 58; March 28, 2005, review of *Who Loves Me?,* p. 79; August 20, 2007, review of *Fiona Loves the Night,* p. 67; May 12, 2008, review of *Such a Silly Baby!,* p. 53.

School Library Journal, October, 2004, Mary Hazelton, review of *Rules of the Wild,* p. 120; May, 2005, Catherine Threadgill, review of *Who Loves Me?,* p. 90. September, 2007, Mary Jean Smith, review of *Fiona Loves the Night,* p. 171; May, 2008, Kathleen Kelly MacMillan, review of *Such a Silly Baby!,* p. 103.

ONLINE

Amanda Shepherd Home Page, http://www.paintdog.com (May 15, 2009).*

*   *   *

SHUSTERMAN, Neal 1962-

Personal

Born November 12, 1962, in New York, NY; son of Milton and Charlotte Shusterman; married Elaine Jones (a teacher and photographer), January 31, 1987; children: Brendan, Jarrod, Joelle, Erin. *Education:* University of California—Irvine, B.A. (psychology and drama), 1985.

Addresses

Home—Dove Canyon, CA. *Office*—P.O. Box 18516, Irvine, CA 92623-8516. *E-mail*—Nstoryman@aol.com.

Neal Shusterman (Reproduced by permission.)

Career

Screenwriter, playwright, and novelist.

Member

PEN, Society of Children's Book Writers and Illustrators, Writers Guild of America (West).

Awards, Honors

Children's Choice Award, International Reading Association, 1988, and Volunteer State Book Award, Tennessee Library Association, 1990, both for *The Shadow Club;* American Library Association (ALA) Best Book designation, Children's Choice Award, International Reading Association (IRA), and Outstanding Fiction for Young Adults Award, all 1992, Young Adult Choice Award, IRA, 1993, and Oklahoma Sequoyah Award, 1994, all for *What Daddy Did;* C.I.N.E. Golden Eagle awards for writing and directing educational films, 1992, for *Heart on a Chain,* and d1994, for *What About the Sisters?;* New York Public Library Best Book for the Teen Age list, 1992, and California Young Reader Medal nomination, 1995-96, both for *Speeding Bullet;* ALA Best Books for Reluctant Readers designation, 1993, for *The Eyes of Kid Midas;* ALA Best Book for Young Adults and Quick Pick list nominations, 1996, and New York Public Library Best Book for the Teen Age listee, 1997, both for *Scorpion Shards;* Best Books for Reluctant Readers listee, 1997, for *MindQuakes;* ALA Quick Pick Top Ten listee and Best Book for Young Adults, both 1998, Outstanding Book of the Year, Southern California Council on Literature for Children

and Young People, 1999, and included on state award lists in California, New York, Maine, South Carolina, Oklahoma, Texas, Utah, Indiana, Illinois, and Nebraska, 2000, all for *The Dark Side of Nowhere;* Texas Lone Star Award Book, 2000-01, for *Downsiders.*

Writings

FOR YOUNG ADULTS

It's Okay to Say No to Cigarettes and Alcohol (nonfiction), Tor Books (New York, NY), 1988.
The Shadow Club (novel), Little, Brown (Boston, MA), 1988.
Dissidents (novel), Little, Brown (Boston, MA), 1989.
(With Cherie Currie) *Neon Angel: The Cherie Currie Story,* Price, Stern, 1989.
Speeding Bullet (novel), Little, Brown (Boston, MA), 1990.
What Daddy Did (novel), Little, Brown (Boston, MA), 1990.
Kid Heroes: True Stories of Rescuers, Survivors, and Achievers, Tor Books (New York, NY), 1991.
The Eyes of Kid Midas (fantasy), Little, Brown (Boston, MA), 1992.
Darkness Creeping: Tales to Trouble Your Sleep (horror), illustrated by Michael Coy, Lowell House (Los Angeles, CA), 1993.
Piggyback Ninja (fiction), illustrated by Joe Boddy, Lowell House (Los Angeles, CA), 1994.
Darkness Creeping II: More Tales to Trouble Your Sleep (horror), Lowell House (Los Angeles, CA), 1995.
The Dark Side of Nowhere (novel), Little, Brown (Boston, MA), 1996.
MindQuakes: Stories to Shatter Your Brain, Tor Books (New York, NY), 1996.
MindStorms: Stories to Blow Your Mind, Tor Books (New York, NY), 1996.
MindTwisters: Stories to Play with Your Head, Tor Books (New York, NY), 1997.
Downsiders (fiction), Simon & Schuster (New York, NY), 1999.
MindBenders: Stories to Warp Your Brain, Tor Books (New York, NY), 2000.
The Shadow Club, Penguin Putnam (New York, NY), 2002.
The Shadow Club Rising, Penguin Putnam (New York, NY), 2002.
Full Tilt, Simon & Schuster (New York, NY), 2003.
The Schwa Was Here, Dutton (New York, NY), 2004.
Everlost, Simon & Schuster (New York, NY), 2006.
Darkness Creeping: Twenty Twisted Tales, Puffin (New York, NY), 2007.
Unwind, Simon & Schuster (New York, NY), 2007.
Antsy Does Time, Dutton (New York, NY), 2008.
Everwild, Simon & Schuster (New York, NY), 2009.

Also author of television adaptations, including *Night of the Living Dummy III* and *The Werewolf of Fever Swamp* for R.L. Stine's "Goosebumps" series; staffwriter for *Animorphs* television series; author of educational films for Learning Corporation of America, including *Heart on a Chain* and *What About the Sisters?* Creator of "How to Host a Mystery" and "How to Host a Murder" games.

"STAR SHARDS TRILOGY"; FOR YOUNG ADULTS

Scorpion Shards, Forge (New York, NY), 1995.
The Thief of Souls, Tor Books (New York, NY), 1999.
The Shattered Sky, Tor Books (New York, NY), 2002.

"DARK FUSION" SERIES; FOR YOUNG ADULTS

Dread Locks, Dutton (New York, NY), 2005.
Red Rider's Hood, Dutton (New York, NY), 2005.
Duckling Ugly, Dutton (New York, NY), 2006.

Adaptations

Downsiders was optioned for a television movie by the Disney Channel, with a script by Shusterman.

Sidelights

"Writers are a lot like vampires," noted author Neal Shusterman on his home page. "A vampire will never come into your house, unless invited—and once you invite one in, he'll grab you by the throat, and won't let go. A writer is much the same." Shusterman, an award-winning author of books for young adults, screenplays, stage plays, music, and games, works in genres ranging from biographies and realistic fiction to fantastic mysteries, science fiction, and thrillers. Following the publication of *Dissidents,* Shusterman's third book, *Bulletin of the Center for Children's Books* critic Roger Sutton called the author "a strong storyteller and a significant new voice in YA fiction." Lyle Blake, writing in *School Library Journal,* found *The Eyes of Kid Midas* to be "inspired and hypnotically readable." In his many books for young readers, including his popular "Dark Fusion" series for older teens, Shusterman acts the part of benevolent vampire, "feeding on your turmoil, as well as feeding on your peace," as the author explained on his home page.

It was this power of books to not only entertain and inform but to totally captivate that Shusterman himself experienced as a young reader. "Books played an important part in my life when I was growing up," he once noted. "I always loved reading. I remember there was this trick I would play for my friends. They'd blindfold me, then shove a book under my nose, and I could tell them the name of the publisher by the smell of the paper and ink." At age ten, Shusterman, who was born and raised in Brooklyn, went off to summer camp. One particular book, *Jonathan Livingston Seagull* by Richard Bach, which he discovered in the rafters of one of the cabins, swept him away in time and place, as did Roald Dahl's *Charlie and the Chocolate Factory* not

long after. "I remember wishing that I could create something as imaginative as *Charlie and the Chocolate Factory,* and as meaningful as *Jonathan Livingston Seagull,*" Shusterman said. Writing his own stories came soon thereafter; inspired by the movie *Jaws,* he wrote the scenario of a similarly beleaguered small town, substituting giant sand worms for the shark.

Shusterman moved with his family to Mexico City, where he finished high school, and then went on to the University of California—Irvine, where he earned degrees in drama and psychology and set out to write his own novels. Returning to the same summer camp he had attended as a boy—now as a counselor—he tried out his stories on youthful ears and left another copy of *Jonathan Livingston Seagull* in the rafters for some other imaginative youth to discover. At age twenty-two Shusterman became the youngest syndicated columnist in the country when his humor column was picked up by Syndicated Writer's Group.

Shusterman gained extensive recognition for his first novel, *The Shadow Club,* published in 1988. It tells the story of seven middle-school friends who grow tired of living in the shadows of their rivals. Each one is second-best at something, and they form a secret club in order to get back at the students who are number one. At first they restrict their activities to harmless practical jokes like putting a snake in an actress's thermos or filling a trumpet player's horn with green slime. Before long, however, their pranks become more destructive and violent. The mystery involves whether the members of the club have unleashed "a power that feeds on a previously hidden cruel or evil side of their personalities," as David Gale wrote in *School Library Journal,* or whether another student has been responsible for the more dangerous actions. In *Voice of Youth Advocates,* Lesa M. Holstine predicted that *The Shadow Club* would be popular with young adults, since it would likely resemble their own experience with "rivalries and constantly changing friendships." A long-awaited sequel, *The Shadow Club Rising,* was published in 2002.

In *Dissidents,* Derek is a rebellious fifteen year old who is shipped off to Moscow to live with his disinterested mother, the U.S. ambassador to Russia, after his father dies in a car accident. Derek misses his father, hates all the restrictions of his new life, has trouble making friends at school, and acts out his frustrations in wild behavior. He soon becomes fascinated with Anna, the daughter of an exiled Soviet dissident, after he sees her in a television interview. Anna's mother is dying, and Derek comes up with a scheme to reunite her with her father. Although a *Publishers Weekly* contributor found Shusterman's portrayal of U.S.-Soviet relations to be somewhat "simplistic," the reviewer went on to praise the book as "a briskly paced, intriguing" adventure. Kristiana Gregory, writing in the *Los Angeles Times Book Review,* called *Dissidents* "an excellent glimpse of life on the other side of the globe."

According to *Horn Book* reviewer Ellen Fader, Shusterman's novel *Speeding Bullet* treats readers to a "gritty, fast-paced, and, at times, funny" tale. Nick is an angst-ridden tenth grader who does poorly in school and has no luck with girls. His life changes dramatically one day when, without thinking, he puts himself in danger to rescue a little girl who is about to be hit by a subway train. He becomes a hero and is thanked personally by the mayor of New York City. Nick then decides to make saving people his mission in life, and before long he also rescues an old man from a burning building. His newfound celebrity status gets the attention of Linda, the beautiful but deceitful daughter of a wealthy developer, and the two begin dating. Nick continues rescuing people, but he soon discovers that Linda has set up the situations and paid actors to portray people in distress. His next real rescue attempt results in Nick being shot, but he recovers and ends up with a better outlook on life. In *School Library Journal,* Lucinda Snyder Whitehurst called Shusterman's book "a complex, multilayered novel" that will provide young adults with "much material for contemplation," while a writer for *Publishers Weekly* found it to be "a fast-paced modern parable with compelling characters and true-to-life dialogue."

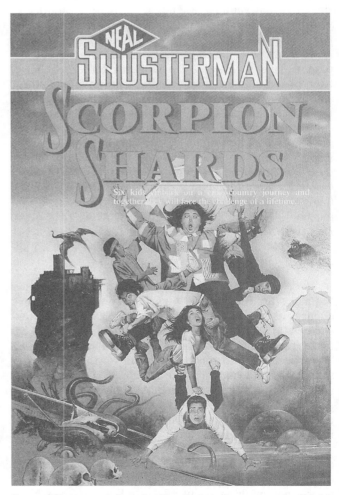

Cover of Shusterman's **Scorpion Shards,** *featuring cover art by Gabriel Picart.* (Tor Books, 1995. Reproduced by permission of St. Martin's Press, Inc.)

Humor and reality also mix in the novels *The Schwa Was Here* and *Antsy Does Time,* both of which focus on quick-witted Brooklyn middle-schooler Antsy Bonano. In *The Schwa Was Here* Antsy and his pals befriend a shy boy named Calvin Schwa, then become fascinated by Calvin's ability to be totally overlooked in most social situations. A scheme is hatched to take advantage of their new friend's talent, but things go too far the boys must endure a punishment that ultimately yields Antsy a new friend. When friend Gunnar is diagnosed with a fatal disease in *Antsy Does Time,* Antsy signs four weeks of his own life over to the boy in a moment of compasion. A date with Gunnar's attractive sister is a surprising result, but Antsy's unselfish act also has more annoying consequences. In *Booklist* John Peters praised Shusterman's young hero as a teen "whose glib tongue and big heart are as apt to get him into trouble as out of it," while *Horn Book* critic Sarah Ellis called Antsy "a fresh and winning amalgam of smart aleck and schlemiel." Shusterman's young characters "are infused with the kind of controlled, precocious improbability that magically vivifies the finest children's classics," concluded Jeffrey Hastings in a *School Library Journal* review of *The Schwa Was Here.*

Shusterman's novel *What Daddy Did* is based on a true story that the author presents as the diary of fourteen-year-old Preston. After his father kills his mother during a heated argument, Preston confronts complex emotions as he deals with the tragedy, learns to live without his parents, and then struggles with his father's release from prison. Preston finally comes to forgive his father, and even serves as best man when his father remarries. Dorothy M. Broderick, writing in *Voice of Youth Advocates,* called *What Daddy Did* "a compelling, spellbinding story of a family gone wrong," adding that it might inspire young adults to "actually stop and think about their own relationship with their parents." Although Gerry Larson commented in *School Library Journal* that "too many issues are not sufficiently resolved" in the book, Rita M. Fontinha wrote in *Kliatt* that *What Daddy Did* "is an important book for many reasons: violence, love, faith, growth, denial, forgiveness are all explored and resolved."

In *The Eyes of Kid Midas* Shusterman takes an amusing fantasy situation and follows the frightening consequences as things spin out of control. Kevin Midas, the smallest kid in the seventh grade, is continually picked on by class bullies and annoyed by his family at home. Then he climbs to the top of a mysterious hill on a school trip and finds a magical pair of sunglasses that make all his wishes come true. At first, Kevin uses the sunglasses for simple things such as making an ice cream cone appear in his hand or making a bully jump into a lake. Over time, however, he becomes addicted to the power, even though he realizes that his wishes can be dangerous and irreversible. When even his dreams start turning into reality and no one seems to notice that anything is out of the ordinary besides him, Kevin must find a way to return things to normal before

Cover of Shusterman's young-adult novel The Schwa Was Here, *featuring artwork by Steven Guarnaccia.* (Cover Illustration copyright © 2006 by Steven Guarnaccia. Reproduced by permission of Puffin Books, a division of Penguin Putnam Books for Young Readers.)

it is too late. *Voice of Youth Advocates* contributor Judith A. Sheriff stated that events in the novel "provide much for thought and discussion, yet do not get in the way of a well-told and intriguing story." Writing in *Wilson Library Bulletin,* Frances Bradburn noted that "Shusterman has written a powerful fantasy based on every adolescent's desire to control his or her life," while a contributor for *Publishers Weekly* called the book "imaginative and witty," and one that "convincingly proves the dangers of the narcissistic ethos of having it all."

In *Scorpion Shards* Shusterman takes special powers one step beyond, enlisting the science-fiction/fantasy genre and the realms of the supernatural in the first installment in his three-part "Star Shards" series. A *Publishers Reviewer* writer noted that in *Scorpion Shards* "Shusterman takes on an outlandish comic-book concept and, through the sheer audacity and breadth if his imagination, makes it stunningly believable." In the story, six teens are outcasts because of the usual afflictions of adolescence, such as acne, obesity, and the fear

of being different. However, their exaggerated sense of their own problems is also accompanied by something special: supernatural powers. Tory's acne causes her to taint everything she touches; Travis likes to break things and ultimately destroys several homes in a landslide. Soon these six divide into two groups: those who want to get rid of such powers and those who wish to cultivate them. "This is a classic story about the battle between [good] and evil made especially gripping as the teenagers struggle with opposing forces literally within themselves," wrote *Kliatt* reviewer Donna L. Scanlon. In *Booklist* Bill Ott noted that, "with all the symbols, metaphors, archetypes—so much meaning—clanging around in this book, it's hard for the characters to draw a breath." However, Ott went on to note of *Scorpion Shards* that "the horror story is suspenseful and compelling."

The second novel in the "Star Shards" trilogy, *Thief of Souls,* follows five of the teens who have discovered the origins of their superhuman powers. Although attempting to live normal lives, Dianna, Tory, Lourdes, Winston, and Michael are now drawn to San Simeon, California, by their sixth companion, Dillon, and enlist to become what a reviewer for *Publishers Weekly* described as "misguided miracle workers." "Echoes of classical and Christian mythology reverberate throughout this tale of fallible messiahs and fallen creatures," noted the reviewer, "giving it an uncommonly solid subtext." Jackie Cassada, reviewing *Thief of Souls* in *Library Journal,* commented that Shusterman's "economy of style and bare-bones characterization propel his tale to its climax with few distractions."

The futuristic "Star Shards" series concludes with *The Sheltered Sky,* which focus on the battle between the six teens and the evil soul eater called Okoya. Now Earth is invaded by three Vectors, travelers from another dimension that survive extinction by feasting on souls. Okoya is kin to these new invaders, and he is worried that he will be killed by his alien comrades should the invasion succeed. Okoya attempts to strike a bargain with Dillon, one of the most powerful shards and one of the few who has not been compromised. Noting that *The Sheltered Sky* is "not for the squeamish" due to it graphic descriptions, a *Publishers Weekly* critic nonetheless wrote that the book's "strong themes of morality, vengeance and the emotional cost of great power should intrigue thoughtful readers."

A second novel trilogy, Shusterman's "Dark Fusion" series, weaves traditional folk stories and mythology into its compelling plots. In series opener *Dread Locks* readers meet wealthy, overindulged fourteen-year-old Parker Baer. When beautiful, golden-haired Brit Tara Herpecheveux and her family move in next door, Parker is fascinated, and although Tara has some odd habits, she quickly becomes one of the most sought-after girls at school . . . even though her new friends all contract a strange illness that eventually turns them to stone. Noting that Shusterman's novel presents an "updated meld-

ing" of the Goldilocks story and the tale of the legendary Medusa, *Kliatt* critic Paula Rohrlick deemed *Dread Locks* "a fast-moving, spine-chilling story" mixing both horror and fantasy. In *School Library Journal* Molly S. Kinney praised the novel, writing that "most books of this genre rarely deliver a message so powerfully," and in *Booklist* Debbie Carton dubbed *Dread Locks* a "fast-paced, short read [that] will be a big hit with fans of Daren Shan."

Shusterman's "Dark Fusion" series continues with *Red Rider's Hood* and *Duckling Ugly,* both of which draw on the dark side of traditional fairy stories. In *Red Rider's Hood* the story of Little Red Riding Hood melds with the werewolf legend in the author's tale of a street-smart urban teen who infiltrates a gang called the Wolves in order to avenge his grandmother's mugging. When he does so, however, he finds that a strange force is drawing him toward accepting the gang's nocturnal lifestyle. In *Duckling Ugly* Shusterman weaves a fictional mix that includes strands of "The Ugly Duck-

Cover of Shusterman's middle-grade thriller **The Dark Side of Knowhere,** *featuring eerie cover art by David Gaadt.* (Tor Books, 1997. Copyright © 1997 by Neal Shusterman. Reproduced by permission of St. Martin's Press.)

ing," "Beauty and the Beast," and "Sleeping Beauty" into a story about Cara de Fido, a teen whose ugly appearance and odd behaviors make her an outcast among her peers. Cara still has normal teen feelings, however, and that includes a crush on a handsome boy. When she is rejected, the teen runs away, determined to find her destiny even though it may cause suffering to others. In *School Library Journal* Sharon Rawlins called *Duckling Ugly* a "a dark, edgy, and suspenseful tale," and Rohrlick wrote that *Red Rider's Hood* "features lots of action and creepy details," making it attractive to reluctant readers.

The Dark Side of Nowhere, a science-fiction thriller, finds teenager Jason feeling trapped in his small town until he discovers an awful secret about himself. Jason undergoes an identity crisis and a crucial choice after discovering that he is the son of aliens who stayed on Earth following an unsuccessful invasion. In *Booklist* Carolyn Phelan noted that the novel contains "a fast-paced story, giving Jason many vivid, original turns of phrase, letting the plot get weird enough to keep readers enthralled, then coming back to the human emotions

Cover of Downsiders, *Schusterman's young-adult thriller featuring cover artwork by Greg Harlin.* (Illustration copyright © 1999 by Greg Harlin, Wood Ronsaville Harlin, Inc. Reproduced by permission.)

at the heart of it all." A writer for *Kirkus Reviews* felt that "Shusterman delivers a tense thriller that doesn't duck larger issues," and also "seamlessly combines gritty, heart-stopping plotting with a wealth of complex issues." *School Library Journal* contributor Bruce Anne Shook concluded that *The Dark Side of Nowhere* serves up "great science fiction."

With *Downsiders* Shusterman again skirts the boundaries between reality and science fiction/fantasy. Talon is a young New Yorker—with a difference. His people live underground—the "Downsiders" of the title—in the sewers and subways beneath the city. His people never mix with "Topsiders" until Talon falls for Lindsay. Their fragile romance is threatened, however, when Lindsay's father, a city engineer, begins work on an underground aqueduct and one of Talon's friends denounces him for his collaboration with the Topsiders. "Facts . . . are blended with fantasy until it is difficult to tell where truth stops and fiction begins," wrote Shook in a *School Library Journal* review of the book. Shook went on to call *Downsiders* "an exciting and entertaining story that will please fans of adventure, science fiction, and fantasy." Janice M. Del Negro, reviewing the same title for the *Bulletin of the Center for Children's Books,* commented specifically on the "quick and suspenseful" pace of the novel and on the "believable underground culture" that Shusterman creates. The novelist "twines suspense and satire through this ingenious tale of a secret community living deep beneath the streets of New York," wrote a contributor for *Kirkus Reviews.* The same reviewer concluded that "urban readers . . . will be checking the storm drains for peering faces in the wake of this cleverly envisioned romp."

Described as a "surreal, scary fantasy, packed with suspenseful psychological drama" by *Booklist* contributor Ed Sullivan, *Full Tilt* finds sixteen-year-old Blake embroiled in a mystery after he receives an invitation from a beautiful young woman. The invitation is to a private carnival, and when Blake's older brother Quinn goes in Blake's stead, the young man winds up in a comatose state. When Blake learns that Quinn has lost his very soul, he learns that to set things right he must endure a test that includes seven horrifying carnival rides, all of which tap into his deepest childhood fears. *Full Tilt* "will have readers glued to the pages," concluded Rohrlick, the critic also praising the book's "clever dialogue and . . . carnival ride action."

Other novels by Shusterman include *Everlost,* which finds two teens trapped together in a strange limbo world after dying in a car accident, and *Unwind,* a near-future fable inspired by the abortion debate. Shusterman's "action-packed plot moves quickly," noted Susan Dove Lempke in her *Horn Book* review of *Everlost,* "and the characters grow and change as they learn to cope with their new existence."

In *Unwind,* unwanted children over age thirteen are relegated to use as a collection of harvest-ready body parts

Cover of Shusterman's novel **Antsy Does Time,** *featuring artwork by* **Steven Guarnaccia.** (Illustration copyright © 2008 by Steven Guarnaccia. Reproduced by permission of Dutton Children's Books, a division of Penguin Putnam Books for Young Readers.)

through a process known as retroactive pregnancy termination. When Connor, Lev, and Risa are scheduled for "unwinding," the teens escape in the hope that they can find a place to safely live out their natural lives. Shusterman "manages to create and balance three separate and compelling journeys of self-discovery," according to Claire E. Gross in her *Horn Book* review of the novel, and in *School Library Journal* Amy J. Chow praised the book's "gripping, omniscient" narration. Commenting on the provocative premise underlining *Unwind,* Ned Vizzini wrote in his *New York Times Book Review* that, "ultimately, . . . the power of the novel lies in what it doesn't do: come down explicitly on one side or the other" of the socially sanctioned taking of human life.

In addition to novels, Shusterman also explores the supernatural with the short stories in his "MindQuakes" series—including *MindQuakes: Stories to Shatter Your Brain, MindTwisters: Stories to Play with Your Head, MindStorms: Stories to Blow Your Mind,* and *Mind-Benders: Stories to Warp Your Brian*—as well as books such as *Darkness Creeping: Twenty Twisted Tales.* The "MindQuakes" books are guaranteed to "snare even re-

luctant readers," according to a contributor for *Publishers Weekly.* Reviewing the second installment in the series, *MindStorms,* Scanlon noted that "these stories range from humorous to poignant and capture the reader's imagination," while in their "quirky, off-the-wall" style they resemble the *Twilight Zone* television series. A contributor to *Voice of Youth Advocates,* writing about *MindTwisters,* warned readers to "prepare to have your mind twisted and your reality warped by this exciting collection of weird tales," while *School Library Journal* critic Mara Alpert dubbed *Darkness Creeping* "extremely readable and elegantly creepy."

In addition to his novels for teen readers, Shusterman has also written for television and film, as well as directed educational short films. In all of his ventures, he takes the creative process and its responsibilities to heart. "I often think about the power of the written word," he explained on his home page. "Being a writer is like being entrusted with . . . or, more accurately stealing the power of flames, and then sling-shotting it into the air to see who catches fire. I think writers have a responsibility not to launch those fireballs indiscriminately, although occasionally we do. Still, what a power to find yourself responsible for, because words can change the world. I've always felt that stories aimed at adolescents and teens are the most important stories that can be written, because it is adolescence that defines who we are going to be."

Biographical and Critical Sources

PERIODICALS

Booklist, February 1, 1996, Bill Ott, review of *Scorpion Shards,* p. 926; April 1, 1997, Carolyn Phelan, review of *The Dark Side of Nowhere,* p. 1322; May 15, 2003, Ed Sullivan, review of *Full Tilt,* p. 1656; December 1, 2004, Frances Bradburn, review of *The Schwa Was Here,* p. 648; June 1, 2005, Debbie Carton, review of *Dread Locks,* p. 1792; September 15, 2006, Holly Koelling, review of *Everlost,* p. 57; May 15, 2007, Jennifer Mattson, review of *Darkness Creeping: Twenty Twisted Tales,* p. 60; September 1, 2008, John Peters, review of *Antsy Does Time,* p. 96.
Bulletin of the Center for Children's Books, June, 1989, Roger Sutton, review of *Dissidents,* p. 264; September, 1999, Janice M. Del Negro, review of *Downsiders,* p. 31.
Horn Book, May-June, 1991, Ellen Fader, review of *Speeding Bullet,* p. 340; June 1, 2005, Debbie Carton, review of *Dread Locks,* p. 1792; December, 2006, Susan Dove Lempke, review of *Everlost,* p. 725; March-April, 2008, Claire E. Gross, review of *Unwind,* p. 219; September-October, 2008, Sarah Ellis, review of *Antsy Does Time,* p. 597.
Journal of Adolescent and Adult Literacy, October, 2001, Sally Emery, review of *Downsiders,* p. 173

Kirkus Reviews, March 15, 1997, review of *The Dark Side of Nowhere,* p. 468; June 1, 1999, review of *Downsiders,* p. 889; April 15, 2002, review of *Shattered Sky,* p. 533; October 1, 2004, review of *The Schwa Was Here,* p. 969; January 15, 2006, review of *Duckling Ugly,* p. 90.

Kliatt, May, 1993, Rita M. Fontinha, review of *What Daddy Did,* p. 10; January, 1997, Donna L. Scanlon, review of *Scorpion Shards,* pp. 10-11, and *Mind-Storms: Stories to Blow Your Mind,* p. 16; May, 2003, Paula Rohrlick, review of *Full Tilt,* p. 14; May, 2005, Paula Rohrlick, review of *Dread Locks,* p. 18; November, 2005, Paula Rohrlick, review of *Red Rider's Hood,* p. 10; September, 2006, Paula Rohrlick, review of *Everlost,* p. 18.

Library Journal, March 15, 1999, Jackie Cassada, review of *Thief of Souls,* p. 113; July 15, 2002, Jackie Cassada, review of *Shattered Sky,* p. 99.

Los Angeles Times Book Review, July 23, 1989, Kristiana Gregory, review of *Dissidents,* p. 11.

New York Times Book Review, March 16, 2008, Ned Vizzini, review of *Unwind,* p. 15.

Publishers Weekly, May 12, 1989, review of *Dissidents,* p. 296; December 14, 1990, review of *Speeding Bullet,* p. 67; November 16, 1992, review of *The Eyes of Kid Midas,* p. 65; December 4, 1995, review of *Scorpion Shards,* p. 63; May 27, 1996, review of *MindQuakes: Stories to Shatter Your Brain,* p. 79; February 8, 1999, review of *Thief of Souls,* p. 199; April 8, 2002, review of *Shattered Sky,* p. 210; November 26, 2007, review of *Unwind,* p. 54.

School Library Journal, May, 1988, David Gale, review of *The Shadow Club,* p. 113; February, 1991, Lucinda Snyder Whitehurst, review of *Speeding Bullet,* p. 94; June, 1991, Gerry Larson, review of *What Daddy Did,* p. 128; December, 1992, Lyle Blake, review of *The Eyes of Kid Midas,* p. 133; July, 1997, Bruce Anne Shook, review of *The Dark Side of Nowhere,* p. 9; July, 1999, Bruce Anne Shook, review of *Downsiders,* p. 100; October, 2004, Jeffrey Hastings, review of *The Schwa Was Here,* p. 176; June, 2005, Molly S. Kinney, review of *Dread Locks,* p. 169; December, 2005, Kimberly L. Paone, review of *Red Rider's Hood,* p. 155; July, 2006, Sharon Rawlins, review of *Duckling Ugly,* p. 112; July, 2007, Mara Alpert, review of *Darkness Creeping,* p. 111; January, 2008, Amy J. Chow, review of *Unwind,* p. 126.

Voice of Youth Advocates, June, 1988, Lesa M. Holstine, review of *The Shadow Club,* p. 90; June, 1991, Dorothy M. Broderick, review of *What Daddy Did,* p. 103; February, 1993, Judith A. Sheriff, review of *The Eyes of Kid Midas,* p. 358; April, 1998, review of *MindTwisters: Stories to Play with Your Head,* p. 14.

Wilson Library Bulletin, March, 1993, Frances Bradburn, review of *The Eyes of Kid Midas,* p. 85.

ONLINE

Neal Shusterman Home Page, http://www.storyman.com (May 15, 2009).*

SINGER, Marilyn 1948-

Personal

Born October 3, 1948, in New York, NY; daughter of Abraham (a photoengraver) and Shirley Singer; married Steven Aronson (a financial manager), July 31, 1971. *Education:* Attended University of Reading, 1967-68; Queens College of the City University of New York, B.A. (cum laude), 1969; New York University, M.A., 1979. *Hobbies and other interests:* Dog obedience and agility, reading, hiking, theater, film, bird watching and caring for animals, gardening, meditation, computer adventure games.

Addresses

Home and office—42 Berkeley Pl., Brooklyn, NY 11217. *E-mail*—writerbabe@aol.com.

Career

Daniel S. Mead Literary Agency, New York, NY, editor, 1967; *Where* (magazine), New York, NY, assistant editor, 1969; New York City Public High Schools, New York, NY, teacher of English and speech, 1969-74; writer, 1974—.

Member

Society of Children's Book Writers and Illustrators, Authors Guild, American Library Association, Dog Writers Association of America, PEN American Center, Nature Conservancy, North American Dog Agility Council, New York Zoological Society, Staten Island Companion Dog Training Club, Phi Beta Kappa.

Awards, Honors

Children's Choice Award, International Reading Association, 1977, for *The Dog Who Insisted He Wasn't,* 1979, for *It Can't Hurt Forever,* 1988, for *Ghost Host,* and 1991, for *Nine o'Clock Lullaby;* Maud Hart Lovelace Award, Friends of the Minnesota Valley Regional Library, 1983, for *It Can't Hurt Forever;* American Library Association (ALA) Best Book for Young Adults citation, 1983, for *The Course of True Love Never Did Run Smooth;* Parents' Choice Award, Parents' Choice Foundation, 1983, for *The Fido Frame-Up,* and 2001, for *A Pair of Wings; New York Times* Best Illustrated Children's Book citation, and *Time* Best Children's Book citation, both 1989, Notable Trade Book in the Language Arts designation, National Council of Teachers of English, 1990, and Texas Bluebonnet Award nomination, 1992, all for *Turtle in July;* South Carolina Book Award nomination, 1992-93, for *Twenty Ways to Lose Your Best Friend;* Iowa Teen Award nomination, 1993, for *Charmed;* Notable Children's Trade Book in the Field of Social Studies, National Council for the Social Studies/Children's Book Council (CBC), 1995, for *Family Reunion,* and 2000, for *On the Same Day in March;* Washington Children's Choice Picture Book

Marilyn Singer (Reproduced by permission.)

Award nomination, 1996, for *Chester the Out-of-Work Dog;* Dorothy Canfield Fisher Award nomination, 1997-98, for *All We Needed to Say;* Society of School Librarians International Best Books designation, 1997-98, for *Deal with a Ghost,* 1998-99, for *Bottoms Up,* and 2001, for *Tough Beginnings;* Best Books for the Teen Age selection, New York Public Library, 1998, for *Stay True,* 2001, for *I Believe in Water,* 2005, for *Face Relations,* 2006, for *Make Me Over;* Edgar Allan Poe Award nominee, Mystery Writers of America 1998, for *Deal with a Ghost;* Popular Paperbacks for Young Adults selection, Young Adult Library Services Association, 2000, for *Stay True;* Animal Behavior Society Award, 2002, for *A Pair of Wings;* Canadian Children's Book Centre Our Choice designation, 2002, for *Didi and Daddy on the Promenade;* Outstanding Science Trade Book for Students, National Science Teachers Association/CBC, 2002, for *Tough Beginnings;* Children's Book of Distinction honor, *Riverbank Review,* 2003, for *Footprints on the Roof;* Honor Book designation, Lee Bennett Hopkins Poetry Award, 2005, for *Creature Carnival;* ALA Honor Book designation, 2005, for *Central Heating;* *Time* magazine Top Ten Children's Books designation, 2007, for *City Lullaby;* Bank Street College of Education Best Children's Book designation, 2007, for *Let's Build a Clubhouse;* Chicago Public Library Best of the Best designation, 2009, for *First Food Fight This Fall, and Other Poems about School.*

Writings

PICTURE BOOKS

The Dog Who Insisted He Wasn't, illustrated by Kelly Oechsli, Dutton (New York, NY), 1976.

The Pickle Plan, illustrated by Steven Kellogg, Dutton (New York, NY), 1978.

Will You Take Me to Town on Strawberry Day?, illustrated by Trinka Hakes Noble, Harper (New York, NY), 1981.

Archer Armadillo's Secret Room, illustrated by Beth Lee Weiner, Macmillan (New York, NY), 1985.

Minnie's Yom Kippur Birthday, illustrated by Ruth Rosner, Harper (New York, NY), 1989.

Nine o'Clock Lullaby, illustrated by Frané Lessac, Harper-Collins (New York, NY), 1991.

The Golden Heart of Winter, illustrated by Robert Rayevsky, Morrow (New York, NY), 1991.

Chester the Out-of-Work Dog, illustrated by Cat Bowman Smith, Holt (New York, NY), 1992.

The Painted Fan, illustrated by Wenhai Ma, Morrow (New York, NY), 1994.

The Maiden on the Moor, illustrated by Troy Howell, Morrow (New York, NY), 1995.

In the Palace of the Ocean King, illustrated by Ted Rand, Atheneum (New York, NY), 1995.

Good Day, Good Night, illustrated by Ponder Goembel, Marshall Cavendish (New York, NY), 1998.

Solomon Sneezes, illustrated by Brian Floca, HarperFestival (New York, NY), 1999.

On the Same Day in March: A Tour of the World's Weather, illustrated by Frané Lessac, HarperCollins (New York, NY), 2000.

The One and Only Me, illustrated by Nicole Rubel, HarperFestival (New York, NY), 2000.

Fred's Bed, illustrated by JoAnn Adinolfi, HarperFestival (New York, NY), 2001.

Didi and Daddy on the Promenade, illustrated by Marie-Louise Gay, Clarion (New York, NY), 2001.

Boo-Hoo, Boo-Boo!, illustrated by Elivia Savadier, HarperFestival (New York, NY), 2002.

Quiet Night, illustrated by John Manders, Clarion (New York, NY), 2002.

Block Party Today!, illustrated by Stephanie Roth, Knopf (New York, NY), 2004.

So Many Kinds of Kisses, illustrated by Emily Arnold McCully, Atheneum (New York, NY), 2004.

Monday on the Mississippi, illustrated by Frané Lessac, Holt (New York, NY), 2005.

City Lullaby, illustrated by Carll Cneut, Clarion Books (New York, NY), 2007.

Eggs, illustrated by Emma Stevenson, Holiday House (New York, NY), 2008.

Shoe Bop!, illustrated by Hiroe Nakata, Dutton Children's Books (New York, NY), 2008.

Checkup, illustrated by David Milgrim, Clarion Books (New York, NY), 2009.

I'm Your Bus, illustrated by Evan Polenghi, Scholastic Press (New York, NY), 2009.

CHILDREN'S FICTION

It Can't Hurt Forever, illustrated by Leigh Grant, Harper (New York, NY), 1978.

Tarantulas on the Brain, illustrated by Leigh Grant, Harper (New York, NY), 1982.

Lizzie Silver of Sherwood Forest (sequel to *Tarantulas on the Brain*), illustrated by Miriam Nerlove, Harper (New York, NY), 1986.

The Lightey Club, illustrated by Kathryn Brown, Four Winds (New York, NY), 1987.

Mitzi Meyer, Fearless Warrior Queen, Scholastic (New York, NY), 1987.

Charmed (fantasy), Atheneum (New York, NY), 1990.

Twenty Ways to Lose Your Best Friend, illustrated by Jeffrey Lindberg, Harper (New York, NY), 1990.

California Demon, Hyperion (New York, NY), 1992.

Big Wheel, Hyperion (New York, NY), 1993.

Josie to the Rescue, illustrated by S.D. Schindler, Scholastic (New York, NY), 1999.

The Circus Lunicus, Holt (New York, NY), 2000.

Let's Build a Clubhouse, illustrated by Timothy Bush, Clarion Books (New York, NY), 2006

What Stinks?, Darby Creek Pub. (Plain City, OH), 2006.

CHILDREN'S POETRY

Turtle in July, illustrated by Jerry Pinkney, Macmillan (New York, NY), 1989.

In My Tent, illustrated by Emily Arnold McCully, Macmillan (New York, NY), 1992.

It's Hard to Read a Map with a Beagle on Your Lap, illustrated by Clement Oubrerie, Holt (New York, NY), 1993.

Sky Words, illustrated by Deborah K. Ray, Macmillan (New York, NY), 1994.

Family Reunion, illustrated by R.W. Alley, Macmillan (New York, NY), 1994.

Please Don't Squeeze Your Boa, Noah!, illustrated by Clement Oubrerie, Holt (New York, NY), 1995.

The Morgans Dream, illustrated by Gary Drake, Holt (New York, NY), 1995.

All That We Needed to Say: Poems about School from Tanya and Sophie, photographs by Lorna Clark, Atheneum (New York, NY), 1996.

Monster Museum, illustrated by Chris Grimly, Hyperion (New York, NY), 2001.

Footprints on the Roof: Poems about the Earth, illustrated by Meilo So, Random House (New York, NY), 2002.

The Company of Crows, illustrated by Linda Saport, Clarion (New York, NY), 2002.

How to Cross a Pond: Poems about Water, illustrated by Meilo So, Knopf (New York, NY), 2003.

Fireflies at Midnight, illustrated by Ken Robbins, Atheneum (New York, NY), 2003.

Creature Carnival, illustrated by Gris Grimley, Hyperion (New York, NY), 2004.

Central Heating: Poems about Fire and Warmth, illustrated by Meilo So, Alfred A. Knopf (New York, NY), 2005.

First Food Fight This Fall, and Other School Poems, illustrated by Sachiko Yoshikawa, Sterling (New York, NY), 2008.

"SAM AND DAVE" MYSTERY SERIES

Leroy Is Missing, illustrated by Judy Glasser, Harper (New York, NY), 1984.

The Case of the Sabotaged School Play, illustrated by Judy Glasser, Harper (New York, NY), 1984.

A Clue in Code, illustrated by Judy Glasser, Harper (New York, NY), 1985.

The Case of the Cackling Car, illustrated by Judy Glasser, Harper (New York, NY), 1985.

The Case of the Fixed Election, illustrated by Richard Williams, Harper (New York, NY), 1989.

The Hoax on You, illustrated by Richard Williams, Harper (New York, NY), 1989.

"SAMANTHA SPAYED" MYSTERY SERIES

The Fido Frame-Up, illustrated by Andrew Glass, Warne (New York, NY), 1983.

A Nose for Trouble, illustrated by Andrew Glass, Holt (New York, NY), 1985.

Where There's a Will, There's a Wag, illustrated by Andrew Glass, Holt (New York, NY), 1986.

YOUNG-ADULT FICTION

No Applause, Please, Dutton (New York, NY), 1977.

The First Few Friends, Harper (New York, NY), 1981.

The Course of True Love Never Did Run Smooth, Harper (New York, NY), 1983.

Horsemaster (fantasy), Atheneum (New York, NY), 1985.

Ghost Host, Harper (New York, NY), 1987.

Several Kinds of Silence, Harper (New York, NY), 1988.

Storm Rising, Scholastic (New York, NY), 1989.

Deal with a Ghost, Holt (New York, NY), 1997.

EDITOR

Stay True: Short Stories for Strong Girls, Scholastic (New York, NY), 1998.

I Believe in Water: Twelve Brushes with Religion (short stories), HarperCollins (New York, NY), 2000.

Face Relations: Eleven Stories about Seeing beyond Color (short stories), Simon & Schuster (New York, NY), 2004.

Make Me Over: Eleven Stories about Transforming Ourselves (short stories), Dutton (New York, NY), 2005.

NONFICTION

(Editor and author of introduction) *A History of Avant-Garde Cinema,* American Federation of Arts, 1976.

(Editor and contributor) *New American Filmmakers,* American Federation of Arts, 1976.

The Fanatic's Ecstatic, Aromatic Guide to Onions, Garlic, Shallots and Leeks, illustrated by Marian Perry, Prentice-Hall (Englewood Cliffs, NJ), 1981.

Exotic Birds (for children), illustrated by James Needham, Doubleday (New York, NY), 1990.

A Wasp Is Not a Bee (for children), illustrated by Patrick O'Brien, Holt (New York, NY), 1995.

Bottoms Up! (for children), illustrated by Patrick O'Brien, Holt (New York, NY), 1998.

Prairie Dogs Kiss and Lobsters Wave (for children), illustrated by Normand Chartier, Holt (New York, NY), 1998.

A Dog's Gotta Do What a Dog's Gotta Do: Dogs at Work (for children), Holt (New York, NY), 2000.

A Pair of Wings (for children), illustrated by Anne Wertheim, Holiday House, 2001.

Tough Beginnings: How Baby Animals Survive (for children), illustrated by Anna Vojtech, Holt (New York, NY), 2001.

Cats to the Rescue: True Tales of Heroic Felines, illustrated by Jean Cassels, Henry Holt (New York, NY), 2006

OTHER

Also author of teacher's guides, catalogs, and program notes on films and filmstrips, including Jacob Bronowski's *The Ascent of Man* and David Attenborough's *The Tribal Eye*. Writer of scripts for the children's television show *The Electric Company*. Contributor to books, including *Children's Writers and Illustrators Market,* 2003. Contributor of short stories to books, including *Shattered,* edited by Jennifer Armstrong, Knopf; and *Sport Shorts: Eight Stories about Sports,* edited by Tanya Dean, Darby Creek Publishing. Contributor of poetry to books, including *Food Fight,* edited by Michael J. Rosen, *Book of Valentine Hearts: Holiday Poetry* and *Oh, No! Where Are My Pants? and Other Disasters: Poems,* both edited by Lee Bennett Hopkins, and to periodicals, including *Yes, Archer, Encore, Corduroy, Tamesis, Storyworks,* and *Gyre*. Writer of articles for magazines, including *Click* and *American Kennel Club Gazette*.

Sidelights

Marilyn Singer is an award-winning author of children's books in a wide variety of genres, including fiction and nonfiction picture books, juvenile novels and mysteries, young-adult fantasies, and poetry. Among her many characters are a dog who insists he is not a dog, an armadillo, a young heart-surgery patient, obsessive Lizzie Silver, Stryker the poltergeist, twin detectives Sam and Dave, and even a dog detective. Singer's ability to write for so many different audiences has won her awards in each area, from Children's Choice awards to Edgar Allan Poe award nominations for her mysteries, to awards for science titles as well as various Best Books citations.

Singer began her writing career creating teaching guides on film and filmstrips. Although she enjoyed the work for a while, she was not entirely satisfied and began looking into magazine writing. Her article proposals were not very successful, but she did manage to have some of her poetry published. Then came a major turning point. She was sitting in the Brooklyn Botanic Garden with a pad of paper and a pen in case she wanted to write a new poem, when she suddenly found herself writing a story instead. Upon seeing this first story, her husband encouraged her to write more, so Singer wrote a number of children's stories featuring animals and mailed them off to publishers. In the meantime, she

Cover of Singer's teen novel The Circus Lunicus, *featuring artwork by* **Janet Drew.** (Illustration copyright © 2000 by Janet Drew. Reprinted by permission of Henry Holt & Company, LLC.)

joined a workshop for unpublished children's authors at Bank Street College and continued writing. Then one day she received a letter from Dutton, telling her that they wanted to publish one of her books—*The Dog Who Insisted He Wasn't*. This was the beginning of Singer's new career.

In *The Dog Who Insisted He Wasn't* Singer tells the story of Konrad, a dog who is absolutely positive that he is not a dog but a person instead. He is lucky enough to find Abigail, who convinces her family to go along with Konrad's whim and treat him as if he were a human. Konrad sits at the table to eat, takes baths, and even goes to school. When the other dogs in the neighborhood decide that they too want to be treated like people, all chaos breaks loose. They are eventually convinced to go back to their carefree lives as dogs, and Konrad compromises by agreeing to pretend that he is a dog. A reviewer for the *Bulletin of the Center for Children's Books* praised Singer's portrayal of conversations between animals and humans and further observed that "the adult-child relationships are exemplary."

Singer often features dogs in her work, including the nonfiction book *A Dog's Gotta Do What a Dog's Gotta*

Do: Dogs at Work and the poetry collection *It's Hard to Read a Map with a Beagle on Your Lap.* In another dog-based title, *Chester the Out-of-Work Dog,* a border collie loses his job when he and his family move from their farm to the city. Writing in *Booklist,* Ilene Cooper noted that *Chester the out-of-Work Dog* "has it all—slapstick comedy, a touch of pathos, and an actual story with a beginning, a middle, and an end." Just to balance the scales, Singer also addresses felines in *Cats to the Rescue: True Tales of Heroic Felines,* a picture book illustrated by Jean Cassels that relates several stories about cats who have led exemplary lives—such as a mouser who has kept a Scottish distiller free of an estimated 30,000 rodents. "Written with affection and a bit of amazement," *Cats to the Rescue* "is a pleasure to read," concluded Cooper of the picture book.

Singer's writing for younger children also addresses a variety of people and places in the world. In *Nine o'Clock Lullaby* she explores what children around the world are doing at the time a child in Brooklyn is going to sleep. Complemented by the illustrations of Frané Lessac, the book provides a simple introduction to time zones and children of other cultures, as well as serving as a "rhythmic, pleasing lullaby," according to a *Pub-*

Cover of Singer's ode to working canines: A Dog's Gotta Do What a Dog's Gotta Do, *featuring photography by Mary Bloom.* (Photograph copyright © by AKC/ Mary Bloom. Reprinted by permission of Henry Holt & Company, LLC.)

lishers Weekly critic. Patricia Dooley, writing in *School Library Journal,* praised the way *Nine o'Clock Lullaby* demonstrates "the connectedness of the inhabitants of our global village."

Singer and Lessac again team up for *On the Same Day in March,* a picture-book look at weather in seventeen locations around the world. For each location, "Singer provides a few lines of lyrical text that vividly create the climate," noted *Booklist* reviewer Michael Cart, the critic concluding that the book "doubles as a delightfully agreeable introduction to both climatology and geography." Jody McCoy, writing in *School Library Journal,* called the same title a "useful and engaging addition." Another collaboration by Singer and Lessac, *Monday on the Mississippi* takes readers on a trip down the fabled Mississippi river from its source at Lake Itasca, Minnesota, to the Gulf of Mexico.

Young readers are drawn into the land of myth in *The Golden Heart of Winter,* Singer's original folktale about three sons sent off to bring back a prize to their aging father. "The rich prose and haunting illustrations of this original story give it the texture of a folktale," wrote Miriam Martinez in *Language Arts.* In *The Painted Fan* readers are transported to ancient China where a cruel ruler destroys all the fans in the kingdom after a soothsayer tells him a painted fan will be his undoing. This is a story told with "simplicity and dignity," according to Carolyn Phelan in *Booklist.*

Medieval England serves as the setting of *Maiden on the Moor,* a story about two shepherd brothers who find a young maiden on a snowy moor. Donna L. Scanlon, reviewing the picture book in *School Library Journal,* felt the tale "is sure to spark imaginations as it transcends ordinary fairy-tale conventions." Scanlon also noted that Singer "knows how to distill words into images, and she conveys the bleak beauty of the setting with clarity and precision." Singer presents another original fairy tale in *The Palace of the Ocean King,* in which traditional roles are reversed: it is the maiden who must save the imprisoned young prince.

Young readers enter the bustling streets of multicultural Brooklyn in the pages of *Didi and Daddy on the Promenade,* as an eager preschooler joins her father on a Sunday morning outing. In contrast, *City Lullaby* brings to life the many layers of sounds that fade from the urban landscape with the coming of night. Shelle Rosenfeld, writing in *Booklist,* commented of *Didi and Daddy on the Promenade* that both young and adult readers will "recognize and enjoy Didi's humorous enthusiasm (and Daddy's good-natured participation) as the walk brings anticipated joys and unexpected surprises." Noting Singer's use of onomatopoeia in *City Lullaby,* Engberg added that the author "writes in infectious, rhyming poetry that scans smoothly to a rapid beat." Also set in Brooklyn, *Block Party Today!* finds a girl letting go of her anger at being left out by her friends in order to enjoy the fun of a neighborhood gathering. "Both text

and art beautifully catch the excitement of an event that transforms ho-hum surroundings into a playground," wrote Jennifer Mattson in her review of *Block Party Today!* for *Booklist,* and in *School Library Journal* Genevieve Gallagher deemed Singer's picture book "a fun choice for welcoming summer or for exploring friendships."

In addition to picture books, Singer has also produced a wide array of nonfiction works for young readers. In *Exotic Birds* she provides a "fact-filled but readable introduction" to the subject, according to *Booklist* contributor Leone McDermott. Ellen Dibner, reviewing the same title in *School Library Journal,* concluded that *Exotic Birds* is a "most satisfying book for browsing, general information, and exotic bird watching." Other flying creatures are dealt with in *A Wasp Is Not a Bee* and *A Pair of Wings,* while their growth is the subject of the simply titled *Eggs.* Describing *Eggs* as "handsome" due to its artwork by Emma Stevenson, Phelan added that Singer's "smoothly written . . . text creates an even, almost conversational flow from page to page." Moving close to the ground, *Venom* ranges from pond to forest, profiling spiders, snakes, and other creatures that defend and attack using poisons. "Browsers . . . will enthusiastically dig their teeth into this substantial survey," concluded John Peters in his review of Singer's detailed look at the darker side of nature.

Some of Singer's nonfiction titles came about because she was annoyed: "When I heard one too many folks call a wasp a 'bee,' a gorilla a 'monkey,' and even a heron a 'duck,' I got bugged enough to write *A Wasp Is Not a Bee,*" she explained in an article for *School Library Journal.* "Then there was the time at the Prospect Park Zoo when a little boy asked his mom why baboons have such big red butts. Despite a series of placards explaining the reason for these simian endowments, the mother loudly replied, 'Because they're sick.' Instead of howling at her, I came up with *Bottoms Up!: A Book about Rear Ends.* Focusing on animal anatomy, *Bottoms Up!* was described as a "cheerful book about behinds and their uses" by *Booklist* reviewer Ilene Cooper. In *Prairie Dogs Kiss and Lobsters Wave,* Singer shows how animals greet one another. The book, according to *Booklist* contributor Hazel Rochman, is noteworthy for its "friendly, immediate text and active, colorful pictures."

Of her several poetry books for young readers, Singer's personal favorite is the award-winning *Turtle in July,* "a lovely picture book of poetry that moves through the seasons," according to Janet Hickman in *Language Arts.* Nancy Vasilakis, reviewing *Turtle in July* for *Horn Book,* felt that Singer and illustrator Jerry Pinkney create a "vivid picture book that is visually as well as auditorily pleasing," and that Singer's use of the first person "captures the essence of each animal."

Fireflies at Midnight has been considered a companion title to *Turtle in July* by several critics. Set over the course of a single day, *Fireflies at Midnight* features poems on the various animals who live near a pond, beginning with the robin who wakes earliest in the morning, stopping to visit a lordly frog, and continuing on until at midnight, the fireflies are encountered. *Fireflies at Midnight* "is well suited for storytime," advised Marge Loch-Wouters in *School Library Journal,* and *Booklist* reviewer Gillian Engberg commented that "Singer clearly imagines the voices and personalities of familiar animals in exuberant lines." A *Kirkus Reviews* critic cited the book for featuring "luminous poems that will stand the test of time."

With Meilo So as her illustrator, Singer has produced three inter-related poetry collections: *Footprints on the Roof: Poems about Earth, How to Cross a Pond: Poems about Water,* and *Central Heating: Poems about Fire and Warmth. Footprints on the Roof* features nineteen poems dealing with various topics about the Earth, from volcanoes and mud to burrows and trees. Although the illustrations make the collection accessible for a younger audience, Engberg recommended the title to "middle-school and teen writers," and Kathleen Whalin called it "a welcome addition to nature-poetry collections." *How to Cross a Pond* focuses on watery topics ranging from oceans to tears, discussing how dearly water is valued when it is hard to get in poems such as "Wells." Hazel Rochman reviewed the collection for *Booklist,* wrote that, "never pretentious, she celebrates the physical joy of splashing . . . as well as the wonder of the rain forest." *Central Heating* covers birthday candles, marshmallow roasts, and a fire that destroys an old, abandoned house. "Its engaging design will surely entice readers to open and read," noted a contributor to *Kirkus Reviews.*

Unlike her more environmentally based collections, the poetry book *Creature Carnival* covers animals that are anything but natural. Featuring monsters and other creatures from myth, legend, and popular movies, Singer introduces new readers to famous monsters such as the Pegasus of Greek mythology and Godzilla of monster-movie fame. "The poems will bring appreciative smiles from readers who know the stories," promised Kathleen Whalin in *School Library Journal,* noting that unfamiliar readers can use a glossary in the back of the book to identify each monster. Engberg wrote in *Booklist* that, even with the glossary, some references "may fly over kids' heads." Engberg concluded, however, that the book as a whole is "a playful collection of shivery delights." A *Kirkus Reviews* critic praised, "This attention-getting menagerie will have readers and listeners sitting on the edges—and probably falling out—of their seats." *Creature Carnival* was named a Lee Bennett Hopkins Poetry Award honor book.

Singer's first middle-grade novel, *It Can't Hurt Forever,* recounts a trauma she experienced as a child. In this fictionalized version of her experience, Ellie Simon is to enter the hospital for the same corrective heart surgery Singer had. Unlike Singer, however, Ellie is told what is going to happen to her, with the exception of

the catheterization she must undergo. When she learns about it, she argues with the doctors and her parents, just as Singer wished she had done. Singer "provides an honest and thorough look at pre-and post-operative care and at the concerns of a girl facing a major trauma," pointed out Karen Harris in *School Library Journal*. A *Kirkus Reviews* contributor concluded that *It Can't Hurt Forever* is "sharp, fast, funny, genuinely serious, and helpfully informative."

Singer's other books for middle-grade children are two novels about the obsessions of a young girl named Lizzie Silver. *Tarantulas on the Brain* has ten-year-old Lizzie doing everything she can to earn enough money to buy a pet tarantula. She tries having a junk sale and even works as a magician's assistant to get the necessary money, lying to her mother about what she is doing. In the end, her secret desire and activities are discovered and everyone is much more sympathetic than Lizzie imagined they would be. The pace of *Tarantulas on the Brain* "is fast and exciting; the characters are sufficiently quirky to keep the readers engrossed and narrator Lizzie Silver, 10, wins their affections," asserted a *Publishers Weekly* reviewer. In the sequel to *Tarantulas on the Brain, Lizzie Silver of Sherwood Forest*, Lizzie's new preoccupations include her desires to be one of Robin Hood's merry followers and to learn how to play the harp so she can attend the same music school as her best friend. *Lizzie Silver of Sherwood Forest* is a "funny, touching sequel," stated another *Publishers Weekly* contributor, adding: "This is an adroitly balanced and enjoyable tale about a naive and eager girl."

A fantasy novel for younger readers, *Charmed* introduces Miranda, a twelve year old with an active imagination. The girl travels to worlds around the galaxy in a quest to collect the "Correct Combination": a group of characters who must unite to destroy an evil being known as the Charmer. Besides Miranda and the humanoid named Iron Dog, the group includes Bastable, Miranda's invisible feline friend, Rattus, a clever rodent, and the wise cobra-goddess, Naja the Ever-Changing. The fact that the characters manage to work together even though some of them represent animals that are natural enemies was appreciated by *Voice of Youth Advocates* contributor Jennifer Langlois, who stated that the plot of *Charmed* is "a good way to show young people that just because someone is different doesn't mean they are bad." Sally Estes declared in *Booklist* that in *Charmed* "the various worlds created by Singer are fascinating," and *School Library Journal* reviewer Susan L. Rogers lauded the fantasy's "somewhat surprising and quite satisfying conclusion."

Other middle-grade and juvenile novels by Singer include *Twenty Ways to Lose Your Best Friend, California Demon, Big Wheel, Josie to the Rescue,* and *The Circus Lunicus.* Rosie Rivera opens up the wrong bottle in her mother's magic shop and unleashes a genie in *California Demon,* a book in which "humor keeps the story

buoyant, magic gives it sparkle," according to Kathryn Jennings in *Bulletin of the Center for Children's Books.* Wheel Wiggins, a leader of a gang, is trying to organize a Fourth of July Carnival, but is running into problems from a rival in *Big Wheel,* a "surefire story from a popular author," as a writer for *Kirkus Reviews* noted.

More magic and fantasy is served up in *The Circus Lunicus* when young Solly's toy lizard turns into a fairy godmother and helps him to learn some home truths about himself, his supposedly dead mother, and his evil stepmother and siblings. "This loony, fast-paced mystery-fantasy . . . is full of surprises and clever plot twists," observed Cart in *Booklist,* "and it's as much fun as a three-ring circus." A *Kirkus Reviews* critic described *The Circus Lunicus* as "luminous and humorous."

Mysteries and young-adult fantasy novels are also among Singer's writings. The "Sam and Dave" series stars a pair of twins who solve mysteries, some set in school, some further afield. *A Clue in Code* has the detectives in search of the thief who stole the class trip money. There is an obvious suspect who insists he is innocent, so Sam and Dave embark on an investigation. "Singer's ability to subtly incorporate the necessary facts of the case into the narrative demonstrates her respect for young readers eager for satisfying mysteries they can solve on their own," pointed out a *Booklist* reviewer.

Elements of the supernatural are introduced into Singer's young-adult novel *Ghost Host.* Bart Hawkins seems to have an ideal life—he is the quarterback of the high school football team and dates Lisa, the captain of the cheerleading squad. He secretly loves to read, though, and fears that if this gets out he will be labeled a nerd. When he discovers that his new house is haunted by Stryker, a nasty poltergeist, his life is thrown into chaos and he must enlist the help of a friendly ghost and the class brain to pacify Stryker. "*Ghost Host* is above all else fun to read," maintained Randy Brough in *Voice of Youth Advocates.* "Singer's deft introduction of the supernatural into the world of a high school junior, his family, and friends creates headaches for everyone, ghosts included."

Ghosts are also at the center of *Deal with a Ghost,* as fifteen-year-old Delia thinks she is terribly sophisticated until she comes face to face with a ghost who knows her name. *Booklist* critic Chris Sherman described this novel as "fast-paced" and "engrossing."

Other books by Singer that are geared for older teen readers include *The Course of True Love Never Did Run Smooth,* which deals with the difficulties encountered by Becky and Nemi, a girl and boy who, during the production of a high-school production of *A Midsummer Night's Dream,* find that their friendship is changing from one of childhood buddies to something more sexually charged. "Singer neatly uses Shakes-

peare's comedic mix-up as a foil for the tangled web woven by her teenage protagonists," noted Estes in a *Booklist* review of the novel. Highlighting Singer's writing style, *Bulletin of the Center for Children's Book* reviewer Zena Sutherland found much merit in *The Course of True Love Never Did Run Smooth,* noting that "the minor characters are sharply defined [and] the familial relations are strongly drawn, with perceptive treatment of the dynamics of the acting group and especially of its gay members."

In *Several Kinds of Silence* Singer tackles the theme of prejudice when young Franny falls in love with a Japanese boy, while *Storm Rising* tells an inter-generational tale of lonely Storm, who finds comfort with an older woman who possesses unusual powers.

In addition to her many book-length works, Singer has edited several volumes of short stories for young-adult readers, including *Stay True: Short Stories for Young Girls, I Believe in Water: Twelve Brushes with Religion,* and *Make Me Over: Eleven Original Stories about Transforming Ourselves.* Calling Singer "an experienced anthologist," *Booklist* contributor Cindy Dobrez described *Make Me Over* as a "diverse, solid group of stories" featuring young people who use adolescence as a time to recreate some aspect of their life to change their future. "Every story is a winner," asserted a *Kirkus Reviews* writer, the critic praising Singer for choosing contributors on the order of Margaret Peterson Haddix and Joyce Sweeney.

Reflecting her own desire for social change, Singer also donated the proceeds from the sale of her anthology *Face Relations: Eleven Stories about Seeing beyond Color* to the Southern Poverty Law Center's Teaching Tolerance project. Featuring stories by such well-known authors as M.E. Kerr, Rita Williams-Garcia, Jess Mowry, and Naomi Shihab Nye, *Face Relations* focuses on characters striving to overcome racial differences to build a relationship with another character. While commenting that some pieces in the collection are stronger than others, a critic for *Kirkus Reviews* commented that the best stories "will engage teens point blank, though all will be appreciated in a classroom setting." Kathleen Isaacs in her *School Library Journal* review also commented on the educational value of the collection, noting that the stories "raise questions that could lead to good classroom discussion." A *Publishers Weekly* reviewer noted that the stories offer "upbeat conclusions and an even balance of funny and sad moments" concluding that the collection is "as much about appreciating color as it is about looking beyond it."

According to an essayist for *St. James Guide to Young-Adult Writers,* "Singer's stories include such a variety of genres—mysteries, medical tales, romances, fantasies, as well as picture books for children—one doesn't know what she is going to write next. Every young adult knows, however, that whatever Singer writes for them will be enjoyable, entertaining reading." When

discussing why she writes in an article for *School Library Journal,* Singer explained that she was enchanted by words as a child, "and I still am. And what better to do with such enchantment than to bring the magic to others, children in particular, by becoming a writer?"

Biographical and Critical Sources

BOOKS

Authors of Books for Young People, 3rd edition, edited by Martha E. Ward, Scarecrow Press (Metuchen, NJ), 1990.
Children's Literature Review, Volume 48, Gale (Detroit, MI), 1998.
St. James Guide to Young Adult Writers, 2nd edition, edited by Tom Pendergast and Sara Pendergast, St. James (Detroit, MI), 1999.

PERIODICALS

Booklist, May 15, 1983, Sally Estes, review of *The Course of True Love Never Did Run Smooth,* p. 1197; September 15, 1985, review of *A Clue in Code,* p. 140; January 1, 1991, Sally Estes, review of *Charmed,* p. 922; February 1, 1991, Leone McDermott, review of *Exotic Birds,* pp. 1126-1127; October 15, 1992, Ilene Cooper, review of *Chester the Out-of-Work Dog,* p. 425; May 1, 1994, Carolyn Phelan, review of *The Painted Fan,* p. 1609; June 1, 1997, Chris Sherman, review of *Deal with a Ghost,* pp. 1686-1687; March 15, 1998, Ilene Cooper, review of *Bottoms Up!,* pp. 1242-1243; December 1, 1998, Hazel Rochman, review of *Prairie Dogs Kiss and Lobsters Wave,* p. 681; February 15, 2000, Michael Cart, review of *On the Same Day in March: A Tour of the World's Weather,* p. 1116; December 1, 2000, Michael Cart, review of *The Circus Lunicus,* p. 708; April 1, 2001, Shelle Rosenfeld, review of *Didi and Daddy on the Promenade,* p. 1480; March 15, 2002, Gillian Engberg, review of *Footprints on the Roof: Poems about the Earth,* p. 1250, Stephanie Zvirin, review of *Quiet Night,* p. 1264; November 15, 2002, John Peters, review of *The Company of Crows: A Book of Poems,* p. 606; April 1, 2003, Gillian Engbert, review of *Fireflies at Midnight,* p 1408; August, 2003, Hazel Rochman, review of *How to Cross a Pond: Poems about Water,* pp. 1975-1976; April 1, 2004, Gillian Engberg, review of *Creature Carnival,* p. 1367; May 15, 2004, Jennifer Mattson, review of *Block Party Today!,* p. 1627; December 1, 2004, Hazel Rochman, review of *Central Heating: Poems about Fire and Warmth,* p. 650; September 15, 2005, Cindy Dobrez, review of *Make Me Over: Eleven Original Stories about Transforming Ourselves,* p. 60; September 15, 2006, Ilene Cooper, review of *Cats to the Rescue: True Tales of Heroic Felines,* p. 62; December 15, 2006, Carolyn Phelan, review of *Let's Build a Clubhouse,* p. 52; October 1, 2007, John Peters, review of *Venom,* p. 58; October 15, 2007, Gil-

lian Engberg, review of *City Lullaby,* p. 51; April 1, 2008, Carolyn Phelan, review of *Eggs,* p. 52; October 15, 2008, Randall Enos, review of *First Food Fight This Fall and Other School Poems,* p. 45.

Bulletin of the Center for Children's Books, January, 1977, review of *The Dog Who Insisted He Wasn't,* p. 82; May, 1983, Zena Sutherland, review of *The Course of True Love Never Did Run Smooth,* p. 179; February, 1993, Kathryn Jennings, review of *California Demon,* p. 191.

Horn Book, January-February, 1990, Nancy Vasilakis, review of *Turtle in July,* pp. 82-83; January-February, 2008, Sarah Ellis, review of *City Lullaby,* p. 79; May-June, 2008, Danielle J. Ford, review of *Eggs,* p. 341.

Kirkus Reviews, October 15, 1978, review of *It Can't Hurt Forever,* p. 1140; December 1, 1993, review of *Big Wheel,* p. 1529; September 15, 2000, review of *The Circus Lunicus;* January 15, 2002, review of *Footprints on the Roof,* p. 110; April 1, 2002, review of *Quiet Night,* pp. 498-499, review of *Boo Hoo Boo-Boo,* p. 579; August 15, 2002, review of *The Company of Crows,* p. 1237; March 15, 2003, review of *Fireflies at Midnight,* p. 479; July 1, 2003, review of *How to Cross a Pond,* p. 915; February 15, 2004, review of *Creature Carnival,* p. 185; April 15, 2004, review of *Block Party Today!* p. 401; May 1, 2004, review of *Face Relations,* p. 449; December 15, 2004, review of *Central Heating,* p. 1207; March 15, 2005, review of *Monday on the Mississippi,* p. 358; August 15, 2005, review of *Make Me Over,* p. 922; September 15, 2007, review of *Venom.*

Language Arts, April, 1990, Janet Hickman, review of *Turtle in July,* pp. 430-431; January, 1992, Miriam Martinez, review of *The Golden Heart of Winter,* p. 67.

Publishers Weekly, July 9, 1982, review of *Tarantulas on the Brain,* p. 49; June 27, 1986, review of *Lizzie Silver of Sherwood Forest,* pp. 91-92; March 1, 1991, review of *Nine o'Clock Lullaby,* p. 72; January 24, 2000, review of *On the Same Day in March,* p. 311; February 25, 2002, review of *Quiet Night,* p. 64; August 19, 2002, review of *The Company of Crows,* p. 89; July 12, 2004, review of *Face Relations,* p. 65; November 12, 2007, review of *City Lullaby,* p. 54; June 9, 2008, review of *Shoe Bop!,* p. 50.

School Library Journal, September, 1978, Karen Harris, review of *It Can't Hurt Forever,* p. 149; August, 1983, Joan McGrath, review of *The Course of True Love Never Did Run Smooth,* p. 80; December, 1990, Susan L. Rogers, review of *Charmed,* p. 111; June, 1991, Ellen Dibner, review of *Exotic Birds,* p. 120; July, 1991, Patricia Dooley, review of *Nine o'Clock Lullaby,* p. 64; April, 1995, Donna L. Scanlon, review of *The Maiden on the Moor,* p. 146; April, 2000, Jody McCoy, review of *On the Same Day in March,* p. 126; July, 2000, p. 87; March, 2002, Catherine Threadgill, review of *Quiet Night,* p. 204; May, 2002, Kathleen Whalin, review of *Footprints on the Roof,* p. 144; January, 2003, Marilyn Singer, "Nurturing Wonder," pp. 42-43; May, 2003, Marge Loch-Wouters, review of *Fireflies at Midnight,* p. 142; August, 2003, Sally R. Dow, review of *How to Cross a Pond,* p. 152; April,

2004, Kathleen Whalin, review of *Creature Carnival,* p. 142; May, 2004, Genevieve Gallagher, review of *Block Party Today!* p. 124; June, 2004, Kathleen Isaacs, review of *Face Relations,* p. 150; September, 2004, Marilyn Singer, "A Blast of Poetry," pp. 41-42; January, 2005, Lee Bock, review of *Central Heating,* p. 156; November, 2006, Kara Schaff Dean, review of *Cats to the Rescue,* p. 164; December, 2006, Nancy Silverrod, review of *Let's Build a Clubhouse,* p. 116; July, 2008, Kathleen Kelly MacMillan, review of *Shoe Bop!,* p. 92; October, 2008, Sally R. Dow, review of *First Food Fight This Fall and Other School Poems,* p. 137.

Voice of Youth Advocates, June, 1987, Randy Brough, review of *Ghost Host,* p. 83; December, 1990, Jennifer Langlois, review of *Charmed,* p. 32.

ONLINE

Marilyn Singer Home Page, http://www.marilynsinger.net (June 8, 2009).*

* * *

SMITH, Cat Bowman 1939-
(Catherine Bowman)

Personal

Born 1939. *Education:* Rochester Institute of Technology, B.F.A., 1961.

Addresses

Office—Cat Bowman Smith Co., 84 Deer Creek Rd., Pittsford, NY 14534.

Career

Illustrator. Former editorial illustrator for Rochester, NY, Gannett newspapers; Rochester Institute of Technology, instructor in illustration.

Writings

ILLUSTRATOR

John Reynolds Gardiner, *General Butterfingers,* Houghton Mifflin (Boston, MA), 1986.

Jane Werner Watson, *My Friend the Dentist,* Crown (New York, NY), 1987.

Jane Werner Watson, *My Friend the Doctor,* Crown (New York, NY), 1987.

Linda Gondosch, *The Monsters of Marble Avenue,* Little, Brown (Boston, MA), 1988.

Jane Werner Watson, *Sometimes a Family Has to Split Up,* Crown (New York, NY), 1988.

Mary Jane Auch, *Angel and Me and the Bayside Bombers,* Little, Brown (Boston, MA), 1989.

Sandy Asher, *Princess Bee and the Royal Good-night Story,* Whitman (Niles, IL), 1990.

Charlotte Herman, *Max Malone and the Great Cereal Rip-off,* Holt (New York, NY), 1990.

Ruth Hooker, *Matthew the Cowboy,* Whitman (Niles, IL), 1990.

Charlotte Herman, *Max Malone Makes a Million,* Holt (New York, NY), 1991.

Constance Hiser, *Ghosts in the Fourth Grade,* Holiday House (New York, NY), 1991.

Constance Morgenstern, *Good Night, Feet,* Holt (New York, NY), 1991.

Frances Ward Weller, *The Closet Gorilla,* Macmillan (New York, NY), 1991.

Charlotte Herman, *Max Malone, Superstar,* Holt (New York, NY), 1992.

Constance Hiser, *Critter Sitters,* Holiday House (New York, NY), 1992.

Julie Anne Peters, *The Stinky Sneakers Contest,* Little, Brown (Boston, MA), 1992.

Louis Sachar, *Monkey Soup,* Knopf (New York, NY), 1992.

Marilyn Singer, *Chester, the Out-of-Work Dog,* Holt (New York, NY), 1992.

Sallie Wolf, *Peter's Trucks,* Whitman (Morton Grove, IL), 1992.

Andy Gregg, *Great Rabbit and the Long-tailed Wildcat,* Whitman (Morton Grove, IL), 1993.

Charlotte Herman, *Max Malone the Magnificent,* Holt (New York, NY), 1993.

Constance Hiser, *Scoop Snoops,* Holiday House (New York, NY), 1993.

Mary Jane Auch, *The Latchkey Dog,* Little, Brown (Boston, MA), 1994.

Duncan Ball, *Grandfather's Wheelything,* Simon & Schuster (New York, NY), 1994.

Stephen H. Lemberg, *Scardey Dog,* Knopf (New York, NY), 1994.

Cynthia Stowe, *Not-so-Normal Norman,* Whitman (Morton Grove, IL), 1994.

Marty Rhodes Figley, *Mary and Martha,* Eerdmans (Grand Rapids, MI), 1995.

Marty Rhodes Figley, *The Story of Zacchaeus,* Eerdmans (Grand Rapids, MI), 1995.

Tynia Thomassie, *Feliciana Feydra LeRoux: A Cajun Tall Tale,* Little, Brown (Boston, MA), 1995.

Karen Waggoner, *Partners,* Simon & Schuster (New York, NY), 1995.

Leah Komaiko, *On Sally Perry's Farm,* Simon & Schuster (New York, NY), 1996.

Sonia Levitin, *Nine for California,* Orchard (New York, NY), 1996.

Amy MacDonald, *No More Nice,* Orchard (New York, NY), 1996.

Mary Quattlebaum, *A Year on My Street: Poems,* Delacorte (New York, NY), 1996.

Mary Quattlebaum, *Underground Train,* Doubleday (New York, NY), 1997.

Sonia Levitin, *Boom Town,* Orchard (New York, NY), 1998.

Tynia Thomassie, *Feliciana Meets d'Loup Garou: A Cajun Tall Tale,* Little, Brown (Boston, MA), 1998.

Sonia Levitin, *Taking Charge,* Orchard Books (New York, NY), 1999.

Ruth Freeman Swain, *Bedtime!,* Holiday House (New York, NY), 1999.

Marguerite W. Davol, *The Loudest, Fastest, Best Drummer in Kansas,* Orchard (New York, NY), 2000.

Martha Freeman, *The Trouble with Cats,* Holiday House (New York, NY), 2000.

Stuart J. Murphy, *Dave's Down-to-Earth Rock Shop,* HarperCollins (New York, NY), 2000.

Amy MacDonald, *No More Nasty,* Farrar Straus & Giroux (New York, NY), 2001.

Jennifer Brutschy, *Just One More Story,* Orchard (New York, NY), 2002.

Martha Freeman, *The Trouble with Babies,* Holiday House (New York, NY), 2002.

Ruth Freeman Swain, *Hairdo!: What We Do and Did to Our Hair,* Holiday House (New York, NY), 2002.

Cynthia C. DeFelice, *Old Granny and the Bean Thief,* Farrar, Straus & Giroux (New York, NY), 2003.

Cynthia Voigt, *The Rosie Stories,* Holiday House (New York, NY), 2003.

Stephanie Greene, *Owen Foote, Mighty Scientist,* Clarion (New York, NY), 2004.

Tres Seymour, *Auction!,* Candlewick Press (Cambridge, MA), 2005.

Peggy Thomas, *Joshua the Giant Frog,* Pelican (Gretna, LA), 2005.

Martha Freeman, *The Trouble with Twins,* Holiday House (New York, NY), 2007.

John Reynolds Gardiner, *General Butterfingers,* Houghton Mifflin (Boston, MA), 2007.

Amy MacDonald, *Too Much Flapdoodle!,* Farrar, Straus & Giroux (New York, NY), 2008.

Sidelights

New York-based illustrator and artist Cat Bowman Smith has provided the pictures for dozens of books for young children and middle-grade readers. Smith began her art at a very young age and worked as an editorial illustrator for newspapers before beginning her career in picture-book illustration in 1985.

Smith's pen-and-ink sketches are featured in a number of chapter books for beginning readers. A *Publishers Weekly* contributor noted that "a generous selection of Smith's engaging black-and-white illustrations" for Cynthia Stowe's *Not-so-Normal Norman* are one feature that will likely entice reluctant readers. Reviewing *The Trouble with Cats,* by Martha Freeman, Carolyn Phelan noted in *Booklist* that "Smith's many line drawings set a lively, humorous tone" for the story. Describing her work in the related reader *The Trouble with Twins,* Ilene Cooper in the same periodical wrote that Smith's illustrations "kick it up a notch," while Kathleen Meulen, writing in *School Library Journal* about the same title, cited Smith's "winsome full-page illustrations."

Water color is Smith's medium of choice for her picture-book illustration. Janice Del Negro, in a *Booklist* review of Tynia Thomassie's *Feliciana Feydra LeRoux: A*

Cat Bowman Smith teams up with writer Amy MacDonald to produce the engaging picture book Too Much Flapdoodle! (Illustration copyright © 2008 by Cat Bowman Smith. All rights reserved. Reproduced by permission of Melanie Kroupa Books, a division of Farrar, Straus & Giroux, LLC.)

Cajun Tall Tale, wrote that the book "combines breezy watercolors and a swinging text." Reviewing the same title, Lauren Adams noted in *Horn Book* that "Smith's spirited illustrations in swampy greens and browns complement the jaunty tale." A sequel, *Feliciana Meets d'Loup Garou: A Cajun Tall Tale,* features similar setting elements; according to John Peters in *Booklist,* "Smith sets her ski-nosed figures against a lush and, after dark, appropriately eerie-looking swamp." In Sonia Levitin's *Boom Town,* Smith's illustrations reflect the humor in the first-person narrative; Margaret A. Bush wrote in *Horn Book* that her "energetic watercolor sketches in sandy tones are comic and informative." Featuring the same characters as *Boom Town,* Smith's pictures for Levitin's *Taking Charge* "are brimming with action and color," according to Phelan. Noting Smith's work for *Joshua the Giant Frog,* a *Kirkus Reviews* contributor explained that the book's "realistically executed watercolors depicting the giant frog and his helpful nature" will help children suspend their disbelief while reading Peggy Thomas's fanciful tall tale.

Smith also uses gouache—opaque water color—in her picture-book art. In *The Loudest, Fastest, Best Drummer in Kansas,* this medium gives Marguerite W. Davol's text a vintage feel: according to Todd Morning

in *Booklist,* Smith's "pictures have a bright, cartoony, old-fashioned look." A *Publishers Weekly* reviewer, critiquing the same title, called the same illustrations "chipper yet quaint renderings of small-town USA from days gone by." Smith also employs gouache to depict a desert setting in her illustrations for Cynthia C. DeFelice's *Old Granny and the Bean Thief.* A *Publishers Weekly* critic, reviewing this work, cited the book's "down-home, spirited gouache spreads and vignettes."

In addition to appearing in picture books and chapter books, Smith's illustrations have been used in educational titles such as Stuart J. Murphy's *Dave's Down-to-Earth Rock Shop.* Kay Weisman, writing in *Booklist,* noted that the "full-color illustrations capture the excitement of rock hunting and include many geological and equipment details." In Ruth Freeman Swain's picture-book history of hair, *Hairdo!: What We Do and Did to Our Hair,* Smith's "art provides apt, often witty, accompaniment," according to Shelle Rosenfeld in her *Booklist* appraisal.

Biographical and Critical Sources

PERIODICALS

Booklist, February 1, 1994, Kay Weisman, review of *The Latchkey Dog,* p. 1005; January 15, 1995, Mary Harris Veeder, review of *Not-so-Normal Norman,* p. 930; April 1, 1995, Janice Del Negro, review of *Feliciana Feydra LeRoux: A Cajun Tall Tale,* p. 1429; December 1, 1997, Ilene Cooper, review of *Underground Train,* p. 643; John Peters, April 15, 1998, review of *Feliciana Meets d'Loup Garou: A Cajun Tall Tale,* p. 1454; March, 1999, Margaret A. Bush, review of *Taking Charge,* p. 196; April 15, 1999, Carolyn Phelan, review of *Taking Charge,* p. 1536; March 15, 2000, Todd Morning, review of *The Loudest, Fastest, Best Drummer in Kansas,* p. 1386; March 15, 2000, Carolyn Phelan, review of *The Trouble with Cats,* p. 1376; May 1, 2000, Kay Weisman, review of *Dave's Down-to-Earth Rock Shop,* p. 1672; September 1, 2001, Chris Sherman, review of *No More Nasty,* p. 106; December 15, 2002, Shelle Rosenfeld, review of *Hairdo! What We Do and Did to Our Hair,* p. 765; July, 2002, Ilene Cooper, review of *The Trouble with Babies,* p. 1844; December 1, 2003, Louise Bruggemann, review of *The Rosie Stories,* p. 686; July, 2003, GraceAnne A. DeCandido, review of *Old Granny and the Bean Thief,* p. 1896; December 1, 2007, Ilene Cooper, review of *The Trouble with Twins,* p. 42.

Horn Book, September-October, 1995, Lauren Adams, review of *Feliciana Feydra LeRoux,* p. 592; March-April, 1998, Margaret A. Bush, review of *Boom Town,* p. 215; November-December, 2001, Martha V. Parravano, review of *No More Nasty,* p. 754; September-October, 2004, Roger Sutton, review of *Owen Foote, Mighty Scientist,* p. 583.

Kirkus Reviews, April 15, 2002, review of *Just One More Story,* p. 564; June 15, 2002, review of *The Trouble*

with Babies, p. 880; March 15, 2005, review of *Joshua the Giant Frog,* p. 359; April 15, 2005, review of *Auction!,* p. 481.

Publishers Weekly, November 22, 1993, review of *The Latchkey Dog,* p. 63; December 12, 1994, review of *Not-so-Normal Norman,* p. 62; November 24, 1997, review of *Underground Train,* p. 73; February 15, 1998, review of *Boom Town,* p. 210; April 20, 1998, review of *Feliciana Meets d'Loup Garou,* p. 66; March 6, 2000, review of *The Loudest, Fastest, Best Drummer in Kansas,* p. 110; May 13, 2002, review of *Just One More Story,* p. 70; August 11, 2003, review of *Old Granny and the Bean Thief,* p. 279.

School Library Journal, July, 2000, Denise Brna, review of *The Trouble with Cats,* p. 72; April, 2000, Jackie Hechtkopf, review of *Dave's Down-to-Earth Rock Shop,* p. 123; December, 2003, Laura Scott, review of *The Rosie Stories,* p. 129; October, 2004, Linda Zeil-

stra Sawyer, review of *Owen Foote, Mighty Scientist,* p. 114; April, 2005, Linda Staskus, review of *Joshua the Giant Frog,* p. 113; June, 2005, Lynda Ritterman, review of *Auction!,* p. 128; March, 2008, Kathleen Meulen, review of *The Trouble with Twins,* p. 162.

ONLINE

Pelican Publishing Web site, http://pelicanpub.com/ (May 13, 2009), profile of Smith.*

* * *

SOO, Kean

Personal

Born in England.

Kean Soo contributes his quirky images to his self-illustrated picture book Jellaby.

Addresses

Home—Canada. *E-mail*—kean@keaner.net.

Career

Author and cartoonist. Assistant editor, *Flight* anthologies. Formerly worked as an electrical engineer.

Member

Iron Ring (Canada).

Writings

(Self-illustrated) *Jellaby* (graphic novel), Hyperion (New York, NY), 2008.

"Jellaby" stories have also appeared in *Flight Explorer* and the "Flight" anthologies. Coauthor, with Kevin Fanning, of Web comic "Baby's First Internet."

Sidelights

Born in England, raised in Hong Kong, and now making his home in Canada, Kean Soo turned his hand to comics in the mid-2000s, developing the Web comic "Jellaby." Soo's comic stars ten-year-old Portia Bennett, who struggles to fit in with her new surroundings, as well as with the absence of her father, after moving to a new neighborhood with her mother. Overly intelligent and mature for her age, Portia feels isolated and alone until she meets Jellaby, an oversized, lovable purple monster. Taking care of Jellaby adds excitement to Portia's day, as she keeps her new friend a secret from everyone, even her mother. Befriending a similarly ostracized classmate, Portia gains another new friend in Jason, and together the two children decide to help Jellaby return home, although their task is made especially challenging because the creature cannot speak.

Originally published online, the "Jellaby" comic appeared in print in *Flight,* an anthology series devoted to short graphic novels. In 2008, Soo collected his early "Jellaby" comics and added new ones to produce *Jellaby,* the first part of an anticipated two-volume collection. Writing in *Booklist,* Kat Kan noted that Soo maintains a good balance between a monster "too cute to be scary" and a "a fairly gritty contemporary reality" where children must endure the threats of bullies at school. In *School Library Journal,* Lisa Goldstein described *Jellaby* as both "sophisticated and thoughtful," also commenting that Soo's illustrations "give the story a cinematic look and a dramatic pace." A *Kirkus Reviews* critic also found great promise in Soo's first graphic novel for children, describing *Jellaby* as "a simply wonderful tale of friendship and whimsy, masterfully constructed with depth and moxie."

Biographical and Critical Sources

PERIODICALS

Booklist, March 15, 2008, Kat Kan, review of *Jellaby,* p. 69.
Kirkus Reviews, January 1, 2008, review of *Jellaby.*
School Library Journal, January, 2008, Lisa Goldstein, review of *Jellaby,* p. 153.

ONLINE

Kean Soo Web Log, http://keaner.net/index.php (May 14, 2009).
Secret Friend Society Web site, http://www.secretfriendsociety.com/ (May 15, 2009), "Kean Soo."*

*   *   *

SUAREZ, Maribel 1952-

Personal

Born 1952, in Mexico; children: three.

Addresses

Home and office—Mexico City, Mexico. *E-mail*—marisubel@hotmail.com.

Career

Illustrator.

Writings

Las frutas/ Fruits, Grijalbo (Mexico City, Mexico), 1999.

ILLUSTRATOR

Ermilo Abreu Gómez, *Doña estrella y sus luceros,* Cidcli (Mexico City, Mexico), 1987.
Margarita Robleda Moguel, *El carrito de Monchito,* Houghton Mifflin (Boston, MA), 1993.
Margarita Robleda Moguel, *Ramon y su ratón/ Ramon and His Mouse,* Editorial Margarita Robleda (Mexico City, Mexico), 2000.
Margarita Robleda Moguel, *Sueños/ Dreams,* Editorial Margarita Robleda (Mexico City, Mexico), 2000.
Margarita Robleda Moguel, *Rana, Rema, Rima,* Editorial Margarita Robleda (Mexico City, Mexico), 2000.
Diane Namm, *Pick a Pet,* Children's Press (New York, NY), 2004.
Alma Flor Ada and F. Isabel Campoy, *Mamá Goose: A Latino Nursery Treasury/ Un tensor de rimas infantiles,* Hyperion (New York, NY), 2004.

Lisa Wheeler, *Te amo, bebé, Little One,* Little, Brown (New York, NY), 2004.

Margarita Robleda Moguel, *Patito, donde estás?,* Alfaguara (Miami, FL), 2006.

Margarita Robleda Moguel, *Jugando con las vocales,* Alfaguara (Miami, FL), 2006.

Margarita Robleda Moguel, *Este soy yo,* Alfaguara (Miami, FL), 2006.

Margarita Robleda Moguel, *Muñeca de trapo,* Alfaguara (Miami, FL), 2006.

Kate Petty, *Gus Goes to School,* QEB (Laguna Hills, CA), 2007.

Pat Mora, *Wiggling Pockets/ Los bolsillos saltarines,* Rayo (New York, NY), 2008.

Pat Mora, *Sweet Dreams/ Dulces sueños,* Rayo (New York, NY), 2008.

Pat Mora, *Let's Eat!/ A comer!,* HarperCollins (New York, NY), 2008.

Pat Mora, *Here, Kitty, Kitty!/ Ven, gatita, ven!,* HarperCollins (New York, NY), 2008.

Sidelights

Mexican illustrator Maribel Suarez has collaborated with authors including Pat Mora and Alma Flor Ada on more than a dozen books for young readers. Many of the titles Suarez has illustrated are bilingual, making them enjoyable for children in both native English-and Spanish-speaking audiences. Others, such as *Te amo, bebé, Little One,* incorporate Spanish words into an English text. Regardless of the language, Suarez uses "bright, bold colors" in her water color art, according to Sheilah Kosco in a *School Library Journal* review.

Teaming up with Alma Flor Ada and F. Isabel Campoy, Suarez contributes "clear, charming watercolor cartoon illustrations" to *Mamá Goose: A Latino Nursery Treasury/ Un tesoro de rimas infantiles,* according to *School Library Journal* critic Ann Welton. Noting that these images range from full-page illustrations to small accent images, a *Kirkus Reviews* contributor described Suarez's cast of characters as "smiling, round-faced, sweet-looking children and animals bouncing about exuberantly."

Mexican author Margarita Robleda Moguel creates the text for *Ramon y su ratón/ Ramon and His Mouse,* in which Suarez's characteristic brightly hued art brings to life the characters of Ramon, an old man, and his mouse companion. Describing the images Suarez creates for Robleda Moguel's *Sueños/ Dreams,* a *School Library Journal* critic called them "soft and friendly."

Suarez teams up with writer Pat Mora on the "My Family/ Mi Familia" series, bilingual books about familiar ideas and family themes. In *Here, Kitty, Kitty!/ Ven, gatita, ven!,* Suarez's "line-and-watercolor pictures" weave together the kitten's adventures and happy family scenes in what *Booklist* reviewer Hazel Rochman called a "joyful picture book." Again employing line and water color, Suarez depicts another happy family in *Let's Eat!/ A comer!* Here her "lively double-page illustrations" feature traditional Hispanic foods, including beans, chilis, and tortillas, that are part of the mean eaten by a family that includes three children, two parents, and a grandmother. To help readers sort out the Spanish-language vocabulary words—presented in Spanish on one page and English on the facing page—each dish in the meal is clearly drawn on a white background. *Sweet Dreams/ Dulces Sueños* finds a grandmother describing animals that fall asleep at night to her three children.

Along with her illustration, Suarez has also created the original, self-illustrated picture book *Las frutas/ Fruits.* Featuring fourteen fruits common to Mexico, *Las frutas/ Fruits* features one fruit per page and pairs each item with "amusing watercolors," according to *Booklist* critic Isabel Schon. "The details of the watercolor pictures are nicely linked to the text," noted a *Kirkus Reviews* contributor in appraising Suarez's *Las frutas/ Fruits.*

Biographical and Critical Sources

PERIODICALS

Booklist, February 1, 1999, Isabel Schon, review of *Las frutas/ Fruits,* p. 981; August, 2004, Hazel Rochman, *Te amo, bebé, Little One,* p. 1946; April 1, 2008, Hazel Rochman, review of *Let's Eat!/ A comer!,* p. 58; October 15, 2008, Hazel Rochman, review of *Here, Kitty, Kitty!/ Ven, gatita, ven!,* p. 46.

Kirkus Reviews, March 1, 2005, review of *Mamá Goose: A Latino Nursery Treasury/ Un tensor de rimas infantiles,* p. 283; February 15, 2008, review of *Let's Eat!/ A comer!*

School Library Journal, August, 2001, reviews of *Sueños/ Dreams,* and *Ramon y su ratón/ Ramon and His Mouse,* p. S68; May, 2004, Sheilah Kosco, review of *Te amo, bebé, Little One,* p. 126; May, 2005, Ann Welton, review of *Mamá Goose,* p. 118; April, 2008, Donna Atmur, review of *Let's Eat!/ A comer!,* p. 117; July, 2008, Madeline Walton-Hadlock, review of *Sweet Dreams/ Dulces sueños,* p. 78.

ONLINE

HarperCollins Web site, http://www.harpercollins.com/ (May 13, 2009), "Maribel Suarez."*

T-U

TAMAKI, Jillian 1980-

Personal
Born 1980, in Canada.

Addresses
Home—Brooklyn, NY. *E-mail*—jill@jilltamaki.com.

Career
Educator and illustrator.

Awards, Honors
Doug Wright Award nomination for Best Book, 2007, for *Gilded Lilies.*

Illustrator
Gilded Lilies, Conundrum Press (Montreal, Quebec, Canada), 2006.

Mariko Tamaki, *Skim,* (graphic novel), Groundwood Books (Toronto, Ontario, Canada), 2008.

Sidelights
Canadian-born illustrator Jillian Tamaki teams up with her cousin, author Mariko Tamaki, to create the highly praised graphic novel *Skim,* which *Booklist* critic Jesse Karp deemed a "pungent commentary on racial, cultural, and sexual issues." In the book, which is set in the early 1990s, Kimberly Keiko "Skim" Cameron feels like an outsider in her private Canadian high school, and enduring her parents' divorce has made her feel even less secure. In response, the overweight teen attempts to find her place through the affectation of a "goth" lifestyle, the study of Wicca, and her strong love connection with her beloved drama teacher, Ms. Archer.

Writing that the "inky art lifts the story into a more poetic, elegiac realm" and "sets it apart from the coming-of-age pack," a *Publishers Weekly* critic added of *Skim*

that Tamaki's "swooping, gorgeous pen line" is "expressive, vibrant and precise all at once." The artist's renderings for her cousin's tale echo "the spare, gloomy emotional landscape in which Skim exists," noted Karp, and in the *New York Times Book Review* Elizabeth Spires observed that Tamaki's "nuanced" images "convey . . . a great deal of information often without the help of the text." A *Kirkus Reviews* writer cited the illustrator's use of "long, languid lines," and *Kliatt* contributor George Galuschak wrote that "the little details [in Tamaki's artwork] are wonderful."

Jillian Tamaki creates the artwork for sister Mariko Tamaki's graphic novel Skim, *which focuses on the lives of modern U.S. teens.* (Illustration copyright © 2008 by Jillian Tamaki. All rights reserved. Reproduced by permission.)

Biographical and Critical Sources

PERIODICALS

Booklist, March 15, 2008, Jesse Karp, review of *Skim,* p. 62.

Horn Book, July-August, 2008, Claire E. Gross, review of *Skim,* p. 459.

Kirkus Reviews, February 15, 2008, review of *Skim.*

Kliatt, May, 2008, George Galuschak, review of *Skim,* p. 31.

New York Times Book Review, November 9, 2008, Elizabeth Spires, review of *Skim,* p. 37.

Publishers Weekly, February 4, 2008, review of *Skim,* p. 44.

School Library Journal, May, 2008, Dave Inabnitt, review of *Skim,* p. 160.

ONLINE

Jillian Tamaki Home Page, http://www.jilliantamaki.com (May 15, 2009).*

*   *   *

TOWNSEND, Wendy 1962-

Personal

Born 1962. *Education:* Vermont College, M.F.A.; attended Empire State College. *Hobbies and other interests:* Nature, reptiles.

Addresses

Home—Callicoon, NY. *E-mail*—contact@wendy townsend.com.

Career

Author. Empire State College, New Paltz, NY, leader of summer writing workshops, 2004—.

Writings

(Coauthor and illustrator) *Iguanas: A Guide to Their Biology and Captive Care,* 1993.
Lizard Love, Front Street (Asheville, NC), 2008.

Contributor of nonfiction articles to periodicals, including *Reptiles.*

Sidelights

After coauthoring a nonfiction work on reptiles, Wendy Townsend realized her fondness for writing and set out to pursue a career as a children's author. After earning a master's degree from Vermont College, she completed her first novel, *Lizard Love,* and saw the book published in 2008. Entering the eighth grade in this coming-of-age story, Grace finds a recent move to New York City difficult. Accustomed to her grandparents' farm in rural Indiana, Grace feels lost in the concrete and high rises of Manhattan. She also misses the quiet contact with nature that comes with living in the country. A fortuitous discovery of a reptile shop offers the middle schooler some comfort in her new environment, and she spends her free time helping the owners of Fang and Claw take care of their animals for sale. New challenges face Grace, however, as she visits her grandparents for the summer and sees their health begin to decline.

"In her debut novel, Townsend displays a remarkable narrative gift," according to *Booklist* critic Thom Barthelmess, the reviewer stating admiration for the author's ability to write about nature as well as create well-developed characters. Despite voicing some reservations about the believability of Grace's affection for reptiles, a *Kirkus Reviews* critic wrote that in *Lizard Love* Townsend "draws gorgeous portraits of scaly creatures." Also recommending *Lizard Love* for preteens who enjoy animals, *School Library Journal* contributor Suzanne Gordon dubbed the novel "a worthwhile choice for young folks shedding the skin of childhood."

Cover of Wendy Townsend's novel Lizard Love, *a coming-of-age novel featuring reptiles.* (Cover Photographs: © 2008 by JupiterImages Corporation.)

Biographical and Critical Sources

PERIODICALS

Booklist, May 1, 2008, Thom Barthelmess, review of *Lizard Love,* p. 88.
Kirkus Reviews, March 15, 2008, review of *Lizard Love.*
School Library Journal, August, 2008, Suzanne Gordon, review of *Lizard Love,* p. 135.
Voice of Youth Advocates, June, 2008, Lisa A. Hazlett, review of *Lizard Love,* p. 154.

ONLINE

Wendy Townsend Home Page, http://wendytownsendwriter. com (May 18, 2009).*

*   *   *

TROUT, Kilgore
See FARMER, Philip José

*   *   *

ULMER, Wendy K. 1950-

Personal

Born 1950. *Education:* College degree.

Addresses

Home—Arrowsic, ME. *E-mail*—wulmer@clinic.net.

Career

Educator and business owner. Former teacher of English and music; owner of a quilt shop, Arrowsic, ME.

Writings

A Campfire for Cowboy Billy, illustrated by Kenneth J. Spengler, Northland Pub. (Flagstaff, AZ), 1997.
A Isn't for Fox: An Isn't Alphabet, illustrated by Laura Knorr, Sleeping Bear Press (Chelsea, MI), 2007.

Sidelights

Before she turned to writing picture books for young children, Wendy K. Ulmer taught both music and English. Now she combines the best of both of these disciplines, creating rhythmic texts full of humor and wordplay in her picture books *A Campfire for Cowboy Billy* and *A Isn't for Fox: An Isn't Alphabet.* Praising *A Campfire for Cowboy Billy,* the story of an imaginative young boy who deals with the loss of his beloved Grandpa by creating a wild-west landscape amid his New York City neighborhood, *School Library Journal* contributor Barbara Chatton wrote that Ulmer "includes sympathetic adults who support bully's fantasy" in her multigenerational tale. "Ulmer lightens Billy's grief without trivializing it," observed John Peters in a *Booklist* review of the same picture book, and in *Publishers Weekly* a critic suggested that *A Campfire for Cowboy Billy* "may well spark a reassuring adult-child dialogue about the death of a loved one."

In *A Isn't for Fox* Ulmer's simple rhythmic text focuses on every letter in the alphabet, listing two rhyming words that do NOT begin with the letter and then finishing with a simple sentence that completes the rhyme and also contains a word beginning with the letter in question. Her examples are "clear and clever," according to a *Kirkus Reviews* writer, the critic adding that *A Isn't for Fox* features a rhythmic text that is "just right for a rambunctions read-aloud." Ulmer's "playful alphabet book" also impressed *Booklist* contributor Carolyn Phelan, a reviewer who also praised illustrator Laura Knorr's detailed artwork as "energetic, colorful, and often jovial." The author's "playful verse and an inventive concept set [*A Isn't for Fox*] . . . apart," noted Jayne Damron in *School Library Journal,* the critic citing the book's imaginative cast of characters: "winking cats, smiling jellyfish, trumpeting lions, and pillow-fighting llamas."

Biographical and Critical Sources

PERIODICALS

Booklist, December 1, 1997, John Peters, review of *A Campfire for Cowboy Billy,* p. 644; April 15, 2008, Carolyn Phelan, review of *A Isn't for Fox: An Isn't Alphabet* p. 49.
Kirkus Reviews, February 1, 2008, review of *A Isn't for Fox.*
Publishers Weekly, September 1, 1997, review of *A Campfire for Cowboy Billy,* p. 105.
School Library Journal, January, 1998, Barbara Chatton, review of *A Campfire for Cowboy Billy,* p. 94; July, 2008, Jayne Damron, review of *A Isn't for Fox,* p. 82.*

V

VAIL, Rachel 1966-

Personal
Born July 25, 1966, in New York, NY; married, husband's name Mitchell (a physician); children: Zachary, Liam. *Education:* Georgetown University, B.A. (English and theatre), 1988.

Addresses
Home—New York, NY. *Office*—c/o Writers House, 21 W. 26th St., New York, NY 10010. *E-mail*—Rachelvailbooks@gmail.com.

Career
Writer.

Member
Authors Guild.

Awards, Honors
Editor's Choice designation, *Booklist,* 1991, for *Wonder,* and 1992, for *Do-Over;* Pick-of-the-List designation, American Booksellers Association, 1991, for *Wonder;* Blue Ribbon designation, *Bulletin of the Center for Children's Books,* 1992, for *Do-Over;* Books for the Teen Age selection, New York Public Library, 1992, for *Do-Over,* and 1994, for *Ever After;* Best Books designation, *School Library Journal,* 1996, for *Daring to Be Abigail.*

Writings

YOUNG-ADULT NOVELS

Wonder, Orchard Books (New York, NY), 1991.
Do-Over, Orchard Books (New York, NY), 1992.
Ever After, Orchard Books (New York, NY), 1994.

Rachel Vail (Photograph by Bill Harris. Reproduced by permission of Rachel Vail.)

Daring to Be Abigail, Orchard Books (New York, NY), 1996.
(With Avi) *Never Mind!: A Twin Novel,* HarperCollins (New York, NY), 2004.
If We Kiss, HarperCollins (New York, NY), 2005.
You, Maybe: The Profound Asymmetry of Love in High School, HarperCollins (New York, NY), 2006.
Lucky, HarperTeen (New York, NY), 2008.
Gorgeous, HarperTeen (New York, NY), 2008.

"FRIENDSHIP RING" SERIES; YOUNG-ADULT NOVELS

Please, Please, Please, Scholastic (New York, NY), 1998.
Not That I Care, Scholastic (New York, NY), 1998.
If You Only Knew, Scholastic (New York, NY), 1998.
Fill in the Blank, Scholastic (New York, NY), 2000.
Popularity Contest, Scholastic (New York, NY), 2000.

"MAMA REX AND T" SERIES; PICTURE BOOKS

Mama Rex and T Shop for Shoes, illustrated by Steve Björkman, Scholastic (New York, NY), 2000.
Mama Rex and T Lose a Waffle, illustrated by Steve Björkman, Scholastic (New York, NY), 2000.
Mama Rex and T Run out of Tape, illustrated by Steve Björkman, Scholastic (New York, NY), 2001.
The Horrible Play Date, illustrated by Steve Björkman, Scholastic (New York, NY), 2001.
The Sort-of-Super Snowman, illustrated by Steve Björkman, Scholastic (New York, NY), 2002.
Mama Rex and T Turn off the TV, illustrated by Steve Björkman, Scholastic (New York, NY), 2002.
Mama Rex and T Have Homework Trouble, illustrated by Steve Björkman, Scholastic (New York, NY), 2002.
The (Almost) Perfect Mother's Day, illustrated by Steve Björkman, Scholastic (New York, NY), 2002.
Halloween Knight, illustrated by Steve Björkman, Scholastic (New York, NY), 2003.
The Reading Champion, illustrated by Steve Björkman, Orchard Books (New York, NY), 2003.
The Prize, illustrated by Steve Björkman, Orchard Books (New York, NY), 2003.
Mama Rex and T Stay up Late, illustrated by Steve Björkman, Orchard Books (New York, NY), 2003.

PICTURE BOOKS

Over the Moon, Orchard Books (New York, NY), 1998.
Sometimes I'm Bombaloo, illustrated by Yumi Heo, Scholastic Press (New York, NY), 2002.
Righty and Lefty: A Tale of Two Feet, illustrated by Matthew Cordell, Scholastic Press (New York, NY), 2007.
Jibberwillies at Night, illustrated by Yumi Heo, Scholastic Press (New York, NY), 2008.

Sidelights

Born in New York City, children's book author Rachel Vail grew up in nearby New Rochelle, New York. In her youth she never intended to be a writer, but with the encouragement of various teachers, both in high school and later at Georgetown University, she worked to develop her talent. In an autobiographical sketch for *Horn Book,* Vail recalled one instructor in particular named Doc Murphy. A theater professor, Murphy encouraged her to focus on the essentials of character. Vail observed, "I think writing would be so much more exciting and less daunting to children if the emphasis were put on the details, the questions that propel the

Vail's picture book Sometimes I'm Bombaloo *captures the feelings of a frustrated child in illustrations by Yumi Heo.* (Scholastic Press, 2002. Illustrations copyright © 2002 by Yumi Heo. Reproduced by permission of Scholastic Inc.)

writer to create astonishing, unique characters who, by their juxtaposition with other astonishing, unique characters, make stories happen."

Vail's emphasis on character is apparent to readers of her first novel for children, the coming-of-age story *Wonder.* As twelve-year-old Jessica enters seventh grade, she finds that she has suddenly become unpopular. Sheila, her former best friend, and five other girls succeed in ostracizing Jessica, giving her the humiliating nickname "Wonder" after one of the girls describes Jessica's new polka-dot dress as "a Wonder Bread explosion." With determination, and with the welcome attentions of Conor O'Malley, the object of her first crush, Jessica perseveres.

Lauded by critics for its skillful rendering of character, *Wonder* proved to be a highly successful debut novel for its author. "Vail has the measure of this vulnerable age and its painful concern about identity within the group," noted a *Kirkus Reviews* commentator. *School Library Journal* contributor Debra S. Gold also spoke favorably of *Wonder*'s title character, commenting that "Jessica's first-person account reveals a three-dimensional character with whom readers will laugh and empathize." Deborah Abbott noted in *Booklist:* "Piercing and funny, Vail's breezy story describes the hazards of junior high, sketched with the emotional chasms universal to the age."

One of Jessica's schoolmates, Whitman Levy, becomes the hero of Vail's next story, *Do-Over.* Eighth grader Whitman faces some severe family problems, including his parents' imminent break-up, while also struggling to deal with his first real crush and get a handle on his acting role in an upcoming school play. Vail balances

her comical tale of the teen's various escapades with several thorny issues, including Whitman's discovery that his best friend Doug is a bigot. Eventually the self-conscious and somewhat bewildered Whitman comes to understand how to deal with all that confronts him in a moment of self-realization while on stage: "I could screw up or I could be amazing, and there's no turning back, no do-overs."

Reviewers noted that *Do-Over* again highlights Vail's skill in dealing with character and dialog. *School Library Journal* contributor Jacqueline Rose called the author "a master at portraying adolescent self-absorption, awkwardness, and fickleness, all with freshness and humor." In the *Bulletin of the Center for Children's Books,* Roger Sutton compared Vail favorably with popular children's book writer Judy Blume, noting that she "is funnier than Blume, and more moving, partly because of her natural ear for teenaged talk, and partly because she never, ever preaches. This is the real thing." Stephanie Zvirin, in *Booklist,* likewise spoke of the "sharp and genuine" dialogue in *Do-Over,* commending Vail's "remarkable talent for capturing so perfectly the pleasure and pain of being thirteen—in a real kids' world."

In *Ever After* Vail employs a new narrative technique, presenting much of her story in the form of diary entries written by fourteen-year-old Molly. Best friends Molly and Vicky live year-round on a small Massachusetts island. The presence of a new friend, summer visitor Grace, causes Vicky to feel insecure and puts a strain on her relationship with Molly. Vicky's possessiveness begins to disturb Molly, and ultimately destroys the girls' friendship when Molly learns that Vicky has been reading her personal journal without permission. "That Vicky and Molly's rift is likely to be permanent . . . is just one hallmark of the authenticity of this carefully conceived story," noted a *Publishers Weekly* reviewer. A *Kirkus Reviews* commentator praised *Ever After* as "an unusually immediate portrayal of a thoughtful teen finding her balance among her peers while making peace with her own capabilities." *School Library Journal* contributor Ellen Fader characterized the book as "a breezy, smart-talking novel that explores the ever-fascinating arena of young teen friendship," while Hazel Rochman, writing in *Booklist,* expressed a common critical refrain in noting that "the contemporary teenage voice is exactly right."

Another fourteen year old is the central character in *Lucky,* the first volume in a trilogy of novels for young teens that also includes *Gorgeous* and *Brilliant.* When readers meet her in *Lucky,* Phoebe Avery is living a comfortable life with her upper-middle-class family, and as middle-school graduation approaches she looks forward to a fancy party during which she plans to wear an expensive new designer dress. Her world turns upside down, however, when Mrs. Avery loses her job and Phoebe's family is forced to economize. For the teen, the biggest concern will be how to hide her sud-

den ill fortune from her still-affluent friends. In *Booklist* Jennifer Hubert called *Lucky* "entertaining, albeit predictable," and noted that Vail's novel will attract teen girls who enjoy books by popular YA novelist Meg Cabot. The author's "insightful characterizations" of middle-grade girls "and their shifting loyalties is right on target," Hubert added. "What rings so true is Phoebe's complete ignorance about money," noted Genevieve Gallagher, the critic adding in her *School Library Journal* review of *Lucky* that "kindness and understanding emerge in unexpected, fresh, and satisfying ways" in Vail's upbeat story.

The other two Avery sisters are the focus of the remaining novels in Vail's novel trilogy. In *Gorgeous* readers meet Allison Avery, while *Brilliant* focuses on Phoebe's oldest sister, Quinn. freshman in high school, dark-haired Allison is tired of being the overlooked middle sister flanked by two attractive blondes, and she negotiates with the devil in order to be viewed as stand-out gorgeous. Soon Allison is attracting the attention of a cute boy, and she has been voted a finalist in a magazine beauty contest. These accomplishments seem hollow, though, because the teen knows that they were achieved with supernatural help. Also, beauty will not help her family pay its bills. "Vail does a particularly nice job" in describing Allison's female friendships, noted *Bulletin of the Center for Children's Books* contributor Deborah Stevenson, the critic adding that other interpersonal relationships in *Gorgeous* are depicted in a "sharp and perceptive [manner] as well."

Daring to Be Abigail features a narrative format similar to that of *Ever After.* The novel unfolds through the letters of Abby Silverman, an eleven year old who has decided to "reinvent herself" while away at Camp Nashaquitsa for the summer. Abby's newly acquired boldness wins the acceptance of her fellow campers, but also seems to require that Abby—now Abigail—forsake Dana, an unpopular girl in her cabin. Although she likes Dana, Abigail succumbs to peer pressure by accepting a dare to urinate in Dana's mouthwash. Unable to stop Dana before she uses the rinse, Abigail is thrown out of camp. She addresses a final, poignant letter to her dead father, whose apparent disappointment with his daughter was the central reason for her crisis of identity and her efforts at "reinvention."

Deborah Stevenson, writing in the *Bulletin of the Center for Children's Books,* noted that Abigail's "vulnerability and her poignantly, desperately upbeat letters home will engender reader sympathy and understanding." *Booklist* reviewer Stephanie Zvirin praised Vail for once again being "right on target when it comes to the reality of preadolescent girls, catching how they act and what they say, their nastiness and envy and sweetness, and how confusing it is to long for independence, yet be afraid of the freedom and responsibility that come with it." Lauren Adams, reviewing *Daring to Be Abigail* for *Horn Book,* commented: "As in her other

books, Vail displays her talent for capturing the humor and angst of early adolescence; this latest novel . . . is her most sophisticated yet."

Also geared for preteens, Vail's "Friendship Ring" series consists of small-format books (each volume is about the size of a compact disc case, with bright neon covers to match) that chronicle the middle-school travails of a group of friends trying to cope with adolescence. "Each book is like an episode in a sitcom, told in the first person by a different member of the group," Rochman explained in a *Booklist* review of one book in the series, *If You Only Knew,* Throughout the series "Vail backtracks over the same events, viewing them from a different character's perspective," Christine M. Heppermann explained in her review of the series for *Horn Book.* "It's a technique designed to correct the misconceptions of any seventh grader who regards her peers' apparently carefree lives with envy and feels totally alone at the bottom of 'the pit,'" the critic added. Like all middle schoolers, Vail's characters have many insecurities. Are they popular enough? Are they pretty and feminine enough to get boyfriends? They also have typical teen family problems; one girl's son's father abandoned her family, leaving her mother bitter and depressed; another has an older sister and a father who fight constantly. Vail addresses these issues "with complexity and humor," Rochman noted in a review of *Not That I Care,* "in a quick-talking, immediate, sitcom mode that offers no formula happy ending."

Vail teams up with fellow young-adult novelist Avi for *Never Mind!: A Twin Novel.* The book's perspective alternates between two fraternal twins. Meg, a hard-working student, will be attending a more prestigious school for seventh grade, while her twin brother Edward, does only as much schoolwork as is required. The popular and athletic Meg is worried that the girls at her new school will think less of her if they realize she has a scrawny "loser" brother, so she lies and tells them that he is a budding rock star. Predictably, this one little lie quickly spirals into a giant, hilarious mess. "As screwball comedies go, this one is consistently entertaining," Heppermann commented of *Never Mind!* in a *Horn Book* review, "and the dual narrators remain sympathetic and genuine-sounding." Edward in particular "is hilarious—wry, touching, and very smart," declared *Booklist* reviewer Rochman.

Vail turns to older teens in *If We Kiss,* a story about a high school freshman named Charlie (short for Charlotte) and her attempts to understand the grown-up feelings of love and lust. Charlie gets her long-awaited first kiss from Kevin Lazarus outside the school one day, but this quickly turns into much more than just a kiss. Charlie, shocked by Kevin's surprise move and unsure of how she feels about it, tells no one about the experience. Then her best friend, Tess, unaware of this complication, becomes involved with Kevin, and Charlie's mother begins dating Kevin's father.

Vail's "frank representation of teen sentiments and razorsharp wit will keep readers turning pages to see how Charlie will handle her dilemmas," wrote a *Publishers Weekly* contributor in a review of *If We Kiss.* Several critics praised Vail's prose style, Angela M. Boccuzzi-Reichert commenting in *School Library Journal* that "Charlie tells her story in a fresh voice." A *Publishers Weekly* critic declared of the novel's heroine that Charlie is "much funnier and more knowing than any ninth-grader on the planet."

The hit that self-esteem can take when love goes wrong is the focus of Vail's *You, Maybe: The Profound Asymmetry of Love in High School.* Independent-minded and flirtatious, Josie watches silly girls in her sophomore class fall apart after they are dumped by their boyfriends, and she knows that she will never stoop that low. Then she falls for dishy Carson Gold, and when he decides to move on to another romantic conquest after dating her for several months, Josie is left with her confidence at low ebb. The teen's "wit and intelligence hold the [novel's] first-person narrative together," wrote Heppermann in a review of *You, Maybe,* and in *Kliatt* Myrna Marler called Josie's voice "interesting and appealing." Also praising Vail's novel, a *Kirkus Reviews* writer noted of *You, Maybe* that the book treats readers to "some great lines . . . , a terrific voice and some thoughtful ideas about love and friendship."

In addition to her middle-grade and young-adult novels, Vail has also written several picture books for younger readers. Many of these books feature Mama Rex and T, a mother-and-child dinosaur duo whose difficulties will be familiar to young children and their parents. In *Mama Rex and T Have Homework Trouble,* T forgets about a diorama he has to make for school until the day before it is due; in *The Horrible Play Date,* he and friend Walter have trouble playing together nicely. The latter tale "will strike resonant chords among its readers, no doubt," predicted a *Kirkus Reviews* contributor, while another critic for the same magazine praised the "droll sense of humor" in *Mama Rex and T Have Homework Trouble.*

Vail spins another picture-book tale about childhood difficulties in *Sometimes I'm Bombaloo,* a picture book featuring artwork by Yumi Heo. The story finds a little girl named Katie Honors struggles to control her temper tantrums with the help of her loving, caring parents. "Vail gets right inside a kid's psyche," Ilene Cooper noted in *Booklist,* "captures the intensity of emotion that children . . . feel when they are angry, and then distills it with laughter." A *Publishers Weekly* contributor also praised the book, noting that Vail's "kid-friendly phrasing and language add immediacy and some humor to the proceedings." Katie returns, courtesy of Vail and Heo, in *Jibberwillies at Night,* a story about nighttime fears that *Booklist* contributor Kristen McKulski dubbed "fresh and compelling" due to Vail's imaginative text and Heo's "distinctive mixed-media" illustrations.

Biographical and Critical Sources

PERIODICALS

Booklist, September 1, 1991, Deborah Abbott, review of *Wonder,* p. 54; August, 1992, Stephanie Zvirin, review of *Do-Over,* p. 2013; March 1, 1994, Hazel Rochman, review of *Ever After,* p. 1254; March 1, 1996, Stephanie Zvirin, review of *Daring to Be Abigail,* p. 1184; September 15, 1998, Kathleen Squires, review of *Over the Moon,* p. 241; October 15, 1998, Hazel Rochman, review of *If You Only Knew,* p. 422; November 15, 1998, Hazel Rochman, review of *Not That I Care,* p. 591; February 1, 2002, Ilene Cooper, review of *Sometimes I'm Bombaloo,* p. 940; April 1, 2004, Hazel Rochman, review of *Never Mind!: A Twin Novel,* p. 1365; March 15, 2005, Ilene Cooper, review of *If We Kiss,* p. 1285; March 1, 2008, Jennifer Hubert, review of *Lucky,* p. 60; November 1, 2008, Kristen McKulski, review of *Jibberwillies at Night,* p. 43.

Bulletin of the Center for Children's Books, September, 1991, review of *Wonder,* p. 24; December, 1992, Roger Sutton, review of *Do-Over,* pp. 125-126; February, 1996, Deborah Stevenson, review of *Daring to Be Abigail,* p. 207; June, 2009, Deborah Stevenson, review of *Gorgeous.*

Horn Book, November-December, 1992, Ellen Fader, review of *Do-Over,* p. 731; May-June, 1994, Rachel Vail, "Making Stories Happen," pp. 301-304; May-June, 1996, Lauren Adams, review of *Daring to Be Abigail,* pp. 337-339; January-February, 1999, Christine M. Heppermann, review of *If You Only Knew* and *Not That I Care,* p. 71; May-June, 2004, Christine M. Heppermann, review of *Never Mind!,* p. 324; May-June, 2006, Christine M. Heppermann, review of *You, Maybe: The Profound Asymmetry of Love in High School,* p. 335.

Kirkus Reviews, August 8, 1991, review of *Wonder,* p. 1095; April 1, 1994, review of *Ever After,* p. 486; January 1, 2002, review of *Sometimes I'm Bombaloo,* p. 53; July 1, 2002, review of *The Horrible Play Date,* p. 964; July 15, 2002, review of *Mama Rex and T Have Homework Trouble,* p. 1046; April 15, 2005, review of *If We Kiss,* p. 483; April 1, 2006, review of *You, Maybe,* p. 358; October 1, 2007, review of *Righty and Lefty: A Tale of Two Feet;* April 15, 2008, review of *Lucky.*

Kliatt, May, 2004, Michele Winship, review of *Never Mind!,* p. 5; May, 2005, Heidi Hauser Green, review of *Ever After,* p. 31; May, 2006, Myrna Marler, review of *You, Maybe,* p. 16.

Publishers Weekly, August 9, 1991, review of *Wonder,* p. 58; December 20, 1991, "Flying Starts," p. 24; February 21, 1994, review of *Ever After,* pp. 255-256; June 8, 1998, review of *The Friendship Ring,* p. 61; July 20, 1998, review of *Over the Moon,* p. 218; December 24, 2001, review of *Sometimes I'm Bombaloo,* p. 63; May 10, 2004, review of *Never Mind!,* p. 60; April 11, 2005, review of *If We Kiss,* p. 56; November 5, 2007, review of *Righty and Lefty,* p. 62; September 1, 2008, review of *Jibberwillies at Night,* p. 53.

School Library Journal, August, 1991, Debra S. Gold, review of *Wonder,* p. 196; September, 1992, Jacqueline Rose, review of *Do-Over,* p. 282; May, 1994, Ellen Fader, review of *Ever After,* p. 136; March, 1996, Connie Tyrrell Burns, review of *Daring to Be Abigail,* p. 198; March, 2002, Nina Lindsay, review of *Sometimes I'm Bombaloo,* p. 204; May, 2005, Angela M. Boccuzzi-Reichert, review of *If We Kiss,* p. 140; November, 2007, Maryann H. Owen, review of *Righty and Lefty,* p. 102; April, 2008, Genevieve Gallagher, review of *Lucky,* p. 150; October, 2008, Joan Kindig, review of *Jibberwillies at Night,* p. 128.

Voice of Youth Advocates, August, 2004, Pam Carlson, review of *Never Mind!,* p. 207.

Washington Post Book World, July 18, 2004, Elizabeth Ward, review of *Never Mind!,* p. 11.

ONLINE

BookPage.com, http://www.bookpage.com/ (July 18, 2005), Heidi Henneman, interview with Vail and Avi.

Rachel Vail Home Page, http://www.rachelvail.com (June 8, 2009).

Teenreads.com, http://www.teenreads.com/ (July 1, 2006), Kristi Olson, review of *If We Kiss;* "Rachel Vail."*

*   *   *

van LIESHOUT, Maria

Personal

Born in the Netherlands; married.

Addresses

Home—San Francisco, CA.

Career

Author, artist, and illustrator. Designer of cards and art prints.

Awards, Honors

Canadian Children's Book Centre Best Books designation, and Blue Spruce Award finalist, Ontario Library Association, both 2008, and *Storytelling World* Honor designation, all for *The List* by Hazel Hutchins.

Writings

SELF-ILLUSTRATED

Bloom!: A Little Book about Finding Love, Feiwel & Friends (New York, NY), 2008.

Splash!: A Little Book about Bouncing Back, Feiwel & Friends (New York, NY), 2008.

Peep!: A Little Book about Taking a Leap, Feiwel & Friends (New York, NY), 2009.

Author's work has been translated into German and Korean.

ILLUSTRATOR

Hazel Hutchins, *The List,* Annick Press (Toronto, Ontario, Canada), 2007.

Maryann Cusimano Love, *Sleep, Baby, Sleep,* Philomel Books (New York, NY), 2009.

Sidelights

Although she now lives in San Francisco, artist and author Maria van Lieshout is inspired by the work of well-known illustrators such a Dick Bruna, who is popular among children in Holland, where she grew up. She shares that expressive art with children in several small-format picture books: *Bloom!: A Little Book about Finding Love, Splash!: A Little Book about Bouncing Back,* and *Peep!: A Little Book about Taking a Leap.*

In *Bloom!* a pink pig with an intense passion for flowers discovers that the best kind of love is the love that is returned, while the blue seal in *Splash!* learns that caring for others is the best way to raise his own low spirits. The little chick that stars in *Peep!* finally summons up the courage to take a risky leap, with the encouragement of his mother and siblings, his story is documented by van Lieshout's characteristic clear, spare watercolor images.

Reviewing *Bloom!* in *Publishers Weekly,* a contributor predicted that, "as light and sweet as cotton candy," van Lieshout's peppermint-pink-and-blue-tinged story "will win over kids and grownups alike." Tinted in a blue reflecting its hero's own mood, *Splash!* features a "deceptively simple" text that successfully "conveys feelings from a child's point of view," according to *School Library Journal* critic Marian Creamer.

Maria Van Lieshout's gently tinted drawings bring to life an equally gentle story in her original picture book **Bloom!** (Copyright © 2008 by Maria van Lieshout. All rights reserved. Reproduced by permission of St. Martin's Press.)

Biographical and Critical Sources

PERIODICALS

Kirkus Reviews, December 1, 2007, review of *Bloom!: A Little Book about Finding Love;* September 15, 2008, review of *Splash!: A Little Book about Bouncing Back.*

Publishers Weekly, December 10, 2007, review of *Bloom!,* p. 54.

School Library Journal, April, 2008, Julie Roach, review of *Bloom!,* p. 152; November, 2008, Marian Creamer, review of *Splash!,* p. 102.

ONLINE

Maria Van Lieshout Home Page, http://www.mariavanlieshout.com (June 8, 2009).*

*   *   *

VOTAW, Carol 1961-

Personal

Born 1961.

Addresses

Home—CA.

Career

Author.

Writings

Good Morning, Little Polar Bear, illustrated by Susan Banta, NorthWood Books for Young Readers (Minnetonka, MN), 2005.

Waking up Down Under, illustrated by Susan Banta, NorthWood Books for Young Readers (Minnetonka, MN), 2007.

Biographical and Critical Sources

PERIODICALS

Kirkus Reviews, September 15, 2007, review of *Waking up Down Under.*

School Library Journal, November, 2005, Anjela J. Reynolds, review of *Good Morning, Little Polar Bear,* p. 122; December, 2007, Martha Simpson, review of *Waking up Down Under,* p. 116.*

W-Y

WATSON, John H.
See FARMER, Philip José

*   *   *

WEIGELT, Udo 1960-

Personal
Born 1960.

Addresses
E-mail—info@uweigelt.de.

Career
Writer of children's books.

Writings

FOR CHILDREN

Ich bin die stärkste Maus der Welt, illustrated by Nicholas d'Aujourd'hui, Nord-Süd (Zürich, Switzerland), 1998, translated by J. Alison James as *The Strongest Mouse in the World,* North-South Books (New York, NY), 1998.

Wer hat dem Hamster das Gold gestohlen?, illustrated by Julia Gukova, Findling (Germany), 1998, translated by J. Alison James as *Who Stole the Gold?,* North-South Books (New York, NY), 2000.

Alle Wetter, illustrated by Nicholas d'Aujourd'hui, Nord-Süd (Zürich, Switzerland), 1999, translated by J. Alison James as *All-Weather Friends,* North-South Books (New York, NY), 1999.

Rodolfo kommt, illustrated by Alexander Reichstein, Nord-Süd (Zürich, Switzerland), 1999, translated by J. Alison James as *Hiding Horatio,,* North-South Books (New York, NY), 1999.

Die verflixten Besuche, illustrated by Nicholas d'Aujourd'hui, Nord-Süd (Zürich, Switzerland), 2000.

Der Osterkuckuck, illustrated by Rolf Siegenthaler, Nord-Süd (Zürich, Switzerland), 2000.

Die Räberspatzenbande, illustrated by Julia Gukova, Nord-Süd (Zürich, Switzerland), 2001, translated by J. Alison James as *Ben and the Buccaneers,* North-South Books (New York, NY), 2001.

Ein ei für den Osterhasen, illustrated by Rolf Siegenthaler, Nord-Süd (Zürich, Switzerland), 2001, translated by J. Alison James as *The Easter Bunny's Baby,* North-South Books (New York, NY), 2001.

Ich wars nicht! (sequel to *Who Stole the Gold?*), illustrated by Julia Gukova, Nord-Süd (Zürich, Switzerland), 2001, translated by J. Alison James as *It Wasn't Me!* North-South Books (New York, NY), 2001.

Wenn der wilde Wombat kommt, illustrated by Anne-Katrin Piepenbrink, Michael Neugebauer (Zurich, Switzerland), 2001, translated by J. Alison James as *The Wild Wombat,* North-South Books (New York, NY), 2002.

Stimmt das alles, was man hört?, illustrated by Maja Dusikova, Nord-Süd (Zürich, Switzerland), 2002, translated by J. Alison James as *What Lies on the Other Side?,* North-South Books (New York, NY), 2002.

Keiner hört mir zu!, illustrated by Manuela Simoncelli, Nord-Süd (Zürich, Switzerland), 2002.

Im Wald ist Platz für alle!, illustrated by Gianluca Garofalo, Nord-Süd (Zürich, Switzerland), 2002, translated by Martina Rasdeuschek-Simmons as *There's Room in the Forest for Everyone,* North-South Books (New York, NY), 2003.

Ber Biber geht fort, illustrated by Bernadette Watts, Nord-Süd (Zürich, Switzerland), 2002, translated by J. Alison James as *Old Beaver,* North-South Books (New York, NY), 2002.

Alex war's!, illustrated by Cristina Kadmon, Nord-Süd (Zürich, Switzerland), 2002, translated by J. Alison James as *Alex Did It!,* North-South Books (New York, NY), 2002.

Zwei Eulen und die kluge dicke Maus, illustrated by Bernhard Oberdieck, Nord-Süd (Zürich, Switzerland), 2002.

Marike wird die Geister los, illustrated by Christa Unzner, Nord-Süd (Zürich, Switzerland), 2002, translated by Marisa Miller as *Miranda's Ghosts,* North-South Books (New York, NY), 2002.

Der alte Bär muss Abschied nehman, illustrated by Cristina Kadmon, Nord-Süd (Zürich, Switzerland), 2003, translated by Sibylle Kazeroid as *Bear's Last Journey,* North-South Books (New York, NY), 2003.

Sandmännchens Mondfahrt, illustrated by Sibylle Heusser, Nord-Süd (Zürich, Switzerland), 2003, translated by J. Alison James as *The Sandman,* North-South Books (New York, NY), 2003.

Der falsche Freund, illustrated by Nora Hilb, Nord-Süd (Zürich, Switzerland), 2003, translated by J. Alison James as *Fair-Weather Friend,* North-South Books (New York, NY), 2003.

Der Nikolaustaler, illustrated by Rolf Siegenthaler, Nord-Süd (Zürich, Switzerland), 2004, translated by Marianne Martens as *Santa's Lucky Charm,* North-South Books (New York, NY), 2004.

Sleepy Bear's Christmas, illustrated by Christina Kadmon, translation by J. Alison James, North-South Books (New York, NY), 2004.

Das sagenhafte Einhorn, illustrated by Julia Gukova, Nord-Süd (Zürich, Switzerland), 2004, translated by J. Alison James as *The Legendary Unicorn,* North-South Books (New York, NY), 2004.

Das Eihörnchen, illustrated by Rolf Siegenthaler, Findlin (Germany), 2004.

Die phantastischen Reisen des kleinen Löwen, illustrated by Julia Gukova, Nord-Süd (Zürich, Switzerland), 2004.

Mole's Journey, illustrated by Jakob Kirchmayr, translation by Sibylle Kazeroid, North-South Books (New York, NY), 2004.

Joschi's grösster Wunsch, illustrated by Pirkko Vainio, Nord-Süd (Zürich, Switzerland), 2005, translated by Marianne Martens as *Little Donkey's Wish,* North-South Books (New York, NY), 2005.

Alvina und die fünf Räuberhüte, illustrated by Wolfgang Slawski, Nord-Süd (Zürich, Switzerland), 2006.

Spring Fever, illustrated by Sarah Emmanuelle Burg, translated by Marianne Martens, North-South Books (New York, NY), 2006.

Wer hilft dir Osterhase?, illustrated by Cristina Kadmon, Nord-Süd (Zürich, Switzerland), 2006, translated by J. Alison James as *Hide Easter Bunny, Hide!,* North-South Books (New York, NY), 2007.

Wanja und die wilden Tiere, illustrated by Svjetlan Junakovic, Bohem Press (Germany), 2006.

Wundermeerschwein rettet die Welt, illustrated by Nina Spranger, Sauerländer (Germany), 2006, translated as *Super Guinea Pig to the Rescue,* Walker Books (New York, NY), 2007.

Immer dieser Bär!, illustrated by Kristina Andres, Nord-Süd (Zürich, Switzerland), 2007.

Paula leiht sich was, illustrated by Astrid Henn, Nord-Süd (Zürich, Switzerland), 2008, translated by J. Alison James as *Becky the Borrower,* North-South Books (New York, NY), 2008.

Der Tierklauer, illustrated by Susanne Smajic, edelkids, 2008.

Die schönste Tasse der Welt, illustrated by Yusuke Yonezu, Minedition, 2008.

Der alte Bär muss Abschied nehmen, illustrated by Cristina Kadmon, Nord-Süd (Zürich, Switzerland), 2008.

Wenn der wilde Wombat kommt, illustrated by Melanie Freund, Minedition, 2009.

Sidelights

German writer Udo Weigelt is the author of many children's picture books, and his gently humorous tales are brought to life through the art of illustrators such as Julie Gukova, Cristina Kadmon, Rolf Siegenthaler, and Nina Spranger. While most of Weigelt's stories, such as *The Strongest Mouse in the World, Bear's Last Journey, Little Donkey's Wish,* and *Spring Fever,* feature an all-animal cast of characters, *Becky the Borrower* is a standout due to its focus on a human child. The story of a little girl who borrows all manner of things from her kindergarten classmates and then forgets where the things came from or to whom they belong, *Becky the Borrower* "conveys a typical childhood dilemma in simple prose accompanied by [Astrid Henn's] charming illustrations," according to *School Library Journal* contributor Lisa Egly Lehmuller. According to a *Publishers Weekly* critic, in *Little Donkey's Wish* Weigelt tells a "pleasant tale of self-esteem and encouragement," while in *Booklist* Ilene Cooper predicted of *The Strongest Mouse in the World* that "little ones will empathize with Lizzie [the mouse]'s desire to be strong" enough to help her friends.

In *Ben and the Buccaneers* a young sparrow wants to join the adventurous Buccaneers, a group of older sparrows that enjoys taunting a neighborhood cat. The Buccaneers daringly fly, in formation, just out of the cat's reach, and they dodge and flip away from him as he tries to catch them with his claws. When the cat suggests a way for Ben to join the Buccaneers, the sparrow readily agrees, only to find out later that he has been tricked; all the Buccaneers are now endangered because of him, and he must show courage to save their lives. Shelley Townsend-Hudson, writing in *Booklist,* noted that "children will root for the brave little sparrow" in *Ben and the Buccaneers,* while *School Library Journal* reviewer Susan Marie Pitard concluded that Weigelt's tale "will ring true with many young children."

In *Alex Did It!* three clever rabbits invent an imaginary friend named Alex, whom they can blame for all their own mischief. The ruse works fine, allowing the rabbits to get away with all sorts of pranks. However, when a new rabbit whose name really is Alex moves into the forest, the three troublemakers must come clean and confess to their misdeeds. A critic for *Kirkus Reviews* called *Alex Did It!* "a playful tale of mischief and redemption," while a *Publishers Weekly* reviewer concluded that "Weigelt's premise will hook readers."

A house cat is the star of *Spring Fever,* another picture book by Weigelt. Finally allowed to go outside now that the weather has warmed, Freddy the Cat is busy

Udo Weigelt introduces an unusual superhero in his engaging picture book Super Guinea Pig to the Rescue, *featuring illustrations by Nina Spranger.* (Illustration copyright © 2007 by Nina Spranger. Reprinted by permission of Walker Books. All rights reserved.)

hunting and scouting out the changes in his family's yard when he suddenly feels a yearning for love . . . and a neighbor cat sunning herself on a window sill catches Freddy's fancy. In *Super Guinea Pig to the Rescue,* a guinea pig is inspired by watching his oversized rodent superhero, but when he tries to impress his animal friends, he winds up needing rescuing himself. Noting that "Weigelt compassionately and humorously relates" his tale, *Booklist* critic Shelle Rosenfeld added that in *Super Guinea Pig to the Rescue* Nina Spranger's "expressive watercolor-and-acrylic illustrations" accentuate the characters' "affectionate, sometimes indulgent friendship."

Weigelt turns to legend in *The Sandman* and describes the character who spreads the magical sand each night that sends every person and animal to sleep. One night, as he is floating above the world in his blue dirigible, the Sandman realizes that he is lonely because everyone around him falls asleep. Finally, the Sandman realizes that the moon, which has been patiently watching him as he works, is also awake and looking for a friend. A critic for *Kirkus Reviews* called *The Sandman* "a simply told, quietly beautiful tale."

In *The Legendary Unicorn,* the forest animals gather to tell stories every evening. One day, the hedgehog sees a unicorn as he is on his way to the storytelling. When he tells his friends, they refuse to believe him; after all, the unicorn is a creature from legends and is not real. This refusal to believe brings about a change in the forest.

Life seems more dull and dreary, and things become less interesting to do. Worse, no one can think up an interesting new story to tell at story time. Though the animals search for the unicorn, they cannot find her. Only by creating a new story together do they prove they still believe in magic, and enable the unicorn to return to the forest. A reviewer for the *Children's Bookwatch* called *The Legendary Unicorn* "a simple, joyful picturebook," and in *School Library Journal* Susan Hepler dubbed Julia Gukova's illustrations" delightful."

Biographical and Critical Sources

PERIODICALS

Booklist, April 15, 1998, Ilene Cooper, review of *The Strongest Mouse in the World,* p. 1455; April 1, 2001, Shelley Townsend-Hudson, review of *The Easter Bunny's Baby,* p. 1480; August, 2001, Shelley Townsend-Hudson, review of *Ben and the Buccaneers,* p. 2133; January 1, 2002, John Peters, review of *It Wasn't Me!,* p. 868; October 1, 2007, Shelle Rosenfeld, review of *Super Guinea Pig to the Rescue,* p. 67.

Childhood Education, spring, 2003, review of *Old Beaver,* p. 180.

Children's Bookwatch, December, 2004, review of *The Legendary Unicorn.*

Kirkus Reviews, February 1, 2002, review of *Alex Did It!,* p. 191; February 1, 2003, review of *The Sandman,* p. 243; March 15, 2003, review of *Bear's Last Journey,* p. 481; December 1, 2005, review of *Spring Fever,* p. 1281; September 15, 2007, review of *Super Guinea Pig to the Rescue;* August 15, 2008, review of *Becky the Borrower.*

Publishers Weekly, January 14, 2002, review of *Alex Did It!,* p. 60; September 23, 2002, review of *Miranda's Ghosts,* p. 72; September 26, 2005, review of *Little Donkey's Wish,* p. 89.

School Librarian, autumn, 1998, review of *The Strongest Mouse in the World,* p. 134; spring, 2001, review of *Who Stole the Gold?,* p. 19; autumn, 2001, review of *Ben and the Buccaneers,* p. 134; summer, 2003, review of *The Wild Wombat,* p. 76, and review of *Miranda's Ghosts,* p. 78; autumn, 2003, review of *The Sandman,* p. 134; summer, 2005, Sarah Merrett, review of *The Legendary Unicorn,* p. 78.

School Library Journal, January, 2001, Maryann H. Owen, review of *Who Stole the Gold?,* p. 112; April, 2001, Blair Christolon, review of *The Easter Bunny's Baby,* p. 126; August, 2001, Susan Marie Pitard, review of *Ben and the Buccaneers,* p. 164; February, 2002, Susan Hepler, review of *It Wasn't Me!,* p. 116; June, 2002, Maryann H. Owen, review of *Old Beaver,* p. 114; July, 2002, Patricia Pearl Dole, review of *Alex Did It!,* p. 100; September, 2002, Be Astengo, review of *What Lies on the Other Side?,* p. 208; December, 2002, Gay Lynn Van Vleck, *The Wild Wombat,* p. 112; February, 2003, Kathleen Kelly, review of *Miranda's Ghosts,* p. 124; October, 2003, Lisa Dennis, review of *Bear's Last Journey,* p. 141, Shelley B. Sutherland,

review of *The Sandman,* p. 142, and Tali Balas, review of *There's Room in the Forest for Everyone,* p. 142; February, 2005, Susan Hepler, review of *The Legendary Unicorn,* p. 110; February, 2006, Maryann H. Owen, review of *Spring Fever,* p. 112; September, 2008, Lisa Egly Lehmuller, review of *Becky the Borrower,* p. 161.

ONLINE

Udo Weigelt Home Page, http://www.uweigelt.de (February 21, 2006).*

* * *

WINSTON, Sherri 1964(?)-

Personal

Born c. 1964; children: two daughters. *Education:* Michigan State University, earned degree.

Addresses

Home—Fort Lauderdale, FL. *E-mail*—swinston@sunsentinel.com.

Career

Young-adult novelist. *Hartford Courant,* Hartford, CT, sports copyeditor; *South Florida Sun-Sentinel,* Fort Lauderdale, FL, columnist; also worked at ESPN sports cable network.

Writings

Acting, Marshall Cavendish (New York, NY), 2004.
The Kayla Chronicles, Little, Brown (New York, NY), 2009.

Sidelights

A columnist for the *South Florida Sun-Sentinel,* Sherri Winston has also published two novels for teen readers: *Acting* and *The Kayla Chronicles.* Told from the perspective of Eve, a sixteen year old from a small Michigan town, *Acting* shares the story of twin girls who both wish to enter the world of acting but take decidedly different paths as they mature into young adults. After Al announces to the family that she is pregnant, Eve tries to compensate for her twin's mistake by overpleasing her parents. Attraction to a young man named Lucious, however, complicates Eve's desire to be a "good" girl. Despite noting some problems with the plot, *Booklist* critic Hazel Rochman predicted that young teens will appreciate *Acting* "for the truth it tells about romance and sex" as well as for Winston's "honest" portrayal of a tight-knit African-American family.

Writing in *Kirkus Reviews,* a critic praised *Acting* for offering "a forthright examination of sex that makes plain how hard it is to keep the hormones from raging."

The Kayla Chronicles features a young African-American girl who is growing up in an upper-middleclass Florida family. A sophomore in high school, Kayla has remained best friends with Rosalie for many years. However, Rosalie's increasingly strident feminist views have the fourteen year old questioning the future of their relationship. In an attempt to illustrate the exploitation of women based on their physical beauty, Rosalie convinces Kayla to try out for the school's dance team, assuming that her friend will not be selected on account of her appearance. Much to everyone's surprise, however, Kayla earns a spot on the Lady Lions dance squad, forcing the adolescent to begin thinking about making her own decisions in life rather than being manipulated by Rosalie. As other members of the dance team turn out to be intelligent and friendly toward Kayla, she realizes that part of maturing into adulthood includes thinking for oneself and not making misguided assumptions about others.

Calling *The Kayla Chronicles* a "refreshing departure" from the abundance of books featuring disadvantaged

Cover of Sherri Winston's young-adult novel The Kayla Chronicles, *featuring a photograph by Patrick Bernard.* (Little, Brown & Company, 2007. Patrick Bernard/Getty Images.)

African-American characters, *Booklist* critic Jennifer Mattson applauded Winston's ability to create a well-developed narrator, writing that Kayla's "smart, gently self-mocking voice will transcend racial lines to hit home with a large number of young women." In *Kliatt* Claire Rosser described the novel as "frequently funny, earthy, and as fast paced as Kayla's dance moves," and *School Library Journal* contributor Sheilah Kosco called *The Kayla Chronicles* "a fun, sassy, lighthearted story."

Biographical and Critical Sources

PERIODICALS

Booklist, October 1, 2004, Hazel Rochman, review of *Acting*, p. 324; February 1, 2008, Jennifer Mattson, review of *The Kayla Chronicles*, p. 52.

Kirkus Reviews, September 15, 2004, review of *Acting*, p. 923.

Kliatt, January, 2008, Claire Rosser, review of *The Kayla Chronicles*, p. 13.

School Library Journal, April, 2008, Sheilah Kosco, review of *The Kayla Chronicles*, p. 154.*

*   *   *

WUMMER, Amy 1955-

Personal

Born 1955; married; husband's name Mark; children: three.

Addresses

Home—Reading, PA. *Agent*—Deborah Wolfe, Ltd.

Career

Illustrator of books for children, beginning mid-1990s.

Illustrator

Patti Farmer, *Bartholomew's Dream,* Barron's (Hauppauge, NY), 1994.

Catherine McMarrow, *The Jellybean Principle,* Random House (New York, NY), 1994.

Jennifer Dussling, *Bug Off!,* Grosset & Dunlap (New York, NY), 1997.

Sid Fleischman, *McBroom Tells the Truth,* Price Stern Sloan (New York, NY), 1998.

Sid Fleischman, *McBroom's Ghost,* Price Stern Sloan (New York, NY), 1998.

Sid Fleischman, *McBroom Tells a Lie,* Price Stern Sloan (New York, NY), 1999.

Sid Fleischman, *McBroom the Rainmaker,* Price Stern Sloan (New York, NY), 1999.

Louis Sachar, *Marvin Redpost: A Flying Birthday Cake,* Random House (New York, NY), 1999.

Louis Sachar, *Marvin Redpost: Class President,* Random House (New York, NY), 1999.

Susan Hood, *Look! I Can Read!,* Grosset & Dunlap (New York, NY), 2000.

Louis Sachar, *A Magic Crystal?,* Random House (New York, NY), 2000.

Louis Sachar, *Marvin Redpost: Super Fast, out of Control!,* Random House (New York, NY), 2000.

Rita Book, *My Soccer Mom from Mars,* Grosset & Dunlap (New York, NY), 2001.

Marcia Thornton Jones and Debbie Dadey, *Ghost Dog,* Volo (New York, NY), 2001.

Marcia Thornton Jones and Debbie Dadey, *Playground Bully,* Volo (New York, NY), 2001.

Marcia Thornton Jones and Debbie Dadey, *Puppy Trouble,* Volo (New York, NY), 2001.

Marcia Thornton Jones and Debbie Dadey, *Snow Day,* Volo (New York, NY), 2001.

Marcia Thronton Jones and Debbie Dadley, *Top Dog,* Volo (New York, NY), 2001.

Johnny Ray Moore, *The Story of Martin Luther King, Jr.,* Candy Cane Press (Nashville, TN), 2001.

Barbara J. Neasi, *Listen to Me,* Children's Press (New York, NY), 2001.

Marcia Thornton Jones and Debbie Dadey, *Tattle Tales,* Volo (New York, NY), 2002.

Johnny Ray Moore, *Meet Martin Luther King, Jr.,* Ideals Children's Books (Nashville, TN), 2002.

Jennie Bishop, *Jesus Must Be Really Special,* Standard (Cincinnati, OH), 2002.

Susan Hood, *Look, I Can Tie My Shoes!,* Grosset & Dunlap (New York, NY), 2002.

Marcia Thornton Jones and Debbie Dadey, *Blue-Ribbon Blues,* Volo (New York, NY), 2002.

Marcia Thornton Jones and Debbie Dadey, *Buried Treasure,* Volo (New York, NY), 2002.

Marcia Thornton Jones and Debbie Dadey, *Puppies on Parade,* Volo (New York, NY), 2002.

Marcia Thornton Jones and Debbie Dadey, *Puppy Love,* Volo, (New York, NY), 2002.

Marcia Thornton Jones and Debbie Dadey, *Santa Dog,* Volo (New York, NY), 2002.

Marcia Thornton Jones and Debbie Dadey, *Sticks and Stones and Doggie Bones,* Volo (New York, NY), 2002.

Michelle Knudsen, *The Case of Vampire Vivian,* Kane Press (New York, NY), 2003.

Karen Ann Moore, *Dear God, Let's Talk about You,* Standard (Cincinnati, OH), 2003.

Karen Ann Moore, *Hi God, Let's Talk about My Life,* Standard (Cincinnati, OH), 2003.

Jennifer Dussling, *Whatcha Got?,* Kane Press (New York, NY), 2004.

Pansie Hart Flood, *It's Test Day, Tiger Turcotte,* Carolrhoda Books (Minneapolis, MN), 2004.

Pamela Kennedy, *Five-Minute Devotions for Children: Celebrating God's World as a Family,* Ideals Childrens Books (Nashville, TN), 2004.

Pamela Kennedy, *More Five-Minute Devotions for Children: Celebrating God's World as a Family,* Ideals Childrens Books (Nashville, TN), 2004.

Lynn Plourde, *Mother, May I?,* Dutton Children's Books (New York, NY), 2004.

Sarah Willson, *Hocus Focus,* Kane Press (New York, NY), 2004.

Michelle Medlock Adams, *What Is Easter?,* CandyCane Press (Nashville, TN), 2005.

Chris Auer, *Molly and the Good Shepherd,* Zonderkidz (Grand Rapids, MI), 2005.

Pansie Hart Flood, *Tiger Turcotte Takes on the Know-It-All,* Carolrhoda (Minneapolis, MN), 2005.

Taylor Jordan, *Movin' on In,* Kane Press (New York, NY), 2005.

Marie Karns, *The Incredible Peepers of Penelope Budd,* Gibbs Smith Publisher (Salt Lake City, UT), 2005.

Lynn Plourde, *Dad, Aren't You Glad?,* Dutton Children's Books (New York, NY), 2005.

Michelle Medlock Adams, *What Is Christmas?,* Candy-Cane Press (Nashville, TN), 2006.

Laura Driscoll, *Sally's Big Save,* Kane Press (New York, NY), 2006.

Jamie Gilson, *Gotcha!,* Clarion Books (New York, NY), 2006.

Pamela Kennedy, *Granny's Cozy Quilt of Memories: Remembering Grandmother's Love through Her Lasting Gift,* GPKids (Nashville, TN), 2006.

Pamela Kennedy, *A Sister for Matthew: A Story about Adoption,* GPKids (Nashville, TN), 2006.

Jill Roman Lord, *If Jesus Lived inside My Heart,* Candy-Cane Press (Nashville, TN), 2006.

Amy Wummer's illustration work includes her humorous drawings for Sid Fleischman's beginning reader **McBroom the Rainmaker.** (Illustration copyright © 1999 by Amy Wummer. Reproduced by permission of Amy Wummer.)

Nan Walker, *Stressbusters,* Kane Press (New York, NY), 2006.

Michelle Medlock Adams, *What Is Halloween?,* Candy-Cane Press (Nashville, TN), 2007.

Jennie Bishop, *Jesus Must Be Really Special,* Standard (Cincinnati, OH), 2007.

Laura Driscoll, *Real Heroes Don't Wear Capes,* Kane Press (New York, NY), 2007.

Denise Eliana Gruska, *The Only Boy in Ballet Class,* Gibbs Smith (Layton, UT), 2007.

Pamela Kennedy and Douglas Kennedy, *My Book of Five-Minute Devotions: Celebrating God's World,* Ideals Children's Books (Nashville, TN), 2007.

Eleanor May, *Ty's Triple Trouble,* Kane Press (New York, NY), 2007.

Margaret Sutherland, *Valentines Are for Saying I Love You,* Grosset & Dunlap (New York, NY), 2007.

Jamie Gilson, *Chess! I Love It, I Love It, I Love It!,* Clarion Books (New York, NY), 2008.

Pamela Kennedy, *Two Homes for Tyler: A Story about Understanding Divorce,* GPKids (Nashville, TN), 2008.

Suzy Kline, *Horrible Harry and the Dead Letters,* Viking Childrens Books (New York, NY), 2008.

Eleanor May, *Keesha's Bright Idea,* Kane Press (New York, NY), 2008.

Nan Walker, *The Bay School Blogger,* Kane Press (New York, NY), 2008.

Toni Buzzeo, *Adventure Girl Goes to Work,* Dial Books for Young Readers (New York, NY), 2009.

Suzy Kline, *Horrible Harry on the Ropes,* Viking Children's Books (New York, NY), 2009.

Lewis B. Montgomery, *The Case of the Amazing Zelda,* Kane Press (New York, NY), 2009.

Lewis B. Montgomery, *The Case of the Haunted Haunted House,* Kane Press (New York, NY), 2009.

Lewis B. Montgomery, *The Case of the Poisoned Pig,* Kane Press (New York, NY), 2009.

Lewis B. Montgomery, *The Case of the Stinky Socks,* Kane Press (New York, NY), 2009.

Natasha Wing, *The Night before New Year's,* Grosset & Dunlap (New York, NY), 2009.

Natasha Wing, *The Night before St. Patrick's Day,* Grosset & Dunlap (New York, NY), 2009.

Sidelights

A prolific artist, Amy Wummer has contributed her amusing cartoon images to picture books, chapter books, and easy readers since the mid-1990s. Often working on several books at the same time, Wummer creates illustrations that have been paired with texts by writers ranging from Sid Fleishman and Louis Sachar to Eleanor May and Suzy Kline, the last for whom she has brought to life the amusing "Horrible Harry" easy readers series.

Commenting on Wummer's work for *It's Test Day, Tiger Turcotte,* a chapter book by Pansie Hart Flood, Sharon R. Pearce wrote in *School Library Journal* that the artist's pencil illustrations capture the characters' emotions." In her artwork for Jamie Gilson's *Gotcha!,* Wummer "spices up" Gilson's story by contributing

Wummer teams up with author Margaret Sutherland to create the warmhearted picture-book **Valentines Are for Saying I Love You.** (Illustration copyright © 2007 by Amy Wummer. All rights reserved. Reproduced by permission of Grosset & Dunlap, a division of Penguin Putnam Books for Young Readers.)

"humorous line drawings, engaging readers in the zany story," according to Debbie Whitbeck, also in *School Library Journal.*

A story about a boy named Tucker whose love of dance allows him to brave socially trying circumstances, Denise Gruska's *The Only Boy in Ballet Class* features "sprightly" pen-and-ink and water-color illustrations "that capture Tucker's fancy footwork and the characters' varied expressions," according to *School Library Journal* critic Linda Ludke. The "cheerful cartoons" Wummer creates for Marie Karns' *The Incredible Peepers of Penelope Budd* "capture the child's free spirit . . . [and] the beauty in everyday objects," Suzanne Myers Harold concluded in another *School Library Journal* review, while in *Booklist* Ilene Cooper wrote that the illustrator's "delightful watercolor-and-ink" cartoon renderings leap off the page "and match . . . the gusto of the text."

Biographical and Critical Sources

PERIODICALS

Booklist, December 1, 2000, Ilene Cooper, review of *Look! I Can Read!,* p. 725; March 15, 2004, Carolyn Phelan, review of *Hocus Focus,* p. 1312.
Kirkus Reviews, January 1, 2004, review of *Mother May I?,* p. 40.
School Library Journal, February, 2003, Nancy Gifford, review of *Look! I Can Tie My Shoes!,* p. 113; March, 2004, Rosalyn Pierini, review of *Mother May I?,* p. 180; July, 2004, Sharon R. Pearce, review of *It's Test*

Day, Tiger Turcotte, p. 75; March, 2005, Wendy Woodfill, review of *Dad, Aren't You Glad?,* p. 186; January, 2006, Suzanne Myers Harold, review of *The Incredible Peepers of Penelope Budd,* p. 104; April, 2006, Debbie Whitbeck, review of *Gotcha!,* p. 106; June, 2007, Gina Powell, review of *Ty's Triple Trouble,* p. 94; September, 2007, Linda L. Walkins, review of *Real Heroes Don't Wear Capes,* p. 164; November, 2007, Linda Ludke, review of *The Only Boy in Ballet Class,* p. 92; May, 2008, Sarah O'Halla, review of *Chess!: I Love It I Love It I Love It!,* p. 98.*

*   *   *

YOUNG, Selina 1971-2006

Personal

Born April 7, 1971, in Surrey, England; committed suicide February 8, 2006, in New Zealand; daughter of Eoin (a writer) and Sandra Young; children: Alfie. *Education:* Attended Epsom Art College; attended Cambridge University art school.

Career

Author and illustrator. *Exhibitions:* Works exhibited at galleries in London and Cambridge, England.

Awards, Honors

Pan-Macmillan Award for Best Children's Book; *New Zealand Post* Book Award, 1998, for *A Summery Saturday Morning* by Margaret Mahy.

Writings

SELF-ILLUSTRATED

Ned, Thomasson-Grant (Charlottesville, VA), 1993.
Whistling in the Woods, Tambourine Books (New York, NY), 1994.
Adam Pig's Everything Fun Book: Stories to Read, Pictures to Look at, and Things to Do, Doubleday Book for Young Readers (New York, NY), 1996.
My Favorite Word Book: Words and Pictures for the Very Young, Random House (New York, NY), 1999.
Big Dog and Little Dog Visit the Moon, Crabtree (New York, NY), 2002.
Big Dog and Little Dog Go Sailing, Crabtree (New York, NY), 2002.
All about Me: A Hundred Things That Happened to Me between 0 and 3, Orion Children's Books (London, England), 2005.

ILLUSTRATOR

Judy Hindley, *Maybe Its a Pirate,* Thomasson-Grant (Charlottesville, VA), 1992.

Julia Eccleshare, editor, *First Poems,* P. Bedrick Books (New York, NY), 1994.

Georgie Adams, *Nanny Fox and the Christmas Surprise,* Doubleday Book for Young Readers (New York, NY), 1996.

Georgie Adams, *A Year Full of Stories: 366 Days of Story and Rhyme,* Doubleday Book for Young Readers (New York, NY), 1997.

Margaret Mahy, *A Summery Saturday Morning,* Viking (New York, NY), 1998.

Joyce Dunbar, *The Pig Who Wished,* Dorling Kindersley (New York, NY), 1999.

Shen Roddie, *Not Now, Mrs. Wolf!,* Dorling Kindersley (New York, NY), 2000.

Paul May, *You're a Big Bear Now, Winston Brown!,* Dorling Kindersley (New York, NY), 2001.

Ros Asquith, *Mrs. Pig's Night Out,* Hodder & Stoughton (New York, NY), 2003.

Georgie Adams, *Three Bears on Vacation,* Gingham Dog Press (New York, NY), 2003.

Tony Mitton *Once upon a Tide,* David Ficking Books (New York, NY), 2006.

Sidelights

Her career tragically cut short by her untimely death, Selina Young was an award-winning artist and illustrator whose work included illustrating Margaret Mahy's text for the award-winning picture book *A Summery Saturday Morning.* An author as well as an artist, Young created a number of original self-illustrated books for children, such as *Adam Pig's Everything Fun Book: Stories to Read, Pictures to Look at, and Things to Do* and *My Favorite Word Book: Words and Pictures for the Very Young.* Reviewing *Adam Pig's Everything Fun*

Selina Young's humorous cartoons bring to life Ros Asquith's picture-book text for **Mrs. Pig's Night Out.** (Illustration copyright © 2003 by Selina Young. Reproduced by permission of Hodder & Stoughton, Ltd.)

Book, a compendium of stories, lists, and how-to projects, a *Publishers Weekly* contributor concluded that "the book's greatest asset is Young's perky, whimsically cluttered art," while in *Booklist* Shelley Townsend-Hudson praised the "delightful" young characters that are brought to life through Young's "whimsical, exuberant drawings" for *My Favorite Word Book.* Inspired by her son's own childhood and featuring "stream of consciousness at its best," according to a *Kirkus Reviews* writer, Young's *All about Me: A Hundred Things That Happened to Me between 0 and 3* characterizes her work in the children's-literature field; it captivates audiences with a wealth of "little vignettes and delightful details that will tickle readers' fancies."

Born in Surrey, England, Young began her illustration career after graduating from Epsom Art School. She quickly found her niche in children's book illustration and developed her unique style further at Cambridge University. Winning England's prestigious Pan-McMillan prize for best children's book illustrator cemented Young's career, and she continued to create picture books and illustrations even after her move to New Zealand's Banks Peninsula. Serendipitously, one of Young's new neighbors was Mahy, and their collaborations reflected the seaside home town they shared.

In Mahy's rhyming text for *A Summery Saturday Morning,* a group of children spend the morning chasing cats and other things during a walk to the ocean, until the tables are turned and the rambunctious group is pursued by a mother goose and her flock. Reviewing the book in *Publishers Weekly,* a contributor described Young's "bustling watercolors" for Mahy's tale as "bouncing with comic discombobulation" and "full of fun."

Biographical and Critical Sources

PERIODICALS

Booklist, July, 1994, Hazel Rochman, review of *First Poems,* p. 1950; July, 1996, Julie Corsaro, review of *Adam Pig's Everything Fun Book: Stories to REad, Pictures to Look at, and Things to Do,* p. 1831; November 1, 1996, Ilene Cooper, review of *Nanny Fox and the Christmas Surprise,* p. 506; June 1, 1998, GraceAnne DeCandido, review of *A Summery Saturday Morning,* p. 1781; April 15, 1999, Carolyn Phelan, review of *The Pig Who Wished,* p. 1534; January 1, 2000, Shelley Townsend-Hudson, review of *My Favorite Word Book: Words and Pictures for the Very Young,* p. 935; May 15, 2003, Ilene Cooper, review of *Mrs. Pig's Night Out,* p. 1668; July, 2004, Hazel Rochman, review of *First Poems,* p. 1950.

Kirkus Reviews, June 1, 2003, review of *Mrs. Pig's Night Out,* p. 800; January 1, 2008, review of *All about Me: A Hundred Things That Happened to Me between 0 and 3.*

Publishers Weekly, November 9, 1992, review of *Maybe It's a Pirate,* p. 82; September 27, 1993, review of *Ned,* p. 62; May 9, 1994, review of *First Poems,* p.

A typical day in the life of a typical rambunctious toddler is captured in Young's self-illustrated picture book **All about Me.** (Illustration copyright © 2005 by Selina Young. All rights reserved. Reproduced by permission of The Orion Publishing Group, Ltd.)

73; March 11, 1996, review of *Adam Pig's Everything Fun Book,* p. 62; September 30, 1996, review of *Nanny Fox and the Christmas Surprise,* p. 91; June 1, 1998, Margaret Mahy, review of *A Summery Saturday Morning,* p. 48; May 12, 2003, review of *Mrs. Pig's Night Out,* p. 65.

School Library Journal, December, 2000. Linda K. Kenton, review of *Not Now, Mrs. Wolf!,* p. 104; August, 2003, Be Astengo, review of *Adam Pig's Everything Fun Book,* p. 122; May, 2006, Judith Constantinides, review of *Once upon a Tide,* p. 95; June, 2008, Jane Marino, review of *All about Me,* p. 117.

ONLINE

Grownups Web site, http://www.grownups.co.nz/ (June 8, 2009), Eoin Young "The Art of Selina Young."*

Illustrations Index

(In the following index, the number of the *volume* in which an illustrator's work appears is given *before* the colon, and the *page number* on which it appears is given *after* the colon. For example, a drawing by Adams, Adrienne appears in Volume 2 on page 6, another drawing by her appears in Volume 3 on page 80, another drawing in Volume 8 on page 1, and so on and so on. . . .)

YABC

Index references to *YABC* refer to listings appearing in the two-volume *Yesterday's Authors of Books for Children,* also published by Gale, Cengage Learning. *YABC* covers prominent authors and illustrators who died prior to 1960.

A

Aas, Ulf 5: 174
Abbe, S. van
 See van Abbe, S.
Abel, Raymond 6: 122; 7: 195; 12: 3; 21: 86; 25: 119
Abelliera, Aldo 71: 120
Abolafia, Yossi 60: 2; 93: 163; 152: 202
Abrahams, Hilary 26: 205; 29: 24, 25; 53: 61
Abrams, Kathie 36: 170
Abrams, Lester 49: 26
Abulafia, Yossi 154: 67; 177: 3
Accardo, Anthony 191: 3, 8
Accornero, Franco 184: 8
Accorsi, William 11: 198
Acs, Laszlo 14: 156; 42: 22
Acuna, Ed 198: 79
Adams, Adrienne 2: 6; 3: 80; 8: 1; 15: 107; 16: 180; 20: 65; 22: 134, 135; 33: 75; 36: 103, 112; 39: 74; 86: 54; 90: 2, 3
Adams, Connie J. 129: 68
Adams, John Wolcott 17: 162
Adams, Lynn 96: 44
Adams, Norman 55: 82
Adams, Pam 112: 1, 2
Adams, Sarah 98: 126; 164: 180
Adamson, George 30: 23, 24; 69: 64
Addams, Charles 55: 5
Addison, Kenneth 192: 173
Addy, Sean 180: 8
Ade, Rene 76: 198; 195: 162
Adinolfi, JoAnn 115: 42; 176: 2
Adkins, Alta 22: 250
Adkins, Jan 8: 3; 69: 4; 144: 2, 3, 4
Adler, Kelynn 195: 47
Adler, Peggy 22: 6; 29: 31
Adler, Ruth 29: 29
Adlerman, Daniel 163: 2
Adragna, Robert 47: 145
Agard, Nadema 18: 1
Agee, Jon 116: 8, 9, 10; 157: 4; 196: 3, 4, 5, 6, 7, 8
Agre, Patricia 47: 195
Aguirre, Alfredo 152: 218
Ahl, Anna Maria 32: 24
Ahlberg, Allan 68: 6, 7, 9; 165: 5
Ahlberg, Janet 68: 6, 7, 9
Aicher-Scholl, Inge 63: 127
Aichinger, Helga 4: 5, 45

Aitken, Amy 31: 34
Akaba, Suekichi 46: 23; 53: 127
Akasaka, Miyoshi YABC 2: 261
Akib, Jamel 181: 13; 182: 99
Akino, Fuku 6: 144
Alain 40: 41
Alajalov 2: 226
Albert, Chris 200: 64
Alborough, Jez 86: 1, 2, 3; 149: 3
Albrecht, Jan 37: 176
Albright, Donn 1: 91
Alcala, Alfredo 91: 128
Alcantará, Felipe Ugalde 171: 186
Alcorn, John 3: 159; 7: 165; 31: 22; 44: 127; 46: 23, 170
Alcorn, Stephen 110: 4; 125: 106; 128: 172; 150: 97; 160: 188; 165: 48; 201: 113
Alcott, May 100: 3
Alda, Arlene 44: 24; 158: 2
Alden, Albert 11: 103
Aldridge, Andy 27: 131
Aldridge, George 105: 125
Aldridge, Sheila 192: 4
Alejandro, Cliff 176: 75
Alex, Ben 45: 25, 26
Alexander, Ellen 91: 3
Alexander, Lloyd 49: 34
Alexander, Martha 3: 206; 11: 103; 13: 109; 25: 100; 36: 131; 70: 6, 7; 136: 3, 4, 5; 169: 120
Alexander, Paul 85: 57; 90: 9
Alexeieff, Alexander 14: 6; 26: 199
Alfano, Wayne 80: 69
Aliki
 See Brandenberg, Aliki
Allamand, Pascale 12: 9
Allan, Judith 38: 166
Alland, Alexandra 16: 255
Allen, Gertrude 9: 6
Allen, Graham 31: 145
Allen, Jonathan 131: 3, 4; 177: 8, 9, 10
Allen, Joy 168: 185
Allen, Pamela 50: 25, 26, 27, 28; 81: 9, 10; 123: 4, 5
Allen, Rowena 47: 75
Allen, Thomas B. 81: 101; 82: 248; 89: 37; 104: 9
Allen, Tom 85: 176
Allender, David 73: 223
Alley, R.W. 80: 183; 95: 187; 156: 100, 153; 169: 4, 5; 179: 17

Allison, Linda 43: 27
Allon, Jeffrey 119: 174
Allport, Mike 71: 55
Almquist, Don 11: 8; 12: 128; 17: 46; 22: 110
Aloise, Frank 5: 38; 10: 133; 30: 92
Alsenas, Linas 186: 2
Althea
 See Braithwaite, Althea
Altschuler, Franz 11: 185; 23: 141; 40: 48; 45: 29; 57: 181
Alvin, John 117: 5
Ambrus, Victor G. 1: 6, 7, 194; 3: 69; 5: 15; 6: 44; 7: 36; 8: 210; 12: 227; 14: 213; 15: 213; 22: 209; 24: 36; 28: 179; 30: 178; 32: 44, 46; 38: 143; 41: 25, 26, 27, 28, 29, 30, 31, 32; 42: 87; 44: 190; 55: 172; 62: 30, 144, 145, 148; 86: 99, 100, 101; 87: 66, 137; 89: 162; 134: 160
Ames, Lee J. 3: 12; 9: 130; 10: 69; 17: 214; 22: 124; 151: 13
Amon, Aline 9: 9
Amoss, Berthe 5: 5
Amstutz, Andre 152: 102
Amundsen, Dick 7: 77
Amundsen, Richard E. 5: 10; 24: 122
Ancona, George 12: 11; 55: 144; 145: 7
Anderson, Alasdair 18: 122
Andersen, Bethanne 116: 167; 162: 189; 175: 17; 191: 4, 5
Anderson, Bob 139: 16
Anderson, Brad 33: 28
Anderson, C.W. 11: 10
Anderson, Carl 7: 4
Anderson, Catherine Corley 72: 2
Anderson, Cecil 127: 152
Anderson, David Lee 118: 176
Anderson, Derek 169: 9; 174: 180
Anderson, Doug 40: 111
Anderson, Erica 23: 65
Anderson, Laurie 12: 153, 155
Anderson, Lena 99: 26
Anderson, Peggy Perry 179: 2
Anderson, Sara 173: 3
Anderson, Scoular 138: 13; 201: 6
Anderson, Susan 90: 12
Anderson, Tara 188: 132
Anderson, Wayne 23: 119; 41: 239; 56: 7; 62: 26; 147: 6
Andreasen, Daniel 86: 157; 87: 104; 103: 201, 202; 159: 75; 167: 106, 107; 168: 184; 180: 247; 186: 9

Andrew, Ian *111:* 37; *116:* 12; *166:* 2
Andrew, John *22:* 4
Andrews, Benny *14:* 251; *31:* 24; *57:* 6, 7; *183:* 8
Andrews, Vaughn *166:* 28
Anelay, Henry *57:* 173
Angel, Marie *47:* 22
Angelo, Valenti *14:* 8; *18:* 100; *20:* 232; *32:* 70
Anglund, Joan Walsh *2:* 7, 250, 251; *37:* 198, 199, 200
Anholt, Catherine *74:* 8; *131:* 7; *141:* 5
Anholt, Laurence *141:* 4
Anno, Mitsumasa *5:* 7; *38:* 25, 26, 27, 28, 29, 30, 31, 32; *77:* 3, 4; *157:* 10, 11
Antal, Andrew *1:* 124; *30:* 145
Antram, David *152:* 133
Apostolou, Christy Hale
  See Hale, Christy
Apple, Margot *33:* 25; *35:* 206; *46:* 81; *53:* 8; *61:* 109; *64:* 21, 22, 24, 25, 27; *71:* 176; *77:* 53; *82:* 245; *92:* 39; *94:* 180; *96:* 107; *152:* 4, 5; *162:* 192, 194; *173:* 44
Appleyard, Dev *2:* 192
Aragones, Sergio *48:* 23, 24, 25, 26, 27
Araneus *40:* 29
Arbo, Cris *103:* 4
Archambault, Matt *85:* 173; *138:* 19, 20; *143:* 33; *145:* 144; *179:* 103; *187:* 7
Archer, Janet *16:* 69; *178:* 156
Ardizzone, Edward *1:* 11, 12; *2:* 105; *3:* 258; *4:* 78; *7:* 79; *10:* 100; *15:* 232; *20:* 69,178; *23:* 223; *24:* 125; *28:* 25, 26, 27, 28, 29, 30, 31,33, 34, 35, 36, 37; *31:* 192, 193; *34:* 215, 217; *60:* 173; *64:* 145; *87:* 176; *YABC 2:* 25
Arena, Jill *176:* 49
Arenella, Roy *14:* 9
Argemi, David *197:* 2
Argent, Kerry *103:* 56; *138:* 17; *158:* 134
Arihara, Shino *201:* 98
Arisman, Marshall *162:* 50
Armer, Austin *13:* 3
Armer, Laura Adams *13:* 3
Armer, Sidney *13:* 3
Armitage, David *47:* 23; *99:* 5; *155:* 4
Armitage, Eileen *4:* 16
Armstrong, George *10:* 6; *21:* 72
Armstrong, Shelagh *102:* 114
Armstrong-Ellis, Carey *185:* 196
Arno, Enrico *1:* 217; *2:* 22, 210; *4:* 9; *5:* 43; *6:* 52; *29:* 217, 219; *33:* 152; *35:* 99; *43:* 31, 32, 33; *45:* 212, 213, 214; *72:* 72; *74:* 166; *100:* 169
Arnold, Alli *187:* 40, 41
Arnold, Caroline *174:* 5
Arnold, Emily *76:* 7, 9, 10
Arnold, Katya *115:* 11; *168:* 2, 3
Arnold, Tedd *116:* 14; *133:* 152; *160:* 5
Arnosky, Jim *22:* 20; *70:* 9, 10, 11; *118:* 3, 5; *160:* 8, 10; *189:* 5, 7, 8, 9, 10
Arnsteen, Katy Keck *105:* 97; *116:* 145
Arrowood, Clinton *12:* 193; *19:* 11; *65:* 210
Artell, Mike *89:* 8
Arting, Fred J. *41:* 63
Artzybasheff, Boris *13:* 143; *14:* 15; *40:* 152, 155
Aruego, Ariane *6:* 4
Aruego, José *4:* 140; *6:* 4; *7:* 64; *33:* 195; *35:* 208; *68:* 16, 17; *75:* 46; *93:* 91, 92; *94:* 197; *109:* 65, 67; *125:* 2, 3, 4, 5; *127:* 188; *143:* 25; *178:* 17, 19, 74; *188:* 166
Arzoumanian, Alik *177:* 12; *194:* 115
Asare, Meshack *86:* 9; *139:* 19
Ascensios, Natalie *105:* 139
Asch, Frank *5:* 9; *66:* 2, 4, 6, 7, 9, 10; *102:* 18, 19,21; *154:* 12
Ashby, Gail *11:* 135
Ashby, Gil *146:* 4
Ashby, Gwynneth *44:* 26
Ashley, C.W. *19:* 197
Ashmead, Hal *8:* 70

Aska, Warabe *56:* 10
Assel, Steven *44:* 153; *77:* 22, 97
Astrop, John *32:* 56
Atene, Ann *12:* 18
Atherton, Lisa *38:* 198
Atkinson, Allen *60:* 5
Atkinson, J. Priestman *17:* 275
Atkinson, Janet *86:* 147; *103:* 138
Atkinson, Mike *127:* 74
Atkinson, Wayne *40:* 46
Attard, Karl *196:* 22, 23
Attebery, Charles *38:* 170
Atwell, Debby *150:* 6
Atwood, Ann *7:* 9
Aubrey, Meg Kelleher *77:* 159
Auch, Herm *173:* 7, 8
Auch, Mary Jane *173:* 7
Augarde, Steve *25:* 22; *159:* 7
Austerman, Miriam *23:* 107
Austin, Margot *11:* 16
Austin, Robert *3:* 44
Austin, Virginia *81:* 205; *127:* 221
Auth, Tony *51:* 5; *192:* 18
Avendano, Dolores *158:* 74
Avedon, Richard *57:* 140
Averill, Esther *1:* 17; *28:* 39, 40, 41
Axeman, Lois *2:* 32; *11:* 84; *13:* 165; *22:* 8; *23:* 49; *61:* 116; *101:* 124
Axtel, David *155:* 110
Ayer, Jacqueline *13:* 7
Ayer, Margaret *15:* 12; *50:* 120
Ayers, Alan *91:* 58; *107:* 169
Ayliffe, Alex *95:* 164
Ayto, Russell *111:* 5; *112:* 54
Azarian, Mary *112:* 9, 10; *114:* 129; *117:* 171; *137:* 163; *171:* 4, 5; *181:* 161; *188:* 128

B

B.T.B.
  See Blackwell, Basil T.
Babbitt, Bradford *33:* 158
Babbitt, Natalie *6:* 6; *8:* 220; *68:* 20; *70:* 242, 243; *194:* 8, 9
Baca, Maria *104:* 5
Bacchus, Andy *94:* 87
Bacha, Andy *109:* 169
Bachelet, Gilles *196:* 18
Bachem, Paul *48:* 180; *67:* 65; *144:* 206
Back, Adam *63:* 125
Back, George *31:* 161
Backes, Nick *190:* 72
Backhouse, Colin *78:* 142
Bacon, Bruce *4:* 74
Bacon, Paul *7:* 155; *8:* 121; *31:* 55; *50:* 42; *56:* 175; *62:* 82, 84
Bacon, Peggy *2:* 11, 228; *46:* 44
Baek, Matthew J. *169:* 95
Baer, Julie *161:* 2
Baicker-McKee, Carol *177:* 15; *180:* 215
Bailey, Peter *58:* 174; *87:* 221; *194:* 12
Bailey, Sheila *155:* 11
Baker, Alan *22:* 22; *61:* 134; *93:* 11, 12; *146:* 6, 7, 10
Baker, Charlotte *2:* 12
Baker, Garin *89:* 65
Baker, Jeannie *23:* 4; *88:* 18, 19, 20
Baker, Jim *22:* 24
Baker, Joe *82:* 188; *111:* 55; *124:* 70; *197:* 73
Baker, Keith *179:* 6, 7
Baker, Leslie *112:* 214; *132:* 103, 246; *180:* 74, 246
Baldacci, Rudy *184:* 9
Baldridge, Cyrus LeRoy *19:* 69; *44:* 50
Baldus, Zachary *152:* 231; *187:* 60
Balet, Jan *11:* 22
Balian, Lorna *9:* 16; *91:* 16
Balit, Christina *102:* 24; *159:* 9; *162:* 118, 119
Ballantyne, R.M. *24:* 34

Ballis, George *14:* 199
Balouch, Kristen *176:* 11
Baltzer, Hans *40:* 30
Banbery, Fred *58:* 15
Banfill, A. Scott *98:* 7; *112:* 59
Bang, Molly Garrett *24:* 37, 38; *69:* 8, 9, 10; *111:* 7,9, 10, 11; *140:* 11; *158:* 37, 38, 39; *195:* 3
Banik, Yvette Santiago *21:* 136
Banner, Angela
  See Maddison, Angela Mary
Bannerman, Helen *19:* 13, 14
Bannon, Laura *6:* 10; *23:* 8
Bantock, Nick *74:* 229; *95:* 6
Banyai, Istvan *185:* 209; *193:* 14, 16
Baptist, Michael *37:* 208
Baracca, Sal *135:* 206
Baranaski, Marcin *182:* 113
Barasch, Lynne *126:* 16; *186:* 15
Barbarin, Lucien C., Jr. *89:* 88
Barbour, Karen *96:* 5; *74:* 209; *170:* 16
Bare, Arnold Edwin *16:* 31
Bare, Colleen Stanley *32:* 33
Barger, Jan *147:* 11
Bargery, Geoffrey *14:* 258
Barkat, Jonathan *149:* 177; *164:* 254; *181:* 106; *184:* 186; *196:* 11; *198:* 148
Barker, Carol *31:* 27
Barker, Cicely Mary *49:* 50, 51
Barkley, James *4:* 13; *6:* 11; *13:* 112
Barks, Carl *37:* 27, 28, 29, 30, 31, 32, 33, 34
Barling, Joy *62:* 148
Barling, Tom *9:* 23
Barlow, Gillian *62:* 20
Barlow, Perry *35:* 28
Barlowe, Dot *30:* 223
Barlowe, Wayne *37:* 72; *84:* 43; *105:* 5
Barnard, Bryn *88:* 53; *13:* 55; *169:* 13; *193:* 194
Barner, Bob *29:* 37; *128:* 33; *136:* 19, 20; *177:* 27
Barnes, Hiram P. *20:* 28
Barnes, Tim *137:* 28
Barnes-Murphy, Rowan *88:* 22
Barnett, Charles II *175:* 150
Barnett, Ivan *70:* 14
Barnett, Moneta *16:* 89; *19:* 142; *31:* 102; *33:* 30, 31, 32; *41:* 153; *61:* 94, 97
Barney, Maginel Wright *39:* 32, 33, 34; *YABC 2:* 306
Barnum, Jay Hyde *11:* 224; *20:* 5; *37:* 189, 190
Baron, Alan *80:* 3; *89:* 123
Barr, George *60:* 74; *69:* 64
Barragan, Paula S. *134:* 116; *186:* 158
Barrall, Tim *115:* 152
Barraud, Martin *189:* 38
Barrauds *33:* 114
Barrer-Russell, Gertrude *9:* 65; *27:* 31
Barret, Robert *85:* 134
Barrett, Angela *40:* 136, 137; *62:* 74; *75:* 10; *76:* 142; *144:* 137; *145:* 14
Barrett, Jennifer *58:* 149
Barrett, John E. *43:* 119
Barrett, Moneta *74:* 10
Barrett, Peter *55:* 169; *86:* 111
Barrett, Robert *62:* 145; *77:* 146; *82:* 35
Barrett, Ron *14:* 24; *26:* 35
Barron, John N. *3:* 261; *5:* 101; *14:* 220
Barrow, Ann *136:* 27
Barrows, Walter *14:* 268
Barry, Ethelred B. *37:* 79; *YABC 1:* 229
Barry, James *14:* 25
Barry, Katharina *2:* 159; *4:* 22
Barry, Robert E. *6:* 12
Barry, Scott *32:* 35
Bartenbach, Jean *40:* 31
Barth, Ernest Kurt *2:* 172; *3:* 160; *8:* 26; *10:* 31
Bartholomew, Marie *200:* 66
Bartlett, Alison *101:* 88; *165:* 93

Barton, Byron *8:* 207; *9:* 18; *23:* 66; *80:* 181; *90:* 18, 19, 20, 21; *126:* 29, 30
Barton, Harriett *30:* 71
Barton, Jill *129:* 108; *135:* 120; *145:* 185, 189; *184:* 177
Bartram, Robert *10:* 42
Bartsch, Jochen *8:* 105; *39:* 38
Bascove, Barbara *45:* 73
Base, Graeme *101:* 15, 16, 17, 18; *162:* 8, 10, 12
Baseman, Gary *174:* 12
Bash, Barbara *132:* 9
Baskin, Leonard *30:* 42, 43, 46, 47; *49:* 125, 126, 128, 129,133; *173:* 120
Bass, Saul *49:* 192
Bassett, Jeni *40:* 99; *64:* 30
Basso, Bill *99:* 139; *189:* 134
Batchelor, Joy *29:* 41, 47, 48
Bate, Norman *5:* 16
Bates, Amy June *188:* 170; *189:* 27, 28
Bates, Leo *24:* 35
Batet, Carmen *39:* 134
Batherman, Muriel *31:* 79; *45:* 185
Battaglia, Aurelius *50:* 44
Batten, John D. *25:* 161, 162
Batten, Mary *162:* 14, 15
Battles, Asa *32:* 94, 95
Bauer, Carla *193:* 6
Bauer, Jutta *150:* 32
Bauernschmidt, Marjorie *15:* 15
Baum, Allyn *20:* 10
Baum, Willi *4:* 24, 25; *7:* 173
Bauman, Leslie *61:* 121
Baumann, Jill *34:* 170
Baumhauer, Hans *11:* 218; *15:* 163, 165, 167
Baxter, Glen *57:* 100
Baxter, Leon *59:* 102
Baxter, Robert *87:* 129
Bayer, Herbert *181:* 16
Bayley, Dorothy *37:* 195
Bayley, Nicola *40:* 104; *41:* 34, 35; *69:* 15; *129:* 33, 34, 35
Baylin, Mark *158:* 233
Baynes, Pauline *2:* 244; *3:* 149; *13:* 133, 135,137, 141; *19:* 18, 19, 20; *32:* 208, 213, 214; *36:* 105, 108; *59:* 12, 13, 14, 16, 17, 18, 20; *100:* 158, 159, 243; *133:* 3, 4
Beach, Lou *150:* 150
Beame, Rona *12:* 40
Bean, Jonathan *196:* 102
Bear's Heart *73:* 215
Beard, Dan *22:* 31, 32
Beard, J.H. *YABC 1:* 158
Bearden, Romare *9:* 7; *22:* 35
Beardshaw, Rosalind *169:* 22; *190:* 22
Beardsley, Aubrey *17:* 14; *23:* 181; *59:* 130, 131
Bearman, Jane *29:* 38
Beaton, Cecil *24:* 208
Beaton, Clare *125:* 28
Beauce, J.A. *18:* 103
Beaujard, Sophie *81:* 54
Beccia, Carlyn *189:* 29
Beck, Charles *11:* 169; *51:* 173
Beck, Ian *138:* 27; *182:* 150; *190:* 25
Beck, Ruth *13:* 11
Becker, Harriet *12:* 211
Beckett, Sheilah *25:* 5; *33:* 37, 38
Beckhoff, Harry *1:* 78; *5:* 163
Beckhorn, Susan Williams *189:* 32
Beckman, Kaj *45:* 38, 39, 40, 41
Beckman, Per *45:* 42, 43
Beddows, Eric *72:* 70
Bedford, F.D. *20:* 118, 122; *33:* 170; *41:* 220, 221,230, 233
Bee, Joyce *19:* 62
Bee, William *188:* 6
Beeby, Betty *25:* 36
Beech, Carol *9:* 149
Beech, Mark *192:* 122
Beek *25:* 51, 55, 59

Beeke, Tiphanie *177:* 127
Beekman, Doug *125:* 146, 148
Beerbohm, Max *24:* 208
Beeson, Bob *108:* 57
Begin, Maryjane *82:* 13
Beha, Philippe *172:* 85
Behr, Joyce *15:* 15; *21:* 132; *23:* 161
Behrens, Hans *5:* 97
Beier, Ellen *135:* 170; *139:* 47; *183:* 164
Beinicke, Steve *69:* 18
Beisner, Monika *46:* 128, 131; *112:* 127
Belden, Charles J. *12:* 182
Belina, Renate *39:* 132
Bell, Corydon *3:* 20
Bell, Graham *54:* 48
Bell, Julia *151:* 214
Bell, Julie *159:* 172; *165:* 18
Bell, Thomas P. *76:* 182
Bellamy, Glen *127:* 15
Bemelmans, Ludwig *15:* 19, 21; *100:* 27
Ben-Ami, Doron *75:* 96; *84:* 107; *108:* 132; *110:* 63; *159:* 157; *197:* 142
Bendall-Brunello, John *150:* 4; *157:* 163; *185:* 3, 4
Benda, Wladyslaw T. *15:* 256; *30:* 76, 77; *44:* 182
Bender, Robert *77:* 162; *79:* 13; *160:* 23
Bendick, Jeanne *2:* 24; *68:* 27, 28
Benioff, Carol *121:* 42; *175:* 23
Benner, Cheryl *80:* 11
Bennett, Charles H. *64:* 6
Bennett, Erin Susanne *165:* 216
Bennett, F.I. *YABC 1:* 134
Bennett, James *146:* 240
Bennett, Jill *26:* 61; *41:* 38, 39; *45:* 54
Bennett, Rainey *15:* 26; *23:* 53
Bennett, Richard *15:* 45; *21:* 11, 12, 13; *25:* 175
Bennett, Susan *5:* 55
Benny, Mike *142:* 78
Benoit, Elise *77:* 74
Benson, Linda *60:* 130; *62:* 91; *75:* 101; *79:* 156; *134:* 129
Benson, Patrick *68:* 162; *147:* 17, 18, 19, 20
Bentley, Carolyn *46:* 153
Bentley, James *149:* 30
Bentley, Roy *30:* 162
Benton, Jim *172:* 22
Benton, Thomas Hart *2:* 99
Berelson, Howard *5:* 20; *16:* 58; *31:* 50
Berenstain, Jan *12:* 47; *64:* 33, 34, 36, 37, 38, 40, 42, 44; *135:* 25, 28, 31, 35
Berenstain, Stan *12:* 47; *64:* 33, 34, 36, 37, 38, 40, 42, 44; *135:* 25, 28, 31, 35
Berenzy, Alix *65:* 13; *73:* 6; *78:* 115
Berg, Joan *1:* 115; *3:* 156; *6:* 26, 58
Berg, Ron *36:* 48, 49; *48:* 37, 38; *67:* 72
Bergen, David *115:* 44
Berger, Barbara *77:* 14
Berger, Carin *185:* 6
Berger, William M. *14:* 143; *YABC 1:* 204
Bergherr, Mary *74:* 170; *151:* 123
Bergin, Mark *114:* 8, 9; *143:* 95; *160:* 26, 27
Bergstreser, Douglas *69:* 76
Bergum, Constance R. *121:* 14, 15
Bering, Claus *13:* 14
Berkeley, Jon *139:* 218
Berkowitz, Jeanette *3:* 249
Berman, Paul *66:* 14
Bernal, Richard *154:* 176
Bernadette
  See Watts, Bernadette
Bernardin, James *112:* 24; *167:* 94
Bernasconi, Pablo *183:* 10, 11
Bernath, Stefen *32:* 76
Bernhard, Durga *80:* 13
Bernstein, Michel J. *51:* 71
Bernstein, Ted *38:* 183; *50:* 131
Bernstein, Zena *23:* 46
Berridge, Celia *86:* 63

Berrill, Jacquelyn *12:* 50
Berry, Erick
  See Best, Allena
Berry, William D. *14:* 29; *19:* 48
Berry, William A. *6:* 219
Berson, Harold *2:* 17, 18; *4:* 28, 29, 220; *9:* 10; *12:* 19; *17:* 45; *18:* 193; *22:* 85; *34:* 172; *44:* 120; *46:* 42; *80:* 240
Bertholf, Bret *187:* 9; *189:* 32, 33
Berton, Patsy *99:* 16
Bertschmann, Harry *16:* 1
Besco, Don *70:* 99
Beskow, Elsa *20:* 13, 14, 15
Bess, Clayton *63:* 94
Best, Allena *2:* 26; *34:* 76
Betera, Carol *74:* 68
Bethell, Thomas N. *61:* 169
Bethers, Ray *6:* 22
Bettina
  See Ehrlich, Bettina
Betts, Ethel Franklin *17:* 161, 164, 165; *YABC 2:* 47
Betz, Rudolf *59:* 161
Bewick, Thomas *16:* 40, 41, 43, 44, 45, 47; *54:* 150; *YABC 1:* 107
Beyer, Paul J. III *74:* 24
Bezencon, Jacqueline *48:* 40
Biamonte, Daniel *40:* 90
Bianchi, John *91:* 19
Bianco, Pamela *15:* 31; *28:* 44, 45, 46
Bible, Charles *13:* 15
Bice, Clare *22:* 40
Biedrzycki, David *186:* 170
Bierman, Don *57:* 184
Biggers, John *2:* 123
Biggs, Brian *192:* 38; *196:* 15
Bikadoroff, Roxanna *201:* 74
Bileck, Marvin *3:* 102; *40:* 36, 37
Bilibin, Ivan *61:* 8, 9, 12, 13, 14, 15, 151, 152, 154, 162
Billington, Patrick *98:* 71
Billout, Guy *144:* 38, 39
Bimen, Levent *5:* 179
Binch, Caroline *81:* 18; *140:* 15, 16; *144:* 115
Binder, Hannes *169:* 163
Bing, Christopher *126:* 34
Binger, Bill *121:* 46
Binks, Robert *25:* 150
Binzen, Bill *24:* 47
Birch, Reginald *15:* 150; *19:* 33, 34, 35, 36; *37:* 196,197; *44:* 182; *46:* 176; *YABC 1:* 84; *2:* 34, 39
Birchall, Mark *123:* 188
Bird, Esther Brock *1:* 36; *25:* 66
Birdsong, Keith *167:* 85
Birkett, Rachel *78:* 206
Birling, Paul *109:* 30
Birmingham, Christian *132:* 243; *143:* 114
Birmingham, Lloyd P. *12:* 51; *83:* 13
Biro, Val *1:* 26; *41:* 42; *60:* 178; *67:* 23, 24; *84:* 242, 243
Bischoff, Ilse *44:* 51
Bishop, Don *199:* 133
Bishop, Gavin *97:* 17, 18; *144:* 42, 44
Bishop, Kathleen Wong *115:* 67
Bishop, Rich *56:* 43
Bite, I. *60:* 14
Bittinger, Ned *93:* 117
Bjorklund, Lorence *3:* 188, 252; *7:* 100; *9:* 113; *10:* 66; *19:* 178; *33:* 122, 123; *35:* 36, 37, 38, 39,41, 42, 43; *36:* 185; *38:* 93; *47:* 106; *66:* 194; *YABC 1:* 242
Bjorkman, Steve *91:* 199; *160:* 110; *198:* 18
Black Sheep *164:* 100
Blackburn, Loren H. *63:* 10
Blackall, Sophie *194:* 140
Blackford, John *137:* 105; *180:* 36
Blackwell, Basil T. *YABC 1:* 68, 69
Blackwood, Freya *199:* 9
Blackwood, Gary L. *118:* 17

Blades, Ann *16:* 52; *37:* 213; *50:* 41; *69:* 21; *99:* 215
Blair, Jay *45:* 46; *46:* 155
Blaisdell, Elinore *1:* 121; *3:* 134; *35:* 63
Blake, Anne Catharine *189:* 71
Blake, Francis *198:* 4
Blake, Quentin *3:* 170; *10:* 48; *13:* 38; *21:* 180; *26:* 60; *28:* 228; *30:* 29, 31; *40:* 108; *45:* 219; *46:* 165, 168; *48:* 196; *52:* 10, 11, 12,13, 14, 15, 16, 17; *73:* 41, 43; *78:* 84, 86; *80:* 250, 251; *84:* 210, 211, 212; *87:* 177; *96:* 24, 26, 28; *124:* 79; *125:* 32, 34; *181:* 139
Blake, Robert J. *37:* 90; *53:* 67; *54:* 23; *160:* 28, 29
Blake, William *30:* 54, 56, 57, 58, 59, 60
Blanchard, N. Taylor *82:* 140
Blass, Jacqueline *8:* 215
Blazek, Scott R. *91:* 71
Bleck, Cathie *118:* 116
Blegvad, Erik *2:* 59; *3:* 98; *5:* 117; *7:* 131; *11:* 149; *14:* 34, 35; *18:* 237; *32:* 219; *60:* 106; *66:* 16, 17, 18, 19; *70:* 233; *76:* 18; *82:* 106; *87:* 45; *100:* 188; *129:* 125; *132:* 17, 18, 19, 20; *176:* 14; *200:* 100; *YABC 1:* 201
Blessen, Karen *93:* 126
Bliss, Corinne Demas *37:* 38
Bliss, Harry *196:* 27, 28, 29
Blitt, Barry *179:* 199; *187:* 13
Bloch, Lucienne *10:* 12
Blondon, Herve *129:* 48; *183:* 22
Bloom, Lloyd *35:* 180; *36:* 149; *47:* 99; *62:* 117; *68:* 231; *72:* 136; *75:* 185; *83:* 99; *108:* 19
Bloom, Suzanne *172:* 23, 24
Blossom, Dave *34:* 29
Bluthenthal, Diana Cain *93:* 32; *104:* 106; *177:* 26
Blythe, Benjamin *128:* 7
Blythe, Gary *112:* 52; *181:* 166; *182:* 64; *185:* 7; *186:* 116, 117
Boake, Kathy *176:* 185
Board, Perry *171:* 99
Boardman, Gwenn *12:* 60
Bober, Richard *125:* 145; *132:* 40
Bobri *30:* 138; *47:* 27
Bock, Vera *1:* 187; *21:* 41
Bock, William Sauts *8:* 7; *14:* 37; *16:* 120; *21:* 141; *36:* 177; *62:* 203
Bodecker, N(iels) M(ogens) *8:* 13; *14:* 2; *17:* 55, 56, 57; *73:* 22, 23, 24
Boehm, Linda *40:* 31
Bogacki, Tomek *138:* 31, 32; *144:* 123
Bogan, Paulette *197:* 152; *201:* 17
Bogdan, Florentina *107:* 43
Bohdal, Susi *22:* 44; *101:* 20
Bohlen, Nina *58:* 13
Boies, Alex *96:* 53
Bolam, Emily *101:* 216; *159:* 12
Bolian, Polly *3:* 270; *4:* 30; *13:* 77; *29:* 197
Bolle, Frank *87:* 100
Bollen, Roger *79:* 186; *83:* 16
Bolling, Vickey *114:* 44
Bollinger, Peter *101:* 7; *128:* 198; *172:* 26
Bolognese, Don *2:* 147, 231; *4:* 176; *7:* 146; *17:* 43; *23:* 192; *24:* 50; *34:* 108; *36:* 133; *71:* 24, 25; *103:* 131; *129:* 39, 40
Bolster, Rob *186:* 169
Bolton, A.T. *57:* 158
Bond, Arnold *18:* 116
Bond, Barbara Higgins *21:* 102
Bond, Bruce *52:* 97
Bond, Felicia *38:* 197; *49:* 55, 56; *89:* 170; *90:* 171; *126:* 37
Bond, Higgins *177:* 22, 23
Bonn, Pat *43:* 40
Bonner, Hannah *197:* 13, 14

Bonners, Susan *41:* 40; *85:* 36; *94:* 99, 100; *151:* 105, 106
Bono, Mary *184:* 73
Bonsall, Crosby *23:* 6
Boon, Debbie *103:* 6; *144:* 188
Boon, Emilie *86:* 23, 24
Boone, Debbie *165:* 77
Boore, Sara *60:* 73
Bootman, Colin *155:* 13; *159:* 35; *174:* 192
Booth, Franklin *YABC 2:* 76
Booth, George *191:* 13
Booth, Graham *32:* 193; *37:* 41, 42
Borda, Juliette *102:* 188
Bordier, Georgette *16:* 54
Boren, Tinka *27:* 128
Borges, Jose Francisco *119:* 62
Borja, Robert *22:* 48
Born, Adolf *49:* 63
Bornstein, Ruth *14:* 44; *88:* 45, 46; *107:* 30
Borten, Helen *3:* 54; *5:* 24
Bosin, Blackbear *69:* 104
Bossom, Naomi *35:* 48
Bostock, Mike *83:* 221; *114:* 14; *188:* 205
Boston, Peter *19:* 42
Bosustow, Stephen *34:* 202
Boszko, Ron *75:* 47
Bottner, Barbara *14:* 46
Boucher, Joelle *41:* 138
Boulat, Pierre *44:* 40
Boulet, Susan Seddon *50:* 47
Bouma, Paddy *118:* 25; *128:* 16
Bour, Daniele *66:* 145
Bourke-White, Margaret *15:* 286, 287; *57:* 102
Boutavant, Marc *200:* 136
Boutet de Monvel, M. *30:* 61, 62, 63, 65
Bowen, Betsy *105:* 222
Bowen, Richard *42:* 134
Bowen, Ruth *31:* 188
Bower, Ron *29:* 33
Bowers, David *95:* 38; *115:* 20; *127:* 169, 170; *165:* 57
Bowers, Tim *185:* 35; *201:* 41
Bowman, Claire *174:* 177
Bowman, Eric *151:* 23
Bowman, Leslie *85:* 203; *105:* 108; *116:* 76; *128:* 234; *182:* 24, 25
Bowman, Peter *146:* 214, 215; *150:* 115
Bowser, Carolyn Ewing *22:* 253
Boxall, Ed *178:* 28
Boyd, Aaron *158:* 242
Boyd, Patti *45:* 31
Boyle, Eleanor Vere *28:* 50, 51
Boynton, Sandra *57:* 13, 14, 15; *107:* 36, 37; *152:* 12, 13, 14
Bozzo, Frank *4:* 154
Brabbs, Derry *55:* 170
Brace, Eric *132:* 193, 194; *152:* 71; *184:* 195; *197:* 6; *201:* 54
Brackers de Hugo, Pierre *115:* 21
Bradford, June *158:* 138
Bradford, Ron *7:* 157
Bradley, David P. *69:* 105
Bradley, Richard D. *26:* 182
Bradley, William *5:* 164
Brady, Irene *4:* 31; *42:* 37; *68:* 191
Bragg, Michael *32:* 78; *46:* 31
Bragg, Ruth Gembicki *77:* 18
Brainerd, John W. *65:* 19
Braithwaite, Althea *23:* 12, 13; *119:* 16
Brak, Syd *146:* 187
Bralds, Braldt *90:* 28; *91:* 151
Bram, Elizabeth *30:* 67
Bramley, Peter *4:* 3
Brandenberg, Aliki *2:* 36, 37; *24:* 222; *35:* 49, 50, 51,52, 53, 54, 56, 57; *75:* 15, 17; *92:* 205; *113:* 18, 19, 20; *157:* 28; *156:* 111
Brandenburg, Alexa *75:* 19
Brandenburg, Jim *47:* 58; *150:* 212
Brandi, Lillian *31:* 158
Brandon, Brumsic, Jr. *9:* 25
Bransom, Paul *17:* 121; *43:* 44

Braren, Loretta Trezzo *87:* 193
Brassard, France *186:* 22
Braun, Wendy *80:* 17, 18
Brautigam, Don *115:* 175, 176
Brazell, Derek *75:* 105; *79:* 9
Breathed, Berkeley *86:* 27, 28, 29; *161:* 13, 14
Breckenreid, Julia *192:* 209
Breen, Steve *186:* 23
Brennan, Steve *83:* 230; *101:* 184
Brenner, Fred *22:* 85; *36:* 34; *42:* 34
Brett, Bernard *22:* 54
Brett, Harold M. *26:* 98, 99, 100
Brett, Jan *30:* 135; *42:* 39; *71:* 31, 32; *130:* 23, 24, 25, 26, 27; *171:* 15, 16
Brewer, Paul *106:* 115; *145:* 202
Brewer, Sally King *33:* 44
Brewster, Patience *40:* 68; *45:* 22, 183; *51:* 20; *66:* 144; *89:* 4; *97:* 30, 31
Brick, John *10:* 15
Brickman, Robin D. *131:* 88; *142:* 150; *155:* 18; *178:* 109; *184:* 32
Bridge, David R. *45:* 28
Bridgman, L.J. *37:* 77
Bridwell, Norman *4:* 37; *138:* 36, 37, 40
Brierley, Louise *91:* 22; *96:* 165; *183:* 51
Briggs, Harry *172:* 187
Briggs, Raymond *10:* 168; *23:* 20, 21; *66:* 29, 31, 32; *131:* 28, 29; *184:* 15, 16
Brigham, Grace A. *37:* 148
Bright, Robert *24:* 55
Brighton, Catherine *107:* 39
Brinckloe, Julie *13:* 18; *24:* 79, 115; *29:* 35; *63:* 140; *81:* 131
Brion *47:* 116
Brisley, Joyce L. *22:* 57
Brisson, James F. *110:* 60
Brittingham, Geoffrey *88:* 37
Brix-Henker, Silke *81:* 194
Brock, Charles E. *15:* 97; *19:* 247, 249; *23:* 224, 225; *36:* 88; *42:* 41, 42, 43, 44, 45; *100:* 189; *YABC 1:* 194, 196, 203
Brock, Emma *7:* 21
Brock, Henry Matthew *15:* 81; *16:* 141; *19:* 71; *34:* 115; *40:* 164; *42:* 47, 48, 49; *49:* 66
Brocksopp, Arthur *57:* 157
Broda, Ron *136:* 180; *174:* 123
Brodkin, Gwen *34:* 135
Brodovitch, Alexi *52:* 22
Bromhall, Winifred *5:* 11; *26:* 38
Bromley, Lizzy *159:* 179
Bronson, Linda *150:* 210; *174:* 133
Brooke, L. Leslie *16:* 181, 182, 183, 186; *17:* 15, 16, 17; *18:* 194
Brooker, Christopher *15:* 251
Brooker, Kyrsten *111:* 94; *140:* 28; *162:* 111; *175:* 108; *186:* 42, 225; *199:* 12; *201:* 30
Brooks, Erik *166:* 52; *182:* 30
Brooks, Karen Stormer *186:* 110
Brooks, Maya Itzna *92:* 153
Brooks, Ron *94:* 15; *197:* 188
Brooks, S.G. *178:* 127
Broomfield, Maurice *40:* 141
Brotman, Adolph E. *5:* 21
Brown, Buck *45:* 48
Brown, Calef *179:* 18
Brown, Christopher *62:* 124, 125, 127, 128
Brown, Craig McFarland *73:* 28; *84:* 65
Brown, Dan *61:* 167; *115:* 183, 184; *116:* 28, 29; *193:* 190; *200:* 21, 23
Brown, David *7:* 47; *48:* 52
Brown, Denise *11:* 213
Brown, Don *172:* 29
Brown, Elbrite *195:* 39; *198:* 5
Brown, Ford Madox *48:* 74
Brown, Hunter *191:* 111, 112
Brown, Judith Gwyn *1:* 45; *7:* 5; *8:* 167; *9:* 182, 190; *20:* 16, 17, 18; *23:* 142; *29:* 117; *33:* 97; *36:* 23, 26; *43:* 184; *48:* 201, 223; *49:* 69; *86:* 227; *110:* 188; *153:* 7
Brown, Kathryn *98:* 26
Brown, Lisa *187:* 175

Brown, Laurie Krasny 99: 30
Brown, Marc (Tolon) 10: 17, 197; 14: 263; 51: 18; 53: 11, 12, 13, 15, 16, 17; 75: 58; 80: 24, 25, 26; 82: 261; 99: 29; 145: 22, 23, 25, 27; 162: 198
Brown, Marcia 7: 30; 25: 203; 47: 31, 32, 33, 34, 35,36, 37, 38, 39, 40, 42, 43, 44; YABC 1: 27
Brown, Margery W. 5: 32, 33; 10: 3
Brown, Martin 101: 43
Brown, Mary Barrett 97: 74
Brown, Palmer 36: 40
Brown, Paul 25: 26; 26: 107
Brown, Richard 61: 18; 67: 30
Brown, Rick 78: 71; 150: 154
Brown, Robert S. 85: 33
Brown, Rod 157: 142
Brown, Ruth 55: 165; 86: 112, 113; 105: 16, 17, 18; 171: 178
Brown, Trevor 99: 160; 139: 247; 189: 206
Browne, Anthony 45: 50, 51, 52; 61: 21, 22, 23, 24, 25; 105: 21, 22, 23, 25
Browne, Dik 8: 212; 67: 32, 33, 35, 37, 39
Browne, Gordon 16: 97; 64: 114, 116, 117, 119, 121
Browne, Hablot K. 15: 65, 80; 21: 14, 15, 16, 17, 18, 19,20; 24: 25
Browne, Jane 165: 222
Browning, Coleen 4: 132
Browning, Mary Eleanor 24: 84
Bruce, Robert 23: 23
Brude, Dick 48: 215
Bruel, Nick 166: 41
Brule, Al 3: 135
Brumbeau, Jeff 157: 29
Bruna, Dick 43: 48, 49, 50; 76: 27, 28
Brundage, Frances 19: 244
Brunhoff, Jean de 24: 57, 58
Brunhoff, Laurent de 24: 60; 71: 35, 36, 37
Brunkus, Denise 84: 50; 123: 117; 178: 209; 193: 99
Brunson, Bob 43: 135
Bryan, Ashley 31: 44; 72: 27, 28, 29; 107: 92; 116: 192; 132: 24; 178: 33, 34, 35
Bryant, Laura J. 176: 36; 183: 168
Bryant, Michael 93: 74
Brychta, Alex 21: 21
Bryer, Diana 107: 121
Bryson, Bernarda 3: 88, 146; 39: 26; 44: 185; 131: 40
Buba, Joy 12: 83; 30: 226; 44: 56
Buchanan, George 166: 198
Buchanan, Lilian 13: 16
Buchanan, Rachel 171: 71
Bucholtz-Ross, Linda 44: 137
Buchs, Thomas 40: 38
Buck, Margaret Waring 3: 30
Buckhardt, Marc 172: 59
Buckley, Mike 166: 180
Budwine, Greg 175: 172
Buehner, Mark 104: 12, 15; 105: 160; 119: 98; 157: 188; 159: 39, 40, 43; 192: 111
Buehr, Walter 3: 31
Buff, Conrad 19: 52, 53, 54
Buff, Mary 19: 52, 53
Bull, Charles Livingston 18: 207; 88: 175, 176
Bullen, Anne 3: 166, 167
Bullock, Kathleen 77: 24
Bumgarner-Kirby, Claudia 77: 194
Burbank, Addison 37: 43
Burchard, Peter Duncan 3: 197; 5: 35; 6: 158, 218; 143: 17
Burckhardt, Marc 94: 48; 110: 89; 196: 41; 199: 116
Burger, Carl 3: 33; 45: 160, 162
Burgeson, Marjorie 19: 31
Burgess, Anne 76: 252
Burgess, Gelett 32: 39, 42
Burgess, Mark 157: 31
Burke, Jim 179: 19; 185: 63
Burke, Phillip 95: 117

Burkert, Nancy Ekholm 18: 186; 22: 140; 24: 62, 63,64, 65; 26: 53; 29: 60, 61; 46: 171; YABC 1: 46
Burkhardt, Bruce 142: 86
Burkhardt, Melissa A. 142: 86
Burleson, Joe 104: 35; 172: 139
Burn, Doris 6: 172
Burn, Jeffrey 89: 125; 152: 132
Burn, Ted
  See Burn, Thomas E.
Burn, Thomas E. 151: 41
Burnard, Damon 115: 23
Burnett, Virgil 44: 42
Burningham, John 9: 68; 16: 60, 61; 59: 28, 29, 30,31, 32, 33, 35; 111: 18, 19, 21; 160: 37
Burns, Howard M. 12: 173
Burns, Jim 47: 70; 86: 32; 91: 197; 123: 16
Burns, M.F. 26: 69
Burns, Raymond 9: 29
Burns, Robert 24: 106
Burr, Dan 65: 28; 108: 134; 164: 203; 182: 68
Burr, Dane 12: 2
Burra, Edward YABC 2: 68
Burrell, Galen 56: 76
Burri, Rene 41: 143; 54: 166
Burridge, Marge Opitz 14: 42
Burris, Burmah 4: 81
Burroughs, John Coleman 41: 64
Burroughs, Studley O. 41: 65
Burton, Marilee Robin 46: 33
Burton, Virginia Lee 2: 43; 44: 49, 51; 100: 46, 47; YABC 1: 24; 147: 56
Busoni, Rafaello 1: 186; 3: 224; 6: 126; 14: 5; 16: 62, 63
Butchkes, Sidney 50: 58
Butler, Geoff 94: 20
Butler, Ralph 116: 212
Butterfield, Ned 1: 153; 27: 128; 79: 63
Butterworth, Ian 184: 48, 49
Butterworth, Nick 106: 43, 44; 149: 34
Buxton, John 123: 12
Buzelli, Christopher 105: 149
Buzonas, Gail 29: 88
Buzzell, Russ W. 12: 177
Byard, Carole 39: 44; 57: 18, 19, 20; 60: 60; 61: 93, 96; 69: 210; 78: 246; 79: 227
Byars, Betsy 46: 35
Byfield, Barbara Ninde 8: 18
Byfield, Graham 32: 29
Bynum, Janie 176: 50
Byrd, Robert 13: 218; 33: 46; 158: 70
Byrd, Samuel 123: 104

C

Cabat, Erni 74: 38
Cabban, Vanessa 138: 73; 176: 39; 185: 65
Cabrera, Jane 103: 24; 152: 27; 182: 33, 34
Caceres, Ana Palmero 198: 106
Caddy, Alice 6: 41
Cady, Harrison 17: 21, 23; 19: 57, 58
Caffrey, Aileen 72: 223; 141: 154
Cairns, Julia 177: 37
Caldecott, Randolph 16: 98, 103; 17: 32, 33, 36, 38, 39; 26: 90; 100: 49, 50; YABC 2: 172
Calder, Alexander 18: 168
Calderón, Gloria 179: 5
Calderon, W. Frank 25: 160
Caldwell, Ben 105: 75; 149: 60; 195: 61
Caldwell, Clyde 98: 100; 116: 39
Caldwell, Doreen 23: 77; 71: 41
Caldwell, John 46: 225
Call, Greg 126: 135; 165: 49; 182: 105, 163; 197: 18, 19; 200: 159
Callahan, Kevin 22: 42
Callahan, Philip S. 25: 77
Callan, Jamie 59: 37

Calvin, James 61: 92
Camburn-Bracalente, Carol A. 118: 22
Cameron, Chad 190: 144
Cameron, Julia Margaret 19: 203
Cameron, Scott 99: 18
Camm, Martin 140: 208, 209, 210
Campbell, Ann 11: 43; 123: 182; 183: 68
Campbell, Bill 89: 39
Campbell, Ken 126: 143
Campbell, Robert 55: 120
Campbell, Rod 51: 27; 98: 34
Campbell, Walter M. YABC 2: 158
Camps, Luis 28: 120, 121; 66: 35
Canga, C.B. 187: 165
Caniglia, Jeremy 201: 89
Cann, Helen 124: 50; 141: 78; 170: 138; 179: 22, 23
Cannell, Jon 196: 43
Cannon, Janell 78: 25; 128: 40
Canright, David 36: 162
Cantone, AnnaLaura 182: 146; 196: 80
Canty, Thomas 85: 161; 92: 47; 113: 192; 134: 60; 185: 117
Canyon, Christopher 150: 44; 151: 112
Caporale, Wende 70: 42
Capp, Al 61: 28, 30, 31, 40, 41, 43, 44
Cappon, Manuela 154: 64
Caras, Peter 36: 64
Caraway, Caren 57: 22
Caraway, James 3: 200, 201
Carbe, Nino 29: 183
Cares, Linda 67: 176
Carigiet, Alois 24: 67
Carle, Eric 4: 42; 11: 121; 12: 29; 65: 32,33, 34, 36; 73: 63, 65; 163: 55, 56
Carling, Amelia Lau 164: 46
Carlino, Angela 168: 43; 188: 20
Carlson, Nancy L. 41: 116; 56: 25; 90: 45; 144: 48, 50
Carlluccio, Maria 175: 129
Carmi, Giora 79: 35; 149: 40
Carpenter, Nancy 76: 128; 86: 173; 89: 171; 131: 186; 134: 8; 138: 215; 153: 204; 159: 93; 165: 232
Carr, Archie 37: 225
Carrick, Donald 5: 194; 39: 97; 49: 70; 53: 156; 63: 15, 16, 17, 18, 19, 21; 80: 131; 86: 151; 118: 24
Carrick, Malcolm 28: 59, 60
Carrick, Paul 118: 26; 194: 28
Carrick, Valery 21: 47
Carrier, Lark 71: 43
Carroll, Jim 88: 211; 140: 177; 153: 99; 195: 75
Carroll, Lewis
  See Dodgson, Charles L.
Carroll, Michael 72: 5
Carroll, Pamela 84: 68; 128: 214; 199: 130
Carroll, Ruth 7: 41; 10: 68
Carter, Abby 81: 32; 97: 121; 102: 61; 163: 139; 164: 125; 184: 22, 23; 191: 85
Carter, Barbara 47: 167, 169
Carter, David A. 114: 24, 25; 170: 42, 43
Carter, Don 124: 54; 184: 100; 192: 43, 44, 45
Carter, Harry 22: 179
Carter, Helene 15: 38; 22: 202, 203; YABC 2: 220, 221
Carter, Penny 173: 91
Cartlidge, Michelle 49: 65; 96: 50, 51
Cartwright, Reg 63: 61, 62; 78: 26; 143: 4
Cartwright, Shannon 176: 81
Carty, Leo 4: 196; 7: 163; 58: 131
Cary 4: 133; 9: 32; 20: 2; 21: 143
Cary, Page 12: 41
Casale, Paul 71: 63; 109: 122; 136: 28
Case, Sandra E. 16: 2
Caseley, Judith 87: 36; 159: 47, 48, 49
Casilla, Robert 78: 7; 167: 124
Casino, Steve 85: 193
Cassel, Lili
  See Wronker, Lili Cassel

Cassel-Wronker, Lili
  See Wronker, Lili Cassel
Cassels, Jean *8:* 50; *150:* 119; *173:* 37; *186:* 182
Cassen, Melody *140:* 51
Cassity, Don *104:* 24
Cassler, Carl *75:* 137, 138; *82:* 162
Casson, Hugh *65:* 38, 40, 42, 43
Castellon, Federico *48:* 45, 46, 47, 48
Castle, Jane *4:* 80
Castro, Antonio *84:* 71
Casu, Danny "casroc" *201:* 10
Catalano, Dominic *94:* 79; *163:* 60, 61; *162:* 54
Catalanotto, Peter *63:* 170; *70:* 23; *71:* 182; *72:* 96; *74:* 114; *76:* 194, 195; *77:* 7; *79:* 157; *80:* 28, 67; *83:* 157; *85:* 27; *108:* 11; *113:* 30, 31, 33, 34, 36; *114:* 27, 28, 29; *117:* 53; *124:* 168; *159:* 54, 55; *195:* 19, 20, 21, 22, 24, 174; *200:* 156
Catania, Tom *68:* 82
Cather, Carolyn *3:* 83; *15:* 203; *34:* 216
Catrow, David *117:* 179; *152:* 31, 33; *173:* 24
Cauley, Lorinda Bryan *44:* 135; *46:* 49
Cayard, Bruce *38:* 67
Cazet, Denys *52:* 27; *99:* 39, 40; *163:* 65, 66; *191:* 25, 27, 28
Ceccoli, Nicoletta *181:* 39; *188:* 99; *199:* 118
Cecil, Randy *127:* 132, 133; *187:* 16, 17; *191:* 168
Cellini, Joseph *2:* 73; *3:* 35; *16:* 116; *47:* 103
Cepeda, Joe *90:* 62; *109:* 91; *134:* 172; *159:* 57, 58, 164; *197:* 157
Chabrian, Debbi *45:* 55
Chabrian, Deborah *51:* 182; *53:* 124; *63:* 107; *75:* 84; *79:* 85; *82:* 247; *89:* 93; *101:* 197
Chagnon, Mary *37:* 158
Chalmers, Mary *3:* 145; *13:* 148; *33:* 125; *66:* 214
Chamberlain, Christopher *45:* 57
Chamberlain, Margaret *46:* 51; *106:* 89; *188:* 193
Chamberlain, Nigel *78:* 140
Chambers, C.E. *17:* 230
Chambers, Dave *12:* 151
Chambers, Jill *134:* 110
Chambers, Mary *4:* 188
Chambliss, Maxie *42:* 186; *56:* 159; *93:* 163, 164; *103:* 178; *186:* 33, 34; *196:* 39
Champlin, Dale *136:* 124
Chan, Harvey *96:* 236; *99:* 153; *143:* 218; *179:* 144
Chandler, David P. *28:* 62
Chaney, Howard *139:* 27
Chang, Warren *101:* 209
Chapel, Jody *68:* 20
Chapman, C.H. *13:* 83, 85, 87
Chapman, Frederick T. *6:* 27; *44:* 28
Chapman, Gaynor *32:* 52, 53
Chapman, Jane *145:* 186; *150:* 56; *166:* 220; *174:* 202; *176:* 43, 44; *179:* 131
Chapman, Lynne *175:* 31; *197:* 25
Chappell, Warren *3:* 172; *21:* 56; *27:* 125
Charles, Donald *30:* 154, 155
Charlip, Remy *4:* 48; *34:* 138; *68:* 53, 54; *119:* 29, 30
Charlot, Jean *1:* 137, 138; *8:* 23; *14:* 31; *48:* 151; *56:* 21
Charlot, Martin *64:* 72
Charlton, Michael *34:* 50; *37:* 39
Charmatz, Bill *7:* 45
Chartier, Normand *9:* 36; *52:* 49; *66:* 40; *74:* 220; *145:* 169; *168:* 91; *177:* 108
Chase, Lynwood M. *14:* 4
Chast, Roz *97:* 39, 40
Chastain, Madye Lee *4:* 50
Chateron, Ann *152:* 19
Chatterton, Martin *68:* 102; *152:* 19
Chau, Tungwai *140:* 35
Chauncy, Francis *24:* 158
Chayka, Doug *145:* 97; *177:* 150; *196:* 46

Chee, Cheng-Khee *79:* 42; *81:* 224; *180:* 245
Chen, Chih-sien *90:* 226
Chen, Tony *6:* 45; *19:* 131; *29:* 126; *34:* 160
Chen, Yong *183:* 34
Cheney, T.A. *11:* 47
Cheng, Judith *36:* 45; *51:* 16
Chermayeff, Ivan *47:* 53
Cherry, David *93:* 40
Cherry, Lynne *34:* 52; *65:* 184; *87:* 111; *99:* 46, 47
Chesak, Lina *135:* 118
Chess, Victoria *12:* 6; *33:* 42, 48, 49; *40:* 194; *41:* 145; *69:* 80; *72:* 100; *92:* 33, 34; *104:* 167
Chessare, Michele *41:* 50; *56:* 48; *69:* 145
Chesterton, G.K. *27:* 43, 44, 45, 47
Chestnutt, David *47:* 217
Chesworth, Michael *75:* 24, 152; *88:* 136; *94:* 25; *98:* 155; *160:* 42
Chetham, Celia *134:* 34
Chetwin, Grace *86:* 40
Cheung, Irving *158:* 96
Chevalier, Christa *35:* 66
Chew, Ruth *7:* 46; *132:* 147
Chewning, Randy *92:* 206
Chichester Clark, Emma *72:* 121; *77:* 212; *78:* 209; *87:* 143; *117:* 37, 39, 40; *144:* 138; *156:* 24, 25
Chifflart *47:* 113, 127
Child, Lauren *119:* 32; *183:* 30, 31
Chin, Alex *28:* 54
Chitwood, Susan Tanner *163:* 16
Cho, Shinta *8:* 126
Chodos-Irvine, Margaret *52:* 102, 103, 107; *152:* 44
Choi, Yangsook *171:* 134; *173:* 135; *178:* 38, 39, 40
Chollat, Emilie *170:* 203
Chollick, Jay *25:* 175
Choma, Christina *99:* 169
Chomey, Steve *188:* 53
Chorao, Kay *7:* 200, 201; *8:* 25; *11:* 234; *33:* 187; *35:* 239; *69:* 35; *70:* 235; *123:* 174; *193:* 179
Chowdhury, Subrata *62:* 130; *162:* 22, 23
Christelow, Eileen *38:* 44; *83:* 198, 199; *90:* 57, 58; *184:* 26
Christensen, Bonnie *93:* 100; *153:* 67
Christensen, Gardell Dano *1:* 57
Christensen, James C. *140:* 226
Christiana, David *90:* 64; *135:* 13; *171:* 7; *195:* 26, 27
Christiansen, Per *40:* 24
Christie, R. Gregory *116:* 107; *127:* 20, 21; *162:* 179; *164:* 114; *165:* 137; *174:* 157; *179:* 172; *185:* 17, 18, 19; *200:* 2
Christy, Howard Chandler *17:* 163, 164, 165, 168, 169; *19:* 186, 187; *21:* 22, 23, 24, 25
Christy, Jana *194:* 21
Chronister, Robert *23:* 138; *63:* 27; *69:* 167
Church, Caroline Jayne *179:* 27
Church, Frederick *YABC 1:* 155
Chute, Marchette *1:* 59
Chwast, Jacqueline *1:* 63; *2:* 275; *6:* 46, 47; *11:* 125; *12:* 202; *14:* 235
Chwast, Seymour *3:* 128, 129; *18:* 43; *27:* 152; *92:* 79; *96:* 56, 57, 58; *146:* 32, 33; *197:* 99
Cieslawksi, Steve *101:* 142; *127:* 116; *158:* 169, 171; *190:* 174
Cinelli, Lisa *146:* 253
Cirlin, Edgard *2:* 168
Clairin, Georges *53:* 109
Clapp, John *105:* 66; *109:* 58; *126:* 7; *129:* 148; *130:* 165; *195:* 48
Clark, Brenda *119:* 85; *153:* 55
Clark, David *77:* 164; *134:* 144, 145
Clark, Emma Chichester
  See Chichester Clark, Emma
Clark, Victoria *35:* 159
Clarke, Greg *169:* 134

Clarke, Gus *72:* 226; *134:* 31
Clarke, Harry *23:* 172, 173
Clarke, Peter *75:* 102
Claverie, Jean *38:* 46; *88:* 29
Clavis, Philippe Goossens *182:* 167
Clayton, Elaine *159:* 60
Clayton, Robert *9:* 181
Cleary, Brian P. *186:* 37
Cleaver, Elizabeth *8:* 204; *23:* 36
Cleland, T.M. *26:* 92
Clemens, Peter *61:* 125
Clement, Charles *20:* 38
Clement, Gary *186:* 79; *191:* 32
Clement, Janet *182:* 50
Clement, Nathan *200:* 30
Clement, Rod *97:* 42
Clement, Stephen *88:* 3
Clementson, John *84:* 213
Clemesha, David *192:* 49, 50
Clevin, Jorgen *7:* 50
Clifford, Judy *34:* 163; *45:* 198
Clokey, Art *59:* 44
Clouse, Dennis *187:* 158
Clouse, James *84:* 15
Clouse, Nancy L. *78:* 31; *114:* 90
Clover, Peter *152:* 45
Cneut, Carll *156:* 166; *165:* 67; *197:* 26
Coalson, Glo *9:* 72, 85; *25:* 155; *26:* 42; *35:* 212; *53:* 31; *56:* 154; *94:* 37, 38, 193
Cober, Alan E. *17:* 158; *32:* 77; *49:* 127
Cober-Gentry, Leslie *92:* 111
Cocca-Leffler, Maryann *80:* 46; *136:* 60; *139:* 193; *194:* 31, 33, 34
Cochran, Bobbye *11:* 52
CoConis, Ted *4:* 41; *46:* 41; *51:* 104
Cocozza, Chris *87:* 18; *110:* 173; *111:* 149
Cockroft, Jason *152:* 20
Coerr, Eleanor *1:* 64; *67:* 52
Coes, Peter *25:* 172
Cogancherry, Helen *52:* 143; *69:* 131; *77:* 93; *78:* 220; *109:* 204; *110:* 129
Coggins, Jack *2:* 69
Cohen, Alix *7:* 53
Cohen, Miriam *155:* 23, 24
Cohen, Nancy R. *165:* 35
Cohen, Santiago *164:* 26
Cohen, Sheldon *105:* 33, 34; *166:* 46, 47
Cohen, Vincent O. *19:* 243
Cohen, Vivien *11:* 112
Coker, Paul *51:* 172
Colbert, Anthony *15:* 41; *20:* 193
Colby, C.B. *3:* 47
Cole, Babette *58:* 172; *96:* 63, 64; *155:* 29
Cole, Brock *68:* 223; *72:* 36, 37, 38, 192; *127:* 23; *136:* 64, 65; *197:*
Cole, Gwen *87:* 185
Cole, Henry *178:* 120; *181:* 42, 43; *189:* 60
Cole, Herbert *28:* 104
Cole, Michael *59:* 46
Cole, Olivia H.H. *1:* 134; *3:* 223; *9:* 111; *38:* 104
Colin, Paul *102:* 59; *123:* 118; *126:* 152; *192:* 129
Collicott, Sharleen *98:* 39; *143:* 29, 30
Collier, Bryan *126:* 54; *151:* 166; *174:* 16, 17, 18
Collier, David *13:* 127
Collier, John *27:* 179
Collier, Steven *50:* 52
Collier-Morales, Roberta *168:* 61
Collins, Heather *66:* 84; *67:* 68; *81:* 40; *98:* 192, 193; *129:* 95, 96, 98
Collins, Matt *167:* 90
Collins, Ross *140:* 23, 24; *200:* 36, 37
Colman, Audrey *146:* 161
Colón, Raul *108:* 112; *113:* 5; *117:* 167; *134:* 112; *146:* 23; *159:* 92; *166:* 73; *180:* 107; *186:* 156; *190:* 6; *193:* 24, 205
Colonna, Bernard *21:* 50; *28:* 103; *34:* 140; *43:* 180; *78:* 150

Comport, Sally Wern *117:* 169; *169:* 104; *190:* 42

Conde, J.M. *100:* 120

Condon, Grattan *54:* 85 Condon, Ken *161:* 44; *195:* 28, 29

Cone, Ferne Geller *39:* 49

Cone, J. Morton *39:* 49

Conklin, Paul *43:* 62

Connelly, James *198:* 12

Connolly, Howard *67:* 88

Connolly, Jerome P. *4:* 128; *28:* 52

Connolly, Peter *47:* 60

Conoly, Walle *110:* 224

Conover, Chris *31:* 52; *40:* 184; *41:* 51; *44:* 79

Contreras, Gerry *72:* 9

Converse, James *38:* 70

Conway *62:* 62

Conway, Michael *69:* 12; *81:* 3; *92:* 108

Cook, Ande *188:* 135

Cook, G.R. *29:* 165

Cook, Joel *108:* 160

Cookburn, W.V. *29:* 204

Cooke, Donald E. *2:* 77

Cooke, Tom *52:* 118

Coomaraswamy, A.K. *50:* 100

Coombs, Charles *43:* 65

Coombs, Deborah *139:* 175

Coombs, Patricia *2:* 82; *3:* 52; *22:* 119; *51:* 32, 33, 34, 35, 36, 37, 38, 39, 40, 42, 43

Cooney, Barbara *6:* 16, 17, 50; *12:* 42; *13:* 92; *15:* 145; *16:* 74, 111; *18:* 189; *23:* 38, 89, 93; *32:* 138; *38:* 105; *59:* 48, 49, 51, 52, 53; *74:* 222; *81:* 100; *91:* 25; *96:* 71, 72, 74; *100:* 149; *YABC2:* 10

Cooper, Elisha *157:* 38, 39

Cooper, Floyd *79:* 95; *81:* 45; *84:* 82; *85:* 74; *91:* 118; *96:* 77, 78; *103:* 149; *144:* 54; *145:* 151; *159:* 198; *176:* 133, 134; *187:* 26, 27, 28, 29; *188:* 22; *199:* 175

Cooper, Heather *50:* 39

Cooper, Helen *102:* 42, 43, 44

Cooper, Mario *24:* 107

Cooper, Marjorie *7:* 112

Cope, Jane *61:* 201; *108* 52

Copeland, Mark *180:* 12

Copelman, Evelyn *8:* 61; *18:* 25

Copley, Heather *30:* 86; *45:* 57

Corbett, Grahame *30:* 114; *43:* 67

Corbino, John *19:* 248

Corcos, Lucille *2:* 223; *10:* 27; *34:* 66

Cordell, Matthew *197:* 93; *199:* 20, 21

Corey, Robert *9:* 34

Corlass, Heather *10:* 7

Cornell, James *27:* 60

Cornell, Jeff *11:* 58

Cornell, Laura *94:* 179; *95:* 25

Corrigan, Barbara *8:* 37

Corrigan, Patrick *145:* 149

Corwin, Judith Hoffman *10:* 28

Corwin, Oliver *191:* 119

Cory, Fanny Y. *20:* 113; *48:* 29

Cosentino, Ralph *169:* 32

Cosgrove, Margaret *3:* 100; *47:* 63; *82:* 133

Costabel, Eva Deutsch *45:* 66, 67

Costanza, John *58:* 7, 8, 9

Costello, Chris *86:* 78

Costello, David F. *23:* 55

Côté, Geneviéve *184:* 37, 39

Cote, Nancy *126:* 139; *156:* 101; *174:* 101; *182:* 53, 54, 55

Cottenden, Jeff *190:* 45

Couch, Greg *94:* 124; *110:* 13; *162:* 31; *168:* 149; *199:* 22

Councell, Ruth Tietjen *79:* 29

Courtney, Cathy *58:* 69, 144; *59:* 15; *61:* 20, 87

Courtney, R. *35:* 110

Counihan, Claire *133:* 106

Cousineau, Normand *89:* 180; *112:* 76

Cousins, Lucy *172:* 53, 54

Couture, Christin *41:* 209

Covarrubias, Miguel *35:* 118, 119, 123, 124, 125

Coville, Katherine *32:* 57; *36:* 167; *92:* 38

Covington, Neverne *113:* 87

Cowdrey, Richard *169:* 170; *178:* 205

Cowell, Cressida *140:* 39

Cowell, Lucinda *77:* 54

Cox *43:* 93

Cox, Charles *8:* 20

Cox, David *56:* 37; *90:* 63; *119:* 38

Cox, Palmer *24:* 76, 77

Cox, Steve *140:* 96

Coxe, Molly *69:* 44

Coxon, Michele *158:* 80

Crabb, Gordon *70:* 39

Crabtree, Judith *98:* 42

Craft, Kinuko *22:* 182; *36:* 220; *53:* 122, 123, 148,149; *74:* 12; *81:* 129; *86:* 31; *89:* 139; *127:* 27, 28, 29; *132:* 142; *139:* 38

Craig, Daniel *177:* 67; *180:* 11; *185:* 203

Craig, David *136:* 198

Craig, Helen *49:* 76; *62:* 70, 71, 72; *69:* 141; *94:* 42, 43, 44; *112:* 53; *135:* 101, 102

Crane, Alan H. *1:* 217

Crane, H.M. *13:* 111

Crane, Jack *43:* 183

Crane, Jordan *174:* 21

Crane, Walter *18:* 46, 47, 48, 49, 53, 54, 56, 57, 59, 60, 61; *22:* 128; *24:* 210, 217; *100:* 70, 71

Cravath, Lynne W. *98:* 45; *182:* 58, 59

Crawford, Denise *137:* 213

Crawford, Will *43:* 77

Credle, Ellis *1:* 69

Czernecki, Stefan *154:* 104; *178:* 68, 69

Crespi, Francesca *87:* 90

Cressy, Michael *124:* 55

Crews, Donald *32:* 59, 60; *76:* 42, 43, 44

Crews, Nina *97:* 49

Crichlow, Ernest *74:* 88; *83:* 203

Croft, James *150:* 57

Crofut, Bob *80:* 87; *81:* 47

Crofut, Susan *23:* 61

Croll, Carolyn *80:* 137; *102:* 52

Cross, Peter *56:* 78; *63:* 60, 65

Crowe, Elizabeth *88:* 144

Crowell, Pers *3:* 125

Cruikshank, George *15:* 76, 83; *22:* 74, 75, 76, 77, 78, 79,80, 81, 82, 84, 137; *24:* 22, 23

Crump, Fred H. *11:* 62

Cruz, Ray *6:* 55; *70:* 234; *123:* 173; *172:* 192

Csatari, Joe *44:* 82; *55:* 152; *63:* 25, 28; *102:* 58

Cuetara, Mittie *158:* 85

Cuffari, Richard *4:* 75; *5:* 98; *6:* 56; *7:* 13,84, 153; *8:* 148, 155; *9:* 89; *11:* 19; *12:* 55, 96,114; *15:* 51, 202; *18:* 5; *20:* 139; *21:* 197; *22:* 14, 192; *23:* 15, 106; *25:* 97; *27:* 133; *28:* 196; *29:* 54; *30:* 85; *31:* 35; *36:* 101; *38:* 171; *42:* 97; *44:* 92, 192; *45:* 212, 213; *46:* 36, 198; *50:* 164; *54:* 80, 136, 137, 145; *56:* 17; *60:* 63; *66:* 49, 50; *70:* 41; *71:* 132; *77:* 157; *78:* 58, 149; *79:* 120; *85:* 2, 152

Cugat, Xavier *19:* 120

Cumings, Art *35:* 160

Cummings, Chris *29:* 167

Cummings, Michael *159:* 142

Cummings, Pat *42:* 61; *61:* 99; *69:* 205; *71:* 57,58; *78:* 24, 25; *93:* 75; *107:* 49, 50; *164:* 259

Cummings, Richard *24:* 119

Cunette, Lou *20:* 93; *22:* 125

Cunningham, Aline *25:* 180

Cunningham, David *11:* 13

Cunningham, Imogene *16:* 122, 127

Cunningham, Kelley *176:* 159

Cupples, Pat *107:* 12; *126:* 109; *182:* 13; *198:* 68

Curlee, Lynn *98:* 48; *141:* 39; *190:* 48

Currey, Anna *190:* 145

Curry, John Steuart *2:* 5; *19:* 84; *34:* 36; *144:* 126

Curry, Tom *127:* 131; *185:* 25, 26

Curtis, Bruce *23:* 96; *30:* 88; *36:* 22

Curtis, Neil *167:* 30

Cusack, Margaret *58:* 49, 50, 51

Cushman, Doug *65:* 57; *101:* 39, 40; *133:* 179; *157:* 45; *186:* 157

Cutting, Ann *196:* 194

Cyrus, Kurt *132:* 39; *179:* 36, 37

Czechowski, Alicia *95:* 21; *171:* 37

Czernecki, Stefan *117:* 173

D

Dabcovich, Lydia *25:* 105; *40:* 114; *99:* 75, 76

Dacey, Bob *82:* 175; *152:* 65

d'Achille, Gino *127:* 175, 176

Dailey, Don *78:* 197

Dain, Martin J. *35:* 75

Dale, Penny *127:* 224; *151:* 57; *160:* 89; *197:* 75

Dale, Rae *72:* 197

Daley, Joann *50:* 22

Dalton, Anne *40:* 62; *63:* 119

Daly, Deborah M. *74:* 213

Daly, Jim *103:* 60; *150:* 48

Daly, Jude *138:* 118, 119

Daly, Nicholas *37:* 53; *76:* 48, 49

Daly, Niki *107:* 15; *114:* 38, 39, 40; *164:* 86; *192:* 53; *198:* 26, 27

Daly, Paul *97:* 205

Dalziel, Brothers *33:* 113

D'Amato, Alex *9:* 48; *20:* 25

D'Amato, Janet *9:* 48; *20:* 25; *26:* 118

D'Amico, Steve *170:* 52

Danalis, Johnny *167:* 27

D'Andrea, Domenick *183:* 108

Daniel, Alan *23:* 59; *29:* 110; *76:* 50, 53, 55, 56; *153:* 76 *115:* 74; *134:* 70

Daniel, Lea *76:* 53, 55; *153:* 76

Daniel, Lewis C. *20:* 216

Daniels, Beau *73:* 4

Daniels, Steve *22:* 16

Daniels, Stewart *56:* 12

Dann, Bonnie *31:* 83

Dann, Penny *82:* 128

Danska, Herbert *24:* 219

Danyell, Alice *20:* 27

Darley, F.O.C. *16:* 145; *19:* 79, 86, 88, 185; *21:* 28,36; *35:* 76, 77, 78, 79, 80, 81; *YABC 2:* 175

Darling, Lois *3:* 59; *23:* 30, 31

Darling, Louis *1:* 40, 41; *2:* 63; *3:* 59; *23:* 30,31; *43:* 54, 57, 59; *121:* 53

Darrow, David R. *84:* 101

Darrow, Whitney, Jr. *13:* 25; *38:* 220, 221

Darwin, Beatrice *43:* 54

Darwin, Len *24:* 82

Dastolfo, Frank *33:* 179

Dauber, Liz *1:* 22; *3:* 266; *30:* 49

Daugherty, James *3:* 66; *8:* 178; *13:* 27, 28, 161; *18:* 101; *19:* 72; *29:* 108; *32:* 156; *42:* 84; *YABC 1:* 256; *2:* 174

d'Aulaire, Edgar Parin *5:* 51; *66:* 53

d'Aulaire, Ingri Parin *5:* 51; *66:* 53

Davalos, Felipe *99:* 197; *159:* 66; *174:* 163

Davenier, Christine *125:* 88; *127:* 32; *128:* 152; *179:* 39, 40

Davick, Linda *151:* 124

David, Jacques-Louis *193:* 22

David, Jonathan *19:* 37

Davidson, Kevin *28:* 154

Davidson, Raymond *32:* 61

Davie, Helen K. *77:* 48, 49

Davis, Allen *20:* 11; *22:* 45; *27:* 222; *29:* 157; *41:* 99; *47:* 99; *50:* 84; *52:* 105

Davis, Bette J. *15:* 53; *23:* 95

Davis, Dimitris *45:* 95

Davis, Hendon *151:* 122
Davis, Jack E. *145:* 139; *175:* 84, 85
Davis, Jim *32:* 63, 64
Davis, Katie *152:* 52, 53, 54
Davis, Lambert *110:* 23, 24; *176:* 58
Davis, Marguerite *31:* 38; *34:* 69, 70; *100:* 34; *YABC 1:* 126, 230
Davis, Nelle *69:* 191
Davis, Paul *78:* 214
Davis, Yvonne LeBrun *94:* 144
Davisson, Virginia H. *44:* 178
DaVolls, Andy *85:* 53
Dawson, Diane *24:* 127; *42:* 126; *52:* 130; *68:* 104
Day, Alexandra *67:* 59; *97:* 54; *166:* 65; *169:* 40; *197:* 50, 51, 52, 54
Day, Larry *169:* 88; *185:* 59
Day, Rob *94:* 110; *127:* 24; *197:* 32
Dean, Bob *19:* 211
Dean, David *192:* 55
de Angeli, Marguerite *1:* 77; *27:* 62, 65, 66, 67, 69, 70, 72; *100:* 75, 76; *YABC 1:* 166
DeArmond, Dale *70:* 47
Deas, Michael *27:* 219, 221; *30:* 156; *67:* 134; *72:* 24; *75:* 155; *84:* 206; *88:* 124
Deas, Rich *191:* 87; *193:* 10
deBarros, Jim *196:* 60
Debon, Nicolas *151:* 60; *177:* 46
de Bosschere, Jean *19:* 252; *21:* 4; *186:* 44, 45
De Bruyn, M(onica) G. *13:* 30, 31
Decker, C.B. *172:* 120
De Cuir, John F. *1:* 28, 29
Deeter, Catherine *74:* 110; *103:* 150; *137:* 50
Degen, Bruce *40:* 227, 229; *57:* 28, 29; *56:* 156; *75:* 229; *76:* 19; *81:* 36, 37; *92:* 26; *93:* 199; *97:* 56, 58, 59; *124:* 40; *147:* 39, 40, 41; *168:* 23
De Grazia *14:* 59; *39:* 56, 57
DeGrazio, George *88:* 40
deGroat, Diane *9:* 39; *18:* 7; *23:* 123; *28:* 200, 201; *31:* 58, 59; *34:* 151; *41:* 152; *43:* 88; *46:* 40, 200; *49:* 163; *50:* 89; *52:* 30, 34; *54:* 43; *63:* 5; *70:* 136; *71:* 99; *73:* 117,156; *77:* 34; *85:* 48; *86:* 201; *87:* 142; *90:* 72, 73, 143; *95:* 182; *111:* 123; *118:* 160; *126:* 8; *130:* 130; *138:* 93, 94; *169:* 46, 47
de Groot, Lee *6:* 21
Deines, Brian *110:* 139
DeJohn, Marie *89:* 78
Dekhteryov, B. *61:* 158
de Kiefte, Kees *94:* 107
Delacre, Lulu *36:* 66; *156:* 35
Delaney, A. *21:* 78
Delaney, Michael *180:* 16
Delaney, Molly *80:* 43
Delaney, Ned *28:* 68; *56:* 80; *102:* 11
DeLange, Alex Pardo *179:* 128
DeLapine, Jim *79:* 21
De La Roche Saint Andre, Anne *75:* 37
de Larrea, Victoria *6:* 119, 204; *29:* 103; *72:* 203; *87:* 199
Delessert, Étienne *7:* 140; *46:* 61, 62, 63, 65, 67, 68; *130:* 38, 39, 40, 41, 42; *179:* 46, 47, 48, 49; *YABC 2:* 209
Delezenne, Christine *186:* 126
Del Negro, Janice *196:* 161
DeLorenzo, Christopher *154:* 149
Delulio, John *15:* 54
DeLuna, Tony *88:* 95
Demarest, Chris L. *45:* 68, 69, 70; *73:* 172, 173, 176; *78:* 106; *82:* 48, 49; *89:* 212; *92:* 86; *128:* 57, 58; *175:* 46, 48
De Mejo, Oscar *40:* 67
Demi *11:* 135; *15:* 245; *66:* 129, 130; *89:* 216; *102:* 66, 67, 68
Denetsosie, Hoke *13:* 126; *82:* 34
Denise, Christopher *147:* 43, 44; *176:* 101; *193:* 35, 36, 37; *201:* 37
Dennis, Morgan *18:* 68, 69; *64:* 89

Dennis, Wesley *2:* 87; *3:* 111; *11:* 132; *18:* 71, 72, 73, 74; *22:* 9; *24:* 196, 200; *46:* 178; *69:* 94, 96; *129:* 62
Denslow, W.W. *16:* 84, 85, 86, 87; *18:* 19, 20, 24; *29:* 211; *100:* 21
Denton, Kady MacDonald *110:* 82; *130:* 70; *181:* 54, 55, 56; *192:* 75
Denton, Terry *72:* 163; *174:* 26; *186:* 52; *196:* 83, 84
DePalma, Mary Newell *132:* 114; *139:* 75; *185:* 30, 31; *186:* 121
dePaola, Tomie *8:* 95; *9:* 93; *11:* 69; 25; 103; *28:* 157; *29:* 80; *39:* 52, 53; *40:* 226; *46:* 187; *59:* 61, 62, 63, 64, 65, 66, 67, 68, 69, 71, 72, 74; *62:* 19; *108:* 63, 67, 68, 70; *155:* 62, 64, 66; *180:* 105; *200:* 47, 48, 49, 50
Deraney, Michael J. *77:* 35; *78:* 148
deRosa, Dee *70:* 48; *71:* 210; *91:* 78
DeSaix, Deborah Durland *180:* 15; *188:* 24
De Saulles, Tony *119:* 39
de Seve, Peter *146:* 261
Deshaprabhu, Meera Dayal *86:* 192
Desimini, Lisa *86:* 68; *94:* 47, 96: 7; *104:* 107; *125:* 194; *131:* 180; *172:* 56
de St. Menin, Charles *70:* 17
Detmold, Edward J. *22:* 104, 105, 106, 107; *35:* 120; *64:* 5; *YABC 2:* 203
Detrich, Susan *20:* 133
Deutermann, Diana *77:* 175
DeVelasco, Joseph E. *21:* 51
de Veyrac, Robert *YABC 2:* 19
DeVille, Edward A. *4:* 235
de Visser, John *55:* 119
Devito, Bert *12:* 164
Devlin, Harry *11:* 74; *74:* 63, 65; *136:* 77, 78
Dewan, Ted *108:* 73; *157:* 55; *165:* 129
Dewar, Nick *133:* 122
Dewdney, Anna *184:* 43, 44
Dewey, Ariane *7:* 64; *33:* 195; *35:* 208; *68:* 16,17; *75:* 46; *93:* 91; *94:* 197; *109:* 65, 66, 67; *125:* 2, 3, 4, 5; *127:* 188; *143:* 25; *178:* 17, 19, 74; *188:* 166
Dewey, Jennifer (Owings) *58:* 54; *64:* 214; *65:* 207; *88:* 169; *103:* 45
Dewey, Kenneth *39:* 62; *51:* 23; *56:* 163
de Zanger, Arie *30:* 40
Diakité, Baba Wagué *174:* 28
Diamond, Donna *21:* 200; *23:* 63; *26:* 142; *35:* 83, 84, 85, 86, 87, 88, 89; *38:* 78; *40:* 147; *44:* 152; *50:* 144; *53:* 126; *69:* 46, 47, 48, 201; *71:* 133; *123:* 19
Dias, Ron *71:* 67
Diaz, David *80:* 213; *96:* 83, 84; *108:* 228; *110:* 29; *149:* 106; *150:* 63; *179:* 160; *184:* 95, 97; *189:* 51, 52, 53
Dibley, Glin *138:* 83; *141:* 128
DiCesare, Joe *70:* 38; *71:* 63, 106; *79:* 214; *93:* 147; *116:* 217; *143:* 111; *166:* 57
Dick, John Henry *8:* 181
Dickens, Frank *34:* 131
Dickey, Robert L. *15:* 279
Dickson, Mora *84:* 21
Didier, Sam *166:* 114
Dietz, James *128:* 223; *193:* 136
di Fate, Vincent *37:* 70; *90:* 11; *93:* 60; *109:* 219, 220
Di Fiori, Lawrence *10:* 51; *12:* 190; *27:* 97; *40:* 219; *93:* 57; *130:* 45
Digby, Desmond *97:* 180
Dignan, James *196:* 143
Di Grazia, Thomas *32:* 66; *35:* 241
Dillard, Annie *10:* 32
Dillard, Sarah *136:* 186
Dillon, Corinne B. *1:* 139
Dillon, Diane *4:* 104, 167; *6:* 23; *13:* 29; *15:* 99; *26:* 148; *27:* 136, 201; *51:* 29, 48, 51, 52, 53, 54,55, 56, 57, 58, 59, 60, 61, 62; *54:* 155; *56:* 69; *58:* 127,128; *61:* 95; *62:* 27; *64:* 46; *68:* 3; *69:* 209; *74:* 89; *79:* 92; *86:*

89; *92:* 28, 177; *93:* 7, 210; *94:* 239, 240; *97:* 167; *106:* 58, 59,61, 64; *107:* 3; *139:* 246; *167:* 77; *189:* 202; *191:* 191; *194:* 45, 46, 48, 49
Dillon, Leo *4:* 104, 167; *6:* 23; *13:* 29; *15:* 99; *26:* 148; *27:* 136, 201; *51:* 29, 48, 51, 52, 53, 54,55, 56, 57, 58, 59, 60, 61, 62; *54:* 155; *56:* 69; *58:* 127,128; *61:* 95; *62:* 27; *64:* 46; *68:* 3; *69:* 209; *74:* 89; *79:* 92; *86:* 89; *92:* 28, 177; *93:* 7, 210; *94:* 239, 240; *97:* 167; *106:* 58, 59,61, 64; *107:* 3; *139:* 246; *167:* 77; *189:* 202; *191:* 191; *194:* 45, 46, 48, 49
Dillon, Sharon Saseen *59:* 179, 188
DiMaccio, Gerald *121:* 80
DiMaggio, Joe *36:* 22
DiMassi, Gina *169:* 17
Dinan, Carol *25:* 169; *59:* 75
Dines, Glen *7:* 66, 67
Dinesen, Thomas *44:* 37
Dinh, Pham Viet *167:* 184
Dinnerstein, Harvey *42:* 63, 64, 65, 66, 67, 68; *50:* 146
Dinsdale, Mary *10:* 65; *11:* 171
Dinyer, Eric *86:* 148; *109:* 163; *110:* 239; *124:* 11; *150:* 69; *170:* 4; *171:* 30
Dion, Nathalie *170:* 124
DiRocco, Carl *181:* 23
DiSalvo-Ryan, DyAnne *59:* 77; *62:* 185; *117:* 46; *144:* 64; *150:* 153; *186:* 162
Disney, Walt *28:* 71, 72, 73, 76, 77, 78, 79, 80, 81, 87, 88, 89,90, 91, 94
DiTerlizzi, Tony *105:* 7; *147:* 22; *154:* 31, 32, 33
Divito, Anna *83:* 159
Dixon, Don *74:* 17; *109:* 196
Dixon, Larry *127:* 125
Dixon, Maynard *20:* 165
Doares, Robert G. *20:* 39
Dobias, Frank *22:* 162
Dobrin, Arnold *4:* 68
Dobson, Steven Gaston *102:* 103
Dockray, Tracy *139:* 77
Docktor, Irv *43:* 70
Dodd, Ed *4:* 69
Dodd, Julie *74:* 73
Dodd, Lynley *35:* 92; *86:* 71; *132:* 45, 46, 47
Dodge, Bill *96:* 36; *118:* 7, 8, 9; *133:* 135
Dodgson, Charles L. *20:* 148; *33:* 146; *YABC 2:* 98
Dodson, Bert *9:* 138; *14:* 195; *42:* 55; *54:* 8; *60:* 49; *101:* 125
Dodson, Liz Brenner *105:* 117; *111:* 15
Dohanos, Stevan *16:* 10
Dolce, J. Ellen *74:* 147; *75:* 41
Dolch, Marguerite P. *50:* 64
Dolesch, Susanne *34:* 49
Dollar, Diane *57:* 32
Dolobowsky, Mena *81:* 54
Dolson, Hildegarde *5:* 57
Domanska, Janina *6:* 66, 67; *YABC 1:* 166
Domi *134:* 113
Dominguez, El *53:* 94
Domjan, Joseph *25:* 93
Domm, Jeffrey C. *84:* 69; *135:* 70
Donahey, William *68:* 209
Donahue, Dorothy *76:* 170
Donahue, Vic *2:* 93; *3:* 190; *9:* 44
Donald, Elizabeth *4:* 18
Donalty, Alison *149:* 195, 196, 197
Donato *85:* 59; *149:* 204; *191:* 19
Donato, Michael A. *200:* 143
Doney, Todd L.W. *87:* 12; *93:* 112; *98:* 135; *101:* 57; *104:* 40; *118:* 163; *135:* 162, 163; *151:* 18
Donna, Natalie *9:* 52
Donohue, Dorothy *95:* 2; *132:* 30; *176:* 54, 55; *178:* 77, 78, 79
Dooling, Michael *82:* 19; *105:* 55; *106:* 224; *125:* 135; *171:* 46; *172:* 12; *176:* 120; *197:* 89

Doran, Ben-Ami *128:* 189
Dore, Gustave *18:* 169, 172, 175; *19:* 93, 94, 95, 96, 97, 98,99, 100, 101, 102, 103, 104, 105; *23:* 188; *25:* 197, 199
Doremus, Robert *6:* 62; *13:* 90; *30:* 95, 96, 97; *38:* 97
Dorfman, Ronald *11:* 128
Doriau *86:* 59; *91:* 152
Dorman, Brandon *197:* 35
Dormer, Frank W. *200:* 55
Dorros, Arthur *78:* 42, 43; *91:* 28
Doruyter, Karel *165:* 105
dos Santos, Joyce Audy *57:* 187, 189
Doty, Roy *28:* 98; *31:* 32; *32:* 224; *46:* 157; *82:* 71; *142:* 7
Doucet, Bob *132:* 238; *169:* 159
Dougherty, Charles *16:* 204; *18:* 74
Doughty, Rebecca *177:* 174
Doughty, Thomas *118:* 31; *140:* 60
Douglas, Aaron *31:* 103
Douglas, Carole Nelson *73:* 48
Douglas, Goray *13:* 151
Dow, Brian *150:* 92
Dowd, Jason *132:* 51, 52; *164:* 244
Dowd, Vic *3:* 244; *10:* 97
Dowden, Anne Ophelia *7:* 70, 71; *13:* 120
Dowdy, Mrs. Regera *29:* 100
Downes, Belinda *180:* 29
Downing, Julie *60:* 140; *81:* 50; *86:* 200; *99:* 129
Doyle, Janet *56:* 31
Doyle, Richard *21:* 31, 32, 33; *23:* 231; *24:* 177; *31:* 87
Draper, Angie *43:* 84
Drath, Bill *26:* 34
Drawson, Blair *17:* 53; *126:* 65
Dray, Matt *177:* 47
Drescher, Henrik *105:* 60, 62, 63; *172:* 72
Drescher, Joan *30:* 100, 101; *35:* 245; *52:* 168; *137:* 52
Dressell, Peggy *186:* 41
Drew, Janet *201:* 177
Drew, Patricia *15:* 100
Dronzek, Laura *199:* 28, 29
Drummond, V.H. *6:* 70
Drury, Christian Potter *105:* 97; *186:* 224
Dubanevich, Arlene *56:* 44
Dubois, Claude K. *196:* 2
Dubois, Gerard *182:* 9
DuBurke, Randy *187:* 89
Ducak, Danilo *99:* 130; *108:* 214
Duchesne, Janet *6:* 162; *79:* 8
Duda, Jana *102:* 155
Dudash, Michael *32:* 122; *77:* 134; *82:* 149
Duer, Douglas *34:* 177
Duewell, Kristina *195:* 76
Duffy, Daniel Mark *76:* 37; *101:* 196; *108:* 147, 148
Duffy, Joseph *38:* 203
Duffy, Pat *28:* 153
Dugan, Karen *181:* 26
Dugin, Andrej *77:* 60
Dugina, Olga *77:* 60
Duke, Chris *8:* 195; *139:* 164
Duke, Kate *87:* 186; *90:* 78, 79, 80, 81; *192:* 21, 59, 60, 61, 63
Duke, Marion *165:* 87
Dulac, Edmund *19:* 108, 109, 110, 111, 112, 113, 114, 115, 117; *23:* 187; *25:* 152; *YABC 1:* 37; *2:* 147
Dulac, Jean *13:* 64
Dumas, Philippe *52:* 36, 37, 38, 39, 40, 41, 42, 43, 45; *119:* 40, 41, 42
Dunaway, Nancy *108:* 161
Dunbar, James *76:* 63
Dunbar, Polly *181:* 60, 61
Duncan, Beverly *72:* 92
Duncan, John *116:* 94
Dunn, H.T. *62:* 196
Dunn, Harvey *34:* 78, 79, 80, 81
Dunn, Iris *5:* 175

Dunn, Phoebe *5:* 175
Dunne, Jeanette *72:* 57, 173, 222
Dunnick, Regan *176:* 51; *178:* 83, 84
Dunnington, Tom *3:* 36; *18:* 281; *25:* 61; *31:* 159; *35:* 168; *48:* 195; *79:* 144; *82:* 230
Dunn-Ramsey, Marcy *117:* 131
Dunrea, Olivier *59:* 81; *118:* 53, 54; *124:* 43
Duntze, Dorothee *88:* 28; *160:* 76
Dupasquier, Philippe *86:* 75; *104:* 76; *151:* 63
DuQuette, Keith *90:* 83; *155:* 73, 74
Durand, Delphine *200:* 56
Durham, Sarah *192:* 248
Duroussy, Nathalie *146:* 150
Durrell, Julie *82:* 62; *94:* 62
Dutz *6:* 59
Duvoisin, Roger *2:* 95; *6:* 76, 77; *7:* 197; *28:* 125; *30:* 101, 102, 103, 104, 105, 107; *47:* 205; *84:* 254
Dyer, Dale *141:* 71
Dyer, Jane *75:* 219; *129:* 28; *147:* 49, 50, 51; *168:* 121; *190:* 4; *191:* 57, 59, 60
Dypold, Pat *15:* 37

E

E.V.B.
  See Boyle, Eleanor Vere (Gordon)
Eachus, Jennifer *29:* 74; *82:* 201; *164:* 153
Eadie, Bob *63:* 36
Eagle, Bruce *95:* 119
Eagle, Ellen *82:* 121; *89:* 3
Eagle, Jeremy *141:* 71
Eagle, Michael *11:* 86; *20:* 9; *23:* 18; *27:* 122; *28:* 57; *34:* 201; *44:* 189; *73:* 9; *78:* 235; *85:* 43
Earl-Bridges, Michele *159:* 128
Earle, Edwin *56:* 27
Earle, Olive L. *7:* 75
Earle, Vana *27:* 99
Earley, Lori *132:* 2; *186:* 4; *195:* 8
Early, Margaret *72:* 59
East, Stella *131:* 223
Eastman, P.D. *33:* 57
Easton, Reginald *29:* 181
Eaton, Tom *4:* 62; *6:* 64; *22:* 99; *24:* 124
Ebbeler, Jeffrey *193:* 62
Ebel, Alex *11:* 89
Eberbach, Andrea *192:* 115
Ebert, Len *9:* 191; *44:* 47
Echevarria, Abe *37:* 69
Echo Hawk, Bunky *187:* 192
Eckersley, Maureen *48:* 62
Eckert, Horst *72:* 62
Ede, Janina *33:* 59
Edens, Cooper *49:* 81, 82, 83, 84, 85; *112:* 58
Edens, John *109:* 115
Edgar, Sarah E. *41:* 97
Edgerton, Perky *195:* 144
Edliq, Emily S. *131:* 107
Edrien *11:* 53
Edwards, Freya *45:* 102
Edwards, George Wharton *31:* 155
Edwards, Gunvor *2:* 71; *25:* 47; *32:* 71; *54:* 106
Edwards, Jeanne *29:* 257
Edwards, Linda Strauss *21:* 134; *39:* 123; *49:* 88, 89
Edwards, Michelle *152:* 62, 63
Edwards, Wallace *170:* 55
Egan, Tim *155:* 76, 77, 78
Egge, David *102:* 71
Eggenhofer, Nicholas *2:* 81
Eggleton, Bob *74:* 40; *81:* 190, 191; *105:* 6; *121:* 183; *149:* 203; *166:* 215
Egielski, Richard *11:* 90; *16:* 208; *33:* 236; *38:* 35; *49:* 91, 92, 93, 95, 212, 213, 214, 216; *79:* 122; *106:* 67, 68, 69; *134:* 135; *144:* 244; *163:* 82, 84

Ehlert, Lois *35:* 97; *69:* 51; *112:* 7; *113:* 208; *128:* 63, 64, 65; *172:* 77, 79, 80
Ehrlich, Bettina *1:* 83
Eitan, Ora *160:* 165
Eichenberg, Fritz *1:* 79; *9:* 54; *19:* 248; *23:* 170; *24:* 200; *26:* 208; *50:* 67, 68, 69, 70, 71, 72, 73,74, 75, 77, 79, 80, 81; *60:* 165; *100:* 137; *YABC 1:* 104, 105; *2:* 213
Einsel, Naiad *10:* 35; *29:* 136
Einsel, Walter *10:* 37
Einzig, Susan *3:* 77; *43:* 78; *67:* 155; *129:* 154
Eisner, Will *165:* 82, 83
Eitzen, Allan *9:* 56; *12:* 212; *14:* 226; *21:* 194; *38:* 162; *76:* 218
Eldridge, H. *54:* 109
Eldridge, Harold *43:* 83
Elgaard, Greta *19:* 241
Elgin, Kathleen *9:* 188; *39:* 69
Ellacott, S.E. *19:* 118
Elliot, David *192:* 26
Elliott, Mark *93:* 69; *105:* 108; *107:* 123; *140:* 53; *165:* 189; *173:* 67; *195:* 95
Elliott, Sarah M. *14:* 58
Ellis, Dianne *130:* 208
Ellis, Jan Davey *88:* 50; *115:* 80
Ellis, Richard *130:* 47, 48
Ellison, Chris *196:* 66; *199:* 131
Ellison, Pauline *55:* 21
Elmer, Richard *78:* 5
Elmore, Larry *90:* 8
Elschner, Géraldine *183:* 38
Elwell, Peter *195:* 150
Elwell, Tristan *110:* 39; *121:* 182; *127:* 46; *137:* 144; *141:* 173; *151:* 236; *158:* 264; *167:* 119, 120, 121; *169:* 20; *190:* 12
Elzbieta *88:* 80, 81
Emberley, Ed *8:* 53; *70:* 53, 54; *146:* 65, 69, 70
Emberley, Michael *34:* 83; *80:* 72; *119:* 47, 48; *147:* 100; *158:* 115; *189:* 62, 64
Emerling, Dorothy *104:* 27
Emery, Leslie *49:* 187
Emmett, Bruce *49:* 147; *80:* 175; *101:* 206
Emry-Perrott, Jennifer *61:* 57
Emshwiller, Ed *174:* 45
Endle, Kate *191:* 167
Engel, Diana *70:* 57
Engle, Mort *38:* 64
Englebert, Victor *8:* 54
English, Mark *101:* 207
Enik, Ted *142:* 39
Enos, Randall *20:* 183
Enright, Maginel Wright *19:* 240, 243; *39:* 31, 35, 36
Enrique, Romeo *34:* 135
Ensor, Barbara *180:* 30
Epstein, Stephen *50:* 142, 148
Erdogan, Buket *174:* 179
Erdrich, Louise *141:* 62
Erhard, Walter *1:* 152
Erickson, Jim *196:* 190
Erickson, Phoebe *11:* 83; *59:* 85
Erikson, Mel *31:* 69
Eriksson, Eva *63:* 88, 90, 92, 93
Ering, Timothy Basil *131:* 100; *176:* 63, 64
Erlbruch, Wolf *181:* 66
Ernst, Lisa Campbell *47:* 147; *95:* 47; *154:* 46, 47, 48; *164:* 88
Esco, Jo *61:* 103
Escourido, Joseph *4:* 81
Escrivá, Viví *119:* 51; *181:* 36
Essakalli, Julie Klear *200:* 58
Este, Kirk *33:* 111
Estep, David *73:* 57
Estes, Eleanor *91:* 66
Estoril, Jean *32:* 27
Estrada, Pau *74:* 76
Estrada, Ric *5:* 52, 146; *13:* 174
Etchemendy, Teje *38:* 68
Etheredges, the *73:* 12
Etienne, Kirk-Albert *145:* 184

Ets, Marie Hall *2:* 102
Ettlinger, Doris *171:* 98; *186:* 106; *197:* 126
Eulalie *YABC 2:* 315
Evans, Greg *73:* 54, 55, 56; *143:* 40, 41
Evans, Katherine *5:* 64
Evans, Leslie *144:* 227
Evans, Shane W. *159:* 142; *160:* 190; *168:* 39; *188:* 88; *189:* 66, 67, 68
Everitt, Betsy *151:* 110
Ewart, Claire *76:* 69; *145:* 59, 60
Ewing, Carolyn *66:* 143; *79:* 52
Ewing, Juliana Horatia *16:* 92
Eyolfson, Norman *98:* 154

F

Fabian, Limbert *136:* 114
Facklam, Paul *132:* 62
Falconer, Ian *125:* 66; *179:* 59
Falconer, Pearl *34:* 23
Falkenstern, Lisa *70:* 34; *76:* 133; *78:* 171; *127:* 16; *191:* 151
Falls, C.B. *1:* 19; *38:* 71, 72, 73, 74
Falter, John *40:* 169, 170
Falwell, Cathryn *118:* 77; *137:* 185; *196:* 71, 72
Fancher, Lou *138:* 219; *141:* 64; *144:* 199; *177:* 51
Fanelli, Sara *89:* 63; *126:* 69
Faria, Rosana *150:* 143
Faricy, Patrick *185:* 182
Farmer, Andrew *49:* 102
Farmer, Peter *24:* 108; *38:* 75
Farnsworth, Bill *93:* 189; *116:* 147; *124:* 8; *135:* 52; *146:* 242, 243, 244; *182:* 176; *186:* 31, 83, 84, 85; *191:* 197
Farquharson, Alexander *46:* 75
Farrell, David *40:* 135
Farrell, Russell *196:* 38
Farris, David *74:* 42
Fasolino, Teresa *118:* 145
Fatigati, Evelyn *24:* 112
Fatus, Sophie *182:* 74; *190:* 218
Faul-Jansen, Regina *22:* 117
Faulkner, Jack *6:* 169
Faulkner, Matt *161:* 174; *167:* 75
Fava, Rita *2:* 29
Fax, Elton C. *1:* 101; *4:* 2; *12:* 77; *25:* 107
Fay *43:* 93
Fearnley, Jan *153:* 82, 83
Fearrington, Ann *146:* 80
Federspiel, Marian *33:* 51
Fedorov, Nickolai Ivanovich *110:* 102
Feelings, Tom *5:* 22; *8:* 56; *12:* 153; *16:* 105; *30:* 196; *49:* 37; *61:* 101; *69:* 56, 57; *93:* 74; *105:* 88
Fehr, Terrence *21:* 87
Feiffer, Jules *3:* 91; *8:* 58; *61:* 66, 67, 70, 74, 76,77, 78; *111:* 47, 48, 49, 50; *132:* 122; *157:* 62; *201:* 48, 49, 50
Feigeles, Neil *41:* 242
Feldman, Elyse *86:* 7
Feller, Gene *33:* 130
Fellows, Muriel H. *10:* 42
Felstead, Cathie *116:* 85
Felts, Shirley *33:* 71; *48:* 59
Fennell, Tracy *171:* 69
Fennelli, Maureen *38:* 181
Fenton, Carroll Lane *5:* 66; *21:* 39
Fenton, Mildred Adams *5:* 66; *21:* 39
Ferguson, Peter *177:* 30, 31; *181:* 154; *197:* 4; *199:* 40
Ferguson, Walter W. *34:* 86
Fernandes, Eugenie *77:* 67
Fernandes, Stanislaw *70:* 28
Fernandez, Fernando *77:* 57
Fernandez, Laura *77:* 153; *101:* 117; *131:* 222; *170:* 119; *175:* 182
Ferrari, Alex *188:* 121

Ferrington, Susan *172:* 22
Fetz, Ingrid *11:* 67; *12:* 52; *16:* 205; *17:* 59; *29:* 105; *30:* 108, 109; *32:* 149; *43:* 142; *56:* 29; *60:* 34; *85:* 48; *87:* 146
Fiammenghi, Gioia *9:* 66; *11:* 44; *12:* 206; *13:* 57, 59; *52:* 126, 129; *66:* 64; *85:* 83; *91:* 161; *166:* 169
Fiedler, Joseph Daniel *96:* 42; *113:* 173; *129:* 164; *146:* 17; *159:* 68; *162:* 104
Field, Rachel *15:* 113
Fielding, David *70:* 124
Fieser, Stephen *152:* 36
Fine, Howard *145:* 159; *159:* 64; *165:* 134; *174:* 129; *181:* 68
Fine, Peter K. *43:* 210
Finger, Helen *42:* 81
Fink, Sam *18:* 119
Finlay, Winifred *23:* 72
Finney, Pat *79:* 215
Fiore, Peter *99:* 196; *125:* 139; *144:* 225; *160:* 169; *180:* 72
Fiorentino, Al *3:* 240
Firehammer, Karla *174:* 202
Firmin, Charlotte *29:* 75; *48:* 70
Firmin, Peter *58:* 63, 64, 65, 67, 68, 70, 71
Firth, Barbara *81:* 208; *127:* 218; *179:* 62
Fischel, Lillian *40:* 204
Fischer, Hans *25:* 202
Fischer-Nagel, Andreas *56:* 50
Fischer-Nagel, Heiderose *56:* 50
Fisher, Carolyn *154:* 50
Fisher, Chris *79:* 62; *158:* 248; *188:* 195
Fisher, Cynthia *117:* 45; *137:* 118; *195:* 40
Fisher, Jeffrey *142:* 80
Fisher, Leonard Everett *3:* 6; *4:* 72, 86; *6:* 197; *9:* 59; *16:* 151, 153; *23:* 44; *27:* 134; *29:* 26; *34:* 87, 89, 90, 91, 93, 94, 95, 96; *40:* 206; *50:* 150; *60:* 158; *73:* 68, 70, 71, 72, 73; *176:* 71, 72, 73; *YABC 2:* 169
Fisher, Lois *20:* 62; *21:* 7
Fisher, Valorie *177:* 55
Fisk, Nicholas *25:* 112
Fitschen, Marilyn *2:* 20, 21; *20:* 48
Fitz-Maurice, Jeff *175:* 2
Fitzgerald, F.A. *15:* 116; *25:* 86, 87
Fitzhugh, Louise *1:* 94; *9:* 163; *45:* 75, 78
Fitzgerald, Joanne *157:* 153, 154; *198:* 34, 35
Fitzhugh, Susie *11:* 117
Fitzpatrick, Jim *109:* 130
Fitzpatrick, Marie-Louise *125:* 69, 70; *189:* 72, 73
Fitzsimmons, Arthur *14:* 128
Fix, Philippe *26:* 102
Flack, Marjorie *21:* 67; *100:* 93; *YABC 2:* 122
Flagg, James Montgomery *17:* 227
Flavin, Teresa *132:* 115; *186:* 119
Flax, Zeona *2:* 245
Fleetwood, Tony *171:* 51
Fleishman, Seymour *14:* 232; *24:* 87
Fleming, Denise *71:* 179; *81:* 58; *126:* 71, 72, 73; *173:* 52, 53
Fleming, Guy *18:* 41
Flesher, Vivienne *85:* 55
Fletcher, Claire *80:* 106; *157:* 159
Flint, Russ *74:* 80
Floate, Helen *111:* 163
Floca, Brian *155:* 88, 89; *190:* 10, 66, 67
Floethe, Richard *3:* 131; *4:* 90
Floherty, John J., Jr. *5:* 68
Flook, Helen *160:* 81
Flora, James *1:* 96; *30:* 111, 112
Florczak, Robert *166:* 51
Florian, Douglas *19:* 122; *83:* 64, 65; *125:* 71, 72, 74, 76; *128:* 130; *177:* 58, 60
Flory, Jane *22:* 111
Flower, Renee *125:* 109
Floyd, Gareth *1:* 74; *17:* 245; *48:* 63; *62:* 35,36, 37, 39, 40, 41; *74:* 245; *79:* 56
Fluchere, Henri A. *40:* 79
Flynn, Alice *183:* 2
Flynn, Barbara *7:* 31; *9:* 70

Fogarty, Thomas *15:* 89
Foley, Greg *190:* 69
Folger, Joseph *9:* 100
Folkard, Charles *22:* 132; *29:* 128, 257, 258
Foott, Jeff *42:* 202
Forberg, Ati *12:* 71, 205; *14:* 1; *22:* 113; *26:* 22; *48:* 64, 65
Ford, George *24:* 120; *31:* 70, 177; *58:* 126; *81:* 103; *107:* 91; *136:* 100; *194:* 47
Ford, Gilbert *199:* 10
Ford, H.J. *16:* 185, 186
Ford, Jason *174:* 119
Ford, Pamela Baldwin *27:* 104
Fordham, John *168:* 160, 161
Foreman, Michael *2:* 110, 111; *67:* 99; *73:* 78, 79, 80,81, 82; *93:* 146; *135:* 55, 56, 57; *184:* 58, 59
Forrester, Victoria *40:* 83
Forsey, Chris *140:* 210
Fortnum, Peggy *6:* 29; *20:* 179; *24:* 211; *26:* 76, 77, 78; *39:* 78; *58:* 19, 21, 23, 27; *YABC 1:* 148
Fortune, Eric *191:* 52
Foster, Brad W. *34:* 99
Foster, Genevieve *2:* 112
Foster, Gerald L. *7:* 78; *198:* 40
Foster, Jon *146:* 18; *198:* 7
Foster, Laura Louise *6:* 79
Foster, Marian Curtis *23:* 74; *40:* 42
Foster, Sally *58:* 73, 74
Foucher, Adele *47:* 118
Foust, Mitch *168:* 50
Fowler, Jim *184:* 190
Fowler, Mel *36:* 127
Fowler, Richard *87:* 219
Fowles, Selley *165:* 127
Fox, Charles Phillip *12:* 84
Fox, Christyan *188:* 36
Fox, Jim *6:* 187
Fox-Davies, Sarah *76:* 150; *182:* 63; *199:* 42, 43
Frace, Charles *15:* 118
Frailey, Joy *72:* 108
Frame, Paul *2:* 45, 145; *9:* 153; *10:* 124; *21:* 71; *23:* 62; *24:* 123; *27:* 106; *31:* 48; *32:* 159; *34:* 195; *38:* 136; *42:* 55; *44:* 139; *60:* 39, 40, 41, 42, 43, 44, 46; *73:* 183
Frampton, David *85:* 72; *102:* 33; *139:* 182; *152:* 37; *189:* 171
Francis, Guy *198:* 164
Francois, Andre *25:* 117
Francoise
   See Seignobosc, Françoise
Frank, Lola Edick *2:* 199
Frank, Mary *4:* 54; *34:* 100
Franke, Phil *45:* 91
Frankel, Alona *66:* 70
Frankel, Julie *40:* 84, 85, 202
Frankenberg, Robert *22:* 116; *30:* 50; *38:* 92, 94, 95; *68:* 111
Frankfeldt, Gwen *84:* 223; *110:* 92
Frankland, David *169:* 137; *182:* 164; *201:* 159
Franklin, Ashton *165:* 144
Franklin, John *24:* 22
Franson, Leanne R. *111:* 57, 58; *151:* 7
Frascino, Edward *9:* 133; *29:* 229; *33:* 190; *48:* 80, 81, 82, 83, 84, 85, 86
Frasconi, Antonio *6:* 80; *27:* 208; *53:* 41, 43, 45, 47,48; *68:* 145; *73:* 226; *131:* 68
Fraser, Betty *2:* 212; *6:* 185; *8:* 103; *31:* 72,73; *43:* 136; *111:* 76
Fraser, Eric *38:* 78; *41:* 149, 151
Fraser, F.A. *22:* 234
Fraser, James *171:* 68
Fraser, Mary Ann *137:* 63
Frasier, Debra *69:* 60; *112:* 67; *182:* 81, 82, 83
Fraustino, Lisa Rowe *146:* 87
Frazee, Marla *72:* 98; *105:* 79, 80; *151:* 67, 68; *164:* 165; *171:* 190, 191; *187:* 53, 54,55, 56, 143

Frazetta, Frank *41:* 72; *58:* 77, 78, 79, 80, 81, 82, 83
Frazier, Craig *177:* 63
Freas, John *25:* 207
Fredrickson, Mark *103:* 33
Freeland, Michael J. *118:* 115
Freeman, Don *2:* 15; *13:* 249; *17:* 62, 63, 65, 67, 68; *18:* 243; *20:* 195; *23:* 213, 217; *32:* 155; *55:* 129
Freeman, Irving *67:* 150
Freeman, Laura *144:* 111; *200:* 62, 63
Freeman, Pietri *140:* 223
Freeman, Tom *167:* 118
Freeman, Tor *164:* 93
Fregosi, Claudia *24:* 117
Fremaux, Charlotte Murray *138:* 29; *141:* 95
French, Fiona *6:* 82, 83; *75:* 61; *109:* 170; *132:* 79, 80, 81, 82
French, Martin *163:* 4
Frendak, Rodney *126:* 97, 98
Freschet, Gina *175:* 73
Freynet, Gilbert *72:* 221
Friedman, Judith *43:* 197; *131:* 221
Friedman, Marvin *19:* 59; *42:* 86
Frinta, Dagmar *36:* 42
Frith, Michael K. *15:* 138; *18:* 120
Fritz, Ronald *46:* 73; *82:* 124
Fromm, Lilo *29:* 85; *40:* 197
Frost, A.B. *17:* 6, 7; *19:* 123, 124, 125, 126, 127, 128, 129,130; *100:* 119; *YABC 1:* 156, 157, 160; *2:* 107
Frost, Helen *183:* 51
Frost, Kristi *118:* 113
Frost, Michael *151:* 209
Froud, Brian *150:* 82, 83
Froud, Wendy *151:* 237
Fry, Guy *2:* 224
Fry, Rosalie *3:* 72; *YABC 2:* 180, 181
Fry, Rosalind *21:* 153, 168
Fryer, Elmer *34:* 115
Fuchs, Bernie *110:* 10; *162:* 46
Fuchs, Erich *6:* 84
Fuchshuber, Annegert *43:* 96
Fufuka, Mahiri *32:* 146
Fuge, Charles *144:* 91, 93
Fujikawa, Gyo *39:* 75, 76; *76:* 72, 73, 74
Fulford, Deborah *23:* 159
Fuller, Margaret *25:* 189
Fulweiler, John *93:* 99
Funai, Mamoru *38:* 105
Funfhausen, Christian *196:* 30
Funk, Tom *7:* 17, 19
Furchgott, Terry *29:* 86
Furness, William Henry, Jr. *94:* 18
Furukawa, Mel *25:* 42
Fusari, Erika *164:* 227

G

Gaadt, David *78:* 212; *121:* 166; *201:* 171
Gaadt, George *71:* 9
Gaber, Susan *99:* 33; *115:* 57, 58; *164:* 195; *169:* 61, 62, 63; *185:* 50, 51; *188:* 124
Gaberell, J. *19:* 236
Gable, Brian *195:* 68, 69
Gabler, Mirko *99:* 71; *195:* 32
Gackenbach, Dick *19:* 168; *41:* 81; *48:* 89, 90, 91, 92,93, 94; *54:* 105; *79:* 75, 76, 77
Gad, Victor *87:* 161
Gaetano, Nicholas *23:* 209
Gaffney-Kessell, Walter *94:* 219; *174:* 188
Gag, Flavia *17:* 49, 52
Gag, Wanda *100:* 101, 102; *YABC 1:* 135, 137, 138, 141, 143
Gagnon, Cecile *11:* 77; *58:* 87
Gaillard, Jason *200:* 69
Gal, Laszlo *14:* 127; *52:* 54, 55, 56; *65:* 142; *68:* 150; *81:* 185; *96:* 104, 105
Galazinski, Tom *55:* 13

Galbraith, Ben *200:* 70
Galdone, Paul *1:* 156, 181, 206; *2:* 40, 241; *3:* 42,144; *4:* 141; *10:* 109, 158; *11:* 21; *12:* 118, 210; *14:* 12; *16:* 36, 37; *17:* 70, 71, 72, 73, 74; *18:* 111, 230; *19:* 183; *21:* 154; *22:* 150, 245; *33:* 126; *39:* 136, 137; *42:* 57; *51:* 169; *55:* 110; *66:* 80, 82, 139; *72:* 73; *100:* 84
Gale, Cathy *140:* 22; *143:* 52
Gall, Chris *176:* 79, 80
Gallagher, Jack *187:* 100
Gallagher, S. Saelig *105:* 154; *198:* 91
Gallagher, Sears *20:* 112
Galloway, Ewing *51:* 154
Galouchka, Annouchka Gravel *95:* 55; *182:* 40
Galster, Robert *1:* 66
Galsworthy, Gay John *35:* 232
Galvez, Daniel *125:* 182
Gamble, Kim *112:* 64, 65; *124:* 77; *183:* 40, 42, 43, 56, 57; *187:* 170
Gammell, Stephen *7:* 48; *13:* 149; *29:* 82; *33:* 209; *41:* 88; *50:* 185, 186, 187; *53:* 51, 52, 53, 54, 55, 56,57, 58; *54:* 24, 25; *56:* 147, 148, 150; *57:* 27, 66; *81:* 62, 63; *87:* 88; *89:* 10; *106:* 223; *126:* 2; *128:* 71, 73, 74, 77; *154:* 34
Gamper, Ruth *84:* 198
Gampert, John *58:* 94
Ganly, Helen *56:* 56
Gannett, Ruth Chrisman *3:* 74; *18:* 254; *33:* 77, 78
Gantschev, Ivan *45:* 32
Garafano, Marie *73:* 33
Garbot, Dave *131:* 106
Garbutt, Bernard *23:* 68
Garcia *37:* 71
Garcia, Manuel *74:* 145
Garcia-Franco, Rebecca *173:* 46
Gardiner, Lindsey *178:* 128; *186:* 137
Gardner, Earle *45:* 167
Gardner, Joan *40:* 87
Gardner, Joel *40:* 87, 92
Gardner, John *40:* 87
Gardner, Lucy *40:* 87
Gardner, Richard
    See Cummings, Richard
Gardner, Sally *171:* 177; *177:* 66, 68
Gargiulo, Frank *84:* 158
Garland, Michael *36:* 29; *38:* 83; *44:* 168; *48:* 78, 221, 222; *49:* 161; *60:* 139; *71:* 6, 11; *72:* 229; *74:* 142; *89:* 187; *93:* 183; *104:* 110; *131:* 55; *139:* 209; *168:* 56
Garland, Peggy *60:* 139
Garland, Sarah *62:* 45; *135:* 67, 68; *171:* 118
Garn, Aimee *75:* 47
Garner, Joan *128:* 170
Garneray, Ambroise Louis *59:* 140
Garnett, Eve *3:* 75
Garnett, Gary *39:* 184
Garns, Allen *80:* 125; *84:* 39; *165:* 231
Garófoli, Viviana *186:* 123
Garraty, Gail *4:* 142; *52:* 106
Garrett, Agnes *46:* 110; *47:* 157
Garrett, Edmund H. *20:* 29
Garrett, Tom *107:* 194
Garrick, Jacqueline *67:* 42, 43; *77:* 94
Garrison, Barbara *19:* 133; *104:* 146; *109:* 87
Garro, Mark *108:* 131; *128:* 210
Garvey, Robert *98:* 222
Garza, Carmen Lomas *80:* 211; *182:* 86
Garza, Xavier *184:* 64
Gates, Frieda *26:* 80
Gaughan, Jack *26:* 79; *43:* 185
Gaver, Becky *20:* 61
Gawing, Toby *72:* 52
Gay, Marie-Louise *68:* 76, 77, 78; *102:* 136; *126:* 76, 78, 81, 83; *127:* 55, 56; *179:* 70, 72, 73, 74
Gay, Zhenya *19:* 135, 136
Gaydos, Tim *62:* 201
Gazsi, Ed *80:* 48

Gazso, Gabriel *73:* 85
Geary, Clifford N. *1:* 122; *9:* 104; *51:* 74
Geary, Rick *142:* 44, 46
Gee, Frank *33:* 26
Geehan, Wayne *157:* 181
Geer, Charles *1:* 91; *3:* 179; *4:* 201; *6:* 168; *7:* 96; *9:* 58; *10:* 72; *12:* 127; *39:* 156,157, 158, 159, 160; *42:* 88, 89, 90, 91; *55:* 111, 116
Geerinck, Manuel *173:* 128
Gehm, Charlie *36:* 65; *57:* 117; *62:* 60, 138
Geis, Alissa Imre *189:* 77
Geisel, Theodor Seuss *1:* 104, 105, 106; *28:* 108, 109, 110,111, 112, 113; *75:* 67, 68, 69, 70, 71; *89:* 127, 128; *100:* 106, 107, 108
Geisert, Arthur *92:* 67, 68; *133:* 72, 73, 74; *165:* 97, 98; *171:* 64, 65
Geldart, William *15:* 121; *21:* 202
Genia *4:* 84
Gentry, Cyrille R. *12:* 66
Genzo, John Paul *136:* 74
George, Jean *2:* 113
George, Lindsay Barrett *95:* 57; *155:* 97, 98
Geraghty, Paul *130:* 60, 61
Gerard, Jean Ignace *45:* 80
Gerard, Rolf *27:* 147, 150
Gerber, Mark *61:* 105
Gerber, Mary Jane *112:* 124; *171:* 56
Gerber, Stephanie *71:* 195
Gerdstein, Mordecai *169:* 105
Gergely, Tibor *54:* 15, 16
Geritz, Franz *17:* 135
Gerlach, Geff *42:* 58
Gerrard, Roy *47:* 78; *90:* 96, 97, 98, 99
Gerritsen, Paula *177:* 69
Gershinowitz, George *36:* 27
Gerstein, Mordicai *31:* 117; *47:* 80, 81, 82, 83, 84, 85, 86; *51:* 173; *69:* 134; *107:* 122; *142:* 49, 52; *165:* 209; *176:* 119; *178:* 95, 97, 99
Gervase *12:* 27
Geter, Tyrone *146:* 249; *150:* 86
Getz, Arthur *32:* 148
Gévry, Claudine *188:* 47
Gewirtz, Bina *61:* 81
Giancola, Donato *95:* 146; *164:* 226
Gibbons, Gail *23:* 78; *72:* 77, 78, 79; *82:* 182; *104:* 65; *160:* 99, 100; *201:* 59, 60, 62
Gibbs, Tony *40:* 95
Gibran, Kahlil *32:* 116
Gider, Iskender *81:* 193
Giebfried, Rosemary *170:* 135
Giesen, Rosemary *34:* 192, 193
Giffard, Hannah *83:* 70
Giguere, George *20:* 111
Gilbert, John *19:* 184; *54:* 115; *YABC 2:* 287
Gilbert, W.S. *36:* 83, 85, 96
Gilbert, Yvonne *116:* 70; *128:* 84; *149:* 119; *185:* 69; *192:* 25; *195:* 81
Gilchrist, Jan Spivey *72:* 82, 83, 84, 85, 87; *77:* 90; *105:* 89, 91; *130:* 63, 64; *155:* 105, 107; *182:* 67
Giles, Will *41:* 218
Gili, Phillida *70:* 73
Gill, Margery *4:* 57; *7:* 7; *22:* 122; *25:* 166; *26:* 146, 147
Gillen, Denver *28:* 216
Gillette, Henry J. *23:* 237
Gilliam, Stan *39:* 64, 81
Gillies, Chuck *62:* 31
Gilliland, Jillian *87:* 58
Gillman, Alec *98:* 105
Gilman, Esther *15:* 124
Gilman, Phoebe *104:* 70, 71
Ginsberg, Sari *111:* 184
Ginsburg, Max *62:* 59; *68:* 194 Girard, Roge *161:* 30
Girouard, Patrick *155:* 100
Giovanopoulos, Paul *7:* 104; *60:* 36
Giovine, Sergio *79:* 12; *93:* 118; *139:* 118
Githens, Elizabeth M. *5:* 47
Gladden, Scott *99:* 108; *103:* 160; *193:* 46, 47
Gladstone, Gary *12:* 89; *13:* 190

Gladstone, Lise *15:* 273
Glanzman, Louis S. *2:* 177; *3:* 182; *36:* 97, 98; *38:* 120, 122; *52:* 141, 144; *71:* 191; *91:* 54, 56
Glaser, Byron *154:* 59, 60
Glaser, Milton *3:* 5; *5:* 156; *11:* 107; *30:* 26; *36:* 112; *54:* 141; *151:* 70
Glass, Andrew *36:* 38; *44:* 133; *48:* 205; *65:* 3; *68:* 43, 45; *90:* 104, 105; *150:* 89
Glass, Marvin *9:* 174
Glasser, Judy *41:* 156; *56:* 140; *69:* 79; *72:* 101
Glattauer, Ned *5:* 84; *13:* 224; *14:* 26
Glauber, Uta *17:* 76
Gleeson, J.M. *YABC 2:* 207
Glegg, Creina *36:* 100
Glienke, Amelie *63:* 150
Gliewe, Unada *3:* 78, 79; *21:* 73; *30:* 220
Gliori, Debi *72:* 91; *138:* 82; *162:* 37; *189:* 79, 81, 82
Glovach, Linda *7:* 105
Gobbato, Imero *3:* 180, 181; *6:* 213; *7:* 58; *9:* 150; *18:* 39; *21:* 167; *39:* 82, 83; *41:* 137, 251; *59:* 177
Goble, Paul *25:* 121; *26:* 86; *33:* 65; *69:* 68, 69; *131:* 79, 80
Goble, Warwick *46:* 78, 79; *194:* 143
Godal, Eric *36:* 93
Godkin, Celia *145:* 84, 86
Godfrey, Michael *17:* 279
Godon, Ingrid *166:* 163; *186:* 99
Goembel, Ponder *42:* 124
Goffe, Toni *61:* 83, 84, 85; *89:* 11; *90:* 124; *178:* 118
Goffstein, M.B. *8:* 71; *70:* 75, 76, 77
Golbin, Andre *15:* 125
Gold, Robert *166:* 151, 152
Goldfeder, Cheryl *11:* 191
Goldfinger, Jennifer P. *185:* 71
Goldsborough, June *5:* 154, 155; *8:* 92, *14:* 226; *19:* 139; *54:* 165
Goldsmith, Robert *110:* 77
Goldstein, Barry *198:* 147
Goldstein, Leslie *5:* 8; *6:* 60; *10:* 106
Goldstein, Nathan *1:* 175; *2:* 79; *11:* 41, 232; *16:* 55
Goldstrom, Robert *98:* 36; *145:* 51, 52
Golembe, Carla *79:* 80, 81; *136:* 91; *144:* 113; *193:* 53
Golin, Carlo *74:* 112
Gomez, Elena *188:* 122; *191:* 72
Gomez, Elizabeth *127:* 70; *133:* 76
Gomi, Taro *64:* 102; *103:* 74, 76
Gon, Adriano *101:* 112
Gonsalve, Ron *178:* 213
Gonzalez, Maya Christina *104:* 3; *136:* 92
Goodall, John S. *4:* 92, 93; *10:* 132; *66:* 92, 93; *YABC 1:* 198
Goode, Diane *15:* 126; *50:* 183; *52:* 114, 115; *76:* 195; *84:* 94; *99:* 141; *114:* 76, 77, 78; *170:* 99, 101
Goodelman, Aaron *40:* 203
Goodenow, Earle *40:* 97
Goodfellow, Peter *62:* 95; *94:* 202
Goodman, Joan Elizabeth *50:* 86
Goodman, Vivienne *82:* 251; *146:* 181, 182
Goodnow, Patti *117:* 33
Goodwin, Harold *13:* 74
Goodwin, Philip R. *18:* 206
Goor, Nancy *39:* 85, 86
Goor, Ron *39:* 85, 86
Goossens, Philippe *195:* 71
Gorbachev, Valeri *89:* 96; *112:* 97; *143:* 63, 64; *184:* 66, 67, 68, 101
Gordon, Gwen *12:* 151
Gordon, Margaret *4:* 147; *5:* 48, 49; *9:* 79
Gordon, Mike *101:* 62, 63, 64
Gordon, Russell *136:* 204; *137:* 214
Gordon, Walter *138:* 9

Gore, Leonid *89:* 51; *94:* 74; *136:* 8; *158:* 117; *166:* 136; *168:* 36; *170:* 107; *181:* 94; *185:* 73
Gorecka-Egan, Erica *18:* 35
Gorey, Edward *1:* 60, 61; *13:* 169; *18:* 192; *20:* 201; *29:* 90, 91, 92, 93, 94, 95, 96, 97, 98, 99, 100; *30:* 129; *32:* 90; *34:* 200, 65: 48; *68:* 24, 25; *69:* 79; *70:* 80, 82, 83, 84; *85:* 136; *127:* 62
Gorsline, Douglas *1:* 98; *6:* 13; *11:* 113; *13:* 104; *15:* 14; *28:* 117, 118; *YABC 1:* 15
Gorton, Julia *108:* 94; *178:* 81, 82
Gosfield, Josh *118:* 165, 166; *149:* 67
Gosner, Kenneth *5:* 135
Gosney, Joy *167:* 142
Gotlieb, Jules *6:* 127
Goto, Scott *115:* 86; *136:* 69
Gott, Barry *197:* 95
Gottlieb, Dale *67:* 162; *107:* 16; *149:* 6
Goudey, Ray *97:* 86
Gough, Alan *91:* 57
Gough, Philip *23:* 47; *45:* 90
Gould, Chester *49:* 112, 113, 114, 116, 117, 118
Gould, Jason *151:* 232
Gourbault, Martine *177:* 159
Govern, Elaine R. *26:* 94
Gower, Teri *102:* 184
Gowing, Toby *60:* 25; *63:* 33; *78:* 70, 252; *83:* 228; *86:* 187; *93:* 145; *108:* 133; *110:* 217; *184:* 125
Grabianski *20:* 144
Grabianski, Janusz *39:* 92, 93, 94, 95
Graboff, Abner *35:* 103, 104
Graef, Renee *61:* 188; *72:* 207
Grafe, Max *156:* 173; *178:* 237; *192:* 240; *198:* 51
Graham, A.B. *11:* 61
Graham, Bob *101:* 66, 67, 68; *151:* 74, 75; *187:* 65, 67, 68, 70
Graham, Georgia *188:* 3; *190:* 75
Graham, L. *7:* 108
Graham, Margaret Bloy *11:* 120; *18:* 305, 307
Graham, Mark *88:* 208; *159:* 153; *182:* 3
Grahame-Johnstone, Janet *13:* 61
Grahame-Johnstone, Anne *13:* 61
Grainger, Sam *42:* 95
Gralley, Jean *166:* 86
Gramatky, Hardie *1:* 107; *30:* 116, 119, 120, 122, 123
Gran, Julie *168:* 118
Granahan, Julie *84:* 84
GrandPré, Mary *84:* 131; *109:* 199; *118:* 76; *180:* 65; *184:* 70, 71, 180; *192:* 87
Grandström, Brita *176:* 139
Grandville, J.J. *45:* 81, 82, 83, 84, 85, 86, 87, 88; *47:* 125; *64:* 10
Granger, Paul *39:* 153
Granström, Brita *162:* 35; *167:* 46
Grant, (Alice) Leigh *10:* 52; *15:* 131; *20:* 20; *26:* 119; *48:* 202
Grant, Gordon *17:* 230, 234; *25:* 123, 124, 125, 126; *52:* 69; *YABC 1:* 164
Grant, Melvyn *159:* 186, 187; *170:* 48, 49
Grant, Renee *77:* 40
Grant, Shirley *109:* 45
Graves, Elizabeth *45:* 101
Graves, Keith *167:* 89; *191:* 74
Gray, Harold *33:* 87, 88
Gray, Les *82:* 76; *83:* 232
Gray, Reginald *6:* 69
Greco, Tony *184:* 6
Greder, Armin *76:* 235
Green, Ann Canevari *62:* 48
Green, Eileen *6:* 97
Green, Elizabeth Shippen *139:* 109
Green, Jonathan *86:* 135; *105:* 109
Green, Ken *111:* 68
Green, Michael *32:* 216
Green, Robina *87:* 138
Green, Jonathan *157:* 105

Greene, Jeffrey *117:* 93
Greenaway, Kate *17:* 275; *24:* 180; *26:* 107; *41:* 222, 232; *100:* 115, 116; *YABC 1:* 88, 89; *2:* 131, 133, 136,138, 139, 141
Greenberg, Melanie Hope *72:* 93; *80:* 125; *101:* 174; *133:* 180; *186:* 189
Greenseid, Diane *178:* 106, 107
Greenstein, Elaine *150:* 100
Greenwald, Sheila *1:* 34; *3:* 99; *8:* 72
Greger, Carol *76:* 86
Gregorian, Joyce Ballou *30:* 125
Gregory, Emilian *177:* 146; *187:* 10
Gregory, Fran *130:* 4; *140:* 93
Gregory, Frank M. *29:* 107
Greiffenhagen, Maurice *16:* 137; *27:* 57; *YABC 2:* 288
Greiner, Robert *6:* 86
Gretter, J. Clemens *31:* 134
Gretz, Susanna *7:* 114
Gretzer, John *1:* 54; *3:* 26; *4:* 162; *7:* 125; *16:* 247; *18:* 117; *28:* 66; *30:* 85, 211; *33:* 235; *56:* 16
Grey, Mini *166:* 90; *192:* 71
Grey Owl *24:* 41
Gri *25:* 90
Grieder, Walter *9:* 84
Griesbach/Martucci *59:* 3
Grifalconi, Ann *2:* 126; *3:* 248; *11:* 18; *13:* 182; *46:* 38; *50:* 145; *66:* 99, 100, 101, 104, 106; *69:* 38; *70:* 64; *87:* 128; *90:* 53; *93:* 49; *128:* 48; *133:* 79, 81
Griffin, Gillett Good *26:* 96
Griffin, James *30:* 166
Griffin, John Howard *59:* 186
Griffin, Rachel *131:* 23
Griffith, Gershom *94:* 214
Griffiths, Dave *29:* 76
Griffiths, Dean *168:* 180; *169:* 182
Grimly, Gris *186:* 102; *192:* 112; *197:* 86
Grimsdell, Jeremy *83:* 75
Grimwood, Brian *82:* 89
Gringhuis, Dirk *6:* 98; *9:* 196
Gripe, Harald *2:* 127; *74:* 98
Grisha *3:* 71
Grobler, Piet *201:* 100
Grohmann, Susan *84:* 97
Gropper, William *27:* 93; *37:* 193
Gros *60:* 199
Grose, Helen Mason *YABC 1:* 260; *2:* 150
Grossman, Nancy *24:* 130; *29:* 101
Grossman, Robert *11:* 124; *46:* 39
Groth, John *15:* 79; *21:* 53, 54; *83:* 230
Grover, Lorie Ann *168:* 59
Grubb, Lisa *160:* 116
Grue, Lisa *187:* 193
Gruelle, Johnny *35:* 107
Gschwind, William *11:* 72
Guarnaccia, Steven *201:* 170, 173
Guay-Mitchell, Rebecca *110:* 95, 96; *135:* 240; *180:* 76; *181:* 71, 73
Guback, Georgia *88:* 102
Guerguerion, Claudine *105:* 73
Guevara, Susan *97:* 87; *167:* 49; *194:* 54
Guggenheim, Hans *2:* 10; *3:* 37; *8:* 136
Guhathaakurta, Ajanta *183:* 199
Guida, Lisa Chauncy *172:* 188
Guilbeau, Honore *22:* 69
Guillette, Joseph *137:* 37
Guisewite, Cathy *57:* 52, 53, 54, 56, 57
Gukova, Julia *95:* 104; *154:* 103; *168:* 195
Gundersheimer, Karen *35:* 240; *82:* 100
Gunderson, Nick *57:* 120
Gunnella *192:* 144
Gurney, James *76:* 97; *86:* 32
Gurney, John Steven *75:* 39, 82; *110:* 175; *143:* 67, 68; *169:* 172
Gusman, Annie *38:* 62
Gustafson, Scott *34:* 111; *43:* 40
Gustavson, Adam *104:* 10; *171:* 183; *176:* 87; *197:* 94
Guthridge, Bettina *108:* 79; *186:* 92

Guthrie, R. Dale *64:* 143
Guthrie, Robin *20:* 122
Gutierrez, Akemi *172:* 87
Gutierrez, Alan *136:* 31, 32
Gutierrez, Rudy *97:* 162
Gutmann, Bessie Pease *73:* 93, 94
Gwynne, Fred *41:* 94, 95
Gyberg, Bo-Erik *38:* 131

H

Haas, Irene *17:* 77; *87:* 46; *96:* 117
Hack, Konrad *51:* 127
Hader, Berta H. *16:* 126
Hader, Elmer S. *16:* 126
Haeffele, Deborah *76:* 99
Haemer, Alan *62:* 109
Hafner, Marylin *22:* 196, 216; *24:* 44; *30:* 51;
    35: 95; *51:* 25, 160, 164; *86:* 16; *105:* 196;
    121: 93, 94; *149:* 208, 209; *179:* 82, 83, 84,
    115; *190:* 200; *201:* 29
Hagerty, Sean *62:* 181
Hague, Michael *32:* 128; *48:* 98, 99, 100, 101,
    103, 105,106, 107, 108, 109, 110; *49:* 121;
    51: 105; *64:* 14, 15; *79:* 134; *80:* 91, 92; *83:*
    135; *100:* 241; *102:* 29; *129:* 101, 103, 104;
    185: 80, 81, 82
Hair, Jonathan *115:* 135
Halas, John *29:* 41, 47, 48
Haldane, Roger *13:* 76; *14:* 202
Hale, Christy *79:* 124; *84:* 200; *114:* 201; *128:*
    2, 3; *146:* 203; *158:* 243; *167:* 99; *179:* 87
Hale, Irina *26:* 97
Hale, James Graham *88:* 207
Hale, Kathleen *17:* 79; *66:* 114, 116, 118
Haley, Gail E. *43:* 102, 103, 104, 105; *78:* 65,
    67; *136:* 106, 107
Hall, Amanda *96:* 110
Hall, Chuck *30:* 189
Hall, Douglas *15:* 184; *43:* 106, 107; *86:* 100;
    87: 82; *129:* 72
Hall, H. Tom *1:* 227; *30:* 210
Hall, Melanie *116:* 48, 49; *169:* 77, 78
Hall, Sydney P. *31:* 89
Hall, Tim *164:* 196
Hall, Vicki *20:* 24
Hallinan, P.K. *39:* 98
Hallman, Tom *98:* 166
Hally, Greg *101:* 200; *151:* 224
Halperin, Wendy Anderson *96:* 151; *125:* 96,
    97, 98, 99; *139:* 22; *140:* 84; *200:* 77, 78
Halpern, Joan *10:* 25
Halpern, Shari *174:* 172
Halsey, Megan *96:* 172; *114:* 185; *180:* 8; *185:*
    85
Halstead, Virginia *125:* 105
Halverson, Janet *49:* 38, 42, 44
Hallensleben, Georg *134:* 5, 6; *172:* 17
Hamanaka, Sheila *71:* 100
Hamann, Brad *78:* 151
Hamann, Sigune *104:* 115
Hamberger, John *6:* 8; *8:* 32; *14:* 79; *34:* 136;
    88: 78
Hamil, Tom *14:* 80; *43:* 163
Hamilton, Bill and Associates *26:* 215
Hamilton, Helen S. *2:* 238
Hamilton, J. *19:* 83, 85, 87
Hamilton, Laurie *116:* 210
Hamilton, Todd Cameron *84:* 15
Hamlin, Janet *97:* 136; *124:* 90; *137:* 157;
    182: 117
Hamlin, Louise *71:* 135
Hammond, Chris *21:* 37
Hammond, Elizabeth *5:* 36, 203
Hampshire, Michael *5:* 187; *7:* 110, 111; *48:*
    150; *51:* 129
Hampson, Denman *10:* 155; *15:* 130
Hampton, Blake *41:* 244
Handford, Martin *64:* 105, 106, 107, 109

Handforth, Thomas *42:* 100, 101, 102, 103,
    104, 105, 107
Handville, Robert *1:* 89; *38:* 76; *45:* 108, 109
Hane, Roger *17:* 239; *44:* 54
Haney, Elizabeth Mathieu *34:* 84
Hanke, Ted *71:* 10
Hankinson, Phil *181:* 164
Hanley, Catherine *8:* 161
Hann, Jacquie *19:* 144
Hanna, Cheryl *91:* 133
Hanna, Wayne A. *67:* 145
Hannon, Mark *38:* 37
Hansen, Gaby *159:* 11; *186:* 25
Hansen, Mia *149:* 76
Hanson, Joan *8:* 76; *11:* 139
Hanson, Peter E. *52:* 47; *54:* 99, 100; *73:* 21;
    84: 79; *116:* 144
Hansson, Gunilla *64:* 111, 112
Hardcastle, Nick *121:* 82; *175:* 185
Hardy, David A. *9:* 96; *119:* 74
Hardy, Paul *YABC 2:* 245 *Haring, Keith 145:*
    65
Harlan, Jerry *3:* 96
Harlin, Greg *89:* 194; *103:* 82; *118:* 161; *121:*
    167; *182:* 76; *201:* 172
Harness, Cheryl *106:* 80; *131:* 87; *178:* 111;
    200: 39
Harnischfeger *18:* 121
Harper, Arthur *YABC 2:* 121
Harper, Betty *126:* 90
Harper, Jamie *174:* 71
Harper, Piers *79:* 27; *105:* 102; *161:* 67
Harrington, Glenn *82:* 18; *94:* 66, 68; *185:*
    118
Harrington, Jack *83:* 162
Harrington, Richard *5:* 81
Harris, Andrew N. *191:* 78
Harris, Jim *127:* 130; *183:* 4
Harris, John *83:* 25
Harris, Nick *86:* 177
Harris, Susan Yard *42:* 121
Harrison, Florence *20:* 150, 152
Harrison, Harry *4:* 103
Harrison, Jack *28:* 149
Harrison, Mark *105:* 157; *165:* 190
Harrison, Ted *56:* 73
Harsh, Fred *72:* 107
Harston, Jerry *105:* 143
Hart, Lewis *98:* 115
Hart, Thomas *181:* 165
Hart, William *13:* 72
Hartland, Jessie *171:* 80, 81; *186:* 165
Hartung, Susan Kathleen *150:* 107, 108; *173:*
    106; *175:* 106; *192:* 78
Hartelius, Margaret *10:* 24
Hartshorn, Ruth *5:* 115; *11:* 129
Harvey, Amanda *145:* 44
Harvey, Bob *48:* 219
Harvey, Gerry *7:* 180
Harvey, Lisa *97:* 21
Harvey, Paul *88:* 74
Harvey, Roland *71:* 88; *123:* 63; *179:* 94
Haskamp, Steve *195:* 36
Hassall, Joan *43:* 108, 109
Hassell, Hilton *YABC 1:* 187
Hassett, John *162:* 59
Hasselriis, Else *18:* 87; *YABC 1:* 96
Hastings, Glenn *89:* 183
Hastings, Ian *62:* 67
Hauman, Doris *2:* 184; *29:* 58, 59; *32:* 85, 86,
    87
Hauman, George *2:* 184; *29:* 58, 59; *32:* 85,
    86, 87
Hausherr, Rosmarie *15:* 29
Hawkes, Kevin *78:* 72; *104:* 198; *105:* 197;
    112: 109; *126:* 87; *144:* 88; *149:* 210; *150:*
    110, 135; *156:* 94; *164:* 35; *186:* 18; *190:*
    197; *198:* 152; *201:* 70, 71, 72
Hawkins, Jacqui *112:* 86; *162:* 64
Hawkinson, John *4:* 109; *7:* 83; *21:* 64
Hawkinson, Lucy *21:* 64

Hawthorne, Mike *140:* 228
Haxton, Elaine *28:* 131
Haydock, Robert *4:* 95
Hayes, Geoffrey *26:* 111; *44:* 133; *91:* 85
Haynes, Max *72:* 107
Hays, Michael *73:* 207; *83:* 93; *139:* 197; *146:*
    202, 250
Haywood, Carolyn *1:* 112; *29:* 104
Heale, Jonathan *104:* 117
Healy, Daty *12:* 143
Healy, Deborah *58:* 181, 182; *101:* 111
Heap, Sue *102:* 207; *150:* 113, 114; *187:* 84,
    85, 87
Hearn, Diane Dawson *79:* 99; *113:* 13
Hearon, Dorothy *34:* 69
Heaslip, William *57:* 24, 25
Hechtkopf, H. *11:* 110
Heck, Ed *173:* 81
Hedderwick, Mairi *30:* 127; *32:* 47; *36:* 104;
    77: 86; *145:* 91, 93, 95
Heffernan, Phil *146:* 197; *195:* 172
Hefter, Richard *28:* 170; *31:* 81, 82; *33:* 183
Hehenberger, Shelly *126:* 91
Heigh, James *22:* 98
Heighway, Richard *25:* 160; *64:* 4
Heighway-Bury, Robin *159:* 89
Heine, Helme *67:* 86; *135:* 91, 92
Heinly, John *45:* 113
Hellard, Susan *81:* 21
Hellebrand, Nancy *26:* 57
Heller, Linda *46:* 86
Heller, Ruth M. *66:* 125; *77:* 30, 32
Hellmuth, Jim *38:* 164
Helms, Georgeann *33:* 62
Helquist, Brett *142:* 203; *146:* 133, 134; *156:*
    10; *173:* 25; *180:* 106; *187:* 90, 91; *193:* 12
Helweg, Hans *41:* 118; *50:* 93; *58:* 22, 26
Hemphill, Helen *179:* 95
Henba, Bobbie *90:* 195
Henderson, Dave *73:* 76; *75:* 191, 192, 193,
    194; *82:* 4
Henderson, Douglas *103:* 68
Henderson, Kathy *55:* 32; *155:* 118
Henderson, Keith *35:* 122
Henderson, Meryl *127:* 58, 60; *169:* 81
Hendrix, John *187:* 133
Hendry, Linda *80:* 104; *83:* 83; *164:* 216
Hengeveld, Dennis *142:* 86
Henkes, Kevin *43:* 111; *108:* 106, 107, 108
Henneberger, Robert *1:* 42; *2:* 237; *25:* 83
Henriksen, Harold *35:* 26; *48:* 68
Henriquez, Celeste *103:* 137
Henriquez, Elsa *82:* 260
Henriquez, Emile F. *89:* 88
Henry, Everett *29:* 191
Henry, Matthew *117:* 58
Henry, Paul *93:* 121; *194:* 125
Henry, Thomas *5:* 102
Hensel *27:* 119
Henshaw, Jacqui *141:* 127
Henstra, Friso *8:* 80; *36:* 70; *40:* 222; *41:* 250;
    73: 100, 101
Henterly, Jamichael *93:* 4
Heo, Yumi *89:* 85, 86; *94:* 89, 90; *146:* 40,
    137, 138; *163:* 227; *201:* 192
Hepple, Norman *28:* 198
Herbert, Helen *57:* 70
Herbert, Jennifer *189:* 47
Herbert, Wally *23:* 101
Herbster, Mary Lee *9:* 33
Herder, Edwin *182:* 104
Herge
    See Remi, Georges
Hermansen, Pal *133:* 113
Hermanson, Dennis *10:* 55
Hermes, Gertrude *54:* 161
Herr, Margo *57:* 191
Herr, Susan *83:* 163
Herriman, George *140:* 74, 75, 76, 77, 78
Herriman, Lisa *87:* 190
Herring, Michael *121:* 76; *182:* 103

Herrington, Roger *3:* 161
Herscovici, C. *165:* 240
Hescox, Richard *85:* 86; *90:* 30; *139:* 35
Heslop, Mike *38:* 60; *40:* 130
Hess, Lydia J. *85:* 17
Hess, Mark *111:* 146; *113:* 207
Hess, Paul *134:* 47; *166:* 133; *193:* 13
Hess, Richard *42:* 31
Hester, Ronnie *37:* 85
Heuser, Olga J. *121:* 116
Heusser, Sibylle *168:* 195
Heustis, Louise L. *20:* 28
Hewgill, Jodi *201:* 90
Hewitson, Jennifer *74:* 119; *124:* 167
Hewitt, Kathryn *80:* 126; *149:* 105; *184:* 93; *196:* 36
Hewitt, Margaret *84:* 112
Heyduck-Huth, Hilde *8:* 82
Heyer, Carol *74:* 122; *130:* 72, 73; *192:* 35
Heyer, Hermann *20:* 114, 115
Heyer, Marilee *102:* 108
Heyman, Ken *8:* 33; *34:* 113
Heyne, Ulrike *146:* 151
Heywood, Karen *48:* 114
Hickling, P.B. *40:* 165
Hickman, Stephen *85:* 58; *136:* 33; *171:* 128
Hierstein, Judy *56:* 40; *162:* 168
Higashi, Sandra *154:* 59, 60
Higginbottom, J. Winslow *8:* 170; *29:* 105, 106
Higgins, Chester *101:* 79
Higham, David *50:* 104
Hilb, Nora *176:* 8
Hildebrandt, Greg *8:* 191; *55:* 35, 36, 38, 39, 40, 42, 46; *172:* 110
Hildebrandt, Tim *8:* 191; *55:* 44, 45, 46
Hilder, Rowland *19:* 207
Hill, Eric *66:* 127, 128; *133:* 91
Hill, Gregory *35:* 190
Hill, Pat *49:* 120
Hillenbrand, Will *84:* 115; *92:* 76, 80; *93:* 131; *104:* 168; *128:* 137; *145:* 187; *146:* 184; *147:* 105, 106, 107; *152:* 59; *184:* 179; *195:* 34, 180; *196:* 125
Hilliard, Richard *183:* 74
Hillier, Matthew *45:* 205
Hillman, Priscilla *48:* 115
Hills, Tad *113:* 4; *137:* 147; *173:* 83
Himler, Ronald *6:* 114; *7:* 162; *8:* 17, 84, 125; *14:* 76; *19:* 145; *26:* 160; *31:* 43; *38:* 116; *41:* 44, 79; *43:* 52; *45:* 120; *46:* 43; *54:* 44, 83; *58:* 180; *59:* 38; *68:* 146; *69:* 231; *70:* 98; *71:* 177, 178; *77:* 219; *79:* 212; *83:* 62; *89:* 5; *91:* 160; *92:* 91, 92, 93; *94:* 93; *95:* 69, 174, 194; *99:* 99, 112; *113:* 92; *118:* 114; *137:* 73, 74, 77, 167; *163:* 99; *165:* 138; *178:* 9, 220; *183:* 77, 79, 80, 81; *184:* 80, 83
Himmelman, John *47:* 109; *65:* 87; *94:* 96, 97; *159:* 85
Hinds, Bill *37:* 127, 130
Hines, Anna Grossnickle *51:* 90; *74:* 124; *95:* 78, 79,80, 81
Hines, Bob *135:* 149, 150
Hiroko *99:* 61
Hiroshige *25:* 71
Hirsh, Marilyn *7:* 126
Hiscock, Bruce *137:* 80, 81
Hissey, Jane *103:* 90; *130:* 81
Hitch, Jeff *99:* 206; *128:* 86
Hitz, Demi *11:* 135; *15:* 245; *66:* 129, 130; *152:* 94, 95
Hnizdovsky, Jacques *32:* 96; *76:* 187
Ho, Kwoncjan *15:* 132
Hoban, Lillian *1:* 114; *22:* 157; *26:* 72; *29:* 53; *40:* 105, 107, 195; *41:* 80; *69:* 107, 108; *71:* 98; *77:* 168; *106:* 50; *113:* 86; *136:* 118
Hoban, Tana *22:* 159; *104:* 82, 83, 85
Hobbie, Jocelyn *190:* 78; *196:* 92
Hobbie, Nathaniel *196:* 92
Hobbs, Leigh *166:* 95
Hoberman, Norman *5:* 82

Hobson, Sally *77:* 185
Hockerman, Dennis *39:* 22; *56:* 23
Hodgell, P.C. *42:* 114
Hodges, C. Walter *2:* 139; *11:* 15; *12:* 25; *23:* 34; *25:* 96; *38:* 165; *44:* 197; *45:* 95; *100:* 57; *YABC 2:* 62, 63
Hodges, David *9:* 98
Hodgetts, Victoria *43:* 132
Hofbauer, Imre *2:* 162
Hoff, Syd *9:* 107; *10:* 128; *33:* 94; *72:* 115,116, 117, 118; *138:* 114, 115
Hoffman, Rosekrans *15:* 133; *50:* 219; *63:* 97
Hoffman, Sanford *38:* 208; *76:* 174; *88:* 160, 161; *151:* 156
Hoffmann, Felix *9:* 109
Hoffnung, Gerard *66:* 76, 77
Hofsinde, Robert *21:* 70
Hogan, Inez *2:* 141
Hogan, Jamie *192:* 94; *198:* 177
Hogarth, Burne *41:* 58; *63:* 46, 48, 49, 50, 52, 53, 54, 55,56
Hogarth, Paul *41:* 102, 103, 104; *YABC 1:* 16
Hogarth, William *42:* 33
Hogenbyl, Jan *1:* 35
Hogner, Nils *4:* 122; *25:* 144
Hogrogian, Nonny *3:* 221; *4:* 106, 107; *5:* 166; *7:* 129; *15:* 2; *16:* 176; *20:* 154; *22:* 146; *25:* 217; *27:* 206; *74:* 127, 128, 129, 149, 152; *127:* 99; *YABC 2:* 84, 94
Hokanson, Lars *93:* 111; *172:* 137
Hokusai *25:* 71
Hol, Colby *126:* 96
Holberg, Richard *2:* 51
Holbrook, Kathy *107:* 114
Holdcroft, Tina *38:* 109
Holden, Caroline *55:* 159
Holder, Heidi *36:* 99; *64:* 9
Holder, Jimmy *151:* 224
Holiday, Henry *YABC 2:* 107
Holl, F. *36:* 91
Holland, Brad *45:* 59, 159
Holland, Gay W. *128:* 105
Holland, Janice *18:* 118
Holland, Marion *6:* 116
Holldobler, Turid *26:* 120
Holliday, Keaf *144:* 236
Holling, Holling C. *15:* 136, 137
Hollinger, Deanne *12:* 116
Holm, Sharon Lane *114:* 84; *115:* 52
Holmes, B. *3:* 82
Holmes, Bea *7:* 74; *24:* 156; *31:* 93
Holmes, Dave *54:* 22
Holmes, Lesley *135:* 96
Holmgren, George Ellen *45:* 112
Holmlund, Heather D. *150:* 140
Holt, Norma *44:* 106
Holt, Pater *151:* 188
Holtan, Gene *32:* 192
Holub, Joan *149:* 72
Holyfield, John *149:* 231
Holz, Loretta *17:* 81
Hom, Nancy *182:* 195
Homar, Lorenzo *6:* 2
Homer, Winslow *128:* 8; *YABC 2:* 87
Honey, Elizabeth *112:* 95, 96; *137:* 93, 94
Honeywood, Varnette P. *110:* 68, 70
Hong, Lily Toy *76:* 104
Honigman, Marian *3:* 2
Honore, Paul *42:* 77, 79, 81, 82
Hood, Alun *69:* 145, 218; *72:* 41; *80:* 226; *87:* 4; *95:* 139
Hood, Susan *12:* 43
Hook, Christian *104:* 103
Hook, Frances *26:* 188; *27:* 127
Hook, Jeff *14:* 137; *103:* 105
Hook, Richard *26:* 188
Hooks *63:* 30
Hooper, Hadley *177:* 145
Hoover, Carol A. *21:* 77
Hoover, Russell *12:* 95; *17:* 2; *34:* 156
Hope, James *141:* 116

Hopkins, Chris *99:* 127
Hopman, Philip *178:* 184
Hoppin, Augustus *34:* 66
Horacek, Petr *163:* 117
Horder, Margaret *2:* 108; *73:* 75
Horen, Michael *45:* 121
Horne, Daniel *73:* 106; *91:* 153; *109:* 127; *110:* 232; *164:* 176
Horne, Richard *111:* 80
Horse, Harry *128:* 195; *169:* 86
Horvat, Laurel *12:* 201
Horvath, David *192:* 95
Horvath, Ferdinand Kusati *24:* 176
Horvath, Maria *57:* 171
Horwitz, Richard *57:* 174
Hotchkiss, De Wolfe *20:* 49
Hough, Charlotte *9:* 112; *13:* 98; *17:* 83; *24:* 195
Houlihan, Ray *11:* 214
House, Caroline *183:* 121
Housman, Laurence *25:* 146, 147
Houston, James *13:* 107; *74:* 132, 134, 135
Hovland, Gary *88:* 172; *171:* 148
Hoyt, Eleanor *158:* 231
How, W.E. *20:* 47
Howard, Alan *16:* 80; *34:* 58; *45:* 114
Howard, Arthur *165:* 111, 112; *190:* 5
Howard, J.N. *15:* 234
Howard, John *33:* 179
Howard, Kim *116:* 71
Howard, Paul *142:* 126, 129; *144:* 187
Howard, Rob *40:* 161
Howarth, Daniel *170:* 34
Howe, John *115:* 47; *176:* 106
Howe, John F. *79:* 101; *80:* 150
Howe, Phillip *79:* 117; *175:* 115
Howe, Stephen *1:* 232
Howell, Karen *119:* 123
Howell, Pat *15:* 139
Howell, Troy *23:* 24; *31:* 61; *36:* 158; *37:* 184; *41:* 76, 235; *48:* 112; *56:* 13; *57:* 3; *59:* 174; *63:* 5; *74:* 46; *89:* 188; *90:* 231; *95:* 97; *98:* 130; *99:* 189; *153:* 156, 157, 158; *176:* 104; *199:* 96, 98
Howes, Charles *22:* 17
Hoyt, Ard *145:* 141; *190:* 82
Hranilovich, Barbara *127:* 51
Hu, Ying-Hwa *116:* 107; *152:* 236; *173:* 171
Huang, Benrei *137:* 55
Huang, Zhong-Yang *117:* 30, 32
Hubbard, Woodleigh Marx *98:* 67; *115:* 79; *160:* 138
Hubley, Faith *48:* 120, 121, 125, 130, 131, 132, 134
Hubley, John *48:* 125, 130, 131, 132, 134
Hudak, Michal *143:* 74
Hudnut, Robin *14:* 62
Huerta, Catherine *76:* 178; *77:* 44, 45; *90:* 182
Huffaker, Sandy *10:* 56
Huffman, Joan *13:* 33
Huffman, Tom *13:* 180; *17:* 212; *21:* 116; *24:* 132; *33:* 154; *38:* 59; *42:* 147
Hughes, Arthur *20:* 148, 149, 150; *33:* 114, 148, 149
Hughes, Darren *95:* 44
Hughes, David *36:* 197
Hughes, Shirley *1:* 20, 21; *7:* 3; *12:* 217; *16:* 163; *29:* 154; *63:* 118; *70:* 102, 103, 104; *73:* 169; *88:* 70; *110:* 118, 119; *159:* 103
Hugo, Victor *47:* 112
Hull, Cathy *78:* 29
Hull, Richard *95:* 120; *123:* 175; *172:* 195
Hulsmann, Eva *16:* 166
Hume, Lachie *189:* 93
Hummel, Berta *43:* 137, 138, 139
Hummel, Lisl *29:* 109; *YABC 2:* 333, 334
Humphrey, Henry *16:* 167
Humphreys, Graham *25:* 168
Humphries, Tudor *76:* 66; *80:* 4; *124:* 4, 5
Huneck, Stephen *183:* 88, 89
Hunt, James *2:* 143

Hunt, Jonathan *84:* 120
Hunt, Paul *119:* 104; *129:* 135; *139:* 160; *173:* 112
Hunt, Robert *110:* 206, 235; *147:* 136, 137; *170:* 3
Hunt, Scott *190:* 143
Hunter, Anne *133:* 190; *178:* 150
Huntington, Amy *180:* 99
Hurd, Clement *2:* 148, 149; *64:* 127, 128, 129, 131, 133, 134,135, 136; *100:* 37, 38
Hurd, Peter *24:* 30, 31,; *YABC 2:* 56
Hurd, Thacher *46:* 88, 89; *94:* 114, 115, 116; *123:* 81, 82, 84
Hurlimann, Ruth *32:* 99
Hurst, Carol Otis *185:* 92
Hurst, Philip *196:* 79
Hurst, Tracey *192:* 238
Hussar, Michael *114:* 113; *117:* 159
Hustler, Tom *6:* 105
Hutchins, Laurence *55:* 22
Hutchins, Pat *15:* 142; *70:* 106, 107, 108; *178:* 131, 132
Hutchinson, Sascha *95:* 211
Hutchinson, William M. *6:* 3, 138; *46:* 70
Hutchison, Paula *23:* 10
Hutton, Clarke *YABC 2:* 335
Hutton, Kathryn *35:* 155; *89:* 91
Hutton, Warwick *20:* 91
Huyette, Marcia *29:* 188
Hyatt, John *54:* 7
Hyatt, Mitch *178:* 162
Hyde, Maureen *82:* 17; *121:* 145, 146
Hyman, David *117:* 64
Hyman, Trina Schart *1:* 204; *2:* 194; *5:* 153; *6:* 106; *7:* 138, 145; *8:* 22; *10:* 196; *13:* 96; *14:* 114; *15:* 204; *16:* 234; *20:* 82; *22:* 133; *24:* 151; *25:* 79, 82; *26:* 82; *29:* 83; *31:* 37, 39; *34:* 104; *38:* 84, 100, 128; *41:* 49; *43:* 146; *46:* 91, 92, 93, 95, 96, 97, 98, 99, 100, 101, 102, 103, 104, 105,108, 109, 111, 197; *48:* 60, 61; *52:* 32; *60:* 168; *66:* 38; *67:* 214; *72:* 74; *75:* 92; *79:* 57; *82:* 95, 238; *89:* 46; *95:* 91, 92, 93; *100:* 33, 199; *132:* 12; *147:* 33, 35, 36; *167:* 58, 60; *177:* 189, 190

I

Ibarra, Rosa *147:* 91
Ibatoulline, Bagram *156:* 48; *174:* 33, 82
Ichikawa, Satomi *29:* 152; *41:* 52; *47:* 133, 134,135, 136; *78:* 93, 94; *80:* 81; *146:* 143, 145, 146
Ide, Jacqueline *YABC 1:* 39
Ilsley, Velma *3:* 1; *7:* 55; *12:* 109; *37:* 62; *38:* 184
Imai, Ayano *190:* 85, 86
in den Bosch, Nicole *150:* 204
Inga *1:* 142
Ingman, Bruce *134:* 50; *182:* 91, 92
Ingpen, Robert *109:* 103, 104; *132:* 138; *137:* 177; *166:* 103; *181:* 140
Ingraham, Erick *21:* 177; *84:* 256; *103:* 66
Inkpen, Mick *99:* 104, 105; *106:* 44
Innerst, Stacy *149:* 104
Innocenti, Roberto *21:* 123; *96:* 122; *159:* 111, 197; *199:* 176
Inoue, Yosuke *24:* 118
Iofin, Michael *97:* 157
Iosa, Ann *63:* 189
Ipcar, Dahlov *1:* 124, 125; *49:* 137, 138, 139, 140, 141, 142,143, 144, 145; *147:* 122, 124, 126
Irvin, Fred *13:* 166; *15:* 143, 144; *27:* 175
Irving, Jay *45:* 72
Irving, Laurence *27:* 50
Isaac, Joanne *21:* 76
Isaacs, Gary *170:* 188
Isadora, Rachel *43:* 159, 160; *54:* 31; *79:* 106, 107,108; *121:* 100, 102; *165:* 116, 117

Ishmael, Woodi *24:* 111; *31:* 99
Ives, Ruth *15:* 257
Iwai, Melissa *149:* 233; *183:* 92; *199:* 115

J

Jabar, Cynthia *101:* 201
Jackness, Andrew *94:* 237
Jackson, Julian *91:* 104, 106
Jackson, Michael *43:* 42
Jackson, Shelley *79:* 71; *99:* 109; *187:* 82
Jacob, Murv *89:* 30
Jacobi, Kathy *62:* 118
Jacobs, Barbara *9:* 136
Jacobs, Lou, Jr. *9:* 136; *15:* 128
Jacobsen, Laura *176:* 98; *177:* 85, 86
Jacobson, Rick *131:* 222; *170:* 119
Jacobus, Tim *79:* 140; *109:* 126; *129:* 180
Jacques, Robin *1:* 70; *2:* 1; *8:* 46; *9:* 20; *15:* 187; *19:* 253; *32:* 102, 103, 104; *43:* 184; *73:* 135; *YABC 1:* 42
Jaeggi, Yoshiko *186:* 184
Jaffee, Al *66:* 131, 132
Jagr, Miloslav *13:* 197
Jahn-Clough, Lisa *88:* 114; *152:* 104; *193:* 70, 71
Jahnke, Robert *84:* 24
Jainschigg, Nicholas *80:* 64; *91:* 138; *95:* 63; *99:* 25; *108:* 50; *171:* 41
Jakesavic, Nenad *85:* 102
Jakobsen, Kathy *116:* 83
Jakubowski, Charles *14:* 192
Jambor, Louis *YABC 1:* 11
James, Ann *73:* 50; *82:* 113; *158:* 61; *183:* 44
James, Brian *140:* 91
James, Curtis E. *182:* 93
James, Derek *35:* 187; *44:* 91; *61:* 133; *74:* 2; *80:* 57; *86:* 88; *130:* 30; *179:* 29
James, Gilbert *YABC 1:* 43
James, Gordon C. *195:* 89
James, Harold *2:* 151; *3:* 62; *8:* 79; *29:* 113; *51:* 195; *74:* 90
James, Kennon *126:* 211
James, Robin *50:* 106; *53:* 32, 34, 35
James, Will *19:* 150, 152, 153, 155, 163
Janosch
  See Eckert, Horst
Janovitch, Marilyn *68:* 168
Janovitz, Marilyn *87:* 187; *130:* 198; *194:* 91
Jansons, Inese *48:* 117
Jansson, Tove *3:* 90; *41:* 106, 108, 109, 110, 111, 113, 114
Jaques, Faith *7:* 11, 132, 133; *21:* 83, 84; *69:* 114,116; *73:* 170
Jaques, Frances Lee *29:* 224
Jarrett, Clare *201:* 77
Jauss, Anne Marie *1:* 139; *3:* 34; *10:* 57, 119; *11:* 205; *23:* 194
Jay, Alison *158:* 97, 98; *183:* 126, 127; *196:* 95, 96, 97, 98; *200:* 72, 73, 74
Jeffers, Oliver *175:* 111
Jeffers, Susan *17:* 86, 87; *25:* 164, 165; *26:* 112; *50:* 132, 134, 135; *70:* 111, 112, 113; *137:* 107, 108, 109, 110, 111
Jefferson, Louise E. *4:* 160
Jenkin-Pearce, Susie *78:* 16
Jenkins, Debra Reid *85:* 202; *114:* 89; *173:* 134
Jenkins, Jean *98:* 79, 102
Jenkins, Leonard *157:* 169; *167:* 128; *189:* 96, 97; *190:* 89
Jenkins, Patrick *72:* 126
Jenkins, Steve *124:* 177; *154:* 90, 91, 92, 93; *185:* 194; *188:* 81, 82, 83, 84, 85, 86
Jenks, Aleta *73:* 117; *124:* 225
Jenkyns, Chris *51:* 97
Jensen, Bruce *95:* 39
Jensinius, Kirsten *56:* 58

Jeram, Anita *89:* 135; *102:* 122, 123; *129:* 112; *154:* 96, 97, 98; *164:* 154
Jernigan, E. Wesley *85:* 92
Jerome, Karen A. *72:* 194
Jeruchim, Simon *6:* 173; *15:* 250
Jeschke, Susan *20:* 89; *39:* 161; *41:* 84; *42:* 120
Jessel, Camilla *29:* 115
Jessell, Tim *159:* 3; *177:* 87; *181:* 95
Jeyaveeran, Ruth *182:* 100
Jiang, Cheng An *109:* 108
Jiang, Wei *109:* 108
Jimenez, Maria *77:* 158; *93:* 127
Jobling, Curtis *138:* 74
Jocelyn, Marthe *118:* 83; *137:* 219; *163:* 119, 120; *198:* 62
Joerns, Consuelo *38:* 36; *44:* 94
John, Diana *12:* 209
John, Helen *1:* 215; *28:* 204
Johns, Elizabeth *127:* 33
Johns, Jasper *61:* 172
Johns, Jeanne *24:* 114
Johnson, Adrian *143:* 50
Johnson, Bruce *9:* 47
Johnson, Cathy *92:* 136
Johnson, Crockett
  See Leisk, David
Johnson, D. William *23:* 104
Johnson, D.B. *183:* 98, 139
Johnson, David *175:* 18; *191:* 91
Johnson, Gillian *119:* 175; *164:* 217
Johnson, Harper *1:* 27; *2:* 33; *18:* 302; *19:* 61; *31:* 181; *44:* 46, 50, 95
Johnson, Ingrid *37:* 118
Johnson, James Ralph *1:* 23, 127
Johnson, James David *12:* 195
Johnson, Jane *48:* 136
Johnson, Joel Peter *98:* 18; *128:* 111; *201:* 13
Johnson, John E. *34:* 133
Johnson, Kevin *72:* 44
Johnson, Kevin Eugene *109:* 215
Johnson, Larry *47:* 56; *123:* 107; *159:* 203
Johnson, Layne *187:* 94
Johnson, Margaret S. *35:* 131
Johnson, Meredith Merrell *71:* 181; *83:* 158; *89:* 103; *104:* 88
Johnson, Milton *1:* 67; *2:* 71; *26:* 45; *31:* 107; *60:* 112; *68:* 96
Johnson, Pamela *16:* 174; *52:* 145; *62:* 140; *73:* 116; *85:* 64
Johnson, Paul Brett *83:* 95; *132:* 119
Johnson, Stephen T. *80:* 15; *131:* 35; *141:* 96; *145:* 40; *164:* 187; *175:* 32; *189:* 99, 100
Johnson, Steve *138:* 219; *141:* 64; *144:* 199; *177:* 51
Johnson, William R. *38:* 91
Johnson-Petrov, Arden *115:* 206
Johnston, David McCall *50:* 131, 133
Johnston, Lynne *118:* 85, 87, 89
Johnstone, Anne *8:* 120; *36:* 89
Johnstone, Janet Grahame *8:* 120; *36:* 89
Jonas, Ann *50:* 107, 108, 109; *135:* 113
Jones, Bob *71:* 5; *77:* 199
Jones, Carol *5:* 131; *72:* 185, 186; *153:* 111, 112
Jones, Chuck *53:* 70, 71
Jones, Davy *89:* 176
Jones, Douglas B. *185:* 192
Jones, Elizabeth Orton *18:* 124, 126, 128, 129
Jones, Harold *14:* 88; *52:* 50
Jones, Holly *127:* 3
Jones, Jeff *41:* 64
Jones, Laurian *25:* 24, 27
Jones, Margaret *74:* 57
Jones, Noah Z. *182:* 37
Jones, Randy *131:* 104
Jones, Richard *127:* 222
Jones, Robert *25:* 67
Jones, Wilfred *35:* 115; *YABC 1:* 163
Jordan, Charles *89:* 58
Jordan, Jess *158:* 136

Jordan, Martin George *84:* 127
Jordan, Richard *84:* 36
Jorgenson, Andrea *91:* 111
Jorisch, Stéphane *153:* 56, 193; *177:* 29; *178:* 138, 139; *187:* 23
Joseph, James *53:* 88
Joudrey, Ken *64:* 145; *78:* 6
Joyce, William *72:* 131, 132, 133, 134; *73:* 227; *145:* 37
Joyner, Jerry *34:* 138
Juan, Ana *175:* 38; *179:* 111, 112
Jucker, Sita *5:* 93
Judge, Lita *192:* 99
Judkis, Jim *37:* 38
Juhasz, Victor *31:* 67
Jullian, Philippe *24:* 206; *25:* 203
Jung, Tom *91:* 217
Junge, Alexandra *183:* 37
Junge, Walter *67:* 150
Jupo, Frank *7:* 148, 149
Jurisch, Stephane *154:* 105
Justice, Martin *34:* 72

K

Kabatova-Taborska, Zdenka *107:* 153
Kachik, John *165:* 230
Kaczman, James *156:* 98
Kadair, Deborah Ousley *184:* 45, 89
Kahl, David *74:* 95; *97:* 35; *109:* 174; *110:* 213; *198:* 15
Kahl, M.P. *37:* 83
Kahl, Virginia *48:* 138
Kahn, Katherine Janus *90:* 135
Kakimoo, Kozo *11:* 148
Kalett, Jim *48:* 159, 160, 161
Kalin, Victor *39:* 186
Kalman, Maira *96:* 131, 132; *137:* 115
Kalmenoff, Matthew *22:* 191
Kalow, Gisela *32:* 105
Kamen, Gloria *1:* 41; *9:* 119; *10:* 178; *35:* 157; *78:* 236; *98:* 82
Kaminsky, Jef *102:* 153
Kandell, Alice *35:* 133
Kane, Henry B. *14:* 90; *18:* 219, 220
Kane, Robert *18:* 131
Kanfer, Larry *66:* 141
Kangas, Juli *200:* 88
Kappes, Alfred *28:* 104
Karalus, Bob *41:* 157
Karas, G. Brian *80:* 60; *99:* 179; *115:* 41; *118:* 50; *136:* 168; *145:* 166; *149:* 245; *159:* 65; *171:* 192; *178:* 142, 143
Karasz, Ilonka *128:* 163
Karlin, Eugene *10:* 63; *20:* 131
Karlin, Nurit *63:* 78; *103:* 110
Karpinski, Tony *134:* 160
Kasamatsu, Shiro *139:* 155
Kasparavicius, Kestutis *139:* 210
Kassian, Olena *64:* 94
Kastner, Jill *79:* 135; *117:* 84, 85
Kasuya, Masahiro *41:* 206, 207; *51:* 100
Kasza, Keiko *191:* 99, 100, 101, 102, 103
Katona, Robert *21:* 85; *24:* 126
Katz, Avi *199:* 55
Katz, Karen *158:* 123
Kauffer, E. McKnight *33:* 103; *35:* 127; *63:* 67
Kaufman, Angelika *15:* 156
Kaufman, Joe *33:* 119
Kaufman, John *13:* 158
Kaufman, Stuart *62:* 64; *68:* 226; *137:* 44
Kaufmann, John *1:* 174; *4:* 159; *8:* 43, 1; *10:* 102; *18:* 133, 134; *22:* 251
Kaye, Graham *1:* 9; *67:* 7, 8
Kaye, M.M. *62:* 95
Kazalovski, Nata *40:* 205
Keane, Bil *4:* 135
Kearney, David *72:* 47; *121:* 83
Keating, Pamel T. *77:* 37

Keats, Ezra Jack *3:* 18, 105, 257; *14:* 101, 102; *33:* 129; *57:* 79, 80, 82, 83, 84, 87
Keegan, Charles *166:* 211
Keegan, Marcia *9:* 122; *32:* 93
Keeler, Patricia A. *81:* 56; *183:* 102, 103
Keely, Jack *119:* 95
Keely, John *26:* 104; *48:* 214
Keen, Eliot *25:* 213
Keep, Richard C. *170:* 122
Keeping, Charles *9:* 124, 185; *15:* 28, 134; *18:* 115; *44:* 194, 196; *47:* 25; *52:* 3; *54:* 156; *69:* 123, 124; *74:* 56; *155:* 9
Keeter, Susan *168:* 46; *183:* 192
Keith, Eros *4:* 98; *5:* 138; *31:* 29; *43:* 220; *52:* 91, 92, 93, 94; *56:* 64, 66; *60:* 37; *79:* 93
Keleinikov, Andrei *65:* 101, 102
Kelen, Emery *13:* 115
Keller, A.J. *62:* 198
Keller, Arthur I. *26:* 106
Keller, Dick *36:* 123, 125
Keller, Holly *45:* 79; *76:* 118, 119, 120, 121; *108:* 137, 138, 140; *157:* 117, 118, 119
Keller, Katie *79:* 222; *93:* 108
Keller, Laurie *196:* 105, 106
Keller, Ronald *45:* 208
Kelley, Gary *183:* 105
Kelley, True *41:* 114, 115; *42:* 137; *75:* 35; *92:* 104, 105; *124:* 62; *130:* 100, 101; *179:* 120, 121, 122; *192:* 251
Kellogg, Steven *8:* 96; *11:* 207; *14:* 130; *20:* ; *201:* 38 58; *29:* 140, 141; *30:* 35; *41:* 141; *57:* 89, 90, 92,93, 94, 96; *59:* 182; *73:* 141; *77:* 129; *130:* 105, 106; *177:* 94, 95, 96, 97; *199:* 57; *YABC 1:* 65, 73
Kelly, Billy *158:* 143
Kelly, Geoff *97:* 196; *112:* 25
Kelly, Irene *147:* 134
Kelly, John *194:* 186
Kelly, Joseph *174:* 94
Kelly, Kathleen M. *71:* 109
Kelly, Laura *89:* 217
Kelly, True *163:* 87
Kelly, Walt *18:* 136, 137, 138, 139, 140, 141, 144, 145, 146, 148, 149
Kemble, E.W. *34:* 75; *44:* 178; *YABC 2:* 54, 59
Kemp-Welsh, Lucy *24:* 197; *100:* 214
Kendall, Jane *150:* 105; *186:* 109
Kendall, Peter *152:* 85
Kendrick, Dennis *79:* 213
Kennaway, Adrienne *60:* 55, 56; *171:* 88, 89
Kennedy, Doug *189:* 104
Kennedy, Paul Edward *6:* 190; *8:* 132; *33:* 120
Kennedy, Richard *3:* 93; *12:* 179; *44:* 193; *100:* 15; *YABC 1:* 57
Kent, Jack *24:* 136; *37:* 37; *40:* 81; *84:* 89; *86:* 150; *88:* 77
Kent, Rockwell *5:* 166; *6:* 129; *20:* 225, 226, 227,229; *59:* 144
Kenyon, Tony *81:* 201; *127:* 74
Kepes, Juliet *13:* 119
Kerins, Anthony *76:* 84
Kerr, Judity *24:* 137
Kerr, Phyllis Forbes *72:* 141
Kessler, Leonard *1:* 108; *7:* 139; *14:* 107, 227; *22:* 101; *44:* 96; *67:* 79; *82:* 123
Kest, Kristin *168:* 99; *173:* 23
Kesteven, Peter *35:* 189
Ketcham, Hank *28:* 140, 141, 142
Kettelkamp, Larry *2:* 164
Key, Alexander *8:* 99
Khalsa, Dayal Kaur *62:* 99
Kiakshuk *8:* 59
Kidd, Chip *94:* 23
Kidd, Richard *152:* 110
Kidd, Tom *64:* 199; *81:* 189; *185:* 173
Kiddell-Monroe, Joan *19:* 201; *55:* 59, 60; *87:* 174; *121:* 112
Kidder, Harvey *9:* 105; *80:* 41
Kidwell, Carl *43:* 145
Kieffer, Christa *41:* 89

Kiesler, Kate *110:* 105; *136:* 142
Kiff, Ken *40:* 45
Kilbride, Robert *37:* 100
Kilby, Don *141:* 144
Kim, David *201:* 79
Kim, Glenn *99:* 82
Kimball, Anton *78:* 114; *119:* 105
Kimball, Yeffe *23:* 116; *37:* 88
Kimber, Murray *171:* 91
Kimmel, Warren *176:* 112
Kincade, Orin *34:* 116
Kindersley, Barnabas *96:* 110
Kindred, Wendy *7:* 151
King, Colin *53:* 3
King, Robin *10:* 164, 165
King, Stephen Michael *141:* 31; *197:* 191
King, Tara Calahan *139:* 172
King, Tony *39:* 121
Kingman, Dong *16:* 287; *44:* 100, 102, 104
Kingsley, Charles *YABC 2:* 182
Kingston, Julie *147:* 14
Kingston, Maxine Hong *53:* 92
Kinney, Jeff *187:* 97
Kipling, John Lockwood *YABC 2:* 198
Kipling, Rudyard *YABC 2:* 196
Kipniss, Robert *29:* 59
Kirchherr, Astrid *55:* 23
Kirchhoff, Art *28:* 136
Kirk, Daniel *153:* 115, 116, 117; *173:* 101; *196:* 113, 114, 115, 116
Kirk, David *117:* 88, 89; *161:* 97, 98
Kirk, Ruth *5:* 96
Kirk, Steve *170:* 37
Kirk, Tim *32:* 209, 211; *72:* 89; *83:* 49
Kirmse, Marguerite *15:* 283; *18:* 153
Kirsch, Vincent X. *124:* 207
Kirschner, Ruth *22:* 154
Kirwan, Wednesday *198:* 73
Kish, Ely *73:* 119; *79:* 2
Kitamura, Satoshi *62:* 102; *98:* 91; *101:* 147; *138:* 2; *143:* 83, 85, 86; *201:* 83
Kiss, Andrew *168:* 115
Kitchel, JoAnn E. *133:* 32
Kitchen, Bert *70:* 126; *193:* 49
Kittelsen, Theodor *62:* 14
Kiuchi, Tatsuro *114:* 71
Kiwak, Barbara *172:* 135
Klahr, Susan *176:* 196
Klapholz, Mel *13:* 35
Klein, Bill *89:* 105
Klein, Robert *55:* 77
Klein, Suzanna *63:* 104
Kleinman, Zalman *28:* 143
Kleven, Elisa *173:* 96, 97
Kliban, B. *35:* 137, 138
Kline, Michael *127:* 66
Klise, M. Sarah *180:* 117, 118; *181:* 97
Knabel, Lonnie *73:* 103; *75:* 187, 228; *194:* 216
Kneen, Maggie *140:* 139
Knight, Ann *34:* 143
Knight, Christopher *13:* 125
Knight, Hilary *1:* 233; *3:* 21; *15:* 92, 158, 159; *16:* 258, 259, 260; *18:* 235; *19:* 169; *35:* 242; *46:* 167; *52:* 116; *69:* 126, 127; *132:* 129; *YABC 1:* 168, 169, 172
Knorr, Laura *200:* 91
Knorr, Peter *126:* 92, 93
Knotts, Howard *20:* 4; *25:* 170; *36:* 163
Knutson, Barbara *112:* 134
Knutson, Kimberley *115:* 90
Kobayashi, Ann *39:* 58
Kochalka, James *196:* 120, 121, 122
Kocsis, J.C.
    See Paul, James
Kodman, Stanislawa *201:* 85
Koehler, Hanne Lore *176:* 203
Koehn, Ilse *34:* 198; *79:* 123
Koelsch, Michael *99:* 182; *107:* 164; *109:* 239; *138:* 142; *150:* 94; *176:* 105; *187:* 63; *198:* 63

Koering, Ursula *3:* 28; *4:* 14; *44:* 5; *64:* 140,141; *85:* 46
Koerner, Henry
    See Koerner, W.H.D.
Koerner, W.H.D. *14:* 216; *21:* 88, 89, 90, 91; *23:* 211
Koetsch, Mike *166:* 68
Koffler, Camilla *36:* 113
Kogan, Deborah Ray *161:* 101, 102
Koide, Yasuko *50:* 114
Kolado, Karen *102:* 228
Komoda, Kiyo *9:* 128; *13:* 214
Kompaneyets, Marc *169:* 92
Konashevich, Vladimir *61:* 160
Konashevicha, V. *YABC 1:* 26
Konigsburg, E.L. *4:* 138; *48:* 141, 142, 144, 145; *94:* 129, 130; *126:* 129, 130, 131; *194:* 95, 98
Kono, Erin Eitter *177:* 99
Kooiker, Leonie *48:* 148
Koonook, Simon *65:* 157
Koontz, Robin Michal *136:* 155
Koopmans, Loek *101:* 121
Kopelke, Lisa *154:* 107
Kopper, Lisa *72:* 152, 153; *105:* 135, 136
Korach, Mimi *1:* 128, 129; *2:* 52; *4:* 39; *5:* 159; *9:* 129; *10:* 21; *24:* 69
Koren, Edward *5:* 100; *65:* 65, 67
Kosaka, Fumi *164:* 130
Koscielniak, Bruce *99:* 122; *153:* 120, 121, 122
Koshkin, Alexander *92:* 180
Kossin, Sandy *10:* 71; *23:* 105
Kostin, Andrej *26:* 204
Kosturko, Bob *164:* 56
Kotzky, Brian *68:* 184
Kovacevic, Zivojin *13:* 247
Kovalski, Maryann *58:* 120; *84:* 88; *97:* 124, 125, 126; *158:* 3; *186:* 80
Krahn, Fernando *2:* 257; *34:* 206; *49:* 152
Kramer, Anthony *33:* 81
Kramer, David *96:* 162; *109:* 132; *150:* 220
Kramer, Frank *6:* 121
Krantz, Kathy *35:* 83
Kratter, Paul *139:* 65
Kraus, Robert *13:* 217; *65:* 113; *93:* 93, 94
Krause, Jon *176:* 62
Krauss, Trisha *174:* 10
Kredel, Fritz *6:* 35; *17:* 93, 94, 95, 96; *22:* 147; *24:* 175; *29:* 130; *35:* 77; *YABC 2:* 166, 300
Kreloff, Eliot *189:* 107, 108
Krementz, Jill *17:* 98; *49:* 41
Krenina, Katya *117:* 106; *125:* 133; *176:* 117
Kresin, Robert *23:* 19
Krieger, Salem *54:* 164
Kriegler, Lyn *73:* 29
Krinitz, Esther Nisenthal *193:* 196
Krommes, Beth *128:* 141; *149:* 136; *181:* 100, 101; *184:* 105; *188:* 125
Krone, Mike *101:* 71
Kronheimer, Ann *135:* 119
Krosoczka, Jarrett J. *155:* 142; *200:* 93, 94
Kruck, Gerald *88:* 181
Krudop, Walter Lyon *199:* 19
Krupinski, Loretta *67:* 104; *102:* 131; *161:* 105, 106
Krupp, Robin Rector *53:* 96, 98
Krush, Beth *1:* 51, 85; *2:* 233; *4:* 115; *9:* 61; *10:* 191; *11:* 196; *18:* 164, 165; *32:* 72; *37:* 203; *43:* 57; *60:* 102, 103, 107, 108, 109
Krush, Joe *2:* 233; *4:* 115; *9:* 61; *10:* 191; *11:* 196; *18:* 164, 165; *32:* 72, 91; *37:* 203; *43:* 57; *60:* 102, 103, 107, 108, 109
Krych, Duane *91:* 43
Krykorka, Vladyana *96:* 147; *143:* 90, 91; *168:* 14
Kubick, Dana *165:* 91
Kubinyi, Laszlo *4:* 116; *6:* 113; *16:* 118; *17:* 100; *28:* 227; *30:* 172; *49:* 24, 28; *54:* 23; *167:* 149

Kubricht, Mary *73:* 118
Kucharik, Elena *139:* 31
Kuchera, Kathleen *84:* 5
Kuhn, Bob *17:* 91; *35:* 235
Kulikov, Boris *163:* 185; *185:* 23
Kulka, Joe *188:* 110
Kukalis, Romas *90:* 27; *139:* 37
Kuklin, Susan *63:* 82, 83, 84
Kunhardt, Dorothy *53:* 101
Kunhardt, Edith *67:* 105, 106
Kunstler, Mort *10:* 73; *32:* 143
Kurchevsky, V. *34:* 61
Kurczok, Belinda *121:* 118
Kurelek, William *8:* 107
Kuriloff, Ron *13:* 19
Kurisu, Jane *160:* 120
Kuskin, Karla *2:* 170; *68:* 115, 116; *111:* 116
Kutzer, Ernst *19:* 249
Kuzma, Steve *57:* 8; *62:* 93
Kuznetsova, Berta *74:* 45
Kvasnosky, Laura McGee *93:* 103; *142:* 83; *182:* 108
Kwas, Susan Estelle *179:* 116
Kyong, Yunmee *165:* 139

L

LaBlanc, Andre *24:* 146
Laboccetta, Mario *27:* 120
LaBrose, Darcie *157:* 134
Labrosse, Darcia *58:* 88; *108:* 77; *178:* 89
LaCava, Vince *95:* 118
Laceky, Adam *32:* 121
Lacis, Astra *85:* 117
Lacome, Julie *174:* 96, 97
La Croix *YABC 2:* 4
Ladwig, Tim *98:* 212; *117:* 76
La Farge, Margaret *47:* 141
LaFave, Kim *64:* 177; *72:* 39; *97:* 146; *99:* 172; *106:* 123; *149:* 126; *196:* 128, 129
Lafontaine, Roger *167:* 158
Lafrance, Marie *197:* 109
Lagarrigue, Jerome *136:* 102; *187:* 81
Laimgruber, Monika *11:* 153
Laite, Gordon *1:* 130, 131; *8:* 209; *31:* 113; *40:* 63; *46:* 117
Laliberté, Louise-Andrée *169:* 98
LaMarche, Jim *46:* 204; *61:* 56; *94:* 69; *114:* 22; *129:* 163; *162:* 78, 80
Lamb, Jim *10:* 117
Lambase, Barbara *101:* 185; *150:* 221; *166:* 234
Lambert, J.K. *38:* 129; *39:* 24
Lambert, Sally Anne *133:* 191
Lambert, Saul *23:* 112; *33:* 107; *54:* 136
Lambert, Stephen *109:* 33; *174:* 99
Lambo, Don *6:* 156; *35:* 115; *36:* 146
Lamontagne, Jacques *166:* 227
Lamut, Sonja *57:* 193
Lamut, Sonya *85:* 102
Landa, Peter *11:* 95; *13:* 177; *53:* 119
Landau, Jacob *38:* 111
Landis, Joan *104:* 23
Landon, Lucinda *79:* 31
Landshoff, Ursula *13:* 124
Landström, Lena *146:* 165, 166
Landström, Olof *146:* 166, 168; *170:* 22
Lane, Daniel *112:* 60
Lane, John R. *8:* 145
Lane, John *15:* 176, 177; *30:* 146
Lane, Nancy *166:* 74
Lang, G.D. *48:* 56
Lang, Gary *73:* 75
Lang, Jerry *18:* 295
Langdo, Bryan *186:* 187; *191:* 113, 114, 115
Lange, Dorothea *50:* 141
Langley, Jonathan *162:* 128
Langner, Nola *8:* 110; *42:* 36
Lanino, Deborah *105:* 148

Lantz, Paul *1:* 82, 102; *27:* 88; *34:* 102; *45:* 123
Larkin, Bob *84:* 225
Laroche, Giles *126:* 140; *146:* 81
LaRochelle, David *171:* 97
Larrecq, John *44:* 108; *68:* 56
Larsen, Suzanne *1:* 13
Larson, Gary *57:* 121, 122, 123, 124, 125, 126, 127
Larsson, Carl *35:* 144, 145, 146, 147, 148, 149, 150, 152, 153, 154
Larsson, Karl *19:* 177
Lartitegui, Ana G. *105:* 167
LaRue, Jenna *167:* 20
La Rue, Michael D. *13:* 215
Lasker, Joe *7:* 186, 187; *14:* 55; *38:* 115; *39:* 47; *83:* 113, 114, 115
Latham, Barbara *16:* 188, 189; *43:* 71
Lathrop, Dorothy *14:* 117, 118, 119; *15:* 109; *16:* 78, 79, 81; *32:* 201, 203; *33:* 112; *YABC 2:* 301
Lattimore, Eleanor Frances *7:* 156
Lauden, Claire *16:* 173
Lauden, George, Jr. *16:* 173
Laune, Paul *2:* 235; *34:* 31
Laure, Jason *49:* 53; *50:* 122
Lauter, Richard *63:* 29; *67:* 111; *77:* 198
Lavallee, Barbara *74:* 157; *92:* 154; *96:* 126; *145:* 193; *166:* 125, 126; *186:* 155; *192:* 172
Lave, Fitz Hugh *59:* 139
Lavis, Stephen *43:* 143; *87:* 137, 164, 165
Layton, Neal *152:* 120, 121; *182:* 65; *187:* 103, 105, 106
Law, Jenny *201:* 31
Lawrason, June *168:* 30
Lawrence, John *25:* 131; *30:* 141; *44:* 198, 200
Lawrence, Stephen *20:* 195
Lawson, Carol *6:* 38; *42:* 93, 131; *174:* 56; *189:* 89
Lawson, George *17:* 280
Lawson, Robert *5:* 26; *6:* 94; *13:* 39; *16:* 11; *20:* 100, 102, 103; *54:* 3; *66:* 12; *100:* 144, 145; *YABC 2:* 222, 224, 225, 227, 228, 229, 230, 231, 232, 233, 234, 235, 237, 238, 239, 240, 241
Layfield, Kathie *60:* 194
Lazare, Jerry *44:* 109; *74:* 28
Lazarevich, Mila *17:* 118
Lazarus, Claire *103:* 30
Lazarus, Keo Felker *21:* 94
Lazzaro, Victor *11:* 126
Lea, Bob *166:* 208
Lea, Tom *43:* 72, 74
Leacroft, Richard *6:* 140
Leaf, Munro *20:* 99
Leake, Donald *70:* 41
Leander, Patricia *23:* 27
Lear, Edward *18:* 183, 184, 185
Lear, Rebecca *149:* 46
Lebenson, Richard *6:* 209; *7:* 76; *23:* 145; *44:* 191; *87:* 153
Le Cain, Errol *6:* 141; *9:* 3; *22:* 142; *25:* 198; *28:* 173; *68:* 128, 129; *86:* 49
Lechon, Daniel *113:* 211
Leder, Dora *129:* 172
Ledger, Bill *181:* 58
Leduc, Bernard *102:* 36
Lee, Alan *62:* 25, 28
Lee, Bryce *99:* 60; *101:* 195; *196:* 53
Lee, Chinlun *181:* 138; *182:* 112
Lee, Declan *191:* 20
Lee, Dom *83:* 118, 120; *93:* 123; *121:* 121, 126; *146:* 174, 175, 206, 207; *174:* 204
Lee, Doris *13:* 246; *32:* 183; *44:* 111
Lee, Hector Viveros *115:* 96
Lee, Ho Baek *200:* 160
Lee, Jeanne M. *158:* 56
Lee, Jared *93:* 200; *157:* 229
Lee, Jody *81:* 121; *82:* 225; *91:* 155; *100:* 182

Lee, Jody A. *127:* 124, 126, 127
See also Lee, Jody
Lee, Manning de V. *2:* 200; *17:* 12; *27:* 87; *37:* 102, 103, 104; *YABC 2:* 304
Lee, Marie G. *138:* 157
Lee, Paul *97:* 100; *105:* 72, 209; *109:* 177; *128:* 113
Lee, Robert J. *3:* 97; *67:* 124
Lee, Victor *96:* 228; *105:* 182; *140:* 196
Leech, Dorothy *98:* 76
Leech, John *15:* 59
Leedy, Loreen *84:* 142; *128:* 144, 145, 146; *175:* 125, 126, 127
Leeman, Michael *44:* 157
Leeming, Catherine *87:* 39
Lees, Harry *6:* 112
LeFever, Bill *88:* 220, 221
Legenisel *47:* 111
Legrand, Edy *18:* 89, 93
Lehman, Barbara *73:* 123; *170:* 130
Lehrman, Rosalie *2:* 180
Leichman, Seymour *5:* 107
Leighton, Clare *25:* 130; *33:* 168; *37:* 105, 106, 108,109
Leisk, David *1:* 140, 141; *11:* 54; *30:* 137, 142, 143,144
Leister, Brian *89:* 45; *106:* 37; *114:* 67; *149:* 236
Leloir, Maurice *18:* 77, 80, 83, 99
Lemaître, Pascal *144:* 175; *176:* 130; *189:* 135
Lemieux, Michele *100:* 148; *139:* 153
Lemke, Horst *14:* 98; *38:* 117, 118, 119
Lemke, R.W. *42:* 162
Lemon, David Gwynne *9:* 1
LeMoult, Adolph *82:* 116
Lenn, Michael *136:* 89
Lennon, John *114:* 100
Lennox, Elsie *95:* 163; *143:* 160
Lenski, Lois *1:* 144; *26:* 135, 137, 139, 141; *100:* 153, 154
Lent, Blair *1:* 116, 117; *2:* 174; *3:* 206, 207; *7:* 168, 169; *34:* 62; *68:* 217; *133:* 101; *183:* 60
Leonard, Richard *91:* 128
Leone, Leonard *49:* 190
Lerner, Carol *86:* 140, 141, 142
Lerner, Judith *116:* 138
Lerner, Sharon *11:* 157; *22:* 56
Leroux-Hugon, Helene *132:* 139
Leslie, Cecil *19:* 244
Lessac, Frane *80:* 182, 207; *96:* 182
Lessing, Erich *167:* 52; *173:* 60
Lester, Alison *50:* 124; *90:* 147, 148; *129:* 130
Lethcoe, Jason *191:* 116, 117
Le Tord, Bijou *49:* 156; *95:* 112
Leutz, Emanuel *165:* 27
Levai, Blaise *39:* 130
Levin, Ted *12:* 148
Levine, David *43:* 147, 149, 150, 151, 152; *64:* 11
Levine, Joe *71:* 88
Levine, Marge *81:* 127
Levinson, David *178:* 232
Levit, Herschel *24:* 223
Levstek, Ljuba *131:* 192; *134:* 216; *149:* 65; *168:* 180
Levy, Jessica Ann *19:* 225; *39:* 191
Levy, Lina *117:* 126
Lewin, Betsy *32:* 114; *48:* 177; *90:* 151; *91:* 125; *92:* 85; *115:* 105; *169:* 110, 111; *178:* 47; *186:* 188; *194:* 201
Lewin, Ted *4:* 77; *8:* 168; *20:* 110; *21:* 99,100; *27:* 110; *28:* 96, 97; *31:* 49; *45:* 55; *48:* 223; *60:* 20, 119, 120; *62:* 139; *66:* 108; *71:* 12; *72:* 21; *74:* 226; *76:* 139, 140; *77:* 82; *79:* 87; *85:* 49, 177; *86:* 55; *88:* 182; *93:* 28, 29; *94:* 34, 182, 194; *99:* 156; *104:* 8; *115:* 123; *118:* 74; *119:* 114, 116; *131:* 54; *145:* 99; *165:* 151; *177:* 75; *178:* 42; *190:* 30; *192:* 86; *195:* 101, 102
Lewis, Allen *15:* 112

Lewis, E.B. *88:* 143; *93:* 109; *119:* 79; *124:* 113; *128:* 49; *151:* 167; *168:* 110; *173:* 121; *174:* 66; *176:* 7; *184:* 150; *185:* 191
Lewis, H.B. *170:* 124
Lewis, J. Patrick *162:* 83
Lewis, Jan *81:* 22
Lewis, Kim *136:* 165
Lewis, Richard W. *52:* 25
Lewis, Robin Baird *98:* 193
Leydon, Rita Floden *21:* 101
Li, Xiojun *187:* 172
Lichtenheld, Tom *152:* 125, 126
Lieblich, Irene *22:* 173; *27:* 209, 214
Lieder, Rick *108:* 197; *199:* 58, 59, 60
Lies, Brian *92:* 40; *141:* 101; *150:* 138; *190:* 97, 98, 99,
Liese, Charles *4:* 222
Life, Kay *79:* 49
Lifton, Robert Jay *66:* 154
Lightburn, Ron *86:* 153; *91:* 122
Lightfoot, Norman R. *45:* 47
Lignell, Lois *37:* 114
Lill, Debra *121:* 70
Lilly, Charles *8:* 73; *20:* 127; *48:* 53; *72:* 9,16; *77:* 98; *102:* 94
Lilly, Ken *37:* 224
Lim, John *43:* 153
Limona, Mercedes *51:* 183
Lin, Grace *143:* 217; *162:* 86, 87; *174:* 185
Lincoln, Patricia Henderson *27:* 27; *78:* 127
Lindahn, Ron *84:* 17
Lindahn, Val *84:* 17
Lindberg, Howard *10:* 123; *16:* 190
Lindberg, Jeffrey *64:* 77; *77:* 71; *79:* 54; *80:* 149; *174:* 109; *179:* 52
Linden, Seymour *18:* 200, 201; *43:* 140
Lindenbaum, Pija *144:* 143; *183:* 113
Linder, Richard *27:* 119
Lindman, Maj *43:* 154
Lindsay, Norman *67:* 114
Lindsay, Vachel *40:* 118
Lindstrom, Jack *145:* 118
Line, Les *27:* 143
Linell
See Smith, Linell
Lionni, Leo *8:* 115; *72:* 159, 160, 161
Lipinsky, Lino *2:* 156; *22:* 175
Lippincott, Gary A. *70:* 35; *119:* 118
Lippman, Peter *8:* 31; *31:* 119, 120, 160
Lisi, Victoria *89:* 145
Lisker, Emily *169:* 114
Lisker, Sonia O. *16:* 274; *31:* 31; *44:* 113, 114
Lisowski, Gabriel *47:* 144; *49:* 157
Lissim, Simon *17:* 138
Little, Ed *89:* 145; *151:* 53
Little, Harold *16:* 72
Little, Mary E. *28:* 146
Littlewood, Karen *165:* 126
Litty, Julie *111:* 63
Litzinger, Rosanne *151:* 101; *176:* 118; *196:* 133, 134, 135
Liu, Lesley *143:* 72
Livesly, Lorna *19:* 216
Livingston, Susan *95:* 22
Liwska, Renata *164:* 113; *199:* 25, 69
Ljungkvist, Laura *180:* 120
Llerena, Carlos Antonio *19:* 181
Lloyd, Errol *11:* 39; *22:* 178
Lloyd, Megan *77:* 118; *80:* 113; *97:* 75; *117:* 94, 95; *189:* 121, 122
Lloyd, Sam *183:* 116, 117
Lo, Beth *165:* 154
Lo, Koon-chiu *7:* 134
Loates, Glen *63:* 76
Lobel, Anita *6:* 87; *9:* 141; *18:* 248; *55:* 85,86, 87, 88, 93, 104; *60:* 67; *78:* 263; *82:* 110; *96:* 157, 159; *101:* 84; *132:* 35; *162:* 93, 94

Lobel, Arnold *1:* 188, 189; *5:* 12; *6:* 147; *7:* 167, 209; *18:* 190, 191; *25:* 39, 43; *27:* 40; *29:* 174; *52:* 127; *55:* 89, 91, 94, 95, 97, 98, 99, 100, 101, 102,103, 105, 106; *60:* 18, 31; *66:* 181, 183; *75:* 57; *82:* 246; *136:* 146
Lobel, Gillian *190:* 21
Locker, Thomas *109:* 134
Lodge, Bernard *107:* 125, 126; *153:* 93
Loeb, Jeph *153:* 177
Lodge, Jo *112:* 119
Loefgren, Ulf *3:* 108
Loescher, Ann *20:* 108
Loescher, Gil *20:* 108
Loew, David *93:* 184; *171:* 120
Lofting, Hugh *15:* 182, 183; *100:* 161, 162
Lofts, Pamela *60:* 188
Loh, George *38:* 88
Lomberg, Jon *58:* 160
Lonette, Reisie *11:* 211; *12:* 168; *13:* 56; *36:* 122; *43:* 155
Long, Ethan *168:* 146; *178:* 12; *182:* 120, 121; *196:* 124
Long, Laurel *162:* 135; *190:* 11
Long, Loren *99:* 176; *172:* 65; *182:* 78; *188:* 114, 115
Long, Melinda *152:* 128
Long, Miles *115:* 174
Long, Sally *42:* 184
Long, Sylvia *74:* 168; *132:* 63; *179:* 134
Longoni, Eduardo *73:* 85
Longtemps, Ken *17:* 123; *29:* 221; *69:* 82
Looser, Heinz *YABC 2:* 208
Lopez, Loretta *190:* 100
López, Rafael *197:* 160; *198:* 85
Lopshire, Robert *6:* 149; *21:* 117; *34:* 166; *73:* 13
Lord, John Vernon *21:* 104; *23:* 25; *51:* 22
Lorenz, Albert *40:* 146; *115:* 127
Loretta, Sister Mary *33:* 73
Lorraine, Walter H. *3:* 110; *4:* 123; *16:* 192; *103:* 119
Los, Marek *146:* 22; *193:* 23
Loss, Joan *11:* 163
Louderback, Walt *YABC 1:* 164
Lousada, Sandra *40:* 138
Louth, Jack *149:* 252; *151:* 191, 192
Love, Judy *173:* 43; *196:* 40
Low, Joseph *14:* 124, 125; *18:* 68; *19:* 194; *31:* 166; *80:* 239
Low, William *62:* 175; *80:* 147; *112:* 194; *150:* 202; *169:* 177; *177:* 110; *192:* 27
Lowe, Vicky *177:* 130
Lowenheim, Alfred *13:* 65, 66
Lowenstein, Sallie *116:* 90, 91
Lowitz, Anson *17:* 124; *18:* 215
Lowrey, Jo *8:* 133
Lubach, Vanessa *142:* 152
Lubell, Winifred *1:* 207; *3:* 15; *6:* 151
Lubin, Leonard B. *19:* 224; *36:* 79, 80; *45:* 128, 129,131, 132, 133, 134, 135, 136, 137, 139, 140, 141; *70:* 95; *YABC2:* 96
Lucht, Irmgard *82:* 145
Ludwig, Helen *33:* 144, 145
Lufkin, Raymond *38:* 138; *44:* 48
Luhrs, Henry *7:* 123; *11:* 120
Lujan, Tonita *82:* 33
Lupo, Dom *4:* 204
Lustig, Loretta *30:* 186; *46:* 134, 135, 136, 137
Luthardt, Kevin *172:* 125, 126
Luxbacher, Irene *153:* 145
Luzak, Dennis *52:* 121; *99:* 142
Lydbury, Jane *82:* 98
Lydecker, Laura *21:* 113; *42:* 53
Lynch, Charles *16:* 33
Lynch, Marietta *29:* 137; *30:* 171
Lynch, P.J. *126:* 228; *129:* 110; *132:* 247; *183:* 64
Lyne, Alison Davis *188:* 118, 198
Lyon, Carol *102:* 26
Lyon, Elinor *6:* 154

Lyon, Fred *14:* 16
Lyon, Tammie *175:* 170
Lyons, Oren *8:* 193
Lyster, Michael *26:* 41

M

Maas, Dorothy *6:* 175
Maas, Julie *47:* 61
Macaulay, David *46:* 139, 140, 141, 142, 143, 144, 145, 147, 149, 150; *72:* 167, 168, 169; *137:* 129, 130, 131, 132
MacCarthy, Patricia *69:* 141
Macdonald, Alister *21:* 55
Macdonald, Roberta *19:* 237; *52:* 164
MacDonald, Norman *13:* 99
MacDonald, Ross *201:* 103
MacDonald, Suse *54:* 41; *109* 138; *130:* 156; *193:* 106, 107, 109, 110
Mace, Varian *49:* 159
Macguire, Robert Reid *18:* 67
Machetanz, Fredrick *34:* 147, 148
MacInnes, Ian *35:* 59
MacIntyre, Elisabeth *17:* 127, 128
Mack, Jeff *161:* 128; *194:* 119, 120
Mack, Stan *17:* 129; *96:* 33
Mackay, Donald *17:* 60
MacKaye, Arvia *32:* 119
Mackenzie, Stuart *73:* 213
MacKenzie, Garry *33:* 159
Mackie, Clare *87:* 134
Mackinlay, Miguel *27:* 22
MacKinstry, Elizabeth *15:* 110; *42:* 139, 140, 141, 142, 143,144, 145
MacLeod, Lee *91:* 167
Maclise, Daniel *YABC 2:* 257
Macnaughton, Tina *182:* 145
MacRae, Tom *181:* 112
Madden, Don *3:* 112, 113; *4:* 33, 108, 155; *7:* 193; *78:* 12; *YABC 2:* 211
Maddison, Angela Mary *10:* 83
Madsen, Jim *146:* 259; *152:* 237; *184:* 106; *197:* 21
Maestro, Giulio *8:* 124; *12:* 17; *13:* 108; *25:* 182; *54:* 147; *59:* 114, 115, 116, 117, 118, 121, 123, 124, 125,126, 127; *68:* 37, 38; *106:* 129, 130, 131, 136, 137, 138
Maffia, Daniel *60:* 200
Maggio, Viqui *58:* 136, 181; *74:* 150; *75:* 90; *85:* 159; *90:* 158; *109:* 184; *193:* 113
Magnus, Erica *77:* 123
Magnuson, Diana *28:* 102; *34:* 190; *41:* 175
Magoon, Scott *181:* 104
Magovern, Peg *103:* 123
Maguire, Sheila *41:* 100
Magurn, Susan *91:* 30
Mahony, Will *37:* 120
Mahony, Will *85:* 116
Mahood, Kenneth *24:* 141
Mahurin, Matt *164:* 225; *175:* 95; *189:* 37; *196:* 14
Maik, Henri *9:* 102
Maione, Heather *106:* 5; *178:* 8; *189:* 126, 127; *193:* 58
Maisto, Carol *29:* 87
Maitland, Antony *1:* 100, 176; *8:* 41; *17:* 246; *24:* 46; *25:* 177, 178; *32:* 74; *60:* 65, 195; *67:* 156; *87:* 131; *101:* 110
Majewski, Dawn W. *169:* 95
Mak, Kam *72:* 25; *75:* 43; *87:* 186; *97:* 24; *102:* 154; *149:* 195; *186:* 28
Makie, Pam *37:* 117
Maktima, Joe *116:* 191
Maland, Nick *99:* 77
Male, Alan *132:* 64
Malone, James Hiram *84:* 161
Malone, Nola Langner *82:* 239
Malone, Peter *191:* 121, 122, 123
Malsberg, Edward *51:* 175

Malvern, Corinne *2:* 13; *34:* 148, 149
Manchess, Gregory *165:* 241
Mancusi, Stephen *63:* 198, 199
Mandelbaum, Ira *31:* 115
Manders, John *138:* 152, 155; *188:* 171; *190:* 92; *199:* 5
Manet, Edouard *23:* 170
Mangiat, Jeff *173:* 127
Mangurian, David *14:* 133
Manham, Allan *42:* 109; *77:* 180; *80:* 227
Manley, Matt *103:* 167; *117:* 98; *172:* 49
Manna, Giovanni *178:* 44
Manniche, Lise *31:* 121
Manning, Jane *96:* 203
Manning, Jo *63:* 154
Manning, Lawrence *191:* 153
Manning, Mick *176:* 139
Manning, Samuel F. *5:* 75
Mantel, Richard *57:* 73; *63:* 106; *82:* 255
Maraja *15:* 86; *YABC 1:* 28; *2:* 115
Marcellino, Fred *20:* 125; *34:* 222; *53:* 125; *58:* 205; *61:* 64, 121, 122; *68:* 154, 156, 157, 158, 159; *72:* 25; *86:* 184; *98:* 181; *118:* 129, 130, 131; *149:* 218; *194:* 7
Marchesi, Stephen *34:* 140; *46:* 72; *50:* 147; *66:* 239; *70:* 33; *73:* 18, 114, 163; *77:* 47, 76,147; *78:* 79; *80:* 30; *81:* 6; *89:* 66; *93:* 21,130; *94:* 94; *97:* 66; *98:* 96; *114:* 115, 116
Marchiori, Carlos *14:* 60
Marciano, John Bemelmans *118:* 133; *167:* 110, 111, 112
Marcus, Barry David *139:* 248; *145:* 18
Maren, Julie *199:* 73
Margules, Gabriele *21:* 120
Mariana
    See Foster, Marian Curtis
Mariano, Michael *52:* 108
Marino, Dorothy *6:* 37; *14:* 135
Mario, Heide Stetson *101:* 202
Maris, Ron *71:* 123
Maritz, Nicolaas *85:* 123
Mark, Mona *65:* 105; *68:* 205; *116:* 213
Markham, R.L. *17:* 240
Marks, Alan *104:* 104; *109:* 182; *164:* 92; *185:* 134; *187:* 120, 121, 122
Marks, Cara *54:* 9
Marokvia, Artur *31:* 122
Marquez, Susan *108:* 121
Marrella, Maria Pia *62:* 116
Marriott, Pat *30:* 30; *34:* 39; *35:* 164, 165, 166; *44:* 170; *48:* 186, 187, 188, 189, 191, 192, 193; *91:* 92
Mars, W.T. *1:* 161; *3:* 115; *4:* 208, 225; *5:* 92, 105, 186; *8:* 214; *9:* 12; *13:* 121; *27:* 151; *31:* 180; *38:* 102; *48:* 66; *62:* 164, 165; *64:* 62; *68:* 229; *79:* 55
Marschall, Ken *85:* 29
Marsh, Christine *3:* 164
Marsh, James *73:* 137
Marsh, Reginald *17:* 5; *19:* 89; *22:* 90, 96
Marshall, Anthony D. *18:* 216
Marshall, Felicia *170:* 190
Marshall, James *6:* 160; *40:* 221; *42:* 24, 25, 29; *51:* 111, 112, 113, 114, 115, 116, 117, 118, 119, 120, 121; *64:* 13; *75:* 126, 127, 128, 129; *102:* 10, 12
Marshall, Janet *97:* 154
Marstall, Bob *55:* 145; *84:* 153, 170; *104:* 145; *154:* 166, 167, 168
Martchenko, Michael *50:* 129, 153, 155, 156, 157; *83:* 144,145; *154:* 137, 138, 139
Marten, Ruth *129:* 52
Martin, Brad *199:* 186
Martin, Charles E. *70:* 144
Martin, David Stone *24:* 232; *62:* 4
Martin, Fletcher *18:* 213; *23:* 151
Martin, Rene *7:* 144; *42:* 148, 149, 150
Martin, Richard E. *51:* 157; *131:* 203
Martin, Ron *32:* 81
Martin, Stefan *8:* 68; *32:* 124, 126; *56:* 33

Martin, Whitney *166:* 137
Martinez, Ed *58:* 192; *72:* 231; *77:* 33; *80:* 214; *167:* 123
Martinez, John *6:* 113; *118:* 13; *139:* 143
Martinez, Sergio *158:* 190
Martini, Angela *183:* 161
Martiniere, Stephan *171:* 130
Marton, Jirina *95:* 127, 128; *144:* 145
Martorell, Antonio *84:* 6; *97:* 161
Martucci, Griesbach *52:* 106
Marvin, Frederic *83:* 86
Marx, Robert F. *24:* 143
Marzollo, Jean *190:* 127
Masefield, Judith *19:* 208, 209
Masheris, Robert *78:* 51
Masiello, Ralph *186:* 171
Mason, George F. *14:* 139
Mason, Robert *84:* 96
Massey, Barbara *68:* 142
Massie, Diane Redfield *16:* 194
Massie, Kim *31:* 43
Mataya, David *121:* 66
Mathers, Petra *119:* 135; *163:* 104; *176:* 143, 144; *187:* 142; *196:* 101
Mathewuse, James *51:* 143
Mathieu, Joseph *14:* 33; *39:* 206; *43:* 167; *56:* 180; *79:* 126; *94:* 147; *185:* 140
Matje, Martin *169:* 177, 178; *172:* 180
Matsubara, Naoko *12:* 121
Matsuda, Shizu *13:* 167
Matsuoka, Mei *192:* 135
Matte, L'Enc *22:* 183
Mattelson, Marvin *36:* 50, 51
Mattheson, Jenny *180:* 132
Matthews, Elizabeth *194:* 128
Matthews, F. Leslie *4:* 216
Matthews, Tina *190:* 130
Mattingly, David *71:* 76, 77; *82:* 64; *91:* 216, 217; *109:* 25
Matulay, Laszlo *5:* 18; *43:* 168
Matus, Greta *12:* 142
Maughan, William *181:* 31
Mauldin, Bill *27:* 23
Mauterer, Erin Marie *119:* 5
Mawicke, Tran *9:* 137; *15:* 191; *47:* 100
Mawson, Matt *74:* 115
Max, Peter *45:* 146, 147, 148, 149, 150
Maxie, Betty *40:* 135
Maxwell, John Alan *1:* 148
Mayan, Earl *7:* 193
Mayer, Bill *200:* 138
Mayer, Danuta *117:* 103
Mayer, Marianna *32:* 132
Mayer, Mercer *11:* 192; *16:* 195, 196; *20:* 55, 57; *32:* 129, 130, 132, 133, 134; *41:* 144, 248, 252; *58:* 186; *73:* 140, 142, 143; *137:* 137, 138
Mayforth, Hal *166:* 77
Mayhew, James *85:* 121; *138:* 187; *149:* 140
Mayhew, Richard *3:* 106
Mayo, Gretchen Will *38:* 81; *84:* 166
Mays, Victor *5:* 127; *8:* 45, 153; *14:* 245; *23:* 50; *34:* 155; *40:* 79; *45:* 158; *54:* 91; *66:* 240
Mazal, Chanan *49:* 104
Maze, Deborah *71:* 83
Mazellan, Ron *75:* 97, 98
Mazetti, Alan *112:* 72
Mazille, Capucine *96:* 168
Mazza, Adriana Saviozzi *19:* 215
Mazzella, Mary Jo *82:* 165
Mazzetti, Alan *45:* 210
McAfee, Steve *135:* 146; *167:* 176; *191:* 84
McAlinden, Paul *112:* 128
McBride, Angus *28:* 49; *103:* 40
McBride, Will *30:* 110
McCaffery, Janet *38:* 145
McCallum, Graham *78:* 78
McCallum, Stephen *141:* 143; *156:* 5; *166:* 228
McCann, Gerald *3:* 50; *4:* 94; *7:* 54; *41:* 121

McCarthy, Dan *174:* 74
McCarthy, Linda *177:* 128
McCarthy, Meghan *168:* 134; *199:* 74
McCauley, Adam *157:* 36; *184:* 199; *193:* 100
McCay, Winsor *41:* 124, 126, 128, 129, 130, 131; *134:* 77, 79
McClary, Nelson *1:* 111
McClements, George *196:* 146
McClintock, Barbara *57:* 135; *95:* 130; *146:* 190
McClintock, Theodore *14:* 141
McCloskey, Robert *1:* 184, 185; *2:* 186, 187; *17:* 209; *39:* 139, 140, 141, 142, 143, 146, 147, 148; *85:* 150, 151; *100:* 172, 173, 174
McClung, Robert *2:* 189; *68:* 166, 167
McClure, Gillian *31:* 132; *150:* 53
McConnel, Jerry *31:* 75, 187
McConnell, Mary *102:* 49
McCord, Kathleen Garry *78:* 236
McCormack, John *66:* 193
McCormick, A.D. *35:* 119
McCormick, Dell J. *19:* 216
McCrady, Lady *16:* 198; *39:* 127
McCrea, James *3:* 122; *33:* 216
McCrea, Ruth *3:* 122; *27:* 102; *33:* 216
McCue, Lisa *65:* 148, 149; *77:* 54; *80:* 132; *175:* 33; *177:* 133, 135
McCully, Emily Arnold *2:* 89; *4:* 120, 121, 146, 197; *5:* 2, 129; *7:* 191; *11:* 122; *15:* 210; *33:* 23; *35:* 244; *37:* 122; *39:* 88; *40:* 103; *50:* 30,31, 32, 33, 34, 35, 36, 37; *52:* 89, 90; *57:* 6; *62:* 3; *70:* 195; *86:* 82; *96:* 192; *97:* 93; *110:* 143,144; *117:* 47; *167:* 96
McCurdy, Michael *13:* 153; *24:* 85; *81:* 160; *82:* 157, 158; *86:* 125; *97:* 92; *117:* 178; *132:* 6; *147:* 159, 160
McCusker, Paul *99:* 19
McDaniel, Jerry *132:* 135
McDaniel, Preston *160:* 206; *170:* 139
McDermott, Beverly Brodsky *11:* 180
McDermott, Gerald *16:* 201; *74:* 174, 175; *163:* 150, 151
McDermott, Mike *96:* 187
McDonald, Jill *13:* 155; *26:* 128
McDonald, Mercedes *169:* 118
McDonald, Ralph J. *5:* 123, 195
McDonnell, Flora *146:* 199, 200
McDonnell, Patrick *179:* 153, 154
McDonough, Don *10:* 163
McElligott, Matt *196:* 147
McElmurry, Jill *137:* 148; *163:* 141
McElrath-Eslick, Lori *129:* 145; *142:* 21; *173:* 123
McEntee, Dorothy *37:* 124
McEwan, Keith *88:* 116; *165:* 122, 123
McEwen, Katharine *169:* 34
McFall, Christie *12:* 144
McFeely, Daniel *160:* 213
McGaw, Laurie *109:* 243; *143:* 216
McGee, Barbara *6:* 165
McGee, Marni *163:* 153
McGillvray, Kim *158:* 171; *165:* 213; *186:* 183; *190:* 175
McGinley-Nally, Sharon *131:* 19
McGinnis, Robert *110:* 113; *177:* 80
McGovern, Tara *98:* 171
McGraw, Sheila *83:* 146
McGregor, Barbara *200:* 155
McGregor, Malcolm *23:* 27
McGrory, Anik *193:* 120
McGuirk, Leslie *152:* 159
McHale, John *138:* 190
McHenry, E.B. *193:* 122
McHugh, Tom *23:* 64
McIntosh, Jon *42:* 56
McKay, Donald *2:* 118; *32:* 157; *45:* 151, 152
McKean, Dave *150:* 71; *174:* 156; *197:* 83, 118
McKeating, Eileen *44:* 58

McKee, David *10:* 48; *21:* 9; *70:* 154, 155; *107:* 139, 140, 141; *134:* 218; *158:* 148, 149, 150, 151
McKee, Diana *109:* 185
McKelvey, Patrick *164:* 141
McKendry, Joe *170:* 136
McKeveny, Tom *164:* 60; *173:* 79
McKie, Roy *7:* 44
McKillip, Kathy *30:* 153
McKinney, Ena *26:* 39
McKinnon, James *136:* 75
McKowen, Scott *172:* 63
McLachlan, Edward *5:* 89
McLaren, Chesley *133:* 53
McLaren, Kirsty *123:* 99; *124:* 226
Mclean, Andrew *113:* 117, 118, 120, 121; *172:* 130, 131
Mclean, Janet *172:* 130
McLean, Meg *94:* 196
McLean, Sammis *32:* 197
McLean, Wilson *90:* 29; *113:* 195
McLoughlin, John C. *47:* 149
McLoughlin, Wayne *102:* 230; *134:* 178
McMahon, Robert *36:* 155; *69:* 169
McManus, Shawn *85:* 71
McMenemy, Sarah *156:* 139
McMillan, Bruce *22:* 184
McMullan, James *40:* 33; *67:* 172; *87:* 142; *99:* 63, 64; *189:* 133; *196:* 51
McMullen, Nigel *146:* 177
McNeely, Tom *162:* 55
McNaught, Harry *12:* 80; *32:* 136
McNaughton, Colin *39:* 149; *40:* 108; *92:* 144, 145, 146; *134:* 104, 106
McNicholas, Maureen *38:* 148
McNicholas, Shelagh *173:* 61; *191:* 125, 126
McPhail, David *14:* 105; *23:* 135; *37:* 217, 218, 220,221; *47:* 151, 152, 153, 154, 155, 156, 158, 159, 160, 162, 163, 164; *71:* 211; *81:* 139, 140, 142; *86:* 123; *132:* 150; *140:* 129, 131, 132; *183:* 134, 135, 137; *189:* 132
McPhee, Richard B. *41:* 133
McPheeters, Neal *78:* 132; *86:* 90; *99:* 162; *111:* 141; *142:* 162
McQuade, Jacqueline *124:* 223
McQueen, Lucinda *28:* 149; *41:* 249; *46:* 206; *53:* 103
McQuillan, Mary *153:* 97; *200:* 140
McVay, Tracy *11:* 68
McVicker, Charles *39:* 150
Mead, Ben Carlton *43:* 75
Meade, Holly *90:* 102; *94:* 101; *149:* 8; *151:* 107
Mecray, John *33:* 62
Meddaugh, Susan *20:* 42; *29:* 143; *41:* 241; *77:* 50; *84:* 173, 174, 175, 176, 177, 178; *125:* 160, 161, 162; *176:* 148, 149, 150, 151
Meehan, Dennis B. *56:* 144
Meents, Len W. *73:* 147, 150
Meers, Tony *99:* 113
Meisel, Paul *98:* 137; *124:* 18; *162:* 180; *179:* 16; *181:* 62; *194:* 154
Melanson, Luc *149:* 229; *198:* 97, 98
Melendez, Francisco *72:* 180
Melnychuk, Monika *153:* 65
Melo, Esperança *196:* 90
Melo, John *16:* 285; *58:* 203
Meloni, Maria Teresa *98:* 62
Meltzer, Ericka
  See O'Rourke, Ericka
Menasco, Milton *43:* 85
Menchin, Scott *188:* 129
Mendelson, Steven T. *86:* 154
Mendelsohn, Felix *19:* 170
Mendola, Christopher *88:* 223
Meng, Heinz *13:* 158
Merian, Maria Sibylla *140:* 88
Mero, Lee *34:* 68
Merrill, Frank T. *16:* 147; *19:* 71; *YABC 1:* 226, 229,273
Merriman, Rachel *98:* 108; *114:* 122; *149:* 142

Merveille, David *200:* 142
Meryman, Hope *27:* 41
Meryweather, Jack *10:* 179
Meseldzija, Petar *168:* 97
Meserve, Jess *184:* 137
Messick, Dale *64:* 150, 151, 152
Meth, Harold *24:* 203
Meyer, Herbert *19:* 189
Meyer, Renate *6:* 170
Meyers, Bob *11:* 136
Meyers, Nancy *172:* 124
Meynell, Louis *37:* 76
Micale, Albert *2:* 65; *22:* 185
Miccuci, Charles *82:* 163; *144:* 150
Micich, Paul *164:* 163
Middleton, Jeffrey *177:* 173
Middleton-Sandford, Betty *2:* 125
Mieke, Anne *45:* 74
Mighell, Patricia *43:* 134
Miglio, Paige *101:* 203; *151:* 223; *201:* 118, 119
Mikolaycak, Charles *9:* 144; *12:* 101; *13:* 212; *21:* 121; *22:* 168; *30:* 187; *34:* 103, 150; *37:* 183; *43:* 179; *44:* 90; *46:* 115, 118, 119; *49:* 25; *78:* 121, 122, 205, 207; *81:* 4
Milelli, Pascal *129:* 66; *135:* 153; *187:* 45
Miles, Elizabeth *117:* 77
Miles, Jennifer *17:* 278
Milgrim, David *158:* 157; *187:* 125, 126, 128
Milhous, Katherine *15:* 193; *17:* 51
Millais, John E. *22:* 230, 231
Millar, H.R. *YABC 1:* 194, 195, 203
Millard, C.E. *28:* 186
Millard, Kerry *105:* 124
Miller, Don *15:* 195; *16:* 71; *20:* 106; *31:* 178
Miller, Edna *29:* 148
Miller, Edward *115:* 64; *183:* 140, 141
Miller, Frank J. *25:* 94
Miller, Grambs *18:* 38; *23:* 16
Miller, Ian *99:* 128
Miller, Jane *15:* 196
Miller, Marcia *13:* 233
Miller, Marilyn *1:* 87; *31:* 69; *33:* 157
Miller, Mitchell *28:* 183; *34:* 207
Miller, Phil *175:* 150
Miller, Shane *5:* 140
Miller, Virginia *81:* 206
Millman, Isaac *172:* 18
Mills, Elaine *72:* 181
Mills, Judith Christine *130:* 168, 169
Mills, Lauren *92:* 170
Mills, Yaroslava Surmach *35:* 169, 170; *46:* 114
Millsap, Darrel *51:* 102
Milone, Karen *89:* 169
Milord, Susan *147:* 163, 164; *200:* 144
Milton, Debbie *162:* 161
Mims, Ashley *170:* 51
Miner, Julia *98:* 69
Minor, Wendell *39:* 188; *52:* 87; *56:* 171; *58:* 116; *62:* 56; *66:* 109; *74:* 93; *78:* 129; *94:* 67; *117:* 12, 13; *124:* 84, 86; *136:* 121; *164:* 168, 169; *170:* 71; *199:* 79, 80, 81, 82
Minter, Daniel *176:* 154; *179:* 177
Mirocha, Paul *81:* 133; *192:* 148; *194:* 36
Misako Rocks! *192:* 149, 150
Mitchell, Judith *109:* 117
Mitchell, Mark *91:* 208
Mitchell, Tracy *190:* 15
Mitgutsch, Ali *76:* 161
Mitsuhashi, Yoko *45:* 153
Miyake, Yoshi *38:* 141
Mizumura, Kazue *10:* 143; *18:* 223; *36:* 159
Mochi, Ugo *8:* 122; *38:* 150
Mock, Paul *55:* 83; *123:* 32
Modarressi, Mitra *90:* 236; *126:* 168; *173:* 165, 166; *200:* 147, 148
Modell, Frank *39:* 152
Mogenson, Jan *74:* 183
Mohn, Susan *89:* 224
Mohr, Mark *133:* 201

Mohr, Nicholasa 8: 139; 113: 127
Molan, Christine 60: 177; 84: 183
Moldon, Peter L. 49: 168
Molk, Laurel 92: 150
Mollica, Gene 197: 11
Momaday, N. Scott 48: 159
Mombourquette, Paul 112: 91; 126: 142
Monk, Julie 165: 231; 191: 96
Monks, Lydia 189: 136, 137
Monroy, Manuel 199: 192
Montgomery, Lucy 150: 126
Montgomery-Higham, Amanda 169: 131
Monteiel, David 201: 95
Montiel, David 69: 106; 84: 145
Montijo, Rhode 193: 164
Montresor, Beni 2: 91; 3: 138; 38: 152, 153, 154,155, 156, 157, 158, 159, 160; 68: 63
Montserrat, Pep 128: 135; 181: 119; 184: 53
Moon, Carl 25: 183, 184, 185
Moon, Eliza 14: 40
Moon, Ivan 22: 39; 38: 140
Moore, Adrienne 67: 147
Moore, Agnes Kay Randall 43: 187
Moore, Cyd 117: 107, 108; 159: 137, 138; 186: 148, 149, 151
Moore, Gustav 127: 181, 182; 170: 162, 163
Moore, Jackie 128: 79
Moore, Janet 63: 153
Moore, Margie 176: 156
Moore, Mary 29: 160
Moore, Patrick 184: 121
Moore, Yvette 101: 11, 12; 154: 141
Mora, Giovanni 179: 127; 184: 11
Mora, Raul Mina 20: 41
Moraes, Odilon 102: 144
Morales, Yuyi 154: 144
Moran, Rosslyn 111: 26
Moran, Tom 60: 100
Mordan, C.B. 193: 115
Mordvinoff, Nicolas 15: 179
Moreno, René King 169: 59; 190: 133, 209
Morgan, Barbara 169: 116
Morgan, Jacqui 58: 57
Morgan, Mary 114: 133, 134, 135; 123: 11
Morgan, Tom 42: 157
Morgan, Pierr 173: 148
Morgenstern, Michael 158: 7, 57; 171: 103; 174: 60
Morice, Dave 93: 142
Morin, Paul 73: 132; 79: 130; 88: 140; 137: 143
Moriuchi, Mique 177: 203
Morozumi, Atsuko 110: 155
Morrill, Leslie 18: 218; 29: 177; 33: 84; 38: 147; 42: 127; 44: 93; 48: 164, 165, 167, 168, 169, 170,171; 49: 162; 63: 136, 180; 70: 72; 71: 70, 91,92; 72: 228; 80: 163, 164, 165; 90: 121; 121: 88; 178: 117
Morrill, Rowena A. 84: 16; 98: 163
Morris 47: 91
Morris, Frank 55: 133; 60: 28; 76: 2
Morris, Harry O. 119: 138
Morris, Jackie 128: 194; 144: 119; 151: 146
Morris, Jennifer E. 179: 157
Morris, Oradel Nolen 128: 180
Morris, Tony 62: 146; 70: 97
Morrison, Bill 42: 116; 66: 170; 69: 40
Morrison, Gordon 87: 150; 113: 93; 128: 181, 182; 183: 144, 145, 146
Morrison, Frank 169: 162
Morrison, Taylor 159: 144, 145; 187: 131
Morrow, Gray 2: 64; 5: 200; 10: 103, 114; 14: 175
Morse, Scott 200: 149, 150
Morton, Lee Jack 32: 140
Morton, Marian 3: 185
Mosberg, Hilary 117: 195; 118: 164; 149: 55
Moser, Barry 56: 68, 117, 118, 119, 120, 121, 122, 123, 124; 59: 141; 60: 160; 79: 91, 147, 149, 151, 152; 82: 81; 90: 118; 91: 35;

95: 210; 97: 91, 93; 102: 152; 126: 4; 128: 175; 133: 141; 138: 167, 171, 174; 153: 205; 174: 130; 185: 152, 154; 195: 163
Moser, Cara 90: 118; 138: 167
Moses, Grandma 18: 228
Moses, Will 178: 170, 171
Moskof, Martin Stephen 27: 152
Mosley, Francis 57: 144
Moss, Donald 11: 184
Moss, Geoffrey 32: 198
Moss, Marissa 71: 130; 104: 127; 163: 156
Most, Bernard 48: 173; 91: 142, 143; 134: 120
Mowll, Joshua 188: 133
Mowry, Carmen 50: 62
Moxley, Sheila 96: 174; 169: 26
Moyers, William 21: 65
Moyler, Alan 36: 142
Mozley, Charles 9: 87; 20: 176, 192, 193; 22: 228; 25: 205; 33: 150; 43: 170, 171, 172, 173, 174; YABC2: 89
Mueller, Hans Alexander 26: 64; 27: 52, 53
Mugnaini, Joseph 11: 35; 27: 52, 53; 35: 62
Mujica, Rick 72: 67; 88: 95; 111: 53; 180: 185; 197: 70
Mullen, Douglas 180: 178
Muller, Robin 86: 161
Muller, Steven 32: 167
Muller, Jorg 35: 215; 67: 138, 139
Mulock, Julie 163: 112
Mullins, Edward S. 10: 101
Mullins, Patricia 51: 68
Multer, Scott 80: 108
Munari, Bruno 15: 200
Munch, Edvard 140: 143
Munowitz, Ken 14: 148; 72: 178, 179
Munro, Roxie 58: 134; 136: 177; 137: 218; 184: 133, 134
Munsinger, Lynn 33: 161; 46: 126; 71: 92; 82: 80; 89: 218; 92: 125; 94: 157, 158, 159, 160; 98: 196; 103: 198; 142: 143; 145: 133, 134, 136; 153: 203; 176: 162; 177: 140, 141, 142; 189: 113, 114, 116, 117; 201: 42
Munson, Russell 13: 9
Munster, Sebastian 166: 107
Munoz, William 42: 160
Munzar, Barbara 149: 75
Murdocca, Salvatore 73: 212; 98: 132; 111: 168; 157: 228; 164: 257
Murphy, Bill 5: 138; 130: 170
Murphy, Jill 37: 142; 70: 166; 142: 132, 134
Murphy, Kelly 130: 212; 143: 119; 176: 158; 190: 135
Murphy, Mary 196: 158
Murphy, Tom 192: 40
Murr, Karl 20: 62
Murray, Joe 175: 37
Murray, Ossie 43: 176
Mussino, Attilio 29: 131; 100: 164
Mutchler, Dwight 1: 25
Myers, Bernice 9: 147; 36: 75; 81: 146, 147, 148
Muth, Jon J. 165: 169; 167: 109; 190: 227; 193: 59
Myers, Christopher 183: 150; 193: 139
Myers, Duane O. 99: 145
Myers, Tim 147: 168
Myers, V.G. 142: 41
Myers, Lou 11: 2

N

Nachreiner, Tom 29: 182
Nacht, Merle 65: 49
Nadler, Ellis 88: 91
Nagle, Shane 180: 223
Nagy, Ian 195: 64
Najaka, Marlies 62: 101
Nakai, Michael 30: 217; 54: 29
Nakata, Hiroe 157: 156; 162: 30

Nakatani, Chiyoko 12: 124
Narahashi, Keiko 77: 188; 82: 213; 115: 142, 143, 144
Nascimbene, Yan 133: 128; 173: 132, 133
Nash, Lesa 87: 135
Nash, Linell 46: 175
Nash, Scott 130: 36; 188: 196
Naso, John 33: 183
Nason, Thomas W. 14: 68
Nasser, Muriel 48: 74
Nast, Thomas 21: 29; 28: 23; 51: 132, 133, 134, 135,136, 137, 138, 139, 141
Nasta, Vincent 78: 185
Natale, Vincent 76: 3; 78: 125; 112: 47; 166: 81; 174: 189; 185: 212; 197: 59
Natchev, Alexi 96: 177
Nathan, Charlott 125: 151
Nathan, Cheryl 150: 104; 186: 112
Natti, Susanna 20: 146; 32: 141, 142; 35: 178; 37: 143; 71: 49; 93: 98; 125: 166, 168; 126: 228; 151: 6; 178: 8; 188: 106
Navarra, Celeste Scala 8: 142
Naylor, Penelope 10: 104
Nazz, James 72: 8
Nebel, M. 45: 154
Neebe, William 7: 93
Needham, Dave 196: 85
Needler, Jerry 12: 93
Neel, Alice 31: 23
Neely, Beth 119: 184
Neely, Keith R. 46: 124
Neff, Leland 78: 74
Negri, Rocco 3: 213; 5: 67; 6: 91, 108; 12: 159
Negrin, Fabian 174: 125; 175: 15
Neidigh, Sherry 128: 53
Neilan, Eujin Kim 180: 241; 200: 151, 152
Neill, John R. 18: 8, 10, 11, 21, 30; 100: 22
Neilsen, Cliff 158: 131; 177: 112, 121
Neilsen, Terese 116: 74
Nelson, Craig 62: 151; 153; 183: 86
Nelson, Gail White 68: 140
Nelson, Jennifer 129: 152; 199: 132
Nelson, Kadir 151: 185; 154: 146, 147; 157: 189, 222; 181: 122, 124; 197: 155
Nelson, S.D. 131: 34; 181: 126, 127
Ness, Evaline 1: 164, 165; 2: 39; 3: 8; 10: 147; 12: 53; 26: 150, 151, 152, 153; 49: 30, 31, 32; 56: 30; 60: 113
Neubecker, Robert 170: 143
Neville, Vera 2: 182
Nevins, Daniel 191: 173
Nevwirth, Allan 79: 168
Newberry, Clare Turlay 1: 170
Newbold, Greg 108: 125; 145: 199; 151: 23; 193: 178; 197: 10; 199: 92, 93
Newfeld, Frank 14: 121; 26: 154
Newman, Andy 149: 61; 195: 63
Newman, Ann 43: 90
Newman, Barbara Johansen 191: 137, 138
Newsham, Ian 143: 162
Newsom, Carol 40: 159; 44: 60; 47: 189; 65: 29; 70: 192; 80: 36; 85: 137, 138; 92: 167; 191: 82
Newsom, Tom 49: 149; 71: 13, 62; 75: 156; 91: 113
Newton, Jill 83: 105; 200: 154
Ng, Michael 29: 171
Ng, Simon 167: 7
Nguyen, Vincent 189: 49
Nicholson, William 15: 33, 34; 16: 48
Nickens, Bessie 104: 153
Nicklaus, Carol 45: 194; 62: 132, 133
Nickle, John 181: 128
Nickless, Will 16: 139
Nicholas, Corasue 154: 20
Nicolas 17: 130, 132, 133; YABC 2: 215
Niebrugge, Jane 6: 118

Nielsen, Cliff *95:* 207, 208; *105:* 58; *114:* 112; *124:* 12; *125:* 91, 92; *132:* 224; *135:* 187; *136:* 40; *137:* 168; *145:* 54; *149:* 28; *158:* 129; *165:* 64, 158; *168:* 169; *170:* 6; *175:* 114, 116; *187:* 75, 76; *194:* 107; *197:* 172; *201:* 14
Nielsen, Jon *6:* 100; *24:* 202
Nielsen, Kay *15:* 7; *16:* 211, 212, 213, 215, 217; *22:* 143; *YABC 1:* 32, 33
Niemann, Christoph *191:* 141
Nikola-Lisa, W. *180:* 180
Niland, Deborah *25:* 191; *27:* 156; *135:* 50; *172:* 143
Niland, Kilmeny *25:* 191; *75:* 143
Nino, Alex *59:* 145
Ninon *1:* 5; *38:* 101, 103, 108
Nissen, Rie *44:* 35
Nithael, Mark *158:* 237
Nivola, Claire A. *78:* 126; *140:* 147
Nixon, K. *14:* 152
Nobati, Eugenia *194:* 118
Noble, Louise *61:* 170
Noble, Marty *97:* 168; *125:* 171
Noble, Trinka Hakes *39:* 162; *84:* 157
Noda, Takayo *168:* 143
Noguchi, Yoshie *30:* 99
Nolan, Dennis *42:* 163; *67:* 163; *78:* 189; *82:* 225; *83:* 26; *92:* 169, 170; *103:* 166; *111:* 35; *112:* 213; *127:* 171; *166:* 161; *194:* 218
Noll, Sally *82:* 171
Nolte, Larry *121:* 63, 65
Nones, Eric Jon *61:* 111; *76:* 38; *77:* 177
Noonan, Daniel *100:* 224
Noonan, Julia *4:* 163; *7:* 207; *25:* 151; *91:* 29; *95:* 149
Norcia, Ernie *108:* 155; *140:* 47
Nordenskjold, Birgitta *2:* 208
Noreika, Robert *173:* 20
Norling, Beth *149:* 153, 154
Norman, Elaine *77:* 72, 176; *94:* 35; *136:* 63; *178:* 42
Norman, Mary *36:* 138, 147
Norman, Michael *12:* 117; *27:* 168
Northway, Jennifer *85:* 96
Nostlinger, Christiana *162:* 131
Novak, Linda *166:* 205
Novak, Matt *104:* 132, 133; *165:* 173, 174
Novelli, Luca *61:* 137
Nugent, Cynthia *106:* 189
Numeroff, Laura Joffe *28:* 161; *30:* 177
Nurse, Chris *164:* 91
Nussbaumer, Paul *16:* 219; *39:* 117
Nutt, Ken *72:* 69; *97:* 170
Nyce, Helene *19:* 219
Nygren, Tord *30:* 148; *127:* 164

O

Oakley, Graham *8:* 112; *30:* 164, 165; *84:* 188,189, 190, 191, 192
Oakley, Thornton *YABC 2:* 189
Oberheide, Heide *118:* 37
Obligado, Lilian *2:* 28, 66, 67; *6:* 30; *14:* 179; *15:* 103; *25:* 84; *61:* 138, 139, 140, 141, 143
Oblinski, Rafael *190:* 139
Obrant, Susan *11:* 186
O'Brien, Anne Sibley *53:* 116, 117; *155:* 115
O'Brien, John *41:* 253; *72:* 12; *89:* 59, 60; *98:* 16; *161:* 185; *169:* 16; *180:* 196
O'Brien, Patrick *193:* 142, 143, 144
O'Brien, Teresa *87:* 89
O'Brien, Tim *93:* 25; *136:* 94; *164:* 57; *169:* 57; *173:* 55; *175:* 86; *184:* 192; *191:* 134; *193:* 137
O'Clair, Dennis *127:* 25
O'Connor, George *183:* 153
Odell, Carole *35:* 47
Odem, Mel *99:* 164; *167:* 84, 87
O'Donohue, Thomas *40:* 89

Oechsli, Kelly *5:* 144, 145; *7:* 115; *8:* 83, 183; *13:* 117; *20:* 94; *81:* 199
Offen, Hilda *42:* 207
Ogden, Bill *42:* 59; *47:* 55
Ogg, Oscar *33:* 34
Ogle, Nancy Gray *163:* 144
Ohi, Ruth *90:* 175, 177; *131:* 63; *135:* 106; *175:* 107; *179:* 55
Ohlsson, Ib *4:* 152; *7:* 57; *10:* 20; *11:* 90; *19:* 217; *41:* 246; *82:* 106; *92:* 213
Ohtomo, Yasuo *37:* 146; *39:* 212, 213
O'Keefe, Jennifer *136:* 184
O'Kelley, Mattie Lou *36:* 150
Olbinski, Rafal *149:* 27; *158:* 77
Oliver, Isaac *171:* 182
Oliver, Jenni *23:* 121; *35:* 112
Oliver, Narelle *152:* 192; *197:* 129, 130
Oller, Erika *128:* 186; *134:* 126
Olschewski, Alfred *7:* 172
Olsen, Ib Spang *6:* 178, 179; *81:* 164
Olson, Alan *77:* 229
Olson-Brown, Ellen *183:* 154
Olugebefola, Ademola *15:* 205
O'Malley, Kevin *94:* 180; *106:* 8; *113:* 108; *136:* 70; *157:* 193; *191:* 146
O'Neil, Dan IV *7:* 176
O'Neill, Catharine *72:* 113; *84:* 78; *134:* 153
O'Neill, Jean *22:* 146
O'Neill, Martin *187:* 39
O'Neill, Michael J. *54:* 172
O'Neill, Rose *48:* 30, 31
O'Neill, Steve *21:* 118
Ono, Chiyo *7:* 97
Orbaan, Albert *2:* 31; *5:* 65, 171; *9:* 8; *14:* 241; *20:* 109
Orbach, Ruth *21:* 112
Orback, Craig *197:* 132
Orfe, Joan *20:* 81
Org, Ed *119:* 93
Ormai, Stella *72:* 129
Ormerod, Jan *55:* 124; *70:* 170, 171; *90:* 39; *132:* 172, 173, 174; *147:* 98
Ormsby, Virginia H. *11:* 187
O'Rourke, Ericka *108:* 216; *117:* 194; *111:* 142; *119:* 194; *137:* 152; *150:* 134; *167:* 64; *172:* 164; *188:* 163; *191:* 172; *201:* 15
O'Rourke, Ericka Meltzer
  See O'Rourke, Ericka
Orozco, Jose Clemente *9:* 177
Orr, Forrest W. *23:* 9
Orr, N. *19:* 70
Ortiz, Vilma *88:* 158
Osborn, Kathy *152:* 232; *199:* 101, 102
Osborn, Robert *65:* 49
Osborne, Billie Jean *35:* 209
Osmond, Edward *10:* 111
O'Sullivan, Tom *3:* 176; *4:* 55; *78:* 195
Otani, June *124:* 42; *156:* 53
Otis, Rebecca *185:* 92
Ottley, Matt *147:* 221; *171:* 133
Otto, Svend *22:* 130, 141; *67:* 188, 189
Oudry, J.B. *18:* 167
Oughton, Taylor *5:* 23; *104:* 136
Overeng, Johannes *44:* 36
Overlie, George *11:* 156
Owens, Carl *2:* 35; *23:* 521
Owens, Gail *10:* 170; *12:* 157; *19:* 16; *22:* 70; *25:* 81; *28:* 203, 205; *32:* 221, 222; *36:* 132; *46:* 40; *47:* 57; *54:* 66, 67, 68, 69, 70, 71, 72, 73; *71:* 100; *73:* 64; *77:* 157; *80:* 32; *82:* 3; *99:* 226
Owens, Mary Beth *113:* 202, 203; *191:* 148, 149
Owens, Nubia *84:* 74
Oxenbury, Helen *3:* 150, 151; *24:* 81; *68:* 174, 175,176; *81:* 209; *84:* 213, 245; *129:* 56; *149:* 159; *184:* 181
Oz, Robin *88:* 167; *185:* 181

P

Padgett, Jim *12:* 165
Page, Homer *14:* 145
Page, Mark *162:* 70
Paget, Sidney *24:* 90, 91, 93, 95, 97
Paget, Walter *64:* 122
Paillot, Jim *173:* 89
Pajouhesh, Noushin *160:* 121
Pak *12:* 76
Pak, Yu Cha *86:* 174
Paladino, Lance *134:* 30
Palazzo, Tony *3:* 152, 153
Palecek, Josef *56:* 136; *89:* 158
Palen, Debbie *135:* 88; *195:* 148, 149
Palencar, John Jude *84:* 12, 45; *85:* 87; *92:* 187; *99:* 128; *110:* 204; *150:* 122; *171:* 86
Palin, Nicki *81:* 201; *89:* 161
Palladini, David *4:* 113; *40:* 176, 177, 178, 179, 181,224, 225; *50:* 138; *78:* 186
Pallarito, Don *43:* 36
Palmer, Carol *158:* 230; *195:* 187
Palmer, Heidi *15:* 207; *29:* 102
Palmer, Jan *42:* 153; *82:* 161
Palmer, Judd *153:* 160, 161
Palmer, Juliette *6:* 89; *15:* 208
Palmer, Kate Salley *104:* 143; *154:* 169
Palmer, Lemuel *17:* 25, 29
Palmisciano, Diane *110:* 62; *162:* 26
Palmquist, Eric *38:* 133
Panesis, Nicholas *3:* 127
Panter, Gary *182:* 191
Panton, Doug *52:* 99
Paparone, Pamela *129:* 174
Papas, William *11:* 223; *50:* 160
Papin, Joseph *26:* 113
Papish, Robin Lloyd *10:* 80
Papp, Robert *198:* 41
Paradis, Susan *40:* 216
Paraquin, Charles H. *18:* 166
Paris, Peter *31:* 127
Parisi, Elizabeth B. *141:* 82; *164:* 57
Park, Nick *113:* 143
Park, Seho *39:* 110
Park, W.B. *22:* 189
Parker, Ant *82:* 87, 88; *104:* 121
Parker, Lewis *2:* 179
Parker, Nancy Winslow *10:* 113; *22:* 164; *28:* 47, 144; *52:* 7; *69:* 153; *91:* 171, 174; *132:* 175
Parker, Robert *4:* 161; *5:* 74; *9:* 136; *29:* 39
Parker, Robert Andrew *11:* 81; *29:* 186; *39:* 165; *40:* 25; *41:* 78; *42:* 123; *43:* 144; *48:* 182; *54:* 140; *74:* 141; *91:* 24; *111:* 115; *151:* 201; *154:* 156; *200:* 163, 164
Parker-Rees, Guy *149:* 145; *193:* 149, 150
Parkin, Trevor *140:* 151
Parkins, David *114:* 123; *146:* 176; *176:* 168; *192:* 107
Parkinson, Kathy *71:* 143; *144:* 234
Parkinson, Keith *70:* 66
Parks, Gordon, Jr. *33:* 228
Parnall, Peter *5:* 137; *16:* 221; *24:* 70; *40:* 78; *51:* 130; *69:* 17, 155; *136:* 22, 23, 24
Parnall, Virginia *40:* 78
Parow, Lorraine *158:* 127
Parr, Todd *134:* 139, 140; *179:* 163, 164, 165
Parrish, Anne *27:* 159, 160
Parrish, Dillwyn *27:* 159
Parrish, Maxfield *14:* 160, 161, 164, 165; *16:* 109; *18:* 12, 13; *YABC 1:* 149, 152, 267; *2:* 146, 149
Parry, David *26:* 156
Parry, Marian *13:* 176; *19:* 179
Parsons, Garry *197:* 135
Partch, Virgil *45:* 163, 165
Pascal, David *14:* 174
Paschkis, Julie *177:* 153, 154
Pasquier, J.A. *16:* 91
Pastel, Elyse *201:* 123

Pasternak, Robert *119:* 53
Paterson, Diane *13:* 116; *39:* 163; *59:* 164, 165, 166,167; *72:* 51, 53; *129:* 175; *177:* 156, 157
Paterson, Helen *16:* 93
Patkau, Karen *112:* 123
Paton, Jane *15:* 271; *35:* 176
Patrick, John *139:* 190
Patrick, Pamela *90:* 160; *93:* 211; *105:* 12
Patrick, Tom *190:* 103
Patterson, Geoffrey *54:* 75
Patterson, Robert *25:* 118
Patti, Joyce *187:* 145, 146
Patz, Nancy *111:* 40; *154:* 161
Paul, James *4:* 130; *23:* 161
Paul, Korky *102:* 85
Paull, Grace *24:* 157; *87:* 127
Paulsen, Ruth Wright *79:* 160, 164; *189:* 146
Pavlov, Elena *80:* 49
Payne, Adam S. *135:* 166
Payne, C.F. *145:* 138, 140; *179:* 168
Payne, Joan Balfour *1:* 118
Payne, Tom *170:* 27
Payson, Dale *7:* 34; *9:* 151; *20:* 140; *37:* 22
Payzant, Charles *21:* 147
Peacock, Ralph *64:* 118
Peake, Mervyn *22:* 136, 149; *23:* 162, 163, 164; *YABC2:* 307
Pearson, Larry *38:* 225
Pearson, Tracey Campbell *64:* 163, 164, 167, 168, 169; *118:* 51; *156:* 169, 171, 172; *163:* 140
Peat, Fern B. *16:* 115
Peck, Anne Merriman *18:* 241; *24:* 155
Peck, Beth *66:* 242; *79:* 166; *80:* 136; *91:* 34; *95:* 9; *101:* 77; *164:* 197; *190:* 170
Peddicord, Jane Ann *199:* 106
Pedersen, Janet *193:* 152
Pedersen, Judy *66:* 217; *121:* 36; *172:* 67
Pedersen, Vilhelm *YABC 1:* 40
Pederson, Sharleen *12:* 92
Pedlar, Elaine *161:* 45
Peek, Merle *39:* 168
Peet, Bill *2:* 203; *41:* 159, 160, 161, 162, 163; *78:* 158, 159, 160, 161
Peguero, Adrian *116:* 133
Peguero, Gerard *116:* 133
Pels, Winslow Pinney *55:* 126
Peltier, Leslie C. *13:* 178
Penberthy, Mark *171:* 78
Pendle, Alexy *7:* 159; *13:* 34; *29:* 161; *33:* 215; *86:* 62
Pendola, Joanne *76:* 203; *81:* 125; *105:* 181; *178:* 152, 153
Pene du Bois, William *4:* 70; *10:* 122; *26:* 61; *27:* 145, 211; *35:* 243; *41:* 216; *68:* 180, 181; *73:* 45
Penfound, David *102:* 185
Pennington, Eunice *27:* 162
Peppe, Mark *28:* 142
Peppe, Rodney *4:* 164, 165; *74:* 187, 188, 189
Pepper, Hubert *64:* 143
Percy, Graham *63:* 2
Pericoli, Matteo *178:* 177
Perini, Ben *173:* 77
Perkins, David *60:* 68
Perkins, Lucy Fitch *72:* 199
Perkins, Lynne Rae *172:* 146
Perl, Susan *2:* 98; *4:* 231; *5:* 44, 45, 118; *6:* 199; *8:* 137; *12:* 88; *22:* 193; *34:* 54, 55; *52:* 128; *YABC 1:* 176
Perrone, Donna *78:* 166
Perry, Marie Fritz *165:* 180
Perry, Patricia *29:* 137; *30:* 171
Perry, Roger *27:* 163
Perske, Martha *46:* 83; *51:* 108, 147
Persson, Stina *175:* 166
Pesek, Ludek *15:* 237
Petach, Heidi *149:* 166; *200:* 207
Peters, David *72:* 205; *182:* 116
Petersen, Jeff *181:* 95

Petersham, Maud *17:* 108, 147, 148, 149, 150, 151, 152, 153
Petersham, Miska *17:* 108, 147, 148, 149, 150, 151, 152, 153
Peterson, Eric *109:* 125
Peterson, Nisse *99:* 27
Peterson, R.F. *7:* 101
Peterson, Russell *7:* 130
Petie, Haris *2:* 3; *10:* 41, 118; *11:* 227; *12:* 70
Petricic, Dusan *153:* 75, 76, 77; *170:* 12; *172:* 13; *176:* 170; *179:* 56
Petrides, Heidrun *19:* 223
Petrone, Valeria *159:* 160; *171:* 92; *186:* 173
Petrosino, Tamara *177:* 40; *193:* 154, 155
Petruccio, Steven James *67:* 159; *127:* 5
Pettingill, Ondre *64:* 181; *70:* 64
Peyo *40:* 56, 57
Peyton, K.M. *15:* 212
Pfeifer, Herman *15:* 262
Pfister, Marcus *83:* 165, 166, 167; *146:* 152; *150:* 160
Pfloog, Jan *124:* 60
Pham, LeUyen *160:* 48; *175:* 154, 156; *179:* 149; *201:* 124, 125, 126, 127
Phelan, Matt *182:* 160; *184:* 222
Phillips, Craig *70:* 151
Phillips, Douglas *1:* 19
Phillips, F.D. *6:* 202
Phillips, Louise *133:* 67
Phillips, Matt *184:* 173
Phillips, Thomas *30:* 55
Philpot, Glyn *54:* 46
Phiz
See Browne, Hablot K.
Piatti, Celestino *16:* 223
Pica, Steve *115:* 181
Picarella, Joseph *13:* 147
Picart, Gabriel *121:* 165; *201:* 169
Pichon, Liz *174:* 139
Pickard, Charles *12:* 38; *18:* 203; *36:* 152
Picken, George A. *23:* 150
Pickens, David *22:* 156
Pickering, Jimmy *195:* 152; *197:* 163
Pienkowski, Jan *6:* 183; *30:* 32; *58:* 140, 141, 142,143, 146, 147; *73:* 3; *87:* 156, 157; *131:* 189
Pieper, Christiane *200:* 168
Pignataro, Anna *163:* 220 *Pileggi, Steve 145:* 122
Pilkey, Dav *68:* 186; *115:* 164, 166; *166:* 173, 174, 175
Pimlott, John *10:* 205
Pincus, Harriet *4:* 186; *8:* 179; *22:* 148; *27:* 164, 165; *66:* 202
Pini, Wendy *89:* 166
Pinkett, Neil *60:* 8
Pinkney, Brian *81:* 184, 185; *94:* 107; *113:* 146, 147; *117:* 121, 166; *132:* 145; *158:* 108, 191; *160:* 189; *200:* 8
Pinkney, Jerry *8:* 218; *10:* 40; *15:* 276; *20:* 66; *24:* 121; *33:* 109; *36:* 222; *38:* 200; *41:* 165, 166, 167, 168, 169, 170, 171, 173, 174; *44:* 198; *48:* 51; *53:* 20; *56:* 61, 68; *58:* 184; *60:* 59; *61:* 91; *71:* 146, 148, 149; *72:* 17; *73:* 149; *74:* 159,192; *75:* 45; *80:* 206; *81:* 44; *85:* 144; *95:* 50; *107:* 158, 159, 160; *108:* 164; *112:* 114, 115; *133:* 58; *195:* 140
Pinkwater, Daniel Manus *46:* 180, 181, 182, 185, 188, 189, 190; *151:* 161 *76:* 178, 179, 180
Pinkwater, Manus *8:* 156; *46:* 180
See also Pinkwater, Daniel Manus
Pinkwater, Jill *114:* 160, 161; *158:* 179; *188:* 143, 145, 146
Pinto, Ralph *10:* 131; *45:* 93
Pinto, Sara *200:* 165
Pinon, Mark *74:* 22
Piven, Hanoch *173:* 142
Pistolesi *73:* 211
Pitcairn, Ansel *188:* 10
Pittman, Helena Clare *71:* 151

Pitz, Henry C. *4:* 168; *19:* 165; *35:* 128; *42:* 80; *YABC 2:* 95, 176
Pitzenberger, Lawrence J. *26:* 94
Pitzer, Susanna *181:* 131
Player, Stephen *82:* 190
Plecas, Jennifer *84:* 201; *106:* 124; *149:* 168
Ploog, Mike *180:* 19
Plowden, David *52:* 135, 136
Plume, Ilse *170:* 149
Plummer, William *32:* 31
Podevin, Jean François *184:* 185
Podwal, Mark *56:* 170, 173; *101:* 154, 155, 157; *149:* 176; *160:* 194
Pogany, Willy *15:* 46, 49; *19:* 222, 256; *25:* 214; *44:* 142, 143, 144, 145, 146, 147, 148
Pohrt, Tom *67:* 116; *104:* 80; *152:* 199; *195:* 154; *199:* 85
Poirson, V.A. *26:* 89
Polacco, Patricia *74:* 195, 196, 197, 198; *123:* 121, 122, 123; *180:* 189, 190, 191, 193, 194
Polgreen, John *21:* 44
Politi, Leo *1:* 178; *4:* 53; *21:* 48; *47:* 173,174, 176, 178, 179, 180, 181
Pollema-Cahill, Phyllis *123:* 126
Pollen, Samson *64:* 80
Polonsky, Arthur *34:* 168
Polseno, Jo *1:* 53; *3:* 117; *5:* 114; *17:* 154; *20:* 87; *32:* 49; *41:* 245
Pomaska, Anna *117:* 148
Pons, Bernadette *184:* 100
Ponter, James *5:* 204
Poole, Colin *111:* 27
Poortvliet, Rien *6:* 212; *65:* 165, 166, 167
Pope, Kevin *183:* 158
Popp, Wendy *72:* 122; *158:* 68
Poppel, Hans *71:* 154, 155
Porfirio, Guy *76:* 134
Portal, Colette *6:* 186; *11:* 203
Porter, George *7:* 181
Porter, Janice Lee *136:* 175; *164:* 37
Porter, John *113:* 47
Porter, Pat Grant *84:* 112; *125:* 101
Porter, Sue *146:* 246, 247
Porter, Walter *124:* 175
Posada, Mia *187:* 151
Posen, Michael *175:* 82
Posthuma, Sieb *150:* 163
Postma, Lidia *79:* 17
Potter, Beatrix *100:* 194, 195; *132:* 179, 180, 181, 182; *YABC 1:* 208, 209, 210, 212, 213
Potter, Giselle *117:* 123; *143:* 44; *144:* 170, 197; *149:* 7; *150:* 165; *187:* 152, 153; *190:* 198; *196:* 152; *200:* 12
Potter, Katherine *104:* 147; *171:* 135; *173:* 136
Potter, Miriam Clark *3:* 162
Poulin, Stephane *98:* 140, 141
Poullis, Nick *146:* 210
Powell, Constance Buffington *174:* 141
Powell, Gary *151:* 208
Powell, Ivan *67:* 219
Power, Margaret *105:* 122
Powers, Daniel *161:* 173
Powers, Richard M. *1:* 230; *3:* 218; *7:* 194; *26:* 186
Powledge, Fred *37:* 154
Powzyk, Joyce *74:* 214
Poydar, Nancy *96:* 149; *190:* 180, 181, 182
Pracher, Richard *91:* 166
Prachaticka, Marketa *126:* 126
Prange, Beckie *181:* 169
Prap, Lila *177:* 165
Prater, John *103:* 142, 143, 144; *149:* 172
Pratt, Charles *23:* 29
Pratt, George *116:* 208
Pratt, Pierre *150:* 73; *166:* 183; *168:* 172; *201:* 27
Prebenna, David *73:* 174
Preiss-Glasser, Robin *123:* 176; *152* 40; *172:* 194
Press, Jenny *116:* 95
Preston, Mark *152:* 162

Pretro, Korinna *91:* 126
Price, Christine *2:* 247; *3:* 163, 253; *8:* 166
Price, Cynthia *118:* 156
Price, Edward *33:* 34
Price, Garrett *1:* 76; *2:* 42
Price, Hattie Longstreet *17:* 13
Price, Norman *YABC 1:* 129
Price, Willard *48:* 184
Priceman, Marjorie *81:* 171; *136:* 169; *156:* 200; *168:* 153, 154; *188:* 45
Priestley, Alice *168:* 33
Priestley, Chris *198:* 144
Primavera, Elise *26:* 95; *58:* 151; *73:* 37; *80:* 79; *86:* 156; *105:* 161
Primrose, Jean *36:* 109
Prince, Alison *86:* 188, 189
Prince, Leonora E. *7:* 170
Pritchett, Shelley *116:* 148
Prittie, Edwin J. *YABC 1:* 120
Proimos, James *176:* 4
Proimos, John *173:* 144
Prosmitsky, Jenya *132:* 33
Provensen, Alice *37:* 204, 215, 222; *70:* 176, 177, 178, 180; *71:* 213; *147:* 184; *191:* 190
Provensen, Martin *37:* 204, 215, 222; *70:* 176, 177, 178, 180; *71:* 213; *191:* 190
Pucci, Albert John *44:* 154
Pudlo *8:* 59
Puggaard, Ulla *196:* 25
Pulver, Harry, Jr. *129:* 159
Pulver, Robin *160:* 4
Punchatz, Don *99:* 57
Purdy, Susan *8:* 162
Pursell, Weimer *55:* 18
Purtscher, Alfons *97:* 6
Puskas, James *5:* 141
Pyk, Jan *7:* 26; *38:* 123
Pyle, Chuck *99:* 149; *191:* 83
Pyle, Howard *16:* 225, 226, 227, 228, 230, 231, 232, 235; *24:* 27; *34:* 124, 125, 127, 128; *59:* 132; *100:* 198

Q

Quackenbush, Robert *4:* 190; *6:* 166; *7:* 175, 178; *9:* 86; *11:* 65, 221; *41:* 154; *43:* 157; *70:* 185, 186; *71:* 137; *85:* 47; *92:* 148; *133:* 154, 164, 169
Qualls, Sean *177:* 167, 168; *193:* 43
Quennell, Marjorie (Courtney) *29:* 163, 164
Quidor, John *19:* 82
Quirk, John *62:* 170
Quirk, Thomas *12:* 81

R

Rackham, Arthur *15:* 32, 78, 214-227; *17:* 105, 115; *18:* 233; *19:* 254; *20:* 151; *22:* 129, 131, 132, 133; *23:* 175; *24:* 161, 181; *26:* 91; *32:* 118; *64:* 18; *100:* 9, 16, 203, 204; *YABC 1:* 25, 45, 55, 147; *2:* 103, 142, 173, 210
Racz, Michael *56:* 134
Raczka, Bob *191:* 155, 156
Radcliffe, Andrew *82:* 215
Rader, Laura *101:* 219; *197:* 147
Radunsky, Vladimir *177:* 170; *192:* 30
Rafilson, Sidney *11:* 172
Raglin, Tim *125:* 24
Raible, Alton *1:* 202, 203; *28:* 193; *35:* 181; *110:* 207
Raine, Patricia *82:* 74; *88:* 154
Ramá, Sue *173:* 45; *185:* 186; *190:* 184
Ramhorst, John *117:* 11
Ramirez, Gladys *177:* 19
Ramsey, James *16:* 41

Ramsey, Marcy Dunn *82:* 11; *180:* 186
Ramus, Michael *51:* 171
Rand, Paul *6:* 188
Rand, Ted *67:* 9, 10, 121, 123; *74:* 190; *84:* 170; *103:* 170; *112:* 6; *114:* 73; *139:* 168; *143:* 194; *156:* 154; *161:* 9, 10; *200:* 38
Randazzo, Tony *81:* 98
Randell, William *55:* 54
Rane, Walter *93:* 144; *143:* 109; *184:* 126
Rankin, Joan *163:* 40
Rankin, Laura *176:* 173, 174; *179:* 150
Ransome, Arthur *22:* 201
Ransome, James E. *74:* 137; *75:* 80; *84:* 181; *94:* 108; *117:* 115; *123:* 128, 129, 130; *158:* 101, 102; *159:* 205; *178:* 188, 189, 190
Rantz, Don *119:* 184
Rao, Anthony *28:* 126
Raphael, Elaine *23:* 192; *71:* 24, 25
Rappaport, Eva *6:* 190
Raschka, Chris *80:* 187, 189, 190; *97:* 211; *115:* 210; *117:* 151, 152, 153, 154; *143:* 195; *145:* 153; *166:* 190, 191; *170:* 114
Rash, Andy *158:* 178; *162:* 172
Raskin, Ellen *2:* 208, 209; *4:* 142; *13:* 183; *22:* 68; *29:* 139; *36:* 134; *38:* 173, 174, 175, 176, 177, 178,179, 180, 181; *60:* 163; *86:* 81
Rathmann, Peggy *93:* 32; *94:* 168; *157:* 212, 214
Ratkus, Tony *77:* 133
Ratzkin, Lawrence *40:* 143
Rau, Margaret *9:* 157
Raverat, Gwen *YABC 1:* 152
Ravid, Joyce *61:* 73
Ravielli, Anthony *1:* 198; *3:* 168; *11:* 143
Ravilious, Robin *77:* 169
Rawlins, Donna *72:* 198; *73:* 15, 129
Rawlins, Janet *76:* 79
Rawlings, Steve *143:* 139; *151:* 54
Rawlinson, Debbie *75:* 132
Ray, Deborah Kogan *8:* 164; *29:* 238; *50:* 112, 113; *62:* 119; *78:* 191
Ray, Jane *96:* 166; *97:* 104; *152:* 208; *190:* 221; *196:* 165
Ray, Ralph *2:* 239; *5:* 73
Rayann, Omar *162:* 205; *186:* 29, 30
Rayevsky, Robert *64:* 17; *70:* 173; *80:* 204; *117:* 79; *190:* 187, 188
Raymond, Larry *31:* 108; *97:* 109
Rayner, Hugh *151:* 170
Rayner, Mary *22:* 207; *47:* 140; *72:* 191; *87:* 171, 172; *192:* 104
Rayner, Shoo
   See Rayner, Hugh
Raynes, John *71:* 19
Raynor, Dorka *28:* 168
Raynor, Paul *24:* 73
Rayyan, Omar *110:* 222; *112:* 17; *125:* 131
Razzi, James *10:* 127
Read, Alexander D. *20:* 45
Reader, Dennis *71:* 157
Reasoner, Charles *53:* 33, 36, 37
Reczuch, Karen *115:* 132; *145:* 131
Redlich, Ben *163:* 221; *198:* 193
Reed, Joseph *116:* 139
Reed, Lynn Rowe *115:* 173; *171:* 146
Reed, Tom *34:* 171
Reeder, Colin *74:* 202; *77:* 113
Rees, Mary *134:* 219
Reese, Bob *60:* 135
Reeve, Philip *171:* 50
Reeves, Eira B. *130:* 173, 174; *141:* 151
Reeves, Rick *181:* 179
Regan, Dana *117:* 116
Regan, Laura *103:* 198; *153:* 206
Reichert, Renée *169:* 127
Reid, Barbara *82:* 178; *92:* 17; *93:* 169, 170
Reid, Stephen *19:* 213; *22:* 89
Reim, Melanie *104:* 151; *150:* 98
Reinert, Kirk *89:* 138; *195:* 129
Reinertson, Barbara *44:* 150; *62:* 103
Reiniger, Lotte *40:* 185

Reisberg, Mira *119:* 2
Reisch, Jesse *158:* 130
Reiser, Lynn *81:* 175; *138:* 184; *180:* 200
Reiss, John J. *23:* 193
Relf, Douglas *3:* 63
Relyea, C.M. *16:* 29; *31:* 153
Remi, Georges *13:* 184
Remington, Frederic *19:* 188; *41:* 178, 179, 180, 181, 183,184, 185, 186, 187, 188; *62:* 197
Remkiewicz, Frank *67:* 102; *77:* 171; *80:* 130; *113:* 107; *152:* 116; *152:* 211, 212; *157:* 148
Rendon, Maria *116:* 141; *192:* *134:* 152
Renfro, Ed *79:* 176
Renlie, Frank *11:* 200
Reschofsky, Jean *7:* 118
Rethi *60:* 181
Rethi, Lili *2:* 153; *36:* 156
Reusswig, William *3:* 267
Revell, Cindy *195:* 93
Rex, Adam *156:* 172; *169:* 91; *186:* 178, 179
Rex, Michael *157:* 147; *191:* 159, 160
Rey, H.A. *1:* 182; *26:* 163, 164, 166, 167, 169; *69:* 172, 173, 174, 175; *86:* 195, 196, 197; *100:* 211; *YABC 2:* 17
Rey, Luis V. *201:* 162
Reynolds, Adrian *192:* 159, 160
Reynolds, Doris *5:* 71; *31:* 77
Reynolds, Peter H. *142:* 12; *179:* 175, 176
Rhead, Louis *31:* 91; *100:* 228
Rhodes, Andrew *38:* 204; *50:* 163; *54:* 76; *61:* 123, 124; *87:* 200
Ribbons, Ian *10:* 37; *37:* 161; *40:* 76
Ricci, Regolo *93:* 22; *164:* 148
Rice, Elizabeth *2:* 53, 214
Rice, Eve *34:* 174, 175; *91:* 172
Rice, James *22:* 210; *93:* 173
Rich, Martha *195:* 16
Richards, Chuck *170:* 154
Richards, George *40:* 116, 119, 121; *44:* 179
Richards, Henry *YABC 1:* 228, 231
Richardson, Ernest *2:* 144
Richardson, Frederick *18:* 27, 31
Richardson, John *110:* 88
Richman, Hilda *26:* 132
Richmond, George *24:* 179
Riddell, Chris *114:* 170, 195; *166:* 179; *199:* 164, 166, 167
Riddle, Tohby *74:* 204; *151:* 179
Riding, Peter *63:* 195
Rieniets, Judy King *14:* 28
Riger, Bob *2:* 166
Riggio, Anita *73:* 191; *85:* 63; *137:* 184; *172:* 165
Riley, Jon *74:* 70
Riley, Kenneth *22:* 230
Riley-Webb, Charlotte *153:* 143
Rinaldi, Angelo *165:* 60, 69
Ringgold, Faith *71:* 162; *114:* 173, 174, 176; *187:* 160, 161, 163
Ringi, Kjell *12:* 171
Rios, Tere
   See Versace, Marie
Ripper, Charles L. *3:* 175
Ripplinger, Henry *117:* 31
Ritchie, William *74:* 183
Ritter, John *175:* 14
Ritz, Karen *41:* 117; *72:* 239; *87:* 125; *102:* 7; *106:* 6
Rivers, Ruth *178:* 193
Rivkin, Jay *15:* 230
Rivoche, Paul *45:* 125
Roach, Marilynne *9:* 158
Robbin, Jodi *44:* 156, 159
Robbins, Frank *42:* 167
Robbins, Ken *147:* 191, 192
Robbins, Ruth *52:* 102
Roberts, Cliff *4:* 126
Roberts, David *154:* 4, 6; *191:* 162; *196:* 184; *197:* 105
Roberts, Doreen *4:* 230; *28:* 105

Roberts, Jim *22:* 166; *23:* 69; *31:* 110
Roberts, Tony *109:* 195, 214
Roberts, W. *22:* 2, 3
Robertson, M.P. *197:* 153
Robins, Arthur *137:* 172; *151:* 225
Robinson, Aminah Brenda Lynn *86:* 205; *103:* 55; *159:* 175
Robinson, Charles [1870-1937] *17:* 157, 171, 172, 173, 175, 176; *24:* 207; *25:* 204; *YABC 2:* 308, 309, 310, 331
Robinson, Charles *3:* 53; *5:* 14; *6:* 193; *7:* 150; *7:* 183; *8:* 38; *9:* 81; *13:* 188; *14:* 248, 249; *23:* 149; *26:* 115; *27:* 48; *28:* 191; *32:* 28; *35:* 210; *36:* 37; *48:* 96; *52:* 33; *53:* 157; *56:* 15; *62:* 142; *77:* 41; *111:* 148
Robinson, Jerry *3:* 262
Robinson, Joan G. *7:* 184
Robinson, Lolly *90:* 227
Robinson, T.H. *17:* 179, 181, 182, 183; *29:* 254
Robinson, W. Heath *17:* 185, 187, 189, 191, 193, 195, 197, 199, 202; *23:* 167; *25:* 194; *29:* 150; *YABC 1:* 44; *2:* 183
Rocco, John *187:* 4; *188:* 151
Roche, Christine *41:* 98
Roche, Denis *99:* 184; *180:* 32; *196:* 168
Roche, P.K. *57:* 151, 152
Rocker, Fermin *7:* 34; *13:* 21; *31:* 40; *40:* 190,191
Rocklen, Margot *101:* 181
Rockwell, Anne *5:* 147; *33:* 171, 173; *71:* 166, 167,168; *114:* 183, 184; *194:* 152, 155
Rockwell, Gail *7:* 186
Rockwell, Harlow *33:* 171, 173, 175
Rockwell, Lizzy *114:* 182; *162:* 182; *185:* 189
Rockwell, Norman *23:* 39, 196, 197, 199, 200, 203, 204, 207; *41:* 140, 143; *123:* 47; *YABC 2:* 60
Rockwood, Richard *119:* 75
Rodanas, Kristina *156:* 183, 184
Rodegast, Roland *43:* 100
Rodgers, Frank *69:* 177
Rodriguez, Albert G. *182:* 50
Rodriguez, Christina *184:* 12
Rodriguez, Joel *16:* 65
Rodriguez, Robert *145:* 145
Rodriguez-Howard, Pauline *177:* 18
Roeckelein, Katrina *134:* 223
Roennfeldt, Robert *66:* 243
Roever, J.M. *4:* 119; *26:* 170
Roffey, Maureen *33:* 142, 176, 177
Rogasky, Barbara *46:* 90
Rogé *173:* 160
Rogers, Carol *2:* 262; *6:* 164; *26:* 129
Rogers, Chris M. *150:* 59; *196:* 61
Rogers, Forest *87:* 160; *101:* 76
Rogers, Frances *10:* 130
Rogers, Gregory *104:* 76; *126:* 57; *171:* 26
Rogers, Jacqueline *78:* 249; *80:* 34; *86:* 54 *103:* 70; *115:* 72; *129:* 173; *131:* 57, 225; *143:* 211; *153:* 100; *193:* 186
Rogers, Sherry *191:* 66
Rogers, Walter S. *31:* 135, 138; *67:* 65, 168; *100:* 81
Rogers, William A. *15:* 151, 153, 154; *33:* 35
Rogoff, Barbara *95:* 20
Rohmann, Eric *103:* 152; *198:* 151
Rojankovsky, Feodor *6:* 134, 136; *10:* 183; *21:* 128,129, 130; *25:* 110; *28:* 42; *68:* 120
Rolfsen, Alf *62:* 15
Romain, Trevor *134:* 157
Roman, Barbara J. *103:* 171
Romas *114:* 111; *165:* 63
Romano, Robert *64:* 68
Romero, Alejandro *187:* 185
Roos, Maryn *168:* 198
Root, Barry *80:* 212; *90:* 196; *146:* 78; *156:* 165; *159:* 161; *182:* 18, 172
Root, Kimberly Bulcken *86:* 72; *98:* 21; *108:* 111; *127:* 114; *159:* 162; *176:* 134; *192:* 163
Roper, Bob *65:* 153

Roraback, Robin *111:* 156
Rorer, Abigail *43:* 222; *85:* 155
Rosales, Melodye *80:* 35
Rosamilia, Patricia *36:* 120
Rose, Carl *5:* 62
Rose, David S. *29:* 109; *70:* 120
Rose, Gerald *68:* 200, 201; *86:* 48
Rose, Ted *93:* 178
Rosenbaum, Jonathan *50:* 46
Rosenberg, Amye *74:* 207, 208
Rosenberry, Vera *87:* 22, 26; *144:* 212, 213; *158:* 120
Rosenblum, Richard *11:* 202; *18:* 18
Rosier, Lydia *16:* 236; *20:* 104; *21:* 109; *22:* 125; *30:* 151, 158; *42:* 128; *45:* 214; *77:* 227, 228
Rosing, Jens *85:* 142
Ross
  See Thomson, Ross
Ross, Christine *83:* 172, 173
Ross, Clare Romano *3:* 123; *21:* 45; *48:* 199
Ross, Dave *32:* 152; *57:* 108
Ross, Graham *199:* 4
Ross, Herbert *37:* 78
Ross, John *3:* 123; *21:* 45
Ross, Johnny *32:* 190
Ross, Larry *47:* 168; *60:* 62
Ross, Ruth *109:* 233
Ross, Tony *17:* 204; *56:* 132; *65:* 176, 177, 179; *90:* 123; *123:* 186, 187, 190; *130:* 188, 190, 191, 192; *132:* 242; *174:* 159; *176:* 181, 182, 183
Rossetti, Dante Gabriel *20:* 151, 153
Rostant, Larry *180:* 221; *194:* 108; *195:* 96; *197:* 12
Roth, Arnold *4:* 238; *21:* 133
Roth, Julie Jersild *180:* 206
Roth, Marci *135:* 223
Roth, R.G. *184:* 50
Roth, Rob *105:* 98; *146:* 41
Roth, Robert *176:* 159
Roth, Roger *61:* 128; *190:* 192
Roth, Stephanie *136:* 171, 172
Roth, Susan L. *80:* 38; *93:* 78; *134:* 165, 166; *181:* 145, 146
Rothenberg, Joani Keller *162:* 190, 191
Rothman, Michael *139:* 62; *184:* 34 Rotman, Jeffrey L. *145:* 30
Rotondo, Pat *32:* 158
Roughsey, Dick *35:* 186
Rouille, M. *11:* 96
Rounds, Glen *8:* 173; *9:* 171; *12:* 56; *32:* 194; *40:* 230; *51:* 161, 162, 166; *56:* 149; *70:* 198, 199; *YABC 1:* 1, 2, 3; *112:* 163
Roundtree, Katherine *114:* 88; *168:* 102
Rovetch, Lissa *201:* 164
Rowan, Evadne *52:* 51
Rowe, Eric *111:* 161
Rowe, Gavin *27:* 144; *72:* 47; *88:* 201
Rowe, John *132:* 70, 71; *180:* 126
Rowell, Kenneth *40:* 72
Rowen, Amy *52:* 143
Rowena *116:* 101
Rowland, Andrew *164:* 136
Rowland, Jada *83:* 73
Rowles, Daphne *58:* 24
Roy, Jeroo *27:* 229; *36:* 110
Royo *118:* 32; *144:* 105, 106, 108; *165:* 19; *166:* 166
Rubel, Nicole *18:* 255; *20:* 59; *81:* 66, 67; *95:* 169, 170; *119:* 60; *135:* 177, 179, 180; *169:* 68; *181:* 150
Rubel, Reina *33:* 217
Rud, Borghild *6:* 15
Ruddell, Gary *110:* 238; *116:* 207
Rudolph, Norman Guthrie *17:* 13
Rue, Leonard Lee III *37:* 164
Rueda, Claudia *183:* 170, 171
Ruelle, Karen Gray *126:* 193
Ruff, Donna *50:* 173; *72:* 203; *78:* 49; *80:* 120,121; *93:* 162; *164:* 121

Ruffins, Reynold *10:* 134, 135; *41:* 191, 192, 193, 194, 195, 196; *125:* 187, 188, 189; *162:* 197
Ruhlin, Roger *34:* 44
Ruiz, Art *95:* 154; *110:* 91
Rumford, James *193:* 167
Runnerstroem, Bengt Arne *75:* 161
Ruse, Margaret *24:* 155
Rush, Ken *98:* 74
Rush, Peter *42:* 75
Russell, Charles M. *167:* 171
Russell, E.B. *18:* 177, 182
Russell, Jim *53:* 134
Russell, P. Craig *80:* 196; *146:* 102; *162:* 186
Russo, Marisabina *84:* 51; *106:* 164; *151:* 183, 188; *153:* 154, 155, 156
Russo, Susan *30:* 182; *36:* 144
Russon, Mary *87:* 145
Ruth, Greg *183:* 125
Ruth, Rod *9:* 161
Rutherford, Alexa *110:* 108
Rutherford, Jenny *78:* 5
Rutherford, Meg *25:* 174; *34:* 178, 179; *69:* 73; *72:* 31
Rutland, Jonathan *31:* 126
Ruurs, Margriet *147:* 195
Ruzzier, Sergio *159:* 176, 177; *163:* 184
Ryan, Amy *188:* 50
Ryan, Will *86:* 134
Ryden, Hope *8:* 176
Rylant, Cynthia *112:* 170, 172
Rymer, Alta M. *34:* 181
Ryniak, Christopher *178:* 11
Rystedt, Rex *49:* 80

S

Saaf, Chuck *49:* 179
Saaf, Donald *101:* 220; *124:* 180
Sabaka, Donna R. *21:* 172
Sabin, Robert *45:* 35; *60:* 30; *99:* 161
Sabuda, Robert *170:* 166, 167, 168
Sacker, Amy *16:* 100
Saelig, S.M. *129:* 73; *173:* 59
Saffioti, Lino *36:* 176; *48:* 60
Saflund, Birgitta *94:* 2
Sagsoorian, Paul *12:* 183; *22:* 154; *33:* 106; *87:* 152
Sahara, Tony *168:* 106; *177:* 181; *178:* 228; *186:* 132
Sahlberg, Myron *57:* 165
Saidens, Amy *145:* 162; *191:* 131
Saint Exupery, Antoine de *20:* 157
Saint James, Synthia *152:* 220; *188:* 90; *200:* 7
Saldutti, Denise *39:* 186; *57:* 178
Sale, Morton *YABC 2:* 31
Sale, Tim *153:* 177
Salerno, Steven *150:* 79; *176:* 188
Salter, George *72:* 128, 130
Saltzberg, Barney *135:* 184, 185; *194:* 160
Saltzman, David *86:* 209
Salwowski, Mark *71:* 54
Salzman, Yuri *86:* 12
Sambourne, Linley *YABC 2:* 181
Sampson, Katherine *9:* 197
Samson, Anne S. *2:* 216
San Souci, Daniel *40:* 200; *96:* 199, 200; *113:* 171; *157:* 149; *170:* 69; *192:* 167, 168
Sancha, Sheila *38:* 185
Sanchez, Enrique O. *155:* 84
Sand, George X. *45:* 182
Sandberg, Lasse *15:* 239, 241
Sanders, Beryl *39:* 173
Sanderson, Ruth *21:* 126; *24:* 53; *28:* 63; *33:* 67; *41:* 48, 198, 199, 200, 201, 202, 203; *43:* 79; *46:* 36,44; *47:* 102; *49:* 58; *62:* 121, 122; *85:* 3; *109:* 207, 208, 209, 210; *172:* 157, 158

Sandia *119:* 74
Sandin, Joan *4:* 36; *6:* 194; *7:* 177; *12:* 145,185; *20:* 43; *21:* 74; *26:* 144; *27:* 142; *28:* 224, 225; *38:* 86; *41:* 46; *42:* 35; *59:* 6; *80:* 136; *94:* 188; *140:* 116; *153:* 179, 180; *197:* 168
Sandland, Reg *39:* 215
Sandoz, Edouard *26:* 45, 47
Sanford, John *66:* 96, 97
Sankey, Tom *72:* 103
Sano, Kazuhiko *153:* 208; *195:* 171
Santat, Dan *188:* 160
Santore, Charles *54:* 139; *200:* 171, 172
Santoro, Christopher *74:* 215
Santos, Jesse J. *99:* 24
Sapieha, Christine *1:* 180
Saport, Linda *123:* 137, 138
Sara
  See De La Roche Saint Andre, Anne
Sardinha, Rick *175:* 151
Sarg, Tony *YABC 2:* 236
Sargent, Claudia *64:* 181
Sargent, Robert *2:* 217
Saris *1:* 33
Sarony *YABC 2:* 170
Sasaki, Goro *170:* 46
Sasek, Miroslav *16:* 239, 240, 241, 242
Sassman, David *9:* 79
Satty *29:* 203, 205
Sauber, Robert *40:* 183; *76:* 256; *78:* 154; *87:* 92
Saunders, Dave *85:* 163, 164, 165
Savadier, Elivia *84:* 50; *145:* 45; *164:* 206
Savage, Naomi *56:* 172
Savage, Steele *10:* 203; *20:* 77; *35:* 28
Savage, Stephen *174:* 182
Savio *76:* 4
Savitt, Sam *8:* 66, 182; *15:* 278; *20:* 96; *24:* 192; *28:* 98
Sawyer, Kem Knapp *84:* 228, 229
Say, Allen *28:* 178; *69:* 182, 183, 232; *110:* 194, 195,196; *161:* 154, 155
Sayles, Elizabeth *82:* 93; *105:* 155; *109:* 116; *180:* 64
Scabrini, Janet *13:* 191; *44:* 128
Scanlan, Peter *83:* 27; *153:* 165; *187:* 149
Scanlon, Paul *83:* 87
Scannell, Reece *105:* 105
Scarry, Huck *35:* 204, 205
Scarry, Richard *2:* 220, 221; *18:* 20; *35:* 193, 194, 195,196, 197, 198, 199, 200, 201, 202; *75:* 165, 167, 168
Schachner, Judith Byron *88:* 180; *92:* 163; *93:* 102; *142:* 82; *178:* 199, 200; *190:* 140
Schaeffer, Mead *18:* 81, 94; *21:* 137, 138, 139; *47:* 128
Schaffer, Amanda *90:* 206
Schanzer, Rosalyn *138:* 192, 193
Scharl, Josef *20:* 132; *22:* 128
Scheel, Lita *11:* 230
Scheffler, Axel *180:* 23, 24
Scheib, Ida *29:* 28
Schermer, Judith *30:* 184
Schick, Eleanor *82:* 210, 211; *144:* 222
Schick, Joel *16:* 160; *17:* 167; *22:* 12; *27:* 176; *31:* 147, 148; *36:* 23; *38:* 64; *45:* 116, 117; *52:* 5, 85; *104:* 159
Schields, Gretchen *75:* 171, 203
Schindelman, Joseph *1:* 74; *4:* 101; *12:* 49; *26:* 51; *40:* 146; *56:* 158; *73:* 40
Schindler, Edith *7:* 22
Schindler, S.D. *38:* 107; *46:* 196; *74:* 162; *75:* 172, 173; *99:* 133; *112:* 177; *118:* 185, 186; *121:* 71; *136:* 159; *143:* 45; *149:* 120; *156:* 30; *169:* 135; *171:* 161, 162, 163; *172:* 9; *186:* 163; *194:* 109; *195:* 35; *198:* 170, 171, 172
Schlesinger, Bret *7:* 77
Schmid, Eleanore *12:* 188; *126:* 196, 197
Schmiderer, Dorothy *19:* 224
Schmidt, Bill *73:* 34; *76:* 220, 222, 224

Schmidt, Elizabeth *15:* 242
Schmidt, George Paul *132:* 122
Schmidt, Karen Lee *54:* 12; *71:* 174; *92:* 56; *94:* 190, 191; *127:* 103
Schmidt, Lynette *76:* 205
Schneider, Christine M. *171:* 165
Schneider, Howie *181:* 159
Schneider, Rex *29:* 64; *44:* 171
Schnurr, Edward *170:* 62
Schoberle, Cecile *80:* 200; *92:* 134
Schoenherr, Ian *32:* 83; *173:* 41
Schoenherr, John *1:* 146, 147, 173; *3:* 39, 139; *17:* 75; *29:* 72; *32:* 83; *37:* 168, 169, 170; *43:* 164, 165; *45:* 160, 162; *51:* 127; 66; 196, 197, 198; *68:* 83; *72:* 240; *75:* 225; *88:* 176
Scholder, Fritz *69:* 103
Schomburg, Alex *13:* 23
Schongut, Emanuel *4:* 102; *15:* 186; *47:* 218, 219; *52:* 147, 148, 149, 150; *185:* 27
Schoonover, Frank *17:* 107; *19:* 81, 190, 233; *22:* 88,129; *24:* 189; *31:* 88; *41:* 69; *YABC 2:* 282, 316
Schories, Pat *164:* 210
Schottland, Miriam *22:* 172
Schramm, Ulrik *2:* 16; *14:* 112
Schreiber, Elizabeth Anne *13:* 193
Schreiber, Ralph W. *13:* 193
Schreiter, Rick *14:* 97; *23:* 171; *41:* 247; *49:* 131
Schroeder, Binette *56:* 128, 129
Schroeder, E. Peter *12:* 112
Schroeder, Ted *11:* 160; *15:* 189; *30:* 91; *34:* 43
Schrotter, Gustav *22:* 212; *30:* 225
Schubert, Dieter *101:* 167, 168
Schubert-Gabrys, Ingrid *101:* 167, 168
Schucker, James *31:* 163
Schuett, Stacey *72:* 137
Schulder, Lili *146:* 29
Schulke, Debra *57:* 167
Schulke, Flip *57:* 167
Schulz, Barbara *167:* 24
Schulz, Charles M. *10:* 137, 138, 139, 140, 141, 142; *118:* 192, 193, 194, 196, 199
Schutzer, Dena *109:* 32
Schwark, Mary Beth *51:* 155; *72:* 175
Schwartz, Amy *47:* 191; *82:* 100; *83:* 178, 179, 180,181; *129:* 107; *131:* 197, 198; *189:* 166, 168
Schwartz, Carol *124:* 41; *130:* 199
Schwartz, Charles *8:* 184
Schwartz, Daniel *46:* 37
Schwartz, Joanie *124:* 170
Schwartzberg, Joan *3:* 208
Schweitzer, Iris *2:* 137; *6:* 207
Schweninger, Ann *29:* 172; *82:* 246; *159:* 202; *168:* 166
Schwinger, Laurence *84:* 44; *91:* 61
Scofield, Penrod *61:* 107; *62:* 160
Scott, Anita Walker *7:* 38
Scott, Art *39:* 41
Scott, Frances Gruse *38:* 43
Scott, Julian *34:* 126
Scott, Roszel *33:* 238
Scott, Sally *87:* 27
Scott, Steve *166:* 230, 231; *171:* 93
Scott, Trudy *27:* 172
Scrace, Carolyn *143:* 95, 96
Scrambly, Crab *198:* 196
Scribner, Joanne *14:* 236; *29:* 78; *33:* 185; *34:* 208; *78:* 75; *164:* 237
Scrofani, Joseph *31:* 65; *74:* 225
Scroggs, Kirk *187:* 169
Seaman, Mary Lott *34:* 64
Searle, Ronald *24:* 98; *42:* 172, 173, 174, 176, 177, 179; *66:* 73, 74; *70:* 205, 206, 207
Searle, Townley *36:* 85
Sebree, Charles *18:* 65
Sedacca, Joseph M. *11:* 25; *22:* 36
Seder, Jason *108:* 102

Seeger, Laura Vaccaro *172:* 162
Seegmiller, Don *174:* 57
Seely, David *164:* 173
Seeley, Laura L. *97:* 105
Segal, John *178:* 202
Segar, E.C. *61:* 179, 181
Segur, Adrienne *27:* 121
Seibold, J. Otto *83:* 188, 190, 191; *149:* 212, 214, 215, 216; *196:* 177, 179
Seignobosc, Francoise *21:* 145, 146
Sejima, Yoshimasa *8:* 187
Selig, Sylvie *13:* 199
Seltzer, Isadore *6:* 18; *133:* 59
Seltzer, Meyer *17:* 214
Selven, Maniam *144:* 133
Selway, Martina *169:* 157
Selznick, Brian *79:* 192; *104:* 25; *117:* 175; *126:* 156; *134:* 171; *158:* 76, 78; *169:* 70; *171:* 172, 173; *191:* 106; *192:* 130; *197:* 158
Sempe, Jean-Jacques *47:* 92; *YABC 2:* 109
Sendak, Maurice *1:* 135, 190; *3:* 204; *7:* 142; *15:* 199; *17:* 210; *27:* 181, 182, 183, 185, 186, 187, 189,190, 191, 192, 193, 194, 195, 197, 198, 199, 203; *28:* 181, 182; *32:* 108; *33:* 148, 149; *35:* 238; *44:* 180, 181; *45:* 97, 99; *46:* 174; *73:* 225; *91:* 10, 11 *YABC1:* 167; *113:* 163, 165, 167, 168; *118:* 153; *127:* 161
Senders, Marci *180:* 79
Sengler, Johanna *18:* 256
Senn, Steve *60:* 145
Seredy, Kate *1:* 192; *14:* 20, 21; *17:* 210
Sergeant, John *6:* 74
Servello, Joe *10:* 144; *24:* 139; *40:* 91; *70:* 130, 131; *146:* 159
Seton, Ernest Thompson *18:* 260-269, 271
Seuss, Dr.
  See Geisel, Theodor
Severin, John Powers *7:* 62
Sewall, Marcia *15:* 8; *22:* 170; *37:* 171, 172, 173; *39:* 73; *45:* 209; *62:* 117; *69:* 185, 186; *71:* 212; *90:* 232; *96:* 127; *102:* 101; *107:* 129; *119:* 176, 177, 178, 180
Seward, James *70:* 35
Seward, Prudence *16:* 243
Sewell, Helen *3:* 186; *15:* 308; *33:* 102; *38:* 189, 190, 191, 192
Seymour, Stephen *54:* 21
Sfar, Joann *182:* 183
Shachat, Andrew *82:* 179
Shahn, Ben *39:* 178; *46:* 193
Shalansky, Len *38:* 167
Shanks, Anne Zane *10:* 149
Shannon, David *57:* 137; *107:* 184; *112:* 216; *135:* 12; *152:* 223, 224, 225; *158:* 192
Sharp, Paul *52:* 60
Sharp, William *6:* 131; *19:* 241; *20:* 112; *25:* 141
Sharratt, Nick *102:* 207, 208; *104:* 163; *153:* 198; *175:* 176; *192:* 208; *199:* 141, 142, 143, 184, 187, 188
Shaw, Barclay *74:* 14, 16; *118:* 138
Shaw, Charles *21:* 135; *38:* 187; *47:* 124; *126:* 219
Shaw, Charles G. *13:* 200
Shaw-Smith, Emma *144:* 117
Shea, Edmund *56:* 19
Shearer, Ted *43:* 193, 194, 195, 196
Sheban, Chris *182:* 185; *190:* 102, 104
Shecter, Ben *16:* 244; *25:* 109; *33:* 188, 191; *41:* 77
Shed, Greg *74:* 94; *84:* 204; *129:* 149; *167:* 91; *179:* 192
Sheeban, Chris *144:* 190; *158:* 163
Shefcik, James *48:* 221, 222; *60:* 141
Shefelman, Karl *58:* 168
Shefts, Joelle *48:* 210
Shein, Bob *139:* 189
Shekerjian, Haig *16:* 245
Shekerjian, Regina *16:* 245; *25:* 73
Sheldon, David *184:* 174; *185:* 204

Shelley, John *186:* 223
Shemie, Bonnie *96:* 207
Shenton, Edward *45:* 187, 188, 189; *YABC 1:* 218, 219, 221
Shepard, Ernest H. *3:* 193; *4:* 74; *16:* 101; *17:* 109; *25:* 148; *33:* 152, 199, 200, 201, 202, 203, 204, 205, 206,207; *46:* 194; *98:* 114; *100:* 111, 178, 179, 217, 219, 220,221; *YABC 1:* 148, 153, 174, 176, 180, 181
Shepard, Mary *4:* 210; *22:* 205; *30:* 132, 133; *54:* 150, 152, 153, 157, 158; *59:* 108, 109, 111; *100:* 246
Shepherd, Amanda *198:* 14
Shepherd, Irana *171:* 112
Sheppard, Kate *195:* 176
Shepperson, Rob *96:* 153; *177:* 163; *178:* 204; *197:* 34
Sheridan, Brian *196:* 193
Sherman, Theresa *27:* 167
Sherwan, Earl *3:* 196
Shields, Charles *10:* 150; *36:* 63
Shields, Leonard *13:* 83, 85, 87
Shiffman, Lena *139:* 167; *168:* 136
Shigley, Neil K. *66:* 219
Shillabeer, Mary *35:* 74
Shilston, Arthur *49:* 61; *62:* 58
Shimin, Symeon *1:* 93; *2:* 128, 129; *3:* 202; *7:* 85; *11:* 177; *12:* 139; *13:* 202, 203; *27:* 138; *28:* 65; *35:* 129; *36:* 130; *48:* 151; *49:* 59; *56:* 63, 65, 153
Shine, Andrea *104:* 165; *128:* 34
Shinn, Everett *16:* 148; *18:* 229; *21:* 149, 150, 151; *24:* 218
Shinn, Florence Scovel *63:* 133, 135
Shore, Robert *27:* 54; *39:* 192, 193; *YABC 2:* 200
Shortall, Leonard *4:* 144; *8:* 196; *10:* 166; *19:* 227, 228, 229, 230; *25:* 78; *28:* 66, 167; *33:* 127; *52:* 125; *73:* 12, 212
Shortt, T.M. *27:* 36
Shpitalnik, Vladimir *83:* 194
Shropshire, Sandy *170:* 191
Shtainments, Leon *32:* 161
Shulevitz, Uri *3:* 198, 199; *17:* 85; *22:* 204; *27:* 212; *28:* 184; *50:* 190, 191, 192, 193, 194, 195, 196,197, 198, 199, 201; *106:* 181, 182, 183; *165:* 203, 205; *166:* 138
Shulman, Dee *180:* 140
Shupe, Bobbi *139:* 80, 81
Shute, A.B. *67:* 196
Shute, Linda *46:* 59; *74:* 118
Siberell, Anne *29:* 193
Sibley, Don *1:* 39; *12:* 196; *31:* 47
Sibthorp, Fletcher *94:* 111, 112
Sidjakov, Nicolas *18:* 274
Siebel, Fritz *3:* 120; *17:* 145
Siebold, J. Otto *158:* 227
Siegel, Hal *74:* 246
Sieger, Ted *189:* 172
Siegl, Helen *12:* 166; *23:* 216; *34:* 185, 186
Silin-Palmer, Pamela *184:* 102
Sill, John *140:* 194; *141:* 157
Sills, Joyce *5:* 199
Silva, Simon *108:* 122
Silver, Maggie *85:* 210
Silveria, Gordon *96:* 44
Silverstein, Alvin *8:* 189
Silverstein, Shel *33:* 211; *92:* 209, 210
Silverstein, Virginia *8:* 189
Silvey, Joe *135:* 203
Simard, Remy *95:* 156
Simmons, Elly *110:* 2; *127:* 69; *134:* 181
Simon, Eric M. *7:* 82
Simon, Hilda *28:* 189
Simon, Howard *2:* 175; *5:* 132; *19:* 199; *32:* 163, 164, 165
Simont, Marc *2:* 119; *4:* 213; *9:* 168; *13:* 238,240; *14:* 262; *16:* 179; *18:* 221; *26:* 210; *33:* 189, 194; *44:* 132; *58:* 122; *68:* 117; *73:* 204, 205, 206; *74:* 221; *126:* 199, 200; *133:* 195; *164:* 128

Sims, Agnes *54:* 152
Sims, Blanche *44:* 116; *57:* 129; *75:* 179, 180; *77:* 92; *104:* 192; *152:* 117; *156:* 160; *160:* 70; *168:* 174, 175; *198:* 17
Singer, Edith G. *2:* 30
Singer, Gloria *34:* 56; *36:* 43
Singer, Julia *28:* 190
Singh, Jen *178:* 146
Siomades, Lorianne *134:* 45
Simont, Marc *163:* 40
Siracusa, Catherine *68:* 135; *82:* 218
Sís, Peter *67:* 179, 181, 183, 184, 185; *96:* 96, 98; *106:* 193, 194, 195; *149:* 224, 226; *180:* 177; *192:* 180, 182
Sivard, Robert *26:* 124
Sivertson, Liz *116:* 84
Skardinski, Stanley *23:* 144; *32:* 84; *66:* 122; *84:* 108
Slack, Michael *185:* 108; *189:* 173, 174
Slackman, Charles B. *12:* 201
Slade, Christian *193:* 187
Slade, Paul *61:* 170
Slark, Albert *99:* 212
Slater, Rod *25:* 167
Slavin, Bill *182:* 14, 15; *196:* 90; *199:* 148, 149, 150
Sloan, Joseph *16:* 68
Sloane, Eric *21:* 3; *52:* 153, 154, 155, 156, 157, 158, 160
Sloat, Teri *164:* 231
Slobodkin, Louis *1:* 200; *3:* 232; *5:* 168; *13:* 251; *15:* 13, 88; *26:* 173, 174, 175, 176, 178, 179; *60:* 180
Slobodkina, Esphyr *1:* 201
Slonim, David *166:* 167, 168
Small, David *50:* 204, 205; *79:* 44; *95:* 189, 190, 191; *126:* 203, 204; *136:* 119; *143:* 201, 202, 203; *144:* 246; *150:* 5; *161:* 176; *183:* 181, 182, 183, 184; *200:* 211
Small, W. *33:* 113
Smalley, Janet *1:* 154
Smath, Jerry *198:* 179, 180
Smedley, William T. *34:* 129
Smee, David *14:* 78; *62:* 30
Smee, Nicola *167:* 156
Smith, A.G., Jr. *35:* 182
Smith, Alvin *1:* 31, 229; *13:* 187; *27:* 216; *28:* 226; *48:* 149; *49:* 60
Smith, Andy *188:* 20
Smith, Anne *194:* 147
Smith, Anne Warren *41:* 212
Smith, Barry *75:* 183
Smith, Brian *200:* 183
Smith, Carl *36:* 41
Smith, Cat Bowman *146:* 39; *164:* 219; *201:* 55, 184
Smith, Craig *97:* 197; *172:* 175
Smith, Donald A. *178:* 7
Smith, Doris Susan *41:* 139
Smith, Douglas *189:* 159
Smith, Duane *171:* 152
Smith, E. Boyd *19:* 70; *22:* 89; *26:* 63; *YABC 1:* 4, 5, 240, 248, 249
Smith, Edward J. *4:* 224
Smith, Elwood H. *157:* 231; *181:* 79
Smith, Eunice Young *5:* 170
Smith, Gary *113:* 216
Smith, George *102:* 169
Smith, Howard *19:* 196
Smith, J. Gerard *95:* 42
Smith, Jacqueline Bardner *27:* 108; *39:* 197
Smith, Jay J. *61:* 119
Smith, Jeff *93:* 191
Smith, Jessie Willcox *15:* 91; *16:* 95; *18:* 231; *19:* 57, 242; *21:* 29, 156, 157, 158, 159, 160, 161; *34:* 65; *100:* 223; *YABC 1:* 6; *2:* 180, 185, 191, 311, 325
Smith, Jos. A. *52:* 131; *72:* 120; *74:* 151; *84:* 147, 148; *85:* 146; *87:* 96; *94:* 219; *96:* 97; *104:* 33; *108:* 126, 127, 128; *111:* 140; *136:* 145; *181:* 173; *200:* 213; *201:* 94

Smith, Kenneth R. *47:* 182
Smith, Kevin Warren *89:* 112
Smith, L.H. *35:* 174
Smith, Lane *76:* 211, 213; *88:* 115; *105:* 202, 203,204, 205; *131:* 207; *160:* 217, 221; *179:* 183, 184, 185, 186; *199:* 122, 123, 124, 126
Smith, Lee *29:* 32
Smith, Linell Nash *2:* 195
Smith, Maggie Kaufman *13:* 205; *35:* 191; *110:* 158; *178:* 226; *190:* 204
Smith, Mavis *101:* 219
Smith, Moishe *33:* 155
Smith, Philip *44:* 134; *46:* 203
Smith, Ralph Crosby *2:* 267; *49:* 203
Smith, Robert D. *5:* 63
Smith, Sally J. *84:* 55
Smith, Susan Carlton *12:* 208
Smith, Terry *12:* 106; *33:* 158
Smith, Virginia *3:* 157; *33:* 72
Smith, William A. *1:* 36; *10:* 154; *25:* 65
Smith-Moore, J.J. *98:* 147
Smolinski, Dick *84:* 217
Smoljan, Joe *112:* 201
Smollin, Mike *39:* 203
Smyth, Iain *105:* 207
Smyth, M. Jane *12:* 15
Smythe, Fiona *151:* 213
Smythe, Theresa *141:* 37
Snair, Andy *176:* 4
Sneed, Brad *125:* 25; *191:* 175, 176
Snyder, Andrew A. *30:* 212
Snyder, Jerome *13:* 207; *30:* 173
Snyder, Joel *28:* 163
So, Meilo *162:* 201
Soentpiet, Chris K. *97:* 208; *110:* 33; *159:* 184; *161:* 10; *163:* 130
Sofia *1:* 62; *5:* 90; *32:* 166; *86:* 43
Sofilas, Mark *93:* 157
Sohn, Jiho *182:* 78
Sokol, Bill *37:* 178; *49:* 23
Sokolov, Kirill *34:* 188
Solbert, Ronni *1:* 159; *2:* 232; *5:* 121; *6:* 34; *17:* 249
Solomon, Michael *174:* 115
Solonevich, George *15:* 246; *17:* 47
Soma, Liana *81:* 118
Soman, David *90:* 122; *102:* 126; *140:* 120; *93;* *188:* 43, 89; *200:* 180, 181
Sommer, Robert *12:* 211
Soo, Kean *201:* 185
Sorel, Edward *4:* 61; *36:* 82; *65:* 191, 193; *126:* 214
Sorensen, Henri *196:* 58
Sorensen, Henrik *62:* 16
Sorensen, Svend Otto *22:* 130, 141; *67:* 188, 189
Sorra, Kristin *155:* 80
Sosa, Hernan *198:* 66
Sostre, Maria *187:* 36
Sotomayor, Antonio *11:* 215
Souhami, Jessica *112:* 128; *176:* 193
Souza, Diana *71:* 139
Sovak, Jan *115:* 190
Soyer, Moses *20:* 177
Spaenkuch, August *16:* 28
Spafford, Suzy *160:* 228
Spain, Valerie *105:* 76
Spain, Sunday Sahara *133:* 204
Spalenka, Greg *149:* 69; *151:* 228; *184:* 195; *191:* 21; *196:* 12; *198:* 181, 182, 201
Spanfeller, James *1:* 72, 149; *2:* 183; *19:* 230, 231,232; *22:* 66; *36:* 160, 161; *40:* 75; *52:* 166; *76:* 37
Sparks, Mary Walker *15:* 247
Spears, Rick *182:* 187
Speidel, Sandra *78:* 233; *94:* 178; *134:* 180
Speirs, John *67:* 178
Spence, Geraldine *21:* 163; *47:* 196
Spence, Jim *38:* 89; *50:* 102
Spencer, Laurie *113:* 12
Spencer, Mark *57:* 170

Spengler, Kenneth J. *146:* 256
Sperling, Andrea *133:* 182
Spiegel, Beth *184:* 203
Spiegel, Doris *29:* 111
Spiegelman, Art *109:* 227
Spier, Jo *10:* 30
Spier, Peter *3:* 155; *4:* 200; *7:* 61; *11:* 78; *38:* 106; *54:* 120, 121, 122, 123, 124, 125, 126, 127, 128, 129, 130,131, 132, 133, 134
Spilka, Arnold *5:* 120; *6:* 204; *8:* 131
Spirin, Gennady *95:* 196, 197; *113:* 172; *128:* 9; *129:* 49; *134:* 210; *153:* 9
Spivak, I. Howard *8:* 10; *13:* 172
Spohn, David *72:* 233
Spohn, Kate *87:* 195; *147:* 201, 202
Spollen, Christopher J. *12:* 214
Spooner, Malcolm *40:* 142
Spowart, Robin *82:* 228; *92:* 149; *133:* 131; *176:* 163; *177:* 183, 184
Sprague, Kevin *150:* 60; *196:* 62
Spranger, Nina *201:* 199
Sprattler, Rob *12:* 176
Spring, Bob *5:* 60
Spring, Ira *5:* 60
Springer, Harriet *31:* 92
Spudvilas, Anne *110:* 74; *197:* 192; *199:* 154
Spurll, Barbara *78:* 199; *88:* 141, 142; *99:* 215
Spurrier, Steven *28:* 198
Spuvilas, Anne *85:* 114
Spy
    See Ward, Leslie
Squires, Stuart *127:* 74
St. Aubin, Bruno *179:* 54
St. John, J. Allen *41:* 62
Stabin, Victor *101:* 131; *164:* 158
Stadler, John *62:* 33
Staffan, Alvin E. *11:* 56; *12:* 187
Stahl, Ben *5:* 181; *12:* 91; *49:* 122; *71:* 128; *87:* 206; *112:* 107
Stair, Gobin *35:* 214
Stallwood, Karen *73:* 126
Stamaty, Mark Alan *12:* 215
Stammen, JoEllen McAllister *113:* 14
Stampnick, Ken *51:* 142
Stanbridge, Joanne *150:* 91
Stanley, Diane *3:* 45; *37:* 180; *80:* 217, 219
Stanley, Sanna *145:* 228
Starcke, Helmut *86:* 217
Stark, Ken *197:* 102
Starr, Branka *73:* 25
Stasiak, Krystyna *49:* 181; *64:* 194
Staub, Leslie *103:* 54
Staunton, Ted *112:* 192
Stawicki, Matt *164:* 250
Stead, L. *55:* 51, 56
Steadman, Broeck *97:* 185, 186; *99:* 56; *121:* 48
Steadman, Ralph *32:* 180; *123:* 143, 145
Stearn, Nick *183:* 26
Steckler, June *90:* 178
Steele, Robert Gantt *169:* 174
Steichen, Edward *30:* 79
Steig, William *18:* 275, 276; *70:* 215, 216, 217, 218; *111:* 173, 174, 175, 176, 177
Stein, Harve *1:* 109
Steinberg, Saul *47:* 193
Steinel, William *23:* 146
Steiner, Charlotte *45:* 196
Steiner, Joan *110:* 219; *199:* 160, 161
Steirnagel, Michael *80:* 56
Stemp, Eric *60:* 184
Stephens, Alice Barber *66:* 208, 209
Stephens, Charles H. *YABC 2:* 279
Stephens, Pam *198:* 69
Stephens, Pat *126:* 110; *128:* 101
Stephens, William M. *21:* 165
Steptoe, Javaka *151:* 203, 204; *190:* 169
Steptoe, John *8:* 197; *57:* 9; *63:* 158, 159, 160, 161,163, 164, 165, 166, 167; *96:* 4; *105:* 87
Stern, Simon *15:* 249, 250; *17:* 58; *34:* 192, 193

Sterret, Jane *53:* 27
Stetsios, Debbie *165:* 108, 109
Steven, Kat *158:* 237
Stevens, David *62:* 44
Stevens, Helen *189:* 31
Stevens, Janet *40:* 126; *57:* 10, 11; *80:* 112; *90:* 221, 222; *109:* 156; *130:* 34; *166:* 202; *176:* 53, 116; *193:* 199, 200, 202
Stevens, Mary *11:* 193; *13:* 129; *43:* 95
Stevenson, Harvey *66:* 143; *80:* 201, 221; *153:* 60; *191:* 166
Stevenson, James *42:* 182, 183; *51:* 163; *66:* 184; *71:* 185, 187, 188; *78:* 262; *87:* 97; *113:* 182, 183,184, 185; *161:* 182, 183
Stevenson, Sucie *92:* 27; *104:* 194, 195; *112:* 168; *160:* 202; *194:* 172, 173; *195:* 166
Stewart, April Blair *75:* 210
Stewart, Arvis *33:* 98; *36:* 69; *60:* 118; *75:* 91; *127:* 4
Stewart, Charles *2:* 205
Stewart, Joel *151:* 205
Stieg, William *172:* 58
Stiles, Fran *26:* 85; *78:* 56; *82:* 150
Stillman, Susan *44:* 130; *76:* 83
Stimpson, Tom *49:* 171
Stinemetz, Morgan *40:* 151
Stinson, Paul *110:* 86
Stirnweis, Shannon *10:* 164
Stites, Joe *86:* 96
Stobbs, William *1:* 48, 49; *3:* 68; *6:* 20; *17:* 117, 217; *24:* 150; *29:* 250; *60:* 179; *87:* 204, 205,206
Stock, Catherine *37:* 55; *65:* 198; *72:* 7; *99:* 225; *114:* 197, 198, 199; *126:* 3; *145:* 161; *161:* 82; *173:* 149
Stockman, Jack *113:* 24
Stoeke, Janet Morgan *90:* 225; *136:* 196
Stoerrle, Tom *55:* 147
Stolp, Jaap *49:* 98
Stolp, Todd *89:* 195
Stone, David L. *87:* 154
Stone, David *9:* 173
Stone, David K. *4:* 38; *6:* 124; *9:* 180; *43:* 182; *60:* 70
Stone, Helen V. *6:* 209
Stone, Helen *44:* 121, 122, 126
Stone, Kazuko G. *134:* 43
Stone, Phoebe *86:* 212; *134:* 213; *162:* 188
Stone, Steve *166:* 213
Stone, Tony *150:* 34, 35
Storrings, Michael *191:* 108
Stoud, Virginia A. *89:* 31
Stover, Jill *82:* 234
Stratton, Helen *33:* 151
Stratton-Porter, Gene *15:* 254, 259, 263, 264, 268, 269
Straub, Matt *192:* 176
Straub, Phillip *197:* 22
Streano, Vince *20:* 173
Street, Janet Travell *84:* 235
Streeter, Clive *121:* 2
Stringer, Lauren *129:* 187; *154:* 172, 173; *161:* 127; *183:* 187, 188
Strodl, Daniel *47:* 95
Strogart, Alexander *63:* 139
Stromoski, Rick *111:* 179; *124:* 161, 190
Strong, Joseph D., Jr. *YABC 2:* 330
Stroyer, Poul *13:* 221
Strugnell, Ann *27:* 38
Struzan, Drew *117:* 6
Stubbs, William *73:* 196
Stubis, Talivaldis *5:* 182, 183; *10:* 45; *11:* 9; *18:* 304; *20:* 127
Stubley, Trevor *14:* 43; *22:* 219; *23:* 37; *28:* 61; *87:* 26
Stuck, Marion *104:* 44
Stuecklen, Karl W. *8:* 34, 65; *23:* 103
Stull, Betty *11:* 46
Stutzman, Mark *119:* 99
Stutzmann, Laura *73:* 185
Suarez, Maribel *162:* 208; *200:* 202

Suba, Susanne *4:* 202, 203; *14:* 261; *23:* 134; *29:* 222; *32:* 30
Sueling, Barbara *98:* 185
Sueling, Gwenn *98:* 186
Sugarman, Tracy *3:* 76; *8:* 199; *37:* 181, 182
Sugimoto, Yugo *170:* 144
Sugita, Yutaka *36:* 180, 181
Suh, John *80:* 157
Sullivan, Dorothy *89:* 113
Sullivan, Edmund J. *31:* 86
Sullivan, James F. *19:* 280; *20:* 192
Sully, Tom *104:* 199, 200; *182:* 77
Sumichrast, Jozef *14:* 253; *29:* 168, 213
Sumiko *46:* 57
Summers, Leo *1:* 177; *2:* 273; *13:* 22
Summers, Mark *118:* 144
Summers, Mike *190:* 176
Sutton, Judith *94:* 164
Svarez, Juan *56:* 113
Svendsen, Mark *181:* 176
Svolinsky, Karel *17:* 104
Swain, Carol *172:* 182
Swain, Su Zan Noguchi *21:* 170
Swan, Susan *22:* 220, 221; *37:* 66; *60:* 146; *145:* 205; *181:* 168
Swann, Susan *86:* 55
Swanson, Karl *79:* 65; *89:* 186
Swayne, Sam *53:* 143, 145
Swayne, Zoa *53:* 143, 145
Swearingen, Greg *152:* 56; *165:* 135; *173:* 2
Sweat, Lynn *25:* 206; *57:* 176; *73:* 184; *168:* 178
Sweet, Darrell K. *60:* 9; *69:* 86; *74:* 15; *75:* 215; *76:* 130, 131; *81:* 96, 122; *82:* 253; *83:* 11; *84:* 14; *85:* 37; *89:* 140; *90:* 6; *91:* 137,139; *95:* 160, 161; *126:* 25; *185:* 175; *195:* 132
Sweet, Darrell K. *1:* 163; *4:* 136; *164:* 175
Sweet, Melissa *71:* 94; *72:* 172; *111:* 82; *139:* 53, 58; *141:* 88; *142:* 231; *155:* 121; *159:* 121, 122; *172:* 185; *188:* 127
Sweet, Ozzie *31:* 149, 151, 152
Sweetland, Robert *12:* 194
Swiatkowska, Gabi *132:* 43; *175:* 139; *180:* 218; *183:* 176
Swope, Martha *43:* 160; *56:* 86, 87, 89
Sylvada, Peter *154:* 174
Sylvester, Natalie G. *22:* 222
Szafran, Gene *24:* 144
Szasz, Susanne *13:* 55, 226; *14:* 48
Szekeres, Cyndy *2:* 218; *5:* 185; *8:* 85; *11:* 166; *14:* 19; *16:* 57, 159; *26:* 49, 214; *34:* 205; *60:* 150, 151, 152, 153, 154; *73:* 224; *74:* 218; *131:* 213, 215
Szpura, Beata *81:* 68; *119:* 65; *168:* 201

T

Taback, Simms *40:* 207; *52:* 120; *57:* 34; *80:* 241; *104:* 202, 203; *170:* 176, 177
Taber, Patricia *75:* 124
Tabor, Nancy Maria Grande *89:* 210; *161:* 188
Taddei, Richard *112:* 13, 14
Tadgell, Nicole *150:* 77; *161:* 20; *177:* 186
Tadiello, Ed *133:* 200
Tafuri, Nancy *39:* 210; *75:* 199, 200; *92:* 75; *130:* 215, 216, 217
Tailfeathers, Gerald *86:* 85
Tait, Douglas *12:* 220; *74:* 105, 106
Takabayashi, Mari *113:* 112; *130:* 22; *156:* 169
Takahashi, Hideko *136:* 160; *187:* 6
Takakjian, Portia *15:* 274
Takashima, Shizuye *13:* 228
Talarczyk, June *4:* 173
Talbott, Hudson *84:* 240; *163:* 100
Tallarico, Tony *116:* 197
Tallon, Robert *2:* 228; *43:* 200, 201, 202, 203, 204, 205,206, 207, 209
Tamaki, Jillian *201:* 188

Tamas, Szecsko *29:* 135
Tamburine, Jean *12:* 222
Tandy, H.R. *13:* 69
Tandy, Russell H. *65:* 9; *100:* 30, 131
Tang, Charles *81:* 202; *90:* 192
Tang, Susan *80:* 174; *108:* 158
Tang, You-shan *63:* 100
Tankersley, Paul *69:* 206; *133:* 219
Tannenbaum, Robert *48:* 181
Tanner, Jane *87:* 13; *97:* 37
Tanner, Tim *72:* 192; *84:* 35
Tanobe, Miyuki *23:* 221
Tarabay, Sharif *110:* 149; *113:* 123; *169:* 83
Tarkington, Booth *17:* 224, 225
Tarlow, Phyllis *61:* 198
Tate, Don *159:* 141, 191; *183:* 69; *186:* 120
Tauss, Herbert *95:* 179
Tauss, Marc *117:* 160; *126:* 155; *178:* 221; *197:* 7
Tavares, Matt *159:* 192, 193; *198:* 188, 189, 190; *199:* 86
Taylor, Ann *41:* 226
Taylor, Dahl *129:* 157
Taylor, Geoff *93:* 156; *197:* 173, 175
Taylor, Isaac *41:* 228
Taylor, Mike *143:* 99, 100
Teague, Mark *83:* 6; *139:* 241; *170:* 180, 181
Teale, Edwin Way *7:* 196
Teason, James *1:* 14
Teckentrup, Britta *200:* 191, 192
Teeple, Lyn *33:* 147
Tee-Van, Helen Damrosch *10:* 176; *11:* 182
Teicher, Dick *50:* 211
Teichman, Mary *77:* 220; *124:* 208; *127:* 22; *197:* 33
Temertey, Ludmilla *96:* 232; *104:* 43, 45; *109:* 244
Tempest, Margaret *3:* 237, 238; *88:* 200
Temple, Frances *85:* 185, 186, 187
Temple, Herbert *45:* 201
Templeton, Owen *11:* 77
ten Cate, Marijke *183:* 193
Tenggren, Gustaf *18:* 277, 278, 279; *19:* 15; *28:* 86; *YABC2:* 145
Tennent, Julie *81:* 105
Tenneson, Joyce *153:* 166
Tenney, Gordon *24:* 204
Tenniel, John *74:* 234, 235; *100:* 89; *YABC 2:* 99; *153:* 63
Tepper, Matt *116:* 80
Terkel, Ari *103:* 162
Terry, Michael *180:* 209
Terry, Will *131:* 73
Teskey, Donald *71:* 51
Tessler, Manya *200:* 193
Thacher, Mary M. *30:* 72
Thackeray, William Makepeace *23:* 224, 228
Thamer, Katie *42:* 187
Tharlet, Eve *146:* 149
Thelwell, Norman *14:* 201
Theobalds, Prue *40:* 23
Theurer, Marilyn Churchill *39:* 195
Thiesing, Lisa *89:* 134; *95:* 202; *156:* 190; *159:* 195
Thiewes, Sam *133:* 114
Thistlethwaite, Miles *12:* 224
Thollander, Earl *11:* 47; *18:* 112; *22:* 224
Thomas, Allan *22:* 13
Thomas, Art *48:* 217
Thomas, Eric *28:* 49
Thomas, Harold *20:* 98
Thomas, Jacqui *125:* 95
Thomas, Jan *197:* 180
Thomas, Mark *42:* 136
Thomas, Martin *14:* 255
Thomas, Middy *177:* 114
Thompson, Arthur *34:* 107
Thompson, Carol *85:* 189; *95:* 75; *102:* 86; *147:* 166; *189:* 179, 180, 181; *190:* 84
Thompson, Colin *95:* 204

Thompson, Ellen *51:* 88, 151; *60:* 33; *67:* 42; *77:* 148; *78:* 75, 219; *79:* 122, 170; *84:* 219; *85:* 97; *87:* 37; *88:* 192, 194; *89:* 80; *93:* 37; *98:* 59; *132:* 14
Thompson, George W. *22:* 18; *28:* 150; *33:* 135
Thompson, John *58:* 201; *102:* 226; *124:* 154; *128:* 228; *129:* 157; *150:* 49; *185:* 160; *191:* 192
Thompson, Julie *44:* 158
Thompson, Katherine *132:* 146
Thompson, K. Dyble *84:* 6
Thompson, Miles *152:* 77
Thomson, Sharon *74:* 113; *158:* 60; *165:* 87
Thomson, Arline K. *3:* 264
Thomson, Bill *186:* 160
Thomson, Hugh *26:* 88
Thomson, Ross *36:* 179
Thorkelson, Gregg *95:* 183, 184; *98:* 58; *165:* 30, 31
Thorn, Lori *189:* 119
Thornberg, Dan *104:* 125
Thornburgh, Rebecca McKillip *143:* 37
Thorne, Diana *25:* 212
Thornhill, Jan *77:* 213
Thorpe, Peter *58:* 109
Thorvall, Kerstin *13:* 235
Threadgall, Colin *77:* 215
Thurber, James *13:* 239, 242, 243, 245, 248, 249
Thurman, Mark *63:* 173; *168:* 116
Tibbles, Jean-Paul *115:* 200
Tibbles, Paul *45:* 23
Tibo, Gilles *67:* 207; *107:* 199, 201
Tichenor, Tom *14:* 207
Tichnor, Richard *90:* 218
Tiegreen, Alan *36:* 143; *43:* 55, 56, 58; *77:* 200; *94:* 216, 217; *121:* 54, 59
Tierney, Tom *113:* 198, 200, 201
Tilley, Debbie *102:* 134; *133:* 226; *137:* 101; *159:* 96; *190:* 211, 212
Tilney, F.C. *22:* 231
Timbs, Gloria *36:* 90
Timmins, Harry *2:* 171
Timmons, Bonnie *194:* 189
Tinkelman, Murray *12:* 225; *35:* 44
Titherington, Jeanne *39:* 90; *58:* 138; *75:* 79; *135:* 161
Tobin, Nancy *145:* 197
Toddy, Irving *172:* 144
Tokunbo, Dimitrea *181:* 183; *187:* 182, 183
Tolbert, Jeff *128:* 69
Toledo, Francisco *197:* 182; *198:* 199
Toledo, Natalia *197:* 182
Tolford, Joshua *1:* 221
Tolkien, J.R.R. *2:* 243; *32:* 215
Tolman, Marije *195:* 43
Tolmie, Ken *15:* 292
Tomei, Lorna *47:* 168, 171
Tomes, Jacqueline *2:* 117; *12:* 139
Tomes, Margot *1:* 224; *2:* 120, 121; *16:* 207; *18:* 250; *20:* 7; *25:* 62; *27:* 78, 79; *29:* 81, 199; *33:* 82; *36:* 186, 187, 188, 189, 190; *46:* 129; *56:* 71; *58:* 183; *70:* 228; *75:* 73, 75; *80:* 80; *83:* 97; *90:* 205
Tommaso, Rich *200:* 198
Toner, Raymond John *10:* 179
Tong, Gary *66:* 215
Tongier, Stephen *82:* 32
Tooke, Susan *173:* 162
Toothill, Harry *6:* 54; *7:* 49; *25:* 219; *42:* 192
Toothill, Ilse *6:* 54
Topolski, Feliks *44:* 48
Torbert, Floyd James *22:* 226
Torgersen, Don *55:* 157
Torline, Kevin *169:* 171
Tormey, Bertram M. *75:* 3, 4
Torrecilla, Pablo *176:* 207
Torres, Leyla *156:* 199, 201
Torrey, Helen *87:* 41
Torrey, Marjorie *34:* 105

Torrey, Richard *189:* 182
Toschik, Larry *6:* 102
Totten, Bob *13:* 93
Toy, Julie *128:* 112
Trachok, Cathy *131:* 16
Tracy, Libba *82:* 24
Trago, Keith *158:* 253
Trail, Lee *55:* 157
Trang, To Ngoc *167:* 180
Trang, Winson *89:* 151
Trapani, Iza *116:* 202
Travers, Bob *49:* 100; *63:* 145
Treatner, Meryl *95:* 180
Tremain, Ruthven *17:* 238
Tresilian, Stuart *25:* 53; *40:* 212
Trez, Alain *17:* 236
Trezzo, Loretta *86:* 45
Trier, Walter *14:* 96
Trimby, Elisa *47:* 199
Trinkle, Sally *53:* 27
Triplett, Gina *182:* 193; *188:* 100; *198:* 38
Tripp, F.J. *24:* 167
Tripp, Wallace *2:* 48; *7:* 28; *8:* 94; *10:* 54,76; *11:* 92; *31:* 170, 171; *34:* 203; *42:* 57; *60:* 157; *73:* 182
Trivas, Irene *53:* 4; *54:* 168; *82:* 46, 101
Trnka, Jiri *22:* 151; *43:* 212, 213, 214, 215; *YABC 1:* 30, 31
Trondheim, Lewis *182:* 183
Troughton, Joanna *37:* 186; *48:* 72
Troyer, Johannes *3:* 16; *7:* 18
Trudeau, G.B. *35:* 220, 221, 222; *48:* 119, 123, 126, 127,128, 129, 133; *168:* 189
Trueman, Matthew *165:* 208; *183:* 191
Truesdell, Sue *55:* 142; *108:* 219, 220
Tryon, Leslie *84:* 7; *139:* 214; *143:* 10; *181:* 10
Tseng, Jean *72:* 195; *94:* 102; *119:* 126; *151:* 106; *173:* 138, 139; *200:* 158
Tseng, Mou-sien *72:* 195; *94:* 102; *119:* 126; *151:* 106; *173:* 138, 139; *200:* 158
Tsinajinie, Andy *2:* 62
Tsinganos, Jim *180:* 142
Tsugami, Kyuzo *18:* 198, 199
Tucker, Ezra *156:* 31
Tuckwell, Jennifer *17:* 205
Tudor, Bethany *7:* 103
Tudor, Tasha *18:* 227; *20:* 185, 186, 187; *36:* 111; *69:* 196, 198; *100:* 44; *YABC 2:* 46, 314; *160:* 234
Tuerk, Hanne *71:* 201
Tugeau, Jeremy *199:* 170
Tulloch, Maurice *24:* 79
Tunis, Edwin *1:* 218, 219; *28:* 209, 210, 211, 212
Tunnicliffe, C.F. *62:* 176; 177; 178, 179; 181
Turkle, Brinton *1:* 211, 213; *2:* 249; *3:* 226; *11:* 3; *16:* 209; *20:* 22; *50:* 23; *67:* 50; *68:* 65; *79:* 205, 206, 207; *128:* 47; *YABC 1:* 79
Turnbull, Christopher J. *143:* 99, 100
Turner, Gwenda *59:* 195
Turska, Krystyna *12:* 103; *31:* 173, 174, 175; *56:* 32,34; *100:* 66
Tusa, Tricia *72:* 242; *111:* 180, 181; *157:* 165; *164:* 186; *189:* 40; *201:* 9
Tusan, Stan *6:* 58; *22:* 236, 237
Tworkov, Jack *47:* 207
Tyers, Jenny *89:* 220
Tylden-Wright, Jenny *114:* 119
Tyrol, Adelaide Murphy *103:* 27
Tyrrell, Frances *107:* 204
Tzimoulis, Paul *12:* 104

U

Uchida, Yoshiko *1:* 220
Uderzo *47:* 88
Udovic, David *189:* 185; *195:* 201
Ueno, Noriko *59:* 155

Ugliano, Natascia *196:* 186
Ulm, Robert *17:* 238
Ulrich, George *73:* 15; *75:* 136, 139; *99:* 150
Ulriksen, Mark *101:* 58; *182:* 43
Unada *84:* 67
    See Gliewe, Unada
Underhill, Liz *53:* 159
Underwood, Beck *192:* 36
Underwood, Clarence *40:* 166
Unger, Jim *67:* 208
Ungerer, Tomi *5:* 188; *9:* 40; *18:* 188; *29:* 175; *33:* 221, 222, 223, 225; *71:* 48; *106:* 209, 210, 211, 212
Unwin, Nora S. *3:* 65, 234, 235; *4:* 237; *44:* 173, 174; *YABC 1:* 59; *2:* 301
Upitis, Alvis *145:* 179
Urban, Helle *149:* 243
Urbanovic, Jackie *86:* 86; *189:* 186, 187
Uris, Jill *49:* 188, 197
Ursell, Martin *50:* 51
Utpatel, Frank *18:* 114
Utz, Lois *5:* 190

V

Vagin, Vladimir *66:* 10; *142:* 215
Vaillancourt, Francois *107:* 199
Vainio, Pirkko *123:* 157, 158
Valério, Geraldo *180:* 225; *194:* 116
Vallejo, Boris *62:* 130; *72:* 212; *91:* 38; *93:* 61
Van Abbe, S. *16:* 142; *18:* 282; *31:* 90; *YABC 2:* 157, 161
Van Allsburg, Chris *37:* 205, 206; *53:* 161, 162, 163, 165,166, 167, 168, 169, 170, 171; *105:* 215, 216, 217, 218; *156:* 176, 177, 178
Vance, James *65:* 28
Van Der Linde, Henry *99:* 17
van der Meer, Ron *98:* 204, 205
van der Meer, Atie *98:* 204, 205
Vandivert, William *21:* 175
Van Dongen, H.R. *81:* 97
Van Dusen, Chris W. *173:* 169
Van Everen, Jay *13:* 160; *YABC 1:* 121
Van Fleet, John *165:* 12, 13
Van Frankenhuyzen, Gijsbert *145:* 230; *149:* 164; *184:* 151
van Genechten, Guido *165:* 226
van Haeringen, Annemarie *193:* 206
Van Horn, William *43:* 218
van Hout, Mies *195:* 191
van Kampen, Vlasta *194:* 217
van Lawick, Hugo *62:* 76, 79
Van Lieshout, Maria *201:* 196
Van Loon, Hendrik Willem *18:* 285, 289, 291
Van Munching, Paul *83:* 85
van Ommen, Sylvia *186:* 192
Van Patter, Bruce *183:* 195
Van Rynbach, Iris *102:* 192
Van Sciver, Ruth *37:* 162
VanSeveren, Joe *63:* 182
Van Stockum, Hilda *5:* 193
Van Wely, Babs *16:* 50; *79:* 16
Van Wright, Cornelius *72:* 18; *102:* 208; *116:* 107; *152:* 236; *173:* 170, 171; *199:* 185
Van Zyle, Jon *103:* 125; *160:* 181, 182; *176:* 199, 200
Vardzigulyants, Ruben *90:* 54
Varga, Judy *29:* 196
Vargo, Kurt *79:* 224
Varley, Susan *61:* 199; *63:* 176, 177; *101:* 148; *134:* 220
Varon, Sara *195:* 208
Vasconcellos, Daniel *80:* 42
Vasiliu, Mircea *2:* 166, 253; *9:* 166; *13:* 58; *68:* 42
Vaughn, Frank *34:* 157
Vavra, Robert *8:* 206
Vawter, Will *17:* 163
Vayas, Diana *71:* 61

Vazquez, Carlos *125:* 184
Veeder, Larry *18:* 4
Velasquez, Eric *45:* 217; *61:* 45; *63:* 110, 111; *88:* 162; *90:* 34, 144; *94:* 213; *107:* 147; *132:* 192; *138:* 213; *159:* 126; *181:* 184; *184:* 96; *191:* 16; *192:* 234
Velasquez, Jose A. *63:* 73
Velez, Walter *71:* 75; *91:* 154; *121:* 181; *168:* 49
Velthuijs, Max *110:* 228, 229
Vendrell, Carme Sole *42:* 205
Venezia, Mike *54:* 17
Venti, Anthony Bacon *124:* 103; *126:* 26
Venturo, Piero *61:* 194, 195
Ver Beck, Frank *18:* 16, 17
Verkaaik, Ben *110:* 209
Verling, John *71:* 27
Verney, John *14:* 225; *75:* 8
Verrier, Suzanne *5:* 20; *23:* 212
Versace, Marie *2:* 255
Verstraete, Randy *108:* 193
Vestal, H.B. *9:* 134; *11:* 101; *27:* 25; *34:* 158
Vestergaard, Hope *190:* 203
Vicatan *59:* 146
Vickrey, Robert *45:* 59, 64
Victor, Joan Berg *30:* 193
Viereck, Ellen *3:* 242; *14:* 229
Vigna, Judith *15:* 293; *102:* 194, 195, 196, 197
Vilato, Gaspar E. *5:* 41
Villiard, Paul *51:* 178
Vimnera, A. *23:* 154
Vincent, Eric *34:* 98
Vincent, Felix *41:* 237
Vincent, Gabrielle *121:* 175
Vip *45:* 164
Viskupic, Gary *83:* 48
Vitale, Stefano *109:* 71, 107; *114:* 219, 220; *123:* 106; *138:* 232; *180:* 228, 229
Vivas, Julie *51:* 67, 69; *96:* 225; *197:* 190; *199:* 71
Voake, Charlotte *114:* 221, 222; *180:* 232
Vo-Dinh, Mai *16:* 272; *60:* 191
Vogel, Ilse-Margret *14:* 230
Voigt, Erna *35:* 228
Vojnar, Kamil *95:* 31; *114:* 4; *115:* 62; *121:* 90; *124:* 72; *130:* 31; *141:* 81; *146:* 196; *150:* 123; *158:* 5, 6; *158:* 154; *171:* 119, 188; *179:* 15; *180:* 112
Vojtech, Anna *42:* 190; *108:* 222, 223; *150:* 203; *174:* 173
von Buhler, Cynthia *149:* 237; *162:* 177; *177:* 205; *180:* 77; *185:* 214, 215, 216
von Roehl, Angela *126:* 191
von Schmidt, Eric *8:* 62; *50:* 209, 210
von Schmidt, Harold *30:* 80
Vosburgh, Leonard *1:* 161; *7:* 32; *15:* 295, 296; *23:* 110; *30:* 214; *43:* 181
Voss, Tom *127:* 104
Voter, Thomas W. *19:* 3, 9
Vroman, Tom *10:* 29
Vulliamy, Clara *72:* 65

W

Waber, Bernard *47:* 209, 210, 211, 212, 213, 214; *95:* 215, 216, 217; *156:* 203, 205, 206, 207
Wachenje, Benjamin *194:* 170
Wack, Jeff *95:* 140; *110:* 90
Wagner, John *8:* 200; *52:* 104
Wagner, Ken *2:* 59
Waide, Jan *29:* 225; *36:* 139
Wainwright, Jerry *14:* 85
Waites, Joan C. *171:* 2
Wakeen, Sandra *47:* 97
Wakiyama, Hanako *171:* 96; *192:* 236; *200:* 16
Waldherr, Kris *81:* 186
Waldman, Bruce *15:* 297; *43:* 178

Waldman, Neil *35:* 141; *50:* 163; *51:* 180; *54:* 78; *77:* 112; *79:* 162; *82:* 174; *84:* 5, 56, 106; *94:* 232, 233, 234; *96:* 41; *111:* 139; *113:* 9; *118:* 30; *142:* 220, 223
Waldrep, Richard *111:* 147; *198:* 202
Walker, Brian *144:* 128
Walker, Charles *1:* 46; *4:* 59; *5:* 177; *11:* 115; *19:* 45; *34:* 74; *62:* 168; *72:* 218
Walker, Dugald Stewart *15:* 47; *32:* 202; *33:* 112
Walker, Gil *8:* 49; *23:* 132; *34:* 42
Walker, Jeff *55:* 154; *123:* 116
Walker, Jim *10:* 94
Walker, Mort *8:* 213
Walker, Norman *41:* 37; *45:* 58
Walker, Stephen *12:* 229; *21:* 174
Wallace, Beverly Dobrin *19:* 259
Wallace, Cly *87:* 93
Wallace, Ian *53:* 176, 177; *56:* 165, 166; *58:* 4; *98:* 4; *101:* 191; *112:* 124; *141:* 197, 198, 199, 200; *151:* 212
Wallace, John *105:* 228
Wallace, Nancy Elizabeth *141:* 204; *186:* 195, 197, 199
Wallenta, Adam *123:* 180
Waller, S.E. *24:* 36
Wallner, Alexandra *15:* 120; *156:* 183
Wallner, John C. *9:* 77; *10:* 188; *11:* 28; *14:* 209; *31:* 56, 118; *37:* 64; *51:* 186, 187, 188, 189, 190, 191,192, 193, 194, 195; *52:* 96; *53:* 23, 26; *71:* 99; *73:* 158; *89:* 215; *141:* 9
Wallner, John *162:* 17
Wallower, Lucille *11:* 226
Walotsky, Ron *93:* 87
Walsh, Ellen Stoll *99:* 209; *147:* 219; *194:* 194, 195, 196
Walsh, Rebecca *158:* 193
Walsh, Vivian *149:* 215; *158:* 227
Walters, Audrey *18:* 294
Walther, Tom *31:* 179
Walton, Garry *69:* 149
Walton, Tony *11:* 164; *24:* 209; *153:* 8; *177:* 73
Waltrip, Lela *9:* 195
Waltrip, Mildred *3:* 209; *37:* 211
Waltrip, Rufus *9:* 195
Wan *12:* 76
Wang, Suling *191:* 183
Warburton, Sarah *154:* 187
Wappers, G. *121:* 40
Ward, Fred *52:* 19
Ward, Helen *72:* 244; *144:* 240, 242
Ward, John *42:* 191; *96:* 54; *97:* 110; *123:* 105; *124:* 71; *173:* 66
Ward, Keith *2:* 107; *132:* 69
Ward, Leslie *34:* 126; *36:* 87
Ward, Lynd *1:* 99, 132, 133, 150; *2:* 108, 158, 196, 259; *18:* 86; *27:* 56; *29:* 79, 187, 253, 255; *36:* 199,200, 201, 202, 203, 204, 205, 206, 207, 209; *43:* 34; *56:* 28; *60:* 116; *100:* 65
Ward, Peter *37:* 116
Waring, Geoff *172:* 84
Warhola, James *92:* 5; *115:* 85, 87; *118:* 174, 175, 177; *176:* 84; *187:* 189, 190
Warner, Ben *159:* 171
Warner, Peter *14:* 87
Warnes, Tim *175:* 159
Warnick, Elsa *113:* 223
Warren, Betsy *2:* 101
Warren, Jim *85:* 81
Warren, Marion Cray *14:* 215
Warshaw, Jerry *30:* 197, 198; *42:* 165
Wasden, Kevin *102:* 162
Washington, Nevin *20:* 123
Washington, Phyllis *20:* 123
Wasserman, Amy L. *92:* 110
Waterman, Stan *11:* 76
Watkins-Pitchford, D.J. *6:* 215, 217
Watling, James *67:* 210; *78:* 112; *101:* 81; *117:* 189, 190; *127:* 119, 120

Watson, Aldren A. *2:* 267; *5:* 94; *13:* 71; *19:* 253; *32:* 220; *42:* 193, 194, 195, 196, 197, 198, 199, 200, 201; *YABC 2:* 202
Watson, G. *83:* 162
Watson, Gary *19:* 147; *36:* 68; *41:* 122; *47:* 139
Watson, J.D. *22:* 86
Watson, Jesse Joshua *197:* 124; *199:* 181
Watson, Karen *11:* 26
Watson, Mary *117:* 193
Watson, Richard Jesse *62:* 188, 189
Watson, Wendy *5:* 197; *13:* 101; *33:* 116; *46:* 163; *64:* 12; *74:* 242, 243; *91:* 21; *142:* 228
Watt, Mélanie *136:* 206; *193:* 211
Wattenberg, Jane *174:* 200; *185:* 46; *187:* 108
Watterson, Bill *66:* 223, 225, 226
Watts, Bernadette *4:* 227; *103:* 182, 183
Watts, James *59:* 197; *74:* 145; *86:* 124
Watts, John *37:* 149
Watts, Leslie Elizabeth *150:* 207; *165:* 106
Watts, Stan *116:* 205
Weatherby, Mark Alan *77:* 141
Webb, Jennifer *110:* 79
Webb, Lanny *142:* 175
Webb, Sophie *135:* 214
Webber, Helen *3:* 141
Webber, Irma E. *14:* 238
Weber, Erik *56:* 19, 20
Weber, Florence *40:* 153
Weber, Jill *127:* 227, 228; *189:* 163
Weber, Roland *61:* 204
Weber, Sam *190:* 227
Weber, William J. *14:* 239
Webster, Jean *17:* 241
Weeks, Sarah *162:* 39
Wegman, William *78:* 243
Wegner, Fritz *14:* 250; *20:* 189; *44:* 165; *86:* 62
Weidenear, Reynold H. *21:* 122
Weigel, Jeff *170:* 193
Weihs, Erika *4:* 21; *15:* 299; *72:* 201; *107:* 207, 208
Weil, Lisl *7:* 203; *10:* 58; *21:* 95; *22:* 188,217; *33:* 193
Weiman, Jon *50:* 162, 165; *52:* 103; *54:* 78, 79, 81; *78:* 80; *82:* 107; *93:* 82; *97:* 69; *105:* 179; *193:* 65
Weiner, Sandra *14:* 240
Weiner, Scott *55:* 27
Weinhaus, Karen Ann *53:* 90; *71:* 50; *86:* 124
Weinman, Brad *197:* 20
Weisgard, Leonard *1:* 65; *2:* 191, 197, 204, 264, 265; *5:* 108; *21:* 42; *30:* 200, 201, 203, 204; *41:* 47; *44:* 125; *53:* 25; *85:* 196, 198, 200, 201; *100:* 139,207; *YABC 2:* 13
Weisman, David *173:* 47
Weiss, Ellen *44:* 202
Weiss, Emil *1:* 168; *7:* 60
Weiss, Harvey *1:* 145, 223; *27:* 224, 227; *68:* 214; *76:* 245, 246, 247
Weiss, Nicki *33:* 229
Weissman, Bari *49:* 72; *90:* 125; *139:* 142
Weitzman, David L. *172:* 199
Welch, Sheila Kelly *130:* 221
Welkes, Allen *68:* 218
Wellington, Monica *99:* 223; *157:* 259, 260, 261
Welliver, Norma *76:* 94
Wellner, Fred *127:* 53
Wells, Frances *1:* 183
Wells, H.G. *20:* 194, 200
Wells, Haru *53:* 120, 121
Wells, Robert E. *184:* 208
Wells, Rosemary *6:* 49; *18:* 297; *60:* 32; *66:* 203; *69:* 215, 216; *114:* 227; *118:* 149, 150; *156:* 188, 189, 190, 191
Wells, Rufus III *56:* 111, 113
Wells, Susan *22:* 43
Wendelin, Rudolph *23:* 234
Wengenroth, Stow *37:* 47
Weninger, Brigitte *189:* 192, 194

Werenskiold, Erik *15:* 6; *62:* 17
Werner, Honi *24:* 110; *33:* 41; *88:* 122
Werth, Kurt *7:* 122; *14:* 157; *20:* 214; *39:* 128
Wesson, West, Harry A. *124:* 38
Westcott, Nadine Bernard *68:* 46; *84:* 49; *86:* 133; *106:* 199; *111:* 78; *113:* 111; *130:* 224; *139:* 54; *158:* 256; *194:* 199
Westerberg, Christine *29:* 226
Westerduin, Anne *105:* 229
Westerman, Johanna *162:* 206
Weston, Martha *29:* 116; *30:* 213; *33:* 85, 100; *53:* 181, 182, 183, 184; *77:* 95; *80:* 152; *119:* 196,197, 198, 199; *127:* 189; *133:* 196
Wetherbee, Margaret *5:* 3
Wexler, Jerome *49:* 73; *150:* 129
Whalley, Peter *50:* 49
Whatley, Bruce *186:* 93, 95
Wheatley, Arabelle *11:* 231; *16:* 276
Wheeler, Cindy *49:* 205
Wheeler, Dora *44:* 179
Wheelright, Rowland *15:* 81; *YABC 2:* 286
Whelan, Michael *56:* 108; *70:* 27, 29, 67, 68, 148; *74:* 18; *84:* 14; *91:* 195, 196; *95:* 147; *98:* 150, 151; *106:* 157; *113:* 218, 220; *116:* 99, 100
Whelan, Patrick *135:* 145
Whistler, Rex *16:* 75; *30:* 207, 208
White, Craig *110:* 130; *119:* 193; *130:* 33; *179:* 31
White, David Omar *5:* 56; *18:* 6
White, Joan *83:* 225
White, Martin *51:* 197; *85:* 127
Whitear *32:* 26
Whitehead, Beck *86:* 171
Whitehead, S.B. *154:* 132
Whithorne, H.S. *7:* 49
Whitney, George Gillett *3:* 24
Whitney, Jean *99:* 53
Whitson, Paul *102:* 161
Whittam, Geoffrey *30:* 191
Whyte, Mary *96:* 127
Wiberg, Harald *38:* 127; *93:* 215
Wick, Walter *77:* 128
Wickstrom, Sylvie *106:* 87; *169:* 180
Wickstrom, Thor *200:* 205
Widener, Terry *105:* 230; *106:* 7; *163:* 23; *200:* 17
Wiese, Kurt *3:* 255; *4:* 206; *14:* 17; *17:* 18, 19; *19:* 47; *24:* 152; *25:* 212; *32:* 184; *36:* 211,213, 214, 215, 216, 217, 218; *45:* 161; *100:* 92
Wiesner, David *33:* 47; *51:* 106; *57:* 67; *58:* 55; *64:* 78, 79, 81; *69:* 233; *72:* 247, 248, 249, 251,252, 253, 254; *83:* 134; *104:* 31; *117:* 197, 199, 200, 202; *139:* 223, 224; *151:* 51; *181:* 189, 190
Wiesner, William *4:* 100; *5:* 200, 201; *14:* 262
Wiggins, George *6:* 133
Wijngaard, Juan *111:* 36; *114:* 124
Wikkelsoe, Otto *45:* 25, 26
Wikland, Ilon *5:* 113; *8:* 150; *38:* 124, 125, 130; *127:* 162
Wikler, Madeline *114:* 233
Wilbur, C. Keith, M.D. *27:* 228
Wilburn, Kathy *53:* 102; *68:* 234
Wilcox, Cathy *105:* 123
Wilcox, J.A.J. *34:* 122
Wilcox, R. Turner *36:* 219
Wild, Jocelyn *46:* 220, 221, 222; *80:* 117
Wilde, George *7:* 139
Wildsmith, Brian *16:* 281, 282; *18:* 170, 171; *66:* 25; *69:* 224, 225, 227; *77:* 103; *83:* 218; *124:* 214,217, 219
Wildsmith, Mike *140:* 229
Wilhelm, Hans *58:* 189, 191; *73:* 157; *77:* 127; *135:* 229, 230, 233, 234; *196:* 209
Wilkin, Eloise *36:* 173; *49:* 208, 209, 210
Wilkinson, Barry *50:* 213
Wilkinson, Gerald *3:* 40

Wilkon, Jozef *31:* 183, 184; *71:* 206, 207, 209; *133:* 222
Wilks, Mike *34:* 24; *44:* 203
Willems, Mo *154:* 245, 246, 247; *180:* 236, 237, 239
Willey, Bee *103:* 129; *139:* 159; *173:* 115
Willhoite, Michael A. *71:* 214
William, Maria *168:* 51
Williams, Berkeley, Jr. *64:* 75
Williams, Ferelith Eccles *22:* 238
Williams, Garth *1:* 197; *2:* 49, 270; *4:* 205; *15:* 198, 302, 304, 307; *16:* 34; *18:* 283, 298, 299, 300, 301; *29:* 177, 178, 179, 232, 233, 241, 242, 243, 244, 245, 248; *40:* 106; *66:* 229, 230, 231, 233, 234; *71:* 192; *73:* 218, 219, 220; *78:* 261; *100:* 251, 252, 255; *136:* 117; *YABC 2:* 15, 16, 19
Williams, J. Scott *48:* 28
Williams, Jennifer *102:* 201
Williams, Jenny *60:* 202; *81:* 21; *88:* 71
Williams, Kent *180:* 18
Williams, Kit *44:* 206, 207, 208, 209, 211, 212
Williams, Marcia *97:* 214; *159:* 208, 209
Williams, Maureen *12:* 238
Williams, Patrick *14:* 218
Williams, Richard *44:* 93; *72:* 229; *74:* 133; *78:* 155, 237; *91:* 178; *110:* 212; *136:* 201, 202, 203; *152:* 115
Williams, Sam *124:* 222; *153:* 11; *177:* 201, 202; *180:* 34
Williams, Sophy *135:* 236
Williams, Vera B. *53:* 186, 187, 188, 189; *102:* 201, 202, 203
Williamson, Alex *177:* 180
Williamson, Mel *60:* 9
Willingham, Fred *104:* 206; *154:* 157
Willis, Adam *181:* 75
Willmore, J.T. *54:* 113, 114
Wilsdorf, Anne *180:* 122; *189:* 124; *191:* 195
Wilson, Anne *160:* 114
Wilson, Charles Banks *17:* 92; *43:* 73
Wilson, Connie *113:* 179
Wilson, Dagmar *10:* 47
Wilson, Dawn *67:* 161; *81:* 120; *113:* 158
Wilson, Edward A. *6:* 24; *16:* 149; *20:* 220, 221; *22:* 87; *26:* 67; *38:* 212, 214, 215, 216, 217
Wilson, Forrest *27:* 231
Wilson, Gahan *35:* 234; *41:* 136
Wilson, George *76:* 87
Wilson, Helen Miranda *140:* 61
Wilson, Jack *17:* 139
Wilson, Janet *77:* 154; *96:* 114; *99:* 219, 220; *153:* 64 *106:* 122; *130:* 210; *145:* 178; *173:* 64
Wilson, John *22:* 240
Wilson, Maurice *46:* 224
Wilson, Patten *35:* 61
Wilson, Peggy *15:* 4; *84:* 20
Wilson, Phil *181:* 29
Wilson, Rowland B. *30:* 170
Wilson, Sarah *50:* 215
Wilson, Tom *33:* 232
Wilson, W.N. *22:* 26
Wilson-Max, Ken *170:* 196; *180:* 181
Wilton, Nicholas *103:* 52; *183:* 111
Wilwerding, Walter J. *9:* 202
Wimmer, Mike *63:* 6; *70:* 121; *75:* 186; *76:* 21,22, 23; *91:* 114; *97:* 45, 68; *98:* 28; *107:* 130; *146:* 21; *149:* 47; *173:* 126; *193:* 21, 25; *194:* 204, 205
Winborn, Marsha *78:* 34; *99:* 70; *192:* 20
Winch, John *165:* 233
Winchester, Linda *13:* 231
Wind, Betty *28:* 158
Windham, Kathryn Tucker *14:* 260
Windham, Sophie *184:* 212
Winfield, Alison *115:* 78
Winfield, Wayne *72:* 23
Wing, Gary *64:* 147
Wing, Ron *50:* 85

Wingerter, Linda S. *132:* 199; *174:* 181; *200:* 196
Winick, Judd *124:* 227, 228, 229
Winslow, Will *21:* 124
Winstead, Rosie *180:* 243
Winsten, Melanie Willa *41:* 41
Winter, Jeanette *151:* 240, 241, 242; *184:* 215, 217, 218, 219
Winter, Milo *15:* 97; *19:* 221; *21:* 181, 203, 204, 205; *64:* 19; *YABC 2:* 144
Winter, Paula *48:* 227
Winter, Susan *163:* 177; *182:* 201
Winters, Greg *70:* 117
Winters, Nina *62:* 194
Wise, Louis *13:* 68
Wiseman, Ann *31:* 187
Wiseman, B. *4:* 233
Wishnefsky, Phillip *3:* 14
Wiskur, Darrell *5:* 72; *10:* 50; *18:* 246
Wisniewski, David *95:* 220, 221
Wisniewski, Robert *95:* 10; *119:* 192
Witschonke, Alan *153:* 149, 150
Witt, Dick *80:* 244
Wittmann, Patrick *162:* 204
Wittman, Sally *30:* 219
Wittner, Dale *99:* 43
Wittwer, Hala *158:* 267; *195:* 80
Woehr, Lois *12:* 5
Wohlberg, Meg *12:* 100; *14:* 197; *41:* 255
Wohnoutka, Mike *137:* 68; *190:* 199; *195:* 218
Wojtowycz, David *167:* 168
Woldin, Beth Weiner *34:* 211
Wolf, Elizabeth *133:* 151
Wolf, J. *16:* 91
Wolf, Janet *78:* 254
Wolf, Linda *33:* 163
Wolfe, Corey *72:* 213
Wolfe, Gillian *199:* 193
Wolff, Ashley *50:* 217; *81:* 216; *156:* 216, 217; *170:* 57; *174:* 174; *184:* 72
Wolff, Glenn *178:* 230
Wolfsgruber, Linda *166:* 61
Wondriska, William *6:* 220
Wong, Janet S. *98:* 225; *152:* 43
Wong, Nicole *174:* 13
Wonsetler, John C. *5:* 168
Wood, Audrey *50:* 221, 222, 223; *81:* 219, 221; *198:* 206
Wood, Don *50:* 220, 225, 226, 228, 229; *81:* 218, 220; *139:* 239, 240
Wood, Grant *19:* 198
Wood, Heather *133:* 108
Wood, Ivor *58:* 17
Wood, Muriel *36:* 119; *77:* 167; *171:* 55; *187:* 46
Wood, Myron *6:* 220
Wood, Owen *18:* 187; *64:* 202, 204, 205, 206, 208, 210
Wood, Rob *193:* 48
Wood, Ruth *8:* 11
Woodbridge, Curtis *133:* 138
Wooding, Sharon L. *66:* 237
Woodruff, Liza *132:* 239; *182:* 46, 204
Woodruff, Thomas *171:* 73
Woods, John, Jr. *109:* 142
Woodson, Jack *10:* 201
Woodson, Jacqueline *94:* 242
Woodward, Alice *26:* 89; *36:* 81
Wool, David *26:* 27
Woolley, Janet *112:* 75
Woolman, Steven *106:* 47; *163:* 73
Wooten, Vernon *23:* 70; *51:* 170
Worboys, Evelyn *1:* 166, 167
Word, Reagan *103:* 204
Wormell, Christopher *154:* 251
Worth, Jo *34:* 143
Worth, Wendy *4:* 133

Wosmek, Frances *29:* 251
Wrenn, Charles L. *38:* 96; *YABC 1:* 20, 21
Wright, Barbara Mullarney *98:* 161
Wright, Cliff *168:* 203
Wright, Dare *21:* 206
Wright-Frierson, Virginia *58:* 194; *110:* 246
Wright, George *YABC 1:* 268
Wright, Joseph *30:* 160
Wronker, Lili Cassel *3:* 247; *10:* 204; *21:* 10
Wu, Donald *200:* 18
Wummer, Amy *154:* 181; *168:* 150; *176:* 85; *201:* 202, 203
Wyant, Alexander Helwig *110:* 19
Wyatt, David *97:* 9; *101:* 44; *114:* 194; *140:* 20; *167:* 13; *188:* 48
Wyatt, Stanley *46:* 210
Wyeth, Andrew *13:* 40; *YABC 1:* 133, 134
Wyeth, Jamie *41:* 257
Wyeth, N.C. *13:* 41; *17:* 252, 253, 254, 255, 256, 257, 258, 259, 264, 265, 266, 267, 268; *18:* 181; *19:* 80, 191, 200; *21:* 57, 183; *22:* 91; *23:* 152; *24:* 28, 99; *35:* 61; *41:* 65; *100:* 206; *YABC1:* 133, 223; *2:* 53, 75, 171, 187, 317
Wyman, Cherie R. *91:* 42

X

Xuan, YongSheng *119:* 202, 207, 208; *140:* 36; *187:* 21

Y

Yaccarino, Dan *141:* 208, 209; *147:* 171; *192:* 244, 245
Yakovetic, Joe *59:* 202; *75:* 85
Yalowitz, Paul *93:* 33
Yamaguchi, Marianne *85:* 118
Yamasaki, James *167:* 93
Yang, Belle *170:* 198
Yang, Jay *1:* 8; *12:* 239
Yap, Weda *6:* 176
Yaroslava
   See Mills, Yaroslava Surmach
Yashima, Taro *14:* 84
Yates, John *74:* 249, 250
Yayo *178:* 88
Yee, Cora *166:* 233
Yee, Wong Herbert *115:* 216, 217; *172:* 204, 205; *194:* 59
Yeo, Brad *135:* 121; *192:* 106
Yerxa, Leo *181:* 195
Yezerski, Thomas F. *162:* 29
Ylla
   See Koffler, Camilla
Yohn, F.C. *23:* 128; *YABC 1:* 269
Yoo, Taeeun *191:* 198
Yorinks, Adrienne *144:* 248; *200:* 214
Yorke, David *80:* 178
Yoshida, Toshi *77:* 231
Yoshikawa, Sachiko *168:* 104; *177:* 28; *181:* 196, 197
Youll, Paul *91:* 218
Youll, Stephen *92:* 227; *118:* 136, 137; *164:* 248
Young, Amy L. *185:* 218; *190:* 46
Young, Cybéle *167:* 9
Young, Ed *7:* 205; *10:* 206; *40:* 124; *63:* 142; *74:* 250, 251, 252, 253; *75:* 227; *81:* 159; *83:* 98; *94:* 154; *115:* 160; *137:* 162; *YABC 2:* 242; *173:* 174, 175, 176

Young, Mary O'Keefe *77:* 95; *80:* 247; *134:* 214; *140:* 213
Young, Noela *8:* 221; *89:* 231; *97:* 195
Young, Paul *190:* 222
Young, Selina *153:* 12; *201:* 204, 205
Yun, Cheng Mung *60:* 143

Z

Zacharow, Christopher *88:* 98
Zacks, Lewis *10:* 161
Zaffo, George *42:* 208
Zagwyn, Deborah Turney *138:* 227
Zahares, Wade *193:* 219
Zaid, Barry *50:* 127; *51:* 201
Zaidenberg, Arthur *34:* 218, 219, 220
Zalben, Jane Breskin *7:* 211; *79:* 230, 231, 233; *170:* 202
Zallinger, Jean *4:* 192; *8:* 8, 129; *14:* 273; *68:* 36; *80:* 254; *115:* 219, 220, 222
Zallinger, Rudolph F. *3:* 245
Zakrajsek, Molly *177:* 146
Zappa, Ahmet *180:* 250
Zebot, George *83:* 214
Zeck, Gerry *40:* 232
Zeff, Joe *181:* 98
Zeifert, Harriet *154:* 265, 267
Zeiring, Bob *42:* 130
Zeldich, Arieh *49:* 124; *62:* 120
Zeldis, Malcah *86:* 239; *94:* 198; *146:* 265, 266
Zelinsky, Paul O. *14:* 269; *43:* 56; *49:* 218-223; *53:* 111; *68:* 195; *102:* 219, 222, 221, 222; *154:* 255, 256, 257; *171:* 141; *185:* 96
Zelvin, Diana *72:* 190; *76:* 101; *93:* 207
Zemach, Kaethe *149:* 250
Zemach, Margot *3:* 270; *8:* 201; *21:* 210, 211; *27:* 204, 205, 210; *28:* 185; *49:* 22, 183, 224; *53:* 151; *56:* 146; *70:* 245, 246; *92:* 74
Zeman, Ludmila *153* 212
Zemsky, Jessica *10:* 62
Zepelinsky, Paul *35:* 93
Zerbetz, Evon *127:* 34; *158:* 109
Zezejl, Daniel *197:* 74
Zhang, Ange *101:* 190; *172:* 41
Zhang, Son Nang *163:* 113; *170:* 206
Ziegler, Jack *84:* 134
Zimdars, Berta *129:* 155
Zimet, Jay *147:* 94; *152:* 74; *196:* 75
Zimic, Tricia *72:* 95
Zimmer, Dirk *38:* 195; *49:* 71; *56:* 151; *65:* 214; *84:* 159; *89:* 26; *147:* 224
Zimmer, Tracie Vaughn *169:* 183
Zimmerman, Andrea *192:* 49, 50
Zimmermann, H. Werner *101:* 223; *112:* 197
Zimnik, Reiner *36:* 224
Zingone, Robin *180:* 134
Zinkeisen, Anna *13:* 106
Zinn, David *97:* 97
Zoellick, Scott *33:* 231
Zollars, Jaime *190:* 190
Zonia, Dhimitri *20:* 234, 235
Zorn, Peter A., Jr. *142:* 157
Zudeck, Darryl *58:* 129; *63:* 98; *80:* 52
Zug, Mark *88:* 131
Zulewski, Tim *164:* 95
Zuma *99:* 36
Zvorykin, Boris *61:* 155
Zweifel, Francis *14:* 274; *28:* 187
Zwerger, Lisbeth *54:* 176, 178; *66:* 246, 247, 248; *130:* 230, 231, 232, 233; *181:* 92; *194:* 224, 225, 226
Zwinger, Herman H. *46:* 227
Zwolak, Paul *67:* 69, 71, 73, 74

Author Index

The following index gives the number of the volume in which an author's biographical sketch, Autobiography Feature, Brief Entry, or Obituary appears.

This index includes references to all entries in the following series, which are also published by The Gale Group.

YABC—*Yesterday's Authors of Books for Children: Facts and Pictures about Authors and Illustrators of Books for Young People from Early Times to 1960*
CLR—*Children's Literature Review: Excerpts from Reviews, Criticism, and Commentary on Books for Children*
SAAS—*Something about the Author Autobiography Series*

A

Aardema, Verna 1911-2000 .... *107*
  Obituary *119*
  Earlier sketches in SATA *:4, 68*
  See also CLR *17*
  See also SAAS *8*
Aaron, Chester 1923- *74*
  Earlier sketch in SATA *9*
  See also SAAS *12*
Aaseng, Nate
  See Aaseng, Nathan
Aaseng, Nathan 1953- *172*
  Brief entry *38*
  Earlier sketches in SATA *51, 88*
  See also CLR *54*
  See also SAAS *12*
Abadzis, Nick 1965- *193*
abalos, Rafael 1956- *197*
Abbas, Jailan 1952- *91*
Abbey, Lynn
  See Abbey, Marilyn Lorraine
Abbey, Marilyn Lorraine 1948- *156*
Abbott, Alice
  See Borland, Kathryn Kilby
  and Speicher, Helen Ross S(mith)
Abbott, Jacob 1803-1879 .... *22*
Abbott, Manager Henry
  See Stratemeyer, Edward L.
Abbott, R(obert) Tucker 1919-1995 .... *61*
  Obituary *87*
Abbott, Sarah
  See Zolotow, Charlotte
Abbott, Tony 1952- *159*
Abdelsayed, Cindy 1962- *123*
Abdul, Raoul 1929- *12*
Abeele, Veronique van den *196*
Abel, Raymond 1911- *12*
Abell, Kathleen 1938- *9*
Abelove, Joan *110*
Abels, Harriette S(heffer) 1926- *50*
Abercrombie, Barbara 1939- *182*
  Earlier sketch in SATA *16*
Abercrombie, Barbara Mattes
  See Abercrombie, Barbara
Abercrombie, Lynn
  See Sorrells, Walter
Abernethy, Robert G(ordon) 1927- *5*
Abisch, Roslyn Kroop 1927- *9*

Abisch, Roz
  See Abisch, Roslyn Kroop
Ablow, Gail 1962- *198*
Abodaher, David J. (Naiph) 1919- *17*
Abolafia, Yossi 1944-
  See Abulafia, Yossi
Abouzeid, Chris *175*
Abrahall, Clare Hoskyns
  See Hoskyns-Abrahall, Clare (Constance Drury)
Abrahams, Hilary (Ruth) 1938- *29*
Abrahams, Peter 1947- *194*
Abrahams, Robert David 1905-1998 .... *4*
Abramovitz, Anita (Zeltner Brooks) 1914- *5*
Abrams, Joy 1941- *16*
Abrams, Lawrence F. *58*
  Brief entry *47*
Abrashkin, Raymond 1911-1960 .... *50*
Abulafia, Yossi 1944- *177*
  Brief entry *46*
  Earlier sketch in SATA *60*
Acampora, Paul *175*
Accardo, Anthony *191*
Achebe, Albert Chinualumogu
  See Achebe, Chinua
Achebe, Chinua 1930- *40*
  Brief entry *38*
  Earlier sketch in SATA *38*
  See also CLR *20*
Ackerman, Diane 1948- *102*
Ackerman, Eugene (Francis) 1888-1974 ...... *10*
Ackerman, Karen 1951- *126*
Ackerman, Susan Yoder 1945- *92*
Ackison, Wendy Wassink 1956- *103*
Ackley, Peggy Jo 1955- *58*
Ackroyd, Peter 1949- *153*
Acorn, John (Harrison) 1958- *79*
Acredolo, Linda (Potter) 1947- *159*
Acs, Laszlo (Bela) 1931- *42*
  Brief entry *32*
Acuff, Selma Boyd 1924- *45*
Ada, Alma Flor 1938- *181*
  Earlier sketches in SATA *43, 84, 143*
  See also CLR *62*
Adair, Gilbert 1944- *98*
Adair, Ian 1942- *53*
Adair, Margaret Weeks (?)-1971 .... *10*
Adam, Cornel
  See Lengyel, Cornel Adam

Adam, Mark
  See Alexander, Marc
Adam, Robert 1948- *93*
Adams, Adrienne 1906- *90*
  Earlier sketch in SATA *8*
  See also CLR *73*
Adams, Andy 1859-1935
  See YABC *1*
Adams, Barbara Johnston 1943- *60*
Adams, Bruin
  See Ellis, Edward S(ylvester)
Adams, Captain Bruin
  See Ellis, Edward S(ylvester)
Adams, Captain J. F. C.
  See Ellis, Edward S(ylvester)
Adams, Dale
  See Quinn, Elisabeth
Adams, Daniel
  See Nicole, Christopher (Robin)
Adams, Debra
  See Speregen, Devra Newberger
Adams, Douglas 1952-2001 .... *116*
  Obituary *128*
Adams, Douglas Noel
  See Adams, Douglas
Adams, Edith
  See Shine, Deborah
Adams, Florence 1932- *61*
Adams, Harriet S(tratemeyer) 1892(?)-1982 .. *1*
  Obituary *29*
Adams, Harrison
  See Rathborne, St. George (Henry)
  and Stratemeyer, Edward L.
Adams, Hazard 1926- *6*
Adams, Hazard Simeon
  See Adams, Hazard
Adams, John Anthony 1944- *67*
Adams, Laurie 1941- *33*
Adams, Lowell
  See Joseph, James (Herz)
Adams, Nicholas
  See Pine, Nicholas
Adams, Nicholas
  See Smith, Sherwood
Adams, Nicholas
  See Doyle, Debra
  and Macdonald, James D.
Adams, Pam 1919- *112*

Adams, Pamela
  See Adams, Pam
Adams, Richard (George) 1920- *69*
  Earlier sketch in SATA *7*
  See also CLR *121*
Adams, Ruth Joyce *14*
Adams, Tricia
  See Kite, Pat
Adams, William Taylor 1822-1897 .... *28*
Adam Smith, Janet (Buchanan) 1905-1999 .. *63*
Adamson, Gareth 1925-1982(?) *46*
  Obituary *30*
Adamson, George 1906-1989
  Obituary *63*
Adamson, George (Worsley) 1913-2005 ...... *30*
Adamson, Graham
  See Groom, Arthur William
Adamson, Joy(-Friederike Victoria)
  1910-1980 .... *11*
  Obituary *22*
Adamson, Wendy Writson 1942- *22*
Addison, Kenneth 1949(?)-2005 .... *187*
Addison, Kenneth L.
  See Addison, Kenneth
Addona, Angelo F. 1925- *14*
Addy, Sharon Hart 1943- *192*
  Earlier sketch in SATA *108*
Addy, Ted
  See Winterbotham, R(ussell) R(obert)
Adelberg, Doris
  See Orgel, Doris
Adelson, Leone 1908- *11*
Adinolfi, JoAnn *176*
Adkins, Jan 1944- *144*
  Earlier sketches in SATA *8, 69*
  See also CLR *77*
  See also SAAS *19*
Adler, C(arole) S(chwerdtfeger) 1932- *126*
  Earlier sketches in SATA *26, 63, 102*
  See also CLR *78*
  See also SAAS *15*
Adler, David A. 1947- *178*
  Earlier sketches in SATA *14, 70, 106, 151*
  See also CLR *108*
Adler, Irene
  See Penzler, Otto
  and Storr, Catherine (Cole)
Adler, Irving 1913- *29*
  Autobiography Feature *164*
  Earlier sketch in SATA *1*
  See also CLR *27*
  See also SAAS *15*
Adler, Larry 1939- *36*
Adler, Peggy *22*
Adler, Ruth 1915-1968 .... *1*
Adlerman, Daniel (Ezra) 1963- *163*
  Earlier sketch in SATA *96*
Adlerman, Kim
  See Adlerman, Kimberly M(arie)
Adlerman, Kimberly M(arie) 1964- *163*
  Earlier sketch in SATA *96*
Adoff, Arnold 1935- *96*
  Earlier sketches in SATA *5, 57*
  See also CLR *7*
  See also SAAS *15*
Adoff, Jaime (Levi) *163*
Adorjan, Carol (Madden) 1934- *71*
  Earlier sketch in SATA *10*
Adrian, Frances
  See Polland, Madeleine A(ngela Cahill)
Adrian, Mary
  See Jorgensen, Mary Venn
Adshead, Gladys L(ucy) 1896-1985 .... *3*
Aesop 620(?)B.C.-560(?)B.C. *64*
  See also CLR *14*
Aesop, Abraham
  See Newbery, John
Affabee, Eric
  See Stine, R.L.
Agapida, Fray Antonio
  See Irving, Washington

Agard, John 1949- *138*
Agard, Nadema 1948- *18*
Agarwal, Deepa 1947- *141*
Agee, Jon 1960- *196*
  Earlier sketches in SATA *116, 157*
Agell, Charlotte 1959- *150*
  Earlier sketch in SATA *99*
Agent Orange
  See Moseley, James W(illett)
Aghill, Gordon
  See Garrett, Randall
  and Silverberg, Robert
Agle, Nan Hayden 1905- *3*
  See also SAAS *10*
Agnew, Edith J(osephine) 1897-1988 .... *11*
Agonito, Joseph *177*
Agonito, Rosemary 1937- *177*
Ahern, Margaret McCrohan 1921- *10*
Ahl, Anna Maria 1926- *32*
Ahlberg, Allan 1938- *165*
  Brief entry *35*
  Earlier sketches in SATA *68, 120*
  See also CLR *18*
Ahlberg, Janet 1944-1994 .... *120*
  Brief entry *32*
  Obituary *83*
  Earlier sketch in SATA *68*
  See also CLR *18*
Aichinger, Helga 1937- *4*
Aiken, Clarissa (M.) Lorenz 1899-1992 .... *12*
  Obituary *109*
Aiken, Conrad (Potter) 1889-1973 .... *30*
  Earlier sketch in SATA *3*
Aiken, Joan (Delano) 1924-2004 .... *73*
  Autobiography Feature *109*
  Obituary *152*
  Earlier sketches in SATA *2, 30*
  See also CLR *90*
  See also SAAS *1*
Aillaud, Cindy Lou 1955- *184*
Ainsley, Alix
  See Steiner, Barbara A(nnette)
Ainsworth, Catherine Harris 1910- *56*
Ainsworth, Norma 1911-1987 .... *9*
Ainsworth, Ruth (Gallard) 1908- *73*
  Earlier sketch in SATA *7*
Ainsworth, William Harrison 1805-1882 ..... *24*
Aistrop, Jack 1916- *14*
Aitken, Amy 1952- *54*
  Brief entry *40*
Aitken, Dorothy 1916- *10*
Aitmatov, Chingiz 1928-2008 .... *56*
Aitmatov, Chingiz Torekulovich
  See Aitmatov, Chingiz
Akaba, Suekichi 1910- *46*
Akers, Floyd
  See Baum, L(yman) Frank
Akib, Jamel *181*
Aks, Patricia 1926-1994 .... *68*
Alagoa, Ebiegberi Joe 1933- *108*
Alain
  See Brustlein, Daniel
Alajalov, Constantin 1900-1987
  Obituary *53*
Alan, David
  See Horsfield, Alan
Alan, Robert
  See Silverstein, Robert Alan
Alarcon, Francisco X(avier) 1954- *104*
Albert, Burton 1936- *22*
Albert, Louise 1928- *157*
Albert, Richard E. 1909-1999 .... *82*
Albert, Susan Wittig 1940- *107*
Alberts, Frances Jacobs 1907-1989 .... *14*
Albertson, Susan
  See Wojciechowski, Susan
Albion, Lee Smith *29*
Alborough, Jez 1959- *149*
  Earlier sketch in SATA *86*
Albrecht, Lillie (Vanderveer H.)
  1894-1985 .... *12*

Albyn, Carole Lisa 1955- *83*
Alchemy, Jack
  See Gershator, David
Alcock, Gudrun 1908- *56*
  Brief entry *33*
Alcock, Vivien (Dolores) 1924-2003 .... *76*
  Brief entry *38*
  Obituary *148*
  Earlier sketch in SATA *45*
  See also CLR *26*
Alcorn, John 1935- *31*
  Brief entry *30*
Alcorn, Stephen 1958- *110*
Alcott, Louisa May 1832-1888 .... *100*
  See also YABC *1*
  See also CLR *109*
Alda, Arlene 1933- *158*
  Brief entry *36*
  Earlier sketches in SATA *44, 106*
  See also CLR *93*
Alden, Isabella (Macdonald) 1841-1930 ..... *115*
  See also YABC *2*
Alden, Sue
  See Francis, Dorothy
Alderman, Clifford Lindsey 1902-1988 .... *3*
Alderson, Sue Ann 1940- *59*
  Brief entry *48*
Alding, Peter
  See Jeffries, Roderic
Aldis, Dorothy (Keeley) 1896-1966 .... *2*
Aldiss, Brian W. 1925- *34*
Aldiss, Brian Wilson
  See Aldiss, Brian W.
Aldon, Adair
  See Meigs, Cornelia Lynde
Aldous, Allan (Charles) 1911- *27*
Aldrich, Ann
  See Meaker, Marijane
Aldrich, Bess Streeter 1881-1954
  See CLR *70*
Aldrich, Thomas (Bailey) 1836-1907 .... *114*
  Earlier sketch in SATA *17*
Aldridge, (Harold Edward) James 1918- *87*
Aldridge, Josephine Haskell *14*
Aldridge, Sheila 1974- *192*
Aleas, Richard
  See Appelt, Kathi
Alegria, Malin 1974(?)- *190*
Alegria, Ricardo E(nrique) 1921- *6*
Aleksin, Anatolii Georgievich 1924- *36*
Alenov, Lydia 1948- *61*
Alex, Ben (a pseudonym) 1946- *45*
Alex, Marlee (a pseudonym) 1948- *45*
Alexander, Anna B(arbara Cooke) 1913- *1*
Alexander, Anne
  See Alexander, Anna B(arbara Cooke)
Alexander, Ellen 1938- *91*
Alexander, Frances (Laura) 1888-1979 .... *4*
Alexander, Janet 1907-1994 .... *97*
  Earlier sketch in SATA *1*
Alexander, Jocelyn Anne Arundel 1930- *22*
Alexander, Linda 1935- *2*
Alexander, Lloyd 1924-2007 .... *135*
  Obituary *182*
  Earlier sketches in SATA *3, 49, 81, 129*
  See also CLR *48*
  See also SAAS *19*
Alexander, Lloyd Chudley
  See Alexander, Lloyd
Alexander, Marc 1929- *117*
Alexander, Martha 1920- *136*
  Earlier sketches in SATA *11, 70*
Alexander, Rae Pace
  See Alexander, Raymond Pace
Alexander, Raymond Pace 1898-1974 .... *22*
Alexander, Robert *200*
  See Gross, Michael (Robert)
  and Zimmerman, R. D.
Alexander, Rod
  See Pellowski, Michael (Joseph)
Alexander, Sally Hobart 1943- *84*

Alexander, Sue 1933-2008 136
   Obituary 195
   Earlier sketches in SATA *12, 89*
   See also SAAS *15*
Alexander, Vincent Arthur 1925-1980
   Obituary 23
Alexeieff, Alexandre A. 1901-1979 .... *14*
Alger, Horatio, Jr.
   See Stratemeyer, Edward L.
Alger, Horatio, Jr. 1832-1899 .... *16*
   See also CLR *87*
Alger, Leclaire (Gowans) 1898-1969 .... *15*
Aliki
   See Brandenberg, Aliki
Alkema, Chester Jay 1932- *12*
Al-Khalili, Jim 1962- *124*
Alkiviades, Alkis 1953- *105*
Alkouatli, Claire *186*
Allaby, John Michael
   See Allaby, Michael
Allaby, Michael 1933- *167*
Allamand, Pascale 1942- *12*
Allan, Mabel Esther 1915-1998 .... *75*
   Earlier sketches in SATA *5, 32*
   See also CLR *43*
   See also SAAS *11*
Allan, Nicholas 1956- *123*
   Earlier sketch in SATA *79*
Allan-Meyer, Kathleen 1918- *51*
   Brief entry *46*
Allard, Harry
   See Allard, Harry G(rover), Jr.
Allard, Harry G(rover), Jr. 1928- *102*
   Earlier sketch in SATA *42*
   See also CLR *85*
Allee, Marjorie Hill 1890-1945 .... *17*
Allen, Adam
   See Epstein, Beryl (M. Williams)
   and Epstein, Samuel
Allen, Alex B.
   See Heide, Florence Parry
Allen, Allyn
   See Eberle, Irmengarde
Allen, Betsy
   See Harrison, Elizabeth (Allen) Cavanna
Allen, Bob 1961- *76*
Allen, Gertrude E(lizabeth) 1888-1984 .... *9*
Allen, Grace
   See Hogarth, Grace (Weston Allen)
Allen, Jeffrey (Yale) 1948- *42*
Allen, John
   See Perry, Ritchie (John Allen)
Allen, Jonathan 1957- *177*
   Earlier sketch in SATA *131*
Allen, Jonathan Dean
   See Allen, Jonathan
Allen, Judy (Christina) 1941- *124*
   Earlier sketch in SATA *80*
Allen, Kenneth S. 1913-1981 .... *56*
Allen, Leroy 1912- *11*
Allen, Linda 1925- *33*
Allen, Marjorie 1931- *22*
Allen, Maury 1932- *26*
Allen, Merritt Parmelee 1892-1954 .... *22*
Allen, Nancy Kelly 1949- *171*
   Earlier sketch in SATA *127*
Allen, Nina (Stroemgren) 1935- *22*
Allen, Pamela (Kay) 1934- *123*
   Earlier sketches in SATA *50, 81*
   See also CLR *44*
Allen, Rodney F. 1938-1999 .... *27*
Allen, Roger MacBride 1957- *105*
Allen, Ruth
   See Peterson, Esther (Allen)
Allen, Samuel W(ashington) 1917- *9*
Allen, T. D.
   See Allen, Terril Diener
Allen, Terril Diener 1908- *35*
Allen, Terry D.
   See Allen, Terril Diener

Allen, Thomas B. 1929- *193*
   Earlier sketches in SATA *45, 140*
Allen, Thomas B. 1929- *193*
Allen, Thomas Benton
   See Allen, Thomas B.
Allen, Tom
   See Allen, Thomas B.
Allende, Isabel 1942- *163*
   See also CLR *99*
Allerton, Mary
   See Govan, (Mary) Christine Noble
Alley, Robert W.
   See Alley, R.W.
Alley, R.W. *169*
Alleyn, Ellen
   See Rossetti, Christina
Allington, Richard L(loyd) 1947- *39*
   Brief entry *35*
Allison, Amy 1956- *138*
Allison, Bob *14*
Allison, Diane Worfolk *78*
Allison, Jennifer *173*
Allison, Linda 1948- *43*
Allison, Margaret
   See Klam, Cheryl
Allman, Barbara 1950- *137*
Allmendinger, David F(rederick), Jr. 1938- . *35*
Allred, Alexandra Powe 1965- *144*
Allred, Gordon T(hatcher) 1930- *10*
Allsop, Kenneth 1920-1973 .... *17*
Allsopp, Sophie *188*
Alma, Ann 1946- *201*
Almedingen, E. M.
   See Almedingen, Martha Edith von
Almedingen, Martha Edith von 1898-1971 .... *3*
Almon, Russell
   See Clevenger, William R.
   and Downing, David A(lmon)
Almond, David 1951- *158*
   Earlier sketch in SATA *114*
   See also CLR *85*
Almond, Linda Stevens 1881(?)-1987
   Obituary *50*
Almquist, Don 1929- *11*
Alonzo, Sandra *199*
Alphin, Elaine Marie 1955- *139*
   Autobiography Feature *139*
   Earlier sketches in SATA *80, 130*
Alsenas, Linas 1979- *186*
Alsop, Mary O'Hara 1885-1980 .... *34*
   Obituary *24*
   Earlier sketch in SATA *2*
Alter, Anna 1974- *135*
Alter, Judith (MacBain) 1938- *101*
   Earlier sketch in SATA *52*
Alter, Judy
   See Alter, Judith (MacBain)
Alter, Robert Edmond 1925-1965 .... *9*
Alter, Stephen 1956- *187*
Althea
   See Braithwaite, Althea
Altman, Linda Jacobs 1943- *21*
Altman, Suzanne
   See Orgel, Doris
   and Schecter, Ellen
Alton, Steve *169*
Altschuler, Franz 1923- *45*
Altsheler, Joseph A(lexander) 1862-1919
   See YABC *1*
Alvarez, John
   See del Rey, Lester
Alvarez, Joseph A. 1930- *18*
Alvarez, Julia 1950- *129*
al-Windawi, Thura
   See Windawi, Thura al-
Alyer, Philip A.
   See Stratemeyer, Edward L.
Amado, Elisa *193*
Amann, Janet 1951- *79*
Amato, Carol A. 1942- *92*

Amato, Mary 1961- *178*
   Earlier sketch in SATA *140*
Ambrose, Stephen E. 1936-2002 .... *138*
   Earlier sketch in SATA *40*
Ambrose, Stephen Edward
   See Ambrose, Stephen E.
Ambrus, Gyozo Laszlo 1935- *1*
   See also SAAS *4*
Ambrus, Victor G.
   See Ambrus, Gyozo Laszlo
Amend, Bill 1962- *147*
Amerman, Lockhart 1911-1969 .... *3*
Ames, Evelyn 1908-1990 .... *13*
   Obituary *64*
Ames, Gerald 1906-1993 .... *11*
   Obituary *74*
Ames, Lee J(udah) 1921- *151*
   Earlier sketch in SATA *3*
Ames, Mildred 1919-1994 .... *85*
   Earlier sketches in SATA *22, 81*
Amico, Tom 1960(?)- *176*
Ammon, Richard 1942- *124*
Amon, Aline 1928- *9*
Amoss, Berthe 1925- *112*
   Earlier sketch in SATA *5*
Anastasio, Dina 1941- *94*
   Brief entry *30*
   Earlier sketch in SATA *37*
Anaya, Rudolfo A. 1937-
   See CLR *129*
Anaya, Rudolpho Alfonso
   See Anaya, Rudolfo A.
Anckarsvard, Karin Inez Maria 1915-1969 .... *6*
Ancona, George 1929- *192*
   Earlier sketches in SATA *12, 85, 145*
   See also SAAS *18*
Anders, C. J.
   See Bennett, Cherie
Anders, Isabel 1946- *101*
Anders, Lou *176*
Andersdatter, Karla M(argaret) 1938- *34*
Andersen, Bethanne 1954- *191*
Andersen, Hans Christian 1805-1875 .... *100*
   See also YABC *1*
   See also CLR *113*
Andersen, Ted
   See Boyd, Waldo T.
Andersen, Yvonne 1932- *27*
Anderson, Bernice G(oudy) 1894-1997 .... *33*
Anderson, Bob 1944- *139*
   Earlier sketch in SATA *136*
Anderson, Brad(ley Jay) 1924- *33*
   Brief entry *31*
Anderson, C. C.
   See Anderson, Catherine Corley
Anderson, C(larence) W(illiam) 1891-1971 . *11*
Anderson, Catherine C.
   See Anderson, Catherine Corley
Anderson, Catherine Corley 1909-2001 .... *72*
Anderson, Clifford
   See Gardner, Richard (M.)
Anderson, Daryl Shon 1963- *93*
Anderson, Dave
   See Anderson, David
Anderson, David 1929- *60*
Anderson, Derek 1969- *169*
Anderson, Eloise Adell 1927- *9*
Anderson, George
   See Groom, Arthur William
Anderson, Grace Fox 1932- *43*
Anderson, J(ohn) R(ichard) L(ane)
   1911-1981 .... *15*
   Obituary *27*
Anderson, Jodi Lynn *182*
Anderson, John David 1975- *197*
Anderson, John L. 1905- *2*
Anderson, Joy 1928- *1*
Anderson, Kevin J. 1962- *117*
   Earlier sketch in SATA *74*
Anderson, Kevin James
   See Anderson, Kevin J.

Anderson, Kirsty 1978- *108*
Anderson, K.J.
  See Moesta, Rebecca
Anderson, Laurie Halse 1961- *186*
  Earlier sketches in SATA *95, 132*
  See also CLR *138*
Anderson, LaVere Francis Shoenfelt
  1907-1998 .... *27*
Anderson, Leone Castell 1923- *53*
  Brief entry *49*
Anderson, Lisa G. 1963- *108*
Anderson, Lonzo
  See Anderson, John L.
Anderson, Lucia (Lewis) 1922- *10*
Anderson, Madelyn Klein 1926-2005 .... *28*
Anderson, Margaret J(ean) 1931- *27*
  See also SAAS *8*
Anderson, Marilyn D. 1943- *144*
Anderson, Mary 1939- *82*
  Earlier sketch in SATA *7*
  See also SAAS *23*
Anderson, Matthew Tobin
  See Anderson, M.T.
Anderson, Mona 1910-2004 .... *40*
Anderson, Mrs. Melvin
  See Anderson, Catherine Corley
Anderson, M.T. 1968- *182*
  Earlier sketches in SATA *97, 146*
Anderson, Norman Dean 1928- *22*
Anderson, Peggy Perry 1953- *179*
  Earlier sketch in SATA *84*
Anderson, Poul 1926-2001 .... *90*
  Autobiography Feature *106*
  Brief entry *39*
  See also CLR *58*
Anderson, Poul William
  See Anderson, Poul
Anderson, Rachel 1943- *86*
  Earlier sketch in SATA *34*
  See also SAAS *18*
Anderson, Rebecca M.
  See Moesta, Rebecca
Anderson, Rebecca Moesta
  See Moesta, Rebecca
Anderson, Richard
  See Anderson, J(ohn) R(ichard) L(ane)
Anderson, Sara *173*
Anderson, Scoular *201*
Anderson, (Tom) Scoular *138*
Anderson, Susan 1952- *90*
Anderson, Thomas Scoular
  See Anderson, Scoular
Anderson, W. B.
  See Schultz, James Willard
Anderson, Wayne 1946- *147*
  Earlier sketch in SATA *56*
Andersson, Kenneth 1970- *200*
Andre, Evelyn M(arie) 1924- *27*
Andreasen, Dan *186*
Andreassen, Karl
  See Boyd, Waldo T.
Andreassi, K. Robert
  See DeCandido, Keith R.A.
Andree, Louise
  See Coury, Louise Andree
Andrew, Ian 1962- *166*
  Earlier sketch in SATA *116*
Andrew, Ian Peter
  See Andrew, Ian
Andrew, Prudence (Hastings) 1924- *87*
Andrews, Benny 1930-2006 .... *31*
  Obituary *178*
Andrews, Eleanor Lattimore
  See Lattimore, Eleanor Frances
Andrews, Elton V.
  See Pohl, Frederik
Andrews, F(rank) Emerson 1902-1978 .... *22*
Andrews, J(ames) S(ydney) 1934- *4*
Andrews, Jan 1942- *167*
  Brief entry *49*
  Earlier sketches in SATA *58, 98*

Andrews, Julie 1935- *153*
  Earlier sketch in SATA *7*
  See also CLR *85*
Andrews, Laura
  See Coury, Louise Andree
Andrews, Roy Chapman 1884-1960 .... *19*
Andrews, Tamra 1959- *129*
Andrews, V(irginia) C(leo) 1924(?)-1986
  Obituary *50*
Andrews, Wendy
  See Sharmat, Marjorie Weinman
Andrews, William G(eorge) 1930- *74*
Andrezel, Pierre
  See Blixen, Karen
Andriani, Renee
  See Williams-Andriani, Renee
Andriola, Alfred J. 1912-1983
  Obituary *34*
Andrist, Ralph K. 1914-2004 .... *45*
Andronik, Catherine M. *189*
Andryszewski, Tricia 1956- *148*
  Earlier sketch in SATA *88*
Angel, Ann 1952- *192*
Angel, Carl *178*
Angel, Marie 1923- *47*
Angeles, Peter A. 1931- *40*
Angeletti, Roberta 1964- *124*
Angeli, Marguerite (Lofft) de
  See de Angeli, Marguerite (Lofft)
Angell, Judie 1937- *78*
  Earlier sketch in SATA *22*
  See also CLR *33*
Angell, Madeline 1919- *18*
Angelo, Valenti 1897- *14*
Angelou, Maya 1928- *136*
  Earlier sketch in SATA *49*
  See also CLR *53*
Angier, Bradford -1997 .... *12*
Angle, Paul M(cClelland) 1900-1975
  Obituary *20*
Anglund, Joan Walsh 1926- *2*
  See also CLR *94*
Ango, Fan D.
  See Longyear, Barry B(rookes)
Angrist, Stanley W(olff) 1933- *4*
Anholt, Catherine 1958- *131*
  Earlier sketch in SATA *74*
Anholt, Laurence 1959- *141*
  Earlier sketch in SATA *74*
Anita
  See Daniel, Anita
Anmar, Frank
  See Nolan, William F(rancis)
Annett, Cora
  See Scott, Cora Annett (Pipitone)
Annie-Jo
  See Blanchard, Patricia
  and Suhr, Joanne
Annixter, Jane
  See Sturtzel, Jane Levington
Annixter, Paul
  See Sturtzel, Howard A(llison)
Anno, Mitsumasa 1926- *157*
  Earlier sketches in SATA *5, 38, 77*
  See also CLR *122*
Anrooy, Francine Van
  See Van Anrooy, Francine
Ansary, Mir Tamim 1948- *140*
Anstey, Caroline 1958- *81*
Antell, Will D. 1935- *31*
Anthony, Barbara
  See Barber, Antonia
Anthony, C. L.
  See Smith, Dorothy Gladys
Anthony, Edward 1895-1971 .... *21*
Anthony, John
  See Beckett, Ronald Brymer
  and Ciardi, John (Anthony)
  and Sabini, John Anthony
Anthony, Joseph Patrick 1964- *103*
Anthony, Patricia 1947- *109*

Anthony, Piers 1934- *129*
  Autobiography Feature *129*
  Earlier sketch in SATA *84*
  See also CLR *118*
  See also SAAS *22*
Anthony, Susan C(arol) 1953- *87*
Anticaglia, Elizabeth 1939- *12*
Antilles, Kem
  See Moesta, Rebecca
Antle, Nancy 1955- *102*
Antolini, Margaret Fishback 1904-1985
  Obituary *45*
Anton, Michael J(ames) 1940- *12*
Antonacci, Robert J(oseph) 1916- *45*
  Brief entry *37*
Anvil, Christopher
  See Crosby, Harry C., Jr.
Anzaldua, Gloria (Evanjelina) 1942-2004
  Obituary *154*
Aoki, Hisako 1942- *45*
Apfel, Necia H(alpern) 1930- *51*
  Brief entry *41*
Aphrodite, J.
  See Livingston, Carole
Apikuni
  See Schultz, James Willard
Apostolina, M. *184*
Apostolina, Michael
  See Apostolina, M.
Apostolou, Christine Hale 1955- *179*
  Earlier sketches in SATA *82, 128*
Appel, Allen (R.) 1945- *115*
Appel, Benjamin 1907-1977 .... *39*
  Obituary *21*
Appel, Martin 1948- *45*
Appel, Martin Eliot
  See Appel, Martin
Appel, Marty
  See Appel, Martin
Appelbaum, Diana Muir Karter 1953- *132*
Appelt, Kathi 1954- *190*
  Earlier sketches in SATA *83, 129*
Apperley, Dawn 1969- *135*
Appiah, Peggy 1921-2006 .... *84*
  Earlier sketch in SATA *15*
  See also SAAS *19*
Apple, Margot *152*
  Brief entry *42*
  Earlier sketch in SATA *64*
Applebaum, Stan 1922- *45*
Applegate, K.A.
  See Applegate, Katherine
Applegate, Katherine 1956- *196*
  Earlier sketches in SATA *109, 162*
  See also CLR *90*
Applegate, Katherine Alice
  See Applegate, Katherine
Appleton, Victor
  See Barrett, Neal, Jr.
  and Doyle, Debra
  and Macdonald, James D.
  and Stratemeyer, Edward L.
  and Vardeman, Robert E(dward)
Appleton, Victor II
  See Goulart, Ron
Apsler, Alfred 1907-1982 .... *10*
Aragones, Sergio 1937- *48*
  Brief entry *39*
Araujo, Frank P. 1937- *86*
Arbo, Cris 1950- *103*
Arbuckle, Dorothy Fry 1910-1982
  Obituary *33*
Arbuthnot, May Hill 1884-1969 .... *2*
Archambault, John *163*
  Earlier sketches in SATA *67, 112*
Archbold, Rick 1950- *97*
Archer, Colleen Rutherford 1949- *164*
Archer, Frank
  See O'Connor, Richard

Archer, Jules 1915- 85
   Earlier sketch in SATA 4
   See also SAAS 5
Archer, Lily 1981- 193
Archer, Marion Fuller 1917- 11
Archer, Nathan
   See Watt-Evans, Lawrence
Archer, Peggy 1947- 199
Archibald, Joe
   See Archibald, Joseph S(topford)
Archibald, Joseph S(topford) 1898-1986 3
   Obituary 47
Ard, William
   See Jakes, John
Ardagh, Philip 1961- 154
Ardai, Charles 1969- 85
Arden, Barbi
   See Stoutenburg, Adrien (Pearl)
Arden, William
   See Lynds, Dennis
Ardizzone, Edward (Jeffrey Irving)
   1900-1979 28
   Obituary 21
   Earlier sketch in SATA 1
   See also CLR 3
Ardley, Neil (Richard) 1937- 121
   Earlier sketch in SATA 43
Arehart-Treichel, Joan 1942- 22
Arena, Felice 1968- 151
Arenella, Roy 1939- 14
Argent, Kerry 1960- 138
Argueta, Jorge 179
Arihara, Shino 1973- 201
Arkin, Alan 1934- 59
   Brief entry 32
Arkin, Alan Wolf
   See Arkin, Alan
Arksey, Neil 158
Arlen, Leslie
   See Nicole, Christopher (Robin)
Arley, Robert
   See Jackson, Mike
Armer, Alberta (Roller) 1904-1986 9
Armer, Laura Adams 1874-1963 13
Armistead, John 1941- 130
Armitage, David 1943- 155
   Brief entry 38
   Earlier sketch in SATA 99
Armitage, Frank
   See Carpenter, John (Howard)
Armitage, Ronda (Jacqueline) 1943- 155
   Brief entry 38
   Earlier sketches in SATA 47, 99
Armour, Richard (Willard) 1906-1989 14
   Obituary 61
Armstrong, Alan 1939- 172
Armstrong, Alan W.
   See Armstrong, Alan
Armstrong, George D. 1927- 10
Armstrong, Gerry (Breen) 1929- 10
Armstrong, Jeannette (C.) 1948- 102
Armstrong, Jennifer 1961- 165
   Autobiography Feature 120
   Earlier sketches in SATA 77, 111
   See also CLR 66
   See also SAAS 24
Armstrong, Louise 43
   Brief entry 33
Armstrong, Martin Donisthorpe
   1882-1974 115
Armstrong, Matthew 1975- 188
Armstrong, Matthew S.
   See Armstrong, Matthew
Armstrong, Ralph Richard
   See Armstrong, Richard
Armstrong, Richard 1903-1986 11
Armstrong, William H(oward) 1914-1999 4
   Obituary 111
   See also CLR 117
   See also SAAS 7
Armstrong-Ellis, Carey (Fraser) 1956- 145

Arndt, Ursula (Martha H.) 56
   Brief entry 39
Arneson, D(on) J(on) 1935- 37
Arnett, Caroline
   See Cole, Lois Dwight
Arnett, Jack
   See Goulart, Ron
Arnette, Robert
   See Silverberg, Robert
Arno, Enrico 1913-1981 43
   Obituary 28
Arnold, Caroline 1944- 174
   Brief entry 34
   Earlier sketches in SATA 36, 85, 131
   See also CLR 61
   See also SAAS 23
Arnold, Elizabeth 1944- 164
Arnold, Elliott 1912-1980 5
   Obituary 22
Arnold, Emily 1939- 134
   Autobiography Feature 134
   Earlier sketches in SATA 5, 50, 76, 110
   See also CLR 46
   See also SAAS 7
Arnold, Katya 1947- 168
   Earlier sketches in SATA 82, 115
Arnold, Louise 175
Arnold, Marsha Diane 1948- 147
   Earlier sketch in SATA 93
Arnold, Nick 1961- 113
Arnold, Oren 1900-1980 4
Arnold, Susan (Riser) 1951- 58
Arnold, Tedd 1949- 160
   Earlier sketches in SATA 69, 116
Arnoldy, Julie
   See Bischoff, Julia Bristol
Arnosky, James Edward 1946- 189
   Earlier sketches in SATA 70, 118
   See also CLR 93
Arnosky, Jim
   See Arnosky, James Edward
Arnott, Kathleen 1914- 20
Arnov, Boris, Jr. 1926- 12
Arnow, Harriette (Louisa) Simpson
   1908-1986 42
   Obituary 47
Arnsteen, Katy Keck 1934- 68
Arnstein, Helene S(olomon) 1915- 12
Arntson, Herbert E(dward) 1911-1982 12
Aroner, Miriam 82
Aronin, Ben 1904-1980
   Obituary 25
Aronson, Marc 1950- 189
   Autobiography Feature 189
   Earlier sketches in SATA 126, 175
Aronson, Marc Henry
   See Aronson, Marc
Aronson, Sarah 196
Aronson, Virginia 1954- 122
Arora, Shirley (Lease) 1930- 2
Arrasmith, Patrick 176
Arrick, Fran
   See Angell, Judie
Arrigan, Mary 1943- 142
Arrington, Aileen 183
Arrington, Stephen L. 1948- 97
Arrington, Stephen Lee
   See Arrington, Stephen L.
Arrley, Richmond
   See Delany, Samuel R., Jr.
Arrowood, (McKendrick Lee) Clinton
   1939- 19
Arrowsmith, Pat 1930- 59
Artell, Mike 1948- 183
   Earlier sketches in SATA 89, 134
Arthur, Robert (Andrew) 1909-1969
   See Arthur, Robert, (Jr.)
Arthur, Robert, (Jr.) 1909-1969 118
Arthur, Ruth M(abel) 1905-1979 26
   Earlier sketch in SATA 7
Artis, Vicki Kimmel 1945- 12

Artzybasheff, Boris (Miklailovich)
   1899-1965 14
Aruego, Ariane
   See Dewey, Ariane
Aruego, Jose 1932- 178
   Earlier sketches in SATA 6, 68, 125
   See also CLR 5
Aruego, Jose Espiritu
   See Aruego, Jose
Arundel, Honor (Morfydd) 1919-1973 4
   Obituary 24
   See also CLR 35
Arundel, Jocelyn
   See Alexander, Jocelyn Anne Arundel
Arvey, Michael 1948- 79
Arzoumanian, Alik 177
Asare, Meshack (Yaw) 1945- 139
   Earlier sketch in SATA 86
Asaro, Catherine 1955- 165
   Earlier sketch in SATA 101
Asaro, Catherine Ann 1955-
   See Asaro, Catherine
Asay, Donna Day 1945- 127
Asbjornsen, Peter Christen 1812-1885 15
   See also CLR 104
Asch, Frank 1946- 154
   Earlier sketches in SATA 5, 66, 102
Ash, Jutta 1942- 38
Ashabranner, Brent 1921- 166
   Earlier sketches in SATA 1, 67, 130
   See also CLR 28
   See also SAAS 14
Ashabranner, Brent Kenneth
   See Ashabranner, Brent
Ashbless, William
   See Blaylock, James P.
   and Powers, Tim
Ashby, Gil 1958- 146
Ashby, Gwynneth 1922- 44
Ashby, Ruth 170
Ashby, Yvonne 1955- 121
Ashe, Arthur (Robert, Jr.) 1943-1993 65
   Obituary 87
Ashe, Geoffrey (Thomas) 1923- 17
   Autobiography Feature 125
Ashe, Mary Ann
   See Lewis, Mary
Asher, Bridget
   See Baggott, Julianna
Asher, Sandra Fenichel
   See Asher, Sandy
Asher, Sandy 1942- 71
   Autobiography Feature 158
   Brief entry 34
   Earlier sketch in SATA 36
   See also SAAS 13
Asheron, Sara
   See Moore, Lilian
Ashey, Bella
   See Breinburg, Petronella
Ashford, Daisy
   See Ashford, Margaret Mary
Ashford, Jeffrey
   See Jeffries, Roderic
Ashford, Margaret Mary 1881-1972 10
Ashley, Bernard (John) 1935- 155
   Brief entry 39
   Earlier sketches in SATA 47, 79
   See also CLR 4
Ashley, Elizabeth
   See Salmon, Annie Elizabeth
Ashley, Ray
   See Abrashkin, Raymond
Ashman, Linda 1960- 150
Ashton, Lorayne
   See Gottfried, Theodore Mark
Ashton, Warren T.
   See Adams, William Taylor
Asimov, Isaac 1920-1992 74
   Earlier sketches in SATA 1, 26
   See also CLR 79

Asinof, Eliot 1919-2008 6
Asinof, Eliot Tager
  See Asinof, Eliot
Aska, Warabe
  See Masuda, Takeshi
Asprin, Robert L. 1946-2008 92
Asprin, Robert Lynn
  See Asprin, Robert L.
Asquith, Cynthia Mary Evelyn (Charteris)
  1887-1960 107
Asquith, Ros 153
Astley, Juliet
  See Lofts, Norah (Robinson)
Aston, Dianna Hutts 1964- 176
Aston, James
  See White, T(erence) H(anbury)
Ata, Te 1895-1995 119
Atene, Ann
  See Atene, (Rita) Anna
Atene, (Rita) Anna 1922- 12
Atheling, William, Jr.
  See Blish, James (Benjamin)
Atkins, Catherine 160
Atkins, Jeannine 1953- 172
  Earlier sketch in SATA 113
Atkinson, Allen G. 1953(?)-1987 60
  Brief entry 46
  Obituary 55
Atkinson, M. E.
  See Frankau, Mary Evelyn Atkinson
Atkinson, Margaret Fleming 14
Atteberry, Kevan J. 186
Attema, Martha 1949- 156
  Earlier sketch in SATA 94
Atticus
  See Davies, Hunter
  and Fleming, Ian
  and Pawle, Gerald Strachan
  and Wilson, (Thomas) Woodrow
Atwater, Florence (Hasseltine Carroll)
  1896-1979 66
  Earlier sketch in SATA 16
  See also CLR 19
Atwater, Montgomery Meigs 1904-1976 15
Atwater, Richard (Tupper) 1892-1948 66
  Brief entry 27
  Earlier sketch in SATA 54
  See also CLR 19
Atwater-Rhodes, Amelia 1984- 170
  Earlier sketch in SATA 124
Atwell, Debby 1953- 150
  Earlier sketch in SATA 87
Atwood, Ann (Margaret) 1913-1992 7
Atwood, Margaret 1939- 170
  Earlier sketch in SATA 50
Atwood, Margaret Eleanor
  See Atwood, Margaret
Aubrey, Meg Kelleher 1963- 83
Aubry, Claude B. 1914-1984 29
  Obituary 40
Auch, Herm 173
Auch, Mary Jane 173
  Earlier sketch in SATA 138
Auch, M.J.
  See Auch, Mary Jane
Auclair, Joan 1960- 68
Auel, Jean M(arie) 1936- 91
Auer, Martin 1951- 77
Augarde, Steve 1950- 159
  Earlier sketch in SATA 25
Augelli, John P(at) 1921- 46
Augustine, Mildred
  See Benson, Mildred
Ault, Phil
  See Ault, Phillip H(alliday)
Ault, Phillip H(alliday) 1914- 23
Ault, Rosalie Sain 1942- 38
Ault, Roz
  See Ault, Rosalie Sain
Aung, (Maung) Htin 1909- 21

Auntie Deb
  See Coury, Louise Andree
Auntie Louise
  See Coury, Louise Andree
Aunt Weedy
  See Alcott, Louisa May
Auseon, Andrew 1976- 166
Austen, Carrie
  See Bennett, Cherie
Austin, Carrie
  See Seuling, Barbara
Austin, Elizabeth S. 1907-1977 5
Austin, Harry
  See McInerny, Ralph
Austin, Margot 1909(?)-1990 11
  Obituary 66
Austin, Michael 178
Austin, Oliver L(uther), Jr. 1903-1988 7
  Obituary 59
Austin, Patricia 1950- 137
Austin, R. G.
  See Gelman, Rita Golden
  and Lamb, Nancy
Austin, Virginia 1951- 152
  Earlier sketch in SATA 80
Auteur, Hillary
  See Gottfried, Theodore Mark
Auth, Tony
  See Auth, William Anthony, Jr.
Auth, William Anthony, Jr. 1942- 192
Autry, Gloria Diener
  See Allen, Terril Diener
Auvil, Peggy A 1954- 122
Auvil, Peggy Appleby
  See Auvil, Peggy A
Aveni, Anthony F. 1938- 181
Aveni, Anthony Francis
  See Aveni, Anthony F.
Averbeck, Jim 1963- 201
Averill, Esther (Holden) 1902-1992 28
  Obituary 72
  Earlier sketch in SATA 1
Avery, A. A.
  See Montgomery, Rutherford George
Avery, Al
  See Montgomery, Rutherford George
Avery, Gillian (Elise) 1926- 137
  Autobiography Feature 137
  Earlier sketches in SATA 7, 75
  See also SAAS 6
Avery, Kay 1908- 5
Avery, Lorraine
  See Older, Effin
  and Older, Jules
Avery, Lynn
  See Cole, Lois Dwight
Avi 1937- 190
  Earlier sketches in SATA 14, 71, 108, 156
  See also CLR 68
Avishai, Susan 1949- 82
Avril, Francois 1961- 191
Avril, Lynne
  See Cravath, Lynne W.
Awdry, Christopher Vere 1940- 67
Awdry, Wilbert Vere 1911-1997 94
  See also CLR 23
Axelrod, Amy 131
Axelsen, Stephen 1953- 165
Axton, David
  See Koontz, Dean R.
Ayars, James S(terling) 1898-1986 4
Aye, A. K.
  See Edwards, Hazel (Eileen)
Ayer, Eleanor H. 1947-1998 121
  Earlier sketch in SATA 78
Ayer, Jacqueline 1930- 13
Ayer, Margaret (?)-1981 15
Aylesworth, Jim 1943- 139
  Earlier sketches in SATA 38, 89
  See also CLR 89

Aylesworth, Thomas G(ibbons) 1927-1995 .. 88
  Earlier sketch in SATA 4
  See also CLR 6
  See also SAAS 17
Ayliffe, Alex 190
Aylward, Marcus
  See Alexander, Marc
Aymar, Brandt 1911- 22
Ayme, Marcel (Andre) 1902-1967 91
  See also CLR 25
Ayres, Becky
  See Hickox, Rebecca (Ayres)
Ayres, Katherine 1947- 187
Ayres, Pam 1947- 90
Ayres, Patricia Miller 1923-1985
  Obituary 46
Aytmatov, Chingiz
  See Aitmatov, Chingiz
Ayto, Russell 1960- 166
  Earlier sketch in SATA 111
Azaid
  See Zaidenberg, Arthur
Azar, Penny 1952- 121
Azarian, Mary 1940- 171
  Earlier sketch in SATA 112
Azore, Barbara 1934- 188

B

Baastad, Babbis Friis
  See Friis-Baastad, Babbis Ellinor
Bab
  See Gilbert, W(illiam) S(chwenck)
Babbis, Eleanor
  See Friis-Baastad, Babbis Ellinor
Babbitt, Lucy Cullyford 1960- 85
Babbitt, Natalie 1932- 194
  Earlier sketches in SATA 6, 68, 106
  See also CLR 141
  See also SAAS 5
Babbitt, Natalie Zane Moore
  See Babbitt, Natalie
Babcock, Chris 1963- 83
Babcock, Dennis 1948- 22
Babcock, Dennis Arthur
  See Babcock, Dennis
Baber, Carolyn Stonnell 1936- 96
Baboni, Elena 198
Baca, Ana 1967- 191
Baca, Maria 1951- 104
Bach, Alice (Hendricks) 1942- 93
  Brief entry 27
  Earlier sketch in SATA 30
Bach, Bellamy
  See Windling, Terri
Bach, Mary 1960- 125
Bach, Richard 1936- 13
Bach, Richard David
  See Bach, Richard
Bache, Ellyn 1942- 124
Bachel, Beverly K. 1957- 142
Bachelet, Gilles 1952- 196
Bachman, Fred 1949- 12
Bachman, Richard
  See King, Stephen
Bachrach, Deborah 80
Backus, James Gilmore 1913-1989
  Obituary 63
Backus, Jim
  See Backus, James Gilmore
Bacmeister, Rhoda W(arner) 1893-1991 11
Bacon, Betty
  See Bacon, Elizabeth
Bacon, Elizabeth 1914-2001 3
  Obituary 131
Bacon, Joan Chase
  See Bowden, Joan Chase
Bacon, Josephine Dodge (Daskam)
  1876-1961 48

Bacon, Margaret Frances
See Bacon, Peggy
Bacon, Margaret Hope 1921- 6
Bacon, Martha Sherman 1917-1981 18
Obituary 27
See also CLR 3
Bacon, Melvin 1950- 93
Bacon, Melvin L.
See Bacon, Melvin
Bacon, Peggy 1895-1987 50
Bacon, R(onald) L(eonard) 1924- 84
Earlier sketch in SATA 26
Baden, Robert 1936- 70
Baden-Powell, Robert (Stephenson Smyth)
1857-1941 16
Badt, Karin L(uisa) 1963- 91
Bae, Hyun-Joo 186
Baehr, Kingsley M. 1937- 89
Baehr, Patricia 1952- 65
Baehr, Patricia Goehner
See Baehr, Patricia
Baer, Jill
See Gilbert, (Agnes) Joan (Sewell)
Baer, Judy 1951- 71
Baer, Julie 1960- 161
Baer-Block, Roxanna 172
Baerg, Harry J(ohn) 1909-1996 12
Baeten, Lieve 1954- 83
Bagert, Brod 1947- 191
Earlier sketch in SATA 80
Baggette, Susan K. 1942- 126
Baggott, Julianna 1969- 197
Bagnold, Enid 1889-1981 25
Earlier sketch in SATA 1
Baguley, Elizabeth 1959- 199
Bahlke, Valerie Worth -1994
See Worth, Valerie
Bahous, Sally 1939- 86
Bahr, Mary (Madelyn) 1946- 95
Bahr, Robert 1940- 38
Bahti, Tom 1926-1972 57
Brief entry 31
Baicker-McKee, Carol 1958- 177
Bailey, Alice Cooper 1890-1978 12
Bailey, Anne 1958- 71
Bailey, Bernadine (Freeman) 1901-1995 14
Bailey, Carolyn Sherwin 1875-1961 14
Bailey, Debbie 1954- 123
Bailey, Donna (Veronica Anne) 1938- 68
Bailey, Jane H(orton) 1916- 12
Bailey, John (Robert) 1940- 52
Bailey, Len 193
Bailey, Linda 1948- 182
Earlier sketch in SATA 107
Bailey, Maralyn Collins (Harrison) 1941- 12
Bailey, Matilda
See Radford, Ruby L(orraine)
Bailey, Maurice Charles 1932- 12
Bailey, Pearl (Mae) 1918-1990 81
Bailey, Peter 1946- 194
Bailey, Ralph Edgar 1893-1982 11
Bailey, Sheila (Lucas) 1960- 155
Baillie, Allan 1943- 151
Earlier sketch in SATA 87
See also CLR 49
See also SAAS 21
Baillie, Allan Stuart
See Baillie, Allan
Baines, John (David) 1943- 71
Bains, Larry
See Sabin, Louis
Baird, Alison 1963- 138
Baird, Bil 1904-1987 30
Obituary 52
Baird, Thomas (P.) 1923-1990 45
Brief entry 39
Obituary 64
Baird, William Britton
See Baird, Bil
Baity, Elizabeth Chesley 1907-1989 1
Baiul, Oksana 1977- 108

Bajoria, Paul 1964- 187
Bakeless, John (Edwin) 1894-1978 9
Bakeless, Katherine Little 1895-1992 9
Baker, Alan 1951- 146
Earlier sketches in SATA 22, 93
Baker, Augusta 1911-1998 3
Baker, Barbara 1947- 192
Baker, Betty Lou 1928-1987 73
Obituary 54
Earlier sketch in SATA 5
Baker, Carin Greenberg 1959- 79
Baker, Charlotte 1910- 2
Baker, Christina
See Kline, Christina Baker
Baker, Christopher W. 1952- 144
Baker, Deirdre 1955- 195
Baker, E.D. 190
Baker, (Mary) Elizabeth (Gillette) 1923- 7
Baker, Gayle Cunningham 1950- 39
Baker, James W. 1924- 65
Earlier sketch in SATA 22
Baker, James W. 1926- 122
Baker, Janice E(dla) 1941- 22
Baker, Jeanette 178
Baker, Jeannie 1950- 156
Earlier sketches in SATA 23, 88
See also CLR 28
Baker, Jeffrey J(ohn) W(heeler) 1931- 5
Baker, Jim
See Baker, James W.
Baker, Keith 1953- 179
Baker, Ken 1962- 133
Baker, Laura Nelson 1911- 3
Baker, Margaret 1890-1965 4
Baker, Margaret J(oyce) 1918- 12
See also SAAS 8
Baker, Mary Gladys Steel 1892-1974 12
Baker, (Robert) Michael (Graham) 1938- 4
Baker, Nina (Brown) 1888-1957 15
Baker, Pamela J. 1947- 66
Baker, Rachel 1904-1978 2
Obituary 26
Baker, Rosalie F. 1945- 166
Baker, Samm Sinclair 1909-1997 12
Obituary 96
Baker, Susan (Catherine) 1942-1991 29
Balaam
See Lamb, G(eoffrey) F(rederick)
Balan, Bruce 1959- 113
Balcavage, Dynise 1965- 137
Balch, Glenn 1902-1989 3
Obituary 83
See also SAAS 11
Baldacci, David 1960- 184
Baldacci, David G.
See Baldacci, David
and Baldacci, David
Balderose, Nancy Ward 1952- 93
Balderson, Margaret 1935- 151
Baldry, Cherith 1947- 167
Earlier sketch in SATA 72
Balducci, Carolyn 1946- 5
Balducci, Carolyn Feleppa
See Balducci, Carolyn
Baldwin, Alex
See Griffin, W.E.B
Baldwin, Anne Norris 1938- 5
Baldwin, Clara 11
Baldwin, Gordo
See Baldwin, Gordon C(ortis)
Baldwin, Gordon C(ortis) 1908-1983 12
Baldwin, James 1841-1925 24
Baldwin, James 1924-1987 9
Obituary 54
Baldwin, Louis 1919- 110
Baldwin, Margaret
See Weis, Margaret
Baldwin, Stan(ley C.) 1929- 62
Brief entry 28
Bales, Carol Ann 1940- 57
Brief entry 29

Balet, Jan (Bernard) 1913- 11
Balgassi, Haemi 1971- 131
Balian, Lorna 1929- 91
Earlier sketch in SATA 9
Balit, Christina 1961- 159
Earlier sketch in SATA 102
Ball, Duncan 1941- 73
Ball, Zachary
See Janas, Frankie-Lee
and Masters, Kelly R(ay)
Ballantine, Lesley Frost
See Frost, Lesley
Ballantyne, R(obert) M(ichael) 1825-1894 ... 24
See also CLR 137
Ballard, James G.
See Ballard, J.G.
Ballard, James Graham
See Ballard, J.G.
Ballard, Jane
See Gorman, Carol
Ballard, J.G. 1930-2009 93
Ballard, Jim G.
See Ballard, J.G.
Ballard, John 1945- 110
Ballard, Lowell C(lyne) 1904-1986 12
Obituary 49
Ballard, (Charles) Martin 1929- 1
Ballard, Mignon F. 1934- 64
Brief entry 49
Ballard, Mignon Franklin
See Ballard, Mignon F.
Ballard, Robert D(uane) 1942- 85
See also CLR 60
Ballard, Robin 1965- 126
Balliett, Blue 1955- 156
Ballinger, Bryan 1968- 161
Ballouhey, Pierre 1944- 90
Balogh, Penelope 1916-1975 1
Obituary 34
Balouch, Kristen 176
Balow, Tom 1931- 12
Baltazzi, Evan S(erge) 1921- 90
Balterman, Marcia Ridlon 1942- 22
Baltimore, J.
See Catherall, Arthur
Baltzer, Hans (Adolf) 1900- 40
Balzano, Jeanne (Koppel) 1912- 7
Bambara, Toni Cade 1939-1995 112
Bamfylde, Walter
See Bevan, Tom
Bamman, Henry A. 1918- 12
Banat, D. R.
See Bradbury, Ray
Bancroft, Griffing 1907-1999 6
Bancroft, Laura
See Baum, L(yman) Frank
Bandel, Betty 1912- 47
Baner, Skulda Vanadis 1897-1964 10
Banerjee, Anjali 174
Banfill, A. Scott 1956- 98
Bang, Betsy 1912- 48
Brief entry 37
Bang, Garrett
See Bang, Molly
Bang, Molly 1943- 158
Earlier sketches in SATA 24, 69, 111
See also CLR 8
Bang, Molly Garrett
See Bang, Molly
Bang-Campbell, Monika 1975(?)- 195
Earlier sketch in SATA 140
Banjo, The
See Paterson, A(ndrew) B(arton)
Banke, Cecile de
See de Banke, Cecile
Banks, Kate 1960- 200
Earlier sketches in SATA 134, 172
Banks, Laura Stockton Voorhees 1908(?)-1980
Obituary 23
Banks, Lynne Reid
See Reid Banks, Lynne

Banks, Merry *197*
Banks, Michael A. 1951- *101*
Banks, Paul 1952- *174*
Banks, Sara (Jeanne Gordon Harrell) *26*
　See Harrell, Sara (Jeanne) Gordon
Bannatyne-Cugnet, Elizabeth Jo-Anne
　See Bannatyne-Cugnet, Jo
Bannatyne-Cugnet, Jo 1951- *101*
Banner, Angela
　See Maddison, Angela Mary
Bannerman, Helen (Brodie Cowan Watson)
　1862(?)-1946 .... *19*
　See also CLR *144*
Banning, Evelyn I. 1903-1993 .... *36*
Bannon, Laura (?)-1963 .... *6*
Bannor, Brett 1959- *143*
Banta, Susan *181*
Bantock, Nick 1950(?)- *95*
Banyai, Istvan *193*
Barakat, Ibtisam 1963- *186*
Barasch, Lynne 1939- *186*
　Earlier sketches in SATA *74, 126*
Barbalet, Margaret 1949- *77*
Barbary, James
　See Baumann, Amy Beeching
　and Beeching, Jack
Barbash, Shepard 1957- *84*
Barbe, Walter Burke 1926- *45*
Barber, Antonia 1932- *163*
　Earlier sketch in SATA *29*
Barber, Atiim Kiambu
　See Barber, Tiki
Barber, Lynda
　See Graham-Barber, Lynda
Barber, Lynda Graham
　See Graham-Barber, Lynda
Barber, Richard (William) 1941- *35*
Barber, Ronde 1975- *182*
Barber, Tiki 1975- *182*
Barbera, Joe 1911-2006 .... *51*
　Obituary *179*
Barbera, Joseph
　See Barbera, Joe
Barbera, Joseph Roland
　See Barbera, Joe
Barberis, Juan C(arlos) 1920- *61*
Barbour, Karen 1956- *170*
　Earlier sketches in SATA *63, 121*
Barbour, Ralph Henry 1870-1944 .... *16*
Barclay, Bill
　See Moorcock, Michael
Barclay, Isabel
　See Dobell, I(sabel) M(arian) B(arclay)
Barclay, William Ewert
　See Moorcock, Michael
Bardhan-Quallen, Sudipta *168*
Bardoe, Cheryl *181*
Bare, Arnold Edwin 1920- *16*
Bare, Colleen Stanley *32*
Bar-el, Dan *199*
Barenholtz, Bernard 1914-1989
　Obituary *64*
Bargar, Gary W. 1947-1985 .... *63*
Barger, Jan 1948- *147*
Barish, Matthew 1907-2000 .... *12*
Barkan, Joanne *127*
　Earlier sketch in SATA *77*
Barker, Albert W. 1900- *8*
Barker, Carol (Minturn) 1938- *31*
Barker, Cicely Mary 1895-1973 .... *49*
　Brief entry *39*
　See also CLR *88*
Barker, Melvern 1907-1989 .... *11*
Barker, S(quire) Omar 1894-1985 .... *10*
Barker, Will 1913-1983 .... *8*
Barkin, Carol 1944- *52*
　Earlier sketch in SATA *42*
Barklem, Jill 1951- *96*
　See also CLR *31*
Barkley, Brad *178*
Barkley, James Edward 1941- *6*

Barks, Carl 1901-2000 .... *37*
Barley, Janet Crane 1934- *95*
Barnaby, Ralph S(tanton) 1893-1986 .... *9*
Barnard, A. M.
　See Alcott, Louisa May
Barnard, Bryn 1956- *169*
　Earlier sketch in SATA *115*
Barne, Kitty
　See Barne, Marion Catherine
Barne, Marion Catherine 1883-1957 .... *97*
Barner, Bob 1947- *136*
　Earlier sketch in SATA *29*
Barnes, Dawn 1957- *175*
Barnes, Derrick *191*
Barnes, Derrick D.
　See Barnes, Derrick
Barnes, (Frank) Eric Wollencott 1907-1962 . *22*
Barnes, Joyce Annette 1958- *85*
Barnes, Laura T. 1958- *119*
Barnes, Loutricia
　See Barnes-Svarney, Patricia L(ou)
Barnes, Malcolm 1909(?)-1984
　Obituary *41*
Barnes, Michael 1934- *55*
Barnes-Murphy, Frances 1951- *88*
Barnes-Murphy, Rowan 1952- *88*
Barnes-Svarney, Patricia L(ou) 1953- *67*
Barnet, Nancy 1954- *84*
Barnett, Ivan 1947- *70*
Barnett, Lincoln (Kinnear) 1909-1979 .... *36*
Barnett, Moneta 1922-1976 .... *33*
Barnett, Naomi 1927- *40*
Barney, Maginel Wright 1881(?)-1966 .... *39*
　Brief entry *32*
Barnhart, Clarence L(ewis) 1900-1993 .... *48*
　Obituary *78*
Barnouw, Adriaan Jacob 1877-1968
　Obituary *27*
Barnouw, Victor 1915-1989 .... *43*
　Brief entry *28*
Barnstone, Willis 1927- *20*
Barnum, Jay Hyde 1888(?)-1962 .... *20*
Barnum, P. T., Jr.
　See Stratemeyer, Edward L.
Barnum, Richard *67*
　Earlier sketch in SATA *1*
Barnum, Theodore
　See Stratemeyer, Edward L.
Barnwell, Ysaye M. 1946- *200*
Baron, Kathy 1954- *90*
Baron, Virginia Olsen 1931- *46*
　Brief entry *28*
Barr, Donald 1921-2004 .... *20*
　Obituary *152*
Barr, George 1907-1992 .... *2*
Barr, Jene 1922-1985 .... *16*
　Obituary *42*
Barr, Nevada 1952- *126*
　Earlier sketch in SATA *115*
Barrer, Gertrude
　See Barrer-Russell, Gertrude
Barrer-Russell, Gertrude 1921- *27*
Barrett, Angela (Jane) 1955- *145*
　Earlier sketch in SATA *75*
Barrett, Ethel *87*
　Brief entry *44*
Barrett, Joyce Durham 1943- *138*
Barrett, Judi
　See Barrett, Judith
Barrett, Judith 1941- *26*
　See also CLR *98*
Barrett, Robert T(heodore) 1949- *92*
Barrett, Ron 1937- *14*
Barrett, Susan (Mary) 1938- *113*
Barrett, Tracy 1955- *156*
　Earlier sketches in SATA *84, 115*
Barrett, William E(dmund) 1900-1986
　Obituary *49*
Barretta, Gene *176*
Barretton, Grandall
　See Garrett, Randall

Barrie, J(ames) M(atthew) 1860-1937 .... *100*
　See also YABC *1*
　See also CLR *124*
Barringer, William 1940-1996 .... *153*
Barrington, Michael
　See Moorcock, Michael
Barris, George 1925- *47*
Barrol, Grady
　See Bograd, Larry
Barron, Rex 1951- *84*
Barron, T.A. 1952- *192*
　Earlier sketches in SATA *83, 126*
　See also CLR *86*
Barron, Thomas Archibald
　See Barron, T.A.
Barron, Tom
　See Barron, T.A.
Barrow, Lloyd H. 1942- *73*
Barrows, Annie 1962- *180*
Barry, Dan 1958- *177*
Barry, Dana (Marie Malloy) 1949- *139*
Barry, James P(otvin) 1918- *14*
Barry, Katharina Watjen 1936- *4*
Barry, Robert (Everett) 1931- *6*
Barry, Scott 1952- *32*
Barry, Sheila Anne -2003 .... *91*
Bartell, Susan S. *175*
Bartenbach, Jean 1918- *40*
Barth, Edna 1914-1980 .... *7*
　Obituary *24*
Barth, Kelly L. 1964- *152*
Barthelme, Donald 1931-1989 .... *7*
　Obituary *62*
Barth-Grozinger, Inge 1950- *185*
Bartholomew, Barbara 1941- *86*
　Brief entry *42*
Bartholomew, Jean
　See Beatty, Patricia (Robbins)
Bartlett, Alison *153*
Bartlett, Philip A. *1*
Bartlett, Robert Merrill 1899-1995 .... *12*
Bartoletti, Susan Campbell 1958- *173*
　Earlier sketches in SATA *88, 129, 135*
Barton, Byron 1930- *126*
　Earlier sketches in SATA *9, 90*
Barton, Jill(ian) 1940- *75*
Barton, May Hollis *67*
　Earlier sketch in SATA *1*
Barton, Pat
　See Arrowsmith, Pat
Bartos-Hoeppner, Barbara 1923- *5*
Bartram, Simon *156*
Bartsch, Jochen 1906- *39*
Baruch, Dorothy W(alter) 1899-1962 .... *21*
Barunga, Albert 1912(?)-1977 .... *120*
Baryshnikov, Mikhail 1948- *192*
Bas, Rutger
　See Rutgers van der Loeff-Basenau, An(na)
　Maria Margaretha
Base, Graeme (Rowland) 1958- *162*
　Earlier sketches in SATA *67, 101*
　See also CLR *22*
Baseman, Gary 1960- *174*
Bash, Barbara 1948- *132*
Bashevis, Isaac
　See Singer, Isaac Bashevis
Bashevis, Yitskhok
　See Singer, Isaac Bashevis
Basile, Gloria Vitanza 1929- *180*
Baskin, Leonard 1922-2000 .... *120*
　Brief entry *27*
　Earlier sketch in SATA *30*
Baskin, Nora Raleigh 1961- *189*
　Earlier sketch in SATA *129*
Bason, Lillian 1913- *20*
Bass, L. G.
　See Geringer, Laura
Bassett, Jeni 1959- *64*
　Brief entry *43*
Bassett, John Keith
　See Keating, Lawrence A.

Bassett, Lisa 1958- 61
Bassil, Andrea
   See Nilsen, Anna
Bastyra, Judy 108
Bat-Ami, Miriam 1950- 150
   Autobiography Feature 150
   Earlier sketches in SATA 82, 122
Bate, Lucy 1939-1993 18
Bate, Norman (Arthur) 1916- 5
Bateman, Colin 1962- 172
Bateman, Donna M. 190
Bateman, Teresa 1957- 168
   Earlier sketch in SATA 112
Bates, Amy June 189
Bates, Barbara S(nedeker) 1919- 12
Bates, Betty
   See Bates, Elizabeth
Bates, Dianne 1948- 147
Bates, Elizabeth 1921- 19
Bates, Ivan 175
Bates, Katharine Lee 1859-1929 113
Bates, Martine
   See Leavitt, Martine
Bateson, Catherine 1960- 197
   Earlier sketch in SATA 157
Batey, Tom 1946- 52
   Brief entry 41
Bath, Kevin P.
   See Bath, K.P.
Bath, K.P. 1959- 171
Batherman, Muriel
   See Sheldon, Muriel
Batson, Larry 1930- 35
Batt, Tanya Robyn 1970- 131
Battaglia, Aurelius 1910- 50
   Brief entry 33
Batten, H(arry) Mortimer 1888-1958 25
Batten, Mary 1937- 162
   Earlier sketches in SATA 5, 102
Batterberry, Ariane Ruskin 1935- 13
Batterberry, Michael Carver 1932- 32
Battle-Lavert, Gwendolyn 1951- 155
   Earlier sketches in SATA 85, 131
Battles, (Roxy) Edith 1921- 7
Baudouy, Michel-Aime 1909- 7
Bauer, A.C.E. 201
Bauer, Caroline Feller 1935- 98
   Brief entry 46
   Earlier sketch in SATA 52
   See also SAAS 24
Bauer, Fred 1934- 36
Bauer, Helen 1900-1988 2
Bauer, Joan 1951- 160
   Earlier sketch in SATA 117
Bauer, Jutta 1955- 150
Bauer, Marion Dane 1938- 192
   Autobiography Feature 144
   Earlier sketches in SATA 20, 69, 113, 144
   See also SAAS 9
Bauer, Michael Gerard 1955(?)- 167
Bauer, Steven 1948- 125
Bauerschmidt, Marjorie 1926- 15
Baughman, Dorothy 1940- 61
Baum, Allyn Z(elton) 1924-1997 98
   Earlier sketch in SATA 20
Baum, L. Frank
   See Thompson, Ruth Plumly
Baum, L(yman) Frank 1856-1919 100
   Earlier sketch in SATA 18
   See also CLR 107
Baum, Louis 1948- 182
   Brief entry 52
   Earlier sketch in SATA 64
Baum, Louis F.
   See Baum, L(yman) Frank
Baum, Maxie 188
Baum, Willi 1931- 4
Baumann, Amy Beeching 1922- 10
Baumann, Amy Brown Beeching
   See Baumann, Amy Beeching

Baumann, Hans 1914- 2
   See also CLR 35
Baumann, Kurt 1935- 21
Baumgartner, Barbara 1939- 86
Baurys, Flo(rence) 1938- 122
Bausum, Ann 173
Bawden, Nina 1925- 132
   Earlier sketches in SATA 4, 72
   See also CLR 51
   See also SAAS 16
Bawden, Nina Mary Mabey
   See Bawden, Nina
Baxter, Valerie
   See Meynell, Laurence Walter
Bay, Jeanette Graham 1928- 88
Bayer, Harold
   See Gregg, Andrew K.
Bayer, Jane E. (?)-1985
   Obituary 44
Bayley, Nicola 1949- 129
   Earlier sketches in SATA 41, 69
Baylor, Byrd 1924- 136
   Earlier sketches in SATA 16, 69
   See also CLR 3
Baynes, Pauline 1922-2008 133
   Obituary 196
   Earlier sketches in SATA 19, 59
Baynes, Pauline Diana
   See Baynes, Pauline
Bayoc, Cbabi 186
BB
   See Watkins-Pitchford, Denys James
Beach, Charles
   See Reid, (Thomas) Mayne
Beach, Charles Amory 1
Beach, Edward L. 1918-2002 12
   Obituary 140
Beach, Edward Latimer
   See Beach, Edward L.
Beach, Lisa 1957- 111
Beach, Lynn
   See Lance, Kathryn
Beach, Stewart T(aft) 1899-1979 23
Beachcroft, Nina 1931- 18
Beagle, Peter S. 1939- 130
   Earlier sketch in SATA 60
Beagle, Peter Soyer
   See Beagle, Peter S.
Beaglehole, Helen 1946- 117
Beale, Fleur 107
Bealer, Alex W(inkler III) 1921-1980 8
   Obituary 22
Beales, Valerie 1915- 74
Beals, Carleton 1893-1979 12
Beals, Frank Lee 1881-1972
   Obituary 26
Beam, Matt 1970- 187
Beame, Rona 1934- 12
Beamer, (George) Charles (Jr.) 1942- 43
Bean, Jonathan 1979- 194
Bean, Normal
   See Burroughs, Edgar Rice
Beaney, Jan
   See Udall, Jan Beaney
Beaney, Jane
   See Udall, Jan Beaney
Bear, Carolyn
   See Rayban, Chloe
Bear, Greg(ory Dale) 1951- 105
   Earlier sketch in SATA 65
Bearanger, Marie
   See Messier, Claire
Beard, Charles A(ustin) 1874-1948 18
Beard, Dan(iel Carter) 1850-1941 22
Beard, Darleen Bailey 1961- 96
Bearden, Romare (Howard) 1914(?)-1988 ... 22
   Obituary 56
Beardmore, Cedric
   See Beardmore, George
Beardmore, George 1908-1979 20
Beardshaw, Rosalind 1969- 190

Beardsley, Martyn R. 1957- 150
Bearman, Jane (Ruth) 1917- 29
Beaton, Clare 1947- 125
Beatty, Elizabeth
   See Holloway, Teresa (Bragunier)
Beatty, Hetty Burlingame 1907-1971 5
Beatty, Jerome, Jr. 1918- 5
Beatty, John (Louis) 1922-1975 6
   Obituary 25
Beatty, Patricia (Robbins) 1922-1991 73
   Obituary 68
   Earlier sketches in SATA 1, 30
   See also SAAS 4
Beaty, Andrea 186
Beaty, Mary (T.) 1947- 146
Beccia, Carlyn 189
Bechard, Margaret 1953- 164
   Earlier sketch in SATA 85
Bechtel, Louise Seaman 1894-1985 4
   Obituary 43
Beck, Barbara L. 1927- 12
Beck, Ian 1947- 190
   Earlier sketch in SATA 138
   See Beck, Ian Archibald
Beck, Peggy 1949- 171
Beck, Scott 197
Becker, Beril 1901-1999 11
Becker, Bonny 184
Becker, Deborah Zimmett 1955- 138
Becker, Helaine 1961- 142
Becker, John (Leonard) 1901- 12
Becker, John E(mil) 1942- 148
Becker, Joyce 1936- 39
Becker, May Lamberton 1873-1958 33
Becker, Neesa 1951- 123
Becker, Shari 174
Beckerman, Chad W. 198
Beckett, Sheilah 1913- 33
Beckhorn, Susan Williams 1953- 189
Beckles Willson, Robina 1930- 27
Beckman, Delores 1914-1994 51
Beckman, Gunnel 1910- 6
   See also CLR 25
   See also SAAS 9
Beckman, Kaj
   See Beckman, Karin
Beckman, Karin 1913- 45
Beckman, Per (Frithiof) 1913- 45
Bedard, Michael 1949- 154
   Earlier sketch in SATA 93
   See also CLR 35
Beddor, Frank 194
Beddows, Eric
   See Nutt, Ken
Bedford, A. N.
   See Watson, Jane Werner
Bedford, Annie North
   See Watson, Jane Werner
Bedford, David 159
Bedoukian, Kerop 1907-1981 53
Bee, Jay
   See Brainerd, John W(hiting)
Bee, William 188
Beebe, B. F.
   See Johnson, B. F.
Beebe, (Charles) William 1877-1962 19
Beeby, Betty 1923- 25
Beech, Mark 1971- 191
Beech, Webb
   See Griffin, W.E.B
Beecham, Jahnna 161
Beechcroft, William
   See Hallstead, William F(inn III)
Beeching, Jack 1922- 14
Beeke, Tiphanie 163
Beeler, Janet
   See Shaw, Janet
Beeler, Nelson F(rederick) 1910-1978 13
Beere, Peter 1951- 97
Beers, Dorothy Sands 1917- 9
Beers, Lorna 1897-1989 14

Beers, V(ictor) Gilbert 1928- *130*
   Earlier sketch in SATA *9*
Beeton, Max
   See Redding, Robert Hull
Begay, Shonto 1954- *137*
Begaye, Lisa Shook
   See Beach, Lisa
Begin, Maryjane 1963- *82*
Begin-Callanan, Maryjane
   See Begin, Maryjane
Begley, Kathleen A. 1948- *21*
Begley, Kathleen Anne
   See Begley, Kathleen A.
Behan, Leslie
   See Gottfried, Theodore Mark
Behler, Deborah A. 1947- *145*
Behler, John L. 1943-2006 .... *145*
   Obituary *173*
Behler, John Luther
   See Behler, John L.
Behn, Harry 1898-1973 .... *2*
   Obituary *34*
Behnke, Frances L. *8*
Behr, Joyce 1929- *15*
Behrens, June York 1925- *19*
Behrman, Carol H(elen) 1925- *144*
   Earlier sketch in SATA *14*
Beifuss, John, (Jr.) 1959- *92*
Beil, Karen Magnuson 1950- *124*
Beiler, Edna 1923- *61*
Beinicke, Steve 1956- *69*
Beirne, Barbara 1933- *71*
Beiser, Arthur 1931- *22*
Beiser, Germaine 1931- *11*
Belair, Richard L. 1934- *45*
Belaney, Archibald Stansfeld 1888-1938 ...... *24*
   See also CLR *32*
Belbin, David 1958- *164*
   Earlier sketch in SATA *106*
Belden, Wilanne Schneider 1925- *56*
Belfrage, Sally 1936-1994 .... *65*
   Obituary *79*
Belknap, B. H.
   See Ellis, Edward S(ylvester)
Belknap, Boynton
   See Ellis, Edward S(ylvester)
Belknap, Boynton M.D.
   See Ellis, Edward S(ylvester)
Bell, Anthea 1936- *148*
   Earlier sketch in SATA *88*
Bell, Clare (Louise) 1952- *99*
Bell, Corydon Whitten 1894-1980 .... *3*
Bell, David Owen 1949- *99*
Bell, Emerson
   See Stratemeyer, Edward L.
Bell, Emily Mary
   See Cason, Mabel Earp
Bell, Frank
   See Benson, Mildred
Bell, Gertrude (Wood) 1911-1987 .... *12*
Bell, Gina
   See Balzano, Jeanne (Koppel)
Bell, Hilari 1958- *197*
   Earlier sketch in SATA *151*
Bell, Jadrien
   See Golden, Christie
Bell, Janet
   See Clymer, Eleanor
Bell, Janet Cheatham 1937- *127*
Bell, Krista 1950- *126*
Bell, Krista Anne Blakeney
   See Bell, Krista
Bell, Margaret E(lizabeth) 1898-1990 .... *2*
Bell, Mary Reeves 1946- *88*
Bell, Norman (Edward) 1899- *11*
Bell, Raymond Martin 1907-1999 .... *13*
Bell, Siobhan *177*
Bell, Thelma Harrington 1896-1985 .... *3*
Bell, William 1945- *90*
   See also CLR *91*

Bellairs, John (Anthony) 1938-1991 .... *160*
   Obituary *66*
   Earlier sketches in SATA *2, 68*
   See also CLR *37*
Beller, Susan Provost 1949- *128*
   Earlier sketch in SATA *84*
   See also CLR *106*
Bellingham, Brenda 1931- *99*
   Brief entry *51*
Bello, Rosario de
   See De Bello, Rosario
Belloc, (Joseph) Hilaire (Pierre Sebastien Rene
   Swanton) 1870-1953 .... *112*
   See also YABC *1*
   See also CLR *102*
Belloc, Joseph Peter Rene Hilaire
   See Belloc, (Joseph) Hilaire (Pierre Sebastien
   Rene Swanton)
Belloc, Joseph Pierre Hilaire
   See Belloc, (Joseph) Hilaire (Pierre Sebastien
   Rene Swanton)
Belloli, Andrea P. A. 1947- *86*
Bell-Rehwoldt, Sheri 1962- *199*
Bellville, Cheryl Walsh 1944- *54*
   Brief entry *49*
Bell-Zano, Gina
   See Balzano, Jeanne (Koppel)
Belpre, Pura 1899-1982 .... *16*
   Obituary *30*
Belting, Natalia Maree 1915-1997 .... *6*
Belton, John Raynor 1931- *22*
Belton, Sandra 1939- *186*
   Earlier sketches in SATA *85, 134*
Belton, Sandra Yvonne
   See Belton, Sandra
Belton, Sandra Yvonne
   See Belton, Sandra
Beltran, Alberto 1923- *43*
Beltran-Hernandez, Irene 1945- *74*
Belvedere, Lee
   See Grayland, Valerie (Merle Spanner)
Bemelmans, Ludwig 1898-1962 .... *100*
   Earlier sketch in SATA *15*
   See also CLR *93*
Benander, Carl D. 1941- *74*
Benary, Margot
   See Benary-Isbert, Margot
Benary-Isbert, Margot 1889-1979 .... *2*
   Obituary *21*
   See also CLR *12*
Benasutti, Marion 1908-1992 .... *6*
Benatar, Raquel 1955- *167*
Benchley, Nathaniel (Goddard) 1915-1981 .. *25*
   Obituary *28*
   Earlier sketch in SATA *3*
Benchley, Peter 1940-2006 .... *164*
   Earlier sketches in SATA *3, 89*
Benchley, Peter Bradford
   See Benchley, Peter
Bendall-Brunello, John *185*
Bender, Edna 1941- *92*
Bender, Esther 1942- *88*
Bender, Lucy Ellen 1942- *22*
Bender, Robert 1962- *160*
   Earlier sketch in SATA *79*
Bendick, Jeanne 1919- *135*
   Earlier sketches in SATA *2, 68*
   See also CLR *5*
   See also SAAS *4*
Bendick, Robert L(ouis) 1917- *11*
Benedetto, William R. 1928- *180*
Benedetto, William Ralph
   See Benedetto, William R.
Benedict, Andrew
   See Arthur, Robert, (Jr.)
Benedict, Dorothy Potter 1889-1979 .... *11*
   Obituary *23*
Benedict, Lois Trimble 1902-1967 .... *12*
Benedict, Rex 1920-1995 .... *8*
Benedict, Stewart H(urd) 1924- *26*
Beneduce, Ann Keay *128*

Benet, Laura 1884-1979 .... *3*
   Obituary *23*
Benet, Stephen Vincent 1898-1943
   See YABC *1*
Benet, Sula 1906-1982 .... *21*
   Obituary *33*
Ben-Ezer, Ehud 1936- *122*
Benezra, Barbara (Beardsley) 1921- *10*
Benham, Leslie 1922- *48*
Benham, Lois (Dakin) 1924- *48*
Benham, Mary Lile 1914-1991 .... *55*
Benjamin, E. M. J.
   See Bache, Ellyn
Benjamin, Nora
   See Kubie, Nora Gottheil Benjamin
Benjamin, Saragail Katzman 1953- *86*
Benner, Cheryl 1962- *80*
Benner, Judith Ann 1942- *94*
Bennett, Alice
   See Ziner, Florence
Bennett, Cherie 1960- *158*
   Earlier sketch in SATA *97*
Bennett, Dorothea
   See Young, Dorothea Bennett
Bennett, Holly 1957- *181*
Bennett, Holly 1957- *181*
Bennett, James (W.) 1942- *153*
   Autobiography Feature *153*
   Earlier sketches in SATA *93, 148*
Bennett, Jay 1912- *87*
   Brief entry *27*
   Earlier sketch in SATA *41*
   See also SAAS *4*
Bennett, Jill (Crawford) 1934- *41*
Bennett, John 1865-1956
   See YABC *1*
Bennett, Penelope (Agnes) 1938- *94*
Bennett, Rachel
   See Hill, Margaret (Ohler)
Bennett, Rainey 1907-1998 .... *15*
   Obituary *111*
Bennett, Richard 1899- *21*
Bennett, Russell H(oradley) 1896- *25*
Bennett, Veronica 1953- *178*
Bennett, William (John) 1943- *102*
Benning, Elizabeth
   See Rice, Bebe Faas
Benson, Elizabeth P(olk) 1924- *65*
Benson, Kathleen 1947- *183*
   Earlier sketches in SATA *62, 111*
Benson, Linda M(aria) 1959- *84*
Benson, Mildred 1905-2002 .... *100*
   Obituary *135*
   Earlier sketches in SATA *1, 65, 67*
Benson, Mildred Augustine Wirt
   See Benson, Mildred
Benson, Mildred Wirt
   See Benson, Mildred
Benson, Millie
   See Benson, Mildred
Benson, Patrick 1956- *147*
Benson, Sally 1900-1972 .... *35*
   Obituary *27*
   Earlier sketch in SATA *1*
Bentley, Judith (McBride) 1945- *89*
   Earlier sketch in SATA *40*
Bentley, Karen
   See Taschek, Karen
Bentley, Nancy (L.) 1946- *78*
Bentley, Nicolas Clerihew 1907-1978
   Obituary *24*
Bentley, Phyllis Eleanor 1894-1977 .... *6*
   Obituary *25*
Bentley, Roy 1947- *46*
Bentley, William (George) 1916- *84*
Benton, Jim 1963- *172*
ben Uzair, Salem
   See Horne, Richard Henry Hengist
Bercaw, Edna Coe 1961- *124*
Berck, Judith 1960- *75*
Berelson, Howard 1940- *5*

Berends, Polly Berrien 1939- *50*
    Brief entry *38*
Berenstain, Jan 1923- *135*
    Earlier sketches in SATA *12, 64, 129*
    See also CLR *19*
    See also SAAS *20*
Berenstain, Janice
    See Berenstain, Jan
Berenstain, Michael 1951- *45*
Berenstain, Mike
    See Berenstain, Michael
Berenstain, Stan 1923-2005 .... *135*
    Obituary *169*
    Earlier sketches in SATA *12, 64, 129*
    See also CLR *19*
    See also SAAS *20*
Berenstain, Stanley
    See Berenstain, Stan
Berenzy, Alix 1957- *168*
    Earlier sketch in SATA *65*
Beresford, Elisabeth 1928- *141*
    Earlier sketches in SATA *25, 86*
    See also SAAS *20*
Berg, Adriane G(ilda) 1948- *152*
Berg, Dave
    See Berg, David
Berg, David 1920-2002 .... *27*
    Obituary *137*
Berg, Elizabeth 1948- *104*
Berg, Jean Horton 1913-1995 .... *6*
Berg, Joan
    See Victor, Joan Berg
Berg, Ron 1952- *48*
Bergaust, Erik 1925-1978 .... *20*
Bergel, Colin J. 1963- *137*
Bergen, Joyce 1949- *95*
Berger, Barbara (Helen) 1945- *77*
Berger, Carin *185*
Berger, Gilda 1935- *88*
    Brief entry *42*
Berger, Josef 1903-1971 .... *36*
Berger, Melvin H. 1927- *158*
    Autobiography Feature *124*
    Earlier sketches in SATA *5, 88*
    See also CLR *32*
    See also SAAS *2*
Berger, Phil 1942-2001 .... *62*
Berger, Samantha (Allison) 1969- *140*
Berger, Terry 1933- *8*
Bergey, Alyce (Mae) 1934- *45*
Bergin, Mark 1961- *160*
    Earlier sketch in SATA *114*
Berglin, Ruth Marie 1970- *181*
Bergman, Donna 1934- *73*
Bergman, Mara 1956- *196*
Bergman, Tamar 1939- *95*
Bergren, Lisa T.
    See Bergren, Lisa Tawn
Bergren, Lisa Tawn *200*
Bergsma, Jody Lynn *163*
Bergum, Constance R. 1952- *121*
Berkebile, Fred D(onovan) 1900-1978
    Obituary *26*
Berkes, Marianne *173*
Berkey, Barry Robert 1935- *24*
Berkowitz, Freda Pastor 1908-1994 .... *12*
Berkus, Clara Widess 1909- *78*
Berlan, Kathryn Hook 1946- *78*
Berlfein, Judy Reiss 1958- *79*
Berlin, Eric *195*
Berliner, Don 1930- *33*
Berliner, Franz 1930- *13*
Berlitz, Charles (L. Frambach) 1914-2003 ... *32*
    Obituary *151*
Berman, Linda 1948- *38*
Berman, Paul (Lawrence) 1949- *66*
Berna, Paul 1910-1994 .... *15*
    Obituary *78*
    See also CLR *19*
Bernadette
    See Watts, (Anna) Bernadette

Bernard, Bruce 1928-2000 .... *78*
    Obituary *124*
Bernard, George I. 1949- *39*
Bernard, Jacqueline (de Sieyes) 1921-1983 ... *8*
    Obituary *45*
Bernard, Patricia 1942- *181*
    Earlier sketch in SATA *106*
Bernard, Trish
    See Bernard, Patricia
Bernardin, James (B.) 1966- *112*
Bernardo, Anilu *184*
Bernards, Neal 1963- *71*
Bernasconi, Pablo 1973- *183*
Bernays, Anne 1930- *32*
Bernhard, Durga T. 1961- *80*
Bernhard, Emery 1950- *80*
Bernheimer, Kate *201*
Bernstein, Daryl (Evan) 1976- *81*
Bernstein, Joanne E(ckstein) 1943- *15*
Bernstein, Margery 1933- *114*
Bernstein, Nina 1949- *180*
Bernstein, Theodore M(enline) 1904-1979 ... *12*
    Obituary *27*
Berrien, Edith Heal
    See Heal, Edith
Berrill, Jacquelyn (Batsel) 1905- *12*
Berrington, John
    See Brownjohn, Alan
Berry, B. J.
    See Berry, Barbara J.
Berry, Barbara J. 1937- *7*
Berry, Erick
    See Best, (Evangel) Allena Champlin
Berry, James 1924- *110*
    Earlier sketch in SATA *67*
    See also CLR *143*
Berry, Jane Cobb 1915(?)-1979
    Obituary *22*
Berry, Joy
    See Berry, Joy Wilt
Berry, Joy Wilt 1944- *58*
    Brief entry *46*
Berry, Lynne *190*
Berry, William D(avid) 1926- *14*
Bersani, Shennen 1961- *164*
Berson, Harold 1926- *4*
Bertagna, Julie 1962- *151*
Bertholf, Bret *189*
Bertin, Charles-Francois
    See Berlitz, Charles (L. Frambach)
Bertolet, Paul
    See McLaughlin, Frank
Berton, Pierre (Francis de Marigny)
    1920-2004 .... *99*
    Obituary *158*
Bertrand, Cecile 1953- *76*
Bertrand, Diane Gonzales 1956- *177*
    Earlier sketch in SATA *106*
Bertrand, Lynne 1963- *164*
    Earlier sketch in SATA *81*
Beskow, Elsa (Maartman) 1874-1953 .... *20*
    See also CLR *17*
Bess, Clayton
    See Locke, Robert
Besson, Luc 1959- *199*
Best, (Evangel) Allena Champlin 1892-1974 . *2*
    Obituary *25*
Best, Cari 1951- *200*
    Earlier sketches in SATA *107, 149*
Best, (Oswald) Herbert 1894-1980 .... *2*
Bestall, A(lfred) E(dmeades) 1892-1986 .... *97*
    Obituary *48*
Betancourt, Jeanne 1941- *148*
    Brief entry *43*
    Earlier sketches in SATA *55, 96*
Beth, Mary
    See Miller, Mary Beth
Bethancourt, T. Ernesto
    See Paisley, Tom
Bethel, Dell 1929- *52*
Bethell, Jean (Frankenberry) 1922- *8*

Bethers, Ray 1902-1973 .... *6*
Bethke, Bruce Raymond 1955- *114*
Bethlen, T.D.
    See Silverberg, Robert
Bethune, J. G.
    See Ellis, Edward S(ylvester)
Bethune, J. H.
    See Ellis, Edward S(ylvester)
Betteridge, Anne
    See Potter, Margaret
Bettina
    See Ehrlich, Bettina Bauer
Bettmann, Otto Ludwig 1903-1998 .... *46*
Bettoli, Delana *187*
Betts, James
    See Haynes, Betsy
Betz, Eva Kelly 1897-1968 .... *10*
Bevan, Tom 1868-1930(?)
    See YABC *2*
Bewick, Thomas 1753-1828 .... *16*
Beyer, Audrey White 1916- *9*
Beyer, Paul J. III 1950- *74*
Beynon, John
    See Harris, John (Wyndham Parkes Lucas)
    Beynon
Bezencon, Jacqueline (Buxcel) 1924- *48*
Bhatia, Jamunadevi 1919- *48*
Bhatia, June
    See Bhatia, Jamunadevi
Bial, Morrison David 1917- *62*
Bial, Raymond 1948- *165*
    Earlier sketches in SATA *76, 116*
Biala
    See Brustlein, Janice Tworkov
Biale, Rachel 1952- *99*
Bialk, Elisa
    See Krautter, Elisa (Bialk)
Bianchi, John 1947- *91*
Bianchi, Robert S(teven) 1943- *92*
Bianco, Margery
    See Bianco, Margery Williams
Bianco, Margery Williams 1881-1944 .... *15*
    See also CLR *19*
Bianco, Pamela 1906- *28*
Bibby, Violet 1908-1996 .... *24*
Bible, Charles 1937- *13*
Bibo, Bobette
    See Gugliotta, Bobette
Bice, Clare 1909-1976 .... *22*
Bickerstaff, Isaac
    See Swift, Jonathan
Bidner, Jenni 1963- *193*
Biegel, Paul 1925- *79*
    Earlier sketch in SATA *16*
    See also CLR *27*
    See also SAAS *18*
Biemiller, Carl L(udwig), Jr.) 1912-1979 ..... *40*
    Obituary *21*
Bienenfeld, Florence L(ucille) 1929- *39*
Bierhorst, John (William) 1936- *149*
    Autobiography Feature *149*
    Earlier sketches in SATA *6, 91*
    See also SAAS *10*
Biggar, Joan R(awlins) 1936- *120*
Biggle, Lloyd, Jr. 1923-2002 .... *65*
Biggs, Brian 1968- *192*
Bilal, Abdel W(ahab) 1970- *92*
Bilbrough, Norman 1941- *111*
Bildner, Phil *173*
Bileck, Marvin 1920- *40*
Bilibin, Ivan (Iakovlevich) 1876-1942 .... *61*
Bill, Alfred Hoyt 1879-1964 .... *44*
Billam, Rosemary 1952- *61*
Billings, Charlene W(interer) 1941- *41*
Billingsley, Franny 1954- *132*
Billington, Elizabeth T(hain) *50*
    Brief entry *43*
Billout, Guy (Rene) 1941- *144*
    Earlier sketch in SATA *10*
    See also CLR *33*
Bilson, Geoffrey 1938-1987 .... *99*

Binch, Caroline (Lesley) 1947- *140*
  Earlier sketch in SATA *81*
Bing, Christopher (H.) *126*
Bingham, Caroline 1962- *158*
Bingham, Jane M. 1941- *163*
Bingham, Jane Marie
  See Bingham, Jane M.
Bingham, Janet 1959- *200*
Bingham, Sam(uel A.) 1944- *96*
Bingley, Margaret (Jane Kirby) 1947- *72*
Binkley, Anne
  See Rand, Ann (Binkley)
Binzen, Bill
  See Binzen, William
Binzen, William *24*
Birch, David (W.) 1913-1996 .... *89*
Birch, Reginald B(athurst) 1856-1943 .... *19*
Birchman, David 1949- *72*
Birchmore, Daniel A. 1951- *92*
Bird, Carmel 1940- *124*
Bird, E(lzy) J(ay) 1911- *58*
Birdsall, Jeanne 1952(?)- *170*
Birdseye, Tom 1951- *148*
  Earlier sketches in SATA *66, 98*
Birenbaum, Barbara 1941- *65*
Birmingham, Lloyd P(aul) 1924- *83*
  Earlier sketch in SATA *12*
Birmingham, Ruth
  See Sorrells, Walter
Birney, Betty G. 1947- *169*
  Earlier sketch in SATA *98*
Biro, B.
  See Biro, B. S.
Biro, B. S. 1921- *1*
  See also CLR *28*
  See also SAAS *13*
Biro, Val
  See Biro, B. S.
Bischoff, Julia Bristol 1899-1970 .... *12*
Bishop, Bonnie 1943- *37*
Bishop, Claire Huchet 1899(?)-1993 .... *14*
  Obituary *74*
  See also CLR *80*
Bishop, Courtney
  See Ruemmler, John D(avid)
Bishop, Curtis (Kent) 1912-1967 .... *6*
Bishop, Elizabeth 1911-1979
  Obituary *24*
Bishop, Gavin 1946- *144*
  Earlier sketch in SATA *97*
Bishop, Kathleen Wong 1954- *120*
Bishop, Kathy
  See Bishop, Kathleen Wong
Bishop, Nic 1955- *161*
  Earlier sketch in SATA *107*
Bisset, Donald 1910-1995 .... *86*
  Earlier sketch in SATA *7*
Bisson, Terry 1942- *99*
Bisson, Terry Ballantine
  See Bisson, Terry
Bitter, Gary G(len) 1940- *22*
Bixby, William (Courtney) 1920-1986 .... *6*
  Obituary *47*
Bjoerk, Christina 1938- *99*
  Earlier sketch in SATA *67*
  See also CLR *22*
Bjork, Christina
  See Bjoerk, Christina
Bjorklund, Lorence F. 1913-1978 .... *35*
  Brief entry *32*
Bjorkman, Steve *163*
Black, Algernon David 1900-1993 .... *12*
  Obituary *76*
Black, Holly 1971- *147*
Black, Irma Simonton 1906-1972 .... *2*
  Obituary *25*
Black, Mansell
  See Trevor, Elleston
Black, MaryAnn
  See Easley, MaryAnn
Black, Susan Adams 1953- *40*

Blackall, Bernie 1956- *126*
Blackall, Sophie *182*
Blackall, Claire
  See Altman, Linda Jacobs
Blackburn, John(ny) Brewton 1952- *15*
Blackburn, Joyce Knight 1920- *29*
Blacker, Terence 1948- *194*
Blacker, Tina
  See Louise, Tina
Blackett, Veronica Heath 1927- *12*
Blackie, Jean Cutler 1943- *79*
Blacklin, Malcolm
  See Chambers, Aidan
Blacklock, Dyan 1951- *112*
Blackman, Malorie 1962- *196*
  Earlier sketches in SATA *83, 128*
Blackton, Peter
  See Wilson, Lionel
Blackwood, Alan 1932- *70*
Blackwood, Freya *199*
Blackwood, Gary L. 1945- *169*
  Earlier sketches in SATA *72, 118*
Blade, Alexander
  See Garrett, Randall
  and Hamilton, Edmond
  and Silverberg, Robert
Blades, Ann (Sager) 1947- *69*
  Earlier sketch in SATA *16*
  See also CLR *15*
Bladow, Suzanne Wilson 1937- *14*
Blaine, Chris
  See Gardner, Craig Shaw
Blaine, John
  See Goodwin, Harold L(eland)
Blaine, Marge
  See Blaine, Margery Kay
Blaine, Margery Kay 1937- *11*
Blair, Alison
  See Lerangis, Peter
Blair, Anne Denton 1914-1993 .... *46*
Blair, David Nelson 1954- *80*
Blair, Eric 1903-1950 .... *29*
  See also CLR *68*
Blair, Jay 1953- *45*
Blair, Lucile
  See Yeakley, Marjory Hall
Blair, Margaret Whitman 1951- *124*
Blair, Mary 1911-1978 .... *195*
Blair, Pauline Hunter
  See Clarke, Pauline
Blair, Ruth Van Ness 1912-1999 .... *12*
Blair, Shannon
  See Kaye, Marilyn
Blair, Walter 1900-1992 .... *12*
  Obituary *72*
Blaisdell, Bob
  See Blaisdell, Robert
Blaisdell, Robert 1959- *105*
Blake, Bronwyn 1940- *149*
Blake, Francis *198*
Blake, Jon 1954- *171*
  Earlier sketch in SATA *78*
Blake, Olive
  See Supraner, Robyn
Blake, Quentin (Saxby) 1932- *125*
  Earlier sketches in SATA *9, 52, 96*
  See also CLR *31*
Blake, Robert 1949- *42*
Blake, Robert J. *160*
Blake, Walker E.
  See Griffin, W.E.B
Blake, William 1757-1827 .... *30*
  See also CLR *52*
Blakely, Gloria 1950- *139*
Blakely, Roger K. 1922- *82*
Blakeney, Jay D.
  See Chester, Deborah
Blakey, Nancy 1955- *94*
Blanc, Esther S. 1913-1997 .... *66*
Blanc, Mel 1908-1989
  Obituary *64*

Blanchard, Patricia *125*
Blanchet, M(uriel) Wylie 1891-1961 .... *106*
Blanco, Richard L(idio) 1926- *63*
Bland, E.
  See Nesbit, E.
Bland, Edith Nesbit
  See Nesbit, E.
Bland, Fabian
  See Nesbit, E.
Blane, Gertrude
  See Blumenthal, Gertrude
Blank, Clarissa Mabel 1915-1965 .... *62*
Blankenship, LeeAnn 1944- *181*
Blassingame, Wyatt Rainey 1909-1985 .... *34*
  Obituary *41*
  Earlier sketch in SATA *1*
Blatchford, Claire H. 1944- *94*
Blauer, Ettagale 1940- *49*
Bledsoe, Glen L. 1951- *108*
Bledsoe, Glen Leonard
  See Bledsoe, Glen L.
Bledsoe, Karen E. 1962- *167*
  Earlier sketch in SATA *108*
Bledsoe, Karen Elizabeth
  See Bledsoe, Karen E.
Bledsoe, Lucy Jane 1957- *162*
  Earlier sketch in SATA *97*
Bleeker, Sonia
  See Zim, Sonia Bleeker
Blegen, Daniel M. 1950- *92*
Blegvad, Erik 1923- *132*
  Earlier sketches in SATA *14, 66*
Blegvad, Lenore 1926- *176*
  Earlier sketches in SATA *14, 66*
Bley, Anette 1967- *188*
Blish, James (Benjamin) 1921-1975 .... *66*
Blishen, Edward (William) 1920-1996 .... *66*
  Obituary *93*
  Earlier sketch in SATA *8*
Bliss, Corinne Demas 1947- *131*
  Earlier sketch in SATA *37*
Bliss, Frederick
  See Card, Orson Scott
Bliss, Gillian
  See Paton Walsh, Jill
Bliss, Harry 1964- *196*
  Earlier sketch in SATA *156*
Bliss, Reginald
  See Wells, H(erbert) G(eorge)
Bliss, Ronald G(ene) 1942- *12*
Blitt, Barry *187*
Bliven, Bruce, Jr. 1916-2002 .... *2*
Blixen, Karen 1885-1962 .... *44*
Blizzard, Gladys S. (?)-1992 .... *79*
Blobaum, Cindy 1966- *123*
Bloch, Lucienne 1909-1999 .... *10*
Bloch, Marie Halun 1910-1998 .... *6*
  See also SAAS *9*
Bloch, Robert (Albert) 1917-1994 .... *12*
  Obituary *82*
Blochman, Lawrence G(oldtree)
  1900-1975 .... *22*
Block, Francesca Lia 1962- *158*
  Earlier sketches in SATA *80, 116*
  See also CLR *116*
  See also SAAS *21*
Block, Irvin 1917- *12*
Blomgren, Jennifer (Alice) 1954- *136*
Blood, Charles Lewis 1929- *28*
Bloom, Barbara Lee 1943- *146*
Bloom, Freddy 1914-2000 .... *37*
  Obituary *121*
Bloom, Lloyd 1947- *108*
  Brief entry *43*
Bloom, Suzanne 1950- *172*
Bloomfield, Michaela 1966- *70*
Bloor, Edward 1950- *201*
  Earlier sketches in SATA *98, 155*
Bloor, Edward William
  See Bloor, Edward

Blos, Joan W. 1928- *153*
   Autobiography Feature *153*
   Brief entry *27*
   Earlier sketches in SATA *33, 69, 109*
   See also CLR *18*
   See also SAAS *11*
Blos, Joan Winsor
   See Blos, Joan W.
Blough, Glenn O(rlando) 1907-1995 .... *1*
Blue, Rose 1931- *166*
   Autobiography Feature *117*
   Earlier sketches in SATA *5, 91, 93*
   See also SAAS *24*
Blue, Zachary
   See Stine, R.L.
Bluggage, Oranthy
   See Alcott, Louisa May
Blumberg, Leda 1956- *59*
Blumberg, Rhoda 1917- *123*
   Earlier sketches in SATA *35, 70*
   See also CLR *21*
Blume, Judy 1938- *195*
   Earlier sketches in SATA *2, 31, 79, 142*
   See also CLR *69*
Blume, Judy Sussman
   See Blume, Judy
Blume, Lesley M.M. 1975- *180*
Blumenthal, Deborah *161*
Blumenthal, Gertrude 1907-1971
   Obituary *27*
Blumenthal, Shirley 1943- *46*
Blutig, Eduard
   See Gorey, Edward (St. John)
Bly, Janet (Chester) 1945- *43*
Bly, Stephen A(rthur) 1944- *116*
   Earlier sketch in SATA *43*
Blyler, Allison Lee 1966- *74*
Blythe, Gary 1959- *185*
Blyton, Carey 1932-2002 .... *9*
   Obituary *138*
Blyton, Enid 1897-1968 .... *25*
   See also CLR *31*
Blyton, Enid Mary
   See Blyton, Enid
Bo, Ben
   See Richardson, V.A.
Boardman, Fon Wyman, Jr. 1911-2000 .... *6*
Boardman, Gwenn R.
   See Petersen, Gwenn Boardman
Boase, Wendy 1944-1999 .... *28*
   Obituary *110*
Boatner, Mark Mayo III 1921- *29*
Bobbe, Dorothie de Bear 1905-1975 .... *1*
   Obituary *25*
Bober, Natalie S. 1930- *134*
   Earlier sketch in SATA *87*
   See also SAAS *23*
Bobette, Bibo
   See Gugliotta, Bobette
Bobri, Vladimir V. 1898-1986 .... *47*
   Brief entry *32*
Bobritsky, Vladimir
   See Bobri, Vladimir V.
Bochak, Grayce 1956- *76*
Bock, Hal
   See Bock, Harold I.
Bock, Harold I. 1939- *10*
Bock, William Sauts Netamux'we 1939- *14*
Bodanis, David *179*
Bode, Janet 1943-1999 .... *96*
   Obituary *118*
   Earlier sketch in SATA *60*
Bode, N.E.
   See Baggott, Julianna
Bodecker, N(iels) M(ogens) 1922-1988 .... *73*
   Obituary *54*
   Earlier sketch in SATA *8*
Boden, Hilda
   See Bodenham, Hilda Morris
Bodenham, Hilda Morris 1901- *13*
Bodett, Thomas Edward 1955- *70*

Bodett, Tom
   See Bodett, Thomas Edward
Bodie, Idella F(allaw) 1925- *89*
   Earlier sketch in SATA *12*
Bodker, Cecil 1927- *133*
   Earlier sketch in SATA *14*
   See also CLR *23*
Bodker, Cecil 1927-
   See Bodker, Cecil
Bodsworth, (Charles) Fred(erick) 1918- *27*
Boeckman, Charles 1920- *12*
Boegehold, Betty (Doyle) 1913-1985
   Obituary *42*
Boelts, Maribeth 1964- *200*
   Earlier sketches in SATA *78, 163*
Boerst, William J. 1939- *170*
   Earlier sketch in SATA *121*
Boesch, Mark J(oseph) 1917- *12*
Boesen, Victor 1908- *16*
Bogacki, Tomek 1950- *138*
Bogaerts, Gert 1965- *80*
Bogan, Paulette 1960- *201*
   Earlier sketch in SATA *129*
Bogart, Jo Ellen 1945- *92*
   See also CLR *59*
Boggs, Ralph Steele 1901-1994 .... *7*
Bograd, Larry 1953- *89*
   Earlier sketch in SATA *33*
   See also SAAS *21*
Bogue, Gary 1938- *195*
Bogue, Gary L.
   See Bogue, Gary
Bohdal, Susi 1951- *101*
   Earlier sketch in SATA *22*
Bohlen, Nina 1931- *58*
Bohlmeijer, Arno 1956- *94*
Bohner, Charles (Henry) 1927- *62*
Bohnhoff, Maya Kaathryn 1954- *88*
Boiger, Alexandra *178*
Boissard, Janine 1932- *59*
Bojunga, Lygia
   See Nunes, Lygia Bojunga
Bojunga-Nunes, Lygia
   See Nunes, Lygia Bojunga
Boland, Janice *98*
Bolden, Tonya 1959- *188*
   Earlier sketches in SATA *79, 138*
Bolden, Tonya Wilyce
   See Bolden, Tonya
Boles, Paul Darcy 1916-1984 .... *9*
   Obituary *38*
Bolian, Polly 1925- *4*
Bollen, Roger 1941(?)- *83*
   Brief entry *29*
Bolliger, Max 1929- *7*
Bollinger, Max 1929- *167*
Bollinger, Peter *172*
Bolognese, Don(ald Alan) 1934- *129*
   Earlier sketches in SATA *24, 71*
Bolognese, Elaine 1933- *23*
Bolotin, Norman (Phillip) 1951- *93*
Bolton, Carole 1926- *6*
Bolton, Elizabeth
   See St. John, Nicole
Bolton, Evelyn
   See Bunting, Eve
Bonar, Veronica
   See Bailey, Donna (Veronica Anne)
Bond, B. J.
   See Heneghan, James
Bond, Bruce 1939- *61*
Bond, Felicia 1954- *126*
   Earlier sketch in SATA *49*
Bond, Gladys Baker 1912- *14*
Bond, Higgins 1951- *177*
   Earlier sketch in SATA *83*
Bond, J. Harvey
   See Winterbotham, R(ussell) R(obert)

Bond, (Thomas) Michael 1926- *157*
   Earlier sketches in SATA *6, 58*
   See also CLR *95*
   See also SAAS *3*
Bond, Nancy 1945- *159*
   Autobiography Feature *159*
   Earlier sketches in SATA *22, 82*
   See also CLR *11*
   See also SAAS *13*
Bond, Nancy Barbara
   See Bond, Nancy
Bond, Rebecca 1972- *130*
Bond, Ruskin 1934- *87*
   Earlier sketch in SATA *14*
Bondie, J. D.
   See Cunningham, Chet
Bondoux, Anne-Laure 1971- *175*
Bone, Ian 1956- *158*
   Earlier sketch in SATA *117*
Bonehill, Captain Ralph
   See Stratemeyer, Edward L.
Bonestell, Chesley 1888-1986
   Obituary *48*
Bonham, Barbara Thomas 1926- *7*
Bonham, Frank 1914-1989 .... *49*
   Obituary *62*
   Earlier sketch in SATA *1*
   See also SAAS *3*
Boniface, William 1963- *182*
   Earlier sketch in SATA *102*
Bonino, Louise
   See Williams, Louise Bonino
Bonk, John J. *189*
Bonn, Pat
   See Bonn, Patricia Carolyn
Bonn, Patricia Carolyn 1948- *43*
Bonner, Hannah *197*
Bonner, Mary Graham 1890-1974 .... *19*
Bonner, Mike 1951- *121*
Bonners, Susan 1947- *85*
   Brief entry *48*
Bonnett-Rampersaud, Louise *173*
Bonning, Tony 1948- *169*
Bonsall, Crosby Barbara (Newell)
   1921-1995 .... *23*
   Obituary *84*
Bonsall, Joseph S. 1948- *119*
Bonsignore, Joan 1959- *140*
Bontemps, Arna(ud Wendell) 1902-1973 ..... *44*
   Obituary *24*
   Earlier sketch in SATA *2*
   See also CLR *6*
Bonzon, Paul-Jacques 1908-1978 .... *22*
Boock, Paula 1964- *134*
Booher, Dianna Daniels 1948- *33*
Book, Rick 1949- *119*
Book, Rita
   See Holub, Joan
Bookman, Charlotte
   See Zolotow, Charlotte
Boon, Debbie 1960- *103*
Boon, Emilie (Laetitia) 1958- *86*
Boone, Charles Eugene
   See Boone, Pat
Boone, Pat 1934- *7*
Boorman, Linda (Kay) 1940- *46*
Boorstin, Daniel J(oseph) 1914-2004 .... *52*
Booth, Coe *187*
Booth, Ernest Sheldon 1915-1984 .... *43*
Booth, George 1926- *191*
Booth, Graham (Charles) 1935- *37*
Bootman, Colin *159*
Borden, Louise 1949- *190*
   Autobiography Feature *141*
   Earlier sketches in SATA *68, 104, 141*
Bordier, Georgette 1924- *16*
Borgman, James
   See Borgman, Jim
Borgman, James Mark
   See Borgman, Jim
Borgman, Jim 1954- *122*

Borgo, Lacy Finn 1972- *194*
Boring, Mel 1939- *168*
  Earlier sketch in SATA *35*
Borja, Corinne 1929- *22*
Borja, Robert 1923- *22*
Borland, Hal
  See Borland, Harold Glen
Borland, Harold Glen 1900-1978 .... *5*
  Obituary *24*
Borland, Kathryn Kilby 1916- *16*
Borlenghi, Patricia 1951- *79*
Born, Adolf 1930- *49*
Bornstein, Ruth Lercher
  See Bornstein-Lercher, Ruth
Bornstein-Lercher, Ruth 1927- *88*
  Autobiography Feature *107*
  Earlier sketch in SATA *14*
Borski, Lucia Merecka *18*
Borten, Helen Jacobson 1930- *5*
Bortolotti, Dan 1969- *157*
Borton, Elizabeth
  See Trevino, Elizabeth B(orton) de
Borton, Lady 1942- *98*
Borton de Trevino, Elizabeth
  See Trevino, Elizabeth B(orton) de
Bortstein, Larry 1942- *16*
Bortz, Alfred B(enjamin) 1944- *139*
  Earlier sketch in SATA *74*
Bortz, Fred
  See Bortz, Alfred B(enjamin)
Bosch, Pseudonymous *199*
Bosco, Jack
  See Holliday, Joseph
Boshell, Gordon 1908-1991 .... *15*
Boshinski, Blanche 1922- *10*
Bosman, Paul 1929- *107*
Bosse, Malcolm (Joseph, Jr.) 1926-2002 .... *136*
  Earlier sketch in SATA *35*
Bosserman, (Charles) Phillip 1931- *84*
Bossom, Naomi 1933- *35*
Bostock, Mike 1962- *114*
Boston, L(ucy) M(aria Wood) 1892-1990 ... *19*
  Obituary *64*
  See also CLR *3*
Bostrom, Kathleen (Susan) Long 1954- *139*
Bostrom, Kathy
  See Bostrom, Kathleen (Susan) Long
Bosworth, J. Allan 1925- *19*
Bothwell, Jean (?)-1977 .... *2*
Botkin, B(enjamin) A(lbert) 1901-1975 .... *40*
Botsford, Ward 1927-2004 .... *66*
Botting, Douglas (Scott) 1934- *43*
Bottner, Barbara 1943- *170*
  Autobiography Feature *121*
  Earlier sketches in SATA *14, 93*
  See also SAAS *26*
Bottone, Frank G., Jr. 1969- *141*
Bouchard, David 1952- *117*
Boucher, (Clarence) Carter 1954- *129*
Boudelang, Bob
  See Pell, Ed(ward)
Boughton, Richard 1954- *75*
Boulet, Susan Seddon 1941- *50*
Boulle, Pierre (Francois Marie-Louis)
  1912-1994 .... *22*
  Obituary *78*
Boulton, Jane 1921- *91*
Bouma, Paddy 1947- *128*
Bour, Daniele 1939- *62*
Bourbonniere, Sylvie 1966- *182*
Bourdon, David 1934-1998 .... *46*
Bourgeois, Paulette 1951- *153*
Bourne, Lesley
  See Marshall, Evelyn
Bourne, Miriam Anne 1931-1989 .... *16*
  Obituary *63*
Boutavant, Marc 1970- *200*
Boutet de Monvel, (Louis) M(aurice)
  1850(?)-1913 .... *30*
  See also CLR *32*

Bova, Ben 1932- *133*
  Earlier sketches in SATA *6, 68*
  See also CLR *96*
Bova, Benjamin William
  See Bova, Ben
Bovaird, Anne E(lizabeth) 1960- *90*
Bow, Patricia 1946- *168*
Bowden, Joan Chase 1925- *51*
  Brief entry *38*
Bowe, Julie 1962- *194*
Bowen, Alexandria Russell *97*
Bowen, Andy Russell
  See Bowen, Alexandria Russell
Bowen, Anne 1952- *170*
Bowen, Betty Morgan
  See West, Betty
Bowen, Catherine (Shober) Drinker
  1897-1973 .... *7*
Bowen, David
  See Bowen, Joshua David
Bowen, Fred 1953- *136*
Bowen, Joshua David 1930- *22*
Bowen, Rhys
  See Quin-Harkin, Janet
Bowen, Robert Sydney 1900-1977 .... *52*
  Obituary *21*
Bowermaster, Jon 1954- *135*
  Earlier sketch in SATA *77*
Bowers, Terrell L. 1945- *101*
Bowers, Terry
  See Bowers, Terrell L.
Bowers, Tim *185*
Bowie, C. W.
  See Old, Wendie C(orbin)
  and Wirths, Claudine (Turner) G(ibson)
Bowie, Jim
  See Norwood, Victor G(eorge) C(harles)
  and Stratemeyer, Edward L.
Bowkett, Stephen 1953- *67*
Bowler, Jan Brett
  See Brett, Jan
Bowler, Tim 1953- *149*
Bowman, Catherine
  See Smith, Cat Bowman
Bowman, Crystal 1951- *105*
Bowman, James Cloyd 1880-1961 .... *23*
Bowman, John S(tewart) 1931- *16*
Bowman, Kathleen (Gill) 1942- *52*
  Brief entry *40*
Bowman, Leslie
  See Bowman, Leslie W.
Bowman, Leslie W. *182*
Bowsher, Melodie *195*
Boxall, Ed *178*
Boyce, Frank Cottrell *182*
Boyce, George A(rthur) 1898- *19*
Boyd, Candy Dawson 1946- *72*
  See also CLR *50*
Boyd, Pauline
  See Schock, Pauline
Boyd, Selma
  See Acuff, Selma Boyd
Boyd, Waldo T. 1918- *18*
Boyden, Linda 1948- *143*
Boyer, Allen B. 1963- *153*
Boyer, Robert E(rnst) 1929- *22*
Boyes, Vivien 1952- *106*
Boyes, Vivien Elizabeth
  See Boyes, Vivien
Boyle, Ann (Peters) 1916- *10*
Boyle, Eleanor Vere (Gordon) 1825-1916 .... *28*
Boyle, Robert H. 1928- *65*
Boylston, Helen Dore 1895-1984 .... *23*
  Obituary *39*
Boyne, John 1971- *181*
Boynton, Sandra (Keith) 1953- *152*
  Brief entry *38*
  Earlier sketches in SATA *57, 107*
  See also CLR *105*
Boz
  See Dickens, Charles (John Huffam)

Braasch, Gary *201*
Bracken, Charles
  See Pellowski, Michael (Joseph)
Brackers de Hugo, Pierre 1960- *115*
Brackett, Dolli Tingle 1911-1993 .... *137*
Brackett, Virginia 1950- *166*
  Earlier sketch in SATA *121*
Brackett, Virginia Roberts Meredith
  See Brackett, Virginia
Bradbury, Bianca (Ryley) 1908-1982 .... *56*
  Earlier sketch in SATA *3*
Bradbury, Edward P.
  See Moorcock, Michael
Bradbury, Ray 1920- *123*
  Earlier sketches in SATA *11, 64*
Bradbury, Ray Douglas
  See Bradbury, Ray
Bradby, Marie *161*
Bradfield, Carl 1942- *91*
Bradford, Ann (Liddell) 1917- *56*
  Brief entry *38*
Bradford, Barbara Taylor 1933- *66*
Bradford, Karleen 1936- *96*
  Earlier sketch in SATA *48*
Bradford, Lois J(ean) 1936- *36*
Bradford, Richard (Roark) 1932-2002 .... *59*
  Obituary *135*
Bradley, Duane
  See Sanborn, Duane
Bradley, Kimberly Brubaker 1967- *179*
Bradley, Marion Zimmer 1930-1999 .... *139*
  Obituary *116*
  Earlier sketch in SATA *90*
Bradley, Timothy J. *193*
Bradley, Virginia 1912- *23*
Bradley, Will
  See Strickland, Brad
Bradman, Tony 1954- *152*
  Earlier sketch in SATA *81*
Bradshaw, Gillian (Joan) 1949- *118*
Bradshaw, Gillian 1956- *127*
Bradshaw, Gillian Marucha
  See Bradshaw, Gillian
Bradstreet, T. J.
  See Thesman, Jean
Brady, Esther Wood 1905-1987 .... *31*
  Obituary *53*
Brady, Irene 1943- *4*
Brady, Kimberley S. 1953- *101*
Brady, Kimberley Smith
  See Brady, Kimberley S.
Brady, Lillian 1902- *28*
Bragdon, Elspeth MacDuffie 1897-1980 .... *6*
Bragdon, Lillian Jacot *24*
Brager, Bruce L. 1949- *146*
Bragg, Mabel Caroline 1870-1945 .... *24*
Bragg, Michael 1948- *46*
Bragg, Ruth Gembicki 1943- *77*
Brahm, Sumishta 1954- *58*
Brailsford, Frances
  See Wosmek, Frances
Brainerd, John W(hiting) 1918- *65*
Braithwaite, Althea 1940- *23*
  Autobiography Feature *119*
  See also SAAS *24*
Bram, Elizabeth 1948- *30*
Brancato, Robin F(idler) 1936- *97*
  See also CLR *32*
  See also SAAS *9*
Branch, Muriel Miller 1943- *152*
  Earlier sketch in SATA *94*
Brand, Christianna
  See Lewis, Mary
Brand, Rebecca
  See Charnas, Suzy McKee
Brande, Robin *194*
Brandel, Marc 1919- *71*
Brandenberg, Alexa (Demetria) 1966- *97*
Brandenberg, Aliki 1929- *157*
  Earlier sketches in SATA *2, 35, 75, 113*
  See also CLR *71*

Brandenberg, Franz 1932- 75
　Earlier sketches in SATA *8, 35*
Brandenburg, Jim 1945- 87
Brandhorst, Carl T(heodore) 1898-1988 23
Brandis, Marianne 1938- 149
　Earlier sketches in SATA *59, 96*
Brandon, Brumsic, Jr. 1927- 9
Brandon, Curt
　See Bishop, Curtis (Kent)
Brandreth, Gyles 1948- 28
Brandreth, Gyles Daubeney
　See Brandreth, Gyles
Brandt, Catharine 1905-1997 40
Brandt, Keith
　See Sabin, Louis
Brandt, Sue R(eading) 1916- 59
Branfield, John (Charles) 1931- 11
Branford, Henrietta 1946-1999 106
Branley, Franklyn M(ansfield) 1915-2002 .. 136
　Earlier sketches in SATA *4, 68*
　See also CLR *13*
　See also SAAS *16*
Branscum, Robbie (Tilley) 1937-1997 72
　Obituary 96
　Earlier sketch in SATA *23*
　See also SAAS *17*
Bransom, (John) Paul 1885-1979 43
Brashares, Ann 1967- 188
　Earlier sketch in SATA *145*
　See also CLR *113*
Brassard, France 1963- 186
Braswell, E.J.
　See Lynn, Tracy
Braswell, Elizabeth J.
　See Lynn, Tracy
Braswell, Liz
　See Lynn, Tracy
Bratton, Helen 1899-1986 4
Bratun, Katy 1950- 160
　Earlier sketch in SATA *83*
Braude, Michael 1936- 23
Braun, Lilian Jackson 1916(?)- 109
Brautigan, Richard (Gary) 1935-1984 56
Bray, Libba 159
Bray, Martha E.
　See Bray, Libba
Braymer, Marjorie Elizabeth 1911-1988 6
Breathed, Berke 1957- 161
　Earlier sketch in SATA *86*
Breathed, Guy Berkeley
　See Breathed, Berke
Brecht, Edith 1895-1975 6
　Obituary 25
Breck, Vivian
　See Breckenfeld, Vivian Gurney
Breckenfeld, Vivian Gurney 1895-1992 1
Breda, Tjalmar
　See DeJong, David C(ornel)
Bredeson, Carmen 1944- 163
　Earlier sketch in SATA *98*
Breen, Steve 1970- 186
Breinburg, Petronella 1927- 11
　See also CLR *31*
Breisky, William J(ohn) 1928- 22
Brenaman, Miriam 172
Brennan, Caitlin
　See Tarr, Judith
Brennan, Gale (Patrick) 1927- 64
　Brief entry 53
Brennan, Herbie 1940- 183
　Earlier sketch in SATA *140*
Brennan, James Herbert
　See Brennan, Herbie
Brennan, Jan
　See Brennan, Herbie
Brennan, J.H.
　See Brennan, Herbie
Brennan, Joseph Lomas 1903-2000 6
Brennan, Linda Crotta 1952- 130
Brennan, Tim
　See Conroy, John Wesley

Brenner, Anita 1905-1974 56
Brenner, Barbara (Johnes) 1925- 124
　Earlier sketches in SATA *4, 42, 76*
　See also SAAS *14*
Brenner, Fred 1920- 36
　Brief entry 34
Brent, Hope 1935(?)-1984
　Obituary 39
Brent, Stuart 14
Breskin, Jane
　See Zalben, Jane Breskin
Breslin, Theresa 128
　Autobiography Feature 128
　Earlier sketch in SATA *70*
Breslow, Maurice 1935- 72
Breslow, Maurice A
　See Breslow, Maurice
Breslow, Susan 1951- 69
Brett, Bernard 1925- 22
Brett, Grace N(eff) 1900-1975 23
Brett, Jan 1949- 171
　Earlier sketches in SATA *42, 71, 130*
　See also CLR *27*
Brett, Jan Churchill
　See Brett, Jan
Brett Bowler, Jan
　See Brett, Jan
Brewer, Heather 1973- 196
Brewer, James D. 1951- 108
Brewer, Sally King 1947- 33
Brewster, Benjamin
　See Folsom, Franklin (Brewster)
Brewster, Hugh 1950- 191
　Earlier sketch in SATA *95*
Brewster, Patience 1952- 97
Brewton, John E(dmund) 1898-1982 5
Brian, Janeen (Paulette) 1948- 141
Briant, Ed 180
Brick, John 1922-1973 10
Brickman, Robin D. 1954- 155
Bride, Nadja
　See Nobisso, Josephine
Bridgers, Sue Ellen 1942- 90
　Autobiography Feature 109
　Earlier sketch in SATA *22*
　See also CLR *18*
　See also SAAS *1*
Bridges, Laurie
　See Bruck, Lorraine
Bridges, Ruby (Nell) 1954- 131
Bridges, William (Andrew) 1901-1984 5
Bridwell, Norman (Ray) 1928- 138
　Earlier sketches in SATA *4, 68*
　See also CLR *96*
Brier, Howard M(axwell) 1903-1969 8
Brierley, (Louise) 1958- 59
Briggs, Katharine Mary 1898-1980 101
　Obituary 25
Briggs, Peter 1921-1975 39
　Obituary 31
Briggs, Raymond 1934- 184
　Earlier sketches in SATA *23, 66, 131*
　See also CLR *10*
Briggs, Raymond Redvers
　See Briggs, Raymond
Bright, Paul 1949- 182
Bright, Robert (Douglas Sr.) 1902-1988 63
　Obituary 60
　Earlier sketch in SATA *24*
Bright, Sarah
　See Shine, Deborah
Brightfield, Richard 1927- 65
　Brief entry 53
Brightfield, Rick
　See Brightfield, Richard
Brighton, Catherine 1943- 107
　Earlier sketch in SATA *65*
Brill, Marlene Targ 1945- 124
　Earlier sketch in SATA *77*
Brimberg, Stanlee 1947- 9

Brimner, Larry Dane 1949- 170
　Autobiography Feature 112
　Earlier sketch in SATA *79*
Brin, David 1950- 65
Brin, Ruth Firestone 1921- 22
Brinckloe, Julie 1950- 13
Brinckloe, Julie Lorraine
　See Brinckloe, Julie
Brindel, June (Rachuy) 1919- 7
Brindle, Max
　See Fleischman, Sid
Brindze, Ruth 1903-1984 23
Brink, Carol Ryrie 1895-1981 100
　Obituary 27
　Earlier sketches in SATA *1, 31*
　See also CLR *30*
Brinsmead, H. F.
　See Brinsmead, H(esba) F(ay)
Brinsmead, H. F(ay)
　See Brinsmead, H(esba) F(ay)
Brinsmead, H(esba) F(ay) 1922- 78
　Earlier sketch in SATA *18*
　See also CLR *47*
　See also SAAS *5*
Briquebec, John
　See Rowland-Entwistle, (Arthur) Theodore
　(Henry)
Brisbane, Henry R.
　See Ellis, Edward S(ylvester)
Brisco, P. A.
　See Matthews, Patricia
Brisco, Patty
　See Matthews, Patricia
　and Matthews, Clayton (Hartley)
Briscoe, Jill (Pauline) 1935- 56
　Brief entry 47
Brisley, Joyce Lankester 1896-1978 22
　Obituary 84
Brissenden, Connie
　See Brissenden, Constance
Brissenden, Constance 1947- 150
Brisson, Pat 1951- 177
　Autobiography Feature 133
　Earlier sketches in SATA *67, 128, 133*
Britt, Albert 1874-1969
　Obituary 28
Britt, Dell 1934- 1
Brittain, Bill
　See Brittain, William
Brittain, C. Dale 1948- 82
Brittain, William 1930- 76
　Earlier sketch in SATA *36*
　See also SAAS *7*
Brittingham, Geoffrey (Hugh) 1959- 76
Britton, Kate
　See Stegeman, Janet Allais
Britton, Louisa
　See McGuire, Leslie (Sarah)
Britton, Rick 1952- 82
Bro, Margueritte (Harmon) 1894-1977 19
　Obituary 27
Broach, Elise 1963- 173
Broadhead, Helen Cross 1913- 25
Brochmann, Elizabeth 1938- 41
Brock, Betty (Carter) 1923-2003 4
　Obituary 150
Brock, C(harles) E(dmund) 1870-1938 42
　Brief entry 32
Brock, Delia
　See Ephron, Delia
Brock, Emma L(illian) 1886-1974 8
Brock, H(enry) M(atthew) 1875-1960 42
Brockett, Eleanor Hall 1913-1967 10
Brockman, C(hristian) Frank 1902-1985 26
Brockmeier, Kevin 1972- 176
Broderick, Dorothy M. 1929- 5
Brodeur, Ruth Wallace
　See Wallace-Brodeur, Ruth
Brodie, Sally
　See Cavin, Ruth (Brodie)

Brodsky, Beverly
    See McDermott, Beverly Brodsky
Brody, Wendy
    See Staub, Wendy Corsi
Broeger, Achim 1944- *31*
Broekel, Rainer Lothar 1923- *38*
Broekel, Ray
    See Broekel, Rainer Lothar
Broekstra, Lorette 1964- *189*
    Earlier sketch in SATA *124*
Brogden, Sherryl
    See Jordan, Sherryl
Broger, Achim
    See Broeger, Achim
Broida, Marian *154*
Brokamp, Marilyn 1920- *10*
Broman, Fred
    See Moseley, James W(illett)
Bromhall, Winifred *26*
Brommer, Gerald F(rederick) 1927- *28*
Brondfield, Jerome 1913-1998 .... *22*
Brondfield, Jerry
    See Brondfield, Jerome
Bronner, Stephen Eric 1949- *101*
Bronowski, Jacob 1908-1974 .... *55*
Bronson, Alice
    See Watkins, Dawn L.
Bronson, Lynn
    See Lampman, Evelyn Sibley
Bronson, Wilfrid Swancourt 1894-1985
    Obituary *43*
Brook, Judith (Penelope) 1926- *59*
    Brief entry *51*
Brook, Judy
    See Brook, Judith (Penelope)
Brooke, L(eonard) Leslie 1862-1940 .... *17*
    See also CLR *20*
Brooke, William J. 1946- *139*
Brooke-Haven, P.
    See Wodehouse, P(elham) G(renville)
Brooker, Kyrsten *199*
Brookins, Dana 1931- *28*
Brooks, Anita
    See Abramovitz, Anita (Zeltner Brooks)
Brooks, Bill 1939- *59*
Brooks, Bruce 1950- *112*
    Brief entry *53*
    Earlier sketch in SATA *72*
    See also CLR *25*
Brooks, Caryl 1924- *84*
Brooks, Charlotte K(endrick) 1918-1998 ..... *24*
    Obituary *112*
Brooks, Erik 1972- *182*
    Earlier sketch in SATA *152*
Brooks, George
    See Baum, L(yman) Frank
Brooks, Gwendolyn 1917-2000 .... *6*
    Obituary *123*
    See also CLR *27*
Brooks, Gwendolyn Elizabeth
    See Brooks, Gwendolyn
Brooks, Jerome 1931- *23*
Brooks, Kevin 1959- *197*
    Earlier sketch in SATA *150*
Brooks, Kevin M.
    See Brooks, Kevin
Brooks, Lester 1924- *7*
Brooks, Martha 1944- *134*
    Autobiography Feature *134*
    Earlier sketches in SATA *68, 121*
Brooks, Maurice (Graham) 1900- *45*
Brooks, Polly Schoyer 1912- *12*
Brooks, Ron 1948- *94*
    Brief entry *33*
Brooks, Ronald George
    See Brooks, Ron
Brooks, Terry 1944- *60*
Brooks, Walter R(ollin) 1886-1958 .... *17*
Brooks-Hill, Helen (Mason) 1908-1994 .... *59*
Broome, Errol 1937- *158*
    Earlier sketch in SATA *105*

Brophy, Nannette 1963- *73*
Brosnan, James Patrick 1929- *14*
Brosnan, Jim
    See Brosnan, James Patrick
Brostoff, Anita 1931- *132*
Brothers Grimm
    See Grimm, Jacob Ludwig Karl
    and Grimm, Wilhelm Karl
Brothers Hildebrandt, The
    See Hildebrandt, Greg
    and Hildebrandt, Tim
Broun, Emily
    See Sterne, Emma Gelders
Brouwer, S. W.
    See Brouwer, Sigmund (W.)
Brouwer, Sigmund (W.) 1959- *109*
Brow, Thea 1934- *60*
Brower, Millicent *8*
Brower, Pauline 1929- *22*
Browin, Frances Williams 1898-1986 .... *5*
Brown, Alexis
    See Baumann, Amy Beeching
Brown, Anne Ensign 1937- *61*
Brown, Beverly Swerdlow *97*
Brown, Bill
    See Brown, William L(ouis)
Brown, Billye Walker
    See Cutchen, Billye Walker
Brown, Bob
    See Brown, Robert Joseph
Brown, Buck 1936- *45*
Brown, Calef *179*
Brown, Cassie 1919-1986 .... *55*
Brown, Charlotte Lewis *181*
Brown, Conrad 1922- *31*
Brown, Craig McFarland 1947- *73*
Brown, David
    See Brown, David A(lan)
    and Myller, Rolf
Brown, Dee 1908-2002 .... *110*
    Obituary *141*
    Earlier sketch in SATA *5*
Brown, Dee Alexander
    See Brown, Dee
Brown, Don 1949- *200*
    Earlier sketch in SATA *172*
Brown, Drew T. III 1955- *83*
Brown, Drollene P. 1939- *53*
Brown, Elbrite *198*
Brown, Eleanor Frances 1908-1987 .... *3*
Brown, Elizabeth Ferguson 1937- *153*
Brown, Elizabeth M(yers) 1915- *43*
Brown, Fern G. 1918- *34*
Brown, (Robert) Fletch 1923- *42*
Brown, Fornan 1901-1996 .... *71*
    Obituary *88*
Brown, George Earl 1883-1964 .... *11*
Brown, George Mackay 1921-1996 .... *35*
Brown, Irene Bennett 1932- *3*
Brown, Irving
    See Adams, William Taylor
Brown, Ivor (John Carnegie) 1891-1974 .... *5*
    Obituary *26*
Brown, Jane Clark 1930- *81*
Brown, Janet Mitsui *87*
Brown, Jo 1964- *170*
Brown, Joanne 1933- *147*
Brown, Joe David 1915-1976 .... *44*
Brown, Joseph E(dward) 1929- *59*
    Brief entry *51*
Brown, Judith Gwyn 1933- *20*
Brown, Kathryn 1955- *168*
    Earlier sketch in SATA *98*
Brown, Kathy
    See Brown, Kathryn
Brown, Ken (James) *129*
Brown, Kevin 1960- *101*
Brown, Laurene Krasny 1945- *99*
    Earlier sketch in SATA *54*
Brown, Laurie Krasny
    See Brown, Laurene Krasny

Brown, Lloyd Arnold 1907-1966 .... *36*
Brown, Mahlon A.
    See Ellis, Edward S(ylvester)
Brown, Marc (Tolon) 1946- *145*
    Earlier sketches in SATA *10, 53, 80*
    See also CLR *29*
Brown, Marcia (Joan) 1918- *47*
    Earlier sketch in SATA *7*
    See also CLR *12*
Brown, Margaret Wise 1910-1952 .... *100*
    See also YABC *2*
    See also CLR *107*
Brown, Margery (Wheeler) *78*
    Earlier sketch in SATA *5*
Brown, Marion Marsh 1908-2001 .... *6*
Brown, Myra Berry 1918- *6*
Brown, Palmer 1919- *36*
Brown, Pamela (Beatrice) 1924-1989 .... *5*
    Obituary *61*
Brown, Peter 1979- *178*
Brown, Reeve Lindbergh
    See Lindbergh, Reeve
Brown, Richard E. 1946- *61*
Brown, Robert Joseph 1907-1989 .... *14*
Brown, Roderick (Langmere) Haig-
    See Haig-Brown, Roderick (Langmere)
Brown, Rosalie
    See Moore, Rosalie (Gertrude)
Brown, Roswell
    See Webb, Jean Francis (III)
Brown, Roy (Frederick) 1921-1982 .... *51*
    Obituary *39*
Brown, Ruth 1941- *170*
    Earlier sketch in SATA *105*
Brown, Scott 1971- *134*
Brown, Sue Ellen 1954- *81*
Brown, Tricia 1954- *114*
Brown, Vinson 1912-1991 .... *19*
Brown, Walter R(eed) 1929- *19*
Brown, Will
    See Ainsworth, William Harrison
Brown, William L(ouis) 1910-1964 .... *5*
Browne, Anthony 1946- *163*
    Brief entry *44*
    Earlier sketches in SATA *45, 61, 105*
    See also CLR *19*
Browne, Anthony Edward Tudor
    See Browne, Anthony
Browne, Dik
    See Browne, Richard Arthur Allen
Browne, Hablot Knight 1815-1882 .... *21*
Browne, Matthew
    See Rands, William Brighty
Browne, Nicki M.
    See Browne, N.M.
Browne, Nicky Matthews
    See Browne, N.M.
Browne, N.M. 1960- *167*
Browne, Richard Arthur Allen 1917-1989 ... *67*
    Brief entry *38*
Browne, Vee F(rances) 1956- *90*
Browning, Robert 1812-1889
    See YABC *1*
    See also CLR *97*
Brownjohn, Alan 1931- *6*
Brownlee, Walter 1930- *62*
Brownlie, Betty 1946- *159*
Brownlow, Kevin 1938- *65*
Brownlow, Mike *183*
Brownridge, William R(oy) 1932- *94*
Broyles, Anne 1953- *201*
Bruce, Dorita Fairlie 1885-1970
    Obituary *27*
Bruce, (William) Harry 1934- *77*
Bruce, Mary 1927- *1*
Bruchac, Joseph III
    See Bruchac, Joseph
Bruchac, Joseph 1942- *176*
    Autobiography Feature *176*
    Earlier sketches in SATA *42, 89, 131*
    See also CLR *46*

Bruchac, Margaret M.
  See Bruchac, Marge
Bruchac, Marge 181
Bruck, Lorraine 1921- 55
  Brief entry 46
Bruel, Nick 166
Bruel, Robert O. 1929-2002 189
Bruemmer, Fred 1929- 47
Brugman, Alyssa (F.) 1974- 152
Brumbeau, Jeff 1955- 157
Bruna, Dick 1927- 76
  Brief entry 30
  Earlier sketch in SATA 43
  See also CLR 7
Brunhoff, Jean de 1899-1937 24
  See also CLR 116
Brunhoff, Laurent de 1925- 150
  Earlier sketches in SATA 24, 71
  See also CLR 116
Brunskill, Elizabeth Ann Flatt
  See Flatt, Lizann
Brush, Karen A(lexandra) 1960- 85
Brussel-Smith, Bernard 1914- 58
Brust, Steven 1955- 121
  Earlier sketch in SATA 86
Brust, Steven K. Zoltan
  See Brust, Steven
Brustlein, Daniel 1904- 40
Brustlein, Janice Tworkov -2000 40
  Obituary 126
Brutschy, Jennifer 1960- 84
Bryan, Ashley 1923- 178
  Earlier sketches in SATA 31, 72, 132
  See also CLR 66
Bryan, Ashley F.
  See Bryan, Ashley
Bryan, Dorothy M. 1896(?)-1984
  Obituary 39
Bryan, Jennifer 190
Bryan, Sean 192
Bryant, Bernice (Morgan) 1908-1976 11
Bryant, Jen 1960- 175
  Earlier sketch in SATA 94
Bryant, Jennifer Fisher
  See Bryant, Jen
Bryant, Laura J. 176
Brychta, Alex 1956- 21
Brynie, Faith H. 1946- 113
Brynie, Faith Hickman
  See Brynie, Faith H.
Bryson, Bernarda 1903-2004 9
Buba, Joy Flinsch 1904- 44
Buchan, Bryan 1945- 36
Buchan, John 1875-1940
  See YABC 2
Buchan, Stuart 1942-1987
  Obituary 54
Buchanan, Debby 1952- 82
Buchanan, Deborah Leevonne
  See Buchanan, Debby
Buchanan, Jane 1956- 160
Buchanan, Paul 1959- 116
Buchanan, Sue 1939- 139
Buchheimer, Naomi Barnett
  See Barnett, Naomi
Buchignani, Walter 1965- 84
Buchmann, Stephen L. 194
Buchwald, Art 1925-2007 10
Buchwald, Arthur
  See Buchwald, Art
Buchwald, Emilie 1935- 7
Buck, Gisela 1941- 101
Buck, Lewis 1925- 18
Buck, Margaret Waring 1905-1997 3
Buck, Nola
  See Godwin, Laura
Buck, Pearl S(ydenstricker) 1892-1973 25
  Earlier sketch in SATA 1
Buck, Siegfried 1941- 101

Buckeridge, Anthony (Malcolm)
  1912-2004 85
  Earlier sketch in SATA 6
Buckholtz, Eileen (Garber) 1949- 54
  Brief entry 47
Buckler, Ernest 1908-1984 47
Buckless, Andrea K. 1968- 117
Buckley, Helen E(lizabeth) 1918- 90
  Earlier sketch in SATA 2
Buckley, James, Jr. 1963- 166
  Earlier sketch in SATA 114
Buckley, Michael 177
Buckley, Susan 184
Buckley, Susan Washburn
  See Buckley, Susan
Buckley-Archer, Linda 185
Buckmaster, Henrietta
  See Stephens, Henrietta Henkle
Bucks, Brad
  See Holub, Joan
Budd, E. S.
  See Sirimarco, Elizabeth
Budd, Lillian (Peterson) 1897-1989 7
Budhos, Marina 173
Buehler, Stephanie Jona 1956- 83
Buehner, Caralyn (M.) 1963- 159
  Earlier sketch in SATA 104
Buehner, Mark 1959- 159
  Earlier sketch in SATA 104
Buehr, Walter Franklin 1897-1971 3
Buell, Ellen Lewis
  See Cash, Ellen Lewis Buell
Buell, Janet 1952- 185
  Earlier sketch in SATA 106
Buergel, Paul-Hermann H. 1949- 83
Buettner, Dan 1960- 95
Buff, Conrad 1886-1975 19
Buff, Mary (E. Marsh) 1890-1970 19
Buffett, Jimmy 1946- 110
  Earlier sketch in SATA 76
Buffie, Margaret 1945- 161
  Earlier sketches in SATA 71, 107
  See also CLR 39
Bugbee, Emma 1888(?)-1981
  Obituary 29
Bugni, Alice 1951- 122
Buhhos, Marina Tamar
  See Budhos, Marina
Bujold, Lois McMaster 1949- 136
Bulfinch, Thomas 1796-1867 35
Bulion, Leslie 1958- 161
Bull, Angela (Mary) 1936- 45
Bull, Emma 1954- 190
  Autobiography Feature 103
  Earlier sketch in SATA 99
Bull, Norman John 1916- 41
Bull, Peter (Cecil) 1912-1984
  Obituary 39
Bull, Schuyler M. 1974- 138
Bulla, Clyde R. 1914-2007 139
  Obituary 182
  Earlier sketches in SATA 2, 41, 91
  See also SAAS 6
Bullard, Lisa 1961- 142
Bullock, Kathleen (Mary) 1946- 77
Bullock, Robert (D.) 1947- 92
Bulpin, (Barbara) Vicki 92
Bumstead, Kathleen Mary 1918-1987 53
Bundles, A'Lelia Perry 1952- 76
Bunin, Catherine 1967- 30
Bunin, Sherry 1925- 30
Bunkers, Suzanne L. 1950- 136
Bunting, A.E.
  See Bunting, Eve
Bunting, Anne Evelyn
  See Bunting, Eve
Bunting, Eve 1928- 196
  Earlier sketches in SATA 18, 64, 110, 158
  See also CLR 82
Bunting, Glenn (Davison) 1957- 22

Bunyan, John 1628-1688
  See CLR 124
Bupp, Walter
  See Garrett, Randall
Burack, Sylvia K. 1916-2003 35
  Obituary 143
Burbank, Addison (Buswell) 1895-1961 37
Burch, Joann J(ohansen) 75
Burch, Robert J(oseph) 1925- 74
  Earlier sketch in SATA 1
  See also CLR 63
Burchard, Peter Duncan 1921- 143
  Earlier sketches in SATA 5, 74
  See also SAAS 13
Burchard, S. H.
  See Burchard, Sue
Burchard, Sue 1937- 22
Burchardt, Nellie 1921- 7
Burckhardt, Marc 1962- 196
Burdett, Lois 117
Burdick, Eugene (Leonard) 1918-1965 22
Burford, Eleanor
  See Hibbert, Eleanor Alice Burford
Burgan, Michael 1960- 167
  Earlier sketch in SATA 118
Burger, Carl 1888-1967 9
Burgess, Ann Marie
  See Gerson, Noel Bertram
Burgess, Barbara Hood 1926- 69
Burgess, Em
  See Burgess, Mary Wyche
Burgess, (Frank) Gelett 1866-1951 32
  Brief entry 30
Burgess, Mark 157
Burgess, Mary Wyche 1916- 18
Burgess, Melvin 1954- 198
  Earlier sketches in SATA 96, 146
Burgess, Michael
  See Gerson, Noel Bertram
Burgess, Robert F(orrest) 1927- 4
Burgess, Starling
  See Tudor, Tasha
Burgess, Thornton Waldo 1874-1965 17
Burgess, Trevor
  See Trevor, Elleston
Burgwyn, Mebane Holoman 1914-1992 7
Burke, David 1927- 46
Burke, Diana G.
  See Gallagher, Diana G.
Burke, Diana Gallagher
  See Gallagher, Diana G.
Burke, Dianne O'Quinn 1940- 89
Burke, Janine 1952- 139
Burke, Jim 1973- 179
Burke, John
  See O'Connor, Richard
Burke, Katie 1953- 168
Burke, Patrick 1958- 114
Burke, Ralph
  See Garrett, Randall
  and Silverberg, Robert
Burkert, Nancy Ekholm 1933- 24
  See also SAAS 14
Burkett, D. Brent 194
Burke-Weiner, Kimberly 1962- 95
Burks, Brian 1955- 95
Burland, Brian (Berkeley) 1931- 34
Burland, C. A.
  See Burland, Cottie (Arthur)
Burland, Cottie (Arthur) 1905-1983 5
Burleigh, Robert 1936- 193
  Earlier sketches in SATA 55, 98, 146
Burlingame, (William) Roger 1889-1967 2
Burman, Alice Caddy 1896(?)-1977
  Obituary 24
Burman, Ben Lucien 1896-1984 6
  Obituary 40
Burn, Doris 1923- 1
Burn, Ted
  See Burn, Thomas E.
Burn, Thomas E. 1940- 150

Burnard, Damon 1963- *115*
Burnett, Constance Buel 1893-1975 .... *36*
Burnett, Frances (Eliza) Hodgson
    1849-1924 .... *100*
    See also YABC 2
    See also CLR *122*
Burnett Bossi, Lisa *193*
Burney, Anton
    See Hopkins, (Hector) Kenneth
Burnford, Sheila (Philip Cochrane Every)
    1918-1984 .... *3*
    Obituary *38*
    See also CLR *2*
Burnham, Gretchen
    See Sprague, Gretchen
Burnham, Nicole 1970- *161*
Burnham, Niki
    See Burnham, Nicole
Burnham, Sophy 1936- *65*
Burningham, John 1936- *160*
    Earlier sketches in SATA *16, 59, 111*
    See also CLR *9*
Burns, Diane L. 1950- *81*
    See also SAAS *24*
Burns, Eloise Wilkin
    See Wilkin, Eloise
Burns, Florence M. 1905-1988 .... *61*
Burns, Khephra 1950- *92*
Burns, Loree Griffin *193*
Burns, Marilyn 1941- *96*
    Brief entry *33*
Burns, Olive Ann 1924-1990 .... *65*
Burns, Paul C. *5*
Burns, Ray
    See Burns, Raymond (Howard)
Burns, Raymond (Howard) 1924- *9*
Burns, Theresa 1961- *84*
Burns, William A. 1909-1999 .... *5*
Burr, Dan 1951- *65*
Burr, Lonnie 1943- *47*
Burrell, Roy E(ric) C(harles) 1923- *72*
Burroughs, Edgar Rice 1875-1950 .... *41*
Burroughs, Jean Mitchell 1908- *28*
Burroughs, Polly 1925- *2*
Burroway, Janet (Gay) 1936- *23*
Burstein, Chaya M(alamud) 1923- *64*
Burstein, Fred 1950- *83*
Burstein, John 1949- *54*
    Brief entry *40*
Burstein, Stanley M.
    See Burstein, Stanley Mayer
Burstein, Stanley Mayer 1941- *175*
Bursztynski, Sue 1953- *114*
Burt, Jesse Clifton 1921-1976 .... *46*
    Obituary *20*
Burt, Olive Woolley 1894-1981 .... *4*
Burtinshaw, Julie *185*
Burton, Gennett 1945- *95*
Burton, Hester (Wood-Hill) 1913-2000 .... *74*
    Earlier sketch in SATA *7*
    See also CLR *1*
    See also SAAS *8*
Burton, Leslie
    See McGuire, Leslie (Sarah)
Burton, Marilee Robin 1950- *82*
    Earlier sketch in SATA *46*
Burton, Maurice 1898-1992 .... *23*
Burton, Rebecca 1970- *183*
Burton, Robert (Wellesley) 1941- *22*
Burton, Virginia Lee 1909-1968 .... *100*
    Earlier sketch in SATA *2*
    See also CLR *11*
Burton, William H(enry) 1890-1964 .... *11*
Busby, Ailie *192*
Busby, Cylin 1970- *118*
Busby, Edith (A. Lake) (?)-1964
    Obituary *29*
Buscaglia, (Felice) Leo(nardo) 1924-1998 ... *65*
Buscaglia, Leo F.
    See Buscaglia, (Felice) Leo(nardo)
Busch, Phyllis S. 1909- *30*

Bush, Anne Kelleher
    See Kelleher, Anne
Bush, Catherine 1961- *128*
Bushmiller, Ernest Paul 1905-1982 .... *31*
Bushmiller, Ernie
    See Bushmiller, Ernest Paul
Bushnell, Jack 1952- *86*
Busoni, Rafaello 1900-1962 .... *16*
Buss, Helen M.
    See Clarke, Margaret
Busse, Sarah Martin *194*
Busselle, Rebecca 1941- *80*
Bustard, Anne 1951- *173*
Butcher, Kristin 1951- *140*
Butenko, Bohdan 1931- *90*
Butler, Beverly Kathleen 1932- *7*
Butler, Bill
    See Butler, William Vivian
    and Butler, Ernest Alton
    and Butler, William Huxford
Butler, Charles 1963- *175*
    Earlier sketch in SATA *121*
Butler, Charles Cadman
    See Butler, Charles
Butler, Dori Hillestad 1965- *164*
Butler, Dorothy 1925- *73*
Butler, Geoff 1945- *94*
Butler, M. Christina 1934- *170*
    Earlier sketch in SATA *72*
Butler, Octavia E. 1947-2006 .... *84*
    See also CLR *65*
Butler, Octavia Estelle
    See Butler, Octavia E.
Butler, Vivian
    See Butler, William Vivian
Butler, William
    See Butler, William Vivian
Butler, William Vivian 1927-1987 .... *79*
Butters, Dorothy Gilman
    See Gilman, Dorothy
Butterworth, Emma Macalik 1928- *43*
Butterworth, Nick 1946- *149*
    Earlier sketch in SATA *106*
Butterworth, Oliver 1915-1990 .... *1*
    Obituary *66*
Butterworth, W.E.
    See Griffin, W.E.B
Butterworth, William E.
    See Griffin, W.E.B
Butterworth, William Edmund III
    See Griffin, W.E.B
Butts, Ed 1951- *177*
Butts, Edward P.
    See Butts, Ed
Butts, Ellen R(ubinstein) 1942- *93*
Buxton, Ralph
    See Silverstein, Alvin
    and Silverstein, Virginia B(arbara Opshelor)
Buzzeo, Toni 1951- *135*
Byalick, Marcia 1947- *141*
    Earlier sketch in SATA *97*
Byard, Carole (Marie) 1941- *57*
Byars, Betsy 1928- *163*
    Autobiography Feature *108*
    Earlier sketches in SATA *4, 46, 80*
    See also CLR *72*
    See also SAAS *1*
Byars, Betsy Cromer
    See Byars, Betsy
Byfield, Barbara Ninde 1930- *8*
Byman, Jeremy 1944- *129*
Bynum, Janie *133*
Byrd, Elizabeth 1912-1989 .... *34*
Byrd, Nicole
    See Zach, Cheryl (Byrd)
Byrd, Robert (John) 1942- *158*
    Earlier sketches in SATA *33, 112*
Byrne, Mary Gregg 1951- *162*

C

C. 3. 3.
    See Wilde, Oscar
C. E. M.
    See Mastrangelo, Charles E(lmer)
Cabaniss, J(ames) Allen 1911-1997 .... *5*
Cabat, Erni 1914- *74*
Cabban, Vanessa 1971- *176*
Cable, Mary 1920- *9*
Cabot, Meg 1967- *175*
    Earlier sketch in SATA *127*
    See also CLR *85*
Cabot, Meggin
    See Cabot, Meg
Cabot, Meggin Patricia
    See Cabot, Meg
Cabot, Patricia
    See Cabot, Meg
Cabral, O. M.
    See Cabral, Olga
Cabral, Olga 1909- *46*
Cabrera, Cozbi A. 1963- *177*
Cabrera, Jane 1968- *182*
    Earlier sketches in SATA *103, 152*
Cabrera, Marcela 1966- *90*
Caddy, Alice
    See Burman, Alice Caddy
Cade, Toni
    See Bambara, Toni Cade
Cadmus and Harmonia
    See Buchan, John
Cadnum, Michael 1949- *165*
    Earlier sketches in SATA *87, 121*
    See also CLR *78*
Caduto, Michael J. 1955- *103*
Cadwallader, Sharon 1936- *7*
Cady, (Walter) Harrison 1877(?)-1970 .... *19*
Caffey, Donna (J.) 1954- *110*
Cagle, Malcolm W(infield) 1918- *32*
Cahn, Rhoda 1922- *37*
Cahn, William 1912-1976 .... *37*
Cain, Arthur H(omer) 1913-1981 .... *3*
Cain, Christopher
    See Fleming, Thomas
Cain, Sheridan 1952- *186*
Caine, Geoffrey
    See Walker, Robert W.
Caines, Jeannette (Franklin) 1938- *78*
    Brief entry *43*
    See also CLR *24*
Cairns, Trevor 1922- *14*
Calabro, Marian 1954- *79*
Caldecott, Moyra 1927- *22*
Caldecott, Randolph (J.) 1846-1886 .... *100*
    Earlier sketch in SATA *17*
    See also CLR *110*
Calder, Charlotte 1952- *125*
Calder, David 1932-1997 .... *105*
Calder, Lyn
    See Calmenson, Stephanie
Calder, Marie D(onais) 1948- *96*
Calderone-Stewart, Lisa
    See Calderone-Stewart, Lisa-Marie
Calderone-Stewart, Lisa-Marie 1958- *123*
Caldwell, Doreen (Mary) 1942- *71*
Caldwell, John C(ope) 1913-1984 .... *7*
Caletti, Deb 1963- *171*
Calhoun, B. B. 1961- *98*
Calhoun, Chad
    See Barrett, Neal, Jr.
    and Cunningham, Chet
    and Goulart, Ron
Calhoun, Dia 1959- *183*
    Earlier sketch in SATA *129*
Calhoun, Mary
    See Wilkins, Mary Huiskamp
Calhoun, T.B.
    See Bisson, Terry
Cali, Davide 1972- *190*
Calif, Ruth 1922- *67*

Calkins, Franklin
    See Stratemeyer, Edward L.
Call, Greg *197*
Call, Hughie Florence 1890-1969 .... *1*
Callahan, Dorothy M(onahan) 1934- *39*
    Brief entry *35*
Callahan, Philip Serna 1923- *25*
Callan, Jamie 1954- *59*
Callan, Jim 1951- *181*
Callaway, Bernice (Anne) 1923- *48*
Callaway, Kathy 1943- *36*
Callen, Larry
    See Callen, Lawrence Willard, Jr.
Callen, Lawrence Willard, Jr. 1927- *19*
Calley, Karin 1965- *92*
Calmenson, Stephanie 1952- *139*
    Brief entry *37*
    Earlier sketches in SATA *51, 84*
Calvert, Elinor H.
    See Lasell, Elinor H.
Calvert, John
    See Leaf, (Wilbur) Munro
Calvert, Patricia 1931- *132*
    Earlier sketches in SATA *45, 69*
    See also SAAS *17*
Camburn, Carol A.
    See Camburn-Bracalente, Carol A.
Camburn-Bracalente, Carol A. 1962- *118*
Cameron, Ann 1943- *129*
    Earlier sketches in SATA *27, 89*
    See also SAAS *20*
Cameron, Edna M. 1905-1999 .... *3*
Cameron, Eleanor (Frances) 1912-1996 .... *25*
    Obituary *93*
    Earlier sketch in SATA *1*
    See also CLR *72*
    See also SAAS *10*
Cameron, Elizabeth
    See Nowell, Elizabeth Cameron
Cameron, Elizabeth Jane 1910-1976 .... *32*
    Obituary *30*
Cameron, Ian
    See Payne, Donald Gordon
Cameron, M(alcolm) G(ordon) Graham
    See Graham-Cameron, M(alcolm) G(ordon)
Cameron, M. Graham
    See Graham-Cameron, M(alcolm) G(ordon)
Cameron, Mike Graham
    See Graham-Cameron, M(alcolm) G(ordon)
Cameron, Polly 1928- *2*
Cameron, Scott 1962- *84*
Camp, Charles L. 1893-1975
    Obituary *31*
Camp, Lindsay 1957- *133*
Camp, Madeleine L'Engle
    See L'Engle, Madeleine
Camp, Walter (Chauncey) 1859-1925
    See YABC *1*
Campbell, (Elizabeth) Andrea 1963- *50*
Campbell, Ann R. 1925- *11*
Campbell, Bill 1960- *89*
Campbell, Bruce
    See Epstein, Samuel
Campbell, Camilla 1905-1992 .... *26*
Campbell, Carole R. 1939- *125*
Campbell, Hope 1925- *20*
Campbell, Hugh 1930- *90*
Campbell, Jane
    See Edwards, Jane Campbell
Campbell, Julie
    See Tatham, Julie Campbell
Campbell, Patricia J(ean) 1930- *45*
Campbell, Patty
    See Campbell, Patricia J(ean)
Campbell, Peter A. 1948- *99*
Campbell, R. W.
    See Campbell, Rosemae Wells
Campbell, Robin
    See Strachan, Ian

Campbell, Rod 1945- *98*
    Brief entry *44*
    Earlier sketch in SATA *51*
Campbell, Rosemae Wells 1909- *1*
Camper, Cathy 1956- *170*
Campion, Nardi Reeder 1917-2007 .... *22*
Campling, Elizabeth 1948- *53*
Campoy, F. Isabel 1946- *181*
    Earlier sketch in SATA *143*
Camps, Luis 1928- *66*
Canales, Viola 1957- *141*
Candell, Victor 1903-1977
    Obituary *24*
Canfield, Dorothea F.
    See Fisher, Dorothy (Frances) Canfield
Canfield, Dorothea Frances
    See Fisher, Dorothy (Frances) Canfield
Canfield, Dorothy
    See Fisher, Dorothy (Frances) Canfield
Canfield, Jack 1944- *164*
Canfield, Jane White 1897-1984 .... *32*
    Obituary *38*
Canfield, Muriel 1935- *94*
Caniff, Milton 1907-1988
    Obituary *58*
Caniff, Milton Arthur Paul
    See Caniff, Milton
Cann, Helen 1969- *179*
    Earlier sketch in SATA *124*
Cann, Kate 1954- *152*
    Earlier sketch in SATA *103*
Cannan, Joanna
    See Pullein-Thompson, Joanna Maxwell
Cannell, Jon *196*
Cannell, Jonathan C.
    See Cannell, Jon
Cannon, A(nn) E(dwards) *163*
    Earlier sketch in SATA *93*
Cannon, Bettie (Waddell) 1922- *59*
Cannon, Curt
    See Hunter, Evan
Cannon, Eileen E(mily) 1948- *119*
Cannon, Frank
    See Mayhar, Ardath
Cannon, Janell 1957- *128*
    Earlier sketch in SATA *78*
    See also CLR *120*
Cannon, Marian G. 1923- *85*
Cannon, Taffy
    See Cannon, Eileen E(mily)
Cantone, AnnaLaura *182*
Canusi, Jose
    See Barker, S(quire) Omar
Canyon, Christopher 1966- *150*
    Earlier sketch in SATA *104*
Capek, Michael 1947- *142*
    Earlier sketch in SATA *96*
Capes, Bernard (Edward Joseph)
    1854-1918 .... *116*
Caple, Kathy *193*
Caple, Laurie 1958- *201*
Caplin, Alfred Gerald 1909-1979 .... *61*
    Obituary *21*
Caponigro, John Paul 1965- *84*
Capote, Truman 1924-1984 .... *91*
Capp, Al
    See Caplin, Alfred Gerald
Cappel, Constance 1936- *22*
Cappetta, Cynthia 1949- *125*
Cappo, Nan Willard 1955- *143*
Capps, Benjamin (Franklin) 1922- *9*
Cappy Dick
    See Cleveland, George
Captain Kangaroo
    See Keeshan, Robert J.
Captain Wheeler
    See Ellis, Edward S(ylvester)
Captain Young of Yale
    See Stratemeyer, Edward L.
Capucilli, Alyssa Satin 1957- *163*
    Earlier sketch in SATA *115*

Capucine
    See Mazille, Capucine
Caraher, Kim(berley Elizabeth) 1961- *105*
Caraker, Mary 1929- *74*
Caras, Roger A(ndrew) 1928-2001 .... *12*
    Obituary *127*
Caravantes, Peggy 1935- *140*
Caraway, Caren 1939- *57*
Carbone, Elisa 1954- *173*
    Earlier sketches in SATA *81, 137*
Carbone, Elisa Lynn
    See Carbone, Elisa
Carbonnier, Jeanne 1894-1974 .... *3*
    Obituary *34*
Card, Orson Scott 1951- *127*
    Earlier sketch in SATA *83*
    See also CLR *116*
Care, Felicity
    See Coury, Louise Andree
Carew, Jan 1925- *51*
    Brief entry *40*
Carew, Jan Rynveld
    See Carew, Jan
Carey, Bonnie
    See Marshall, Bonnie C.
Carey, Charles W., Jr. 1951- *170*
Carey, Ernestine Gilbreth 1908-2006 .... *2*
    Obituary *177*
Carey, Janet Lee 1954(?)- *185*
Carey, Lisa *110*
Carey, M. V.
    See Carey, Mary V(irginia)
Carey, Mary V(irginia) 1925-1994 .... *44*
    Brief entry *39*
Carey, Peter 1943- *94*
Carey, Peter Philip
    See Carey, Peter
Carey, Valerie Scho 1949- *60*
Carheden, Goorel Kristina
    See Naaslund, Goorel Kristina
Carigiet, Alois 1902-1985 .... *24*
    Obituary *47*
    See also CLR *38*
Carini, Edward 1923- *9*
Carkeet, David 1946- *75*
Carle, Eric 1929- *163*
    Earlier sketches in SATA *4, 65, 120*
    See also CLR *72*
    See also SAAS *6*
Carleton, Captain L. C.
    See Ellis, Edward S(ylvester)
Carleton, Captain Latham C.
    See Ellis, Edward S(ylvester)
Carleton, Latham C.
    See Ellis, Edward S(ylvester)
Carley, V(an Ness) Royal 1906-1976
    Obituary *20*
Carling, Amelia Lau 1949- *164*
    Earlier sketch in SATA *119*
Carlisle, Carolyn
    See Hawes, Louise
Carlisle, Clark
    See Holding, James (Clark Carlisle, Jr.)
Carlisle, Olga Andreyev 1930- *35*
Carlock, Miriam
    See Eyerly, Jeannette
Carls, Claudia 1978- *198*
Carlsen, G(eorge) Robert 1917- *30*
Carlsen, Ruth C(hristoffer) 1918- *2*
Carlson, Bernice Wells 1910- *8*
Carlson, Dale (Bick) 1935- *1*
Carlson, Daniel (Bick) 1960- *27*
Carlson, Kirsten 1968- *192*
Carlson, Kirsten M.
    See Carlson, Kirsten
Carlson, Laurie 1952- *173*
    Earlier sketch in SATA *101*
Carlson, Laurie Winn
    See Carlson, Laurie
Carlson, Melody 1956- *171*
    Earlier sketch in SATA *113*

Carlson, Nancy L.
    See Carlson, Nancy L(ee)
Carlson, Nancy L(ee) 1953- *144*
    Brief entry *45*
    Earlier sketches in SATA *56, 90*
Carlson, Natalie Savage 1906-1997 .... *68*
    Earlier sketch in SATA *2*
    See also SAAS *4*
Carlson, Susan Johnston 1953- *88*
Carlson, Vada F. 1897- *16*
Carlstrom, Nancy White 1948- *156*
    Brief entry *48*
    Earlier sketches in SATA *53, 92*
Carlton, Keith
    See Robertson, Keith (Carlton)
Carlton, Susan 1960- *195*
Carlyon, Richard *55*
Carman, Patrick 1966- *197*
    Earlier sketch in SATA *161*
Carmer, Carl (Lamson) 1893-1976 .... *37*
    Obituary *30*
Carmer, Elizabeth Black 1904- *24*
Carmi, Giora 1944- *149*
    Earlier sketch in SATA *79*
Carmichael, Carrie
    See Carmichael, Harriet
Carmichael, Harriet *40*
Carmody, Isobelle 1958- *191*
    Earlier sketch in SATA *161*
Carmody, Isobelle Jane
    See Carmody, Isobelle
Carney, Elizabeth 1981- *199*
Carney, Jeff 1962- *196*
Carney, Mary Lou 1949- *170*
Carol, Bill J.
    See Knott, William C(ecil, Jr.)
Caron, Romi
    See Caron-Kyselkova', Romana
Caron-Kyselkova', Romana 1967- *94*
Caroselli, Remus F(rancis) 1916- *36*
Carpelan, Bo 1926- *8*
Carpelan, Bo Gustaf Bertelsson
    See Carpelan, Bo
Carpenter, (John) Allan 1917- *81*
    Earlier sketch in SATA *3*
Carpenter, Angelica Shirley 1945- *153*
    Earlier sketch in SATA *71*
Carpenter, Frances 1890-1972 .... *3*
    Obituary *27*
Carpenter, John (Howard) 1948- *58*
Carpenter, Johnny
    See Carpenter, John (Howard)
Carpenter, Patricia (Healy Evans) 1920- *11*
Carr, Glyn
    See Styles, (Frank) Showell
Carr, Harriett H(elen) 1899-1977 .... *3*
Carr, Jan 1953- *132*
    Earlier sketch in SATA *89*
Carr, M. J.
    See Carr, Jan
Carr, Mary Jane 1899-1988 .... *2*
    Obituary *55*
Carr, Philippa
    See Hibbert, Eleanor Alice Burford
Carr, Roger Vaughan 1937- *95*
Carrel, Annette Felder 1929- *90*
Carrick, Carol (Hatfield) 1935- *118*
    Earlier sketches in SATA *7, 63*
    See also SAAS *18*
Carrick, Donald (F.) 1929-1989 .... *63*
    Earlier sketch in SATA *7*
Carrick, Malcolm 1945- *28*
Carrick, Paul 1972- *194*
Carrier, Lark 1947- *71*
    Brief entry *50*
Carrier, Roch 1937- *166*
    Earlier sketch in SATA *105*
Carrighar, Sally 1898-1985 .... *24*
Carrington, G. A.
    See Cunningham, Chet

Carrington, Marsha Gray 1954- *168*
    Earlier sketch in SATA *111*
Carris, Joan 1938- *182*
    Brief entry *42*
    Earlier sketch in SATA *44*
Carris, Joan Davenport
    See Carris, Joan
Carroll, Curt
    See Bishop, Curtis (Kent)
Carroll, Elizabeth
    See Barkin, Carol
    and James, Elizabeth
Carroll, Jenny
    See Cabot, Meg
Carroll, (Archer) Latrobe 1894-1996 .... *7*
Carroll, Laura
    See Parr, Lucy
Carroll, Lewis 1832-1898 .... *100*
    See also YABC *2*
    See also CLR *108*
Carroll, Raymond 1924- *86*
    Brief entry *47*
Carruth, Hayden 1921-2008 .... *47*
    Obituary *197*
Carryl, Charles E. 1841-1920 .... *114*
Carryl, Charles Edward
    See Carryl, Charles E.
Carse, Robert 1902-1971 .... *5*
Carson, J(ohn) Franklin 1920-1981 .... *1*
    Obituary *107*
Carson, Mary Kay 1964- *200*
    Earlier sketch in SATA *150*
Carson, Rachel
    See Carson, Rachel Louise
Carson, Rachel Louise 1907-1964 .... *23*
Carson, Rosalind
    See Chittenden, Margaret
Carson, S. M.
    See Gorsline, (Sally) Marie
Carson, William C. 1928- *154*
Carter, Abby *184*
Carter, Alden R 1947- *137*
    Earlier sketch in SATA *67*
    See also CLR *22*
    See also SAAS *18*
Carter, Alden Richardson
    See Carter, Alden R
Carter, Andy 1948- *134*
Carter, Angela 1940-1992 .... *66*
    Obituary *70*
Carter, Angela Olive
    See Carter, Angela
Carter, Anne Laurel 1953- *135*
Carter, Asa Earl
    See Carter, Forrest
Carter, Avis Murton
    See Allen, Kenneth S.
Carter, Bruce
    See Hough, Richard (Alexander)
Carter, Carol S(hadis) 1948- *124*
Carter, David A. 1957- *170*
    Earlier sketch in SATA *114*
Carter, Don 1958- *192*
    Earlier sketch in SATA *124*
Carter, Dorothy Sharp 1921- *8*
Carter, Forrest 1927(?)-1979 .... *32*
Carter, Helene 1887-1960 .... *15*
Carter, (William) Hodding, Jr. 1907-1972 ...... *2*
    Obituary *27*
Carter, James Earl, Jr.
    See Carter, Jimmy
Carter, Jimmy 1924- *79*
Carter, Katharine J(ones) 1905-1984 .... *2*
Carter, Lin(wood Vrooman) 1930-1988 .... *91*
Carter, Mike 1936- *138*

Carter, Nick
    See Avallone, Michael (Angelo, Jr.)
    and Ballard, (Willis) Todhunter
    and Crider, Bill
    and Cassiday, Bruce (Bingham)
    and Chastain, Thomas
    and Dey, Frederic (Merrill) Van Rensselaer
    and Garside, (Clifford) Jack
    and Hayes, Ralph E(ugene)
    and Henderson, M(arilyn) R(uth)
    and Lynds, Dennis
    and Lynds, Gayle (Hallenbeck)
    and Randisi, Robert J.
    and Rasof, Henry
    and Stratemeyer, Edward L.
    and Smith, Martin Cruz
    and Swain, Dwight V(reeland)
    and Vardeman, Robert E(dward)
    and Wallmann, Jeffrey M(iner)
    and White, Lionel
Carter, Peter 1929- *57*
Carter, Phyllis Ann
    See Eberle, Irmengarde
Carter, Samuel (Thomson) III 1904-1988 .... *37*
    Obituary *60*
Carter, William E. 1926-1983 .... *1*
    Obituary *35*
Cartlidge, Michelle 1950- *96*
    Brief entry *37*
    Earlier sketch in SATA *49*
Cartner, William Carruthers 1910- *11*
Cartwright, Ann 1940- *78*
Cartwright, Reg(inald Ainsley) 1938- *64*
Cartwright, Sally 1923- *9*
Carusone, Al 1949- *89*
Carvell, Marlene *172*
Carver, John
    See Gardner, Richard (M.)
Carwell, L'Ann
    See McKissack, Patricia C.
Cary
    See Cary, Louis F(avreau)
Cary, Barbara Knapp 1912(?)-1975
    Obituary *31*
Cary, Kate 1967(?)- *174*
Cary, Louis F(avreau) 1915- *9*
Caryl, Jean
    See Kaplan, Jean Caryl Korn
Casanova, Mary 1957- *186*
    Earlier sketches in SATA *94, 136*
Cascone, A.G.
    See Cascone, Annette
    and Cascone, Gina
Cascone, Annette 1960- *103*
Cascone, Gina 1955- *103*
Case, Marshal T(aylor) 1941- *9*
Case, Michael
    See Howard, Robert West
Caseley, Judith 1951- *159*
    Brief entry *53*
    Earlier sketch in SATA *87*
Casewit, Curtis W(erner) 1922-2002 .... *4*
Casey, Barbara (Louise) 1944- *147*
    Earlier sketch in SATA *79*
Casey, Brigid 1950- *9*
Casey, Tina 1959- *141*
Cash, Ellen Lewis Buell 1905-1989
    Obituary *64*
Cash, Megan Montague *160*
Casilla, Robert 1959- *146*
    Earlier sketch in SATA *75*
Cason, Mabel Earp 1892-1965 .... *10*
Cass, Joan E(velyn) *1*
Cass-Beggs, Barbara 1904- *62*
Cassedy, Patrice (Rinaldo) 1953- *149*
Cassedy, Sylvia 1930-1989 .... *77*
    Obituary *61*
    Earlier sketch in SATA *27*
    See also CLR *26*
Cassel, Lili
    See Wronker, Lili Cassel

Cassels, Jean 173
Cassidy, Anne 1952- 166
Cassidy, Cathy 1962- 183
Casson, Hugh Maxwell 1910-1999 65
  Obituary 115
Cassutt, Michael 1954- 78
Cassutt, Michael Joseph
  See Cassutt, Michael
Castaldi, Elicia 194
Castaldo, Nancy Fusco 1962- 151
  Earlier sketch in SATA *93*
Castaneda, Omar S. 1954- 71
Castell, Megan
  See Williams, Jeanne
Castellanos, Jane Mollie Robinson
  1913-2001 9
Castellon, Federico 1914-1971 48
Castellucci, Cecil 1969- 176
Castillo, Edmund L. 1924-2005 1
  Obituary 167
Castillo, Lauren 195
Castle, Lee
  See Ogan, George F.
  and Ogan, Margaret E. (Nettles)
Castle, Paul
  See Howard, Vernon (Linwood)
Castle, Robert
  See Hamilton, Edmond
Castrovilla, Selene 1966- 186
Caswell, Brian 1954- 171
  Earlier sketch in SATA *97*
Caswell, Helen (Rayburn) 1923- 12
Catalano, Dominic 1956- 163
  Earlier sketch in SATA *76*
Catalano, Grace (A.) 1961- 99
Catalanotto, Peter 1959- 195
  Autobiography Feature 113
  Earlier sketches in SATA *70, 114, 159*
  See also CLR *68*
  See also SAAS *25*
Catanese, P.W. 1961- 179
Cate, Annette LeBlanc 196
Cate, Dick
  See Cate, Richard Edward Nelson
Cate, Richard Edward Nelson 1932- 28
Cather, Willa (Sibert) 1873-1947 30
  See also CLR *98*
Catherall, Arthur 1906-1980 74
  Earlier sketches in SATA *3, 4*
Cathon, Laura E(lizabeth) 1908-1991 27
Catlett, Elizabeth 1919(?)- 82
Catlin, Wynelle 1930- 13
Catlow, Nikalas
  See Catlow, Niki
Catlow, Niki 1975- 193
Cato, Heather 105
Cato, Sheila 114
Catran, Ken 1944- 190
Catrow, David
  See Catrow, David J. III
Catrow, David J. III 152
Catt, Louis
  See French, Vivian
Cattell, James 1954- 123
Catton, (Charles) Bruce 1899-1978 2
  Obituary 24
Catz, Max
  See Glaser, Milton
Caudell, Marian 1930- 52
Caudill, Rebecca 1899-1985 1
  Obituary 44
Cauley, Lorinda Bryan 1951- 46
  Brief entry 43
Caulfield, Peggy F. 1926-1987
  Obituary 53
Cauman, Samuel 1910-1971 48
Causley, Charles (Stanley) 1917-2003 66
  Obituary 149
  Earlier sketch in SATA *3*
  See also CLR *30*
Cavallaro, Ann (Abelson) 1918- 62

Cavallo, Diana 1931- 7
Cavanagh, Helen (Carol) 1939- 98
  Brief entry 37
  Earlier sketch in SATA *48*
Cavanah, Frances 1899-1982 31
  Earlier sketch in SATA *1*
Cavanna, Betty
  See Harrison, Elizabeth (Allen) Cavanna
Cavanna, Elizabeth
  See Harrison, Elizabeth (Allen) Cavanna
Cave, Kathryn 1948- 123
  Earlier sketch in SATA *76*
Cavendish, Peter
  See Horler, Sydney
Cavin, Ruth (Brodie) 1918- 38
Cavoukian, Raffi 1948- 68
Cawley, Winifred 1915- 13
Caxton, Pisistratus
  See Lytton, Edward G(eorge) E(arle) L(ytton)
  Bulwer-Lytton Baron
Cazeau, Charles J(ay) 1931- 65
Cazet, Denys 1938- 191
  Brief entry 41
  Earlier sketches in SATA *52, 99, 163*
Cazzola, Gus 1934- 73
Cebulash, Mel 1937- 91
  Earlier sketch in SATA *10*
Ceccoli, Nicoletta 181
Cecil, Randy 1968- 187
Cecka, Melanie 199
Ceder, Georgiana Dorcas -1985 10
Celenza, Anna Harwell 133
Celestino, Martha Laing
  See Laing, Martha
Cepeda, Joe 159
Cerf, Bennett (Alfred) 1898-1971 7
Cerf, Christopher (Bennett) 1941- 2
Cermak, Martin
  See Duchacek, Ivo D(uka)
Cerullo, Mary M. 1949- 145
  Earlier sketch in SATA *86*
Cervon, Jacqueline
  See Moussard, Jacqueline
Cetin, Frank Stanley 1921- 2
Chabon, Michael 1963- 145
Chaconas, D.J.
  See Chaconas, Dori
Chaconas, Dori 1938- 175
  Earlier sketch in SATA *145*
Chaconas, Doris J.
  See Chaconas, Dori
Chadwick, Lester 67
  Earlier sketch in SATA *1*
Chaffee, Allen 3
Chaffin, Lillie D(orton) 1925- 4
Chaikin, Miriam 1924- 152
  Earlier sketches in SATA *24, 102*
Chall, Marsha Wilson 150
Challand, Helen J(ean) 1921- 64
Challans, Mary 1905-1983 23
  Obituary 36
Chalmers, Mary (Eileen) 1927- 6
  See also SAAS *14*
Chamberlain, Barbara A.
  See Azore, Barbara
Chamberlain, Margaret 1954- 46
Chamberlin, Kate 1945- 105
Chamberlin, Mary 1960- 177
Chamberlin, Rich 177
Chamberlin, Richard
  See Chamberlin, Rich
Chambers, Aidan 1934- 171
  Earlier sketches in SATA *1, 69, 108*
  See also SAAS *12*
Chambers, Bradford 1922-1984
  Obituary 39
Chambers, Catherine E.
  See St. John, Nicole
Chambers, John W. 1933- 57
  Brief entry 46

Chambers, Kate
  See St. John, Nicole
Chambers, Margaret Ada Eastwood 1911- 2
Chambers, Peggy
  See Chambers, Margaret Ada Eastwood
Chambers, Robert W(illiam) 1865-1933 107
Chambliss, Maxie 186
Chan, Gillian 1954- 147
  Earlier sketch in SATA *102*
Chance, James T.
  See Carpenter, John (Howard)
Chance, John T.
  See Carpenter, John (Howard)
Chance, Stephen
  See Turner, Philip (William)
Chandler, Caroline A(ugusta) 1906-1979 22
  Obituary 24
Chandler, David P(orter) 1933- 28
Chandler, Edna Walker 1908-1982 11
  Obituary 31
Chandler, Jennifer
  See Westwood, Jennifer
Chandler, Karen 1959- 122
Chandler, Linda S(mith) 1929- 39
Chandler, Pauline 175
Chandler, Robert 1953- 40
Chandler, Ruth Forbes 1894-1978 2
  Obituary 26
Chandonnet, Ann F. 1943- 92
Chaney, Jill 1932- 87
Chang, Chih-Wei 1966- 111
Chang, Cindy 1968- 90
Chang, Margaret 1941- 71
Chang, Margaret Scrogin
  See Chang, Margaret
Chang, Raymond 1939- 142
  Earlier sketches in SATA *71, 142 PEN*
Chanin, Michael 1952- 84
Channel, A. R.
  See Catherall, Arthur
Chapian, Marie 1938- 29
Chapin, Alene Olsen Dalton 1915(?)-1986
  Obituary 47
Chapin, Tom 1945- 83
Chapman, Allen 67
  Earlier sketch in SATA *1*
Chapman, Cheryl O(rth) 1948- 80
Chapman, (Constance) Elizabeth (Mann)
  1919- 10
Chapman, Gaye 1970- 200
Chapman, Gaye Coralie
  See Chapman, Gaye
Chapman, Gaynor 1935- 32
Chapman, Gillian 1955- 120
Chapman, Jane 1970- 176
  Earlier sketch in SATA *122*
Chapman, Jean 104
  Earlier sketch in SATA *34*
  See also CLR *65*
Chapman, John Stanton Higham 1891-1972
  Obituary 27
Chapman, Lee
  See Bradley, Marion Zimmer
Chapman, Lynne 1960- 197
Chapman, Lynne F(erguson) 1963- 150
  Earlier sketch in SATA *94*
Chapman, Maristan
  See Chapman, John Stanton Higham
Chapman, Vera (Ivy May) 1898-1996 33
Chapman, Walker
  See Silverberg, Robert
Chappell, Audrey 1954- 72
Chappell, Crissa-Jean 198
Chappell, Warren 1904-1991 68
  Obituary 67
  Earlier sketch in SATA *6*
  See also SAAS *10*
Chapra, Mimi 182
Charbonneau, Eileen 1951- 118
  Earlier sketch in SATA *84*
Charbonnet, Gabrielle 1961- 81

Chardiet, Bernice (Kroll) 1927(?)- 27
Charest, Emily MacLachlan 198
Charles, Donald
See Meighan, Donald Charles
Charles, Louis
See Stratemeyer, Edward L.
Charles, Nicholas J.
See Kuskin, Karla
Charles, Norma 153
Charles, Veronika Martenova 182
Charlip, Remy 1929- 119
Earlier sketches in SATA 4, 68
See also CLR 8
Charlot, Jean 1898-1979 8
Obituary 31
Charlot, Martin (Day) 1944- 64
Charlton, Michael (Alan) 1923- 34
Charlton-Trujillo, e.E. 189
Charmatz, Bill 1925-2005 7
Charnas, Suzy McKee 1939- 110
Earlier sketch in SATA 61
Charosh, Mannis 1906- 5
Chartier, Normand L. 1945- 66
Chase, Alice
See McHargue, Georgess
Chase, Alyssa 1965- 92
Chase, Andra 1942- 91
Chase, Emily
See Aks, Patricia
and Garwood, Julie
and Sachs, Judith
and White, Carol
Chase, Mary (Coyle) 1907-1981 17
Obituary 29
Chase, Mary Ellen 1887-1973 10
Chase, Richard 1904-1988 64
Obituary 56
Chase, Samantha
See Glick, Ruth (Burtnick)
Chast, Roz 1954- 97
Chastain, Madye Lee 1908-1989 4
Chataway, Carol 1955- 140
Chatterjee, Debjani 1952- 83
Chauncy, Nan(cen Beryl Masterman)
1900-1970 6
See also CLR 6
Chaundler, Christine 1887-1972 1
Obituary 25
Chayka, Doug 196
Chbosky, Stephen 1972- 164
Cheaney, Janie B.
See Cheaney, J.B.
Cheaney, J.B. 1950- 188
Chee, Cheng-Khee 1934- 79
Cheese, Chloe 1952- 118
Chekhonte, Antosha
See Chekhov, Anton (Pavlovich)
Chekhov, Anton (Pavlovich) 1860-1904 90
Chelushkin, Kirill 1968- 186
Chen, Anthony 1929- 6
Chen, Chih-Yuan 1975- 155
Chen, Ju-Hong 1941- 78
Chen, Sara
See Odgers, Sally Farrell
Chen, Tony
See Chen, Anthony
Chen, Yong 1963- 183
Chen, Yuan-tsung 1932- 65
Chenault, Nell
See Smith, Linell Nash
Chenery, Janet (Dai) 1923- 25
Cheney, Cora 1916-1999 3
Obituary 110
Cheney, Glenn (Alan) 1951- 99
Cheney, Lynne V. 1941- 152
Cheney, Ted
See Cheney, Theodore Albert
Cheney, Theodore A. Rees
See Cheney, Theodore Albert
Cheney, Theodore Albert 1928- 11

Cheng, Andrea 1957- 172
Earlier sketch in SATA 128
Cheng, Christopher 1959- 173
Earlier sketch in SATA 106
Cheng, Judith 1955- 36
Cheng, Shan
See Jiang, Cheng An
Cheripko, Jan 1951- 155
Earlier sketch in SATA 83
Chermayeff, Ivan 1932- 47
Chernenko, Dan
See Chernenko, Dan
Chernoff, Dorothy A.
See Ernst, (Lyman) John
Chernoff, Goldie Taub 1909- 10
Cherry, Carolyn Janice
See Cherryh, C.J.
Cherry, Lynne 1952- 99
Earlier sketch in SATA 34
Cherryh, C.J. 1942- 172
Earlier sketch in SATA 93
Cherryholmes, Anne
See Price, Olive
Cheshire, Simon 172
Chesler, Bernice 1932-2002 59
Chess, Victoria (Dickerson) 1939- 92
Earlier sketch in SATA 33
Chessa, Francesca 191
Chester, Deborah 1957- 85
Chester, Kate
See Guccione, Leslie Davis
Chesterton, G(ilbert) K(eith) 1874-1936 27
Chesworth, Michael 160
Chetin, Helen 1922- 6
Chetwin, Grace 86
Brief entry 50
Chevalier, Christa 1937- 35
Chevalier, Tracy 1962- 128
Chew, Ruth 1920- 7
Chichester Clark, Emma 1955- 69
Earlier sketches in SATA 117, 156
Chidsey, Donald Barr 1902-1981 3
Obituary 27
Chiefari, Janet D. 1942- 58
Chien, Catia 193
Chien-min, Lin
See Rumford, James
Child, L. Maria
See Child, Lydia Maria
Child, Lauren 1965- 183
Earlier sketches in SATA 119, 160
Child, Lincoln 1957- 113
Child, Lincoln B.
See Child, Lincoln
Child, Lydia Maria 1802-1880 67
Child, Mrs.
See Child, Lydia Maria
Child, Philip 1898-1978 47
Children's Shepherd, The
See Westphal, Arnold Carl
Childress, Alice 1920-1994 81
Earlier sketches in SATA 7, 48
See also CLR 14
Childs, H(alla) Fay (Cochrane) 1890-1971 1
Obituary 25
Chilton, Charles (Frederick William)
1917- 102
Chima, Cinda Williams 192
Chimaera
See Farjeon, Eleanor
Chin, Richard (M.) 1946- 52
Chinery, Michael 1938- 26
Chin-Lee, Cynthia 1958- 102
Chin-Lee D., Cynthia
See Chin-Lee, Cynthia
Chippendale, Lisa A. 158
Chipperfield, Joseph Eugene 1912-1980(?) .. 87
Earlier sketch in SATA 2
Chisholm, P. F.
See Finney, Patricia
Chislett, Gail (Elaine) 1948- 58

Chittenden, Elizabeth F. 1903-1999 9
Chittenden, Margaret 1935- 28
Chittum, Ida 1918- 7
Chitwood, Suzanne Tanner 1958- 160
Chmielarz, Sharon Lee 1940- 72
Choate, Judith (Newkirk) 1940- 30
Chocolate, Debbi 1954- 96
Chocolate, Deborah M. Newton
See Chocolate, Debbi
Chodos-Irvine, Margaret 152
Choi, Sook Nyul 1937- 73
Autobiography Feature 126
See also CLR 53
Choi, Yangsook 178
Choldenko, Gennifer 1957- 182
Earlier sketch in SATA 135
Chorao, (Ann Mc)Kay (Sproat) 1936- 162
Earlier sketches in SATA 8, 69
Choron, Sandra (Zena Samelson) 1950- 146
Choung, Eun-hee 199
Chown, Marcus 1959- 137
Choyce, Lesley 1951- 165
Earlier sketch in SATA 94
Chrisman, Arthur Bowie 1889-1953 124
See also YABC 1
Christelow, Eileen 1943- 184
Autobiography Feature 120
Brief entry 35
Earlier sketches in SATA 38, 90
Christensen, Bonnie 1951- 157
Earlier sketch in SATA 110
Christensen, Gardell Dano 1907-1991 1
Christensen, Laurie
See Steding, Laurie
Christesen, Barbara 1940- 40
Christgau, Alice Erickson 1902-1977 13
Christian, Mary Blount 1933- 9
Christiana, David 195
Christie, Agatha (Mary Clarissa)
1890-1976 36
Christie, Ann Philippa
See Pearce, Philippa
Christie, Gregory
See Christie, R. Gregory
Christie, Philippa
See Pearce, Philippa
Christie, R. Gregory 1971- 185
Earlier sketch in SATA 127
Christopher, John
See Youd, Samuel
Christopher, Louise
See Hale, Arlene
Christopher, Matt(hew Frederick)
1917-1997 80
Obituary 99
Earlier sketches in SATA 2, 47
See also CLR 119
See also SAAS 9
Christopher, Milbourne 1914(?)-1984 46
Christy, Howard Chandler 1873-1952 21
Chrustowski, Rick 176
Chrystie, Frances N(icholson) 1904-1986 60
Chu, Daniel 1933- 11
Chukovsky, Kornei (Ivanovich) 1882-1969 . 34
Earlier sketch in SATA 5
Church, Caroline Jayne 179
Church, Richard 1893-1972 3
Churchill, E(lmer) Richard 1937- 11
Churchill, Elizabeth
See Hough, Richard (Alexander)
Chute, B(eatrice) J(oy) 1913-1987 2
Obituary 53
Chute, Marchette (Gaylord) 1909-1994 1
Chwast, Jacqueline 1932- 6
Chwast, Seymour 1931- 146
Earlier sketches in SATA 18, 96
Ciardi, John (Anthony) 1916-1986 65
Obituary 46
Earlier sketch in SATA 1
See also CLR 19
See also SAAS 26

Ciccone, Madonna Louise Veronica
    See Madonna
Ciment, James D. 1958- *140*
Cirrone, Dorian *182*
Cisneros, Sandra 1954-
    See CLR *123*
Citra, Becky 1954- *137*
Citrin, Michael 1965(?)- *183*
Clair, Andree *19*
Clampett, Bob 1914(?)-1985 .... *44*
    Obituary *38*
Clampett, Robert
    See Clampett, Bob
Clapp, John 1968- *109*
Clapp, Patricia 1912- *74*
    Earlier sketch in SATA *4*
    See also SAAS *4*
Clare, Ellen
    See Sinclair, Olga
Clare, Helen
    See Clarke, Pauline
Claremont, Chris 1950- *87*
Claremont, Christopher Simon
    See Claremont, Chris
Clark, Ann Nolan 1896-1995 .... *82*
    Obituary *87*
    Earlier sketch in SATA *4*
    See also CLR *16*
    See also SAAS *16*
Clark, Champ 1923-2002 .... *47*
Clark, Christopher (Anthony) Stuart
    See Stuart-Clark, Christopher (Anthony)
Clark, Clara Gillow 1951- *154*
    Earlier sketch in SATA *84*
Clark, David
    See Hardcastle, Michael
Clark, David Allen
    See Ernst, (Lyman) John
Clark, Emma Chichester
    See Chichester Clark, Emma
Clark, Frank J(ames) 1922- *18*
Clark, Garel
    See Garelick, May
Clark, Halsey
    See Deming, Richard
Clark, Joan
    See Benson, Mildred
Clark, Joan 1934- *182*
    Earlier sketches in SATA *59, 96*
Clark, Leonard 1905-1981 .... *30*
    Obituary *29*
Clark, M. R.
    See Clark, Mavis Thorpe
Clark, Margaret (D.) 1943- *126*
Clark, Margaret Goff 1913- *82*
    Earlier sketch in SATA *8*
Clark, Mary Higgins 1929- *46*
Clark, Mavis Thorpe 1909-1999 .... *74*
    Earlier sketch in SATA *8*
    See also CLR *30*
    See also SAAS *5*
Clark, Merle
    See Gessner, Lynne
Clark, Patricia Denise 1921- *117*
Clark, Patricia Finrow 1929- *11*
Clark, Ronald Harry 1904-1999 .... *193*
Clark, Ronald William 1916-1987 .... *2*
    Obituary *52*
Clark, Sherryl 1956- *149*
Clark, Van D(eusen) 1909-1974 .... *2*
Clark, Virginia
    See Gray, Patricia (Clark)
Clark, Walter Van Tilburg 1909-1971 .... *8*
Clarke, Arthur
    See Clarke, Arthur C.
Clarke, Arthur C. 1917-2008 .... *115*
    Obituary *191*
    Earlier sketches in SATA *13, 70*
    See also CLR *119*
Clarke, Arthur Charles
    See Clarke, Arthur C.

Clarke, Clorinda 1917- *7*
Clarke, Gus 1948- *134*
Clarke, J.
    See Clarke, Judith
Clarke, James Hall
    See Rowland-Entwistle, (Arthur) Theodore
    (Henry)
Clarke, Joan B. 1921- *42*
    Brief entry *27*
Clarke, John
    See Laklan, Carli
    and Sontup, Dan(iel)
Clarke, Judith 1943- *164*
    Earlier sketches in SATA *75, 110*
    See also CLR *61*
Clarke, Julia 1950- *138*
Clarke, Kenneth 1957- *107*
Clarke, Lea
    See Rowland-Entwistle, (Arthur) Theodore
    (Henry)
Clarke, Margaret 1941-
    See CLR *99*
Clarke, Mary Stetson 1911-1994 .... *5*
Clarke, Michael
    See Newlon, (Frank) Clarke
Clarke, Pauline 1921- *131*
    Earlier sketch in SATA *3*
    See also CLR *28*
Clarke-Rich, Elizabeth L. 1934- *103*
Clarkson, E(dith) Margaret 1915- *37*
Clarkson, Ewan 1929- *9*
Claudia, Susan
    See Goulart, Ron
    and Johnston, William
Claverie, Jean 1946- *38*
Clay, Patrice 1947- *47*
Clayman, Deborah Paula
    See Da Costa, Deborah
Claypool, Jane
    See Miner, Jane Claypool
Clayton, Elaine 1961- *159*
    Earlier sketch in SATA *94*
Clayton, Lawrence (Otto, Jr.) 1945- *75*
Clayton, Sandra 1951- *110*
Clea, Super
    See Hantman, Clea
Cleary, Beverly 1916- *121*
    Earlier sketches in SATA *2, 43, 79*
    See also CLR *72*
    See also SAAS *20*
Cleary, Beverly Atlee Bunn
    See Cleary, Beverly
Cleary, Brian P. 1959- *186*
    Earlier sketches in SATA *93, 132*
Cleaver, Bill
    See Cleaver, William J.
Cleaver, Carole 1934- *6*
Cleaver, Elizabeth (Ann Mrazik)
    1939-1985 .... *23*
    Obituary *43*
    See also CLR *13*
Cleaver, Hylton Reginald 1891-1961 .... *49*
Cleaver, Vera (Allen) 1919-1993 .... *76*
    Earlier sketch in SATA *22*
    See also CLR *6*
Cleaver, William J. 1920-1981 .... *22*
    Obituary *27*
    See also CLR *6*
Cleishbotham, Jebediah
    See Scott, Sir Walter
Cleland, Mabel
    See Widdemer, Mabel Cleland
Clem, Margaret H(ollingsworth) 1923- *90*
Clemens, Samuel Langhorne
    See Twain, Mark
Clemens, Virginia Phelps 1941- *35*
Clement, Gary *191*
Clement, Janet *182*
Clement, Nathan 1966- *200*
Clement, Priscilla Ferguson 1942- *171*
Clement, Rod *97*

Clement-Moore, Rosemary *188*
Clements, Andrew 1949- *158*
    Earlier sketch in SATA *104*
Clements, Bruce 1931- *178*
    Earlier sketches in SATA *27, 94*
Clemesha, David *192*
Clemons, Elizabeth
    See Nowell, Elizabeth Cameron
Clerk, N. W.
    See Lewis, C.S.
Cleveland, Bob
    See Cleveland, George
Cleveland, George 1903(?)-1985
    Obituary *43*
Cleveland-Peck, Patricia *80*
Cleven, Cathrine
    See Cleven, Kathryn Seward
Cleven, Kathryn Seward *2*
Clevenger, William R. 1954- *84*
Clevenger, William Russell
    See Clevenger, William R.
Clevin, Joergen 1920- *7*
Clevin, Jorgen
    See Clevin, Joergen
Clewes, Dorothy (Mary) 1907-2003 .... *86*
    Obituary *138*
    Earlier sketch in SATA *1*
Clifford, David
    See Rosenberg, Eth Clifford
Clifford, Eth
    See Rosenberg, Eth Clifford
Clifford, Harold B(urton) 1893-1988 .... *10*
Clifford, Margaret Cort 1929- *1*
Clifford, Martin
    See Hamilton, Charles (Harold St. John)
Clifford, Mary Louise Beneway 1926- *23*
Clifford, Peggy
    See Clifford, Margaret Cort
Clifford, Rachel Mark
    See Lewis, Brenda Ralph
Clifton, Lucille 1936- *128*
    Earlier sketches in SATA *20, 69*
    See also CLR *5*
Clifton, Thelma Lucille
    See Clifton, Lucille
Climo, Shirley 1928- *166*
    Autobiography Feature *110*
    Brief entry *35*
    Earlier sketches in SATA *39, 77*
    See also CLR *69*
Cline-Ransome, Lesa *201*
Clinton, Cathryn 1957- *136*
Clinton, Dirk
    See Silverberg, Robert
Clinton, Jon
    See Prince, J(ack) H(arvey)
Clippinger, Carol *193*
Clish, (Lee) Marian 1946- *43*
Clive, Clifford
    See Hamilton, Charles (Harold St. John)
Clokey, Art 1921- *59*
Cloudsley-Thompson, J(ohn) L(eonard)
    1921- *19*
Clouse, Nancy L. 1938- *78*
Clover, Peter 1952- *152*
Clutha, Janet Paterson Frame
    See Frame, Janet
Clymer, Eleanor 1906-2001 .... *85*
    Obituary *126*
    Earlier sketch in SATA *9*
    See also SAAS *17*
Clyne, Patricia (Edwards) *31*
Cneut, Carll 1969- *197*
Coalson, Glo 1946- *94*
    Earlier sketch in SATA *26*
Coates, Anna 1958- *73*
Coates, Belle 1896-1986 .... *2*
Coates, Ruth Allison 1915- *11*
Coats, Alice M(argaret) 1905-1976 .... *11*

Coatsworth, Elizabeth (Jane) 1893-1986 .... *100*
  Obituary *49*
  Earlier sketches in SATA *2, 56*
  See also CLR *2*
Cobalt, Martin
  See Mayne, William (James Carter)
Cobb, Jane
  See Berry, Jane Cobb
Cobb, Mary 1931- *88*
Cobb, Vicki 1938- *136*
  Autobiography Feature *136*
  Earlier sketches in SATA *8, 69, 131*
  See also CLR *2*
  See also SAAS *6*
Cobbett, Richard
  See Pluckrose, Henry (Arthur)
Cober, Alan E(dwin) 1935-1998 .... *7*
  Obituary *101*
Cobham, Sir Alan
  See Hamilton, Charles (Harold St. John)
Coburn, Jake 1978- *155*
Cocagnac, Augustin Maurice(-Jean) 1924- *7*
Cocca-Leffler, Maryann 1958- *194*
  Earlier sketches in SATA *80, 136*
Cochran, Bill *187*
Cochran, Bobbye A. 1949- *11*
Cochran, Thomas 1955- *198*
Cockett, Mary *3*
Coddell, Esme Raji
  See Codell, Esme Raji
Codell, Esme Raji 1968- *160*
Cody, C. S.
  See Waller, Leslie
Cody, Jess
  See Cunningham, Chet
Coe, Anne (E.) 1949- *95*
Coe, Douglas
  See Epstein, Beryl (M. Williams)
  and Epstein, Samuel
Coe, Lloyd 1899(?)-1976
  Obituary *30*
Coen, Rena Neumann 1925- *20*
Coerr, Eleanor (Beatrice) 1922- *67*
  Earlier sketch in SATA *1*
Cofer, Judith Ortiz 1952- *164*
  Earlier sketch in SATA *110*
Coffelt, Nancy 1961- *189*
Coffey, Brian
  See Koontz, Dean R.
Coffin, Geoffrey
  See Mason, F(rancis) van Wyck
Coffin, M. T.
  See Stanley, George Edward
Coffman, Ramon Peyton 1896-1989 .... *4*
Cogan, Karen 1954- *125*
Coggins, Jack (Banham) 1911-2006 .... *2*
Cohen, Barbara 1932-1992 .... *77*
  Obituary *74*
  Earlier sketch in SATA *10*
  See also SAAS *7*
Cohen, Daniel (E.) 1936- *70*
  Earlier sketch in SATA *8*
  See also CLR *43*
  See also SAAS *4*
Cohen, Deborah Bodin 1968- *180*
Cohen, Jan Barger
  See Barger, Jan
Cohen, Jene Barr
  See Barr, Jene
Cohen, Joan Lebold 1932- *4*
Cohen, Judith Love 1933- *78*
Cohen, Miriam 1926-1955 .... *155*
  Earlier sketches in SATA *29, 106*
  See also SAAS *11*
Cohen, Nora *75*
Cohen, Paul S. 1945- *58*
Cohen, Peter Zachary 1931- *150*
  Earlier sketch in SATA *4*
Cohen, Robert Carl 1930- *8*
Cohen, Sholom 1951- *94*
Cohn, Angelo 1914-1997 .... *19*

Cohn, Diana *194*
Cohn, Rachel 1968- *161*
Coit, Margaret Louise 1922-2003 .... *2*
  Obituary *142*
Colato Laínez, Rene 1970- *176*
Colbert, Anthony 1934-2007 .... *15*
Colbert, Nancy A. 1936- *139*
Colby, C(arroll) B(urleigh) 1904-1977 .... *35*
  Earlier sketch in SATA *3*
Colby, Jean Poindexter 1909-1993 .... *23*
Cole, Annette
  See Steiner, Barbara A(nnette)
Cole, Babette 1949- *155*
  Earlier sketches in SATA *61, 96*
Cole, Betsy 1940- *83*
Cole, Brock 1938- *200*
  Earlier sketches in SATA *72, 136*
  See also CLR *18*
Cole, Davis
  See Elting, Mary
Cole, Hannah 1954- *74*
Cole, Henry 1955- *181*
Cole, Jack -1974
  See Stewart, John
Cole, Jackson
  See Curry, Thomas Albert
  and Germano, Peter B.
  and Heckelmann, Charles N(ewman)
  and Newton, D(wight) B(ennett)
  and Schisgall, Oscar
Cole, Jennifer
  See Zach, Cheryl (Byrd)
Cole, Joanna 1944- *168*
  Brief entry *37*
  Earlier sketches in SATA *49, 81, 120*
  See also CLR *40*
Cole, Lois Dwight 1903-1979 .... *10*
  Obituary *26*
Cole, Michael 1947- *59*
Cole, Samantha
  See Cole, Stephen
Cole, Sheila 1939- *171*
  Earlier sketches in SATA *24, 95*
Cole, Sheila R.
  See Cole, Sheila
Cole, Sheila Rotenberg
  See Cole, Sheila
Cole, Stephen 1971- *161*
Cole, William (Rossa) 1919-2000 .... *71*
  Earlier sketch in SATA *9*
  See also SAAS *9*
Coleman, Andrew
  See Pine, Nicholas
Coleman, Clare
  See Bell, Clare (Louise)
  and Easton, M(alcolm) Coleman
Coleman, Janet Wyman *184*
Coleman, Loren 1947- *164*
Coleman, Loren Elwood, Jr.
  See Coleman, Loren
Coleman, Mary Ann 1928- *83*
Coleman, Michael 1946- *199*
  Autobiography Feature *133*
  Earlier sketches in SATA *108, 133*
Coleman, Rowan *187*
Coleman, William L(eRoy) 1938- *49*
  Brief entry *34*
Coles, Robert (Martin) 1929- *23*
Colfer, Eoin 1965- *197*
  Earlier sketch in SATA *148*
  See also CLR *112*
Colin, Ann
  See Ure, Jean
Collard, Sneed B. III 1959- *184*
  Earlier sketches in SATA *84, 139*
Colledge, Anne 1939- *142*
Collicott, Sharleen 1937- *143*
  Earlier sketch in SATA *98*
Collier, Bryan *174*
  Earlier sketch in SATA *126*

Collier, Christopher 1930- *70*
  Earlier sketch in SATA *16*
  See also CLR *126*
Collier, Ethel 1903-1999 .... *22*
Collier, James Lincoln 1928- *166*
  Earlier sketches in SATA *8, 70*
  See also CLR *126*
  See also SAAS *21*
Collier, Jane
  See Collier, Zena
Collier, Kristi *182*
Collier, Steven 1942- *61*
Collier, Zena 1926- *23*
Collings, Gillian 1939- *102*
Collington, Peter 1948- *99*
  Earlier sketch in SATA *59*
Collins, Ace 1953- *82*
Collins, Andrew J.
  See Collins, Ace
Collins, David R(aymond) 1940-2001 .... *121*
  Earlier sketch in SATA *7*
Collins, Heather 1946- *81*
Collins, Hunt
  See Hunter, Evan
Collins, Michael
  See Lynds, Dennis
Collins, Michael 1930- *58*
Collins, Pat(ricia) Lowery 1932- *151*
  Earlier sketch in SATA *31*
Collins, Paul 1954- *126*
Collins, Ross 1972- *200*
Collins, Ruth Philpott 1890-1975
  Obituary *30*
Collins, Suzanne *180*
Collins, Yvonne *194*
Collinson, A. S.
  See Collinson, Alan S.
Collinson, Alan S. 1934- *80*
Collinson, Roger (Alfred) 1936- *133*
Collison, Linda 1953- *185*
Collodi, Carlo
  See Lorenzini, Carlo
Colloms, Brenda 1919- *40*
Colman, Hila *53*
  Earlier sketch in SATA *1*
  See also SAAS *14*
Colman, Morris 1899(?)-1981
  Obituary *25*
Colman, Penny (Morgan) 1944- *160*
  Autobiography Feature *160*
  Earlier sketches in SATA *77, 114*
Colman, Warren (David) 1944- *67*
Colombo, John Robert 1936- *50*
Colon, Raul *156*
Colonius, Lillian 1911-1992 .... *3*
Colorado, Antonio J.
  See Colorado (Capella), Antonio J(ulio)
Colorado (Capella), Antonio J(ulio)
  1903-1994 .... *23*
  Obituary *79*
Colquhoun, Glenn 1964- *165*
Colston, Fifi E. 1960- *150*
Colt, Martin
  See Epstein, Beryl (M. Williams)
  and Epstein, Samuel
Colum, Padraic 1881-1972 .... *15*
  See also CLR *36*
Columbus, Chris 1959- *97*
Columbus, Christopher
  See Columbus, Chris
Columella
  See Moore, Clement Clarke
Colver, Anne 1908- *7*
Colvin, James
  See Moorcock, Michael
Colwell, Eileen (Hilda) 1904-2002 .... *2*
Colwyn, Stewart
  See Pepper, Frank S.
Coman, Carolyn 1951- *197*
  Earlier sketch in SATA *127*

Combs, Lisa M.
  See McCourt, Lisa
Combs, Robert
  See Murray, John
Comfort, Jane Levington
  See Sturtzel, Jane Levington
Comfort, Mildred Houghton 1886-1976 .... *3*
Comins, Ethel M(ae) *11*
Comins, Jeremy 1933- *28*
Commager, Henry Steele 1902-1998 .... *23*
  Obituary *102*
Comora, Madeleine *190*
Compere, Mickie
  See Davidson, Margaret
Compestine, Ying Chang 1963- *187*
  Earlier sketch in SATA *140*
Comport, Sally Wern *190*
Compton, Patricia A. 1936- *75*
Comte, The Great
  See Hawkesworth, Eric
Comus
  See Ballantyne, R(obert) M(ichael)
Comyns, Nance
  See Comyns-Toohey, Nantz
Comyns-Toohey, Nantz 1956- *86*
Conan Doyle, Arthur
  See Doyle, Sir Arthur Conan
Condit, Martha Olson 1913- *28*
Condon, Bill 1949- *142*
Condon, Judith *83*
Condon, Ken *195*
Condy, Roy 1942- *96*
Cone, Ferne Geller 1921- *39*
Cone, Molly (Lamken) 1918- *151*
  Autobiography Feature *151*
  Earlier sketches in SATA *1, 28, 115*
  See also SAAS *11*
Cone, Patrick 1954- *89*
Coney, Michael G. 1932-2005 .... *61*
  Obituary *170*
Coney, Michael Greatrex
  See Coney, Michael G.
Coney, Mike
  See Coney, Michael G.
Conford, Ellen 1942- *162*
  Earlier sketches in SATA *6, 68, 110*
  See also CLR *71*
Conger, Lesley
  See Suttles, Shirley (Smith)
Conklin, Gladys Plemon 1903- *2*
Conklin, Paul S. 1929(?)-2003 .... *43*
  Brief entry *33*
  Obituary *147*
Conkling, Hilda 1910-1986 .... *23*
Conlan, Kathleen Elizabeth 1950- *145*
Conlan, Kathy
  See Conlan, Kathleen Elizabeth
Conley, Robyn 1963- *125*
Conley-Weaver, Robyn
  See Conley, Robyn
Conlon-McKenna, Marita 1956- *71*
Conly, Jane Leslie 1948- *164*
  Earlier sketches in SATA *80, 112*
Conly, Robert Leslie 1918(?)-1973 .... *23*
  See also CLR *2*
Connell, Kirk
  See Chapman, John Stanton Higham
Connelly, Marc(us Cook) 1890-1980
  Obituary *25*
Connolly, Jerome P(atrick) 1931- *8*
Connolly, Pat 1943- *74*
Connolly, Peter 1935- *105*
  Earlier sketch in SATA *47*
Conover, Chris 1950- *31*
Conquest, Owen
  See Hamilton, Charles (Harold St. John)
Conrad, Joseph 1857-1924 .... *27*

Conrad, Pam 1947-1996 .... *133*
  Brief entry *49*
  Obituary *90*
  Earlier sketches in SATA *52, 80*
  See also CLR *18*
  See also SAAS *19*
Conroy, Jack
  See Conroy, John Wesley
Conroy, John Wesley 1899-1990 .... *19*
  Obituary *65*
Conroy, Robert
  See Goldston, Robert (Conroy)
Constable, Kate 1966- *172*
Constant, Alberta Wilson 1908-1981 .... *22*
  Obituary *28*
Constantin, Pascale *185*
Conway, Diana C(ohen) 1943- *91*
Conway, Gordon
  See Hamilton, Charles (Harold St. John)
Cook, Ande *192*
Cook, Bernadine 1924- *11*
Cook, Fred J(ames) 1911-2003 .... *2*
  Obituary *145*
Cook, Glen 1944- *171*
  Earlier sketch in SATA *108*
Cook, Glen Charles
  See Cook, Glen
Cook, Hugh 1956- *85*
Cook, Hugh, Walter Gilbert
  See Cook, Hugh
Cook, Jean Thor 1930- *94*
Cook, Joel 1934- *79*
Cook, Joseph Jay 1924- *8*
Cook, Lisa Broadie *157*
Cook, Lyn
  See Waddell, Evelyn Margaret
Cook, Roy
  See Silverberg, Robert
Cook, Trish *175*
Cooke, Ann
  See Cole, Joanna
Cooke, Arthur
  See Lowndes, Robert A(ugustine) W(ard)
Cooke, Barbara
  See Alexander, Anna B(arbara Cooke)
Cooke, David Coxe 1917- *2*
Cooke, Donald Ewin 1916-1985 .... *2*
  Obituary *45*
Cooke, Frank E. 1920- *87*
Cooke, Jean (Isobel Esther) 1929- *74*
Cooke, John Estes
  See Baum, L(yman) Frank
Cooke, Trish 1962- *129*
Cookson, Catherine (McMullen) 1906-1998 .. *9*
  Obituary *116*
Cooley, Regina Francoise 1940- *177*
Coolidge, Olivia E(nsor) 1908- *26*
  Earlier sketch in SATA *1*
Cooling, Wendy *169*
  Earlier sketch in SATA *111*
Coombs, Charles I(ra) 1914-1994 .... *43*
  Earlier sketch in SATA *3*
  See also SAAS *15*
Coombs, Chick
  See Coombs, Charles I(ra)
Coombs, Kate *190*
Coombs, Patricia 1926- *51*
  Earlier sketch in SATA *3*
  See also SAAS *22*
Cooney, Barbara 1917-2000 .... *96*
  Obituary *123*
  Earlier sketches in SATA *6, 59*
  See also CLR *23*
Cooney, Caroline B. 1947- *179*
  Brief entry *41*
  Earlier sketches in SATA *48, 80, 113, 130*
Cooney, Doug *181*
Cooney, Nancy Evans 1932- *42*
Coontz, Otto 1946- *33*
Cooper, Ann (Catharine) 1939- *104*

Cooper, Dutch
  See Kuyper, Sjoerd
Cooper, Elisha 1971- *157*
  Earlier sketch in SATA *99*
Cooper, Elizabeth Keyser -1992 .... *47*
Cooper, Floyd *187*
  Earlier sketches in SATA *96, 144*
  See also CLR *60*
Cooper, Gordon 1932- *23*
Cooper, Helen 1963- *169*
  Earlier sketch in SATA *102*
Cooper, Henry S(potswood) F(enimore), Jr.
  1933- *65*
Cooper, Ilene 1948- *145*
  Earlier sketches in SATA *66, 97*
Cooper, James Fenimore 1789-1851 .... *19*
  See also CLR *105*
Cooper, John R. *1*
Cooper, Kay 1941- *11*
Cooper, Lee Pelham 1926- *5*
Cooper, Lester (Irving) 1919-1985 .... *32*
  Obituary *43*
Cooper, Lettice (Ulpha) 1897-1994 .... *35*
  Obituary *82*
Cooper, Louise 1952- *152*
Cooper, M.E.
  See Lerangis, Peter
Cooper, M.E.
  See Davis, Maggie S.
Cooper, Melrose
  See Kroll, Virginia L.
Cooper, Michael L. 1950- *181*
  Earlier sketches in SATA *79, 117*
Cooper, Patrick 1949- *134*
Cooper, Susan 1935- *151*
  Earlier sketches in SATA *4, 64, 104*
  See also CLR *67*
  See also SAAS *6*
Cooper, Susan Mary
  See Cooper, Susan
Cope, Jane U(rsula) 1949- *108*
Copeland, Helen 1920- *4*
Copeland, Mark 1956- *180*
Copeland, Paul W. *23*
Coplans, Peta 1951- *84*
Copley, (Diana) Heather Pickering 1918- *45*
Coppard, A(lfred) E(dgar) 1878-1957
  See YABC *1*
Copper, Melinda 1952- *172*
Copper, Melinda McConnaughey
  See Copper, Melinda
Coralie
  See Anderson, Catherine Corley
Corbett, Grahame *43*
  Brief entry *36*
Corbett, Scott 1913- *42*
  Earlier sketch in SATA *2*
  See also CLR *1*
  See also SAAS *2*
Corbett, Sue *174*
Corbett, W(illiam) J(esse) 1938- *102*
  Brief entry *44*
  Earlier sketch in SATA *50*
  See also CLR *19*
Corbin, Sabra Lee
  See Malvern, Gladys
Corbin, William
  See McGraw, William Corbin
Corbman, Marjorie 1987- *179*
Corby, Dan
  See Catherall, Arthur
Corcoran, Barbara (Asenath) 1911- *77*
  Autobiography Feature *125*
  Earlier sketch in SATA *3*
  See also CLR *50*
  See also SAAS *20*
Corcos, Lucille 1908-1973 .... *10*
Cordell, Alexander
  See Graber, Alexander
Cordell, Alexander
  See Graber, (George) Alexander

Cordell, Matthew 1975- *199*
Corder, Zizou
 See Young, Louisa
Corella, Joseph
 See Odgers, Sally Farrell
Coren, Alan 1938-2007 32
 Obituary *187*
Corey, Dorothy 23
Corey, Shana 1974- *133*
Corfe, Thomas Howell 1928- 27
Corfe, Tom
 See Corfe, Thomas Howell
Corfield, Robin Bell 1952- 74
Corlett, William 1938-2005 46
 Brief entry *39*
Cormack, M(argaret) Grant 1913- *11*
Cormack, Maribelle B. 1902-1984 39
Cormier, Robert 1925-2000 83
 Obituary *122*
 Earlier sketches in SATA *10, 45*
 See also CLR *55*
Cormier, Robert Edmund
 See Cormier, Robert
Cornelius, Carol 1942- 40
Cornelius, Kay 1933- *157*
Cornell, J.
 See Cornell, Jeffrey
Cornell, James (Clayton, Jr.) 1938- 27
Cornell, Jean Gay 1920- 23
Cornell, Jeffrey 1945- *11*
Cornell, Laura *189*
Cornish, D.M. 1972- *185*
Cornish, Sam(uel James) 1935- 23
Cornwall, Nellie
 See Sloggett, Nellie
Cornwell, Autumn *195*
Corr, Christopher 1955- *189*
Correy, Lee
 See Stine, G(eorge) Harry
Corrick, James A. 1945- 76
Corrigan, (Helen) Adeline 1909- 23
Corrigan, Barbara 1922- 8
Corrigan, Eireann 1977- *163*
Corrin, Sara 1918- 86
 Brief entry 48
Corrin, Stephen 86
 Brief entry 48
Corsi, Wendy
 See Staub, Wendy Corsi
Cort, M. C.
 See Clifford, Margaret Cort
Cort, Margaret
 See Clifford, Margaret Cort
Corwin, Judith H(offman) 1946- *10*
Cory, Rowena
 See Lindquist, Rowena Cory
Cosby, Bill 1937- *110*
 Earlier sketch in SATA *66*
Cosby, William Henry, Jr.
 See Cosby, Bill
 and Cosby, Bill
Cosentino, Ralph *169*
Cosgrave, John O'Hara II 1908-1968
 Obituary 21
Cosgrove, Margaret (Leota) 1926- 47
Cosgrove, Stephen E(dward) 1945- 53
 Brief entry 40
Coskey, Evelyn 1932- 7
Cosner, Shaaron 1940- 43
Cossi, Olga 1921- *102*
 Earlier sketch in SATA *67*
Costabel, Eva Deutsch 1924- 45
Costabel-Deutsch, Eva
 See Costabel, Eva Deutsch
Coste, Marion 1938- *183*
Costello, David *174*
Costello, David F(rancis) 1904-1990 23
Cte, Genevieve 1964- *184*
Cote, Nancy 1952- *182*
Cott, Jonathan 1942- 23
Cottam, Clarence 1899-1974 25

Cotten, Cynthia *188*
Cottle, Joan 1960- *135*
Cottler, Joseph 1899-1996 22
Cottonwood, Joe 1947- 92
Cottrell, Leonard 1913-1974 24
Cottringer, Anne 1952- *150*
 Earlier sketch in SATA *97*
Couch, Greg *199*
Coulman, Valerie 1969- *161*
Couloumbis, Audrey *173*
Counsel, June 1926- 70
Countryman, The
 See Whitlock, Ralph
Courlander, Harold 1908-1996 6
 Obituary 88
Coursen, Valerie 1965(?)- *102*
Courtis, Stuart Appleton 1874-1969
 Obituary 29
Courtland, Tyler
 See Stevens, Serita
Courtney, Dayle
 See Goldsmith, Howard
Coury, Louise Andree 1895(?)-1983
 Obituary 34
Cousins, Linda 1946- 90
Cousins, Lucy 1964- *172*
Cousins, Margaret 1905-1996 2
 Obituary 92
Cousteau, Jacques-Yves 1910-1997 98
 Earlier sketch in SATA *38*
Couture, Christin 1951- 73
Couvillon, Jacques *195*
Covert, Ralph 1968- *197*
Coville, Bruce 1950- *155*
 Autobiography Feature *155*
 Earlier sketches in SATA *32, 77, 118*
Covington, Dennis *109*
Covington, Linda
 See Windsor, Linda
Cowan, Catherine *121*
Cowan, Rebecca M.
 See Moesta, Rebecca
Cowan, Rebecca Moesta
 See Moesta, Rebecca
Coward, Fiona 1963- *178*
Cowell, Cressida 1966- *140*
Cowen, Eve
 See Werner, Herma
Cowen, Ida 1898-1993 64
Cowie, Leonard W(allace) 1919- 4
Cowles, Kathleen
 See Krull, Kathleen
Cowley, Cassia Joy
 See Cowley, Joy
Cowley, Joy 1936- *164*
Cowley, (Cassia) Joy 1936- 90
 Autobiography Feature *118*
 Earlier sketch in SATA *4*
 See also CLR *55*
 See also SAAS *26*
Cowley, Marjorie 1925- *111*
Cox, (Christopher) Barry 1931- 62
Cox, Clinton 1934- *108*
 Earlier sketch in SATA *74*
Cox, David (Dundas) 1933- 56
Cox, Donald William 1921- 23
Cox, Jack
 See Cox, John Roberts
Cox, John Roberts 1915-1981 .... *191*
 Earlier sketch in SATA *9*
Cox, Judy 1954- *198*
 Earlier sketches in SATA *117, 160*
Cox, Marion Monroe 1898-1983
 Obituary 34
Cox, Palmer 1840-1924 24
 See also CLR *24*
Cox, Vic 1942- 88
Cox, Vicki 1945- *158*
Cox, Victoria
 See Garretson, Victoria Diane
Cox, Wallace 1924-1973 25

Cox, Wally
 See Cox, Wallace
Cox, William R(obert) 1901-1988 46
 Brief entry *31*
 Obituary *57*
Coxe, Molly 1959- *101*
 Earlier sketch in SATA *69*
Coxon, Michele 1950- *158*
 Earlier sketch in SATA *76*
Coy, Harold 1902-1986 .... *3*
Coy, John 1958- *171*
 Earlier sketch in SATA *120*
Craats, Rennay 1973- *131*
Crabtree, Judith 1928- 98
 Earlier sketch in SATA *63*
Cracker, Edward E.B.
 See Odgers, Sally Farrell
Craft, K. Y.
 See Craft, Kinuko Y(amabe)
Craft, Kinuko
 See Craft, Kinuko Y(amabe)
Craft, Kinuko Y(amabe) 1940- *127*
 Earlier sketch in SATA *65*
Craft, Ruth 1935- 87
 Brief entry *31*
Craig, A. A.
 See Anderson, Poul
Craig, Alisa
 See MacLeod, Charlotte (Matilda)
Craig, Helen 1934- 94
 Earlier sketches in SATA *46, 49*
Craig, Joe 1979- *198*
Craig, Joe Alexander
 See Craig, Joe
Craig, John Eland
 See Chipperfield, Joseph Eugene
Craig, John Ernest 1921- 23
Craig, Kit
 See Reed, Kit
Craig, M. F.
 See Craig, Mary (Francis) Shura
Craig, M. Jean *17*
Craig, M. S.
 See Craig, Mary (Francis) Shura
Craig, Margaret (Maze) 1911-1964 .... *9*
Craig, Mary
 See Craig, Mary (Francis) Shura
Craig, Mary Shura
 See Craig, Mary (Francis) Shura
Craig, Mary (Francis) Shura 1923-1991 86
 Obituary 65
 Earlier sketch in SATA *6*
 See also SAAS *7*
Craig, Ruth 1922- 95
Craik, Mrs.
 See Craik, Dinah Maria (Mulock)
Craik, Dinah Maria (Mulock) 1826-1887 34
Crandall, Court 1965- *175*
Crandell, Rachel 1943- *152*
Crane, Barbara (Joyce) 1934- 31
Crane, Caroline 1930- *11*
Crane, Jordan 1973- *174*
Crane, M. A.
 See Wartski, Maureen (Ann Crane)
Crane, Royston Campbell 1901-1977
 Obituary 22
Crane, Stephen (Townley) 1871-1900
 See YABC *2*
 See also CLR *132*
Crane, Walter 1845-1915 .... *100*
 Earlier sketch in SATA *18*
 See also CLR *56*
Crane, William D(wight) 1892-1976 .... *1*
Cranfield, Ingrid 1945- 74
Cranshaw, Stanley
 See Fisher, Dorothy (Frances) Canfield
Crary, Elizabeth (Ann) 1942- 99
 Brief entry *43*
Crary, Margaret (Coleman) 1906-1986 .... *9*
Craste, Marc *201*

Cravath, Lynne Avril
 See Cravath, Lynne W.
Cravath, Lynne W. 1951- 182
 Earlier sketches in SATA 98, 148
Craven, Thomas 1889-1969 22
Crawford, Charles P. 1945- 28
Crawford, Deborah 1922- 6
Crawford, John E(dmund) 1904-1971 3
Crawford, K(aren) Michael 1959- 155
Crawford, Mel 1925- 44
 Brief entry 33
Crawford, Phyllis 1899- 3
Crawley, Dave 177
Cray, Roberta
 See Emerson, Ru
Crayder, Dorothy 7
Crayder, Teresa
 See Colman, Hila
Crayon, Geoffrey
 See Irving, Washington
Craz, Albert G. 1926- 24
Crebbin, June 1938- 169
 Earlier sketch in SATA 80
Crecy, Jeanne
 See Williams, Jeanne
Credle, Ellis 1902-1998 1
Creech, Sharon 1945- 172
 Earlier sketches in SATA 94, 139
 See also CLR 89
Creeden, Sharon 1938- 91
Creel, Ann Howard 1953- 187
Creighton, (Mary) Helen 1899-1989
 Obituary 64
Creighton, Jill 1949- 96
Crenson, Victoria 1952- 159
 Earlier sketch in SATA 88
Cresp, Gael 1954- 119
Crespo, George 1962- 82
Cresswell, Helen 1934-2005 79
 Obituary 168
 Earlier sketches in SATA 1, 48
 See also CLR 18
 See also SAAS 20
Cressy, Michael 1955- 124
Cressy, Mike
 See Cressy, Michael
Cretan, Gladys (Yessayan) 1921- 2
Cretzmeyer, Stacy (Megan) 1959- 124
Crew, Gary 1947- 163
 Earlier sketches in SATA 75, 110
 See also CLR 42
Crew, Helen (Cecilia) Coale 1866-1941
 See YABC 2
Crew, Linda (Jean) 1951- 137
 Earlier sketch in SATA 71
Crews, Donald 1938- 76
 Brief entry 30
 Earlier sketch in SATA 32
 See also CLR 7
Crews, Nina 1963- 158
 Earlier sketch in SATA 97
Crichton, John Michael
 See Crichton, Michael
Crichton, Michael 1942-2008 88
 Obituary 199
 Earlier sketch in SATA 9
Crider, Allen Billy
 See Crider, Bill
Crider, Bill 1941- 99
Crilley, Mark 1966- 148
 Autobiography Feature 148
 Earlier sketch in SATA 120
Crimi, Carolyn 1959- 176
Cripps, Enid Margaret
 See Appiah, Peggy
Crisler, Curtis L. 188
Crisman, Ruth 1914- 73
Crisp, Marta Marie 1947- 128
Crisp, Marty
 See Crisp, Marta Marie
Crispin, A(nn) C(arol) 1950- 86

Crist, James J. 1961- 168
Cristall, Barbara 79
Crist-Evans, Craig 1954- 153
Crocker, Carter 193
Crocker, Nancy 1956- 185
Crofford, Emily (Ardell) 1927- 61
Crofut, William E. III 1934- 23
Croggon, Alison 1962- 194
Croll, Carolyn 1945- 102
 Brief entry 52
 Earlier sketch in SATA 56
Croman, Dorothy Young
 See Rosenberg, Dorothy
Cromie, Alice Hamilton 1914-2000 24
Cromie, William J(oseph) 1930- 4
Crompton, Anne Eliot 1930- 73
 Earlier sketch in SATA 23
Crompton, Richmal
 See Lamburn, Richmal Crompton
Cronbach, Abraham 1882-1965 11
Crone, Ruth 1919-2003 4
Cronin, A(rchibald) J(oseph) 1896-1981 47
 Obituary 25
Cronin, Doreen (A.) 125
Cronin, Doreen 1966(?)- 178
 See also CLR 136
Cronin, Doreen A.
 See Cronin, Doreen
Crook, Beverly Courtney 38
 Brief entry 35
Crook, Connie Brummel 1930- 168
 Earlier sketch in SATA 98
Crook, Constance
 See Crook, Connie Brummel
Crosby, Alexander L. 1906-1980 2
 Obituary 23
Crosby, Harry C., Jr. 102
Crosby, Margaret
 See Rathmann, Peggy
Crosher, G. R. 14
Cross, Gilbert B. 1939- 60
 Brief entry 51
Cross, Gillian 1945- 178
 Autobiography Feature 178
 Earlier sketches in SATA 38, 71, 110, 165
 See also CLR 28
Cross, Gillian Clare
 See Cross, Gillian
Cross, Helen Reeder
 See Broadhead, Helen Cross
Cross, Peter 1951- 95
Cross, Shauna 1976(?)- 196
Cross, Tom 1954- 146
Cross, Verda 1914- 75
Cross, Wilbur Lucius III 1918- 2
Crossland, Caroline 1964- 83
Crossley-Holland, Kevin 1941- 165
 Earlier sketches in SATA 5, 74, 120
 See also CLR 84
 See also SAAS 20
Crossley-Holland, Kevin John William
 See Crossley-Holland, Kevin
Crouch, Marcus 1913-1996 4
Crout, George C(lement) 1917- 11
Crow, Donna Fletcher 1941- 40
Crow, Francis Luther
 See Luther, Frank
Crowe, Andrew 111
Crowe, John
 See Lynds, Dennis
Crowe, (Bettina) Peter Lum 1911- 6
Crowell, Grace Noll 1877-1969 34
Crowell, Pers 1910-1990 2
Crowell, Robert Leland 1909-2001 63
Crowfield, Christopher
 See Stowe, Harriet (Elizabeth) Beecher
Crowley, Arthur McBlair 1945- 38
Crowley, John 1942- 140
 Earlier sketch in SATA 65
Crowley, Suzanne 1963- 196

Crowley, Suzanne Carlisle
 See Crowley, Suzanne
Crownfield, Gertrude 1867-1945
 See YABC 1
Crowther, James Gerald 1899-1983 14
Crowther, Robert 1948- 163
Cruikshank, George 1792-1878 22
 See also CLR 63
Cruise, Robin 1951- 179
Crum, Shutta 192
 Earlier sketch in SATA 134
Crummel, Susan Stevens 1949- 176
 Earlier sketch in SATA 130
Crump, Fred H., Jr. 1931- 76
 Earlier sketch in SATA 11
Crump, J(ames) Irving 1887-1979 57
 Obituary 21
Crump, William D(rake) 1949- 138
Crunden, Reginald
 See Cleaver, Hylton Reginald
Crunk, T.
 See Crunk, Tony
Crunk, Tony 1956- 130
Crutcher, Chris 1946- 196
 Earlier sketches in SATA 52, 99, 153
 See also CLR 28
Crutcher, Christopher C.
 See Crutcher, Chris
Cruz, Ray(mond) 1933- 6
Cruz Martinez, Alejandro (?)-1987 74
Crystal, Billy 1947- 154
Ctvrtek, Vaclav 1911-1976
 Obituary 27
Cuetara, Mittie 1957- 158
 Earlier sketch in SATA 106
Cuffari, Richard 1925-1978 66
 Obituary 25
 Earlier sketch in SATA 6
Cuffe-Perez, Mary 1946- 199
Cullen, Countee 1903-1946 18
Cullen, Lynn 190
Culliford, Pierre 1928-1992 40
 Obituary 74
Cullinan, Bernice E(llinger) 1926- 135
Culp, Louanna McNary 1901-1965 2
Culper, Felix
 See McCaughrean, Geraldine
Cumbaa, Stephen 1947- 72
Cumming, Peter 1951- 168
Cumming, Primrose Amy 1915- 24
Cumming, Robert 1945- 65
Cummings, Betty Sue 1918- 15
 See also SAAS 9
Cummings, Mary 1951- 185
Cummings, Parke 1902-1987 2
 Obituary 53
Cummings, Pat (Marie) 1950- 107
 Earlier sketches in SATA 42, 71
 See also CLR 48
 See also SAAS 13
Cummings, Phil 1957- 123
 Earlier sketch in SATA 74
Cummings, Priscilla 1951- 170
 Earlier sketch in SATA 129
Cummings, Richard
 See Gardner, Richard (M.)
Cummins, Julie 200
Cummins, Maria Susanna 1827-1866
 See YABC 1
Cuneo, Mary Louise -2001 85
Cunliffe, John Arthur 1933- 86
 Earlier sketch in SATA 11
Cunliffe, Marcus (Falkner) 1922-1990 37
 Obituary 66
Cunnane, Kelly 175
Cunningham, Bob
 See May, Julian
Cunningham, Captain Frank
 See Glick, Carl (Cannon)
Cunningham, Cathy
 See Cunningham, Chet

Cunningham, Chet 1928- 23
Cunningham, Dale S(peers) 1932- 11
Cunningham, Dru 91
Cunningham, E. V.
  See Fast, Howard
Cunningham, Julia (Woolfolk) 1916- 132
  Earlier sketches in SATA 1, 26
  See also SAAS 2
Cunningham, Lawrence J. 1943- 125
Cunningham, Virginia
  See Holmgren, Virginia C(unningham)
Curiae, Amicus
  See Fuller, Edmund (Maybank)
Curie, Eve 1904-2007 1
  Obituary 188
Curlee, Lynn 1947- 190
  Earlier sketches in SATA 98, 141
Curley, Daniel 1918-1988 23
  Obituary 61
Curley, Marianne 1959- 175
  Earlier sketch in SATA 131
Currey, Anna 194
Currie, Robin 1948- 120
Currie, Stephen 1960- 132
  Earlier sketch in SATA 82
Curry, Ann (Gabrielle) 1934- 72
Curry, Jane L(ouise) 1932- 138
  Autobiography Feature 138
  Earlier sketches in SATA 1, 52, 90
  See also CLR 31
  See also SAAS 6
Curry, Peggy Simson 1911-1987 8
  Obituary 50
Curry, Tom 185
Curtis, Bruce (Richard) 1944- 30
Curtis, Chara M(ahar) 1950- 78
Curtis, Christopher Paul 1954(?)- 187
  Earlier sketches in SATA 93, 140
  See also CLR 68
Curtis, Gavin 1965- 107
Curtis, Jamie Lee 1958- 144
  Earlier sketch in SATA 95
  See also CLR 88
Curtis, Jennifer Keats 185
Curtis, Marci 160
Curtis, Patricia 1921- 101
  Earlier sketch in SATA 23
Curtis, Peter
  See Lofts, Norah (Robinson)
Curtis, Philip (Delacourt) 1920- 62
Curtis, Richard (Alan) 1937- 29
Curtis, Richard Hale
  See Deming, Richard
  and Levinson, Leonard
  and Rothweiler, Paul Roger
Curtis, Wade
  See Pournelle, Jerry (Eugene)
Curtiss, A(rlene) B. 1934- 90
Cusack, Margaret 1945- 58
Cushman, Doug 1953- 157
  Earlier sketches in SATA 65, 101
Cushman, Jerome 2
Cushman, Karen 1941- 147
  Earlier sketch in SATA 89
  See also CLR 55
Cusick, Richie Tankersley 1952- 140
  Earlier sketch in SATA 67
Cutbill, Andy 1972- 201
Cutchen, Billye Walker 1930- 15
Cutchins, Judy 1947- 59
Cutler, Daniel S(olomon) 1951- 78
Cutler, Ebbitt 1923- 9
Cutler, Ivor 1923-2006 24
  Obituary 174
Cutler, Jane 1936- 162
  Earlier sketches in SATA 75, 118
Cutler, May Ebbitt
  See Cutler, Ebbitt
Cutler, Samuel
  See Folsom, Franklin (Brewster)
Cutlip, Kimbra L(eigh-Ann) 1964- 128

Cutrate, Joe
  See Spiegelman, Art
Cutt, W(illiam) Towrie 1898-1981 16
  Obituary 85
Cuyler, Margery 1948- 195
  Earlier sketches in SATA 39, 99, 156
Cuyler, Margery Stuyvesant
  See Cuyler, Margery
Cuyler, Stephen
  See Bates, Barbara S(nedeker)
Cyrus, Kurt 1954- 179
  Earlier sketch in SATA 132
Czernecki, Stefan 1946- 178

D

Dabba Smith, Frank 174
Dabcovich, Lydia 99
  Brief entry 47
  Earlier sketch in SATA 58
Dace, Dolores B(oelens) 1929- 89
Da Costa, Deborah 193
Daddo, Andrew 1967- 198
Dadey, Debbie 1959- 136
  Earlier sketch in SATA 73
Dahl, Borghild (Margarethe) 1890-1984 7
  Obituary 37
Dahl, Roald 1916-1990 73
  Obituary 65
  Earlier sketches in SATA 1, 26
  See also CLR 111
Dahlberg, Maurine F. 1951- 171
Dahlstedt, Marden (Stewart) 1921-1983 8
  Obituary 110
Dain, Martin J. 1924-2000 35
Dakos, Kalli 1950- 115
  Earlier sketch in SATA 80
Dale, Anna 1971- 170
Dale, Gary
  See Reece, Colleen L.
Dale, George E.
  See Asimov, Isaac
Dale, Jack
  See Holliday, Joseph
Dale, Kim 1957- 123
Dale, Margaret J(essy) Miller 1911- 39
Dale, Mitzi
  See Hemstock, Gillian
Dale, Norman
  See Denny, Norman (George)
Dale, Penny 1954- 151
  Earlier sketch in SATA 70
Daley, Michael J. 170
Dalgliesh, Alice 1893-1979 17
  Obituary 21
  See also CLR 62
Dalkey, Kara 1953- 132
Dalkey, Kara Mia
  See Dalkey, Kara
Dallas, Ruth 1919- 86
Dalmas, John
  See Jones, John R(obert)
Dalton, Alene
  See Chapin, Alene Olsen Dalton
Dalton, Annie 1948- 140
  Earlier sketch in SATA 40
Dalton, Kit
  See Cunningham, Chet
Dalton, Pamela
  See Johnson, Pamela
Dalton, Sean
  See Chester, Deborah
Dalton, Sheila 1949- 108
Daly, Jim
  See Stratemeyer, Edward L.
Daly, Jude 1951- 177
Daly, Kathleen N(orah) 124
  Brief entry 37

Daly, Maureen 1921-2006 129
  Obituary 176
  Earlier sketch in SATA 2
  See also CLR 96
  See also SAAS 1
Daly, Nicholas 1946- 164
  Earlier sketches in SATA 37, 76, 114
  See also CLR 41
  See also SAAS 21
  See Daly, Niki
Daly, Niki 1946- 198
  See Daly, Nicholas
D'Amato, Alex 1919- 20
D'Amato, Janet (Potter) 1925- 9
Damerow, Gail 1944- 83
Damerow, Gail Jane
  See Damerow, Gail
D'Amico, Carmela 170
D'Amico, Steve 170
Damrell, Liz 1956- 77
Damrosch, Helen
  See Tee-Van, Helen Damrosch
Dana, Barbara 1940- 22
Dana, Richard Henry, Jr. 1815-1882 26
Danachair, Caoimhin O
  See Danaher, Kevin
Danaher, Kevin 1913-2002 22
Danakas, John 1963- 94
Dandi
  See Mackall, Dandi Daley
D'Andrea, Kate
  See Steiner, Barbara A(nnette)
Dangerfield, Balfour
  See McCloskey, (John) Robert
Daniel, Alan 1939- 76
  Brief entry 53
Daniel, Anita 1893(?)-1978 23
  Obituary 24
Daniel, Anne
  See Steiner, Barbara A(nnette)
Daniel, Becky 1947- 56
Daniel, Claire 1949- 164
Daniel, Colin
  See Windsor, Patricia
Daniel, Hawthorne 1890- 8
Daniel, (Donna) Lee 1944- 76
Daniel, Rebecca
  See Daniel, Becky
Daniels, Guy 1919-1989 11
  Obituary 62
Daniels, Lucy
  See Oldfield, Jenny
Daniels, Max
  See Gellis, Roberta
Daniels, Olga
  See Sinclair, Olga
Daniels, Patricia 1955- 93
Daniels, Zoe
  See Laux, Constance
Dank, Gloria Rand 1955- 56
  Brief entry 46
Dank, Leonard D(ewey) 1929- 44
Dank, Milton 1920- 31
Dann, Max 1955- 62
Danneberg, Julie 1958- 173
Dantz, William R.
  See Philbrick, Rodman
Danziger, Paula 1944-2004 149
  Brief entry 30
  Obituary 155
  Earlier sketches in SATA 36, 63, 102
  See also CLR 20
Darby, Gene Kegley
  See Darby, Jean (Kegley)
Darby, J. N.
  See Govan, (Mary) Christine Noble
Darby, Jean (Kegley) 1921- 68
Darby, Patricia (Paulsen) 14
Darby, Ray(mond) 1912-1982 7
d'Arcy, Willard
  See Cox, William R(obert)

Dare, Geena
See McNicoll, Sylvia (Marilyn)
Darian, Shea 1959- 97
Daringer, Helen Fern 1892-1986 1
Darke, Marjorie 1929- 87
Earlier sketch in SATA 16
Darley, F(elix) O(ctavius) C(arr)
1822-1888 35
Darling, David J. 1953- 60
Brief entry 44
Darling, Kathy
See Darling, Mary Kathleen
Darling, Lois (MacIntyre) 1917-1989 3
Obituary 64
Darling, Louis, (Jr.) 1916-1970 3
Obituary 23
Darling, Mary Kathleen 1943- 124
Earlier sketches in SATA 9, 79
Darling, Sandra Louise Woodward
See Day, Alexandra
Darnell, K(athryn) L(ynne) 1955- 150
Darroll, Sally
See Odgers, Sally Farrell
Darrow, Sharon 181
Darrow, Whitney, (Jr.) 1909-1999 13
Obituary 115
Darwin, Len
See Darwin, Leonard
Darwin, Leonard 1916- 24
Dasent, Sir George Webbe 1817-1896 62
Brief entry 29
Dash, Joan 1925- 142
Daskam, Josephine Dodge
See Bacon, Josephine Dodge (Daskam)
D'ath, Justin 1953- 174
Earlier sketch in SATA 106
Dauer, Rosamond 1934- 23
Daugherty, Charles Michael 1914- 16
Daugherty, James (Henry) 1889-1974 13
See also CLR 78
Daugherty, Richard D(eo) 1922- 35
Daugherty, Sonia Medwedeff (?)-1971
Obituary 27
d'Aulaire, Edgar Parin 1898-1986 66
Obituary 47
Earlier sketch in SATA 5
See also CLR 21
d'Aulaire, Ingri (Mortenson Parin)
1904-1980 66
Obituary 24
Earlier sketch in SATA 5
See also CLR 21
Dave, Dave
See Berg, David
Daveluy, Paule Cloutier 1919- 11
Davenier, Christine 1961- 179
Earlier sketch in SATA 127
Davenport, John 1960- 156
Daves, Michael 1938- 40
David, A. R.
See David, A(nn) Rosalie
David, A(nn) Rosalie 1946- 103
David, Jonathan
See Ames, Lee J(udah)
David, Lawrence 1963- 165
Earlier sketch in SATA 111
David, Peter 1956- 72
David, Peter Allen
See David, Peter
David, Rosalie
See David, A(nn) Rosalie
Davidson, Alice Joyce 1932- 54
Brief entry 45
Davidson, Basil 1914- 13
Davidson, (Marie) Diane 1924- 91
Davidson, Hugh
See Hamilton, Edmond
Davidson, Jessica 1915-1986 5
Davidson, Judith 1953- 40
Davidson, Lionel 1922- 87
Davidson, Margaret 1936- 5

Davidson, Marion
See Garis, Howard R(oger)
Davidson, Mary R. 1885-1973 9
Davidson, Mary S. 1940- 61
Davidson, Mickie
See Davidson, Margaret
Davidson, Nicole
See Jensen, Kathryn
Davidson, R.
See Davidson, Raymond
Davidson, Raymond 1926- 32
Davidson, Rosalie 1921- 23
Davie, Helen K(ay) 1952- 148
Earlier sketch in SATA 77
Davies, Andrew (Wynford) 1936- 27
Davies, Andy Robert 200
Davies, Bettilu D(onna) 1942- 33
Davies, Hunter 1936- 55
Brief entry 45
Davies, Jacqueline 1962- 186
Earlier sketch in SATA 155
Davies, Joan 1934- 50
Brief entry 47
Davies, Nicola 1958- 182
Earlier sketches in SATA 99, 150
Davies, Peter J(oseph) 1937- 52
Davies, Sumiko 1942- 46
Davis, (A.) Aubrey 1949- 153
Davis, Barbara Steincrohn
See Davis, Maggie S.
Davis, Bette J. 1923- 15
Davis, Burke 1913- 4
Davis, Christopher 1928- 6
Davis, D(elbert) Dwight 1908-1965 33
Davis, Daniel S(heldon) 1936- 12
Davis, David R. 1948- 106
Davis, Donald 1944- 169
Earlier sketch in SATA 93
Davis, Donald D.
See Davis, Donald
Davis, Emma
See Davis, Maggie S.
Davis, Gibbs 1953- 102
Brief entry 41
Earlier sketch in SATA 46
Davis, Grania 1943- 88
Brief entry 50
Davis, H(arold) L(enoir) 1896-1960 114
Davis, Hubert J(ackson) 1904-1997 31
Davis, James Robert 1945- 32
Davis, Jenny 1953- 74
Davis, Jim
See Davis, James Robert
Davis, Julia 1900(?)-1993 6
Obituary 75
Davis, Karen (Elizabeth) 1944- 109
Davis, Katie 1959(?)- 152
Davis, Lambert 176
Davis, Leslie
See Guccione, Leslie Davis
Davis, Louise Littleton 1921- 25
Davis, Maggie S. 1943- 57
Davis, Marguerite 1889- 34
Davis, Mary L(ee) 1935- 9
Davis, Mary Octavia 1901-1976 6
Davis, Nelle 1958- 73
Davis, Ossie 1917-2005 81
See also CLR 56
Davis, Paxton 1925-1994 16
Davis, Robert 1881-1949
See YABC 1
Davis, Robin W(orks) 1962- 87
Davis, Russell Gerard 1922- 3
Davis, Tim(othy N.) 1957- 94
Davis, Verne Theodore 1889-1973 6
Davis, Yvonne 1927- 115
Davol, Marguerite W. 1928- 146
Earlier sketch in SATA 82
DaVolls, Andy (P.) 1967- 85
DaVolls, Linda 1966- 85

Davys, Sarah
See Manning, Rosemary
Dawes, Claiborne 1935- 111
Dawson, Elmer A. 67
Earlier sketch in SATA 1
Dawson, Imogen (Zoe) 1948- 126
Earlier sketch in SATA 90
Dawson, Janine 1957- 196
Dawson, Mary 1919- 11
Day, A(rthur) Grove 1904-1994 59
Day, Alexandra 1941- 197
Autobiography Feature 197
Earlier sketches in SATA 67, 97, 169
See also CLR 22
See also SAAS 19
Day, Beth (Feagles) 1924- 33
Day, Donna
See Asay, Donna Day
Day, Edward C. 1932- 72
Day, Jon 1936(?)- 79
Day, Karen 187
Day, Larry 1956- 181
Day, Nancy 1953- 140
Day, Nancy Raines 1951- 148
Earlier sketch in SATA 93
Day, Shirley 1962- 94
Day, Thomas 1748-1789
See YABC 1
Day, Trevor 1955- 124
Dazey, Agnes J(ohnston) 2
Dazey, Frank M. 2
Deacon, Alexis 1978- 139
Deacon, Eileen
See Geipel, Eileen
Deacon, Richard
See McCormick, (George) Donald (King)
Deadman, Ronald 1919-1988(?)
Obituary 56
Deak, Erzsi 1959- 152
Dean, Anabel 1915- 12
Dean, Carolee 1962- 148
Dean, David 1976- 192
Dean, Karen Strickler 1923- 49
Dean, Ruth (Brigham) 1947- 145
Dean, Zoey
See Bennett, Cherie
de Angeli, Marguerite (Lofft) 1889-1987 ... 100
Obituary 51
Earlier sketches in SATA 1, 27
See also CLR 1
Deans, Karen 195
Deans, Sis Boulos 1955- 136
Earlier sketch in SATA 78
DeArmand, Frances Ullmann 1904(?)-1984 . 10
Obituary 38
DeArmond, Dale 1914- 70
DeArmond, Dale Burlison
See DeArmond, Dale
Deary, Terry 1946- 171
Brief entry 41
Earlier sketches in SATA 51, 101
Deaver, Julie Reece 1953- 68
de Banke, Cecile 1889-1965 11
De Bello, Rosario 1923- 89
Debon, Nicolas 186
Earlier sketch in SATA 151
de Bono, Edward 1933- 66
de Brissac, Malcolm
See Dickinson, Peter (Malcolm de Brissac)
de Brunhoff, Jean
See Brunhoff, Jean de
De Brunhoff, Laurent
See Brunhoff, Laurent de
De Bruyn, Monica G. 1952- 13
De Bruyn, Monica Jean Grembowicz
See De Bruyn, Monica G.
DeBry, Roger K. 1942- 91
de Camp, Catherine Crook 1907-2000 83
Earlier sketch in SATA 12
de Camp, L(yon) Sprague 1907-2000 83
Earlier sketch in SATA 9

DeCandido, Keith R.A. *112*
Dechausay, Sonia E. *94*
Decker, C.B. *172*
Decker, Cynthia B.
    See Decker, C.B.
Decker, Duane 1910-1964 .... *5*
Decker, Timothy 1974- *197*
DeClements, Barthe (Faith) 1920- *131*
    Earlier sketches in SATA *35, 71*
    See also CLR 23
de Clercq Zubli, Rita la Fontaine 1929- *199*
de Conte, Sieur Louis
    See Twain, Mark
Dedman, Stephen *108*
Dee, Catherine 1964- *138*
Dee, Ruby
    See Wallace, Ruby Ann
Deedy, Carmen Agra 1960- *196*
Deedy, John 1923- *24*
Deegan, Paul Joseph 1937- *48*
    Brief entry *38*
Deem, James M. 1950- *191*
    Autobiography Feature *191*
    Earlier sketches in SATA *75, 134*
Deem, James Morgan
    See Deem, James M.
Deeter, Catherine 1947- *137*
DeFelice, Cynthia 1951- *165*
    Earlier sketches in SATA *79, 121*
DeFelice, Cynthia C.
    See DeFelice, Cynthia
Defoe, Daniel 1660(?)-1731 .... *22*
    See also CLR 61
DeFord, Deborah H. *123*
deFrance, Anthony
    See DiFranco, Anthony (Mario)
Degen, Bruce 1945- *147*
    Brief entry *47*
    Earlier sketches in SATA *57, 97*
DeGering, Etta (Belle) Fowler 1898-1996 ..... *7*
De Goldi, Kate
    See De Goldi, Kathleen Domenica
De Goldi, Kathleen Domenica 1959- *123*
de Goursac, Olivier 1959- *184*
De Grazia, Ettore 1909-1982 .... *39*
De Grazia, Ted
    See De Grazia, Ettore
deGroat, Diane 1947- *169*
    Earlier sketches in SATA *31, 90*
deGros, J. H.
    See Villiard, Paul
de Grummond, Lena Young *62*
    Earlier sketch in SATA *6*
de Hamel, Joan Littledale 1924- *86*
De Haven, Tom 1949- *72*
de Hugo, Pierre
    See Brackers de Hugo, Pierre
Deiss, Joseph Jay 1915- *12*
de Jenkins, Lyll Becerra 1925-1997 .... *102*
DeJong, David C(ornel) 1905-1967 .... *10*
de Jong, Dola 1911-2003
    See de Jong, Dorothea Rosalie
de Jong, Dorothea Rosalie 1911-2003 .... *7*
    Obituary *149*
DeJong, Meindert 1906-1991 .... *2*
    Obituary *68*
    See also CLR 73
DeJonge, Joanne E. 1943- *56*
Deka, Connie
    See Laux, Constance
de Kay, Ormonde (Jr.) 1923-1998 .... *7*
    Obituary *106*
de Kiriline, Louise
    See Lawrence, Louise de Kiriline
Dekker, Carl
    See Laffin, John (Alfred Charles)
    and Lynds, Dennis
deKruif, Paul (Henry) 1890-1971 .... *50*
    Earlier sketch in SATA *5*
Delacre, Lulu 1957- *156*
    Earlier sketch in SATA *36*

DeLaCroix, Alice 1940- *195*
    Earlier sketch in SATA *75*
de la Cruz, Melissa 1971- *179*
De la Garza, Phyllis 1942- *169*
De Lage, Ida 1918- *11*
de la Mare, Walter (John) 1873-1956 .... *16*
    See also CLR 23
Delaney, Harry 1932- *3*
Delaney, Joseph 1945- *172*
Delaney, M.C.
    See Delaney, Michael
Delaney, Michael 1955- *180*
    Earlier sketch in SATA *96*
Delaney, Michael Clark
    See Delaney, Michael
Delaney, Ned
    See Delaney, Thomas Nicholas III
Delaney, Thomas Nicholas III 1951- *28*
Delano, Hugh 1933- *20*
Delany, Samuel R., Jr. 1942- *92*
Delany, Samuel Ray
    See Delany, Samuel R., Jr.
De La Ramee, Marie Louise 1839-1908 ...... *20*
de la Roche, Mazo 1879-1961 .... *64*
De La Roche Saint Andre, Anne 1950- *75*
Delaune, (Jewel) Lynn (de Grummond) *7*
DeLaurentis, Louise Budde 1920- *12*
del Barco, Lucy Salamanca 1900(?)-1989
    Obituary *64*
Delderfield, Eric R(aymond) 1909-1995 ...... *14*
Delderfield, Ronald Frederick 1912-1972 ... *20*
DeLeeuw, Adele (Louise) 1899-1988 .... *30*
    Obituary *56*
    Earlier sketch in SATA *1*
De Leon, Nephtali 1945- *97*
Delessert, Etienne 1941- *179*
    Brief entry *27*
    Earlier sketches in SATA *46, 130*
    See also CLR 81
Delgado, James P. 1958- *122*
de Lint, Charles 1951- *157*
    Earlier sketch in SATA *115*
de Lint, Charles Henri Diederick Hofsmit
    See de Lint, Charles
Delmar, Roy
    See Wexler, Jerome (LeRoy)
Del Negro, Janice M. *197*
Deloria, Vine, Jr. 1933-2005 .... *21*
    Obituary *171*
Deloria, Vine Victor, Jr.
    See Deloria, Vine, Jr.
del Rey, Lester 1915-1993 .... *22*
    Obituary *76*
Delrio, Martin
    See Doyle, Debra
    and Macdonald, James D.
Delton, Judy 1931-2001 .... *77*
    Obituary *130*
    Earlier sketch in SATA *14*
    See also SAAS 9
Delulio, John 1938- *15*
Delving, Michael
    See Williams, Jay
de Marcken, Gail *186*
Demarest, Chris L. 1951- *175*
    Brief entry *44*
    Earlier sketches in SATA *45, 82, 128*
Demarest, Christopher Lynn
    See Demarest, Chris L.
Demarest, Doug
    See Barker, Will
De Mari, Silvana 1953- *193*
Demas, Corinne
    See Bliss, Corinne Demas
Demas, Vida 1927- *9*
DeMatteis, J.M. 1953- *180*
DeMatteis, John Marc
    See DeMatteis, J.M.
De Mejo, Oscar 1911-1992 .... *40*
Demers, Dominique 1956- *177*
de Messieres, Nicole 1930- *39*

Demi
    See Hitz, Demi
Demijohn, Thom
    See Disch, Thomas M.
    and Sladek, John
Deming, Richard 1915-1983 .... *24*
Deming, Sarah *191*
de Monfreid, Dorothee 1973- *189*
Demuth, Patricia Brennan 1948- *84*
    Brief entry *51*
Dendinger, Roger E. 1952- *158*
Denenberg, Barry 1940- *175*
Dengler, Marianna (Herron) 1935- *103*
Dengler, Sandy 1939- *54*
    Brief entry *40*
Denim, Sue
    See Pilkey, Dav
Denise, Christopher 1968- *193*
    Earlier sketch in SATA *147*
Denman, K.L. 1957- *186*
Denmark, Harrison
    See Zelazny, Roger
Dennard, Deborah 1953- *136*
    Earlier sketch in SATA *78*
Denney, Diana 1910-2000 .... *25*
    Obituary *120*
Dennis, Morgan 1891(?)-1960 .... *18*
Dennis, Wesley 1903-1966 .... *18*
Denniston, Elinore 1900-1978
    Obituary *24*
Denny, Norman (George) 1901-1982 .... *43*
Denslow, Sharon Phillips 1947- *142*
    Earlier sketch in SATA *68*
Denslow, W(illiam) W(allace) 1856-1915 .... *16*
    See also CLR 15
Dent, Grace 1973- *187*
Denton, Kady MacDonald *181*
    Earlier sketches in SATA *66, 110*
    See also CLR 71
Denton, Terry 1950- *186*
Denver, Walt
    See Redding, Robert Hull
    and Sherman, Jory (Tecumseh)
Denzel, Justin F(rancis) 1917-1999 .... *46*
    Brief entry *38*
Denzer, Ann Wiseman
    See Wiseman, Ann (Sayre)
DePalma, Mary Newell 1961- *185*
    Earlier sketch in SATA *139*
De Palma, Toni *199*
dePaola, Thomas Anthony 1934- *155*
    Earlier sketches in SATA *11, 59, 108*
    See also CLR 81
    See also SAAS 15
    See dePaola, Tomie
dePaola, Tomie *200*
    See dePaola, Thomas Anthony
deParrie, Paul 1949- *74*
DePauw, Linda Grant 1940- *24*
DeRan, David 1946- *76*
Derby, Ken 1956- *181*
Derby, Kenneth R.
    See Derby, Ken
Derby, Pat 1942- *172*
Derby, Sally 1934- *189*
    Earlier sketches in SATA *89, 132*
de Regniers, Beatrice Schenk (Freedman)
    1914-2000 .... *68*
    Obituary *123*
    Earlier sketch in SATA *2*
    See also SAAS 6
Dereske, Jo 1947- *72*
Derleth, August (William) 1909-1971 .... *5*
Derman, Martha (Winn) *74*
Derman, Sarah Audrey 1915- *11*
DeRoberts, Lyndon
    See Silverstein, Robert Alan
de Roo, Anne Louise 1931-1997 .... *84*
    Earlier sketch in SATA *25*
    See also CLR 63
deRosa, Dee *70*

Derrick, Lionel
  See Cunningham, Chet
Derrickson, Jim 1959- *141*
Derry Down Derry
  See Lear, Edward
Dervaux, Isabelle 1961- *106*
Derwent, Lavinia *14*
Desai, Anita 1937- *126*
  Earlier sketch in SATA *63*
DeSaix, Deborah Durland *188*
De Saulles, Tony 1958- *119*
Desbarats, Peter 1933- *39*
de Selincourt, Aubrey 1894-1962 .... *14*
de Seve, Randall *198*
Deshpande, Chris 1950- *69*
Desimini, Lisa 1964- *148*
  Earlier sketch in SATA *86*
Desjarlais, John 1953- *71*
Desjarlais, John J.
  See Desjarlais, John
Desmoinaux, Christel 1967- *149*
  Earlier sketch in SATA *103*
Desmond, Adrian J(ohn) 1947- *51*
Desmond, Alice Curtis 1897-1990 .... *8*
Desnoettes, Caroline *183*
DeSpain, Pleasant 1943- *87*
Desputeaux, Helene 1959- *95*
Dessen, Sarah 1970- *172*
  Earlier sketch in SATA *120*
Detine, Padre
  See Olsen, Ib Spang
de Trevino, Elizabeth B.
  See Trevino, Elizabeth B(orton) de
de Trevino, Elizabeth Borton
  See Trevino, Elizabeth B(orton) de
Detwiler, Susan Dill 1956- *58*
Deuker, Carl 1950- *196*
  Earlier sketches in SATA *82, 150*
Deutsch, Babette 1895-1982 .... *1*
  Obituary *33*
Deutsch, Eva Costabel
  See Costabel, Eva Deutsch
Deutsch, Helen 1906-1992 .... *76*
Deutsch, Kurt
  See Singer, Kurt D.
De Valera, Sinead 1879(?)-1975
  Obituary *30*
Devaney, John 1926-1994 .... *12*
de Varennes, Monique 1947- *168*
de Varona, Frank J. 1943- *83*
Devereux, Frederick L(eonard), Jr.
  1914-1993 .... *9*
Devi, Nila
  See Woody, Regina Jones
deVinck, Christopher 1951- *85*
DeVita, James *195*
DeVito, Cara 1956- *80*
Devlin, Dorothy Wende
  See Devlin, Wende
Devlin, Harry 1918-2001 .... *136*
  Earlier sketches in SATA *11, 74*
Devlin, Wende 1918-2002 .... *74*
  Earlier sketch in SATA *11*
Devon, Paddie 1953- *92*
Devons, Sonia 1974- *72*
Devorah-Leah *111*
de Vos, Gail 1949- *122*
DeVries, Douglas 1933- *122*
De Waard, E(lliott) John 1935- *7*
Dewan, Ted 1961- *157*
  Earlier sketch in SATA *108*
Dewdney, Anna *184*
Dewdney, Selwyn (Hanington) 1909-1979 ... *64*
DeWeese, Gene
  See DeWeese, Thomas Eugene
DeWeese, Jean
  See DeWeese, Thomas Eugene
DeWeese, Thomas Eugene 1934- *46*
  Brief entry *45*
Dewey, Ariane 1937- *178*
  Earlier sketches in SATA *7, 109*

Dewey, Jennifer (Owings) 1941- *103*
  Brief entry *48*
  Earlier sketch in SATA *58*
Dewey, Kenneth Francis 1940- *39*
De Wire, Elinor 1953- *180*
deWit, Dorothy (May Knowles) 1916-1980 . *39*
  Obituary *28*
Dexter, Alison 1966- *125*
Dexter, John
  See Bradley, Marion Zimmer
Deyneka, Anita 1943- *24*
Deyrup, Astrith Johnson 1923- *24*
Dezern, Chad *201*
Dhami, Narinder 1958- *152*
Dhondy, Farrukh 1944- *152*
  Earlier sketch in SATA *65*
  See also CLR *41*
Diakite, Baba Wague 1961- *174*
Diakite, Penda 1993(?)- *174*
Diamond, Arthur 1957- *76*
Diamond, Donna 1950- *69*
  Brief entry *30*
  Earlier sketch in SATA *35*
Diamond, Petra
  See Sachs, Judith
Diamond, Rebecca
  See Sachs, Judith
Dias, Earl Joseph 1916- *41*
Dias, Ron 1937- *71*
Diaz, David 1959(?)- *189*
  Earlier sketches in SATA *96, 150*
  See also CLR *65*
Dibley, Glin
DiCamillo, Kate 1964- *163*
  Earlier sketch in SATA *121*
  See also CLR *117*
Di Certo, J(oseph) J(ohn) 1933- *60*
DiCianni, Ron 1952- *107*
Dick, Trella Lamson 1889-1974 .... *9*
Dickens, Charles (John Huffam)
  1812-1870 .... *15*
  See also CLR *95*
Dickens, Frank
  See Huline-Dickens, Frank William
Dickens, Monica (Enid) 1915-1992 .... *4*
  Obituary *74*
Dickerson, Roy Ernest 1886-1965
  Obituary *26*
Dickinson, Emily (Elizabeth) 1830-1886 ..... *29*
Dickinson, Mary 1949- *48*
  Brief entry *41*
Dickinson, Mary-Anne
  See Rodda, Emily
Dickinson, Peter (Malcolm de Brissac)
  1927- *150*
  Earlier sketches in SATA *5, 62, 95*
  See also CLR *125*
Dickinson, Susan 1931- *8*
Dickinson, Terence 1943- *102*
Dickinson, W(illiam) Croft 1897-1963 .... *13*
Dickson, Gordon R. 1923-2001 .... *77*
Dickson, Gordon Rupert
  See Dickson, Gordon R.
Dickson, Helen
  See Reynolds, Helen Mary Greenwood Camp-
  bell
Dickson, Naida 1916- *8*
Diehn, Gwen 1943- *80*
Dierssen, Andreas 1962- *190*
Diesen, Deborah 1967- *200*
Dieterich, Michele M. 1962- *78*
Dietz, David H(enry) 1897-1984 .... *10*
  Obituary *41*
Dietz, Lew 1907-1997 .... *11*
  Obituary *95*
Diffily, Deborah *159*
Di Fiori, Larry
  See Di Fiori, Lawrence
Di Fiori, Lawrence 1934- *130*
DiFranco, Anthony (Mario) 1945- *42*
Digby, Anne 1935- *72*

Digges, Jeremiah
  See Berger, Josef
Digman, Kristina 1959- *176*
D'Ignazio, Fred(erick) 1949- *39*
  Brief entry *35*
Di Grazia, Thomas (?)-1983 .... *32*
Dijkstra, Lida 1961- *195*
Dikty, Julian May
  See May, Julian
Dillard, Annie 1945- *140*
  Earlier sketch in SATA *10*
Dillard, Kristine 1964- *113*
Dillard, Polly Hargis 1916- *24*
Diller, Harriett 1953- *78*
Dillon, Barbara 1927- *44*
  Brief entry *39*
Dillon, Diane 1933- *194*
  Earlier sketches in SATA *15, 51, 106*
  See also CLR *44*
Dillon, Diane Claire
  See Dillon, Diane
Dillon, Eilis 1920-1994 .... *74*
  Autobiography Feature *105*
  Obituary *83*
  Earlier sketch in SATA *2*
  See also CLR *26*
Dillon, Jana (a pseudonym) 1952- *117*
Dillon, Leo 1933- *194*
  Earlier sketches in SATA *15, 51, 106*
  See also CLR *44*
Dillon, Sharon Saseen
  See Saseen, Sharon (Dillon)
Dils, Tracey E. 1958- *83*
Dilson, Jesse 1914-1988 .... *24*
Dinan, Carolyn *59*
  Brief entry *47*
Dines, Carol 1956- *175*
Dines, (Harry) Glen 1925-1996 .... *7*
Dinesen, Isak
  See Blixen, Karen
Dinessi, Alex
  See Schembri, Jim
Dinneen, Betty 1929- *61*
Dinnerstein, Harvey 1928- *42*
Dinsdale, Tim(othy Kay) 1924-1987 .... *11*
Diop, Birago (Ismael) 1906-1989
  Obituary *64*
Diouf, Sylviane A. *168*
Diouf, Sylviane Anna
  See Diouf, Sylviane A.
DiPucchio, Kelly *159*
Dirk
  See Gringhuis, Richard H.
Dirks, Wilhelmina 1916- *59*
Dirks, Willy
  See Dirks, Wilhelmina
Dirtmeister
  See Tomecek, Steve
DiSalvo, DyAnne 1960- *144*
  Earlier sketch in SATA *59*
DiSalvo-Ryan, DyAnne
  See DiSalvo, DyAnne
Disch, Thomas M. 1940-2008 .... *92*
  Obituary *195*
  See also CLR *18*
  See also SAAS *15*
Disch, Thomas Michael
  See Disch, Thomas M.
Disch, Tom
  See Disch, Thomas M.
Disher, Garry 1949- *125*
  Earlier sketch in SATA *81*
Disney, Walt(er Elias) 1901-1966 .... *28*
  Brief entry *27*
Ditchfield, Christin 1973- *189*
DiTerlizzi, Tony 1969- *154*
Divakaruni, Chitra Banerjee 1956- *160*
Di Valentin, Maria (Amelia) Messuri
  1911-1985 .... *7*
Divine, Arthur Durham 1904-1987
  Obituary *52*

Divine, David
  See Divine, Arthur Durham
Dixon, Ann R. 1954- *127*
  Earlier sketch in SATA 77
Dixon, Ann Renee
  See Dixon, Ann R.
Dixon, Dougal 1947- *190*
  Earlier sketches in SATA 45, 127
Dixon, Franklin W.
  See Barrett, Neal, Jr.
  and Goulart, Ron
  and Lantz, Francess L(in)
  and Lerangis, Peter
  and McFarlane, Leslie
  and Stanley, George Edward
  and Stratemeyer, Edward L.
Dixon, Jeanne 1936- *31*
Dixon, Paige
  See Corcoran, Barbara (Asenath)
Dixon, Peter L(ee) 1931- *6*
Dixon, Rachel 1952- *74*
Djoleto, (Solomon Alexander) Amu 1929- ... *80*
d'lacey, Chris 1949- *165*
Doak, Annie
  See Dillard, Annie
Doane, Pelagie 1906-1966 .... *7*
Dobell, I(sabel) M(arian) B(arclay)
  1909-1998 .... *11*
Dobie, J(ames) Frank 1888-1964 .... *43*
Dobkin, Alexander 1908-1975
  Obituary *30*
Dobler, Lavinia G. 1910- *6*
Dobrin, Arnold 1928- *4*
Dobson, Jill 1969- *140*
Dobson, Julia 1941- *48*
Dobson, Mary 1954- *117*
Dockery, Wallene T. 1941- *27*
Dockray, Tracy 1962- *139*
Dockrey, Karen 1955- *103*
Doctor, Bernard
  See Doctor, Bernard Aquina
Doctor, Bernard Aquina 1950- *81*
Doctor X
  See Nourse, Alan E(dward)
Dodd, Ed(ward Benton) 1902-1991 .... *4*
  Obituary *68*
Dodd, Lynley (Stuart) 1941- *132*
  Earlier sketches in SATA 35, 86
  See also CLR 62
Dodd, Marty 1921- *142*
Dodd, Quentin 1972- *137*
Dodds, Bill 1952- *78*
Dodds, Dayle Ann 1952- *201*
  Earlier sketches in SATA 75, 150
Doder, Josh 1968- *187*
Dodge, Bertha S(anford) 1902-1995 .... *8*
Dodge, Fremont
  See Grimes, Lee
Dodge, Gil
  See Hano, Arnold
Dodge, Mary (Elizabeth) Mapes
  1831(?)-1905 .... *100*
  Earlier sketch in SATA 21
  See also CLR 62
Dodgson, Charles Lutwidge
  See Carroll, Lewis
Dodson, Kenneth MacKenzie 1907-1999 ..... *11*
Dodson, Susan 1941- *50*
  Brief entry *40*
Dogyear, Drew
  See Gorey, Edward (St. John)
Doherty, Berlie 1943- *111*
  Earlier sketch in SATA 72
  See also CLR 21
  See also SAAS 16
Doherty, Charles Hugh 1913- *6*
Doherty, Craig A. 1951- *169*
  Earlier sketch in SATA 83
Doherty, Katherine M(ann) 1951- *83*
Doherty, Kieran 1945- *164*
Dokey, Cameron 1956- *97*

Dolan, Edward F(rancis), Jr. 1924- *94*
  Brief entry *31*
  Earlier sketch in SATA 45
Dolan, Ellen M(eara) 1929-1998 .... *88*
Dolan, Sean J. 1958- *74*
Dolce, J. Ellen 1948- *75*
Dolch, Edward William 1889-1961 .... *50*
Dolch, Marguerite Pierce 1891-1978 .... *50*
Dollar, Diane (Hills) 1933- *57*
Dolson, Hildegarde
  See Lockridge, Hildegarde (Dolson)
Domanska, Janina 1913(?)-1995 .... *68*
  Obituary *84*
  Earlier sketch in SATA 6
  See also CLR 40
  See also SAAS 18
Dominguez, Angel 1953- *76*
Domino, John
  See Averill, Esther (Holden)
Domjan, Joseph (Spiri) 1907-1992 .... *25*
Domm, Jeffrey C. 1958- *84*
Donahue, Dorothy *178*
Donald, Rhonda Lucas 1962- *147*
Donalds, Gordon
  See Shirreffs, Gordon D(onald)
Donaldson, Bryna
  See Stevens, Bryna
Donaldson, Gordon 1913-1993 .... *64*
  Obituary *76*
Donaldson, Joan 1953- *78*
Donaldson, Julia 1948- *180*
  Earlier sketches in SATA 82, 132
Donaldson, Stephen R. 1947- *121*
Donaldson, Stephen Reeder
  See Donaldson, Stephen R.
Doner, Kim 1955- *91*
Doney, Todd L. W. 1959- *104*
Dong-Sung, Kim 1970- *195*
Dong-Sung Kim
  See Dong-Sung, Kim
Donkin, Nance (Clare) 1915- *95*
Donna, Natalie 1934-1979 .... *9*
Donnelly, Elfie 1950-
  See CLR 104
Donnelly, Jennifer 1963- *154*
Donnelly, Matt 1972- *148*
Donnio, Sylviane *188*
Donoghue, Emma 1969- *101*
Donohue, Moira Rose 1954- *201*
Donoughue, Carol 1935- *139*
Donovan, Frank (Robert) 1906-1975
  Obituary *30*
Donovan, John 1928-1992 .... *72*
  Brief entry *29*
  See also CLR 3
Donovan, Mary Lee 1961- *86*
Donovan, William
  See Berkebile, Fred D(onovan)
Donze, Mary Terese 1911- *89*
Doob, Leonard W(illiam) 1909-2000 .... *8*
Dooley, Norah 1953- *74*
Dooling, Michael 1958- *105*
Dor, Ana
  See Ceder, Georgiana Dorcas
Dore, (Louis Christophe Paul) Gustave
  1832-1883 .... *19*
Doremus, Robert 1913- *30*
Doren, Marion (Walker) 1928- *57*
Dorenkamp, Michelle 1957- *89*
Dorflinger, Carolyn 1953- *91*
Dorfman, Joaquin 1979- *180*
Dorfman, Joaquin Emiliano
  See Dorfman, Joaquin
Dorian, Edith M(cEwen) 1900-1983 .... *5*
Dorian, Harry
  See Hamilton, Charles (Harold St. John)
Dorian, Marguerite *7*
Dorin, Patrick C(arberry) 1939- *59*
  Brief entry *52*
Dorman, Brandon *194*
Dorman, Michael 1932- *7*

Dorman, N. B. 1927- *39*
Dormer, Frank W. *200*
Dorris, Michael 1945-1997 .... *75*
  Obituary *94*
  See also CLR 58
Dorris, Michael A.
  See Dorris, Michael
Dorris, Michael Anthony
  See Dorris, Michael
Dorritt, Susan
  See Schlein, Miriam
Dorros, Alex 1991- *194*
Dorros, Arthur 1950- *168*
  Earlier sketches in SATA 78, 122
  See also CLR 42
  See also SAAS 20
Dorros, Arthur M.
  See Dorros, Arthur
Dorson, Richard M(ercer) 1916-1981 .... *30*
Doss, Helen (Grigsby) 1918- *20*
Doss, Margot Patterson *6*
dos Santos, Joyce Audy 1949- *57*
  Brief entry *42*
Dothers, Anne
  See Chess, Victoria (Dickerson)
Dotlich, Rebecca Kai 1951- *182*
Dottig
  See Grider, Dorothy
Dotts, Maryann J. 1933- *35*
Doty, Jean Slaughter 1929- *28*
Doty, Roy 1922- *28*
Doubtfire, Dianne (Abrams) 1918- *29*
Doucet, Sharon Arms 1951- *144*
  Autobiography Feature *144*
  Earlier sketch in SATA 125
Dougherty, Charles 1922- *18*
Dougherty, Terri (L.) 1964- *146*
Doughty, Rebecca 1955- *174*
Douglas, Blaise 1960- *101*
Douglas, Carole Nelson 1944- *73*
Douglas, Garry
  See Kilworth, Garry
Douglas, James McM.
  See Griffin, W.E.B
Douglas, Kathryn
  See Ewing, Kathryn
Douglas, Leonard
  See Bradbury, Ray
Douglas, Lola
  See Zeises, Lara M.
Douglas, Marjory Stoneman 1890-1998 .... *10*
Douglas, Michael
  See Bright, Robert (Douglas Sr.)
Douglas, Michael
  See Crichton, Michael
Douglas, Shirley Stewart
  See Tepper, Sheri S.
Douglass, Barbara 1930- *40*
Douglass, Frederick 1817(?)-1895 .... *29*
Douglass, Keith
  See Cunningham, Chet
Douty, Esther M(orris) 1909-1978 .... *8*
  Obituary *23*
Dow, Emily R. 1904-1987 .... *10*
Dow, Vicki
  See McVey, Vicki
Dowd, John David 1945- *78*
Dowdell, Dorothy (Florence) Karns 1910- ... *12*
Dowden, Anne Ophelia Todd 1907-2007 .... *7*
  Obituary *180*
  See also SAAS 10
Dowdey, Landon Gerald 1923- *11*
Dowdy, Mrs. Regera
  See Gorey, Edward (St. John)
Dowell, Frances O'Roark *157*
Dower, Laura *185*
Dowling, Terry 1947- *101*
Downer, Ann 1960- *155*
Downer, Marion 1892(?)-1971 .... *25*
Downes, Belinda 1962- *180*

Downey, Fairfax D(avis) 1893-1990 .... *3*
   Obituary *66*
Downey, Lynn 1961- *185*
Downham, Jenny 1964- *192*
Downie, John 1931- *87*
Downie, Mary Alice 1934- *171*
   Earlier sketches in SATA *13, 87*
Downie, Mary Alice Dawe
   See Downie, Mary Alice
Downing, David A(lmon) 1958- *84*
Downing, Johnette *184*
Downing, Julie 1956- *148*
   Earlier sketch in SATA *81*
Downing, Paula E. 1951- *80*
Downing, Warwick 1931- *138*
Downing, Wick
   See Downing, Warwick
Dowswell, Paul 1957- *184*
Doyle, A. Conan
   See Doyle, Sir Arthur Conan
Doyle, Sir Arthur Conan 1859-1930 .... *24*
   See also CLR *106*
Doyle, Brian 1935- *156*
   Earlier sketches in SATA *67, 104*
   See also CLR *22*
   See also SAAS *16*
Doyle, Charlotte 1937- *178*
   Earlier sketch in SATA *94*
Doyle, Charlotte Lackner
   See Doyle, Charlotte
Doyle, Conan
   See Doyle, Sir Arthur Conan
Doyle, Debra 1952- *165*
   Earlier sketch in SATA *105*
Doyle, Donovan
   See Boegehold, Betty (Doyle)
Doyle, John
   See Graves, Robert
Doyle, Malachy 1954- *165*
   Earlier sketch in SATA *120*
   See also CLR *83*
Doyle, Richard 1824-1883 .... *21*
Doyle, Sir A. Conan
   See Doyle, Sir Arthur Conan
Dr. A
   See Asimov, Isaac
   and Silverstein, Alvin
   and Silverstein, Virginia B(arbara Opshelor)
Dr. Alphabet
   See Morice, Dave
Dr. Fred
   See Bortz, Alfred B(enjamin)
Dr. Laura
   See Schlessinger, Laura (Catherine)
Dr. Seuss
   See Geisel, Theodor Seuss
   and LeSieg, Theo.
   and Seuss, Dr.
   and Stone, Rosetta
Dr. Zed
   See Penrose, Gordon
Drabble, Margaret 1939- *48*
Drackett, Phil(ip Arthur) 1922- *53*
Draco, F.
   See Davis, Julia
Dracup, Angela 1943- *74*
Dragisic, Patricia *116*
Dragonwagon, Crescent 1952- *186*
   Autobiography Feature *186*
   Earlier sketches in SATA *11, 41, 75, 133*
   See also SAAS *14*
Drake, David 1945- *85*
Drake, David Allen
   See Drake, David
Drake, Frank
   See Hamilton, Charles (Harold St. John)
Drake, Jane 1954- *82*
Drakeford, Dale B 1952- *113*
Drakeford, Dale Benjamin
   See Drakeford, Dale B

Draper, Hastings
   See Jeffries, Roderic
Draper, Sharon
   See Draper, Sharon M.
Draper, Sharon M. 1948- *195*
   Autobiography Feature *146*
   Earlier sketches in SATA *98, 146*
   See also CLR *57*
Draper, Sharon Mills
   See Draper, Sharon M.
Drapier, M. B.
   See Swift, Jonathan
Drawson, Blair 1943- *126*
   Earlier sketch in SATA *17*
Dray, Matt 1967- *177*
Dray, Matthew Frederick
   See Dray, Matt
Dresang, Eliza (Carolyn Timberlake) 1941- . *19*
Drescher, Henrik 1955- *172*
   Earlier sketches in SATA *67, 105*
   See also CLR *20*
Drescher, Joan E(lizabeth) 1939- *137*
   Earlier sketch in SATA *30*
Dressen-McQueen, Stacey *191*
Dreves, Veronica R. 1927-1986
   Obituary *50*
Drew, Patricia (Mary) 1938- *15*
Drewery, Mary 1918- *6*
Drewery, Melanie 1970- *165*
Drewry, Henry N(athaniel) 1924- *138*
Dreyer, Ellen *177*
Drial, J. E.
   See Laird, Jean E(louise)
Drimmer, Frederick 1916-2000 .... *60*
   Obituary *124*
Driskill, J. Lawrence 1920- *90*
Driskill, Larry
   See Driskill, J. Lawrence
Driving Hawk, Virginia
   See Sneve, Virginia Driving Hawk
Dron, Laura
   See Matthews, L.S.
Dronzek, Laura *199*
Drucker, Malka 1945- *111*
   Brief entry *29*
   Earlier sketch in SATA *39*
Drucker, Olga Levy 1927- *79*
Druitt, Tobias
   See Purkiss, Diane
Drummond, V(iolet) H(ilda) 1911-2000 .... *6*
Drummond, Walter
   See Silverberg, Robert
Drury, Clare Marie
   See Hoskyns-Abrahall, Clare (Constance Drury)
Drury, Roger W(olcott) 1914-1996 .... *15*
Druse, Eleanor
   See King, Stephen
Dryden, Pamela
   See St. John, Nicole
D.T., Hughes
   See Hughes, Dean
Duane, Diane (Elizabeth) 1952- *145*
   Brief entry *46*
   Earlier sketches in SATA *58, 95*
Dubanevich, Arlene 1950- *56*
Dubelaar, Thea 1947- *60*
du Blane, Daphne
   See Groom, Arthur William
Duble, Kathleen Benner 1958- *164*
Dubois, Claude K. 1960- *196*
DuBois, Rochelle Holt 1946- *41*
Du Bois, Shirley Graham 1907(?)-1977 .... *24*
   See Graham, Shirley
Du Bois, W(illiam) E(dward) B(urghardt) 1868-1963 .... *42*
du Bois, William Pene
   See Pene du Bois, William (Sherman)
Duboise, Novella 1911-1999 .... *88*
Dubosarsky, Ursula 1961- *193*
   Earlier sketches in SATA *107, 147*

DuBose, LaRocque (Russ) 1926- *2*
Dubrovin, Vivian 1931- *139*
   Earlier sketch in SATA *65*
DuBurke, Randy *172*
Ducey, Jean Sparks 1915- *93*
Duchacek, Ivo D(uka) 1913-1988
   Obituary *55*
Du Chaillu, Paul (Belloni) 1835(?)-1903 ..... *26*
Ducharme, Dede Fox
   See Ducharme, Lilian Fox
Ducharme, Lilian Fox 1950- *122*
Ducornet, Erica 1943- *7*
Ducornet, Rikki
   See Ducornet, Erica
Duden, Jane 1947- *136*
Duder, Tessa 1940- *117*
   Earlier sketch in SATA *80*
   See also CLR *43*
   See also SAAS *23*
Dudley, Helen
   See Hope Simpson, Jacynth
Dudley, Martha Ward 1909(?)-1985
   Obituary *45*
Dudley, Nancy
   See Cole, Lois Dwight
Dudley, Robert
   See Baldwin, James
Dudley, Ruth H(ubbell) 1905-2001 .... *11*
Dudley-Smith, T.
   See Trevor, Elleston
Due, Linnea A. 1948- *64*
Dueck, Adele 1955- *97*
Dueland, Joy V(ivian) *27*
Duerr, Gisela 1968- *89*
Duey, Kathleen 1950- *199*
   Earlier sketch in SATA *132*
Dufault, Joseph Ernest Nephtali
   See James, Will(iam Roderick)
Duff, Annis (James) 1904(?)-1986
   Obituary *49*
Duff, Maggie
   See Duff, Margaret K(app)
Duff, Margaret K(app) 1916-2003 .... *37*
   Obituary *144*
Duffey, Betsy (Byars) 1953- *131*
   Earlier sketch in SATA *80*
Duffie, Charles 1960- *144*
Duffield, Katy S. 1961- *147*
Duffy, Carol Ann 1955- *165*
   Earlier sketch in SATA *95*
Dugan, Jack
   See Griffin, W.E.B
Dugan, John Kevin
   See Griffin, W.E.B
Dugan, Michael (Gray) 1947- *15*
Duggan, Alfred Leo 1903-1964 .... *25*
Duggan, Maurice (Noel) 1922-1974 .... *40*
   Obituary *30*
Duggleby, John 1952- *94*
Dugin, Andrej 1955- *77*
Dugina, Olga 1964- *77*
du Jardin, Rosamond Neal 1902-1963 .... *2*
Duka, Ivo
   See Duchacek, Ivo D(uka)
Duke, Kate 1956- *192*
   Earlier sketches in SATA *90, 148*
   See also CLR *51*
Duke, Will
   See Gault, William Campbell
Dulac, Edmund 1882-1953 .... *19*
Dumas, Alexandre (pere) 1802-1870 .... *18*
   See also CLR *134*
Dumas, Jacqueline 1946- *55*
Dumas, Philippe 1940- *119*
   Earlier sketch in SATA *52*
du Maurier, Daphne 1907-1989 .... *27*
   Obituary *60*
Dumbleton, Mike 1948- *124*
   Earlier sketch in SATA *73*
Dunbar, Fiona 1961- *167*

Dunbar, Joyce 1944- 162
  Earlier sketches in SATA 76, 112
Dunbar, Paul Laurence 1872-1906 34
Dunbar, Polly 1980(?)- 181
Dunbar, Robert E(verett) 1926- 32
Duncan, Alexandra
  See Moore, Ishbel (Lindsay)
Duncan, Alice Faye 1967- 168
  Earlier sketch in SATA 95
Duncan, Gregory
  See McClintock, Marshall
Duncan, Jane
  See Cameron, Elizabeth Jane
Duncan, Julia K.
  See Benson, Mildred
Duncan, Lois 1934- 141
  Autobiography Feature 141
  Earlier sketches in SATA 1, 36, 75, 133
  See also CLR 129
  See also SAAS 2
Duncan, Norman 1871-1916
  See YABC 1
Duncan, Terence
  See Nolan, William F(rancis)
Duncombe, Frances (Riker) 1900-1994 25
  Obituary 82
Dunham, Montrew 1919- 162
Dunham, Montrew Goetz
  See Dunham, Montrew
Dunkle, Clare B. 1964- 155
Dunlap, Julie 1958- 84
Dunleavy, Deborah 1951- 133
Dunlop, Agnes M. R. (?)-1982 87
Dunlop, Eileen (Rhona) 1938- 76
  Earlier sketch in SATA 24
  See also SAAS 12
Dunmore, Helen 1952- 201
Dunn, Anne M. 1940- 107
Dunn, Harvey T(homas) 1884-1952 34
Dunn, Herb
  See Gutman, Dan
Dunn, John M. (III) 1949- 93
Dunn, Judy
  See Spangenberg, Judith Dunn
Dunn, Mary Lois 1930- 6
Dunnahoo, Terry Janson 1927- 7
Dunne, Jeanette 1952- 72
Dunne, Kathleen 1933- 126
Dunne, Marie
  See Clark, Ann Nolan
Dunne, Mary Collins 1914- 11
Dunne, Mary Jo
  See Dunne, Mary Collins
Dunnett, Kaitlyn
  See Emerson, Kathy Lynn
Dunnett, Margaret (Rosalind) 1909-1977 42
Dunnick, Regan 178
Dunrea, Olivier 1953- 160
  Brief entry 46
  Earlier sketches in SATA 59, 118
Dunrea, Olivier Jean-Paul Dominique
  See Dunrea, Olivier
Dunton, Dorothy 1912- 92
Dupasquier, Philippe 1955- 151
  Earlier sketch in SATA 86
DuPrau, Jeanne 1944- 144
Dupuy, T(revor) N(evitt) 1916-1995 4
  Obituary 86
DuQuette, Keith 1960- 155
  Earlier sketch in SATA 90
Duran, Gloria 1924- 171
Duran, Gloria Bradley
  See Duran, Gloria
Duranceau, Suzanne 1952- 162
Durand, Delphine 1971- 200
Durango, Julia 1967- 173
Durant, Alan 1958- 165
  Earlier sketch in SATA 121
Durant, John 1902- 27
Durbin, William 1951- 174
  Earlier sketch in SATA 143

Durell, Ann 1930- 66
Durkee, Sarah 173
Durrant, Lynda 1954- 148
  Earlier sketch in SATA 96
Durrell, Gerald (Malcolm) 1925-1995 8
  Obituary 84
Durrell, Julie 1955- 94
Durrett, Deanne 1940- 144
  Earlier sketch in SATA 92
Du Soe, Robert C. 1892-1958
  See YABC 2
Dussling, Jennifer 1970- 143
  Earlier sketch in SATA 96
DuTemple, Lesley A. 1952- 113
Dutton, Sandra 191
Dutz
  See Davis, Mary Octavia
Duval, Katherine
  See James, Elizabeth
Duval, Kathy 1946- 181
Duvall, Aimee
  See Thurlo, Aimee
  and Thurlo, David
Duvall, Evelyn Millis 1906- 9
Duvall, Jill D(onovan) 1932- 102
Duvoisin, Roger (Antoine) 1904-1980 30
  Obituary 23
  Earlier sketch in SATA 2
  See also CLR 23
Dwiggins, Don(ald J.) 1913-1988 4
  Obituary 60
Dwight, Allan
  See Cole, Lois Dwight
Dwyer, Deanna
  See Koontz, Dean R.
Dwyer, K.R.
  See Koontz, Dean R.
Dyck, Peter J. 1914- 75
Dyer, James (Frederick) 1934- 37
Dyer, Jane 191
  Earlier sketch in SATA 147
Dyess, John (Foster) 1939- 76
Dygard, Thomas J. 1931-1996 97
  Obituary 92
  Earlier sketch in SATA 24
  See also SAAS 15
Dyke, John 1935- 35

E

E. V. L.
  See Lucas, E(dward) V(errall)
Eagar, Frances (Elisabeth Stuart)
  1940-1978 11
  Obituary 55
Eager, Edward (McMaken) 1911-1964 17
  See also CLR 43
Eager, George 1921- 56
Eager, George B.
  See Eager, George
Eagle, Ellen 1953- 61
Eagle, Kin
  See Adlerman, Daniel (Ezra)
  and Adlerman, Kimberly M(arie)
Eagle, Mike 1942- 11
Earle, Olive L(ydia) 1888-1982 7
Earle, William
  See Johns, W(illiam) E(arle)
Earls, Nick 1963- 156
  Earlier sketch in SATA 95
Early, Jack
  See Scoppettone, Sandra
Early, Jon
  See Johns, W(illiam) E(arle)
Early, Margaret 1951- 72
Earnshaw, Brian 1929- 17
Earnshaw, Micky
  See Earnshaw, Spencer Wright
Earnshaw, Spencer Wright 1939- 88

Easley, MaryAnn 94
Eason, Alethea 1957- 197
Eastman, Charles A(lexander) 1858-1939
  See YABC 1
Eastman, P(hilip) D(ey) 1909-1986 33
  Obituary 46
Easton, Kelly 1960- 192
  Earlier sketch in SATA 141
Eastwick, Ivy (Ethel) O(live) 3
Eaton, Anne T(haxter) 1881-1971 32
Eaton, Anthony 1971- 167
Eaton, George L.
  See Verral, Charles Spain
Eaton, Janet
  See Givens, Janet E(aton)
Eaton, Jeanette 1886-1968 24
Eaton, Maxwell III 1981- 199
Eaton, Tom 1940- 22
Ebel, Alex 1927- 11
Eber, Dorothy (Margaret) Harley 1930- 27
Eberhart, Sheri S.
  See Tepper, Sheri S.
Eberle, Irmengarde 1898-1979 2
  Obituary 23
Eble, Diane 1956- 74
Eboch, Chris 113
Eccles Williams, Ferelith 1920- 22
Echlin, Kim 1955- 166
Eckblad, Edith Berven 1923- 23
Ecke, Wolfgang 1927-1983
  Obituary 37
Eckert, Allan W. 1931- 91
  Brief entry 27
  Earlier sketch in SATA 29
  See also SAAS 21
Eckert, Horst 1931- 72
  Earlier sketch in SATA 8
  See also CLR 26
Ecklar, Julia (Marie) 1964- 112
Eddings, David 1931-2009 91
Eddings, David Carroll
  See Eddings, David
Ede, Janina 1937- 33
Edell, Celeste 12
Edelman, Lily (Judith) 1915-1981 22
Edelson, Edward 1932- 51
Edens, Cooper 1945- 166
  Earlier sketches in SATA 49, 112
Edens, (Bishop) David 1926- 39
Edey, Maitland A(rmstrong) 1910-1992 25
  Obituary 71
Edgerton, Perky 196
Edgeworth, Maria 1768-1849 21
Edgy, Wardore
  See Gorey, Edward (St. John)
Edison, Theodore
  See Stratemeyer, Edward L.
Edler, Tim(othy) 1948- 56
Edmiston, Jim 1948- 80
Edmonds, I(vy) G(ordon) 1917- 8
Edmonds, Walter D(umaux) 1903-1998 27
  Obituary 99
  Earlier sketch in SATA 1
  See also SAAS 4
Edmund, Sean
  See Pringle, Laurence
Edsall, Marian (Stickney) 1920- 8
Edwards, Al
  See Nourse, Alan E(dward)
Edwards, Anne 1927- 35
Edwards, Audrey 1947- 52
  Brief entry 31
Edwards, Becky (Jane) 1966- 125
Edwards, Bertram
  See Edwards, Herbert Charles
Edwards, Bronwen Elizabeth
  See Rose, Wendy
Edwards, Cecile Pepin 1916- 25
Edwards, David 1962- 198

Edwards, Dorothy 1914-1982 .... *88*
  Obituary *31*
  Earlier sketch in SATA *4*
Edwards, F. E.
  See Nolan, William F(rancis)
Edwards, Frank B. 1952- *93*
Edwards, Gunvor *32*
Edwards, Harvey 1929- *5*
Edwards, Hazel (Eileen) 1945- *135*
Edwards, Herbert Charles 1912- *12*
Edwards, Jane Campbell 1932- *10*
Edwards, Julia
  See Stratemeyer, Edward L.
Edwards, Julie
  See Andrews, Julie
Edwards, Julie Andrews
  See Andrews, Julie
Edwards, June
  See Bhatia, Jamunadevi
Edwards, Linda Strauss 1948- *49*
  Brief entry *42*
Edwards, Margaret (Alexander) 1902-1988
  Obituary *56*
Edwards, Michelle 1955- *152*
  Earlier sketch in SATA *70*
Edwards, Monica le Doux Newton
  1912-1998 .... *12*
Edwards, Olwen
  See Gater, Dilys
Edwards, Page (Lawrence, Jr.) 1941-1999 ... *59*
Edwards, Pamela Duncan *189*
Edwards, R. T.
  See Goulart, Ron
Edwards, Sally (Cary) 1929- *7*
Edwards, Samuel
  See Gerson, Noel Bertram
Edwards, Wallace 1957(?)- *170*
Egan, E(dward) W(elsted) 1922- *35*
Egan, Kerry *175*
Egan, Lorraine Hopping 1960- *134*
  Earlier sketch in SATA *91*
Egan, Tim 1957- *191*
  Earlier sketches in SATA *89, 155*
Egermeier, Elsie E(milie) 1890-1986 .... *65*
Eggenberger, David 1918- *6*
Eggleston, Edward 1837-1902 .... *27*
Egielski, Richard 1952- *163*
  Earlier sketches in SATA *11, 49, 106*
Egypt, Ophelia Settle 1903-1984 .... *16*
  Obituary *38*
Ehlert, Lois 1934- *172*
  Earlier sketches in SATA *35, 69, 128*
  See also CLR *28*
Ehlert, Lois Jane
  See Ehlert, Lois
Ehling, Katalin Olah 1941- *93*
Ehrenfreund, Norbert 1921- *86*
Ehrenhaft, Daniel 1970- *185*
Ehrhardt, Karen 1963- *184*
Ehrlich, Amy 1942- *132*
  Earlier sketches in SATA *25, 65, 96*
Ehrlich, Bettina Bauer 1903-1985 .... *1*
Ehrlich, H. M.
  See Ziefert, Harriet
Eichenberg, Fritz 1901-1990 .... *50*
  Earlier sketch in SATA *9*
Eichler, Margrit 1942- *35*
Eichner, James A. 1927- *4*
Eidson, Thomas 1944- *112*
Eifert, Virginia (Louise) S(nider) 1911-1966 . *2*
Eige, (Elizabeth) Lillian 1915- *65*
Eiken, J. Melia 1967- *125*
Einsel, Naiad *10*
Einsel, Walter 1926- *10*
Einzig, Susan 1922- *43*
Eiseman, Alberta 1925- *15*
Eisenberg, Azriel (Louis) 1903-1985 .... *12*
Eisenberg, Lisa 1949- *155*
  Brief entry *50*
  Earlier sketch in SATA *57*
Eisenberg, Phyllis Rose 1924- *41*

Eisner, Vivienne
  See Margolis, Vivienne
Eisner, Will 1917-2005 .... *165*
  Earlier sketch in SATA *31*
Eisner, William Erwin
  See Eisner, Will
Eitzen, Allan 1928- *9*
Eitzen, Ruth (Carper) 1924- *9*
Ekwensi, C. O. D.
  See Ekwensi, Cyprian
Ekwensi, Cyprian 1921-2007 .... *66*
Ekwensi, Cyprian Odiatu Duaka
  See Ekwensi, Cyprian
Elam, Richard M(ace, Jr.) 1920- *9*
Elborn, Andrew
  See Clements, Andrew
  and Clements, Andrew
Elboz, Stephen 1956- *152*
Eldin, Peter 1939- *154*
Eldon, Kathy 1946- *107*
Eldridge, Marion *199*
Elfman, Blossom 1925- *8*
Elgin, Kathleen 1923- *39*
Elia
  See Lamb, Charles
Eliot, A. D.
  See Jewett, (Theodora) Sarah Orne
Eliot, Alice
  See Jewett, (Theodora) Sarah Orne
Eliot, Anne
  See Cole, Lois Dwight
Eliot, Dan
  See Silverberg, Robert
Elish, Dan 1960- *129*
  Earlier sketch in SATA *68*
Elisha, Ron 1951- *104*
Elisofon, Eliot 1911-1973
  Obituary *21*
Elkeles, Simone *187*
Elkin, Benjamin 1911-1995 .... *3*
Elkins, Dov Peretz 1937- *5*
Ellacott, S(amuel) E(rnest) 1911- *19*
Elleman, Barbara 1934- *147*
Ellen, Jaye
  See Nixon, Joan Lowery
Eller, Scott
  See Holinger, William (Jacques)
  and Shepard, Jim
Ellestad, Myrvin
  See Ellestad, Myrvin H.
Ellestad, Myrvin H. 1921- *120*
Elliot, David 1952- *122*
Elliott, Bruce
  See Field, Edward
Elliott, David 1947- *201*
  Earlier sketch in SATA *163*
Elliott, Don
  See Silverberg, Robert
Elliott, Elizabeth Shippen Green
  See Green, Elizabeth Shippen
Elliott, Janice 1931-1995 .... *119*
Elliott, Joey
  See Houk, Randy
Elliott, Laura Malone 1957- *197*
Elliott, Louise *111*
Elliott, Odette 1939- *75*
Elliott, Patricia 1946- *176*
Elliott, Sarah M(cCarn) 1930- *14*
Elliott, (Robert) Scott 1970- *153*
Elliott, William
  See Bradbury, Ray
Ellis, (Mary) Amabel (Nassau Strachey)
  Williams
  See Williams-Ellis, (Mary) Amabel (Nassau
  Strachey)
Ellis, Anyon
  See Rowland-Entwistle, (Arthur) Theodore
  (Henry)
Ellis, Carson 1975- *190*
Ellis, Carson Friedman
  See Ellis, Carson

Ellis, Deborah 1960- *187*
  Earlier sketch in SATA *129*
Ellis, E. S.
  See Ellis, Edward S(ylvester)
Ellis, Edward S(ylvester) 1840-1916
  See YABC *1*
Ellis, Ella Thorp 1928- *127*
  Earlier sketch in SATA *7*
  See also SAAS *9*
Ellis, Harry Bearse 1921-2004 .... *9*
Ellis, Herbert
  See Wilson, Lionel
Ellis, Mel(vin Richard) 1912-1984 .... *7*
  Obituary *39*
Ellis, Richard 1938- *130*
Ellis, Sarah 1952- *179*
  Earlier sketches in SATA *68, 131*
  See also CLR *42*
Ellison, Chris *196*
Ellison, Emily *114*
Ellison, Lucile Watkins 1907(?)-1979 .... *50*
  Obituary *22*
Ellison, Virginia H(owell) 1910- *4*
Ellsberg, Edward 1891-1983 .... *7*
Ellsworth, Loretta 1954- *199*
Ellsworth, Mary Ellen (Tressel) 1940- *146*
Elmer, Robert 1958- *154*
  Earlier sketch in SATA *99*
Elmore, (Carolyn) Patricia 1933- *38*
  Brief entry *35*
El-Moslimany, Ann P(axton) 1937- *90*
Elschner, Geraldine 1954- *183*
Elspeth
  See Bragdon, Elspeth MacDuffie
Elster, Jean Alicia 1953- *150*
Elting, Mary 1906- *88*
  Earlier sketch in SATA *2*
  See also SAAS *20*
Elvgren, Jennifer Riesmeyer *179*
Elwart, Joan Potter 1927- *2*
Elwood, Ann 1931- *55*
  Brief entry *52*
Elwood, Roger 1943-2007 .... *58*
Elya, Susan M(iddleton) 1955- *159*
  Earlier sketch in SATA *106*
Elzbieta *88*
Ember, Kathi *190*
Emberley, Barbara A(nne) 1932- *146*
  Earlier sketches in SATA *8, 70*
  See also CLR *5*
Emberley, Ed(ward Randolph) 1931- *146*
  Earlier sketches in SATA *8, 70*
  See also CLR *81*
Emberley, Michael 1960- *189*
  Earlier sketches in SATA *34, 80, 119*
Embry, Margaret Jacob 1919-1975 .... *5*
Emecheta, Buchi 1944- *66*
Emecheta, Florence Onye Buchi
  See Emecheta, Buchi
Emerson, Alice B.
  See Benson, Mildred
Emerson, Kathy Lynn 1947- *63*
Emerson, Ru 1944- *107*
  Earlier sketch in SATA *70*
Emerson, Sally 1952- *111*
Emerson, William K(eith) 1925- *25*
Emert, Phyllis R(aybin) 1947- *93*
Emery, Anne (McGuigan) 1907- *33*
  Earlier sketch in SATA *1*
Emmens, Carol Ann 1944- *39*
Emmett, Jonathan 1965- *188*
  Earlier sketch in SATA *138*
Emmons, Della (Florence) Gould 1890-1983
  Obituary *39*
Emory, Jerry 1957- *96*
Emrich, Duncan (Black Macdonald)
  1908-1970(?) *11*
Emshwiller, Carol 1921- *174*
  Autobiography Feature *174*
Emshwiller, Carol Fries
  See Emshwiller, Carol

Emslie, M. L.
   See Simpson, Myrtle L(illias)
Ende, Michael (Andreas Helmuth)
   1929-1995 .... *130*
   Brief entry *42*
   Obituary *86*
   Earlier sketch in SATA *61*
   See also CLR *138*
Enderle, Dotti 1954- *145*
Enderle, Judith (Ann) Ross 1941- *89*
   Autobiography Feature *114*
   Earlier sketch in SATA *38*
   See also SAAS *26*
Enell, Trinka (Gochenour) 1951- *79*
Enfield, Carrie
   See Smith, Susan Vernon
Engdahl, Sylvia Louise 1933- *4*
   Autobiography Feature *122*
   See also CLR *2*
   See also SAAS *5*
Engel, Diana 1947- *70*
Engelbreit, Mary 1952- *169*
Engelhart, Margaret S. 1924- *59*
Engelmann, Kim (V.) 1959- *87*
England, George Allan 1877-1936 .... *102*
Englart, Mindi Rose 1965- *146*
Engle, Eloise
   See Paananen, Eloise (Katherine)
Engle, Margarita 1951- *193*
Englebert, Victor 1933- *8*
English, James W(ilson) 1915- *37*
Engstrom, Elizabeth 1951- *110*
Enright, D(ennis) J(oseph) 1920-2002 .... *25*
   Obituary *140*
Enright, Dominique *194*
Enright, Elizabeth (Wright) 1909-1968 .... *9*
   See also CLR *4*
Ensor, Barbara *180*
Ensor, Robert (T.) 1922- *93*
Enthoven, Sam 1974- *187*
Entwistle, (Arthur) Theodore (Henry) Rowland
   See Rowland-Entwistle, (Arthur) Theodore
   (Henry)
Enys, Sarah L.
   See Sloggett, Nellie
Epanya, Christian A(rthur Kingue) 1956- *91*
Ephraim, Shelly S(chonebaum) 1952- *97*
Ephron, Delia 1944- *197*
   Brief entry *50*
   Earlier sketch in SATA *65*
Epler, Doris M. 1928- *73*
Epp, Margaret A(gnes) 1913- *20*
Eppenstein, Louise (Kohn) 1892-1987
   Obituary *54*
Epple, Anne Orth 1927- *20*
Epstein, Anne Merrick 1931- *20*
Epstein, Beryl (M. Williams) 1910- *31*
   Earlier sketch in SATA *1*
   See also CLR *26*
   See also SAAS *17*
Epstein, Perle S(herry) 1938- *27*
Epstein, Rachel S. 1941- *102*
Epstein, Samuel 1909-2000 .... *31*
   Earlier sketch in SATA *1*
   See also CLR *26*
   See also SAAS *17*
Erdman, Loula Grace 1905(?)-1976 .... *1*
Erdoes, Richard 1912- *33*
   Brief entry *28*
Erdogan, Buket *187*
Erdrich, Karen Louise
   See Erdrich, Louise
Erdrich, Louise 1954- *141*
   Earlier sketch in SATA *94*
Erickson, Betty J. 1923- *97*
Erickson, Betty Jean
   See Erickson, Betty J.
Erickson, John R. 1943- *136*
   Earlier sketch in SATA *70*
Erickson, Jon 1948- *141*
Erickson, Phoebe *59*

Erickson, Russell E(verett) 1932- *27*
Erickson, Sabra Rollins 1912-1995 .... *35*
Erickson, Walter
   See Fast, Howard
Ericson, Walter
   See Fast, Howard
Ericsson, Jennifer A. *170*
Erikson, Mel 1937- *31*
Ering, Timothy Basil *176*
Erlanger, Baba
   See Trahey, Jane
Erlbach, Arlene 1948- *160*
   Earlier sketches in SATA *78, 115*
Erlbruch, Wolf 1948- *181*
Erlich, Lillian (Feldman) 1910-1983 .... *10*
Erlings, Fridrik 1962- *196*
Erlingsson, Frierik
   See Erlings, Fridrik
Ermatinger, James W. 1959- *170*
Ernest, William
   See Berkebile, Fred D(onovan)
Ernst, (Lyman) John 1940- *39*
Ernst, Kathleen
   See Ernst, Kathleen A.
Ernst, Kathleen A. 1959- *162*
Ernst, Kathryn (Fitzgerald) 1942- *25*
Ernst, Lisa Campbell 1957- *154*
   Brief entry *44*
   Earlier sketches in SATA *55, 95*
Erskine, Kathryn *193*
Ervin, Janet Halliday 1923- *4*
Erwin, Will
   See Eisner, Will
Esbaum, Jill *174*
Esbensen, Barbara J(uster) 1925-1996 .... *97*
   Brief entry *53*
   Earlier sketch in SATA *62*
Eschbacher, Roger *160*
Eschmeyer, R. E. 1898-1989 .... *29*
Escriva, Vivi *182*
Eseki, Bruno
   See Mphahlele, Es'kia
Esekie, Bruno
   See Mphahlele, Es'kia
Eshmeyer, Reinhart Ernst
   See Eschmeyer, R. E.
Eskridge, Ann E. 1949- *84*
Espeland, Pamela (Lee) 1951- *128*
   Brief entry *38*
   Earlier sketch in SATA *52*
Espriella, Don Manuel Alvarez
   See Southey, Robert
Espy, Willard R(ichardson) 1910-1999 .... *38*
   Obituary *113*
Essakalli, Julie Klear *200*
Essrig, Harry 1912- *66*
Estep, Irene Compton *5*
Esterl, Arnica 1933- *77*
Estes, Eleanor (Ruth) 1906-1988 .... *91*
   Obituary *56*
   Earlier sketch in SATA *7*
   See also CLR *70*
Estoril, Jean
   See Allan, Mabel Esther
Estrada, Pau 1961- *200*
   Earlier sketch in SATA *74*
Etchemendy, Nancy 1952- *166*
   Earlier sketch in SATA *38*
Etchemendy, Nancy Elise Howell
   See Etchemendy, Nancy
Etchison, Birdie L(ee) 1937- *38*
Etchison, Craig 1945- *133*
Etherington, Frank 1945- *58*
Eton, Robert
   See Meynell, Laurence Walter
Ets, Marie Hall 1893-1984 .... *2*
   See also CLR *33*
Ettlinger, Doris 1950- *173*
Eunson, (John) Dale 1904-2002 .... *5*
   Obituary *132*
Evan, Frances Y. 1951- *167*

Evanoff, Vlad 1916- *59*
Evans, Cambria 1981- *178*
Evans, Douglas 1953- *144*
   Earlier sketch in SATA *93*
Evans, Eva (Knox) 1905-1998 .... *27*
Evans, Freddi Williams 1957- *134*
Evans, Greg 1947- *143*
   Earlier sketch in SATA *73*
Evans, Hubert Reginald 1892-1986 .... *118*
   Obituary *48*
Evans, Katherine (Floyd) 1901-1964 .... *5*
Evans, Larry
   See Evans, Laurence Chubb
Evans, Laurence Chubb 1939- *88*
Evans, Lawrence Watt
   See Watt-Evans, Lawrence
Evans, Lezlie *180*
Evans, Mari 1923- *10*
Evans, Mark *19*
Evans, Nancy 1950- *65*
Evans, Nate *201*
Evans, Patricia Healy
   See Carpenter, Patricia (Healy Evans)
Evans, (Alice) Pearl 1927- *83*
Evans, Shane W. *189*
Evans, Shirlee 1931- *58*
Evans, Tabor
   See Cameron, Lou
   and Knott, William C(ecil, Jr.)
   and Wallmann, Jeffrey M(iner)
   and Whittington, Harry (Benjamin)
Evarts, Esther
   See Benson, Sally
Evarts, Hal G., (Jr.) 1915-1989 .... *6*
Everett, Gail
   See Hale, Arlene
Evernden, Margery 1916- *5*
Eversole, Robyn 1971- *74*
Eversole, Robyn H.
   See Eversole, Robyn
Eversole, Robyn Harbert
   See Eversole, Robyn
Evslin, Bernard 1922-1993 .... *83*
   Brief entry *28*
   Obituary *77*
   Earlier sketch in SATA *45*
Ewart, Claire 1958- *145*
   Earlier sketch in SATA *76*
Ewen, David 1907-1985 .... *4*
   Obituary *47*
Ewing, Juliana (Horatia Gatty) 1841-1885 ... *16*
   See also CLR *78*
Ewing, Kathryn 1921- *20*
Eyerly, Jeannette 1908-2008 .... *86*
   Obituary *196*
   Earlier sketch in SATA *4*
   See also SAAS *10*
Eyerly, Jeannette Hyde
   See Eyerly, Jeannette
Eyre, Dorothy
   See McGuire, Leslie (Sarah)
Eyre, Frank 1910-1988
   Obituary *62*
Eyre, Katherine Wigmore 1901-1970 .... *26*
Ezzell, Marilyn 1937- *42*
   Brief entry *38*

F

Fabe, Maxene 1943- *15*
Faber, Doris (Greenberg) 1924- *78*
   Earlier sketch in SATA *3*
Faber, Harold 1919- *5*
Fabre, Jean Henri (Casimir) 1823-1915 .... *22*
Facklam, Margery (Metz) 1927- *132*
   Earlier sketches in SATA *20, 85*
Fadden, David Kanietakeron *196*
Fadiman, Clifton (Paul) 1904-1999 .... *11*
   Obituary *115*

Fagan, Cary 1957- *186*
Fahs, Sophia Blanche Lyon 1876-1978 ...... *102*
Failing, Barbara Larmon *182*
Fair, David 1952- *96*
Fair, Sylvia 1933- *13*
Fairfax-Lucy, Brian (Fulke Cameron-Ramsay)
  1898-1974 .... *6*
  Obituary *26*
Fairfield, Flora
  See Alcott, Louisa May
Fairlie, Gerard 1899-1983
  Obituary *34*
Fairman, Joan A(lexandra) 1935- *10*
Faithfull, Gail 1936- *8*
Falcone, L(ucy) M. 1951- *155*
Falcone, Ian 1959- *179*
  Earlier sketch in SATA *125*
  See also CLR *90*
Falconer, James
  See Kirkup, James
Falconer, Lee N.
  See May, Julian
Falkner, Leonard 1900-1977 .... *12*
Fall, Andrew
  See Arthur, Robert, (Jr.)
Fall, Thomas
  See Snow, Donald Clifford
Faller, Regis 1968- *187*
Falls, C(harles) B(uckles) 1874-1960 .... *38*
  Brief entry *27*
Falstein, Louis 1909-1995 .... *37*
Falwell, Cathryn 1952- *196*
Fancher, Lou 1960- *177*
Fanelli, Sara 1969- *126*
  Earlier sketch in SATA *89*
Fanning, Leonard M(ulliken) 1888-1967 .... *5*
Faralla, Dana 1909- *9*
Faralla, Dorothy W.
  See Faralla, Dana
Farb, Peter 1929-1980 .... *12*
  Obituary *22*
Farber, Norma 1909-1984 .... *75*
  Obituary *38*
  Earlier sketch in SATA *25*
Fardell, John 1967- *195*
Farish, Terry 1947- *146*
  Earlier sketch in SATA *82*
Farjeon, (Eve) Annabel 1919-2004 .... *11*
  Obituary *153*
Farjeon, Eleanor 1881-1965 .... *2*
  See also CLR *34*
Farley, Carol (J.) 1936- *137*
  Earlier sketch in SATA *4*
Farley, Terri *165*
Farley, Walter (Lorimer) 1915-1989 .... *132*
  Earlier sketches in SATA *2, 43*
Farlow, James O(rville, Jr.) 1951- *75*
Farmer, Nancy 1941- *161*
  Earlier sketches in SATA *79, 117*
Farmer, Patti 1948- *79*
Farmer, Penelope (Jane) 1939- *105*
  Brief entry *39*
  Earlier sketch in SATA *40*
  See also CLR *8*
  See also SAAS *22*
Farmer, Peter 1950- *38*
Farmer, Philip Jose
  See Farmer, Philip Jose
Farmer, Philip Jose 1918-2009 .... *93*
  Obituary *201*
Farmer, Philipe Jos
  See Farmer, Philip Jose
Farnham, Burt
  See Clifford, Harold B(urton)
Farnsworth, Bill 1958- *186*
  Earlier sketches in SATA *84, 135*
Farquhar, Margaret C(utting) 1905-1988 ...... *13*
Farquharson, Alexander 1944- *46*
Farquharson, Martha
  See Finley, Martha

Farr, Diana *82*
  Earlier sketch in SATA *3*
Farr, Finis (King) 1904-1982 .... *10*
Farrar, Jill
  See Morris, Jill
Farrar, Susan Clement 1917- *33*
Farrell, Ben
  See Cebulash, Mel
Farrell, Patrick
  See Odgers, Sally Farrell
Farrell, Sally
  See Odgers, Sally Farrell
Farrer, Vashti *167*
Farrington, Benjamin 1891-1974
  Obituary *20*
Farrington, S(elwyn) Kip, Jr. 1904-1983 ..... *20*
Farshtey, Greg(ory T.) 1965- *148*
Farthing, Alison 1936- *45*
  Brief entry *36*
Farthing-Knight, Catherine 1933- *92*
Fassler, Joan (Grace) 1931- *11*
Fast, Howard 1914-2003 .... *7*
  Autobiography Feature *107*
Fast, Howard Melvin
  See Fast, Howard
Fasulo, Michael 1963- *83*
Fatchen, Max 1920- *84*
  Earlier sketch in SATA *20*
  See also SAAS *20*
Fate, Marilyn
  See Collins, Paul
Father Goose
  See Ghigna, Charles
Fatigati, (Frances) Evelyn 1948- *24*
Fatio, Louise 1904-1993 .... *6*
Fatus, Sophie 1957- *182*
Faulhaber, Martha 1926- *7*
Faulkner, Anne Irvin 1906- *23*
Faulkner, Frank
  See Ellis, Edward S(ylvester)
Faulkner, Nancy
  See Faulkner, Anne Irvin
Faulknor, Cliff(ord Vernon) 1913- *86*
Favole, Robert J(ames) 1950- *125*
Fax, Elton Clay 1909-1993 .... *25*
Faxon, Lavinia
  See Russ, Lavinia (Faxon)
Feagles, Anita M(acRae) 1927- *9*
Feagles, Elizabeth
  See Day, Beth (Feagles)
Feague, Mildred H. 1915- *14*
Fearnley, Jan 1965- *153*
Fearrington, Ann (Peyton) 1945- *146*
Fecher, Constance
  See Heaven, Constance (Christina)
Feder, Chris Welles 1938- *81*
Feder, Harriet K. 1928- *73*
Feder, Paula (Kurzband) 1935- *26*
Federici, Debbie 1965- *175*
Federici, Debbie Tanner
  See Federici, Debbie
Feelings, Muriel (Lavita Grey) 1938- *16*
  See also CLR *5*
  See also SAAS *8*
Feelings, Thomas 1933-2003 .... *69*
  Obituary *148*
  Earlier sketch in SATA *8*
  See also CLR *58*
  See also SAAS *19*
Feelings, Tom
  See Feelings, Thomas
Fehler, Gene 1940- *201*
  Earlier sketch in SATA *74*
Fehrenbach, T(heodore) R(eed, Jr.) 1925- *33*
Feiffer, Jules 1929- *201*
  Earlier sketches in SATA *8, 61, 111, 157*
Feiffer, Jules Ralph
  See Feiffer, Jules
Feiffer, Kate 1964- *170*
Feig, Barbara Krane 1937- *34*

Feikema, Feike
  See Manfred, Frederick (Feikema)
Feil, Hila 1942- *12*
Feilen, John
  See May, Julian
Feinberg, Barbara Jane 1938- *123*
  Earlier sketch in SATA *58*
Feinberg, Barbara Silberdick
  See Feinberg, Barbara Jane
Feinstein, John 1956- *195*
  Earlier sketch in SATA *163*
Feldman, Anne (Rodgers) 1939- *19*
Feldman, Elane *79*
Feldman, Jody *200*
Felin, M. Sindy *194*
Felix
  See Vincent, Felix
Fell, Derek 1939- *167*
Fell, Derek John
  See Fell, Derek
Fellowes, Julian 1950- *198*
Fellows, Muriel H. *10*
Fellows, Stan 1957- *177*
Fellows, Stanley
  See Fellows, Stan
Felsen, Henry Gregor 1916-1995 .... *1*
  See also SAAS *2*
Felstead, Cathie 1954- *192*
Feltenstein, Arlene (H.) 1934- *119*
Felton, Harold William 1902-1991 .... *1*
Felton, Ronald Oliver 1909- *3*
Felts, Shirley 1934- *33*
Fenderson, Lewis H., Jr. 1907-1983 .... *47*
  Obituary *37*
Fenner, Carol (Elizabeth) 1929-2002 .... *89*
  Obituary *132*
  Earlier sketch in SATA *7*
  See also SAAS *24*
Fenner, Phyllis R(eid) 1899-1982 .... *1*
  Obituary *29*
Fensham, Elizabeth *169*
Fenten, Barbara D(oris) 1935- *26*
Fenten, D(onald) X. 1932- *4*
Fenton, Carroll Lane 1900-1969 .... *5*
Fenton, Edward 1917-1995 .... *7*
  Obituary *89*
Fenton, Mildred Adams 1899-1995 .... *21*
Fenwick, Patti
  See Grider, Dorothy
Feravolo, Rocco Vincent 1922- *10*
Ferber, Brenda A. 1967- *184*
Ferber, Edna 1887-1968 .... *7*
Fergus, Charles *114*
Ferguson, Alane 1957- *182*
  Earlier sketch in SATA *85*
Ferguson, Bob
  See Ferguson, Robert Bruce
Ferguson, Cecil 1931- *45*
Ferguson, Peter 1968- *199*
Ferguson, Robert Bruce 1927-2001 .... *13*
Ferguson, Sarah 1959- *180*
  Earlier sketches in SATA *66, 110*
Ferguson, Sarah Margaret
  See Ferguson, Sarah
Ferguson, Walter (W.) 1930- *34*
Fergusson, Erna 1888-1964 .... *5*
Fermi, Laura 1907-1977 .... *6*
  Obituary *28*
Fern, Eugene A. 1919-1987 .... *10*
  Obituary *54*
Fernandes, Eugenie 1943- *139*
  Earlier sketch in SATA *77*
Fernandez, Laura 1960- *171*
Ferrari, Maria *123*
Ferreiro, Carmen 1958- *158*
Ferrell, Nancy Warren 1932- *70*
Ferri, Giuliano 1965- *197*
Ferrier, Lucy
  See Penzler, Otto
Ferris, Helen Josephine 1890-1969 .... *21*

Ferris, James Cody
  See McFarlane, Leslie
Ferris, Jean 1939- *149*
  Brief entry *50*
  Earlier sketches in SATA *56, 105*
Ferris, Jeri Chase 1937- *84*
Ferry, Charles 1927- *92*
  Earlier sketch in SATA *43*
  See also CLR *34*
  See also SAAS *20*
Fetz, Ingrid 1915- *30*
Feydy, Anne Lindbergh
  See Sapieyevski, Anne Lindbergh
Fiammenghi, Gioia 1929- *66*
  Earlier sketch in SATA *9*
Fiarotta, Noel
  See Ficarotta, Noel
Fiarotta, Phyllis
  See Ficarotta, Phyllis
Ficarotta, Noel 1944- *15*
Ficarotta, Phyllis 1942- *15*
Fichter, George S. 1922-1993 .... *7*
Ficocelli, Elizabeth *189*
Fidler, Kathleen (Annie) 1899-1980 .... *87*
  Obituary *45*
  Earlier sketch in SATA *3*
Fiedler, Jean(nette Feldman) *4*
Fiedler, Joseph Daniel *159*
Fiedler, Lisa *185*
Field, Dorothy 1944- *97*
Field, Edward 1924- *109*
  Earlier sketch in SATA *8*
Field, Elinor Whitney 1889-1980
  Obituary *28*
Field, Eugene 1850-1895 .... *16*
Field, Gans T.
  See Wellman, Manly Wade
Field, James 1959- *113*
Field, Peter
  See Drago, Harry Sinclair
  and Dresser, Davis
  and Mann, E(dward) B(everly)
Field, Rachel (Lyman) 1894-1942 .... *15*
  See also CLR *21*
Fielding, Kate
  See Oldfield, Jenny
Fields, Bryan W. 1958(?)- *188*
Fields, Terri 1948- *191*
Fields, T.S.
  See Fields, Terri
Fienberg, Anna 1956- *183*
  Earlier sketch in SATA *112*
Fife, Dale (Odile Hollerbach) 1901- *18*
Fighter Pilot, A
  See Johnston, H(ugh) A(nthony) S(tephen)
Figler, Jeanie 1949- *123*
Figley, Marty Rhodes 1948- *158*
  Earlier sketch in SATA *88*
Figueredo, D(anilo) H. 1951- *155*
Figueroa, Pablo 1938- *9*
Fijan, Carol 1918- *12*
Filderman, Diane E(lizabeth) 1959- *87*
Files, Meg 1946- *107*
Fillmore, Parker H(oysted) 1878-1944
  See YABC *1*
Filstrup, Chris
  See Filstrup, E(dward) Christian
Filstrup, E(dward) Christian 1942- *43*
Filstrup, Janie
  See Merrill, Jane
Finchler, Judy 1943- *93*
Finder, Martin
  See Salzmann, Siegmund
Findlay, Jamieson 1958- *169*
Findon, Joanne 1957- *161*
Fine, Anne 1947- *197*
  Earlier sketches in SATA *29, 72, 111, 160*
  See also CLR *25*
  See also SAAS *15*
Fine, Edith Hope *169*
Fine, Howard 1961- *181*

Fine, Jane
  See Ziefert, Harriet
Finger, Charles J(oseph) 1869(?)-1941 .... *42*
Fink, William B(ertrand) 1916- *22*
Finke, Blythe Foote 1922- *26*
Finkel, George (Irvine) 1909-1975 .... *8*
Finkelstein, Norman H. 1941- *137*
  Earlier sketch in SATA *73*
Finkelstein, Norman Henry
  See Finkelstein, Norman H.
Finlay, Alice Sullivan 1946- *82*
Finlay, Winifred Lindsay Crawford
  (McKissack) 1910-1989 .... *23*
Finlayson, Ann 1925- *8*
Finley, Martha 1828-1909 .... *43*
Finley, Mary Peace 1942- *83*
Finney, Jack
  See Finney, Walter Braden
Finney, Patricia 1958- *163*
Finney, Shan 1941- *65*
Finney, Walter Braden 1911-1995 .... *109*
Firer, Ben Zion
  See Firer, Benzion
Firer, Benzion 1914- *64*
Fireside, Bryna J. 1932- *73*
Firmin, Charlotte 1954- *29*
Firmin, Peter 1928- *58*
  Earlier sketch in SATA *15*
Firth, Barbara *179*
Fischbach, Julius 1894-1988 .... *10*
Fischer, John
  See Fluke, Joanne
Fischer, R.J.
  See Fluke, Joanne
Fischer, Scott M. 1971- *195*
Fischer-Nagel, Andreas 1951- *56*
Fischer-Nagel, Heiderose 1956- *56*
Fischler, Shirley (Walton) *66*
Fischler, Stan(ley I.) *66*
  Brief entry *36*
Fischtrom, Harvey 1933-1974 .... *3*
Fishback, Margaret
  See Antolini, Margaret Fishback
Fishbone, Greg R. *195*
Fisher, Aileen (Lucia) 1906-2002 .... *73*
  Obituary *143*
  Earlier sketches in SATA *1, 25*
  See also CLR *49*
Fisher, Barbara 1940- *44*
  Brief entry *34*
Fisher, Carolyn 1968- *154*
Fisher, Catherine 1957- *155*
Fisher, Chris 1958- *80*
Fisher, Clavin C(argill) 1912- *24*
Fisher, Cynthia *195*
Fisher, Dorothy (Frances) Canfield 1879-1958
  See YABC *1*
  See also CLR *71*
Fisher, Gary L. 1949- *86*
Fisher, John 1909-1996 .... *15*
Fisher, John Oswald Hamilton
  See Fisher, John
Fisher, Laura Harrison 1934- *5*
Fisher, Leonard Everett 1924- *176*
  Autobiography Feature *122*
  Earlier sketches in SATA *4, 34, 73, 120*
  See also CLR *18*
  See also SAAS *1*
Fisher, Lois I. 1948- *38*
  Brief entry *35*
Fisher, Margery (Turner) 1913-1992 .... *20*
  Obituary *74*
Fisher, Marshall Jon 1963- *113*
Fisher, Nikki
  See Strachan, Ian
Fisher, Robert (Tempest) 1943- *47*
Fisher, Suzanne
  See Staples, Suzanne Fisher
Fisher, Valorie *177*
Fishman, Cathy Goldberg 1951- *106*

Fisk, Nicholas
  See Higginbottom, David
Fisk, Pauline 1948- *160*
  Earlier sketch in SATA *66*
Fiske, Tarleton
  See Bloch, Robert (Albert)
Fisscher, Catharina G. M. 1958- *142*
Fisscher, Tiny
  See Fisscher, Catharina G. M.
Fitch, Clarke
  See Sinclair, Upton
Fitch, John IV
  See Cormier, Robert
Fitch, Sheree 1956- *178*
  Earlier sketch in SATA *108*
Fitschen, Dale 1937- *20*
Fitzalan, Roger
  See Trevor, Elleston
Fitzgerald, Captain Hugh
  See Baum, L(yman) Frank
FitzGerald, Cathleen 1932-1987
  Obituary *50*
Fitzgerald, Dawn *175*
Fitzgerald, Edward Earl 1919-2001 .... *20*
Fitzgerald, F(rancis) A(nthony) 1940- *15*
Fitzgerald, Joanne 1956- *198*
Fitzgerald, John D(ennis) 1907(?)-1988 .... *20*
  Obituary *56*
  See also CLR *1*
Fitzgerald, Merni Ingrassia 1955- *53*
Fitzgibbon, Terry 1948- *121*
Fitzhardinge, Joan Margaret 1912- *73*
  Earlier sketch in SATA *2*
  See also CLR *5*
  See also SAAS *3*
Fitzhugh, Louise (Perkins) 1928-1974 .... *45*
  Obituary *24*
  Earlier sketch in SATA *1*
  See also CLR *72*
Fitzhugh, Percy Keese 1876-1950 .... *65*
Fitzpatrick, Marie-Louise 1962- *189*
  Earlier sketch in SATA *125*
FitzRalph, Matthew
  See McInerny, Ralph
Fitz-Randolph, Jane (Currens) 1915- *51*
Fitzsimons, Cecilia 1952- *97*
Fitzsimons, Cecilia A.L.
  See Fitzsimons, Cecilia
Flack, Marjorie 1897-1958 .... *100*
  See also YABC *2*
  See also CLR *28*
Flack, Naomi John White -1999 .... *40*
  Brief entry *35*
Flake, Sharon G. *166*
Flanagan, John 1944- *180*
Flanagan, John Anthony
  See Flanagan, John
Flannery, Kate
  See De Goldi, Kathleen Domenica
Flatt, Lizann 1966- *88*
Fleagle, Gail S(hatto) 1940- *117*
Fleetwood, Jenni 1947- *80*
Fleischer, Jane
  See Oppenheim, Joanne
Fleischhauer-Hardt, Helga 1936- *30*
Fleischman, Albert Sidney
  See Fleischman, Sid
Fleischman, John 1948- *145*
Fleischman, Paul 1952- *156*
  Brief entry *32*
  Earlier sketches in SATA *39, 72, 110*
  See also CLR *66*
  See also SAAS *20*
Fleischman, Sid 1920- *185*
  Earlier sketches in SATA *8, 59, 96, 148*
  See also CLR *15*
Fleischner, Jennifer 1956- *188*
  Earlier sketch in SATA *93*
Fleisher, Paul 1948- *132*
  Earlier sketch in SATA *81*

Fleisher, Robbin 1951-1977 52
    Brief entry 49
Fleishman, Seymour 1918- 66
    Brief entry 32
Fleming, A. A.
    See Arthur, Robert, (Jr.)
Fleming, Alice Mulcahey 1928- 9
Fleming, Candace 1962- 190
    Earlier sketches in SATA *94, 143*
Fleming, Denise 1950- 173
    Earlier sketches in SATA *81, 126*
Fleming, Elizabeth P. 1888-1985
    Obituary 48
Fleming, Ian 1908-1964 9
Fleming, Ian Lancaster
    See Fleming, Ian
Fleming, Ronald Lee 1941- 56
Fleming, Sally
    See Walker, Sally M(acArt)
Fleming, Stuart
    See Knight, Damon (Francis)
Fleming, Susan 1932- 32
Fleming, Thomas 1927- 8
Fleming, Thomas James
    See Fleming, Thomas
Fleming, Virginia (Edwards) 1923- 84
Flesch, Y.
    See Flesch, Yolande (Catarina)
Flesch, Yolande (Catarina) 1950- 55
Fletcher, Charlie May Hogue 1897-1977 3
Fletcher, Colin 1922-2007 28
Fletcher, Dirk
    See Cunningham, Chet
Fletcher, George U.
    See Pratt, (Murray) Fletcher
Fletcher, Helen Jill 1910- 13
Fletcher, Ralph 1953- 195
    Earlier sketches in SATA *105, 149*
    See also CLR *104*
Fletcher, Ralph J.
    See Fletcher, Ralph
Fletcher, Richard E. 1917(?)-1983
    Obituary 34
Fletcher, Rick
    See Fletcher, Richard E.
Fletcher, Susan 1951- 181
    Earlier sketches in SATA *70, 110*
Fletcher, Susan Clemens
    See Fletcher, Susan
Fleur, Paul
    See Pohl, Frederik
Flexner, James Thomas 1908-2003 9
Flinn, Alex 1966- 198
    Earlier sketch in SATA *159*
Flint, Helen 1952- 102
Flint, Russ 1944- 74
Flitner, David P(erkins), Jr. 1949- 7
Floca, Brian 190
    Earlier sketch in SATA *155*
Floethe, Louise Lee 1913-1988 4
Floethe, Richard 1901-1998 4
Floherty, John Joseph 1882-1964 25
Flood, Bo
    See Flood, Nancy Bo
Flood, Nancy Bo 1945- 130
Flood, Pansie Hart 1964- 140
Flood, William 1942- 129
Floogelbuckle, Al
    See Spiegelman, Art
Flora, James (Royer) 1914-1998 30
    Obituary 103
    Earlier sketch in SATA *1*
    See also SAAS *6*
Flores-Galbis, Enrique 1952- 186
Florian, Douglas 1950- 177
    Earlier sketches in SATA *19, 83, 125*
Flory, Jane Trescott 1917- 22
Flournoy, Valerie 1952- 95
Flournoy, Valerie Rose
    See Flournoy, Valerie
Flowerdew, Phyllis -1994 33

Flowers, Pam 1946- 136
Flowers, Sarah 1952- 98
Floyd, Gareth 1940- 62
    Brief entry 31
Fluchere, Henri 1914-1991 40
Fluke, Joanne 1943- 88
Flutsztejn-Gruda, Ilona 1930- 170
Flynn, Barbara 1928- 9
Flynn, Jackson
    See Bensen, Donald R.
    and Shirreffs, Gordon D(onald)
Flynn, Nicholas
    See Odgers, Sally Farrell
Flynn, Rachel 1953- 171
    Earlier sketch in SATA *109*
Flynn, Warren (G.) 1950- 154
Fodor, R(onald) V(ictor) 1944- 25
Fogelin, Adrian 1951- 175
    Earlier sketch in SATA *129*
Foley, (Anna) Bernice Williams 1902-1987 . 28
Foley, Greg E. 1969- 190
Foley, June 1944- 44
Foley, (Mary) Louise Munro 1933- 106
    Brief entry 40
    Earlier sketch in SATA *54*
Foley, Rae
    See Denniston, Elinore
Folke, Will
    See Bloch, Robert (Albert)
Follett, Helen Thomas 1884(?)-1970
    Obituary 27
Folsom, Franklin (Brewster) 1907-1995 5
    Obituary 88
Folsom, Michael (Brewster) 1938-1990 40
    Obituary 88
Fontenot, Mary Alice 1910- 91
    Earlier sketch in SATA *34*
Fontes, Justine 172
Fontes, Ron 1952- 183
Foon, Dennis 1951- 119
Fooner, Michael 22
Foote, Timothy (Gilson) 1926- 52
Forberg, Ati
    See Forberg, Beate Gropius
Forberg, Beate Gropius 1925- 22
Forbes, Anna 1954- 101
Forbes, Bryan 1926- 37
Forbes, Cabot L.
    See Hoyt, Edwin P(almer), Jr.
Forbes, Esther 1891-1967 100
    Earlier sketch in SATA *2*
    See also CLR *27*
Forbes, Graham B. 1
Forbes, Kathryn
    See McLean, Kathryn (Anderson)
Forbes, Robert
    See Arthur, Robert, (Jr.)
Ford, Albert Lee
    See Stratemeyer, Edward L.
Ford, Barbara 56
    Brief entry 34
Ford, Brian J(ohn) 1939- 49
Ford, Carolyn (Mott) 1938- 98
Ford, Christine 1953- 176
Ford, David
    See Baldacci, David
    and Baldacci, David
Ford, David B.
    See Baldacci, David
Ford, David Baldacci
    See Baldacci, David
Ford, Elbur
    See Hibbert, Eleanor Alice Burford
Ford, Ellen 1949- 89
Ford, George (Jr.) 31
Ford, Hilary
    See Youd, Samuel
Ford, Hildegarde
    See Morrison, Velma Ford
Ford, Jerome W. 1949- 78

Ford, Jerry
    See Ford, Jerome W.
Ford, Juwanda G(ertrude) 1967- 102
Ford, Marcia
    See Radford, Ruby L(orraine)
Ford, Nancy K(effer) 1906-1961
    Obituary 29
Ford, Peter 1936- 59
Ford, S. M.
    See Uhlig, Susan
Forde, Catherine 1961- 170
Foreman, Mark 199
Foreman, Michael 1938- 184
    Earlier sketches in SATA *2, 73, 129, 135*
    See also CLR *32*
    See also SAAS *21*
Foreman, Wilmoth 1939- 153
Forest, Antonia 1915-2003 29
    Obituary 149
Forest, Dial
    See Gault, William Campbell
Forest, Heather 1948- 185
    Earlier sketch in SATA *120*
Forester, C(ecil) S(cott) 1899-1966 13
Forman, Brenda 1936- 4
Forman, James
    See Forman, James D.
Forman, James D. 1932- 70
    Earlier sketch in SATA *8*
Forman, James Douglas
    See Forman, James D.
Forman, Ruth 1970- 186
Forrest, Elizabeth
    See Salsitz, Rhondi Vilott
Forrest, Mary
    See Pausacker, Jenny
Forrest, Sybil
    See Markun, Patricia Maloney
Forrestal, Elaine 1941- 165
    Earlier sketch in SATA *117*
Forrester, Frank H. 1919(?)-1986
    Obituary 52
Forrester, Helen
    See Bhatia, Jamunadevi
Forrester, Jade
    See Pausacker, Jenny
Forrester, Marian
    See Schachtel, Roger
Forrester, Sandra 1949- 166
    Earlier sketch in SATA *90*
Forrester, Victoria 1940- 40
    Brief entry 35
Forsee, (Frances) Aylesa -1986 1
Forsey, Chris 1950- 59
Forshay-Lunsford, Cin 1965- 60
Forster, E(dward) M(organ) 1879-1970 57
Forsyth, Kate 1966- 154
Fort, Paul
    See Stockton, Francis Richard
Forte, Maurizio 1961- 110
Fortey, Richard 1946- 109
Fortey, Richard A.
    See Fortey, Richard
Fortey, Richard Alan
    See Fortey, Richard
Forth, Melissa D(eal) 96
Fortnum, Peggy
    See Nuttall-Smith, Margaret Emily Noel
Fortune, Eric 182
Forward, Robert L(ull) 1932-2002 82
Foster, Alan Dean 1946- 70
Foster, Brad W. 1955- 34
Foster, Doris Van Liew 1899-1993 10
Foster, E(lizabeth) C(onnell) 1902- 9
Foster, Elizabeth 1902- 12
Foster, Elizabeth 1905-1963 10
Foster, F. Blanche 1919- 11
Foster, G(eorge) Allen 1907-1969 26
Foster, Genevieve (Stump) 1893-1979 2
    Obituary 23
    See also CLR *7*

Foster, Gerald L. *198*
Foster, Hal
  See Foster, Harold
Foster, Harold 1892-1982 .... *31*
Foster, Jeanne
  See Williams, Jeanne
Foster, John
  See Foster, John L(ouis)
  and Furcolo, Foster
Foster, John (Thomas) 1925- *8*
Foster, John L(ouis) 1941- *102*
Foster, Juliana *196*
Foster, Laura Louise (James) 1918- *6*
Foster, Leila Merrell 1929- *73*
Foster, Lynne 1937- *74*
Foster, Margaret Lesser 1899(?)-1979
  Obituary *21*
Foster, Marian Curtis 1909-1978 .... *23*
Foster, Mark 1961- *197*
Foster, Sally *58*
Fotheringham, Edwin *201*
Foulds, E. V.
  See Foulds, Elfrida Vipont
Foulds, Elfrida Vipont 1902-1992 .... *52*
Fountas, Angela Jane *180*
Fourie, Corlia 1944- *91*
Fourth Brother, The
  See Aung, (Maung) Htin
Fowke, Edith (Margaret) 1913-1996 .... *14*
Fowles, John 1926-2005 .... *22*
  Obituary *171*
Fowles, John Robert
  See Fowles, John
Fox, Aileen 1907-2005 .... *58*
  Obituary *170*
Fox, Aileen Mary
  See Fox, Aileen
Fox, Annie 1950- *175*
Fox, Charles Philip 1913-2003 .... *12*
  Obituary *150*
Fox, Christyan *188*
Fox, Diane *188*
Fox, Eleanor
  See St. John, Wylly Folk
Fox, Fontaine Talbot, Jr. 1884-1964
  Obituary *23*
Fox, Fred 1903(?)-1981
  Obituary *27*
Fox, Freeman
  See Hamilton, Charles (Harold St. John)
Fox, Geoffrey 1941- *73*
Fox, Grace
  See Anderson, Grace Fox
Fox, Helen 1962- *181*
Fox, Larry *30*
Fox, Lorraine 1922-1976 .... *27*
  Earlier sketch in SATA *11*
Fox, Louisa
  See Kroll, Virginia L.
Fox, Mary Virginia 1919- *152*
  Brief entry *39*
  Earlier sketches in SATA *44, 88*
Fox, Mem
  See Fox, Merrion Frances
Fox, Merrion Frances 1946- *155*
  Earlier sketches in SATA *51, 103*
  See also CLR *80*
Fox, Michael W(ilson) 1937- *15*
Fox, Paula 1923- *167*
  Earlier sketches in SATA *17, 60, 120*
  See also CLR *96*
Fox, Robert J. 1927- *33*
Fox-Davies, Sarah 1956- *199*
Foyt, Victoria .... *187*.
Fradin, Dennis
  See Fradin, Dennis Brindell
Fradin, Dennis Brindell 1945- *185*
  Earlier sketches in SATA *29, 90, 135*
Fradin, Judith Bloom 1945- *185*
  Earlier sketches in SATA *90, 152*
Frailey, Paige (Menefee) 1965- *82*

Frame, Janet 1924-2004 .... *119*
Frame, Paul 1913-1994 .... *60*
  Brief entry *33*
  Obituary *83*
Frances, Miss
  See Horwich, Frances R(appaport)
Franchere, Ruth *18*
Francis, Charles
  See Holme, Bryan
Francis, Dee
  See Haas, Dorothy F.
Francis, Dorothy 1926- *127*
  Earlier sketch in SATA *10*
Francis, Dorothy B.
  See Francis, Dorothy
Francis, Dorothy Brenner
  See Francis, Dorothy
Francis, Jaye
  See Pausacker, Jenny
Francis, Pamela (Mary) 1926- *11*
Franck, Eddie
  See Cooke, Frank E.
Franco, Betsy *188*
  Earlier sketch in SATA *150*
Franco, Eloise (Bauder) 1910- *62*
Franco, Johan (Henri Gustave) 1908-1988 ... *62*
Franco, Marjorie *38*
Francois, Andre 1915-2005 .... *25*
Francoise
  See Seignobosc, Francoise
Frank, Anne(lies Marie) 1929-1945 .... *87*
  Brief entry *42*
  See also CLR *101*
Frank, Daniel B. 1956- *55*
Frank, Emily R.
  See Frank, E.R.
Frank, E.R. 1967- *157*
Frank, Helene
  See Vautier, Ghislaine
Frank, Hillary 1976- *148*
Frank, John *199*
Frank, Josette 1893-1989 .... *10*
  Obituary *63*
Frank, Lucy 1947- *166*
  Earlier sketch in SATA *94*
Frank, Mary 1933- *34*
Frank, R., Jr.
  See Ross, Frank (Xavier), Jr.
Frankau, Mary Evelyn Atkinson 1899-1974 .. *4*
Frankel, Alona 1937- *66*
Frankel, Bernice *9*
Frankel, Edward 1910- *44*
Frankel, Ellen 1951- *78*
Frankel, Julie 1947- *40*
  Brief entry *34*
Frankenberg, Robert 1911- *22*
Franklin, Cheryl J. 1955- *70*
Franklin, Harold 1926- *13*
Franklin, Kristine L. 1958- *124*
  Earlier sketch in SATA *80*
Franklin, Lance
  See Lantz, Francess L(in)
Franklin, Madeleine
  See L'Engle, Madeleine
Franklin, Madeleine L'Engle
  See L'Engle, Madeleine
Franklin, Madeleine L'Engle Camp
  See L'Engle, Madeleine
Franklin, Max
  See Deming, Richard
Franklin, Steve
  See Stevens, Franklin
Franson, Leanne R. 1963- *111*
Franson, Scott E. 1966- *192*
Franzen, Nils-Olof 1916- *10*
Frascino, Edward *48*
  Brief entry *33*
  See also SAAS *9*
Frasconi, Antonio 1919- *131*
  Earlier sketches in SATA *6, 53*
  See also SAAS *11*

Fraser, Betty
  See Fraser, Elizabeth Marr
Fraser, Elizabeth Marr 1928- *31*
Fraser, Eric (George) 1902-1983 .... *38*
Fraser, Mary Ann 1959- *137*
  Earlier sketch in SATA *76*
  See also SAAS *23*
Fraser, Wynnette (McFaddin) 1925- *90*
Frasier, Debra 1953- *182*
  Earlier sketches in SATA *69, 112*
Fraustino, Lisa Rowe 1961- *146*
  Autobiography Feature *146*
  Earlier sketch in SATA *84*
Frazee, Marla 1958- *187*
  Earlier sketches in SATA *105, 151*
Frazetta, Frank 1928- *58*
Frazier, Craig 1955- *177*
Frazier, Neta (Osborn) Lohnes 1890-1990 ..... *7*
Frazier, Sundee T. 1968- *198*
Frazier, Sundee Tucker
  See Frazier, Sundee T.
Frederic, Mike
  See Cox, William R(obert)
Fredericks, Anthony D. 1947- *113*
Freed, Alvyn M. 1913-1993 .... *22*
Freedman, Benedict 1919- *27*
Freedman, Claire *185*
Freedman, Deborah 1960- *191*
Freedman, Jeff 1953- *90*
Freedman, Nancy 1920- *27*
Freedman, Russell 1929- *175*
  Earlier sketches in SATA *16, 71, 123*
  See also CLR *71*
Freedman, Russell Bruce
  See Freedman, Russell
Freeman, Barbara C. 1906-1999 .... *28*
Freeman, Barbara Constance
  See Freeman, Barbara C.
Freeman, Bill
  See Freeman, William Bradford
Freeman, Don 1908-1978 .... *17*
  See also CLR *90*
Freeman, Ira Maximilian 1905-1987 .... *21*
Freeman, Laura *200*
Freeman, Lucy (Greenbaum) 1916-2004 ...... *24*
Freeman, Mae 1907-1985 .... *25*
Freeman, Mae Blacker
  See Freeman, Mae
Freeman, Marcia S. 1937- *102*
Freeman, Martha 1956- *201*
  Earlier sketches in SATA *101, 152*
Freeman, Nancy 1932- *61*
Freeman, Peter J.
  See Calvert, Patricia
Freeman, Sarah (Caroline) 1940- *66*
Freeman, Tor 1977- *164*
Freeman, VicToria
  See Freeman, Tor
Freeman, William Bradford 1938- *58*
  Brief entry *48*
Fregosi, Claudia (Anne Marie) 1946- *24*
French, Allen 1870-1946
  See YABC *1*
French, Dorothy Kayser 1926- *5*
French, Fiona 1944- *132*
  Earlier sketches in SATA *6, 75*
  See also CLR *37*
  See also SAAS *21*
French, Jackie *186*
  Autobiography Feature *139*
  Earlier sketches in SATA *108, 139*
  See French, Jackie Anne
  and French, Jacqueline Anne
French, Kathryn
  See Mosesson, Gloria R(ubin)
French, Martin *176*
French, Michael 1944- *49*
  Brief entry *38*
French, Paul
  See Asimov, Isaac

French, Simon 1957- *147*
  Earlier sketch in SATA *86*
French, Vivian *165*
Frenette, Liza *126*
Freschet, Gina 1960- *175*
  Earlier sketch in SATA *139*
Frewer, Glyn (M.) 1931- *11*
Frey, Darcy *98*
Freymann, Saxton 1958(?)- *178*
Freymann-Weyr, (Rhoda) Garret (Michaela)
  1965- *145*
Frick, C. H.
  See Irwin, Constance (H.) Frick
Frick, Constance
  See Irwin, Constance (H.) Frick
Fricke, Aaron 1962- *89*
Fridell, Ron 1943- *124*
Fried, Janice *197*
Friedlander, Joanne K(ohn) 1930- *9*
Friedman, Aimee 1979- *189*
Friedman, D. Dina 1957- *180*
Friedman, Debra 1955- *150*
Friedman, Estelle (Ehrenwald) 1920- *7*
Friedman, Frieda 1905- *43*
Friedman, Ina R(osen) 1926- *136*
  Brief entry *41*
  Earlier sketch in SATA *49*
Friedman, Jerrold David
  See Gerrold, David
Friedman, Judi 1935- *59*
Friedman, Laurie 1964- *179*
  Earlier sketch in SATA *138*
Friedman, Marvin 1930- *42*
  Brief entry *33*
Friedman, Robin 1968- *162*
Friedmann, Stan 1953- *80*
Friedrich, Otto (Alva) 1929-1995 .... *33*
Friedrich, Priscilla 1927- *39*
Friend, Catherine 1957(?)- *194*
Friend, David Michael 1975- *195*
Friend, Natasha 1972- *184*
Friendlich, Dick
  See Friendlich, Richard J.
Friendlich, Richard J. 1909- *11*
Friermood, Elisabeth Hamilton 1903-1992 ..... *5*
Friesen, Bernice (Sarah Anne) 1966- *105*
Friesen, Gayle 1960- *200*
  Earlier sketch in SATA *109*
Friesner, Esther M. 1951- *168*
  Earlier sketch in SATA *71*
Friis-Baastad, Babbis Ellinor 1921-1970 .... *7*
Frimmer, Steven 1928- *31*
Frischmuth, Barbara 1941- *114*
Friskey, Margaret (Richards) 1901-1995 .... *5*
Fritts, Mary Bahr
  See Bahr, Mary (Madelyn)
Fritz, Jean (Guttery) 1915- *163*
  Autobiography Feature *122*
  Earlier sketches in SATA *1, 29, 72, 119*
  See also CLR *96*
  See also SAAS *2*
Froehlich, Margaret W(alden) 1930- *56*
Frois, Jeanne 1953- *73*
Froissart, Jean 1338(?)-1410(?) *28*
Froman, Elizabeth Hull 1920-1975 .... *10*
Froman, Robert (Winslow) 1917- *8*
Fromm, Lilo 1928- *29*
Frommer, Harvey 1937- *41*
Frost, A(rthur) B(urdett) 1851-1928 .... *19*
Frost, Elizabeth
  See Frost-Knappman, Elizabeth
Frost, Erica
  See Supraner, Robyn
Frost, Helen 1949- *194*
  Autobiography Feature *194*
  Earlier sketches in SATA *157, 183*
Frost, Helen Marie
  See Frost, Helen
Frost, Lesley 1899-1983 .... *14*
  Obituary *34*

Frost, Robert 1874-1963 .... *14*
  See also CLR *67*
Frost, Robert Lee
  See Frost, Robert
Frost, Shelley 1960- *138*
Frost-Knappman, Elizabeth 1943- *179*
Froud, Brian 1947- *150*
Fry, Annette R(iley) *89*
Fry, Christopher 1907-2005 .... *66*
Fry, Edward Bernard 1925- *35*
Fry, Rosalie Kingsmill 1911-1992 .... *3*
  See also SAAS *11*
Fry, Virginia Lynn 1952- *95*
Frye, Sally
  See Moore, Elaine
Fuchs, Bernie 1932- *162*
  Earlier sketch in SATA *95*
Fuchs, Erich 1916- *6*
Fuchshuber, Annegert 1940- *43*
Fuerst, Jeffrey B. 1956- *143*
Fuertes, Gloria 1918-1998 .... *115*
Fuge, Charles 1966- *144*
  Earlier sketch in SATA *74*
Fujikawa, Gyo 1908-1998 .... *76*
  Brief entry *30*
  Obituary *110*
  Earlier sketch in SATA *39*
  See also CLR *25*
  See also SAAS *16*
Fujita, Tamao 1905-1999 .... *7*
Fujiwara, Kim 1957- *81*
Fujiwara, Michiko 1946- *15*
Fuka, Vladimir 1926-1977
  Obituary *27*
Fulcher, Jennifer
  See Westwood, Jennifer
Fuller, Catherine Leuthold 1916- *9*
Fuller, Edmund (Maybank) 1914- *21*
Fuller, Iola
  See McCoy, Iola Fuller
Fuller, John G(rant, Jr.) 1913-1990 .... *65*
Fuller, Kathleen
  See Gottfried, Theodore Mark
Fuller, Lois Hamilton 1915- *11*
Fuller, Margaret
  See Ossoli, Sarah Margaret
Fuller, Maud
  See Petersham, Maud (Sylvia Fuller)
Fuller, Roy (Broadbent) 1912-1991 .... *87*
Fuller, Sarah Margaret
  See Ossoli, Sarah Margaret
Fults, John Lee 1932- *33*
Funk, Thompson 1911- *7*
Funk, Tom
  See Funk, Thompson
Funke, Cornelia 1958- *174*
  Earlier sketch in SATA *154*
Funke, Cornelia Caroline
  See Funke, Cornelia
Funke, Lewis 1912-1992 .... *11*
Fuqua, Jonathon Scott 1966- *141*
Furbee, Mary R.
  See Furbee, Mary Rodd
Furbee, Mary Rodd 1954- *138*
Furchgott, Terry 1948- *29*
Furlong, Monica (Mavis) 1930-2003 .... *86*
  Obituary *142*
Furman, Gertrude Lerner Kerman 1909- *21*
Furniss, Tim 1948- *49*
Furrow, Robert 1985- *172*
Furukawa, Toshi 1924- *24*
Fusillo, Archimede 1962- *137*
Futcher, Jane P. 1947- *76*
Futehali, Zahida
  See Whitaker, Zai
Fyleman, Rose (Amy) 1877-1957 .... *21*
Fyson, Jenny Grace
  See Fyson, J.G.
Fyson, J.G. 1904-1998 .... *42*

G

Gaan, Margaret 1914- *65*
Gaber, Susan 1956- *169*
  Earlier sketch in SATA *115*
Gaberman, Judie Angell
  See Angell, Judie
Gabhart, Ann
  See Gabhart, Ann H.
Gabhart, Ann H. 1947- *75*
Gable, Brian 1949- *195*
Gabler, Mirko 1951- *77*
Gabriel, Adriana
  See Rojany, Lisa
Gabrys, Ingrid Schubert
  See Schubert-Gabrys, Ingrid
Gackenbach, Dick 1927- *79*
  Brief entry *30*
  Earlier sketch in SATA *48*
Gadd, Jeremy 1949- *116*
Gaddis, Vincent H. 1913-1997 .... *35*
Gadler, Steve J. 1905-1985 .... *36*
Gaeddert, Lou Ann (Bigge) 1931- *103*
  Earlier sketch in SATA *20*
Gaeddert, Louann
  See Gaeddert, Lou Ann (Bigge)
Gaer, Joseph 1897-1969 .... *118*
Gaer, Yossef
  See Gaer, Joseph
Gaetz, Dayle Campbell 1947- *138*
Gaffney, Timothy R. 1951- *170*
  Earlier sketch in SATA *69*
Gaffron, Norma (Bondeson) 1931- *97*
Gag, Flavia 1907-1979
  Obituary *24*
Gag, Wanda (Hazel) 1893-1946 .... *100*
  See also YABC *1*
  See also CLR *4*
Gage, Brian *162*
Gage, Wilson
  See Steele, Mary Q(uintard Govan)
Gagliano, Eugene M. 1946- *150*
Gagliardo, Ruth Garver 1895(?)-1980
  Obituary *22*
Gagnon, Cecile 1936- *58*
Gaillard, Jason 1965- *200*
Gaiman, Neil 1960- *197*
  Earlier sketches in SATA *85, 146*
  See also CLR *109*
Gaiman, Neil Richard
  See Gaiman, Neil
Gainer, Cindy 1962- *74*
Gaines, Ernest J. 1933- *86*
  See also CLR *62*
Gaines, Ernest James
  See Gaines, Ernest J.
Gaither, Gloria 1942- *127*
Gal, Laszlo 1933- *96*
  Brief entry *32*
  Earlier sketch in SATA *52*
  See also CLR *61*
Galbraith, Ben 1980- *200*
Galbraith, Kathryn O(sebold) 1945- *85*
Galdone, Paul 1907(?)-1986 .... *66*
  Obituary *49*
  Earlier sketch in SATA *17*
  See also CLR *16*
Galinsky, Ellen 1942- *23*
Gall, Chris 1961- *176*
Gallagher, Diana G. 1946- *153*
Gallagher, Lurlene Nora
  See McDaniel, Lurlene
Gallant, Roy A(rthur) 1924- *110*
  Earlier sketches in SATA *4, 68*
  See also CLR *30*
Gallardo, Evelyn 1948- *78*
Gallaz, Christophe 1948- *162*
  See also CLR *126*
Gallego Garcia, Laura 1977- *173*
Gallico, Paul (William) 1897-1976 .... *13*

Gallo, Donald R. 1938- *112*
  Autobiography Feature *104*
Gallo, Donald Robert
  See Gallo, Donald R.
Galloway, Owateka (S.) 1981- *121*
Galloway, Priscilla 1930- *112*
  Earlier sketch in SATA *66*
Gallup, Joan 1957- *128*
Galouchko, Annouchka Gravel 1960- *95*
Galt, Thomas Franklin, Jr. 1908-1989 .... *5*
Galt, Tom
  See Galt, Thomas Franklin, Jr.
Galvin, Matthew R. 1950- *93*
Galvin, Matthew Reppert
  See Galvin, Matthew R.
Gamble, Kim 1952- *183*
  Earlier sketches in SATA *81, 124*
Gambrell, Jamey *82*
Gamerman, Martha 1941- *15*
Gammell, Stephen 1943- *128*
  Earlier sketches in SATA *53, 81*
  See also CLR *83*
Ganly, Helen (Mary) 1940- *56*
Gannett, Ruth Chrisman (Arens)
  1896-1979 .... *33*
Gannett, Ruth Stiles 1923- *3*
Gannon, Robert Haines 1931- *8*
Gano, Lila 1949- *76*
Gans, Roma 1894-1996 .... *45*
  Obituary *93*
Gant, Matthew
  See Hano, Arnold
Gantner, Susan (Verble) 1939- *63*
Gantos, Jack 1951- *169*
  Earlier sketches in SATA *20, 81, 119*
  See also CLR *85*
Gantos, John Bryan, Jr.
  See Gantos, Jack
Ganz, Yaffa 1938- *61*
  Brief entry *52*
Garafano, Marie 1942- *84*
Garant, Andre J. 1968- *123*
Garbe, Ruth Moore
  See Moore, Ruth (Ellen)
Garber, Esther
  See Lee, Tanith
Garcia, Emma 1969- *198*
Garcia, Yolanda P. 1952- *113*
Garcia, Yolanda Pacheco
  See Garcia, Yolanda P.
Gard, Janice
  See Latham, Jean Lee
Gard, Joyce
  See Reeves, Joyce
Gard, Robert Edward 1910-1992 .... *18*
  Obituary *74*
Gard, (Sanford) Wayne 1899-1986
  Obituary *49*
Gardam, Jane 1928- *130*
  Brief entry *28*
  Earlier sketches in SATA *39, 76*
  See also CLR *12*
  See also SAAS *9*
Gardam, Jane Mary
  See Gardam, Jane
Gardella, Tricia 1944- *96*
Garden, Nancy 1938- *147*
  Autobiography Feature *147*
  Earlier sketches in SATA *12, 77, 114*
  See also CLR *51*
  See also SAAS *8*
Gardiner, John Reynolds 1944-2006 .... *64*
  Obituary *174*
Gardiner, Lindsey 1971- *144*
Gardner, Craig Shaw 1949- *99*
Gardner, Dic
  See Gardner, Richard (M.)
Gardner, Graham *159*
Gardner, Hugh 1910-1986
  Obituary *49*
Gardner, Jane Mylum 1946- *83*

Gardner, Jeanne LeMonnier 1925- *5*
Gardner, John, Jr. 1933-1982 .... *40*
  Obituary *31*
Gardner, John Champlin, Jr.
  See Gardner, John, Jr.
Gardner, John E(dward) 1917- *192*
Gardner, Lyn *192*
Gardner, Martin 1914- *142*
  Earlier sketch in SATA *16*
Gardner, Miriam
  See Bradley, Marion Zimmer
Gardner, Richard (M.) 1931- *24*
Gardner, Richard A(lan) 1931-2003 .... *13*
  Obituary *144*
Gardner, Sally *177*
Gardner, Sandra 1940- *70*
Gardner, Scot 1968- *143*
Gardner, Sheldon 1934- *33*
Gardner, Ted
  See Gardner, Theodore Roosevelt II
Gardner, Theodore Roosevelt
  See Gardner, Theodore Roosevelt II
Gardner, Theodore Roosevelt II 1934- *84*
Garelick, May 1910-1989 .... *19*
Garfield, James B. 1881-1984 .... *6*
  Obituary *38*
Garfield, Leon 1921-1996 .... *76*
  Obituary *90*
  Earlier sketches in SATA *1, 32*
  See also CLR *21*
Garfinkle, Debra L.
  See Garfinkle, D.L.
Garfinkle, D.L. *187*
Garis, Howard R(oger) 1873-1962 .... *13*
Garland, Mark 1953- *79*
Garland, Mark A.
  See Garland, Mark
Garland, Michael 1952- *168*
Garland, Sarah 1944- *135*
  Earlier sketch in SATA *62*
Garland, Sherry 1948- *145*
  Autobiography Feature *145*
  Earlier sketches in SATA *73, 114*
Garner, Alan 1934- *69*
  Autobiography Feature *108*
  Earlier sketch in SATA *18*
  See also CLR *130*
Garner, David 1958- *78*
Garner, Eleanor Ramrath 1930- *122*
Garner, James Finn 1960(?)- *92*
Garnet, A. H.
  See Slote, Alfred
Garnett, Eve C. R. 1900-1991 .... *3*
  Obituary *70*
Garofoli, Viviana 1970- *186*
Garou, Louis P.
  See Bowkett, Stephen
Garraty, John A. 1920-2007 .... *23*
  Obituary *189*
Garraty, John Arthur
  See Garraty, John A.
Garren, Devorah-Leah
  See Devorah-Leah
Garret, Maxwell R. 1917- *39*
Garretson, Victoria Diane 1945- *44*
Garrett, Helen 1895- *21*
Garrett, Randall 1927-1987 .... *180*
Garrett, Richard 1920- *82*
Garrigue, Sheila 1931- *21*
Garrison, Barbara 1931- *163*
  Earlier sketch in SATA *19*
Garrison, Frederick
  See Sinclair, Upton
Garrison, Mary 1952- *146*
Garrison, Peter
  See Gardner, Craig Shaw
Garrison, Webb B(lack) 1919-2000 .... *25*
Garrity, Jennifer Johnson 1961- *124*
Garrity, Linda K. 1947- *128*
Garsee, Jeannine *199*
Garst, Doris Shannon 1894-1981 .... *1*

Garst, Shannon
  See Garst, Doris Shannon
Garth, Will
  See Hamilton, Edmond
  and Kuttner, Henry
Garthwaite, Marion H(ook) 1893-1981 .... *7*
Garton, Malinda D(ean) (?)-1976
  Obituary *26*
Garvie, Maureen 1944- *175*
Garvie, Maureen McCallum
  See Garvie, Maureen
Garza, Carmen Lomas 1948- *182*
Garza, Xavier *184*
Gascoigne, Bamber 1935- *62*
Gaskins, Pearl Fuyo 1957- *134*
Gasperini, Jim 1952- *54*
  Brief entry *49*
Gater, Dilys 1944- *41*
Gates, Doris 1901-1987 .... *34*
  Obituary *54*
  Earlier sketch in SATA *1*
  See also SAAS *1*
Gates, Frieda 1933- *26*
Gates, Susan 1950- *153*
Gates, Viola R. 1931- *101*
Gathorne-Hardy, Jonathan G. 1933- *124*
  Earlier sketch in SATA *26*
Gatti, Anne 1952- *103*
Gatty, Juliana Horatia
  See Ewing, Juliana (Horatia Gatty)
Gauch, Patricia Lee 1934- *80*
  Earlier sketch in SATA *26*
  See also CLR *56*
  See also SAAS *21*
Gaudasinska, Elzbieta 1943- *190*
Gaul, Randy 1959- *63*
Gault, Clare 1925- *36*
Gault, Frank 1926-1982 .... *36*
  Brief entry *30*
Gault, William Campbell 1910-1995 .... *8*
Gauthier, Gail 1953- *160*
  Earlier sketch in SATA *118*
Gaver, Becky
  See Gaver, Rebecca
Gaver, Rebecca 1952- *20*
Gavin, Jamila 1941- *125*
  Earlier sketch in SATA *96*
Gay, Amelia
  See Hogarth, Grace (Weston Allen)
Gay, Francis
  See Gee, H(erbert) L(eslie)
Gay, Kathlyn 1930- *144*
  Earlier sketch in SATA *9*
Gay, Marie-Louise 1952- *179*
  Earlier sketches in SATA *68, 126*
  See also CLR *27*
  See also SAAS *21*
Gay, Michel 1947- *162*
Gay, Zhenya 1906-1978 .... *19*
Gaze, Gillian
  See Barklem, Jill
Gear, Kathleen M. O'Neal
  See Gear, Kathleen O'Neal
Gear, Kathleen O'Neal 1954- *166*
  Earlier sketch in SATA *71*
Gear, W. Michael 1955- *166*
  Earlier sketch in SATA *71*
Geary, Rick 1946- *142*
Geason, Susan 1946- *122*
Gedalof, Robin
  See McGrath, Robin
Gedge, Pauline (Alice) 1945- *101*
Gee, H(erbert) L(eslie) 1901-1977
  Obituary *26*
Gee, Maurice 1931- *101*
  Earlier sketch in SATA *46*
  See also CLR *56*
Gee, Maurice Gough
  See Gee, Maurice
Geehan, Wayne (E.) 1947- *107*

Geer, Charles 1922- *42*
   Brief entry *32*
Geeslin, Campbell 1925- *163*
   Earlier sketch in SATA *107*
Gehman, Mary W. 1923- *86*
Gehr, Mary 1910(?)-1997 .... *32*
   Obituary *99*
Geipel, Eileen 1932- *30*
Geis, Alissa Imre 1976- *189*
Geis, Darlene Stern 1918(?)-1999 .... *7*
   Obituary *111*
Geisel, Helen 1898-1967 .... *26*
Geisel, Theodor Seuss 1904-1991 .... *100*
   Obituary *67*
   Earlier sketches in SATA *1, 28, 75*
   See also CLR *100*
Geisert, Arthur 1941- *171*
   Brief entry *52*
   Earlier sketches in SATA *56, 92, 133*
   See also CLR *87*
   See also SAAS *23*
Geisert, Arthur Frederick
   See Geisert, Arthur
Geisert, Bonnie 1942- *165*
   Earlier sketch in SATA *92*
Geist, Ken *191*
Geldart, William 1936- *15*
Gelinas, Paul J. 1904-1996 .... *10*
Gellis, Roberta 1927- *128*
Gellis, Roberta Leah Jacobs
   See Gellis, Roberta
Gellman, Marc *112*
Gelman, Amy 1961- *72*
Gelman, Jan 1963- *58*
Gelman, Rita Golden 1937- *131*
   Brief entry *51*
   Earlier sketch in SATA *84*
Gelman, Steve 1934- *3*
Gemming, Elizabeth 1932- *11*
Gendel, Evelyn W. 1916(?)-1977
   Obituary *27*
Gennaro, Joseph F(rancis), Jr. 1924- *53*
Gentile, Petrina 1969- *91*
Gentle, Mary 1956- *48*
Gentleman, David (William) 1930- *7*
Geoghegan, Adrienne 1962- *143*
George, Barbara
   See Katz, Bobbi
George, Emily
   See Katz, Bobbi
George, Gail
   See Katz, Bobbi
George, Jean
   See George, Jean Craighead
George, Jean Craighead 1919- *170*
   Earlier sketches in SATA *2, 68, 124*
   See also CLR *136*
George, John L(othar) 1916- *2*
George, Kristine O'Connell 1954- *156*
   Earlier sketch in SATA *110*
George, Lindsay Barrett 1952- *155*
   Earlier sketch in SATA *95*
George, S(idney) C(harles) 1898- *11*
George, Sally
   See Orr, Wendy
George, Twig C. 1950- *114*
George, W(illiam) Lloyd 1900(?)-1975
   Obituary *30*
Georgiou, Constantine 1927- *7*
Georgiou, Theo
   See Odgers, Sally Farrell
Geraghty, Paul 1959- *130*
Gerard, Jean Ignace Isidore 1803-1847 .... *45*
Geras, Adele 1944- *180*
   Autobiography Feature *180*
   Earlier sketches in SATA *23, 87, 129, 173*
   See also SAAS *21*
Geras, Adele Daphne Weston
   See Geras, Adele

Gerber, Merrill Joan 1938- *170*
   Autobiography Feature *170*
   Earlier sketches in SATA *64, 127*
Gerber, Perren 1933- *104*
Gerberg, Mort 1931- *64*
Gergely, Tibor 1900-1978 .... *54*
   Obituary *20*
Geringer, Laura 1948- *164*
   Earlier sketches in SATA *29, 94*
Gerler, William R(obert) 1917-1996 .... *47*
Gerrard, Jean 1933- *51*
Gerrard, Roy 1935-1997 .... *90*
   Brief entry *45*
   Obituary *99*
   Earlier sketch in SATA *47*
   See also CLR *23*
Gerritsen, Paula 1956- *177*
Gerrold, David 1944- *144*
   Earlier sketch in SATA *66*
Gershator, David 1937- *180*
Gershator, Phillis 1942- *188*
   Earlier sketches in SATA *90, 158*
Gershon, Dann 1955- *187*
Gershon, Gina 1962- *187*
Gerson, Corinne 1927- *37*
Gerson, Mary-Joan *136*
   Earlier sketch in SATA *79*
Gerson, Noel Bertram 1914-1988 .... *22*
   Obituary *60*
Gerstein, Mordicai 1935- *178*
   Brief entry *36*
   Earlier sketches in SATA *47, 81, 142*
   See also CLR *102*
Gertridge, Allison 1967- *132*
Gervais, Bernadette 1959- *80*
Gervay, Susanne *183*
Gesner, Clark 1938-2002 .... *40*
   Obituary *143*
Gessner, Lynne 1919- *16*
Geter, Tyrone *150*
Getz, David 1957- *91*
Getzinger, Donna 1968- *128*
Gevirtz, Eliezer 1950- *49*
Gevry, Claudine *188*
Gewe, Raddory
   See Gorey, Edward (St. John)
Ghan, Linda (R.) 1947- *77*
Ghent, Natale 1962- *148*
Gherman, Beverly 1934- *123*
   Earlier sketch in SATA *68*
Ghigna, Charles 1946- *153*
   Earlier sketch in SATA *108*
Giacobbe, Beppe 1953- *174*
Giambastiani, Kurt R. A. 1958- *141*
Giannini, Enzo 1946- *68*
Gibbons, Alan 1953- *198*
   Earlier sketch in SATA *124*
Gibbons, Faye 1938- *103*
   Earlier sketch in SATA *65*
Gibbons, Gail 1944- *201*
   Earlier sketches in SATA *23, 72, 104, 160*
   See also CLR *8*
   See also SAAS *12*
Gibbons, Gail Gretchen
   See Gibbons, Gail
Gibbons, Kaye 1960- *117*
Gibbs, Adrea 1960- *126*
Gibbs, Alonzo (Lawrence) 1915-1992 .... *5*
Gibbs, (Cecilia) May 1877-1969
   Obituary *27*
Gibbs, Tony
   See Gibbs, Wolcott, Jr.
Gibbs, Wolcott, Jr. 1935- *40*
Giblin, James Cross 1933- *197*
   Earlier sketches in SATA *33, 75, 122*
   See also CLR *29*
   See also SAAS *12*
Gibson, Andrew (William) 1949- *72*
Gibson, Betty 1911- *75*
Gibson, Jo
   See Fluke, Joanne

Gibson, Josephine
   See Hine, Sesyle Joslin
   and Hine, Al(fred Blakelee)
Gibson, William 1914-2008 .... *66*
   Obituary *199*
Gibson, William Ford
   See Gibson, William
Gidal, Nachum
   See Gidal, Tim Nachum
Gidal, Sonia (Epstein) 1922- *2*
Gidal, Tim Nachum 1909-1996 .... *2*
Gidalewitsch, Nachum
   See Gidal, Tim Nachum
Gideon, Melanie 1963- *175*
Giegling, John A(llan) 1935- *17*
Gifaldi, David 1950- *76*
Giff, Patricia Reilly 1935- *160*
   Earlier sketches in SATA *33, 70, 121*
Giffard, Hannah 1962- *83*
Gifford, Clive 1966- *198*
Gifford, Griselda 1931- *171*
   Earlier sketch in SATA *42*
Gifford, Kerri 1961- *91*
Gifford, Peggy 1952- *191*
Gilbert, Ann
   See Taylor, Ann
Gilbert, Anne Yvonne 1951- *185*
Gilbert, Barbara Snow 1954- *97*
Gilbert, Catherine
   See Murdock, Catherine Gilbert
Gilbert, Frances
   See Collings, Gillian
Gilbert, Harriett 1948- *30*
Gilbert, (Agnes) Joan (Sewell) 1931- *10*
Gilbert, John (Raphael) 1926- *36*
Gilbert, Nan
   See Gilbertson, Mildred Geiger
Gilbert, Roby Goodale 1966- *90*
Gilbert, Ruth Gallard Ainsworth
   See Ainsworth, Ruth (Gallard)
Gilbert, Sara (Dulaney) 1943- *82*
   Earlier sketch in SATA *11*
Gilbert, Sheri L. *157*
Gilbert, Suzie 1956- *97*
Gilbert, W(illiam) S(chwenck) 1836-1911 ... *36*
Gilbert, Yvonne
   See Gilbert, Anne Yvonne
Gilbertson, Mildred Geiger 1908-1988 .... *2*
Gilbreath, Alice 1921- *12*
Gilbreth, Frank B(unker), Jr. 1911-2001 .... *2*
Gilchrist, Jan Spivey 1949- *130*
   Earlier sketch in SATA *72*
Gilden, Mel 1947- *97*
Giles, Gail *196*
   Earlier sketch in SATA *152*
Gilfond, Henry *2*
Gilge, Jeanette 1924- *22*
Gili, Phillida 1944- *70*
Gill, Derek (Lewis Theodore) 1919-1997 ...... *9*
Gill, Margery Jean 1925- *22*
Gill, Shelley *176*
Gill, Stephen 1932- *63*
Gillespie, Carol Ann 1951- *158*
Gillett, Mary (Bledsoe) *7*
Gillette, Henry Sampson 1915- *14*
Gillette, J(an) Lynett 1946- *103*
Gilley, Jeremy 1969- *174*
Gillham, Bill
   See Gillham, W(illiam) E(dwin) C(harles)
Gillham, W(illiam) E(dwin) C(harles)
   1936- *42*
Gilliam, Stan 1946- *39*
   Brief entry *35*
Gilliland, Alexis A(rnaldus) 1931- *72*
Gilliland, (Cleburne) Hap 1918- *92*
Gilliland, Judith Heide *180*
Gillmor, Don 1954- *127*
Gilman, Dorothy 1923- *5*
Gilman, Esther 1925- *15*
Gilman, Laura Anne *178*

Gilman, Phoebe 1940-2002 .... *104*
   Obituary *141*
   Earlier sketch in SATA *58*
Gilmore, Iris 1900-1982 .... *22*
Gilmore, Kate 1931- *87*
Gilmore, Mary (Jean Cameron) 1865-1962 . *49*
Gilmore, Susan 1954- *59*
Gilpin, Stephen *177*
Gilroy, Beryl (Agatha) 1924- *80*
Gilson, Barbara
   See Gilson, Charles James Louis
Gilson, Charles James Louis 1878-1943
   See YABC *2*
Gilson, Jamie 1933- *176*
   Brief entry *34*
   Earlier sketches in SATA *37, 91*
Ginsburg, Mirra 1909-2000 .... *92*
   Earlier sketch in SATA *6*
   See also CLR *45*
Giovanni, Nikki 1943- *107*
   Earlier sketch in SATA *24*
   See also CLR *73*
Giovanni, Yolanda Cornelia
   See Giovanni, Nikki
Giovanni, Yolanda Cornelia
   See Giovanni, Nikki
Giovanni, Yolande Cornelia, Jr.
   See Giovanni, Nikki
Giovanopoulos, Paul (Arthur) 1939- *7*
Gipson, Fred(erick Benjamin) 1908-1973 ...... *2*
   Obituary *24*
Girard, Linda (Walvoord) 1942- *41*
Girion, Barbara 1937- *78*
   Earlier sketch in SATA *26*
   See also SAAS *14*
Girouard, Patrick 1957- *155*
Girzone, Joseph F. 1930- *76*
Girzone, Joseph Francis
   See Girzone, Joseph F.
Gise, Joanne
   See Mattern, Joanne
Gittings, Jo (Grenville) Manton 1919- *3*
Gittings, Robert (William Victor) 1911-1992 . *6*
   Obituary *70*
Givens, Janet E(aton) 1932- *60*
Givner, Joan 1936- *171*
Givner, Joan Mary
   See Givner, Joan
Gladstone, Eve
   See Werner, Herma
Gladstone, Gary 1935- *12*
Gladstone, M(yron) J. 1923- *37*
Glanville, Brian (Lester) 1931- *42*
Glanzman, Louis S. 1922- *36*
Glaser, Byron 1954- *154*
Glaser, Dianne E(lizabeth) 1937- *50*
   Brief entry *31*
Glaser, Isabel Joshlin 1929- *94*
Glaser, Milton 1929- *151*
   Earlier sketch in SATA *11*
Glaser, Shirley *151*
Glaspell, Susan 1882(?)-1948
   See YABC *2*
Glass, Andrew 1949- *150*
   Brief entry *46*
   Earlier sketch in SATA *90*
Glass, Linzi *175*
Glass, Linzi Alex
   See Glass, Linzi
Glasscock, Amnesia
   See Steinbeck, John (Ernst)
Glassman, Bruce 1961- *76*
Glauber, Uta (Heil) 1936- *17*
Glazer, Thomas (Zachariah) 1914-2003 .... *9*
Glazer, Tom
   See Glazer, Thomas (Zachariah)
Gleasner, Diana (Cottle) 1936- *29*
Gleason, Judith 1929- *24*
Gleason, Katherine (A.) 1960- *104*

Gleeson, Libby 1950- *142*
   Autobiography Feature *142*
   Earlier sketches in SATA *82, 118*
Gleiter, Jan 1947- *111*
Gleitzman, Morris 1953- *156*
   Earlier sketch in SATA *88*
   See also CLR *88*
Glen, Maggie 1944- *88*
Glendinning, Richard 1917-1988 .... *24*
Glendinning, Sally
   See Glendinning, Sara W(ilson)
Glendinning, Sara W(ilson) 1913-1993 .... *24*
Glenn, John W. *195*
Glenn, Mel 1943- *93*
   Brief entry *45*
   Earlier sketch in SATA *51*
   See also CLR *51*
Glenn, Patricia Brown 1953- *86*
Glenn, Sharlee *159*
Glenn, Sharlee Mullins
   See Glenn, Sharlee
Glennon, Karen M. 1946- *85*
Gles, Margaret Breitmaier 1940- *22*
Glick, Carl (Cannon) 1890-1971 .... *14*
Glick, Ruth (Burtnick) 1942- *125*
Glick, Virginia Kirkus 1893-1980
   Obituary *23*
Gliewe, Unada (Grace) 1927- *3*
Glimmerveen, Ulco 1958- *85*
Glines, Carroll V(ane), Jr. 1920- *19*
Gliori, Debi 1959- *189*
   Earlier sketches in SATA *72, 138*
Globe, Leah Ain 1900- *41*
Glori Ann
   See Blakely, Gloria
Glovach, Linda 1947- *105*
   Earlier sketch in SATA *7*
Glover, Denis (James Matthews) 1912-1980 . *7*
Glubok, Shirley (Astor) *146*
   Autobiography Feature *146*
   Earlier sketches in SATA *6, 68*
   See also CLR *1*
   See also SAAS *7*
Gluck, Felix 1923-1981
   Obituary *25*
Glyman, Caroline A. 1967- *103*
Glynne-Jones, William 1907-1977 .... *11*
Gobbato, Imero 1923- *39*
Gobbletree, Richard
   See Quackenbush, Robert M(ead)
Goble, Dorothy *26*
Goble, Paul 1933- *131*
   Earlier sketches in SATA *25, 69*
   See also CLR *21*
Goble, Warwick (?)-1943 .... *46*
Godden, (Margaret) Rumer 1907-1998 .... *36*
   Obituary *109*
   Earlier sketch in SATA *3*
   See also CLR *20*
   See also SAAS *12*
Gode, Alexander
   See Gode von Aesch, Alexander (Gottfried
   Friedrich)
Gode von Aesch, Alexander (Gottfried
   Friedrich) 1906-1970 .... *14*
Godfrey, Jane
   See Bowden, Joan Chase
Godfrey, Martyn
   See Godfrey, Martyn N.
   and Godfrey, Martyn N.
Godfrey, Martyn N. 1949-2000 .... *95*
   See also CLR *57*
Godfrey, William
   See Youd, Samuel
Godkin, Celia (Marilyn) 1948- *145*
   Earlier sketch in SATA *66*
Godon, Ingrid 1958- *186*
Godwin, Laura 1956- *179*
Godwin, Sam
   See Pirotta, Saviour
Goedecke, Christopher (John) 1951- *81*

Goekler, Susan
   See Wooley, Susan Frelick
Goertzen, Glenda *172*
Goettel, Elinor 1930- *12*
Goetz, Delia 1898-1996 .... *22*
   Obituary *91*
Goffe, Toni 1936- *61*
Goffstein, Brooke
   See Goffstein, M(arilyn) B(rooke)
Goffstein, M(arilyn) B(rooke) 1940- *70*
   Earlier sketch in SATA *8*
   See also CLR *3*
Goforth, Ellen
   See Francis, Dorothy
Gogol, Sara 1948-2004 .... *80*
Goh, Chan Hon 1969- *145*
Going, Kelly L.
   See Going, K.L.
Going, Kelly Louise
   See Going, K.L.
Going, K.L. *199*
   Earlier sketch in SATA *156*
Golann, Cecil Paige 1921-1995 .... *11*
Golbin, Andree 1923- *15*
Gold, Alison Leslie 1945- *104*
Gold, Bernice *150*
Gold, Phyllis
   See Goldberg, Phyllis
Gold, Robert S(tanley) 1924- *63*
Gold, Sharlya *9*
Gold, Susan
   See Gold, Susan Dudley
Gold, Susan Dudley 1949- *147*
Goldberg, Grace 1956- *78*
Goldberg, Herbert S. 1926- *25*
Goldberg, Jacob 1943- *94*
Goldberg, Jake
   See Goldberg, Jacob
Goldberg, Phyllis 1941- *21*
Goldberg, Stan J. 1939- *26*
Goldberg, Susan 1948- *71*
Goldberg, Whoopi 1955- *119*
Goldberger, Judith M. 1948- *80*
Goldblatt, Stacey 1969(?)- *191*
Golden, Christie 1963- *167*
   Earlier sketch in SATA *116*
Goldentyer, Debra 1960- *84*
Goldfeder, Cheryl
   See Pahz, Cheryl Suzanne
Goldfeder, James
   See Pahz, James Alon
Goldfeder, Jim
   See Pahz, James Alon
Goldfinger, Jennifer P. 1963- *185*
Goldfrank, Helen Colodny 1912- *6*
Goldin, Augusta 1906-1999 .... *13*
Goldin, Barbara Diamond 1946- *129*
   Autobiography Feature *129*
   Earlier sketch in SATA *92*
   See also SAAS *26*
Goldin, David 1963- *101*
Golding, Julia 1969- *188*
Golding, Theresa Martin 1960- *150*
Golding, William 1911-1993
   See CLR *130*
Golding, William Gerald
   See Golding, William
Goldman, Alex J. 1917- *65*
Goldman, E(leanor) M(aureen) 1943- *103*
Goldman, Elizabeth 1949- *90*
Goldring, Ann 1937- *149*
Goldsborough, June 1923- *19*
Goldsmith, Connie 1945- *147*
Goldsmith, Howard 1943- *108*
   Earlier sketch in SATA *24*
Goldsmith, John Herman Thorburn 1903-1987
   Obituary *52*
Goldsmith, Oliver 1730(?)-1774 .... *26*
Goldsmith, Ruth M. 1919- *62*
Goldstein, Nathan 1927- *47*
Goldstein, Philip 1910-1997 .... *23*

Goldston, Robert (Conroy) 1927- 6
Goldstone, Bruce *183*
Goldstone, Lawrence A.
 See Treat, Lawrence
Goldszmit, Henryk 1878-1942 65
Golembe, Carla 1951- 79
Golenbock, Peter 1946- 99
Goll, Reinhold W(eimar) 1897-1993 26
Gollub, Matthew 1960- *134*
 Earlier sketch in SATA *83*
Gomes, Filomena 1965- *183*
Gomez, Elena *191*
Gomez, Elizabeth *133*
Gomez-Freer, Elizabeth
 See Gomez, Elizabeth
Gomi, Taro 1945- *103*
 Earlier sketch in SATA *64*
 See also CLR *57*
Gondosch, Linda 1944- 58
Gonyea, Mark *194*
Gonzalez, Catherine Troxell 1917-2000 87
Gonzalez, Christina
 See Gonzalez, Maya Christina
Gonzalez, Gloria 1940- 23
Gonzalez, Julie 1958- *174*
Gonzalez, Maya
 See Gonzalez, Maya Christina
Gonzalez, Maya Christina 1964- *175*
 Earlier sketch in SATA *115*
Gonzalez, Rigoberto 1970- *147*
Goobie, Beth 1959- *128*
Good, Alice 1950- 73
Good, Clare
 See Romano, Clare
Goodall, Daphne Machin
 See Machin Goodall, Daphne (Edith)
Goodall, Jane 1934- *111*
Goodall, John S(trickland) 1908-1996 66
 Obituary 91
 Earlier sketch in SATA *4*
 See also CLR *25*
Goodbody, Slim
 See Burstein, John
Goode, Diane 1949- *170*
 Earlier sketches in SATA *15, 84, 114*
Goode, Diane Capuozzo
 See Goode, Diane
Goode, Stephen Ray 1943- 55
 Brief entry 40
Goodenow, Earle 1913- 40
Goodhart, Pippa 1958- *196*
 Earlier sketch in SATA *153*
Goodhue, Thomas W. 1949- *143*
Goodin, Sallie (Brown) 1953- 74
Goodman, Alison 1966- *111*
Goodman, Deborah Lerme 1956- 50
 Brief entry 49
Goodman, Elaine 1930- 9
Goodman, Joan Elizabeth 1950- *162*
 Earlier sketches in SATA *50, 94*
Goodman, Susan E. 1952- *181*
Goodman, Walter 1927-2002 9
Goodrich, Samuel Griswold 1793-1860 23
Goodsell, Jane Neuberger 1921(?)-1988
 Obituary 56
GoodWeather, Hartley
 See King, Thomas
Goodweather, Hartley
 See King, Thomas
Goodwin, Hal
 See Goodwin, Harold L(eland)
Goodwin, Harold L(eland) 1914-1990 .... *51*
 Obituary 65
 Earlier sketch in SATA *13*
Goodwin, William 1943- *117*
Goor, Nancy (Ruth Miller) 1944- 39
 Brief entry 34
Goor, Ron(ald Stephen) 1940- 39
 Brief entry 34
Goossen, Agnes
 See Epp, Margaret A(gnes)

Goossens, Philippe 1963- *195*
Gootman, Marilyn E. 1944- *179*
Gopnik, Adam 1956- *171*
Gorbachev, Valeri 1944- *184*
 Autobiography Feature *143*
 Earlier sketches in SATA *98, 143*
Gordion, Mark
 See Turtledove, Harry
Gordon, Ad
 See Hano, Arnold
Gordon, Amy 1949- *197*
 Earlier sketches in SATA *115, 156*
Gordon, Bernard Ludwig 1931- 27
Gordon, Colonel H. R.
 See Ellis, Edward S(ylvester)
Gordon, David
 See Garrett, Randall
Gordon, Donald
 See Payne, Donald Gordon
Gordon, Dorothy 1893-1970 20
Gordon, Esther S(aranga) 1935- 10
Gordon, Frederick *1*
Gordon, Gaelyn 1939-1997
 See CLR *75*
Gordon, Garrett
 See Garrett, Randall
Gordon, Gary
 See Edmonds, I(vy) G(ordon)
Gordon, Hal
 See Goodwin, Harold L(eland)
Gordon, Jeffie Ross
 See Enderle, Judith (Ann) Ross
 and Gordon, Stephanie Jacob
Gordon, John
 See Gesner, Clark
Gordon, John (William) 1925- 84
Gordon, Lew
 See Baldwin, Gordon C(ortis)
Gordon, Margaret (Anna) 1939- 9
Gordon, Mike 1948- *101*
Gordon, Mildred 1912-1979
 Obituary 24
Gordon, Selma
 See Lanes, Selma Gordon
Gordon, Sheila 1927- 88
 See also CLR *27*
Gordon, Shirley 1921- 48
 Brief entry 41
Gordon, Sol 1923- 11
Gordon, Stephanie Jacob 1940- 89
 Autobiography Feature *114*
 Earlier sketch in SATA *64*
 See also SAAS *26*
Gordon, Stewart
 See Shirreffs, Gordon D(onald)
Gordons, The
 See Gordon, Mildred
 and Gordon, Gordon
Gore, Leonid *185*
Gorelick, Molly C(hernow) 1920-2003 9
 Obituary *153*
Gorey, Edward (St. John) 1925-2000 70
 Brief entry 27
 Obituary *118*
 Earlier sketch in SATA *29*
 See also CLR *36*
Gorham, Charles Orson 1868-1936 36
Gorham, Michael
 See Folsom, Franklin (Brewster)
Gorman, Carol *187*
 Earlier sketch in SATA *150*
Gorman, Jacqueline Laks 1955- *148*
Gormley, Beatrice 1942- *127*
 Brief entry 35
 Earlier sketch in SATA *39*
Gorog, Judith (Katharine Allen) 1938- 75
 Earlier sketch in SATA *39*
Gorrell, Gena K. 1946- *170*
Gorsline, Douglas (Warner) 1913-1985 .... *11*
 Obituary 43
Gorsline, (Sally) Marie 1928- 28

Gorsline, S. M.
 See Gorsline, (Sally) Marie
Gorton, Kaitlyn
 See Emerson, Kathy Lynn
Gorton, Kathy Lynn
 See Emerson, Kathy Lynn
Goryan, Sirak
 See Saroyan, William
Goscinny, Rene 1926-1977 47
 Brief entry 39
 See also CLR *37*
Goss, Clay(ton E.) 1946- 82
Goss, Gary 1947- *124*
Goss, Mini 1963- *186*
Gott, Barry *197*
Gottesman, S. D.
 See Kornbluth, C(yril) M.
 and Lowndes, Robert A(ugustine) W(ard)
 and Pohl, Frederik
Gottfried, Ted
 See Gottfried, Theodore Mark
Gottfried, Theodore Mark 1928- *150*
 Earlier sketch in SATA *85*
Gottlieb, Gerald 1923- 7
Gottlieb, William P. 1917-2006 24
Gottlieb, William Paul
 See Gottlieb, William P.
Goudey, Alice E(dwards) 1898-1993 20
Goudge, Eileen 1950- 88
Goudge, Elizabeth (de Beauchamp)
 1900-1984 2
 Obituary 38
 See also CLR *94*
Gough, Catherine
 See Mulgan, Catherine
Gough, Philip 1908-1986 45
Gough, Sue 1940- *106*
Goulart, Ron 1933- 67
 Earlier sketch in SATA *1*
Goulart, Ronald Joseph
 See Goulart, Ron
Gould, Alberta 1945- 96
Gould, Chester 1900-1985 49
 Obituary 43
Gould, Jean R(osalind) 1909-1993 11
 Obituary 77
Gould, Lilian 6
Gould, Marilyn 1928- 76
 Earlier sketch in SATA *15*
Gould, Robert *154*
Gould, Steven 1955- 95
Gould, Steven Charles
 See Gould, Steven
Gourley, Catherine 1950- *190*
 Earlier sketch in SATA *95*
Gourse, Leslie 1939-2004 89
Govan, (Mary) Christine Noble 1898-1985 ... 9
Gove, Doris 1944- 72
Govenar, Alan 1952- *189*
Govenar, Alan Bruce
 See Govenar, Alan
Govern, Elaine 1939- 26
Gowen, L. Kris 1968- *156*
Graaf, Peter
 See Youd, Samuel
Graber, Alexander 1914-1997 98
 Earlier sketch in SATA *7*
Graber, (George) Alexander 1914-1997 98
Graber, Janet 1942- *170*
Graber, Richard (Fredrick) 1927- 26
Grabianski, Janusz 1928-1976 39
 Obituary 30
Graboff, Abner 1919-1986 35
Grace, Fran(ces Jane) 45
Grace, N.B.
 See Harper, Suzanne
Grace, Theresa
 See Mattern, Joanne
Gracza, Margaret Young 1928- 56
Graduate of Oxford, A
 See Ruskin, John

Grady, Denise 1952- *189*
Graeber, Charlotte Towner *106*
  Brief entry *44*
  Earlier sketch in SATA *56*
Graeme, Roderic
  See Jeffries, Roderic
Graf, Michael
  See Graf, Mike
Graf, Mike 1960- *164*
Grafe, Max *198*
Graff, Lisa 1981- *188*
Graff, Polly Anne Colver
  See Colver, Anne
Graff, (S.) Stewart 1908- *9*
Graham, Ada 1931- *11*
Graham, Alastair 1945- *74*
Graham, Arthur Kennon
  See Harrison, David L.
Graham, Bob 1942- *187*
  Earlier sketches in SATA *63, 101, 151*
  See also CLR *31*
Graham, Brenda Knight 1942- *32*
Graham, Charlotte
  See Bowden, Joan Chase
Graham, Eleanor 1896-1984 .... *18*
  Obituary *38*
Graham, Ennis
  See Molesworth, Mary Louisa
Graham, Frank, Jr. 1925- *11*
Graham, Georgia 1959- *190*
Graham, Ian 1953- *112*
Graham, John 1926-2007 .... *11*
Graham, Kennon
  See Harrison, David L.
Graham, Larry
  See Graham, Lawrence
Graham, Lawrence 1962- *63*
Graham, Lawrence Otis
  See Graham, Lawrence
Graham, Linda
  See Graham-Barber, Lynda
Graham, Lorenz (Bell) 1902-1989 .... *74*
  Obituary *63*
  Earlier sketch in SATA *2*
  See also CLR *10*
  See also SAAS *5*
Graham, Margaret Bloy 1920- *11*
Graham, Robin Lee 1949- *7*
Graham, Shirley 1896(?)-1977
  See Du Bois, Shirley Graham
Graham-Barber, Lynda 1944- *159*
  Earlier sketch in SATA *42*
Graham-Cameron, M.
  See Graham-Cameron, M(alcolm) G(ordon)
Graham-Cameron, M(alcolm) G(ordon)
  1931- *53*
  Brief entry *45*
Graham-Cameron, Mike
  See Graham-Cameron, M(alcolm) G(ordon)
Grahame, Kenneth 1859-1932 .... *100*
  See also YABC *1*
  See also CLR *135*
Gralley, Jean *166*
Gramatky, Hardie 1907-1979 .... *30*
  Obituary *23*
  Earlier sketch in SATA *1*
  See also CLR *22*
Grambling, Lois G. 1927- *148*
  Earlier sketch in SATA *71*
Grambo, Rebecca L(ynn) 1963- *109*
Grammer, June Amos 1927- *58*
Grand, Samuel 1912-1988 .... *42*
Grandits, John 1949- *192*
GrandPré, Mary 1954- *184*
Grandville, J. J.
  See Gerard, Jean Ignace Isidore
Grandville, Jean Ignace Isidore Gerard
  See Gerard, Jean Ignace Isidore
Granfield, Linda 1950- *160*
  Earlier sketch in SATA *96*

Grange, Peter
  See Nicole, Christopher (Robin)
Granger, Margaret Jane 1925(?)-1977
  Obituary *27*
Granger, Michele 1949- *88*
Granger, Peggy
  See Granger, Margaret Jane
Granowsky, Alvin 1936- *101*
Granstaff, Bill 1925- *10*
Granstrom, Brita 1969- *167*
  Earlier sketch in SATA *111*
Grant, Bruce 1893-1977 .... *5*
  Obituary *25*
Grant, Cynthia D. 1950- *147*
  Earlier sketches in SATA *33, 77*
Grant, Eva 1907-1996 .... *7*
Grant, Evva H. 1913-1977
  Obituary *27*
Grant, Gordon 1875-1962 .... *25*
Grant, Gwen(doline Ellen) 1940- *47*
Grant, Katie M.
  See Grant, K.M.
Grant, K.M. *175*
Grant, (Alice) Leigh 1947- *10*
Grant, Matthew G.
  See May, Julian
Grant, Maxwell
  See Gibson, Walter B(rown)
  and Lynds, Dennis
Grant, Melvyn *183*
Grant, Myrna (Lois) 1934- *21*
Grant, Neil 1938- *154*
  Earlier sketch in SATA *14*
Grant, Nicholas
  See Nicole, Christopher (Robin)
Grant, Richard 1948- *80*
Grant, Skeeter
  See Spiegelman, Art
Grater, Michael 1923- *57*
Gravel, Fern
  See Hall, James Norman
Gravelle, Karen 1942- *166*
  Earlier sketch in SATA *78*
Graves, Charles Parlin 1911-1972 .... *4*
Graves, Keith *191*
  Earlier sketch in SATA *156*
Graves, Robert 1895-1985 .... *45*
Graves, Robert von Ranke
  See Graves, Robert
Graves, Valerie
  See Bradley, Marion Zimmer
Gravett, Emily 1972(?)- *189*
Gray, Betsy
  See Poole, Gray Johnson
Gray, Caroline
  See Nicole, Christopher (Robin)
Gray, Dianne E. *183*
Gray, Elizabeth Janet
  See Vining, Elizabeth Gray
Gray, Genevieve S(tuck) 1920-1995 .... *4*
Gray, Harold (Lincoln) 1894-1968 .... *33*
  Brief entry *32*
Gray, Jenny
  See Gray, Genevieve S(tuck)
Gray, John Lee
  See Jakes, John
Gray, Judith A. 1949- *93*
Gray, Judith Anne
  See Gray, Judith A.
Gray, Keith *151*
Gray, Kes 1960- *153*
Gray, Les 1929- *82*
Gray, Libba Moore 1937- *83*
Gray, Luli 1945- *149*
  Earlier sketch in SATA *90*
Gray, Marian
  See Pierce, Edith Gray
Gray, Nicholas Stuart 1922-1981 .... *4*
  Obituary *27*
Gray, Nigel 1941- *104*
  Earlier sketch in SATA *33*

Gray, (Lucy) Noel (Clervaux) 1898-1983 .... *47*
Gray, Patricia (Clark) *7*
Gray, Patsey
  See Gray, Patricia (Clark)
Gray, Rita *184*
Graydon, Shari 1958- *158*
Grayland, V. Merle
  See Grayland, Valerie (Merle Spanner)
Grayland, Valerie (Merle Spanner) *7*
Grayson, Devin (Kalile) 1970- *119*
Grayson, Kristine
  See Rusch, Kristine Kathryn
Grayson, Paul 1946- *79*
Graystone, Lynn
  See Brennan, Joseph Lomas
Great Comte, The
  See Hawkesworth, Eric
Greaves, Margaret 1914-1995 .... *87*
  Earlier sketch in SATA *7*
Greaves, Nick 1955- *77*
Gree, Alain 1936- *28*
Green, Adam
  See Weisgard, Leonard (Joseph)
Green, Anne Canevari 1943- *62*
Green, Brian
  See Card, Orson Scott
Green, Cliff(ord) 1934- *126*
Green, Connie Jordan 1938- *80*
Green, D.
  See Casewit, Curtis W(erner)
Green, Elizabeth Shippen 1871-1954 .... *139*
Green, Hannah
  See Greenberg, Joanne (Goldenberg)
Green, Jane 1937- *9*
Green, John 1977(?)- *170*
Green, Mary Moore 1906- *11*
Green, Morton 1937- *8*
Green, Norma B(erger) 1925- *11*
Green, Phyllis 1932- *20*
Green, Roger (Gilbert) Lancelyn 1918-1987 . *2*
  Obituary *53*
Green, (James Le)Roy 1948- *89*
Green, Sheila Ellen 1934- *148*
  Earlier sketches in SATA *8, 87*
Green, Timothy 1953- *91*
Greenaway, Kate 1846-1901 .... *100*
  See also YABC *2*
  See also CLR *111*
Greenbank, Anthony Hunt 1933- *39*
Greenberg, David 1954- *171*
Greenberg, David T.
  See Greenberg, David
Greenberg, Harvey R. 1935- *5*
Greenberg, Jan 1942- *125*
  Earlier sketch in SATA *61*
Greenberg, Joanne (Goldenberg) 1932- *25*
Greenberg, Melanie Hope 1954- *72*
Greenberg, Polly 1932- *52*
  Brief entry *43*
Greenblat, Rodney Alan 1960- *106*
Greenburg, Dan 1936- *175*
  Earlier sketch in SATA *102*
Greene, Bette 1934- *161*
  Earlier sketches in SATA *8, 102*
  See also CLR *140*
  See also SAAS *16*
Greene, Carla 1916- *67*
  Earlier sketch in SATA *1*
Greene, Carol *102*
  Brief entry *44*
  Earlier sketch in SATA *66*
Greene, Constance C(larke) 1924- *72*
  Earlier sketch in SATA *11*
  See also CLR *62*
  See also SAAS *11*
Greene, Edgar
  See Papademetriou, Lisa
Greene, Ellin 1927- *23*
Greene, Graham 1904-1991 .... *20*
Greene, Graham Henry
  See Greene, Graham

Greene, Jacqueline Dembar 1946- *131*
  Earlier sketch in SATA *76*
Greene, Laura Offenhartz 1935- *38*
Greene, Meg
  See Malvasi, Meg Greene
Greene, Michele 1962- *178*
Greene, Michele Dominguez
  See Greene, Michele
Greene, Rhonda Gowler 1955- *160*
  Earlier sketch in SATA *101*
Greene, Stephanie 1953- *173*
  Earlier sketch in SATA *127*
Greene, Wade 1933- *11*
Greene, Yvonne
  See Flesch, Yolande (Catarina)
Greenfeld, Howard (Scheinman) 1928- *140*
  Earlier sketch in SATA *19*
Greenfeld, Josh(ua Joseph) 1928- *62*
Greenfield, Eloise 1929- *155*
  Earlier sketches in SATA *19, 61, 105*
  See also CLR *38*
  See also SAAS *16*
Greenhaus, Thelma Nurenberg 1903-1984
  Obituary *45*
Greenhut, Josh
  See Mercer, Sienna
Greenhut, Josh
  See Mercer, Sienna
Greening, Hamilton
  See Hamilton, Charles (Harold St. John)
Greenlaw, M. Jean 1941- *107*
Greenleaf, Barbara Kaye 1942- *6*
Greenleaf, Peter 1910-1997 .... *33*
Greenlee, Sharon 1935- *77*
Greeno, Gayle 1949- *81*
Greenseid, Diane 1948- *178*
  Earlier sketch in SATA *93*
Greenspun, Adele Aron 1938- *142*
  Earlier sketch in SATA *76*
Greenstein, Elaine 1959- *150*
  Earlier sketch in SATA *82*
Greenwald, Sheila
  See Green, Sheila Ellen
Greenwood, Barbara 1940- *129*
  Earlier sketch in SATA *90*
Greenwood, Pamela D. 1944- *115*
Greer, Richard
  See Garrett, Randall
  and Silverberg, Robert
Gregg, Andrew K. 1929- *81*
Gregg, Charles T(hornton) 1927- *65*
Gregg, Walter H(arold) 1919- *20*
Gregor, Arthur 1923- *36*
Gregor, Lee
  See Pohl, Frederik
Gregori, Leon 1919- *15*
Gregorian, Joyce Ballou 1946-1991 .... *30*
  Obituary *83*
Gregorich, Barbara 1943- *184*
  Earlier sketch in SATA *66*
Gregorowski, Christopher 1940- *30*
Gregory, Diana (Jean) 1933- *49*
  Brief entry *42*
Gregory, Harry
  See Gottfried, Theodore Mark
Gregory, Jean
  See Ure, Jean
Gregory, Kristiana 1951- *136*
  Earlier sketch in SATA *74*
Gregory, Nan 1944- *192*
  Earlier sketch in SATA *148*
Gregory, Philippa 1954- *122*
Gregory, Stephen
  See Penzler, Otto
Gregory, Valiska 1940- *82*
Greif, Jean-Jacques 1944- *195*
Greisman, Joan Ruth 1937- *31*
Grendon, Stephen
  See Derleth, August (William)
Grenville, Pelham
  See Wodehouse, P(elham) G(renville)

Gretz, Susanna 1937- *7*
Gretzer, John *18*
Grewdead, Roy
  See Gorey, Edward (St. John)
Grey, Carol
  See Lowndes, Robert A(ugustine) W(ard)
Grey, Christopher *191*
Grey, Christopher Peter
  See Grey, Christopher
Grey, Jerry 1926- *11*
Grey, Mini *166*
Greybeard the Pirate
  See Macintosh, Brownie
Grey Owl
  See Belaney, Archibald Stansfeld
Gri
  See Denney, Diana
Gribbin, John 1946- *159*
Gribbin, John R.
  See Gribbin, John
Grice, Frederick 1910-1983 .... *6*
Grider, Dorothy 1915- *31*
Gridley, Marion E(leanor) 1906-1974 .... *35*
  Obituary *26*
Grieco-Tiso, Pina 1954- *108*
Grieder, Walter 1924- *9*
Griego, Tony A. 1955- *77*
Griese, Arnold A(lfred) 1921- *9*
Griessman, Annette 1962- *170*
  Earlier sketch in SATA *116*
Grieve, James 1934- *146*
Grifalconi, Ann 1929- *133*
  Earlier sketch in SATA *2, 66*
  See also CLR *35*
  See also SAAS *16*
Griffin, Adele 1970- *195*
  Earlier sketches in SATA *105, 153*
Griffin, Elizabeth May 1985- *89*
Griffin, Gillett Good 1928- *26*
Griffin, Judith Berry *34*
Griffin, Kitty 1951- *137*
Griffin, Peni R. 1961- *193*
  Earlier sketches in SATA *67, 99*
Griffin, Steven A. 1953- *89*
Griffin, Steven Arthur
  See Griffin, Steven A.
Griffin, W.E.B 1929- *5*
Griffith, Connie 1946- *89*
Griffith, Gershom 1960- *85*
Griffith, Helen V(irginia) 1934- *87*
  Autobiography Feature *107*
  Earlier sketch in SATA *39*
Griffith, Jeannette
  See Eyerly, Jeannette
Griffith, Saul 1974- *200*
Griffiths, Andy 1961- *196*
  Earlier sketch in SATA *152*
Griffiths, G(ordon) D(ouglas) 1910-1973
  Obituary *20*
Griffiths, Helen 1939- *86*
  Earlier sketch in SATA *5*
  See also CLR *75*
  See also SAAS *5*
Grigson, Jane (McIntire) 1928-1990 .... *63*
Grimes, Lee 1920- *68*
Grimes, Nikki 1950- *174*
  Earlier sketches in SATA *93, 136*
  See also CLR *42*
Grimly, Gris *186*
Grimm, Jacob Ludwig Karl 1785-1863 .... *22*
  See also CLR *112*
Grimm, Wilhelm Karl 1786-1859 .... *22*
  See also CLR *112*
Grimm, William C(arey) 1907-1992 .... *14*
Grimm and Grim
  See Grimm, Jacob Ludwig Karl
  and Grimm, Wilhelm Karl
Grimm Brothers
  See Grimm, Jacob Ludwig Karl
  and Grimm, Wilhelm Karl
Grimsdell, Jeremy 1942- *83*

Grimshaw, Nigel (Gilroy) 1925- *23*
Grimsley, Gordon
  See Groom, Arthur William
Grindley, Jane Sally
  See Grindley, Sally
Grindley, Sally 1953- *148*
Gringhuis, Dirk
  See Gringhuis, Richard H.
Gringhuis, Richard H. 1918-1974 .... *6*
  Obituary *25*
Grinnell, David
  See Wollheim, Donald A(llen)
Grinnell, George Bird 1849-1938 .... *16*
Grinspoon, David
  See Grinspoon, David H.
Grinspoon, David H. 1959- *156*
Grinspoon, David Harry
  See Grinspoon, David H.
Gripe, Maria 1923- *74*
  Earlier sketch in SATA *2*
  See also CLR *5*
Gripe, Maria Kristina
  See Gripe, Maria
Grobler, Piet 1959- *201*
Groch, Judith (Goldstein) 1929- *25*
Grode, Redway
  See Gorey, Edward (St. John)
Groener, Carl
  See Lowndes, Robert A(ugustine) W(ard)
Groening, Matt 1954- *116*
  Earlier sketch in SATA *81*
Grohmann, Susan 1948- *84*
Grohskopf, Bernice *7*
Grol, Lini R(icharda) 1913- *9*
Grollman, Earl A. 1925- *22*
Groom, Arthur William 1898-1964 .... *10*
Grooms, Duffy 1964- *169*
Gross, Alan 1947- *54*
  Brief entry *43*
Gross, Ernie 1913- *67*
Gross, Philip 1952- *164*
  Earlier sketch in SATA *84*
Gross, Philip John
  See Gross, Philip
Gross, Ruth Belov 1929- *33*
Gross, Sarah Chokla 1906-1976 .... *9*
  Obituary *26*
Grosser, Morton 1931- *74*
Grosser, Vicky 1958- *83*
Grossman, Bill 1948- *126*
  Earlier sketch in SATA *72*
Grossman, Nancy 1940- *29*
Grossman, Patricia 1951- *73*
Grossman, Robert 1940- *11*
Grote, JoAnn A. 1951- *113*
Groten, Dallas 1951- *64*
Groth, John (August) 1908-1988 .... *21*
  Obituary *56*
Groth-Fleming, Candace
  See Fleming, Candace
Grove, Vicki 1948- *151*
  Autobiography Feature *151*
  Earlier sketch in SATA *122*
Grover, Lorie Ann 1964- *168*
Grover, Wayne 1934- *69*
Groves, Georgina
  See Symons, (Dorothy) Geraldine
Groves, Maketa 1950- *107*
Groves, Seli *77*
Grubb, Lisa *160*
Gruber, Michael 1940- *173*
Gruber, Terry (deRoy) 1953- *66*
Gruelle, John 1880-1938 .... *35*
  Brief entry *32*
  See also CLR *34*
Gruelle, Johnny
  See Gruelle, John
Gruenberg, Sidonie Matsner 1881-1974 .... *2*
  Obituary *27*
Gruhzit-Hoyt, Olga (Margaret) 1922- *127*
  Earlier sketch in SATA *16*

Grummer, Arnold E(dward) 1923- *49*
Grunewalt, Pine
  See Kunhardt, Edith
Grunwell, Jeanne Marie 1971- *147*
Grupper, Jonathan *137*
Gryski, Camilla 1948- *72*
Guarino, Dagmar
  See Guarino, Deborah
Guarino, Deborah 1954- *68*
Guay, Georgette (Marie Jeanne) 1952- *54*
Guback, Georgia *88*
Guccione, Leslie Davis 1946- *111*
  Earlier sketch in SATA *72*
Guck, Dorothy 1913-2002 .... *27*
Guerny, Gene
  See Gurney, Gene
Guest, Elissa Haden 1953- *125*
Guest, Jacqueline 1952- *135*
Guevara, Susan *167*
  Earlier sketch in SATA *97*
Gugler, Laurel Dee *95*
Gugliotta, Bobette 1918-1994 .... *7*
Guianan, Eve 1965- *102*
Guiberson, Brenda Z. 1946- *124*
  Earlier sketch in SATA *71*
Guibert, Emmanuel 1964- *181*
Guile, Melanie 1949- *152*
  Earlier sketch in SATA *104*
Guillaume, Jeanette G. Flierl 1899-1990 .... *8*
Guillot, Rene 1900-1969 .... *7*
  See also CLR *22*
Guisewite, Cathy (Lee) 1950- *57*
Gulbis, Stephen 1959- *142*
Gulley, Judie 1942- *58*
Gump, P. Q.
  See Card, Orson Scott
Gump, P.Q.
  See Card, Orson Scott
Gundrey, Elizabeth 1924- *23*
Gunn, James E. 1923- *35*
Gunn, James Edwin
  See Gunn, James E.
Gunn, Robin Jones 1955- *84*
Gunnella 1956- *197*
Gunning, Monica Olwen 1930- *161*
Gunston, Bill
  See Gunston, William Tudor
Gunston, William Tudor 1927- *9*
Gunterman, Bertha Lisette 1886(?)-1975
  Obituary *27*
Gunther, John 1901-1970
Guravich, Dan 1918- *74*
Gurko, Leo 1914- *9*
Gurko, Miriam 1910(?)-1988 .... *9*
  Obituary *58*
Gurney, Gene 1924- *65*
Gurney, James 1958- *120*
  Earlier sketch in SATA *76*
Gurney, John Steven 1962- *143*
  Earlier sketch in SATA *75*
Gustafson, Sarah R.
  See Riedman, Sarah R(egal)
Gustafson, Scott 1956- *34*
Gustavson, Adam *176*
Guthrie, A(lfred) B(ertram), Jr. 1901-1991 .. *62*
  Obituary *67*
Guthrie, Anne 1890-1979 .... *28*
Guthrie, Donna W. 1946- *105*
  Earlier sketch in SATA *63*
Gutierrez, Akemi *172*
Gutman, Bill *128*
  Brief entry *43*
  Earlier sketch in SATA *67*
Gutman, Dan 1955- *188*
  Earlier sketches in SATA *77, 139*
Gutman, Naham 1899(?)-1981
  Obituary *25*
Gutmann, Bessie Pease 1876-1960 .... *73*
Guy, Geoffrey 1942- *153*
Guy, Ginger Foglesong 1954- *171*

Guy, Rosa (Cuthbert) 1925- *122*
  Earlier sketches in SATA *14, 62*
  See also CLR *137*
Guy, Susan 1948- *149*
Guymer, (Wilhelmina) Mary 1909- *50*
Guzman, Lila 1952- *168*
Guzman, Rick 1957- *168*
Gwaltney, Doris 1932- *181*
Gwynne, Fred(erick Hubbard) 1926-1993 .... *41*
  Brief entry *27*
  Obituary *75*
Gwynne, Oscar A.
  See Ellis, Edward S(ylvester)
Gwynne, Oswald A.
  See Ellis, Edward S(ylvester)

H

Haab, Sherri 1964- *169*
  Earlier sketch in SATA *91*
Haar, Jaap ter
  See ter Haar, Jaap
Haarsma, P.J. *183*
Haas, Carolyn Buhai 1926- *43*
Haas, Dan 1957- *105*
Haas, Dorothy F. *46*
  Brief entry *43*
  See also SAAS *17*
Haas, Irene 1929- *96*
  Earlier sketch in SATA *17*
Haas, James E(dward) 1943- *40*
Haas, (Katherine) Jessie 1959- *135*
  Autobiography Feature *135*
  Earlier sketch in SATA *98*
Haas, Merle S. 1896(?)-1985
  Obituary *41*
Habenstreit, Barbara 1937- *5*
Haber, Karen 1955- *78*
Haber, Louis 1910-1988 .... *12*
Hacker, Randi 1951- *185*
Hacker, Randi Dawn
  See Hacker, Randi
Hackett, John Winthrop 1910-1997 .... *65*
Hacks, Peter 1928-2003
  Obituary *151*
Haddix, Margaret Peterson 1964- *187*
  Earlier sketches in SATA *94, 125*
Haddon, Mark 1962- *155*
Hader, Berta (Hoerner) 1891(?)-1976 .... *16*
Hader, Elmer (Stanley) 1889-1973 .... *16*
Hadithi, Mwenye
  See Hobson, Bruce
Hadley, Franklin
  See Winterbotham, R(ussell) R(obert)
Hadley, Lee 1934-1995 .... *89*
  Brief entry *38*
  Obituary *86*
  Earlier sketch in SATA *47*
  See also CLR *40*
  See also SAAS *14*
Haeffele, Deborah 1954- *76*
Haenel, Wolfram 1956- *89*
  See also CLR *64*
Hafner, Marylin 1925- *179*
  Earlier sketches in SATA *7, 121*
Haft, Erin
  See Ehrenhaft, Daniel
Hager, Alan 1940- *176*
Hager, Alice Rogers 1894-1969
  Obituary *26*
Hager, Betty 1923- *89*
Hager, Sarah *171*
Hager, Thomas 1953- *119*
Hager, Tom
  See Hager, Thomas
Hagerup, Klaus 1946- *186*
Haggard, H(enry) Rider 1856-1925 .... *16*
Haggerty, James J(oseph) 1920- *5*

Hagon, Priscilla
  See Allan, Mabel Esther
Hague, (Susan) Kathleen 1949- *49*
  Brief entry *45*
Hague, Michael 1948- *185*
  Brief entry *32*
  Earlier sketches in SATA *48, 80, 129*
Hague, Michael R.
  See Hague, Michael
Hahn, Emily 1905-1997 .... *3*
  Obituary *96*
Hahn, Hannelore *8*
Hahn, James (Sage) 1947- *9*
Hahn, (Mona) Lynn 1949- *9*
Hahn, Mary Downing 1937- *157*
  Autobiography Feature *157*
  Brief entry *44*
  Earlier sketches in SATA *50, 81, 138*
  See also SAAS *12*
Hahn, Michael T. 1953- *92*
Haig-Brown, Roderick (Langmere)
  1908-1976 .... *12*
  See also CLR *31*
Haight, Anne Lyon 1895-1977
  Obituary *30*
Haight, Rip
  See Carpenter, John (Howard)
Haight, Sandy 1949- *79*
Haij, Vera
  See Jansson, Tove (Marika)
Haines, Gail Kay 1943- *11*
Haines, Margaret Ann Beck
  See Beck, Peggy
Haining, Peter 1940-2007 .... *14*
  Obituary *188*
Haining, Peter Alexander
  See Haining, Peter
Hains, Harriet
  See Watson, Carol
Hajdusiewicz, Babs Bell *163*
Hakim, Joy 1931- *173*
  Earlier sketch in SATA *83*
Halacy, D. S., Jr. 1919-2002 .... *36*
  See also SAAS *8*
Halacy, Dan
  See Halacy, D. S., Jr.
Halam, Ann
  See Jones, Gwyneth A(nn)
Haldane, Roger John 1945- *13*
Hale, Arlene 1924-1982 .... *49*
Hale, Bruce 1957- *123*
Hale, Christy
  See Apostolou, Christine Hale
Hale, Edward Everett 1822-1909 .... *16*
Hale, Glenn
  See Walker, Robert W.
Hale, Helen
  See Mulcahy, Lucille Burnett
Hale, Irina 1932- *26*
Hale, Kathleen 1898-2000 .... *66*
  Obituary *121*
  Earlier sketch in SATA *17*
Hale, Linda (Howe) 1929- *6*
Hale, Lucretia P.
  See Hale, Lucretia Peabody
Hale, Lucretia Peabody 1820-1900 .... *26*
  See also CLR *105*
Hale, Marian *194*
Hale, Nancy 1908-1988 .... *31*
  Obituary *57*
Hale, Shannon *200*
  Earlier sketch in SATA *158*
Haley, Gail E(inhart) 1939- *161*
  Autobiography Feature *161*
  Brief entry *28*
  Earlier sketches in SATA *43, 78, 136*
  See also CLR *21*
  See also SAAS *13*
Haley, Neale *52*
Hall, Adam
  See Trevor, Elleston

Hall, Adele 1910- 7
Hall, Anna Gertrude 1882-1967 8
Hall, Barbara 1960- 68
Hall, Becky 1950- 186
Hall, Beverly B. 1918- 95
Hall, Borden
    See Yates, Raymond F(rancis)
Hall, Brian P(atrick) 1935- 31
Hall, Cameron
    See del Rey, Lester
Hall, Caryl
    See Hansen, Caryl (Hall)
Hall, Donald 1928- 97
    Earlier sketch in SATA 23
Hall, Donald Andrew, Jr.
    See Hall, Donald
Hall, Douglas 1931- 43
Hall, Elizabeth 1929- 77
Hall, Elvajean 1910-1984 6
Hall, Francie 1940- 166
Hall, James Norman 1887-1951 21
Hall, Jesse
    See Boesen, Victor
Hall, Katy
    See McMullan, Kate
Hall, Kirsten Marie 1974- 67
Hall, Lynn 1937- 79
    Earlier sketches in SATA 2, 47
    See also SAAS 4
Hall, Malcolm 1945- 7
Hall, Marjory
    See Yeakley, Marjory Hall
Hall, Melanie W. 1949- 169
    Earlier sketches in SATA 78, 116
Hall, Patricia 1940- 136
Hall, Rosalys Haskell 1914- 7
Hall, Willis 1929-2005 66
Hallard, Peter
    See Catherall, Arthur
Hallas, Richard
    See Knight, Eric
Hall-Clarke, James
    See Rowland-Entwistle, (Arthur) Theodore
    (Henry)
Hallensleben, Georg 1958- 173
Haller, Dorcas Woodbury 1946- 46
Hallett, Mark 1947- 83
Halliburton, Richard 1900-1939(?) 81
Halliburton, Warren J. 1924- 19
Halliday, Brett
    See Dresser, Davis
    and Johnson, (Walter) Ryerson
    and Terrall, Robert
Halliday, William R(oss) 1926- 52
Hallin, Emily Watson 1916-1995 6
Hallinan, P(atrick) K(enneth) 1944- 39
    Brief entry 37
Hallman, Ruth 1929- 43
    Brief entry 28
Hallowell, Tommy
    See Hill, Thomas
Hall-Quest, (Edna) Olga W(ilbourne)
    1899-1986 11
    Obituary 47
Halls, Kelly Milner 1957- 131
Hallstead, William F(inn III) 1924- 11
Hallward, Michael 1889-1982 12
Halperin, Michael 156
Halperin, Wendy Anderson 1952- 200
    Earlier sketch in SATA 80, 125
Halpern, Julie 1975- 198
Halpin, Brendan 1968- 193
Halpin, Marlene 1927- 88
Halsell, Grace (Eleanor) 1923-2000 13
Halsey, Megan 185
Halsted, Anna Roosevelt 1906-1975
    Obituary 30
Halter, Jon C(harles) 1941- 22
Halvorson, Marilyn 1948- 123
Hamalian, Leo 1920- 41
Hamberger, John 1934- 14

Hamblin, Dora Jane 1920- 36
Hambly, Barbara 1951- 108
Hambly, Barbara Joan
    See Hambly, Barbara
Hamer, Martyn
    See Eldin, Peter
Hamerstrom, Frances 1907-1998 24
Hamil, Thomas Arthur 1928- 14
Hamill, Ethel
    See Webb, Jean Francis (III)
Hamilton, (John) Alan 1943- 66
Hamilton, Alice
    See Cromie, Alice Hamilton
Hamilton, Anita 1919- 92
Hamilton, Buzz
    See Hemming, Roy G.
Hamilton, Carol (Jean Barber) 1935- 94
Hamilton, Charles (Harold St. John)
    1876-1961 13
Hamilton, Charles 1913-1996 65
    Obituary 93
Hamilton, Clive
    See Lewis, C.S.
Hamilton, Dorothy (Drumm) 1906-1983 12
    Obituary 35
Hamilton, Edith 1867-1963 20
Hamilton, Edmond 1904-1977 118
Hamilton, (Muriel) Elizabeth (Mollie)
    1906- 23
Hamilton, Emma Walton 1962- 177
Hamilton, Franklin
    See Silverberg, Robert
Hamilton, Gail
    See Corcoran, Barbara (Asenath)
    and Dodge, Mary Abigail
Hamilton, Kersten 1958- 134
Hamilton, Martha 1953- 183
    Earlier sketch in SATA 123
Hamilton, Mary (E.) 1927- 55
Hamilton, Mollie
    See Kaye, M.M.
Hamilton, Morse 1943-1998 101
    Earlier sketch in SATA 35
Hamilton, Peter F. 1960- 109
Hamilton, Priscilla
    See Gellis, Roberta
Hamilton, Ralph
    See Stratemeyer, Edward L.
Hamilton, Virginia 1936-2002 123
    Obituary 132
    Earlier sketches in SATA 4, 56, 79
    See also CLR 127
Hamilton, Virginia Esther
    See Hamilton, Virginia
Hamilton-Paterson, James 1941- 82
Hamlet, Ova
    See Lupoff, Richard A(llen)
Hamley, Dennis 1935- 69
    Earlier sketch in SATA 39
    See also CLR 47
    See also SAAS 22
Hamlin, Peter J. 1970- 84
Hamm, Diane Johnston 1949- 78
Hammer, Charles 1934- 58
Hammer, Richard 1928- 6
Hammerman, Gay M(orenus) 1926- 9
Hammond, Andrew 1970- 181
Hammond, Ralph
    See Hammond Innes, Ralph
Hammond, Winifred G(raham) 1899-1992 29
    Obituary 107
Hammond Innes, Ralph 1913-1998 116
Hammontree, Marie (Gertrude) 1913- 13
Hample, Zack 1977- 161
Hampshire, Joyce Gregorian
    See Gregorian, Joyce Ballou
Hampshire, Susan 1942- 98
Hampson, (Richard) Denman 1929- 15
Hampson, Frank 1918(?)-1985
    Obituary 46

Hampton, Wilborn 1940- 196
    Earlier sketch in SATA 156
Hamre, Leif 1914- 5
Hamsa, Bobbie 1944- 52
    Brief entry 38
Han, Jenny 1981- 175
Han, Lu
    See Stickler, Soma Han
Han, Soma
    See Stickler, Soma Han
Han, Suzanne Crowder 1953- 89
Hancock, Mary A. 1923- 31
Hancock, Sibyl 1940- 9
Hand, Elizabeth 1957- 167
    Earlier sketch in SATA 118
Handford, Martin (John) 1956- 64
    See also CLR 22
Handforth, Thomas (Schofield) 1897-1948 42
Handler, Daniel
    See Snicket, Lemony
Handville, Robert (Tompkins) 1924- 45
Hane, Roger 1940-1974
    Obituary 20
Hanel, Wolfram
    See Haenel, Wolfram
Haney, Lynn 1941- 23
Hanff, Helene 1916-1997 97
    Earlier sketch in SATA 11
Hanft, Josh 1956- 197
Hanft, Joshua E.
    See Hanft, Josh
Hanley, Boniface Francis 1924- 65
Hanlon, Emily 1945- 15
Hann, Jacquie 1951- 19
Hann, Judith 1942- 77
Hanna, Bill
    See Hanna, William (Denby)
Hanna, Cheryl 1951- 84
Hanna, Dan 200
Hanna, Jack (Bushnell) 1947- 74
Hanna, Nell(ie L.) 1908- 55
Hanna, Paul R(obert) 1902-1988 9
Hanna, William (Denby) 1910-2001 51
    Obituary 126
Hannam, Charles 1925- 50
Hannan, Peter 1954- 187
Hannigan, Katherine 170
Hannon, Ezra
    See Hunter, Evan
Hann-Syme, Marguerite 127
Hano, Arnold 1922- 12
Hano, Renee Roth
    See Roth-Hano, Renee
Hanover, Terri
    See Huff, Tanya
Hansen, Ann Larkin 1958- 96
Hansen, Brooks 1965- 104
Hansen, Caryl (Hall) 1929- 39
Hansen, Ian V. 1929- 113
Hansen, Jennifer 1972- 156
Hansen, Joyce 1942- 172
    Autobiography Feature 172
    Brief entry 39
    Earlier sketches in SATA 46, 101
    See also CLR 21
    See also SAAS 15
Hansen, Joyce Viola
    See Hansen, Joyce
Hansen, Mark Victor 112
Hansen, Ron(ald Thomas) 1947- 56
Hanser, Richard (Frederick) 1909-1981 13
Hanson, Joan 1938- 8
Hanson, Joseph E. 1894(?)-1971
    Obituary 27
Hanson, Mary Elizabeth 188
Hanson, Warren 1949- 155
Hansson, Gunilla 1939- 64
Hantman, Clea 200
Harald, Eric
    See Boesen, Victor

Harcourt, Ellen Knowles 1890(?)-1984
    Obituary *36*
Hard, Charlotte (Ann) 1969- *98*
Hardcastle, Michael 1933- *47*
    Brief entry *38*
Harding, Lee 1937- *32*
    Brief entry *31*
Hardt, Helga Fleischhauer
    See Fleischhauer-Hardt, Helga
Hardwick, Richard Holmes, Jr. 1923- *12*
Hardy, Alice Dale *67*
    Earlier sketch in SATA *1*
Hardy, David A(ndrews) 1936- *9*
Hardy, Jon 1958- *53*
Hardy, LeAnne 1951- *154*
Hardy, Stuart
    See Schisgall, Oscar
Hare, Norma Q(uarles) 1924- *46*
    Brief entry *41*
Harel, Nira 1936- *154*
Harford, Henry
    See Hudson, W(illiam) H(enry)
Hargrave, Leonie
    See Disch, Thomas M.
Hargreaves, (Charles) Roger 1935-1988
    Obituary *56*
Hargrove, James 1947- *57*
    Brief entry *50*
Hargrove, Jim
    See Hargrove, James
Hariton, Anca I. 1955- *79*
Hark, Mildred
    See McQueen, Mildred Hark
Harkaway, Hal
    See Stratemeyer, Edward L.
Harkins, Philip 1912-1997 .... *6*
    Obituary *129*
Harlan, Elizabeth 1945- *41*
    Brief entry *35*
Harlan, Glen
    See Cebulash, Mel
Harlan, Judith 1949- *135*
    Earlier sketch in SATA *74*
    See also CLR *81*
Harland, Richard 1947- *152*
Harlee, J. V.
    See Leese, Jennifer L.B.
Harler, Ann
    See Van Steenwyk, Elizabeth (Ann)
Harley, Avis *183*
Harley, Bill 1954- *87*
Harlow, Joan Hiatt 1932- *157*
Harman, Fred 1902(?)-1982
    Obituary *30*
Harman, Hugh 1903-1982
    Obituary *33*
Harmelink, Barbara (Mary) *9*
Harmer, Mabel 1894-1992 .... *45*
Harmon, Dan
    See Harmon, Daniel E(lton)
Harmon, Daniel E(lton) 1949- *157*
Harmon, Margaret 1906- *20*
Harmon, Michael 1969- *189*
Harmon, William (Ruth) 1938- *65*
Harnan, Terry 1920- *12*
Harness, Cheryl 1951- *178*
    Earlier sketch in SATA *131*
Harnett, Cynthia (Mary) 1893-1981 .... *5*
    Obituary *32*
Harper, Anita 1943- *41*
Harper, Betty 1946- *126*
Harper, Charise
    See Harper, Charise Mericle
Harper, Charise Mericle *179*
Harper, Elaine
    See Hallin, Emily Watson
Harper, Ellen
    See Noble, Marty
Harper, Jamie *174*
Harper, Jessica (R.) 1949- *148*

Harper, Jo 1932- *169*
    Earlier sketch in SATA *97*
Harper, Lee *201*
Harper, Mary Wood
    See Dixon, Jeanne
Harper, Piers 1966- *161*
    Earlier sketch in SATA *105*
Harper, Suzanne *194*
Harper, Wilhelmina 1884-1973 .... *4*
    Obituary *26*
Harrah, Madge 1931- *154*
Harrah, Michael 1940- *41*
Harrah, Monique
    See Harrah, Madge
Harrar, George E. 1949- *124*
Harrell, Beatrice Orcutt 1943- *93*
Harrell, Janice 1945- *70*
Harries, Joan 1922- *39*
Harrill, Ronald 1950- *90*
Harrington, Denis J(ames) 1932- *88*
Harrington, Evelyn Davis 1911- *5*
Harrington, Janice N. 1956- *187*
Harrington, Lyn
    See Harrington, Evelyn Davis
Harris, Alan 1944- *71*
Harris, Aurand 1915-1996 .... *37*
    Obituary *91*
Harris, Bob
    See Harris, Robert J.
Harris, Carol Flynn 1933- *135*
Harris, Catherine
    See Ainsworth, Catherine Harris
Harris, Christie
    See Harris, Christie (Lucy) Irwin
Harris, Christie (Lucy) Irwin 1907-2002 ...... *74*
    Autobiography Feature *116*
    Earlier sketch in SATA *6*
    See also CLR *47*
    See also SAAS *10*
Harris, Christine 1955- *105*
Harris, Colver
    See Colver, Anne
Harris, David 1942- *118*
Harris, David William
    See Harris, David
Harris, Dorothy Joan 1931- *153*
    Earlier sketch in SATA *13*
Harris, Geraldine (Rachel) 1951- *54*
Harris, Jacqueline L. 1929- *62*
Harris, Janet 1932-1979 .... *4*
    Obituary *23*
Harris, Jesse
    See Standiford, Natalie
Harris, Joan 1946- *146*
Harris, Joe 1928- *201*
Harris, Joel Chandler 1848-1908 .... *100*
    See also YABC *1*
    See also CLR *128*
Harris, John (Wyndham Parkes Lucas) Beynon
    1903-1969 .... *118*
Harris, Johnson
    See Harris, John (Wyndham Parkes Lucas)
    Beynon
Harris, Jonathan 1921-1997 .... *52*
Harris, Larry Vincent 1939- *59*
Harris, Lavinia
    See St. John, Nicole
Harris, Leon A., Jr. 1926-2000 .... *4*
Harris, Lois V. *199*
Harris, Lorle K(empe) 1912-2001 .... *22*
Harris, Marilyn
    See Springer, Marilyn Harris
Harris, Mark Jonathan 1941- *84*
    Earlier sketch in SATA *32*
Harris, Mary K(athleen) 1905-1966 .... *119*
Harris, Robert J. 1955- *195*
Harris, Robie H. 1940- *147*
    Brief entry *53*
    Earlier sketch in SATA *90*
Harris, Robin
    See Shine, Deborah

Harris, Rosemary (Jeanne) *82*
    Earlier sketch in SATA *4*
    See also CLR *30*
    See also SAAS *7*
Harris, Ruth Elwin 1935- *164*
Harris, Sherwood 1932- *25*
Harris, Steven Michael 1957- *55*
Harris, Trudy 1949- *191*
    Earlier sketch in SATA *128*
Harris-Filderman, Diane
    See Filderman, Diane E(lizabeth)
Harrison, C(hester) William 1913-1994 .... *35*
Harrison, Carol
    See Harrison, Carol Thompson
Harrison, Carol Thompson *113*
Harrison, David L. 1937- *186*
    Earlier sketches in SATA *26, 92, 150*
Harrison, Deloris 1938- *9*
Harrison, Edward Hardy 1926- *56*
Harrison, Elizabeth (Allen) Cavanna
    1909-2001 .... *30*
    Earlier sketch in SATA *1*
    See also SAAS *4*
Harrison, Harry 1925- *4*
Harrison, Harry Max
    See Harrison, Harry
Harrison, Mette Ivie 1970- *149*
Harrison, Michael 1939- *106*
Harrison, Molly (Hodgett) 1909-2002 .... *41*
Harrison, Sarah 1946- *63*
Harrison, Ted
    See Harrison, Edward Hardy
Harsh, Fred (T.) 1925- *72*
Harshaw, Ruth H(etzel) 1890-1968 .... *27*
Harshman, Marc 1950- *109*
    Earlier sketch in SATA *71*
Hart, Alexandra 1939- *14*
Hart, Alison
    See Leonhardt, Alice
Hart, Bruce 1938-2006 .... *57*
    Brief entry *39*
Hart, Carole 1943- *57*
    Brief entry *39*
Hart, Carolyn 1936- *74*
Hart, Carolyn G.
    See Hart, Carolyn
Hart, Carolyn Gimpel
    See Hart, Carolyn
Hart, Jan Siegel 1940- *79*
Hart, Joyce 1954- *148*
Hart, Karen *185*
Hart, Lenore *171*
Hart, Philip S. 1944- *180*
Hart, Virginia 1949- *83*
Harte, (Francis) Bret(t) 1836(?)-1902 .... *26*
Harter, Debbie 1963- *107*
Hartfield, Claire 1957- *147*
Hartinger, Brent 1964- *174*
    Earlier sketch in SATA *145*
Hartland, Jessie *171*
Hartley, Ellen (Raphael) 1915-1980 .... *23*
Hartley, Fred Allan III 1953- *41*
Hartley, William B(rown) 1913-1980 .... *23*
Hartling, Peter
    See Hartling, Peter
Hartling, Peter 1933- *66*
    See also CLR *29*
Hartman, Evert 1937- *38*
    Brief entry *35*
Hartman, Jane E(vangeline) 1928- *47*
Hartman, Louis F(rancis) 1901-1970 .... *22*
Hartman, Rachel *174*
Hartman, Victoria 1942- *91*
Hartnett, Sonya 1968- *176*
    Earlier sketches in SATA *93, 130*
Hartshorn, Ruth M. 1928- *11*
Hartung, Susan Kathleen *192*
    Earlier sketch in SATA *150*
Hartwig, Manfred 1950- *81*
Harvey, Brett 1936- *61*

Harvey, Edith 1908(?)-1972
  Obituary 27
Harvey, Gill 189
Harvey, Karen D. 1935- 88
Harvey, Roland 1945- 179
  Earlier sketches in SATA 71, 123
Harvey-Fitzhenry, Alyxandra 1974- 189
Harwick, B. L.
  See Keller, Beverly L(ou)
Harwin, Brian
  See Henderson, LeGrand
Harwood, Pearl Augusta (Bragdon)
  1903-1998 9
Haseley, Dennis 1950- 157
  Brief entry 44
  Earlier sketches in SATA 57, 105
Hashmi, Kerri 1955- 108
Haskell, Arnold L(ionel) 1903-1981(?) 6
Haskins, James
  See Haskins, James S.
Haskins, James S. 1941-2005 132
  Autobiography Feature 132
  Earlier sketches in SATA 9, 69, 105
  See also CLR 39
  See also SAAS 4
Haskins, Jim
  See Haskins, James S.
Hasler, Eveline 1933- 181
Hasler, Joan 1931- 28
Hass, Robert 1941- 94
Hassall, Joan 1906-1988 43
  Obituary 56
Hassett, Ann 1958- 162
Hassett, John 162
Hassler, Jon 1933-2008 19
  Obituary 191
Hassler, Jon Francis
  See Hassler, Jon
Hastings, Beverly
  See Barkin, Carol
  and James, Elizabeth
Hastings, Graham
  See Jeffries, Roderic
Hastings, Ian 1912- 62
Hastings, Victor
  See Disch, Thomas M.
Haszard, Patricia Moyes 1923-2000 63
Hatch, Lynda S. 1950- 90
Hathaway, Barbara 164
Hathorn, Elizabeth
  See Hathorn, Elizabeth Helen
Hathorn, Elizabeth Helen 1943- 156
  Autobiography Feature 156
  Earlier sketches in SATA 74, 120
Hathorn, Libby 1943-
  See Hathorn, Elizabeth Helen
Hatkoff, Craig 1954- 192
Hatlo, Jimmy 1898-1963
  Obituary 23
Haugaard, Erik Christian 1923- 68
  Earlier sketch in SATA 4
  See also CLR 11
  See also SAAS 12
Haugaard, Kay 117
Haugen, Hayley Mitchell 1968- 172
Haugen, Tormod 1945- 66
Hauman, Doris 1898-1984 32
Hauman, George 1890-1961 32
Hauptly, Denis J(ames) 1945- 57
Hauser, Jill Frankel 1950- 127
Hauser, Margaret L(ouise) 1909- 10
Hausherr, Rosmarie 1943- 86
Hausman, Gerald 1945- 180
  Earlier sketches in SATA 13, 90, 132
  See also CLR 89
Hausman, Gerry
  See Hausman, Gerald
Hauth, Katherine B. 1940- 99
Hautman, Pete 1952- 173
  Earlier sketches in SATA 82, 128

Hautman, Peter Murray
  See Hautman, Pete
Hautzig, Deborah 1956- 106
  Earlier sketch in SATA 31
Hautzig, Esther Rudomin 1930- 148
  Earlier sketches in SATA 4, 68
  See also CLR 22
  See also SAAS 15
Havel, Geoff 1955- 152
Havel, Jennifer
  See Havill, Juanita
Havelin, Kate 1961- 143
Havighurst, Walter (Edwin) 1901-1994 1
  Obituary 79
Haviland, Virginia 1911-1988 6
  Obituary 54
Havill, Juanita 1949- 155
  Earlier sketch in SATA 74
Hawes, Judy 1913- 4
Hawes, Louise 1943- 180
  Earlier sketch in SATA 60
Hawke, Rosanne 1953- 165
  Earlier sketch in SATA 124
Hawke, Rosanne Joy
  See Hawke, Rosanne
Hawkes, Kevin 1959- 201
  Earlier sketches in SATA 78, 150
Hawkes, Nigel 1943- 119
Hawkesworth, Eric 1921- 13
Hawking, Lucy 1969- 197
Hawkins, Arthur 1903-1985 19
Hawkins, Colin 1945- 162
  Earlier sketch in SATA 112
Hawkins, Jacqui 162
  Earlier sketch in SATA 112
Hawkins, Jimmy 1941- 188
Hawkins, Laura 1951- 74
Hawkins, (Helena Ann) Quail 1905-2002 6
  Obituary 141
Hawkinson, John (Samuel) 1912-1994 4
Hawkinson, Lucy (Ozone) 1924-1971 21
Hawks, Robert 1961- 85
Hawley, Mabel C. 67
  Earlier sketch in SATA 1
Hawthorne, Captain R. M.
  See Ellis, Edward S(ylvester)
Hawthorne, Nathaniel 1804-1864
  See YABC 2
  See also CLR 103
Hay, Jeff T. 154
Hay, John 1915- 13
Hay, Timothy
  See Brown, Margaret Wise
Hayashi, Leslie Ann 1954- 115
Hayashi, Nancy 1939- 186
  Earlier sketch in SATA 80
Haycak, Cara 1961- 180
Haycock, Kate 1962- 77
Haycraft, Howard 1905-1991 6
  Obituary 70
Haycraft, Molly Costain 1911- 6
Hayden, Gwendolen Lampshire 1904- 35
Hayden, Robert C(arter), Jr. 1937- 47
  Brief entry 28
Hayden, Robert E(arl) 1913-1980 19
  Obituary 26
Hayden, Torey L. 1951- 163
  Earlier sketch in SATA 65
Hayden, Torey Lynn
  See Hayden, Torey L.
Hayes, Carlton J(oseph) H(untley)
  1882-1964 11
Hayes, Daniel 1952- 109
  Earlier sketch in SATA 73
Hayes, Geoffrey 1947- 91
  Earlier sketch in SATA 26
Hayes, Joe 1945- 131
  Earlier sketch in SATA 88
Hayes, John F. 1904-1980 11
Hayes, Rosemary 158

Hayes, Sheila 1937- 51
  Brief entry 50
Hayes, Will 7
Hayes, William D(imitt) 1913-1976 8
Haynes, Betsy 1937- 94
  Brief entry 37
  Earlier sketch in SATA 48
  See also CLR 90
Haynes, David 1955- 97
Haynes, Linda
  See Swinford, Betty (June Wells)
Haynes, Mary 1938- 65
Haynes, Max 1956- 72
Hays, H(offmann) R(eynolds) 1904-1980 26
Hays, Thomas Anthony 1957- 84
Hays, Tony
  See Hays, Thomas Anthony
Hays, Wilma Pitchford 1909- 28
  Earlier sketch in SATA 1
  See also CLR 59
  See also SAAS 3
Hayward, Linda 1943- 185
  Brief entry 39
  Earlier sketch in SATA 101
Haywood, Carolyn 1898-1990 75
  Obituary 64
  Earlier sketches in SATA 1, 29
  See also CLR 22
Hazell, Rebecca (Eileen) 1947- 141
Hazen, Barbara Shook 1930- 178
  Earlier sketches in SATA 27, 90
Head, Gay
  See Hauser, Margaret L(ouise)
Head, Tom 1978- 167
Headley, Elizabeth
  See Harrison, Elizabeth (Allen) Cavanna
Headley, Justina Chen 1968- 176
Headstrom, (Birger) Richard 1902-1985 8
Heady, Eleanor B(utler) 1917-1979 8
Heagy, William D. 1964- 76
Heal, Edith 1903-1995 7
Heal, Gillian 1934- 89
Heale, Jay (Jeremy Peter Wingfield) 1937- .. 84
Healey, Brooks
  See Albert, Burton
Healey, Larry 1927- 44
  Brief entry 42
Heap, Sue 1954- 187
  Earlier sketch in SATA 150
Heaps, Willard A(llison) 1908-1987 26
Hearn, Diane Dawson 1952- 79
Hearn, Emily
  See Valleau, Emily
Hearn, Julie 1958- 152
Hearn, Lian
  See Rubinstein, Gillian
Hearn, Sneed
  See Gregg, Andrew K.
Hearne, Betsy 1942- 146
  Earlier sketches in SATA 38, 95
Heath, Charles D(ickinson) 1941- 46
Heath, Veronica
  See Blackett, Veronica Heath
Heaven, Constance (Christina) 1911- 7
Hebert-Collins, Sheila 1948- 111
Hecht, George J(oseph) 1895-1980
  Obituary 22
Hecht, Henri Joseph 1922- 9
Hechtkopf, Henryk 1910- ....
Heck, Bessie (Mildred) Holland 1911-1995 . 26
Heck, Ed 1963- 173
Heckert, Connie K(aye Delp) 1948- 82
Hedderwick, Mairi 1939- 145
  Earlier sketches in SATA 30, 77
Hedges, Sid(ney) G(eorge) 1897-1974 28
Hedrick, Irene Hope 1920- 175
Heelan, Jamee Riggio 1965- 146
Heerboth, Sharon
  See Leon, Sharon
Heffernan, John 1949- 168
  Earlier sketch in SATA 121

Heffron, Doris 1944- 68
Hefter, Richard 1942- 31
Hegarty, Reginald Beaton 1906-1973 10
Hehenberger, Shelly 1968- 126
Heidbreder, Robert 1947- 196
    Earlier sketch in SATA 130
Heidbreder, Robert K.
    See Heidbreder, Robert
Heide, Florence Parry 1919- 192
    Earlier sketches in SATA 32, 69, 118
    See also CLR 60
    See also SAAS 6
Heiderstadt, Dorothy 1907-2001 6
Heidi Louise
    See Erdrich, Louise
Heidler, David S(tephen) 1955- 132
Heidler, Jeanne T. 1956- 132
Heilbroner, Joan Knapp 1922- 63
Heilbrun, Lois Hussey 1922(?)-1987
    Obituary 54
Heiligman, Deborah 1958- 193
    Earlier sketches in SATA 90, 144
Heilman, Joan Rattner 50
Heimann, Rolf 1940- 164
    Earlier sketch in SATA 120
Hein, Lucille Eleanor 1915-1994 20
Heine, Helme 1941- 135
    Earlier sketch in SATA 67
    See also CLR 18
Heinlein, Robert A. 1907-1988 69
    Obituary 56
    Earlier sketch in SATA 9
    See also CLR 75
Heinlein, Robert Anson
    See Heinlein, Robert A.
Heins, Ethel L(eah) 1918-1997 101
Heins, Paul 1909- 13
Heintze, Carl 1922- 26
Heinz, Bill
    See Heinz, W.C.
Heinz, Brian J. 1946- 181
    Earlier sketch in SATA 95
Heinz, Brian James
    See Heinz, Brian J.
Heinz, W.C. 1915-2008 26
Heinz, Wilfred Charles
    See Heinz, W.C.
Heinzen, Mildred
    See Masters, Mildred
Heisel, Sharon E(laine) 1941- 125
    Earlier sketch in SATA 84
Heitzmann, William Ray 1948- 73
Heitzmann, Wm. Ray
    See Heitzmann, William Ray
Helakoski, Leslie 178
Helberg, Shirley Adelaide Holden 1919- ... 138
Helfer, Andrew 187
Helfer, Ralph 1937- 177
Helfman, Elizabeth S(eaver) 1911-2001 3
Helfman, Harry Carmozin 1910-1995 3
Helgerson, Joseph 1950- 181
Hellard, Susan 182
Hellberg, Hans-Eric 1927- 38
Heller, Linda 1944- 46
    Brief entry 40
Heller, Mike
    See Hano, Arnold
Heller, Ruth M. 1924- 112
    Earlier sketch in SATA 66
Hellman, Hal
    See Hellman, Harold
Hellman, Harold 1927- 4
Helman, Andrea (Jean) 1946- 160
    Earlier sketch in SATA 107
Helmer, Diana Star 1962- 86
Helmer, Marilyn 160
    Earlier sketch in SATA 112
Helps, Racey 1913-1971 2
    Obituary 25
Helquist, Brett 187
    Earlier sketch in SATA 146

Helweg, Hans H. 1917- 50
    Brief entry 33
Helyar, Jane Penelope Josephine 1933- 5
    Autobiography Feature 138
    See also SAAS 2
Hemmant, Lynette 1938- 69
Hemming, Roy G. 1928-1995 11
    Obituary 86
Hemphill, Helen 1955- 179
Hemphill, Kris (Harrison) 1963- 118
Hemphill, Martha Locke 1904-1973 37
Hemphill, Stephanie 190
Hemstock, Gillian 1956- 173
Henba, Bobbie 1926- 87
Henbest, Nigel 1951- 55
    Brief entry 52
Henderley, Brooks 1
Henderson, Aileen Kilgore 1921- 178
Henderson, Aileen Mary
    See Fox, Aileen
Henderson, Gordon 1950- 53
Henderson, Kathy 1949- 155
    Brief entry 53
    Earlier sketches in SATA 55, 95
Henderson, Lauren 1966- 201
Henderson, LeGrand 1901-1965 9
Henderson, Nancy Wallace 1916- 22
Henderson, Zenna (Chlarson) 1917-1983 5
Hendrickson, Walter Brookfield, Jr. 1936- 9
Hendry, Diana 1941- 106
    Earlier sketch in SATA 68
Hendry, Frances Mary 1941- 171
    Earlier sketch in SATA 110
Hendry, Linda (Gail) 1961- 83
Heneghan, James 1930- 160
    Earlier sketches in SATA 53, 97
Henkes, Kevin 1960- 154
    Earlier sketches in SATA 43, 76, 108
    See also CLR 108
Hennessy, Barbara G.
    See Hennessy, B.G.
Hennessy, Barbara Gulbrandsen
    See Hennessy, B.G.
Hennessy, B.G. 1951- 175
Henney, Carolee Wells 1928- 102
Henriod, Lorraine 1925- 26
Henriquez, Emile F. 1937- 170
    Earlier sketch in SATA 89
Henry, April 1959- 174
Henry, Ernest 1948- 107
Henry, Joanne Landers 1927- 6
Henry, Maeve 1960- 75
Henry, Marguerite 1902-1997 100
    Obituary 99
    See also CLR 4
    See also SAAS 7
Henry, Marie H. 1935- 65
Henry, Marilyn 1939- 117
Henry, Marion
    See del Rey, Lester
Henry, O. 1862-1910
    See YABC 2
Henry, Oliver
    See Henry, O.
Henry, T. E.
    See Rowland-Entwistle, (Arthur) Theodore
    (Henry)
Henschel, Elizabeth Georgie 56
Henson, James Maury
    See Henson, Jim
Henson, Jim 1936-1990 43
    Obituary 65
Henstra, Friso 1928- 73
    Earlier sketch in SATA 8
    See also SAAS 14
Hentoff, Nat(han Irving) 1925- 133
    Brief entry 27
    Earlier sketches in SATA 42, 69
    See also CLR 52
Henty, G(eorge) A(lfred) 1832-1902 64
    See also CLR 76

Heo, Yumi 1964- 146
    Earlier sketch in SATA 94
Hepler, Heather 177
Herald, Kathleen
    See Peyton, Kathleen Wendy
Herb, Angela M. 1970- 92
Herbert, Cecil
    See Hamilton, Charles (Harold St. John)
Herbert, Don 1917-2007 2
    Obituary 184
Herbert, Donald Jeffrey
    See Herbert, Don
Herbert, Frank 1920-1986 37
    Obituary 47
    Earlier sketch in SATA 9
Herbert, Frank Patrick
    See Herbert, Frank
Herbert, Helen (Jean) 1947- 57
Herbert, Janis 1956- 139
Herbert, Wally 1934-2007 23
Herbert, Walter William
    See Herbert, Wally
Herbst, Judith 1947- 74
Herda, D.J. 1948- 80
Herge
    See Remi, Georges
Heritage, Martin
    See Horler, Sydney
Herkimer, L(awrence) R(ussell) 1925(?)- 42
Herlihy, Dirlie Anne 1935- 73
Herman, Charlotte 1937- 99
    Earlier sketch in SATA 20
Hermanson, Dennis (Everett) 1947- 10
Hermes, Jules 1962- 92
Hermes, Patricia 1936- 191
    Earlier sketches in SATA 31, 78, 141
Hermes, Patricia Mary
    See Hermes, Patricia
Hernandez, Natalie Nelson 1929- 123
Herndon, Ernest 91
Herold, Ann Bixby 1937- 72
Herrera, Juan Felipe 1948- 127
Herrick, Steven 1958- 156
    Earlier sketch in SATA 103
Herriman, George (Joseph) 1880-1944 140
Herriot, James 1916-1995
    See Wight, James Alfred
Herrmanns, Ralph 1933- 11
Herrold, Tracey
    See Dils, Tracey E.
Herron, Edward A(lbert) 1912- 4
Herschler, Mildred Barger 130
Hersey, John 1914-1993 25
    Obituary 76
Hersey, John Richard
    See Hersey, John
    and Hersey, John
Hershberger, Priscilla (Gorman) 1951- 81
Hershenhorn, Esther 1945- 151
Hershey, Kathleen M. 1934- 80
Hershey, Mary 173
Hersom, Kathleen 1911- 73
Hertz, Grete Janus 1915- 23
Herzig, Alison Cragin 1935- 87
Herzog, Brad 1968- 131
Heslewood, Juliet 1951- 82
Hess, Lilo 1916- 4
Hess, Paul 1961- 134
Hesse, Hermann 1877-1962 50
Hesse, Karen 1952- 158
    Autobiography Feature 113
    Earlier sketches in SATA 74, 103
    See also CLR 141
    See also SAAS 25
Hest, Amy 1950- 193
    Earlier sketches in SATA 55, 82, 129
Heuer, Kenneth John 1927- 44
Heuman, William 1912-1971 21
Heuston, Kimberley 1960- 167
Heuston, Kimberley Burton
    See Heuston, Kimberley

Hewes, Agnes Danforth 1874-1963 .... *35*
Hewett, Anita 1918-1989 .... *13*
Hewett, Joan 1930- *140*
  Earlier sketch in SATA *81*
Hewett, Richard 1929- *81*
Hewitson, Jennifer 1961- *97*
Hewitt, Margaret 1961- *84*
Hewitt, Sally 1949- *127*
Hext, Harrington
  See Phillpotts, Eden
Hey, Nigel S(tewart) 1936- *20*
Heyduck-Huth, Hilde 1929- *8*
Heyer, Carol 1950- *130*
  Earlier sketch in SATA *74*
Heyer, Marilee 1942- *102*
  Earlier sketch in SATA *64*
Heyerdahl, Thor 1914-2002 .... *52*
  Earlier sketch in SATA *2*
Heyes, (Nancy) Eileen 1956- *150*
  Earlier sketch in SATA *80*
Heyliger, William 1884-1955
  See YABC *1*
Heyman, Ken(neth Louis) 1930- *114*
  Earlier sketch in SATA *34*
Heyward, (Edwin) DuBose 1885-1940 .... *21*
Heywood, Karen 1946- *48*
Hezlep, William (Earl) 1936- *88*
Hibbert, Arthur Raymond
  See Hibbert, Christopher
Hibbert, Christopher 1924-2008 .... *4*
  Obituary *201*
Hibbert, Eleanor Alice Burford 1906-1993 .... *2*
  Obituary *74*
Hickman, Estella (Lee) 1942- *111*
Hickman, Janet 1940- *127*
  Earlier sketch in SATA *12*
Hickman, Martha Whitmore 1925- *26*
Hickman, Pamela 1958- *186*
  Earlier sketch in SATA *128*
Hickock, Will
  See Harrison, C(hester) William
Hickok, Lorena A. 1893-1968 .... *20*
Hickox, Rebecca (Ayres) *116*
Hicks, Barbara Jean 1953- *165*
Hicks, Betty *191*
Hicks, Clifford B. 1920- *50*
Hicks, Eleanor B.
  See Coerr, Eleanor (Beatrice)
Hicks, Harvey
  See Stratemeyer, Edward L.
Hicks, Peter 1952- *111*
Hicyilmaz, Gaye 1947- *157*
  Earlier sketch in SATA *77*
Hieatt, Constance B(artlett) 1928- *4*
Hiebert, Ray Eldon 1932- *13*
Higdon, Hal 1931- *4*
Higginbottom, David 1923- *87*
  Earlier sketch in SATA *25*
Higginbottom, J(effrey) Winslow 1945- *29*
Higgins, Joanna 1945- *125*
Higgins, Simon (Richard) 1958- *105*
Higginsen, Vy *79*
High, Linda Oatman 1958- *188*
  Autobiography Feature *188*
  Earlier sketches in SATA *94, 145*
High, Philip E. 1914- *119*
High, Philip Empson
  See High, Philip E.
Higham, David (Michael) 1949- *50*
Higham, Jon Atlas
  See Higham, Jonathan Huw
Higham, Jonathan Huw 1960- *59*
Highet, Helen
  See MacInnes, Helen (Clark)
Hightman, Jason 1971(?)- *189*
Hightman, J.P.
  See Hightman, Jason
Hightower, Florence Cole 1916-1981 .... *4*
  Obituary *27*

Highwater, Jamake (Mamake)
  1942(?)-2001 .... *69*
  Brief entry *30*
  Earlier sketch in SATA *32*
  See also CLR *17*
Hilb, Nora 1953- *178*
Hildebrandt, Greg 1939- *172*
  Brief entry *33*
  Earlier sketch in SATA *55*
Hildebrandt, Tim 1939-2006 .... *55*
  Brief entry *33*
Hildebrandt, Timothy
  See Hildebrandt, Tim
Hildebrandts, The
  See Hildebrandt, Greg
  and Hildebrandt, Tim
Hilder, Rowland 1905-1993 .... *36*
  Obituary *77*
Hildick, E. W.
  See Hildick, Wallace
Hildick, Wallace 1925-2001 .... *68*
  Earlier sketch in SATA *2*
  See also SAAS *6*
Hilgartner, Beth 1957- *58*
Hill, Alexis
  See Craig, Mary (Francis) Shura
  and Glick, Ruth (Burtnick)
Hill, Anthony R. 1942- *164*
  Earlier sketch in SATA *91*
Hill, Anthony Robert
  See Hill, Anthony R.
Hill, David 1942- *152*
  Earlier sketch in SATA *103*
Hill, Donna (Marie) 1921- *124*
  Earlier sketch in SATA *24*
Hill, Douglas 1935-2007 .... *78*
  Earlier sketch in SATA *39*
Hill, Douglas Arthur
  See Hill, Douglas
Hill, Elizabeth Starr 1925- *143*
  Earlier sketch in SATA *24*
Hill, Eric 1927- *133*
  Brief entry *53*
  Earlier sketch in SATA *66*
  See also CLR *13*
Hill, Gordon
  See Eldin, Peter
Hill, Grace Brooks *67*
  Earlier sketch in SATA *1*
Hill, Grace Livingston 1865-1947
  See YABC *2*
Hill, Helen M(orey) 1915- *27*
Hill, John
  See Koontz, Dean R.
Hill, Johnson
  See Kunhardt, Edith
Hill, Judy I. R.
  See Roberts, Judy I.
Hill, Kathleen Louise 1917- *4*
Hill, Kay
  See Hill, Kathleen Louise
Hill, Kirkpatrick 1938- *188*
  Earlier sketches in SATA *72, 126*
Hill, Laban Carrick *170*
Hill, Lee Sullivan 1958- *96*
Hill, Lorna 1902-1991 .... *12*
Hill, Margaret (Ohler) 1915- *36*
Hill, Meg
  See Hill, Margaret (Ohler)
Hill, Meredith
  See Craig, Mary (Francis) Shura
Hill, Monica
  See Watson, Jane Werner
Hill, Pamela Smith 1954- *112*
Hill, Ralph Nading 1917-1987 .... *65*
Hill, Robert W(hite) 1919-1982 .... *12*
  Obituary *31*
Hill, Ruth A.
  See Viguers, Ruth Hill
Hill, Ruth Livingston
  See Munce, Ruth Hill

Hill, Stuart 1958- *186*
Hill, Susan 1942- *183*
Hill, Susan Elizabeth
  See Hill, Susan
Hill, Susanna Leonard 1965- *193*
Hill, Thomas 1960- *82*
Hillcourt, William 1900-1992 .... *27*
Hillenbrand, Will 1960- *147*
  Earlier sketch in SATA *84*
Hiller, Ilo (Ann) 1938- *59*
Hillerman, Anthony Grove
  See Hillerman, Tony
Hillerman, Tony 1925-2008 .... *6*
  Obituary *198*
Hillert, Margaret 1920- *91*
  Earlier sketch in SATA *8*
Hilliard, Richard *183*
Hillman, Elizabeth 1942- *75*
Hillman, John 1952- *120*
Hillman, Martin
  See Hill, Douglas
Hillman, Priscilla 1940- *48*
  Brief entry *39*
Hillman, Shane *200*
Hills, C.A.R. 1955- *39*
Hills, Charles Albert Reis
  See Hills, C.A.R.
Hills, Tad *173*
Hilton, Irene Pothus -1979 .... *7*
Hilton, James 1900-1954 .... *34*
Hilton, Margaret Lynette 1946- *105*
  Earlier sketch in SATA *68*
  See also CLR *25*
  See also SAAS *21*
Hilton, Nette
  See Hilton, Margaret Lynette
Hilton, Ralph 1907-1982 .... *8*
Hilton, Suzanne 1922- *4*
Hilton-Bruce, Anne
  See Hilton, Margaret Lynette
Him, George 1937-1982
  Obituary *30*
Himelblau, Linda -2005 .... *179*
Himelstein, Shmuel 1940- *83*
Himler, Ann 1946- *8*
Himler, Ronald 1937- *183*
  Earlier sketches in SATA *6, 92, 137*
Himler, Ronald Norbert
  See Himler, Ronald
Himmelman, John C(arl) 1959- *159*
  Earlier sketches in SATA *47, 94*
Hinckley, Helen
  See Jones, Helen Hinckley
Hind, Dolores (Ellen) 1931- *53*
  Brief entry *49*
Hindin, Nathan
  See Bloch, Robert (Albert)
Hindley, Judy 1940- *179*
  Earlier sketch in SATA *120*
Hinds, P(atricia) Mignon *98*
Hine, Sesyle Joslin 1929- *2*
Hines, Anna Grossnickle 1946- *141*
  Brief entry *45*
  Earlier sketches in SATA *51, 95*
  See also SAAS *16*
Hines, Gary (Roger) 1944- *136*
  Earlier sketch in SATA *74*
Hinojosa, Maria (de Lourdes) 1961- *88*
Hinton, Nigel 1941- *166*
Hinton, Sam 1917- *43*
Hinton, S.E. 1950- *160*
  Earlier sketches in SATA *19, 58, 115*
  See also CLR *23*
Hinton, Susan Eloise
  See Hinton, S.E.
Hintz, Martin 1945- *128*
  Brief entry *39*
  Earlier sketch in SATA *47*
Hintz, Stephen V. 1975- *129*
Hippopotamus, Eugene H.
  See Kraus, (Herman) Robert

Hirano, Cathy 1957- 68
Hirsch, Karen 1941- 61
Hirsch, Odo 157
   Earlier sketch in SATA *111*
Hirsch, Phil 1926- 35
Hirsch, S. Carl 1913-1990 2
   See also SAAS *7*
Hirschfelder, Arlene B. 1943- 138
   Earlier sketch in SATA *80*
Hirschi, Ron 1948- 192
   Earlier sketches in SATA *56, 95*
Hirschmann, Linda (Ann) 1941- 40
Hirsh, Marilyn 1944-1988 7
   Obituary 58
Hirshberg, Al(bert Simon) 1909-1973 38
Hiscock, Bruce 1940- 137
   Earlier sketch in SATA *57*
Hiser, Constance 1950- 71
Hiser, Iona Seibert -1998 4
Hislop, Julia Rose Catherine 1962- 74
Hissey, Jane 1952- 130
   Autobiography Feature 130
   Earlier sketches in SATA *58, 103*
Hissey, Jane Elizabeth
   See Hissey, Jane
Hitchcock, Alfred (Joseph) 1899-1980 27
   Obituary 24
Hite, Sid 1954- 175
   Earlier sketches in SATA *75, 136*
Hitte, Kathryn 1919- 16
Hitz, Demi 1942- 152
   Earlier sketches in SATA *11, 66, 102*
   See also CLR *58*
Hitzeroth, Deborah L. 1961- 78
Hnizdovsky, Jacques 1915- 32
Ho, Louise 185
Ho, Minfong 1951- 151
   Earlier sketches in SATA *15, 94*
   See also CLR *28*
Hoagland, Edward (Morley) 1932- 51
Hoare, Robert J(ohn) 1921-1975 38
Hoban, Lillian 1925-1998 69
   Obituary 104
   Earlier sketch in SATA *22*
   See also CLR *67*
Hoban, Russell 1925- 136
   Earlier sketches in SATA *1, 40, 78*
   See also CLR *139*
Hoban, Russell Conwell
   See Hoban, Russell
Hoban, Tana 1917(?)-2006 104
   Obituary 173
   Earlier sketches in SATA *22, 70*
   See also CLR *76*
   See also SAAS *12*
Hobart, Lois (Elaine) 7
Hobbie, Holly 1944- 178
   See also CLR *88*
Hobbie, Jocelyn 190
Hobbie, Nathaniel 196
Hobbs, Leigh 1953- 166
Hobbs, Valerie 1941- 193
   Autobiography Feature 145
   Earlier sketches in SATA *93, 145*
Hobbs, Will 1947- 177
   Autobiography Feature 127
   Earlier sketches in SATA *72, 110*
   See also CLR *59*
Hobbs, William Carl
   See Hobbs, Will
Hoberman, Mary Ann 1930- 158
   Earlier sketches in SATA *5, 72, 111*
   See also CLR *22*
   See also SAAS *18*
Hobson, Bruce 1950- 62
Hobson, Burton (Harold) 1933- 28
Hobson, Laura Z(ametkin) 1900-1986 52
Hobson, Sally 1967- 172
   Earlier sketch in SATA *84*
Hoce, Charley E. 174
Hochschild, Arlie Russell 1940- 11

Hockaby, Stephen
   See Mitchell, Gladys (Maude Winifred)
Hockenberry, Hope
   See Newell, Hope Hockenberry
Hodge, Deborah 1954- 163
   Earlier sketch in SATA *122*
Hodge, P. W.
   See Hodge, Paul W(illiam)
Hodge, Paul W(illiam) 1934- 12
Hodgell, P(atricia) C(hristine) 1951- 42
Hodges, C. Walter 1909-2004 2
   Obituary 158
Hodges, Carl G. 1902-1964 10
Hodges, Cyril Walter
   See Hodges, C. Walter
Hodges, Elizabeth Jamison 1
Hodges, Margaret 1911-2005 167
   Obituary 172
   Earlier sketches in SATA *1, 33, 75, 117*
   See also SAAS *9*
Hodges, Margaret Moore
   See Hodges, Margaret
Hodgetts, Blake Christopher 1967- 43
Hodgkins, Fran 1964- 199
Hodgman, Ann 1956- 198
Hodgson, Harriet (W.) 1935- 84
Hoehne, Marcia 1951- 89
Hoellwarth, Cathryn Clinton
   See Clinton, Cathryn
Hoestlandt, Jo 1948- 94
Hoestlandt, Jocelyne
   See Hoestlandt, Jo
Hoexter, Corinne K. 1927- 6
Hoeye, Michael 1947- 136
Hoff, Carol 1900-1979 11
Hoff, Mary (King) 1956- 157
   Earlier sketch in SATA *74*
Hoff, Syd(ney) 1912-2004 138
   Obituary 154
   Earlier sketches in SATA *9, 72*
   See also CLR *83*
   See also SAAS *4*
Hoffman, Edwin D. 49
Hoffman, Elizabeth P(arkinson) 1921-2003
   Obituary 153
Hoffman, Mary 1945- 144
   Earlier sketches in SATA *59, 97*
   See also SAAS *24*
Hoffman, Mat 1972- 150
Hoffman, Nina Kiriki 1955- 160
Hoffman, Phyllis M(iriam) 1944- 4
Hoffman, Rosekrans 1926- 15
Hoffmann, E(rnst) T(heodor) A(madeus)
   1776-1822 27
   See also CLR *133*
Hoffmann, Felix 1911-1975 9
Hoffmann, Heinrich 1809-1894
   See CLR *122*
Hoffmann, Margaret Jones 1910- 48
Hoffmann, Peggy
   See Hoffmann, Margaret Jones
Hofher, Catherine Baxley 1954- 130
Hofher, Cathy
   See Hofher, Catherine Baxley
Hofmeyr, Dianne (Louise) 138
Hofsepian, Sylvia A. 1932- 74
Hofsinde, Robert 1902-1973 21
Hogan, Bernice Harris 1929- 12
Hogan, Inez 1895-1973 2
Hogan, James P(atrick) 1941- 81
Hogan, Jamie 192
Hogan, Linda 1947- 132
Hogarth, Burne 1911-1996 89
   Earlier sketch in SATA *63*
Hogarth, Grace (Weston Allen) 1905-1995 .. 91
Hogarth, Jr.
   See Kent, Rockwell
Hogarth, (Arthur) Paul 1917-2001 41
Hogg, Garry 1902-1976 2
Hogg, Gary 1957- 172
   Earlier sketch in SATA *105*

Hogner, Dorothy Childs 4
Hogner, Nils 1893-1970 25
Hogrogian, Nonny 1932- 74
   Autobiography Feature 127
   Earlier sketch in SATA *7*
   See also CLR *95*
   See also SAAS *1*
Hoh, Diane 1937- 102
   Brief entry 48
   Earlier sketch in SATA *52*
Hoke, Helen
   See Watts, Helen L. Hoke
Hoke, Helen L.
   See Watts, Helen L. Hoke
Hoke, John (Lindsay) 1925- 7
Hokenson, Terry 1948- 193
Hol, Coby 1943- 126
Holabird, Katharine 1948- 135
   Earlier sketch in SATA *62*
Holaday, Bobbie 1922- 153
Holbeach, Henry
   See Rands, William Brighty
Holberg, Ruth L(angland) 1889-1984 1
Holbrook, Kathy 1963- 107
Holbrook, Peter
   See Glick, Carl (Cannon)
Holbrook, Sabra
   See Erickson, Sabra Rollins
Holbrook, Sara 131
Holbrook, Stewart Hall 1893-1964 2
Holcomb, Jerry (Leona) Kimble 1927- 113
Holcomb, Nan
   See McPhee, Norma H.
Holden, Elizabeth Rhoda
   See Lawrence, Louise
Holding, James (Clark Carlisle, Jr.)
   1907-1997 3
Holeman, Linda 1949- 136
   Autobiography Feature 136
   Earlier sketch in SATA *102*
Holinger, William (Jacques) 1944- 90
Holisher, Desider 1901-1972 6
Holl, Adelaide Hinkle 1910- 8
Holl, Kristi D(iane) 1951- 51
Holland, Gay W. 1941- 128
Holland, Isabelle (Christian) 1920-2002 70
   Autobiography Feature 103
   Obituary 132
   Earlier sketch in SATA *8*
   See also CLR *57*
Holland, Janice 1913-1962 18
Holland, John L(ewis) 1919- 20
Holland, Joyce
   See Morice, Dave
Holland, Julia 1954- 106
Holland, Lynda (H.) 1959- 77
Holland, Lys
   See Gater, Dilys
Holland, Marion 1908-1989 6
   Obituary 61
Hollander, John 1929- 13
Hollander, Nicole 1940(?)- 101
Hollander, Paul
   See Silverberg, Robert
Hollander, Phyllis 1928- 39
Hollander, Zander 1923- 63
Holldobler, Turid 1939- 26
Holliday, Joe
   See Holliday, Joseph
Holliday, Joseph 1910- 11
Holling, Holling C(lancy) 1900-1973 15
   Obituary 26
   See also CLR *50*
Hollingsworth, Alvin C(arl) 1930- 39
Hollingsworth, Mary 1947- 166
   Earlier sketch in SATA *91*
Holloway, Teresa (Bragunier) 1906- 26
Holm, (Else) Anne (Lise) 1922-1998 1
   See also CLR *75*
   See also SAAS *7*

Holm, Jennifer L. 1968(?)- *183*
  Earlier sketches in SATA *120, 163*
Holm, Matthew 1974- *174*
Holm, Sharon Lane 1955- *114*
  Earlier sketch in SATA *78*
Holman, Felice 1919- *82*
  Earlier sketch in SATA *7*
  See also SAAS *17*
Holm and Hamel
  See Holm, Jennifer L.
Holme, Bryan 1913-1990 .... *26*
  Obituary *66*
Holmes, Barbara Ware 1945- *127*
  Earlier sketch in SATA *65*
Holmes, Elizabeth 1957- *191*
Holmes, Elizabeth Ann
  See Holmes, Elizabeth
Holmes, John
  See Souster, (Holmes) Raymond
Holmes, Marjorie (Rose) 1910-2002 .... *43*
Holmes, Martha 1961- *72*
Holmes, Mary Tavener 1954- *199*
Holmes, Mary Z(astrow) 1943- *80*
Holmes, Oliver Wendell 1809-1894 .... *34*
Holmes, Peggy 1898- *60*
Holmes, Raymond
  See Souster, (Holmes) Raymond
Holmes, Rick
  See Hardwick, Richard Holmes, Jr.
Holmes, Sara Lewis *186*
Holmgren, Helen Jean 1930- *45*
Holmgren, Sister George Ellen
  See Holmgren, Helen Jean
Holmgren, Virginia C(unningham) 1909- *26*
Holmquist, Eve 1921- *11*
Holt, Kimberly Willis 1960- *179*
  Earlier sketch in SATA *122*
Holt, Margaret 1937- *4*
Holt, Margaret Van Vechten (Saunders)
  1899-1963 .... *32*
Holt, Michael (Paul) 1929- *13*
Holt, Rackham
  See Holt, Margaret Van Vechten (Saunders)
Holt, Rochelle L.
  See DuBois, Rochelle Holt
Holt, Stephen
  See Thompson, Harlan
Holt, Victoria
  See Hibbert, Eleanor Alice Burford
Holton, Leonard
  See Wibberley, Leonard (Patrick O'Connor)
Holtze, Sally Holmes 1952- *64*
Holtzman, Jerome 1926-2008 .... *57*
  Obituary *194*
Holub, Joan 1956- *149*
  Earlier sketch in SATA *99*
Holub, Josef 1926- *175*
Holubitsky, Katherine 1955- *165*
  Earlier sketch in SATA *121*
Holyer, Erna Maria 1925- *22*
Holyer, Ernie
  See Holyer, Erna Maria
Holz, Loretta (Marie) 1943- *17*
Homel, David 1952- *97*
Homze, Alma C. 1932- *17*
Honey, Elizabeth 1947- *137*
  Autobiography Feature *137*
  Earlier sketch in SATA *112*
Honeycutt, Natalie 1945- *97*
Hong, Lily Toy 1958- *76*
Hong, Maxine Ting Ting
  See Kingston, Maxine Hong
Honig, Donald 1931- *18*
Honness, Elizabeth H. 1904- *2*
Hoobler, Dorothy 1941- *161*
  Earlier sketches in SATA *28, 109*
Hoobler, Thomas *161*
  Earlier sketches in SATA *28, 109*
Hood, Joseph F. 1925- *4*
Hood, Robert E. 1926- *21*

Hood, Sarah
  See Killough, (Karen) Lee
Hook, Brendan 1963- *105*
Hook, Frances 1912-1983 .... *27*
Hook, Geoffrey R(aynor) 1928- *103*
Hook, Jeff
  See Hook, Geoffrey R(aynor)
Hook, Martha 1936- *27*
Hooker, Richard
  See Heinz, W.C.
Hooker, Ruth 1920-1998 .... *21*
hooks, bell 1952(?)- *170*
  Earlier sketch in SATA *115*
Hooks, William H(arris) 1921- *94*
  Earlier sketch in SATA *16*
Hoon, Patricia Easterly 1954- *90*
Hooper, Byrd
  See St. Clair, Byrd Hooper
Hooper, Mary 1948- *160*
Hooper, Maureen Brett 1927- *76*
Hooper, Meredith 1939- *159*
  Earlier sketches in SATA *28, 101*
Hooper, Meredith Jean
  See Hooper, Meredith
Hooper, Patricia 1941- *95*
Hoopes, Lyn Littlefield 1953- *49*
  Brief entry *44*
Hoopes, Ned E(dward) 1932- *21*
Hoopes, Roy 1922- *11*
Hoose, Phillip M. 1947- *137*
Hoover, H(elen) M(ary) 1935- *132*
  Brief entry *33*
  Earlier sketches in SATA *44, 83*
  See also SAAS *8*
Hoover, Helen (Drusilla Blackburn)
  1910-1984 .... *12*
  Obituary *39*
Hope, Christopher 1944- *62*
Hope, Christopher David Tully
  See Hope, Christopher
Hope, Laura Lee
  See Goulart, Ron
  and Stanley, George Edward
Hope Simpson, Jacynth 1930- *12*
Hopf, Alice (Martha) L(ightner) 1904-1988 ... *5*
  Obituary *55*
Hopkins, A. T.
  See Turngren, Annette
Hopkins, C. M.
  See Hopkins, Cathy
Hopkins, Cathy 1953- *165*
Hopkins, Cathy M.
  See Hopkins, Cathy
Hopkins, Clark 1895-1976
  Obituary *34*
Hopkins, Ellen 1955- *128*
  See Hopkins, Ellen L.
Hopkins, Ellen L.
  See Hopkins, Ellen
Hopkins, Jackie
  See Hopkins, Jackie Mims
Hopkins, Jackie Mims 1952- *178*
  Earlier sketch in SATA *92*
Hopkins, Joseph G(erard) E(dward) 1909- ... *11*
Hopkins, (Hector) Kenneth 1914-1988
  Obituary *58*
Hopkins, Lee Bennett 1938- *168*
  Earlier sketches in SATA *3, 68, 125*
  See also CLR *44*
  See also SAAS *4*
Hopkins, Lyman
  See Folsom, Franklin (Brewster)
Hopkins, Marjorie 1911-1999 .... *9*
Hopkins, Mary R(ice) 1956- *97*
Hopkinson, Amanda 1948- *84*
Hopkinson, Deborah 1952- *180*
  Autobiography Feature *180*
  Earlier sketches in SATA *76, 108, 159*
  See also CLR *118*
Hopman, Philip 1961- *177*
Hoppe, Joanne 1932- *42*

Hoppe, Matthias 1952- *76*
Hopper, Nancy J. 1937- *38*
  Brief entry *35*
Hopping, Lorraine Jean
  See Egan, Lorraine Hopping
Horacek, Petr *163*
Horenstein, Henry 1947- *108*
Horgan, Paul (George Vincent O'Shaughnessy)
  1903-1995 .... *13*
  Obituary *84*
Horlak, E.E.
  See Tepper, Sheri S.
Horler, Sydney 1888-1954 .... *102*
Horn, Sandra Ann 1944- *154*
Hornblow, Arthur, Jr. 1893-1976 .... *15*
Hornblow, Leonora 1920-2005 .... *18*
  Obituary *171*
Hornblow, Leonora Schinasi
  See Hornblow, Leonora
Horne, Constance 1927- *149*
Horne, Richard 1960-2007 .... *169*
  Obituary *180*
  Earlier sketch in SATA *111*
Horne, Richard Henry Hengist
  1802(?)-1884 .... *29*
Horner, Althea (Jane) 1926- *36*
Horner, Dave 1934- *12*
Horner, Jack
  See Horner, John R(obert)
Horner, John R(obert) 1946- *106*
Hornik, Laurie Miller *159*
Horniman, Joanne 1951- *167*
  Earlier sketch in SATA *98*
Hornos, Axel 1907-1994 .... *20*
Hornstein, Reuben Aaron 1912- *64*
Horowitz, Anthony 1955- *195*
  Earlier sketch in SATA *137*
Horowitz, Dave 1973(?)- *172*
Horowitz, Ruth 1957- *136*
Horrocks, Anita 1958- *169*
Horse, Harry
  See Horne, Richard
Horsfield, Alan 1939- *153*
Hort, Lenny *179*
Horton, James O. 1943- *173*
Horton, James Oliver
  See Horton, James O.
Horton, Madelyn (Stacey) 1962- *77*
Horvath, Betty 1927- *4*
Horvath, David 1972(?)- *192*
Horvath, Polly 1957- *194*
  Earlier sketches in SATA *85, 140*
  See also CLR *90*
Horwich, Frances R(appaport) 1908-2001 .... *11*
  Obituary *130*
Horwitz, Elinor Lander *45*
  Brief entry *33*
Horwood, William 1944- *85*
Hosford, Dorothy (Grant) 1900-1952 .... *22*
Hosford, Jessie 1892-1990 .... *5*
Hoshi, Shin'ichi 1926- *101*
Hoshino, Felicia 1968- *189*
Hoskyns-Abrahall, Clare (Constance
  Drury) *13*
Hosler, Danamarie 1978- *184*
Hossack, Sylvia 1939- *83*
Hossack, Sylvie Adams
  See Hossack, Sylvia
Hosseini, Khaled 1965- *156*
Hossell, Karen Price
  See Price, Karen
Hosta, Dar *192*
Hostetler, Marian 1932- *91*
Houck, Carter 1924- *22*
Hough, Charlotte 1924-2008 .... *9*
Hough, Helen Charlotte
  See Hough, Charlotte
Hough, Judy Taylor 1932- *63*
  Brief entry *51*
  Earlier sketch in SATA *56*
Hough, Richard (Alexander) 1922-1999 ...... *17*

Houghton, Eric 1930- 7
Houk, Randy 1944- 97
Houlehen, Robert J. 1918- 18
Houlton, Peggy Mann 1925(?)-1990 6
Household, Geoffrey (Edward West)
    1900-1988 14
    Obituary 59
Housman, Laurence 1865-1959 25
Houston, Dick 1943- 74
Houston, Gloria 138
    Autobiography Feature 138
    Earlier sketch in SATA *81*
Houston, James A(rchibald) 1921-2005 74
    Obituary 163
    Earlier sketch in SATA *13*
    See also CLR *3*
    See also SAAS *17*
Houston, James D. 1933-2009 78
Houston, James Dudley
    See Houston, James D.
Houston, Jeanne Toyo Wakatsuki
    See Houston, Jeanne Wakatsuki
Houston, Jeanne Wakatsuki 1934- 168
    Autobiography Feature 168
    Earlier sketch in SATA *78*
Houston, Juanita C. 1921- 129
Houton, Kathleen
    See Kilgore, Kathleen
Houts, Amy F. 164
Hovey, Kate 158
Howard, Alan 1922- 45
Howard, Alyssa
    See Buckholtz, Eileen (Garber)
    and Glick, Ruth (Burtnick)
    and Titchener, Louise
Howard, Arthur 1948- 165
Howard, Arthur Charles
    See Howard, Arthur
Howard, Elizabeth Fitzgerald 1927- 119
    Earlier sketch in SATA *74*
Howard, Ellen 1943- 184
    Earlier sketches in SATA *67, 99*
Howard, Jane R(uble) 1924- 87
Howard, Norman Barry 1949- 90
Howard, P. M.
    See Howard, Pauline Rodriguez
Howard, Paul 1967- 190
    Earlier sketch in SATA *118*
Howard, Pauline Rodriguez 1951- 124
Howard, Prosper
    See Hamilton, Charles (Harold St. John)
Howard, Robert West 1908-1988 5
Howard, Todd 1964- 135
Howard, Tristan
    See Currie, Stephen
Howard, Vernon (Linwood) 1918-1992 40
    Obituary 73
Howard, Warren F.
    See Pohl, Frederik
Howarth, Daniel 188
Howarth, David (Armine) 1912-1991 6
    Obituary 68
Howarth, Lesley 1952- 94
Howe, Deborah 1946-1978 29
Howe, James 1946- 161
    Earlier sketches in SATA *29, 71, 111*
    See also CLR *9*
Howe, John F. 1957- 79
Howe, Norma 1930- 126
Howell, Pat 1947- 15
Howell, S.
    See Styles, (Frank) Showell
Howell, Virginia
    See Ellison, Virginia H(owell)
Howes, Barbara 1914-1996 5
Howie, Diana 1945- 122
Howie, Diana Melson
    See Howie, Diana

Howker, Janni 1957- 72
    Brief entry 46
    See also CLR *14*
    See also SAAS *13*
Howland, Ethan 1963- 131
Hoy, Linda 1946- 65
Hoy, Nina
    See Roth, Arthur J(oseph)
Hoyle, Geoffrey 1942- 18
Hoyt, Ard 190
Hoyt, Edwin P(almer), Jr. 1923- 28
Hoyt, Erich 1950- 140
    Earlier sketch in SATA *65*
Hoyt, Olga
    See Gruhzit-Hoyt, Olga (Margaret)
Hrdlitschka, Shelley 1956- 167
    Earlier sketch in SATA *111*
Hrdlitschka, Shelley Joanne
    See Hrdlitschka, Shelley
Htin Aung, U.
    See Aung, (Maung) Htin
Hu, Ying-Hwa 173
Huang, Benrei 1959- 86
Hubalek, Linda K. 1954- 111
Hubbard, Margaret Ann
    See Priley, Margaret (Ann) Hubbard
Hubbard, Michelle Calabro 1953- 122
Hubbard, Patricia 1945- 124
Hubbard, Woodleigh Marx 160
    Earlier sketch in SATA *98*
Hubbell, Patricia 1928- 186
    Earlier sketches in SATA *8, 132*
Hubery, Julia 195
Hubley, Faith Elliot 1924-2001 48
    Obituary 133
Hubley, John 1914-1977 48
    Obituary 24
Huck, Charlotte S. 1922- 136
    Earlier sketch in SATA *82*
Hudak, Michal 1956- 143
Hudson, Cheryl Willis 1948- 160
    Earlier sketch in SATA *81*
Hudson, Jan 1954-1990 77
    See also CLR *40*
Hudson, Jeffery
    See Crichton, Michael
Hudson, Jeffrey
    See Crichton, Michael
Hudson, (Margaret) Kirsty 1947- 32
Hudson, Margaret
    See Shuter, Jane (Margaret)
Hudson, W(illiam) H(enry) 1841-1922 35
Hudson, Wade 1946- 162
    Earlier sketch in SATA *74*
Huelsmann, Eva 1928- 16
Huerlimann, Bettina 1909-1983 39
    Obituary 34
Huerlimann, Ruth 1939- 32
    Brief entry 31
Huff, Barbara A. 1929- 67
Huff, Tanya 1957- 171
    Earlier sketch in SATA *85*
Huff, Tanya Sue
    See Huff, Tanya
Huff, T.S.
    See Huff, Tanya
Huff, Vivian 1948- 59
Huffaker, Sandy 1943- 10
Huffman, Tom 24
Huggins, Nathan Irvin 1927-1989 63
Huggins, Peter 178
Hughes, Carol 1955- 108
Hughes, Dean 1943- 139
    Earlier sketches in SATA *33, 77*
    See also CLR *76*
Hughes, Eden
    See Griffin, W.E.B
Hughes, Edward James
    See Hughes, Ted

Hughes, (James Mercer) Langston
    1902-1967 33
    Earlier sketch in SATA *4*
    See also CLR *17*
Hughes, Libby 71
Hughes, Matilda
    See MacLeod, Charlotte (Matilda)
Hughes, Monica 1925-2003 162
    Earlier sketches in SATA *15, 70, 119*
    See also CLR *60*
    See also SAAS *11*
Hughes, Monica Ince
    See Hughes, Monica
Hughes, Pat 197
Hughes, Richard (Arthur Warren)
    1900-1976 8
    Obituary 25
Hughes, Sara
    See Saunders, Susan
Hughes, Shirley 1927- 159
    Earlier sketches in SATA *16, 70, 110*
    See also CLR *15*
Hughes, Ted 1930-1998 49
    Brief entry 27
    Obituary 107
    See also CLR *131*
Hughes, Thomas 1822-1896 31
Hughes, Virginia
    See Campbell, Hope
Hughes, Walter (Llewellyn) 1910-1993 26
Hughey, Roberta 1942- 61
Hugo, Pierre Brackers de
    See Brackers de Hugo, Pierre
Hugo, Victor (Marie) 1802-1885 47
Huline-Dickens, Frank William 1931- 34
Huling, Jan 172
Huliska-Beith, Laura 175
Hull, Eleanor (Means) 1913- 21
Hull, Eric Traviss
    See Harnan, Terry
Hull, H. Braxton
    See Jacobs, Helen Hull
Hull, Jesse Redding
    See Hull, Jessie Redding
Hull, Jessie Redding 1932- 51
Hull, Katharine 1921-1977 23
Hull, Lise (E.) 1954- 148
Hull, Maureen 1949- 142
Hulme, Joy N. 1922- 161
    Earlier sketches in SATA *74, 112*
Hults, Dorothy Niebrugge 1898-2000 6
Humble, Richard 1945- 60
Hume, Lachie 189
Hume, Lotta Carswell 7
Hume, Ruth Fox 1922-1980 26
    Obituary 22
Hume, Stephen Eaton 1947- 136
Hummel, Berta 1909-1946 43
Hummel, Sister Maria Innocentia
    See Hummel, Berta
Humphrey, Carol Sue 1956- 167
Humphrey, Henry (III) 1930- 16
Humphrey, Kate
    See Forsyth, Kate
Humphrey, Sandra McLeod 1936- 95
Humphreys, Martha 1943- 71
Humphreys, Susan L.
    See Lowell, Susan
Hundal, Nancy 1957- 128
Huneck, Stephen 1949- 183
    Earlier sketch in SATA *129*
Hungerford, Hesba Fay
    See Brinsmead, H(esba) F(ay)
Hungerford, Pixie
    See Brinsmead, H(esba) F(ay)
Hunkin, Timothy Mark Trelawney 1950- 53
Hunt, Angela Elwell 1957- 159
    Earlier sketch in SATA *75*
Hunt, Bernice 1920- 4
Hunt, Francesca
    See Holland, Isabelle (Christian)

Author Index

Hunt, Irene 1907-2001 .... *91*
 Earlier sketch in SATA 2
 See also CLR *1*
Hunt, Janie Louise 1963- *102*
Hunt, Jonathan 1966- *84*
Hunt, Joyce 1927- *31*
Hunt, Linda 1940- *39*
Hunt, Lisa B(ehnke) 1967- *84*
Hunt, Mabel Leigh 1892-1971 .... *1*
 Obituary *26*
Hunt, Morton M(agill) 1920- *22*
Hunt, Nigel
 See Greenbank, Anthony Hunt
Hunt, Peter (Leonard) 1945- *76*
Hunter, Anne B. 1966- *118*
Hunter, Bernice Thurman 1922-2002 .... *85*
 Brief entry *45*
Hunter, Bobbi Dooley 1945- *89*
Hunter, Captain Marcy
 See Ellis, Edward S(ylvester)
Hunter, Chris
 See Fluke, Joanne
Hunter, Clingham M.D.
 See Adams, William Taylor
Hunter, Edith Fisher 1919- *31*
Hunter, Erin
 See Cary, Kate
Hunter, Evan 1926-2005 .... *25*
 Obituary *167*
Hunter, George E.
 See Ellis, Edward S(ylvester)
Hunter, Hilda 1921- *7*
Hunter, Jana
 See Hunter, Jana Novotny
Hunter, Jana Novotny *190*
Hunter, Jim 1939- *65*
Hunter, Kristin
 See Lattany, Kristin Hunter
Hunter, Leigh
 See Etchison, Birdie L(ee)
Hunter, Lieutenant Ned
 See Ellis, Edward S(ylvester)
Hunter, Mel 1927-2004 .... *39*
Hunter, Mollie 1922- *139*
 Autobiography Feature *139*
 Earlier sketches in SATA *2, 54, 106*
 See also CLR *25*
 See also SAAS *7*
Hunter, Ned
 See Ellis, Edward S(ylvester)
Hunter, Norman (George Lorimer)
 1899-1995 .... *84*
 Earlier sketch in SATA *26*
Hunter, Ryan Ann
 See Greenwood, Pamela D.
 and Macalaster, Elizabeth G.
Hunter, Sara Hoagland 1954- *98*
Hunter Blair, Pauline
 See Clarke, Pauline
Huntington, Amy 1956- *180*
 Earlier sketch in SATA *138*
Huntington, Geoffrey *145*
Huntington, Harriet E(lizabeth) 1909- *1*
Huntsberry, William E(mery) 1916- *5*
Hurd, Clement (G.) 1908-1988 .... *64*
 Obituary *54*
 Earlier sketch in SATA *2*
 See also CLR *49*
Hurd, Edith Thacher 1910-1997 .... *64*
 Obituary *95*
 Earlier sketch in SATA *2*
 See also CLR *49*
 See also SAAS *13*
Hurd, (John) Thacher 1949- *94*
 Autobiography Feature *123*
 Brief entry *45*
 Earlier sketch in SATA *46*
Hurley, Jo
 See Dower, Laura
Hurlimann, Bettina
 See Huerlimann, Bettina

Hurlimann, Ruth
 See Huerlimann, Ruth
Hurmence, Belinda 1921- *77*
 See also CLR *25*
 See also SAAS *20*
Hurst, Carol Otis 1933-2007 .... *185*
 Earlier sketch in SATA *130*
Hurt-Newton, Tania 1968- *84*
Hurwin, Davida Wills 1950- *180*
Hurwitz, Johanna 1937- *175*
 Earlier sketches in SATA *20, 71, 113*
 See also SAAS *18*
Hurwood, Bernhardt J. 1926-1987 .... *12*
 Obituary *50*
Husain, Shahrukh 1950- *108*
Huser, Glen 1943- *151*
Hutchens, Paul 1902-1977 .... *31*
Hutchins, Carleen Maley 1911- *9*
Hutchins, Hazel J. 1952- *175*
 Brief entry *51*
 Earlier sketches in SATA *81, 135*
 See also SAAS *24*
Hutchins, Pat 1942- *178*
 Earlier sketches in SATA *15, 70, 111*
 See also CLR *20*
 See also SAAS *16*
Hutchins, Ross Elliott 1906- *4*
Hutchison, Linda 1942- *152*
Huthmacher, J. Joseph 1929- *5*
Hutto, Nelson (Allen) 1904-1985 .... *20*
Hutton, Kathryn 1915- *89*
Hutton, Warwick 1939-1994 .... *20*
 Obituary *83*
 See also SAAS *17*
Huxley, Aldous (Leonard) 1894-1963 .... *63*
Huxley, Elspeth (Josceline Grant)
 1907-1997 .... *62*
 Obituary *95*
Hyde, Catherine R.
 See Hyde, Catherine Ryan
Hyde, Catherine Ryan 1955- *141*
Hyde, Dayton O(gden) *9*
Hyde, Hawk
 See Hyde, Dayton O(gden)
Hyde, Jeannette
 See Eyerly, Jeannette
Hyde, Margaret O. 1917- *139*
 Earlier sketches in SATA *1, 42, 76*
 See also CLR *23*
 See also SAAS *8*
Hyde, Margaret Oldroyd
 See Hyde, Margaret O.
Hyde, Shelley
 See Reed, Kit
Hyde, Wayne Frederick 1922- *7*
Hylander, Clarence J(ohn) 1897-1964 .... *7*
Hyman, Robin P(hilip) 1931- *12*
Hyman, Trina Schart 1939-2004 .... *95*
 Obituary *158*
 Earlier sketches in SATA *7, 46*
 See also CLR *50*
Hymes, Lucia M(anley) 1907-1998 .... *7*
Hyndman, Jane Andrews Lee 1912-1978 ..... *46*
 Obituary *23*
 Earlier sketch in SATA *1*
Hyndman, Robert Utley 1906-1973 .... *18*
Hynes, Pat *98*

I

Iannone, Jeanne
 See Balzano, Jeanne (Koppel)
Ibatoulline, Bagram 1965(?)- *174*
Ibbitson, John Perrie 1955- *102*
Ibbotson, Eva 1925- *156*
 Earlier sketches in SATA *13, 103*
Ibbotson, M. C(hristine) 1930- *5*
Icenoggle, Jodi 1967- *168*

Icenoggle, Jodi O.
 See Icenoggle, Jodi
Ichikawa, Satomi 1949- *146*
 Brief entry *36*
 Earlier sketches in SATA *47, 78*
 See also CLR *62*
Iggulden, Hal 1972- *196*
Ignoffo, Matthew 1945- *92*
Igus, Toyomi 1953- *112*
 Earlier sketch in SATA *76*
Ihimaera, Witi (Tame) 1944- *148*
Ikeda, Daisaku 1928- *77*
Ilowite, Sheldon A. 1931- *27*
Ilsey, Dent
 See Chapman, John Stanton Higham
Ilsley, Dent
 See Chapman, John Stanton Higham
Ilsley, Velma (Elizabeth) 1918- *12*
Imai, Ayano 1980- *190*
Imai, Miko 1963- *90*
Imershein, Betsy 1953- *62*
Immel, Mary Blair 1930- *28*
Immell, Myra H. 1941- *92*
Impey, Rose 1947- *152*
 Earlier sketch in SATA *69*
Ingelow, Jean 1820-1897 .... *33*
Ingermanson, Randall 1958- *134*
Ingermanson, Randy
 See Ingermanson, Randall
Ingersoll, Norman 1928- *79*
Ingham, Colonel Frederic
 See Hale, Edward Everett
Ingman, Bruce 1963- *182*
 Earlier sketch in SATA *134*
Ingman, Nicholas 1948- *52*
Ingold, Jeanette *128*
Ingpen, Robert 1936- *166*
 Earlier sketch in SATA *109*
Ingpen, Robert Roger
 See Ingpen, Robert
Ingraham, Erick 1950- *145*
Ingraham, Leonard W(illiam) 1913-2003 ..... *4*
Ingram, Scott 1948- *167*
 Earlier sketch in SATA *92*
Ingram, W. Scott
 See Ingram, Scott
Ingrams, Doreen 1906-1997 .... *97*
 Earlier sketch in SATA *20*
Ingrid, Charles
 See Salsitz, Rhondi Vilott
Ingves, Gunilla (Anna Maria Folkesdotter)
 1939- *101*
Inkpen, Mick 1952- *154*
 Earlier sketch in SATA *99*
Innes, (Ralph) Hammond
 See Hammond Innes, Ralph
Innes, Ralph Hammond
 See Hammond Innes, Ralph
Innocenti, Roberto 1940- *159*
 Earlier sketch in SATA *96*
 See also CLR *126*
Innocenti and Gallaz
 See Gallaz, Christophe
 and Innocenti, Roberto
Inyart, Gene
 See Namovicz, Gene Inyart
Ionesco, Eugene 1912-1994 .... *7*
 Obituary *79*
Ipcar, Dahlov (Zorach) 1917- *147*
 Autobiography Feature *147*
 Earlier sketches in SATA *1, 49*
 See also SAAS *8*
Ireland, Karin *151*
 Earlier sketch in SATA *101*
Ironside, Jetske 1940- *60*
Irvin, Fred 1914- *15*
Irvine, Georgeanne 1955- *72*
Irvine, Joan 1951- *80*
Irving, Alexander
 See Hume, Ruth Fox

Irving, Robert
  See Adler, Irving
Irving, Washington 1783-1859
  See YABC 2
  See also CLR 97
Irwin, Ann(abelle Bowen) 1915-1998 89
  Brief entry 38
  Obituary 106
  Earlier sketch in SATA 44
  See also CLR 40
  See also SAAS 14
Irwin, Constance (H.) Frick 1913-1995 6
Irwin, Hadley
  See Hadley, Lee
  and Irwin, Ann(abelle Bowen)
Irwin, Keith Gordon 1885-1964 11
Isaac, Joanne 1934- 21
Isaacs, Anne 1949- 185
  Earlier sketch in SATA 90
Isaacs, Jacob
  See Kranzler, George G(ershon)
Isaacson, Philip M(arshal) 1924- 87
Isadora, Rachel 1953(?)- 165
  Brief entry 32
  Earlier sketches in SATA 54, 79, 121
  See also CLR 7
Isbell, Rebecca T(emple) 1942- 125
Isham, Charlotte H(ickock) 1912- 21
Ishida, Jui 176
Ish-Kishor, Judith 1892-1972 11
Ish-Kishor, Sulamith 1896-1977 17
Ishmael, Woodi 1914-1995 31
  Obituary 109
Isle, Sue 1963- 105
Israel, Elaine 1945- 12
Israel, Marion Louise 1882-1973
  Obituary 26
Iterson, S(iny) R(ose) Van
  See Van Iterson, S(iny) R(ose)
Ivanko, John D. 1966- 111
Ivanko, John Duane
  See Ivanko, John D.
Iversen, Jeremy 1980(?)- 174
Iversen, Jeremy Watt
  See Iversen, Jeremy
Iverson, Carol (L.) 1941- 145
Iverson, Diane 1950- 122
Iverson, Eric G.
  See Turtledove, Harry
Ivery, Martha M. 1948- 124
Ives, David 1951- 173
Ives, Morgan
  See Bradley, Marion Zimmer
Iwai, Melissa 183
Iwamatsu, Jun Atsushi 1908-1994 81
  Earlier sketch in SATA 14
  See also CLR 4
Iwasaki (Matsumoto), Chihiro 1918-1974
  See CLR 18

J

Jablonski, Carla 184
Jac, Lee
  See Morton, Lee Jack, Jr.
Jacka, Martin 1943- 72
Jackson, Alison 1953- 160
  Earlier sketches in SATA 73, 108
Jackson, Anne 1896(?)-1984
  Obituary 37
Jackson, Barry
  See Jackson, Barry E.
Jackson, Barry E. 200
Jackson, C(aary) Paul 1902-1991 6
Jackson, Caary
  See Jackson, C(aary) Paul
Jackson, Charlotte E. (Cobden) 1903(?)-1989
  Obituary 62

Jackson, Dave
  See Jackson, J. David
Jackson, Ellen B. 1943- 167
  Earlier sketches in SATA 75, 115
Jackson, Garnet Nelson 1944- 87
Jackson, Geoffrey (Holt Seymour) 1915-1987
  Obituary 53
Jackson, Gina
  See Fluke, Joanne
Jackson, Guida M. 1930- 71
Jackson, J. David 1944- 91
Jackson, Jacqueline 1928- 65
Jackson, Jacqueline Dougan
  See Jackson, Jacqueline
Jackson, Jesse 1908-1983 29
  Obituary 48
  Earlier sketch in SATA 2
  See also CLR 28
Jackson, Marjorie 1928- 127
Jackson, Melanie 1956- 141
Jackson, Mike 1946- 91
Jackson, Neta J. 1944- 91
Jackson, O. B.
  See Jackson, C(aary) Paul
Jackson, Rob 1961- 176
Jackson, Robert B(lake) 1926- 8
Jackson, Robert Bradley
  See Jackson, Rob
Jackson, Sally
  See Kellogg, Jean (Defrees)
Jackson, Shirley 1919-1965 2
Jackson, Woody 1948- 92
Jacob, Helen Pierce 1927- 21
Jacobin
  See Bisson, Terry
Jacobs, Deborah Lynn 187
Jacobs, Flora Gill 1918-2006 5
  Obituary 178
Jacobs, Francine 1935- 150
  Brief entry 42
  Earlier sketch in SATA 43
Jacobs, Frank 1929- 30
Jacobs, Helen Hull 1908-1997 12
Jacobs, Joseph 1854-1916 25
Jacobs, Judy 1952- 69
Jacobs, Laurie A. 1956- 89
Jacobs, Leah
  See Gellis, Roberta
Jacobs, Leland Blair 1907-1992 20
  Obituary 71
Jacobs, Linda
  See Altman, Linda Jacobs
Jacobs, Lou(is), Jr. 1921- 2
Jacobs, Shannon K. 1947- 77
Jacobs, Susan
  See Quinn, Susan
Jacobs, William Jay 1933- 89
  Earlier sketch in SATA 28
Jacobsen, Laura 177
Jacobson, Daniel 1923- 12
Jacobson, Jennifer
  See Jacobson, Jennifer Richard
Jacobson, Jennifer Richard 1958- 170
Jacobson, Morris K(arl) 1906- 21
Jacobson, Rick 170
Jacopetti, Alexandra
  See Hart, Alexandra
Jacques, Brian 1939- 176
  Earlier sketches in SATA 62, 95, 138
  See also CLR 21
Jacques, Robin 1920-1995 32
  Brief entry 30
  Obituary 86
  See also SAAS 5
Jaekel, Susan M. 1948- 89
Jaffe, Michele 179
Jaffe, Michele Sharon
  See Jaffe, Michele
Jaffee, Al(lan) 1921- 66
  Earlier sketch in SATA 37

Jagendorf, Moritz (Adolf) 1888-1981 2
  Obituary 24
Jahn, Michael
  See Jahn, (Joseph) Michael
Jahn, (Joseph) Michael 1943- 28
Jahn, Mike
  See Jahn, (Joseph) Michael
Jahn-Clough, Lisa 1967- 193
  Earlier sketches in SATA 88, 152
Jahsmann, Allan Hart 1916- 28
Jakes, John 1932- 62
Jakes, John William
  See Jakes, John
James, Andrew
  See Kirkup, James
James, Ann 1952- 168
  Earlier sketches in SATA 82, 117
James, Betsy 183
James, Brian 1976- 140
James, Bronte
  See Nash, Renea Denise
James, Captain Lew
  See Stratemeyer, Edward L.
James, Charlie 1961- 185
James, Curtis E. 182
James, Dynely
  See Mayne, William (James Carter)
James, Edwin
  See Gunn, James E.
James, Elizabeth 1942- 97
  Earlier sketches in SATA 39, 45, 52
James, Emily
  See Standiford, Natalie
James, Gordon C. 1973- 195
James, Harry Clebourne 1896-1978 11
James, J. Alison 1962- 146
  Earlier sketch in SATA 83
James, Josephine
  See Sterne, Emma Gelders
James, Mary
  See Meaker, Marijane
James, Matt 201
James, Philip
  See del Rey, Lester
  and Moorcock, Michael
James, Robin 1953- 50
James, Robin Irene
  See James, Robin
James, Tegan
  See Odgers, Sally Farrell
James, T.F.
  See Fleming, Thomas
James, Will(iam Roderick) 1892-1942 19
Jameson, W. C. 1942- 93
Jamieson, Ian R.
  See Goulart, Ron
Jamiolkowski, Raymond M. 1953- 81
Jane, Mary Childs 1909- 6
Jane, Pamela 158
Janeczko, Paul B(ryan) 1945- 155
  Earlier sketches in SATA 53, 98
  See also CLR 47
  See also SAAS 18
Janes, Edward C. 1908-1984 25
Janes, J(oseph) Robert 1935- 148
  Brief entry 50
  Earlier sketch in SATA 101
Janeway, Elizabeth (Hall) 1913-2005 19
Janger, Kathleen N. 1940- 66
Janice
  See Brustlein, Janice Tworkov
Janisch, Heinz 1960- 181
Janosch
  See Eckert, Horst
Janover, Caroline (Davis) 1943- 141
  Earlier sketch in SATA 89
Janovitz, Marilyn 194
Jansen, Jared
  See Cebulash, Mel
Janson, Dora Jane (Heineberg) 1916- 31
Janson, H(orst) W(oldemar) 1913-1982 9

Jansson, Tove (Marika) 1914-2001 .... *41*
  Earlier sketch in SATA *3*
  See also CLR *125*
Janus, Grete
  See Hertz, Grete Janus
Jaques, Faith 1923-1997 .... *97*
  Earlier sketches in SATA *21, 69*
Jaquith, Priscilla 1908- *51*
Jaramillo, Mari-Luci 1928- *139*
Jarman, Julia 1946- *198*
  Earlier sketch in SATA *133*
Jarman, Rosemary Hawley 1935- *7*
Jarrell, Mary Von Schrader 1914- *35*
Jarrell, Randall 1914-1965 .... *7*
  See also CLR *111*
Jarrett, Clare 1952- *201*
Jarrett, Roxanne
  See Werner, Herma
Jarrow, Gail 1952- *185*
  Earlier sketch in SATA *84*
Jarvis, E.K.
  See Ellison, Harlan
  and Silverberg, Robert
Jarvis, Robin 1963- *181*
Jaskol, Julie 1958- *127*
Jasner, W. K.
  See Watson, Jane Werner
Jassem, Kate
  See Oppenheim, Joanne
Jauss, Anne Marie 1902(?)-1991 .... *10*
  Obituary *69*
Javernick, Ellen 1938- *89*
Jay, Alison *196*
Jayne, Lieutenant R. H.
  See Ellis, Edward S(ylvester)
Jaynes, Clare
  See Mayer, Jane Rothschild
Jeake, Samuel, Jr.
  See Aiken, Conrad (Potter)
Jean-Bart, Leslie 1954- *121*
Jeapes, Ben 1965- *174*
Jecan, Gavriel 1962- *200*
Jefferds, Vincent H(arris) 1916- *59*
  Brief entry *49*
Jefferies, (John) Richard 1848-1887 .... *16*
Jeffers, Dawn *189*
Jeffers, Oliver 1977- *175*
Jeffers, Susan 1942- *137*
  Earlier sketches in SATA *17, 70, 129*
  See also CLR *30*
Jefferson, Sarah
  See Farjeon, (Eve) Annabel
Jeffries, Roderic 1926- *4*
Jeffries, Roderic Graeme
  See Jeffries, Roderic
Jenkin-Pearce, Susie 1943- *80*
Jenkins, A.M. *174*
Jenkins, Amanda McRaney
  See Jenkins, A.M.
Jenkins, Debra Reid
  See Reid Jenkins, Debra
Jenkins, Emily 1967- *174*
  Earlier sketch in SATA *144*
Jenkins, Jean *98*
Jenkins, Jerry B. 1949- *149*
Jenkins, Jerry Bruce
  See Jenkins, Jerry B.
Jenkins, Leonard *189*
Jenkins, Marie M(agdalen) 1909- *7*
Jenkins, Patrick 1955- *72*
Jenkins, Steve 1952- *188*
  Earlier sketch in SATA *154*
Jenkins, William A(twell) 1922-1998 .... *9*
Jenkyns, Chris 1924- *51*
Jennings, Christopher S. 1971(?)- *201*
Jennings, Coleman A(lonzo) 1933- *64*
Jennings, C.S.
  See Jennings, Christopher S.
Jennings, Dana Andrew 1957- *93*
Jennings, Elizabeth (Joan) 1926-2001 .... *66*

Jennings, Gary 1928-1999 .... *9*
  Obituary *117*
Jennings, Gary Gayne
  See Jennings, Gary
Jennings, Patrick 1962- *160*
  Earlier sketch in SATA *96*
Jennings, Paul 1943- *165*
  Earlier sketch in SATA *88*
  See also CLR *40*
Jennings, Richard W. 1945- *185*
  Earlier sketch in SATA *136*
Jennings, Robert
  See Hamilton, Charles (Harold St. John)
Jennings, S. M.
  See Meyer, Jerome Sydney
Jennings, Sharon 1954- *95*
Jennings, Sharon Elizabeth
  See Jennings, Sharon
Jennison, C. S.
  See Starbird, Kaye
Jennison, Keith Warren 1911-1995 .... *14*
Jensen, Kathryn 1949- *81*
Jensen, Kristine Mary 1961- *78*
Jensen, Niels 1927- *25*
Jensen, Vickie (Dee) 1946- *81*
Jensen, Virginia Allen 1927- *8*
Jenson-Elliott, Cynthia L(ouise) 1962- *143*
Jeram, Anita 1965- *154*
  Earlier sketches in SATA *71, 102*
Jerman, Jerry 1949- *89*
Jernigan, E. Wesley 1940- *85*
Jernigan, Gisela (Evelyn) 1948- *85*
Jeschke, Susan 1942- *42*
  Brief entry *27*
Jessel, Camilla (Ruth) 1937- *143*
  Earlier sketch in SATA *29*
Jessell, Tim *177*
Jessey, Cornelia
  See Sussman, Cornelia Silver
Jewel
  See Kilcher, Jewel
Jewell, Nancy 1940- *109*
  Brief entry *41*
Jewett, Eleanore Myers 1890-1967 .... *5*
Jewett, (Theodora) Sarah Orne 1849-1909 ... *15*
Jezard, Alison 1919- *57*
  Brief entry *34*
Jiang, Cheng An 1943- *109*
Jiang, Ji-li 1954- *101*
Jiang, Zheng An
  See Jiang, Cheng An
Jiler, John 1946- *42*
  Brief entry *35*
Jimenez, Francisco 1943- *108*
Jinks, Catherine 1963- *155*
  Earlier sketch in SATA *94*
Jobb, Jamie 1945- *29*
Jobling, Curtis *131*
Jocelyn, Ann Henning 1948- *92*
Jocelyn, Marthe 1956- *198*
  Earlier sketches in SATA *118, 163*
Joerns, Consuelo *44*
  Brief entry *33*
Joey D
  See Macaulay, Teresa (E.)
Johansen, Krista V.
  See Johansen, K.V.
Johansen, K.V 1968- *186*
Johansen, K.V. 1968- *186*
  Earlier sketch in SATA *129*
Johansson, Philip *163*
John, Joyce *59*
Johns, Avery
  See Cousins, Margaret
Johns, Elizabeth 1943- *88*
Johns, Janetta
  See Quin-Harkin, Janet
Johns, Linda 1945- *173*
Johns, W(illiam) E(arle) 1893-1968 .... *55*
Johns, Captain W. E.
  See Johns, W(illiam) E(arle)

Johnson, A.
  See Johnson, Annabell
Johnson, A. E.
  See Johnson, Annabell
  and Johnson, Edgar (Raymond)
Johnson, Angela 1961- *188*
  Earlier sketches in SATA *69, 102, 150*
  See also CLR *33*
Johnson, Annabel
  See Johnson, Annabell
Johnson, Annabell 1921- *72*
  Earlier sketch in SATA *2*
Johnson, Art 1946- *123*
Johnson, B. F. 1920- *1*
Johnson, Benjamin F., of Boone
  See Riley, James Whitcomb
Johnson, Bettye 1858-1919
  See Rogers, Bettye
Johnson, Caryn
  See Goldberg, Whoopi
Johnson, Caryn E.
  See Goldberg, Whoopi
Johnson, Caryn Elaine
  See Goldberg, Whoopi
Johnson, Charles R. 1925- *11*
Johnson, Charlotte Buel
  See von Wodtke, Charlotte Buel Johnson
Johnson, Chuck
  See Johnson, Charles R.
Johnson, Crockett
  See Leisk, David (Johnson)
Johnson, D(ana) William 1945- *23*
Johnson, Daniel Shahid 1954- *73*
Johnson, David
  See Johnson, David A.
Johnson, David A. 1951- *191*
Johnson, D.B. 1944- *183*
  Earlier sketch in SATA *146*
Johnson, Dianne 1960- *130*
Johnson, Dinah
  See Johnson, Dianne
Johnson, Dolores 1949- *69*
Johnson, Donald B.
  See Johnson, D.B.
Johnson, Dorothy M(arie) 1905-1984 .... *6*
  Obituary *40*
Johnson, E(ugene) Harper *44*
Johnson, Edgar (Raymond) 1912-1990 .... *72*
  Earlier sketch in SATA *2*
Johnson, Eleanor Murdock 1892-1987
  Obituary *54*
Johnson, Elizabeth 1911-1984 .... *7*
  Obituary *39*
Johnson, Eric W(arner) 1918-1994 ....
  Obituary *82*
  Earlier sketch in SATA *8*
Johnson, Evelyne 1922- *20*
Johnson, Fred 19(?)-1982 .... *63*
Johnson, Gaylord 1884-1972 .... *7*
Johnson, Gerald White 1890-1980 .... *19*
  Obituary *28*
Johnson, Harper
  See Johnson, E(ugene) Harper
Johnson, Harriett 1908-1987
  Obituary *53*
Johnson, James Ralph 1922- *1*
Johnson, James Weldon 1871-1938 .... *31*
  See also CLR *32*
Johnson, Jane 1951- *48*
Johnson, Joan J. 1942- *59*
Johnson, John E(mil) 1929- *34*
Johnson, Johnny 1901-1995
  See Johnson, (Walter) Ryerson
Johnson, Kathleen Jeffrie 1950- *186*
Johnson, La Verne B(ravo) 1925- *13*
Johnson, Layne *187*
Johnson, Lee Kaiser 1962- *78*
Johnson, Lissa H(alls) 1955- *65*
Johnson, Lois Smith 1894-1993 .... *6*
Johnson, Lois Walfrid 1936- *130*
  Earlier sketches in SATA *22, 91*

Johnson, Margaret S(weet) 1893-1964 35
Johnson, Marguerite Annie
    See Angelou, Maya
Johnson, Mary Frances K. 1929(?)-1979
    Obituary 27
Johnson, Maud Battle 1918(?)-1985
    Obituary 46
Johnson, Maureen 1973- 200
Johnson, Meredith Merrell 1952- 104
Johnson, Milton 1932- 31
Johnson, Neil 1954- 135
    Earlier sketch in SATA 73
Johnson, Pamela 1949- 71
Johnson, Patricia Polin 1956- 84
Johnson, Paul Brett 1947- 132
    Earlier sketch in SATA 83
Johnson, Rebecca L. 1956- 147
    Earlier sketch in SATA 67
Johnson, Rick L. 1954- 79
Johnson, (Walter) Ryerson 1901-1995 10
    Obituary 106
Johnson, Scott 1952- 119
    Earlier sketch in SATA 76
Johnson, Sherrie 1948- 87
Johnson, Shirley K(ing) 1927- 10
Johnson, Siddie Joe 1905-1977
    Obituary 20
Johnson, Spencer 1938- 145
    Brief entry 38
Johnson, Stacie
    See Myers, Walter Dean
Johnson, Stephen T. 1964- 189
    Earlier sketches in SATA 84, 141
Johnson, Steve 1960- 177
Johnson, Sue Kaiser 1963- 78
Johnson, Sylvia A. 166
    Brief entry 52
    Earlier sketch in SATA 104
Johnson, William R. 38
Johnson, William Weber 1909-1992 7
Johnson-Feelings, Dianne
    See Johnson, Dianne
Johnston, Agnes Christine
    See Dazey, Agnes J(ohnston)
Johnston, Annie Fellows 1863-1931 37
Johnston, Dorothy Grunbock 1915-1979 54
Johnston, Ginny 1946- 60
Johnston, H(ugh) A(nthony) S(tephen)
    1913-1967 14
Johnston, Janet 1944- 71
Johnston, Jeffry W. 188
Johnston, Johanna 1914(?)-1982 12
    Obituary 33
Johnston, Julie 1941- 110
    Autobiography Feature 128
    Earlier sketch in SATA 78
    See also CLR 41
    See also SAAS 24
Johnston, Lynn 1947- 118
Johnston, Lynn Beverley
    See Johnston, Lynn
Johnston, Mark 194
Johnston, Norma
    See St. John, Nicole
Johnston, Portia
    See Takakjian, Portia
Johnston, Susan Taylor 1942- 180
    Earlier sketches in SATA 8, 83, 128
Johnston, Tim(othy Patrick) 1962- 146
Johnston, Tony
    See Johnston, Susan Taylor
Joinson, Carla 160
Jolin, Paula 186
Jonas, Ann 1932- 135
    Brief entry 42
    Earlier sketch in SATA 50
    See also CLR 74
Jonell, Lynne 1956- 196
    Earlier sketch in SATA 109

Jones, Adrienne 1915-2000 82
    Earlier sketch in SATA 7
    See also SAAS 10
Jones, Annabel
    See Lewis, Mary
Jones, Betty Millsaps 1940- 54
Jones, Carol 1942- 153
    Earlier sketch in SATA 79
Jones, Carrie 1971- 191
Jones, Charles M. 1912-2002 53
    Obituary 133
Jones, Charlotte Foltz 1945- 122
    Earlier sketch in SATA 77
Jones, Chuck
    See Jones, Charles M.
Jones, Constance 112
Jones, Constance A.
    See Jones, Constance
Jones, Diana Wynne 1934- 160
    Earlier sketches in SATA 9, 70, 108
    See also CLR 120
    See also SAAS 7
Jones, Douglas C(lyde) 1924-1998 52
Jones, Elizabeth McDavid 155
Jones, Elizabeth Orton 1910-2005 18
    Obituary 164
Jones, Evan 1915-1996 3
Jones, Geraldine
    See McCaughrean, Geraldine
Jones, Gillingham
    See Hamilton, Charles (Harold St. John)
Jones, Gwyneth A(nn) 1952- 159
Jones, Harold 1904-1992 14
    Obituary 72
Jones, Helen Hinckley 1903-1991 26
Jones, Helen L(ouise) 1903-1973
    Obituary 22
Jones, Hettie 1934- 42
    Brief entry 27
Jones, Hortense P. 1918- 9
Jones, J. Sydney 1948- 101
Jones, Jasmine
    See Papademetriou, Lisa
Jones, Jennifer (Berry) 1947- 90
Jones, Jessie Mae Orton 1887(?)-1983
    Obituary 37
Jones, John R(obert) 1926- 76
Jones, Jon Sydney
    See Jones, J. Sydney
Jones, Kimberly K. 1957- 187
Jones, Marcia Thornton 1958- 115
    Earlier sketch in SATA 73
Jones, Martha T(annery) 1931- 130
Jones, Mary Alice 1898(?)-1980 6
Jones, McClure 34
Jones, Noah Z. 182
Jones, Patrick 1961- 136
Jones, Penelope 1938- 31
Jones, Rebecca C(astaldi) 1947- 99
    Earlier sketch in SATA 33
Jones, Robin D(orothy) 1959- 80
Jones, Sanford W.
    See Thorn, John
Jones, Sylvie 185
Jones, Sylvie Michelle
    See Jones, Sylvie
Jones, Terence Graham Parry 1942- 127
    Brief entry 51
    Earlier sketch in SATA 67
Jones, Terry
    See Jones, Terence Graham Parry
Jones, Tim Wynne
    See Wynne-Jones, Tim
Jones, Traci L. 186
Jones, V(ictoria) M(ary) 1958- 147
Jones, Veda Boyd 1948- 119
Jones, Volcano
    See Mitchell, Adrian
Jones, Weyman (B.) 1928- 4
    See also SAAS 11

Jones, William Glynne
    See Glynne-Jones, William
Jonk, Clarence 1906-1987 10
Jonsberg, Barry 1951- 168
Joos, Francoise 1956- 78
Joos, Frederic 1953- 78
Joosse, Barbara M. 1949- 164
    Earlier sketches in SATA 52, 96
Joosse, Barbara Monnot
    See Joosse, Barbara M.
Jordan, Alexis Hill
    See Glick, Ruth (Burtnick)
    and Titchener, Louise
Jordan, Anne Devereaux 1943- 80
Jordan, Chris
    See Philbrick, Rodman
Jordan, Deloris 191
Jordan, Don
    See Howard, Vernon (Linwood)
Jordan, Hope Dahle 1905-1995 15
Jordan, Jael (Michal) 1949- 30
Jordan, June 1936-2002 136
    Earlier sketch in SATA 4
    See also CLR 10
Jordan, June Meyer
    See Jordan, June
Jordan, Lee
    See Scholefield, Alan
Jordan, Martin George 1944- 84
Jordan, Robert 1948-2007 95
Jordan, Robert K.
    See Jordan, Robert
Jordan, Rosa 1939- 191
Jordan, Roslyn M. 189
Jordan, Sherryl 1949- 122
    Earlier sketch in SATA 71
    See also SAAS 23
Jordan, Shirley 1930- 154
Jordan, Tanis 1946- 84
Jorgensen, Ivar
    See Ellison, Harlan
    and Garrett, Randall
Jorgensen, Mary Venn -1995 36
Jorgensen, Norman 1954- 157
Jorgenson, Ivar
    See Silverberg, Robert
Jorisch, Stephane 178
Joseph, Anne
    See Coates, Anna
Joseph, James (Herz) 1924- 53
Joseph, Joan 1939- 34
Joseph, Joseph M(aron) 1903-1979 22
Joseph, Patrick
    See O'Malley, Kevin
Josephs, Rebecca
    See Talbot, Toby
Josephson, Judith Pinkerton 1943- 198
Josh
    See Twain, Mark
Joshua, Peter
    See Stone, Peter
Joslin, Mary 1953- 176
Joslin, Sesyle
    See Hine, Sesyle Joslin
Journet, Mireille
    See Marokvia, Mireille
Joyce, Bill
    See Joyce, William
Joyce, J(ames) Avery 1902-1987 11
    Obituary 50
Joyce, Peter 1937- 127
Joyce, William 1957- 118
    Brief entry 46
    Earlier sketch in SATA 72
    See also CLR 26
Joyner, Jerry 1938- 34
Juan, Ana 1961- 179
Jubert, Herve 185
Juby, Susan 1969- 156
Jucker, Sita 1921- 5
Judah, Aaron 1923- 118

Judd, Cyril
  See Kornbluth, C(yril) M.
  and Merril, Judith
  and Pohl, Frederik
Judd, Denis (O'Nan) 1938- 33
Judd, Frances K.
  See Benson, Mildred
Jude, Conny 81
Judge, Lita 192
Judson, Clara Ingram 1879-1960 38
  Brief entry 27
Judy, Stephen
  See Tchudi, Stephen N.
Judy, Stephen N.
  See Tchudi, Stephen N.
Juhasz, Victor 1954- 177
Jukes, Mavis 1947- 111
  Brief entry 43
  Earlier sketch in SATA 72
  See also SAAS 12
Jules, Jacqueline 1956- 183
  Earlier sketch in SATA 148
Julesberg, Elizabeth Rider Montgomery
  1902-1985 34
  Obituary 41
  Earlier sketch in SATA 3
Julian, Jane
  See Wiseman, David
Jumpp, Hugo
  See MacPeek, Walter G.
Jungman, Ann 165
Jupo, Frank J. 1904-1981 7
Jurmain, Suzanne 1945- 169
  Earlier sketch in SATA 72
Jurmain, Suzanne Tripp
  See Jurmain, Suzanne
Juster, Norton 1929- 132
  Earlier sketch in SATA 3
  See also CLR 112
Justus, May 1898-1989 1
  Obituary 106
Juvenilia
  See Taylor, Ann

K

Kaaberbol, Lene
  See Kaaberbol, Lene
Kaaberbol, Lene 1960- 159
Kabdebo, Tamas
  See Kabdebo, Thomas
Kabdebo, Thomas 1934- 10
Kabibble, Osh
  See Jobb, Jamie
Kacer, Kathy 1954- 184
  Earlier sketch in SATA 142
Kaczman, James 156
Kadair, Deborah Ousley 184
Kadesch, Robert R(udstone) 1922- 31
Kadohata, Cynthia 1956(?)- 180
  Earlier sketch in SATA 155
  See also CLR 121
Kaempfert, Wade
  See del Rey, Lester
Kaestner, Erich 1899-1974 14
  See also CLR 4
Kahl, Jonathan (D.) 1959- 77
Kahl, M(arvin) P(hilip) 1934- 37
Kahl, Virginia (Caroline) 1919-2004 48
  Brief entry 38
  Obituary 158
Kahn, Joan 1914-1994 48
  Obituary 82
Kahn, Katherine Janus 1942- 167
  Earlier sketch in SATA 90
Kahn, Peggy
  See Katz, Bobbi
Kahn, Roger 1927- 37
Kahukiwa, Robyn 1940- 134

Kains, Josephine
  See Goulart, Ron
Kaizuki, Kiyonori 1950- 72
Kakimoto, Kozo 1915- 11
Kalashnikoff, Nicholas 1888-1961 16
Kalb, Jonah 1926- 23
Kalbacken, Joan 1925- 96
Kalechofsky, Roberta 1931- 92
Kaler, James Otis 1848-1912 15
Kalish, Claire M. 1947- 92
Kallen, Stuart A(rnold) 1955- 126
  Earlier sketch in SATA 86
Kallevig, Christine Petrell 1955- 164
Kalman, Bobbie 1947- 63
Kalman, Maira 1949- 137
  Earlier sketch in SATA 96
  See also CLR 32
Kalnay, Francis 1899-1992 7
Kaloustian, Rosanne 1955- 93
Kalow, Gisela 1946- 32
Kalstein, Dave 175
Kamen, Gloria 1923- 98
  Earlier sketch in SATA 9
Kamerman, Sylvia E.
  See Burack, Sylvia K.
Kamm, Josephine (Hart) 1905-1989 24
Kammerman, Sylvia K.
  See Burack, Sylvia K.
Kandel, Michael 1941- 93
Kandell, Alice S. 1938- 35
Kane, Bob 1916-1998 120
Kane, Henry Bugbee 1902-1971 14
Kane, L. A.
  See Mannetti, Lisa
Kane, Robert W. 1910- 18
Kane, Wilson
  See Bloch, Robert (Albert)
Kanefield, Teri 1960- 135
Kaner, Etta 1947- 198
  Earlier sketch in SATA 126
Kanetzke, Howard W(illiam) 1932- 38
Kangas, Juli 1958- 200
Kann, Elizabeth 180
Kann, Victoria 180
Kanninen, Barbara 196
Kanninen, Barbara J.
  See Kanninen, Barbara
Kanoza, Muriel Canfield
  See Canfield, Muriel
Kantner, Seth 1965- 179
Kanzawa, Toshiko
  See Furukawa, Toshi
Kanzler, John 1963- 188
Kaplan, Andrew 1960- 78
Kaplan, Anne Bernays
  See Bernays, Anne
Kaplan, Bess 1927- 22
Kaplan, Boche 1926- 24
Kaplan, Elizabeth 1956- 83
Kaplan, Elizabeth A.
  See Kaplan, Elizabeth
Kaplan, Irma 1900- 10
Kaplan, Jean Caryl Korn 1926- 10
Kaplow, Robert 1954- 70
Karageorge, Michael
  See Anderson, Poul
Karas, G. Brian 1957- 178
Karas, George Brian
  See Karas, G. Brian
Karasz, Ilonka 1896-1981
  Obituary 29
Karen, Ruth 1922-1987 9
  Obituary 54
Kark, Nina Mary
  See Bawden, Nina
Karl, Herb 1938- 73
Karl, Jean E(dna) 1927-2000 122
  Earlier sketch in SATA 34
  See also SAAS 10
Karlin, Bernie 1927- 68
Karlin, Eugene 1918- 10

Karlin, Nurit 103
  Earlier sketch in SATA 63
Karnes, Frances A. 1937- 110
Karp, Naomi J. 1926- 16
Karpinski, J. Rick
  See Karpinski, John Eric
Karpinski, John Eric 1952- 81
Karpinski, Rick
  See Karpinski, John Eric
Karr, Kathleen 1946- 127
  Earlier sketch in SATA 82
Karr, Phyllis Ann 1944- 119
Karwoski, Gail 1949- 127
Karwoski, Gail Langer
  See Karwoski, Gail
Kashiwagi, Isami 1925- 10
Kaslik, Ibi
  See Kaslik, Ibolya Emma
Kaslik, Ibolya Emma 1973- 185
Kassem, Lou 1931- 62
  Brief entry 51
Kastel, Warren
  See Silverberg, Robert
Kastner, Erich
  See Kaestner, Erich
Kastner, Jill (Marie) 1964- 117
  Earlier sketch in SATA 70
Kasuya, Masahiro 1937- 51
Kasza, Keiko 1951- 191
  Earlier sketch in SATA 124
Kataphusin
  See Ruskin, John
Katchen, Carole 1944- 9
Kathryn
  See Searle, Kathryn Adrienne
Katona, Robert 1949- 21
Katsarakis, Joan Harries
  See Harries, Joan
Katz, Alan 185
Katz, Avi 1949- 199
Katz, Avner 1939- 103
Katz, Bobbi 1933- 179
  Earlier sketch in SATA 12
Katz, Fred(eric Phillip) 1938- 6
Katz, Jane B(resler) 1934- 33
Katz, Karen 1947- 195
  Earlier sketch in SATA 158
Katz, Marjorie P.
  See Weiser, Marjorie P(hillis) K(atz)
Katz, Susan 1945- 156
Katz, Welwyn Wilton 1948- 96
  Autobiography Feature 118
  Earlier sketch in SATA 62
  See also CLR 45
Katz, William 1940- 98
Katz, William Loren 1927- 13
Kaufman, Bel 57
Kaufman, Jeff 1955- 84
Kaufman, Joe 1911-2001 33
Kaufman, Joseph
  See Kaufman, Joe
Kaufman, Mervyn D. 1932- 4
Kaufmann, Angelika 1935- 15
Kaufmann, John 1931- 18
Kaula, Edna Mason 1906-1987 13
Kaur Khalsa, Dayal
  See Khalsa, Dayal Kaur
Kavaler, Lucy 1930- 23
Kavanagh, Jack 1920- 85
Kavanagh, P(atrick) J(oseph Gregory)
  1931- 122
Kavanaugh, Ian
  See Webb, Jean Francis (III)
Kay, Alan N. 1965- 144
Kay, Elizabeth 1949- 165
Kay, Guy Gavriel 1954- 167
  Earlier sketch in SATA 121
Kay, Helen
  See Goldfrank, Helen Colodny
Kay, Jackie 1961- 165
  Earlier sketch in SATA 97

Kay, Jacqueline Margaret
See Kay, Jackie
Kay, Mara *13*
Kay, Verla 1946- *120*
Kaye, Danny 1913-1987
Obituary *50*
Kaye, Geraldine (Hughesdon) 1925- *85*
Earlier sketch in SATA *10*
Kaye, Judy
See Baer, Judy
Kaye, Marilyn 1949- *110*
Earlier sketch in SATA *56*
Kaye, Mary Margaret
See Kaye, M.M.
Kaye, M.M. 1908-2004 .... *62*
Obituary *152*
Kaye, Mollie
See Kaye, M.M.
Kaye, Peggy 1948- *143*
Keach, James P. 1950- *125*
Keams, Geri 1951- *117*
Keane, Bil 1922- *4*
Keaney, Brian 1954- *188*
Earlier sketch in SATA *106*
Kearney, Meg 1964- *178*
Kearny, Jillian
See Goulart, Ron
Keating, Bern
See Keating, Leo Bernard
Keating, Frank 1944- *143*
Keating, Lawrence A. 1903-1966 .... *23*
Keating, Leo Bernard 1915- *10*
Keats, Emma 1899(?)-1979(?) *68*
Keats, Ezra Jack 1916-1983 .... *57*
Obituary *34*
Earlier sketch in SATA *14*
See also CLR *35*
Keefer, Catherine
See Ogan, George F.
and Ogan, Margaret E. (Nettles)
Keefer, Janice Kulyk
See Kulyk Keefer, Janice
Keegan, Marcia 1943- *104*
Earlier sketch in SATA *9*
Keehn, Sally M. 1947- *165*
Earlier sketch in SATA *87*
Keel, Frank
See Keeler, Ronald F(ranklin)
Keeler, Patricia *183*
Keeler, Patricia A.
See Keeler, Patricia
Keeler, Ronald F(ranklin) 1913-1983 .... *47*
Keely, Jack 1951- *119*
Keen, Martin L. 1913-1992 .... *4*
Keenan, Sheila 1953- *95*
Keene, Ann T(odd) 1940- *86*
Keene, Carolyn
See Benson, Mildred
and Goulart, Ron
and Lerangis, Peter
and McFarlane, Leslie
and Stanley, George Edward
and Stratemeyer, Edward L.
Keens-Douglas, Richardo 1953- *154*
Earlier sketch in SATA *95*
Keep, Linda Lowery
See Lowery, Linda
Keep, Richard 1949- *170*
Keep, Richard Cleminson
See Keep, Richard
Keeping, Charles (William James)
1924-1988 .... *69*
Obituary *56*
Earlier sketch in SATA *9*
See also CLR *34*
Keeshan, Robert J. 1927-2004 .... *32*
Obituary *151*
Kehlenbeck, Angela 1959- *186*
Kehret, Peg 1936- *149*
Autobiography Feature *149*
Earlier sketches in SATA *73, 108*

Keillor, Garrison 1942- *58*
Keillor, Gary Edward
See Keillor, Garrison
Keir, Christine
See Pullein-Thompson, Christine
Keister, Douglas 1948- *88*
Keith, Doug 1952- *81*
Keith, Eros 1942- *52*
Keith, Hal 1934- *36*
Keith, Harold (Verne) 1903-1998 .... *74*
Earlier sketch in SATA *2*
Keith, Robert
See Applebaum, Stan
Keleinikov, Andrei 1924- *65*
Kelemen, Julie 1959- *78*
Kelen, Emery 1896-1978 .... *13*
Obituary *26*
Kelleam, Joseph E(veridge) 1913-1975 .... *31*
Kelleher, Anne 1959- *97*
Kelleher, Annette 1950- *122*
Kelleher, Daria Valerian 1955- *79*
Kelleher, Victor (Michael Kitchener)
1939- *129*
Brief entry *52*
Earlier sketch in SATA *75*
See also CLR *36*
Keller, Beverly L(ou) *91*
Earlier sketch in SATA *13*
Keller, Charles 1942- *82*
Earlier sketch in SATA *8*
Keller, Debra 1958- *94*
Keller, Dick 1923- *36*
Keller, Emily *96*
Keller, Gail Faithfull
See Faithfull, Gail
Keller, Holly 1942- *157*
Brief entry *42*
Earlier sketches in SATA *76, 108*
See also CLR *45*
Keller, Irene (Barron) 1927-2002 .... *36*
Obituary *139*
Keller, Laurie 1961(?)- *196*
Kelley, Ellen A. *185*
Kelley, Ellen Chavez
See Kelley, Ellen A.
Kelley, Gary 1945- *183*
Kelley, Leo P(atrick) 1928- *32*
Brief entry *31*
Kelley, Patrick (G.) 1963- *129*
Kelley, Patte 1947- *93*
Kelley, True 1946- *179*
Kelley, True (Adelaide) 1946- *130*
Brief entry *39*
Earlier sketches in SATA *41, 92*
Kelley, True Adelaide
See Kelley, True
Kellin, Sally Moffet 1932- *9*
Kelling, Furn L. 1914-2000 .... *37*
Kellogg, Gene
See Kellogg, Jean (Defrees)
Kellogg, Jean (Defrees) 1916-1978 .... *10*
Kellogg, Steven 1941- *177*
Earlier sketches in SATA *8, 57, 130*
See also CLR *6*
Kellogg, Steven Castle
See Kellogg, Steven
Kellow, Kathleen
See Hibbert, Eleanor Alice Burford
Kelly, C. M. O.
See Gibbs, (Cecilia) May
Kelly, Clint 1950- *140*
Kelly, Eric P(hilbrook) 1884-1960
See YABC *1*
Kelly, Fiona
See Coleman, Michael
and Hendry, Frances Mary
and Oldfield, Jenny
and Welford, Sue
Kelly, Irene 1957- *147*
Kelly, Jeff
See Kelly, Jeffrey

Kelly, Jeffrey 1946- *65*
Kelly, Joanne (W.) 1934- *87*
Kelly, Kate 1958- *91*
Kelly, Kathleen M. 1964- *71*
Kelly, Katy 1955- *169*
Kelly, Lauren
See Oates, Joyce Carol
Kelly, Laurene 1954- *123*
Kelly, Martha Rose 1914-1983 .... *37*
Kelly, Marty
See Kelly, Martha Rose
Kelly, Mij *166*
Kelly, Ralph
See Geis, Darlene Stern
Kelly, Regina Z(immerman) 1898-1986 .... *5*
Kelly, Rosalie (Ruth) *43*
Kelly, Tom 1961- *191*
Kelly, Walt(er Crawford) 1913-1973 .... *18*
Kelsey, Alice Geer 1896-1982 .... *1*
Kelsey, Elin 1961- *159*
Kemly, Kathleen 1958- *197*
Kemnitz, Thomas Milton, Jr. 1984- *152*
Kemnitz, Tom, Jr.
See Kemnitz, Thomas Milton, Jr.
Kemp, Gene 1926- *75*
Earlier sketch in SATA *25*
See also CLR *29*
Kempner, Mary Jean 1913-1969 .... *10*
Kempter, Christa 1945- *187*
Kempton, Jean Welch 1914- *10*
Kenah, Katharine 1949- *182*
Kenda, Margaret 1942- *71*
Kendall, Carol (Seeger) 1917- *74*
Earlier sketch in SATA *11*
See also SAAS *7*
Kendall, Katherine
See Applegate, Katherine
Kendall, Lace
See Stoutenburg, Adrien (Pearl)
Kendall, Martha E. *87*
Kendall, Russ 1957- *83*
Kenealy, James P. 1927- *52*
Brief entry *29*
Kenealy, Jim
See Kenealy, James P.
Kennaway, Adrienne 1945- *171*
Earlier sketch in SATA *60*
Kennedy, Anne 1955- *198*
Kennedy, Anne Vittur
See Kennedy, Anne
Kennedy, Brendan 1970- *57*
Kennedy, Dana Forrest 1917- *74*
Kennedy, Dorothy M(intzlaff) 1931- *53*
Kennedy, Doug 1963- *189*
Earlier sketch in SATA *122*
Kennedy, Frances 1937- *192*
Kennedy, John Fitzgerald 1917-1963 .... *11*
Kennedy, Joseph Charles 1929- *130*
Autobiography Feature *130*
Earlier sketches in SATA *14, 86*
See also CLR *27*
See also SAAS *22*
See Kennedy, X. J.
Kennedy, Kim *189*
Kennedy, Pamela (J.) 1946- *87*
Kennedy, Paul E(dward) 1929- *113*
Earlier sketch in SATA *33*
Kennedy, Richard (Pitt) 1910-1989
Obituary *60*
Kennedy, (Jerome) Richard 1932- *22*
Kennedy, Robert 1938- *63*
Kennedy, T.A. 1953- *42*
Brief entry *35*
Kennedy, Teresa
See Kennedy, T.A.
Kennedy, Teresa A.
See Kennedy, T.A.
Kennedy, William 1928- *57*
Kennedy, William Joseph
See Kennedy, William

Kennedy, X. J.
  See CLR 27
  See also SAAS 22
  See Kennedy, Joseph Charles
Kennell, Ruth Epperson 1893-1977 6
  Obituary 25
Kennemore, Tim 1957- 133
Kennen, Ally 190
Kennett, David 1959- 121
Kenny, Ellsworth Newcomb 1909-1971
  Obituary 26
Kenny, Herbert Andrew 1912-2002 13
Kenny, Jude
  See Daly, Jude
Kenny, Kathryn
  See Bowden, Joan Chase
  and Krull, Kathleen
  and Sanderlin, Owenita (Harrah)
  and Stack, Nicolete Meredith
Kenny, Kevin
  See Krull, Kathleen
Kensinger, George
  See Fichter, George S.
Kensington, Kathryn Wesley
  See Rusch, Kristine Kathryn
Kent, Alexander
  See Reeman, Douglas Edward
Kent, David
  See Lambert, David (Compton)
Kent, Deborah Ann 1948- 155
  Brief entry 41
  Earlier sketches in SATA 47, 104
Kent, Jack
  See Kent, John Wellington
Kent, John Wellington 1920-1985 24
  Obituary 45
Kent, Lisa 1942- 90
Kent, Mallory
  See Lowndes, Robert A(ugustine) W(ard)
Kent, Margaret 1894- 2
Kent, Rockwell 1882-1971 6
Kent, Rose 188
Kent, Sherman 1903-1986 20
  Obituary 47
Kenward, Jean 1920- 42
Kenworthy, Leonard S. 1912-1991 6
Kenyon, Karen (Smith) 1938- 145
Kenyon, Kate
  See Adorjan, Carol (Madden)
  and Ransom, Candice F.
Kenyon, Ley 1913-1990 6
Keown, Elizabeth 78
Kepes, Juliet A(ppleby) 1919-1999 13
Kephart, Beth 1960- 196
Kerby, Mona 1951- 75
Kerigan, Florence 1896-1984 12
Kerley, Barbara 1960- 191
  Earlier sketch in SATA 138
Kerman, Gertrude
  See Furman, Gertrude Lerner Kerman
Kerns, Thelma 1939- 116
Kerr, Anne Louise
  See Mackey, Weezie Kerr
Kerr, Bob 1951- 120
Kerr, Jessica 1901-1991 13
Kerr, (Anne-)Judith 1923-1970 24
Kerr, M. E.
  See Meaker, Marijane
Kerr, P.B.
  See Kerr, Philip
Kerr, Philip 1956- 168
Kerr, Phyllis Forbes 1942- 72
Kerr, Tom 1950- 77
Kerrin, Jessica Scott 174
Kerry, Frances
  See Kerigan, Florence
Kerry, Lois
  See Duncan, Lois
Kershen, (L.) Michael 1982- 82
Kerven, Rosalind 1954- 83

Ker Wilson, Barbara 1929- 121
  Earlier sketches in SATA 20, 70
  See also SAAS 18
Keselman, Gabriela 1953- 128
Kesey, Ken 1935-2001 66
  Obituary 131
Kesey, Ken Elton
  See Kesey, Ken
Kesler, Jay 1935- 65
Kessel, Joyce Karen 1937- 41
Kessler, Cristina 190
Kessler, Ethel 1922- 44
  Brief entry 37
Kessler, Leonard P. 1921- 14
Kest, Kristin 1967- 168
  Earlier sketch in SATA 118
Kesteven, G. R.
  See Crosher, G. R.
Ketcham, Hank
  See Ketcham, Henry King
Ketcham, Henry King 1920-2001 28
  Brief entry 27
  Obituary 128
Ketcham, Sallie 1963- 124
Ketchum, Liza 1946-
  See Murrow, Liza Ketchum
Ketner, Mary Grace 1946- 75
Kettelkamp, Larry (Dale) 1933- 2
  See also SAAS 3
Ketteman, Helen 1945- 167
  Earlier sketches in SATA 73, 115
Kettle, Peter
  See Glover, Denis (James Matthews)
Kevles, Bettyann Holtzmann 1938- 23
Key, Alexander (Hill) 1904-1979 8
  Obituary 23
Key, Samuel M.
  See de Lint, Charles
Key, Watt 1970- 189
Keyes, Daniel 1927- 37
Keyes, Fenton 1915-1999 34
Keyes, Greg 1963- 116
Keyes, J. Gregory
  See Keyes, Greg
Keyser, Marcia 1933- 42
Keyser, Sarah
  See McGuire, Leslie (Sarah)
Khalid, Mohamed Nor
  See Lat
Khalsa, Dayal Kaur 1943-1989 62
  See also CLR 30
Khan, Rukhsana 1962- 165
  Earlier sketch in SATA 118
Khanshendel, Chiron
  See Rose, Wendy
Kheirabadi, Masoud 1951- 158
Khemir, Sabiha 87
Kherdian, David 1931- 74
  Autobiography Feature 125
  Earlier sketch in SATA 16
  See also CLR 24
Khing, T.T. 1933- 192
Kibbe, Pat (Hosley) 60
Kidd, Diana 1933-2000 150
Kidd, Richard 1952-2008 152
  Obituary 194
Kidd, Ronald 1948- 173
  Earlier sketches in SATA 42, 92
Kiddell, John 1922- 3
Kiddell-Monroe, Joan 1908-1972 55
Kidwell, Carl 1910- 43
Kiefer, Irene 1926- 21
Kiefer, Kathleen Balmes 1957- 142
Kiepper, Shirley Morgan 1933- 10
Kierstead, Vera M.
  See Kierstead-Farber, Vera M.
Kierstead-Farber, Vera M. 1913- 121
Kierstead-Farber, Vera May
  See Kierstead-Farber, Vera M.
Kiesel, Stanley 1925- 35

Kiesler, Kate (A.) 1971- 152
  Earlier sketch in SATA 90
Kihn, Greg 1952- 110
Kikukawa, Cecily H(arder) 1919- 44
  Brief entry 35
Kilcher, Jewel 1974- 109
Kile, Joan 1940- 78
Kilgore, Kathleen 1946- 42
Kilian, Crawford 1941- 35
Killdeer, John
  See Mayhar, Ardath
Killien, Christi 1956- 73
Killilea, Marie (Lyons) 1913-1991 2
Killingback, Julia 1944- 63
Killough, (Karen) Lee 1942- 64
Kilreon, Beth
  See Walker, Barbara (Jeanne) K(erlin)
Kilworth, Garry 1941- 94
Kilworth, Garry D.
  See Kilworth, Garry
Kilworth, Garry Douglas
  See Kilworth, Garry
Kim, David 1977- 201
Kim, Helen 1899-1970 98
Kimball, Gayle 1943- 90
Kimball, Violet T(ew) 1932- 126
Kimball, Yeffe 1914-1978 37
Kimber, Murray 1964- 171
Kimble, Warren 176
Kimbrough, Emily 1899-1989 2
  Obituary 59
Kimeldorf, Martin 1948- 121
Kimeldorf, Martin R.
  See Kimeldorf, Martin
Kimenye, Barbara 1940(?)- 121
Kimmel, Elizabeth Cody 170
Kimmel, Eric A. 1946- 176
  Earlier sketches in SATA 13, 80, 125
Kimmel, Margaret Mary 1938- 43
  Brief entry 33
Kimmelman, Burt 1947- 180
Kimmelman, Leslie (Grodinsky) 1958- 156
  Earlier sketch in SATA 85
Kincaid, Jamaica 1949-
  See CLR 63
Kincher, Jonni 1949- 79
Kindl, Patrice 1951- 128
  Earlier sketch in SATA 82
  See also CLR 132
Kindred, Wendy (Good) 1937- 7
Kinerk, Robert 199
Kines, Pat Decker 1937- 12
King, Adam
  See Hoare, Robert J(ohn)
King, Alison
  See Martini, Teri
King, (Maria) Anna 1964- 72
King, Billie Jean 1943- 12
King, Christopher (L.) 1945- 84
King, (David) Clive 1924- 144
  Earlier sketch in SATA 28
King, Colin 1943- 76
King, Cynthia 1925- 7
King, Daniel (John) 1963- 130
King, Daren 1972- 197
King, Elizabeth 1953- 83
King, Frank O. 1883-1969
  Obituary 22
King, Frank R. 1904-1999 127
King, Jane
  See Currie, Stephen
King, Jeanette (Margaret) 1959- 105
King, Larry L. 1929- 66
King, Laurie R. 1952- 88
King, Marian 1900(?)-1986 23
  Obituary 47
King, Martin Luther, Jr. 1929-1968 14
King, Mary Ellen 1958- 93
King, Paul
  See Drackett, Phil(ip Arthur)

King, Paula
 See Downing, Paula E.
King, Stephen 1947- 161
 Earlier sketches in SATA 9, 55
 See also CLR 124
King, Stephen Edwin
 See King, Stephen
King, Stephen Michael 157
King, Steve
 See King, Stephen
King, Thomas 1943- 96
King, Thomas Hunt
 See King, Thomas
King, Tony 1947- 39
Kingman, Dong (Moy Shu) 1911-2000 44
Kingman, Lee
 See Natti, Lee
Kingsland, Leslie William 1912- 13
Kingsley, Charles 1819-1875
 See YABC 2
 See also CLR 77
Kingsley, Emily Perl 1940- 33
Kingsley, Kaza 193
King-Smith, Dick 1922- 192
 Brief entry 38
 Earlier sketches in SATA 47, 80, 135
 See also CLR 40
Kingston, Maxine Hong 1940- 53
Kingston, Maxine Ting Ting Hong
 See Kingston, Maxine Hong
Kinney, C. Cle(land) 1915- 6
Kinney, Harrison 1921- 13
Kinney, Jean Stout 1912- 12
Kinney, Jeff 1971- 187
Kinsey, Elizabeth
 See Clymer, Eleanor
Kinsey, Helen 1948- 82
Kinsey-Warnock, Natalie 1956- 167
 Earlier sketches in SATA 71, 116
Kinzel, Dorothy 1950- 57
Kinzel, Dottie
 See Kinzel, Dorothy
Kipling, (Joseph) Rudyard 1865-1936 100
 See also YABC 2
 See also CLR 65
Kippax, Frank
 See Needle, Jan
Kirby, David K. 1944- 78
Kirby, David Kirk
 See Kirby, David K.
Kirby, Margaret
 See Bingley, Margaret (Jane Kirby)
Kirby, Susan E. 1949- 62
Kirk, Connie Ann 1957- 167
Kirk, Daniel 1952- 196
 Earlier sketches in SATA 107, 153
Kirk, David 1955- 161
 Earlier sketch in SATA 117
Kirk, Heather 1949- 166
Kirk, Ruth (Kratz) 1925- 5
Kirkham, Dinah
 See Card, Orson Scott
Kirkland, Will
 See Hale, Arlene
Kirkpatrick, Katherine (Anne) 1964- 113
Kirkup, James 1918-2009 12
Kirkus, Virginia
 See Glick, Virginia Kirkus
Kirkwood, Kathryn
 See Fluke, Joanne
Kirshenbaum, Binnie 79
Kirshner, David S. 1958- 123
Kirtland, G. B.
 See Hine, Sesyle Joslin
 and Hine, Al(fred Blakelee)
Kirwan, Wednesday 198
Kish, Eleanor M(ary) 1924- 73
Kish, Ely
 See Kish, Eleanor M(ary)
Kishida, Eriko 1929- 12
Kisinger, Grace Gelvin (Maze) 1913-1965 .. 10

Kissin, Eva H. 1923- 10
Kissinger, Rosemary K.
 See Updyke, Rosemary K.
Kistler, John M. 1967- 160
Kitamura, Satoshi 1956- 201
 Earlier sketches in SATA 62, 98, 143
 See also CLR 60
Kitchen, Bert
 See Kitchen, Herbert Thomas
Kitchen, Herbert Thomas 1940- 70
Kite, L. Patricia
 See Kite, Pat
Kite, Pat 1940- 78
Kitt, Tamara
 See de Regniers, Beatrice Schenk (Freedman)
Kittinger, Jo S(usenbach) 1955- 148
 Earlier sketch in SATA 96
Kituomba
 See Odaga, Asenath (Bole)
Kitzinger, Sheila 1929- 57
Kiwak, Barbara 1966- 103
Kjelgaard, James Arthur 1910-1959 17
 See also CLR 81
 See Kjelgaard, Jim
Kjelgaard, Jim
 See Kjelgaard, James Arthur
Kjelle, Marylou Morano 1954- 146
Klages, Ellen 1954- 196
Klagsbrun, Francine (Lifton) 36
Klaits, Barrie 1944- 52
Klam, Cheryl 191
Klaperman, Gilbert 1921- 33
Klaperman, Libby Mindlin 1921-1982 33
 Obituary 31
Klass, David 1960- 142
 Earlier sketch in SATA 88
Klass, Morton 1927-2001 11
Klass, Sheila Solomon 1927- 99
 Autobiography Feature 126
 Earlier sketch in SATA 45
 See also SAAS 26
Klause, Annette Curtis 1953- 175
 Earlier sketch in SATA 79
 See also CLR 104
Klaveness, Jan O'Donnell 1939- 86
Kleberger, Ilse 1921- 5
Kleeberg, Irene (Flitner) Cumming 1932- 65
Klein, Aaron E. 1930-1998 45
 Brief entry 28
Klein, Bill 1945- 89
Klein, David 1919-2001 59
Klein, Frederick C. 1938- 154
Klein, Gerda Weissmann 1924- 44
Klein, H(erbert) Arthur 8
Klein, James 1932- 115
Klein, Leonore (Glotzer) 1916- 6
Klein, Mina C(ooper) 1906-1979 8
Klein, Norma 1938-1989 57
 Earlier sketch in SATA 7
 See also CLR 19
 See also SAAS 1
Klein, Rachel S. 1953- 105
Klein, Robin 1936- 164
 Brief entry 45
 Earlier sketches in SATA 55, 80
 See also CLR 21
Klemin, Diana 65
Klemm, Barry 1945- 104
Klemm, Edward G., Jr. 1910-2001 30
Klemm, Roberta K(ohnhorst) 1884-1975 30
Kleven, Elisa 1958- 173
 Earlier sketch in SATA 76
 See also CLR 85
Klevin, Jill Ross 1935- 39
 Brief entry 38
Kliban, B(ernard) 1935-1990 35
 Obituary 66
Klimowicz, Barbara 1927- 10
Kline, Christina Baker 1964- 101
Kline, James
 See Klein, James

Kline, Jim
 See Kline, Jim
Kline, Lisa Williams 1954- 143
Kline, Suzy 1943- 193
 Autobiography Feature 193
 Brief entry 48
 Earlier sketches in SATA 67, 99, 152
Kliros, Thea 1935- 106
Klise, Kate 181
Klise, M. Sarah 1961- 180
 Earlier sketch in SATA 128
Klots, Alexander Barrett 1903-1989
 Obituary 62
Klug, Ron(ald) 1939- 31
Knaak, Richard A. 1961- 166
 Earlier sketch in SATA 86
Knaak, Richard Allen
 See Knaak, Richard A.
Knapman, Timothy 200
Knapp, Edward
 See Kunhardt, Edith
Knapp, Ron 1952- 34
Knebel, Fletcher 1911-1993 36
 Obituary 75
Kneeland, Linda Clarke 1947- 94
Knickerbocker, Diedrich
 See Irving, Washington
Knifesmith
 See Cutler, Ivor
Knigge, Robert (R.) 1921(?)-1987 50
Knight, Anne (Katherine) 1946- 34
Knight, Brenda 112
Knight, Christopher G. 1943- 96
Knight, Damon (Francis) 1922-2002 9
 Obituary 139
Knight, David C(arpenter) 1925-1984 14
 See also CLR 38
Knight, Eric 1897-1943 18
Knight, Eric Mowbray
 See Knight, Eric
Knight, Francis Edgar 1905- 14
Knight, Frank
 See Knight, Francis Edgar
Knight, Hilary 1926- 132
 Earlier sketches in SATA 15, 69
Knight, Joan (MacPhail) 159
 Earlier sketch in SATA 82
Knight, Joan
 See Knight, Joan (MacPhail)
Knight, Kathryn Lasky
 See Lasky, Kathryn
Knight, Mallory T.
 See Hurwood, Bernhardt J.
Knight, Ruth Adams 1898-1974
 Obituary 20
Knight, Theodore O. 1946- 77
Knobloch, Dorothea 1951- 88
Knoepfle, John (Ignatius) 1923- 66
Knorr, Laura 1971- 200
Knott, Bill
 See Knott, William C(ecil, Jr.)
Knott, William C(ecil, Jr.) 1927- 3
Knotts, Howard (Clayton, Jr.) 1922- 25
Knowles, Anne 1933- 37
Knowles, Jo 1970- 197
Knowles, Johanna Beth
 See Knowles, Jo
Knowles, John 1926-2001 89
 Obituary 134
 Earlier sketch in SATA 8
 See also CLR 98
Knox, Calvin M.
 See Silverberg, Robert
Knox, (Mary) Eleanor Jessie 1909-2000 59
 Earlier sketch in SATA 30
Knox, Elizabeth 1959- 176
Knox, Elizabeth Fiona
 See Knox, Elizabeth
Knox, James
 See Brittain, William
Knox, Jolyne 1937- 76

Knudsen, James 1950- *42*
Knudsen, Michelle *171*
Knudson, R. R.
    See Knudson, Rozanne
Knudson, Richard L(ewis) 1930- *34*
Knudson, Rozanne 1932-2008 .... *79*
    Earlier sketch in SATA *7*
    See also SAAS *18*
Knutson, Barbara 1959-2005 .... *166*
Knutson, Kimberley *115*
Knye, Cassandra
    See Disch, Thomas M.
Kobayashi, Masako Matsuno 1935- *6*
Koch, Dorothy Clarke 1924- *6*
Koch, Kenneth 1925-2002 .... *65*
Koch, Kenneth Jay
    See Koch, Kenneth
Koch, Phyllis (Mae) McCallum 1911- *10*
Kochalka, James 1967- *196*
Kocsis, J. C.
    See Paul, James
Koda-Callan, Elizabeth 1944- *140*
    Earlier sketch in SATA *67*
Kodman, Stanislawa *201*
Koehler, Phoebe 1955- *85*
Koehler-Pentacoff, Elizabeth 1957- *160*
    Earlier sketch in SATA *96*
Koehn, Ilse
    See Van Zwienen, Ilse Charlotte Koehn
Koeller, Carol *192*
Koenig, Viviane 1950- *80*
Koering, Ursula 1921-1976 .... *64*
Koerner, W(illiam) H(enry) D(avid)
    1878-1938 .... *21*
Koertge, Ronald 1940- *131*
    Earlier sketches in SATA *53, 92*
Koestler-Grack, Rachel A. 1973- *156*
Koff, Richard Myram 1926- *62*
Koffinke, Carol 1949- *82*
Kogan, Deborah
    See Kogan Ray, Deborah
Kogan Ray, Deborah 1940- *161*
    Earlier sketches in SATA *8, 50*
Kogawa, Joy Nozomi 1935- *99*
Kogler, Jennifer Anne 1982(?)- *174*
Kohl, Herbert 1937- *47*
Kohl, Herbert R.
    See Kohl, Herbert
Kohl, MaryAnn F(aubion) 1947- *144*
    Earlier sketch in SATA *74*
Kohler, Julilly H(ouse) 1908-1976
    Obituary *20*
Kohn, Bernice
    See Hunt, Bernice
Kohn, Rita (T.) 1933- *89*
Kohner, Frederick 1905-1986 .... *10*
    Obituary *48*
Koide, Tan 1938-1986 .... *50*
Koike, Kay 1940- *72*
Koja, Kathe 1960- *199*
    Earlier sketch in SATA *155*
Koja, Stephan *198*
Kolb, Larry J. 1953- *175*
Kolba, St. Tamara *22*
Kolibalova, Marketa
    See Kolibalova, Marketa
Kolibalova, Marketa 1953- *126*
Koller, Jackie French 1948- *157*
    Earlier sketches in SATA *72, 109*
    See also CLR *68*
Kolodny, Nancy J. 1946- *76*
Kolosov, Jacqueline 1967- *199*
Komaiko, Leah 1954- *164*
    Earlier sketch in SATA *97*
Komisar, Lucy 1942- *9*
Komoda, Beverly 1939- *25*
Komoda, Kiyo 1937- *9*
Kompaneyets, Marc 1974- *169*
Komroff, Manuel 1890-1974 .... *2*
    Obituary *20*

Konigsburg, E.L. 1930- *194*
    Earlier sketches in SATA *4, 48, 94, 126*
    See also CLR *81*
Konigsburg, Elaine Lobl
    See Konigsburg, E.L.
Koning, Hans 1921-2007 .... *5*
    Obituary *182*
Koningsberger, Hans
    See Koning, Hans
Konkle, Janet Everest 1917- *12*
Kono, Erin Eitter 1973- *177*
Konzak, Burt 1946- *151*
Koob, Theodora (J. Foth) 1918- *23*
Kooiker, Leonie
    See Kooyker-Romijn, Johanna Maria
Koons, James
    See Pernu, Dennis
Koontz, Dean
    See Koontz, Dean R.
Koontz, Dean R. 1945- *165*
    Earlier sketch in SATA *92*
Koontz, Dean Ray
    See Koontz, Dean R.
Koontz, Robin Michal 1954- *136*
    Earlier sketch in SATA *70*
Kooyker, Leonie
    See Kooyker-Romijn, Johanna Maria
Kooyker-Romijn, Johanna Maria 1927- *48*
Kooyker-Romyn, Johanna Maria
    See Kooyker-Romijn, Johanna Maria
Kopelke, Lisa 1963- *154*
Kopper, Lisa (Esther) 1950- *105*
    Brief entry *51*
Koppes, Steven N. 1957- *169*
Koppes, Steven Nelson
    See Koppes, Steven N.
Korach, Mimi 1922- *9*
Koralek, Jenny 1934- *140*
    Earlier sketch in SATA *71*
Korczak, Janusz
    See Goldszmit, Henryk
Koren, Edward (Benjamin) 1935- *148*
    Earlier sketch in SATA *5*
Korinets, Iurii Iosifovich
    See Korinetz, Yuri (Iosifovich)
Korinetz, Yuri (Iosifovich) 1923- *9*
    See also CLR *4*
Korman, Bernice 1937- *78*
Korman, Gordon 1963- *167*
    Brief entry *41*
    Earlier sketches in SATA *49, 81, 119*
    See also CLR *25*
Korman, Gordon Richard
    See Korman, Gordon
Korman, Justine 1958- *70*
Kornblatt, Marc 1954- *147*
    Earlier sketch in SATA *84*
Kornprobst, Jacques 1937- *177*
Korte, Gene J. 1950- *74*
Korty, Carol 1937- *15*
Koscielniak, Bruce 1947- *153*
    Earlier sketches in SATA *67, 99*
Koshin, Alexander (A.) 1952- *86*
Kositsky, Lynne 1947- *158*
Koskenmaki, Rosalie
    See Maggio, Rosalie
Koss, Amy Goldman 1954- *158*
    Earlier sketch in SATA *115*
Kossin, Sandy (Sanford) 1926- *10*
Kossman, Nina 1959- *84*
Kostick, Conor 1964- *186*
Kotzwinkle, William 1938- *146*
    Earlier sketches in SATA *24, 70*
    See also CLR *6*
Kouhi, Elizabeth 1917- *54*
    Brief entry *49*
Kouts, Anne 1945- *8*
Koutsky, Jan Dale 1955- *146*
Kovacs, Deborah 1954- *132*
    Earlier sketch in SATA *79*

Kovalski, Maryann 1951- *175*
    Earlier sketches in SATA *58, 97*
    See also CLR *34*
    See also SAAS *21*
Kowalski, Kathiann M. 1955- *151*
    Earlier sketch in SATA *96*
Kraft, Betsy Harvey 1937- *157*
Kraft, Erik P. *193*
Krahn, Fernando 1935- *49*
    Brief entry *31*
    See also CLR *3*
Krakauer, Hoong Yee Lee 1955- *86*
Krakauer, Jon 1954- *108*
Kramer, George
    See Heuman, William
Kramer, Nora 1896(?)-1984 .... *26*
    Obituary *39*
Kramer, Remi (Thomas) 1935- *90*
Krantz, Hazel (Newman) *12*
Kranzler, George G(ershon) 1916- *28*
Kranzler, Gershon
    See Kranzler, George G(ershon)
Krasilovsky, Phyllis 1926- *38*
    Earlier sketch in SATA *1*
    See also CLR *83*
    See also SAAS *5*
Krasne, Betty
    See Levine, Betty K(rasne)
Krasner, Steven 1953- *154*
Krasno, Rena 1923- *104*
Kratman, Tom *175*
Kraus, Joanna Halpert 1937- *87*
Kraus, (Herman) Robert 1925-2001 .... *93*
    Obituary *130*
    Earlier sketches in SATA *4, 65*
    See also SAAS *11*
Krauss, Ruth (Ida) 1911-1993 .... *30*
    Obituary *75*
    Earlier sketch in SATA *1*
    See also CLR *42*
Krautter, Elisa (Bialk) 1912(?)-1990 .... *1*
    Obituary *65*
Krautwurst, Terry 1946- *79*
Kray, Robert Clement 1930- *82*
Krech, Bob 1956- *185*
Krech, Robert
    See Krech, Bob
Kredel, Fritz 1900-1973 .... *17*
Kreikemeier, Gregory Scott 1965- *85*
Kreloff, Elliot *189*
Krementz, Jill 1940- *134*
    Earlier sketches in SATA *17, 71*
    See also CLR *5*
    See also SAAS *8*
Kremer, Marcie
    See Sorenson, Margo
Krenina, Katya 1968- *101*
Krensky, Stephen 1953- *188*
    Brief entry *41*
    Earlier sketches in SATA *47, 93, 136*
Krensky, Stephen Alan
    See Krensky, Stephen
Kresh, Paul 1919-1997 .... *61*
    Obituary *94*
Kress, Nancy 1948- *147*
    Autobiography Feature *147*
    Earlier sketch in SATA *85*
Kricher, John C. 1944- *113*
Krieger, Melanie *96*
Krinitz, Esther Nisenthal 1927-2001 .... *194*
Kripke, Dorothy Karp *30*
Krisher, Trudy 1946- *160*
    Earlier sketch in SATA *86*
Krisher, Trudy B.
    See Krisher, Trudy
Krishnaswami, Uma 1956- *182*
    Earlier sketch in SATA *144*
Kristof, Jane 1932- *8*
Kroeber, Theodora (Kracaw) 1897-1979 .... *1*
Kroeger, Mary Kay 1950- *92*

Krohn, Katherine E(lizabeth) 1961- *125*
  Earlier sketch in SATA *84*
Kroll, Francis Lynde 1904-1973 .... *10*
Kroll, Steven 1941- *135*
  Autobiography Feature *135*
  Earlier sketches in SATA *19, 66, 125*
  See also SAAS *7*
Kroll, Virginia L. 1948- *168*
  Earlier sketches in SATA *76, 114*
Kroll, Virginia Louisa
  See Kroll, Virginia L.
Kromhout, Rindert 1958- *189*
Krommes, Beth 1956- *181*
  Earlier sketch in SATA *128*
Kronenwetter, Michael 1943- *62*
Kroniuk, Lisa
  See Berton, Pierre (Francis de Marigny)
Kropp, Paul 1948- *38*
  Brief entry *34*
  See also CLR *96*
Kropp, Paul Stephan
  See Kropp, Paul
Krosoczka, Jarrett J. 1977- *200*
  Earlier sketch in SATA *155*
Krovatin, Christopher 1985- *171*
Kruess, James
  See Kruss, James
Kruglik, Gerald *187*
Krull, Kathleen 1952- *184*
  Autobiography Feature *106*
  Brief entry *39*
  Earlier sketches in SATA *52, 80, 149*
  See also CLR *44*
Krumgold, Joseph (Quincy) 1908-1980 .... *48*
  Obituary *23*
  Earlier sketch in SATA *1*
Krupinski, Loretta 1940- *161*
  Earlier sketches in SATA *67, 102*
Krupnick, Karen 1947- *89*
Krupp, E(dwin) C(harles) 1944- *123*
  Earlier sketch in SATA *53*
Krupp, Robin Rector 1946- *53*
Krush, Beth 1918- *18*
Krush, Joe 1918-
  See Krush, Joseph P.
Krush, Joseph P. 1918- *18*
Kruss, James 1926-1997 .... *8*
  See also CLR *9*
Kruusval, Catarina 1951- *201*
Krykorka, Vladyana 1945- *96*
Krystoforski, Andrej 1943- *196*
Kubie, Eleanor Gottheil
  See Kubie, Nora Gottheil Benjamin
Kubie, Nora Benjamin
  See Kubie, Nora Gottheil Benjamin
Kubie, Nora Gottheil Benjamin 1899-1988 . *39*
  Obituary *59*
Kubinyi, Laszlo 1937- *94*
  Earlier sketch in SATA *17*
Kudlinski, Kathleen V. 1950- *150*
Kuenstler, Morton 1927- *10*
Kuh, Charlotte 1892(?)-1985
  Obituary *43*
Kuharski, Janice 1947- *128*
Kuhn, Dwight *199*
Kuijer, Guus 1942- *179*
Kujoth, Jean Spealman 1935-1975
  Obituary *30*
Kuklin, Susan 1941- *163*
  Earlier sketches in SATA *63, 95*
  See also CLR *51*
Kulikov, Boris 1966- *170*
Kulka, Joe *188*
Kulling, Monica 1952- *89*
Kullman, Harry 1919-1982 .... *35*
Kulyk Keefer, Janice 1952- *132*
Kumin, Maxine 1925- *12*
Kumin, Maxine Winokur
  See Kumin, Maxine
Kunhardt, Dorothy (Meserve) 1901-1979 .... *53*
  Obituary *22*

Kunhardt, Edith 1937- *67*
Kunjufu, Jawanza 1953- *73*
Kunstler, Morton
  See Kuenstler, Morton
Kuntz, J(ohn) L. 1947- *91*
Kuntz, Jerry 1956- *133*
Kupferberg, Herbert 1918-2001 .... *19*
Kuratomi, Chizuko 1939- *12*
  See also CLR *32*
Kurczok, Belinda 1978- *121*
Kurelek, William 1927-1977 .... *8*
  Obituary *27*
  See also CLR *2*
Kurian, George 1928- *65*
Kurjian, Judi(th M.) 1944- *127*
Kurland, Gerald 1942- *13*
Kurland, Michael 1938- *118*
  Earlier sketch in SATA *48*
Kurland, Michael Joseph
  See Kurland, Michael
Kuroi, Ken 1947- *120*
Kurokawa, Mitsuhiro 1954- *88*
Kurten, Bjorn (Olof) 1924-1988 .... *64*
Kurtz, Jane 1952- *139*
  Earlier sketch in SATA *91*
  See also CLR *123*
Kurtz, Katherine 1944- *182*
  Earlier sketches in SATA *76, 126*
Kurtz, Katherine Irene
  See Kurtz, Katherine
Kurz, Rudolf 1952- *95*
Kushner, Donn (J.) 1927- *52*
  See also CLR *55*
Kushner, Ellen 1955- *98*
Kushner, Ellen Ruth
  See Kushner, Ellen
Kushner, Jill Menkes 1951- *62*
Kushner, Lawrence 1943- *169*
  Earlier sketch in SATA *83*
Kushner, Tony 1956- *160*
Kuskin, Karla 1932- *164*
  Earlier sketches in SATA *2, 68, 111*
  See also CLR *4*
  See also SAAS *3*
Kuskin, Karla Seidman
  See Kuskin, Karla
Kusugak, Michael 1948- *143*
Kusugak, Michael Arvaarluk
  See Kusugak, Michael
Kutner, Merrily 1948- *196*
Kuttner, Paul 1922- *18*
Kuyper, Sjoerd 1952- *177*
Kuzma, Kay 1941- *39*
Kvale, Velma R(uth) 1898-1979 .... *8*
Kvasnosky, Laura McGee 1951- *182*
  Earlier sketches in SATA *93, 142*
Kwasney, Michelle D. 1960- *162*
Kyle, Benjamin
  See Gottfried, Theodore Mark
Kyle, Elisabeth
  See Dunlop, Agnes M. R.
Kyte, Kathy S. 1946- *50*
  Brief entry *44*

L

L., Barry
  See Longyear, Barry B(rookes)
L., Tommy
  See Lorkowski, Thomas V(incent)
Labouisse, Eve Curie
  See Curie, Eve
Labouisse, Eve Denise
  See Curie, Eve
Lace, William W. 1942- *126*
Lacey, Joshua
  See Doder, Josh
Lachner, Dorothea
  See Knobloch, Dorothea

Lachtman, Ofelia Dumas 1919- *179*
Lackey, Mercedes R. 1950- *127*
  Earlier sketch in SATA *81*
Lackey, Mercedes Ritchie
  See Lackey, Mercedes R.
Lacoe, Addie *78*
Lacombe, Benjamin 1982- *198*
Lacome, Julie 1961- *174*
  Earlier sketch in SATA *80*
Lacy, Leslie Alexander 1937- *6*
Ladd, Cheryl (Jean) 1951- *113*
Ladd, Louise 1943- *97*
Ladd, Veronica
  See Miner, Jane Claypool
Laden, Nina 1962- *148*
  Earlier sketch in SATA *85*
Lader, Lawrence 1919-2006 .... *6*
  Obituary *178*
LaDoux, Rita C. 1951- *74*
Lady, A
  See Taylor, Ann
Lady Mears
  See Tempest, Margaret Mary
Lady of Quality, A
  See Bagnold, Enid
La Farge, Oliver 1901-1963 .... *19*
La Farge, Oliver Hazard Perry
  See La Farge, Oliver
La Farge, Phyllis *14*
LaFave, Kim *196*
LaFaye, A. 1970- *156*
  Earlier sketch in SATA *105*
LaFaye, Alexandria R.T.
  See LaFaye, A.
LaFevers, R.L. *191*
LaFevers, Robin L.
  See LaFevers, R.L.
Laffin, John (Alfred Charles) 1922- *31*
LaFontaine, Bruce 1948- *176*
  Earlier sketch in SATA *114*
La Fontaine, Jean de 1621-1695 .... *18*
Lafrance, Marie 1955- *197*
Lager, Claude
  See Lapp, Christiane (Germain)
Lager, Marilyn 1939- *52*
Lagercrantz, Rose (Elsa) 1947- *39*
Lagerloef, Selma
  See Lagerlof, Selma
Lagerlof, Selma 1858-1940 .... *15*
  See also CLR *7*
Laguna, Sofie 1968- *158*
LaHaye, Tim F. 1926- *149*
LaHaye, Timothy F.
  See LaHaye, Tim F.
Laiken, Deirdre S(usan) 1948- *48*
  Brief entry *40*
Laimgruber, Monika 1946- *11*
Lain, Anna
  See Lamb, Nancy
Laing, Alexander (Kinnan) 1903-1976 .... *117*
Laing, Martha 1951- *39*
Laird, Christa 1944- *108*
  Autobiography Feature *120*
  See also SAAS *26*
Laird, Elizabeth (Mary Risk) 1943- *159*
  Earlier sketches in SATA *77, 114*
  See also CLR *65*
Laird, Jean E(louise) 1930- *38*
Laite, Gordon 1925- *31*
Lake, Harriet
  See Taylor, Paula (Wright)
Lakin, Patricia 1944- *190*
Laklan, Carli 1907-1988 .... *5*
Laliberte, Louise-Andree 1958- *169*
Lalicki, Barbara *61*
Lalicki, Tom 1949- *186*
Lally, Soinbhe 1945- *119*
LaMarche, Jim *162*
Lamb, Albert *187*
Lamb, Beatrice Pitney 1904-1997 .... *21*
Lamb, Charles 1775-1834 .... *17*

Lamb, Elizabeth Searle 1917- *31*
Lamb, G(eoffrey) F(rederick) *10*
Lamb, Harold (Albert) 1892-1962 .... *53*
Lamb, Lynton (Harold) 1907-1977 .... *10*
Lamb, Mary Ann 1764-1847 .... *17*
Lamb, Nancy 1939- *80*
Lamb, Robert (Boyden) 1941- *13*
Lamba, Marie *195*
Lambert, David (Compton) 1932- *84*
  Brief entry *49*
Lambert, Janet 1895(?)-1973 .... *25*
Lambert, Martha L. *113*
Lambert, Saul 1928- *23*
Lambert, Stephen *174*
Lamburn, Richmal Crompton 1890-1969 .... *5*
Lamensdorf, Len 1930- *120*
Lamensdorf, Leonard
  See Lamensdorf, Len
Laminack, Lester L. 1956- *163*
  Earlier sketch in SATA *120*
Lamont, Priscilla *200*
Lamorisse, Albert (Emmanuel) 1922-1970 ... *23*
Lampert, Emily 1951- *52*
  Brief entry *49*
Lamplugh, Lois 1921- *17*
Lampman, Evelyn Sibley 1907-1980 .... *87*
  Obituary *23*
  Earlier sketch in SATA *4*
Lamprey, Louise 1869-1951
  See YABC *2*
Lampton, Chris
  See Lampton, Christopher F.
Lampton, Christopher
  See Lampton, Christopher F.
Lampton, Christopher F. *67*
  Brief entry *47*
Lamstein, Sarah 1943- *174*
  Earlier sketch in SATA *126*
Lamstein, Sarah Marwil
  See Lamstein, Sarah
Lanagan, Margo 1960- *201*
  Earlier sketch in SATA *163*
Lancaster, Bruce 1896-1963 .... *9*
Lancaster, Matthew 1973(?)-1983
  Obituary *45*
Lance, Kathryn 1943- *76*
Land, Barbara (Neblett) 1923- *16*
Land, Jane
  See Borland, Kathryn Kilby
  and Speicher, Helen Ross S(mith)
Land, Myrick (Ebben) 1922-1998 .... *15*
Land, Ross
  See Borland, Kathryn Kilby
  and Speicher, Helen Ross S(mith)
Landau, Elaine 1948- *141*
  Earlier sketches in SATA *10, 94*
Landau, Jacob 1917- *38*
Landeck, Beatrice 1904-1978 .... *15*
Landin, Les 1923- *2*
Landis, J(ames) D(avid) 1942- *60*
  Brief entry *52*
Landis, James D.
  See Landis, J(ames) D(avid)
Landis, Jill Marie 1948- *101*
Landmann, Bimba 1968- *176*
Landon, Dena 1978(?)- *168*
Landon, Lucinda 1950- *56*
  Brief entry *51*
Landon, Margaret (Dorothea Mortenson)
  1903-1993 .... *50*
Landshoff, Ursula 1908-1989 .... *13*
Landstrom, Lena 1943- *146*
Landstrom, Olof 1943- *146*
Lane, Carolyn 1926-1993 .... *10*
Lane, Connie
  See Laux, Constance
Lane, Dakota 1959- *166*
  Earlier sketch in SATA *105*
Lane, Jerry
  See Martin, Patricia Miles
Lane, John (Richard) 1932- *15*

Lane, Leena *199*
Lane, Margaret 1907-1994 .... *65*
  Brief entry *38*
  Obituary *79*
Lane, Rose Wilder 1887-1968 .... *29*
  Brief entry *28*
Lanes, Selma Gordon 1929- *3*
Lanfredi, Judy 1964- *83*
Lang, Andrew 1844-1912 .... *16*
  See also CLR *101*
Lang, Aubrey *169*
Lang, Paul 1948- *83*
Lang, Susan S. 1950- *68*
Lang, T.T.
  See Taylor, Theodore
Langart, Darrell T.
  See Garrett, Randall
Langdo, Bryan 1973- *191*
  Earlier sketch in SATA *138*
Lange, John
  See Crichton, Michael
Lange, Karen E. *190*
Lange, Suzanne 1945- *5*
Langley, Andrew 1949- *166*
  Earlier sketch in SATA *104*
Langley, Charles P(itman) III 1949- *103*
Langley, Jonathan 1952- *122*
Langley, Noel 1911-1980
  Obituary *25*
Langley, Wanda *173*
Langner, Nola
  See Malone, Nola Langner
Langone, John (Michael) 1929- *46*
  Brief entry *38*
Langreuter, Jutta 1944- *122*
Langrish, Katherine *177*
Langsen, Richard C. 1953- *95*
Langstaff, John 1920-2005 .... *68*
  Obituary *172*
  Earlier sketch in SATA *6*
  See also CLR *3*
Langstaff, John Meredith
  See Langstaff, John
Langstaff, Launcelot
  See Irving, Washington
Langston, Laura 1958- *186*
Langton, Jane 1922- *200*
  Autobiography Feature *140*
  Earlier sketches in SATA *3, 68, 129, 140*
  See also CLR *33*
  See also SAAS *5*
Lanier, Sidney 1842-1881 .... *18*
Lanier, Sterling E. 1927-2007 .... *109*
Lanier, Sterling Edmund
  See Lanier, Sterling E.
Lanino, Deborah 1964- *123*
Lankford, Mary D. 1932- *112*
  Earlier sketch in SATA *77*
Lannin, Joanne 1951- *121*
Lannin, Joanne A.
  See Lannin, Joanne
Lansdale, Joe R. 1951- *116*
Lansdale, Joe Richard
  See Lansdale, Joe R.
Lansing, Alfred 1921-1975 .... *35*
Lansing, Karen E. 1954- *71*
Lansky, Vicki 1942- *177*
Lantier-Sampon, Patricia 1952- *92*
Lantz, Fran
  See Lantz, Francess L(in)
Lantz, Francess L(in) 1952-2004 .... *153*
  Autobiography Feature *153*
  Obituary *159*
  Earlier sketches in SATA *63, 109*
Lantz, Paul 1908- *45*
Lantz, Walter 1900-1994 .... *37*
  Obituary *79*
Lanza, Barbara 1945- *101*
Lapp, Christiane (Germain) 1948- *74*
Lappin, Peter 1911-1999 .... *32*
Larbalestier, Justine *178*

Lardy, Philippe 1963- *168*
LaReau, Jenna *181*
LaReau, Kara *181*
Larios, Julie 1949- *178*
Larios, Julie Hofstrand
  See Larios, Julie
Larkin, Amy
  See Burns, Olive Ann
Larkin, Maia
  See Wojciechowska, Maia (Teresa)
Laroche, Giles 1956- *126*
  Earlier sketch in SATA *71*
LaRochelle, David 1960- *171*
  Earlier sketch in SATA *115*
Larom, Henry V. 1903(?)-1975
  Obituary *30*
LaRose, Linda *125*
Larrabee, Lisa 1947- *84*
Larrecq, John M(aurice) 1926-1980 .... *44*
  Obituary *25*
Larrick (Crosby), Nancy 1910-2004 .... *4*
Larsen, Anita 1942- *78*
Larsen, Egon 1904- *14*
Larsen, Rebecca 1944- *54*
Larson, Eve
  See St. John, Wylly Folk
Larson, Gary 1950- *57*
Larson, Ingrid D(ana) 1965- *92*
Larson, Jean Russell 1930- *121*
Larson, Kirby 1954- *181*
  Earlier sketch in SATA *96*
Larson, Norita D(ittberner) 1944- *29*
Larson, William H. 1938- *10*
Larsson, Carl (Olof) 1853-1919 .... *35*
LaSalle, Charles A.
  See Ellis, Edward S(ylvester)
LaSalle, Charles E.
  See Ellis, Edward S(ylvester)
Lasell, Elinor H. 1929- *19*
Lasell, Fen H.
  See Lasell, Elinor H.
Lasenby, Jack 1931- *172*
  Earlier sketches in SATA *65, 103*
Laser, Michael 1954- *117*
Lash, Joseph P. 1909-1987 .... *43*
Lasher, Faith B. 1921- *12*
Lasker, David 1950- *38*
Lasker, Joe
  See Lasker, Joseph Leon
Lasker, Joseph Leon 1919- *83*
  Earlier sketch in SATA *9*
  See also SAAS *17*
Laski, Marghanita 1915-1988 .... *55*
Laskin, Pamela L. 1954- *75*
Lasky, Kathryn 1944- *157*
  Earlier sketches in SATA *13, 69, 112*
  See also CLR *140*
Lasky Knight, Kathryn
  See Lasky, Kathryn
Lass, Bonnie *131*
Lassalle, C. E.
  See Ellis, Edward S(ylvester)
Lassiter, Mary
  See Hoffman, Mary
Lassiter, Rhiannon 1977- *157*
Lat 1951- *196*
Latham, Barbara 1896- *16*
Latham, Frank B(rown) 1910-2000 .... *6*
Latham, Jean Lee 1902-1995 .... *68*
  Earlier sketch in SATA *2*
  See also CLR *50*
Latham, Mavis
  See Clark, Mavis Thorpe
Latham, Philip
  See Richardson, Robert S(hirley)
Lathrop, Dorothy P(ulis) 1891-1980 .... *14*
  Obituary *24*
Lathrop, Francis
  See Leiber, Fritz (Reuter, Jr.)
Latimer, Jim 1943- *80*

Latta, Rich
  See Latta, Richard
Latta, Richard 1946- *113*
Latta, Sara L. 1960- *174*
Lattany, Kristin
  See Lattany, Kristin Hunter
Lattany, Kristin (Eggleston) Hunter 1931- . *154*
  Autobiography Feature *154*
  Earlier sketch in SATA *132*
Lattany, Kristin Hunter 1931- *132*
  Earlier sketch in SATA *12*
  See also CLR *3*
  See also SAAS *10*
Lattimore, Eleanor Frances 1904-1986 .... *7*
  Obituary *48*
Lattin, Ann
  See Cole, Lois Dwight
Lauber, Patricia (Grace) 1924- *138*
  Earlier sketches in SATA *1, 33, 75*
  See also CLR *16*
Laugesen, Mary E(akin) 1906-1995 .... *5*
Laughbaum, Steve 1945- *12*
Laughlin, Florence Young 1910-2001 .... *3*
Laughlin, Rosemary 1941- *123*
Laure, Ettagale
  See Blauer, Ettagale
Laure, Jason 1940- *50*
  Brief entry *44*
Laurence, Ester Hauser 1935- *7*
Laurence, Jean Margaret Wemyss
  See Laurence, Margaret
Laurence, Margaret 1926-1987
  Obituary *50*
Laurie, Rona 1916- *55*
Laurin, Anne
  See McLaurin, Anne
Lauritzen, Jonreed 1902-1979 .... *13*
Lauscher, Hermann
  See Hesse, Hermann
Lauture, Denize 1946- *86*
Laux, Connie
  See Laux, Constance
Laux, Constance 1952- *97*
Laux, Dorothy 1920- *49*
Lavallee, Barbara 1941- *166*
  Earlier sketch in SATA *74*
Lavender, David (Sievert) 1910-2003 .... *97*
  Obituary *145*
  Earlier sketch in SATA *64*
Lavender, William D. 1921- *143*
Laverne, Christine *175*
Lavert, Gwendolyn Battle 1951-
  See Battle-Lavert, Gwendolyn
Laverty, Donald
  See Blish, James (Benjamin)
  and Knight, Damon (Francis)
Lavigne, Louis-Dominique *107*
Lavine, David 1928- *31*
Lavine, Sigmund Arnold 1908-1986 .... *82*
  Earlier sketch in SATA *3*
  See also CLR *35*
Lavond, Paul Dennis
  See Kornbluth, C(yril) M.
  and Lowndes, Robert A(ugustine) W(ard)
  and Pohl, Frederik
Lawford, Paula Jane 1960- *57*
  Brief entry *53*
Lawhead, Stephen R. 1950- *109*
Lawhead, Steve
  See Lawhead, Stephen R.
Lawlor, Laurie 1953- *137*
  Earlier sketch in SATA *80*
Lawlor, William
  See Lawlor, William T.
Lawlor, William T. 1951- *183*
Lawrence, Ann (Margaret) 1942-1987 .... *41*
  Obituary *54*
Lawrence, Iain 1955- *183*
  Earlier sketch in SATA *135*

Lawrence, J. T.
  See Rowland-Entwistle, (Arthur) Theodore
  (Henry)
Lawrence, Jerome 1915-2004 .... *65*
Lawrence, John 1933- *30*
Lawrence, Josephine 1890(?)-1978
  Obituary *24*
Lawrence, Louise 1943- *119*
  Earlier sketches in SATA *38, 78*
Lawrence, Louise de Kiriline 1894-1992 ..... *13*
Lawrence, Lynn
  See Garland, Sherry
Lawrence, Margery H. 1889-1969 .... *120*
Lawrence, Michael 1943- *132*
Lawrence, Mildred Elwood 1907-1997 .... *3*
Lawrence, R(onald) D(ouglas) 1921- *55*
Lawrinson, Julia 1969- *141*
Lawson, Amy
  See Gordon, Amy
Lawson, Carol (Antell) 1946- *42*
Lawson, Don(ald Elmer) 1917-1990 .... *9*
Lawson, Joan 1906- *55*
Lawson, Julie 1947- *126*
  Earlier sketch in SATA *79*
  See also CLR *89*
Lawson, Marion Tubbs 1896-1994 .... *22*
Lawson, Robert 1892-1957 .... *100*
  See also YABC *2*
  See also CLR *73*
Lawton, Clive A. 1951- *145*
Laxdal, Vivienne 1962- *112*
Laybourn, Emma *193*
Laycock, George (Edwin) 1921- *5*
Layne, Laura
  See Knott, William C(ecil, Jr.)
Layne, Steven L. *171*
Layton, Neal 1971- *187*
  Earlier sketch in SATA *152*
Layton, Neal Andrew
  See Layton, Neal
Lazare, Gerald John 1927- *44*
Lazare, Jerry
  See Lazare, Gerald John
Lazarevich, Mila 1942- *17*
Lazarus, Keo Felker 1913-1993 .... *21*
  Obituary *129*
Lea, Alec 1907- *19*
Lea, Joan
  See Neufeld, John (Arthur)
Leach, Maria 1892-1977 .... *39*
  Brief entry *28*
Leacock, Elspeth 1946- *131*
Leacroft, Helen (Mabel Beal) 1919- *6*
Leacroft, Richard (Vallance Becher) 1914- *6*
Leaf, Margaret P. 1909(?)-1988
  Obituary *55*
Leaf, (Wilbur) Munro 1905-1976 .... *20*
  See also CLR *25*
Leaf, VaDonna Jean 1929- *26*
Leah, Devorah
  See Devorah-Leah
Leakey, Richard E(rskine Frere) 1944- *42*
Leander, Ed
  See Richelson, Geraldine
Lear, Edward 1812-1888 .... *100*
  Earlier sketch in SATA *18*
  See also CLR *75*
Lears, Laurie 1955- *127*
Leasor, James 1923-2007 .... *54*
Leasor, Thomas James
  See Leasor, James
Leavitt, Jerome E(dward) 1916- *23*
Leavitt, Martine 1953- *170*
LeBar, Mary E(velyn) 1910-1982 .... *35*
LeBlanc, Annette M. 1965- *68*
LeBlanc, L(ee) 1913- *54*
LeBox, Annette 1943- *145*
Lebrun, Claude 1929- *66*
Le Cain, Errol (John) 1941-1989 .... *68*
  Obituary *60*
  Earlier sketch in SATA *6*

Lechner, Jack *201*
Lechner, John 1966- *200*
Lecourt, Nancy (Hoyt) 1951- *73*
Ledbetter, Suzann 1953- *119*
Leder, Jane Mersky 1945- *61*
  Brief entry *51*
Lederer, Muriel 1929- *48*
Lederer, William J(ulius) 1912- *62*
Lee, Amanda
  See Baggett, Nancy
  and Buckholtz, Eileen (Garber)
  and Glick, Ruth (Burtnick)
Lee, Benjamin 1921- *27*
Lee, Betsy 1949- *37*
Lee, Carol
  See Fletcher, Helen Jill
Lee, Carol Ann 1969- *185*
Lee, Chinlun *182*
Lee, Cora
  See Anderson, Catherine Corley
Lee, Dennis (Beynon) 1939- *102*
  Earlier sketch in SATA *14*
  See also CLR *3*
Lee, Dom 1959- *146*
  Autobiography Feature *121*
  Earlier sketch in SATA *83*
  See also SAAS *26*
Lee, Doris Emrick 1905-1983 .... *44*
  Obituary *35*
Lee, Edward
  See Lee, J. Edward
Lee, Elizabeth Rogers 1940- *90*
Lee, Harper 1926- *11*
Lee, Hector Viveros 1962- *115*
Lee, Howard N.
  See Goulart, Ron
Lee, Huy Voun 1969- *129*
Lee, J. Edward 1953- *130*
Lee, Jeanne M. 1943- *138*
Lee, John R(obert) 1923-1976 .... *27*
Lee, Jordan
  See Scholefield, Alan
Lee, Joseph Edward
  See Lee, J. Edward
Lee, Julian
  See Latham, Jean Lee
Lee, Linda
  See Eyerly, Jeannette
Lee, Liz
  See Lee, Elizabeth Rogers
Lee, Lucy
  See Talbot, Charlene Joy
Lee, Lyn 1953- *128*
Lee, Manning de Villeneuve 1894-1980 ...... *37*
  Obituary *22*
Lee, Marian
  See Clish, (Lee) Marian
Lee, Marie G. 1964- *178*
  Earlier sketches in SATA *81, 130*
Lee, Marie Myung-Ok
  See Lee, Marie G.
Lee, Mary Price 1934- *82*
  Earlier sketch in SATA *8*
Lee, Mildred
  See Scudder, Mildred Lee
Lee, Nelle Harper
  See Lee, Harper
Lee, Richard S. 1927- *82*
Lee, Robert C. 1931- *20*
Lee, Robert E(dwin) 1918-1994 .... *65*
  Obituary *82*
Lee, Robert J. 1921- *10*
Lee, Roy
  See Hopkins, Clark
Lee, Sally 1943- *67*
Lee, Suzy *193*
Lee, Tammie
  See Townsend, Thomas L.
Lee, Tanith 1947- *185*
  Earlier sketches in SATA *8, 88, 134*

Leech, Ben
  See Bowkett, Stephen
Leeds, Contance 188
Leedy, Loreen 1959- 175
  Brief entry 50
  Earlier sketches in SATA 54, 84, 128
Leedy, Loreen Janelle
  See Leedy, Loreen
Lee-Hostetler, Jeri 1940- 63
Leekley, Thomas B(riggs) 1910-2001 23
Leeming, Jo Ann
  See Leeming, Joseph
Leeming, Joseph 1897-1968 26
Leemis, Ralph B. 1954- 72
Leese, Jennifer L.B. 1970- 163
Leeson, Muriel 1920- 54
Leeson, R. A.
  See Leeson, Robert (Arthur)
Leeson, Robert (Arthur) 1928- 76
  Earlier sketch in SATA 42
Lee Tae-Jun 1904-1956(?) 194
Lee-Tai, Amy 1964- 189
Leffland, Ella 1931- 65
Leffler, Silke 197
Lefler, Irene (Whitney) 1917- 12
LeFrak, Karen 182
Le Gallienne, Eva 1899-1991 9
  Obituary 68
Legg, Gerald 1947- 143
Legg, Sarah Martha Ross Bruggeman (?)-1982
  Obituary 40
LeGrand
  See Henderson, LeGrand
Le Guin, Ursula K. 1929- 194
  Earlier sketches in SATA 4, 52, 99, 149
  See also CLR 91
Le Guin, Ursula Kroeber
  See Le Guin, Ursula K.
Legum, Colin 1919-2003 10
Lehman, Barbara 1963- 170
  Earlier sketch in SATA 115
Lehman, Bob 91
Lehman, Elaine 91
Lehmann, Debra Lynn
  See Vanasse, Deb
Lehn, Cornelia 1920- 46
Lehne, Judith Logan 1947- 93
Lehr, Delores 1920- 10
Lehr, Norma 1930- 71
Leiber, Fritz (Reuter, Jr.) 1910-1992 45
  Obituary 73
Leibold, Jay 1957- 57
  Brief entry 52
Leichman, Seymour 1933- 5
Leigh, Nila K. 1981- 81
Leigh, Tom 1947- 46
Leigh-Pemberton, John 1911-1997 35
Leighton, Clare (Veronica Hope)
  1899-1989 37
Leighton, Margaret (Carver) 1896-1987 1
  Obituary 52
Leiner, Al(an) 1938- 83
Leiner, Katherine 1949- 93
Leipold, L. Edmond 1902-1983 16
Leisk, David (Johnson) 1906-1975 30
  Obituary 26
  Earlier sketch in SATA 1
  See also CLR 98
Leister, Mary 1917- 29
Leitch, Patricia 1933- 98
  Earlier sketch in SATA 11
Leitner, Isabella 1924- 86
Leland, Bob 1956- 92
Leland, Robert E.
  See Leland, Bob
Lematre, Pascal 1967- 176
Lember, Barbara Hirsch 1941- 92
LeMieux, A.C. 1954- 125
  Earlier sketch in SATA 90
LeMieux, Anne
  See LeMieux, A.C.

LeMieux, Anne Connelly
  See LeMieux, A.C.
Lemieux, Michele 1955- 139
Lemke, Horst 1922- 38
Lenain, Thierry 1959- 201
Lenanton, Carola Mary Anima Oman
  See Oman, Carola (Mary Anima)
Lenard, Alexander 1910-1972
  Obituary 21
L'Engle, Madeleine 1918-2007 128
  Obituary 186
  Earlier sketches in SATA 1, 27, 75
  See also CLR 57
  See also SAAS 15
L'Engle, Madeleine Camp Franklin
  See L'Engle, Madeleine
Lengyel, Cornel Adam 1915- 27
Lengyel, Emil 1895-1985 3
  Obituary 42
Lennon, John (Ono) 1940-1980 114
Leno, Jay 1950- 154
LeNoir, Janice 1941- 89
Lens, Sidney 1912-1986 13
  Obituary 48
Lenski, Lois 1893-1974 100
  Earlier sketches in SATA 1, 26
  See also CLR 26
Lent, Blair 1930-2009 133
  Obituary 200
  Earlier sketch in SATA 2
Lent, Henry Bolles 1901-1973 17
Lent, John 1948- 108
Leodhas, Sorche Nic
  See Alger, Leclaire (Gowans)
Leokum, Arkady 1916(?)- 45
Leon, Sharon 1959- 79
Leonard, Alison 1944- 70
Leonard, Constance (Brink) 1923- 42
  Brief entry 40
Leonard, Dutch
  See Leonard, Elmore
Leonard, Elmore 1925- 163
Leonard, Elmore John, Jr.
  See Leonard, Elmore
Leonard, Jonathan N(orton) 1903-1975 36
Leonard, Laura 1923- 75
Leong, Gor Yun
  See Ellison, Virginia H(owell)
Leonhardt, Alice 1950- 152
Lerangis, Peter 1955- 171
  Earlier sketch in SATA 72
Lerner, Aaron 1920-2007 35
  Obituary 179
Lerner, Aaron Bunsen
  See Lerner, Aaron
Lerner, Carol 1927- 86
  Earlier sketch in SATA 33
  See also CLR 34
  See also SAAS 12
Lerner, Gerda 1920- 65
Lerner, Harriet 1944- 101
Lerner, Marguerite Rush 1924-1987 11
  Obituary 51
Lerner, Sharon (Ruth) 1938-1982 11
  Obituary 29
Leroe, Ellen W(hitney) 1949- 99
  Brief entry 51
  Earlier sketch in SATA 61
Leroux, Gaston 1868-1927 65
Leroux-Hugon, Helene 1955- 132
LeRoy, Gen 52
  Brief entry 36
Lerrigo, Marion Olive 1898-1968
  Obituary 29
LeShan, Eda J(oan) 1922-2002 21
  See also CLR 6
LeSieg, Theo.
  See Dr. Seuss
  and Geisel, Theodor Seuss
  and Seuss, Dr.
  and Stone, Rosetta

Lesinski, Jeanne M. 1960- 120
Leslie, Robert Franklin 1911-1990 7
Leslie, Roger 1961- 168
Leslie, Roger James
  See Leslie, Roger
Leslie, Sarah
  See McGuire, Leslie (Sarah)
LeSourd, Catherine
  See Marshall, (Sarah) Catherine (Wood)
Lessac, Frane
  See Lessac, Frane
Lessac, Frane 1954- 148
  Earlier sketch in SATA 61
Lessem, Dino Don
  See Lessem, Don
Lessem, Don 1951- 182
  Earlier sketches in SATA 97, 155
Lesser, Margaret 1899(?)-1979
  Obituary 22
Lesser, Rika 1953- 53
Lester, Alison 1952- 129
  Earlier sketches in SATA 50, 90
Lester, Helen 1936- 189
  Earlier sketches in SATA 46, 92, 145
Lester, Julius 1939- 157
  Earlier sketches in SATA 12, 74, 112
  See also CLR 143
Lester, Julius Bernard
  See Lester, Julius
Lester, Mike 1955- 131
Le Sueur, Meridel 1900-1996 6
Lethcoe, Jason 191
Le Tord, Bijou 1945- 95
  Earlier sketch in SATA 49
Letts, Billie 1938- 121
Leuck, Laura 1962- 192
  Earlier sketches in SATA 85, 146
Leutscher, Alfred (George) 1913- 23
Levai, Blaise 1919- 39
Levenkron, Steven 1941- 86
Leverich, Kathleen 1948- 103
LeVert, (William) John 1946- 55
Levete, Sarah 1961- 153
Levin, Betty 1927- 201
  Earlier sketches in SATA 19, 84, 137
  See also SAAS 11
Levin, Ira 1929-2007 66
  Obituary 187
Levin, Ira Marvin
  See Levin, Ira
Levin, Ira Marvin
  See Levin, Ira
Levin, Marcia Obrasky 1918- 13
Levin, Meyer 1905-1981 21
  Obituary 27
Levin, Miriam (Ramsfelder) 1962- 97
Levine, Abby 1943- 54
  Brief entry 52
Levine, Betty K(rasne) 1933- 66
Levine, David 1926- 43
  Brief entry 35
Levine, Edna S(imon) 35
Levine, Ellen 1939- 190
Levine, Evan 1962- 77
  Earlier sketch in SATA 74
Levine, Gail Carson 1947- 195
  Earlier sketches in SATA 98, 161
  See also CLR 85
Levine, I(srael) E. 1923-2003 12
  Obituary 146
Levine, Joan Goldman 11
Levine, Joseph 1910- 33
Levine, Marge 1934- 81
Levine, Rhoda 14
Levine, Sarah 1970- 57
Levine, Shar 1953- 131
Levine-Freidus, Gail
  See Provost, Gail Levine
Levinson, Nancy Smiler 1938- 140
  Earlier sketches in SATA 33, 80

Levinson, Riki 99
  Brief entry 49
  Earlier sketch in SATA 52
Levithan, David 1972- 166
Levitin, Sonia 1934- 192
  Autobiography Feature 131
  Earlier sketches in SATA 4, 68, 119, 131
  See also CLR 53
  See also SAAS 2
Levitt, Sidney (Mark) 1947- 68
Levon, O. U.
  See Kesey, Ken
Levoy, Myron 49
  Brief entry 37
Levy, Barrie 112
Levy, Constance 1931- 140
  Earlier sketch in SATA 73
  See also SAAS 22
Levy, Elizabeth 1942- 169
  Earlier sketches in SATA 31, 69, 107
  See also SAAS 18
Levy, Janice 172
Levy, Marilyn 1937- 67
Levy, Nathan 1945- 63
Levy, Robert 1945- 82
Lewees, John
  See Stockton, Francis Richard
Lewin, Betsy 1937- 169
  Autobiography Feature 115
  Earlier sketches in SATA 32, 90
Lewin, Hugh 1939- 72
  Brief entry 40
  See also CLR 9
Lewin, Ted 1935- 195
  Autobiography Feature 115
  Earlier sketches in SATA 21, 76, 119, 165
Lewis, Alice C. 1936- 46
Lewis, Alice Hudson 1895(?)-1971
  Obituary 29
Lewis, Amanda 1955- 80
Lewis, Anthony 1927- 27
Lewis, Anthony 1966- 120
Lewis, Barbara A. 1943- 73
Lewis, Beverly 1949- 80
Lewis, Brenda Ralph 1932- 72
Lewis, Brian 1963- 128
Lewis, Claudia (Louise) 1907-2001 5
Lewis, Clive Staples
  See Lewis, C.S.
Lewis, C.S. 1898-1963 100
  Earlier sketch in SATA 13
  See also CLR 109
Lewis, Cynthia Copeland 1960- 111
Lewis, E. M. 123
  Earlier sketch in SATA 20
Lewis, Earl Bradley
  See Lewis, E.B.
Lewis, E.B. 1956- 168
  Earlier sketches in SATA 93, 124
Lewis, Elizabeth Foreman 1892-1958 121
  See also YABC 2
Lewis, Francine
  See Wells, Helen
Lewis, Hilda (Winifred) 1896-1974
  Obituary 20
Lewis, J. Patrick 1942- 162
  Earlier sketches in SATA 69, 104
Lewis, Jack P(earl) 1919- 65
Lewis, Jean 1924- 61
Lewis, Joseph Anthony
  See Lewis, Anthony
Lewis, Julinda
  See Lewis-Ferguson, Julinda
Lewis, Kevin 173
Lewis, Kim 1951- 136
  Earlier sketch in SATA 84
Lewis, Linda (Joy) 1946- 67
Lewis, Lucia Z.
  See Anderson, Lucia (Lewis)
Lewis, Marjorie 1929- 40
  Brief entry 35

Lewis, Mary 1907(?)-1988 64
  Obituary 56
Lewis, Mervyn
  See Frewer, Glyn (M.)
Lewis, Michael
  See Untermeyer, Louis
Lewis, Naomi 144
  Earlier sketch in SATA 76
Lewis, Paeony 1960- 173
Lewis, Paul
  See Gerson, Noel Bertram
Lewis, Richard 1935- 3
Lewis, Rob 1962- 72
Lewis, Roger
  See Zarchy, Harry
Lewis, Shannon
  See Llywelyn, Morgan
Lewis, Shari 1934-1998 35
  Brief entry 30
  Obituary 104
Lewis, Sylvan R.
  See Aronson, Virginia
Lewis, Thomas P(arker) 1936- 27
Lewis, Wendy A. 1966- 150
Lewis-Ferguson, Julinda 1955- 85
Lewison, Wendy Cheyette 177
Lewiton, Mina 1904-1970 2
Lew-Vriethoff, Joanne 186
Lexau, Joan M. 130
  Earlier sketches in SATA 1, 36
Ley, Willy 1906-1969 2
Leydon, Rita (Floden) 1949- 21
Leyland, Eric (Arthur) 1911- 37
L'Hommedieu, Dorothy Keasley 1885-1961
  Obituary 29
Li, Xiao Jun 1952- 86
Liatsos, Sandra Olson 1942- 103
Libby, Alisa M. 189
Libby, Barbara M. 153
Libby, Bill
  See Libby, William M.
Libby, William M. 1927-1984 5
  Obituary 39
Liberty, Gene 1924- 3
Lichtenheld, Tom 152
Lichtman, Wendy 1946- 193
Liddell, Kenneth 1912-1975 63
Lidz, Jane 120
Lieberman, E(dwin) James 1934- 62
Liebers, Arthur 1913-1984 12
Lieblich, Irene 1923- 22
Liers, Emil E(rnest) 1890-1975 37
Lies, Brian 1963- 190
  Earlier sketch in SATA 131
Liestman, Vicki 1961- 72
Lietz, Gerald S. 1918- 11
Life, Kay (Guinn) 1930- 83
Lifton, Betty Jean 118
  Earlier sketch in SATA 6
Lifton, Robert Jay 1926- 66
Lightburn, Ron 1954- 91
Lightburn, Sandra 1955- 91
Lightner, A. M.
  See Hopf, Alice (Martha) L(ightner)
Lightner, Alice
  See Hopf, Alice (Martha) L(ightner)
Lignell, Lois 1911- 37
Liles, Maurine Walpole 1935- 81
Lillegard, Dee 184
Lilley, Stephen R. 1950- 97
Lilley, Stephen Ray
  See Lilley, Stephen R.
Lillington, Kenneth (James) 1916-1998 39
Lilly, Nate 182
Lilly, Ray
  See Curtis, Richard (Alan)
Lim, John 1932- 43
Liman, Ellen (Fogelson) 1936- 22
Limb, Sue 1946- 158
Limburg, Peter R(ichard) 1929- 13

Lin, Grace 1974- 198
  Earlier sketches in SATA 111, 162
Lincoln, C(harles) Eric 1924-2000 5
Lincoln, Hazel 187
Lincoln, James
  See Bates, Katharine Lee
Lindbergh, Anne
  See Sapieyevski, Anne Lindbergh
Lindbergh, Anne Morrow 1906-2001 33
  Obituary 125
Lindbergh, Anne Spencer Morrow
  See Lindbergh, Anne Morrow
Lindbergh, Charles A(ugustus, Jr.)
  1902-1974 33
Lindbergh, Reeve 1945- 163
  Earlier sketch in SATA 116
Lindblom, Steven (Winther) 1946- 94
  Brief entry 39
  Earlier sketch in SATA 42
Linde, Gunnel 1924- 5
Lindenbaum, Pija 1955- 183
  Earlier sketches in SATA 77, 144
Lindgren, Astrid (Anna Emilia Ericsson)
  1907-2002 38
  Obituary 128
  Earlier sketch in SATA 2
  See also CLR 119
Lindgren, Barbro 1937- 120
  Brief entry 46
  Earlier sketch in SATA 63
  See also CLR 86
Lindman, Maj (Jan) 1886-1972 43
Lindop, Edmund 1925- 5
Lindquist, Jennie Dorothea 1899-1977 13
Lindquist, Rowena Cory 1958- 98
Lindquist, Willis 1908-1988 20
Lindsay, Norman Alfred William
  1879-1969 67
  See also CLR 8
Lindsay, (Nicholas) Vachel 1879-1931 40
Lindsey, Kathleen D(orothy) 1949- 153
Line, David
  See Davidson, Lionel
Line, Les 1935- 27
Lines, Kathleen Mary 1902-1988
  Obituary 61
Linfield, Esther 40
Lingard, Joan (Amelia) 1932- 130
  Autobiography Feature 130
  Earlier sketches in SATA 8, 74, 114
  See also CLR 89
  See also SAAS 5
Link, Martin 1934- 28
Linn, Margot
  See Ziefert, Harriet
Linnea, Sharon 1956- 82
Lion, Melissa 1976- 176
Lionni, Leo(nard) 1910-1999 72
  Obituary 118
  Earlier sketch in SATA 8
  See also CLR 71
Lipinsky de Orlov, Lino S. 1908- 22
Lipkind, William 1904-1974 15
Lipman, David 1931-2008 21
Lipman, Matthew 1923- 14
Lippincott, Bertram 1898(?)-1985
  Obituary 42
Lippincott, Gary A. 1953- 119
  Earlier sketch in SATA 73
Lippincott, Joseph W(harton) 1887-1976 17
Lippincott, Sarah Lee 1920- 22
Lippman, Peter J. 1936- 31
Lipsyte, Robert 1938- 198
  Earlier sketches in SATA 5, 68, 113, 161
  See also CLR 76
Lipsyte, Robert Michael
  See Lipsyte, Robert
Lisandrelli, Elaine Slivinski 1951- 94
Lisker, Sonia O. 1933- 44
Lisle, Holly 1960- 98

Lisle, Janet Taylor 1947- *150*
  Brief entry *47*
  Earlier sketches in SATA *59, 96*
  See also SAAS *14*
Lisle, Rebecca *162*
Lisle, Seward D.
  See Ellis, Edward S(ylvester)
Lisowski, Gabriel 1946- *47*
  Brief entry *31*
Liss, Howard 1922-1995 .... *4*
  Obituary *84*
Lissiat, Amy
  See Thompson, Colin
Lisson, Deborah 1941- *110*
  Earlier sketch in SATA *71*
List, Ilka Katherine 1935- *6*
Liston, Robert A. 1927- *5*
Litchfield, Ada B(assett) 1916-1999 .... *5*
Litchfield, Jo 1973- *116*
Lithgow, John (Arthur) 1945- *145*
Litowinsky, Olga (Jean) 1936- *26*
Littke, Lael J. 1929- *140*
  Earlier sketches in SATA *51, 83*
Little, A. Edward
  See Klein, Aaron E.
Little, Douglas 1942- *96*
Little, (Flora) Jean 1932- *149*
  Earlier sketches in SATA *2, 68, 106*
  See also CLR *4*
  See also SAAS *17*
Little, Lessie Jones 1906-1986 .... *60*
  Obituary *50*
Little, Mary E. 1912-1999 .... *28*
Littlechild, George 1958- *85*
Littledale, Freya (Lota) 1929-1992 .... *74*
  Earlier sketch in SATA *2*
Littlefield, Bill 1948- *83*
Littlefield, Holly 1963- *97*
Littlesugar, Amy 1953- *176*
  Earlier sketch in SATA *122*
Littleton, Mark R. 1950- *142*
  Earlier sketch in SATA *89*
Littman, Sarah Darer *175*
Litty, Julie 1971- *181*
Litzinger, Rosanne 1948- *196*
Lively, Penelope 1933- *164*
  Earlier sketches in SATA *7, 60, 101*
  See also CLR *7*
Lively, Penelope Margaret
  See Lively, Penelope
Liverakos, L.A.
  See Gilman, Laura Anne
Liversidge, (Henry) Douglas 1913- *8*
Livesey, Claire (Warner) 1927- *127*
Livingston, Carole 1941- *42*
Livingston, (M.) Irene 1932- *150*
Livingston, Myra Cohn 1926-1996 .... *68*
  Obituary *92*
  Earlier sketch in SATA *5*
  See also CLR *7*
  See also SAAS *1*
Livingston, Richard R(oland) 1922- *8*
Livo, Norma J. 1929- *76*
Liwska, Renata *199*
Ljungkvist, Laura *180*
Llerena Aguirre, Carlos 1952- *19*
Llerena Aguirre, Carlos Antonio
  See Llerena Aguirre, Carlos
Llewellyn, Claire 1954- *196*
  Earlier sketches in SATA *77, 143*
Llewellyn, Grace 1964- *110*
Llewellyn, Richard
  See Llewellyn Lloyd, Richard Dafydd Vivian
Llewellyn, Sam 1948- *185*
  Earlier sketch in SATA *95*
Llewellyn Lloyd, Richard Dafydd Vivian
  1906-1983 .... *11*
  Obituary *37*
Llewelyn, T. Harcourt
  See Hamilton, Charles (Harold St. John)

Lloyd, Alan
  See Lloyd, A.R.
Lloyd, Alan Richard
  See Lloyd, A.R.
Lloyd, A.R. 1927- *168*
  Earlier sketch in SATA *97*
Lloyd, David
  See Lloyd, David T.
Lloyd, David T. 1954- *167*
Lloyd, E. James
  See James, Elizabeth
Lloyd, Errol 1943- *22*
Lloyd, Hugh
  See Fitzhugh, Percy Keese
Lloyd, James
  See James, Elizabeth
Lloyd, Megan 1958- *189*
  Earlier sketches in SATA *77, 117*
Lloyd, Norman 1909-1980
  Obituary *23*
Lloyd, (Mary) Norris 1908-1993 .... *10*
  Obituary *75*
Lloyd, Sam *183*
Lloyd-Jones, Sally 1960- *179*
Lloyd Webber, Andrew 1948- *56*
Llywelyn, Morgan 1937- *109*
Lo, Ginnie *165*
Lo, Virginia M.
  See Lo, Ginnie
Lobato, Jose Bento Monteiro 1882-1948 ... *114*
Lobel, Anita (Kempler) 1934- *162*
  Earlier sketches in SATA *6, 55, 96*
Lobel, Arnold (Stark) 1933-1987 .... *55*
  Obituary *54*
  Earlier sketch in SATA *6*
  See also CLR *5*
Lobel, Gillian *181*
Lobsenz, Amelia *12*
Lobsenz, Norman M(itchell) 1919- *6*
Lochak, Michele 1936- *39*
Lochlons, Colin
  See Jackson, C(aary) Paul
Locke, Clinton W. *1*
Locke, Elsie (Violet) 1912-2001 .... *87*
Locke, Gary 1963- *197*
Locke, Lucie 1904-1989 .... *10*
Locke, Robert 1944- *63*
  See also CLR *39*
Locker, Thomas 1937- *109*
  Earlier sketch in SATA *59*
  See also CLR *14*
Lockhart, E.
  See Jenkins, Emily
Lockridge, Hildegarde (Dolson)
  1908-1981 .... *121*
  Earlier sketch in SATA *5*
Lockwood, Mary
  See Spelman, Mary
Lodge, Bernard 1933- *107*
  Earlier sketch in SATA *33*
Lodge, Jo 1966- *173*
  Earlier sketch in SATA *112*
Loeb, Jeffrey 1946- *57*
Loeb, Robert H., Jr. 1917- *21*
Loefgren, Ulf 1931- *3*
Loehfelm, Bill 1969- *153*
Loehr, Mallory *184*
Loehr, Patrick 1968(?)- *194*
Loeper, John J(oseph) 1929- *118*
  Earlier sketch in SATA *10*
Loescher, Ann Dull 1942- *20*
Loescher, Gil(burt Damian) 1945- *20*
Loewer, Jean Jenkins
  See Jenkins, Jean
Loewer, (Henry) Peter 1934- *98*
LoFaro, Jerry 1959- *77*
Lofo
  See Heimann, Rolf
Lofthouse, Liz *199*

Lofting, Hugh (John) 1886-1947 .... *100*
  Earlier sketch in SATA *15*
  See also CLR *143*
Lofts, Norah (Robinson) 1904-1983 .... *8*
  Obituary *36*
Logan, Jake
  See Knott, William C(ecil, Jr.)
  and Krepps, Robert W(ilson)
  and Pearl, Jacques Bain
  and Riefe, Alan
  and Rifkin, Shepard
  and Smith, Martin Cruz
Logan, Mark
  See Nicole, Christopher (Robin)
Logan, Rochelle 1954- *169*
Logston, Anne 1962- *112*
Logue, Christopher 1926- *23*
Logue, Mary 1952- *161*
  Earlier sketch in SATA *112*
Logue, Mary Louise
  See Logue, Mary
Loh, Morag 1935- *73*
Lohans, Alison 1949- *101*
Loizeaux, William *185*
Loken, Newton Clayton 1919- *26*
Lomas, Steve
  See Brennan, Joseph Lomas
Lomask, Milton (Nachman) 1909-1991 .... *20*
Lombard, Jenny *178*
Lombino, Salvatore
  See Hunter, Evan
LoMonaco, Palmyra 1932- *102*
London, Jack 1876-1916
  See London, John Griffith
London, Jane
  See Geis, Darlene Stern
London, John Griffith 1876-1916 .... *18*
  See also CLR *108*
London, Jonathan (Paul) 1947- *157*
  Earlier sketches in SATA *74, 113*
Lonergan, (Pauline) Joy (MacLean) 1909- ... *10*
Lonette, Reisie (Dominee) 1924- *43*
Long, Cathryn J. 1946- *89*
Long, Earlene (Roberta) 1938- *50*
Long, Emmett
  See Leonard, Elmore
Long, Ethan 1968(?)- *182*
Long, Helen Beecher *1*
Long, Judith Elaine 1953- *20*
Long, Judy
  See Long, Judith Elaine
Long, Kim 1949- *69*
Long, Laura Mooney 1892-1967
  Obituary *29*
Long, Loren 1966(?)- *188*
  Earlier sketch in SATA *151*
Long, Melinda 1960- *152*
Long, Sylvia 1948- *179*
  Earlier sketch in SATA *120*
Longbeard, Frederick
  See Longyear, Barry B(rookes)
Longfellow, Henry Wadsworth 1807-1882 ... *19*
  See also CLR *99*
Longfellow, Layne (A.) 1937- *102*
Longman, Harold S. 1919- *5*
Longsworth, Polly 1933- *28*
Longtemps, Kenneth 1933- *17*
Longway, A. Hugh
  See Lang, Andrew
Longyear, Barry B(rookes) 1942- *117*
Look, Lenore *180*
Loomans, Diane 1955- *90*
Loomis, Christine *160*
  Earlier sketch in SATA *113*
Loomis, Jennifer A. 1942- *101*
Loomis, Robert D. *5*
Lopez, Angelo (Cayas) 1967- *83*
Lopez, Barry (Holstun) 1945- *67*
Lopez, Jack 1950- *178*
Lopez, Loretta 1963- *190*
Lopez, Lorraine M. 1956- *181*

Lopez, Rafael 1961(?)- *198*
Lopshire, Robert M(artin) 1927- *6*
Loraine, Connie
  See Reece, Colleen L.
Lorbiecki, Marybeth 1959- *172*
  Earlier sketch in SATA *121*
Lord, Athena V. 1932- *39*
Lord, Beman 1924-1991 .... *5*
  Obituary *69*
Lord, Bette Bao 1938- *58*
Lord, Cynthia *182*
Lord, Doreen Mildred Douglas
  See Lord, Douglas
Lord, Douglas 1904-1992 .... *12*
Lord, John Vernon 1939- *21*
Lord, Michele *201*
Lord, Nancy
  See Titus, Eve
Lord, Patricia C. 1927-1988
  Obituary *58*
Lord, Walter 1917-2002 .... *3*
Lorde, Diana
  See Reno, Dawn E(laine)
Lorenz, Albert 1941- *115*
Lorenzini, Carlo 1826-1890 .... *100*
  Earlier sketch in SATA *29*
  See also CLR *120*
Lorey, Dean 1967- *193*
Lorimer, Janet 1941- *60*
Loring, Emilie (Baker) 1864(?)-1951 .... *51*
Lorkowski, Thomas V(incent) 1950- *92*
Lorkowski, Tom
  See Lorkowski, Thomas V(incent)
Lorraine, Walter (Henry) 1929- *16*
Lorrimer, Claire
  See Clark, Patricia Denise
Loss, Joan 1933- *11*
Lothrop, Harriet Mulford Stone 1844-1924 . *20*
Lottridge, Celia Barker 1936- *157*
  Earlier sketch in SATA *112*
LoTurco, Laura 1963- *84*
Lotz, Wolfgang 1912-1981 .... *65*
Louie, Ai-Ling 1949- *40*
  Brief entry *34*
Louis, Catherine 1963- *186*
Louis, Pat
  See Francis, Dorothy
Louisburgh, Sheila Burnford
  See Burnford, Sheila (Philip Cochrane Every)
Louise, Anita
  See Riggio, Anita
Louise, Tina 1934- *191*
Lourie, Helen
  See Storr, Catherine (Cole)
Lourie, Peter 1952- *183*
  Earlier sketches in SATA *82, 142*
Lourie, Peter King
  See Lourie, Peter
Love, Ann 1947- *168*
  Earlier sketch in SATA *79*
Love, D. Anne 1949- *180*
  Earlier sketches in SATA *96, 145*
Love, Douglas 1967- *92*
Love, Judith Dufour
  See Love, Judy
Love, Judy *188*
Love, Katherine (Isabel) 1907- *3*
Love, Kathleen Ann
  See Love, Ann
Love, Sandra (Weller) 1940- *26*
Lovejoy, Jack 1937- *116*
Lovelace, Delos Wheeler 1894-1967 .... *7*
Lovelace, Maud Hart 1892-1980 .... *2*
  Obituary *23*
Lovell, Ingraham
  See Bacon, Josephine Dodge (Daskam)
Loverseed, Amanda (Jane) 1965- *75*
Lovett, Margaret (Rose) 1915- *22*
Low, Alice 1926- *156*
  Earlier sketches in SATA *11, 76*
Low, Elizabeth Hammond 1898-1991 .... *5*

Low, Joseph 1911-2007 .... *14*
Low, Penelope Margaret
  See Lively, Penelope
Low, William *177*
Lowe, Jay, Jr.
  See Loeper, John J(oseph)
Lowell, Pamela *187*
Lowell, Susan 1950- *127*
  Earlier sketch in SATA *81*
Lowenstein, Dyno 1914-1996 .... *6*
Lowenstein, Sallie 1949- *116*
Lowery, Linda 1949- *151*
  Earlier sketch in SATA *74*
Lowitz, Anson C. 1901(?)-1978 .... *18*
Lowitz, Sadyebeth Heath 1901-1969 .... *17*
Lowndes, Robert A(ugustine) W(ard)
  1916-1998 .... *117*
Lowrey, Janette Sebring 1892-1986 .... *43*
Lowry, Lois 1937- *177*
  Autobiography Feature *127*
  Earlier sketches in SATA *23, 70, 111*
  See also CLR *72*
  See also SAAS *3*
Lowry, Lois Hammersberg
  See Lowry, Lois
Lowry, Peter 1953- *7*
Lowther, George F. 1913-1975
  Obituary *30*
Loyie, Larry 1933- *150*
Lozansky, Edward D. 1941- *62*
Lozier, Herbert 1915- *26*
Lubar, David 1954- *190*
  Earlier sketch in SATA *133*
Lubell, Cecil 1912-2000 .... *6*
Lubell, Winifred (A. Milius) 1914- *6*
Lubin, Leonard
  See Lubin, Leonard B.
Lubin, Leonard B. 1943-1994 .... *45*
  Brief entry *37*
Lubka, S. Ruth 1948- *154*
Lubner, Susan *185*
Luby, Thia 1954- *124*
Lucado, Max (Lee) 1955- *104*
Lucas, Cedric 1962- *101*
Lucas, E(dward) V(errall) 1868-1938 .... *20*
Lucas, Eileen 1956- *113*
  Earlier sketch in SATA *76*
Lucas, George 1944- *56*
Lucas, Jerry 1940- *33*
Lucas, Margeaux *186*
Lucas, Victoria
  See Plath, Sylvia
Lucashenko, Melissa 1967- *104*
Luccarelli, Vincent 1923- *90*
Luce, Celia (Geneva Larsen) 1914- *38*
Luce, Willard (Ray) 1914-1990 .... *38*
Lucht, Irmgard 1937- *82*
Luckett, Dave 1951- *167*
  Earlier sketch in SATA *106*
Luckhardt, Mildred Corell 1898-1990 .... *5*
Ludden, Allen (Ellsworth) 1918(?)-1981
  Obituary *27*
Ludel, Jacqueline 1945- *64*
Ludlow, Geoffrey
  See Meynell, Laurence Walter
Ludlum, Mabel Cleland
  See Widdemer, Mabel Cleland
Ludwig, Helen *33*
Ludwig, Lyndell 1923- *63*
Ludwig, Trudy 1959- *166*
Lueders, Edward (George) 1923- *14*
Luenn, Nancy 1954- *79*
  Earlier sketch in SATA *51*
Lufkin, Raymond H. 1897- *38*
Lugard, Flora Louisa Shaw 1852-1929 .... *21*
Luger, Harriett Mandelay 1914- *23*
Luhrmann, Winifred B(ruce) 1934- *11*
Luis, Earlene W. 1929- *11*
Lujan, Jorge *201*
Luke, Pauline *178*

Luke, Pauline R.
  See Luke, Pauline
Lum, Peter
  See Crowe, (Bettina) Peter Lum
Lumry, Amanda (R.) *159*
Lund, Deb *157*
Lund, Doris Herold 1919- *12*
Lung, Chang
  See Jordan, Robert
Lunge-Larsen, Lise 1955- *184*
  Earlier sketch in SATA *138*
Lunn, Carolyn (Kowalczyk) 1960- *67*
Lunn, Janet (Louise Swoboda) 1928- *110*
  Earlier sketches in SATA *4, 68*
  See also CLR *18*
  See also SAAS *12*
Lunsford, Cin Forshay
  See Forshay-Lunsford, Cin
Lupica, Michael 1952- *177*
Lupica, Michael Thomas
  See Lupica, Michael
Lupica, Mike
  See Lupica, Michael
Lupoff, Dick
  See Lupoff, Richard A(llen)
Lupoff, Richard A(llen) 1935- *60*
Lurie, Alison 1926- *112*
  Earlier sketch in SATA *46*
Lurie, Morris 1938- *72*
Lussert, Anneliese 1929- *101*
Lusted, Marcia Amidon 1962- *143*
Lustig, Arnost 1926- *56*
Lustig, Loretta 1944- *46*
Luthardt, Kevin 1973- *172*
Luther, Frank 1905-1980
  Obituary *25*
Luther, Rebekah (Lyn) S(tiles) 1960- *90*
Luttmann, Gail
  See Damerow, Gail
Luttrell, Guy L. 1938- *22*
Luttrell, Ida (Alleene) 1934- *91*
  Brief entry *35*
  Earlier sketch in SATA *40*
Luttrell, William (J. III) 1954- *149*
Lutz, John 1939- *180*
Lutz, John Thomas
  See Lutz, John
Lutz, Norma Jean 1943- *122*
Lutzeier, Elizabeth 1952- *72*
Lutzker, Edythe 1904-1991 .... *5*
Luxbacher, Irene M. 1970- *153*
Luzadder, Patrick 1954- *89*
Luzzati, Emanuele 1921-2007 .... *7*
Luzzatto, Paola Caboara 1938- *38*
Lybbert, Tyler 1970- *88*
Lydon, Michael 1942- *11*
Lutz, John Thomas

Lyfick, Warren
  See Reeves, Lawrence F.
Lyle, Katie Letcher 1938- *8*
Lynch, Chris 1962- *171*
  Earlier sketches in SATA *95, 131*
  See also CLR *58*
Lynch, Lorenzo 1932- *7*
Lynch, Marietta 1947- *29*
Lynch, P(atrick) J(ames) 1962- *122*
  Earlier sketch in SATA *79*
Lynch, Patricia (Nora) 1898-1972 .... *9*
Lynds, Dennis 1924-2005 .... *47*
  Brief entry *37*
Lyne, Alison Davis *188*
Lyngseth, Joan
  See Davies, Joan
Lynn, Elizabeth A(nne) 1946- *99*
Lynn, Mary
  See Brokamp, Marilyn
Lynn, Patricia
  See Watts, Mabel Pizzey
Lynn, Tracy *175*
Lyon, Elinor 1921-2008 .... *6*
  Obituary *192*

Lyon, Elinor Bruce
  See Lyon, Elinor
Lyon, George Ella 1949- 148
  Autobiography Feature 148
  Earlier sketches in SATA *68, 119*
Lyon, Lyman R.
  See de Camp, L(yon) Sprague
Lyons, Dorothy M(arawee) 1907-1997 3
Lyons, Grant 1941- 30
Lyons, Marcus
  See Blish, James (Benjamin)
Lyons, Mary E. 1947- 195
  Autobiography Feature 195
  Earlier sketches in SATA *93, 142*
Lyons, Mary Evelyn
  See Lyons, Mary E.
Lystad, Mary (Hanemann) 1928- 11
Lytle, Elizabeth Stewart 1949- 79
Lytle, Robert A. 1944- 119
Lyttle, Richard B(ard) 1927- 23
Lytton, Edward G(eorge) E(arle) L(ytton)
  Bulwer-Lytton Baron 1803-1873 23

M

Ma, Wenhai 1954- 84
Maar, Leonard (Frank, Jr.) 1927- 30
Maartens, Maretha 1945- 73
Maas, Selve -1997 14
Maass, Robert 195
Mabie, Grace
  See Mattern, Joanne
Mac
  See MacManus, Seumas
  and Maccari, Ruggero
Macalaster, Elizabeth G. 1951- 115
MacAlister, Katie 159
MacAllan, Andrew
  See Leasor, James
MacAodhagain, Eamon
  See Egan, E(dward) W(elstead)
MacArthur-Onslow, Annette Rosemary
  1933- 26
Macaulay, David (Alexander) 1946- 137
  Brief entry 27
  Earlier sketches in SATA *46, 72*
  See also CLR 14
Macaulay, Teresa (E.) 1947- 95
Macavinta, Courtney 176
MacBeth, George (Mann) 1932-1992 4
  Obituary 70
MacBride, Roger Lea 1929-1995 85
MacCarter, Don 1944- 91
MacClintock, Dorcas 1932- 8
MacCready, Robin Merrow 1959(?)- 190
MacCullough, Carolyn 174
MacDonald, Alan 1958- 192
MacDonald, Amy 1951- 156
  Autobiography Feature 156
  Earlier sketches in SATA *76, 136*
MacDonald, Anne Elizabeth Campbell Bard
  -1958
  See MacDonald, Betty
MacDonald, Anson
  See Heinlein, Robert A.
MacDonald, Betty 1908-1958
  See YABC 1
Macdonald, Blackie
  See Emrich, Duncan (Black Macdonald)
Macdonald, Caroline 1948- 86
  Obituary 111
  See also CLR 60
Macdonald, Dwight 1906-1982 29
  Obituary 33
MacDonald, George 1824-1905 100
  Earlier sketch in SATA *33*
  See also CLR 67
MacDonald, Golden
  See Brown, Margaret Wise

Macdonald, Guy 195
Macdonald, James D. 1954- 67
  Earlier sketches in SATA *81, 114, 165, 1*
Macdonald, Marcia
  See Hill, Grace Livingston
MacDonald, Margaret Read 1940- 194
  Earlier sketches in SATA *94, 164*
Macdonald, Marianne 1934- 113
Macdonald, Mary
  See Gifford, Griselda
Macdonald, Maryann 1947- 189
  Earlier sketch in SATA *72*
MacDonald, Ross 1957- 201
Macdonald, Shelagh 1937- 25
MacDonald, Suse 1940- 193
  Brief entry 52
  Earlier sketches in SATA *54, 109*
Macdonald, Zillah K(atherine) 1885-1979 ... 11
MacDonnell, Megan
  See Stevens, Serita
MacDougal, John
  See Blish, James (Benjamin)
Mace, Elisabeth 1933- 27
Mace, Varian 1938- 49
MacEwen, Gwendolyn (Margaret)
  1941-1987 50
  Obituary 55
Macfarlan, Allan A. 1892-1982 35
MacFarlane, Iris 1922- 11
MacGill-Callahan, Sheila 1926-2000 78
MacGregor, Carol Lynn 153
MacGregor, Ellen 1906-1954 39
  Brief entry 27
MacGregor-Hastie, Roy (Alasdhair Niall)
  1929- 3
MacGrory, Yvonne 1948- 142
Machado, Ana Maria 1941- 150
MacHale, D.J. 1956- 175
MacHale, Donald James
  See MacHale, D.J.
Machetanz, Frederick 1908- 34
Machin Goodall, Daphne (Edith) 37
Macht, Norm
  See Macht, Norman L.
Macht, Norman L. 1929- 122
Macht, Norman Lee
  See Macht, Norman L.
MacInnes, Helen (Clark) 1907-1985 22
  Obituary 44
Macintosh, Brownie 1950- 98
MacIntyre, Elisabeth 1916- 17
MacIntyre, Wendy 1947- 196
Mack, Jeff 194
Mack, L.V.
  See Kimmelman, Burt
Mack, Stan(ley) 17
Mack, Todd 168
Mack, Tracy 1968- 183
  Earlier sketch in SATA *128*
Mackall, Dandi D.
  See Mackall, Dandi Daley
Mackall, Dandi Daley 1949- 182
  Earlier sketches in SATA *118, 177*
Mackay, Claire 1930- 97
  Autobiography Feature 124
  Earlier sketch in SATA *40*
  See also CLR 43
Mackay, Constance D'Arcy (?)-1966 125
Mackay, Donald 1914-2005 81
  Obituary 173
Mackay, Donald Alexander
  See Mackay, Donald
MacKaye, Percy (Wallace) 1875-1956 32
Mackel, Kathryn 1950- 162
Mackel, Kathy
  See Mackel, Kathryn
MacKellar, William 1914- 4
Macken, JoAnn Early 1953- 201
Macken, Walter 1915-1967 36
MacKenzie, Jill (Kelly) 1947- 75

Mackey, Ernan
  See McInerny, Ralph
Mackey, Weezie Kerr 188
Mackie, Maron
  See McNeely, Jeannette
Mackin, Edward
  See McInerny, Ralph
MacKinnon, Bernie 1957- 69
MacKinnon Groomer, Vera 1915- 57
MacKinstry, Elizabeth 1879-1956 42
Mackler, Carolyn 1973- 156
MacLachlan, Emily
  See Charest, Emily MacLachlan
MacLachlan, Patricia 1938- 168
  Brief entry 42
  Earlier sketches in SATA *62, 107*
  See also CLR 14
MacLane, Jack
  See Crider, Bill
MacLean, Alistair (Stuart) 1922(?)-1987 23
  Obituary 50
Maclean, Art
  See Shirreffs, Gordon D(onald)
MacLean, Christine Kole 177
MacLean, Glynne 1964- 150
MacLeod, Beatrice 1910- 162
  Earlier sketch in SATA *10*
MacLeod, Beatrice Beach
  See MacLeod, Beatrice
MacLeod, Charlotte (Matilda) 1922-2005 28
  Obituary 160
MacLeod, Doug 1959- 201
  Earlier sketch in SATA *60*
MacLeod, Elizabeth 184
  Earlier sketch in SATA *158*
MacLeod, Ellen Jane (Anderson) 1916- 14
MacManus, James
  See MacManus, Seumas
MacManus, Seumas 1869-1960 25
MacMaster, Eve (Ruth) B(owers) 1942- 46
MacMillan, Annabelle
  See Quick, Annabelle
MacMillan, Dianne M(arie) 1943- 125
  Earlier sketch in SATA *84*
Macnaughton, Tina 182
Macneill, Janet
  See McNeely, Jeannette
MacPeek, Walter G. 1902-1973 4
  Obituary 25
MacPhail, Catherine 1946- 197
  Earlier sketch in SATA *130*
MacPherson, Margaret 1908-2001 9
  See also SAAS 4
MacPherson, Thomas George 1915-1976
  Obituary 30
MacPherson, Winnie 1930- 107
MacRae, Tom 1980- 181
Macrae, Travis
  See Feagles, Anita M(acRae)
MacRaois, Cormac 1944- 72
Macumber, Mari
  See Sandoz, Mari(e Susette)
Macy, Sue 1954- 134
  Earlier sketch in SATA *88*
Madaras, Lynda 1947- 151
Madden, Don 1927- 3
Madden, Kerry 1961- 168
Madden-Lunsford, Kerry
  See Madden, Kerry
Maddern, Eric 1950- 166
Maddigan, Beth 1967- 174
Maddison, Angela Mary 1923- 10
  See also CLR 24
Maddock, Reginald (Bertram) 1912-1994 15
Madenski, Melissa (Ann) 1949- 77
Madian, Jon 1941- 9
Madison, Alan 182
Madison, Arnold 1937- 6
Madison, Winifred 5
Madonna 1958- 149
Madsen, Gunnar 171

Madsen, Ross Martin 1946- 82
Madsen, Susan A. 1954- 90
Madsen, Susan Arrington
    See Madsen, Susan A.
Maehlqvist, Stefan 1943- 30
Maestro, Betsy (Crippen) 1944- 106
    Brief entry 30
    Earlier sketch in SATA *59*
    See also CLR *45*
Maestro, Giulio 1942- 106
    Earlier sketches in SATA *8, 59*
    See also CLR *45*
Maeterlinck, Maurice 1862-1949 66
Magee, Doug 1947- 78
Magee, Wes 1939- 64
Maggio, Rosalie 1943- 69
Magid, Ken(neth Marshall) 65
Magnus, Erica 1946- 77
Magoon, Scott 182
Magorian, James 1942- 92
    Earlier sketch in SATA *32*
Magorian, Michelle 1947- 128
    Earlier sketch in SATA *67*
Magorian, Michelle Jane
    See Magorian, Michelle
Magovern, Peg 103
Maguire, Anne
    See Nearing, Penny
Maguire, Gregory 1954- 200
    Autobiography Feature 200
    Earlier sketches in SATA *28, 84, 129*
    See also SAAS *22*
Maguire, Gregory Peter
    See Maguire, Gregory
Maguire, Jack 1920-2000 74
Maguire, Jesse
    See Smith, Sherwood
Maguire, Jessie
    See Smith, Sherwood
Maher, Ramona 1934- 13
Mahlqvist, Stefan
    See Maehlqvist, Stefan
Mahon, Julia C(unha) 1916- 11
Mahony, Elizabeth Winthrop
    See Winthrop, Elizabeth
Mahood, Kenneth 1930- 24
Mahy, Margaret 1936- 171
    Earlier sketches in SATA *14, 69, 119*
    See also CLR *78*
Mahy, Margaret May
    See Mahy, Margaret
Maiden, Cecil (Edward) 1902-1981 52
Maidoff, Ilka
    See List, Ilka Katherine
Maifair, Linda Lee 1947- 83
Maik, Henri
    See Hecht, Henri Joseph
Maillu, David G(ian) 1939- 111
Maine, Trevor
    See Catherall, Arthur
Mains, Randolph P. 1946- 80
Maione, Heather 189
Maiorano, Robert 1946- 43
Maisner, Heather 1947- 89
Maison, Della
    See Katz, Bobbi
Maitland, Antony Jasper 1935- 25
Maitland, Barbara 102
Mai-Wyss, Tatjana 1972- 187
Major, Kevin (Gerald) 1949- 134
    Earlier sketches in SATA *32, 82*
    See also CLR *11*
Majure, Janet 1954- 96
Makhijani, Pooja 188
Makie, Pam 1943- 37
Makowski, Silk
    See Makowski, Silvia Ann
Makowski, Silvia Ann 1940- 101
Malam, John 1957- 152
    Earlier sketch in SATA *89*
Maland, Nick 195

Malcolm, Dan
    See Silverberg, Robert
Malcolm, Jahnna N.
    See Beecham, Jahnna
Malcolmson, Anne
    See von Storch, Anne B.
Malcolmson, David 1899-1978 6
Maletta, Dr. Arlene
    See Feltenstein, Arlene (H.)
Mali, Jane Lawrence 1937-1995 51
    Brief entry 44
    Obituary 86
Malkin, Nina 1959(?)- 179
Mallett, Jerry J. 1939- 76
Malley, Gemma 198
Malley, G.R.
    See Malley, Gemma
Mallory, Kenneth 1945- 185
    Earlier sketch in SATA *128*
Mallowan, Agatha Christie
    See Christie, Agatha (Mary Clarissa)
Malmberg, Carl 1904-1979 9
Malmgren, Dallin 1949- 65
Malo, John W. 1911-2000 4
Malone, James Hiram 1930- 84
Malone, Nola Langner 1930-2003 8
    Obituary 151
Malone, Patricia 1932- 155
Malone, Peter 1953- 191
Maloney, Pat
    See Markun, Patricia Maloney
Malory, Sir Thomas 1410(?)-1471(?) 59
    Brief entry 33
Maltese, Michael 1909(?)-1981
    Obituary 24
Malvasi, Meg Greene 143
Malvern, Corinne 1905-1956 34
Malvern, Gladys (?)-1962 23
Mama G.
    See Davis, Grania
Mammano, Julie (Lynn) 1962- 107
Mamonova, Tatyana 1943- 93
Manchel, Frank 1935- 10
Manchester, William (Raymond)
    1922-2004 65
Mandabach, Brian 1962(?)- 197
Mandel, Brett H. 1969- 108
Mandel, Peter 1957- 87
Mandel, Sally (Elizabeth) 1944- 64
Mandell, Muriel (Hortense Levin) 1921- 63
Manders, John 1957- 175
Manes, Stephen 1949- 99
    Brief entry 40
    Earlier sketch in SATA *42*
Manfred, Frederick (Feikema) 1912-1994 30
Mangin, Marie France 1940- 59
Mangione, Gerlando 1909-1998 6
    Obituary 104
Mangione, Jerre
    See Mangione, Gerlando
Mango, Karin N. 1936- 52
Mangurian, David 1938- 14
Mania, Cathy 1950- 102
Mania, Robert 1952- 102
Mania, Robert C., Jr.
    See Mania, Robert
Maniatty, Taramesha 1978- 92
Maniscalco, Joseph 1926- 10
Manley, Deborah 1932- 28
Manley, Seon 1921- 15
    See also CLR *3*
    See also SAAS *2*
Mann, Elizabeth 1948- 153
Mann, Josephine
    See Pullein-Thompson, Josephine (Mary
        Wedderburn)
Mann, Kenny 1946- 91
Mann, Pamela 1946- 91
Mann, Patrick
    See Waller, Leslie

Mann, Peggy
    See Houlton, Peggy Mann
Mannetti, Lisa 1953- 57
    Brief entry 51
Mannheim, Grete (Salomon) 1909-1986 10
Manniche, Lise 1943- 31
Manning, Jane K. 185
Manning, Mick 1959- 176
Manning, Rosemary 1911-1988 10
Manning, Sarra 162
Manning-Sanders, Ruth (Vernon)
    1895(?)-1988 73
    Obituary 57
    Earlier sketch in SATA *15*
Mannion, Diane
    See Paterson, Diane
Mannis, Celeste Davidson 173
Mannon, Warwick
    See Hopkins, (Hector) Kenneth
Manos, Helen 199
Mansir, A. Richard 1932- 170
Manson, Ainslie Kertland 1938- 115
Manson, Beverlie 1945- 57
    Brief entry 44
Manthorpe, Helen 1958- 122
Mantinband, Gerda (B.) 1917- 74
Manton, Jo
    See Gittings, Jo (Grenville) Manton
Manuel, Lynn 1948- 179
    Earlier sketch in SATA *99*
Manushkin, Fran 1942- 166
    Earlier sketches in SATA *7, 54, 93*
Manushkin, Frances
    See Manushkin, Fran
Man Without a Spleen, A
    See Chekhov, Anton (Pavlovich)
Manzano, Sonia 1950- 167
Mapes, Mary A.
    See Ellison, Virginia H(owell)
Maple, Marilyn 1931- 80
Mappin, Strephyn 1956- 109
Mara, Barney
    See Roth, Arthur J(oseph)
Mara, Jeanette
    See Cebulash, Mel
Marais, Josef 1905-1978
    Obituary 24
Marasmus, Seymour
    See Rivoli, Mario
Marbach, Ethel
    See Pochocki, Ethel (Frances)
Marcal, Annette B.
    See Callaway, Bernice (Anne)
Marcelino
    See Agnew, Edith J(osephine)
Marcellino, Fred 1939-2001 118
    Obituary 127
    Earlier sketch in SATA *68*
March, Carl
    See Fleischman, Sid
Marchant, Bessie 1862-1941
    See YABC *2*
Marchant, Catherine
    See Cookson, Catherine (McMullen)
Marcher, Marion Walden 1890-1987 10
Marchesi, Stephen 1951- 114
Marchesi, Steve
    See Marchesi, Stephen
    and Older, Effin
    and Older, Jules
Marchetta, Melina 1965- 170
Marciano, John Bemelmans 1970- 167
    Earlier sketch in SATA *118*
    See also CLR *93*
Marco, Lou
    See Gottfried, Theodore Mark
Marcus, Leonard S. 1950- 187
    Earlier sketch in SATA *133*
Marcus, Paul 1953- 82
Marcus, Rebecca B(rian) 1907- 9
Marcuse, Aida E. 1934- 89

Marek, Margot L. 1934(?)-1987
  Obituary 54
Maren, Julie 1970- 199
Margaret, Karla
  See Andersdatter, Karla M(argaret)
Margolin, Harriet
  See Ziefert, Harriet
Margolis, Jeffrey A. 1948- 108
Margolis, Leslie 187
Margolis, Richard J(ules) 1929-1991 86
  Obituary 67
  Earlier sketch in SATA 4
Margolis, Vivienne 1922- 46
Mariana
  See Foster, Marian Curtis
Marie, Geraldine 1949- 61
Mariner, Scott
  See Pohl, Frederik
Marino, Dorothy Bronson 1912- 14
Marino, Jan 1936- 114
Marino, Nick
  See Deming, Richard
Marino, Peter 1960- 179
Mario, Anna
  See Odgers, Sally Farrell
Marion, Henry
  See del Rey, Lester
Maris, Ron 71
  Brief entry 45
Mark, Jan 1943-2006 164
  Obituary 173
  Earlier sketches in SATA 22, 69, 114
  See also CLR 11
Mark, Janet Marjorie
  See Mark, Jan
Mark, Joan T. 1937- 122
Mark, Pauline (Dahlin) 1913-1997 14
Mark, Polly
  See Mark, Pauline (Dahlin)
Mark, Ted
  See Gottfried, Theodore Mark
Markel, Michelle 169
Marker, Sherry 1941- 76
Markert, Jennifer 1965- 83
Markert, Jenny
  See Markert, Jennifer
Markham, Lynne 1947- 102
Markham, Marion M. 1929- 60
Markham, Wendy
  See Staub, Wendy Corsi
Markins, W. S.
  See Jenkins, Marie M(agdalen)
Markle, Sandra L. 1946- 185
  Brief entry 41
  Earlier sketches in SATA 57, 92, 148
Markle, Sandra Lee
  See Markle, Sandra L.
Marko, Katherine D(olores) 28
Markoosie
  See Patsauq, Markoosie
Marks, Alan 1957- 187
  Earlier sketches in SATA 77, 151
Marks, Burton 1930- 47
  Brief entry 43
Marks, Graham 158
Marks, Hannah K.
  See Trivelpiece, Laurel
Marks, J.
  See Highwater, Jamake (Mamake)
Marks, J(ames) M(acdonald) 1921- 13
Marks, Laurie J. 1957- 68
Marks, Margaret L. 1911(?)-1980
  Obituary 23
Marks, Mickey Klar -1986 12
Marks, Peter
  See Smith, Robert Kimmel
Marks, Rita 1938- 47
Marks, Stan(ley) 14
Marks-Highwater, J.
  See Highwater, Jamake (Mamake)
Markun, Patricia Maloney 1924- 15

Markusen, Bruce (Stanley Rodriguez)
  1965- 141
Marley, Louise 1952- 173
  Earlier sketch in SATA 120
Marlin, Hilda
  See Van Stockum, Hilda
Marlow, Max
  See Nicole, Christopher (Robin)
Marlow, Susan K. 1953- 178
Marlowe, Amy Bell 67
  Earlier sketch in SATA 1
Marlowe, Jack
  See Deary, Terry
Marney, Dean 1952- 90
Marokvia, Artur 1909- 31
Marokvia, Mireille 1908-2008 5
  Obituary 197
Marokvia, Mireille Journet
  See Marokvia, Mireille
Marol, Jean-Claude 1946- 125
Marr, John S(tuart) 1940- 48
Marr, Melissa 1972- 189
Marric, J. J.
  See Butler, William Vivian
  and Creasey, John
Marrin, Albert 1936- 193
  Brief entry 43
  Earlier sketches in SATA 53, 90, 126
  See also CLR 53
Marriott, Alice Lee 1910-1992 31
  Obituary 71
Marriott, Janice 1946- 134
Marriott, Pat(ricia) 1920- 35
Marroquin, Patricio
  See Markun, Patricia Maloney
Mars, W. T.
  See Mars, Witold Tadeusz J.
Mars, Witold Tadeusz J. 1912-1985 3
Marsden, Carolyn 1950- 175
  Earlier sketch in SATA 140
Marsden, John 1950- 146
  Earlier sketches in SATA 66, 97
  See also CLR 34
  See also SAAS 22
Marsh, Carole 1946- 127
Marsh, Dave 1950- 66
Marsh, J. E.
  See Marshall, Evelyn
Marsh, James 1946- 73
Marsh, Jean
  See Marshall, Evelyn
Marsh, Joan F. 1923- 83
Marsh, Paul
  See Hopkins, (Hector) Kenneth
Marsh, Valerie 1954- 89
Marshall, Anthony D(ryden) 1924- 18
Marshall, Bonnie C. 1941- 141
  Earlier sketch in SATA 18
Marshall, Bridget M(ary) 1974- 103
Marshall, (Sarah) Catherine (Wood)
  1914-1983 2
  Obituary 34
Marshall, Douglas
  See McClintock, Marshall
Marshall, Edmund
  See Hopkins, (Hector) Kenneth
Marshall, Edward
  See Marshall, James
Marshall, Evelyn 1897-1991 11
Marshall, Felicity 1950- 116
Marshall, Garry 1934- 60
Marshall, H. H.
  See Jahn, (Joseph) Michael
Marshall, James 1942-1992 75
  Earlier sketches in SATA 6, 51
  See also CLR 21
Marshall, James Edward
  See Marshall, James
Marshall, James Vance
  See Payne, Donald Gordon
Marshall, Janet (Perry) 1938- 97

Marshall, Jeff
  See Laycock, George (Edwin)
Marshall, Kim
  See Marshall, Michael (Kimbrough)
Marshall, Michael (Kimbrough) 1948- 37
Marshall, Percy
  See Young, Percy M(arshall)
Marshall, S(amuel) L(yman) A(twood)
  1900-1977 21
Marsoli, Lisa Ann 1958- 101
  Brief entry 53
Marsten, Richard
  See Hunter, Evan
Marston, Elsa 1933- 156
Marston, Hope Irvin 1935- 127
  Earlier sketch in SATA 31
Marszalek, John F. 1939- 167
Marszalek, John Francis, Jr.
  See Marszalek, John F.
Marszalek, John Francis 1939-
  See Marszalek, John F.
Martchenko, Michael 1942- 154
  Earlier sketches in SATA 50, 95
Martel, Aimee
  See Thurlo, Aimee
  and Thurlo, David
Martel, Suzanne 1924- 99
Martignoni, Margaret E. 1908(?)-1974
  Obituary 27
Martin, Ann M. 1955- 192
  Brief entry 41
  Earlier sketches in SATA 44, 70, 126
  See also CLR 32
Martin, Bill, Jr. -2004
  See Martin, William Ivan, Jr.
Martin, Charles E(lmer)
  See Mastrangelo, Charles E(lmer)
Martin, Christopher
  See Hoyt, Edwin P(almer), Jr.
Martin, Claire 1933- 76
Martin, David Stone 1913-1992 39
Martin, Del 1921-2008 47
Martin, Donald
  See Honig, Donald
Martin, Dorothy
  See Martin, Del
Martin, Dorothy L.
  See Martin, Del
Martin, Eugene 1
Martin, Eva M. 1939- 65
Martin, Frances M(cEntee) 1906-1998 36
Martin, Francesca 1947- 101
Martin, Fred 1948- 119
Martin, Fredric
  See Christopher, Matt(hew Frederick)
Martin, George Raymond Richard
  See Martin, George R.R.
Martin, George R.R. 1948- 118
Martin, J(ohn) P(ercival) 1880(?)-1966 15
Martin, Jacqueline Briggs 1945- 188
  Earlier sketches in SATA 98, 149
Martin, Jane Read 1957- 84
Martin, Jeremy
  See Levin, Marcia Obrasky
Martin, Les
  See Schulman, L(ester) M(artin)
Martin, Linda 1961- 82
Martin, Lynne 1923- 21
Martin, Marcia
  See Levin, Marcia Obrasky
Martin, Marvin 1926- 126
Martin, Melanie
  See Pellowski, Michael (Joseph)
Martin, Nancy
  See Salmon, Annie Elizabeth
Martin, Patricia 200
Martin, Patricia A.
  See Martin, Patricia
Martin, Patricia Miles 1899-1986 43
  Obituary 48
  Earlier sketch in SATA 1

Martin, Peter
  See Chaundler, Christine
Martin, Rafe 1946- *175*
Martin, Rene 1891-1977 .... *42*
  Obituary *20*
Martin, Rupert (Claude) 1905- *31*
Martin, S. R.
  See Mappin, Strephyn
Martin, Stefan 1936- *32*
Martin, Vicky
  See Storey, Victoria Carolyn
Martin, Webber
  See Silverberg, Robert
Martin, Wendy
  See Martini, Teri
Martin, William Ivan, Jr. 1916-2004 .... *145*
  Brief entry *40*
  Earlier sketches in SATA *40, 67*
  See also CLR *97*
  See Martin, Bill, Jr.
Martineau, Diane 1940- *178*
Martineau, Harriet 1802-1876
  See YABC *2*
Martinet, Jeanne 1958- *80*
Martinez, Agnes *167*
Martinez, Arturo O. 1933- *192*
Martinez, Ed(ward) 1954- *98*
Martinez, Elizabeth Coonrod 1954- *85*
Martinez, Victor 1954- *95*
Martini, Teri 1930- *3*
Martini, Therese
  See Martini, Teri
Martino, Alfred C. 1964- *174*
Martinson, Janis
  See Herbert, Janis
Marton, Jirina 1946- *144*
  Earlier sketch in SATA *95*
Marton, Pierre
  See Stone, Peter
Martson, Del
  See Lupoff, Richard A(llen)
Martyr, Paula (Jane)
  See Lawford, Paula Jane
Maruki, Toshi 1912-2000 .... *112*
  See also CLR *19*
Marvin, Isabel R(idout) 1924- *84*
Marx, Patricia Windschill 1948- *160*
  Earlier sketch in SATA *112*
Marx, Robert F(rank) 1936- *24*
Marx, Trish
  See Marx, Patricia Windschill
Marzani, Carl (Aldo) 1912-1994 .... *12*
Marzollo, Jean 1942- *190*
  Autobiography Feature *190*
  Earlier sketches in SATA *29, 77, 130*
  See also SAAS *15*
Masefield, John (Edward) 1878-1967 .... *19*
Masoff, Joy 1951- *118*
Mason, Adrienne 1962- *163*
Mason, Cherie *170*
Mason, Edwin A. 1905-1979
  Obituary *32*
Mason, Ernst
  See Pohl, Frederik
Mason, F(rancis) van Wyck 1901-1978 .... *3*
  Obituary *26*
Mason, Frank W.
  See Mason, F(rancis) van Wyck
Mason, George Frederick 1904-2000 .... *14*
Mason, Miriam E(vangeline) 1900-1973 .... *2*
  Obituary *26*
Mason, Prue *195*
Mason, Simon 1962- *178*
Mason, Tally
  See Derleth, August (William)
Mason, Van Wyck
  See Mason, F(rancis) van Wyck
Mass, Wendy 1967- *196*
  Earlier sketch in SATA *158*
Mass, William
  See Gibson, William

Masselman, George 1897-1971 .... *19*
Massie, Dianne Redfield 1938- *125*
  Earlier sketch in SATA *16*
Massie, Elizabeth *108*
Masson, Sophie 1959- *179*
  Earlier sketch in SATA *133*
Masters, Anthony (Richard) 1940-2003 ...... *112*
  Obituary *145*
Masters, Kelly R(ay) 1897-1987 .... *3*
Masters, Mildred 1932- *42*
Masters, William
  See Cousins, Margaret
Masters, Zeke
  See Bensen, Donald R.
  and Goulart, Ron
Mastrangelo, Charles E(lmer) 1910-1995 ..... *70*
  Earlier sketch in SATA *69*
Masuda, Takeshi 1944- *56*
Matas, Carol 1949- *194*
  Autobiography Feature *112*
  Earlier sketch in SATA *93*
  See also CLR *52*
Matchette, Katharine E. 1941- *38*
Math, Irwin 1940- *42*
Mathabane, Mark 1960- *123*
Mather, Kirtley F(letcher) 1888-1978 .... *65*
Mathers, Petra 1945- *176*
  Earlier sketch in SATA *119*
  See also CLR *76*
Matheson, Richard (Christian) 1953- *119*
Matheson, Shirlee Smith 1942- *155*
Mathews, Eleanor
  See Mathews, Ellie
Mathews, Ellie 1946(?)- *193*
Mathews, Janet 1914-1992 .... *41*
Mathews, Judith
  See Goldberger, Judith M.
Mathews, Louise
  See Tooke, Louise Mathews
Mathiesen, Egon 1907-1976
  Obituary *28*
Mathieu, Joe 1949- *185*
  Brief entry *36*
  Earlier sketches in SATA *43, 94*
Mathieu, Joseph P.
  See Mathieu, Joe
Mathis, Sharon Bell 1937- *58*
  Earlier sketch in SATA *7*
  See also CLR *3*
  See also SAAS *3*
Matlin, Marlee 1965- *181*
Matlin, Marlee Beth
  See Matlin, Marlee
Matloff, Gregory 1945- *73*
Matott, Justin 1961- *109*
Matranga, Frances Carfi 1922- *78*
Matray, James I. 1948- *161*
Matray, James Irving
  See Matray, James I.
Matson, Emerson N(els) 1926- *12*
Matsui, Tadashi 1926- *8*
Matsuno, Masako
  See Kobayashi, Masako Matsuno
Matsuoka, Mei 1981- *192*
Matte, (Encarnacion) L'Enc 1936- *22*
Mattern, Joanne 1963- *122*
Mattheson, Jenny *180*
Matthews, Aline
  See De Wire, Elinor
Matthews, Andrew 1948- *138*
Matthews, Caitlin 1952- *122*
Matthews, Downs 1925- *71*
Matthews, Elizabeth 1978- *194*
Matthews, Ellen
  See Bache, Ellyn
Matthews, Ellen 1950- *28*
Matthews, Harold Downs
  See Matthews, Downs
Matthews, Jacklyn Meek
  See Meek, Jacklyn O'Hanlon
Matthews, John (Kentigern) 1948- *116*

Matthews, Laura S.
  See Matthews, L.S.
Matthews, Liz
  See Pellowski, Michael (Joseph)
Matthews, L.S. *183*
Matthews, Morgan
  See Pellowski, Michael (Joseph)
Matthews, Nicola
  See Browne, N.M.
Matthews, Patricia 1927-2006 .... *28*
Matthews, Patricia Anne
  See Matthews, Patricia
Matthews, Tina 1961- *190*
Matthews, Tom L.
  See Lalicki, Tom
Matthews, William Henry III 1919- *45*
  Brief entry *28*
Matthiessen, Peter 1927- *27*
Mattingley, Christobel (Rosemary) 1931- *85*
  Earlier sketch in SATA *37*
  See also CLR *24*
  See also SAAS *18*
Matulay, Laszlo 1912- *43*
Matus, Greta 1938- *12*
Maugham, W. S.
  See Maugham, W(illiam) Somerset
Maugham, W(illiam) Somerset 1874-1965 .. *54*
Maugham, William Somerset
  See Maugham, W(illiam) Somerset
Maurer, Diane Philippoff
  See Maurer-Mathison, Diane V(ogel)
Maurer, Diane Vogel
  See Maurer-Mathison, Diane V(ogel)
Maurer-Mathison, Diane V(ogel) 1944- *89*
Mauser, Pat Rhoads
  See McCord, Patricia
Mauser, Patricia Rhoads
  See McCord, Patricia
Maves, Mary Carolyn 1916- *10*
Maves, Paul B(enjamin) 1913-1994 .... *10*
Mavor, Salley 1955- *125*
Mawicke, Tran 1911- *15*
Max 1906-1989
  See Diop, Birago (Ismael)
Max, Peter 1939- *45*
Maxon, Anne
  See Best, (Evangel) Allena Champlin
Maxwell, Arthur S. 1896-1970 .... *11*
Maxwell, Edith 1923- *7*
Maxwell, Gavin 1914-1969 .... *65*
Maxwell, Katie
  See MacAlister, Katie
Maxwell, William (Keepers, Jr.) 1908-2000
  Obituary *128*
Maxwell-Hyslop, Miranda 1968- *154*
May, Charles Paul 1920- *4*
May, Elaine Tyler 1947- *120*
May, J. C.
  See May, Julian
May, Julian 1931- *11*
May, Robert Lewis 1905-1976
  Obituary *27*
May, Robert Stephen 1929-1996 .... *46*
May, Robin
  See May, Robert Stephen
Mayall, Beth *171*
Mayberry, Florence V(irginia) Wilson *10*
Maybury, Richard J. 1946- *72*
Maybury, Rick
  See Maybury, Richard J.
Mayer, Agatha
  See Maher, Ramona
Mayer, Albert Ignatius, Jr. 1906-1994
  Obituary *29*
Mayer, Ann M(argaret) 1938- *14*
Mayer, Bill *200*
Mayer, Danuta 1958- *117*
Mayer, Hannelore Valencak 1929- *42*
Mayer, Jane Rothschild 1903-2001 .... *38*
Mayer, Marianna 1945- *132*
  Earlier sketches in SATA *32, 83*

Mayer, Mercer 1943- 137
  Earlier sketches in SATA *16, 32, 73, 129*
  See also CLR *11*
Mayerson, Charlotte Leon 36
Mayerson, Evelyn Wilde 1935- 55
Mayfield, Katherine 1958- 118
Mayfield, Sue 1963- 146
  Earlier sketch in SATA *72*
Mayhar, Ardath 1930- 38
Mayhew, James (John) 1964- 149
  Earlier sketch in SATA *85*
Maynard, Olga 1920- 40
Mayne, William (James Carter) 1928- 122
  Earlier sketches in SATA *6, 68*
  See also CLR *123*
  See also SAAS *11*
Maynes, J. O. Rocky, Jr.
  See Maynes, J. Oscar, Jr.
Maynes, J. Oscar, Jr. 1929- 38
Mayo, Gretchen Will 1936- 163
  Earlier sketch in SATA *84*
Mayo, Margaret 1935- 165
  Earlier sketches in SATA *38, 96*
Mayo, Margaret Mary
  See Mayo, Margaret
Mayr, Diane 1949- 197
Mays, Lucinda L(a Bella) 1924- 49
Mays, (Lewis) Victor (Jr.) 1927- 5
Mazer, Anne 1953- 192
  Earlier sketches in SATA *67, 105*
Mazer, Harry 1925- 167
  Earlier sketches in SATA *31, 67, 105*
  See also CLR *16*
  See also SAAS *11*
Mazer, Norma Fox 1931- 198
  Earlier sketches in SATA *24, 67, 105, 168*
  See also CLR *23*
  See also SAAS *1*
Mazille, Capucine 1953- 96
Mazza, Adriana 1928- 19
Mazzio, Joann 1926- 74
Mbugua, Kioi Wa 1962- 83
McAfee, Carol 1955- 81
McAllister, Amanda
  See Dowdell, Dorothy (Florence) Karns
  and Hager, Jean
  and Meaker, Eloise
McAllister, Angela 182
McAllister, Margaret I. 1956- 169
  Earlier sketch in SATA *117*
McAllister, M.I.
  See McAllister, Margaret I.
McArdle, Paula 1971- 198
McArthur, Nancy 96
McAvoy, Jim 1972- 142
McBain, Ed
  See Hunter, Evan
McBain, Georgina 189
McBratney, Sam 1943- 164
  Earlier sketch in SATA *89*
  See also CLR *44*
McBrier, Michael
  See Older, Effin
  and Older, Jules
McCafferty, Jim 1954- 84
McCaffery, Janet 1936- 38
McCaffrey, Anne 1926- 152
  Autobiography Feature 152
  Earlier sketches in SATA *8, 70, 116*
  See also CLR *130*
  See also SAAS *11*
McCaffrey, Anne Inez
  See McCaffrey, Anne
McCaffrey, Mary
  See Szudek, Agnes S(usan) P(hilomena)
McCain, Becky Ray 1954- 138
McCain, Murray (David, Jr.) 1926-1981 7
  Obituary 29
McCall, Edith (Sansom) 1911- 6
McCall, Virginia Nielsen 1909-2000 13

McCall, Wendell
  See Pearson, Ridley
McCallum, Phyllis
  See Koch, Phyllis (Mae) McCallum
McCallum, Stephen 1960- 91
McCampbell, Darlene Z. 1942- 83
McCann, Edson
  See del Rey, Lester
  and Pohl, Frederik
McCann, Gerald 1916- 41
McCann, Helen 1948- 75
McCannon, Dindga 41
McCants, William D. 1961- 82
McCarter, Neely Dixon 1929- 47
McCarthy, Agnes 1933- 4
McCarthy, Colin (John) 1951- 77
McCarthy, Meghan 199
  Earlier sketch in SATA *168*
McCarthy, Ralph F. 1950- 139
McCarthy-Tucker, Sherri N. 1958- 83
McCarty, Peter 1966- 182
McCarty, Rega Kramer 1904-1986 10
McCaslin, Nellie 1914-2005 12
McCaughrean, Geraldine 1951- 173
  Earlier sketches in SATA *87, 139*
  See also CLR *38*
McCaughren, Tom 1936- 75
McCauley, Adam 1965- 128
McCay, (Zenas) Winsor 1869-1934 134
  Earlier sketch in SATA *41*
McClafferty, Carla Killough 1958- 137
McClary, Jane Stevenson 1919-1990
  Obituary 64
McCleery, Patsy R. 1925- 133
  Earlier sketch in SATA *88*
McClements, George 196
McClintock, Barbara 1955- 146
  Earlier sketches in SATA *57, 95*
McClintock, Marshall 1906-1967 3
McClintock, May Garelick
  See Garelick, May
McClintock, Mike
  See McClintock, Marshall
McClintock, Norah 178
McClintock, Theodore 1902-1971 14
McClinton, Leon 1933- 11
McCloskey, Kevin 1951- 79
McCloskey, (John) Robert 1914-2003 100
  Obituary 146
  Earlier sketches in SATA *2, 39*
  See also CLR *7*
McCloy, James F(loyd) 1941- 59
McClung, Robert M(arshall) 1916- 135
  Earlier sketches in SATA *2, 68*
  See also CLR *11*
  See also SAAS *15*
McClure, Gillian Mary 1948- 31
McColley, Kevin 1961- 80
  See also SAAS *23*
McConduit, Denise Walter 1950- 89
McConnell, James Douglas Rutherford
  1915-1988 40
  Obituary 56
McCord, Anne 1942- 41
McCord, David (Thompson Watson)
  1897-1997 18
  Obituary 96
  See also CLR *9*
McCord, Jean 1924- 34
McCord, Pat Mauser
  See McCord, Patricia
McCord, Patricia 1943- 159
  Earlier sketch in SATA *37*
McCord, Patricia Sue Rhoads Mauser
  See McCord, Patricia
McCormick, Brooks
  See Adams, William Taylor
McCormick, Dell J. 1892-1949 19
McCormick, (George) Donald (King)
  1911-1998 14
McCormick, Edith (Joan) 1934- 30

McCormick, Kimberly A. 1960- 153
McCormick, Patricia 1956- 181
  Earlier sketch in SATA *128*
McCourt, Edward (Alexander) 1907-1972
  Obituary 28
McCourt, Lisa 1964- 159
  Earlier sketch in SATA *117*
McCourt, Malachy 1931- 126
McCoy, Iola Fuller 3
McCoy, J(oseph) J(erome) 1917- 8
McCoy, Karen Kawamoto 1953- 82
McCoy, Lois (Rich) 1941- 38
McCrady, Lady 1951- 16
McCrea, James (Craig, Jr.) 1920- 3
McCrea, Ruth (Pirman) 1921- 3
McCreigh, James
  See Pohl, Frederik
McCrumb, Sharyn 1948- 109
McCue, Lisa 1959- 177
  Earlier sketch in SATA *65*
McCue, Lisa Emiline
  See McCue, Lisa
McCullen, Andrew
  See Arthur, Robert, (Jr.)
McCullers, (Lula) Carson (Smith)
  1917-1967 27
McCulloch, Derek (Ivor Breashur) 1897-1967
  Obituary 29
McCulloch, John Tyler
  See Burroughs, Edgar Rice
McCulloch, Sarah
  See Ure, Jean
McCullough, David 1933- 62
McCullough, David Gaub
  See McCullough, David
McCullough, Frances Monson 1938- 8
McCullough, Sharon Pierce 1943- 131
McCully, Emily Arnold
  See Arnold, Emily
McCune, Dan
  See Haas, Dorothy F.
McCunn, Ruthanne Lum 1946- 63
McCurdy, Michael (Charles) 1942- 147
  Earlier sketches in SATA *13, 82*
McCutcheon, Elsie (Mary Jackson) 1937- ... 60
McCutcheon, John 1952- 97
McDaniel, Becky Bring 1953- 61
McDaniel, Lurlene 1944- 146
  Earlier sketch in SATA *71*
McDaniels, Pellom III 1968- 121
McDaniels, Preston 1952- 192
McDearmon, Kay 20
McDermott, Beverly Brodsky 1941- 11
McDermott, Eleni 156
McDermott, Gerald (Edward) 1941- 163
  Earlier sketches in SATA *16, 74*
  See also CLR *9*
McDermott, Michael 1962- 76
McDevitt, Jack 1935- 155
  Earlier sketch in SATA *94*
McDevitt, John Charles
  See McDevitt, Jack
McDole, Carol
  See Farley, Carol (J.)
McDonald, Collin 1943- 79
McDonald, Gerald D(oan) 1905-1970 3
McDonald, Jamie
  See Heide, Florence Parry
McDonald, Janet 1953-2007 148
McDonald, Jill (Masefield) 1927-1982 13
  Obituary 29
McDonald, Joyce 1946- 164
  Earlier sketch in SATA *101*
McDonald, Lucile Saunders 1898-1992 10
McDonald, Mary Ann 1956- 84
McDonald, Megan 1959- 151
  Autobiography Feature 151
  Earlier sketches in SATA *67, 99, 148*
  See also CLR *94*
McDonald, Meme 1954- 112

McDonald, Mercedes 1956- *169*
  Earlier sketch in SATA *97*
McDonald, Rae A. 1952- *201*
McDonell, Chris 1960- *138*
McDonnell, Christine 1949- *115*
  Earlier sketch in SATA *34*
McDonnell, Flora (Mary) 1963- *146*
  Earlier sketch in SATA *90*
McDonnell, Kathleen 1947- *186*
McDonnell, Lois Eddy 1914-2001 .... *10*
McDonnell, Patrick 1956- *179*
McDonough, Yona Zeldis 1957- *73*
McElligott, Matt 1968- *196*
  Earlier sketch in SATA *135*
McElligott, Matthew
  See McElligott, Matt
McElmeel, Sharron L. 1942- *128*
McElmurry, Jill *198*
  Earlier sketch in SATA *159*
McElrath, William N. 1932- *65*
McElrath-Eslick, Lori 1960- *96*
McEntee, Dorothy (Layng) 1902- *37*
McEwen, Katherine *183*
McEwen, Robert (Lindley) 1926-1980
  Obituary *23*
McFadden, Kevin Christopher
  See Pike, Christopher
McFall, Christie 1918- *12*
McFall, Gardner 1952- *183*
McFarlan, Donald M(aitland) 1915- *59*
McFarland, Henry "Hammer"
  See McFarland, Henry O.
McFarland, Henry O. 1934- *143*
McFarland, Kenton D(ean) 1920- *11*
McFarland, Martha
  See Smith-Ankrom, M. E.
McFarlane, Leslie 1902-1977 .... *100*
  Earlier sketches in SATA *31, 1, 65, 67*
  See also CLR *118*
McFarlane, Leslie Charles
  See McFarlane, Leslie
McFarlane, Peter (William) 1940- *95*
McFarlane, Sheryl P. 1954- *86*
McFarlane, Todd 1961- *117*
McGaw, Jessie Brewer 1913-1997 .... *10*
McGee, Barbara 1943- *6*
McGee, Marni *163*
McGhee, Alison 1960- *196*
McGiffin, (Lewis) Lee (Shaffer) 1908-1978 ... *1*
McGill, Alice *159*
McGill, Ormond 1913- *92*
McGinley, Jerry 1948- *116*
McGinley, Phyllis 1905-1978 .... *44*
  Obituary *24*
  Earlier sketch in SATA *2*
McGinnis, Lila S(prague) 1924- *44*
McGinty, Alice B. 1963- *134*
McGivern, Justin 1985- *129*
McGivern, Maureen Daly
  See Daly, Maureen
McGivern, Maureen Patricia Daly
  See Daly, Maureen
McGough, Elizabeth (Hemmes) 1934- *33*
McGovern, Ann 1930- *132*
  Earlier sketches in SATA *8, 69, 70*
  See also CLR *50*
  See also SAAS *17*
McGowen, Thomas E. 1927- *109*
  Earlier sketch in SATA *2*
McGowen, Tom
  See McGowen, Thomas E.
McGrady, Mike 1933- *6*
McGrath, Barbara Barbieri 1953- *169*
  Earlier sketch in SATA *108*
McGrath, Robin 1949- *121*
McGrath, Thomas (Matthew) 1916-1990 ..... *41*
  Obituary *66*
McGraw, Eloise Jarvis 1915-2000 .... *67*
  Obituary *123*
  Earlier sketch in SATA *1*
  See also SAAS *6*

McGraw, William Corbin 1916-1999 .... *3*
McGreal, Elizabeth
  See Yates, Elizabeth
McGregor, Barbara 1959- *82*
McGregor, Craig 1933- *8*
McGregor, Iona 1929- *25*
McGrory, Anik *193*
McGuffey, Alexander Hamilton 1816-1896 . *60*
McGuigan, Mary Ann 1949- *106*
McGuire, Edna 1899- *13*
McGuire, Leslie (Sarah) 1945- *94*
  Brief entry *45*
  Earlier sketch in SATA *52*
McGuire, Robert *187*
McGuirk, Leslie (A.) 1960- *152*
McGurk, Slater
  See Roth, Arthur J(oseph)
McHargue, Georgess 1941- *77*
  Earlier sketch in SATA *4*
  See also CLR *2*
  See also SAAS *5*
McHenry, E.B. 1963(?)- *193*
McHugh, (Berit) Elisabet 1941- *55*
  Brief entry *44*
McIlvaine, Jane
  See McClary, Jane Stevenson
McIlwraith, Maureen Mollie Hunter
  See Hunter, Mollie
McInerney, Judith W(hitelock) 1945- *49*
  Brief entry *46*
McInerny, Ralph 1929- *93*
McInerny, Ralph Matthew
  See McInerny, Ralph
McKaughan, Larry (Scott) 1941- *75*
McKay, Donald 1895- *45*
McKay, Hilary (Jane) 1959- *145*
  Earlier sketch in SATA *92*
  See also SAAS *23*
McKay, Lawrence, Jr. 1948- *114*
McKay, Robert W. 1921- *15*
McKay, Sharon E. 1954- *165*
McKay, Simon
  See Nicole, Christopher (Robin)
McKean, Dave 1963- *197*
McKean, David Jeff
  See McKean, Dave
McKeating, Eileen 1957- *81*
McKee, David (John) 1935- *158*
  Earlier sketches in SATA *70, 107*
  See also CLR *38*
McKee, Tim 1970- *111*
McKeever, Marcia
  See Laird, Jean E(louise)
McKelvey, Carole A. 1942- *78*
McKelvy, Charles 1950- *124*
McKendrick, Melveena (Christine) 1941- *55*
McKendry, Joe 1972- *170*
McKenna, Colleen O'Shaughnessy 1948- .. *136*
  Earlier sketch in SATA *76*
McKenzie, Dorothy Clayton 1910-1981
  Obituary *28*
McKenzie, Ellen Kindt 1928- *80*
McKernan, Victoria 1957- *171*
McKie, Robin *112*
McKillip, Patricia A. 1948- *174*
  Earlier sketches in SATA *30, 80, 126*
McKillip, Patricia Anne
  See McKillip, Patricia A.
McKim, Audrey Margaret 1909-1999 .... *47*
McKimmie, Chris *194*
McKinley, Jennifer Carolyn Robin
  See McKinley, Robin
McKinley, Robin 1952- *195*
  Brief entry *32*
  Earlier sketches in SATA *50, 89, 130*
  See also CLR *127*
McKinney, Barbara Shaw 1951- *116*
McKinney, Nadine 1938- *91*
McKinty, Adrian *186*

McKissack, Fredrick L. 1939- *162*
  Brief entry *53*
  Earlier sketches in SATA *73, 117*
  See also CLR *55*
McKissack, Fredrick Lemuel
  See McKissack, Fredrick L.
McKissack, Patricia C. 1944- *195*
  Earlier sketches in SATA *51, 73, 117, 162*
  See also CLR *129*
McKissack, Patricia L'Ann Carwell
  See McKissack, Patricia C.
McKissack and McKissack
  See McKissack, Fredrick L.
  and McKissack, Patricia C.
McKown, Robin (?)-1976 .... *6*
McKy, Katie 1956- *184*
McLaren, Clemence 1938- *158*
  Earlier sketch in SATA *105*
McLaughlin, Frank 1934- *73*
McLaurin, Anne 1953- *27*
McLean, Andrew 1946- *172*
  Earlier sketch in SATA *113*
McLean, J. Sloan
  See Gillette, Virginia M(ary)
  and Wunsch, Josephine (McLean)
McLean, Jacqueline
  See Kolosov, Jacqueline
McLean, Janet 1946- *113*
McLean, Kathryn (Anderson) 1909-1966 ...... *9*
McLean, Virginia Overton 1946- *90*
McLean-Carr, Carol 1948- *122*
McLeish, Kenneth 1940-1997 .... *35*
McLenighan, Valjean 1947- *46*
  Brief entry *40*
McLennan, Connie *171*
McLennan, Will
  See Wisler, G(ary) Clifton
McLeod, Bob 1951- *173*
McLeod, Chum 1955- *95*
McLeod, Emilie Warren 1926-1982 .... *23*
  Obituary *31*
McLeod, Kirsty
  See Hudson, (Margaret) Kirsty
McLeod, Margaret Vail
  See Holloway, Teresa (Bragunier)
McLerran, Alice 1933- *137*
  Earlier sketch in SATA *68*
McLimans, David 1949- *182*
McLoughlin, John C. 1949- *47*
McManus, Patrick F. 1933- *46*
McManus, Patrick Francis
  See McManus, Patrick F.
McMeekin, Clark
  See McMeekin, Isabel McLennan
McMeekin, Isabel McLennan 1895-1973 .... *3*
McMenemy, Sarah 1965- *156*
McMillan, Bruce 1947- *192*
  Earlier sketches in SATA *22, 70, 129*
  See also CLR *47*
McMillan, Naomi
  See Grimes, Nikki
McMorey, James L.
  See Moyer, Terry J.
McMorrow, Annalisa 1969- *104*
McMullan, Jim 1934- *150*
  Earlier sketch in SATA *87*
McMullan, K. H.
  See McMullan, Kate
McMullan, Kate 1947- *189*
  Brief entry *48*
  Earlier sketches in SATA *52, 87, 132*
McMullan, Kate Hall
  See McMullan, Kate
McMurtrey, Martin A(loysias) 1921- *21*
McNabb, Linda 1963- *147*
McNair, Kate *3*
McNair, Sylvia 1924-2002 .... *74*
McNamara, Margaret C(raig) 1915-1981
  Obituary *24*
McNaught, Harry *32*

McNaughton, Colin 1951- *134*
  Earlier sketches in SATA *39, 92*
  See also CLR *54*
McNaughton, Janet 1953- *162*
  Earlier sketch in SATA *110*
McNeal, Laura *194*
McNeal, Tom *194*
McNeely, Jeannette 1918- *25*
McNeer, May (Yonge) 1902-1994 .... *81*
  Earlier sketch in SATA *1*
McNeese, Tim 1953- *139*
McNeill, Janet
  See Alexander, Janet
McNicholas, Shelagh *191*
McNickle, (William) D'Arcy 1904-1977
  Obituary *22*
McNicoll, Sylvia (Marilyn) 1954- *113*
  See also CLR *99*
McNulty, Faith 1918-2005 .... *168*
  Earlier sketches in SATA *12, 84, 139*
McPhail, David 1940- *183*
  Brief entry *32*
  Earlier sketches in SATA *47, 81, 140*
McPhail, David M.
  See McPhail, David
McPhail, David Michael
  See McPhail, David
McPhee, Norma H. 1928- *95*
McPhee, Richard B(yron) 1934- *41*
McPherson, James M. 1936- *141*
  Earlier sketch in SATA *16*
McPherson, James Munro
  See McPherson, James M.
McQueen, Lucinda 1950- *58*
  Brief entry *48*
McQueen, Mildred Hark 1908-1978 .... *12*
McQuillan, Mary *200*
McRae, Russell (William) 1934- *63*
McShean, Gordon 1936- *41*
Mc Swigan, Marie 1907-1962 .... *24*
McTavish, Sandy
  See Eyerly, Jeannette
McVeity, Jen *148*
McVey, Vicki 1946- *80*
McVicker, Charles (Taggart) 1930- *39*
McVicker, Chuck
  See McVicker, Charles (Taggart)
McWhirter, A(lan) Ross 1925-1975 .... *37*
  Obituary *31*
McWhirter, Norris (Dewar) 1925-2004 .... *37*
McWilliams, Karen 1943- *65*
Mdurvwa, Hajara E. 1962- *92*
Meacham, Margaret 1952- *95*
Meachum, Virginia 1918- *133*
  Earlier sketch in SATA *87*
Mead, Alice 1952- *146*
  Earlier sketch in SATA *94*
Mead, Margaret 1901-1978
  Obituary *20*
Mead, Russell (M., Jr.) 1935- *10*
Mead, Stella (?)-1981
  Obituary *27*
Meade, Ellen
  See Roddick, Ellen
Meade, Marion 1934- *127*
  Earlier sketch in SATA *23*
Meader, Stephen W(arren) 1892-1977 .... *1*
Meadmore, Susan
  See Sallis, Susan (Diana)
Meadow, Charles T(roub) 1929- *23*
Meadowcroft, Enid LaMonte
  See Wright, Enid Meadowcroft (LaMonte)
Meadows, Graham (W.) 1934- *161*
Meaker, M. J.
  See Meaker, Marijane
Meaker, Marijane 1927- *160*
  Autobiography Feature *111*
  Earlier sketches in SATA *20, 61, 99*
  See also CLR *29*
  See also SAAS *1*

Meaker, Marijane Agnes
  See Meaker, Marijane
Means, Florence Crannell 1891-1980 .... *1*
  Obituary *25*
  See also CLR *56*
Mearian, Judy Frank 1936- *49*
Mecca, Judy Truesdell 1955- *127*
Mechling, Lauren 1978(?)- *194*
Medary, Marjorie 1890-1980 .... *14*
Meddaugh, Susan 1944- *176*
  Earlier sketches in SATA *29, 84, 125*
Medearis, Angela Shelf 1956- *123*
  Earlier sketch in SATA *72*
Medearis, Mary 1915- *5*
Medina, Jane 1953- *167*
  Earlier sketch in SATA *122*
Medina, Nico 1982- *193*
Medlicott, Mary 1946- *88*
Mee, Charles L., Jr. 1938- *72*
  Earlier sketch in SATA *8*
Meek, Jacklyn O'Hanlon 1933- *51*
  Brief entry *34*
Meek, S(terner St.) P(aul) 1894-1972
  Obituary *28*
Meeker, Clare Hodgson 1952- *96*
Meeker, Oden 1919(?)-1976 .... *14*
Meeker, Richard
  See Brown, Fornan
Meeks, Esther MacBain *1*
Meggs, Libby Phillips 1943- *130*
Mehdevi, Alexander (Sinclair) 1947- *7*
Mehdevi, Anne (Marie) Sinclair 1947- *8*
Meidell, Sherry 1951- *73*
Meier, Minta 1906- *55*
Meighan, Donald Charles 1929- *30*
Meigs, Cornelia Lynde 1884-1973 .... *6*
  See also CLR *55*
Meilach, Dona Z(weigoron) 1926- *34*
Meilman, Philip W(arren) 1951- *79*
Meinstereifel, Ronald L. 1960- *134*
Meisel, Paul *184*
Melanson, Luc *198*
Melcher, Daniel 1912-1985
  Obituary *43*
Melcher, Frederic Gershom 1879-1963
  Obituary *22*
Melcher, Marguerite Fellows 1879-1969 ...... *10*
Melendez, Francisco 1964- *72*
Melhuish, Eva *199*
Melin, Grace Hathaway 1892-1973 .... *10*
Mellersh, H(arold) E(dward) L(eslie)
  1897- *10*
Melling, David *186*
Melmoth, Sebastian
  See Wilde, Oscar
Melnikoff, Pamela (Rita) *97*
Meltzer, Milton 1915- *201*
  Autobiography Feature *124*
  Earlier sketches in SATA *1, 50, 80, 128*
  See also CLR *13*
  See also SAAS *1*
Melville, Anne
  See Potter, Margaret
Melville, Herman 1819-1891 .... *59*
Melwood, Mary
  See Lewis, E. M.
Melzack, Ronald 1929- *5*
Memling, Carl 1918-1969 .... *6*
Menchin, Scott *188*
Mendel, Jo
  See Bond, Gladys Baker
  and Gilbertson, Mildred Geiger
Mendelson, Steven T. 1958-1995 .... *86*
Mendelson-Stevens, Serita Deborah
  See Stevens, Serita
Mendes, Valerie 1939- *157*
Mendez, Raymond A. 1947- *66*
Mendonca, Susan
  See Smith, Susan Vernon

Mendoza, George 1934- *41*
  Brief entry *39*
  See also SAAS *7*
Menendez, Shirley (C.) 1937- *146*
Meng, Cece *194*
Meng, Heinz (Karl) 1924- *13*
Mennen, Ingrid 1954- *85*
Menotti, Gian Carlo 1911-2007 .... *29*
  Obituary *180*
Menuhin, Sir Yehudi 1916-1999 .... *40*
  Obituary *113*
Menville, Douglas 1935- *64*
Menzel, Barbara Jean 1946- *63*
Mercati, Cynthia *164*
Mercati, Cynthia J.
  See Mercati, Cynthia
Mercer, Charles (Edward) 1917-1988 .... *16*
  Obituary *61*
Mercer, Jessie *21*
Mercer, Sienna *192*
Meredith, Arnold
  See Hopkins, (Hector) Kenneth
Meredith, David William
  See Miers, Earl Schenck
Meringoff, Laurene Krasny
  See Brown, Laurene Krasny
Meriwether, Louise 1923- *52*
  Brief entry *31*
Merlin, Arthur
  See Blish, James (Benjamin)
Merlin, Christina
  See Heaven, Constance (Christina)
Merriam, Eve 1916-1992 .... *73*
  Earlier sketches in SATA *3, 40*
  See also CLR *14*
Merrill, Jane 1946- *42*
Merrill, Jane Merrill
  See Merrill, Jane
Merrill, Jean (Fairbanks) 1923- *82*
  Earlier sketch in SATA *1*
  See also CLR *52*
Merrill, Phil
  See Merrill, Jane
Merriman, Alex
  See Silverberg, Robert
Merriman, Rachel 1971- *149*
  Earlier sketch in SATA *98*
Merrit, Elizabeth
  See Goudge, Eileen
Merski, Patricia K.
  See Merski, P.K.
Merski, P.K. *172*
Mertz, Barbara
  See Peters, Elizabeth
Mertz, Barbara Gross
  See Peters, Elizabeth
Merveille, David *200*
Merz, Jennifer J. *196*
Meschel, Susan V. 1936- *83*
Messenger, Charles (Rynd Milles) 1942- *59*
Messick, Dale 1906-2005 .... *64*
  Brief entry *48*
Messier, Claire 1956- *103*
Messieres, Nicole de
  See de Messieres, Nicole
Messinger, Carla *198*
Messmer, Otto 1892(?)-1983 .... *37*
Mesta, Gabriel
  See Moesta, Rebecca
Metcalf, Doris H(unter) *91*
Metcalf, Suzanne
  See Baum, L(yman) Frank
Metos, Thomas H(arry) 1932- *37*
Metter, Bert(ram Milton) 1927- *56*
Metzenthen, David 1958- *167*
  Earlier sketch in SATA *106*
Meunier, Brian 1954- *195*
Meyer, Barbara 1939- *77*

Meyer, Carolyn 1935- *142*
  Autobiography Feature *142*
  Earlier sketches in SATA *9, 70, 118*
  See also SAAS *9*
Meyer, Carolyn Mae
  See Meyer, Carolyn
Meyer, Edith Patterson 1895-1993 .... *5*
Meyer, F(ranklyn) E(dward) 1932- *9*
Meyer, Jean Shepherd *11*
Meyer, Jerome Sydney 1895-1975 .... *3*
  Obituary *25*
Meyer, June
  See Jordan, June
Meyer, Kerstin 1966- *190*
Meyer, L. A.
  See Meyer, Louis A(lbert), Jr.
Meyer, Louis A(lbert), Jr. 1942- *144*
  Earlier sketch in SATA *12*
Meyer, Renate 1930- *6*
Meyer, Stephenie 1973- *193*
  See also CLR *142*
Meyer, Susan E. 1940- *64*
Meyers, Susan 1942- *164*
  Earlier sketches in SATA *19, 108*
Meynell, Laurence Walter 1899-1989
  Obituary *61*
Meynier, Yvonne (Pollet) 1908- *14*
Mezey, Robert 1935- *33*
Micale, Albert 1913- *22*
Michael, James
  See Scagnetti, Jack
Michael, Livi 1960- *172*
Michael, Manfred
  See Winterfeld, Henry
Michael, Olivia
  See Michael, Livi
Michaels, Barbara
  See Peters, Elizabeth
Michaels, Jamie *195*
Michaels, Joanne Louise
  See Teitelbaum, Michael
Michaels, Kristin
  See Williams, Jeanne
Michaels, Molly
  See Untermeyer, Louis
Michaels, Neal
  See Teitelbaum, Michael
Michaels, Rune *194*
Michaels, Ski
  See Pellowski, Michael (Joseph)
Michaels, Steve 1955- *71*
Michaels, William M. 1917- *77*
Michel, Anna 1943- *49*
  Brief entry *40*
Michel, Francois 1948- *82*
Michelin, Linda *183*
Michelson, Richard *198*
  Earlier sketch in SATA *173*
Micich, Paul *74*
Micklish, Rita 1931- *12*
Micklos, John, Jr. 1956- *173*
  Earlier sketch in SATA *129*
Micklos J., John, Jr. 1956-
  See Micklos, John, Jr.
Micucci, Charles (Patrick, Jr.) 1959- *144*
  Earlier sketch in SATA *82*
Middleton, Haydn 1955- *152*
  Earlier sketch in SATA *85*
Miers, Earl Schenck 1910-1972 .... *1*
  Obituary *26*
Migdale, Lawrence 1951- *89*
Miglio, Paige 1966- *201*
Mikaelsen, Ben 1952- *173*
  Earlier sketches in SATA *73, 107*
Mikaelsen, Benjamin John
  See Mikaelsen, Ben
Miklowitz, Gloria D. 1927- *129*
  Earlier sketches in SATA *4, 68*
  See also SAAS *17*

Mikolaycak, Charles 1937-1993 .... *78*
  Obituary *75*
  Earlier sketch in SATA *9*
  See also SAAS *4*
Mild, Warren (Paul) 1922- *41*
Milelli, Pascal 1965- *135*
Miles, Betty 1928- *78*
  Earlier sketch in SATA *8*
  See also SAAS *9*
Miles, Miska
  See Martin, Patricia Miles
Miles, (Mary) Patricia 1930- *29*
Miles, Patricia A.
  See Martin, Patricia Miles
Miles, Victoria 1966- *188*
Milgrim, David *187*
  Earlier sketch in SATA *158*
Milgrom, Harry 1912-1978 .... *25*
Milhous, Katherine 1894-1977 .... *15*
Milich, Zoran *174*
Milios, Rita 1949- *79*
Militant
  See Sandburg, Carl (August)
Millais, Raoul 1901- *77*
Millar, Barbara F. 1924- *12*
Millar, Margaret (Ellis Sturm) 1915-1994 .... *61*
  Obituary *79*
Millbank, Captain H. R.
  See Ellis, Edward S(ylvester)
Millen, C(ynthia) M. 1955- *114*
Miller, Albert G(riffith) 1905-1982 .... *12*
  Obituary *31*
Miller, Alice Ann 1958- *150*
Miller, Alice P(atricia McCarthy) *22*
Miller, Debbie 1951- *160*
  Earlier sketch in SATA *103*
Miller, Debbie S.
  See Miller, Debbie
Miller, Deborah Uchill 1944- *61*
Miller, Don 1923- *15*
Miller, Doris R.
  See Mosesson, Gloria R(ubin)
Miller, Eddie
  See Miller, Edward
Miller, Edna Anita 1920- *29*
Miller, Edward 1905-1974 .... *8*
Miller, Edward 1964- *183*
Miller, Elizabeth 1933- *41*
Miller, Ellanita 1957- *87*
Miller, Eugene 1925- *33*
Miller, Frances A. 1937- *52*
  Brief entry *46*
Miller, Helen M(arkley) -1984 .... *5*
Miller, Helen Topping 1884-1960
  Obituary *29*
Miller, Jane (Judith) 1925-1989 .... *15*
Miller, Jewel 1956- *73*
Miller, John
  See Samachson, Joseph
Miller, Judi *117*
Miller, Kate 1948- *193*
Miller, Kirsten 1973- *185*
Miller, Louise (Rolfe) 1940- *76*
Miller, M. L. *85*
Miller, Madge 1918- *63*
Miller, Margaret J.
  See Dale, Margaret J(essy) Miller
Miller, Marilyn (Jean) 1925- *33*
Miller, Marvin *65*
Miller, Mary
  See Northcott, (William) Cecil
Miller, Mary Beth 1942- *9*
Miller, Mary Beth 1964- *185*
Miller, Maryann 1943- *73*
Miller, Natalie 1917-1976 .... *35*
Miller, Robert H. 1944- *91*
Miller, Ron 1947- *185*
Miller, Ruth White
  See White, Ruth C.
Miller, Sandra
  See Miller, Sandy

Miller, Sandra Peden
  See Miller, Sandy
Miller, Sandy 1948- *41*
  Brief entry *35*
Miller, Sarah 1969- *175*
Miller, Virginia
  See Austin, Virginia
Miller, William R. 1959- *116*
Milligan, Bryce 1953- *170*
Milligan, Spike
  See Milligan, Terence Alan
Milligan, Terence Alan 1918-2002 .... *29*
  Obituary *134*
  See also CLR *92*
Millington, Ada
  See Deyneka, Anita
Millman, Isaac 1933- *140*
Mills, Adam
  See Stanley, George Edward
Mills, Claudia 1954- *191*
  Brief entry *41*
  Earlier sketches in SATA *44, 89, 145*
Mills, Elaine (Rosemary) 1941- *72*
Mills, G. Riley *196*
Mills, Joyce C. 1944- *102*
Mills, Judith Christine 1956- *130*
Mills, Yaroslava Surmach 1925- *35*
Millspaugh, Ben P. 1936- *77*
Millstead, Thomas E. *30*
Milne, A. A. 1882-1956 .... *100*
  See also YABC *1*
  See also CLR *108*
Milne, Alan Alexander
  See Milne, A. A.
Milne, Lorus J. *5*
  See also CLR *22*
  See also SAAS *18*
Milne, Margery *5*
  See also CLR *22*
  See also SAAS *18*
Milne, Terry
  See Milne, Theresa Ann
Milne, Theresa Ann 1964- *84*
Milnes, Irma McDonough 1924- *101*
Milonas, Rolf
  See Myller, Rolf
Milord, Susan 1954- *200*
  Earlier sketches in SATA *74, 147*
Milotte, Alfred G(eorge) 1904-1989 .... *11*
  Obituary *62*
Milstein, Linda 1954- *80*
Milton, Ann *134*
Milton, Hilary (Herbert) 1920- *23*
Milton, John R(onald) 1924- *24*
Milton, Joyce 1946- *101*
  Brief entry *41*
  Earlier sketch in SATA *52*
Milverton, Charles A.
  See Penzler, Otto
Minahan, John A. 1956- *92*
Minar, Barbra (Goodyear) 1940- *79*
Minard, Rosemary 1939- *63*
Minarik, Else Holmelund 1920- *127*
  Earlier sketch in SATA *15*
  See also CLR *33*
Miner, Jane Claypool 1933- *103*
  Brief entry *37*
  Earlier sketch in SATA *38*
Miner, Lewis S. 1909-1971 .... *11*
Mines, Jeanette 1948- *61*
Mines, Jeanette Marie
  See Mines, Jeanette
Minier, Nelson
  See Stoutenburg, Adrien (Pearl)
Minnitt, Ronda Jacqueline
  See Armitage, David
Minor, Wendell 1944- *199*
  Earlier sketches in SATA *78, 109, 164*
Minter, Daniel 1961- *176*
Mintonye, Grace *4*

Miranda, Anne 1954- *109*
   Earlier sketch in SATA *71*
Mirocha, Paul *192*
Mirsky, Jeannette 1903-1987 .... *8*
   Obituary *51*
Mirsky, Reba Paeff 1902-1966 .... *1*
Misako Rocks! *192*
Mishica, Clare 1960- *91*
Miskovits, Christine 1939- *10*
Miss Frances
   See Horwich, Frances R(appaport)
Miss Read
   See Saint, Dora Jessie
Mister Rogers
   See Rogers, Fred McFeely
Mitchard, Jacquelyn 1956- *168*
   Earlier sketch in SATA *98*
Mitchell, Adrian 1932-2008 .... *166*
   Obituary *200*
   Earlier sketch in SATA *104*
Mitchell, Allison
   See Griffin, W.E.B
Mitchell, Betty Jo
   See Mitchell, B.J.
Mitchell, B.J. 1931- *120*
Mitchell, Clyde
   See Ellison, Harlan
   and Silverberg, Robert
Mitchell, Cynthia 1922- *29*
Mitchell, (Sibyl) Elyne (Keith) 1913- *10*
Mitchell, Gladys (Maude Winifred)
   1901-1983 .... *46*
   Obituary *35*
Mitchell, Jay
   See Roberson, Jennifer
Mitchell, Joyce Slayton 1933- *142*
   Brief entry *43*
   Earlier sketch in SATA *46*
Mitchell, K. L.
   See Lamb, Elizabeth Searle
Mitchell, Kathy 1948- *59*
Mitchell, Lori 1961- *128*
Mitchell, Margaree King 1953- *84*
Mitchell, Marianne 1947- *145*
Mitchell, Rhonda *89*
Mitchell, Stephen 1943- *199*
Mitchell, Todd 1974- *191*
Mitchell, Yvonne 1925-1979
   Obituary *24*
Mitchelson, Mitch
   See Mitchelson, Peter Richard
Mitchelson, Peter Richard 1950- *104*
Mitchison, Naomi (Margaret Haldane)
   1897-1999 .... *24*
   Obituary *112*
Mitchnik, Helen 1901-1982 .... *41*
   Brief entry *35*
Mitchum, Hank
   See Knott, William C(ecil, Jr.)
   and Murray, Stuart A. P.
   and Newton, D(wight) B(ennett)
   and Sherman, Jory (Tecumseh)
Mitgutsch, Ali 1935- *76*
Mitsuhashi, Yoko *45*
   Brief entry *33*
Mitton, Jacqueline 1948- *162*
   Earlier sketches in SATA *66, 115*
Mitton, Simon 1946- *66*
Mitton, Tony 1951- *149*
   Earlier sketch in SATA *104*
Miura, Taro 1968- *181*
Mizner, Elizabeth Howard 1907- *27*
Mizumura, Kazue *18*
Mlynowski, Sarah 1977(?)- *180*
Mobin-Uddin, Asma *172*
Mobley, Joe A. 1945- *91*
Moche, Dinah (Rachel) L(evine) 1936- *44*
   Brief entry *40*
Mochi, Ugo (A.) 1889-1977 .... *38*

Mochizuki, Ken 1954- *146*
   Earlier sketch in SATA *81*
   See also SAAS *22*
Modarressi, Mitra 1967- *200*
   Earlier sketch in SATA *126*
Modell, Frank B. 1917- *39*
   Brief entry *36*
Modesitt, Jeanne 1953- *143*
   Earlier sketch in SATA *92*
Modesitt, L.E., Jr. 1943- *164*
   Earlier sketch in SATA *91*
Modesitt, Leland Exton, Jr.
   See Modesitt, L.E., Jr.
Modrell, Dolores 1933- *72*
Moe, Barbara 1937- *20*
Moe, Jorgen (Ingebretsen) 1813-1882
   See CLR *104*
Moed-Kass, Pnina *169*
Moerbeek, Kees 1955- *98*
Moeri, Louise 1924- *93*
   Earlier sketch in SATA *24*
   See also SAAS *10*
Moesta, Rebecca 1956- *182*
Moffett, Jami 1952- *84*
Moffett, Martha (Leatherwood) 1934- *8*
Mogensen, Suzanne A(ncher) 1946- *129*
Mohammed, Khadra *197*
Mohn, Peter B(urnet) 1934- *28*
Mohn, Viola Kohl 1914- *8*
Mohr, Nicholasa 1938- *97*
   Autobiography Feature *113*
   Earlier sketch in SATA *8*
   See also CLR *22*
   See also SAAS *8*
Mok, Esther 1953- *93*
Molan, Christine 1943- *84*
Molarsky, Osmond 1909- *16*
Moldon, Peter L(eonard) 1937- *49*
Mole, John 1941- *103*
   Earlier sketch in SATA *36*
   See also CLR *61*
Molesworth, Mary Louisa 1839-1921 .... *98*
Molin, Charles
   See Mayne, William (James Carter)
Molina, Silvia 1946- *97*
Molk, Laurel 1957- *162*
   Earlier sketch in SATA *92*
Mollel, Tololwa M. 1952- *88*
Molloy, Anne Baker 1907-1999 .... *32*
Molloy, Michael (John) 1940- *162*
Molloy, Paul (George) 1924- *5*
Moloney, James 1954- *144*
   Autobiography Feature *144*
   Earlier sketch in SATA *94*
Momaday, N. Scott 1934- *48*
   Brief entry *30*
Momaday, Navarre Scott
   See Momaday, N. Scott
Monaco, Octavia 1963- *169*
Monagle, Bernie 1957- *121*
Moncure, Jane Belk 1926- *23*
Monjo, F(erdinand) N(icholas III)
   1924-1978 .... *16*
   See also CLR *2*
Monk, Isabell 1952- *136*
Monks, Lydia *189*
Monroe, Lyle
   See Heinlein, Robert A.
Monroe, Marion
   See Cox, Marion Monroe
Monroy, Manuel 1970- *196*
Monsell, Helen Albee 1895-1971 .... *24*
Monson-Burton, Marianne 1975- *139*
Montana, Bob 1920-1975
   Obituary *21*
Montecalvo, Janet *177*
Montenegro, Laura Nyman 1953- *95*
Montero, Gloria 1933- *109*
Montes, Marisa 1951- *144*
Montgomerie, Norah (Mary) 1913- *26*

Montgomery, Constance
   See Cappel, Constance
Montgomery, Elizabeth
   See Julesberg, Elizabeth Rider Montgomery
Montgomery, Elizabeth Rider
   See Julesberg, Elizabeth Rider Montgomery
Montgomery, Hugh (Edward) 1962- *146*
Montgomery, L(ucy) M(aud) 1874-1942 .... *100*
   See also YABC *1*
   See also CLR *91*
Montgomery, Raymond A. (Jr.) 1936- *39*
Montgomery, Rutherford George 1894-1985 . *3*
Montgomery, Sy 1958- *184*
   Autobiography Feature *132*
   Earlier sketches in SATA *114, 132*
Montgomery, Vivian *36*
Monthei, Betty *179*
Montijo, Rhode *179*
Montileaux, Donald F. 1948- *183*
Montpetit, Charles 1958- *101*
Montresor, Beni 1926-2001 .... *38*
   Earlier sketch in SATA *3*
   See also SAAS *4*
Montserrat, Pep *181*
Monty Python
   See Chapman, Graham
   and Cleese, John (Marwood)
   and Gilliam, Terry
   and Idle, Eric
   and Jones, Terence Graham Parry
   and Palin, Michael
Moodie, Craig 1956- *172*
Moodie, Fiona 1952- *133*
Moody, Minerva
   See Alcott, Louisa May
Moody, Ralph Owen 1898-1982 .... *1*
Moon, Carl 1879(?)-1948 .... *25*
Moon, Grace (Purdie) 1877(?)-1947 .... *25*
Moon, Lily
   See Warnes, Tim
Moon, Nicola 1952- *147*
   Earlier sketch in SATA *96*
Moon, Pat 1946- *113*
Moon, Sheila 1910-1991 .... *5*
   Obituary *114*
Moon, Sheila Elizabeth
   See Moon, Sheila
Mooney, Bel 1946- *95*
Mooney, Bill 1936- *122*
Mooney, Elizabeth C(omstock) 1918-1986
   Obituary *48*
Mooney, William
   See Mooney, Bill
Moor, Emily
   See Deming, Richard
Moorcock, Michael 1939- *166*
   Earlier sketch in SATA *93*
Moorcock, Michael John
   See Moorcock, Michael
Moore, Anne Carroll 1871-1961 .... *13*
Moore, Cheri
   See Ladd, Cheryl (Jean)
Moore, Clement Clarke 1779-1863 .... *18*
Moore, Cyd 1957- *186*
   Earlier sketches in SATA *83, 133*
Moore, Don W. 1905(?)-1986
   Obituary *48*
Moore, Elaine 1944- *86*
Moore, Eva 1942- *103*
   Earlier sketch in SATA *20*
Moore, Ishbel (Lindsay) 1954- *140*
Moore, Jack (William) 1941- *46*
   Brief entry *32*
Moore, Janet Gaylord 1905-1992 .... *18*
Moore, Jim 1946- *42*
Moore, John Travers 1908- *12*
Moore, Lilian 1909-2004 .... *137*
   Obituary *155*
   Earlier sketch in SATA *52*
   See also CLR *15*

Moore, Liz
  See Moore, M. Elizabeth
Moore, M. Elizabeth 1959- *156*
Moore, Margaret R(umberger) 1903- *12*
Moore, Margie *176*
Moore, Marianne (Craig) 1887-1972 .... *20*
Moore, Patrick (Alfred Caldwell) 1923- *49*
  Brief entry *39*
  See also SAAS 8
Moore, Patrick 1959- *184*
Moore, Perry *193*
Moore, Peter 1963- *175*
Moore, Peter G.
  See Moore, Peter
Moore, Ray (S.) 1905(?)-1984
  Obituary *37*
Moore, Regina
  See Dunne, Mary Collins
Moore, Rosalie (Gertrude) 1910-2001 .... *9*
Moore, Ruth (Ellen) 1908-1989 .... *23*
Moore, Ruth Nulton 1923- *38*
Moore, S(arah) E. *23*
Moore, Sarah Margaret
  See Hodges, Margaret
Moore, Tara 1950- *61*
Moore, Yvette 1958- *154*
  Earlier sketches in SATA 69, 70
Moores, Dick
  See Moores, Richard (Arnold)
Moores, Richard (Arnold) 1909-1986
  Obituary *48*
Mooser, Stephen 1941- *75*
  Earlier sketch in SATA 28
Mora, Francisco X(avier) 1952- *90*
Mora, Pat 1942- *186*
  Earlier sketches in SATA 92, 134
  See also CLR 58
Mora, Patricia
  See Mora, Pat
Morales, Yuyi *180*
  Earlier sketch in SATA 154
Moran, Tom 1943- *60*
Moranville, Sharelle Byars *196*
  Earlier sketch in SATA 152
Moray Williams, Ursula 1911-2006 .... *3*
  Obituary *177*
  See also SAAS 9
Mordvinoff, Nicolas 1911-1973 .... *17*
More, Caroline
  See Cone, Molly (Lamken)
  and Strachan, Margaret Pitcairn
Moreno, Rene King *190*
Moreton, Andrew Esq.
  See Defoe, Daniel
Morey, Charles
  See Fletcher, Helen Jill
Morey, Walt(er Nelson) 1907-1992 .... *51*
  Obituary *70*
  Earlier sketch in SATA 3
  See also SAAS 9
Morgan, Alfred P(owell) 1889-1972 .... *33*
Morgan, Alison (Mary) 1930- *85*
  Earlier sketch in SATA 30
Morgan, Anne 1954- *121*
Morgan, Christopher 1956- *199*
Morgan, Clay 1950- *198*
Morgan, Douglas
  See Macdonald, James D.
Morgan, Ellen
  See Bumstead, Kathleen Mary
Morgan, Geoffrey 1916- *46*
Morgan, Helen (Gertrude Louise)
  1921-1990 .... *29*
Morgan, Jane
  See Cooper, James Fenimore
  and Franklin, Jane (Morgan)
  and Moren, Sally M(oore)
Morgan, Lenore H. 1908-1976 .... *8*
Morgan, Mary 1957- *114*
  Earlier sketch in SATA 81

Morgan, McKayla
  See Basile, Gloria Vitanza
Morgan, Michaela
  See Basile, Gloria Vitanza
Morgan, Nicola 1961- *161*
Morgan, Nina 1953- *110*
Morgan, Pierr 1952- *122*
  Earlier sketch in SATA 77
Morgan, Robin (Evonne) 1941- *80*
Morgan, Roxanne
  See Gentle, Mary
Morgan, Sarah (Nicola) 1959- *68*
Morgan, Shirley
  See Kiepper, Shirley Morgan
Morgan, Stacy T(owle) 1959- *104*
Morgan, Stevie
  See Davies, Nicola
Morgan, Tom 1942- *42*
Morgan, Wendy
  See Staub, Wendy Corsi
Morgan-Vanroyen, Mary
  See Morgan, Mary
Morgenstern, Susie Hoch 1945- *133*
Mori, Hana 1909-1990(?) *88*
Mori, Kyoko 1957- *122*
  Autobiography Feature *126*
  See also CLR 64
  See also SAAS 26
Moriarty, Jaclyn *162*
Moriarty, William J. 1930- *127*
Morice, Dave 1946- *93*
Morin, Isobel V. 1928- *110*
Morine, Hoder
  See Conroy, John Wesley
Morley, Taia *199*
Morley, Wilfred Owen
  See Lowndes, Robert A(ugustine) W(ard)
Morningstar, Mildred (Whaley) 1912-1997 .. *61*
  Obituary *114*
Morozumi, Atsuko *110*
Morpurgo, Michael 1943- *184*
  Earlier sketches in SATA 93, 143
  See also CLR 51
Morrah, Dave
  See Morrah, David Wardlaw, Jr.
Morrah, David Wardlaw, Jr. 1914-1991 .... *10*
Morreale-de la Garza, Phyllis
  See De la Garza, Phyllis
Morressy, John 1930-2006 .... *23*
Morrill, Leslie H(olt) 1934-2003 .... *48*
  Brief entry *33*
  Obituary *148*
  See also SAAS 22
Morris, Chris(topher Crosby) 1946- *66*
Morris, Deborah 1956- *91*
Morris, Desmond 1928- *14*
Morris, Desmond John
  See Morris, Desmond
Morris, Don 1954- *83*
Morris, Gerald 1963- *150*
  Earlier sketch in SATA 107
Morris, Gerald Paul
  See Morris, Gerald
Morris, Gilbert (Leslie) 1929- *104*
Morris, Jackie *151*
Morris, Janet (Ellen) 1946- *66*
Morris, Jay
  See Tatham, Julie Campbell
Morris, (Margaret) Jean 1924- *98*
Morris, Jeffrey B(randon) 1941- *92*
Morris, Jennifer E. 1969- *179*
Morris, Jill 1936- *165*
  Earlier sketch in SATA 119
Morris, Juddi *85*
Morris, Judy K. 1936- *61*
Morris, Oradel Nolen *128*
Morris, Robert A(da) 1933- *7*
Morris, William 1913-1994 .... *29*
Morrison, Bill 1935- *66*
  Brief entry *37*

Morrison, Chloe Anthony Wofford
  See Morrison, Toni
Morrison, Dorothy Nafus *29*
Morrison, Frank 1971- *185*
Morrison, Gordon 1944- *183*
  Earlier sketches in SATA 87, 128
Morrison, Joan 1922- *65*
Morrison, Lillian 1917- *108*
  Earlier sketch in SATA 3
Morrison, Lucile Phillips 1896- *17*
Morrison, Martha A. 1948- *77*
Morrison, Meighan 1966- *90*
Morrison, P.R. *196*
Morrison, Richard
  See Lowndes, Robert A(ugustine) W(ard)
Morrison, Robert
  See Lowndes, Robert A(ugustine) W(ard)
Morrison, Roberta
  See Webb, Jean Francis (III)
Morrison, Susan Dudley
  See Gold, Susan Dudley
Morrison, Taylor 1971- *187*
  Earlier sketches in SATA 95, 159
Morrison, Toni 1931- *144*
  Earlier sketch in SATA 57
  See also CLR 99
Morrison, Velma Ford 1909- *21*
Morrison, Wilbur Howard 1915- *64*
Morrison, William
  See Samachson, Joseph
Morriss, James E(dward) 1932- *8*
Morrissey, Dean *183*
Morrow, Barbara Olenyik 1952- *167*
Morrow, Betty
  See Bacon, Elizabeth
Morse, C. Scott
  See Morse, Scott
Morse, Carol
  See Yeakley, Marjory Hall
Morse, C.S.
  See Morse, Scott
Morse, Dorothy B(ayley) 1906-1979
  Obituary *24*
Morse, Flo 1921- *30*
Morse, Scott 1973- *200*
Morse, Tony 1953- *129*
Mort, Vivian
  See Cromie, Alice Hamilton
Mortensen, Denise Dowling *179*
Mortimer, Anne 1958- *116*
Mortimer, Mary H.
  See Coury, Louise Andree
Morton, Alexandra (Hubbard) 1957- *144*
Morton, Anthony
  See Arthur, Robert, (Jr.)
Morton, Jane 1931- *50*
Morton, Joseph C. 1932- *156*
Morton, Lee Jack, Jr. 1928- *32*
Morton, Miriam 1918(?)-1985 .... *9*
  Obituary *46*
Mosatche, Harriet
  See Mosatche, Harriet
Mosatche, Harriet 1949- *122*
Moscow, Alvin 1925- *3*
Mosel, Arlene (Tichy) 1921-1996 .... *7*
Moseley, James W(illett) 1931- *139*
Moseng, Elisabeth 1967- *90*
Moser, Barry 1940- *185*
  Earlier sketches in SATA 56, 79, 138
  See also CLR 49
  See also SAAS 15
Moser, Don(ald Bruce) 1932- *31*
Moser, Laura *194*
Moser, Lisa *192*
Moses, Sheila P. 1961- *168*
Moses, Will 1956- *178*
  Earlier sketch in SATA 120
Mosesson, Gloria R(ubin) *24*
Mosher, Richard 1949- *120*
Moskin, Marietta D(unston) 1928- *23*
Moskof, Martin Stephen 1930- *27*

Mosley, Francis 1957- 57
Moss, Don(ald) 1920- 11
Moss, Elaine (Dora) 1924- 57
  Brief entry 31
Moss, Jeff(rey) 1942-1998 73
  Obituary 106
Moss, Marissa 1959- 163
  Earlier sketches in SATA 71, 104
  See also CLR 134
Moss, Miriam 1955- 140
  Earlier sketch in SATA 76
Moss, Thylias 1954- 108
Moss, Thylias Rebecca Brasier
  See Moss, Thylias
Most, Bernard 1937- 134
  Brief entry 40
  Earlier sketches in SATA 48, 91
Mosz, Gosia 1972- 194
Mott, Evelyn Clarke 1962- 133
  Earlier sketch in SATA 75
Motz, Lloyd 1909-2004 20
Mould, Edwin
  See Whitlock, Ralph
Mouly, Francoise 155
Mountain, Robert
  See Montgomery, Raymond A. (Jr.)
Mountfield, David
  See Grant, Neil
Mourlevat, Jean-Claude 1952- 187
Moussard, Jacqueline 1924- 24
Mowat, Claire 1933- 123
Mowat, Claire Angel Wheeler
  See Mowat, Claire
Mowat, Farley 1921- 55
  Earlier sketch in SATA 3
  See also CLR 20
Mowat, Farley McGill
  See Mowat, Farley
Mowll, Joshua 1970(?)- 188
Mowry, Jess 1960- 131
  Autobiography Feature 131
  Earlier sketch in SATA 109
  See also CLR 65
Moxley, Sheila 1966- 96
Moyer, Terry J. 1937- 94
Moyes, Patricia
  See Haszard, Patricia Moyes
Moyler, Alan (Frank Powell) 1926- 36
Mozelle, Shirley 179
Mozley, Charles 1915- 43
  Brief entry 32
Mphahlele, Es'kia 1919-2008 119
  Obituary 198
Mphahlele, Ezekiel
  See Mphahlele, Es'kia
Mphahlele, Zeke
  See Mphahlele, Es'kia
Mr. McGillicuddy
  See Abisch, Roslyn Kroop
Mr. Sniff
  See Abisch, Roslyn Kroop
Mr. Tivil
  See Lorkowski, Thomas V(incent)
Mr. Wizard
  See Herbert, Don
Mrs. Fairstar
  See Horne, Richard Henry Hengist
Muchamore, Robert 1972- 175
Muchmore, Jo Ann 1937- 103
Mude, O.
  See Gorey, Edward (St. John)
Mudgeon, Apeman
  See Mitchell, Adrian
Mueller, Jorg 1942- 67
  See also CLR 43
Mueller, Miranda R. 201
Mueller, Virginia 1924- 28
Muggs
  See Watkins, Lois
Muir, Diana
  See Appelbaum, Diana Muir Karter

Muir, Frank (Herbert) 1920-1998 30
Muir, Helen 1937- 65
Mukerji, Dhan Gopal 1890-1936 40
  See also CLR 10
Mulcahy, Lucille Burnett 12
Mulford, Philippa G. 1948- 112
  Earlier sketch in SATA 43
Mulford, Philippa Greene
  See Mulford, Philippa G.
Mulgan, Catherine 1931- 24
Mulila, Vigad G.
  See Maillu, David G(ian)
Mull, Brandon 1974- 190
Mullen, Michael 1937- 122
Muller, Billex
  See Ellis, Edward S(ylvester)
Muller, Jorg
  See Mueller, Jorg
Muller, (Lester) Robin 1953- 86
Mullin, Caryl Cude 1969- 130
Mullins, Edward S(wift) 1922- 10
Mullins, Hilary 1962- 84
Mulock, Dinah Maria
  See Craik, Dinah Maria (Mulock)
Mulvihill, William Patrick 1923- 8
Mumford, Ruth
  See Dallas, Ruth
Mumy, Bill 1954- 112
Mun
  See Leaf, (Wilbur) Munro
Munari, Bruno 1907-1998 15
  See also CLR 9
Munce, Ruth Hill 1898- 12
Mundy, Simon 1954- 64
Mundy, Simon Andrew James Hainault
  See Mundy, Simon
Munger, Nancy 170
Munowitz, Ken 1935-1977 14
Munoz, William 1949- 92
  Earlier sketch in SATA 42
Munro, Alice 1931- 29
Munro, Alice Anne
  See Munro, Alice
Munro, Eleanor 1928- 37
Munro, Roxie 1945- 184
  Earlier sketches in SATA 58, 136
Munsch, Bob
  See Munsch, Robert (Norman)
Munsch, Robert (Norman) 1945- 120
  Brief entry 48
  Earlier sketches in SATA 50, 83
  See also CLR 19
Munsinger, Lynn 1951- 177
  Earlier sketches in SATA 33, 94
Munson, Derek 1970- 139
Munson, R. W.
  See Karl, Jean E(dna)
Munson-Benson, Tunie 1946- 15
Munsterberg, Peggy 1921- 102
Muntean, Michaela 182
Munthe, Nelly 1947- 53
Munves, James (Albert) 1922- 30
Munzer, Martha E. 1899-1999 4
Murawski, Darlyne A. 193
Murch, Mel
  See Manes, Stephen
Murdoch, David H(amilton) 1937- 96
Murdoch, Patricia 1957- 192
Murdock, Catherine Gilbert 185
Murhall, J(acqueline) J(ane) 1964- 143
Murphy, Barbara Beasley 1933- 130
  Earlier sketch in SATA 5
Murphy, Claire Rudolf 1951- 137
  Earlier sketch in SATA 76
Murphy, E(mmett) Jefferson 1926- 4
Murphy, Jill (Frances) 1949- 142
  Earlier sketches in SATA 37, 70
  See also CLR 39

Murphy, Jim 1947- 185
  Brief entry 32
  Earlier sketches in SATA 37, 77, 124
  See also CLR 53
Murphy, Joseph E., Jr. 1930- 65
Murphy, Kelly 1977- 190
  Earlier sketch in SATA 143
Murphy, Louise 1943- 155
Murphy, Mary 1961- 196
Murphy, Pat
  See Murphy, E(mmett) Jefferson
Murphy, Patricia J. 1963- 132
Murphy, Rita 180
Murphy, Robert (William) 1902-1971 10
Murphy, Shirley Rousseau 1928- 126
  Earlier sketches in SATA 36, 71
  See also SAAS 18
Murphy, Stuart J. 1942- 157
  Earlier sketch in SATA 115
Murphy, Thomas Basil, Jr. 1935- 191
Murphy, Tim
  See Murphy, Jim
Murphy, Tom
  See Murphy, Thomas Basil, Jr.
Murray, John 1923- 39
Murray, Kirsty 1960- 165
  Earlier sketch in SATA 108
Murray, Marguerite 1917- 63
Murray, Marian 5
Murray, Martine 1965- 125
Murray, (Judith) Michele (Freedman)
  1933-1974 7
Murray, Ossie 1938- 43
Murray, Peter
  See Hautman, Pete
Murrow, Liza Ketchum 1946- 132
  Earlier sketch in SATA 78
Musgrave, Florence 1902-1999 3
Musgrove, Margaret W(ynkoop) 1943- 124
  Earlier sketch in SATA 26
Mussey, Virginia Howell
  See Ellison, Virginia H(owell)
Mussey, Virginia T.H.
  See Ellison, Virginia H(owell)
Mutel, Cornelia F. 1947- 74
Muth, Jon J. 165
Mutz
  See Kuenstler, Morton
Mwangi, Meja 1948- 174
My Brother's Brother
  See Chekhov, Anton (Pavlovich)
Myers, Anna 160
Myers, Arthur 1917- 91
  Earlier sketch in SATA 35
Myers, Bernice 81
  Earlier sketch in SATA 9
Myers, Caroline Elizabeth Clark
  1887-1980 28
Myers, Christopher 1975- 183
  See also CLR 97
Myers, Edward 1950- 172
  Earlier sketch in SATA 96
Myers, Elisabeth P(erkins) 1918- 36
Myers, (Mary) Hortense (Powner)
  1913-1987 10
Myers, Jack 1913-2006 83
  Obituary 178
Myers, Jack Edgar
  See Myers, Jack
Myers, Lou 1915-2005 81
  Obituary 171
Myers, Louis
  See Myers, Lou
Myers, R.E. 1924- 119
Myers, Robert Eugene
  See Myers, R.E.
Myers, Tim 1953- 176
  Earlier sketch in SATA 147
Myers, Timothy Joseph
  See Myers, Tim

Myers, Walter Dean 1937- *193*
  Brief entry *27*
  Earlier sketches in SATA *41, 71, 109, 157*
  See also CLR *110*
  See also SAAS *2*
Myers, Walter M.
  See Myers, Walter Dean
Myller, Rolf 1926-2006 .... *27*
  Obituary *175*
Myra, Harold L(awrence) 1939- *46*
  Brief entry *42*
Myracle, Lauren 1969- *162*
Myrus, Donald (Richard) 1927- *23*
Mysterious Traveler, The
  See Arthur, Robert, (Jr.)

N

Na, An *149*
Naaslund, Goorel Kristina 1940- *170*
Nadel, Laurie 1948- *74*
Naden, Corinne J. 1930- *166*
  Earlier sketch in SATA *79*
Nadimi, Suzan *188*
Nagda, Ann Whitehead *199*
Nagel, Andreas Fischer
  See Fischer-Nagel, Andreas
Nagel, Heiderose Fischer
  See Fischer-Nagel, Heiderose
Nagle, Shane *176*
Naidoo, Beverley 1943- *180*
  Earlier sketches in SATA *63, 135*
  See also CLR *29*
Nakae, Noriko 1940- *59*
Nakatani, Chiyoko 1930-1981 .... *55*
  Brief entry *40*
  See also CLR *30*
Nally, Susan W. 1947- *90*
Namioka, Lensey 1929- *157*
  Autobiography Feature *116*
  Earlier sketches in SATA *27, 89*
  See also CLR *48*
  See also SAAS *24*
Namovicz, Gene Inyart 1927- *6*
Nanji, Shenaaz 1954- *131*
Nanogak Agnes 1925- *61*
Napier, Mark
  See Laffin, John (Alfred Charles)
Napoli, Donna Jo 1948- *190*
  Earlier sketches in SATA *92, 137*
  See also CLR *51*
  See also SAAS *23*
Narahashi, Keiko 1959- *115*
  Earlier sketch in SATA *79*
Narayan, Rasipuram Krishnaswami
  See Narayan, R.K.
Narayan, R.K. 1906-2001 .... *62*
Nascimbene, Yan 1949- *173*
  Earlier sketch in SATA *133*
Nash, Bruce M(itchell) 1947- *34*
Nash, Frediric Ogden
  See Nash, Ogden
Nash, Linell
  See Smith, Linell Nash
Nash, Mary (Hughes) 1925- *41*
Nash, Ogden 1902-1971 .... *46*
  Earlier sketch in SATA *2*
Nash, Renea Denise 1963- *81*
Nast, Elsa Ruth
  See Watson, Jane Werner
Nast, Thomas 1840-1902 .... *51*
  Brief entry *33*
Nastick, Sharon 1954- *41*
Natale, Vince *196*
Natarajan, Srividya *187*
Nathan, Adele (Gutman) 1900(?)-1986
  Obituary *48*
Nathan, Amy *155*
  Earlier sketch in SATA *104*

Nathan, Dorothy (Goldeen) (?)-1966 .... *15*
Nathan, Robert (Gruntal) 1894-1985 .... *6*
  Obituary *43*
Nathanson, Laura Walther 1941- *57*
Natti, Lee 1919- *67*
  Earlier sketch in SATA *1*
  See also SAAS *3*
Natti, Susanna 1948- *125*
  Earlier sketch in SATA *32*
Nau, Thomas *186*
Naughtie, Eleanor
  See Updale, Eleanor
Naughton, Bill
  See Naughton, William John (Francis)
Naughton, James Franklin 1957- *85*
Naughton, Jim
  See Naughton, James Franklin
Naughton, William John (Francis)
  1910-1992 .... *86*
Navarra, John Gabriel 1927- *8*
Naylor, Penelope 1941- *10*
Naylor, Phyllis 1933- *152*
  Autobiography Feature *152*
  Earlier sketches in SATA *12, 66, 102*
  See also CLR *135*
  See also SAAS *10*
Naylor, Phyllis Reynolds 1933-
  See Naylor, Phyllis
Nazarian, Nikki
  See Nichols, Cecilia Fawn
Nazaroff, Alexander I(vanovich) 1898-1981 .. *4*
Nazoa, Aquiles 1920-1976 .... *198*
Neal, Harry Edward 1906-1993 .... *5*
  Obituary *76*
Neal, Michael
  See Teitelbaum, Michael
Nearing, Penny 1916- *47*
  Brief entry *42*
Nebel, Gustave E. *45*
  Brief entry *33*
Nebel, Mimouca
  See Nebel, Gustave E.
Nee, Kay Bonner *10*
Needham, Kate 1962- *95*
Needle, Jan 1943- *98*
  Earlier sketch in SATA *30*
  See also CLR *43*
  See also SAAS *23*
Needleman, Jacob 1934- *6*
Neel, David 1960- *82*
Neel, Preston 1959- *93*
Negri, Rocco 1932- *12*
Negrin, Fabian 1963- *189*
Neier, Aryeh 1937- *59*
Neigoff, Anne *13*
Neigoff, Mike 1920- *13*
Neilan, Eujin Kim 1969- *200*
Neilson, Frances Fullerton (Jones)
  1910-2001 .... *14*
Neimark, Anne E. 1935- *145*
  Earlier sketch in SATA *4*
Neimark, Paul G. 1934- *80*
  Brief entry *37*
Neitzel, Shirley 1941- *134*
  Earlier sketch in SATA *77*
Nell
  See Hanna, Nell(ie L.)
Nelscott, Kris
  See Rusch, Kristine Kathryn
Nelson, Blake 1960- *177*
Nelson, Catherine Chadwick 1926- *87*
Nelson, Cordner (Bruce) 1918- *54*
  Brief entry *29*
Nelson, Drew 1952- *77*
Nelson, Esther L. 1928- *13*
Nelson, Jim A.
  See Stotter, Mike
Nelson, Julie L. 1970- *117*
Nelson, Kadir *181*
  Earlier sketch in SATA *154*

Nelson, Kris
  See Rusch, Kristine Kathryn
Nelson, Lawrence E(rnest) 1928-1977
  Obituary *28*
Nelson, Marilyn 1946- *60*
  Autobiography Feature *180*
Nelson, Mary Carroll 1929- *23*
Nelson, O. Terry 1941- *62*
Nelson, Peter N. 1953- *73*
Nelson, R.A. *197*
Nelson, Richard K(ing) 1941- *65*
Nelson, Robin Laura 1971- *141*
Nelson, Roy Paul 1923- *59*
Nelson, S.D. *181*
Nelson, Sharlene (P.) 1933- *96*
Nelson, Suzanne 1976- *184*
Nelson, Ted (W.) 1931- *96*
Nelson, Theresa 1948- *143*
  Autobiography Feature *143*
  Earlier sketch in SATA *79*
Nemeth, Sally *187*
Neri, G. *197*
Neri, Greg
  See Neri, G.
Neri, Gregory
  See Neri, G.
Nerlove, Miriam 1959- *53*
  Brief entry *49*
Nesbit, E. 1858-1924 .... *100*
  See also YABC *1*
  See also CLR *70*
Nesbit, Edith
  See Nesbit, E.
Nesbit, Troy
  See Folsom, Franklin (Brewster)
Nespojohn, Katherine V(eronica) 1912-1975 . *7*
Ness, Evaline (Michelow) 1911-1986 .... *26*
  Obituary *49*
  Earlier sketch in SATA *1*
  See also CLR *6*
  See also SAAS *1*
Nestor, Larry 1940- *149*
Nestor, William P(rodromos) 1947- *49*
Nethery, Mary *93*
Neubecker, Robert *170*
Neuberger, Julia (Babette Sarah) 1950- *142*
  Earlier sketch in SATA *78*
Neufeld, John (Arthur) 1938- *131*
  Autobiography Feature *131*
  Earlier sketches in SATA *6, 81*
  See also CLR *52*
  See also SAAS *3*
Neuhaus, David 1958- *83*
Neumeyer, Peter F(lorian) 1929- *13*
Neurath, Marie (Reidemeister) 1898-1986 ..... *1*
Neuschwander, Cindy 1953- *157*
  Earlier sketch in SATA *107*
Neusner, Jacob 1932- *38*
Neville, Charles
  See Bodsworth, (Charles) Fred(erick)
Neville, Emily Cheney 1919- *1*
  See also SAAS *2*
Neville, Mary
  See Woodrich, Mary Neville
Nevins, Albert (Francis) J(erome)
  1915-1997 .... *20*
Nevius, Carol 1955- *186*
Newberger, Devra
  See Speregen, Devra Newberger
Newberry, Clare Turlay 1903-1970 .... *1*
  Obituary *26*
Newbery, John 1713-1767 .... *20*
Newbery, Linda 1952- *184*
  Earlier sketch in SATA *142*
Newbigging, Martha *198*
Newbold, Greg *199*
Newcomb, Ellsworth
  See Kenny, Ellsworth Newcomb
Newcombe, Eugene A. 1923-1990 .... *45*
  Brief entry *33*

Newcombe, Jack
    See Newcombe, Eugene A.
Newcome, Robert 1955- 91
Newcome, Zita 1959- 88
Newell, Crosby
    See Bonsall, Crosby Barbara (Newell)
Newell, Edythe W(eatherford) 1910-1989 11
Newell, Hope Hockenberry 1896-1965 24
Newfeld, Frank 1928- 26
Newgarden, Mark 1959- 194
Newlon, (Frank) Clarke 1905(?)-1982 6
    Obituary 33
Newman, Barbara Johansen 191
Newman, Daisy 1904-1994 27
    Obituary 78
Newman, Gerald 1939- 46
    Brief entry 42
Newman, Jerry 1935- 82
Newman, Leslea 1955- 134
    Earlier sketches in SATA *71, 128*
Newman, Margaret
    See Potter, Margaret
Newman, Marjorie 146
Newman, Matthew (Harrison) 1955- 56
Newman, Nanette 1934- 162
Newman, Robert (Howard) 1909-1988 87
    Obituary 60
    Earlier sketch in SATA *4*
Newman, Shirlee P(etkin) 144
    Earlier sketches in SATA *10, 90*
Newsom, Carol 1948- 92
    Earlier sketch in SATA *40*
Newsom, Tom 1944- 80
Newth, Mette 1942- 140
Newton, David E(dward) 1933- 67
Newton, James R(obert) 1935- 23
Newton, Jill 1964- 200
Newton, Robert 1965- 191
Newton, Suzanne 1936- 77
    Earlier sketch in SATA *5*
Ney, John 1923- 43
    Brief entry 33
Nez, John 155
Ng, Franklin 82
Nguyen, Vincent 187
Nichol, B(arrie) P(hillip) 1944-1988 66
Nicholas, Louise D.
    See Watkins, Dawn L.
Nicholls, Judith (Ann) 1941- 61
Nichols, Cecilia Fawn 1906-1987 12
Nichols, Grace 1950- 164
    Earlier sketch in SATA *98*
Nichols, Janet (Louise) 1952- 67
Nichols, Judy 1947- 124
Nichols, Leigh
    See Koontz, Dean R.
Nichols, Paul
    See Hawks, Robert
Nichols, Peter
    See Youd, Samuel
Nichols, (Joanna) Ruth 1948- 15
Nicholson, C. R.
    See Nicole, Christopher (Robin)
Nicholson, Christina
    See Nicole, Christopher (Robin)
Nicholson, Joyce Thorpe 1919- 35
Nicholson, Lois P. 1949- 88
Nicholson, Robin
    See Nicole, Christopher (Robin)
Nicholson, William 180
Nicholson, William 1872-1949
    See CLR *76*
Nickel, Barbara 1966- 188
Nickell, Joe 1944- 167
    Earlier sketch in SATA *73*
Nickelsburg, Janet 1893-1983 11
Nickerson, Betty 1922- 14
Nickerson, Elizabeth
    See Nickerson, Betty
Nickl, Barbara (Elisabeth) 1939- 56

Nicklaus, Carol 62
    Brief entry 33
Nickle, John 181
Nickless, Will 1902-1979(?) 66
Nic Leodhas, Sorche
    See Alger, Leclaire (Gowans)
Nicol, Ann
    See Turnbull, Ann
Nicolas
    See Mordvinoff, Nicolas
Nicolay, Helen 1866-1954
    See YABC *1*
Nicole, Christopher (Robin) 1930- 5
Nicoll, Helen 1937- 87
Nicolson, Cynthia Pratt 1949- 141
Ni Dhuibhne, Eilis 1954- 91
Niehaus, Paddy Bouma
    See Bouma, Paddy
Nields, Nerissa 1967- 166
Nielsen, Kay (Rasmus) 1886-1957 16
    See also CLR *16*
Nielsen, Laura F. 1960- 93
Nielsen, Laura Farnsworth
    See Nielsen, Laura F.
Nielsen, Nancy J. 1951- 77
Nielsen, Susin 1964- 195
Nielsen, Virginia
    See McCall, Virginia Nielsen
Nielsen-Fernlund, Susin
    See Nielsen, Susin
Niemann, Christoph 1970- 191
Nieuwsma, Milton J(ohn) 1941- 142
Nightingale, Sandy 1953- 76
Nikolajeva, Maria 1952- 127
Nikola-Lisa, W. 1951- 180
    Earlier sketch in SATA *71*
Niland, Deborah 1951- 172
    Earlier sketch in SATA *27*
Niland, Kilmeny 75
Nilsen, Anna 1948- 174
    Earlier sketch in SATA *96*
Nilsson, Eleanor 1939- 117
    Earlier sketch in SATA *81*
    See also SAAS *23*
Nilsson, Per 1954- 159
Nimmo, Jenny 1944- 144
    Earlier sketch in SATA *87*
    See also CLR *44*
Nishimura, Kae 196
Niven, Larry 1938- 171
    Earlier sketch in SATA *95*
Niven, Laurence VanCott
    See Niven, Larry
Nivola, Claire A. 1947- 140
    Earlier sketch in SATA *84*
Nix, Garth 1963- 143
    Earlier sketch in SATA *97*
    See also CLR *68*
Nixon, Hershell Howard 1923- 42
Nixon, Joan Lowery 1927-2003 115
    Obituary 146
    Earlier sketches in SATA *8, 44, 78*
    See also CLR *24*
    See also SAAS *9*
Nixon, K.
    See Nixon, Kathleen Irene (Blundell)
Nixon, Kathleen Irene (Blundell)
    1894-1988(?) 14
    Obituary 59
Nobati, Eugenia 1968- 201
Nobisso, Josephine 1953- 121
    Earlier sketch in SATA *78*
Noble, Iris (Davis) 1922-1986 5
    Obituary 49
Noble, Marty 1947- 125
    Earlier sketch in SATA *97*
Noble, Trinka Hakes 1944- 197
    Brief entry 37
    Earlier sketch in SATA *123*
Noda, Takayo 1961- 168
Nodelman, Perry 1942- 101

Nodset, Joan L.
    See Lexau, Joan M.
Noel Hume, Ivor 1927- 65
Noestlinger, Christine
    See Nostlinger, Christine
Noguere, Suzanne 1947- 34
Nolan, Dennis 1945- 166
    Brief entry 34
    Earlier sketches in SATA *42, 92*
Nolan, Han 1956- 157
    Earlier sketch in SATA *109*
Nolan, Janet 1956- 191
    Earlier sketch in SATA *145*
Nolan, Jeannette Covert 1897-1974 2
    Obituary 27
Nolan, Paul T(homas) 1919- 48
Nolan, William F(rancis) 1928- 88
    Brief entry 28
Nolen, Jerdine 1953- 157
    Earlier sketch in SATA *105*
Noll, Sally 1946- 82
Noonan, Brandon 1979- 184
Noonan, Diana 1960- 146
Noonan, Julia 1946- 148
    Earlier sketches in SATA *4, 95*
Norac, Carl 1960- 166
Norcross, John
    See Conroy, John Wesley
Nordan, Robert W(arren) 1934-2004 133
Nordhoff, Charles Bernard 1887-1947 23
Nordlicht, Lillian 29
Nordstrom, Ursula 1910-1988 3
    Obituary 57
Nordtvedt, Matilda 1926- 67
Norling, Beth 1969- 149
Norman, Charles 1904-1996 38
    Obituary 92
Norman, Howard
    See Norman, Howard A.
Norman, Howard A. 1949- 81
Norman, James
    See Schmidt, James Norman
Norman, Jay
    See Arthur, Robert, (Jr.)
Norman, Lilith 1927- 120
    Earlier sketch in SATA *86*
Norman, Mary 1931- 36
Norman, Steve
    See Pashko, Stanley
Norment, Lisa 1966- 91
Norris, Gunilla Brodde 1939- 20
North, Andrew
    See Norton, Andre
North, Anthony
    See Koontz, Dean R.
North, Captain George
    See Stevenson, Robert Louis (Balfour)
North, Captain George
    See Stevenson, Robert Louis (Balfour)
North, Howard
    See Trevor, Elleston
North, Joan 1920- 16
North, Milou
    See Erdrich, Louise
North, Robert
    See Withers, Carl A.
North, Sara
    See Bonham, Barbara Thomas
    and Hager, Jean
North, Sherry 201
North, Sterling 1906-1974 45
    Obituary 26
    Earlier sketch in SATA *1*
Northcott, (William) Cecil 1902-1987
    Obituary 55
Northeast, Brenda V(ictoria) 1948- 106
Northmore, Elizabeth Florence 1906-1974 . 122
Norton, Alice Mary
    See Norton, Andre

Norton, Andre 1912-2005 91
  Earlier sketches in SATA *1, 43*
  See also CLR *50*
Norton, Browning
  See Norton, Frank R. B(rowning)
Norton, Frank R. B(rowning) 1909-1989 ..... *10*
Norton, Mary 1903-1992 60
  Obituary *72*
  Earlier sketch in SATA *18*
  See also CLR *140*
Nosredna, Trebor
  See Anderson, Bob
Nostlinger, Christine 1936- *162*
  Brief entry *37*
  Earlier sketch in SATA *64*
  See also CLR *12*
Nourse, Alan E(dward) 1928-1992 .... *48*
  See also CLR *33*
Novak, Matt 1962- *165*
  Brief entry *52*
  Earlier sketches in SATA *60, 104*
Novelli, Luca 1947- *61*
Nowell, Elizabeth Cameron *12*
Noyes, Deborah 1965- *194*
  Earlier sketch in SATA *145*
Nugent, Nicholas 1949- *73*
Numeroff, Laura Joffe 1953- *142*
  Earlier sketches in SATA *28, 90*
  See also CLR *85*
Nunes, Lygia Bojunga 1932- *154*
  Earlier sketch in SATA *75*
Nunn, Laura (Donna) Silverstein 1968- *124*
Nurenberg, Thelma
  See Greenhaus, Thelma Nurenberg
Nurnberg, Maxwell 1897-1984 27
  Obituary *41*
Nussbaumer, Paul (Edmund) 1934- *16*
Nutt, Ken 1951- *163*
  Earlier sketch in SATA *97*
Nuttall-Smith, Margaret Emily Noel 1919- .. *26*
Nuygen, Mathieu 1967- *80*
Nuzum, K.A. *195*
Nyberg, (Everett Wayne) Morgan 1944- 87
Nyce, (Nellie) Helene von Strecker
  1885-1969 .... *19*
Nyce, Vera 1862-1925 .... *19*
Nye, Naomi Shihab 1952- *198*
  Earlier sketches in SATA *86, 147*
  See also CLR *59*
Nye, Robert 1939- 6
Nyikos, Stacy A. 1969- *164*
Nystrom, Carolyn 1940- *130*
  Earlier sketch in SATA *67*

O

Oakes, Elizabeth H. 1964- *132*
Oakes, Vanya 1909-1983 6
  Obituary *37*
Oakley, Don(ald G.) 1927- 8
Oakley, Graham 1929- 84
  Earlier sketch in SATA *30*
  See also CLR *7*
Oakley, Helen (McKelvey) 1906- *10*
Oana, Katherine 1929- 53
  Brief entry *37*
Oates, Eddie H. 1943- 88
Oates, Joyce Carol 1938- *159*
Oates, Stephen B(aery) 1936- 59
Obed, Ellen Bryan 1944- 74
Oberle, Joseph 1958- 69
Oberman, Sheldon 1949-2004 85
  Autobiography Feature *114*
  Obituary *153*
  See also CLR *54*
  See also SAAS *26*
Obligado, Lilian (Isabel) 1931- 61
  Brief entry *45*
Obrant, Susan 1946- *11*

O'Brian, E.G.
  See Clarke, Arthur C.
O'Brien, Anne Sibley 1952- 80
  Brief entry *48*
  Earlier sketch in SATA *53*
O'Brien, E.G.
  See Clarke, Arthur C.
O'Brien, Esse Forrester 1895(?)-1975
  Obituary *30*
O'Brien, Patrick 1960- *193*
O'Brien, Robert C.
  See Conly, Robert Leslie
O'Brien, Thomas C(lement) 1938- *29*
O'Callaghan, Julie 1954- *113*
O'Callahan, Jay 1938- 88
O'Carroll, Ryan
  See Markun, Patricia Maloney
Ochiltree, Dianne 1953- *117*
Ockham, Joan Price
  See Price, Joan
O'Connell, Margaret F(orster) 1935-1977 .... *30*
  Obituary *30*
O'Connell, Peg
  See Ahern, Margaret McCrohan
O'Connell, Rebecca 1968- *130*
O'Connor, Barbara 1950- *193*
  Earlier sketch in SATA *154*
O'Connor, Francine M(arie) 1930- 90
O'Connor, Genevieve A. 1914- 75
O'Connor, George *183*
O'Connor, Ian 1965- *188*
O'Connor, Jane 1947- *186*
  Brief entry *47*
  Earlier sketches in SATA *59, 103, 150*
O'Connor, Karen 1938- 89
  Earlier sketch in SATA *34*
O'Connor, Patrick
  See Wibberley, Leonard (Patrick O'Connor)
O'Connor, Richard 1915-1975
  Obituary *21*
O'Conor, Jane 1958- 78
Odaga, Asenath (Bole) 1937- *130*
  Earlier sketch in SATA *67*
  See also SAAS *19*
O Danachair, Caoimhin
  See Danaher, Kevin
Odanaka, Barbara *159*
O'Daniel, Janet 1921- 24
O'Day, Cathy
  See Crane, Barbara (Joyce)
O'Dell, Scott 1898-1989 .... *134*
  Earlier sketches in SATA *12, 60*
  See also CLR *126*
Odenwald, Robert P(aul) 1899-1965 .... *11*
Odgers, Sally
  See Odgers, Sally Farrell
Odgers, Sally Farrell 1957- *139*
  Earlier sketch in SATA *72*
O'Donnell, Dick
  See Lupoff, Richard A(llen)
  and Thompson, Don(ald Arthur)
Odriozola, Elena *186*
Oechsli, Kelly 1918-1999 5
Oesterle, Virginia Rorby
  See Rorby, Ginny
Ofek, Uriel 1926- 36
  See also CLR *28*
Offenbacher, Ami 1958- 91
Offit, Sidney 1928- 10
Ofosu-Appiah, L(awrence) H(enry) 1920- ... *13*
Ogan, George F. 1912-1983 .... *13*
Ogan, M. G.
  See Ogan, George F.
  and Ogan, Margaret E. (Nettles)
Ogan, Margaret E. (Nettles) 1923-1979 .... *13*
Ogburn, Charlton (Jr.) 1911-1998 3
  Obituary *109*
Ogburn, Jacqueline K. *162*
Ogilvie, Elisabeth May 1917-2006 40
  Brief entry *29*
  Obituary *176*

Ogilvy, Gavin
  See Barrie, J(ames) M(atthew)
Ogilvy, Ian 1943- *177*
Ogilvy, Ian Raymond
  See Ogilvy, Ian
Ogle, Lucille Edith 1904-1988
  Obituary 59
Ogletree, Charles J. 1952- *175*
O'Green, Jennifer
  See Roberson, Jennifer
O'Green, Jennifer Roberson
  See Roberson, Jennifer
O'Hagan, Caroline 1946- 38
O'Hanlon, Jacklyn
  See Meek, Jacklyn O'Hanlon
O'Hara, Elizabeth
  See Ni Dhuibhne, Eilis
O'Hara, Kenneth
  See Morris, (Margaret) Jean
O'Hara, Mary
  See Alsop, Mary O'Hara
O'Hara (Alsop), Mary
  See Alsop, Mary O'Hara
O'Hare, Jeff(rey A.) 1958- *105*
Ohi, Ruth 1964- 95
Ohiyesa
  See Eastman, Charles A(lexander)
Ohlsson, Ib 1935- 7
Ohmi, Ayano 1959- *115*
Ohtomo, Yasuo 1946- 37
o huigin, sean 1942- *138*
  See also CLR *75*
Oiseau
  See Moseley, James W(illett)
Oke, Janette 1935- 97
O'Keefe, Susan Heyboer *176*
  Earlier sketch in SATA *133*
O'Keeffe, Frank 1938- 99
O'Kelley, Mattie Lou 1908-1997 97
  Earlier sketch in SATA *36*
Okimoto, Jean Davies 1942- *103*
  Earlier sketch in SATA *34*
Okomfo, Amasewa
  See Cousins, Linda
olafsdottir, Gudrun Elin
  See Gunnella
Olaleye, Isaac O. 1941- 96
  See also SAAS *23*
Olcott, Frances Jenkins 1872(?)-1963 .... *19*
Old, Wendie C(orbin) 1943- *154*
Old Boy
  See Hughes, Thomas
Oldenburg, E(gbert) William 1936-1974 35
Older, Effin 1942- *114*
Older, Jules 1940- *156*
  Earlier sketch in SATA *114*
Oldfield, Jenny 1949- *140*
Oldfield, Margaret J(ean) 1932- 56
Oldfield, Pamela 1931- 86
Oldham, June 70
Oldham, Mary 1944- 65
Olds, Elizabeth 1896-1991 3
  Obituary 66
Olds, Helen Diehl 1895-1981 9
  Obituary 25
Oldstyle, Jonathan
  See Irving, Washington
O'Leary, Brian (Todd) 1940- 6
O'Leary, Patsy B(aker) 1937- 97
Oliphant, B.J.
  See Tepper, Sheri S.
Oliver, Burton
  See Burt, Olive Woolley
Oliver, Chad
  See Oliver, Symmes C.
Oliver, John Edward 1933- 21
Oliver, Marilyn Tower 1935- 89
Oliver, Narelle 1960- *197*
  Earlier sketch in SATA *152*
Oliver, Shirley (Louise Dawkins) 1958- 74
Oliver, Symmes C. 1928-1993 .... *101*

Oliviero, Jamie 1950- *84*
Olmsted, Lorena Ann 1890-1989 .... *13*
Olney, Ross R. 1929- *13*
Olschewski, Alfred (Erich) 1920- *7*
Olsen, Barbara *148*
Olsen, Carol 1945- *89*
Olsen, Ib Spang 1921- *81*
  Earlier sketch in SATA *6*
Olsen, Violet (Mae) 1922-1991 .... *58*
Olson, Arielle North 1932- *67*
Olson, David J. 1974- *198*
Olson, Gene 1922- *32*
Olson, Gretchen *187*
Olson, Helen Kronberg *48*
Olson, Kay Melchisedech 1948- *175*
Olson, Marianne
  See Mitchell, Marianne
Olson-Brown, Ellen 1967- *183*
Olten, Manuela 1970- *197*
Olugebefola, Ademole 1941- *15*
Oluonye, Mary N(kechi) 1955- *111*
Om
  See Gorey, Edward (St. John)
O'Malley, Kevin 1961- *191*
  Earlier sketch in SATA *157*
Oman, Carola (Mary Anima) 1897-1978 ..... *35*
O'Mara, Carmel 1965- *166*
O'Mara-Horwitz, Carmel
  See O'Mara, Carmel
O'Meara, Walter (Andrew) 1897-1989 .... *65*
Ommanney, F(rancis) D(ownes) 1903-1980 . *23*
O Mude
  See Gorey, Edward (St. John)
Oneal, Elizabeth 1934- *82*
  Earlier sketch in SATA *30*
  See also CLR *13*
O'Neal, Reagan
  See Jordan, Robert
O'Neal, Regan
  See Jordan, Robert
Oneal, Zibby
  See Oneal, Elizabeth
O'Neill, Amanda 1951- *111*
O'Neill, Gerard K(itchen) 1927-1992 .... *65*
O'Neill, Judith (Beatrice) 1930- *34*
O'Neill, Mary L(e Duc) 1908(?)-1990 .... *2*
  Obituary *64*
O'Neill, Reagan
  See Jordan, Robert
Onslow, Annette Rosemary MacArthur
  See MacArthur-Onslow, Annette Rosemary
Onslow, John 1906-1985
  Obituary *47*
Onyefulu, Ifeoma 1959- *157*
  Earlier sketches in SATA *81, 115*
Opie, Iona (Margaret Balfour) 1923- *118*
  Earlier sketches in SATA *3, 63*
  See also SAAS *6*
Opie, Peter (Mason) 1918-1982 .... *118*
  Obituary *28*
  Earlier sketches in SATA *3, 63*
Oppel, Kenneth 1967- *199*
  Earlier sketches in SATA *99, 153*
Oppel, Kenneth Kerry
  See Oppel, Kenneth
Oppenheim, Joanne 1934- *174*
  Earlier sketches in SATA *5, 82, 136*
Oppenheim, Shulamith Levey 1928- *177*
Oppenheimer, Joan L(etson) 1925- *28*
Oppong, Joseph Ransford 1953- *160*
Optic, Oliver
  See Adams, William Taylor
  and Stratemeyer, Edward L.
Oram, Hiawyn 1946- *101*
  Earlier sketch in SATA *56*
Orbach, Ruth Gary 1941- *21*
Orback, Craig *197*
Orczy, Emma
  See Orczy, Baroness Emmuska
Orczy, Emma Magdalena Rosalia Maria Josefa
  See Orczy, Baroness Emmuska

Orczy, Emmuska
  See Orczy, Baroness Emmuska
Orczy, Baroness Emmuska 1865-1947 .... *40*
Orde, A.J.
  See Tepper, Sheri S.
O'Reilly, Jackson
  See Jordan, Robert
Orenstein, Denise Gosliner 1950- *157*
Orgad, Dorit 1936- *199*
Orgel, Doris 1929- *148*
  Earlier sketches in SATA *7, 85*
  See also CLR *48*
  See also SAAS *19*
Orgill, Roxane *198*
Oriolo, Joe
  See Oriolo, Joseph D.
Oriolo, Joseph D. 1913-1985
  Obituary *46*
Orleans, Ilo 1897-1962 .... *10*
Orlev, Uri 1931- *135*
  Earlier sketch in SATA *58*
  See also CLR *30*
  See also SAAS *19*
Ormai, Stella *57*
  Brief entry *48*
Ormerod, Jan 1946- *132*
  Brief entry *44*
  Earlier sketches in SATA *55, 70*
  See also CLR *20*
Ormes, Jackie
  See Ormes, Zelda J.
Ormes, Zelda J. 1914-1986
  Obituary *47*
Ormondroyd, Edward 1925- *14*
Ormsby, Virginia H(aire) 1906-1990 .... *11*
Orona-Ramirez, Kristy 1964- *189*
Orozco, Jose-Luis 1948- *179*
Orr, Katherine S(helley) 1950- *72*
Orr, Wendy 1953- *141*
  Earlier sketch in SATA *90*
Orris
  See Ingelow, Jean
Orth, Richard
  See Gardner, Richard (M.)
Ortiz Cofer, Judith
  See Cofer, Judith Ortiz
Orwell, George
  See Blair, Eric
Orwin, Joanna 1944- *141*
Osborn, Elinor 1939- *145*
Osborn, Kathy 1955(?)- *199*
Osborn, Lois D(orothy) 1915- *61*
Osborne, Charles 1927- *59*
Osborne, Chester G(orham) 1915-1987 .... *11*
Osborne, David
  See Silverberg, Robert
Osborne, George
  See Silverberg, Robert
Osborne, Leone Neal 1914-1996 .... *2*
Osborne, Mary Pope 1949- *144*
  Earlier sketches in SATA *41, 55, 98*
  See also CLR *88*
Osceola
  See Blixen, Karen
Osgood, William E(dward) 1926- *37*
O'Shaughnessy, Darren
  See Shan, Darren
O'Shaughnessy, Ellen Cassels 1937- *78*
O'Shea, Catherine Patricia Shiels
  See O'Shea, Pat
O'Shea, Pat 1931-2007 .... *87*
  See also CLR *18*
Osmond, Edward 1900- *10*
Ossoli, Sarah Margaret 1810-1850 .... *25*
Ostendorf, (Arthur) Lloyd, (Jr.) 1921-2000 .. *65*
  Obituary *125*
Ostow, Micol 1976- *170*
Otfinoski, Steven 1949- *116*
  Earlier sketch in SATA *56*
Otis, James
  See Kaler, James Otis

O'Toole, Thomas 1941- *71*
O'Trigger, Sir Lucius
  See Horne, Richard Henry Hengist
Otten, Charlotte
  See Otten, Charlotte F.
Otten, Charlotte F. 1926- *98*
Otten, Charlotte Fennema
  See Otten, Charlotte F.
Ottley, Matt 1962- *171*
  Earlier sketch in SATA *102*
Ottley, Reginald Leslie 1909-1985 .... *26*
  See also CLR *16*
Otto, Margaret Glover 1909-1976
  Obituary *30*
Otto, Svend
  See Soerensen, Svend Otto
Oughton, Jerrie (Preston) 1937- *131*
  Earlier sketch in SATA *76*
Oughton, (William) Taylor 1925- *104*
Ouida
  See De La Ramee, Marie Louise
Ousley, Odille 1896-1976 .... *10*
Outcalt, Todd 1960- *123*
Overmyer, James E. 1946- *88*
Overton, Jenny (Margaret Mary) 1942- *52*
  Brief entry *36*
Owen, Ann
  See Qualey, Marsha
Owen, Annie 1949- *75*
Owen, Caroline Dale
  See Snedeker, Caroline Dale (Parke)
Owen, Clifford
  See Hamilton, Charles (Harold St. John)
Owen, Dilys
  See Gater, Dilys
Owen, (Benjamin) Evan 1918-1984 .... *38*
Owen, (John) Gareth 1936-2002 .... *162*
  Earlier sketch in SATA *83*
  See also CLR *31*
  See also SAAS *14*
Owen, James A. *185*
Owens, Bryant 1968- *116*
Owens, Dana Elaine
  See Queen Latifah
Owens, Gail 1939- *54*
Owens, Mary Beth *191*
Owens, Thomas S(heldon) 1960- *86*
Owens, Tom
  See Owens, Thomas S(heldon)
Oxenbury, Helen 1938- *149*
  Earlier sketches in SATA *3, 68*
  See also CLR *70*
Oxendine, Bess Holland 1933- *90*
Oz, Frank (Richard) 1944- *60*
Ozer, Jerome S. 1927- *59*

P

Paananen, Eloise (Katherine) 1923-1993 .... *9*
Pace, Lorenzo 1943- *131*
Pace, Mildred Mastin 1907- *46*
  Brief entry *29*
Pachter, Hedwig (?)-1988 .... *63*
Pack, Janet 1952- *77*
Pack, Robert 1929- *118*
Packard, Edward 1931- *148*
  Earlier sketches in SATA *47, 90*
Packer, Kenneth L. 1946- *116*
Packer, Vin
  See Meaker, Marijane
Pad, Peter
  See Stratemeyer, Edward L.
Page, Eileen
  See Heal, Edith
Page, Eleanor
  See Coerr, Eleanor (Beatrice)
Page, Jake 1936- *81*
Page, James Keena, Jr.
  See Page, Jake

Page, Lou Williams 1912-1997 .... *38*
Page, Mary
   See Heal, Edith
Page, Robin 1943- *154*
Pagnucci, Susan 1944- *90*
Pahlen, Kurt 1907-2003
   Obituary *147*
Pahz, Cheryl
   See Pahz, Cheryl Suzanne
Pahz, Cheryl Suzanne 1949- *11*
Pahz, James Alon 1943- *11*
Paice, Margaret 1920- *10*
Paige, Harry W(orthington) 1922- *41*
   Brief entry *35*
Paige, Richard
   See Koontz, Dean R.
Paige, Robin
   See Albert, Susan Wittig
Paine, Penelope Colville 1946- *87*
Paine, Roberta M. 1925- *13*
Paisley, Tom 1932- *11*
   See also CLR *3*
Palatini, Margie *174*
   Earlier sketch in SATA *134*
Palazzo, Anthony D.
   See Palazzo, Tony
Palazzo, Tony 1905-1970 .... *3*
Palder, Edward L. 1922- *5*
Palecek, Josef 1932- *56*
Palecek, Libuse 1937- *89*
Palen, Debbie *195*
Palin, Michael 1943- *67*
Palin, Michael Edward
   See Palin, Michael
Palladini, David (Mario) 1946- *40*
   Brief entry *32*
Pallas, Norvin 1918-1983 .... *23*
Pallister, John C(lare) 1891-1980
   Obituary *26*
Pallotta, Gerard Larry
   See Pallotta, Jerry
Pallotta, Jerry 1953- *186*
Pallotta-Chiarolli, Maria 1960- *117*
Palmer, Bernard (Alvin) 1914-1998 .... *26*
Palmer, C. Everard 1930- *14*
Palmer, (Ruth) Candida 1926- *11*
Palmer, Cyril Everard
   See Palmer, C. Everard
Palmer, Don
   See Benson, Mildred
Palmer, Hap 1942- *68*
Palmer, Heidi 1948- *15*
Palmer, Helen Marion
   See Geisel, Helen
Palmer, Jessica 1953- *120*
Palmer, Judd 1972- *153*
Palmer, Juliette 1930- *15*
Palmer, Kate Salley 1946- *97*
Palmer, Maria
   See Strachan, Ian
Palmer, Maria
   See Brennan, Herbie
Palmer, Robin 1909-2000 .... *43*
Palmero Caceres, Ana *198*
Paltrowitz, Donna 1950- *61*
   Brief entry *50*
Paltrowitz, Donna Milman
   See Paltrowitz, Donna
Paltrowitz, Stuart 1946- *61*
   Brief entry *50*
Pamela, Todd 1950- *124*
Pamintuan, Macky *178*
Panagopoulos, Janie Lynn *149*
Panati, Charles 1943- *65*
Panchyk, Richard 1970- *138*
Panetta, George 1915-1969 .... *15*
Panetta, Joseph N. 1953- *96*
Panik, Sharon 1952- *82*
Panowski, Eileen Thompson 1920- *49*
Pansy
   See Alden, Isabella (Macdonald)

Pantell, Dora (Fuchs) *39*
Panter, Carol 1936- *9*
Paolini, Christopher 1983- *157*
   See also CLR *102*
Papademetriou, Lisa *175*
Paparone, Pam *185*
Paparone, Pamela
   See Paparone, Pam
Papas, Bill
   See Papas, William
Papas, William 1927-2000 .... *50*
Papashvily, George 1898-1978 .... *17*
Papashvily, Helen (Waite) 1906-1996 .... *17*
Pape, D. L.
   See Pape, Donna (Lugg)
Pape, Donna (Lugg) 1930- *82*
   Earlier sketch in SATA *2*
Paperny, Myra (Green) 1932- *51*
   Brief entry *33*
Paradis, Adrian A(lexis) 1912- *67*
   Earlier sketch in SATA *1*
   See also SAAS *8*
Paradis, Marjorie Bartholomew
   1886(?)-1970 .... *17*
Paradiz, Valerie 1963- *176*
Paratore, Coleen
   See Paratore, Coleen Murtagh
Paratore, Coleen Murtagh 1958- *200*
Parenteau, Shirley 1935- *199*
   Brief entry *40*
   Earlier sketch in SATA *47*
Parish, Margaret 1927-1988 .... *73*
   Obituary *59*
   Earlier sketch in SATA *17*
   See also CLR *22*
Parish, Margaret Holt
   See Holt, Margaret
Parish, Peggy
   See Parish, Margaret
Park, Barbara 1947- *123*
   Brief entry *35*
   Earlier sketches in SATA *40, 78*
   See also CLR *34*
Park, Bill
   See Park, W(illiam) B(ryan)
Park, Frances 1955- *171*
Park, Ginger *173*
Park, Janie Jaehyun *150*
Park, Jordan
   See Kornbluth, C(yril) M.
   and Pohl, Frederik
Park, Linda Sue 1960- *200*
   Earlier sketches in SATA *127, 173*
   See also CLR *84*
Park, Nick 1958- *113*
Park, (Rosina) Ruth (Lucia) 1923(?)- *93*
   Earlier sketch in SATA *25*
   See also CLR *51*
Park, W(illiam) B(ryan) 1936- *22*
Parke, Marilyn 1928- *82*
Parker, Barbara Keevil 1938- *157*
Parker, Daniel
   See Ehrenhaft, Daniel
Parker, Elinor Milnor 1906- *3*
Parker, Julie F. 1961- *92*
Parker, Kim 1963- *174*
Parker, Kristy 1957- *59*
Parker, Lois M(ay) 1912-1996 .... *30*
Parker, Margot M. 1937- *52*
Parker, Marjorie Blain 1960- *145*
Parker, Mary Jessie 1948- *71*
Parker, Nancy Winslow 1930- *132*
   Earlier sketches in SATA *10, 69*
   See also SAAS *20*
Parker, Richard 1915-1990 .... *14*
Parker, Robert
   See Boyd, Waldo T.
   and Parker, Robert Andrew
Parker, Robert Andrew 1927- *200*
Parker, Toni Trent 1947-2005 .... *142*
   Obituary *169*

Parker-Rees, Guy *193*
Parkes, Lucas
   See Harris, John (Wyndham Parkes Lucas)
   Beynon
Parkhill, John
   See Cox, William R(obert)
Parkins, David 1955- *176*
Parkinson, Ethelyn M(inerva) 1906-1999 ..... *11*
Parkinson, Kathryn N. 1954- *71*
Parkinson, Kathy
   See Parkinson, Kathryn N.
Parkinson, Siobhan
   See Parkinson, Siobhan
Parkinson, Siobhan 1954- *178*
Parks, Deborah A. 1948- *133*
   Earlier sketch in SATA *91*
Parks, Edd Winfield 1906-1968 .... *10*
Parks, Gordon 1912-2006 .... *108*
   Obituary *175*
   Earlier sketch in SATA *8*
Parks, Gordon Roger Alexander
   See Parks, Gordon
Parks, Peggy J. 1951- *143*
Parks, PJ
   See Parks, Peggy J.
Parks, Rosa 1913-2005 .... *83*
   Obituary *169*
Parks, Rosa Louise Lee
   See Parks, Rosa
Parks, Van Dyke 1943- *62*
Parley, Peter
   See Goodrich, Samuel Griswold
Parlin, John
   See Graves, Charles Parlin
Parme, Fabrice 1966- *191*
Parnall, Peter 1936- *69*
   Earlier sketch in SATA *16*
   See also SAAS *11*
Parotti, Phillip (Elliott) 1941- *109*
Parr, Ann 1943- *144*
Parr, Danny
   See Parr, Ann
Parr, Letitia (Evelyn) 1906-1985(?) *37*
Parr, Lucy 1924- *10*
Parr, Todd *179*
   Earlier sketch in SATA *134*
Parrish, Anne 1888-1957 .... *27*
Parrish, Mary
   See Cousins, Margaret
Parrish, Maxfield
   See Parrish, (Frederick) Maxfield
Parrish, (Frederick) Maxfield 1870-1966 ..... *14*
Parry, Marian 1924- *13*
Parson Lot
   See Kingsley, Charles
Parsons, Alexandra 1947- *92*
Parsons, Ellen
   See Dragonwagon, Crescent
Parsons, Garry *197*
Parsons, Martin 1951- *116*
Parsons, Martin Leslie
   See Parsons, Martin
Parsons, Tom
   See MacPherson, Thomas George
Parsons-Yazzi, Evangeline *172*
Partch, Virgil Franklin II 1916-1984 .... *39*
   Obituary *39*
Parton, Dolly 1946- *94*
Parton, Dolly Rebecca
   See Parton, Dolly
Partridge, Benjamin W., Jr. 1915-2005 .... *28*
   Obituary *163*
Partridge, Benjamin Waring, Jr.
   See Partridge, Benjamin W., Jr.
Partridge, Cora Cheney
   See Cheney, Cora
Partridge, Elizabeth *134*
Partridge, Jenny (Lilian) 1947- *52*
   Brief entry *37*
Pasachoff, Naomi 1947- *147*
Pascal, David 1918- *14*

Pascal, Francine 1938- *143*
  Brief entry *37*
  Earlier sketches in SATA *51, 80*
  See also CLR *25*
Paschal, Nancy
  See Trotter, Grace V(iolet)
Paschkis, Julie 1957- *177*
Pascudniak, Pascal
  See Lupoff, Richard A(llen)
Pashko, Stanley 1913-1982 .... *29*
Passailaigue, Thomas E.
  See Paisley, Tom
Pastel, Elyse *201*
Pateman, Robert 1954- *84*
Patent, Dorothy Hinshaw 1940- *162*
  Autobiography Feature *162*
  Earlier sketches in SATA *22, 69, 120*
  See also CLR *19*
  See also SAAS *13*
Paterson, A(ndrew) B(arton) 1864-1941 .... *97*
Paterson, Banjo
  See Paterson, A(ndrew) B(arton)
Paterson, Diane 1946- *177*
  Brief entry *33*
  Earlier sketch in SATA *59*
Paterson, John (Barstow) 1932- *114*
Paterson, Katherine 1932- *133*
  Earlier sketches in SATA *13, 53, 92*
  See also CLR *127*
Paterson, Katherine Womeldorf
  See Paterson, Katherine
Patience, John 1949- *90*
Patneaude, David 1944- *159*
  Earlier sketch in SATA *85*
Paton, Alan 1903-1988 .... *11*
  Obituary *56*
Paton, Alan Stewart
  See Paton, Alan
Paton, Jane (Elizabeth) 1934- *35*
Paton, Priscilla 1952- *98*
Paton Walsh, Gillian
  See Paton Walsh, Jill
Paton Walsh, Jill 1937- *190*
  Autobiography Feature *190*
  Earlier sketches in SATA *4, 72, 109*
  See also CLR *128*
  See also SAAS *3*
Patrick, Susan
  See Clark, Patricia Denise
Patron, Susan 1948- *182*
  Earlier sketch in SATA *76*
Patsauq, Markoosie 1942-
  See CLR *23*
Patschke, Steve 1955- *125*
Patten, Brian 1946- *152*
  Earlier sketch in SATA *29*
Patterson, Charles 1935- *59*
Patterson, Geoffrey 1943- *54*
  Brief entry *44*
Patterson, James 1947- *197*
  Earlier sketch in SATA *164*
Patterson, James B.
  See Patterson, James
Patterson, Lillie G. -1999 .... *88*
  Earlier sketch in SATA *14*
Patterson, Nancy Ruth 1944- *148*
  Earlier sketch in SATA *72*
Pattison, Darcy (S.) 1954- *126*
  Earlier sketch in SATA *72*
Pattou, Edith *164*
Patz (Blaustein), Nancy *154*
Paul, Aileen 1917- *12*
Paul, Alison *196*
Paul, Ann Whitford 1941- *168*
  Earlier sketches in SATA *76, 110*
Paul, David (Tyler) 1934-1988
  Obituary *56*
Paul, Dominique 1973- *184*
Paul, Elizabeth
  See Crow, Donna Fletcher

Paul, Hamish Vigne Christie 1951- *151*
  See also CLR *87*
Paul, James 1936- *23*
Paul, Korky
  See Paul, Hamish Vigne Christie
Paul, Robert
  See Roberts, John G(aither)
Paul, Tessa 1944- *103*
Pauli, Hertha (Ernestine) 1909-1973 .... *3*
  Obituary *26*
Paull, Grace A. 1898- *24*
Paulsen, Gary 1939- *189*
  Earlier sketches in SATA *22, 50, 54, 79, 111,
  158*
  See also CLR *82*
Paulson, Jack
  See Jackson, C(aary) Paul
Pauquet, Gina Ruck
  See Ruck-Pauquet, Gina
Pausacker, Jenny 1948- *72*
  See also SAAS *23*
Pausewang, Gudrun 1928- *165*
  Earlier sketch in SATA *104*
Pavel, Frances 1907- *10*
Paver, Michelle *170*
Paxton, Thomas R. 1937- *70*
Paxton, Tom
  See Paxton, Thomas R.
Paye, Won-Ldy *185*
Payne, Alan
  See Jakes, John
Payne, Bernal C., Jr. 1941- *60*
Payne, C. Douglas
  See Payne, C.D.
Payne, C.D. 1949- *133*
Payne, C.F. 1956- *179*
Payne, Chris Fox
  See Payne, C.F.
Payne, Donald Gordon 1924- *37*
Payne, Emmy
  See West, Emily Govan
Payne, Nina *135*
Payne, Rachel Ann
  See Jakes, John
Payson, Dale 1943- *9*
Payzant, Charles *18*
Paz, A.
  See Pahz, James Alon
Paz, Natalia Toledo
  See Toledo, Natalia
Paz, Zan
  See Pahz, Cheryl Suzanne
Peace, Mary
  See Finley, Mary Peace
Peacock, Shane 1957- *192*
Peake, Mervyn 1911-1968 .... *23*
Peale, Norman Vincent 1898-1993 .... *20*
  Obituary *78*
Pearce, Ann Philippa
  See Pearce, Philippa
Pearce, Emily Smith 1975- *199*
Pearce, Jacqueline 1962- *146*
Pearce, Margaret *104*
Pearce, Philippa 1920-2006 .... *129*
  Obituary *179*
  Earlier sketches in SATA *1, 67*
  See also CLR *9*
Peare, Catherine Owens 1911- *9*
Pearsall, Shelley 1966- *190*
Pearson, Gayle 1947- *119*
  Earlier sketch in SATA *53*
Pearson, Jean Mary
  See Gardam, Jane
Pearson, Kit 1947- *77*
  Autobiography Feature *117*
  See also CLR *26*
Pearson, Mary E. 1955- *134*
Pearson, Ridley 1953- *182*
Pearson, Susan 1946- *166*
  Brief entry *27*
  Earlier sketches in SATA *39, 91*

Pearson, Tracey Campbell 1956- *155*
  Earlier sketch in SATA *64*
Pease, (Clarence) Howard 1894-1974 .... *2*
  Obituary *25*
Peavy, Linda 1943- *54*
Peck, Anne Merriman 1884-1976 .... *18*
Peck, Beth 1957- *190*
  Earlier sketch in SATA *79*
Peck, Jan *159*
Peck, Jeanie J. 1967- *147*
Peck, Marshall III 1951- *92*
Peck, Richard 1934- *190*
  Autobiography Feature *110*
  Earlier sketches in SATA *18, 55, 97, 110, 158*
  See also CLR *142*
  See also SAAS *2*
Peck, Richard Wayne
  See Peck, Richard
Peck, Robert Newton 1928- *156*
  Autobiography Feature *108*
  Earlier sketches in SATA *21, 62, 111*
  See also CLR *45*
  See also SAAS *1*
Peck, Sylvia 1953- *133*
Peck-Whiting, Jeanie J.
  See Peck, Jeanie J.
Peddicord, Jane Ann *199*
Pedersen, Janet *193*
Pedersen, Sharleen
  See Collicott, Sharleen
Pedler, Caroline *197*
Peebles, Anne
  See Galloway, Priscilla
Peek, Merle 1938- *39*
Peel, John 1954- *79*
Peel, Norman Lemon
  See Hirsch, Phil
Peeples, Edwin A(ugustus, Jr.) 1915-1994 ..... *6*
Peers, Judi 1956- *119*
Peers, Judith May West
  See Peers, Judi
Peet, Bill
  See Peet, William Bartlett
Peet, Creighton B. 1899-1977 .... *30*
Peet, Mal *171*
Peet, Malcolm
  See Peet, Mal
Peet, William Bartlett 1915-2002 .... *78*
  Obituary *137*
  Earlier sketches in SATA *2, 41*
  See also CLR *12*
Peguero, Leone *116*
Pelaez, Jill 1924- *12*
Pelham, David 1938- *70*
Pell, Ed(ward) 1950- *157*
Pelletier, Andrew T. *195*
Pelletier, Andrew Thomas
  See Pelletier, Andrew T.
Pellowski, Anne 1933- *20*
Pellowski, Michael (Joseph) 1949- *151*
  Brief entry *48*
  Earlier sketch in SATA *88*
Pellowski, Michael Morgan
  See Pellowski, Michael (Joseph)
Pelta, Kathy 1928- *18*
Peltier, Leslie C(opus) 1900-1980 .... *13*
Pemberton, Bonnie *191*
Pemberton, John Leigh
  See Leigh-Pemberton, John
Pembury, Bill
  See Groom, Arthur William
Pemsteen, Hans
  See Manes, Stephen
Pendennis, Arthur Esquir
  See Thackeray, William Makepeace
Pender, Lydia Podger 1907- *61*
Pendery, Rosemary (Schmitz) *7*
Pendle, Alexy 1943- *29*
Pendle, George 1906-1977
  Obituary *28*

Pendleton, Don
  See Cunningham, Chet
  and Garside, (Clifford) Jack
  and Jagninski, Tom
  and Krauzer, Steven M(ark)
  and Obstfeld, Raymond
Pendziwol, Jean E. 1965- *177*
Pene du Bois, William (Sherman)
  1916-1993 .... *68*
  Obituary *74*
  Earlier sketch in SATA *4*
  See also CLR *1*
Penn, Audrey 1950- *22*
Penn, Ruth Bonn
  See Rosenberg, Eth Clifford
Pennac, Daniel 1944- *155*
Pennage, E. M.
  See Finkel, George (Irvine)
Penner, Fred 1946- *169*
  Earlier sketch in SATA *67*
Penner, Frederick Ralph Cornelius
  See Penner, Fred
Penney, Grace Jackson 1904-2000 .... *35*
Penney, Ian 1960- *76*
Penney, Sue 1957- *152*
  Earlier sketch in SATA *102*
Pennington, Eunice 1923- *27*
Pennington, Lillian Boyer 1904-2003 .... *45*
Pennypacker, Sara 1951- *187*
Penrose, Gordon 1925- *66*
Penson, Mary E. 1917- *78*
Penzler, Otto 1942- *38*
Pepe, Phil 1935- *20*
Pepe, Philip
  See Pepe, Phil
Peppe, Rodney (Darrell) 1934- *74*
  Earlier sketch in SATA *4*
  See also SAAS *10*
Pepper, Frank S. 1910-1988
  Obituary *61*
Percy, Charles Henry
  See Smith, Dorothy Gladys
Percy, Rachel 1930- *63*
Perdrizet, Marie-Pierre 1952- *79*
Perenyi, Constance 1954- *93*
Perenyi, Constance Marie
  See Perenyi, Constance
Perera, Hilda 1926- *105*
Perera, Thomas Biddle 1938- *13*
Peretti, Frank E. 1951- *141*
  Earlier sketch in SATA *80*
Perez, L. King 1940- *199*
Perez, Lana
  See Perez, Marlene
Perez, Lucia Angela 1973- *182*
Perez, Marlene *170*
Pericoli, Matteo 1968- *178*
Perkins, Al(bert Rogers) 1904-1975 .... *30*
Perkins, Lucy Fitch 1865-1937 .... *72*
Perkins, Lynne Rae 1956- *172*
  Earlier sketch in SATA *131*
Perkins, (Richard) Marlin 1905-1986 .... *21*
  Obituary *48*
Perkins, Mitali 1963- *188*
  Earlier sketch in SATA *88*
Perks, Anne-Marie 1955- *122*
Perl, Erica S. *188*
Perl, Lila *72*
  Earlier sketch in SATA *6*
Perl, Susan 1922-1983 .... *22*
  Obituary *34*
Perlman, Rhea 1948- *183*
Perlmutter, O(scar) William 1920-1975 .... *8*
Pernu, Dennis 1970- *87*
Perrault, Charles 1628-1703 .... *25*
  See also CLR *134*
Perret, Delphine 1980- *190*
Perret, Gene (Richard) 1937- *76*
Perrine, Mary 1913-1976 .... *2*
Perrins, Lesley 1953- *56*
Perrow, Angeli 1954- *121*

Perry, Andrea 1956- *190*
  Earlier sketch in SATA *148*
Perry, Barbara Fisher
  See Fisher, Barbara
Perry, Elizabeth 1959- *174*
Perry, Elizabeth Goodwin
  See Perry, Elizabeth
Perry, Marie Fritz *165*
Perry, Patricia 1949- *30*
Perry, Phyllis J(ean) 1933- *152*
  Earlier sketches in SATA *60, 101*
Perry, Ritchie (John Allen) 1942- *105*
Perry, Roger 1933- *27*
Perry, Steve(n Carl) 1947- *76*
Pershall, Mary K. 1951- *172*
  Earlier sketch in SATA *70*
Pershing, Marie
  See Schultz, Pearle Henriksen
Perske, Robert 1927- *57*
Persun, Morgan Reed
  See Watkins, Dawn L.
Petach, Heidi *149*
Peter
  See Stratemeyer, Edward L.
Peters, Alexander
  See Hollander, Zander
Peters, Andrew Fusek 1965- *169*
  Earlier sketch in SATA *107*
Peters, Caroline
  See Betz, Eva Kelly
Peters, David
  See David, Peter
Peters, Elizabeth 1927- *49*
Peters, Emma
  See Price, Karen
Peters, Gabriel
  See Matott, Justin
Peters, Julie Anne 1952- *197*
  Earlier sketches in SATA *82, 128*
Peters, Linda
  See Catherall, Arthur
Peters, Lisa Westberg 1951- *161*
  Earlier sketches in SATA *74, 115*
Peters, Patricia 1953- *84*
Peters, Russell M. 1929- *78*
Peters, S. H.
  See Henry, O.
  and Proffitt, Nicholas
Petersen, David 1946- *109*
  Earlier sketch in SATA *62*
Petersen, Gwenn Boardman 1924- *12*
Petersen, P(eter) J(ames) 1941- *118*
  Brief entry *43*
  Earlier sketches in SATA *48, 83*
Petersen, Palle 1943- *85*
Petersham, Maud (Sylvia Fuller)
  1890-1971 .... *17*
  See also CLR *24*
Petersham, Miska 1888-1960 .... *17*
  See also CLR *24*
Peterson, Cris 1952- *174*
  Earlier sketches in SATA *84, 145*
Peterson, Dawn 1934- *86*
Peterson, Esther (Allen) 1934- *35*
Peterson, Hans 1922- *8*
Peterson, Harold L(eslie) 1922-1978 .... *8*
Peterson, Helen Stone 1910- *8*
Peterson, Jean Sunde 1941- *108*
Peterson, Jeanne Whitehouse 1939- *159*
  Earlier sketch in SATA *29*
Peterson, Kathleen B. 1951- *119*
Peterson, Lorraine 1940- *56*
  Brief entry *44*
Peterson, Shelley 1952- *146*
Petie, Haris
  See Petty, Roberta
Petricic, Dusan 1946- *176*
Petrides, Heidrun 1944- *19*
Petrie, Catherine 1947- *52*
  Brief entry *41*
Petrone, Valeria *186*

Petrosino, Tamara *193*
Petroski, Catherine (Ann Groom) 1939- *48*
Petrovich, Michael B(oro) 1922- *40*
Petrovskaya, Kyra
  See Wayne, Kyra Petrovskaya
Petruccio, Steven James 1961- *67*
Petry, Ann (Lane) 1908-1997 .... *5*
  Obituary *94*
  See also CLR *12*
Pettit, Jayne 1932- *108*
Petty, J.T. 1977- *189*
Petty, Roberta 1915- *10*
Pevsner, Stella *131*
  Earlier sketches in SATA *8, 77*
  See also SAAS *14*
Peyo
  See Culliford, Pierre
Peyton, K. M.
  See Peyton, Kathleen Wendy
Peyton, Kathleen Wendy 1929- *157*
  Earlier sketches in SATA *15, 62*
  See also CLR *3*
  See also SAAS *17*
Pfanner, (Anne) Louise 1955- *68*
Pfeffer, Susan Beth 1948- *180*
  Earlier sketches in SATA *4, 83*
  See also CLR *11*
  See also SAAS *17*
Pfeffer, Wendy 1929- *142*
  Earlier sketch in SATA *78*
Pfeiffer, Janet (B.) 1949- *96*
Pfister, Marcus *150*
  Earlier sketch in SATA *83*
  See also CLR *42*
Pfitsch, Patricia Curtis 1948- *148*
Pflieger, Pat 1955- *84*
Pham, LeUyen 1973- *201*
  Earlier sketch in SATA *175*
Phelan, Mary Kay 1914- *3*
Phelan, Matt 1970- *172*
Phelan, Terry Wolfe 1941- *56*
Phelps, Ethel Johnston 1914-1984 .... *35*
Philbrick, Rodman 1951- *163*
Philbrick, W. R.
  See Philbrick, Rodman
Philbrick, W. Rodman
  See Philbrick, Rodman
Philbrook, Clem(ent E.) 1917- *24*
Phillips, Aileen Paul
  See Paul, Aileen
Phillips, Betty Lou
  See Phillips, Elizabeth Louise
Phillips, Bob 1940- *95*
Phillips, Douglas A. 1949- *161*
Phillips, Elizabeth Louise *58*
  Brief entry *48*
Phillips, Irv(ing W.) 1905-2000 .... *11*
  Obituary *125*
Phillips, Jack
  See Sandburg, Carl (August)
Phillips, Leon
  See Gerson, Noel Bertram
Phillips, Loretta (Hosey) 1893-1987 .... *10*
Phillips, Louis 1942- *102*
  Earlier sketch in SATA *8*
Phillips, Mark
  See Garrett, Randall
  and Janifer, Laurence M(ark)
Phillips, Mary Geisler 1881-1964 .... *10*
Phillips, Michael
  See Nolan, William F(rancis)
Phillips, (Woodward) Prentice 1894-1981 .... *10*
Phillpotts, Eden 1862-1960 .... *24*
Phin
  See Thayer, Ernest Lawrence
Phipson, Joan
  See Fitzhardinge, Joan Margaret
Phiz
  See Browne, Hablot Knight
Phleger, Fred B. 1909-1993 .... *34*

Phleger, Marjorie Temple 1908(?)-1986 .... _1_
  Obituary .... _47_
Piaget, Jean 1896-1980
  Obituary .... _23_
Piatti, Celestino 1922- .... _16_
Picard, Barbara Leonie 1917- .... _89_
  Earlier sketch in SATA _2_
  See also SAAS _10_
Pichon, Liz .... _174_
Pickard, Charles 1932- .... _36_
Pickering, James Sayre 1897-1969 .... _36_
  Obituary .... _28_
Pickering, Jimmy .... _195_
Pickering, Robert B. 1950- .... _93_
Pielichaty, Helena 1955- .... _142_
Pienkowski, Jan (Michal) 1936- .... _131_
  Earlier sketches in SATA _6, 58_
  See also CLR _6_
Pierce, Edith Gray 1893-1977 .... _45_
Pierce, Katherine
  See St. John, Wylly Folk
Pierce, Meredith Ann 1958- .... _127_
  Brief entry .... _48_
  Earlier sketch in SATA _67_
  See also CLR _20_
Pierce, Ruth (Ireland) 1936- .... _5_
Pierce, Sharon
  See McCullough, Sharon Pierce
Pierce, Tamora 1954- .... _187_
  Brief entry .... _49_
  Earlier sketches in SATA _51, 96, 153_
Pierce, Terry .... _178_
Pierik, Robert 1921- .... _13_
Piernas-Davenport, Gail .... _199_
Piers, Robert
  See Anthony, Piers
Pig, Edward
  See Gorey, Edward (St. John)
Pike, Bob
  See Pike, Robert W(ilson)
Pike, Christopher 1954(?)- .... _156_
  Earlier sketch in SATA _68_
  See also CLR _29_
Pike, Deborah 1951- .... _89_
Pike, E(dgar) Royston 1896-1980 .... _22_
  Obituary .... _56_
Pike, R. William 1956- .... _92_
Pike, Robert W(ilson) 1931- .... _102_
Pilarski, Laura 1926- .... _13_
Pilgrim, Anne
  See Allan, Mabel Esther
Pilkey, Dav 1966- .... _166_
  Earlier sketches in SATA _68, 115_
  See also CLR _48_
Pilkey, David Murray, Jr.
  See Pilkey, Dav
Pilkington, Francis Meredyth 1907-1993 .... _4_
Pilkington, Roger (Windle) 1915-2003 .... _10_
  Obituary .... _144_
Pin, Isabel 1975- .... _183_
Pinchot, David 1914(?)-1983
  Obituary .... _34_
Pincus, Harriet 1938- .... _27_
Pinczes, Elinor J(ane) 1940- .... _81_
Pine, Nicholas 1951- .... _91_
Pine, Tillie S(chloss) 1896-1999 .... _13_
Pini, Richard (Alan) 1950- .... _89_
Pini, Wendy 1951- .... _89_
Pinkerton, Kathrene Sutherland (Gedney)
  1887-1967
  Obituary .... _26_
Pinkett, Jada
  See Smith, Jada Pinkett
Pinkney, Andrea Davis 1963- .... _160_
  Earlier sketch in SATA _113_
Pinkney, (Jerry) Brian 1961- .... _148_
  Earlier sketch in SATA _74_
  See also CLR _54_
Pinkney, Gloria Jean 1941- .... _85_
Pinkney, J. Brian
  See Pinkney, (Jerry) Brian

Pinkney, Jerry 1939- .... _198_
  Autobiography Feature .... _198_
  Brief entry .... _32_
  Earlier sketches in SATA _41, 71, 107, 151_
  See also CLR _43_
  See also SAAS _12_
Pinkney, John .... _97_
Pinkney, Sandra L. .... _193_
  Earlier sketch in SATA _128_
Pinkwater, D. Manus
  See Pinkwater, Daniel
Pinkwater, Daniel 1941- .... _158_
  Earlier sketches in SATA _8, 46, 76, 114_
  See also CLR _4_
  See also SAAS _3_
Pinkwater, Daniel M.
  See Pinkwater, Daniel
Pinkwater, Daniel Manus
  See Pinkwater, Daniel
Pinkwater, Jill .... _188_
Pinkwater, Manus
  See Pinkwater, Daniel
Pinner, Joma
  See Werner, Herma
Pinto, Sara .... _200_
Pioneer
  See Yates, Raymond F(rancis)
Piowaty, Kim Kennelly 1957- .... _49_
Piper, Roger
  See Fisher, John
Pirner, Connie White 1955- .... _72_
Piro, Richard 1934- .... _7_
Pirot, Alison Lohans
  See Lohans, Alison
Pirotta, Saviour .... _184_
Pirsig, Robert M(aynard) 1928- .... _39_
Pita
  See Rendon, Maria
Pitcher, C.
  See Pitcher, Caroline
Pitcher, Caroline 1948- .... _128_
Pitcher, Caroline Nell
  See Pitcher, Caroline
Pitman, (Isaac) James 1901-1985
  Obituary .... _46_
Pitre, Felix 1949- .... _84_
Pitrone, Jean Maddern 1920- .... _4_
Pittman, Helena Clare 1945- .... _71_
Pitz, Henry C(larence) 1895-1976 .... _4_
  Obituary .... _24_
Pitzer, Susanna 1958- .... _181_
Piven, Hanoch 1963- .... _173_
Pixley, Marcella .... _194_
Pizer, Vernon 1918- .... _21_
Place, Marian T(empleton) 1910- .... _3_
Place, Robin (Mary) 1926- .... _71_
Plaidy, Jean
  See Hibbert, Eleanor Alice Burford
Plain, Belva 1919- .... _62_
Plaine, Alfred R. 1898(?)-1981
  Obituary .... _29_
Plath, Sylvia 1932-1963 .... _96_
Platt, Chris 1959- .... _185_
Platt, Kin 1911- .... _86_
  Earlier sketch in SATA _21_
  See also SAAS _17_
Platt, Randall 1948- .... _95_
Platt, Randall Beth
  See Platt, Randall
Platt, Richard 1953- .... _166_
  Earlier sketch in SATA _120_
Playfellow, Robin
  See Ellis, Edward S(ylvester)
Playsted, James
  See Wood, James Playsted
Plecas, Jennifer 1966- .... _149_
  Earlier sketch in SATA _84_
Plimpton, George 1927-2003 .... _10_
  Obituary .... _150_
Plimpton, George Ames
  See Plimpton, George

Plomer, William Charles Franklin
  1903-1973 .... _24_
Plotz, Helen Ratnoff 1913-2000 .... _38_
Plourde, Lynn 1955- .... _168_
  Earlier sketch in SATA _122_
Plowden, David 1932- .... _52_
Plowden, Martha Ward 1948- .... _98_
Plowhead, Ruth Gipson 1877-1967 .... _43_
Plowman, Stephanie 1922- .... _6_
Pluckrose, Henry (Arthur) 1931- .... _141_
  Earlier sketch in SATA _13_
Plum, J.
  See Wodehouse, P(elham) G(renville)
Plum, Jennifer
  See Kurland, Michael
Plumb, Charles P. 1900(?)-1982
  Obituary .... _29_
Plume, Ilse .... _170_
  Brief entry .... _43_
Plumme, Don E.
  See Katz, Bobbi
Plummer, Margaret 1911- .... _2_
Plum-Ucci, Carol .... _184_
Pochocki, Ethel (Frances) 1925- .... _76_
Podendorf, Illa (E.) 1903(?)-1983 .... _18_
  Obituary .... _35_
Podwal, Mark 1945- .... _160_
  Earlier sketch in SATA _101_
Podwal, Mark H.
  See Podwal, Mark
Poe, Edgar Allan 1809-1849 .... _23_
Poe, Ty (Christopher) 1975- .... _94_
Pogany, William Andrew 1882-1955 .... _44_
  Brief entry .... _30_
Pogany, Willy
  See Pogany, William Andrew
Pohl, Frederik 1919- .... _24_
Pohlmann, Lillian (Grenfell) 1902-1997 .... _11_
Pohrt, Tom 1953- .... _195_
  Earlier sketches in SATA _67, 152_
Pointon, Robert
  See Rooke, Daphne
Points, Larry G. 1945- .... _177_
  Earlier sketch in SATA _133_
Points, Larry Gene
  See Points, Larry G.
Pokeberry, P.J.
  See Mitchell, B.J.
POLA
  See Watson, Pauline
Polacco, Patricia 1944- .... _180_
  Earlier sketches in SATA _74, 123_
  See also CLR _40_
Polacco, Patricia Ann
  See Polacco, Patricia
Polak, Monique 1960- .... _178_
Polatnick, Florence T. 1923- .... _5_
Polder, Markus
  See Kruss, James
Polese, Carolyn 1947- .... _58_
Polese, James 1914- .... _87_
Polette, Nancy (Jane) 1930- .... _42_
Polhamus, Jean Burt 1928- .... _21_
Policoff, Stephen Phillip 1948- .... _77_
Polikoff, Barbara G. 1929- .... _162_
  Earlier sketch in SATA _77_
Polikoff, Barbara Garland
  See Polikoff, Barbara G.
Polisar, Barry Louis 1954- .... _134_
  Earlier sketch in SATA _77_
Politi, Leo 1908-1996 .... _47_
  Obituary .... _88_
  Earlier sketch in SATA _1_
  See also CLR _29_
Polking, Kirk 1925- .... _5_
Pollack, Jill S. 1963- .... _88_
Pollack, Merrill S. 1924-1988
  Obituary .... _55_
Polland, Barbara K(ay) 1939- .... _44_

Polland, Madeleine A(ngela Cahill) 1918- ... 68
Earlier sketch in SATA 6
See also SAAS 8
Pollema-Cahill, Phyllis 1958- 123
Pollock, Bruce 1945- 46
Pollock, Mary
See Blyton, Enid
Pollock, Penny 1935- 137
Brief entry 42
Earlier sketch in SATA 44
Pollowitz, Melinda Kilborn 1944- 26
Polner, Murray 1928- 64
Polonsky, Arthur 1925- 34
Polseno, Jo 17
Pomaska, Anna 1946- 117
Pomerantz, Charlotte 1930- 177
Earlier sketches in SATA 20, 80
Pomeroy, Pete
See Roth, Arthur J(oseph)
Pond, Alonzo W(illiam) 1894-1986 5
Pontiflet, Ted 1932- 32
Poole, Gray Johnson 1906- 1
Poole, Josephine
See Helyar, Jane Penelope Josephine
Poole, (Jane Penelope) Josephine
See Helyar, Jane Penelope Josephine
Poole, Lynn 1910-1969 1
Poole, Peggy 1925- 39
Poortvliet, Rien 1932- 65
Brief entry 37
Pope, Elizabeth Marie 1917-1992 38
Brief entry 36
Pope, Kevin 1958- 183
Popescu, Christine
See Pullein-Thompson, Christine
Poploff, Michelle 1956- 67
Popp, K. Wendy 91
Poppel, Hans 1942- 71
Porfirio, Guy 1958- 197
Portal, Colette 1936- 6
Porte, Barbara Ann 1943- 152
Brief entry 45
Earlier sketches in SATA 57, 93
Porter, A(nthony) P(eyton) 1945- 68
Porter, Connie (Rose) 1959(?)- 129
Earlier sketch in SATA 81
Porter, Donald Clayton
See Gerson, Noel Bertram
Porter, Eleanor H(odgman) 1868-1920
See CLR 110
Porter, Gene Stratton
See Stratton-Porter, Gene
Porter, Janice Lee 1953- 108
Earlier sketch in SATA 68
Porter, Katherine Anne 1890-1980 39
Obituary 23
Porter, Kathryn
See Swinford, Betty (June Wells)
Porter, Pamela 1956- 193
Porter, Sheena 1935- 24
See also SAAS 10
Porter, Sue
See Limb, Sue
Porter, Sue 1951- 76
Porter, Tracey 191
Porter, William Sydney
See Henry, O.
Portis, Antoinette 189
Porto, Tony 1960- 153
Portteus, Eleanora Marie Manthei (?)-1983
Obituary 36
Posada, Mia 187
Posell, Elsa Z(eigerman) -1995 3
Posten, Margaret L(ois) 1915- 10
Posthuma, Sieb 1960- 150
Potok, Chaim 1929-2002 106
Obituary 134
Earlier sketch in SATA 33
See also CLR 92
Potok, Herbert Harold -2002
See Potok, Chaim

Potok, Herman Harold
See Potok, Chaim
Potter, Beatrix 1866-1943 132
Earlier sketch in SATA 100
See also YABC 1
See also CLR 73
Potter, Giselle 187
Earlier sketch in SATA 150
Potter, Helen Beatrix
See Potter, Beatrix
Potter, Margaret 1926-1998 21
Obituary 104
Potter, Marian 1915- 9
Potter, Miriam Clark 1886-1965 3
Poulin, Stephane 1961- 98
See also CLR 28
Poulton, Kimberly 1957(?)- 136
Pournelle, Jerry (Eugene) 1933- 161
Earlier sketches in SATA 26, 91
Povelite, Kay 1955- 102
Pow, Tom 1950- 163
Powe-Allred, Alexandra
See Allred, Alexandra Powe
Powell, A. M.
See Morgan, Alfred P(owell)
Powell, Consie 174
Powell, E. Sandy 1947- 72
Powell, E.S.
See Powell, E. Sandy
Powell, Pamela 1960- 78
Powell, Patricia Hruby 1951- 136
Powell, Randy 1956- 118
Powell, Richard Stillman
See Barbour, Ralph Henry
Powell, Robert (Stephenson Smyth) Baden
See Baden-Powell, Robert (Stephenson
Smyth)
Powell, Stephanie 1953- 93
Power, Margaret (M.) 1945- 125
Earlier sketch in SATA 75
Powers, Anne
See Schwartz, Anne Powers
Powers, Bill 1931- 52
Brief entry 31
Powers, Daniel 1959- 164
Powers, Jessica Lynn
See Powers, J.L.
Powers, J.L. 1974- 195
Powers, Margaret
See Heal, Edith
Powers, Tim 1952- 107
Powers, Timothy Thomas
See Powers, Tim
Powledge, Fred 1935- 37
Poydar, Nancy 190
Poynter, Margaret 1927- 27
Prachaticka, Marketa
See Kolibalova, Marketa
Prachatika, Marketa
See Kolibalova, Marketa
Prager, Arthur 44
Prager, Ellen J. 1962- 136
Prange, Beckie 172
Prap, Lila 1955- 177
Praprotnik-Zupancic, Lilijana
See Prap, Lila
Pratchett, Terence David John
See Pratchett, Terry
Pratchett, Terry 1948- 185
Earlier sketches in SATA 82, 139
See also CLR 64
Prater, John 1947- 149
Earlier sketches in SATA 72, 103
Prato, Rodica 184
Pratt, (Murray) Fletcher 1897-1956 102
Pratt, Kristin Joy 1976- 87
Pratt, Pierre 1962- 166
Earlier sketch in SATA 95
Preiss, Byron 1953-2005 166
Brief entry 42
Earlier sketch in SATA 47

Preiss, Byron Cary
See Preiss, Byron
Preller, James 1961- 88
Prelutsky, Jack 1940- 171
Earlier sketches in SATA 22, 66, 118
See also CLR 115
Prentice, Amy
See Kaler, James Otis
Prescott, Casey
See Morris, Chris(topher Crosby)
Presnall, Judith (Ann) Janda 1943- 96
Pressler, Mirjam 1940- 155
Preston, Douglas 1956- 113
Preston, Edna Mitchell 40
Preston, Lillian Elvira 1918- 47
Preussler, Otfried 1923- 24
Prevert, Jacques (Henri Marie) 1900-1977
Obituary 30
Prevost, Guillaume 1964- 192
Price, Beverley Joan 1931- 98
Price, Charlie 187
Price, Christine (Hilda) 1928-1980 3
Obituary 23
Price, Garrett 1896-1979
Obituary 22
Price, Jennifer
See Hoover, Helen (Drusilla Blackburn)
Price, Joan 1931- 124
Price, Jonathan (Reeve) 1941- 46
Price, Karen 1957- 125
Price, Kathy Z. 1957- 172
Price, Lucie Locke
See Locke, Lucie
Price, Olive 1903-1991 8
Price, Susan 1955- 128
Earlier sketches in SATA 25, 85
Price, Willard 1887-1983 48
Brief entry 38
Price-Groff, Claire 127
Priceman, Marjorie 1958- 168
Earlier sketches in SATA 81, 120
Prichard, Katharine Susannah 1883-1969 66
Prideaux, Tom 1908-1993 37
Obituary 76
Priestley, Alice 1962- 95
Priestley, Chris 1958- 198
Priestley, Lee (Shore) 1904-1999 27
Priestly, Doug 1954- 122
Priestly, Douglas Michael
See Priestly, Doug
Prieto, Mariana Beeching 1912-1999 8
Priley, Margaret (Ann) Hubbard 1909-1992
Obituary 130
Primavera, Elise 1954- 185
Brief entry 48
Earlier sketches in SATA 58, 109
Prime, Derek (James) 1931- 34
Prince, Alison (Mary) 1931- 86
Earlier sketch in SATA 28
Prince, April Jones 1975- 180
Prince, J(ack) H(arvey) 1908- 17
Prince, Joshua 188
Prince, Maggie 102
Pringle, Eric 138
Pringle, Laurence 1935- 201
Autobiography Feature 201
Earlier sketches in SATA 4, 68, 104, 154
See also CLR 57
See also SAAS 6
Pringle, Laurence Patrick
See Pringle, Laurence
Prinz, Yvonne 1960- 175
Prior, Natalie Jane 1963- 106
Pritchett, Elaine H(illyer) 1920- 36
Pritchett, Laura 1971- 178
Pritchett, Laura Rose
See Pritchett, Laura
Pritts, Kim Derek 1953- 83
Prochazkova, Iva 1953- 68
Proctor, Everitt
See Montgomery, Rutherford George

Proeysen, Alf 1914-1970 67
    See also CLR 24
Professor Scribbler
    See Hollingsworth, Mary
Proimos, James 1955- 173
Prose, Francine 1947- 198
    Earlier sketches in SATA 101, 149
Protopopescu, Orel 186
Protopopescu, Orel Odinov
    See Protopopescu, Orel
Provensen, Alice 1918- 147
    Earlier sketches in SATA 9, 70
    See also CLR 11
Provensen, Martin (Elias) 1916-1987 70
    Obituary 51
    Earlier sketch in SATA 9
    See also CLR 11
Provenzo, Eugene (F., Jr.) 1949- 142
    Earlier sketch in SATA 78
Provist, d'Alain 1906-1989
    See Diop, Birago (Ismael)
Provost, Gail Levine 1944- 65
Provost, Gary (Richard) 1944-1995 66
Proysen, Alf
    See Proeysen, Alf
Pruett, Candace (J.) 1968- 157
Pryor, Bonnie H. 1942- 69
Pryor, Boori (Monty) 1950- 112
Pryor, Helen Brenton 1897-1972 4
Pryor, Michael 1957- 153
Pucci, Albert John 1920- 44
Pudney, John (Sleigh) 1909-1977 24
Pugh, Ellen (Tiffany) 1920- 7
Pullein-Thompson, Christine 1925-2005 82
    Obituary 172
    Earlier sketch in SATA 3
Pullein-Thompson, Diana
    See Farr, Diana
Pullein-Thompson, Joanna Maxwell
    1898-1961 82
Pullein-Thompson, Josephine (Mary
    Wedderburn) 82
    Earlier sketch in SATA 3
Pullen, Zachary 189
Pullman, Philip 1946- 198
    Earlier sketches in SATA 65, 103, 150
    See also CLR 84
    See also SAAS 17
Pullman, Philip Nicholas
    See Pullman, Philip
Pulver, Harry, Jr. 1960- 129
Pulver, Robin 1945- 133
    Earlier sketch in SATA 76
Puner, Helen W(alker) 1915-1989 37
    Obituary 63
Purdy, Carol 1943- 120
    Earlier sketch in SATA 66
Purdy, Susan G(old) 1939- 8
Purkiss, Diane 1961- 194
Purmell, Ann 1953- 147
Purnell, Idella 1901-1982 120
Purscell, Phyllis 1934- 7
Purtill, Richard L. 1931- 53
Pushker, Gloria 1927- 162
    Earlier sketch in SATA 75
Pushker, Gloria Teles
    See Pushker, Gloria
Pushkin, Aleksandr Sergeevich
    See Pushkin, Alexander
Pushkin, Alexander 1799-1837 61
Putnam, Alice 1916- 61
Putnam, Arthur Lee
    See Alger, Horatio, Jr.
Putnam, Peter B(rock) 1920-1998 30
    Obituary 106
Puttapipat, Niroot 199
Puttock, Simon 178
Puybaret, Eric 1976- 195
Pyle, Howard 1853-1911 100
    Earlier sketch in SATA 16
    See also CLR 117

Pyle, Katharine 1863-1938 66
Pyne, Mable Mandeville 1903-1969 9
Pyrnelle, Louise-Clarke 1850-1907 114

Q

Quackenbush, Robert M(ead) 1929- 133
    Autobiography Feature 133
    Earlier sketches in SATA 7, 70
    See also CLR 122
    See also SAAS 7
Qualey, Marsha 1953- 124
    Earlier sketch in SATA 79
Qualls, Sean 177
Quammen, David 1948- 7
Quark, Jason
    See Eldin, Peter
Quarles, Benjamin (Arthur) 1904-1996 12
Quatermass, Martin
    See Carpenter, John (Howard)
Quattlebaum, Mary 1958- 185
    Earlier sketches in SATA 88, 134
Quay, Emma 173
    Earlier sketch in SATA 119
Queen, Ellery
    See Deming, Richard
    and Dannay, Frederic
    and Davidson, Avram (James)
    and Fairman, Paul W.
    and Flora, Fletcher
    and Holding, James (Clark Carlisle, Jr.)
    and Hoch, Edward D.
    and Kane, Henry
    and Lee, Manfred B.
    and Marlowe, Stephen
    and Powell, (Oval) Talmage
    and Sheldon, Walter J(ames)
    and Sturgeon, Theodore (Hamilton)
    and Tracy, Don(ald Fiske)
    and Vance, Jack
Queen Latifah 1970- 185
Quennell, Marjorie Courtney 1884-1972 29
Quentin
    See Sheldon, David
Quentin, Brad
    See Bisson, Terry
Quest, (Edna) Olga W(ilbourne) Hall
    See Hall-Quest, (Edna) Olga W(ilbourne)
Quick, Annabelle 1922-1986 2
Quigg, Jane (Hulda) (?)-1986
    Obituary 49
Quill, Monica
    See McInerny, Ralph
Quin-Harkin, Janet 1941- 165
    Earlier sketches in SATA 18, 90, 119
Quin-Harkin, Janet Elizabeth
    See Quin-Harkin, Janet
Quinlan, Susan E. 1954- 88
Quinlan, Susan Elizabeth
    See Quinlan, Susan E.
Quinn, Elisabeth 1881-1962 22
Quinn, Pat 1947- 130
Quinn, Patrick 1950- 73
Quinn, Rob 1972- 138
Quinn, Susan 1940- 30
Quinn, Susan Taft
    See Quinn, Susan
Quinn, Theodora K.
    See Kroeber, Theodora (Kracaw)
Quinn, Vernon
    See Quinn, Elisabeth
Quintano, D.M.
    See Sheldon, Dyan
Quirk, Anne (E.) 1956- 99
Quixley, Jim 1931- 56
Quyth, Gabriel
    See Jennings, Gary

R

Ra, Carol F. 1939- 76
Raab, Evelyn 1951- 129
Rabb, Margo 1972- 188
Rabb, M.E.
    See Rabb, Margo
Rabe, Berniece (Louise) 1928- 148
    Autobiography Feature 148
    Earlier sketches in SATA 7, 77
    See also SAAS 10
Rabe, Olive H(anson) (?)-1968 13
Rabin, Staton 1958- 162
    Earlier sketch in SATA 84
Rabinowich, Ellen 1946- 29
Rabinowitz, Sandy 1954- 52
    Brief entry 39
Rachlin, Carol K(ing) 1919- 64
Rachlin, Harvey 1951- 47
Rachlin, Harvey Brant
    See Rachlin, Harvey
Rachlin, Nahid 64
Rachlis, Eugene (Jacob) 1920-1986
    Obituary 50
Rackham, Arthur 1867-1939 100
    Earlier sketch in SATA 15
    See also CLR 57
Raczka, Bob 1963- 191
    Earlier sketch in SATA 163
Radencich, Marguerite C. 1952-1998 79
Rader, Laura 197
Radford, Ruby L(orraine) 1891-1971 6
Radin, Ruth Yaffe 1938- 107
    Brief entry 52
    Earlier sketch in SATA 56
Radlauer, David 1952- 28
Radlauer, Edward 1921- 15
Radlauer, Ruth Shaw 1926- 98
    Earlier sketch in SATA 15
Radley, Gail 1951- 112
    Earlier sketch in SATA 25
Radunsky, Vladimir 177
Rae, Gwynedd 1892-1977 37
Raebeck, Lois 1921- 5
Rael, Elsa Okon 1927-
    See CLR 84
Raffi
    See Cavoukian, Raffi
Raftery, Gerald (Bransfield) 1905-1986 11
Ragan-Reid, Gale 1956- 90
Rahaman, Vashanti 1953- 98
Rahn, Joan Elma 1929- 27
Rai, Bali 1971- 152
Raible, Alton (Robert) 1918- 35
Raiff, Stan 1930- 11
Raines, Shirley C(arol) 1945- 128
Rainey, W. B.
    See Blassingame, Wyatt Rainey
Rake, Jody 1961- 157
Rallison, Janette 1966- 183
Ralston, Jan
    See Dunlop, Agnes M. R.
Rama, Sue 190
Ramal, Walter
    See de la Mare, Walter (John)
Ramanujan, A(ttipat) K(rishnaswami)
    1929-1993 86
Rame, David
    See Divine, Arthur Durham
Ramirez, Jose 1967- 198
Ramirez, Orlando L. 1972- 194
Ramstad, Ralph L. 1919- 115
Rana, Indi
    See Rana, Indira Higham
Rana, Indira Higham 1944- 82
Rana, J.
    See Bhatia, Jamunadevi
Ranadive, Gail 1944- 10
Rand, Ann (Binkley) 30
Rand, Gloria 1925- 156
    Earlier sketch in SATA 101

Rand, Paul 1914-1996 6
Randall, Carrie
    See Ransom, Candice F.
Randall, David 1972- 167
Randall, Florence Engel 1917-1997 5
Randall, Janet
    See Young, Janet Randall
    and Young, Robert W(illiam)
Randall, Robert
    See Garrett, Randall
    and Silverberg, Robert
Randall, Ruth (Elaine) Painter 1892-1971 3
Randell, Beverley
    See Price, Beverley Joan
Randle, Kristen D. 1952- 92
    Autobiography Feature 119
    See also SAAS 24
Randle, Kristen Downey
    See Randle, Kristen D.
Randolph, Boynton M.D.
    See Ellis, Edward S(ylvester)
Randolph, Ellen
    See Rawn, Melanie
Randolph, Geoffrey
    See Ellis, Edward S(ylvester)
Randolph, J. H.
    See Ellis, Edward S(ylvester)
Randolph, Lieutenant J. H.
    See Ellis, Edward S(ylvester)
Rands, William Brighty 1823-1882 17
Raney, Ken 1953- 74
Rankin, Joan 1940- 148
    Earlier sketch in SATA 88
Rankin, Laura 1953(?)- 176
Ranney, Agnes V. 1916-1985 6
Ransom, Candice F. 1952- 183
    Brief entry 49
    Earlier sketches in SATA 52, 89, 135
Ransom, Jeanie Franz 1957- 187
Ransome, Arthur (Michell) 1884-1967 22
    See also CLR 8
Ransome, James E. 1961- 178
    Earlier sketches in SATA 76, 123
    See also CLR 86
Rant, Tol E.
    See Longyear, Barry B(rookes)
Raphael, Elaine
    See Bolognese, Elaine
Raposo, Joseph Guilherme 1938-1989
    Obituary 61
Rapp, Adam 1968(?)- 148
Rappaport, Doreen 151
Rappaport, Eva 1924- 6
Rappoport, Ken 1935- 167
    Earlier sketch in SATA 89
Rarick, Carrie 1911-2002 41
Raschka, Chris 1959- 166
    Earlier sketches in SATA 80, 117
Raschka, Christopher
    See Raschka, Chris
Rascol, Sabina I. 159
Rash, Andy 162
Raskin, Edith Lefkowitz 1908-1987 9
Raskin, Ellen 1928-1984 139
    Earlier sketches in SATA 2, 38
    See also CLR 12
Raskin, Joseph 1897-1982 12
    Obituary 29
Rathjen, Carl Henry 1909-1984 11
Rathmann, Peggy 1953- 157
    Earlier sketch in SATA 94
    See also CLR 77
Ratliff, Thomas M. 1948- 118
Ratner, Sue Lynn
    See Alexander, Sue
Rattigan, Jama Kim 1951- 99
Ratto, Linda Lee 1952- 79
Rattray, Simon
    See Trevor, Elleston
Ratz de Tagyos, Paul 1958- 198
    Earlier sketch in SATA 76

Rau, Dana Meachen 1971- 167
    Earlier sketch in SATA 94
Rau, Margaret 1913- 168
    Earlier sketch in SATA 9
    See also CLR 8
Rauch, Mabel Thompson 1888-1972
    Obituary 26
Raucher, Herman 1928- 8
Raude, Karina 199
Rauh, Sherry
    See North, Sherry
Raum, Elizabeth 1949- 155
Raven, Margot Theis 184
RavenWolf, Silver 1956- 155
Ravielli, Anthony 1916-1997 3
    Obituary 95
Ravilious, Robin 1944- 77
Ravishankar, Anushka 1961- 200
Rawding, F(rederick) W(illiam) 1930- 55
Rawlings, Marjorie Kinnan 1896-1953 100
    See also YABC 1
    See also CLR 63
Rawlinson, Julia 175
Rawls, (Woodrow) Wilson 1913-1984 22
    See also CLR 81
Rawlyk, George Alexander 1935- 64
Rawn, Melanie 1954- 98
Rawn, Melanie Robin
    See Rawn, Melanie
Rawson, Katherine 1955- 190
Ray, Carl 1943-1978 63
Ray, Deborah
    See Kogan Ray, Deborah
Ray, Delia 1963- 179
    Earlier sketch in SATA 70
Ray, Irene
    See Sutton, Margaret Beebe
Ray, Jane 1960- 196
    Earlier sketches in SATA 72, 152
Ray, JoAnne 1935- 9
Ray, Mary (Eva Pedder) 1932- 127
    Earlier sketch in SATA 2
Ray, Mary Lyn 1946- 154
    Earlier sketch in SATA 90
Rayban, Chloe 1944- 167
Rayevsky, Robert 1955- 190
    Earlier sketch in SATA 81
Raymond, James Crossley 1917-1981
    Obituary 29
Raymond, Robert
    See Alter, Robert Edmond
Rayner, Hugh 151
Rayner, Mary 1933- 87
    Earlier sketch in SATA 22
    See also CLR 41
Rayner, Shoo
    See Rayner, Hugh
Rayner, William 1929- 55
    Brief entry 36
Raynor, Dorka 28
Rayson, Steven 1932- 30
Razzell, Arthur (George) 1925- 11
Razzell, Mary (Catherine) 1930- 102
Razzi, James 1931- 10
Read, Elfreida 1920- 2
Read, Nicholas 1956- 146
Read, Piers Paul 1941- 21
Reade, Deborah 1949- 69
Reader, Dennis 1929- 71
Reading, Richard P(atrick) 1962- 161
Readman, Jo 1958- 89
Ready, Kirk L(ewis) 1943- 39
Reaney, James 1926-2008 43
Reaney, James Crerar
    See Reaney, James
Reardon, Joyce
    See Pearson, Ridley
Reaver, Chap 1935-1993 69
    Obituary 77
Reaver, Herbert R.
    See Reaver, Chap

Reaves, J. Michael
    See Reaves, (James) Michael
Reaves, (James) Michael 1950- 99
Reber, Deborah 189
Recorvits, Helen 191
Redding, Robert Hull 1919- 2
Redekopp, Elsa 61
Redlich, Ben 1977- 181
Redsand, Anna 1948- 184
Redway, Ralph
    See Hamilton, Charles (Harold St. John)
Redway, Ridley
    See Hamilton, Charles (Harold St. John)
Reece, Colleen L. 1935- 116
Reece, Gabrielle 1970- 108
Reed, Betty Jane 1921- 4
Reed, E.
    See Evans, Mari
Reed, Gwendolyn E(lizabeth) 1932- 21
Reed, Kit 1932- 184
    Autobiography Feature 184
    Earlier sketches in SATA 34, 116
Reed, Lynn Rowe 171
Reed, Neil 1961- 99
Reed, Talbot Baines 1852-1893
    See CLR 76
Reed, Thomas (James) 1947- 34
Reed, William Maxwell 1871-1962 15
Reeder, Carolyn 1937- 97
    Earlier sketch in SATA 66
    See also CLR 69
Reeder, Colin (Dawson) 1938- 74
Reeder, Colonel Red
    See Reeder, Russell P(otter), Jr.
Reeder, Russell P(otter), Jr. 1902-1998 4
    Obituary 101
Reeder, Stephanie Owen 1951- 102
Reed-Jones, Carol 1955- 112
Reef, Catherine 1951- 189
    Earlier sketches in SATA 73, 128
Reekie, Jocelyn (Margaret) 1947- 145
Reeman, Douglas Edward 1924- 63
    Brief entry 28
Rees, Celia 1949- 124
Rees, David (Bartlett) 1936-1993 69
    Obituary 76
    Earlier sketch in SATA 36
    See also SAAS 5
Rees, Douglas 1947- 169
Rees, Ennis (Samuel, Jr.) 1925- 3
Rees, (George) Leslie (Clarence)
    1905-2000 105
    Obituary 135
Reese, Bob
    See Reese, Robert A.
Reese, Carolyn Johnson 1938- 64
Reese, Della 1931(?)- 114
Reese, Lyn
    See Reese, Carolyn Johnson
Reese, Robert A. 1938- 60
    Brief entry 53
Reese, (John) Terence 1913-1996 59
Reeve, Joel
    See Cox, William R(obert)
Reeve, Kirk 1934- 117
Reeve, Philip 201
    Earlier sketch in SATA 170
Reeve, Rosie 186
Reeve, Rosie 188
Reeves, Faye Couch 1953- 76
Reeves, James
    See Reeves, John Morris
Reeves, Jeni 1947- 111
Reeves, John Morris 1909-1978 87
    Earlier sketch in SATA 15
Reeves, Joyce 1911- 17
Reeves, Lawrence F. 1926- 29
Reeves, Ruth Ellen
    See Ranney, Agnes V.

Regan, Dian Curtis 1950- *149*
   Autobiography Feature *149*
   Earlier sketches in SATA *75, 133*
Regehr, Lydia 1903-1991 .... *37*
Reger, James P. 1952- *106*
Reggiani, Renee 1925- *18*
Rehm, Karl M. 1935- *72*
Reich, Ali
   See Katz, Bobbi
Reich, Susanna 1954- *113*
Reiche, Dietlof 1941- *159*
Reichert, Edwin C(lark) 1909-1988
   Obituary *57*
Reichert, Mickey Zucker
   See Reichert, Miriam Zucker
Reichert, Miriam Zucker 1962- *85*
Reichert, Renee *172*
Reichhold, Jane(t E.) 1937- *147*
Reid, Alastair 1926- *46*
Reid, Barbara 1922- *21*
Reid, Barbara (Jane) 1957- *93*
   See also CLR *64*
Reid, Desmond
   See Moorcock, Michael
   and McNeilly, Wilfred (Glassford)
Reid, Eugenie Chazal 1924- *12*
Reid, John Calvin *21*
Reid, (Thomas) Mayne 1818-1883 .... *24*
Reid, Meta Mayne 1905-1991 .... *58*
   Brief entry *36*
Reid, Robin (Nicole) 1969- *145*
Reid Banks, Lynne 1929- *165*
   Earlier sketches in SATA *22, 75, 111*
   See also CLR *86*
Reider, Katja 1960- *126*
Reid Jenkins, Debra 1955- *87*
Reiff, Stephanie Ann 1948- *47*
   Brief entry *28*
Reig, June 1933- *30*
Reigot, Betty Polisar 1924- *55*
   Brief entry *41*
Reilly, Joan *195*
Reim, Melanie (K.) 1956- *104*
Reinach, Jacquelyn (Krasne) 1930-2000 ...... *28*
Reiner, Carl 1922- *151*
Reiner, William B(uck) 1910-1976 .... *46*
   Obituary *30*
Reinfeld, Fred 1910-1964 .... *3*
Reinhardt, Dana 1971- *175*
Reinhart, Matthew 1971- *197*
   Earlier sketch in SATA *161*
Reiniger, Lotte 1899-1981 .... *40*
   Obituary *33*
Reinsma, Carol 1949- *91*
Reinstedt, Randall A. 1935- *101*
Reinstedt, Randy
   See Reinstedt, Randall A.
Reisberg, Mira 1955- *82*
Reisberg, Veg
   See Reisberg, Mira
Reiser, Lynn 1944- *180*
   Earlier sketches in SATA *81, 138*
Reiser, Lynn Whisnant
   See Reiser, Lynn
Reisgies, Teresa (Maria) 1966- *74*
Reiss, Johanna (de Leeuw) 1929(?)- *18*
   See also CLR *19*
Reiss, John J. *23*
Reiss, Kathryn 1957- *144*
   Earlier sketch in SATA *76*
Reit, Seymour Victory 1918-2001 .... *21*
   Obituary *133*
Reit, Sy
   See Reit, Seymour Victory
Relf, Patricia 1954- *134*
   Earlier sketch in SATA *71*
Remi, Georges 1907-1983 .... *13*
   Obituary *32*
   See also CLR *114*
Remington, Frederic S(ackrider)
   1861-1909 .... *41*

Remkiewicz, Frank 1939- *152*
   Earlier sketch in SATA *77*
Rempt, Fiona 1973- *198*
Remy, Georges
   See Remi, Georges
Renaud, Bernadette 1945- *66*
Renault, Mary
   See Challans, Mary
Rendell, Joan *28*
Rendina, Laura (Jones) Cooper 1902- *10*
Rendon, Marcie R. 1952- *97*
Rendon, Maria 1965- *116*
Renee, Janina 1956- *140*
Renfro, Ed 1924- *79*
Renick, Marion (Lewis) 1905-1983 .... *1*
Renken, Aleda 1907- *27*
Renlie, Frank H. 1936- *11*
Rennert, Richard Scott 1956- *67*
Rennison, Louise 1951- *149*
Reno, Dawn E(laine) 1953- *130*
Rensie, Willis
   See Eisner, Will
Renton, Cam
   See Armstrong, Richard
Renvoize, Jean *5*
Resau, Laura 1973- *190*
Resciniti, Angelo G. 1952- *75*
Resnick, Michael David
   See Resnick, Mike
Resnick, Mike 1942- *159*
   Earlier sketches in SATA *38, 106*
Resnick, Seymour 1920- *23*
Retla, Robert
   See Alter, Robert Edmond
Rettig, Liz *199*
Reuter, Bjarne (B.) 1950- *142*
   Earlier sketch in SATA *68*
Reuter, Carol (Joan) 1931- *2*
Revena
   See Wright, Betty Ren
Revsbech, Vicki
   See Liestman, Vicki
Rex, Adam *186*
Rex, Michael *191*
Rey, H(ans) A(ugusto) 1898-1977 .... *100*
   Earlier sketches in SATA *1, 26, 69*
   See also CLR *93*
Rey, Luis V. 1955- *201*
Rey, Margret (Elisabeth) 1906-1996 .... *86*
   Obituary *93*
   Earlier sketch in SATA *26*
   See also CLR *93*
Reyher, Becky
   See Reyher, Rebecca Hourwich
Reyher, Rebecca Hourwich 1897-1987 .... *18*
   Obituary *50*
Reynold, Ann
   See Bernardo, Anilu
Reynolds, Aaron 1970- *197*
Reynolds, Adrian 1963- *192*
Reynolds, C. Buck 1957- *107*
Reynolds, Dickson
   See Reynolds, Helen Mary Greenwood Campbell
Reynolds, Helen Mary Greenwood Campbell
   1884-1969
   Obituary *26*
Reynolds, Jan 1956- *180*
Reynolds, John
   See Whitlock, Ralph
Reynolds, Madge
   See Whitlock, Ralph
Reynolds, Malvina 1900-1978 .... *44*
   Obituary *24*
Reynolds, Marilyn 1935- *121*
   See also SAAS *23*
Reynolds, Marilyn M.
   See Reynolds, Marilyn
Reynolds, Marilynn 1940- *141*
   Earlier sketch in SATA *80*
Reynolds, Pamela 1923- *34*

Reynolds, Peter H. 1961- *128*
Reynolds, Peter J. 1961- *179*
Reynolds, Susan *179*
Rhine, Richard
   See Silverstein, Alvin
   and Silverstein, Virginia B(arbara Opshelor)
Rhoades, Diane 1952- *90*
Rhodes, Bennie (Loran) 1927- *35*
Rhodes, Donna McKee 1962- *87*
Rhodes, Frank Harold Trevor 1926- *37*
Rhue, Morton
   See Strasser, Todd
Rhyne, Nancy 1926- *66*
Rhynes, Martha E. 1939- *141*
Ribbons, Ian 1924- *37*
   Brief entry *30*
   See also SAAS *3*
Ricciuti, Edward R(aphael) 1938- *10*
Rice, Alice (Caldwell) Hegan 1870-1942 ..... *63*
Rice, Bebe Faas 1932- *89*
Rice, Charles D(uane) 1910-1971
   Obituary *27*
Rice, Dale R. 1948- *42*
Rice, Dale Richard
   See Rice, Dale R.
Rice, Dick
   See Rice, R. Hugh
Rice, Earle (Wilmont), Jr. 1928- *151*
   Earlier sketch in SATA *92*
Rice, Edward 1918-2001 .... *47*
   Brief entry *42*
Rice, Elizabeth 1913-1976 .... *2*
Rice, Eve 1951- *91*
   Earlier sketch in SATA *34*
Rice, Eve Hart
   See Rice, Eve
Rice, Inez 1907- *13*
Rice, James 1934- *93*
   Earlier sketch in SATA *22*
Rice, John F. 1958- *82*
Rice, R. Hugh 1929- *115*
Rice, Richard H.
   See Rice, R. Hugh
Rich, Barbara
   See Graves, Robert
Rich, Elaine Sommers 1926- *6*
Rich, Josephine Bouchard 1912- *10*
Rich, Louise Dickinson 1903-1991 .... *54*
   Obituary *67*
Richard, Adrienne 1921- *5*
   See also SAAS *9*
Richard, James Robert
   See Bowen, Robert Sydney
Richards, Chuck 1957- *170*
Richards, Frank
   See Hamilton, Charles (Harold St. John)
Richards, Hilda
   See Hamilton, Charles (Harold St. John)
Richards, Jackie 1925- *102*
Richards, Jean 1940- *135*
Richards, Justin *169*
Richards, Kay
   See Baker, Susan (Catherine)
Richards, Laura E(lizabeth Howe) 1850-1943
   See YABC *1*
   See also CLR *54*
Richards, Leigh
   See King, Laurie R.
Richards, Marlee
   See Brill, Marlene Targ
Richards, Norman 1932- *48*
Richards, R(onald) C(harles) W(illiam)
   1923- *59*
   Brief entry *43*
Richards, Walter Alden (Jr.) 1907-1988
   Obituary *56*
Richardson, Andrew (William) 1986- *120*
Richardson, Carol 1932- *58*
Richardson, Frank Howard 1882-1970
   Obituary *27*

Richardson, Grace Lee
    See Dickson, Naida
Richardson, Jean (Mary) 59
Richardson, Judith Benet 1941- 77
Richardson, Nigel 1957- 187
Richardson, Robert S(hirley) 1902-1981 8
Richardson, Sandy 1949- 116
Richardson, V.A. 189
Richardson, Willis 1889-1977 60
Richelson, Geraldine 1922- 29
Richemont, Enid 1940- 82
Richler, Mordecai 1931-2001 98
    Brief entry 27
    Earlier sketch in SATA 44
    See also CLR 17
Richman, Sophia 1941- 142
Rich-McCoy, Lois
    See McCoy, Lois (Rich)
Richmond, Robin 1951- 75
Richoux, Pat(ricia) 1927- 7
Richter, Alice 1941- 30
Richter, Conrad (Michael) 1890-1968 3
Richter, Hans Peter 1925-1993 6
    See also CLR 21
    See also SAAS 11
Richter, Jutta 1955- 184
Rickard, Graham 1949- 71
Rico, Don(ato) 1917-1985
    Obituary 43
Riddell, Chris 1962- 166
    Earlier sketch in SATA 114
Riddell, Christopher Barry
    See Riddell, Chris
Riddell, Edwina 1955- 82
Ridden, Brian (John) 1934- 123
Riddle, Tohby 1965- 151
    Earlier sketch in SATA 74
Riddles, Libby 1956- 140
Rideout, Sandy 194
Ridge, Antonia (Florence) (?)-1981 7
    Obituary 27
Ridge, Martin 1923-2003 43
Ridley, Philip 171
    Earlier sketch in SATA 88
Ridlon, Marci
    See Balterman, Marcia Ridlon
Riedman, Sarah R(egal) 1902-1995 1
Riehecky, Janet 1953- 164
Ries, Lori 185
Riesenberg, Felix, Jr. 1913-1962 23
Rieu, E(mile) V(ictor) 1887-1972 46
    Obituary 26
Riffenburgh, Beau 1955- 175
Rigg, Sharon
    See Creech, Sharon
Riggio, Anita 1952- 148
    Earlier sketch in SATA 73
Riggs, Shannon 190
Riggs, Sidney Noyes 1892-1975
    Obituary 28
Riggs, Stephanie 1964- 138
Riglietti, Serena 1969- 189
Rigney, James Oliver, Jr.
    See Jordan, Robert
Rikhoff, Jean 1928- 9
Rikki
    See Ducornet, Erica
Riley, James A. 1939- 97
Riley, James Whitcomb 1849-1916 17
Riley, Jocelyn 1949- 60
    Brief entry 50
Riley, Jocelyn Carol
    See Riley, Jocelyn
Riley, Linda Capus 1950- 85
Riley, Martin 1948- 81
Rimbauer, Steven
    See Pearson, Ridley
Rimes, (Margaret) LeAnn 1982- 154

Rinaldi, Ann 1934- 161
    Brief entry 50
    Earlier sketches in SATA 51, 78, 117
    See also CLR 46
Rinard, Judith E(llen) 1947- 140
    Earlier sketch in SATA 44
Rinder, Lenore 1949- 92
Ring, Elizabeth 1920- 79
Ringdahl, Mark
    See Longyear, Barry B(rookes)
Ringgold, Faith 1930- 187
    Earlier sketches in SATA 71, 114
    See also CLR 30
Ringi, Kjell (Arne Soerensen) 1939- 12
Rinkoff, Barbara Jean (Rich) 1923-1975 4
    Obituary 27
Rinn, Miriam 1946- 127
Riordan, James 1936- 95
Riordan, Rick 174
Rios, Tere
    See Versace, Marie Teresa Rios
Ripken, Cal, Jr. 1960- 114
Ripken, Calvin Edward, Jr.
    See Ripken, Cal, Jr.
Ripley, Catherine 1957- 82
Ripley, Elizabeth Blake 1906-1969 5
Ripper, Charles L(ewis) 1929- 3
Ripper, Chuck
    See Ripper, Charles L(ewis)
Riq
    See Atwater, Richard (Tupper)
Rish, David 1955- 110
Riskind, Mary 1944- 60
Rissinger, Matt 1956- 93
Rissman, Art
    See Sussman, Susan
Rissman, Susan
    See Sussman, Susan
Ritchie, Barbara Gibbons 14
Ritter, Felix
    See Kruss, James
Ritter, John H. 1951- 137
    Earlier sketch in SATA 129
Ritter, Lawrence S(tanley) 1922-2004 58
    Obituary 152
Ritthaler, Shelly 1955- 91
Ritts, Paul 1920(?)-1980
    Obituary 25
Ritz, Karen 1957- 80
Rivera, Geraldo (Miguel) 1943- 54
    Brief entry 28
Rivers, Elfrida
    See Bradley, Marion Zimmer
Rivers, Karen 1970- 131
Riverside, John
    See Heinlein, Robert A.
Rivkin, Ann 1920- 41
Rivoli, Mario 1943- 10
Roach, Marilynne K. 1946- 9
Roach, Marilynne Kathleen
    See Roach, Marilynne K.
Roach, Portia
    See Takakjian, Portia
Robb, Don 1937- 194
Robb, Laura 1937- 95
Robberecht, Thierry 1960- 182
Robbins, Frank 1917-1994(?) 42
    Brief entry 32
Robbins, Ken 1945- 147
    Brief entry 53
    Earlier sketch in SATA 94
Robbins, Raleigh
    See Hamilton, Charles (Harold St. John)
Robbins, Ruth 1917(?)- 14
Robbins, Tony
    See Pashko, Stanley
Robbins, Wayne
    See Cox, William R(obert)
Robel, S. L.
    See Fraustino, Lisa Rowe
Roberson, Jennifer 1953- 72

Roberson, John R(oyster) 1930- 53
Robert, Adrian
    See St. John, Nicole
Roberts, Bethany 133
Roberts, Bruce (Stuart) 1930- 47
    Brief entry 39
Roberts, Charles G(eorge) D(ouglas)
    1860-1943 88
    Brief entry 29
    See also CLR 33
Roberts, David
    See Cox, John Roberts
Roberts, Diane 1937- 184
Roberts, Elizabeth 1944- 80
Roberts, Elizabeth Madox 1886-1941 33
    Brief entry 27
    See also CLR 100
Roberts, Jim
    See Bates, Barbara S(nedeker)
Roberts, John G(aither) 1913-1993 27
Roberts, Judy I. 1957- 93
Roberts, Katherine 1962- 152
Roberts, M. L.
    See Mattern, Joanne
Roberts, Nancy Correll 1924- 52
    Brief entry 28
Roberts, Priscilla 1955- 184
Roberts, Terence
    See Sanderson, Ivan T(erence)
Roberts, Willo Davis 1928-2004 150
    Autobiography Feature 150
    Obituary 160
    Earlier sketches in SATA 21, 70, 133
    See also CLR 95
    See also SAAS 8
Robertson, Barbara (Anne) 1931- 12
Robertson, Don 1929-1999 8
    Obituary 113
Robertson, Dorothy Lewis 1912- 12
Robertson, Ellis
    See Ellison, Harlan
    and Silverberg, Robert
Robertson, James I., Jr. 1930- 182
Robertson, James Irvin
    See Robertson, James I., Jr.
Robertson, Janet (E.) 1935- 68
Robertson, Jennifer Sinclair 1942-1998 12
Robertson, Jenny
    See Robertson, Jennifer Sinclair
Robertson, Keith (Carlton) 1914-1991 85
    Obituary 69
    Earlier sketch in SATA 1
    See also SAAS 15
Robertson, Mark
    See Robertson, M.P.
Robertson, M.P. 1965- 197
Robertson, Stephen
    See Walker, Robert W.
Robertus, Polly M. 1948- 73
Robeson, Kenneth
    See Dent, Lester
    and Goulart, Ron
Robeson, Kenneth
    See Johnson, (Walter) Ryerson
Robinet, Harriette Gillem 1931- 104
    Earlier sketch in SATA 27
    See also CLR 64
Robins, Deri 1958- 166
    Earlier sketch in SATA 117
Robins, Patricia
    See Clark, Patricia Denise
Robins, Rollo, Jr.
    See Ellis, Edward S(ylvester)
Robins, Seelin
    See Ellis, Edward S(ylvester)
Robinson, Adjai 1932- 8
Robinson, Aminah Brenda Lynn 1940- 159
    Earlier sketch in SATA 77
Robinson, Barbara (Webb) 1927- 84
    Earlier sketch in SATA 8

Robinson, C(harles) A(lexander), Jr.
1900-1965 .... *36*
Robinson, Charles 1870-1937 .... *17*
Robinson, Charles 1931- *6*
Robinson, Dorothy W. 1929- *54*
Robinson, Eve
  See Tanselle, Eve
Robinson, Glen 1953- *92*
Robinson, Glendal P.
  See Robinson, Glen
Robinson, Jan M. 1933- *6*
Robinson, Jean O. 1934- *7*
Robinson, Joan (Mary) G(ale Thomas)
1910-1988 .... *7*
Robinson, Kim Stanley 1952- *109*
Robinson, Lee 1948- *110*
Robinson, Lloyd
  See Silverberg, Robert
Robinson, Lynda S(uzanne) 1951- *107*
Robinson, Marileta 1942- *32*
Robinson, Maudie Millian Oller 1914- *11*
Robinson, Maurice R(ichard) 1895-1982
  Obituary *29*
Robinson, Nancy K(onheim) 1942-1994 ...... *91*
  Brief entry *31*
  Obituary *79*
  Earlier sketch in SATA *32*
Robinson, Ray 1920- *23*
Robinson, Raymond Kenneth
  See Robinson, Ray
Robinson, Shari
  See McGuire, Leslie (Sarah)
Robinson, Sharon 1950- *197*
  Earlier sketch in SATA *162*
Robinson, Spider 1948- *118*
Robinson, Sue
  See Robinson, Susan Maria
Robinson, Susan Maria 1955- *105*
Robinson, Suzanne
  See Robinson, Lynda S(uzanne)
Robinson, T(homas) H(eath) 1869-1950 ...... *17*
Robinson, (Wanda) Veronica 1926- *30*
Robinson, W(illiam) Heath 1872-1944 .... *17*
Robison, Bonnie 1924- *12*
Robison, Nancy L(ouise) 1934- *32*
Robles, Harold E. 1948- *87*
Robottom, John 1934- *7*
Robson, Eric 1939- *82*
Roca, Francois 1971- *200*
Rocco, John 1967- *188*
Roche, A. K.
  See Abisch, Roslyn Kroop
  and Kaplan, Boche
Roche, Denis 1967- *196*
  Earlier sketch in SATA *99*
Roche, Denis Mary
  See Roche, Denis
Roche, Luane 1937- *170*
Roche, P(atricia) K. 1935- *57*
  Brief entry *34*
Roche, Terry
  See Poole, Peggy
Rochman, Hazel 1938- *105*
Rock, Lois
  See Joslin, Mary
Rock, Maxine 1940- *108*
Rocker, Fermin 1907- *40*
Rocklin, Joanne 1946- *134*
  Earlier sketch in SATA *86*
Rockwell, Anne F. 1934- *194*
  Earlier sketches in SATA *33, 71, 114, 162*
  See also SAAS *19*
Rockwell, Anne Foote
  See Rockwell, Anne F.
Rockwell, Bart
  See Pellowski, Michael (Joseph)
Rockwell, Harlow 1910-1988 .... *33*
  Obituary *56*
Rockwell, Lizzy 1961- *185*
Rockwell, Norman (Percevel) 1894-1978 .... *23*

Rockwell, Thomas 1933- *70*
  Earlier sketch in SATA *7*
  See also CLR *6*
Rockwood, Joyce 1947- *39*
Rockwood, Roy
  See McFarlane, Leslie
  and Stratemeyer, Edward L.
Rodanas, Kristina 1952- *155*
Rodari, Gianni 1920-1980
  See CLR *24*
Rodd, Kathleen Tennant
  See Rodd, Kylie Tennant
Rodd, Kylie Tennant 1912-1988 .... *57*
  Obituary *55*
  Earlier sketch in SATA *6*
Rodda, Emily 1948- *146*
  Earlier sketch in SATA *97*
  See also CLR *32*
Roddenberry, Eugene Wesley 1921-1991 ..... *45*
  Obituary *69*
Roddenberry, Gene
  See Roddenberry, Eugene Wesley
Roddick, Ellen 1936- *5*
Roddie, Shen *153*
Roddy, Lee 1921- *57*
Rodenas, Paula *73*
Rodgers, Frank 1944- *69*
Rodgers, Mary 1931- *130*
  Earlier sketch in SATA *8*
  See also CLR *20*
Rodman, Emerson
  See Ellis, Edward S(ylvester)
Rodman, Eric
  See Silverberg, Robert
Rodman, Maia
  See Wojciechowska, Maia (Teresa)
Rodman, Mary Ann *185*
Rodman, (Cary) Selden 1909-2002 .... *9*
Rodowsky, Colby 1932- *164*
  Earlier sketches in SATA *21, 77, 120*
  See also SAAS *22*
Rodowsky, Colby F.
  See Rodowsky, Colby
Rodriguez, Alejo 1941- *83*
Rodriguez, Alex 1975- *189*
Rodriguez, Christina 1981- *177*
Rodriguez, Edel 1971- *196*
Rodriguez, Luis J. 1954- *125*
Rodriguez, Rachel *180*
Rodriguez, Rachel Victoria
  See Rodriguez, Rachel
Roeder, Virginia Marsh 1926- *98*
Roehrig, Catharine H. 1949- *67*
Roennfeldt, Robert 1953- *78*
Roessel-Waugh, C. C.
  See Waugh, Carol-Lynn Rossel
  and Waugh, Charles G(ordon)
Roets, Lois F. 1937- *91*
Roever, J(oan) M(arilyn) 1935- *26*
Rofes, Eric 1954-2006 .... *52*
Rofes, Eric Edward 1954-2006
  See Rofes, Eric
Roffey, Maureen 1936- *33*
Rogak, Lisa 1962- *80*
Rogak, Lisa Angowski
  See Rogak, Lisa
Rogan, S. Jones *199*
Rogan, Sally Jones
  See Rogan, S. Jones
Rogasky, Barbara 1933- *144*
  Earlier sketch in SATA *86*
Rogers, (Thomas) Alan (Stinchcombe)
1937- *81*
  Earlier sketch in SATA *2*
Rogers, Bettye 1858-1919 .... *103*
Rogers, Cindy 1950- *89*
Rogers, Emma 1951- *74*
Rogers, Frances 1888-1974 .... *10*
Rogers, Fred McFeely 1928-2003 .... *33*
  Obituary *138*

Rogers, Hal
  See Sirimarco, Elizabeth
Rogers, Jean 1919- *55*
  Brief entry *47*
Rogers, Matilda 1894-1976 .... *5*
  Obituary *34*
Rogers, Pamela 1927- *9*
Rogers, Paul 1950- *98*
  Earlier sketch in SATA *54*
Rogers, Robert
  See Hamilton, Charles (Harold St. John)
Rogers, Sherry *193*
Rogers, W(illiam) G(arland) 1896-1978 .... *23*
Rohan, M. S.
  See Rohan, Michael Scott
Rohan, Michael Scott 1951- *98*
Rohan, Mike Scott
  See Rohan, Michael Scott
Rohmann, Eric 1957- *171*
  See also CLR *100*
Rohmer, Harriet 1938- *56*
Rohrer, Doug 1962- *89*
Rojan
  See Rojankovsky, Feodor (Stepanovich)
Rojankovsky, Feodor (Stepanovich)
1891-1970 .... *21*
Rojany, Lisa *94*
Rokeby-Thomas, Anna E(lma) 1911- *15*
Roland, Albert 1925-2002 .... *11*
Roland, Mary
  See Lewis, Mary
Roleff, Tamara L. 1959- *143*
Rolerson, Darrell A(llen) 1946- *8*
Roll, Winifred 1909-1998 .... *6*
Rollins, Charlemae Hill 1897-1979 .... *3*
  Obituary *26*
Rollock, Barbara T(herese) 1924- *64*
Romack, Janice Reed
  See LeNoir, Janice
Romain, Trevor *134*
Romanenko, Vitaliy 1962- *101*
Romano, Clare 1922- *111*
  Earlier sketch in SATA *48*
Romano, Louis G. 1921- *35*
Romano, Melora A. 1966- *118*
Romano, Ray 1957- *170*
Romano, Raymond
  See Romano, Ray
Romijn, Johanna Maria Kooyker
  See Kooyker-Romijn, Johanna Maria
Romyn, Johanna Maria Kooyker
  See Kooyker-Romijn, Johanna Maria
Rong, Yu 1970- *174*
Rongen, Bjoern 1906- *10*
Rongen, Bjorn
  See Rongen, Bjoern
Ronson, Mark
  See Alexander, Marc
Rood, Ronald (N.) 1920- *12*
Rook, Sebastian
  See Jeapes, Ben
Rooke, Daphne 1914-2009 .... *12*
Rooke, Daphne Marie
  See Rooke, Daphne
Roop, Connie 1951- *167*
  Brief entry *49*
  Earlier sketches in SATA *54, 116*
Roop, Constance Betzer
  See Roop, Connie
Roop, Peter 1951- *167*
  Brief entry *49*
  Earlier sketches in SATA *54, 116*
Roop, Peter G.
  See Roop, Peter
Roop, Peter Geiger
  See Roop, Peter
Roos, Stephen 1945- *128*
  Brief entry *41*
  Earlier sketches in SATA *47, 77*
Roose-Evans, James 1927- *65*
Roosevelt, (Anna) Eleanor 1884-1962 .... *50*

Root, Barry *182*
Root, Betty *84*
Root, Kimberly Bulcken *192*
Root, Phyllis 1949- *184*
  Brief entry *48*
  Earlier sketches in SATA *55, 94, 145*
Root, Shelton L., Jr. 1923-1986
  Obituary *51*
Roper, Laura (Newbold) Wood 1911-2003 .. *34*
  Obituary *150*
Roper, Robert 1946- *142*
  Earlier sketch in SATA *78*
Roraback, Robin (Ellan) 1964- *111*
Rorby, Ginny 1944- *94*
Rorer, Abigail 1949- *85*
Rosamel, Godeleine de 1968- *151*
Roscoe, D(onald) T(homas) 1934- *42*
Rose, Anne *8*
Rose, Deborah Lee 1955- *185*
  Earlier sketches in SATA *71, 124*
Rose, Elizabeth (Jane Pretty) 1933- *68*
  Brief entry *28*
Rose, Florella
  See Carlson, Vada F.
Rose, Gerald (Hembdon Seymour) 1935- *68*
  Brief entry *30*
Rose, Malcolm 1953- *168*
  Earlier sketch in SATA *107*
Rose, Nancy A.
  See Sweetland, Nancy A(nn)
Rose, Ted 1940- *93*
Rose, Wendy 1948- *12*
Rosen, Lillian (Diamond) 1928- *63*
Rosen, Marvin 1933- *161*
Rosen, Michael 1946- *181*
  Brief entry *40*
  Earlier sketches in SATA *48, 84, 137*
  See also CLR *45*
Rosen, Michael J. 1954- *199*
  Earlier sketch in SATA *86*
Rosen, Michael Wayne
  See Rosen, Michael
Rosen, Sidney 1916- *1*
Rosen, Winifred 1943- *8*
Rosenbaum, Maurice 1907-1987 .... *6*
Rosenberg, Amye 1950- *74*
Rosenberg, Dorothy 1906- *40*
Rosenberg, Eth Clifford 1915- *92*
  See also SAAS *22*
Rosenberg, Jane 1949- *58*
Rosenberg, Liz 1958- *129*
  Earlier sketch in SATA *75*
Rosenberg, Maxine B(erta) 1939- *93*
  Brief entry *47*
  Earlier sketch in SATA *55*
Rosenberg, Nancy (Sherman) 1931- *4*
Rosenberg, Sharon 1942- *8*
Rosenberry, Vera 1948- *144*
  Earlier sketch in SATA *83*
Rosenblatt, Arthur
  See Rosenblatt, Arthur S.
Rosenblatt, Arthur S. 1938- *68*
  Brief entry *45*
Rosenblatt, Lily 1956- *90*
Rosenbloom, Joseph 1928- *21*
Rosenblum, Richard 1928- *11*
Rosenburg, John M. 1918- *6*
Rosenfeld, Dina 1962- *99*
Rosenthal, Amy Krouse 1965- *177*
Rosenthal, Betsy R. 1957- *178*
Rosenthal, Harold 1914-1999 .... *35*
Rosenthal, M(acha) L(ouis) 1917-1996 .... *59*
Rosenthal, Marc 1949- *193*
Rosenthal, Mark A(lan) 1946- *64*
Rosing, Norbert 1953- *196*
Rosman, Steven M 1956- *81*
Rosman, Steven Michael
  See Rosman, Steven M
Rosoff, Meg 1956- *160*
Ross, Alan
  See Warwick, Alan R(oss)

Ross, Christine 1950- *172*
  Earlier sketch in SATA *83*
Ross, Clare
  See Romano, Clare
Ross, Dana Fuller
  See Cockrell, Amanda
  and Gerson, Noel Bertram
Ross, Dave
  See Ross, David
Ross, David 1896-1975 .... *49*
  Obituary *20*
Ross, David 1949- *133*
  Earlier sketch in SATA *32*
Ross, Deborah J.
  See Wheeler, Deborah
Ross, Diana
  See Denney, Diana
Ross, Edward S(hearman) 1915- *85*
Ross, Eileen 1950- *115*
Ross, Frank (Xavier), Jr. 1914- *28*
Ross, Jane 1961- *79*
Ross, John 1921- *45*
Ross, Judy 1942- *54*
Ross, Katharine Reynolds
  See Ross, Kathy
Ross, Kathy 1948- *169*
  Earlier sketch in SATA *89*
Ross, Kent 1956- *91*
Ross, Lillian Hammer 1925- *72*
Ross, Michael Elsohn 1952- *170*
  Earlier sketches in SATA *80, 127*
Ross, Pat(ricia Kienzle) 1943- *53*
  Brief entry *48*
Ross, Ramon R(oyal) 1930- *62*
Ross, Stewart 1947- *134*
  Earlier sketch in SATA *92*
  See also SAAS *23*
Ross, Tom 1958- *84*
Ross, Tony 1938- *176*
  Earlier sketches in SATA *17, 65, 130*
Ross, Wilda 1915- *51*
  Brief entry *39*
Rossel, Seymour 1945- *28*
Rossell, Judith 1953- *187*
Rossel-Waugh, C. C.
  See Waugh, Carol-Lynn Rossel
Rossetti, Christina 1830-1894 .... *20*
  See also CLR *115*
Rossetti, Christina Georgina
  See Rossetti, Christina
Rossi, Joyce 1943- *116*
Rossotti, Hazel Swaine 1930- *95*
Rostkowski, Margaret I. 1945- *59*
Roth, Arnold 1929- *21*
Roth, Arthur J(oseph) 1925-1993 .... *43*
  Brief entry *28*
  Obituary *75*
  See also SAAS *11*
Roth, David 1940- *36*
Roth, Julie Jersild *180*
Roth, Matthue 1978(?)- *174*
Roth, Roger *190*
Roth, Susan L. *181*
  Earlier sketch in SATA *134*
Rothberg, Abraham 1922- *59*
Roth-Hano, Renee 1931- *85*
Rothkopf, Carol Z. 1929- *4*
Rothman, Joel 1938- *7*
Rotner, Shelley 1951- *169*
  Earlier sketch in SATA *76*
Rottman, S.L. 1970- *157*
  Earlier sketch in SATA *106*
Rottman, Susan Lynn
  See Rottman, S.L.
Roueche, Berton 1911-1994 .... *28*
Roughsey, Dick 1921(?)-1985 .... *35*
  See also CLR *41*
Roughsey, Goobalathaldin
  See Roughsey, Dick

Rounds, Glen (Harold) 1906-2002 .... *112*
  Obituary *141*
  Earlier sketches in SATA *8, 70*
Rourke, Constance Mayfield 1885-1941
  See YABC *1*
Rovetch, L. Bob
  See Rovetch, Lissa
Rovetch, Lissa *201*
Rowan, Deirdre
  See Williams, Jeanne
Rowe, Jennifer
  See Rodda, Emily
Rowe, John A. 1949- *198*
  Earlier sketch in SATA *146*
Rowe, Viola Carson 1903-1969
  Obituary *26*
Rowh, Mark 1952- *90*
Rowland, Florence Wightman 1900-1997 ...... *8*
  Obituary *108*
Rowland-Entwistle, (Arthur) Theodore (Henry)
  1925- *94*
  Earlier sketch in SATA *31*
Rowling, J.K. 1965- *174*
  Earlier sketch in SATA *109*
  See also CLR *112*
Rowling, Joanne Kathleen
  See Rowling, J.K.
Rowsome, Frank (Howard), Jr. 1914-1983 .. *36*
Roy, Gabrielle 1909-1983 .... *104*
Roy, Jacqueline 1954- *74*
Roy, Jennifer
  See Roy, Jennifer Rozines
Roy, Jennifer Rozines 1967- *178*
Roy, Jessie Hailstalk 1895-1986
  Obituary *51*
Roy, Liam
  See Scarry, Patricia (Murphy)
Roy, Ron(ald) 1940- *110*
  Brief entry *35*
  Earlier sketch in SATA *40*
Roybal, Laura 1956- *85*
Roybal, Laura Husby
  See Roybal, Laura
Royds, Caroline 1953- *55*
Royston, Angela 1945- *169*
  Earlier sketch in SATA *120*
Rozakis, Laurie E. 1952- *84*
Rubel, Nicole 1953- *181*
  Earlier sketches in SATA *18, 95, 135*
Rubin, Eva Johanna 1925- *38*
Rubin, Susan Goldman 1939- *182*
  Earlier sketches in SATA *84, 132*
Rubin, Vicky 1964- *193*
Rubinetti, Donald 1947- *92*
Rubinstein, Gillian 1942- *158*
  Autobiography Feature *116*
  Earlier sketches in SATA *68, 105*
  See also CLR *35*
  See also SAAS *25*
Rubinstein, Gillian Margaret
  See Rubinstein, Gillian
Rubinstein, Patricia -2003
  See Forest, Antonia
Rubinstein, Robert E(dward) 1943- *49*
Rublowsky, John M(artin) 1928- *62*
Rubright, Lynn 1936- *171*
Ruby, Laura *181*
  Earlier sketch in SATA *155*
Ruby, Lois 1942- *184*
  Autobiography Feature *105*
  Brief entry *34*
  Earlier sketches in SATA *35, 95*
Ruby, Lois F.
  See Ruby, Lois
Ruchlis, Hy(man) 1913-1992 .... *3*
  Obituary *72*
Rucker, Mike 1940- *91*
Ruckman, Ivy 1931- *93*
  Earlier sketch in SATA *37*
Ruck-Pauquet, Gina 1931- *40*
  Brief entry *37*

Ruditis, Paul *190*
Rudley, Stephen 1946- *30*
Rudolph, Marguerita 1908- *21*
Rudomin, Esther
  See Hautzig, Esther Rudomin
Rue, Leonard Lee III 1926- *142*
  Earlier sketch in SATA *37*
Rueda, Claudia *183*
Ruedi, Norma Paul
  See Ainsworth, Norma
Ruelle, Karen Gray 1957- *126*
  Earlier sketch in SATA *84*
Ruemmler, John D(avid) 1948- *78*
Ruepp, Krista 1947- *143*
Ruffell, Ann 1941- *30*
Ruffins, Reynold 1930- *125*
  Earlier sketch in SATA *41*
Rugoff, Milton 1913- *30*
Ruhen, Olaf 1911-1989 .... *17*
Rukeyser, Muriel 1913-1980
  Obituary *22*
Rumbaut, Hendle 1949- *84*
Rumford, James 1948- *193*
  Earlier sketch in SATA *116*
Rumsey, Marian (Barritt) 1928- *16*
Rumstuckle, Cornelius
  See Brennan, Herbie
Runnerstroem, Bengt Arne 1944- *75*
Runyan, John
  See Palmer, Bernard (Alvin)
Runyon, Catherine 1947- *62*
Ruoff, A. LaVonne Brown 1930- *76*
Rupp, Rebecca *185*
Rusch, Elizabeth 1966- *198*
Rusch, Kris
  See Rusch, Kristine Kathryn
Rusch, Kristine Kathryn 1960- *113*
Rush, Alison 1951- *41*
Rush, Peter 1937- *32*
Rushdie, Ahmed Salman
  See Rushdie, Salman
Rushdie, Salman 1947-
  See CLR *125*
Rushford, Patricia H(elen) 1943- *134*
Rushmore, Helen 1898-1994 .... *3*
Rushmore, Robert (William) 1926-1986 .... *8*
  Obituary *49*
Ruskin, Ariane
  See Batterberry, Ariane Ruskin
Ruskin, John 1819-1900 .... *24*
Russ, Lavinia (Faxon) 1904-1992 .... *74*
Russell, Charlotte
  See Rathjen, Carl Henry
Russell, Ching Yeung 1946- *107*
Russell, Don(ald Bert) 1899-1986
  Obituary *47*
Russell, Franklin (Alexander) 1926- *11*
Russell, Gertrude Barrer
  See Barrer-Russell, Gertrude
Russell, Helen Ross 1915- *8*
Russell, James 1933- *53*
Russell, Jim
  See Russell, James
Russell, Joan Plummer 1930- *139*
Russell, P(hilip) Craig 1951- *162*
  Earlier sketch in SATA *80*
Russell, Patrick
  See Sammis, John
Russell, Paul (Gary) 1942- *57*
Russell, Sarah
  See Laski, Marghanita
Russell, Sharman Apt 1954- *123*
Russell, Solveig Paulson 1904-1985 .... *3*
Russo, Marisabina 1950- *188*
  Earlier sketches in SATA *106, 151*
Russo, Monica J. 1950- *83*
Russo, Susan 1947- *30*
Russon, Penni 1974- *179*
Rutgers van der Loeff, An
  See Rutgers van der Loeff-Basenau, An(na)
  Maria Margaretha

Rutgers van der Loeff-Basenau, An(na) Maria
  Margaretha 1910- *22*
Ruth, Rod 1912-1987 .... *9*
Rutherford, Douglas
  See McConnell, James Douglas Rutherford
Rutherford, Meg 1932- *34*
Ruthin, Margaret
  See Catherall, Arthur
Rutledge, Jill Zimmerman 1951- *155*
Rutz, Viola Larkin 1932- *12*
Ruurs, Margriet 1952- *147*
  Earlier sketch in SATA *97*
Ruzicka, Rudolph 1883-1978
  Obituary *24*
Ruzzier, Sergio 1966- *159*
Ryan, Betsy
  See Ryan, Elizabeth (Anne)
Ryan, Cheli Duran *20*
Ryan, Darlene 1958- *176*
Ryan, Elizabeth (Anne) 1943- *30*
Ryan, Jeanette
  See Mines, Jeanette
Ryan, John (Gerald Christopher) 1921- *22*
Ryan, Margaret 1950- *166*
  Earlier sketch in SATA *78*
Ryan, Mary E. 1953- *61*
Ryan, Mary Elizabeth
  See Ryan, Mary E.
Ryan, Pam Munoz 1951- *197*
  Earlier sketch in SATA *134*
Ryan, Patrick 1957- *138*
Ryan, Peter (Charles) 1939- *15*
Ryan-Lush, Geraldine 1949- *89*
Rybakov, Anatoli (Naumovich) 1911-1998 .. *79*
  Obituary *108*
Rybakov, Anatolii (Naumovich)
  See Rybakov, Anatoli (Naumovich)
Rybolt, Thomas R. 1954- *62*
Rybolt, Thomas Roy
  See Rybolt, Thomas R.
Rybolt, Tom
  See Rybolt, Thomas R.
Rydberg, Ernest E(mil) 1901-1993 .... *21*
Rydberg, Lou(isa Hampton) 1908- *27*
Rydell, Katy 1942- *91*
Rydell, Wendell
  See Rydell, Wendy
Rydell, Wendy *4*
Ryden, Hope *91*
  Earlier sketch in SATA *8*
Ryder, Joanne (Rose) 1946- *163*
  Brief entry *34*
  Earlier sketches in SATA *65, 122*
  See also CLR *37*
Ryder, Pamela
  See Lamb, Nancy
Rye, Anthony
  See Youd, Samuel
Rylant, Cynthia 1954- *195*
  Brief entry *44*
  Earlier sketches in SATA *50, 76, 112, 160*
  See also CLR *86*
  See also SAAS *13*
Rymer, Alta May 1925- *34*
Rymond, Lynda Gene *199*

S

S. L. C.
  See Twain, Mark
S., Svend Otto
  See Soerensen, Svend Otto
Saaf, Donald W(illiam) 1961- *124*
Saal, Jocelyn
  See Sachs, Judith
Sabbeth, Carol (Landstrom) 1957- *125*
Saberhagen, Fred 1930-2007 .... *89*
  Obituary *184*
  Earlier sketch in SATA *37*

Saberhagen, Fred T.
  See Saberhagen, Fred
Saberhagen, Fred Thomas
  See Saberhagen, Fred
Saberhagen, Frederick Thomas
  See Saberhagen, Fred
Sabin, Edwin L(egrand) 1870-1952
  See YABC *2*
Sabin, Francene *27*
Sabin, Lou
  See Sabin, Louis
Sabin, Louis 1930- *27*
Sabre, Dirk
  See Laffin, John (Alfred Charles)
Sabuda, Robert (James) 1965- *120*
  Earlier sketch in SATA *81*
Sabuda, Robert 1965- *170*
Sabuda, Robert James
  See Sabuda, Robert
Sachar, Louis 1954- *154*
  Brief entry *50*
  Earlier sketches in SATA *63, 104*
  See also CLR *79*
Sachs, Elizabeth-Ann 1946- *48*
Sachs, Judith 1947- *52*
  Brief entry *51*
Sachs, Marilyn 1927- *164*
  Autobiography Feature *110*
  Earlier sketches in SATA *3, 68*
  See also CLR *2*
  See also SAAS *2*
Sachs, Marilyn Stickle
  See Sachs, Marilyn
Sackett, S(amuel) J(ohn) 1928- *12*
Sackson, Sid 1920- *16*
Sacre, Antonio 1968- *152*
Saddler, Allen
  See Richards, R(onald) C(harles) W(illiam)
Saddler, K. Allen
  See Richards, R(onald) C(harles) W(illiam)
Sadie, Stanley 1930-2005 .... *14*
Sadie, Stanley John
  See Sadie, Stanley
Sadiq, Nazneen 1944- *101*
Sadler, Catherine Edwards 1952- *60*
  Brief entry *45*
Sadler, Marilyn (June) 1950- *79*
Sadler, Mark
  See Lynds, Dennis
Saffer, Barbara *144*
Sagan, Carl 1934-1996 .... *58*
  Obituary *94*
Sagan, Carl Edward
  See Sagan, Carl
Sage, Angie *197*
Sage, Juniper
  See Brown, Margaret Wise
  and Hurd, Edith Thacher
Sagsoorian, Paul 1923- *12*
Said, S.F. 1967- *174*
Saidman, Anne 1952- *75*
Saint, Dora Jessie 1913- *10*
St. Anthony, Jane *175*
St. Antoine, Sara L. 1966- *84*
St. Clair, Byrd Hooper 1905-1976
  Obituary *28*
Saint-Exupery, Antoine de 1900-1944 .... *20*
  See also CLR *142*
Saint-Exupery, Antoine Jean Baptiste Marie
  Roger de
  See Saint-Exupery, Antoine de
St. George, Judith 1931- *161*
  Earlier sketches in SATA *13, 99*
  See also CLR *57*
  See also SAAS *12*
St. James, Blakely
  See Gottfried, Theodore Mark
  and Platt, Charles
St. James, Blakely
  See Griffin, W.E.B

St. James, Sierra
  See Rallison, Janette
Saint James, Synthia 1949- *152*
  Earlier sketch in SATA *84*
St. John, Nicole *143*
  Autobiography Feature *143*
  Earlier sketches in SATA *29, 89*
  See also CLR *46*
  See also SAAS *7*
St. John, Patricia Mary 1919-1993
  Obituary *79*
St. John, Philip
  See del Rey, Lester
St. John, Wylly Folk 1908-1985 .... *10*
  Obituary *45*
St. Max, E. S.
  See Ellis, Edward S(ylvester)
St. Meyer, Ned
  See Stratemeyer, Edward L.
St. Mox, E. A.
  See Ellis, Edward S(ylvester)
St. Myer, Ned
  See Stratemeyer, Edward L.
St. Tamara
  See Kolba, St. Tamara
Saito, Michiko
  See Fujiwara, Michiko
Sakaki, Ichiro 1969- *192*
Sakamoto, Miki *198*
Sakers, Don 1958- *72*
Sakharnov, S.
  See Sakharnov, Svyatoslav
Sakharnov, Svyatoslav 1923- *65*
Sakharnov, Svyatoslav Vladimirovich
  See Sakharnov, Svyatoslav
Saksena, Kate *148*
Sakurai, Gail 1952- *153*
  Earlier sketch in SATA *87*
Salamanca, Lucy
  See del Barco, Lucy Salamanca
Salassi, Otto R(ussell) 1939-1993 .... *38*
  Obituary *77*
Salat, Cristina *82*
Saldana, Rene, Jr. *186*
Saldutti, Denise 1953- *39*
Sale, Tim 1956- *153*
Salem, Kay 1952- *92*
Salerno, Steven *176*
Salinger, J.D. 1919- *67*
  See also CLR *18*
Salinger, Jerome David
  See Salinger, J.D.
Salisbury, Graham 1944- *195*
  Earlier sketches in SATA *76, 108, 161*
Salisbury, Joyce E(llen) 1944- *138*
Salkey, (Felix) Andrew (Alexander)
  1928-1995 .... *118*
  Earlier sketch in SATA *35*
Salley, Coleen *166*
Sallis, Susan (Diana) 1929- *55*
Salmon, Annie Elizabeth 1899- *13*
Salonen, Roxane Beauclair 1968- *184*
Salsi, Lynn 1947- *130*
Salsitz, R. A. V.
  See Salsitz, Rhondi Vilott
Salsitz, Rhondi Vilott *115*
Salten, Felix
  See Salzmann, Siegmund
Salter, Cedric
  See Knight, Francis Edgar
Saltman, Judith 1947- *64*
Saltzberg, Barney 1955- *194*
  Earlier sketch in SATA *135*
Saltzman, David (Charles Laertes)
  1967-1990 .... *86*
Salvadori, Mario (George) 1907-1997 .... *97*
  Earlier sketch in SATA *40*
Salwood, F.K.
  See Kilworth, Garry
Salzer, L. E.
  See Wilson, Lionel

Salzman, Marian 1959- *77*
Salzmann, Siegmund 1869-1945 .... *25*
Samachson, Dorothy (Mirkin) 1914-1997 ...... *3*
Samachson, Joseph 1906-1980 .... *3*
  Obituary *52*
Sammis, John 1942- *4*
Sampson, Emma (Keats) Speed 1868-1947 . *68*
Sampson, Fay (Elizabeth) 1935- *151*
  Brief entry *40*
  Earlier sketch in SATA *42*
Sampson, Michael 1952- *143*
  Earlier sketch in SATA *95*
Samson, Anne S(tringer) 1933- *2*
Samson, Joan 1937-1976 .... *13*
Samson, Suzanne M. 1959- *91*
Samuels, Barbara *199*
Samuels, Charles 1902-1982 .... *12*
Samuels, Cynthia K(alish) 1946- *79*
Samuels, Gertrude 1910(?)-2003 .... *17*
  Obituary *147*
Sanborn, Duane 1914-1996 .... *38*
Sancha, Sheila 1924- *38*
Sanchez, Alex 1957- *151*
Sanchez, Sonia 1934- *136*
  Earlier sketch in SATA *22*
  See also CLR *18*
Sanchez-Silva, Jose Maria 1911- *132*
  Earlier sketch in SATA *16*
  See also CLR *12*
Sand, George X. *45*
Sandak, Cass R(obert) 1950-2001 .... *51*
  Brief entry *37*
Sandberg, (Karin) Inger 1930- *15*
Sandberg, Karl C. 1931- *35*
Sandberg, Lasse (E. M.) 1924- *15*
Sandburg, Carl (August) 1878-1967 .... *8*
  See also CLR *67*
Sandburg, Charles
  See Sandburg, Carl (August)
Sandburg, Charles A.
  See Sandburg, Carl (August)
Sandburg, Helga 1918- *3*
  See also SAAS *10*
Sandell, Lisa Ann 1977- *175*
Sander, Heather L. 1947- *157*
Sanderlin, George 1915- *4*
Sanderlin, Owenita (Harrah) 1916- *11*
Sanders, Betty Jane
  See Monthei, Betty
Sanders, Nancy I. 1960- *141*
  Earlier sketch in SATA *90*
Sanders, Scott Russell 1945- *109*
  Earlier sketch in SATA *56*
Sanders, Winston P.
  See Anderson, Poul
Sanderson, Irma 1912- *66*
Sanderson, Ivan T(erence) 1911-1973 .... *6*
Sanderson, Margaret Love
  See Keats, Emma
  and Sampson, Emma (Keats) Speed
Sanderson, Ruth 1951- *172*
  Earlier sketches in SATA *41, 109*
Sanderson, Ruth L.
  See Sanderson, Ruth
Sandin, Joan 1942- *197*
  Earlier sketches in SATA *12, 94, 153*
Sandison, Janet
  See Cameron, Elizabeth Jane
Sandler, Martin W. *160*
Sandom, J. Gregory
  See Welsh, T.K.
Sandom, J.G.
  See Welsh, T.K.
Sandoz, Mari(e Susette) 1900-1966 .... *5*
Sanford, Agnes (White) 1897-1976 .... *61*
Sanford, Doris 1937- *69*
Sanger, Marjory Bartlett 1920- *8*
San Jose, Christine 1929- *167*
Sankey, Alice (Ann-Susan) 1910- *27*
San Souci, Daniel *192*
  Earlier sketch in SATA *96*

San Souci, Robert D. 1946- *158*
  Earlier sketches in SATA *40, 81, 117*
  See also CLR *43*
Santamaria, Benjamin 1955- *184*
Santat, Dan *188*
Santesson, Hans Stefan 1914(?)-1975
  Obituary *30*
Santiago, Esmeralda 1948- *129*
Santore, Charles 1935- *200*
Santos, Helen
  See Griffiths, Helen
Santrey, Louis
  See Sabin, Louis
Santucci, Barbara 1948- *130*
Sapergia, Barbara 1943- *181*
Sapieyevski, Anne Lindbergh 1940-1993 ..... *81*
  Brief entry *32*
  Earlier sketches in SATA *35, 78*
Saport, Linda 1954- *123*
Sapp, Allen 1929- *151*
Sarac, Roger
  See Caras, Roger A(ndrew)
Sarah, Duchess of York
  See Ferguson, Sarah
Sarasin, Jennifer
  See Sachs, Judith
Sardinha, Rick *192*
Sarg, Anthony Frederick
  See Sarg, Tony
Sarg, Tony 1882-1942
  See YABC *1*
Sargent, Pamela 1948- *78*
  Earlier sketch in SATA *29*
Sargent, Robert 1933- *2*
Sargent, Sarah 1937- *44*
  Brief entry *41*
Sargent, Shirley 1927-2004 .... *11*
Sarnoff, Jane 1937- *10*
Saroyan, William 1908-1981 .... *23*
  Obituary *24*
Sarton, Eleanor May
  See Sarton, May
Sarton, May 1912-1995 .... *36*
  Obituary *86*
Sasaki, Chris *182*
Saseen, Sharon (Dillon) 1949- *59*
Sasek, Miroslav 1916-1980 .... *16*
  Obituary *23*
  See also CLR *4*
Sasso, Sandy Eisenberg 1947- *162*
  Earlier sketches in SATA *86, 116*
Sathre, Vivian 1952- *133*
  Earlier sketch in SATA *79*
Satterfield, Charles
  See del Rey, Lester
  and Pohl, Frederik
Sattgast, L. J.
  See Sattgast, Linda J.
Sattgast, Linda J. 1953- *91*
Sattler, Helen Roney 1921-1992 .... *74*
  Earlier sketch in SATA *4*
  See also CLR *24*
Sauer, Julia Lina 1891-1983 .... *32*
  Obituary *36*
Sauerwein, Leigh 1944- *155*
Saul, Carol P. 1947- *117*
  Earlier sketch in SATA *78*
Saul, John III
  See Saul, John
Saul, John 1942- *98*
Saul, John W.
  See Saul, John
Saul, John W. III
  See Saul, John
Saul, John Woodruff III
  See Saul, John
Saul, (Ellen) Wendy 1946- *42*
Saulnier, Karen Luczak 1940- *80*
Saunders, Caleb
  See Heinlein, Robert A.
Saunders, Dave 1939- *85*

Saunders, Julie 1939- 85
Saunders, (William) Keith 1910-1994 12
Saunders, Rubie (Agnes) 1929- 21
Saunders, Susan 1945- 96
    Brief entry 41
    Earlier sketch in SATA 46
Saunders-Smith, Gail 1952- 169
Sauvain, Philip Arthur 1933- 111
Savadier, Elivia 1950- 164
    Earlier sketch in SATA 79
Savage, Alan
    See Nicole, Christopher (Robin)
Savage, Blake
    See Goodwin, Harold L(eland)
Savage, Candace 1949- 142
Savage, Deborah 1955- 76
Savage, Jeff 1961- 97
Savage, Katharine James 1905-1989
    Obituary 61
Savage, Stephen 1965- 194
Savage, Thomas 1915-2003
    Obituary 147
Savageau, Cheryl 1950- 96
Savery, Constance (Winifred) 1897-1999 1
Saville, Andrew
    See Taylor, Andrew
Saville, (Leonard) Malcolm 1901-1982 23
    Obituary 31
Saviozzi, Adriana
    See Mazza, Adriana
Savitt, Sam 1917-2000 8
    Obituary 126
Savitz, Harriet May 1933- 72
    Earlier sketch in SATA 5
    See also SAAS 26
Sawicki, Mary 1950- 90
Sawyer, (Frederick) Don(ald) 1947- 72
Sawyer, Kem Knapp 1953- 84
Sawyer, Robert J. 1960- 149
    Earlier sketch in SATA 81
Sawyer, Robert James
    See Sawyer, Robert J.
Sawyer, Ruth 1880-1970 17
    See also CLR 36
Saxby, H.M.
    See Saxby, (Henry) Maurice
Saxby, (Henry) Maurice 1924- 71
Saxon, Andrew
    See Arthur, Robert, (Jr.)
Saxon, Antonia
    See Sachs, Judith
Say, Allen 1937- 161
    Earlier sketches in SATA 28, 69, 110
    See also CLR 135
Sayers, Frances Clarke 1897-1989 3
    Obituary 62
Sayles, Elizabeth 1956- 163
    Earlier sketch in SATA 108
Saylor-Marchant, Linda 1963- 82
Sayre, April Pulley 1966- 191
    Earlier sketches in SATA 88, 131
Sazer, Nina 1949- 13
Scabrini, Janet 1953- 13
Scagell, Robin 1946- 107
Scagnetti, Jack 1924- 7
Scamander, Newt
    See Rowling, J.K.
Scamell, Ragnhild 1940- 180
    Earlier sketch in SATA 77
Scanlon, Marion Stephany 11
Scannel, John Vernon
    See Scannell, Vernon
Scannell, Vernon 1922-2007 59
    Obituary 188
Scarborough, Elizabeth
    See Scarborough, Elizabeth Ann
Scarborough, Elizabeth Ann 1947- 171
    Earlier sketch in SATA 98
Scarf, Maggi
    See Scarf, Maggie
Scarf, Maggie 1932- 5

Scariano, Margaret M. 1924- 86
Scarlett, Susan
    See Streatfeild, Noel
Scarry, Huck
    See Scarry, Richard McClure, Jr.
Scarry, Patricia (Murphy) 1924- 2
Scarry, Patsy
    See Scarry, Patricia (Murphy)
Scarry, Richard (McClure) 1919-1994 75
    Obituary 90
    Earlier sketches in SATA 2, 35
    See also CLR 41
Scarry, Richard McClure, Jr. 1953- 35
Schachner, Judith Byron 1951- 178
    Earlier sketch in SATA 88
Schachner, Judy
    See Schachner, Judith Byron
Schachtel, Roger 1949- 38
Schachtel, Roger Bernard
    See Schachtel, Roger
Schade, Susan 189
Schaedler, Sally 116
Schaefer, Carole Lexa 173
Schaefer, Jack (Warner) 1907-1991 66
    Obituary 65
    Earlier sketch in SATA 3
Schaefer, Lola M. 1950- 183
    Earlier sketches in SATA 91, 144
Schaeffer, Mead 1898- 21
Schaeffer, Susan Fromberg 1941- 22
Schaer, Brigitte 1958- 112
Schaller, George
    See Schaller, George B.
Schaller, George B. 1933- 30
Schaller, George Beals
    See Schaller, George B.
Schanzer, Rosalyn (Good) 1942- 138
    Earlier sketch in SATA 77
Schatell, Brian 66
    Brief entry 47
Schechter, Betty (Goodstein) 1921- 5
Schechter, Simone
    See Elkeles, Simone
Schecter, Ellen 1944- 85
Scheeder, Louis 1946- 141
Scheer, Julian (Weisel) 1926-2001 8
Scheffer, Victor B(lanchard) 1906- 6
Scheffler, Axel 1957- 180
Scheffler, Ursel 1938- 81
Scheffrin-Falk, Gladys 1928- 76
Scheidl, Gerda Marie 1913- 85
Scheier, Michael 1943- 40
    Brief entry 36
Schell, Mildred 1922- 41
Schell, Orville (Hickok) 1940- 10
Scheller, Melanie 1953- 77
Schellie, Don 1932- 29
Schembri, Jim 1962- 124
Schembri, Pamela 1969- 195
Schemm, Mildred Walker 1905-1998 21
    Obituary 103
Schenker, Dona 1947- 133
    Earlier sketch in SATA 68
Scher, Paula 1948- 47
Scherer, Jeffrey 194
Scherf, Margaret 1908-1979 10
Schermer, Judith (Denise) 1941- 30
Schertle, Alice 1941- 192
    Earlier sketches in SATA 36, 90, 145
Schick, Alice 1946- 27
Schick, Eleanor 1942- 144
    Earlier sketches in SATA 9, 82
Schick, Joel 1945- 31
    Brief entry 30
Schields, Gretchen 1948- 75
Schiff, Ken(neth Roy) 1942- 7
Schiller, Andrew 1919- 21
Schiller, Barbara (Heyman) 1928- 21
Schiller, Pamela (Byrne) 127
Schindel, John 1955- 115
    Earlier sketch in SATA 77

Schindelman, Joseph 1923- 67
    Brief entry 32
Schindler, S.D. 1952- 198
    Brief entry 50
    Earlier sketches in SATA 75, 118, 171
Schindler, Steven D.
    See Schindler, S.D.
Schinto, Jeanne 1951- 93
Schisgall, Oscar 1901-1984 12
    Obituary 38
Schlaepfer, Gloria G. 1931- 154
Schlee, Ann 1934- 44
    Brief entry 36
Schleichert, Elizabeth 1945- 77
Schlein, Miriam 1926-2004 130
    Obituary 159
    Earlier sketches in SATA 2, 87
    See also CLR 41
Schlesinger, Arthur M., Jr. 1917-2007 61
    Obituary 181
    See Schlesinger, Arthur Meier
Schlesinger, Arthur Meier 1888-1965
Schlessinger, Laura (Catherine) 1947- 160
    Earlier sketch in SATA 110
Schlitz, Laura Amy 184
Schloat, G. Warren, Jr. 1914-2000 4
Schmatz, Pat 197
Schmid, Eleonore 1939- 126
    Earlier sketch in SATA 12, 84
Schmiderer, Dorothy 1940- 19
Schmidt, Annie M. G. 1911-1995 67
    Obituary 91
    See also CLR 22
Schmidt, C.A. 196
Schmidt, Diane 1953- 70
Schmidt, Elizabeth 1915- 15
Schmidt, Gary D. 1957- 193
    Earlier sketches in SATA 93, 135
Schmidt, James Norman 1912-1983 21
Schmidt, Karen Lee 1953- 185
    Earlier sketch in SATA 94
Schmidt, Lynette 1952- 76
Schneider, Antonie 1954- 167
    Earlier sketch in SATA 89
Schneider, Christine M. 1972(?)- 171
    Earlier sketch in SATA 120
Schneider, Dick
    See Schneider, Richard H.
Schneider, Elisa
    See Kleven, Elisa
Schneider, Herman 1905-2003 7
    Obituary 148
Schneider, Howie -2007 181
Schneider, Josh 1980- 196
Schneider, Laurie
    See Adams, Laurie
Schneider, Nina 1913-2007 2
    Obituary 186
Schneider, Nina Zimet
    See Schneider, Nina
Schneider, Rex 1937- 44
Schneider, Richard H. 1922- 171
Schneider, Richard Henry
    See Schneider, Richard H.
Schneider, Robyn 1986- 187
Schnirel, James R. 1931- 14
Schnitter, Jane T. 1958- 88
Schnitzlein, Danny 134
Schnur, Steven 1952- 144
    Earlier sketch in SATA 95
Schnurre, Wolfdietrich 1920-1989
    Obituary 63
Schoberle, Cecile 1949- 80
Schock, Pauline 1928- 45
Schoell, William 1951- 160
Schoen, Barbara (Taylor) 1924-1993 13
Schoenherr, Ian 177
Schoenherr, John (Carl) 1935- 66
    Earlier sketch in SATA 37
    See also SAAS 13

Schofield, Sandy
    See Rusch, Kristine Kathryn
Scholastica, Sister Mary
    See Jenkins, Marie M(agdalen)
Scholefield, A. T.
    See Scholefield, Alan
Scholefield, Alan 1931- 66
Scholefield, Edmund O.
    See Griffin, W.E.B
Scholey, Arthur 1932- 28
Scholz, Jackson Volney 1897-1986
    Obituary 49
Schone, Virginia 22
Schongut, Emanuel 1936- 184
    Brief entry 36
    Earlier sketch in SATA 52
Schoonover, Frank (Earle) 1877-1972 24
Schoor, Gene 1921- 3
Schories, Pat 1952- 164
    Earlier sketch in SATA 116
Schorr, Melissa 1972- 194
Schorr, Melissa Robin
    See Schorr, Melissa
Schott, Jane A. 1946- 172
Schotter, Roni 190
    Earlier sketches in SATA 105, 149
Schraff, Anne E(laine) 1939- 92
    Earlier sketch in SATA 27
Schram, Peninnah 1934- 119
Schrank, Joseph 1900-1984
    Obituary 38
Schrecengost, Maity 1938- 118
Schrecengost, S. Maitland
    See Schrecengost, Maity
Schreck, Karen
    See Schreck, Karen Halvorsen
Schreck, Karen Halvorsen 1962- 185
Schrecker, Judie 1954- 90
Schreiber, Elizabeth Anne (Ferguson)
    1947- 13
Schreiber, Ralph W(alter) 1942- 13
Schreiner, Samuel A(gnew), Jr. 1921- 70
Schroeder, Alan 1961- 98
    Earlier sketch in SATA 66
Schroeder, Binette
    See Nickl, Barbara (Elisabeth)
Schroeder, Russell (K.) 1943- 146
Schroeder, Ted 1931(?)-1973
    Obituary 20
Schubert, Dieter 1947- 101
    Earlier sketch in SATA 62
Schubert, Leda 1950(?)- 181
Schubert-Gabrys, Ingrid 1953- 101
    Earlier sketch in SATA 62
Schuelein-Steel, Danielle
    See Steel, Danielle
Schuelein-Steel, Danielle Fernande
    See Steel, Danielle
Schuerger, Michele R. 110
Schuett, Stacey 1960- 168
    Earlier sketch in SATA 75
Schulke, Flip Phelps Graeme 1930- 57
Schulman, Arlene 1961- 105
Schulman, Janet 1933- 137
    Earlier sketch in SATA 22
Schulman, L(ester) M(artin) 1934- 13
Schulte, Elaine L(ouise) 1934- 36
Schultz, Betty K(epka) 1932- 125
Schultz, Gwendolyn 21
Schultz, James Willard 1859-1947
    See YABC 1
Schultz, Pearle Henriksen 1918- 21
Schulz, Charles M. 1922-2000 10
    Obituary 118
Schulz, Charles Monroe
    See Schulz, Charles M.
Schumacher, Julie 1958- 191
Schumaker, Ward 1943- 96
Schuman, Michael A. 1953- 134
    Earlier sketch in SATA 85

Schur, Maxine
    See Schur, Maxine Rose
Schur, Maxine Rose 1948- 135
    Autobiography Feature 135
    Brief entry 49
    Earlier sketches in SATA 53, 98
Schurfranz, Vivian 1925- 13
Schutzer, A. I. 1922- 13
Schuyler, Pamela R. 1948- 30
Schwabach, Karen 185
Schwager, Tina 1964- 110
Schwandt, Stephen (William) 1947- 61
Schwark, Mary Beth 1954- 51
Schwartz, Alvin 1927-1992 56
    Obituary 71
    Earlier sketch in SATA 4
    See also CLR 89
Schwartz, Amy 1954- 189
    Brief entry 41
    Earlier sketches in SATA 47, 83, 131
    See also CLR 25
    See also SAAS 18
Schwartz, Anne Powers 1913-1987 10
Schwartz, Carol 1954- 77
Schwartz, Charles W(alsh) 1914- 8
Schwartz, David M. 1951- 110
    Earlier sketch in SATA 59
Schwartz, David Martin
    See Schwartz, David M.
Schwartz, Elizabeth Reeder 1912- 8
Schwartz, Ellen 1949- 117
Schwartz, Jerome L.
    See Lawrence, Jerome
Schwartz, Joel L. 1940- 54
    Brief entry 51
Schwartz, Joyce R. 1950- 93
Schwartz, Julius 1907-2004 45
Schwartz, Perry 1942- 75
Schwartz, Sheila (Ruth) 1929- 27
Schwartz, Stephen (Lawrence) 1948- 19
Schwartz, Virginia Frances 1950- 184
    Earlier sketch in SATA 131
Schwarz, (Silvia Tessa) Viviane 1977- 141
Schweitzer, Byrd Baylor
    See Baylor, Byrd
Schweitzer, Iris 59
    Brief entry 36
Schweninger, Ann 1951- 168
    Earlier sketches in SATA 29, 98
Schwerin, Doris H(alpern) 1922- 64
Schy, Yael 197
Scieszka, Jon 1954- 199
    Earlier sketches in SATA 68, 105, 160
    See also CLR 107
Scillian, Devin 199
    Earlier sketch in SATA 128
Scioscia, Mary (Hershey) 1926- 63
Sciurba, Katie 1957- 196
Scofield, Penrod 1933- 62
    Obituary 78
Scoggin, Margaret C(lara) 1905-1968 47
    Brief entry 28
Scoltock, Jack 1942- 141
    Earlier sketch in SATA 72
Scoppettone, Sandra 1936- 92
    Earlier sketch in SATA 9
Scot, Michael
    See Rohan, Michael Scott
Scot-Bernard, P.
    See Bernard, Patricia
Scotland, Jay
    See Jakes, John
Scott, Alastair
    See Allen, Kenneth S.
Scott, Ann Herbert 1926- 140
    Autobiography Feature 140
    Brief entry 29
    Earlier sketches in SATA 56, 94
Scott, Bill
    See Scott, William N(eville)

Scott, Bill 1920(?)-1985
    Obituary 46
Scott, Cora Annett (Pipitone) 1931- 11
Scott, Dan
    See Barker, S(quire) Omar
Scott, Elaine 1940- 198
    Earlier sketches in SATA 36, 90, 164
Scott, Elizabeth 194
Scott, Jack Denton 1915-1995 83
    Earlier sketch in SATA 31
    See also CLR 20
    See also SAAS 14
Scott, Jane (Harrington) 1931- 55
Scott, Jessica
    See De Wire, Elinor
Scott, John 1912-1976 14
Scott, John Anthony 1916- 23
Scott, John M(artin) 1913- 12
Scott, Mary
    See Mattern, Joanne
Scott, Melissa 1960- 109
Scott, Richard
    See Rennert, Richard Scott
Scott, Roney
    See Gault, William Campbell
Scott, Sally 1909-1978 43
Scott, Sally 1948- 44
Scott, Sally Elisabeth
    See Scott, Sally
Scott, W. N.
    See Scott, William N(eville)
Scott, Sir Walter 1771-1832
    See YABC 2
Scott, Warwick
    See Trevor, Elleston
Scott, William N(eville) 1923- 87
Scotti, Anna
    See Coates, Anna
Scotton, Rob 1960- 177
Scribner, Charles, Jr. 1921-1995 13
    Obituary 87
Scribner, Joanne L. 1949- 33
Scribner, Kimball 1917- 63
Scrimger, Richard 1957- 164
    Earlier sketch in SATA 119
Scrimsher, Lila Gravatt 1897-1974
    Obituary 28
Scroder, Walter K. 1928- 82
Scroggs, Kirk 187
Scruggs, Sandy 1961- 89
Scudder, Brooke 1959- 154
Scudder, Mildred Lee 1908- 6
    See also SAAS 12
Scull, Marie-Louise 1943-1993 77
Scuro, Vincent 1951- 21
Seabrooke, Brenda 1941- 148
    Earlier sketches in SATA 30, 88
Seaman, Augusta Huiell 1879-1950 31
Seamands, Ruth 1916- 9
Searcy, Margaret Zehmer 1926- 54
    Brief entry 39
Searight, Mary W(illiams) 1918- 17
Searle, Kathryn Adrienne 1942- 10
Searle, Ronald (William Fordham) 1920- 70
    Earlier sketch in SATA 42
Sears, Stephen W. 1932- 4
Sebastian, Lee
    See Silverberg, Robert
Sebestyen, Igen
    See Sebestyen, Ouida
Sebestyen, Ouida 1924- 140
    Earlier sketch in SATA 39
    See also CLR 17
    See also SAAS 10
Sebrey, Mary Ann 1951- 62
Sechrist, Elizabeth Hough 1903-1991 2
Sedges, John
    See Buck, Pearl S(ydenstricker)
Sedgwick, Marcus 1968- 197
    Earlier sketch in SATA 160

Seed, Cecile Eugenie 1930- 86
  Earlier sketch in SATA 8
  See also CLR 76
Seed, Jenny
  See Seed, Cecile Eugenie
Seed, Sheila Turner 1937(?)-1979
  Obituary 23
Seeger, Elizabeth 1889-1973
  Obituary 20
Seeger, Laura Vaccaro 200
  Earlier sketch in SATA 172
Seeger, Pete 1919- 139
  Earlier sketch in SATA 13
Seeger, Peter R.
  See Seeger, Pete
Seeley, Laura L. 1958- 71
Seever, R.
  See Reeves, Lawrence F.
Sefozo, Mary 1925- 82
Sefton, Catherine
  See Waddell, Martin
Segal, John 178
Segal, Joyce 1940- 35
Segal, Lore 1928- 163
  Earlier sketches in SATA 4, 66
  See also SAAS 11
Segal, Lore Groszmann
  See Segal, Lore
Segar, E(lzie) C(risler) 1894-1938 61
Segovia, Andres 1893(?)-1987
  Obituary 52
Seguin, Marilyn W(eymouth) 1951- 91
Seguin-Fontes, Marthe 1924- 109
Seibold, J. Otto 1960- 196
  Earlier sketches in SATA 83, 149
  See also SAAS 22
Seidel, Ross 95
Seidelman, James Edward 1926- 6
Seiden, Art(hur) 107
  Brief entry 42
Seidensticker, John 1944- 200
Seidler, Ann (G.) 1925- 131
Seidler, Tor 1952- 149
  Brief entry 46
  Earlier sketches in SATA 52, 98
Seidman, Laurence Ivan 1925- 15
Seigel, Kalman 1917-1998 12
  Obituary 103
Seignobosc, Francoise 1897-1961 21
Seinfeld, Jerry 1954- 146
Seitz, Jacqueline 1931- 50
Seixas, Judith S. 1922- 17
Sejima, Yoshimasa 1913- 8
Selberg, Ingrid (Maria) 1950- 68
Selden, George
  See Thompson, George Selden
Selden, Neil R(oy) 1931- 61
Self, Margaret Cabell 1902-1996 24
Selfors, Suzanne 1963- 193
Selick, Henry 1952- 183
Selig, Sylvie 1942- 13
Selkirk, Jane
  See Chapman, John Stanton Higham
Sellers, Naomi
  See Flack, Naomi John White
Selman, LaRue W. 1927- 55
Selsam, Millicent E(llis) 1912-1996 29
  Obituary 92
  Earlier sketch in SATA 1
  See also CLR 1
Seltzer, Meyer 1932- 17
Seltzer, Richard 1946- 41
Seltzer, Richard Warren, Jr.
  See Seltzer, Richard
Selvadurai, Shyam 1965(?)- 171
Selway, Martina 1940- 169
  Earlier sketch in SATA 74
Selzer, Adam 1980- 192
Selznick, Brian 1966- 171
  Earlier sketches in SATA 79, 117
Semel, Nava 1954- 107

Semloh
  See Holmes, Peggy
Sendak, Jack 1924(?)-1995 28
Sendak, Maurice 1928- 165
  Earlier sketches in SATA 1, 27, 113
  See also CLR 131
Sendak, Maurice Bernard
  See Sendak, Maurice
Sender, Ruth M(insky) 1926- 62
Sengler, Johanna 1924- 18
Senisi, Ellen B. 1951- 116
Senisi, Ellen Babinec
  See Senisi, Ellen B.
Senn, J(oyce) A(nn) 1941- 115
Senn, Steve 1950- 60
  Brief entry 48
Serafini, Frank 201
Serage, Nancy 1924- 10
Seredy, Kate 1899-1975 1
  Obituary 24
  See also CLR 10
Serfozo, Mary 1925- 194
Seroff, Victor I(ilyitch) 1902-1979 12
  Obituary 26
Serraillier, Ian (Lucien) 1912-1994 73
  Obituary 83
  Earlier sketch in SATA 1
  See also CLR 2
  See also SAAS 3
Serros, Michele 175
Serros, Michele M.
  See Serros, Michele
Servello, Joe 1932- 10
Service, Pamela F. 1945- 64
Service, Robert
  See Service, Robert W.
Service, Robert W. 1874(?)-1958 20
Serwadda, W(illiam) Moses 1931- 27
Serwer-Bernstein, Blanche L(uria)
  1910-1997 10
Sescoe, Vincent E. 1938- 123
Seth, Mary
  See Lexau, Joan M.
Seton, Anya 1904(?)-1990 3
  Obituary 66
Seton, Ernest (Evan) Thompson 1860-1946 . 18
  See also CLR 59
Seton-Thompson, Ernest
  See Seton, Ernest (Evan) Thompson
Seuling, Barbara 1937- 193
  Earlier sketches in SATA 10, 98, 145
  See also SAAS 24
Seuss, Dr.
  See Dr. Seuss
  and Geisel, Theodor Seuss
  and LeSieg, Theo.
  and Stone, Rosetta
Severn, Bill
  See Severn, William Irving
Severn, David
  See Unwin, David S(torr)
Severn, William Irving 1914- 1
Sewall, Marcia 1935- 119
  Earlier sketches in SATA 37, 69
Seward, Prudence 1926- 16
Sewell, Anna 1820-1878 100
  Earlier sketch in SATA 24
  See also CLR 17
Sewell, Helen (Moore) 1896-1957 38
Sexton, Anne (Harvey) 1928-1974 10
Seymour, Alta Halverson 10
Seymour, Jane 1951- 139
Seymour, Tres 1966- 164
  Earlier sketch in SATA 82
Sfar, Joann 1971- 182
Shachtman, Tom 1942- 49
Shackleton, C.C.
  See Aldiss, Brian W.
Shader, Rachel
  See Sofer, Barbara

Shadow, Jak
  See Sutherland, Jon
Shadyland, Sal
  See Cooper, Louise
Shafer, Audrey 183
Shafer, Robert E(ugene) 1925- 9
Shaffer, Terea 1968- 79
Shahan, Sherry 1949- 134
  Earlier sketch in SATA 92
Shahn, Ben(jamin) 1898-1969
  Obituary 21
Shahn, Bernarda Bryson
  See Bryson, Bernarda
Shaik, Fatima 114
Shalant, Phyllis 1949- 150
Shan, Darren 1972- 199
  Earlier sketches in SATA 129, 168
Shan, D.B.
  See Shan, Darren
Shanahan, Lisa 199
Shanberg, Karen
  See Shragg, Karen (I.)
Shane, Harold Gray 1914-1993 36
  Obituary 76
Shange, Ntozake 1948- 157
Shanks, Ann Zane (Kushner) 10
Shannon, David 1959- 152
  Earlier sketch in SATA 107
  See also CLR 87
Shannon, George (William Bones) 1952- ... 143
  Earlier sketches in SATA 35, 94
Shannon, Jacqueline 63
Shannon, Margaret
  See Silverwood, Margaret Shannon
Shannon, Monica 1905(?)-1965 28
Shannon, Terry
  See Mercer, Jessie
Shannon, Terry Miller 1951- 148
Shapiro, Irwin 1911-1981 32
Shapiro, Jody Fickes 1940- 193
Shapiro, Karen Jo 1964- 186
Shapiro, Michelle 1961- 196
Shapiro, Milton J. 1926- 32
Shapiro, Tricia
  See Andryszewski, Tricia
Shapp, Charles M(orris) 1906-1989
  Obituary 61
Shapp, Martha Glauber 1910- 3
Sharenow, Robert 193
Sharfman, Amalie 14
Sharma, Partap 1939- 15
Sharma, Rashmi
  See Singh, Rashmi Sharma
Sharman, Alison
  See Leonard, Alison
Sharmat, Marjorie Weinman 1928- 133
  Earlier sketches in SATA 4, 33, 74
Sharmat, Mitchell 1927- 127
  Earlier sketch in SATA 33
Sharp, Anne Wallace 1947- 144
Sharp, Luke
  See Alkiviades, Alkis
Sharp, Margery 1905-1991 29
  Obituary 67
  Earlier sketch in SATA 1
  See also CLR 27
Sharp, Zerna A. 1889-1981
  Obituary 27
Sharpe, Jon
  See Duncan, Alice
  and Knott, William C(ecil, Jr.)
  and Messman, Jon
Sharpe, Mitchell R(aymond) 1924- 12
Sharpe, Susan 1946- 71
Sharratt, Nick 1962- 199
  Earlier sketches in SATA 104, 153
Shasha, Mark 1961- 80
Shattuck, Roger 1923-2005 64
  Obituary 174
Shattuck, Roger Whitney
  See Shattuck, Roger

Shaw, Arnold 1909-1989 4
  Obituary 63
Shaw, Carolyn V. 1934- 91
Shaw, Charles (Green) 1892-1974 13
Shaw, Evelyn S. 1927- 28
Shaw, Flora Louisa
  See Lugard, Flora Louisa Shaw
Shaw, Janet 1937- 146
  Earlier sketch in SATA 61
  See also CLR 96
Shaw, Janet Beeler
  See Shaw, Janet
Shaw, Lisa
  See Rogak, Lisa
Shaw, Margret 1940- 68
Shaw, Mary 1965- 180
Shaw, Nancy 1946- 162
  Earlier sketch in SATA 71
Shaw, Ray 7
Shaw, Richard 1923- 12
Shawn, Frank S.
  See Goulart, Ron
Shay, Art
  See Shay, Arthur
Shay, Arthur 1922- 4
Shay, Lacey
  See Shebar, Sharon Sigmond
Shea, Bob 188
Shea, George 1940- 54
  Brief entry 42
Shea, Pegi Deitz 1960- 172
  Earlier sketches in SATA 77, 137
Shearer, John 1947- 43
  Brief entry 27
  See also CLR 34
Shearer, Ted 1919- 43
Shearing, Leonie 1972- 184
Sheban, Chris 182
Shebar, Sharon Sigmond 1945- 36
Shecter, Ben 1935- 16
Shedd, Warner 1934- 147
  Earlier sketch in SATA 87
Sheedy, Alexandra Elizabeth 1962- 39
  Earlier sketch in SATA 19
Sheehan, Ethna 1908-2000 9
Sheehan, Patty 1945- 77
Sheehan, Sean 1951- 154
  Earlier sketch in SATA 86
Sheen, Barbara 1949- 143
Shefelman, Janice Jordan 1930- 129
  Earlier sketch in SATA 58
Shefelman, Tom (Whitehead) 1927- 58
Sheffer, H. R.
  See Abels, Harriette S(heffer)
Sheffield, Charles 1935-2002 109
Sheffield, Janet N. 1926- 26
Sheikh, Nazneen
  See Sadiq, Nazneen
Shekerjian, Regina Tor 16
Shelby, Anne 1948- 85
  Autobiography Feature 121
  See also SAAS 26
Sheldon, Ann
  See Antle, Nancy
Sheldon, Ann 67
  Earlier sketch in SATA 1
Sheldon, Aure 1917-1976 12
Sheldon, David 185
Sheldon, Dyan 181
Sheldon, John
  See Bloch, Robert (Albert)
Sheldon, Muriel 1926- 45
  Brief entry 39
Shell, Barry 1951- 176
Shelley, Frances
  See Wees, Frances Shelley
Shelley, Mary Wollstonecraft (Godwin)
  1797-1851 29
  See also CLR 133
Shelton, William Roy 1919-1995 5
  Obituary 129

Shemie, Bonnie (Jean Brenner) 1949- 96
Shemin, Margaretha (Hoeneveld) 1928- 4
Shen, Michele 1953- 173
Shenker, Michele
  See Shen, Michele
Shenton, Edward 1895-1977 45
Shepard, Aaron 1950- 187
  Earlier sketches in SATA 75, 113
Shepard, Ernest Howard 1879-1976 100
  Obituary 24
  Earlier sketches in SATA 3, 33
  See also CLR 27
Shepard, James R.
  See Shepard, Jim
Shepard, Jim 1956- 164
  Earlier sketch in SATA 90
Shepard, Mary
  See Knox, (Mary) Eleanor Jessie
Shephard, Esther 1891-1975 5
  Obituary 26
Shepherd, Amanda 201
Shepherd, Donna Walsh
  See Walsh Shepherd, Donna
Shepherd, Elizabeth 4
Shepherd, Irana 173
Shepherd, Roni
  See Shepherd, Irana
Sheppard, Kate 195
Shepperson, Rob 178
Sherburne, Zoa (Lillian Morin) 1912-1995 3
  See also SAAS 18
Sherk-Savage, Candace
  See Savage, Candace
Sherlock, Patti 71
Sherman, D(enis) R(onald) 1934- 48
  Brief entry 29
Sherman, Diane (Finn) 1928- 12
Sherman, Elizabeth
  See Friskey, Margaret (Richards)
Sherman, Harold (Morrow) 1898-1987 37
  Obituary 137
Sherman, Josepha 163
  Earlier sketch in SATA 75
Sherman, Michael
  See Lowndes, Robert A(ugustine) W(ard)
Sherman, Nancy
  See Rosenberg, Nancy (Sherman)
Sherman, Pat 174
Sherman, Peter Michael
  See Lowndes, Robert A(ugustine) W(ard)
Sherrard, Valerie (Anne) 1957- 141
Sherrod, Jane
  See Singer, Jane Sherrod
Sherry, Clifford J. 1943- 84
Sherry, (Dulcie) Sylvia 1932- 122
  Earlier sketch in SATA 8
Sherwan, Earl 1917- 3
Sherwood, Jonathan
  See London, Jonathan (Paul)
Sheth, Kashmira 186
Shetterly, Will 1955- 78
  Autobiography Feature 106
Shetterly, William Howard
  See Shetterly, Will
Shiefman, Vicky 1942- 22
Shields, Brenda Desmond (Armstrong)
  1914- 37
Shields, Carol Diggory 174
Shields, Charles 1944- 10
Shiels, Barbara
  See Adams, Barbara Johnston
Shiffman, Lena 1957- 101
Shiina, Makoto 1944- 83
Shimin, Symeon 1902-1984 13
Shimko, Bonnie 1941- 191
Shine, Andrea 1955- 104
Shine, Deborah 1932- 71
Shinn, Everett 1876-1953 21
Shinn, Sharon 1957- 164
  Earlier sketch in SATA 110

Shippen, Katherine B(inney) 1892-1980 1
  Obituary 23
  See also CLR 36
Shippey, T. A. 1943- 143
Shippey, Thomas Alan
  See Shippey, T. A.
Shipton, Eric Earle 1907-1977 10
Shipton, Paul 1963- 196
Shiraz, Yasmin 173
Shirer, William L(awrence) 1904-1993 45
  Obituary 78
Shirley, Gayle C 1955- 96
Shirley, Gayle Corbett
  See Shirley, Gayle C
Shirley, Jean 1919- 70
Shirreffs, Gordon D(onald) 1914-1996 11
Shirts, Morris A(lpine) 1922- 63
Shlichta, Joe 1968- 84
Shmurak, Carole B. 1944- 118
Sholokhov, Mikhail (Aleksandrovich)
  1905-1984
  Obituary 36
Shore, Diane Z. 179
Shore, Diane ZuHone
  See Shore, Diane Z.
Shore, June Lewis 30
Shore, Nancy 1960- 124
Shore, Robert 1924- 39
Short, Michael 1937- 65
Short, Roger
  See Arkin, Alan
Shortall, Leonard W. 19
Shortt, Tim(othy Donald) 1961- 96
Shotwell, Louisa Rossiter 1902-1993 3
Shoup, Barbara 1947- 156
  Earlier sketch in SATA 86
  See also SAAS 24
Shoveller, Herb 184
Showalter, Jean B(reckinridge) 12
Showell, Ellen Harvey 1934- 33
Showers, Paul C. 1910-1999 92
  Obituary 114
  Earlier sketch in SATA 21
  See also CLR 6
  See also SAAS 7
Shpakow, Tanya 1959(?)- 94
Shpitalnik, Vladimir 1964- 83
Shragg, Karen (I.) 1954- 142
Shreeve, Elizabeth 1956- 156
Shreve, Susan
  See Shreve, Susan Richards
Shreve, Susan Richards 1939- 152
  Brief entry 41
  Earlier sketches in SATA 46, 95
Shriver, Jean Adair 1932- 75
Shriver, Maria 1955- 134
Shriver, Maria Owings
  See Shriver, Maria
Shrode, Mary
  See Hollingsworth, Mary
Shtainmets, Leon 32
Shub, Elizabeth 1915(?)-2004 5
Shuken, Julia 1948- 84
Shulevitz, Uri 1935- 165
  Earlier sketches in SATA 3, 50, 106
  See also CLR 61
Shulman, Alix Kates 1932- 7
Shulman, Dee 1957- 146
Shulman, Irving 1913-1995 13
Shulman, Mark 1962- 184
Shulman, Max 1919-1988
  Obituary 59
Shulman, Milton 1913-2004
  Obituary 154
Shulman, Neil B(arnett) 1945- 89
Shumsky, Zena
  See Collier, Zena
Shura, Mary Francis
  See Craig, Mary (Francis) Shura

Shusterman, Neal 1962- *201*
  Autobiography Feature *140*
  Earlier sketches in SATA *85, 121, 140*
Shuter, Jane (Margaret) 1955- *151*
  Earlier sketch in SATA *90*
Shuttlesworth, Dorothy Edwards *3*
Shwartz, Susan (Martha) 1949- *94*
Shyer, Christopher 1961- *98*
Shyer, Marlene Fanta *13*
Siberell, Anne *29*
Sibley, Don 1922- *12*
Siburt, Ruth 1951- *121*
Siculan, Daniel 1922- *12*
Siddon, Barbara
  See Bradford, Barbara Taylor
Sidgwick, Ethel 1877-1970 .... *116*
Sidjakov, Nicolas 1924- *18*
Sidman, Joyce 1956- *181*
  Earlier sketch in SATA *145*
Sidney, Frank
  See Warwick, Alan R(oss)
Sidney, Margaret
  See Lothrop, Harriet Mulford Stone
Siebert, Diane 1948- *189*
Siegal, Aranka 1930- *88*
  Brief entry *37*
Siegel, Beatrice *36*
Siegel, Helen
  See Siegl, Helen
Siegel, Robert 1939- *39*
Siegel, Robert Harold
  See Siegel, Robert
Siegel, Siena Cherson 1967(?)- *185*
Siegelson, Kim L. 1962- *114*
Sieger, Ted 1958- *189*
Siegl, Helen 1924- *34*
Siepmann, Mary Aline
  See Wesley, Mary (Aline)
Sierra, Judy 1945- *195*
  Earlier sketches in SATA *104, 162*
Sieswerda, Paul L. 1942- *147*
Sievert, Terri
  See Dougherty, Terri (L.)
Silas
  See McCay, (Zenas) Winsor
Silcock, Sara Lesley 1947- *12*
Silin-Palmer, Pamela *184*
Sill, Cathryn 1953- *141*
  Earlier sketch in SATA *74*
Sill, John 1947- *140*
  Earlier sketch in SATA *74*
Sillitoe, Alan 1928- *61*
Sills, Leslie (Elka) 1948- *129*
Silly, E. S.
  See Kraus, (Herman) Robert
Silsbe, Brenda 1953- *73*
Silva, Joseph
  See Goulart, Ron
Silver, Ruth
  See Chew, Ruth
Silverberg, Robert 1935- *91*
  Autobiography Feature *104*
  Earlier sketch in SATA *13*
  See also CLR *59*
Silverman, Erica 1955- *165*
  Earlier sketches in SATA *78, 112*
Silverman, Janis L. 1946- *127*
Silverman, Mel(vin Frank) 1931-1966 .... *9*
Silverman, Robin L. 1954- *96*
Silverman, Robin Landew
  See Silverman, Robin L.
Silverstein, Alvin 1933- *124*
  Earlier sketches in SATA *8, 69*
  See also CLR *25*
Silverstein, Herma 1945- *106*
Silverstein, Robert Alan 1959- *124*
  Earlier sketch in SATA *77*

Silverstein, Shel 1932-1999 .... *92*
  Brief entry *27*
  Obituary *116*
  Earlier sketch in SATA *33*
  See also CLR *96*
Silverstein, Sheldon Allan
  See Silverstein, Shel
Silverstein, Virginia B(arbara Opshelor)
  1937- *124*
  Earlier sketches in SATA *8, 69*
  See also CLR *25*
Silverthorne, Elizabeth 1930- *35*
Silverwood, Margaret Shannon 1966- *137*
  Earlier sketch in SATA *83*
Silvey, Diane F. 1946- *135*
Sim, David 1953- *162*
Sim, Dorrith M. 1931- *96*
Simak, Clifford D(onald) 1904-1988
  Obituary *56*
Simard, Remy 1959- *168*
Simmie, Lois (Ann) 1932- *106*
Simmonds, Posy 1945- *130*
  See also CLR *23*
Simmons, Andra 1939- *141*
Simmons, Elly 1955- *134*
Simmons, Michael 1970- *185*
Simms, Laura 1947- *117*
Simner, Janni Lee *113*
Simon, Charlie May
  See Fletcher, Charlie May Hogue
Simon, Francesca 1955- *111*
Simon, Gabriel 1972- *118*
Simon, Hilda Rita 1921- *28*
  See also CLR *39*
Simon, Howard 1903-1979 .... *32*
  Obituary *21*
Simon, Joe
  See Simon, Joseph H.
Simon, Joseph H. 1913- *7*
Simon, Martin P(aul William) 1903-1969 .... *12*
Simon, Mina Lewiton
  See Lewiton, Mina
Simon, Norma (Feldstein) 1927- *129*
  Earlier sketches in SATA *3, 68*
Simon, Seymour 1931- *138*
  Earlier sketches in SATA *4, 73*
  See also CLR *63*
Simon, Shirley (Schwartz) 1921- *11*
Simon, Solomon 1895-1970 .... *40*
Simonetta, Linda 1948- *14*
Simonetta, Sam 1936- *14*
Simons, Barbara B(rooks) 1934- *41*
Simont, Marc 1915- *126*
  Earlier sketches in SATA *9, 73*
Simpson, Colin 1908-1983 .... *14*
Simpson, Harriette
  See Arnow, Harriette (Louisa) Simpson
Simpson, Jacynth Hope
  See Hope Simpson, Jacynth
Simpson, Lesley 1963- *150*
Simpson, Margaret 1943- *128*
Simpson, Myrtle L(illias) 1931- *14*
Sims, Blanche *168*
  Earlier sketch in SATA *75*
Sims, Blanche L.
  See Sims, Blanche
Simundsson, Elva 1950- *63*
Sinclair, Clover
  See Gater, Dilys
Sinclair, Emil
  See Hesse, Hermann
Sinclair, Jeff 1958- *77*
Sinclair, Olga 1923- *121*
Sinclair, Rose
  See Smith, Susan Vernon
Sinclair, Upton 1878-1968 .... *9*
Sinclair, Upton Beall
  See Sinclair, Upton
Singer, A.L.
  See Lerangis, Peter
Singer, Arthur 1917-1990 .... *64*

Singer, Isaac
  See Singer, Isaac Bashevis
Singer, Isaac Bashevis 1904-1991 .... *27*
  Obituary *68*
  Earlier sketch in SATA *3*
  See also CLR *1*
Singer, Jane Sherrod 1917-1985 .... *4*
  Obituary *42*
Singer, Julia 1917- *28*
Singer, Kurt D. 1911-2005 .... *38*
  Obituary *172*
Singer, Marilyn 1948- *201*
  Autobiography Feature *158*
  Brief entry *38*
  Earlier sketches in SATA *48, 80, 125, 158*
  See also CLR *48*
  See also SAAS *13*
Singer, Muff 1942-2005 .... *104*
  Obituary *160*
Singer, Nicky 1956- *194*
Singer, Susan (Mahler) 1941- *9*
Singh, Rashmi Sharma 1952- *90*
Singleton, Linda Joy 1957- *166*
  Earlier sketch in SATA *88*
Singleton, L.J.
  See Singleton, Linda Joy
Sinykin, Sheri Cooper 1950- *142*
  Autobiography Feature *142*
  Earlier sketches in SATA *72, 133*
Sipiera, Paul P., (Jr.) 1948- *144*
  Earlier sketch in SATA *89*
Siracusa, Catherine (Jane) 1947- *82*
Sirett, Dawn (Karen) 1966- *88*
Sirimarco, Elizabeth 1966- *158*
Sirof, Harriet 1930- *94*
  Earlier sketch in SATA *37*
Sirois, Allen L. 1950- *76*
Sirvaitis (Chernyaev), Karen (Ann) 1961- ... *79*
Sis, Peter 1949- *192*
  Earlier sketch in SATA *149*
  See also CLR *110*
Sisson, Rosemary Anne 1923- *11*
Sister Mary Terese
  See Donze, Mary Terese
Sita, Lisa 1962- *87*
Sitarski, Anita *200*
Sitomer, Alan Lawrence *174*
Sitomer, Harry 1903-1985 .... *31*
Sitomer, Mindel 1903-1987 .... *31*
Sittenfeld, Curtis 1975(?)- *164*
Sive, Helen R(obinson) 1951- *30*
Sivulich, Sandra (Jeanne) Stroner 1941- *9*
Siy, Alexandra *193*
Skarmeta, Antonio 1940- *57*
Skelly, James R(ichard) 1927- *17*
Skelton, Matthew 1971- *185*
Skinner, Constance Lindsay 1877-1939
  See YABC *1*
Skinner, Cornelia Otis 1901-1979 .... *2*
Skipper, G. C. 1939- *46*
  Brief entry *38*
Sklansky, Amy E(dgar) 1971- *145*
Skofield, James *95*
  Brief entry *44*
Skold, Betty Westrom 1923- *41*
Skorpen, Liesel Moak 1935- *3*
Skott, Maria
  See Nikolajeva, Maria
Skrypuch, Marsha Forchuk 1954- *134*
Skultety, Nancy Laney 1960- *175*
Skurzynski, Gloria 1930- *145*
  Autobiography Feature *145*
  Earlier sketches in SATA *8, 74, 122*
  See also SAAS *9*
Skurzynski, Gloria Joan
  See Skurzynski, Gloria
Skutch, Robert 1925- *89*
Skye, Maggie
  See Werner, Herma
Skye, Obert *200*
  Earlier sketch in SATA *170*

Slack, Michael 1969- *189*
Slackman, Charles B. 1934- *12*
Slade, Arthur G. 1967- *149*
 Earlier sketch in SATA *106*
Slade, Arthur Gregory
 See Slade, Arthur G.
Slade, Christian 1974- *193*
Slade, Richard 1910-1971 .... *9*
Slangerup, Erik Jon 1969- *130*
Slate, Joseph 1928- *174*
 Earlier sketches in SATA *38, 122*
Slate, Joseph Frank
 See Slate, Joseph
Slater, Dashka 1963- *179*
Slater, Ray
 See Lansdale, Joe R.
Slaughter, Hope 1940- *84*
Slaughter, Jean
 See Doty, Jean Slaughter
Slaughter, Tom 1955- *152*
Slavicek, Louise Chipley 1956- *144*
Slavin, Bill 1959- *199*
 Earlier sketches in SATA *76, 148*
Slaymaker, Melissa Eskridge 1958- *158*
Sleator, William 1945- *161*
 Earlier sketches in SATA *3, 68, 118*
 See also CLR *128*
Sleator, William Warner III
 See Sleator, William
Slegers, Liesbet 1975- *154*
Sleigh, Barbara 1906-1982 .... *86*
 Obituary *30*
 Earlier sketch in SATA *3*
Slepian, Jan 1921- *85*
 Brief entry *45*
 Earlier sketch in SATA *51*
 See also SAAS *8*
Slepian, Janice B.
 See Slepian, Jan
Slicer, Margaret O. 1920- *4*
Slier, Debby
 See Shine, Deborah
Sloan, Brian 1966- *172*
Sloan, Carolyn 1937- *116*
 Earlier sketch in SATA *58*
Sloan, Glenna (Davis) 1930- *120*
Sloane, Eric 1910(?)-1985 .... *52*
 Obituary *42*
Sloane, Todd 1955- *88*
Sloat, Teri 1948- *164*
 Earlier sketches in SATA *70, 106*
Slobodkin, Florence Gersh 1905-1994 ...... *5*
 Obituary *107*
Slobodkin, Louis 1903-1975 .... *26*
 Earlier sketch in SATA *1*
Slobodkina, Esphyr 1908-2002 .... *1*
 Obituary *135*
 See also SAAS *8*
Sloggett, Nellie 1851-1923 .... *44*
Sloss, Lesley Lord 1965- *72*
Slote, Alfred 1926- *72*
 Earlier sketch in SATA *8*
 See also CLR *4*
 See also SAAS *21*
Slote, Elizabeth 1956- *80*
Small, David 1945- *183*
 Brief entry *46*
 Earlier sketches in SATA *50, 95, 126*
 See also CLR *53*
Small, Ernest
 See Lent, Blair
Small, Mary 1932- *165*
Small, Terry 1942- *75*
Smallcomb, Pam 1954- *159*
Smallman, Steve *197*
Smalls, Irene
 See Smalls-Hector, Irene
Smalls-Hector, Irene 1950- *146*
 Earlier sketch in SATA *73*
 See also CLR *103*

Smallwood, Norah (Evelyn) 1910(?)-1984
 Obituary *41*
Smaridge, Norah (Antoinette) 1903-1994 ...... *6*
Smath, Jerry 1933- *198*
Smee, Nicola 1948- *167*
 Earlier sketch in SATA *76*
Smiley, Virginia Kester 1923- *2*
Smit, Noelle 1972- *199*
Smith, Alexander McCall 1948- *179*
 Earlier sketch in SATA *73*
Smith, Anne Warren 1938- *41*
 Brief entry *34*
Smith, Barry (Edward Jervis) 1943- *75*
Smith, Beatrice S(chillinger) *12*
Smith, Betsy Covington 1937- *55*
 Earlier sketch in SATA *43*
Smith, Betty (Wehner) 1904-1972 .... *6*
Smith, Bradford 1909-1964 .... *5*
Smith, Brenda 1946- *82*
Smith, C. Pritchard
 See Hoyt, Edwin P(almer), Jr.
Smith, Caesar
 See Trevor, Elleston
Smith, Cat Bowman 1939- *201*
Smith, Charles R., (Jr.) 1969- *159*
Smith, Craig 1955- *172*
 Earlier sketches in SATA *81, 117*
Smith, Cynthia Leitich 1967- *152*
Smith, Datus C(lifford), Jr. 1907-1999 ...... *13*
 Obituary *116*
Smith, Debra 1955- *89*
Smith, Derek 1943- *141*
Smith, Dick King
 See King-Smith, Dick
Smith, Dodie
 See Smith, Dorothy Gladys
Smith, Doris Buchanan 1934-2002 .... *75*
 Obituary *140*
 Earlier sketch in SATA *28*
 See also SAAS *10*
Smith, Dorothy Gladys 1896-1990 .... *82*
 Obituary *65*
Smith, Dorothy Stafford 1905- *6*
Smith, E(lmer) Boyd 1860-1943
 See YABC *1*
Smith, E(dric) Brooks 1917- *40*
Smith, Emma 1923- *52*
 Brief entry *36*
Smith, (Katherine) Eunice (Young)
 1902-1993 .... *5*
Smith, Frances C(hristine) 1904-1986 .... *3*
Smith, Gary R. 1932- *14*
Smith, Geof 1969- *102*
Smith, George Harmon 1920- *5*
Smith, Gordon 1951- *184*
Smith, Greg Leitich *152*
Smith, H(arry) Allen 1907-1976
 Obituary *20*
Smith, Helene 1937- *142*
Smith, Howard E(verett), Jr. 1927- *12*
Smith, Hugh L(etcher) 1921-1968 .... *5*
Smith, Imogene Henderson 1922- *12*
Smith, Jacqueline B. 1937- *39*
Smith, Jada Pinkett 1971- *161*
Smith, James D. 1955- *176*
Smith, James Noel 1950- *193*
Smith, Janet (Buchanan) Adam
 See Adam Smith, Janet (Buchanan)
Smith, Janice Lee 1949- *155*
 Earlier sketch in SATA *54*
Smith, Jean
 See Smith, Frances C(hristine)
Smith, Jean Pajot 1945- *10*
Smith, Jeff(rey Alan) 1960- *161*
 Earlier sketch in SATA *93*
Smith, Jeff Allen
 See Smith, Jeff(rey Alan)
Smith, Jenny 1963- *90*
Smith, Jessie
 See Kunhardt, Edith

Smith, Jessie Willcox 1863-1935 .... *21*
 See also CLR *59*
Smith, Joan (Mary) 1933- *54*
 Brief entry *46*
Smith, Johnston
 See Crane, Stephen (Townley)
Smith, Jos A. 1936- *181*
 Earlier sketches in SATA *73, 120*
Smith, Joseph Arthur
 See Smith, Jos A.
Smith, Judie R. 1936- *80*
Smith, Lafayette
 See Higdon, Hal
Smith, Lane 1959- *179*
 Earlier sketches in SATA *76, 131*
 See also CLR *47*
Smith, Lee
 See Albion, Lee Smith
Smith, Lendon H(oward) 1921- *64*
Smith, Lillian H(elena) 1887-1983
 Obituary *32*
Smith, Linda 1949- *177*
Smith, Linell Nash 1932- *2*
Smith, Lucia B. 1943- *30*
Smith, Maggie 1965- *190*
Smith, Margaret Emily Noel Nuttall
 See Nuttall-Smith, Margaret Emily Noel
Smith, Marion Hagens 1913- *12*
Smith, Marion Jaques 1899-1987 .... *13*
Smith, Mary Ellen *10*
Smith, Marya 1945- *78*
Smith, Mike
 See Smith, Mary Ellen
Smith, Nancy Covert 1935- *12*
Smith, Norman F. 1920- *70*
 Earlier sketch in SATA *5*
Smith, Patricia Clark 1943- *96*
Smith, Pauline C.
 See Arthur, Robert, (Jr.)
Smith, Pauline C(oggeshall) 1908-1994 ..... *27*
Smith, Philip Warren 1936- *46*
Smith, R. Alexander McCall
 See Smith, Alexander McCall
Smith, Rebecca 1946- *123*
Smith, Robert Kimmel 1930- *77*
 Earlier sketch in SATA *12*
Smith, Robert Paul 1915-1977 .... *52*
 Obituary *30*
Smith, Roland 1951- *193*
 Earlier sketches in SATA *115, 161*
Smith, Rosamond
 See Oates, Joyce Carol
Smith, Ruth Leslie 1902- *2*
Smith, Samantha 1972-1985
 Obituary *45*
Smith, Sandra Lee 1945- *75*
Smith, Sarah Stafford
 See Smith, Dorothy Stafford
Smith, Sharon 1947- *82*
Smith, Sherri L. 1971- *156*
Smith, Sherwood 1951- *140*
 Earlier sketch in SATA *82*
Smith, Shirley Raines
 See Raines, Shirley C(arol)
Smith, Susan Carlton 1923- *12*
Smith, Susan Mathias 1950- *43*
 Brief entry *35*
Smith, Susan Vernon 1950- *48*
 Brief entry *45*
Smith, Tim(othy R.) 1945- *151*
Smith, Ursula 1934- *54*
Smith, Vian (Crocker) 1920-1969 .... *11*
Smith, Wanda VanHoy 1926- *65*
Smith, Ward
 See Goldsmith, Howard
Smith, William A. 1918- *10*
Smith, William Jay 1918- *154*
 Autobiography Feature *154*
 Earlier sketches in SATA *2, 68*
 See also SAAS *22*
Smith, Winsome 1935- *45*

Smith, Z.Z.
  See Westheimer, David
Smith-Ankrom, M. E. 1942- 130
Smith-Griswold, Wendy 1955- 88
Smith-Rex, Susan J. 1950- 94
Smithsen, Richard
  See Pellowski, Michael (Joseph)
Smits, Teo
  See Smits, Theodore R(ichard)
Smits, Theodore R(ichard) 1905-1996 45
  Brief entry 28
Smolinski, Dick 1932- 86
Smothers, Ethel Footman 1944- 149
  Earlier sketch in SATA 76
Smucker, Barbara 1915-2003 130
  Earlier sketches in SATA 29, 76
  See also CLR 10
  See also SAAS 11
Smucker, Barbara Claassen
  See Smucker, Barbara
Smyth, Iain 1959- 105
Snedeker, Caroline Dale (Parke) 1871-1956
  See YABC 2
Sneed, Brad 191
Sneider, Marian 1932-2005 197
Snell, Nigel (Edward Creagh) 1936- 57
  Brief entry 40
Snellgrove, L(aurence) E(rnest) 1928- 53
Snelling, Dennis (Wayne) 1958- 84
Sneve, Virginia Driving Hawk 1933- 95
  Earlier sketch in SATA 8
  See also CLR 2
Snicket, Lemony 1970- 187
  Earlier sketch in SATA 126
  See also CLR 79
Sniegoski, Thomas E. 195
Sniegoski, Tom
  See Sniegoski, Thomas E.
Snodgrass, Mary Ellen 1944- 75
Snodgrass, Quentin Curtius
  See Twain, Mark
Snodgrass, Thomas Jefferson
  See Twain, Mark
Snook, Barbara (Lillian) 1913-1976 34
Snow, Alan 1959- 190
Snow, Donald Clifford 1917-1979 16
Snow, Dorothea J(ohnston) 1909- 9
Snow, Richard F(olger) 1947- 52
  Brief entry 37
Snyder, Anne 1922-2001 4
  Obituary 125
Snyder, Bernadette McCarver 1930- 97
Snyder, Carol 1941- 35
Snyder, Gerald S(eymour) 1933- 48
  Brief entry 34
Snyder, Jerome 1916-1976
  Obituary 20
Snyder, Midori 1954- 106
Snyder, Paul A. 1946- 125
Snyder, Zilpha Keatley 1927- 163
  Autobiography Feature 163
  Earlier sketches in SATA 1, 28, 75, 110
  See also CLR 121
  See also SAAS 2
Snyderman, Reuven K. 1922- 5
So, Meilo 162
Sobel, June 1950- 149
Soble, Jennie
  See Cavin, Ruth (Brodie)
Sobol, Donald J. 1924- 132
  Earlier sketches in SATA 1, 31, 73
  See also CLR 4
Sobol, Harriet Langsam 1936- 47
  Brief entry 34
Sobol, Rose 1931- 76
Sobott-Mogwe, Gaele 1956- 97
Soderlind, Arthur E(dwin) 1920- 14
Soentpiet, Chris K. 1970- 159
  Earlier sketch in SATA 97
Soerensen, Svend Otto 1916- 67
Sofer, Barbara 1949- 109

Sofer, Rachel
  See Sofer, Barbara
Softly, Barbara Frewin 1924- 12
Soglow, Otto 1900-1975
  Obituary 30
Sohl, Frederic J(ohn) 1916- 10
Sohr, Daniel 1973- 190
Sokol, Bill
  See Sokol, William
Sokol, William 1923- 37
Sokolov, Kirill 1930- 34
Solbert, Romaine G. 1925- 2
Solbert, Ronni
  See Solbert, Romaine G.
Solheim, James 133
Solomon, Heather M. 188
Solomon, Joan 1930- 51
  Brief entry 40
Solomons, Ikey Esquir
  See Thackeray, William Makepeace
Solonevich, George 1915-2003 15
Solot, Mary Lynn 1939- 12
Soman, David 1965- 200
Somerlott, Robert 1928-2001 62
Somervill, Barbara A(nn) 1948- 140
Sommer, Angela
  See Sommer-Bodenburg, Angela
Sommer, Carl 1930- 175
  Earlier sketch in SATA 126
Sommer, Elyse 1929- 7
Sommer, Robert 1929- 12
Sommer-Bodenburg, Angela 1948- 113
  Earlier sketch in SATA 63
Sommerdorf, Norma 1926- 131
Sommerdorf, Norma Jean
  See Sommerdorf, Norma
Sommerfelt, Aimee 1892-1975 5
Son, John 160
Sones, Sonya 131
Sonneborn, Ruth (Cantor) 1899-1974 4
  Obituary 27
Sonnenblick, Jordan 1969- 185
  See also CLR 144
Sonnenmark, Laura A. 1958- 73
Soo, Kean 201
Sopko, Eugen 1949- 58
Sorel, Edward 1929- 126
  Brief entry 37
  Earlier sketch in SATA 65
Sorensen, Henri 1950- 115
  Earlier sketch in SATA 77
Sorensen, Svend Otto
  See Soerensen, Svend Otto
Sorensen, Virginia 1912-1991 2
  Obituary 72
  See also SAAS 15
Sorenson, Jane 1926- 63
Sorenson, Margo 1946- 96
Sorley Walker, Kathrine 41
Sorra, Kristin 185
Sorrells, Walter 177
Sorrentino, Joseph N. 1937- 6
Sortor, June Elizabeth 1939- 12
Sortor, Toni
  See Sortor, June Elizabeth
Soskin, V. H.
  See Ellison, Virginia H(owell)
Soto, Gary 1952- 174
  Earlier sketches in SATA 80, 120
  See also CLR 38
Sotomayor, Antonio 1902-1985 11
Souci, Robert D. San
  See San Souci, Robert D.
Soudley, Henry
  See Wood, James Playsted
Souhami, Jessica 176
Soule, Gardner (Bosworth) 1913-2000 14
Soule, Jean Conder 1919- 10
Souster, (Holmes) Raymond 1921- 63
South, Sheri Cobb 1959- 82

Southall, Ivan 1921-2008 134
  Autobiography Feature 134
  Earlier sketches in SATA 3, 68
  See also CLR 2
  See also SAAS 3
Southall, Ivan Francis
  See Southall, Ivan
Southey, Robert 1774-1843 54
Southgate, Vera 54
Sovak, Jan 1953- 115
Sowden, Celeste
  See Walters, Celeste
Sowter, Nita 69
Spafford, Suzy 1945- 160
Spagnoli, Cathy 1950- 134
  Earlier sketch in SATA 79
Spain, Sahara Sunday 1991- 133
Spain, Susan Rosson 185
Spalding, Andrea 1944- 150
  Earlier sketch in SATA 101
Spalenka, Greg 1958- 198
Spanfeller, James J. 1930- 19
  See also SAAS 8
Spanfeller, Jim
  See Spanfeller, James J.
Spangenberg, Judith Dunn 1942- 5
Spanyol, Jessica 1965- 137
Spar, Jerome 1918- 10
Sparks, Barbara 1942- 78
Sparks, Beatrice (Mathews) 1918- 44
  Brief entry 28
  See also CLR 139
Sparks, Mary W. 1920- 15
Spaulding, Douglas
  See Bradbury, Ray
Spaulding, Leonard
  See Bradbury, Ray
Spaulding, Norma 107
Speare, Elizabeth George 1908-1994 62
  Obituary 83
  Earlier sketch in SATA 5
  See also CLR 8
Spearing, Judith (Mary Harlow) 1922- 9
Spears, Rick 182
Speck, Katie 196
Speck, Nancy 1959- 104
Specking, Inez 1890-1960(?) 11
Speed, Nell
  See Keats, Emma
  and Sampson, Emma (Keats) Speed
Speed, Nell (Ewing) 1878-1913 68
Speer, Bonnie Stahlman 1929- 113
Speer-Lyon, Tammie L. 1965- 89
Speicher, Helen Ross S(mith) 1915- 8
Speir, Nancy 1958- 81
Spellman, John W(illard) 1934- 14
Spellman, Roger G.
  See Cox, William R(obert)
Spelman, Cornelia Maude 1946- 144
  Earlier sketch in SATA 96
Spelman, Mary 1934- 28
Spelvin, George
  See Lerangis, Peter
  and Phillips, David Atlee
Spence, Cynthia
  See Eble, Diane
Spence, Eleanor (Rachel) 1928- 21
  See also CLR 26
Spence, Geraldine 1931- 47
Spencer, Ann 1918- 10
Spencer, Cornelia
  See Yaukey, Grace S(ydenstricker)
Spencer, Donald D(ean) 1931- 41
Spencer, Elizabeth 1921- 14
Spencer, Leonard G.
  See Garrett, Randall
  and Silverberg, Robert
Spencer, William 1922- 9
Spencer, Zane A(nn) 1935- 35
Sper, Emily 1957- 142
Speregen, Devra Newberger 1964- 84

Sperling, Dan(iel Lee) 1949- 65
Sperry, Armstrong W. 1897-1976 1
    Obituary 27
Sperry, Raymond
    See Garis, Howard R(oger)
Sperry, Raymond, Jr. 1
Spetter, Jung-Hee 1969- 134
Spicer, Dorothy Gladys -1975 32
Spiegel, Beth 184
Spiegelman, Art 1948- 158
    Earlier sketch in SATA 109
Spiegelman, Judith M. 5
Spielberg, Steven 1947- 32
Spier, Peter (Edward) 1927- 54
    Earlier sketch in SATA 4
    See also CLR 5
Spilhaus, Athelstan (Frederick) 1911-1998 .. 13
    Obituary 102
Spilka, Arnold 1917- 6
Spillane, Frank Morrison
    See Spillane, Mickey
Spillane, Mickey 1918-2006 66
    Obituary 176
Spinelli, Eileen 1942- 186
    Earlier sketches in SATA 38, 101, 150
Spinelli, Jerry 1941- 195
    Earlier sketches in SATA 39, 71, 110, 158
    See also CLR 82
Spink, Reginald (William) 1905-1994 11
Spinka, Penina Keen 1945- 72
Spinner, Stephanie 1943- 132
    Earlier sketches in SATA 38, 91
Spinossimus
    See White, William, Jr.
Spiotta-DiMare, Loren 173
Spires, Ashley 1978- 183
Spires, Elizabeth 1952- 111
    Earlier sketch in SATA 71
Spiridellis, Gregg 1971(?)- 199
Spirin, Gennadii
    See Spirin, Gennady
Spirin, Gennadij
    See Spirin, Gennady
Spirin, Gennady 1948- 134
    Earlier sketch in SATA 95
    See also CLR 88
Spivak, Dawnine 101
Spizman, Robyn Freedman 194
Spohn, David 1948- 72
Spohn, Kate 1962- 147
    Earlier sketch in SATA 87
Spollen, Christopher 1952- 12
Spooner, Michael (Tim) 1954- 92
Spowart, Robin 1947- 177
    Earlier sketch in SATA 82
Sprague, Gretchen 1926-2003 27
Sprengel, Artie
    See Lerangis, Peter
Sprigge, Elizabeth (Miriam Squire)
    1900-1974 10
Spring, (Robert) Howard 1889-1965 28
Springer, Margaret 1941- 78
Springer, Marilyn Harris 1931- 47
Springer, Nancy 1948- 172
    Earlier sketches in SATA 65, 110
Springstubb, Tricia 1950- 78
    Brief entry 40
    Earlier sketch in SATA 46
Spudvilas, Anne 1951- 199
    Earlier sketch in SATA 94
Spurll, Barbara 1952- 78
Spurr, Elizabeth 172
Spykman, E(lizabeth) C(hoate) 1896-1965 .. 10
    See also CLR 35
Spyri, Johanna (Heusser) 1827-1901 100
    Earlier sketch in SATA 19
    See also CLR 115
Squires, Phil
    See Barker, S(quire) Omar
Srba, Lynne 98
Sreenivasan, Jyotsna 1964- 101

S-Ringi, Kjell
    See Ringi, Kjell (Arne Soerensen)
Stacey, Cherylyn 1945- 96
Stacy, Donald
    See Pohl, Frederik
Stadtler, Bea 1921- 17
Stafford, Jean 1915-1979
    Obituary 22
Stafford, Liliana 1950- 141
Stafford, Paul 1966- 116
Stahl, Ben(jamin) 1910-1987 5
    Obituary 54
Stahl, Hilda 1938-1993 48
    Obituary 77
Stahler, David, Jr. 162
Stainton, Sue 187
Stair, Gobin (John) 1912- 35
Stalder, Valerie 27
Stamaty, Mark Alan 1947- 12
Stambler, Irwin 1924- 5
Standiford, Natalie 1961- 169
    Earlier sketch in SATA 81
Stanek, Lou Willett 1931- 63
Stang, Judit 1921-1977 29
Stang, Judy
    See Stang, Judit
Stangl, (Mary) Jean 1928- 67
Stanhope, Eric
    See Hamilton, Charles (Harold St. John)
Stankevich, Boris 1928- 2
Stanley, Diane 1943- 164
    Brief entry 32
    Earlier sketches in SATA 37, 80, 115
    See also CLR 46
    See also SAAS 15
Stanley, George Edward 1942- 67
    Earlier sketches in SATA 53, 111, 157, 1
Stanley, Jerry 1941- 127
    Earlier sketch in SATA 79
Stanley, Mandy 165
Stanley, Robert
    See Hamilton, Charles (Harold St. John)
Stanley, Sanna 1962- 145
Stanli, Sue
    See Meilach, Dona Z(weigoron)
Stanstead, John
    See Groom, Arthur William
Stanton, Karen 1960- 190
Stanton, Schuyler
    See Baum, L(yman) Frank
Staples, Suzanne Fisher 1945- 151
    Earlier sketches in SATA 70, 105
    See also CLR 137
Stapleton, Marjorie (Winifred) 1932- 28
Stapp, Arthur D(onald) 1906-1972 4
Starbird, Kaye 1916- 6
    See also CLR 60
Stark, Evan 1942- 78
Stark, James
    See Goldston, Robert (Conroy)
Stark, Ken 1943- 199
Stark, Ulf 1944- 124
Starke, Ruth (Elaine) 1946- 129
Starkey, Marion L(ena) 1901-1991 13
Starr, Ward
    See Manes, Stephen
Starret, William
    See McClintock, Marshall
Starr Taylor, Bridget 1959- 99
Stasiak, Krystyna 49
Staub, Frank 1949- 116
Staub, Frank Jacob
    See Staub, Frank
Staub, Wendy Corsi 1964- 114
Stauffacher, Sue 1961- 199
    Earlier sketch in SATA 155
Stauffer, Don
    See Berkebile, Fred D(onovan)
Staunton, Schuyler
    See Baum, L(yman) Frank

Staunton, Ted 1956- 167
    Earlier sketch in SATA 112
Stead, Rebecca 1968(?)- 188
Steadman, Ralph 1936- 123
    Earlier sketch in SATA 32
Steadman, Ralph Idris
    See Steadman, Ralph
Stearman, Kaye 1951- 118
Stearns, Monroe (Mather) 1913-1987 5
    Obituary 55
Steckler, Arthur 1921-1985 65
Steding, Laurie 1953- 119
Steel, Danielle 1947- 66
Steel, Danielle Fernande
    See Steel, Danielle
Steele, Addison II
    See Lupoff, Richard A(llen)
Steele, Alexander 1958- 116
Steele, Henry Maxwell
    See Steele, Max
Steele, Mary 1930- 94
Steele, Mary Q(uintard Govan) 1922-1992 .. 51
    Obituary 72
    Earlier sketch in SATA 3
Steele, Max 1922-2005 168
    Earlier sketch in SATA 10
Steele, Philip 1948- 140
    Earlier sketch in SATA 81
Steele, William O(wen) 1917-1979 51
    Obituary 27
    Earlier sketch in SATA 1
Steelhammer, Ilona 1952- 98
Steelsmith, Shari 1962- 72
Stefanik, Alfred T. 1939- 55
Steffanson, Con
    See Cassiday, Bruce (Bingham)
    and Goulart, Ron
Steffens, Bradley 1955- 166
    Earlier sketch in SATA 77
Steffensmeier, Alexander 1977- 195
Stegeman, Janet Allais 1923- 49
    Brief entry 49
Steggall, Susan 1967- 182
Steig, William 1907-2003 111
    Obituary 149
    Earlier sketches in SATA 18, 70
    See also CLR 103
Steig, William H.
    See Steig, William
Stein, David Ezra 180
Stein, M(eyer) L(ewis) 1920- 6
Stein, Mathilde 1969- 195
Stein, Mini 2
Stein, R(ichard) Conrad 1937- 154
    Earlier sketches in SATA 31, 82
Stein, Wendy 1951- 77
Steinbeck, John (Ernst) 1902-1968 9
Steinberg, Alfred 1917-1995 9
Steinberg, David 1962- 200
Steinberg, D.J.
    See Steinberg, David
Steinberg, Fannie 1899-1990 43
Steinberg, Fred J. 1933- 4
Steinberg, Phillip Orso 1921- 34
Steinberg, Rafael (Mark) 1927- 45
Steinberg, Saul 1914-1999 67
Steincrohn, Maggie
    See Davis, Maggie S.
Steiner, Barbara A(nnette) 1934- 83
    Earlier sketch in SATA 13
    See also SAAS 13
Steiner, Charlotte 1900-1981 45
Steiner, George 1929- 62
Steiner, Joan 199
    Earlier sketch in SATA 110
Steiner, Jorg
    See Steiner, Jorg
Steiner, Jorg 1930- 35
Steiner, K. Leslie
    See Delany, Samuel R., Jr.

Steiner, Stan(ley) 1925-1987 14
  Obituary 50
Steins, Richard 1942- 79
Stem, Jacqueline 1931- 110
Stemple, Jason 179
Steneman, Shep 1945- 132
Stengel, Joyce A. 1938- 158
Stephanie, Gordon
  See Gordon, Stephanie Jacob
Stephens, Alice Barber 1858-1932 66
Stephens, Casey
  See Wagner, Sharon B.
Stephens, Henrietta Henkle 1909-1993 6
Stephens, J.B.
  See Lynn, Tracy
Stephens, Mary Jo 1935- 8
Stephens, Rebecca 1961- 141
Stephens, Reed
  See Donaldson, Stephen R.
Stephens, Suzanne
  See Kirby, Susan E.
Stephens, William M(cLain) 1925- 21
Stephensen, A. M.
  See Manes, Stephen
Stephenson, Lynda 1941- 179
Stephenson, Lynda A.
  See Stephenson, Lynda
Stepp, Ann 1935- 29
Stepto, Michele 1946- 61
Steptoe, Javaka 1971- 151
Steptoe, John (Lewis) 1950-1989 63
  Earlier sketch in SATA 8
  See also CLR 12
Sterling, Brett
  See Bradbury, Ray
  and Hamilton, Edmond
  and Samachson, Joseph
Sterling, Dorothy 1913-2008 83
  Autobiography Feature 127
  Obituary 200
  Earlier sketch in SATA 1
  See also CLR 1
  See also SAAS 2
Sterling, Helen
  See Watts, Helen L. Hoke
Sterling, Philip 1907-1989 8
  Obituary 63
Sterling, Shirley (Anne) 1948- 101
Stern, Ellen Norman 1927- 26
Stern, Judith M. 1951- 75
Stern, Madeleine
  See Stern, Madeleine B.
Stern, Madeleine B. 1912-2007 14
Stern, Madeleine Bettina
  See Stern, Madeleine B.
Stern, Maggie 1953- 156
Stern, Philip Van Doren 1900-1984 13
  Obituary 39
Stern, Simon 1943- 15
Sterne, Emma Gelders 1894- 6
Steurt, Marjorie Rankin 1888-1978 10
Stevens, Bryna 1924- 65
Stevens, Carla M(cBride) 1928- 13
Stevens, Chambers 1968- 128
Stevens, Diane 1939- 94
Stevens, Franklin 1933- 6
Stevens, Greg
  See Cook, Glen
Stevens, Gwendolyn 1944- 33
Stevens, Jan Romero 1953- 95
Stevens, Janet 1953- 193
  Earlier sketches in SATA 90, 148
Stevens, Kathleen 1936- 49
Stevens, Leonard A. 1920- 67
Stevens, Lucile Vernon 1899-1994 59
Stevens, Margaret Dean
  See Aldrich, Bess Streeter
Stevens, Patricia Bunning 1931- 27
Stevens, Peter
  See Geis, Darlene Stern
Stevens, Serita 1949- 70

Stevens, Serita Deborah
  See Stevens, Serita
Stevens, Serita Mendelson
  See Stevens, Serita
Stevens, Shira
  See Stevens, Serita
Stevenson, Anna (M.) 1905- 12
Stevenson, Augusta 1869(?)-1976 2
  Obituary 26
Stevenson, Burton Egbert 1872-1962 25
Stevenson, Drew 1947- 60
Stevenson, Harvey 1960- 148
  Earlier sketch in SATA 80
Stevenson, James 1929- 195
  Brief entry 34
  Earlier sketches in SATA 42, 71, 113, 161
  See also CLR 17
Stevenson, Janet 1913- 8
Stevenson, Robert Louis (Balfour)
  1850-1894 100
  See also YABC 2
  See also CLR 107
Stevenson, Sucie
  See Stevenson, Sucie
Stevenson, Sucie 1956- 194
  Earlier sketch in SATA 104
Stewart, A(gnes) C(harlotte) 15
Stewart, Amber 181
Stewart, Chantal 1945- 173
  Earlier sketch in SATA 121
Stewart, Charles
  See Zurhorst, Charles (Stewart, Jr.)
Stewart, Eleanor
  See Porter, Eleanor H(odgman)
Stewart, Elisabeth J(ane) 1927- 93
Stewart, Elizabeth Laing 1907- 6
Stewart, Gail B. 1949- 141
Stewart, George Rippey 1895-1980 3
  Obituary 23
Stewart, Jennifer J(enkins) 1960- 128
Stewart, Joel 151
Stewart, John 1920- 14
Stewart, Mary (Florence Elinor) 1916- 12
Stewart, Mary Rainbow
  See Stewart, Mary (Florence Elinor)
Stewart, Melissa 1968- 167
  Earlier sketch in SATA 111
Stewart, Paul 1955- 199
  Earlier sketches in SATA 114, 163
Stewart, Robert Neil 1891-1972 7
Stewart, Sarah 143
Stewart, Scott
  See Zaffo, George J.
Stewart, W(alter) P. 1924- 53
Stewart, Whitney 1959- 167
  Earlier sketch in SATA 92
Stewig, John Warren 1937- 162
  Earlier sketches in SATA 26, 110
Stickler, Soma Han 1942- 128
Stidworthy, John 1943- 63
Stiegemeyer, Julie 180
Stier, Catherine 198
Stiles, Martha Bennett 108
  Earlier sketch in SATA 6
Still, James 1906-2001 29
  Obituary 127
Stille, Darlene R. 1942- 170
  Earlier sketch in SATA 126
Stille, Darlene Ruth
  See Stille, Darlene R.
Stillerman, Marci 104
Stillerman, Robbie 1947- 12
Stilley, Frank 1918- 29
Stilton, Geronimo 158
Stimpson, Gerald
  See Mitchell, Adrian
Stine, Catherine 165
Stine, G(eorge) Harry 1928-1997 136
  Earlier sketch in SATA 10
Stine, Jovial Bob
  See Stine, R.L.

Stine, R.L. 1943- 194
  Earlier sketches in SATA 31, 76, 129
  See also CLR 111
Stine, Robert Lawrence
  See Stine, R.L.
Stinetorf, Louise (Allender) 1900-1992 10
Stinson, Kathy 1952- 98
Stirling, Arthur
  See Sinclair, Upton
Stirling, Ian 1941- 77
Stirling, Nora B(romley) 1900-1997 3
Stirnweis, Shannon 1931- 10
Stobbs, William 1914-2000 17
  Obituary 120
Stock, Carolmarie 1951- 75
Stock, Catherine 1952- 158
  Earlier sketches in SATA 65, 114
Stockdale, Susan 1954- 98
Stockham, Peter (Alan) 1928- 57
Stockton, Francis Richard 1834-1902 44
  Brief entry 32
Stockton, Frank R.
  See Stockton, Francis Richard
Stockwell-Moniz, Marc J. 1954- 164
Stoddard, Edward G. 1923- 10
Stoddard, Hope 1900-1987 6
Stoddard, Sandol 1927- 98
  Earlier sketch in SATA 14
Stoehr, Shelley 1969- 107
Stoeke, Janet Morgan 1957- 136
  Earlier sketch in SATA 90
Stohner, Anu 1952- 179
Stoiko, Michael 1919- 14
Stojic, Manya 1967- 156
Stoker, Abraham 1847-1912 29
Stoker, Bram
  See Stoker, Abraham
Stokes, Cedric
  See Beardmore, George
Stokes, Jack (Tilden) 1923- 13
Stokes, Olivia Pearl 1916- 32
Stolz, Mary 1920-2006 133
  Obituary 180
  Earlier sketches in SATA 10, 71
  See also SAAS 3
Stolz, Mary Slattery
  See Stolz, Mary
Stone, Alan
  See Svenson, Andrew E(dward)
Stone, David K(arl) 1922- 9
Stone, David Lee 1978- 166
Stone, Eugenia 1879-1971 7
Stone, Gene
  See Stone, Eugenia
Stone, Helen V(irginia) 6
Stone, Idella Purnell
  See Purnell, Idella
Stone, Ikey
  See Purnell, Idella
Stone, Irving 1903-1989 3
  Obituary 64
Stone, Jeff 178
Stone, Jon 1931-1997 39
  Obituary 95
Stone, Josephine Rector
  See Dixon, Jeanne
Stone, Lesley
  See Trevor, Elleston
Stone, Peter 1930-2003 65
  Obituary 143
Stone, Phoebe 134
Stone, Raymond 1
Stone, Rosetta
  See Dr. Seuss
  and Geisel, Theodor Seuss
  and LeSieg, Theo.
  and Seuss, Dr.
Stone, Tanya Lee 182
Stonehouse, Bernard 1926- 140
  Earlier sketches in SATA 13, 80
Stones, (Cyril) Anthony 1934- 72

Stong, Phil(ip Duffield) 1899-1957 .... *32*
Stoops, Erik D(aniel) 1966- *142*
    Earlier sketch in SATA *78*
Stoppelmoore, Cheryl Jean
    See Ladd, Cheryl (Jean)
Stops, Sue 1936- *86*
Storace, Patricia *193*
Storad, Conrad J. 1957- *119*
Storey, Margaret 1926- *9*
Storey, Victoria Carolyn 1945- *16*
Storme, Peter
    See Stern, Philip Van Doren
Storr, Catherine (Cole) 1913-2001 .... *87*
    Obituary *122*
    Earlier sketch in SATA *9*
Story, Josephine
    See Loring, Emilie (Baker)
Stotko, Mary-Ann 1960- *154*
Stott, Dorothy (M.) 1958- *99*
    Earlier sketch in SATA *67*
Stott, Dot
    See Stott, Dorothy (M.)
Stotter, Mike 1957- *108*
Stout, William 1949- *132*
Stoutenburg, Adrien (Pearl) 1916-1982 .... *3*
Stoutland, Allison 1963- *130*
Stover, Allan C(arl) 1938- *14*
Stover, Jill (Griffin) 1958- *82*
Stover, Marjorie Filley 1914- *9*
Stowe, Harriet (Elizabeth) Beecher 1811-1896
    See YABC *1*
    See also CLR *131*
Stowe, Leland 1899-1994 .... *60*
    Obituary *78*
Stowe, Rosetta
    See Ogan, George F.
    and Ogan, Margaret E. (Nettles)
Stower, Adam *195*
Strachan, Ian 1938- *85*
Strachan, Linda *167*
Strachan, Margaret Pitcairn 1908-1998 .... *14*
Strahinich, H. C.
    See Strahinich, Helen C.
Strahinich, Helen C. 1949- *78*
Strait, Treva Adams 1909-2002 .... *35*
Strand, Mark 1934- *41*
Strange, Philippa
    See Coury, Louise Andree
Stranger, Joyce
    See Wilson, Joyce M.
Strangis, Joel 1948- *124*
Strannigan, Shawn 1956- *93*
Strannigan, Shawn Alyne
    See Strannigan, Shawn
Strasser, Todd 1950- *153*
    Earlier sketches in SATA *41, 45, 71, 107*
    See also CLR *11*
Stratemeyer, Edward L. 1862-1930 .... *100*
    Earlier sketches in SATA *1, 67*
    See Adams, Harrison
Stratford, Philip 1927- *47*
Stratton, Allan 1951- *178*
Stratton, J. M.
    See Whitlock, Ralph
Stratton, Thomas
    See Coulson, Robert S(tratton)
    and DeWeese, Thomas Eugene
Stratton-Porter, Gene 1863-1924 .... *15*
    See also CLR *87*
Strauss, Gwen 1963- *77*
Strauss, Joyce 1936- *53*
Strauss, Linda Leopold 1942- *127*
Strauss, Susan (Elizabeth) 1954- *75*
Strayer, E. Ward
    See Stratemeyer, Edward L.
Streano, Vince(nt Catello) 1945- *20*
Streatfeild, Mary Noel
    See Streatfeild, Noel
Streatfeild, Noel 1897(?)-1986 .... *20*
    Obituary *48*
    See also CLR *83*

Street, Janet Travell 1959- *84*
Street, Julia Montgomery 1898-1993 .... *11*
Streissguth, Thomas 1958- *116*
Strelkoff, Tatiana 1957- *89*
Stren, Patti 1949- *88*
    Brief entry *41*
    See also CLR *5*
Strete, Craig Kee 1950- *96*
    Earlier sketch in SATA *44*
Stretton, Barbara (Humphrey) 1936- *43*
    Brief entry *35*
Strickland, Brad 1947- *200*
    Earlier sketches in SATA *83, 137, 142*
Strickland, Craig (A.) 1956- *102*
Strickland, Dorothy S(alley) 1933- *89*
Strickland, Michael R. 1965- *144*
    Earlier sketch in SATA *83*
Strickland, Tessa *173*
Strickland, William Bradley
    See Strickland, Brad
Striegel, Jana 1955- *140*
Striegel-Wilson, Jana
    See Striegel, Jana
Striker, Lee
    See Clark, Margaret (D.)
Striker, Susan 1942- *63*
Stringer, Lauren 1957- *183*
    Earlier sketch in SATA *129*
Stroeyer, Poul 1923- *13*
Stromoski, Rick 1958- *111*
Strong, Charles
    See Epstein, Beryl (M. Williams)
    and Epstein, Samuel
Strong, David
    See McGuire, Leslie (Sarah)
Strong, Jeremy 1949- *175*
    Earlier sketches in SATA *36, 105*
Strong, J.J.
    See Strong, Jeremy
Strong, Pat
    See Hough, Richard (Alexander)
Strong, Stacie 1965- *74*
Stroud, Bettye 1939- *165*
    Earlier sketch in SATA *96*
Stroud, Jonathan 1970- *159*
    Earlier sketch in SATA *102*
    See also CLR *134*
Stroyer, Poul
    See Stroeyer, Poul
Strug, Kerri 1977- *108*
Stryer, Andrea Stenn 1938- *192*
Stryker, Daniel
    See Morris, Chris(topher Crosby)
    and Stump, Jane Barr
Stuart, David
    See Hoyt, Edwin P(almer), Jr.
Stuart, Derek
    See Foster, John L(ouis)
Stuart, Forbes 1924- *13*
Stuart, Ian
    See MacLean, Alistair (Stuart)
Stuart, Jesse (Hilton) 1906-1984 .... *2*
    Obituary *36*
Stuart, Ruth McEnery 1849(?)-1917 .... *116*
Stuart, Sheila
    See Baker, Mary Gladys Steel
Stuart-Clark, Christopher (Anthony) 1940- .. *32*
Stubis, Talivaldis 1926- *5*
Stubley, Trevor (Hugh) 1932- *22*
Stucky, Naomi R. 1922- *72*
Stucley, Elizabeth
    See Northmore, Elizabeth Florence
Stultifer, Morton
    See Curtis, Richard (Alan)
Sture-Vasa, Mary
    See Alsop, Mary O'Hara
Sturges, Philemon *174*
Sturtevant, Katherine 1950- *180*
    Earlier sketch in SATA *130*
Sturton, Hugh
    See Johnston, H(ugh) A(nthony) S(tephen)

Sturtzel, Howard A(llison) 1894-1985 .... *1*
Sturtzel, Jane Levington 1903-1996 .... *1*
Stutley, D(oris) J(ean) 1959- *142*
Stutson, Caroline 1940- *104*
Stuve-Bodeen, Stephanie 1965- *158*
    Earlier sketch in SATA *114*
Stux, Erica 1929- *140*
Styles, (Frank) Showell 1908- *10*
Stynes, Barbara White *133*
Suarez, Maribel 1952- *201*
Suba, Susanne *4*
Subond, Valerie
    See Grayland, Valerie (Merle Spanner)
Sudbery, Rodie 1943- *42*
Suen, Anastasia 1956(?)- *157*
Sufrin, Mark 1925- *76*
Sugarman, Joan G. 1917- *64*
Sugarman, Tracy 1921- *37*
Sugita, Yutaka 1930- *36*
Suhl, Yuri (Menachem) 1908-1986 .... *8*
    Obituary *50*
    See also CLR *2*
    See also SAAS *1*
Suhr, Joanne *129*
Suid, Murray 1942- *27*
Sullivan, George (Edward) 1927- *147*
    Earlier sketches in SATA *4, 89*
Sullivan, Jody
    See Rake, Jody
Sullivan, Kathryn A. 1954- *141*
Sullivan, Mary Ann 1954- *63*
Sullivan, Mary W(ilson) 1907- *13*
Sullivan, Pat
    See Messmer, Otto
Sullivan, Paul 1939- *106*
Sullivan, Sarah G. 1953- *179*
Sullivan, Silky
    See Makowski, Silvia Ann
Sullivan, Sue
    See Sullivan, Susan E.
Sullivan, Susan E. 1962- *123*
Sullivan, Thomas Joseph, Jr. 1947- *16*
Sullivan, Tom
    See Sullivan, Thomas Joseph, Jr.
Sully, Tom 1959- *104*
Sumichrast, Jozef 1948- *29*
Sumiko
    See Davies, Sumiko
Summerforest, Ivy B.
    See Kirkup, James
Summers, Barbara 1944- *182*
Summers, James L(evingston) 1910-1973 .... *57*
    Brief entry *28*
Summertree, Katonah
    See Windsor, Patricia
Sun, Chyng Feng 1959- *90*
Sunderlin, Sylvia (S.) 1911-1997 .... *28*
    Obituary *99*
Sung, Betty Lee *26*
Supeene, Shelagh Lynne 1952- *153*
Supraner, Robyn 1930- *101*
    Earlier sketch in SATA *20*
Supree, Burt(on) 1941-1992 .... *73*
Surface, Mary Hall 1958- *126*
Surge, Frank 1931- *13*
Susac, Andrew 1929- *5*
Susi, Geraldine Lee 1942- *98*
Sussman, Cornelia Silver 1914-1999 .... *59*
Sussman, Irving 1908-1996 .... *59*
Sussman, Susan 1942- *48*
Sutcliff, Rosemary 1920-1992 .... *78*
    Obituary *73*
    Earlier sketches in SATA *6, 44*
    See also CLR *138*
Sutcliffe, Jane 1957- *138*
Sutherland, Colleen 1944- *79*
Sutherland, Efua (Theodora Morgue)
    1924-1996 .... *25*
Sutherland, Jon 1958- *167*
Sutherland, Jonathan D.
    See Sutherland, Jon

Sutherland, Jonathan David
  See Sutherland, Jon
Sutherland, Margaret 1941- *15*
Sutherland, Zena Bailey 1915-2002 .... *37*
  Obituary *137*
Suttles, Shirley (Smith) 1922- *21*
Sutton, Ann (Livesay) 1923- *31*
Sutton, Eve(lyn Mary) 1906-1992 .... *26*
Sutton, Felix 1910(?)-1973 .... *31*
Sutton, Jane 1950- *52*
  Brief entry *43*
Sutton, Larry M(atthew) 1931- *29*
Sutton, Margaret Beebe 1903-2001 .... *1*
  Obituary *131*
Sutton, Myron Daniel 1925- *31*
Sutton, Roger 1956- *93*
Suzanne, Jamie
  See Hawes, Louise
  and Lantz, Francess L(in)
  and Singleton, Linda Joy
  and Zach, Cheryl (Byrd)
Suzuki, David 1936- *138*
Suzuki, David Takayoshi
  See Suzuki, David
Svendsen, Mark 1962- *181*
  Earlier sketch in SATA *120*
Svendsen, Mark Nestor
  See Svendsen, Mark
Svenson, Andrew E(dward) 1910-1975 .... *2*
  Obituary *26*
Swaab, Neil 1978- *191*
Swain, Carol 1962- *172*
Swain, Gwenyth 1961- *134*
  Earlier sketch in SATA *84*
Swain, Ruth
  See Swain, Ruth Freeman
Swain, Ruth Freeman 1951- *161*
  Earlier sketch in SATA *119*
Swain, Su Zan (Noguchi) 1916- *21*
Swallow, Pamela Curtis *178*
Swamp, Jake 1941- *98*
Swan, Susan 1944- *108*
  Earlier sketch in SATA *22*
Swann, Brian (Stanley Frank) 1940- *116*
Swann, E. L.
  See Lasky, Kathryn
Swann, Ruth Rice 1920- *84*
Swanson, Helen M(cKendry) 1919- *94*
Swanson, June 1931- *76*
Swanson, Wayne 1942- *167*
Swarthout, Glendon (Fred) 1918-1992 .... *26*
Swarthout, Kathryn 1919- *7*
Swayne, Sam(uel F.) 1907- *53*
Swayne, Zoa (Lourana) 1905- *53*
Sweat, Lynn 1934- *168*
  Earlier sketch in SATA *57*
Swede, George 1940- *67*
Sweeney, James B(artholomew) 1910-1999 . *21*
Sweeney, Joyce 1955- *167*
  Earlier sketches in SATA *65, 68, 108*
Sweeney, Joyce Kay
  See Sweeney, Joyce
Sweeney, Karen O'Connor
  See O'Connor, Karen
Sweeney, Matthew (Gerard) 1952- *156*
Sweet, Melissa 1956- *172*
Sweet, Sarah C.
  See Jewett, (Theodora) Sarah Orne
Sweetland, Nancy A(nn) 1934- *48*
Swenson, Allan A(rmstrong) 1933- *21*
Swenson, May 1919-1989 .... *15*
Swentzell, Rina 1939- *79*
Swiatkowska, Gabi 1971(?)- *180*
Swift, Bryan
  See Knott, William C(ecil, Jr.)
Swift, David
  See Kaufmann, John
Swift, Hildegarde Hoyt 1890(?)-1977
  Obituary *20*
Swift, Jonathan 1667-1745 .... *19*
  See also CLR *53*

Swift, Merlin
  See Leeming, Joseph
Swiger, Elinor Porter 1927- *8*
Swinburne, Laurence (Joseph) 1924- *9*
Swinburne, Stephen R. 1952- *188*
  Earlier sketch in SATA *150*
Swinburne, Steve
  See Swinburne, Stephen R.
Swindells, Robert (Edward) 1939- *150*
  Brief entry *34*
  Earlier sketches in SATA *50, 80*
  See also SAAS *14*
Swinford, Betty (June Wells) 1927- *58*
Swinford, Bob
  See Swinford, Betty (June Wells)
Swithen, John
  See King, Stephen
Switzer, Ellen 1923- *48*
Swope, Sam *156*
Swope, Samuel
  See Swope, Sam
Sybesma, Jetske
  See Ironside, Jetske
Sydney, Frank
  See Warwick, Alan R(oss)
Sylvester, Natalie G(abry) 1922- *22*
Syme, (Neville) Ronald 1913-1992 .... *87*
  Earlier sketch in SATA *2*
Symes, R. F. *77*
Symes, Ruth Louise 1962- *179*
Symons, (Dorothy) Geraldine 1909- *33*
Symons, Stuart
  See Stanley, George Edward
Symynkywicz, Jeffrey B. 1954- *87*
Symynkywicz, Jeffrey Bruce
  See Symynkywicz, Jeffrey B.
Synge, (Phyllis) Ursula 1930- *9*
Sypher, Lucy Johnston 1907- *7*
Szasz, Suzanne (Shorr) 1915-1997 .... *13*
  Obituary *99*
Szekeres, Cyndy 1933- *157*
  Autobiography Feature *157*
  Earlier sketches in SATA *5, 60, 131*
  See also SAAS *13*
Szekessy, Tanja *98*
Szpura, Beata 1961- *93*
Szudek, Agnes S(usan) P(hilomena) *57*
  Brief entry *49*
Szulc, Tad 1926-2001 .... *26*
Szydlow, Jarl
  See Szydlowski, Mary Vigliante
Szydlowski, Mary Vigliante 1946- *94*
Szymanski, Lois 1957- *91*

T

Taback, Simms 1932- *170*
  Brief entry *36*
  Earlier sketches in SATA *40, 104*
  See also CLR *100*
Taber, Gladys (Bagg) 1899-1980
  Obituary *22*
Tabor, Nancy Maria Grande 1949- *161*
  Earlier sketch in SATA *89*
Tabrah, Ruth Milander 1921- *14*
Tackach, James 1953- *123*
Tackach, James M.
  See Tackach, James
Tadgell, Nicole 1969- *177*
Tafuri, Nancy 1946- *192*
  Autobiography Feature *192*
  Earlier sketches in SATA *39, 75, 130*
  See also CLR *74*
  See also SAAS *14*
Tagg, Christine Elizabeth 1962- *138*
Tagliaferro, Linda *173*
Taha, Karen T(erry) 1942- *156*
  Earlier sketch in SATA *71*
Tai, Sharon O. 1963- *153*

Tait, Douglas 1944- *12*
Takabayashi, Mari 1960- *156*
  Earlier sketch in SATA *115*
Takahashi, Rumiko 1957- *163*
Takakjian, Portia 1930- *15*
Takashima, Misako
  See Misako Rocks!
Takashima, Shizuye 1928- *13*
Takayama, Sandi 1962- *106*
Takeda, Pete(r M.) 1964- *148*
Tal, Eve 1947- *176*
Talbert, Marc (Alan) 1953- *154*
  Autobiography Feature *154*
  Earlier sketches in SATA *68, 99*
Talbot, Charlene Joy 1928- *10*
Talbot, Toby 1928- *14*
Talbott, Hudson 1949- *131*
  Earlier sketch in SATA *84*
Taliaferro, Dorothy L.
  See Martin, Del
Talifero, Gerald 1950- *75*
Talker, T.
  See Rands, William Brighty
Tallarico, Tony 1933- *116*
Tallcott, Emogene *10*
Tallec, Olivier 1970- *197*
Tallis, Robyn
  See Smith, Sherwood
Tallon, Robert 1939- *43*
  Brief entry *28*
Talmadge, Marian *14*
Tamaki, Jillian 1980- *201*
Tamar, Erika 1934- *150*
  Earlier sketches in SATA *62, 101*
Tamarin, Alfred H. 1913-1980 .... *13*
Tamburine, Jean 1930- *12*
Tames, Richard (Lawrence) 1946- *102*
  Earlier sketch in SATA *67*
Tamminga, Frederick W(illiam) 1934- *66*
Tammuz, Benjamin 1919-1989
  Obituary *63*
Tan, Amy 1952- *75*
Tan, Amy Ruth
  See Tan, Amy
Tan, Shaun 1974- *198*
Tanaka, Beatrice 1932- *76*
Tanaka, Shelley *136*
Tang, Charles 1948- *81*
Tang, Greg *172*
Tang, You-Shan 1946- *53*
Tania B.
  See Blixen, Karen
Tankard, Jeremy 1973- *191*
Tannen, Mary 1943- *37*
Tannenbaum, Beulah Goldstein 1916- *3*
Tannenbaum, D(onald) Leb 1948- *42*
Tanner, Jane 1946- *74*
Tanner, Louise S(tickney) 1922-2000 .... *9*
Tanobe, Miyuki 1937- *23*
Tanselle, Eve 1933- *125*
Tapio, Pat Decker
  See Kines, Pat Decker
Tapp, Kathy Kennedy 1949- *88*
  Brief entry *50*
Tarbescu, Edith 1939- *107*
Tarkington, (Newton) Booth 1869-1946 ..... *17*
Tarpley, Natasha A(nastasia) 1971- *147*
Tarr, Judith 1955- *149*
  Earlier sketch in SATA *64*
Tarry, Ellen 1906- *16*
  See also CLR *26*
  See also SAAS *16*
Tarshis, Jerome 1936- *9*
Tarshis, Lauren *187*
Tarsky, Sue 1946- *41*
Taschek, Karen 1956- *185*
Tashjian, Janet 1956- *151*
  Earlier sketch in SATA *102*
Tashjian, Virginia A. 1921-2008 .... *3*
Tasker, James 1908- *9*
Tate, Don(ald E.) *159*

Tate, Eleanora E. 1948- *191*
  Earlier sketches in SATA *38, 94*
  See also CLR *37*
Tate, Eleanora Elaine
  See Tate, Eleanora E.
Tate, Ellalice
  See Hibbert, Eleanor Alice Burford
Tate, Joan 1922- *86*
  Earlier sketch in SATA *9*
  See also SAAS *20*
Tate, Mary Anne
  See Hale, Arlene
Tate, Nikki *134*
Tate, Richard
  See Masters, Anthony (Richard)
Tate, Suzanne 1930- *91*
Tatham, Betty *142*
Tatham, Campbell
  See Elting, Mary
Tatham, Julie
  See Tatham, Julie Campbell
Tatham, Julie Campbell 1908-1999 .... *80*
Tavares, Matt *198*
  Earlier sketch in SATA *159*
Tavares, Victor 1971- *176*
Taves, Isabella 1915- *27*
Taylor, Alastair 1959- *130*
Taylor, Andrew 1951- *70*
Taylor, Andrew John Robert
  See Taylor, Andrew
Taylor, Ann 1782-1866 .... *41*
  Brief entry *35*
Taylor, Audilee Boyd 1931- *59*
Taylor, Barbara J. 1927- *10*
Taylor, Ben
  See Strachan, Ian
Taylor, Carl 1937- *14*
Taylor, Cheryl Munro 1957- *96*
Taylor, Cora (Lorraine) 1936- *103*
  Earlier sketch in SATA *64*
  See also CLR *63*
Taylor, Dave 1948- *78*
Taylor, David
  See Taylor, Dave
Taylor, David 1900-1965 .... *10*
Taylor, Debbie A. 1955- *169*
Taylor, Elizabeth 1912-1975 .... *13*
Taylor, Florance Walton *9*
Taylor, Florence M(arian Tompkins)
  1892-1983 .... *9*
Taylor, G(raham) P(eter) 1959(?)- *156*
Taylor, Gage 1942-2000 .... *87*
Taylor, Graham
  See Taylor, G(raham) P(eter)
Taylor, Herb(ert Norman, Jr.) 1942-1987 ..... *22*
  Obituary *54*
Taylor, J. David
  See Taylor, Dave
Taylor, Jane 1783-1824 .... *41*
  Brief entry *35*
Taylor, Jerry D(uncan) 1938- *47*
Taylor, John Robert
  See Taylor, Andrew
Taylor, Judy
  See Hough, Judy Taylor
Taylor, Kenneth N. 1917-2005 .... *26*
Taylor, Kenneth Nathaniel
  See Taylor, Kenneth N.
Taylor, Kim *180*
Taylor, L(ester) B(arbour), Jr. 1932- *27*
Taylor, Lois Dwight Cole
  See Cole, Lois Dwight
Taylor, Louise Todd 1939- *47*
Taylor, Margaret 1950- *106*
Taylor, Mark 1927- *32*
  Brief entry *28*
Taylor, Mildred D. 1943- *135*
  See also CLR *144*
  See also SAAS *5*
Taylor, Mildred Delois
  See Taylor, Mildred D.

Taylor, Paula (Wright) 1942- *48*
  Brief entry *33*
Taylor, Robert Lewis 1912-1998 .... *10*
Taylor, Sean 1965- *192*
Taylor, Sydney (Brenner) 1904(?)-1978 .... *28*
  Obituary *26*
  Earlier sketch in SATA *1*
Taylor, Theodore 1921-2006 .... *128*
  Obituary *177*
  Earlier sketches in SATA *5, 54, 83*
  See also CLR *30*
  See also SAAS *4*
Taylor, William 1938- *164*
  Earlier sketches in SATA *78, 113*
  See also CLR *63*
Tazewell, Charles 1900-1972 .... *74*
Tchana, Katrin
  See Tchana, Katrin Hyman
Tchana, Katrin H.
  See Tchana, Katrin Hyman
Tchana, Katrin Hyman 1963- *177*
  Earlier sketch in SATA *125*
Tchekhov, Anton
  See Chekhov, Anton (Pavlovich)
Tchen, Richard *120*
Tchudi, Stephen N. 1942- *55*
Teague, Bob
  See Teague, Robert
Teague, Mark 1963- *170*
  Earlier sketches in SATA *68, 99*
Teague, Mark Christopher
  See Teague, Mark
Teague, Robert 1929- *32*
  Brief entry *31*
Teal, Val 1902-1997 .... *10*
  Obituary *114*
Teal, Valentine M.
  See Teal, Val
Teale, Edwin Way 1899-1980 .... *7*
  Obituary *25*
Teasdale, Sara 1884-1933 .... *32*
Tebbel, John (William) 1912-2004 .... *26*
Teckentrup, Britta 1969- *200*
Teensma, Lynne Bertrand
  See Bertrand, Lynne
Tee-Van, Helen Damrosch 1893-1976 .... *10*
  Obituary *27*
Tegner, Bruce 1928- *62*
Teitelbaum, Michael 1953- *116*
  Earlier sketch in SATA *59*
Tejima
  See Tejima, Keizaburo
Tejima, Keizaburo 1931- *139*
  See also CLR *20*
Telander, Todd (G.) 1967- *88*
Teleki, Geza 1943- *45*
Telemaque, Eleanor Wong 1934- *43*
Telescope, Tom
  See Newbery, John
Tellis, Annabel 1967- *191*
Temkin, Sara Anne Schlossberg 1913-1996 . *26*
Temko, Florence *13*
Tempest, Margaret Mary 1892-1982
  Obituary *33*
Templar, Maurice
  See Groom, Arthur William
Temple, Arthur
  See Northcott, (William) Cecil
Temple, Charles 1947- *79*
Temple, Frances (Nolting) 1945-1995 .... *85*
Temple, Herbert 1919- *45*
Temple, Paul
  See McConnell, James Douglas Rutherford
Temple, William F(rederick) 1914-1989 .... *107*
Tenggren, Gustaf 1896-1970 .... *18*
  Obituary *26*
Tennant, Kylie
  See Rodd, Kylie Tennant
Tennant, Veronica 1947- *36*

Tenneshaw, S.M.
  See Beaumont, Charles
  and Garrett, Randall
  and Silverberg, Robert
Tenniel, John 1820-1914 .... *74*
  Brief entry *27*
  See also CLR *18*
Tepper, Sheri S. 1929- *113*
Terada, Alice M. 1928- *90*
Terban, Marvin 1940- *54*
  Brief entry *45*
Teresi, Judith M.
  See Goldberger, Judith M.
ter Haar, Jaap 1922- *6*
  See also CLR *15*
Terhune, Albert Payson 1872-1942 .... *15*
Terkel, Susan N(eiburg) 1948- *103*
  Earlier sketch in SATA *59*
Terlouw, Jan (Cornelis) 1931- *30*
Terrell, John Upton 1900-1988
  Obituary *60*
Terrill, Beth *198*
Terrill, Elizabeth
  See Terrill, Beth
Terris, Susan 1937- *77*
  Earlier sketch in SATA *3*
Terry, Luther L(eonidas) 1911-1985 .... *11*
  Obituary *42*
Terry, Margaret
  See Dunnahoo, Terry Janson
Terry, Walter 1913-1982 .... *14*
Terzian, James P. 1915- *14*
Tessendorf, K(enneth) C(harles) 1925-2003 . *75*
  Obituary *142*
Tessler, Manya *200*
Tessler, Stephanie Gordon
  See Gordon, Stephanie Jacob
Tester, Sylvia Root 1939- *64*
  Brief entry *37*
Tether, (Cynthia) Graham 1950- *46*
  Brief entry *36*
Tetzner, Lisa 1894-1963 .... *169*
Thach, James Otis 1969- *195*
Thacher, Mary McGrath 1933- *9*
Thackeray, William Makepeace 1811-1863 .. *23*
Thaler, Michael C.
  See Thaler, Mike
Thaler, Mike 1936- *93*
  Brief entry *47*
  Earlier sketch in SATA *56*
Thaler, Shmuel 1958- *126*
  Earlier sketch in SATA *72*
Thamer, Katie 1955- *42*
Thane, Elswyth 1900-1984(?) *32*
Tharp, Louise (Marshall) Hall 1898-1992 ...... *3*
  Obituary *129*
Tharp, Tim 1957- *189*
Thayer, Ernest Lawrence 1863-1940 .... *60*
Thayer, Jane
  See Woolley, Catherine
Thayer, Marjorie 1908-1992 .... *74*
  Brief entry *37*
Thayer, Peter
  See Wyler, Rose
Thelwell, Norman 1923-2004 .... *14*
Themerson, Stefan 1910-1988 .... *65*
Thermes, Jennifer 1966- *155*
Theroux, Paul 1941- *109*
  Earlier sketch in SATA *44*
Theroux, Paul Edward
  See Theroux, Paul
Thesman, Jean *124*
  Earlier sketch in SATA *74*
The Tjong-Khing
  See Khing, T.T.
Thieda, Shirley Ann 1943- *13*
Thiele, Colin 1920-2006 .... *125*
  Earlier sketches in SATA *14, 72*
  See also CLR *27*
  See also SAAS *2*

Thiele, Colin Milton
  See Thiele, Colin
Thiesing, Lisa 1958- *159*
  Earlier sketch in SATA *95*
Thimmesh, Catherine *189*
Thiry, Joan (Marie) 1926- *45*
Thistlethwaite, Miles 1945- *12*
Thollander, Earl 1922- *22*
Thomas, Abigail 1941- *112*
Thomas, Andrea
  See Hill, Margaret (Ohler)
Thomas, Art(hur Lawrence) 1952- *48*
  Brief entry *38*
Thomas, Carroll
  See Ratliff, Thomas M.
  and Shmurak, Carole B.
Thomas, Dylan (Marlais) 1914-1953 .... *60*
Thomas, Egbert S.
  See Ellis, Edward S(ylvester)
Thomas, Estelle Webb 1899-1982 .... *26*
Thomas, Frances 1943- *171*
  Earlier sketch in SATA *92*
Thomas, H. C.
  See Keating, Lawrence A.
Thomas, Ianthe 1951- *139*
  Brief entry *42*
  See also CLR *8*
Thomas, Jan 1958- *197*
Thomas, Jane Resh 1936- *171*
  Earlier sketches in SATA *38, 90*
Thomas, Jerry D. 1959- *91*
Thomas, J.F.
  See Fleming, Thomas
Thomas, Joan Gale
  See Robinson, Joan (Mary) G(ale Thomas)
Thomas, Joyce Carol 1938- *137*
  Autobiography Feature *137*
  Earlier sketches in SATA *40, 78, 123*
  See also CLR *19*
  See also SAAS *7*
Thomas, Lowell Jackson, Jr. 1923- *15*
Thomas, Margaret
  See Thomas, Peggy
Thomas, Meredith 1963- *119*
Thomas, Michael
  See Wilks, Michael Thomas
Thomas, Middy 1931- *191*
Thomas, Patricia 1934- *199*
  Earlier sketch in SATA *51*
Thomas, Peggy *174*
Thomas, Rob 1965- *97*
Thomas, Scott 1959- *147*
Thomas, Velma Maia 1955- *171*
Thomas, Vernon (Arthur) 1934- *56*
Thomas, Victoria
  See DeWeese, Thomas Eugene
  and Kugi, Constance Todd
Thomasma, Kenneth R. 1930- *90*
Thomassie, Tynia 1959- *92*
Thompson, Brenda 1935- *34*
Thompson, Carol 1951- *189*
  Earlier sketch in SATA *85*
Thompson, China
  See Lewis, Mary
Thompson, Colin 1942- *198*
  Earlier sketches in SATA *95, 163*
Thompson, David H(ugh) 1941- *17*
Thompson, Eileen
  See Panowski, Eileen Thompson
Thompson, George Selden 1929-1989 .... *73*
  Obituary *63*
  Earlier sketch in SATA *4*
  See also CLR *8*
Thompson, Harlan 1894-1987 .... *10*
  Obituary *53*
Thompson, Hilary 1943- *56*
  Brief entry *49*
Thompson, Joanna Maxwell Pullein
  See Pullein-Thompson, Joanna Maxwell

Thompson, Julian F(rancis) 1927- *155*
  Brief entry *40*
  Earlier sketches in SATA *55, 99*
  See also CLR *24*
  See also SAAS *13*
Thompson, K(athryn Carolyn) Dyble
  1952- *82*
Thompson, Kay 1912(?)-1998 .... *16*
  See also CLR *22*
Thompson, Lauren 1962- *200*
  Earlier sketches in SATA *132, 174*
Thompson, Lauren Stevens
  See Thompson, Lauren
Thompson, Megan Lloyd
  See Lloyd, Megan
Thompson, Richard 1951- *184*
Thompson, Ruth Plumly 1891-1976 .... *66*
Thompson, Sharon 1952- *119*
Thompson, Sharon Elaine
  See Thompson, Sharon
Thompson, Stith 1885-1976 .... *57*
  Obituary *20*
Thompson, Vivian L(aubach) 1911- *3*
Thomson, Bill 1963- *187*
Thomson, Celia
  See Lynn, Tracy
Thomson, David (Robert Alexander)
  1914-1988 .... *40*
  Obituary *55*
Thomson, Pat 1939- *122*
  Earlier sketch in SATA *77*
Thomson, Peggy 1922- *31*
Thomson, Sarah L. *178*
Thon, Melanie Rae 1957- *132*
Thong, Roseanne *174*
Thorburn, John
  See Goldsmith, John Herman Thorburn
Thorn, John 1947- *59*
Thorndyke, Helen Louise
  See Benson, Mildred
Thorne, Ian
  See May, Julian
Thorne, Jean Wright
  See May, Julian
Thornhill, Jan 1955- *148*
  Earlier sketch in SATA *77*
Thornton, Hall
  See Silverberg, Robert
Thornton, W. B.
  See Burgess, Thornton Waldo
Thornton, Yvonne S(hirley) 1947- *96*
Thorpe, E(ustace) G(eorge) 1916- *21*
Thorpe, J. K.
  See Nathanson, Laura Walther
Thorvall, Kerstin 1925- *13*
Thorvall-Falk, Kerstin
  See Thorvall, Kerstin
Thrasher, Crystal (Faye) 1921- *27*
Threadgall, Colin 1941- *77*
Three Little Pigs
  See Lantz, Francess L(in)
Thum, Gladys 1920- *26*
Thum, Marcella *28*
  Earlier sketch in SATA *3*
Thundercloud, Katherine
  See Witt, Shirley Hill
Thurber, James (Grover) 1894-1961 .... *13*
Thurlo, Aimee *161*
Thurlo, David *161*
Thurman, Judith 1946- *33*
Thurman, Mark (Gordon Ian) 1948- *63*
Thwaite, Ann (Barbara Harrop) 1932- *14*
Tibbetts, Peggy *127*
Tibbles, Jean-Paul 1958- *115*
Tibo, Gilles 1951- *107*
  Earlier sketch in SATA *67*
Tiburzi, Bonnie 1948- *65*
Ticheburn, Cheviot
  See Ainsworth, William Harrison
Tichenor, Tom 1923-1992 .... *14*
Tichnor, Richard 1959- *90*

Tichy, William 1924- *31*
Tickle, Jack
  See Chapman, Jane
Tiegreen, Alan F. 1935- *94*
  Brief entry *36*
Tierney, Frank M. 1930- *54*
Tierney, Tom 1928- *113*
Tiffault, Benette W. 1955- *77*
Tiller, Ruth L. 1949- *83*
Tilley, Debbie *190*
Tilly, Nancy 1935- *62*
Tilton, Madonna Elaine 1929- *41*
Tilton, Rafael
  See Tilton, Madonna Elaine
Timberlake, Amy *156*
Timberlake, Carolyn
  See Dresang, Eliza (Carolyn Timberlake)
Timmers, Leo 1970- *190*
Timmins, William F(rederick) *10*
Tinbergen, Niko(laas) 1907-1988
  Obituary *60*
Tincknell, Cathy *194*
Tiner, John Hudson 1944- *32*
Tingle, Dolli (?)-
  See Brackett, Dolli Tingle
Tingle, Rebecca *174*
Tingum, Janice 1958- *91*
Tinkelman, Murray 1933- *12*
Tinkham, Kelly A. *188*
Tinkle, (Julien) Lon 1906-1980 .... *36*
Tinling, Marion (Rose) 1904- *140*
Tipene, Tim 1972- *141*
Tippett, James S(terling) 1885-1958 .... *66*
Tirone Smith, Mary-Ann 1944- *143*
Titlebaum, Ellen *195*
Titler, Dale M(ilton) 1926- *35*
  Brief entry *28*
Titmarsh, Michael Angelo
  See Thackeray, William Makepeace
Titus, Eve 1922- *2*
Tjong Khing, The 1933- *76*
Tobias, Katherine
  See Gottfried, Theodore Mark
Tobias, Tobi 1938- *82*
  Earlier sketch in SATA *5*
  See also CLR *4*
Todd, Anne Ophelia
  See Dowden, Anne Ophelia Todd
Todd, Barbara 1961- *173*
Todd, Barbara K(eith) 1917- *10*
Todd, Chuck *195*
Todd, H(erbert) E(atton) 1908-1988 .... *84*
  Earlier sketch in SATA *11*
Todd, Loreto 1942- *30*
Todd, Peter
  See Hamilton, Charles (Harold St. John)
Toews, Miriam 1964- *165*
Tofel, Richard J. 1957- *140*
Toft, Kim Michelle 1960- *170*
Tokunbo, Dimitrea *187*
Tolan, Stephanie S. 1942- *142*
  Earlier sketches in SATA *38, 78*
Toland, John (Willard) 1912-2004 .... *38*
Tolbert, Steve 1944- *143*
Toledo, Francisco 1940- *198*
Toledo, Natalia 1967- *197*
Tolkien, John Ronald Reuel
  See Tolkien, J.R.R
Tolkien, J.R.R 1892-1973 .... *100*
  Obituary *24*
  Earlier sketches in SATA *2, 32*
  See also CLR *56*
Toll, Emily
  See Cannon, Eileen E(mily)
Toll, Nelly S. 1935- *78*
Tolland, W. R.
  See Heitzmann, William Ray
Tolles, Martha 1921- *76*
  Earlier sketch in SATA *8*

Tolliver, Ruby C(hangos) 1922- *110*
   Brief entry *41*
   Earlier sketch in SATA *55*
Tolmie, Kenneth Donald 1941- *15*
Tolstoi, Lev
   See Tolstoy, Leo (Nikolaevich)
Tolstoy, Leo (Nikolaevich) 1828-1910 .... *26*
Tolstoy, Count Leo
   See Tolstoy, Leo (Nikolaevich)
Tomalin, Ruth *29*
Tomaselli, Rosa
   See Pausacker, Jenny
Tomecek, Steve *172*
Tomes, Margot (Ladd) 1917-1991 .... *70*
   Brief entry *27*
   Obituary *69*
   Earlier sketch in SATA *36*
Tomey, Ingrid 1943- *77*
Tomfool
   See Farjeon, Eleanor
Tomkins, Jasper
   See Batey, Tom
Tomline, F. Latour
   See Gilbert, W(illiam) S(chwenck)
Tomlinson, Heather *192*
Tomlinson, Jill 1931-1976 .... *3*
   Obituary *24*
Tomlinson, Reginald R(obert) 1885-1979(?)
   Obituary *27*
Tomlinson, Theresa 1946- *165*
   Earlier sketch in SATA *103*
   See also CLR *60*
Tommaso, Rich 1970(?)- *200*
Tompert, Ann 1918- *139*
   Earlier sketches in SATA *14, 89*
Toner, Raymond John 1908-1986 .... *10*
Tong, Gary S. 1942- *66*
Tong, Paul *188*
Took, Belladonna
   See Chapman, Vera (Ivy May)
Tooke, Louise Mathews 1950- *38*
Tooke, Susan *173*
Toonder, Martin
   See Groom, Arthur William
Toothaker, Roy Eugene 1928- *18*
Tooze, Ruth (Anderson) 1892-1972 .... *4*
Topek, Susan Remick 1955- *78*
Topping, Audrey R(onning) 1928- *14*
Tor, Regina
   See Shekerjian, Regina Tor
Torbert, Floyd James 1922- *22*
Torgersen, Don Arthur 1934- *55*
   Brief entry *41*
Torley, Luke
   See Blish, James (Benjamin)
Torres, Andres Segovia
   See Segovia, Andres
Torres, Daniel 1958- *102*
Torres, John A. 1965- *163*
   Earlier sketch in SATA *94*
Torres, John Albert
   See Torres, John A.
Torres, Laura 1967- *146*
   Earlier sketch in SATA *87*
Torres, Leyla 1960- *155*
Torrey, Rich
   See Torrey, Richard
Torrey, Richard *189*
Torrie, Malcolm
   See Mitchell, Gladys (Maude Winifred)
Toten, Teresa 1955- *99*
Totham, Mary
   See Breinburg, Petronella
Touponce, William F. 1948- *114*
Tournier, Michel 1924- *23*
Tournier, Michel Edouard
   See Tournier, Michel
Towle, Wendy 1963- *79*
Towne, Mary
   See Spelman, Mary

Townley, Rod
   See Townley, Roderick
Townley, Roderick 1942- *177*
Townsend, Brad W. 1962- *91*
Townsend, John Rowe 1922- *132*
   Autobiography Feature *132*
   Earlier sketches in SATA *4, 68*
   See also CLR *2*
   See also SAAS *2*
Townsend, Michael 1981- *194*
Townsend, Sue
   See Townsend, Susan Lilian
Townsend, Susan Lilian 1946- *93*
   Brief entry *48*
   Earlier sketch in SATA *55*
Townsend, Thomas L. 1944- *59*
Townsend, Tom
   See Townsend, Thomas L.
Townsend, Wendy 1962- *201*
Townson, Hazel *134*
Toye, William Eldred 1926- *8*
Traherne, Michael
   See Watkins-Pitchford, Denys James
Trahey, Jane 1923-2000 .... *36*
   Obituary *120*
Trapani, Iza 1954- *116*
   Earlier sketch in SATA *80*
Trapp, Maria Augusta von
   See von Trapp, Maria Augusta
Travers, P(amela) L(yndon) 1899-1996 ...... *100*
   Obituary *90*
   Earlier sketches in SATA *4, 54*
   See also CLR *93*
   See also SAAS *2*
Travis, Lucille *133*
   Earlier sketch in SATA *88*
Treadgold, Mary 1910- *49*
Trease, (Robert) Geoffrey 1909-1998 .... *60*
   Obituary *101*
   Earlier sketch in SATA *2*
   See also CLR *42*
   See also SAAS *6*
Treat, Lawrence 1903-1998 .... *59*
Tredez, Alain 1926- *17*
Tredez, Denise 1930- *50*
Treece, Henry 1912-1966 .... *2*
   See also CLR *2*
Tregarthen, Enys
   See Sloggett, Nellie
Tregaskis, Richard 1916-1973 .... *3*
   Obituary *26*
Treherne, Katie Thamer 1955- *76*
Trell, Max 1900-1996 .... *14*
   Obituary *108*
Tremain, Ruthven 1922- *17*
Trembath, Don 1963- *168*
   Earlier sketch in SATA *96*
Tremens, Del
   See MacDonald, Amy
Trent, Robbie 1894-1988 .... *26*
Trent, Timothy
   See Malmberg, Carl
Treseder, Terry Walton 1956- *68*
Tresilian, (Cecil) Stuart 1891-(?) *40*
Tresselt, Alvin 1916-2000 .... *7*
   See also CLR *30*
Trevino, Elizabeth B(orton) de 1904- *29*
   Earlier sketch in SATA *1*
   See also SAAS *5*
Trevor, Elleston 1920-1995 .... *28*
Trevor, Frances
   See Teasdale, Sara
Trevor, Glen
   See Hilton, James
Trevor, (Lucy) Meriol 1919-2000 .... *113*
   Obituary *122*
   Earlier sketch in SATA *10*
Trewellard, J.M. *195*
Trewellard, Juliet
   See Trewellard, J.M.

Trez, Alain
   See Tredez, Alain
Trez, Denise
   See Tredez, Denise
Trezise, Percy (James) 1923-
   See CLR *41*
Triggs, Tony D. 1946- *70*
Trimble, Marshall I(ra) 1939- *93*
Trimby, Elisa 1948- *47*
   Brief entry *40*
Tring, A. Stephen
   See Meynell, Laurence Walter
Tripp, Eleanor B(aldwin) 1936- *4*
Tripp, Janet 1942- *108*
Tripp, Jenny *188*
Tripp, John
   See Moore, John Travers
Tripp, Nathaniel 1944- *101*
Tripp, Paul 1916-2002 .... *8*
   Obituary *139*
Tripp, Valerie 1951- *168*
   Earlier sketch in SATA *78*
Tripp, Wallace (Whitney) 1940- *31*
Trivelpiece, Laurel 1926- *56*
   Brief entry *46*
Trivett, Daphne Harwood 1940- *22*
Trivizas, Eugene 1946- *84*
Trnka, Jiri 1912-1969 .... *43*
   Brief entry *32*
Trollope, Anthony 1815-1882 .... *22*
Trost, Lucille W(ood) 1938- *149*
   Earlier sketch in SATA *12*
Trott, Betty 1933- *91*
Trotter, Deborah W. *184*
Trotter, Grace V(iolet) 1900-1991 .... *10*
Trottier, Maxine 1950- *175*
   Earlier sketch in SATA *131*
Troughton, Joanna (Margaret) 1947- *37*
Trout, Kilgore
   See Farmer, Philip Jose
Trout, Richard E. *123*
Trudeau, Garretson Beekman
   See Trudeau, G.B.
Trudeau, Garry
   See Trudeau, G.B.
Trudeau, Garry B.
   See Trudeau, G.B.
Trudeau, G.B. 1948- *168*
   Earlier sketch in SATA *35*
Trueit, Trudi
   See Trueit, Trudi Strain
Trueit, Trudi Strain 1963- *179*
Trueman, Matthew *183*
Trueman, Terry 1947- *178*
   Earlier sketch in SATA *132*
Truesdell, Judy
   See Mecca, Judy Truesdell
Truesdell, Sue
   See Truesdell, Susan G.
Truesdell, Susan G. *108*
   Brief entry *45*
Trumbauer, Lisa (Trutkoff) 1963- *149*
Truss, Jan 1925- *35*
Truss, Lynne 1955(?)- *194*
Tryon, Leslie *194*
   Earlier sketch in SATA *139*
Tubb, Jonathan N. 1951- *78*
Tubby, I. M.
   See Kraus, (Herman) Robert
Tucker, Caroline
   See Nolan, Jeannette Covert
Tudor, Edward
   See Browne, Anthony
Tudor, Tasha 1915-2008 .... *160*
   Earlier sketches in SATA *20, 69*
   See also CLR *13*
Tuerk, Hanne 1951- *71*
Tugeau, Jeremy *199*
Tulloch, Richard 1949- *180*
   Earlier sketch in SATA *76*

Tulloch, Richard George
   See Tulloch, Richard
Tulloch, Shirley 169
Tully, John (Kimberley) 1923- 14
Tumanov, Vladimir A. 1961- 138
Tung, Angela 1972- 109
Tunis, Edwin (Burdett) 1897-1973 28
   Obituary 24
   Earlier sketch in SATA 1
   See also CLR 2
Tunis, John R(oberts) 1889-1975 37
   Brief entry 30
Tunnell, Michael
   See Tunnell, Michael O.
Tunnell, Michael O. 1950- 157
   Earlier sketch in SATA 103
Tunnell, Michael O'Grady
   See Tunnell, Michael O.
Tunnicliffe, C(harles) F(rederick)
   1901-1979 62
Turck, Mary C. 1950- 144
Turk, Hanne
   See Tuerk, Hanne
Turk, Ruth 1917- 82
Turkle, Brinton 1915- 79
   Earlier sketch in SATA 2
Turlington, Bayly 1919-1977 5
   Obituary 52
Turnbull, Agnes Sligh 1888-1982 14
Turnbull, Ann 1943- 160
   Earlier sketch in SATA 18
Turnbull, Ann Christine
   See Turnbull, Ann
Turner, Alice K. 1940- 10
Turner, Ann 1945- 188
   Autobiography Feature 188
   Earlier sketches in SATA 14, 77, 113, 178
Turner, Ann Warren
   See Turner, Ann
Turner, Bonnie 1932- 75
Turner, Elizabeth 1774-1846
   See YABC 2
Turner, Glennette Tilley 1933- 183
   Earlier sketch in SATA 71
Turner, Josie
   See Crawford, Phyllis
Turner, Megan Whalen 1965- 174
   Earlier sketch in SATA 94
Turner, Philip (William) 1925- 83
   Earlier sketch in SATA 11
   See also CLR 89
   See also SAAS 6
Turner, Robyn 1947- 77
Turner, Sheila R.
   See Seed, Sheila Turner
Turngren, Annette 1902(?)-1980
   Obituary 23
Turngren, Ellen (?)-1964 3
Turska, Krystyna (Zofia) 1933- 31
   Brief entry 27
Turteltaub, H.N.
   See Turtledove, Harry
Turtledove, Harry 1949- 166
   Earlier sketch in SATA 116
Turtledove, Harry Norman
   See Turtledove, Harry
Tusa, Tricia 1960- 111
   Earlier sketch in SATA 72
Tusiani, Joseph 1924- 45
Twain, Mark 1835-1910 100
   See also YABC 2
   See also CLR 66
Tweit, Susan J 1956- 94
Tweit, Susan Joan
   See Tweit, Susan J
Tweton, D. Jerome 1933- 48
Twinem, Neecy 1958- 92
Twohill, Maggie
   See Angell, Judie
Tworkov, Jack 1900-1982 47
   Obituary 31

Tyche
   See Papademetriou, Lisa
Tyers, Jenny 1969- 89
Tyers, Kathy 1952- 82
Tyler, Anne 1941- 173
   Earlier sketches in SATA 7, 90
Tyler, Linda
   See Tyler, Linda W(agner)
Tyler, Linda W(agner) 1952- 65
Tyler, Vicki 1952- 64
Tyne, Joel
   See Schembri, Jim
Tyrrell, Frances 1959- 107

U

Ubell, Earl 1926-2007 4
   Obituary 182
Uchida, Yoshiko 1921-1992 53
   Obituary 72
   Earlier sketch in SATA 1
   See also CLR 56
   See also SAAS 1
Udall, Jan Beaney 1938- 10
Uden, (Bernard Gilbert) Grant 1910- 26
Uderzo, Albert 1927-
   See CLR 37
Udovic, David 1950- 189
Udry, Janice May 1928- 152
   Earlier sketch in SATA 4
Uegaki, Chieri 1969- 153
Ueno, Noriko
   See Nakae, Noriko
Ugliano, Natascia 196
Uhlberg, Myron 174
Uhlig, Richard 1970- 195
Uhlig, Susan 1955- 129
Ulam, S(tanislaw) M(arcin) 1909-1984 51
Ullman, James Ramsey 1907-1971 7
Ulm, Robert 1934-1977 17
Ulmer, Louise 1943- 53
Ulmer, Wendy K. 1950- 201
Ulyatt, Kenneth 1920- 14
Umansky, Kaye 1946- 188
   Earlier sketch in SATA 158
Unada
   See Gliewe, Unada (Grace)
Uncle Carter
   See Boucher, (Clarence) Carter
Uncle Eric
   See Maybury, Richard J.
Uncle Gus
   See Rey, H(ans) A(ugusto)
Uncle Mac
   See McCulloch, Derek (Ivor Breashur)
Uncle Ray
   See Coffman, Ramon Peyton
Uncle Shelby
   See Silverstein, Shel
Underhill, Alice Mertie (Waterman)
   1900-1971 10
Underhill, Liz 1948- 53
   Brief entry 49
Unger, Harlow G. 1931- 75
Unger, Jim 1937- 67
Ungerer, (Jean) Thomas 1931- 106
   Earlier sketches in SATA 5, 33
   See also CLR 77
Ungerer, Tomi 1931-
   See Ungerer, (Jean) Thomas
Unkelbach, Kurt 1913-1992 4
Unnerstad, Edith (Totterman) 1900-1982 3
   See also CLR 36
Unobagha, Uzo 139
Unrau, Ruth 1922- 9
Unstead, R(obert) J(ohn) 1915-1988 12
   Obituary 56
Unsworth, Walt(er) 1928- 4
Untermeyer, Bryna Ivens 1909-1985 61

Untermeyer, Louis 1885-1977 37
   Obituary 26
   Earlier sketch in SATA 2
Unwin, David S(torr) 1918- 14
Unwin, Nora S(picer) 1907-1982 3
   Obituary 49
Unzner, Christa 1958- 141
   Earlier sketch in SATA 80
Unzner-Fischer, Christa
   See Unzner, Christa
Updale, Eleanor 1953- 175
Updyke, Rosemary K. 1924- 103
Upitis, Alvis 109
Urban, Helle (Denise) 1957- 149
Urban, Linda 199
Urbanovic, Jackie 189
Urbigkit, Cat 1965- 196
Ure, Jean 1943- 192
   Autobiography Feature 192
   Earlier sketches in SATA 48, 78, 129
   See also CLR 34
   See also SAAS 14
U'Ren, Andrea 1968- 142
Uris, Leon 1924-2003 49
   Obituary 146
Uris, Leon Marcus
   See Uris, Leon
Ursu, Anne 177
Ury, Allen B. 1954- 98
Uschan, Michael V. 1948- 129
Usher, Margo Scegge
   See McHargue, Georgess
Uslan, Michael E. 1951- 169
Uston, Ken(neth Senzo) 1935-1987 65
Uttley, Alice Jane 1884-1976 88
   Obituary 26
   Earlier sketch in SATA 3
Uttley, Alison
   See Uttley, Alice Jane
Utz, Lois (Marie) 1932-1986 5
   Obituary 50

V

Vaeth, J. Gordon 1921- 17
Vaeth, Joseph Gordon
   See Vaeth, J. Gordon
Vagin, Vladimir (Vasilevich) 1937- 142
Vail, Rachel 1966- 201
   Earlier sketches in SATA 94, 163
Vainio, Pirkko 1957- 123
   Earlier sketch in SATA 76
Valen, Nanine 1950- 21
Valencak, Hannelore
   See Mayer, Hannelore Valencak
Valens, Amy 1946- 70
Valens, E(vans) G(ladstone), Jr. 1920-1992 ... 1
Valentine, Johnny 72
Valerio, Geraldo 1970- 180
Valgardson, W(illiam) D(empsey) 1939- 151
   Earlier sketch in SATA 101
Valleau, Emily 1925- 51
Van Abbe, Salaman 1883-1955 18
Van Allsburg, Chris 1949- 156
   Earlier sketches in SATA 37, 53, 105
   See also CLR 113
Van Anrooy, Francine 1924- 2
Van Anrooy, Frans
   See Van Anrooy, Francine
Vanasse, Deb 1957- 170
Vance, Eleanor Graham 1908-1985 11
Vance, Gerald
   See Garrett, Randall
   and Silverberg, Robert
Vance, Marguerite 1889-1965 29
VanCleave, Janice 1942- 116
   Autobiography Feature 123
   Earlier sketch in SATA 75
Vandenburg, Mary Lou 1943- 17

Vander Boom, Mae M. *14*
Vander-Els, Betty 1936- *63*
van der Heide, Iris 1970- *183*
van der Linde, Laurel 1952- *78*
van der Meer, Ron 1945- *98*
van de Ruit, John 1975- *199*
Van der Veer, Judy 1912-1982 .... *4*
    Obituary *33*
Vanderwerff, Corrine 1939- *117*
Vander Zee, Ruth *199*
    Earlier sketch in SATA *159*
Vande Velde, Vivian 1951- *141*
    Earlier sketches in SATA *62, 95*
Vandivert, Rita (Andre) 1905-1986 .... *21*
Van Draanen, Wendelin *122*
Van Dusen, Chris *173*
Van Duyn, Janet 1910- *18*
Van Dyne, Edith
    See Baum, L(yman) Frank
    and Sampson, Emma (Keats) Speed
    and van Zantwijk, Rudolf (Alexander
    Marinus)
Vane, Mitch
    See Vane, Mitchelle
Vane, Mitchelle *176*
van Frankenhuyzen, Gijsbert 1951- *132*
Van Genechten, Guido 1957- *165*
van Haeringen, Annemarie *193*
Van Hook, Beverly H. 1941- *99*
Van Horn, William 1939- *43*
van Hout, Mies 1962- *178*
Van Iterson, S(iny) R(ose) *26*
Van Kampen, Vlasta 1943- *163*
    Earlier sketch in SATA *54*
Van Laan, Nancy 1939- *105*
van Lawick-Goodall, Jane
    See Goodall, Jane
Van Leeuwen, Jean 1937- *141*
    Autobiography Feature *141*
    Earlier sketches in SATA *6, 82, 132*
    See also SAAS *8*
van Lhin, Erik
    See del Rey, Lester
van Lieshout, Maria *201*
Van Loon, Hendrik Willem 1882-1944 .... *18*
van Ommen, Sylvia 1978- *186*
VanOosting, James 1951- *170*
Van Orden, M(erton) D(ick) 1921- *4*
Van Patter, Bruce *183*
Van Rensselaer, Alexander (Taylor Mason)
    1892-1962 .... *14*
Van Riper, Guernsey, Jr. 1909-1995 .... *3*
van Rossum, Heleen 1962- *174*
Van Rynbach, Iris 1952- *102*
Vansant, Rhonda Joy Edwards 1950- *92*
Van Steenwyk, Elizabeth (Ann) 1928- *89*
    Earlier sketch in SATA *34*
Van Stockum, Hilda 1908-2006 .... *5*
    Obituary *179*
van Straaten, Harmen 1961- *195*
Van Tuyl, Barbara 1940- *11*
van Vogt, A(lfred) E(lton) 1912-2000 .... *14*
    Obituary *124*
Van Woerkom, Dorothy (O'Brien)
    1924-1996 .... *21*
Van Wormer, Joe
    See Van Wormer, Joseph Edward
Van Wormer, Joseph Edward 1913-1998 .... *35*
Van Wright, Cornelius *173*
Van Zwienen, Ilse Charlotte Koehn
    1929-1991 .... *34*
    Brief entry *28*
    Obituary *67*
Van Zyle, Jon 1942- *176*
    Earlier sketch in SATA *84*
Varela, Barry *180*
Varga, Judy
    See Stang, Judit
Varley, Dimitry V. 1906-1984 .... *10*
Varley, Susan 1961- *134*
    Earlier sketch in SATA *63*

Varon, Sara *195*
Vasileva, Tatiana
    See Wassiljewa, Tatjana
Vasiliev, Valery 1949- *80*
Vasilieva, Tatiana
    See Wassiljewa, Tatjana
Vasiliu, Mircea 1920- *2*
Vass, George 1927- *57*
    Brief entry *31*
Vaughan, Carter A.
    See Gerson, Noel Bertram
Vaughan, Harold Cecil 1923- *14*
Vaughan, Marcia (K.) 1951- *159*
    Earlier sketches in SATA *60, 95*
Vaughan, Richard 1947- *87*
Vaughan, Sam(uel) 1928- *14*
Vaughn, Ruth 1935- *14*
Vaught, Susan 1965- *195*
Vaupel, Robin *198*
Vautier, Ghislaine 1932- *53*
Vavra, Robert James 1935- *8*
Vecsey, George Spencer 1939- *9*
Vedral, Joyce L(auretta) 1943- *65*
Vega, Denise *174*
Vega, Denise B.
    See Vega, Denise
Veglahn, Nancy (Crary) 1937- *5*
Vejjajiva, Jane 1963- *189*
Velasquez, Eric *192*
Velasquez, Gloria 1949- *113*
Velasquez, Gloria 1949-
    See Velasquez, Gloria
Velthuijs, Max 1923-2005 .... *110*
    Obituary *160*
    Earlier sketch in SATA *53*
Venable, Alan (Hudson) 1944- *8*
Venezia, Mike 1945- *150*
Ventura, Anthony
    See Pellowski, Michael (Joseph)
Ventura, Piero (Luigi) 1937- *61*
    Brief entry *43*
    See also CLR *16*
Vequin, Capini
    See Quinn, Elisabeth
Verba, Joan Marie 1953- *78*
Verboven, Agnes 1951- *103*
verDorn, Bethea (Stewart) 1952- *76*
Vere, Ed *197*
Verissimo, Erico (Lopes) 1905-1975 .... *113*
Verne, Jules (Gabriel) 1828-1905 .... *21*
    See also CLR *88*
Verner, Gerald 1897(?)-1980
    Obituary *25*
Verney, John 1913-1993 .... *14*
    Obituary *75*
Verniero, Joan C. 1949- *181*
Vernon, (Elda) Louise A(nderson) 1914- *14*
Vernon, Rosemary
    See Smith, Susan Vernon
Vernor, D.
    See Casewit, Curtis W(erner)
Verr, Harry Coe
    See Kunhardt, Edith
Verral, Charles Spain 1904-1990 .... *11*
    Obituary *65*
Verrillo, Erica 1953- *199*
Verrillo, Erica F.
    See Verrillo, Erica
Verrone, Robert J. 1935(?)-1984
    Obituary *39*
Versace, Marie Teresa Rios 1917- *2*
Vertreace, Martha M(odena) 1945- *78*
Vesey, A(manda) 1939- *62*
Vesey, Mark (David) 1958- *123*
Vesey, Paul
    See Allen, Samuel W(ashington)
Vestergaard, Hope *178*
Vestly, Anne-Cath(arina) 1920- *14*
    See also CLR *99*
Vevers, (Henry) Gwynne 1916-1988 .... *45*
    Obituary *57*

Viator, Vacuus
    See Hughes, Thomas
Vicar, Henry
    See Felsen, Henry Gregor
Vick, Helen Hughes 1950- *88*
Vicker, Angus
    See Felsen, Henry Gregor
Vickers, Sheena 1960- *94*
Vickery, Kate
    See Kennedy, T.A.
Victor, Edward 1914- *3*
Victor, Joan Berg 1942- *30*
Vidrine, Beverly Barras 1938- *188*
    Earlier sketch in SATA *103*
Viereck, Ellen K. 1928- *14*
Viereck, Phillip 1925- *3*
Viertel, Janet 1915- *10*
Vigliante, Mary
    See Szydlowski, Mary Vigliante
Vigna, Judith 1936- *102*
    Earlier sketch in SATA *15*
Viguers, Ruth Hill 1903-1971 .... *6*
Villareal, Ray *187*
Villasenor, Edmundo
    See Villasenor, Victor
Villasenor, Victor 1940- *171*
Villasenor, Victor E. 1940-
    See Villasenor, Victor
Villasenor, Victor Edmundo
    See Villasenor, Victor
Villiard, Paul 1910-1974 .... *51*
    Obituary *20*
Villiers, Alan (John) 1903-1982 .... *10*
Vilott, Rhondi
    See Salsitz, Rhondi Vilott
Vincent, Eric Douglas 1953- *40*
Vincent, Erin 1969- *188*
Vincent, Felix 1946- *41*
Vincent, Gabrielle 1928-2000 .... *121*
    Earlier sketch in SATA *61*
    See also CLR *13*
Vincent, Mary Keith
    See St. John, Wylly Folk
Vincent, William R.
    See Heitzmann, William Ray
Vinegar, Tom
    See Gregg, Andrew K.
Vinest, Shaw
    See Longyear, Barry B(rookes)
Vinge, Joan (Carol) D(ennison) 1948- *113*
    Earlier sketch in SATA *36*
Vining, Elizabeth Gray 1902-1999 .... *6*
    Obituary *117*
Vinson, Kathryn 1911-1995 .... *21*
Vinton, Iris 1906(?)-1988 .... *24*
    Obituary *55*
Viola, Herman J(oseph) 1938- *126*
Viorst, Judith 1931- *172*
    Earlier sketches in SATA *7, 70, 123*
    See also CLR *90*
Vip
    See Partch, Virgil Franklin II
Vipont, Charles
    See Foulds, Elfrida Vipont
Vipont, Elfrida
    See Foulds, Elfrida Vipont
Viscott, David S(teven) 1938-1996 .... *65*
Visser, W(illem) F(rederik) H(endrik)
    1900-1968 .... *10*
Vitale, Stefano 1958- *180*
    Earlier sketch in SATA *114*
Vivas, Julie 1947- *96*
Vivelo, Jackie 1943- *63*
Vivelo, Jacqueline J.
    See Vivelo, Jackie
Vivelo, Jacqueline Jean
    See Vivelo, Jackie
Vizzini, Ned 1981- *179*
    Earlier sketch in SATA *125*
Vlahos, Olivia 1924- *31*

Vlasic, Bob
  See Hirsch, Phil
Voake, Charlotte 180
  Earlier sketch in SATA 114
Voake, Steve 1961- 178
Vo-Dinh, Mai 1933- 16
Vogel, Carole Garbuny 1951- 105
  Earlier sketch in SATA 70
Vogel, Ilse-Margret 1918- 14
Vogel, John H., Jr. 1950- 18
Vogt, Esther Loewen 1915-1999 14
Vogt, Gregory L. 94
Vogt, Marie Bollinger 1921- 45
Voight, Virginia Frances 1909-1989 8
Voigt, Cynthia 1942- 160
  Brief entry 33
  Earlier sketches in SATA 48, 79, 116
  See also CLR 141
Voigt, Erna 1925- 35
Voigt-Rother, Erna
  See Voigt, Erna
Vojtech, Anna 1946- 108
  Earlier sketch in SATA 42
Vollstadt, Elizabeth Weiss 1942- 121
Volponi, Paul 175
Volting, Dr. R.E.
  See Lerangis, Peter
Von Ahnen, Katherine 1922- 93
von Buhler, Cynthia 185
Vondra, J. Gert
  See Vondra, Josef
Vondra, Josef 1941- 121
Vondra, Josef Gert
  See Vondra, Josef
Von Gunden, Kenneth 1946- 113
Von Hagen, Victor Wolfgang 1908-1985 29
von Klopp, Vahrah
  See Malvern, Gladys
von Schmidt, Eric 1931-2007 50
  Brief entry 36
  Obituary 181
von Storch, Anne B. 1910- 1
von Trapp, Maria Augusta 1905-1987 16
von Wodtke, Charlotte Buel Johnson
  1918-1982 46
von Ziegesar, Cecily 1970- 161
Vos, Ida 1931-2006 121
  Earlier sketch in SATA 69
  See also CLR 85
Vosburgh, Leonard (W.) 1912- 15
Votaw, Carol 1961- 201
Voyle, Mary
  See Manning, Rosemary
Vrettos, Adrienne Maria 187
Vriens, Jacques 1946- 151
Vugteveen, Verna Aardema
  See Aardema, Verna
Vulture, Elizabeth T.
  See Gilbert, Suzie
Vuong, Lynette Dyer 1938- 110
  Earlier sketch in SATA 60

W

Waas, Uli
  See Waas-Pommer, Ulrike
Waas-Pommer, Ulrike 1949- 85
Waber, Bernard 1924- 155
  Brief entry 40
  Earlier sketches in SATA 47, 95
  See also CLR 55
Wachtel, Shirley Russak 1951- 88
Wachter, Oralee (Roberts) 1935- 61
  Brief entry 51
Waddell, Evelyn Margaret 1918- 10

Waddell, Martin 1941- 129
  Autobiography Feature 129
  Earlier sketches in SATA 43, 81, 127
  See also CLR 31
  See also SAAS 15
Waddy, Lawrence (Heber) 1914- 91
Wade, Mary Dodson 1930- 151
  Earlier sketch in SATA 79
Wade, Suzanne
  See Kirby, Susan E.
Wade, Theodore E., Jr. 1936- 37
Wademan, Peter John 1946- 122
Wademan, Spike
  See Wademan, Peter John
Wadsworth, Ginger 1945- 157
  Earlier sketch in SATA 103
Wagenheim, Kal 1935- 21
Wagner, Michele R. 1975- 157
Wagner, Sharon B. 1936- 4
Wagoner, David (Russell) 1926- 14
Wahl, Jan (Boyer) 1933- 132
  Earlier sketches in SATA 2, 34, 73
  See also SAAS 3
Wahl, Mats 1945- 186
Waide, Jan 1952- 29
Wainscott, John Milton 1910-1981 53
Wainwright, Richard M. 1935- 91
Wainwright, Ruth
  See Symes, Ruth Louise
Wait, Lea 1946- 137
Waite, Judy 174
Waite, Judy Bernard
  See Bernard, Patricia
Waite, Michael P(hillip) 1960- 101
Waite, P(eter) B(usby) 1922- 64
Waites, Joan C. 187
Waitley, Douglas 1927- 30
Wakefield, Jean L.
  See Laird, Jean E(louise)
Wakin, Daniel (Joseph) 1961- 84
Wakin, Edward 1927- 37
Wakiyama, Hanako 1966- 192
Walck, Henry Z. 1908(?)-1984
  Obituary 40
Walden, Amelia Elizabeth 3
Walden, Mark 188
Waldherr, Kris 1963- 76
Waldman, Bruce 1949- 15
Waldman, Neil 1947- 142
  Earlier sketches in SATA 51, 94
Waldrep, Richard 198
Waldron, Ann Wood 1924- 16
Waldron, Kathleen Cook 176
Walgren, Judy 1963- 118
Walker, Addison
  See Walker, (Addison) Mort
Walker, Alice 1944- 31
Walker, Alice Malsenior
  See Walker, Alice
Walker, Barbara (Jeanne) K(erlin) 1921- 80
  Earlier sketch in SATA 4
Walker, Barbara M(uhs) 1928- 57
Walker, (James) Braz(elton) 1934-1983 45
Walker, David 1965- 197
Walker, David G(ordon) 1926- 60
Walker, David Harry 1911-1992 8
  Obituary 71
Walker, Diana 1925- 9
Walker, Diane Marie Catherine
  See Walker, Kate
Walker, Dick
  See Pellowski, Michael (Joseph)
Walker, Frank 1931-2000 36
Walker, Holly Beth
  See Bond, Gladys Baker
Walker, Kate 1950- 165
  Earlier sketch in SATA 82
Walker, Kathrine Sorley
  See Sorley Walker, Kathrine
Walker, Lou Ann 1952- 66
  Brief entry 53

Walker, Louise Jean 1891-1976
  Obituary 35
Walker, Mary Alexander 1927- 61
Walker, Mildred
  See Schemm, Mildred Walker
Walker, (Addison) Mort 1923- 8
Walker, Pamela 1948- 142
  Earlier sketch in SATA 24
Walker, Paul Robert 1953- 154
Walker, Robert W. 1948- 66
Walker, Sally M(acArt) 1954- 135
Walker, Stephen J. 1951- 12
Walker-Blondell, Becky 1951- 89
Wallace, Barbara Brooks 1922- 136
  Earlier sketches in SATA 4, 78
  See also SAAS 17
Wallace, Beverly Dobrin 1921- 19
Wallace, Bill 1947- 169
  Brief entry 47
  Earlier sketches in SATA 53, 101
Wallace, Daisy
  See Cuyler, Margery
Wallace, Ian 1950- 141
  Earlier sketches in SATA 53, 56
  See also CLR 37
Wallace, John 1966- 155
  Earlier sketch in SATA 105
Wallace, John A(dam) 1915-2004 3
  Obituary 155
Wallace, Karen 1951- 188
  Earlier sketches in SATA 83, 139
Wallace, Nancy Elizabeth 1948- 186
  Earlier sketch in SATA 141
Wallace, Nigel
  See Hamilton, Charles (Harold St. John)
Wallace, Paula S. 153
Wallace, Rich 1957- 196
  Earlier sketches in SATA 117, 158
Wallace, Robert 1932-1999 47
  Brief entry 37
Wallace, Ruby Ann 1923(?)- 77
Wallace, William Keith
  See Wallace, Bill
Wallace-Brodeur, Ruth 1941- 169
  Brief entry 41
  Earlier sketches in SATA 51, 88
Wallenta, Adam 1974- 123
Waller, Leslie 1923-2007 20
Walley, Byron
  See Card, Orson Scott
Wallis, Diz 1949- 77
Wallis, G. McDonald
  See Campbell, Hope
Wallner, Alexandra 1946- 156
  Brief entry 41
  Earlier sketches in SATA 51, 98
Wallner, John C. 1945- 133
  Earlier sketches in SATA 10, 51
Wallower, Lucille 11
Walrod, Amy 1973(?)- 182
Walsh, Ann 1942- 176
  Earlier sketch in SATA 62
Walsh, Ellen Stoll 1942- 194
  Earlier sketches in SATA 49, 99, 147
Walsh, George Johnston 1889-1981 53
Walsh, Gillian Paton
  See Paton Walsh, Jill
Walsh, Jill Paton
  See Paton Walsh, Jill
Walsh, Joanna 1970- 182
Walsh, Lawrence 1942- 170
Walsh, Marissa 1972- 195
Walsh, Mary Caswell 1949- 118
Walsh, Mitzy
  See Walsh, Marissa
Walsh, Suella 170
Walsh, V. L.
  See Walsh, Vivian
Walsh, Vivian 1960- 120
Walsh Shepherd, Donna 1948- 78
Walter, Frances V. 1923- 71

Walter, Mildred Pitts 1922- *133*
    Brief entry *45*
    Earlier sketch in SATA 69
    See also CLR 61
    See also SAAS 12
Walter, Villiam Christian
    See Andersen, Hans Christian
Walter, Virginia
    See Walter, Virginia A.
Walter, Virginia A. *134*
Walters, Audrey 1929- *18*
Walters, Celeste 1938- *126*
Walters, Eric (Robert) 1957- *155*
    Earlier sketch in SATA 99
Walters, Helen B. (?)-1987
    Obituary *50*
Walters, Hugh
    See Hughes, Walter (Llewellyn)
Walther, Thomas A. 1950- *31*
Walther, Tom
    See Walther, Thomas A.
Waltner, Elma 1912-1987 .... *40*
Waltner, Willard H. 1909- *40*
Walton, Darwin McBeth 1926- *119*
Walton, Fiona L. M. 1959- *89*
Walton, Richard J. 1928- *4*
Walton, Rick 1957- *151*
    Earlier sketch in SATA 101
Waltrip, Lela (Kingston) 1904-1995 .... *9*
Waltrip, Mildred 1911- *37*
Waltrip, Rufus (Charles) 1898-1988 .... *9*
Walworth, Nancy Zinsser 1917- *14*
Wangerin, Walter, Jr. 1944- *98*
    Brief entry *37*
    Earlier sketch in SATA 45
Waniek, Marilyn Nelson 1946-
    See Nelson, Marilyn
Wannamaker, Bruce
    See Moncure, Jane Belk
Warbler, J. M.
    See Cocagnac, Augustin Maurice(-Jean)
Warburg, Sandol Stoddard
    See Stoddard, Sandol
Ward, E. D.
    See Gorey, Edward (St. John)
    and Lucas, E(dward) V(errall)
Ward, Ed
    See Stratemeyer, Edward L.
Ward, Helen 1962- *144*
    Earlier sketch in SATA 72
Ward, Jay 1920-1989
    Obituary *63*
Ward, Jennifer 1963- *146*
Ward, John (Stanton) 1917- *42*
Ward, Jonas
    See Ard, William
    and Cox, William R(obert)
    and Garfield, Brian (Francis Wynne)
Ward, Lynd (Kendall) 1905-1985 .... *36*
    Obituary *42*
    Earlier sketch in SATA 2
Ward, Martha (Eads) *5*
Ward, Melanie
    See Curtis, Richard (Alan)
    and Lynch, Marilyn
Ward, Nicholas John
    See Ward, Nick
Ward, Nick 1955- *190*
Ward, Tom
    See Stratemeyer, Edward L.
Wardell, Dean
    See Prince, J(ack) H(arvey)
Wardlaw, Lee 1955- *115*
    Earlier sketch in SATA 79
Ware, Cheryl 1963- *101*
Ware, Chris 1967- *140*
Ware, Leon (Vernon) 1909-1976 .... *4*
Wargin, Kathy-jo 1964- *145*
Warhola, James 1955- *187*
Warner, Frank A. *67*
    Earlier sketch in SATA 1

Warner, Gertrude Chandler 1890-1979 .... *9*
    Obituary *73*
Warner, J(ohn) F. 1929- *75*
Warner, Lucille Schulberg *30*
Warner, Matt
    See Fichter, George S.
Warner, Oliver (Martin Wilson) 1903-1976 . *29*
Warner, Sally 1946- *131*
Warner, Sunny (B.) 1931- *108*
Warnes, Tim 1971- *166*
    Earlier sketch in SATA 116
Warnes, Timothy
    See Warnes, Tim
Warnick, Elsa 1942- *113*
Warren, Andrea 1946- *98*
Warren, Betsy
    See Warren, Elizabeth Avery
Warren, Billy
    See Warren, William Stephen
Warren, Cathy 1951- *62*
    Brief entry *46*
Warren, Elizabeth
    See Supraner, Robyn
Warren, Elizabeth Avery 1916- *46*
    Brief entry *38*
Warren, Jackie M. 1953- *135*
Warren, Joshua P(aul) 1976- *107*
Warren, Joyce W(illiams) 1935- *18*
Warren, Mary Phraner 1929- *10*
Warren, Robert Penn 1905-1989 .... *46*
    Obituary *63*
Warren, Scott S. 1957- *79*
Warren, William Stephen 1882-1968 .... *9*
Warrick, Patricia Scott 1925- *35*
Warriner, John 1907(?)-1987
    Obituary *53*
Warsh
    See Warshaw, Jerry
Warshaw, Jerry 1929- *30*
Warshaw, Mary 1931- *89*
Warshofsky, Fred 1931- *24*
Warshofsky, Isaac
    See Singer, Isaac Bashevis
Wartski, Maureen (Ann Crane) 1940- *50*
    Brief entry *37*
Warwick, Alan R(oss) 1900-1973 .... *42*
Wa-sha-quon-asin
    See Belaney, Archibald Stansfeld
Wa-Sha-Quon-Asin
    See Belaney, Archibald Stansfeld
Washburn, Bradford 1910-2007 .... *38*
    Obituary *181*
Washburn, Henry Bradford, Jr.
    See Washburn, Bradford
Washburn, Jan(ice) 1926- *63*
Washburn, Lucia *193*
Washburne, Carolyn Kott 1944- *86*
Washburne, Heluiz Chandler 1892-1970 ...... *10*
    Obituary *26*
Washington, Booker T(aliaferro)
    1856-1915 .... *28*
Washington, Donna L. 1967- *159*
    Earlier sketch in SATA 98
Wasserstein, Wendy 1950-2006 .... *94*
    Obituary *174*
Wassiljewa, Tatjana 1928- *106*
Watanabe, Shigeo 1928- *131*
    Brief entry *32*
    Earlier sketch in SATA 39
    See also CLR 8
Waters, John F(rederick) 1930- *4*
Waters, Tony 1958- *75*
Waterton, Betty 1923- *99*
    Brief entry *34*
    Earlier sketch in SATA 37
Waterton, Betty Marie
    See Waterton, Betty
Watkins, Dawn L. *126*
Watkins, Gloria Jean
    See hooks, bell
Watkins, Lois 1930- *88*

Watkins, Peter 1934- *66*
Watkins, Yoko Kawashima 1933- *93*
Watkins-Pitchford, Denys James
    1905-1990 .... *87*
    Obituary *66*
    Earlier sketch in SATA 6
    See also SAAS 4
Watling, James 1933- *117*
    Earlier sketch in SATA 67
Watson, Aldren A(uld) 1917- *42*
    Brief entry *36*
Watson, Amy Zakrzewski 1965- *76*
Watson, B. S.
    See Teitelbaum, Michael
Watson, Carol 1949- *78*
Watson, C.G. *193*
Watson, Clyde 1947- *68*
    Earlier sketch in SATA 5
    See also CLR 3
Watson, Helen Orr 1892-1978
    Obituary *24*
Watson, James 1936- *106*
    Earlier sketch in SATA 10
Watson, Jane Werner 1915- *54*
    Earlier sketch in SATA 3
Watson, Jesse Joshua *199*
Watson, John H.
    See Farmer, Philip Jose
Watson, Mary 1953- *117*
Watson, N. Cameron 1955- *81*
Watson, Nancy Dingman *32*
Watson, Pauline 1925- *14*
Watson, Richard F.
    See Silverberg, Robert
Watson, Richard Jesse 1951- *62*
Watson, Sally (Lou) 1924- *3*
Watson, Wendy (McLeod) 1942- *142*
    Earlier sketches in SATA 5, 74
Watson Taylor, Elizabeth 1915- *41*
Watt, Melanie 1975- *193*
    Earlier sketch in SATA 136
Watt, Thomas 1935- *4*
Wattenberg, Jane *174*
Watterson, Bill 1958- *66*
Watt-Evans, Lawrence 1954- *121*
Watts, (Anna) Bernadette 1942- *103*
    Earlier sketch in SATA 4
Watts, Ephraim
    See Horne, Richard Henry Hengist
Watts, Franklin (Mowry) 1904-1978 .... *46*
    Obituary *21*
Watts, Helen L. Hoke 1903-1990
    Obituary *65*
Watts, Irene N(aemi) 1931- *111*
    Earlier sketch in SATA 56
Watts, Isaac 1674-1748 .... *52*
Watts, James K(ennedy) M(offitt) 1955- *59*
Watts, Jeri Hanel 1957- *170*
Watts, Julia 1969- *103*
Watts, Leander 1956- *146*
Watts, Leslie Elizabeth 1961- *168*
Watts, Mabel Pizzey 1906-1994 .... *11*
Watts, Nigel 1957-1999 .... *121*
Waugh, C. C. Roessel
    See Waugh, Carol-Lynn Rossel
    and Waugh, Charles G(ordon)
Waugh, Carol-Lynn Rossel 1947- *41*
Waugh, Dorothy -1996 .... *11*
Waugh, Sylvia 1935- *169*
Waugh, Virginia
    See Sorensen, Virginia
Wax, Wendy A. 1963- *163*
    Earlier sketch in SATA 73
Wayland, April Halprin 1954- *143*
    Earlier sketch in SATA 78
    See also SAAS 26
Wayland, Patrick
    See O'Connor, Richard
Wayne, (Anne) Jenifer 1917-1982 .... *32*
Wayne, Kyra Petrovskaya 1918- *8*

Wayne, Richard
 See Decker, Duane
Wayshak, Deborah Noyes
 See Noyes, Deborah
Waystaff, Simon
 See Swift, Jonathan
Weales, Gerald (Clifford) 1925- *11*
Weary, Ogdred
 See Gorey, Edward (St. John)
Weatherford, Carole Boston 1956- *181*
 Earlier sketch in SATA *138*
Weatherly, Lee 1967- *192*
Weatherly, Myra 1926- *130*
Weatherly, Myra S.
 See Weatherly, Myra
Weaver, Harriett E. 1908-1993 .... *65*
Weaver, John L. 1949- *42*
Weaver, Robyn
 See Conley, Robyn
Weaver, Robyn M.
 See Conley, Robyn
Weaver, Tess *197*
Weaver, Ward
 See Mason, F(rancis) van Wyck
Weaver, Will 1950- *161*
 Earlier sketches in SATA *88, 109*
Weaver, William Weller
 See Weaver, Will
Weaver-Gelzer, Charlotte 1950- *79*
Webb, Christopher
 See Wibberley, Leonard (Patrick O'Connor)
Webb, Jacqueline
 See Pearce, Margaret
Webb, Jacquelyn
 See Pearce, Margaret
 and Pearce, Margaret
Webb, Jean Francis (III) 1910-1991 .... *35*
Webb, Kaye 1914- *60*
Webb, Lois Sinaiko 1922- *82*
Webb, Margot 1934- *67*
Webb, Sharon 1936- *41*
Webb, Sophie 1958- *135*
Webber, Andrew Lloyd
 See Lloyd Webber, Andrew
Webber, Desiree Morrison 1956- *170*
Webber, Irma E(leanor Schmidt)
 1904-1995 .... *14*
Weber, Alfons 1921- *8*
Weber, Bruce 1942- *120*
 Earlier sketch in SATA *73*
Weber, Debora 1955- *58*
Weber, EdNah New Rider 1919(?)- *168*
Weber, Jill 1950- *127*
Weber, Judith E(ichler) 1938- *64*
Weber, Ken(neth J.) 1940- *90*
Weber, Lenora Mattingly 1895-1971 .... *2*
 Obituary *26*
Weber, Michael 1945- *87*
Weber, Sandra 1961- *158*
Weber, William J(ohn) 1927- *14*
Webster, Alice Jane Chandler 1876-1916 ..... *17*
Webster, David 1930- *11*
Webster, Frank V. *67*
 Earlier sketch in SATA *1*
Webster, Gary
 See Garrison, Webb B(lack)
Webster, James 1925-1981 .... *17*
 Obituary *27*
Webster, Jean
 See Webster, Alice Jane Chandler
Wechsler, Doug *189*
Wechsler, Herman J. 1904-1976
 Obituary *20*
Wechter, Nell (Carolyn) Wise 1913-1989 .. *127*
 Earlier sketch in SATA *60*
Weck, Thomas L. 1942- *62*
Wedd, Kate
 See Gregory, Philippa
Weddle, Ethel Harshbarger 1897-1996 .... *11*
Weeks, Sarah *194*
 Earlier sketch in SATA *158*

Weems, David B(urnola) 1922- *80*
Wees, Frances Shelley 1902-1982 .... *58*
Weevers, Peter 1944- *59*
Wegen, Ronald 1946-1985 .... *99*
Wegman, William (George) 1943- *135*
 Earlier sketches in SATA *78, 129*
Wegner, Fritz 1924- *20*
Weidhorn, Manfred 1931- *60*
Weidt, Maryann N. 1944- *85*
Weigel, Jeff 1958- *170*
Weigelt, Udo 1960- *201*
 Earlier sketch in SATA *168*
Weihs, Erika 1917- *107*
 Earlier sketch in SATA *15*
Weik, Mary Hays 1898(?)-1979 .... *3*
 Obituary *23*
Weil, Ann Yezner 1908-1969 .... *9*
Weil, Lisl 1910- *7*
Weilerstein, Sadie Rose 1894-1993 .... *3*
 Obituary *75*
Weill, Cynthia 1959- *167*
Wein, Elizabeth E(ve) 1964- *151*
 Earlier sketch in SATA *82*
Weinberg, Larry
 See Weinberg, Lawrence (E.)
Weinberg, Lawrence (E.) *92*
 Brief entry *48*
Weinberger, Tanya 1939- *84*
Weiner, Sandra 1922- *14*
Weingarten, Violet (Brown) 1915-1976 .... *3*
 Obituary *27*
Weingartner, Charles 1922- *5*
Weinheimer, Beckie 1958- *186*
Weinstein, Ellen Slusky 1959- *200*
Weinstein, Nina 1951- *73*
Weir, Bob 1947- *76*
Weir, Diana (R.) Loiewski 1958- *111*
Weir, Joan S(herman) 1928- *99*
Weir, LaVada *2*
Weir, Rosemary (Green) 1905-1994 .... *21*
Weir, Wendy 1949- *76*
Weis, Margaret 1948- *164*
 Earlier sketches in SATA *38, 92*
Weisberger, Bernard A(llen) 1922- *21*
Weiser, Marjorie P(hillis) K(atz) 1934- *33*
Weisgard, Leonard (Joseph) 1916-2000 .... *85*
 Obituary *122*
 Earlier sketches in SATA *2, 30*
 See also SAAS *19*
Weiss, Adelle 1920- *18*
Weiss, Ann E(dwards) 1943- *69*
 Earlier sketch in SATA *30*
 See also SAAS *13*
Weiss, Edna
 See Barth, Edna
Weiss, Ellen 1953- *44*
Weiss, Harvey 1922- *76*
 Earlier sketches in SATA *1, 27*
 See also CLR *4*
 See also SAAS *19*
Weiss, Jaqueline Shachter 1926- *65*
Weiss, Malcolm E. 1928- *3*
Weiss, Margaret Edith
 See Weis, Margaret
Weiss, Miriam
 See Schlein, Miriam
Weiss, Mitch 1951- *183*
 Earlier sketch in SATA *123*
Weiss, Nicki 1954- *86*
 Earlier sketch in SATA *33*
Weiss, Renee Karol 1923- *5*
Weissberger, Ela 1930- *181*
Weissberger, Ela Stein
 See Weissberger, Ela
Weissenborn, Hellmuth 1898-1982
 Obituary *31*
Weitzman, David L. 1936- *172*
 Earlier sketch in SATA *122*
Wekesser, Carol A. 1963- *76*
Welber, Robert *26*
Welch, Amanda (Jane) 1945- *75*

Welch, D'Alte Aldridge 1907-1970
 Obituary *27*
Welch, Jean-Louise
 See Kempton, Jean Welch
Welch, Pauline
 See Bodenham, Hilda Morris
Welch, Ronald
 See Felton, Ronald Oliver
Welch, Sheila Kelly 1945- *130*
Welch, Willy 1952- *93*
Weldin, Frauke 1969- *188*
Welford, Sue 1942- *75*
Weller, George 1907-2002 .... *31*
 Obituary *140*
Weller, George Anthony
 See Weller, George
Welling, Peter J. 1947- *135*
Wellington, Monica 1957- *157*
 Earlier sketches in SATA *67, 99*
Wellman, Alice 1900-1984 .... *51*
 Brief entry *36*
Wellman, Manly Wade 1903-1986 .... *6*
 Obituary *47*
Wellman, Paul I. 1898-1966 .... *3*
Wellman, Paul Iselin
 See Wellman, Paul I.
Wellman, Sam(uel) 1939- *122*
Wells, H(erbert) G(eorge) 1866-1946 .... *20*
 See also CLR *133*
Wells, Helen
 See Campbell, Hope
Wells, Helen 1910-1986 .... *49*
 Earlier sketch in SATA *2*
Wells, J. Wellington
 See de Camp, L(yon) Sprague
Wells, June
 See Swinford, Betty (June Wells)
Wells, Robert
 See Welsch, Roger L(ee)
Wells, Robert E. *184*
Wells, Rosemary 1943- *156*
 Earlier sketches in SATA *18, 69, 114*
 See also CLR *69*
 See also SAAS *1*
Wells, Susan (Mary) 1951- *78*
Wels, Byron G(erald) 1924-1993 .... *9*
Welsbacher, Anne 1955- *89*
Welsch, Roger L(ee) 1936- *82*
Welsh, David
 See Hills, C.A.R.
Welsh, Mary Flynn 1910(?)-1984
 Obituary *38*
Welsh, T.K. 1956- *184*
Weltner, Linda R(iverly) 1938- *38*
Welton, Jude 1955- *143*
 Earlier sketch in SATA *79*
Welty, S. F.
 See Welty, Susan F.
Welty, Susan F. 1905- *9*
Wemmlinger, Raymond *190*
Wendelin, Rudolph 1910-2000 .... *23*
Weninger, Brigitte 1960- *189*
Wentworth, Robert
 See Hamilton, Edmond
Werlin, Nancy 1961- *161*
 Earlier sketches in SATA *87, 119*
Werner, Elsa Jane
 See Watson, Jane Werner
Werner, Herma 1926- *47*
 Brief entry *41*
Werner, Jane
 See Watson, Jane Werner
Werner, K.
 See Casewit, Curtis W(erner)
Wersba, Barbara 1932- *58*
 Autobiography Feature *103*
 Earlier sketch in SATA *1*
 See also CLR *78*
 See also SAAS *2*
Werstein, Irving 1914(?)-1971 .... *14*
Werth, Kurt 1896-1983 .... *20*

Wesley, Alison
    See Barnes, Michael
Wesley, Kathryn
    See Rusch, Kristine Kathryn
Wesley, Mary (Aline) 1912-2002 .... *66*
Wesley, Valerie Wilson 1947- *168*
    Earlier sketch in SATA *106*
West, Andrew
    See Arthur, Robert, (Jr.)
West, Anna 1938- *40*
West, Barbara
    See Price, Olive
West, Betty 1921- *11*
West, Bruce 1951- *63*
West, C. P.
    See Wodehouse, P(elham) G(renville)
West, Dorothy
    See Benson, Mildred
West, Emily Govan 1919- *38*
West, Emmy
    See West, Emily Govan
West, James
    See Withers, Carl A.
West, Jerry
    See Svenson, Andrew E(dward)
West, (Mary) Jessamyn 1902-1984
    Obituary *37*
West, John
    See Arthur, Robert, (Jr.)
West, Owen
    See Koontz, Dean R.
West, Ward
    See Borland, Harold Glen
Westall, Robert (Atkinson) 1929-1993 .... *69*
    Obituary *75*
    Earlier sketch in SATA *23*
    See also CLR *13*
    See also SAAS *2*
Westaway, Jane 1948- *121*
Westcott, Nadine Bernard 1949- *130*
Westera, Marleen 1962- *187*
Westerberg, Christine 1950- *29*
Westerduin, Anne 1945- *105*
Westerfeld, Scott *161*
Westervelt, Virginia Veeder 1914-2005 .... *10*
Westheimer, David 1917-2005 .... *14*
    Obituary *170*
Westheimer, David Kaplan
    See Westheimer, David
Westmacott, Mary
    See Christie, Agatha (Mary Clarissa)
Westman, Barbara *70*
Westman, Paul (Wendell) 1956- *39*
Westmoreland, William C. 1914-2005 .... *63*
Westmoreland, William Childs
    See Westmoreland, William C.
Weston, Allen
    See Hogarth, Grace (Weston Allen)
    and Norton, Andre
Weston, Carol 1956- *135*
Weston, Carrie *190*
Weston, John (Harrison) 1932- *21*
Weston, Martha 1947- *119*
    Earlier sketch in SATA *53*
Westphal, Arnold Carl 1897- *57*
Westrup, Hugh *102*
Westwood, Jennifer 1940-2008 .... *10*
    Obituary *192*
Wexler, Jerome (LeRoy) 1923- *14*
Weyland, Jack 1940- *81*
Weyn, Suzanne 1955- *164*
    Earlier sketches in SATA *63, 101*
Weyr, Garret
    See Freymann-Weyr, (Rhoda) Garret
    (Michaela)
Wezyk, Joanna 1966- *82*
Whaley, Joyce Irene 1923- *61*
Whalin, W. Terry 1953- *93*
Wharf, Michael
    See Weller, George
Wharmby, Margot *63*

Wharton, Edith (Newbold Jones) 1862-1937
    See CLR *136*
Whatley, Bruce 1954- *177*
Wheatley, Arabelle 1921- *16*
Wheatley, Nadia 1949- *147*
Wheeler, Cindy 1955- *49*
    Brief entry *40*
Wheeler, Deborah 1947- *83*
Wheeler, Janet D. *1*
Wheeler, Jill C. 1964- *136*
    Earlier sketch in SATA *86*
Wheeler, Jody 1952- *148*
    Earlier sketch in SATA *84*
Wheeler, Lisa 1963- *200*
    Earlier sketch in SATA *162*
Wheeler, Opal 1898- *23*
Whelan, Elizabeth M(urphy) 1943- *14*
Whelan, Gloria 1923- *178*
    Earlier sketches in SATA *85, 128*
    See also CLR *90*
Whelan, Gloria Ann
    See Whelan, Gloria
Whipple, A(ddison) B(eecher) C(olvin)
    1918- *64*
Whipple, Cal
    See Whipple, A(ddison) B(eecher) C(olvin)
Whisp, Kennilworthy
    See Rowling, J.K.
Whistler, Reginald John 1905-1944 .... *30*
Whistler, Rex
    See Whistler, Reginald John
Whitaker, Zai *183*
Whitcher, Susan (Godsil) 1952- *96*
Whitcomb, Jon 1906-1988 .... *10*
    Obituary *56*
Whitcomb, Laura *171*
White, Anne Terry 1896-1980 .... *2*
White, Bessie (Felstiner) 1892(?)-1986
    Obituary *50*
White, Carolyn 1948- *130*
White, Dale
    See Place, Marian T(empleton)
White, Dori 1919- *10*
White, E. B. 1899-1985 .... *100*
    Obituary *44*
    Earlier sketches in SATA *2, 29*
    See also CLR *107*
White, Eliza Orne 1856-1947
    See YABC *2*
White, Elwyn Brooks
    See White, E. B.
White, Florence M(eiman) 1910- *14*
White, Laurence B(arton), Jr. 1935- *10*
White, Lee *176*
White, Martin 1943- *51*
White, Nancy 1942- *126*
White, Ramy Allison *67*
    Earlier sketch in SATA *1*
White, Robb 1909-1990 .... *83*
    Earlier sketch in SATA *1*
    See also CLR *3*
    See also SAAS *1*
White, Ruth C. 1942- *186*
    Autobiography Feature *186*
    Earlier sketches in SATA *39, 117, 165*
White, T(erence) H(anbury) 1906-1964 .... *12*
    See also CLR *139*
White, Tekla N. 1934- *115*
White, Timothy (Thomas Anthony)
    1952-2002 .... *60*
White, Tom 1923- *148*
White, William, Jr. 1934- *16*
Whitehead, Don(ald) F. 1908-1981 .... *4*
Whitehead, Jenny 1964- *191*
Whitehead, Kathy 1957- *176*
Whitehouse, Arch
    See Whitehouse, Arthur George Joseph
Whitehouse, Arthur George Joseph
    1895-1979 .... *14*
    Obituary *23*
Whitehouse, Elizabeth S(cott) 1893-1968 .... *35*

Whitehouse, Jeanne
    See Peterson, Jeanne Whitehouse
Whitelaw, Nancy 1933- *166*
    Earlier sketch in SATA *76*
Whitesel, Cheryl Aylward *162*
Whitinger, R. D.
    See Place, Marian T(empleton)
Whitley, Mary Ann
    See Sebrey, Mary Ann
Whitley, Peggy 1938- *140*
Whitlock, Pamela 1921(?)-1982
    Obituary *31*
Whitlock, Ralph 1914-1995 .... *35*
Whitman, Alice
    See Marker, Sherry
Whitman, Sylvia (Choate) 1961- *135*
    Earlier sketch in SATA *85*
Whitman, Walt(er) 1819-1892 .... *20*
Whitmore, Arvella 1922- *125*
Whitney, Alex(andra) 1922- *14*
Whitney, David C(harles) 1921- *48*
    Brief entry *29*
Whitney, Kim Ablon *162*
Whitney, Phyllis A. 1903-2008 .... *30*
    Obituary *189*
    Earlier sketch in SATA *1*
    See also CLR *59*
Whitney, Phyllis Ayame
    See Whitney, Phyllis A.
Whitney, Phyllis Ayame
    See Whitney, Phyllis A.
Whitney, Sharon 1937- *63*
Whitney, Thomas P. 1917-2007 .... *25*
    Obituary *189*
Whitney, Thomas Porter
    See Whitney, Thomas P.
Whittington, Mary K(athrine) 1941- *75*
Whitworth, John 1945- *123*
Whybrow, Ian *132*
Whyte, Mal(colm Kenneth, Jr.) 1933- *62*
Whyte, Mary 1953- *148*
    Earlier sketch in SATA *94*
Whyte, Ron 1942(?)-1989
    Obituary *63*
Whytock, Cherry *177*
Wiater, Stanley 1953- *84*
Wibbelsman, Charles J(oseph) 1945- *59*
Wibberley, Leonard (Patrick O'Connor)
    1915-1983 .... *45*
    Obituary *36*
    Earlier sketch in SATA *2*
    See also CLR *3*
Wiberg, Harald (Albin) 1908- *93*
    Brief entry *40*
Wick, Walter 1953- *148*
Wickberg, Susan
    See Rottman, S.L.
Wickens, Elaine *86*
Wicker, Ireene 1905(?)-1987
    Obituary *55*
Wickstrom, Sylvie 1960- *169*
Wickstrom, Thor 1960- *200*
Widdemer, Mabel Cleland 1902-1964 .... *5*
Widener, Terry 1950- *105*
Widerberg, Siv 1931- *10*
Wiebe, Rudy 1934- *156*
Wiebe, Rudy Henry
    See Wiebe, Rudy
Wieler, Diana (Jean) 1961- *109*
Wiener, Lori 1956- *84*
Wier, Ester (Alberti) 1910-2000 .... *3*
Wiese, Kurt 1887-1974 .... *36*
    Obituary *24*
    Earlier sketch in SATA *3*
    See also CLR *86*
Wiesel, Elie 1928- *56*
Wiesel, Eliezer
    See Wiesel, Elie
Wiesner, David 1956- *181*
    Earlier sketches in SATA *72, 117, 139*
    See also CLR *84*

Wiesner, Portia
 See Takakjian, Portia
Wiesner, William 1899-1984 5
Wiggers, Raymond 1952- 82
Wiggin, Eric E. 1939- 167
 Earlier sketch in SATA *88*
Wiggin, Eric Ellsworth 1939-
 See Wiggin, Eric E.
Wiggin (Riggs), Kate Douglas (Smith)
 1856-1923
 See YABC *1*
 See also CLR *52*
Wiggins, VeraLee (Chesnut) 1928-1995 89
Wight, James Alfred 1916-1995 135
 Brief entry 44
 Earlier sketch in SATA *86*
 See also CLR *80*
Wignell, Edel 1936- 69
Wijnberg, Ellen 85
Wikland, Ilon 1930- 93
 Brief entry 32
Wikler, Madeline 1943- 114
Wilber, Donald N(ewton) 1907-1997 35
Wilbur, C. Keith 1923- 27
Wilbur, Frances 1921- 107
Wilbur, Richard 1921- 108
 Earlier sketch in SATA *9*
Wilbur, Richard Purdy
 See Wilbur, Richard
Wilburn, Kathy 1948- 68
Wilcox, Charlotte 1948- 72
Wilcox, R(uth) Turner 1888-1970 36
Wilcox, Roger
 See Collins, Paul
Wild, Jocelyn 1941- 46
Wild, Kate 1954- 192
Wild, Margaret 1948- 197
 Earlier sketch in SATA *151*
Wild, Robin (Evans) 1936- 46
Wild, Robyn 1947- 117
Wilde, D. Gunther
 See Hurwood, Bernhardt J.
Wilde, Oscar 1854(?)-1900 24
 See also CLR *114*
Wilde, Oscar Fingal O'Flahertie Willis
 See Wilde, Oscar
Wilder, Buck
 See Smith, Tim(othy R.)
Wilder, Laura (Elizabeth) Ingalls
 1867-1957 100
 Earlier sketches in SATA *15, 29*
 See also CLR *111*
Wildsmith, Brian 1930- 124
 Earlier sketches in SATA *16, 69*
 See also CLR *52*
 See also SAAS *5*
Wiles, Deborah 171
Wilhelm, Doug 1952- 190
Wilhelm, Hans 1945- 196
 Autobiography Feature 196
 Earlier sketches in SATA *58, 135*
 See also CLR *46*
 See also SAAS *21*
Wilkie, Katharine E(lliott) 1904-1980 31
Wilkin, Eloise 1904-1987 49
 Obituary 54
Wilkins, Frances 1923- 14
Wilkins, Kim 147
Wilkins, Marilyn (Ruth) 1926- 30
Wilkins, Marne
 See Wilkins, Marilyn (Ruth)
Wilkins, Mary Huiskamp 1926- 2
 See also CLR *42*
Wilkins, Mary Huiskamp Calhoun
 See Wilkins, Mary Huiskamp
Wilkins, Rose 180
Wilkinson, (Thomas) Barry 1923- 50
 Brief entry 32
Wilkinson, Beth 1925- 80

Wilkinson, Brenda 1946- 91
 Earlier sketch in SATA *14*
 See also CLR *20*
Wilkinson, (John) Burke 1913-2000 4
Wilkinson, Sylvia 1940- 56
 Brief entry 39
Wilkon, Jozef 1930- 133
 Earlier sketches in SATA *31, 71*
Wilkowski, Sue 193
Wilks, Michael Thomas 1947- 44
Wilks, Mike
 See Wilks, Michael Thomas
Will
 See Lipkind, William
Willard, Barbara (Mary) 1909-1994 74
 Earlier sketch in SATA *17*
 See also CLR *2*
 See also SAAS *5*
Willard, Mildred Wilds 1911-1978 14
Willard, Nancy 1936- 191
 Brief entry 30
 Earlier sketches in SATA *37, 71, 127*
 See also CLR *5*
Willcox, Isobel 1907-1996 42
Willems, Mo 180
 Earlier sketch in SATA *154*
 See also CLR *114*
Willett, Edward (C.) 1959- 115
Willey, Bee 184
Willey, Margaret 1950- 86
Willey, Robert
 See Ley, Willy
Willhoite, Michael A. 1946- 71
William, Kate
 See Armstrong, Jennifer
Williams, Arlene 171
Williams, Barbara 1925- 107
 Earlier sketch in SATA *11*
 See also CLR *48*
 See also SAAS *16*
Williams, Barbara 1937- 62
Williams, Beryl
 See Epstein, Beryl (M. Williams)
Williams, Brian (Peter) 1943- 54
Williams, Carol Lynch 1959- 110
Williams, Charles
 See Collier, James Lincoln
Williams, Clyde C. 1881-1974 8
 Obituary 27
Williams, Coe
 See Harrison, C(hester) William
Williams, Colleen Madonna Flood 1963- .. 156
Williams, Cynthia G. 1958- 123
Williams, Dar 1967- 168
Williams, Donna Reilly 1945- 83
Williams, Dorothy
 See Williams, Marcia
Williams, Dorothy Snowden
 See Williams, Dar
Williams, Eric (Ernest) 1911-1983 14
 Obituary 38
Williams, Ferelith Eccles
 See Eccles Williams, Ferelith
Williams, Frances B.
 See Browin, Frances Williams
Williams, Garth (Montgomery) 1912-1996 .. 66
 Obituary 90
 Earlier sketch in SATA *18*
 See also CLR *57*
 See also SAAS *7*
Williams, Guy R(ichard) 1920- 11
Williams, Hawley
 See Heyliger, William
Williams, Helen 1948- 77
Williams, J. R.
 See Williams, Jeanne
Williams, J. Walker
 See Wodehouse, P(elham) G(renville)

Williams, Jay 1914-1978 41
 Obituary 24
 Earlier sketch in SATA *3*
 See also CLR *8*
Williams, Jeanne 1930- 5
Williams, Jenny 1939- 60
Williams, Karen Lynn 1952- 99
 Earlier sketch in SATA *66*
Williams, Kit 1946(?)- 44
 See also CLR *4*
Williams, Laura E. 180
Williams, Laura Ellen
 See Williams, Laura E.
Williams, L.E.
 See Williams, Laura Ellen
Williams, Leslie 1941- 42
Williams, Linda 1948- 59
Williams, Louise Bonino 1904(?)-1984
 Obituary 39
Williams, Lynn
 See Hale, Arlene
Williams, Marcia 1945- 159
 Earlier sketches in SATA *71, 97*
Williams, Marcia Dorothy
 See Williams, Marcia
Williams, Margery
 See Bianco, Margery Williams
Williams, Mark
 See Arthur, Robert, (Jr.)
Williams, Mark London 1959- 140
Williams, Maureen 1951- 12
Williams, Michael
 See St. John, Wylly Folk
Williams, Patrick J.
 See Griffin, W.E.B
Williams, Pete
 See Faulknor, Cliff(ord Vernon)
Williams, S. P.
 See Hart, Virginia
Williams, Sam 177
 Earlier sketch in SATA *124*
Williams, Selma R(uth) 1925- 14
Williams, Sherley Anne 1944-1999 78
 Obituary 116
Williams, Sheron 1955- 77
Williams, Shirley
 See Williams, Sherley Anne
Williams, Slim
 See Williams, Clyde C.
Williams, Sophy 1965- 135
Williams, Susan
 See Beckhorn, Susan Williams
Williams, Suzanne (Bullock) 1953- 71
Williams, Ursula Moray
 See Moray Williams, Ursula
Williams, Vera B(aker) 1927- 102
 Brief entry 33
 Earlier sketch in SATA *53*
 See also CLR *9*
Williams-Andriani, Renee 1963- 98
Williams-Ellis, (Mary) Amabel (Nassau
 Strachey) 1894-1984 29
 Obituary 41
Williams-Garcia, Rita 1957- 160
 Earlier sketch in SATA *98*
 See also CLR *36*
Williamson, Gwyneth 1965- 109
Williamson, Henry (William) 1895-1977 37
 Obituary 30
Williamson, Joanne S(mall) 1926- 122
 Earlier sketch in SATA *3*
Williamson, Melanie 196
Willis, Charles
 See Clarke, Arthur C.
Willis, Connie 1945- 110
 See also CLR *66*
Willis, Jeanne 1959- 195
 Earlier sketches in SATA *61, 123*
Willis, Jeanne Mary
 See Willis, Jeanne
Willis, Meredith Sue 1946- 101

Willis, Nancy Carol 1952- 139
  Earlier sketch in SATA 93
Willis, Paul J. 1955- 113
Willms, Russ 95
Willoughby, Lee Davis
  See Avallone, Michael (Angelo, Jr.)
  and Brandner, Gary (Phil)
  and Deming, Richard
  and DeAndrea, William L(ouis)
  and Laymon, Richard (Carl)
  and Streib, Dan(iel Thomas)
  and Toombs, John
  and Webb, Jean Francis (III)
Willson, Robina Beckles
  See Beckles Willson, Robina
Wilma, Dana
  See Faralla, Dana
Wilsdorf, Anne 1954- 191
Wilson, April 80
Wilson, Barbara Ker
  See Ker Wilson, Barbara
Wilson, Beth P(ierre) 8
Wilson, Budge 1927- 55
  Brief entry 51
Wilson, Carletta 1951- 81
Wilson, Carter 1941- 6
Wilson, Charles Morrow 1905-1977 30
Wilson, Christopher B. 1910(?)-1985
  Obituary 46
Wilson, Darryl B(abe) 1939- 90
Wilson, Diane Lee 172
Wilson, Dirk
  See Pohl, Frederik
Wilson, Dorothy Clarke 1904-2003 16
Wilson, Edward A(rthur) 1886-1970 38
Wilson, Ellen (Janet Cameron) (?)-1976 9
  Obituary 26
Wilson, Eric (H.) 1940- 34
  Brief entry 32
Wilson, Erica 51
Wilson, Forrest 1918- 27
Wilson, Gahan 1930- 35
  Brief entry 27
Wilson, Gina 1943- 85
  Brief entry 34
  Earlier sketch in SATA 36
Wilson, (Leslie) Granville 1912- 14
Wilson, Hazel (Hutchins) 1898-1992 3
  Obituary 73
Wilson, J(erry) M. 1964- 121
Wilson, Jacqueline 1945- 199
  Brief entry 52
  Earlier sketches in SATA 61, 102, 153
Wilson, John 1922- 22
Wilson, John 1951- 182
Wilson, John Alexander
  See Wilson, John
Wilson, Johnniece Marshall 1944- 75
Wilson, Jonathan 1950- 181
Wilson, Joyce M. 84
  Earlier sketch in SATA 21
  See also SAAS 24
Wilson, Karma 174
Wilson, Leslie 1952- 166
Wilson, Linda Miller 1936- 116
Wilson, Lionel 1924-2003 33
  Brief entry 31
  Obituary 144
Wilson, Marjorie
  See Wilson, Budge
Wilson, Maurice (Charles John) 1914- 46
Wilson, Nancy Hope 1947- 138
  Earlier sketch in SATA 81
Wilson, Nathan D.
  See Wilson, N.D.
Wilson, N.D. 1978- 194
Wilson, Nick
  See Ellis, Edward S(ylvester)
Wilson, Phil 1948- 181
Wilson, Ron(ald William) 1941- 38

Wilson, Sarah 1934- 142
  Earlier sketch in SATA 50
Wilson, Tom 1931- 33
  Brief entry 30
Wilson, Troy 1970- 169
Wilson, Walt(er N.) 1939- 14
Wilson-Max, Ken 1965- 170
  Earlier sketch in SATA 93
Wilton, Elizabeth 1937- 14
Wilton, Hal
  See Pepper, Frank S.
Wilwerding, Walter Joseph 1891-1966 9
Wimmer, Mike 1961- 194
  Earlier sketch in SATA 70
Winborn, Marsha (Lynn) 1947- 75
Winch, John 1944- 165
  Earlier sketch in SATA 117
Winchester, James H(ugh) 1917-1985 30
  Obituary 45
Winchester, Stanley
  See Youd, Samuel
Windawi, Thura al- 1983(?)- 165
Winders, Gertrude Hecker -1987 3
Windham, Basil
  See Wodehouse, P(elham) G(renville)
Windham, Kathryn T(ucker) 1918- 14
Windham, Sophie 184
Windling, Terri 1958- 151
Windrow, Martin
  See Windrow, Martin Clive
Windrow, Martin C.
  See Windrow, Martin Clive
Windrow, Martin Clive 1944- 68
Windsor, Claire
  See Hamerstrom, Frances
Windsor, Linda 1950- 124
Windsor, Patricia 1938- 78
  Earlier sketch in SATA 30
  See also SAAS 19
Wineman-Marcus, Irene 1952- 81
Winer, Yvonne 1934- 120
Winerip, Michael 175
Winfield, Arthur M.
  See Stratemeyer, Edward L.
Winfield, Edna
  See Stratemeyer, Edward L.
Winfield, Julia
  See Armstrong, Jennifer
Wing, Natasha 1960- 200
  Earlier sketch in SATA 82
Winick, Judd 1970- 124
Winks, Robin William 1930-2003 61
Winn, Alison
  See Wharmby, Margot
Winn, Chris 1952- 42
Winn, Janet Bruce 1928- 43
Winn, Marie 1936(?)- 38
Winnick, Karen B(eth) B(inkoff) 1946- 51
Winn-Lederer, Ilene 198
Winslow, Barbara 1947- 91
Winstead, Rosie 180
Winston, Clara 1921-1983 54
  Obituary 39
Winston, Richard 1917-1979 54
Winston, Sherri 1964(?)- 201
Winter, Janet 1926- 126
Winter, Jeanette 1939- 184
  Earlier sketch in SATA 151
Winter, Jonah 1962- 179
Winter, Milo (Kendall) 1888-1956 21
Winter, Paula Cecelia 1929- 48
Winter, R. R.
  See Winterbotham, R(ussell) R(obert)
Winter, Susan 182
Winterbotham, R(ussell) R(obert)
  1904-1971 10
Winterbotham, Russ
  See Winterbotham, R(ussell) R(obert)
Winterfeld, Henry 1901-1990 55
Winters, J. C.
  See Cross, Gilbert B.

Winters, Jon
  See Cross, Gilbert B.
Winters, Katherine 1936- 153
  Earlier sketch in SATA 103
Winters, Kay
  See Winters, Katherine
Winters, Nina 1944- 62
Winters, Paul A. 1965- 106
Winterson, Jeanette 1959- 190
Winterton, Gayle
  See Adams, William Taylor
Winthrop, Elizabeth 1948- 164
  Autobiography Feature 116
  Earlier sketches in SATA 8, 76
  See also CLR 89
Winton, Ian (Kenneth) 1960- 76
Winton, Tim 1960- 98
Wintz-Litty, Julie
  See Litty, Julie
Wirt, Ann
  See Benson, Mildred
Wirt, Mildred A.
  See Benson, Mildred
Wirtenberg, Patricia Z. 1932-2007 10
Wirtenberg, Patricia Zarrella
  See Wirtenberg, Patricia Z.
Wirth, Beverly 1938- 63
Wirths, Claudine (Turner) G(ibson)
  1926-2000 104
  Earlier sketch in SATA 64
Wise, Bill 1958- 191
Wise, Lenny
  See Wise, Leonard
Wise, Leonard 1940- 167
Wise, Leonard A.
  See Wise, Leonard
Wise, Leonard Allan
  See Wise, Leonard
Wise, William 1923- 163
  Earlier sketch in SATA 4
Wise, Winifred E. 2
Wiseman, Ann (Sayre) 1926- 31
Wiseman, B(ernard) 1922-1995 4
Wiseman, David 1916- 43
  Brief entry 40
Wishinsky, Frieda 1948- 166
  Earlier sketches in SATA 70, 112
Wisler, G(ary) Clifton 1950- 103
  Brief entry 46
  Earlier sketch in SATA 58
Wismer, Donald (Richard) 1946- 59
Wisner, Bill
  See Wisner, William L.
Wisner, William L. 1914(?)-1983 42
Wisnewski, David 1953-2002
  See Wisniewski, David
Wisniewski, David 1953-2002 95
  Obituary 139
  See also CLR 51
Wister, Owen 1860-1938 62
Witham, (Phillip) Ross 1917- 37
Withers, Carl A. 1900-1970 14
Withers, Pam 1956- 182
Withrow, Sarah 1966- 199
  Earlier sketch in SATA 124
Witt, Dick 1948- 80
Witt, Shirley Hill 1934- 17
Wittanen, Etolin 1907- 55
Wittels, Harriet Joan 1938- 31
Wittig, Susan
  See Albert, Susan Wittig
Wittlinger, Ellen 1948- 189
  Autobiography Feature 128
  Earlier sketches in SATA 83, 122
Wittman, Sally (Anne Christensen) 1941- 30
Witty, Paul 1898-1976 50
  Obituary 30
Wodehouse, P(elham) G(renville)
  1881-1975 22
Wodge, Dreary
  See Gorey, Edward (St. John)

Woelfle, Gretchen 1945- *145*
Wohlberg, Meg 1905-1990 .... *41*
  Obituary *66*
Wohlrabe, Raymond A. 1900-1977 .... *4*
Wohnoutka, Mike *195*
Wojciechowska, Maia (Teresa) 1927-2002 ... *83*
  Autobiography Feature *104*
  Obituary *134*
  Earlier sketches in SATA *1, 28*
  See also CLR *1*
  See also SAAS *1*
Wojciechowski, Susan *126*
  Earlier sketch in SATA *78*
Wojnarowski, Adrian 1970- *190*
Wolcott, Patty 1929- *14*
Wold, Allen L. 1943- *64*
Wold, Jo Anne 1938- *30*
Woldin, Beth Weiner 1955- *34*
Wolf, Allan 1963- *192*
Wolf, Bernard 1930- *102*
  Brief entry *37*
Wolf, Erica (Van Varick) 1978- *156*
Wolf, Gita 1956- *101*
Wolf, Janet 1957- *78*
Wolf, J.M.
  See Wolf, Joan M.
Wolf, Joan M. 1966- *193*
Wolf, Sallie 1950- *80*
Wolfe, Art 1952- *76*
Wolfe, Burton H. 1932- *5*
Wolfe, Gene 1931- *165*
  Earlier sketch in SATA *118*
Wolfe, Gene Rodman
  See Wolfe, Gene
Wolfe, Gillian *199*
Wolfe, Louis 1905-1985 .... *8*
  Obituary *133*
Wolfe, Rinna (Evelyn) 1925- *38*
Wolfenden, George
  See Beardmore, George
Wolfer, Dianne 1961- *167*
  Autobiography Feature *117*
  Earlier sketch in SATA *104*
Wolff, Alexander (Nikolaus) 1957- *137*
  Earlier sketch in SATA *63*
Wolff, Ashley 1956- *155*
  Earlier sketches in SATA *50, 81*
Wolff, Diane 1945- *27*
Wolff, Ferida 1946- *164*
  Earlier sketch in SATA *79*
Wolff, Jennifer Ashley
  See Wolff, Ashley
Wolff, Robert Jay 1905-1977 .... *10*
Wolff, Sonia
  See Levitin, Sonia
Wolff, Virginia Euwer 1937- *137*
  Earlier sketch in SATA *78*
  See also CLR *62*
Wolfman, Judy 1933- *138*
Wolfson, Evelyn 1937- *62*
Wolitzer, Hilma 1930- *31*
Wolkoff, Judie (Edwards) *93*
  Brief entry *37*
Wolkstein, Diane 1942- *138*
  Earlier sketches in SATA *7, 82*
Wollheim, Donald A(llen) 1914-1990
  Obituary *69*
Wolny, P.
  See Janeczko, Paul B(ryan)
Wolters, Richard A. 1920-1993 .... *35*
Wondriska, William 1931- *6*
Wong, Jade Snow 1922-2006 .... *112*
  Obituary *175*
Wong, Janet S. 1962- *148*
  Earlier sketch in SATA *98*
  See also CLR *94*
Wood, Anne (Savage) 1937- *64*
Wood, Audrey *198*
  Brief entry *44*
  Earlier sketches in SATA *50, 81, 139*
  See also CLR *26*

Wood, Catherine
  See Etchison, Birdie L(ee)
Wood, David 1944- *87*
Wood, Don 1945- *50*
  Brief entry *44*
  See also CLR *26*
Wood, Douglas 1951- *180*
  Earlier sketches in SATA *81, 132*
Wood, Douglas Eric
  See Wood, Douglas
Wood, Edgar A(llardyce) 1907-1998 .... *14*
Wood, Esther
  See Brady, Esther Wood
Wood, Frances Elizabeth *34*
Wood, Frances M. 1951- *97*
Wood, James Playsted 1905- *1*
Wood, Jenny 1955- *88*
Wood, John Norris 1930- *85*
Wood, June Rae 1946- *120*
  Earlier sketch in SATA *79*
  See also CLR *82*
Wood, Kerry
  See Wood, Edgar A(llardyce)
Wood, Kim Marie *134*
Wood, Laura N.
  See Roper, Laura (Newbold) Wood
Wood, Linda C(arol) 1945- *59*
Wood, Marcia 1956- *80*
Wood, Marcia Mae
  See Wood, Marcia
Wood, Nancy
  See Wood, Nancy C.
Wood, Nancy C. 1936- *178*
  Earlier sketch in SATA *6*
Wood, Nuria
  See Nobisso, Josephine
Wood, Owen 1929- *64*
Wood, Phyllis Anderson 1923- *33*
  Brief entry *30*
Wood, Richard 1949- *110*
Wood, Tim(othy William Russell) 1946- *88*
Wood, Wallace 1927-1981
  Obituary *33*
Woodard, Carol 1929- *14*
Woodburn, John Henry 1914- *11*
Woodbury, David Oakes 1896-1981 .... *62*
Woodford, Peggy 1937- *25*
Woodhouse, Barbara (Blackburn)
  1910-1988 .... *63*
Woodhull, Ann Love *194*
Wooding, Chris 1977- *166*
Wooding, Sharon
  See Wooding, Sharon L(ouise)
Wooding, Sharon L(ouise) 1943- *66*
Woodman, Allen 1954- *76*
Woodrich, Mary Neville 1915- *2*
Woodruff, Elvira 1951- *162*
  Earlier sketches in SATA *70, 106*
Woodruff, Joan Leslie 1953- *104*
Woodruff, Liza 1971(?)- *182*
Woodruff, Marian
  See Goudge, Eileen
Woodruff, Noah 1977- *86*
Woods, George A(llan) 1926-1988 .... *30*
  Obituary *57*
Woods, Geraldine 1948- *111*
  Brief entry *42*
  Earlier sketch in SATA *56*
Woods, Harold 1945- *56*
  Brief entry *42*
Woods, Lawrence
  See Lowndes, Robert A(ugustine) W(ard)
Woods, Margaret 1921- *2*
Woods, Nat
  See Stratemeyer, Edward L.
Woods, Titania
  See Weatherly, Lee
Woodson, Jack
  See Woodson, John Waddie Jr.

Woodson, Jacqueline 1964- *189*
  Earlier sketches in SATA *94, 139*
  See also CLR *49*
Woodson, Jacqueline Amanda
  See Woodson, Jacqueline
Woodson, John Waddie Jr. 1913- *10*
Woodtor, Dee
  See Woodtor, Delores Parmer
Woodtor, Dee Parmer 1945(?)-2002
  See Woodtor, Delores Parmer
Woodtor, Delores Parmer 1945-2002 .... *93*
Wood-Trost, Lucille
  See Trost, Lucille W(ood)
Woodward, (Landon) Cleveland 1900-1986 . *10*
  Obituary *48*
Woodworth, Chris 1957- *168*
Woodworth, Viki 1952- *127*
Woody, Regina Jones 1894-1983 .... *3*
Woodyadd, Charlotte
  See Hough, Charlotte
Woog, Adam 1953- *125*
  Earlier sketch in SATA *84*
Wooldridge, Connie Nordhielm 1950- *143*
  Earlier sketch in SATA *92*
Wooldridge, Frosty 1947- *140*
Wooldridge, Rhoda 1906-1988 .... *22*
Wooley, Susan Frelick 1945- *113*
Woolf, Paula 1950- *104*
Woolfe, Angela 1976- *169*
Woolley, Catherine 1904-2005 .... *3*
  Obituary *166*
Woolman, Steven 1969-2004 .... *163*
  Earlier sketch in SATA *90*
Woolsey, Janette 1904-1989 .... *3*
  Obituary *131*
Worcester, Donald E(mmet) 1915- *18*
Word, Reagan 1944- *103*
Work, Virginia 1946- *57*
  Brief entry *45*
Worline, Bonnie Bess 1914- *14*
Wormell, Christopher 1955- *154*
  Earlier sketch in SATA *103*
Wormell, Mary 1959- *96*
Wormser, Richard 1933- *106*
  Autobiography Feature *118*
  See also SAAS *26*
Wormser, Sophie 1897-1979 .... *22*
Worth, Richard 1945- *59*
  Brief entry *46*
Worth, Valerie 1933-1994 .... *81*
  Earlier sketches in SATA *8, 70*
  See also CLR *21*
Worthington, Leonie 1956- *200*
Wortis, Avi
  See Avi
Wortis, Edward Irving
  See Avi
Wosmek, Frances 1917- *29*
Woychuk, Denis 1953- *71*
Wrede, Patricia C(ollins) 1953- *146*
  Earlier sketch in SATA *67*
Wriggins, Sally Hovey 1922- *17*
Wright, Alexandra 1979- *103*
Wright, Betty Ren 1927- *109*
  Brief entry *48*
  Earlier sketch in SATA *63*
Wright, Cliff 1963- *168*
  Earlier sketch in SATA *76*
Wright, Courtni
  See Wright, Courtni C(rump)
Wright, Courtni C(rump) 1950- *84*
Wright, Courtni Crump
  See Wright, Courtni C(rump)
Wright, Dare 1914(?)-2001 .... *21*
  Obituary *124*
Wright, David K. 1943- *112*
  Earlier sketch in SATA *73*
Wright, Elinor
  See Lyon, Elinor
Wright, Enid Meadowcroft (LaMonte)
  1898-1966 .... *3*

Wright, Esmond 1915-2003 .... *10*
Wright, Frances Fitzpatrick 1897-1982 .... *10*
Wright, J. B.
  See Barkan, Joanne
Wright, Judith 1915-2000 .... *14*
  Obituary *121*
Wright, Judith Arundell
  See Wright, Judith
Wright, Katrina
  See Gater, Dilys
Wright, Kenneth
  See del Rey, Lester
Wright, Kit 1944- *87*
Wright, Leslie B(ailey) 1959- *91*
Wright, Michael 1954- *198*
Wright, Nancy Means *38*
Wright, R(obert) H(amilton) 1906- *6*
Wright, Rachel *134*
Wright, Susan Kimmel 1950- *97*
Wrightfrierson
  See Wright-Frierson, Virginia (Marguerite)
Wright-Frierson, Virginia (Marguerite)
  1949- *110*
  Earlier sketch in SATA *58*
Wrightson, (Alice) Patricia 1921- *112*
  Earlier sketches in SATA *8, 66*
  See also CLR *14*
  See also SAAS *4*
Wroble, Lisa A. 1963- *134*
Wrongo, I.B.
  See Katz, Alan
Wronker, Lili
  See Wronker, Lili Cassel
Wronker, Lili Cassel 1924- *10*
Wryde, Dogear
  See Gorey, Edward (St. John)
Wu, Elizabeth
  See Wu, Liz
Wu, Liz *184*
Wu, Norbert 1961- *155*
  Earlier sketch in SATA *101*
Wulffson, Don 1943- *155*
  Earlier sketches in SATA *32, 88*
Wulffson, Don L.
  See Wulffson, Don
Wummer, Amy 1955- *201*
Wunderli, Stephen 1958- *79*
Wunsch, Josephine (McLean) 1914- *64*
Wuorio, Eva-Lis 1918- *34*
  Brief entry *28*
Wurts, Janny 1953- *98*
Wyatt, B. D.
  See Robinson, Spider
Wyatt, David 1968- *185*
Wyatt, Jane
  See Bradbury, Bianca (Ryley)
Wyatt, Melissa 1963- *177*
Wyeth, Betsy James 1921- *41*
Wyeth, N(ewell) C(onvers) 1882-1945 .... *17*
  See also CLR *106*
Wyler, Rose 1909-2000 .... *18*
  Obituary *121*
Wylie, Betty Jane *48*
Wylie, Laura
  See Matthews, Patricia
Wylie, Laurie
  See Matthews, Patricia
Wyllie, Stephen *86*
Wyman, Andrea *75*
Wyman, Carolyn 1956- *83*
Wymer, Norman (George) 1911- *25*
Wynard, Talbot
  See Hamilton, Charles (Harold St. John)
Wyndham, John
  See Harris, John (Wyndham Parkes Lucas)
  Beynon
Wyndham, Lee
  See Hyndman, Jane Andrews Lee
Wyndham, Robert
  See Hyndman, Robert Utley

Wynne-Jones, Tim 1948- *186*
  Autobiography Feature *136*
  Earlier sketches in SATA *67, 96, 136*
  See also CLR *58*
Wynne-Jones, Timothy
  See Wynne-Jones, Tim
Wynter, Edward (John) 1914- *14*
Wynyard, Talbot
  See Hamilton, Charles (Harold St. John)
Wyss, Johann David Von 1743-1818 .... *29*
  Brief entry *27*
  See also CLR *92*
Wyss, Thelma Hatch 1934- *140*
  Earlier sketch in SATA *10*

X

Xavier, Father
  See Hurwood, Bernhardt J.
Xuan, YongSheng 1952- *116*
  Autobiography Feature *119*

Y

Yaccarino, Dan *192*
  Earlier sketch in SATA *141*
Yadin, (Rav-Aloof) Yigael 1917-1984 .... *55*
Yaffe, Alan
  See Yorinks, Arthur
Yagher, Kevin 1962- *143*
Yakovetic, (Joseph Sandy) 1952- *59*
Yakovetic, Joe
  See Yakovetic, (Joseph Sandy)
Yamada, Utako 1963- *188*
Yamaguchi, Marianne (Illenberger) 1936- *7*
Yamaka, Sara 1978- *92*
Yamanaka, Lois-Ann 1961- *166*
Yancey, Diane 1951- *138*
  Earlier sketch in SATA *81*
Yancey, Richard *193*
Yancey, Rick
  See Yancey, Richard
Yang, Belle 1960- *170*
Yang, James 1960- *190*
Yang, Jay 1941- *12*
Yang, Mingyi 1943- *72*
Yarbrough, Camille 1938- *79*
  See also CLR *29*
Yarbrough, Ira 1910(?)-1983
  Obituary *35*
Yaroslava
  See Mills, Yaroslava Surmach
Yarrow, Peter 1938- *195*
Yashima, Taro
  See Iwamatsu, Jun Atsushi
Yates, Elizabeth 1905-2001 .... *68*
  Obituary *128*
  Earlier sketch in SATA *4*
  See also SAAS *6*
Yates, Janelle K(aye) 1957- *77*
Yates, John 1939- *74*
Yates, Philip 1958- *149*
  Earlier sketch in SATA *92*
Yates, Raymond F(rancis) 1895-1966 .... *31*
Yaukey, Grace S(ydenstricker) 1899-1994 ... *80*
  Earlier sketch in SATA *5*
Ye, Ting-xing 1952- *106*
Yeahpau, Thomas M. 1975- *187*
Yeakley, Marjory Hall 1908- *21*
Yeatman, Linda 1938- *42*
Yee, Brenda Shannon *133*
Yee, Lisa 1959- *160*
Yee, Paul (R.) 1956- *143*
  Earlier sketches in SATA *67, 96*
  See also CLR *44*
Yee, Wong Herbert 1953- *172*
  Earlier sketches in SATA *78, 115*
Yeh, Chun-Chan 1914- *79*

Ye Junjian
  See Yeh, Chun-Chan
Yelchin, Eugene 1956- *196*
Yenawine, Philip 1942- *85*
Yensid, Retlaw
  See Disney, Walt(er Elias)
Yeo, Wilma (Lethem) 1918-1994 .... *81*
  Earlier sketch in SATA *24*
Yeoman, John 1934- *80*
  Earlier sketch in SATA *28*
  See also CLR *46*
Yep, Laurence 1948- *176*
  Earlier sketches in SATA *7, 69, 123*
  See also CLR *132*
Yep, Laurence Michael
  See Yep, Laurence
Yepsen, Roger B(ennet), Jr. 1947- *59*
Yerian, Cameron John *21*
Yerian, Margaret A. *21*
Yerxa, Leo 1947- *181*
Yetska
  See Ironside, Jetske
Yezerski, Thomas F. 1969- *190*
Yin *194*
Ylvisaker, Anne 1965(?)- *172*
Yoder, Carolyn P. 1953- *149*
Yoder, Carolyn Patricia
  See Yoder, Carolyn P.
Yoder, Dorothy Meenen 1921- *96*
Yoder, Dot
  See Yoder, Dorothy Meenen
Yoder, Walter D. 1933- *88*
Yolen, Jane 1939- *194*
  Autobiography Feature *111*
  Earlier sketches in SATA *4, 40, 75, 112, 158*
  See also CLR *44*
  See also SAAS *1*
Yolen, Jane Hyatt
  See Yolen, Jane
Yonezu, Yusuke *196*
Yonge, Charlotte (Mary) 1823-1901 .... *17*
Yoo, Paula 1969(?)- *174*
Yoo, Taeeun *191*
Yorinks, Adrienne 1956- *171*
Yorinks, Arthur 1953- *200*
  Earlier sketches in SATA *33, 49, 85, 144*
  See also CLR *20*
York, Alison
  See Nicole, Christopher (Robin)
York, Andrew
  See Nicole, Christopher (Robin)
York, Carol Beach 1928- *77*
  Earlier sketch in SATA *6*
York, Rebecca
  See Buckholtz, Eileen (Garber)
  and Glick, Ruth (Burtnick)
York, Simon
  See Heinlein, Robert A.
Yoshida, Toshi 1911- *77*
Yoshikawa, Sachiko *181*
Yost, Edna 1889-1971
  Obituary *26*
Youd, C. S.
  See Youd, Samuel
Youd, Samuel 1922- *135*
  Brief entry *30*
  Earlier sketch in SATA *47*
  See also CLR *2*
  See also SAAS *6*
Young, Amy L. *185*
Young, Bob
  See Young, Robert W(illiam)
  and Young, James Robert
Young, Carol 1945- *102*
Young, Catherine
  See Olds, Helen Diehl
Young, Clarence
  See Stratemeyer, Edward L.
Young, Collier
  See Bloch, Robert (Albert)
Young, Dan 1952- *126*

Young, Dianne 1959- *88*
Young, Dorothea Bennett 1924- *31*
Young, Ed 1931- *173*
    Earlier sketches in SATA *10, 74, 122*
    See also CLR 27
Young, Ed Tse-chun
    See Young, Ed
Young, Edward
    See Reinfeld, Fred
Young, Elaine L.
    See Schulte, Elaine L(ouise)
Young, James
    See Graham, Ian
Young, Jan
    See Young, Janet Randall
Young, Janet 1957- *188*
Young, Janet Randall 1919-1994 .... *3*
Young, Janet Ruth
    See Young, Janet
Young, Jeff C. 1948- *132*
Young, John
    See Macintosh, Brownie
Young, Judy 1956- *155*
Young, Judy (Elaine) Dockrey 1949- *72*
Young, Karen Romano 1959- *168*
    Earlier sketch in SATA *116*
Young, Ken 1956- *86*
Young, Lois Horton 1911-1981 .... *26*
Young, Louisa *161*
Young, Louise B. 1919- *64*
Young, Margaret B(uckner) 1922- *2*
Young, Mary 1940- *89*
Young, Miriam 1913-1974 .... *7*
Young, Noela 1930- *89*
Young, (Rodney Lee) Patrick (Jr.) 1937- *22*
Young, Percy M(arshall) 1912-2004 .... *31*
    Obituary *154*
Young, Richard Alan 1946- *72*
Young, Robert W(illiam) 1916-1969 .... *3*
Young, Ross B. 1955- *150*
Young, Ruth 1946- *67*
Young, Sara
    See Pennypacker, Sara
Young, Scott A. 1918-2005 .... *5*
Young, Scott Alexander
    See Young, Scott A.
Young, Selina 1971-2006 .... *201*
Young, Vivien
    See Gater, Dilys
Younger, Barbara 1954- *108*
Youngs, Betty 1934-1985 .... *53*
    Obituary *42*
Younkin, Paula 1942- *77*
Yount, Lisa (Ann) 1944- *124*
    Earlier sketch in SATA *74*
Yourgrau, Barry *179*
Yuditskaya, Tatyana 1964- *75*
Yumoto, Kazumi 1959- *153*

Z

Zach, Cheryl (Byrd) 1947- *98*
    Brief entry *51*
    Earlier sketch in SATA *58*
    See also SAAS 24
Zacharias, Gary L. 1946- *153*
Zaffo, George J. (?)-1984 .... *42*
Zagarenski, Pamela 1969(?)- *183*
Zagwyn, Deborah Turney 1953- *138*
    Earlier sketch in SATA *78*
Zahares, Wade *193*
Zahn, Timothy 1951- *156*
    Earlier sketch in SATA *91*
Zaid, Barry 1938- *51*
Zaidenberg, Arthur 1908(?)-1990 .... *34*
    Obituary *66*

Zalben, Jane Breskin 1950- *170*
    Earlier sketches in SATA *7, 79, 120*
    See also CLR 84
Zallinger, Jean (Day) 1918- *115*
    Earlier sketches in SATA *14, 80*
Zallinger, Peter Franz 1943- *49*
Zambreno, Mary Frances 1954- *140*
    Earlier sketch in SATA *75*
Zanderbergen, George
    See May, Julian
Zappa, Ahmet 1974- *180*
Zappa, Ahmet Emuukha Rodan
    See Zappa, Ahmet
Zappler, Lisbeth 1930- *10*
Zarchy, Harry 1912-1987 .... *34*
Zarin, Cynthia 1959- *192*
    Earlier sketch in SATA *108*
Zaring, Jane (Thomas) 1936- *40*
Zarins, Joyce Audy
    See dos Santos, Joyce Audy
Zaslavsky, Claudia 1917- *36*
Zaugg, Sandra L. 1938- *118*
Zaugg, Sandy
    See Zaugg, Sandra L.
Zaunders, Bo 1939- *137*
Zawadzki, Marek 1958- *97*
Zebra, A.
    See Scoltock, Jack
Zebrowski, George 1945- *67*
Zebrowski, George T.
    See Zebrowski, George
Zeck, Gerald Anthony 1939- *40*
Zeck, Gerry
    See Zeck, Gerald Anthony
Zed, Dr.
    See Penrose, Gordon
Zei, Alki 1925- *24*
    See also CLR 6
Zeier, Joan T(heresa) 1931- *81*
Zeinert, Karen 1942-2002 .... *137*
    Earlier sketch in SATA *79*
Zeises, Lara M. 1976- *184*
    Earlier sketch in SATA *145*
Zelazny, Roger 1937-1995 .... *57*
    Brief entry *39*
Zelazny, Roger Joseph
    See Zelazny, Roger
Zeldis, Malcah 1931- *146*
    Earlier sketch in SATA *86*
Zelinsky, Paul O. 1953- *154*
    Brief entry *33*
    Earlier sketches in SATA *49, 102*
    See also CLR 55
Zellan, Audrey Penn
    See Penn, Audrey
Zemach, Harve
    See Fischtrom, Harvey
Zemach, Kaethe 1958- *149*
    Brief entry *39*
    Earlier sketch in SATA *49*
Zemach, Margot 1931-1989 .... *70*
    Obituary *59*
    Earlier sketch in SATA *21*
Zemach-Bersin, Kaethe
    See Zemach, Kaethe
Zeman, Ludmila 1947- *153*
Zephaniah, Benjamin 1958- *189*
    Earlier sketches in SATA *86, 140*
Zephaniah, Benjamin Obadiah Iqbal
    See Zephaniah, Benjamin
Zephaniah, Benjamin Pbadiah Iqubal
    See Zephaniah, Benjamin
Zephaniah, Benjamin Pbadiah Iqubal
    See Zephaniah, Benjamin
Zerman, Melvyn Bernard 1930- *46*
Zettner, Pat 1940- *70*
Zevin, Gabrielle *176*
Zhang, Christopher Zhong-Yuan 1954- *91*

Zhang, Song Nan 1942- *170*
    Earlier sketch in SATA *85*
Ziefert, Harriet 1941- *154*
    Earlier sketch in SATA *101*
Ziegler, Jack (Denmore) 1942- *60*
Ziemienski, Dennis (Theodore) 1947- *10*
Ziliox, Marc
    See Fichter, George S.
Zillah
    See Macdonald, Zillah K(atherine)
Zim, Herbert S(pencer) 1909-1994 .... *30*
    Obituary *85*
    Earlier sketch in SATA *1*
    See also CLR 2
    See also SAAS 2
Zim, Sonia Bleeker 1909-1971 .... *2*
    Obituary *26*
Zima, Gordon 1920- *90*
Zimelman, Nathan 1921- *65*
    Brief entry *37*
Zimmer, Dirk 1943- *147*
    Earlier sketch in SATA *65*
Zimmer, Tracie Vaughn *169*
Zimmerman, Andrea 1950- *192*
    Earlier sketch in SATA *123*
Zimmerman, Andrea Griffing
    See Zimmerman, Andrea
Zimmerman, H. Werner 1951- *101*
Zimmerman, Heinz Werner
    See Zimmerman, H. Werner
Zimmerman, Naoma 1914-2004 .... *10*
Zimmerman, R. D.
    See Alexander, Robert
Zimmermann, Arnold E. 1909- *58*
Zimmett, Debbie
    See Becker, Deborah Zimmett
Zimmy
    See Stratemeyer, Edward L.
Zimnik, Reiner 1930- *36*
    See also CLR 3
Zindel, Bonnie 1943- *34*
Zindel, Lizabeth *187*
Zindel, Paul 1936-2003 .... *102*
    Obituary *142*
    Earlier sketches in SATA *16, 58*
    See also CLR 85
Ziner, Feenie
    See Ziner, Florence
Ziner, Florence 1921- *5*
Zingara, Professor
    See Leeming, Joseph
Zinger, Yitskhok
    See Singer, Isaac Bashevis
Zion, Eugene 1913-1975 .... *18*
Zion, Gene
    See Zion, Eugene
Zoehfeld, Kathleen Weidner 1954- *193*
Zohorsky, Janet R. 1958- *148*
Zolkower, Edie Stoltz *171*
Zolkowski, Cathy (A.) 1969- *121*
Zollars, Jaime *191*
Zolotow, Charlotte 1915- *138*
    Earlier sketches in SATA *1, 35, 78*
    See also CLR 77
Zolotow, Charlotte Gertrude Shapiro
    See Zolotow, Charlotte
Zolotow, Ellen
    See Dragonwagon, Crescent
Zonderman, Jon 1957- *92*
Zonia, Dhimitri 1921- *20*
Zonta, Pat 1951- *143*
Zubrowski, Bernard 1939- *90*
    Earlier sketch in SATA *35*
Zubrowski, Bernie
    See Zubrowski, Bernard
Zucker, Miriam S.
    See Reichert, Miriam Zucker
Zuckerman, Linda *190*
Zudeck, Darryl 1961- *61*